CHRONOLOGY OF THE
COLD WAR

CHRONOLOGY OF THE COLD WAR 1917–1992

Lester Brune

Richard Dean Burns
Consulting Editor

Routledge
Taylor & Francis Group
New York London

Published in 2006 by
Routledge
Taylor & Francis Group
270 Madison Avenue
New York, NY 10016

Published in Great Britain by
Routledge
Taylor & Francis Group
2 Park Square
Milton Park, Abingdon
Oxon OX14 4RN

© 2006 by Taylor & Francis Group, LLC
Routledge is an imprint of Taylor & Francis Group

Printed in the United States of America on acid-free paper
10 9 8 7 6 5 4 3 2 1

International Standard Book Number-10: 0-415-97339-2 (Hardcover)
International Standard Book Number-13: 978-0-415-97339-7 (Hardcover)

No part of this book may be reprinted, reproduced, transmitted, or utilized in any form by any electronic, mechanical, or other means, now known or hereafter invented, including photocopying, microfilming, and recording, or in any information storage or retrieval system, without written permission from the publishers.

Trademark Notice: Product or corporate names may be trademarks or registered trademarks, and are used only for identification and explanation without intent to infringe.

Library of Congress Cataloging-in-Publication Data

Catalog record is available from the Library of Congress

Taylor & Francis Group is the Academic Division of Informa plc.

Visit the Taylor & Francis Web site at
http://www.taylorandfrancis.com

and the Routledge Web site at
http://www.routledge-ny.com

Contents

Maps

Preface and Acknowledgments

The *Chronology of the Cold War, 1917–1992* is designed as a reference for scholars, librarians, students, researchers, and citizens seeking a straightforward explanation of particular events regarding the United States, the Soviet Union, and other participants in the Cold War. We have tried to provide an understanding of the issues surrounding decisions and events with regard to the two Cold War superpowers, their allies, and their client states. It is based on portions of the three-volume reference *Chronological History of U.S. Foreign Relations* (Routledge, 2003), with material added to round out the international picture of the Cold War. Two new maps were commissioned especially for this volume, and most of the photographs were newly researched for this volume at the National Archives and various presidential libraries.

How to Use This Volume

Some who use this volume will be seeking information about forgotten information on domestic and international activities between 1917 and 1992. Others may prefer to browse through this *Chronology of the Cold War* for a quick overview of activities in a particular year or two to compare time periods. Whatever your concerns, you will find these features useful:

Dual Entry Structure: The entry for each event consists of a short heading describing the event with an explanation of that event. You may scan headings for a timeline or stop at any point to read in-depth descriptions of that event.

Searchers of information about specific Cold War persons, events, or subjects may make use of these features:

Date Heading: The volume's organization is chronological with the entry for each event headed by a date for the month, day, and year of that event. After locating the desired event, one can review events preceding and following to learn about its broad historical context.

Cross-References: Many entries include cross-references to a related event, referred to by date.

Appendix: The appendix has brief biographical entries on key U.S., Soviet, and Communist Chinese figures who played important roles during the Cold War.

Index: The analytical index in the back of the volume lists names, events, and topics.

Acknowledgments

The author would like to thank Routledge's Sylvia Miller for conceiving this project and Richard Dean Burns for suggesting appropriate chronological entries, editing the text, and selecting illustrations.

Introduction

No less than the eighteenth-century Second Hundred Years' War between England and France, the Cold War comprised a major divide in the history of the modern world. In large measure, the Soviet–American rivalry, like that between England and France, seemed to respond to long-term historic trends. Even to some nineteenth-century observers the two landed empires would one day submerge Western Europe to a secondary status in international life. Writing in the 1830s, Alexis de Tocqueville, the brilliant French critic of American society, pointed to the United States and Russia as the two great nations of the future, each "marked out by the will of heaven to sway the destinies of half the globe." "Between the autocracy of Russia on the East, and the democracy of America, aggrandized by the conquest of Mexico, on the West," predicted Paris's *Journal des Debats* in 1845, "Europe may find herself more compressed than she may one day think consistent with her independence and dignity." The trend continued, but not until 1945 did that reality reach fulfillment as the United States and the USSR confronted each other, as victorious allies, across a ruined Europe.

That the American–Soviet relationship as allies would disintegrate to a status of animosity was not preordained. Yet for some Americans the euphoria of victory and peace evaporated quickly. The Soviet Union's total victory over Germany, upsetting the historic European balance of power, mattered little to Americans who had lauded the USSR for its costly and necessary contributions to Allied success. But for a small minority of U.S. officials and writers, all conditioned by their wartime experience, the continuing postwar Soviet occupation of Eastern Europe enhanced that country's strategic position, especially in the Balkans, and rendered bordering regions vulnerable to further Soviet expansion. It required only the Kremlin's postwar demands on Iran and Turkey to unleash visions of Soviet military expansion reminiscent of the Italian, German, and Japanese aggressions that, so recently, had brought war to the world. Responding to Soviet pressures on Turkey for a new Straits settlement in August 1946, Acting Secretary of State Dean Acheson and the Chiefs of Staff, with advice from State Department experts, prepared a memorandum on Turkey for the president. The memorandum warned:

> If the Soviet Union succeeds in its objective of obtaining control over Turkey, it will be extremely difficult, if not impossible, to prevent the Soviet Union from obtaining control over Greece and over the whole Near and Middle East...[including] the territory lying between the Mediterranean and India. When the Soviet Union has once obtained full mastery of this territory it will be in a much stronger position to obtain its objectives in India and China.

Adviser Clark Clifford's September 1946 report to President Harry Truman, reflecting the views of top Washington officials, described a deeply threatened world with similar language.

When suspected Soviet ambitions, in early 1947, seemed to focus on Greece as well as Turkey, the Truman administration framed the famed Truman Doctrine, with its corresponding rhetorical predictions of falling dominoes across Europe,

Africa, or Asia should Greece fall to its Communist-led guerillas. Senator Arthur Vandenberg of Michigan accepted the administration's dire predictions uncritically. "Greece," he wrote on March 12, "must be helped or Greece sinks permanently into the Communist order. Turkey inevitably follows. Then comes the chain reaction which might sweep from the Dardanelles to the China Sea." Never before, critics noted, had U.S. leaders described external dangers in such limitless, imprecise terms. Secretary of State George C. Marshall, Soviet expert George Kennan, and columnist Walter Lippmann objected to the language. Lippmann accused the administration of launching a crusade, not defining a policy. Despite the bitter opposition to the Truman Doctrine within Congress as well, the measure, with its $400 million package of military aid to Greece and Turkey, passed both houses of Congress by wide margins.

The rhetorical portrayals of Soviet territorial ambitions that underwrote the Truman Doctrine far exceeded Soviet military capabilities and intentions. The Kremlin had already demonstrated its extreme reluctance to confront the West militarily along the Iranian and Turkish borders where its strategic advantage was profound. Confronted by the predictable resistance of the non-Soviet world, Kremlin leaders understood that any military venture would end in disaster. Never did the USSR mass forces along any border for the object of invading another country. Indeed, U.S. military officials concluded as early as 1946 that the Soviet Union had no intention of embarking on a career of military aggression. But what seized the country's emerging anti-Communist elite was the fear that the real Soviet danger, one that rendered military aggression irrelevant, lay in the limitless promise of Soviet ideological expansion. For those Americans who took the Soviet rhetoric seriously, the USSR, as the self-assigned leader of world Communism, possessed the power and will to incite or support Communist-led revolutions everywhere, imposing on them its influence, if not its direct control. Such notions of ideological conquest attributed to the Kremlin the power to extend its influence over vast areas without military force. It mattered little whether Soviet troops or even Soviet officials were present at all.

Growth of Western Power and Suspicion

Rhetorical depictions of the Soviet Union's expansive power took slight measure of the West's economic, political, and diplomatic predominance. During the two years that followed Congress's approval of the Truman Doctrine, the Western powers achieved an unbroken succession of diplomatic triumphs that demonstrated their total superiority. The sometimes astonishing successes began in 1948 with the elimination of Communists from the French government to sever any possible ties to the Kremlin. Similarly, Washington's varied electioneering efforts in Italy triumphed in an election that freed the government of all Communists and socialists. In June, Marshall Tito, Yugoslavia's staunch Communist leader, broke with the Kremlin to demonstrate that Communism could not erode the power of nationalism, and that Kremlin control extended only as far as the reach of Soviet armies.

During subsequent months, America's varied policies aimed at the containment of Soviet power emerged victorious. In Greece, the U.S.-supported government, in August 1949, eliminated the Communist-led insurgency, driving the surviving guerrillas into Albania. President Truman proclaimed victory on November 28. Meanwhile, U.S. officers organized and modernized the Turkish army, vastly improved the country's military capabilities with shipments of equipment and aircraft, and constructed new roads and airstrips. Even greater triumphs for European stability came in response to the Czech coup of February 1948, which established a Communist regime in Czechoslovakia and created a momentary threat to European security. Amid that crisis, Congress, which had long resisted the cost, adopted the Marshall Plan to launch Europe on a course of unparalleled economic growth. During May 1949, Stalin lifted the Berlin blockade, which had been instituted a year earlier to prevent the unification of Germany's three western zones. The Paris Foreign Minister's Conference, one month later, announced the formation of the Federal Republic of Germany, an achievement long opposed by the Kremlin. Finally, in April 1949, again in response to the Czech war crisis, twelve Western countries formed the North Atlantic Alliance to underwrite the stability and security of western Europe.

Washington, with the complete cooperation of the European powers, gained the full spectrum of its immediate objectives, in large measure because Europe's postwar challenges gave the economic supremacy of the United States a special relevance. With Europe in ruins and the Soviet Union reeling in near disaster, U.S. economic power was absolute. British writer Harold J. Laski wrote in November 1947:

> America bestrides the world like a colossus; neither Rome at the height of its power nor Great Britain in the period of its economic supremacy enjoyed an influence so direct, so profound, or so pervasive....Today literally hundreds of millions of Europeans and Asiatics know that both the quality and the rhythm of their lives depend upon decisions made in Washington. On the wisdom of those decisions hangs the fate of the next generation.

The war had rained destruction on every major power of Europe and Asia, destroying countless cities, factories, and rail lines. By contrast, the United States, with its many accumulating elements of power, had escaped unscathed. Its undamaged industrial capacity now matched that of the rest of the industrialized world. Its technological superiority was so obvious that the world assumed its existence and set out to acquire or copy American products. During the immediate postwar years, the United States reached the highest point of world power achieved by any nation in modern times.

Abroad, the United States gained its marvelous triumphs where it mattered: the economic rehabilitation of western Europe and Japan, the promotion of international trade and investment, and the maintenance of a defense structure that underwrote the containment effort and played an essential role in Europe's political development and burgeoning confidence. These contributions to the world's unprecedented security and prosperity comprised the essence of the nation's postwar international achievement. By 1949, the USSR faced the greatest manifestation of opposing power in the peacetime history of the world. The persistent Soviet retreats were evidence enough that Europe's balance of forces had turned against it.

In the events of 1948 and 1949, especially in the Czech and Berlin crises, the Cold War in Europe reached its peak. At the same time, the rapid succession of Western victories and Soviet retreats, added to western Europe's astonishing recovery, created the foundations of a profound East–West stability across Europe. If American purpose in Europe was the stability of a divided continent—beyond which no policy would be effective—the United States, in 1949, had achieved its goal. The United States, alone or with its allies, would not assume the risk of war by seeking to change the status quo of Europe; the Soviets had no power to do so. With the major antagonists compelled to accept existing conditions, Britain's Winston Churchill, George Kennan, Walter Lippmann, and countless informed observers, called for negotiations to adjust differences, relieve tensions, and perhaps stall an arms race. For Churchill, delay would serve no purpose. Convinced that the Western position might become weaker, he placed his case before Parliament. "[W]hile I believe there is time for further effort for a lasting peace settlement," he averred, "I cannot feel that it is necessarily a long time, or that its passage will progressively improve our own security." But for Secretary of State Dean Acheson and much of official Washington, the object of diplomacy was not compromise, but the measuring of changing conditions. Settlements, when they came, would simply record the corroding effect of Western power on the ambitions and designs of the Kremlin. Meanwhile, NATO, backed by the power of the United States, would sustain the military division—and thus the stability—of Europe with a vengeance.

Western superiority and unending diplomatic triumphs offered reassurance only to those who believed the Soviet Union well contained, physically and diplomatically. For those whose concern was Soviet ideological expansion, the danger was only emerging. By 1948, the official American world view could detect no visible limits to the Kremlin's expansive power. The National Security Council's study, NSC 7, dated March 30, 1948, defined the Soviet challenge in global terms. "The ultimate objective of Soviet-directed world communism," the document warned, "is the domination of the world. To this end, Soviet-directed world communism employs against its victims in opportunistic coordination the complementary instruments of Soviet aggressive pressure from without and military revolutionary subversion from within." With its control of international Communism, NSC 7 continued, the USSR had engaged the United States in a struggle for power "from which we cannot withdraw short of national suicide." The more pervading NSC 20/4, approved by the president on November 24, 1948, defined the danger in similar terms: "Communist ideology and Soviet behavior clearly demonstrate that the ultimate objective of the leaders of the USSR is the domination of the world."

Designed specifically to kindle the nation's insecurities, NSC 68, of April 1950, comprised the final and most elaborate attempt of the Truman Cold War elite to define a national defense policy. This document, like its predecessors, described the Soviet danger in global, limitless terms. It concluded that the USSR, "unlike previous aspirants to hegemony, is animated by a new fanatic faith, antithetical to our own, and seeks to impose its absolute authority over the rest of the world." For the Soviets, conflict had become endemic, waged through violent and nonviolent means in accordance with the dictates of expediency. "The issues that face us," NSC 68 continued, "are momentous, involving the...destruction not only of the Republic but of civilization itself." Defeat at the hands of the Soviets would be total. Still, neither NSC 68 nor any of its predecessors offered responses commensurate with the dangers they portrayed; none contemplated the need for, or risk of, war. Washington never confronted the Kremlin directly over its alleged efforts to conquer the globe.

Visions of Falling Dominoes in Asia: 1948–1950

Events in East Asia, where the United States faced two unwanted, powerfully-led Communist revolutions in China and Indochina, seemed to confirm the fears of Soviet expansionism.

Washington officials presumed, logically, that both revolutions were under Kremlin control. The State Department's China experts, in a memorandum of October 1948, concluded that the Soviets, through their alleged role in the coming Communist victory in China, had acquired control of that country as firmly "as in the satellite countries behind the Iron Curtain." The USSR, apparently, had acquired control of China without one soldier. Secretary of State Dean Acheson claimed no less. "The Communist leaders," he declared "have foresworn their Chinese heritage and have publicly announced their subservience to a foreign power, Russia..." With the final Chinese Communist victory in late 1949, NSC 48/1 declared: "The USSR is now an Asiatic power of the first magnitude with expanding influence and interests extending throughout continental Asia and into the Pacific."

With a powerful coterie of American Chinese Nationalist supporters, Chiang Kai-shek's exile to the island of Formosa eliminated the final barrier to the Communist conquest of Asia. This rendered those held responsible for Washington's refusal to launch an effective rescue mission guilty of treason. Among those who shared this absolute, unshakable devotion to the Nationalist cause were businessmen, missionaries, members of Congress, and the press, who had strong ties to the old China that they loved. Their position at the core of American anti-Communism gave them incredible access to the country's fears and emotions. It was left for Senator Joseph McCarthy of Wisconsin to launch the crusade against the alleged Communists in government who were responsible for the demise of China's Nationalist regime. The undying crusade for Chiang's return to the mainland sustained Washington's decision to avoid recognition of the new Communist government. However, for the country's leading China experts—indeed, for the world generally—the Communist triumph in China comprised a genuine national revolution. If the United States' pro-Chiang forces exerted a profound influence on American attitudes and policies toward China, they would learn soon enough that their dominance of the American mind was irrelevant to the course of events in China.

Meanwhile, the supposition of Soviet control over Asia's Communist movements brought the United States into direct confrontation with Ho Chi Minh and the Communist-led struggle for Indochinese independence. Ho assumed command of Indochina's independence movement in 1945 and proclaimed his country's freedom from French rule. When France subsequently re-established its control over its former colony, the United States, in April 1946, announced its support of France. What governed this decision was the evolving U.S. conception of Ho, not as a nationalist seeking the independence of his country, but as a Communist serving the interests of the Kremlin. Secretary of State George C. Marshall, in February 1947, warned Paris that the old empires were doomed, and that the French empire was no exception. "On the other hand," he continued, "we do not lose sight of the fact that Ho Chi Minh has direct Communist connections and it should be obvious that we are not interested in seeing colonial administrations supplanted by [the] philosophy and political organizations emanating from and controlled by the Kremlin." Marshall's rationale for supporting the

French faced a serious challenge from officials in the State Department's Division of Southeast Asian Affairs, as well as U.S. diplomats in East Asia, who argued that Ho was a native nationalist, not tied to the Kremlin, no danger to American security, and destined to win.

In 1949, France, in its search for a native nationalist who could challenge Ho for the support of Indochinese nationalism, selected Bao Dai, former King of Annam, as spokesman of the new state of Vietnam. Some U.S. officials doubted that the maneuver would succeed. It was too late, observed State Department adviser Raymond Fosdick, to establish a cheap substitute for French colonialism in the form of the Bao Dai regime. "For the United States to support France in this attempt," he wrote, "will cost us our standing and prestige in all of Southeast Asia." Because Ho was independent of both Russia and China, there was nothing to be gained by supporting French policy. "Whether the French like it or not," Fosdick predicted, "independence is coming to Indochina. Why, therefore, do we tie ourselves to the tail of their battered kite?" Such predictions of disaster had no chance against the United States' official denial that nationalism was the controlling factor in Vietnam's future. Washington, viewing Ho as an agent of the Kremlin, had eliminated all choices except that of following the French to disaster.

With the French withdrawal in 1954 and the perennial failure of the Vietnamese government in Saigon to rid the country of its Communist-led insurgency, the United States, in 1965, assumed command of the disintegrating struggle to save Vietnam. Meanwhile, the alleged dangers emanating from Vietnam reached eastward across Asia to Europe, as well as throughout the Pacific. Senator Thomas J. Dodd of Connecticut warned the Senate in 1965: "We are again confronted by an incorrigible aggressor, fanatically committed to the destruction of the free world, whose agreements are as worthless as Hitler's. If we fail to draw the line in Viet-Nam, in short, we may find ourselves compelled to draw a defense line as far back as Seattle." For the Joint Chiefs of Staff the war in Vietnam was "a planned phase in the Communist timetable for world domination." Visions of falling dominoes continued to discount the power of nationalism or the individuality of nations that in reality rendered the states of East Asia resistant to external encroachments. No Washington official could define the enemy that, having acquired Saigon, would spread Communist conquest across Asia and the Pacific. If Moscow and Beijing were the enemy, fighting Hanoi in the defense of Saigon was irrelevant. If Hanoi's defeat assured the peace and stability of Asia, what was the meaning of falling dominoes? Hanoi, driven by Vietnamese nationalism, possessed the power and will to unite Vietnam; it possessed neither the power nor the intent to expand across Asia and the Pacific.

American policy in East Asia faced its ultimate test in Korea. When North Korea's Communist forces invaded the South on June 25, 1950, Washington officials presumed logically that the Kremlin ordered the attack. Moscow maintained a powerful, unwanted influence in North Korean affairs. It approved the North Korean invasion reluctantly, and only when Kim Il-song, the North Korean leader, assured an easy victory. The Soviets promised aid and advice, but nothing more. Yet Secretary Acheson, following the attack, addressed a note to the U.S. embassy in Moscow that accused the Soviets of possessing "controlling influence over [the] North Korean regime." The note demanded that the Kremlin press the North Korean authorities to withdraw the invading forces immediately. When the American ambassador advised Washington to avoid any identification of the

USSR with the invasion, President Truman, in his June 27 address, defined the Soviet danger more vaguely: "The attack upon Korea makes it plain beyond all doubt that Communism has passed beyond the use of subversion to conquer independent nations and will now use armed invasion and war." Americans agreed with the president that the North Korean attack, unless challenged, presaged another world war. As U.S. forces entered Korea, Washington officials again presumed that they could defeat the Korean enemy, soon threatening rhetorically all southeast Asia as well as the Pacific, without engaging Soviet military forces.

General Douglas MacArthur, following his success at Inchon, received permission to advance to the Yalu and thereby eliminate the North Korean regime. Soon the administration received warnings from American advisers as well as observers throughout Asia that MacArthur's advance would bring China into the war. Again Washington refused to confront the Kremlin when it attributed the predicted Chinese invasion, in late November 1950, to Soviet influence and expansionism. Acheson warned the country in a nationwide radio address on November 29: "Those who control the Soviet Union and the international Communist movement have made clear their fundamental design." Truman declared the following day: "We hope that the Chinese people will not continue to be forced or deceived into serving the ends of Russian colonial policy in Asia." Even *The New York Times* proclaimed on December 8: "The Chinese Communist dictatorship will eventually go down in history as the men who sold out their country to the foreigners, in this case the Russians, rather than as those who rescued China from foreign 'imperialism'." Supported by that terrifying judgment, East Asia would long remain the core of the Cold War, where the United States continued to face such perennial antagonists as North Vietnam, China, and the Soviet Union.

Containment and Coexistence: 1960s–1990

By the mid-1960s, the continuing Cold War, especially in Asia, faced rejection amid the changing realities of international life. Europe had long recovered from the damages of war and had achieved levels of wealth and prosperity unprecedented in its history. Its very stability erased fears of Soviet aggression. The earlier crises over Berlin had long become history. The USSR and China, the Communist giants, had become the world's most bitter rivals, demonstrating that a Communist bloc no longer existed. Revolts behind the Iron Curtain demonstrated the reality that Soviet power and influence in Eastern Europe was limited. Finally, the rhetoric of Soviet expansionism, driven by the alleged quest for world domination, was never reflected in actual Soviet behavior. Through the decades of Cold War, the USSR expanded nowhere through force. Wherever a Soviet presence appeared outside Europe, it did so by invitation. Whatever the anti-Communist warnings that the Communist and non-Communist worlds could not coexist, in actuality they coexisted with sufficient success to create one of the world's golden ages. The two foundations of Western policy—containment and coexistence—emerged triumphant.

Much of the United States' predominant realism had become soft, emphasizing less the demands of security and defense than the need of accommodation with the realities of coexistence. European stability and Asian nationalism presented few options beyond maximizing international relationships in a divided, but fundamentally unchallenging world. Convinced that previous administrations had exaggerated the Soviet threat, President James Earl (Jimmy) Carter set out, in 1977, to establish a more relaxed, flexible, non-ideological relationship with both China and the USSR. After the American failure in Vietnam, the country could no longer maintain the illusion of global power. Carter responded by lessening the strategic importance of Asia, Africa, and Latin America. Nationalism, he believed, limited both Soviet and American influence in the Third World. In his Notre Dame speech of May 1977, he rejected the traditional notion that American interests were global. "Being confident of our own future," he said, "we are now free of that inordinate fear of communism which once led us to embrace any dictator who joined us in that fear." Dismissing the Cold War commitment to global containment, Carter accepted Soviet activity in the Afro-Asian world with profound indifference.

But the Soviet Union's Leonid Brezhnev, in power since 1964, not only perfected the Soviet structure of centralized power, but also diverted his country's new-found wealth from oil and natural gas into new weaponry. What the enhanced military sophistication contributed to Soviet prestige and ambition remained elusive, but its contrast with Carter's readiness to accommodate Communist Third World advances, especially in Africa, launched many Democrats who had favored the soft realism into an anti-Communist crusade, as neoconservatives, to restore America's Cold War role as the world's defender against Communist expansionism. The neoconservatives found themselves aligned with the traditional Republican anti-Communist right. This counterattack on the notion of a receding Cold War received added impetus from CIA director George H.W. Bush, who appointed an outside-government panel to prepare an estimate of Soviet intentions. The Team B report embraced a somber view of the Soviet danger. Carter, finding little merit in the report, ignored it. Another group, the Committee on the Present Danger (CPD), was in the vanguard of those who shared Team B's dread of Soviet power. Members of the press joined the attack on Carter's alleged vacillation and weakness, while much of the country's foreign policy elite challenged the Team B and CPD predictions of doom.

Already facing open challenges to its alleged loss of will, the Carter administration reacted to the Soviet invasion of Afghanistan, in late December 1979, with bewilderment and rage. On January 4, the president revealed his new anti-Soviet mood to the nation. "A Soviet-occupied Afghanistan," he declared, "threatens both Iran and Pakistan, and is a stepping stone to possible control over much of the world's oil supplies." Soviet dominance over Afghanistan and adjacent countries, he warned, would threaten "the stable, strategic and peaceful balance of the entire world." Actually, the Soviets, recognizing the nature of their Afghan opposition, were already seeking an escape. But the widespread assumption that the Soviet invasion of Afghanistan exposed south and southeast Asia to further Soviet encroachment pushed American hawkishness to a new high. Again the new mood of insecurity did not capture all Americans. Many analysts could detect no Soviet threat to the oil fields and sea lanes of the Middle East, or to world peace. For them, the occupation of Afghanistan was, in itself, no measure of Soviet intentions toward the regions beyond.

Ronald Reagan caught the country's post-Afghanistan alarms at full tide, embellished them, and rode them to victory. He entered office in January 1991, with an advisory team committed to the recovery of the country's global leadership. Despite the new administration's tough rhetoric and massive military expansion, it maintained the defense posture of previous administrations. It made no effort to recover the alleged losses of the Carter years—in Afghanistan or elsewhere. Even before Reagan's inauguration, the Soviet Union had entered its long, predictable disintegration that, in 1985, produced Mikhail Gorbachev and the possibility of a genuine U.S.–Soviet détente, one which Reagan and Gorbachev achieved in their four summits. The processes of Soviet disintegration culminated in the collapse of the Soviet satellite empire in Eastern Europe in 1989, and exit from the Cold War during the following year. Reagan supporters attributed the Soviet collapse to the rhetorical toughness and military buildup of the Reagan years. For Soviet experts, the Communist regime's collapse flowed naturally from its internal flaws, its political erosion, and its ideological rejection. After forty years, the Cold War died quietly and without celebration.

Norman Graebner

I. THE COLD PEACE, 1917–1940

The Great War of 1914–1918 witnessed drastic political and economic changes in Europe that also had an impact on America. Russia entered World War I under Nicholas II but ended with a Bolshevik government led by Vladimir Lenin and later Josef Stalin. In contrast, the American republic in the 1780s was born into a world governed by monarchs, while Russia's Communists emerged in a world dominated by capitalists. During the late eighteenth century, Americans believed democracy was the wave of the future, while in the early twentieth century the Bolsheviks were certain that socialism would overthrow the capitalist-imperialist governments and create egalitarian societies. These contrasting political views dominated American-Soviet relations during the next twenty years of the Cold Peace and later.

After the Bolsheviks seized power, they signed the Brest-Litovsk peace treaty with Germany—a move leading to an Allied intervention in Northern Russia, the Crimea, and Siberia. These interventions left a lasting impression on the Communist leaders; Stalin often looked back to those days during the World War II negotiations about the future boundaries of the Soviet Union.

America's domestic reaction to Bolshevism prompted its first "Red Scare" of 1919–1920 that briefly threatened the nation's cherished civil liberties. During the labor unrest of the 1870s and 1880s, many American business and political leaders feared that socialists, anarchists, and union activists threatened the nation's traditional values. After Russia's Bolshevik government emerged, the antiradical American attitude solidified as an anti-Communist one because many Americans feared that socialists, radicals, and labor organizers were inspired, if not led, by Communism. This belief led many Americans to fear that foreign Communism would subvert American society.

In spite of the 1918–1919 influenza epidemic that led to one-fourth of all Americans catching the flu, and nearly a half million dying, the United States recovered from the Great War with its basic economy intact. Although the farmers experienced a sharp decline during the mid-1920s, the economy did not collapse until the Great Depression of 1929.

In contrast, postwar Russia was exhausted and devastated from the Great War, the subsequent civil war and Allied interventions, and the Russo-Polish conflict. These events caused Russia to lose Bessarabia, Estonia, Finland, Latvia, and Lithuania, in addition to the Polish provinces and parts of White Russia. According to James Libbey's *American-Russian Economic Relations*

> The loss of these regions contributed to the 80% drop in factory output and the 63% decline in farm production between 1914 and 1920. Cotton cultivation, for example, plummeted 95%, closing down major segments of the textile industry. The railroad network crumbled, delaying the shipment of raw materials, components, and fuels, disrupting the work of factories and accelerating the economy's downward spiral.
>
> (Libbey, *American-Russian Economic Relations, 1770s–1990s* [1989])

America's only assistance to Russia occurred when Herbert Hoover organized a famine relief operation during 1921–1922. This momentary act of cooperation was followed by the United States' refusal to recognize the Soviet Union until November 1933. Commercial activities continued between the two countries during the uneasy 1920s and 1930s, but without the active support of the American government.

Although Russia's economy suffered after the civil war, the Bolsheviks began as early as March 1919 to express their revolutionary fervor by forming the Third Communist International (Comintern), to direct local Communist parties. Comintern members could form alliances and shift Soviet policies, provided that, as Adam Ulam noted, "the given Communist Party always retained its organizational separateness and its allegiance to the Soviet republic." Consequently, the Comintern aided or joined revolutionary movements in Europe and Asia. After Stalin gained control, a significant change took place in Comintern policies through his emphasis on the idea of "socialism in one country." This did not mean, as Ulam points out, "the abandonment of world Communism, still less leaving the foreign Communists to their own devices. But it meant the subjugation, this time unequivocal, of the interests of the world movement to those of Soviet Russia." Differences arose between the Soviet foreign ministry and the Comintern's international affairs branch that sometimes led to serious contradictions in Soviet foreign affairs.

As World War II approached in the 1930s, President Franklin D. Roosevelt recognized the Soviet government and the two countries exchanged ambassadors, but United States policies often were at odds with the Soviet Union. During the Spanish Civil War, the Soviets assisted the Loyalist government, whereas the United States advocated a neutralist policy that actually aided Franco's Fascist forces, which were backed by Germany and Italy. Because Stalin's policies emphasized the security of the Soviet Union, he negotiated defensive pacts with various European nations such as France and Czechoslovakia. During the spring of 1939, President Roosevelt urged Britain to conclude an alliance with the Soviet Union as a bulwark against Adolph Hitler. However, two factors prevented Britain from making that alliance. First, Prime Minister Neville Chamberlain responded slowly because he believed Hitler would use an alliance with Russia as an excuse to drag Britain into a war that the British public would not support. Second, neither the British nor French were willing to agree to the terms Stalin now demanded—the return of the territories lost during World War I.

Consequently in 1939, Stalin joined with Hitler in the infamous Nazi-Soviet pact, much to the disappointment of the Western nations. Meanwhile, as war broke out in Europe in 1939, Roosevelt gradually began shifting from a policy of neutrality to one of opposing the Axis powers through a lend-lease program.

1917

March 15, 1917

Czar Nicholas II abdicates in favor of his brother Michael, who abdicates on March 16 in favor of Prince Lvov.

The Russian czar abdicated because the nation's economy and government broke down during the winter of 1916–1917. Strikes, riots, and a troop mutiny in Petrograd (St. Petersburg was renamed in 1914) led to the formation of a provisional government under Prince George Lvov, to whom Michael gave authority on March 16. The new government included Paul Miliukov, a Constitutional Democrat; Alexander Guchkov, an Octobrist; and Alexander Kerensky, a Socialist.

The Allies feared the prospect of Russia leaving the war because Germany would be able to move several fresh divisions to the western front for a new offensive. President Wilson learned about the revolution on March 15, and on March 22, American Ambassador David R. Francis formally recognized the provisional government of Alexander Kerensky. On March 18, the provisional government of Kerensky accepted the Allied urging to continue the war against Germany. For Russia, this was an unpopular and fatal decision. The new Russian government's commitment to continue the war placed an unbearable strain on the economy as well as prevented social and political reform.

March 22, 1917

The kaiser declares he cannot negotiate further with America.

Because of rumors that there would be neutral rights negotiations, the German Foreign Office told newsmen there would be no talks by Germany. The rumors came from Vienna, Austria, which still had relations with the United States.

The Berlin message of March 22 stated that the submarine war would be pushed aggressively. American ships in the war zone would have the same risks as any other ships. The message quoted the kaiser as saying, "Now, once and for all, an end to negotiations with America. If Wilson wants war, let him make it, and let him have it."

April 2, 1917

President Wilson calls for a declaration of war against Germany: Congress complies on April 6.

By the middle of March 1917, more and more Americans had reached the opinion that war against Germany appeared necessary. President Wilson moved to this decision only slowly and reluctantly. He knew the Allied war objectives were little better than those of Germany, but he also understood that the democracies would revert to a less militaristic stance after the war whereas the aggressive nature of the Prussian General Staff might continue if it were not defeated.

Public reaction to the news of German attacks on three U.S. ships between March 12 and March 18 convinced Wilson and his cabinet members that war had to be declared. The *Algonquin* was the first American steamer sunk by a German submarine without warning on March 12. No lives were lost, however. Then in quick succession news of the sinking of the *City of Memphis* (March 17), the *Illinois* (March 18), and the *Vigilancia* (March 18) reached American newspapers and an outburst of public demonstrations ensued. On March 22, 12,000 people at Madison Square Garden in New York City cheered for war at a rally of the American Rights Committee. On March 31, thousands paraded at a Philadelphia meeting, while other mass meetings took place in Chicago, Boston, Denver, and Manchester, New Hampshire. The Socialist Eugene Debs and former Secretary of State William Jennings Bryan were among the small minority denouncing the war fever.

While aware that it was best to act at the proper psychological moment, Wilson considered the situation carefully; first in solitude, later, on March 20, in a cabinet meeting. Exactly when he decided to ask for war is uncertain. That all cabinet members supported a declaration of war made the decision less difficult. Even two longtime peace advocates, Secretary of the Navy Josephus Daniels and Postmaster General Albert Burleson, spoke in favor of war. The most eloquent speech favoring war may have been Secretary of State Robert Lansing's. The secretary had favored war against Germany for several months and believed that now the president had reached the best time to act. Wilson's valiant effort at armed neutrality had failed; Germany had carried out its submarine warfare as announced on January 31. In addition, Lansing believed the recent Russian overthrow of autocracy and the statements of German liberals against the vast power of the kaiser and General Staff indicated that forces of liberal democracy were appearing and the United States could lead this alignment for future peace.

Following the cabinet session of March 20, Wilson called for a special session of Congress on April 2. But he was still considering exactly what action he could ask for and how. By March 28, he decided that the United States had to join the Allies in war to end Germany's autocracy and enable the United States to become a leader of postwar peace efforts. These were the underlying themes of the president's April 2 speech to Congress, in which he asked for a declaration of war.

Wilson made his speech to a joint session of Congress at 8:30 P.M. on April 2. Reviewing events since February 1, Wilson pointed out that Germany had made submarine war against neutral commerce, an act against all humankind. The United States, he said, could not submit to the German attacks, and armed neutrality did not function unless U.S. ships could shoot submarines on sight. Thus, the acts of the German government were in fact "war against the government and people of the United States," and America must accept the "status of belligerent which thus has been thrust upon it." The president called for measures to help other governments at war with Germany, to mobilize U.S. resources, and to expand the armed forces "preferably through universal liability to service." The U.S. war aims were to vindicate peace and justice and establish a concert of power among the world's free peoples. He argued that America's quarrel was with the few German leaders, not with the German people, who were pawns of their ambitious leaders. "We have no selfish ends to serve," Wilson declared, we desire no conquest, no indemnities, and no material compensation. "We are but one of the champions of the rights of mankind" and will be satisfied when these are made secure. We shall fight for things "nearest our hearts, for democracy, for the right of those who submit to authority to have a voice in their own Governments," for a concert of free people to make "the world itself at last free."

There was never any doubt that Congress would support the president. On April 4, the Senate approved the war resolution by a vote of 82 to 6, as only five senators spoke against the war. The House discussions took longer because over 100 congressmen wanted to speak in favor of the war, while only 20 spoke in opposition. The House voted on April 6 to favor war

President Woodrow Wilson before Congress, announcing the break in official relations with Germany. National Archives

by 373 to 50. Soon after, a messenger brought the resolution to the White House, where Wilson signed the act immediately at 1:18 P.M. President Wilson then signed a proclamation announcing the declaration of war against Germany as an Associate of the Western allies. He adopted the term "Allied Associated Powers" because he believed Americans were prejudiced against foreign alliances.

War was not declared against Austria-Hungary until December 7, 1917.

April 7, 1917

American Socialist leaders gather for an emergency meeting.

The day after the United States declared war on Germany, socialist leaders such as Eugene Debs met in St. Louis to denounce the conflict as imperialism and promise "continuous, active, and public opposition to the war." This pronouncement gave rise to a renewed antiradicalism propelled by an intolerant American majority and allowed persecution of the radical left, especially the International Workers of the World (IWW), under the Espionage Act of June 1917 that is amended to add the Sedition Act of May 1918.

April 14, 1917

A Committee on Public Information is established by executive order of the president to unite the nation behind the war front.

The president appointed journalist George Creel to chair the Committee on Public Information, which included the secretaries of state, war, and the navy. Later Secretary of State Lansing had difficulties with Creel's aggressive propaganda tactics because he interfered with the State Department's news releases and tried to set up independent American propaganda agencies in foreign countries. As the war went on, the committee became controversial because many observers believed Creel went too far in "censoring" news and "playing" with the truth.

May 15, 1917

The Petrograd Soviet issues a peace proposal, appealing to socialists of all countries.

In contrast to the provisional government's decision to remain in the war, the Russian Communist Party leader Nikolai Lenin and the Petrograd Soviet advocated immediate peace. The Soviet peace formula may be summarized in one of its sentences: "Peace without annexation or indemnities on the basis of self-determination of peoples is the formula adopted unreservedly by the proletarian mind and heart." The Soviet called for a peace conference of socialists of all belligerent nations to form a future world peace.

Nikolai Lenin. National Archives

In 1917, some commentators believed the Soviet's formula was inspired by Woodrow Wilson's appeal to the people of Europe in January 1917. Wilson, of course, believed democratic liberalism, not Communism, was the best political means to achieve these ends.

May 18, 1917

The Selective Service Act provides for recruitment of American men into the armed forces.

The Selective Service Act provided for the registration and drafting into service of men between 21 and 35 years of age. Later, on September 23, 1918, the registration age was changed to be between 18 years and 48 years. In the first registration on June 5, 1917, 9,586,508 men had registered; a year later another 1 million 21 year olds were added. After the change in ages in 1918, another 13,228,762 men enrolled.

During the war, the U.S. army expanded from 200,000 soldiers to over 4 million soldiers. The U.S. navy's wartime strength was 500,000. A total of 2,084,000 U.S. soldiers served in France at some time, with 1,390,000 seeing active combat duty. The American Expeditionary Force was commanded by General John J. Pershing. U.S. naval forces in Europe were commanded by Admiral William S. Sims. The navy convoyed troop and merchant ships, chased submarines, and assisted the British fleet in the North Sea.

May 26, 1917

Elihu Root is appointed head of a special U.S. delegation to visit Russia and give encouragement to the provisional government.

Secretary of State Lansing suggested a special mission to Russia on April 9, as part of an Allied attempt to maintain Russia's participation in the war. Britain and France had each sent delegations, and the American group could meet the new leaders of Russia and personally examine their situation. Characteristically, while Paris and London sent pro-war socialists to represent their views, Wilson wanted to send persons from every walk of life in America. As a former secretary of state, Root held satisfactory credentials, but was not sympathetic to recent developments in Russia. For the rest of the U.S. delegation, Wilson chose, among others, James Duncan, vice president of the American Federation of Labor, and Charles Russell, a right-wing socialist.

Following a four-week visit to Petrograd in July, the Root mission returned to the United States in August and made several recommendations that focused on the German danger in Russia. Alexander Kerensky, who became the leader of the provisional government in July 1917, emphasized this to the American and European delegates as a means for generating support and loans from the Western powers.

Among the Root mission suggestions were (1) an educational campaign to persuade the Russian people to stay in the war and preserve democracy. (The Germans spent $3 million a month for intrigue in Russia. The United States should spend at least $5.5 million over one year through the Committee for Public Information for a news, film, leaflet, advertising, and speaking service); and (2) an effort to build the morale of the Russian army. The 13 million men in the (Russian?) army had never had an organization such as the Young Men's Christian Association to assist their physical, mental, social, and moral betterment. This was the largest area where the United States could help the Russian people, according to the Root mission.

In brief, the Root mission sought a long-range solution to an immediate Russian problem. The mission did not seem to have realized the complete breakdown of the social order; Russia had evolved that social order over the previous one hundred years. Opposed to the Root report, Secretary of State Lansing expressed a concern that, similar to prior revolutions, Russia's provisional government would be overthrown by a military group. To support Kerensky's government, Lansing and the U.S. minister to Russia, David R. Francis, helped arrange $325 million of loans from America between April and November 1917.

The provisional government failed to solve Russia's critical economic problems, however. The decision to continue to fight Germany and the government's failure to institute significant reforms caused its gradual loss of support in Petrograd.

June 15, 1917

The United States passes an Espionage Act to punish and eliminate disloyal or treasonable activity.

This new law stated that persons found guilty of aiding the enemy, obstructing army recruitment or causing troop insubordination, acting disloyally, or refusing service in the armed forces could be fined up to $10,000 and imprisoned for 10 years. Unfortunately, the application of this statute and its frequent revisions (See May 16, 1918) was handled unwisely by overzealous federal district attorneys who delegated several functions of the law to the American Protective League, an official recognized auxiliary. The League consisted of some 250,000 reactionaries who often exceeded orders or engaged "in illegal arrests and searches, impersonation of federal officers, and irresponsible propaganda activities." (See Robert K. Murray, *Red Scare: A Study in National Hysteria, 1919–1920* [1955]).

This statute also provided for government censorship that bore most heavily on left-wing radicals, the IWW, anarchists, and socialists, who opposed the war on philosophical grounds. Postmaster General Albert S. Burleson, could—and did—prohibit use of the mail to newspapers, periodicals, and other publications that allegedly printed treasonable or seditious material. A maximum penalty of five years' imprisonment or a $5,000 fine, or both, was established for attempting to use the mails for distribution of the prohibited materials. Burleson used censorship to destroy the left-wing press, and by September 1918 he had denied mailing privileges to twenty-two Socialist newspapers. (See H.C. Peterson and G.C. Fite, *Opponents of War, 1917–1918* [1957]).

July 19, 1917

The German Reichstag passes a peace resolution.

The peace resolution of July 19 showed the strength of Germany's liberal and socialist parties but did not affect the German kaiser or his ministers. The resolution also indicated the end of Chancellor Bethmann-Hollweg's coalition ministry of center parties that was formed in August 1914. At that time the 110 members of the left-wing Social Democrat Party (SPD) joined the coalition as a method of fighting autocratic Russia and liberalizing the German government. The Russian Revolution of March 1917 ended the work of the Chancellor's coalition on the SPD, and, during the spring of 1917, German parties in the Reichstag realigned. Philipp Scheidemann, the SPD spokesman, united with the Center Party of Matthias Erzberger and the Progressive People's Party of Friedrich von Payer to gain a majority in the Reichstag.

In addition to forming a committee to study constitutional reform, the new coalition overthrew Bethmann's ministry in early July and passed the July 19 peace resolution in an attempt to change German policy. The peace resolution stated the German people were only fighting in self-defense and Germany would not attempt to annex territory or oppress other peoples. The resolution also advocated freedom of the seas and "economic peace." Finally, the resolution stated: "The Reichstag will actively promote the creation of an International Law Organization." Unfortunately, the constitution of 1871 did not make the German kaiser or his ministry responsible to the Reichstag. When Bethmann was overthrown, William II appointed a safe Nationalist Party member, Georg Michaelis, as chancellor. The executive branch controlled the government and opposed the Peace Resolution. In July 1917, German liberals finally realized that Germany had one of Europe's most autocratic governments.

September 2, 1917

President Wilson asks Colonel House to create a group of experts to study problems for a satisfactory peace settlement—"The Inquiry."

Throughout the summer of 1917, many groups and individuals in Europe and America suggested a variety of proposals to establish a more peaceful world when World War I ended. Therefore, on September 2, the president told Colonel House that a group should systematically survey what different parties to the war expected in a peace agreement to enable America to formulate its position and "begin to gather the influences we may employ" from knowledge of other ideas.

In response to Wilson's request, House formed a group known as The Inquiry. Chaired by President Sidney E. Mezes of the College of the City of New York, the group included Dr. Isaiah Bowman, the director of the American Geographic Society; Walter Lippmann, from the staff of the New Republic; David Hunter Miller, an international legal expert; and two history professors, Charles Seymour and James T. Shotwell. For the group's most significant report see December 22, 1917.

October 6, 1917

The Trading with the Enemy Act prohibits commerce with enemy nations and permits the takeover of alien property in the United States.

This law empowered the president to embargo imports and to establish censorship for material passing between America and any foreign nation. It also created the Office of Alien Property Custodian to oversee the possession and disposal of property held in the United States by residents of enemy nations.

November 7, 1917

The Bolshevik Revolution in Russia overthrows the provisional government of Kerensky.

Led by Nikolai Lenin, the Bolshevik revolution began on November 6 (October 24 by the old-style Russian calendar) when Soviet troops arrested members of the provisional government and took over their offices; Kerensky escaped but failed to organize a successful resistance. On November 7, the Second All-Russian Congress of Soviets gave all power to the Bolshevik Party. One slogan of the new government was "peace at any price," and the government sought to end the war with Germany as early as possible. Lenin had returned to Russia from exile in Switzerland on April 16 and organized the Bolsheviks to oppose the provisional government.

The Bolsheviks demanded "peace, land, and bread," reforms that the more moderate provisional leaders refused to institute until the war was over. Kerensky had replaced Prince Lvov as head of the government on July 20, but Kerensky's willingness to remain in the war was contrary to the wishes of most Russians. The events of November 6–7 ended Kerensky's regime.

Once the Bolsheviks were in power, Lenin became leader of the ruling council and appointed Leon Trotsky as commissar of foreign affairs.

November 8, 1917

Russia's Bolshevik government issues a peace decree to "all belligerent peoples and their governments."

The peace decree of Lenin's new regime represented two parts of the Bolshevik strategy for maintaining control in Russia and enlisting socialist revolution in other parts of the world. First, together with the Land Decree of the same day, it represented the practical, immediate Russian need to end the war at any cost so that social, political, and economic order could be restored within the country. Second, it represented the Bolshevik expectation that to succeed in Russia, Communism had to be supported by the class-conscious proletariat of Western Europe. As orthodox

Marxists, both Lenin and Trotsky believed that as Europe's most backward industrial nation, Russia had advanced beyond its masses' political consciousness. Following the Petrograd Formula of May 15, 1917, the Bolsheviks urged workers of other nations to demonstrate for peace, overthrow their bourgeois governments, and form socialist regimes.

The Peace Decree of November 8 bore remarkable similarities to President Wilson's "peace without victory" concept. The Bolshevik decree called for a general peace conference, the conduct of "negotiations absolutely open before the entire people," and no territorial annexations in Europe or "in distant lands beyond the seas." On November 27, Trotsky elaborated on specific aspects of the decree before a group of Allied military attachés in Petrograd. His main points included:

1. Russia desired general peace but would make a separate peace if the Allies refused.
2. Immediate armistice negotiations should begin.
3. If Allied governments did not respond to the decrees, Russia would appeal to the people of the nations at war.

Because the Allies refused to recognize the Bolshevik peace program, Lenin undertook separate talks with Germany. As Russia's commissar of foreign affairs, Trotsky led a campaign to aid foreign Communist parties in subverting their governments and advocating peace. His methods were not secret because he wanted the world to know the Communists' ideological objectives. His decrees denounced secret diplomacy and released documents of the czarist foreign office that disclosed the secret territorial ambitions of the capitalist powers. Trotsky contended that the secret decrees demonstrated that the Allied and German statements about the war were "lies" that betrayed their citizens. The publication of the Allies' secret treaties began on November 23, 1917.

November 25, 1917

Rejecting the Bolshevik government of Russia, President Wilson continues to accept the provisional government's ambassador, Boris Bakhmetev.

The Wilson administration refused to accept the Bolshevik regime in Petrograd, recognizing Ambassador Bakhmetev as the representative of Russia. On November 11, Bakhmetev informed newsmen that he did not represent the Bolsheviks because they were but a temporary aberration. He believed that the liberal groups in Russia would soon regain control. Wilson concurred and on November 25 announced that the United States recognized Bakhmetev's official status. Wilson argued that the Soviet coup was illegal and did not represent the majority of Russia's people.

Even as Lenin solidified his power in Russia, Wilson and, later, President Warren Harding, continued to recognize Bakhmetev as "ambassador of the Russian people." Bakhmetev became custodian of $56 million of the provisional government's funds at the First National City Bank of New York. Initially he used these funds to send nonmilitary goods to both Bolshevik and anti-Bolshevik groups in Russia. Later, however, he purchased military supplies that were sent to Admiral Alexandr Kolchak and other "White" army leaders who sought to overthrow the Bolsheviks (Reds).

Bakhmetev continued to serve as Russia's "representative" until June 1922. After he resigned, the State Department recognized neither the Russian government nor the Union of Soviet Socialist Republics until 1933.

December 3, 1917

Russia begins peace negotiations with the Central Powers at Brest-Litovsk.

Because the Allied powers ignored the Bolshevik peace decree of November 8, Lenin contacted German leaders and arranged an armistice and peace conference for the eastern front of the war. The peace conference with Russia, Austria, and Germany opened on December 3.

At the opening meeting at Brest-Litovsk, the Soviet delegation, headed by Adolf Joffe, submitted six points as the basis of negotiations, summarized as follows:

1. No forcible annexation of territory;
2. Political independence to be restored to people backing independence;
3. Referendums to be conducted for self-determination of a national government, the vote to be free to all residents of a territory;
4. Minority rights to cultural independence and administrative autonomy to be guaranteed;
5. No war indemnities, and private losses to be paid by a fund raised in all belligerent countries;
6. Colonial questions to be settled according to points 1 through 4 above.

Joffe also insisted that conference sessions be open to the public.

December 22, 1917

The Inquiry—organized to advise Wilson on war aims—reports on territorial issues and the politics of war aims.

The Inquiry was formed on September 2, 1917, and its experts completed their most important report for the president by December 22. It was presented to Wilson on January 4, enabling him to consult it while preparing his 14 points address on January 8, 1918. The report indicated that there was a "universal longing for peace" among the common people of the world, who disliked the old diplomacy of secret treaties and armed forces. In addition, it said there was a great hope for a league of nations. Liberals and progressives in the United States and Europe should "show the way" not only in obtaining a better peace but as an "invaluable support for their internal domestic troubles."

Thus, the group's report encouraged Wilson to advocate the liberal idea of a peace designed to aid the people of the world in resolving national and international social and economic goals.

1918

January 5, 1918

Prime Minister Lloyd George announces British war aims.

In a speech to labor union delegates, David Lloyd George indicated that Great Britain recognized a need for a postwar organization to limit armaments and prevent war.

January 8, 1918

France requests American cooperation with an Allied intervention in Siberia: Wilson refuses.

Although on January 1, the British had telegraphed a request to Wilson to consider landing forces at Vladivostok, the French ambassador made the first formal request for American cooperation in Siberia on January 8. French Ambassador Jules Jusserand requested U.S. aid because he said the Bolsheviks committed atrocities in Irkutsk against Russians who were loyal to the war effort. In reality, France and Britain feared the Russians would make a separate peace with Germany. In addition to endangering the large Allied loans made to the czar, a separate peace would permit Germany to shift soldiers from the eastern to the western front in Europe. Wilson considered Jusserand's request, but on January 16 informed the French that America could not support a Siberian intervention. The French request was the first of a series of Allied attempts to persuade Wilson to join an intervention in Russia.

Initially, Wilson's policy on the Russian problem was stated as point six in his Fourteen Points of January 8, 1918.

January 8, 1918

Wilson's 14 points define his views of Allied war aims.

Wilson's speech to Congress on January 8 outlined America's 14 peace objectives in the context of recent developments in Europe and especially in Russia. Since March 1917, liberal and socialist groups had proposed their "new diplomacy" in contrast to the aggressive and militaristic objectives of European warfare.

The German Reichstag resolution of July 19, 1917, the Petrograd Peace Formula of May 15, 1917, and in particular the Bolshevik statement of November 8, 1917 encouraged Wilson to state the position of liberal democracy in future world relations. British and French officials had been reluctant to state their war aims although the Bolshevik's publication of their secret wartime agreements placed pressure on the Allies to assert their peace concepts to answer Trotsky's and Joffe's statements. After Lloyd George's speech to the British labor unions on January 5 established some liberalization of Allied war aims, Wilson considered canceling his speech. Colonel House convinced him to proceed so that Wilson could become the "spokesman for the liberals of the world."

Wilson's speech to Congress began by reviewing recent diplomatic developments. Referring to the Brest-Litovsk negotiations and the Bolshevik statement of peace principles, Wilson criticized the German-Austrian delegates at Brest-Litovsk because they followed a spirit of "conquest and subjugation." Before the Allies made peace with the Central Powers, they needed to know if the German-Austrian delegates spoke "for the Reichstag majority or the military party and the men whose creed is imperial domination." Wilson appealed to the democratic and moderate Germans to rally the people for peace and not permit the socialists to gain control of the peace process.

Drawing on these introductory remarks, Wilson enunciated a program to make the world "fit and safe to live in" for every "peace-loving nation." "All the peoples of the world," he said, "are in effect partners in this interest... The program of the world's peace, therefore, is our program; and that program is the only possible program, as we see it." Point 6 of Wilson's 14 points stated there should be an "evacuation of all Russian territory" and the settlement of Russian questions in free cooperation with other nations to give Russia "an unhampered and unembarrassed opportunity for the independent determination of her own political developments," and to "assure her of a sincere welcome into the society of free nations under institutions of her own choosing." The treatment of Russia by her "sister nations" will be "the acid test of their good will" as separate "from their own interests, and of their intelligent and unselfish sympathy."

American principles, Wilson declared, were based on peace and justice for all peoples and nationalities. The weak and the strong should, he concluded, live on equal terms of "liberty and safety with one another."

January 20, 1918

The Russian Constituent Assembly is dissolved.

The Bolsheviks ordered the Russian Constituent Assembly dissolved after they won only 168 of the 703 seats being contested. This action, and the results of the election, led some Americans, including President Wilson, to believe the Bolshevik government lacked popular support and would soon disappear.

January 28, 1918

A last-chance Allied-Soviet alliance is attempted.

The assistant U.S. military attaché in Petrograd, Captain E. Francis Riggs, informed his superiors in Washington on January 28 that the new Russian government was considering the possibility of reaching an understanding with the United States, France, and Britain to be used against the Germans. On February 18, after the Germans resumed their military advances on the western front, Jacques Sadoul, the French military attaché, succeeded in persuading his government to temporarily suspend their hostility to the Bolsheviks by arguing that cooperation was the only realistic hope of keeping the Russians in the field against the Germans. While the French government authorized Sadoul to investigate the possibility of keeping Russia in the war, it also inquired whether the United States would join the French in their collaboration.

Even though they desired to see the Russians maintain an eastern front, both Secretary Lansing and President Wilson rejected any consideration of collaborating with the French. Lansing was emphatic in opposing the Bolsheviks because he considered them ultimately more dangerous than the Germans in denying national and property rights of the people and promoting worldwide revolution.

See February 22, 1918.

February 10, 1918

Russian government repudiates all Allied debts.

In an apparent effort to distance themselves from the Allies, the Bolshevik government renounced all debts owed to the Allies for wartime aid incurred by all previous Russian governments. These debts included funds the United States had transferred to the Russian Provisional Government. President Wilson notified Secretary of State Lansing that these debts must be acknowledged before he would consider recognition of the new government.

February 19, 1918

The Mexican government decrees that oil is an inalienable natural resource, levying taxes on all oil lands and contracts made before May 1, 1917.

The Mexican constitution of 1917 gave the nation the right to all subsoil resources that included oil (Article 27). Therefore, in addition to taxing oil lands, all prior oil land drilling had to be transformed into concessions for Mexico. British and American companies and their governments protested the Mexican decree but could not effectively act until World War I ended.

American critics soon began to label the Mexican action as the work of local Bolsheviks because they confiscated their earlier grants and claims on the oil land. The American notion of Bolshevik influence in determining Mexican policies on oil grants continued throughout the 1920s.

February 22, 1918

Bolshevik council approves a Red Cross collaboration with the Allies.

Unaware that Wilson and Lansing strongly disapproved of the Bolshevik government, the chief of the Red Cross mission to Russia, Raymond Robbins, continued his efforts to persuade the Bolsheviks to cooperate with the Allies. He appeared to be making some progress. During a contentious session on February 22, the Bolshevik Central Committee voted 6 to 5—with Lenin casting the deciding ballot—to accept military aid from Britain and France.

Thus on the eve of agreeing on a peace treaty with the Germans, Lenin seemed to consider continued fighting against Germany because his military commanders were instructed to prepare their forces for a burnt earth policy should the German forces advance. After signing the Brest-Litovsk Treaty, and before the treaty was considered for ratification by the Soviet Congress, the Bolsheviks used the time to attract Allied support. On March 4, 1918, Leon Trotsky informed U.S. Ambassador David R. Francis that should the peace treaty be ratified the Russians could again take to the field in April or May if Allied military assistance be made available.

Throughout these discussions, Trotsky and Lenin surely understood that the distance and concentration of troops on the western front made it unlikely that the Allies could provide Russia with assistance needed to check any determined German assault. Consequently, they made cautious efforts to determine whether limited cooperation with the Allies was doomed to fail. Contributing to this failure were the vast ideological differences between the Bolsheviks and the Allies.

March 3, 1918

Russia and Germany sign the treaty of Brest-Litovsk to end their war.

The peace negotiations had begun on December 3, 1917, with Adolf Joffe representing Russia's Bolshevik regime. German demands were so severe that on February 10, Russia's commissar of foreign affairs, Trotsky, declared the war over without any peace terms. The Germans renewed the war and after they had advanced to within 100 miles of Petrograd, Lenin insisted that negotiations for a treaty be renewed.

The result was the Treaty of Brest-Litovsk, by which Russia gave up Poland, Lithuania, the Ukraine, the Baltic provinces (Estonia and Latvia), Finland, and Transcaucasia. Later German troops occupied several major Ukrainian cities.

March 6, 1918

Moscow becomes the Russian capital.

Because the Germans' continuing military offensives threatened the capital city of St. Petersburg (later Leningrad), the Bolsheviks relocated the Russian government to Moscow and designated it the capital.

March 11, 1918

President Wilson ignores the Bolshevik government and appeals directly to the Russian people.

Ignoring the possibility of direct negotiations with the Bolshevik government, the president appealed directly to the Russian people. The essence of Wilson's message was that while Americans greatly sympathized with the Russian people for their most difficult times, the U.S. government was not able to offer "the direct and effective aid" it would like to provide. The president implied the Bolsheviks were now allied with the Germans. After Wilson's message was read to the Soviet Congress on March 15, that body voted to support the overthrow of all bourgeoisie governments—including the United States. Gregory Zinoviev, a delegate to the Congress, declared the president's message a slap in the face.

On March 17, the Soviet Congress ratified the Brest-Litovsk Treaty.

April 3, 1918

German forces assist Finns in gaining independence.

German troops landed in Finland on April 8 to support Finns in their quest for independence from the Russian Empire. The German action and their military assistance helped cement relations between the two countries. The recognition of mutual interests between Germans and Finns became evident in the early days of World War II when the Finns sided with the Nazis against the Soviet Union.

May 16, 1918

The U.S. Sedition Act amends the Espionage Act of 1917 to prohibit disloyal language and the promoting of disloyal actions.

The Sedition Act passed in Congress because members of Congress feared that war dissenters were inciting Americans to disloyal actions that could injure the war effort. Under this law sedition was defined to include "false statements interfering with the war; employing disloyal, profane, scurrilous, or abusive language" about the U.S. government, the Constitution, the flag, or the armed forces; urging curtailment of war production; and advocating, teaching, defending, or suggesting disloyal acts.

The Sedition and Espionage acts led to the arrest of many wartime dissenters, especially left-wing radicals who were philosophically opposed to war. Public statements by the administration, even the president, implied these radicals were "friends and partisans of the German Government." This legislation resulted in a series of "free speech" decisions by the U.S. Supreme Court after the war. In *Schenck v. U.S.*, Justice Oliver Wendell Holmes wrote a unanimous court opinion upholding the Espionage Act. By applying the "clear and present danger" ruling to the law, Holmes found that Schenck's pamphlets encouraged resistance to the draft. Holmes argued that free speech is always under restraint, especially in time of war. In the case of *Abrams v. U.S.*, a majority of the court found that pamphlets criticizing the U.S. Expeditionary Force to Siberia fell under the Sedition Act as invoking disloyalty in wartime. Although Justice Holmes dissented in the Abrams case because it was not within the "clear and present danger," Justice John Clarke and the court majority applied the "bad tendency" test to justify Abrams' guilt.

Several hundred people were imprisoned under these laws. Socialist Party leader Eugene Debs, who ran for president five times, was sentenced to 10 years in prison for violating the sedition provisions of the Espionage Act. The administration's dislike of criticism can be found in its continued prosecution under these statutes after November 11, 1918, despite Congress' express desire to terminate them. Indeed, President Wilson vetoed a bill in May 1920 that would have ended the laws.

These statutes, which have been viewed by many scholars as among the most serious infringements on civil liberties in U.S. history, had widespread popular support at the time and intensified the fears that made the first Red Scare possible in 1919.

July 17, 1918

Wilson agrees to send American forces to north Russia and Siberia to protect military stores and assist Czechoslovak soldiers trying to flee Russia through Siberia.

The issue of U.S. intervention in Russia required more and more of President Wilson's time in 1918. Almost every month since January 8, the British or French had requested U.S. aid, but the president refused consistently until late June. He opposed intervention because, as he had stated in point 6 of his 14 points, allowing Russia to settle its own problems was an "acid test" of Western attitudes of good faith toward self-determination. Some of his biographers believe Wilson learned during the Mexican intervention that such actions created more problems than they solved because of nationalistic opposition to foreign forces.

During these same months, Britain and France constantly plotted for a method to intervene against the Bolsheviks and, as they emphasized to Wilson, to maintain a second front against Germany. France especially desired to assist former czarist generals in their effort to defeat the Communist government, and France loaned money to the anti-Bolshevik groups. On December 23, 1917, an Anglo-French agreement divided southern Russia into spheres of action against the "Germans" to aid the former czarists against Lenin's peace plans. The British aided Aleksey Kaledin, who planned a state for the Don Cossacks. This plan faltered on February 11, 1918, when the Cossacks repudiated Kaledin and he committed suicide. The French and British then shifted support first to General Lavr Kornilov, later to General Anatol Denikin. Britain also sent a few troops to Murmansk in northern Russia to protect military stores and to rally anti-Bolshevik and anti-German groups to assist the Allied cause.

The problem facing Anglo-French plans was the lack of British and French soldiers to commit to the intervention in Russia. Thus, they sought troops from the United States and Japan, and even from a Czechoslovak legion that had helped Russia fight the Austrian armies until 1917. The Japanese were eager to move into eastern Asia but preferred not to move unless the United States agreed. Although President Wilson opposed Japanese action, the British persuaded

Tokyo to send a cruiser to Vladivostok on January 12, 1918, to join them in blockading that port. On April 5, following the murder of a Japanese citizen in Vladivostok, a British-Japanese marine force landed to take control of the city. Vladivostok had been a storage area for western supplies to Russia. By 1918, more than 800,000 tons of war matériel had stacked up in Vladivostok because the single track Trans-Siberian Railway overburdened Russia's transportation system. This compared to the 160,000 tons held in north Russia in the spring of 1918.

For Wilson neither the large storage of supplies, the desire to intervene against Lenin, nor Japan's desire to intervene justified Allied action in Russia. By June, however, another development gained Wilson's sympathy for action: the plight of the Czechoslovak Legion in Siberia. The Czech Legion consisted of defectors or prisoners of war from the Austro-Hungarian armies as well as those in the Russian army because they lived in Russian territory in Slovakia before the war. They had formed into one army in the Russian ranks against Germany, but after the Bolshevik Revolution began, the Czech Legion maintained its unity and discipline. It captured stores of arms and munitions that it previously had guarded, and sought some means to evacuate Russia to join the Western armies in France, where they could win independence for Czechoslovakia from both Austria and Russia at the peace conference.

The Czech Legion had been stationed in the Ukraine until 1918, and on March 16 the Soviet commander in Kiev authorized the Czechs to leave for France by way of the Trans-Siberian Railway and Vladivostok. During their journey, Soviet leaders

Vladivostok, Russia. Soldiers and sailors from many nations are lined up in front of the Allies' headquarters building. Note different flags. National Archives

Russia, 1918–1920

often stopped the Czech train but usually allowed it to proceed.

On May 8, however, trouble began for the Czechs. First, the Soviet leaders told them the Allies desired to split their army so that one-half could go to Murmansk. This information was correct because the British hoped the Czechs would assist them in north Russia. The Czech leaders did not believe the Russians because the British had not bothered to send the Czechs direct information. Thus, the Czechs refused to divide and suspected that this was a Soviet attempt to divide and defeat them.

On May 14, the Czechs' suspicions seemed to be confirmed because the Soviets told them to leave the train and disarm. The Soviets stopped their train at the small town of Chelyabinsk, and negotiations began. While the Czech train awaited release, a trainload of Hungarians happened to arrive in the town. The Czechs and Hungarians normally despised each other, but the unexpected visit went well until a Hungarian soldier threw a heavy piece of iron at a Czech and apparently killed him. The Czechs immediately stopped the Hungarian train, captured the Hungarian who threw the iron, and lynched him.

The Czechs refused to be responsible to local rulers for the lynching, and just as trouble brewed, they intercepted a telegram from Moscow in which one of Leon Trotsky's aides ordered the Czechs to be drafted into a labor battalion for the Red Army. Trotsky had ordered that Russia shoot anyone trying to stop the disarming of the Czechs. This series of events caused the Czechs to rebel and fight local Red Army troops. Consequently, although 15,000 Czechs reached Vladivostok on June 25, the remainder of the legion was stalled near Irkutsk. In addition, the Western powers failed to send ships to Siberia to evacuate the Czechs. Some Czechs took control of the city from the British, while others turned back to aid their brothers in central Siberia.

In mid-June 1918, the Czech leader Thomás Masaryk visited President Wilson to describe his nation's desire for independence and the conditions in Siberia. As an articulate liberal democrat, Masaryk gained Wilson's sympathy, and by July 6, Wilson was ready to respond to the Czech pleas for aid. Wilson met with the secretary of war, the army's chief of staff, and the chief of naval operations, and they agreed to use a force of 7,000 Americans and 7,000 Japanese to intervene in Siberia.

Wilson's decision to commit American troops to northern Russia was based on a number of circumstances. During the war, Great Britain sent food and military equipment to Russia by way of Archangel and Murmansk, constructing an 800-mile railway that connected Archangel to the Trans-Siberian Railway near Petrograd. During the summer and fall of 1917, Britain sent 160,000 tons of war matériel to the Russian provisional government in northern Russia and it remained stored there in early 1918. The Russians had not paid for this equipment and Lenin rejected a British offer to exchange food for the military stores in the north.

In February 1918, the Soviet army gained control of Archangel, but at Murmansk the local Soviet was controlled by moderate socialists and cooperated with British Admiral Thomas W. Kemp, who commanded the British naval squadron. On May 24, the Allied Supreme Command at Versailles ordered British troops to take Archangel, and the U.S. navy's cruiser *Olympia* went to Murmansk to assist the movement. In early June, 600 British Royal Marines landed at Murmansk to prepare an attack on Archangel. At this point, in June 1918, the British requested American troops to assist in northern Russia. Wilson agreed provided that the Supreme Allied Commander, Marshal Ferdinand Foch, stated that American troops at Murmansk were critical to the Allied war effort against Germany. Foch made the required statement, and on July 6 Wilson agreed to send U.S. forces to both northern Russia and Siberia.

Wilson's public statement announcing the dispatch of American forces to Russia was made on July 17. This press release gave Wilson's precise reasons for intervention in Russia. The north Russian troops were "to guard the military stores at Kola" in the peninsula where Murmansk was situated. The Americans would not "take part in organized intervention in adequate force from... Murmansk and Archangel." The United States would withdraw its forces if there were developments inconsistent with this policy. Regarding Siberia, Wilson's July 17 statement said that the United States did not intervene to disturb Russia or to win the war against Germany. "The United States could neither take part in such an intervention nor sanction it in principle." The American forces went to Siberia "to help the Czechoslovaks to guard military stores...; and to render such aid as might be acceptable to the Russians." Wilson's memo of July 17 influenced Britain and France less than Wilson desired. In addition, the Japanese considered that Wilson's action approved their intervention in northern China and Siberia to control the Trans-Siberian Railway. Consequently, Japan joined the intervention on its own terms, not Wilson's.

September 1, 1918

General William S. Graves arrives at Vladivostok as Commander of American Forces in Siberia.

Following President Wilson's July 6 decision to commit U.S. troops to Siberia, 9,000 soldiers embarked from the Philippine Islands, arriving at Vladivostok on August 16. About the same time, Japan dispatched forces that by November 11 numbered 72,000, while the British sent 1,000 in August and another 1,000 in December. The Japanese forces took up positions along the Trans-Siberian Railway and the Chinese Eastern Railway between Irkutsk and Vladivostok.

Before leaving Washington, General Graves received instructions on his duties from Secretary of War Newton Baker. He obtained a copy of Wilson's July 17 press release and was told to protect the Czech Legion from German and Austrian prisoners of war but not to interfere in Russia's internal or territorial affairs. The American purpose was to aid the Czechoslovaks and not to intervene against the Soviets. Baker added a final warning: "Watch your step; you will be walking on eggs loaded with dynamite. God bless you and good-bye."

September 4, 1918

American troops arrive at Archangel, not Murmansk, because the British route them to the scene of military action without informing Washington.

In keeping with President Wilson's desire that the north Russian action have a military role under the authority of Supreme Allied Commander Foch, the French general and General Pershing sent 4,500 new American recruits from the 339th Infantry Regiment, the 337th Field Hospital Company, and the 310th Engineer Battalion. As specified by Wilson in his July 17 statement, these troops would protect the military stores at Murmansk but not participate in organized intervention.

The American forces embarked from Newcastle, England, on August 5 under the command of British officers. Before their ship reached Murmansk, the British commander, Major General F. C. Poole, wired the ship's captain, ordering him to go directly to Archangel. The Americans arrived at Archangel on the afternoon of September 4, and within 24 hours approximately one-third of them occupied combat outposts against Bolshevik troops and what the British claimed were their "German Communist officers." Actually, the nearest Germans were in Finland, 500 miles from Archangel. The alleged presence of Germans was part of the British myth that justified military action in north Russia.

General Poole diverted the American troops to Archangel because of developments in that region since June 23, 1918, which had resulted in engagements between British and Bolshevik armies. Late in June, a British patrol riding the railroad south of Murmansk encountered Soviet soldiers *en route* to take control of Murmansk. The British captured the Bolshevik train, disarmed the men, and sent it south once again. Subsequently, the British took over the entire hundred miles of railroad between Murmansk and Kem.

The incident near Murmansk attracted the attention of Lenin, and the Soviets determined they should take control of that city. The Soviet commissar for foreign affairs, Georgy Chicherin, contacted the head of the Murmansk Soviet, Aleksey Yuryev, and demanded that he break with the English, who were to be considered as hostile as the Germans. Yuryev rejected Chicherin's advice, telling the foreign affairs commissar that the English were less evil than the Germans. If Chicherin did not agree, it was only, said Yuryev, because the German ambassador was looking over Chicherin's shoulder. Chicherin became enraged. He denounced Yuryev as an "enemy of the people" and cut off further contact with him. Yuryev and the Murmansk Soviet proceeded to make a formal pact with General Poole, so that the British could claim to act in conjunction with an anti-Soviet in Murmansk.

At Archangel, however, the Bolsheviks had taken over in February 1918, and they began to move the British military stores south to Petrograd as quickly as the spring thaw and Russia's transportation system permitted. Because neither the czar nor the Soviets had paid for these stores, the British wanted to regain them. In May, the Allied War Council planned to transfer half of the Czech Legion from Siberia to Archangel, but this plot failed. Therefore, late in June the British and French decided to capture Archangel. In July, the French sent a battalion to Murmansk, and General Poole proposed to attack Archangel as soon as possible. Poole had contacted a pro-czarist naval officer under the pseudonym Chaplain at Archangel, and Chaplain agreed to stage a rebellion at the same time that British naval units attacked from the sea.

On August 1, the Poole-Chaplain plot succeeded. While an international force of 1,500 British and French and 50 U.S. Marines from the *Olympia* attacked Archangel, Chaplain's supporters carried out a *coup d'état* against the local Soviets. The U.S. Marines and the *Olympia* had come to Murmansk on May 24. The Bolsheviks fled into the forests surrounding Archangel, where they erected barricades to defend themselves from the Allies.

At this moment, the fresh and green American soldiers were diverted from Murmansk by General Poole and arrived at Archangel. One-third were placed

Americans frequently employed reindeer teams in getting about the Archangel region. National Archives

under the command of British General John Finlayson and dispatched on a 100-mile trip by railroad boxcars to the front. Meanwhile, the group of 50 U.S. Marines that had taken part in the original attack on Archangel had seized an engine and railway cars at the suburb of Bakaritsa and chased the Soviet troops down the rail line for 75 miles. The Americans set up a defense line after the Russians burned a railroad bridge that stopped their train.

Although the action by American soldiers at Archangel violated Wilson's directions of July 17, the president did not find out about General Poole's orders until late in October. By that time, Wilson had become engrossed in the armistice discussions and could not immediately protest. The Americans remained in north Russia for another nine months.

September 15, 1918

The Sisson Documents are published, purporting to demonstrate that the leaders of Russia's Bolshevik government—Lenin and Trotsky—are German agents. Although released by the U.S. Committee on Public Information, these documents are later found to be forgeries.

On September 15, newspapers throughout America began printing documents that the Committee on Public Information said demonstrated that Lenin's government was "a German government acting solely in the interests of Germany." Edgar Sisson, a U.S. newsman, visited Petrograd during the winter of 1917–1918, and obtained documents from three sources: (1) from Raymond Robins, an American Red Cross director who found pamphlets being distributed on the streets of Petrograd but did not believe they were authentic; (2) from a Russian newsman, Eugene Semenov (alias Kohn); and (3) from a former czarist army officer, Colonel Samsonov, who claimed to have original documents from the Bolshevik headquarters at the Smolny Institute in Petrograd. The documents given to Sisson by Samsonov were allegedly stolen during a clandestine raid on the Smolny headquarters on the night of March 2–3, 1918.

Believing he held explosive proof regarding German control of the Bolsheviks, Sisson left Petrograd on March 3. He left Russia by going through Finland with a group of refugees, having secreted the documents in the baggage of an unwitting Norwegian courier. The trip was arduous, and Sisson arrived in Washington with the documents on May 6. Sisson delivered the papers to George Creel and Secretary of State Lansing. Lansing decided not to release them to the public until the "proper" time. Subsequently, the papers were released in September when President Wilson ordered Creel to let American newspapers print them.

The Sisson papers were released without consulting with the State Department. Some U.S. Foreign Service officers doubted their authenticity. Secretary Lansing stated that he had preferred to wait to release them until a time that would damage the German war effort. Exactly how and why Wilson released the papers is not certain. Creel's committee arranged their distribution. Probably the president desired further support for his July decision to send U.S. troops to Russia.

The publication of the documents appeared to confirm the rumor that Lenin and Trotsky acted on behalf of Germany. There appears to be substance to the allegation that Lenin had been carried across Germany from Switzerland to Petrograd in a sealed German railway car. The papers claimed that the Bolsheviks had acted as German agents since 1914, and that Lenin withdrew Russia from the war in 1918 to assist Germany at the expense of Russian territory. These rumors, if true, would further justify the British, French, and American interventions against the Bolsheviks at Archangel, south Russia, and Siberia after July 1918.

Because of doubts about the documents' authenticity, Creel asked the National Board for Historical Service to appoint a committee to review them. In late September, the board appointed J. Franklin Jameson, editor of the *American Historical Review*, and Samuel Harper, Professor of Russian language and institutions at the University of Chicago. Jameson and Harper reported within a week that "we have no hesitation in declaring... the genuineness or authenticity" of 53 of the 68 documents examined. These 53 documents were the critically important ones.

The Jameson-Harper report and the Sisson documents were printed and distributed by Creel's committee in October 1918 in a pamphlet entitled "The German-Bolshevik Conspiracy." Other countries printed the documents in later editions. Over the next two years, attempts to authenticate the documents were made by Sisson and Creel. In December 1920, however, Creel stopped the investigation because neither the White House nor Mrs. Wilson, who took charge during her husband's illness, would permit an examination of the original documents.

Between 1952 and 1956, the documents became public. Following a thorough study, the historian George F. Kennan demonstrated that the Sisson documents were forged. Writing in the June 1956 issue of the *Journal of Modern History*, Kennan showed that the documents contained technical errors of language, form, letterhead, seals, handwriting, and typewriting. Incidentally, historians Jameson and Harper later explained that in 1918 they had acted from a sense of duty to support the war effort against Germany.

October 16, 1918

The Alien Act allows the deportation of radicals.

In February 1917, Congress passed, over President Wilson's veto, an immigration act that reaffirmed the exclusion of anarchists and allowed the deportation of radicals. Additionally, it introduced the concept of "guilt by association" into immigration law by denying entry to any immigrant "who is a member of or affiliated with any organization entertaining or teaching disbelief in or opposition to organized government." When these provisions were incorporated into the 1918 statute, Wilson signed it. The law provided a legal basis for Attorney General A. Mitchell Palmer's actions during the first Red Scare.

See November 7, 1919.

November 11, 1918

Germany signs an armistice to end the war amidst the collapse of the old order and the rise of radical elements.

Following receipt of the German peace request on October 6, President Wilson undertook to ascertain that the German government represented the people, that the Allies would accept the peace terms, and that Marshal Foch determined an armistice was appropriate from the military viewpoint. Significantly, only General Pershing of the United States dissented seriously with the Allied commanders regarding the armistice issue. Following the normal U.S. military doctrine developed during the nineteenth century Indian wars, Pershing wanted the Germans to be given no conditions for surrender. The European commanders, whose military doctrine was based on centuries of European conflict among often nearly equal opponents, believed, as Foch said, "One makes war only to get results"; that is, war is for political purposes only insofar as defeating the enemy's military and naval power serves political ends. These ends the European commanders had achieved, and therefore, in their view, an armistice with surrender terms was appropriate. General Foch met with a German Armistice Commission to settle the surrender terms.

German developments between October 6 and November 9 confirmed that the country was in a state of political and economic collapse. These events included (1) on October 28, a sailors' mutiny at Kiel during which the seamen refused to go to sea to fight the British; (2) a revolt in Munich led by Kurt Eisner, an independent socialist who proclaimed the Republic of Bavaria on November 8; (3) the proclamation of the abdication of Emperor William II on November 9 followed by the proclamation of a German republic in Berlin under a ministry of the majority Socialists led by Frederick Ebert and Philipp Scheidemann.

November 11, 1918

The human costs of World War I are significant.

During the war in Europe, the estimated number of battlefield deaths was 8,538,315 and 22,129,492 wounded, with over 6.6 million civilians' deaths attributed to disease, starvation, and other causes. The war's economic costs were staggering and its impact on several nations' traditional political structures was often devastating. Consequently, after the armistices were signed, civil conflict erupted in Central and Eastern Europe.

Russia suffered an estimated 1,700,000 battle deaths and 4,980,000 wounded, while civilian deaths were perhaps two million. At the time the armistice was made, the total of U.S. deaths was 126,432, more than half of these from an influenza pandemic at U.S. military camps. The battle casualties of the American Expeditionary Forces were 48,909 dead and 230,074 wounded.

December 17, 1918

French forces arrive at Odessa in the Ukraine on Premier Georges Clemenceau's orders to isolate and destroy Russian Bolshevism.

The French intervention at Odessa became the Allies' most disastrous operation in Russia between 1918 and 1920. Clemenceau, the most ardent anti-Communist of the Big Three, often chided Lloyd George and Wilson for their weakness in pursuing Russian intervention. The Ukraine offered Clemenceau the opportunity to demonstrate the proper anti-Bolshevism. Yet the French attempt ended in total failure and the desertion of many anti-Communist refugees in the Ukraine. Clemenceau ordered the French intervention on October 27, 1918, contrary to the advice of General Franchet d'Esperey, the French commander in the Danube area who had led French and Greek forces to victory against the Bulgarians on September 30, 1918. The French premier replaced d'Esperey with the more optimistic General Henri Berthelot, who brought 1,700 French troops to Odessa on December 17.

In December 1918, Ukrainian politics were in near anarchy. Following the Bolshevik Revolution of November 1917, Ukrainian nationalists established an independent state and drove out the German and Austrian forces. Soon after, Soviet forces moved into Kiev to prevent the new government from operating. At Brest-Litovsk, Lenin agreed to evacuate the Ukraine, and German troops returned to pillage and loot the province. A Ukrainian nationalist, Simon Petliura, rallied the people and took control when the Germans withdrew on November 11, 1918.

During the winter of 1918–1919, Trotsky delayed sending the Red Army to the Ukraine because of the political problems. Petliura tried to create a dictatorship, numerous Don Cossack atamans fought each

Street corner in Poelcapelle, Belgium, December 19, 1918. National Archives

other to extend their personal power, and a former czarist officer, General Anatol Denikin, sent his officers to the Ukraine to set up an anti-Bolshevik Russian state. Among these many factions, the largest were Petliura's Ukrainian nationalists and the czarist group under Denikin's appointee, General Yuri Grishin-Almazov.

1919

January 15, 1919

The Spartacists uprising in Berlin ends, during which the Communists sought to control the city.

On November 10, a coalition ministry of the Independent and Majority Socialists gained control in Berlin. Soon, however, the Independents joined the extreme left-wing Communists (Spartacists) led by Karl Liebknecht and Rosa Luxemburg to seek dictatorial control and to use violence to effect a radical economic revolution. The majority Socialists (Social Democrats) preferred evolutionary not violent changes for Germany and proposed a national assembly to draw up a constitution.

To forestall control by an assembly, the Spartacists revolted in Berlin and attempted to duplicate Lenin's victory of November 1917. The Social Democratic leader, Friederich Ebert, decided to accept the aid of the German General Staff in putting down the uprising. This tactic met immediate success and the rebellion was silenced by January 15. Liebknecht and Luxemburg were arrested and executed on January 15.

Subsequently, a national constituent assembly was elected on January 19 and began sessions at Weimar on February 6, 1919. The Communists boycotted the election, in which the Social Democrats won 163 seats while other parties won 258.

In February, the Communists staged smaller uprisings in Berlin, Munich, and other cities, but they were suppressed. When a Soviet Republic was declared on April 4 in Bavaria, it was overthrown by the German army of the federal government.

January 18, 1919

The Paris Peace Conference formally opens; Germany, the League, and Bolshevism are major issues.

The Paris Conference was attended by 70 delegates representing 27 victorious powers. The major decisions and policies were made by the "Big Four": Premier Georges Clemenceau of France, Vittorio Orlando of Italy, Prime Minister David Lloyd George of Great Britain, and President Woodrow Wilson of the United States. Germany and its wartime allies were not represented as they were expected to merely concur with agreements when the agreements were arrived at. The Russians were not invited to participate in the conference because they signed the Brest-Litovsk Treaty and the Allied intervention was still underway.

While questions of disarming Germany and forming the League of Nations took center stage, Allied fears of the Bolsheviks lurked not far behind the scenes. The economic and political chaos that followed the Central Powers' defeat created fertile ground for future revolutionary uprisings in Germany and central Europe and disrupted some treaty negotiations. For example, the uprisings and chaos in Hungary prevented an agreement being reached until June 4, 1920, and one with Turkey was not signed until August 10, 1920.

February 12, 1919

The Prinkipo proposal—an Anglo-American suggestion—fails to end the Russian Civil War.

At discussions during the Paris Peace Conference in January 1919, Prime Minister Lloyd George and President Wilson agreed to invite all warring factions of the Red and White Russian armies together to settle their disputes. Georges Clemenceau absolutely refused to invite them to Paris, so Lloyd George

The "Big Four" at the Paris Peace Conference. L-R. David Lloyd George of Great Britain, Vittorio Orlando of Italy, Georges Clemenceau of France, and Woodrow Wilson of the Unites States. National Archives

proposed Prinkipo Island in the Sea of Marmara. Clemenceau agreed to this and the Big Three invited the various Russian factions to attend a Prinkipo conference on February 15.

On February 12, Lenin agreed to an armistice and meeting under prescribed conditions, but Admiral Kolchak and General Denikin, the two principal White leaders, refused. President Wilson learned later that Clemenceau had discreetly advised the pro-czarist leaders not to accept the proposal, undermining any slim hope that the conference might succeed.

February 14, 1919

At the Paris Peace Conference, President Wilson reads the covenant of the League of Nations drafted by a conference commission that he chaired.

Prominent among his 14 Points of 1918, Wilson argued that if a League of Nations were properly formed, it could work out in the long term any immediate shortcomings of the remainder of the peace treaty. Wilson was appointed chairman of the commission to draft the league proposal. After laboring arduously for two weeks, the commission offered its draft to the delegates on February 14. Although the draft underwent a few revisions, the commission report became the basis for the League of Nations as adopted in its final form on April 28, 1919.

March 2, 1919

The Third Communist International is founded in Moscow.

Lenin's government founded the Third Communist International because of the belief that it was important to the Bolsheviks' success in Russia to secure support from workers in other parts of Europe and the world. The First International had been founded by Karl Marx in London during 1864 but was wrecked by a dispute between Marx and Michael Bakunin, who advocated direct action to create anarchy as the method to promote the working-class revolution.

The Second International, organized in 1889, was dominated by moderate socialists who opposed violence and believed in the gradual evolution of socialism as part of economic democracy. The Second International split apart in August 1914, because most delegates joined their nations' war efforts. Late in 1918, Lenin discovered that socialists in Western and Central Europe had plans to revive the Second International. To counteract this possibility and bring the organization under Russian control, Lenin invited delegates from various European nations to send representatives to Moscow to establish the Third International. He especially hoped to get radical socialists from Germany to join the Russian organization.

During its sessions between March 2 and 6, 1919, 35 delegates attended. Most of them represented minority groups of the old Russian Empire. Five foreign representatives came from Germany, Austria, Norway, Sweden, and Holland. The radical German delegates came to oppose a new international group, hoping to keep Germans in control of the Second International. Nevertheless, the Russian delegates dominated the meeting and voted to organize the Third International under Bolshevik leadership.

March 21, 1919

A Socialist-Communist government is formed in Hungary; soon after, the Communist Béla Kun establishes a Communist dictatorship.

On October 17, 1919, Hungary declared complete independence from Austria and declared itself a republic on November 16. On March 21, Hungarian President Michael Karolyi resigned to protest the Allied powers' decision to assign Transylvania to Romania. The same day the socialist Alexander Garbai became president and Kun became minister of foreign affairs. Kun, who had come to Hungary from Russia in November 1918, soon crowded out the socialists and took full control.

April 5, 1919

French forces evacuate Odessa, leaving behind nearly 500,000 anti-Bolshevik refugees who crowded to Odessa to gain French protection.

Premier Clemenceau's October 1918 predictions that he could destroy Bolshevism ended in disaster on April 5, when the French commander in Odessa received orders to evacuate southern Russia. The quick French exit resulted from the hopelessness of the French attempt to back anti-Bolshevik armies in the Ukraine and political circumstances in Paris that required Clemenceau to recall the troops or be voted out of office. If Clemenceau had followed General d'Esperey's advice in 1918, the French debacle would have been avoided.

The French troops in the Ukraine faced internal disputes and anti-Bolshevik Russians who fought each other. Within the French army, Clemenceau's precise objective was not clear. Many French officers did not understand their mission, for as one French general told his men: "We are not here to fight. We cannot anyway since we are not at war with Russia." Other officers grumbled that no Frenchman who had survived Verdun or the Marne against Germany wanted to die in Russia.

Equally serious, the local Russian army leaders preferred fighting each other to fighting the Bolsheviks. Petliura, the Ukrainian national leader, dreamed of controlling an independent state; the White army General Grishin-Almazov wanted to save the province for the new czarist empire of General Denikin. The French could not decide which local leader to support, and attempts to compromise made their status more tenuous.

In the midst of the political confusion at Odessa, the Bolsheviks enlisted a competent military commander to conquer the Ukraine. He was Vladimir Antonov-Ovseenko, the officer whose Soviet troops had arrested the members of Kerensky's government in November 1917, and was a notable Bolshevik until executed by Stalin during the 1938 purges. In 1918, Antonov led Red Army forces in defeating the Petliurists and capturing Kiev on February 4. He then recruited a Cossack, Nikifor Grigorev, and sent him against the French position on the Black Sea.

The telling blow against the French became Grigorev's siege of Odessa, which began on March 12. The French had greater fire power because of their warships along the Black Sea coast. Within the city, troop morale was poor and the city suffered from typhus, food shortages, and overcrowding. Many local Ukrainians were anti-Bolshevik and flocked to Odessa for protection, but this only made living conditions there worse.

In Paris, newspapers and politicians first avoided printing reports on the difficulty in the Ukraine. In Britain, however, the *Manchester Guardian* reported the Bolshevik successes. Even Winston Churchill, whose anti-Communism matched Clemenceau's, confessed that the Ukrainian experience had been a disaster and the French had aroused the ill will of most Russians. French leaders soon had to admit their problems to the Chamber of Deputies. Marshal Foch confessed that Odessa was unimportant and that the only reason for keeping French troops there was to bolster army morale. Finally, on March 29, Clemenceau's delegate announced to the assembly that no more troops would be sent to Russia because an evacuation was being planned.

In Odessa, the April 5 evacuation notice caused panic in the city. Refugees rushed to the docks to secure passage out of the city. Exactly how many escaped is not known. The French took their troops aboard their warships and crowded 40,000 Russians on board before leaving. Many of the remaining refugees committed suicide; some died during the mad rush to board the ships. The fate of the rest was never reported. According to the British historian John Silverlight, French news reports and memoirs on the Ukrainian incident are almost nonexistent. No official French reports were issued. The French attempt never achieved the heights of Clemenceau's anti-Communist rhetoric.

The Odessa incident was the clearest instance of a direct Allied attempt to overthrow the Bolsheviks; it was a disaster.

April 10, 1919

A U.S. attempt to reach a settlement with the Bolsheviks fails: the Bullitt Mission.

Shortly after the White army generals rejected the Prinkipo conference on February 12, 1919, Colonel House and Secretary of State Lansing accepted William C. Bullitt's suggestion that Bullitt make a personal trip to Petrograd and Moscow to assess the situation. A State Department aide at the Paris Conference, Bullitt believed that every effort should be made to reconcile the Russians. Before sending Bullitt to Russia, the Americans obtained Britain's Prime Minister Lloyd George's sanction for the attempt.

On March 16, Bullitt held a personal interview with Lenin and reported to Paris that the Bolsheviks had agreed to terms of negotiation provided the Allies would accept them by April 10. Lenin's terms included an armistice by all Russian groups, amnesty to Russians who supported the Allies, the end of the Allied blockade of Russia, the withdrawal from Russia of Allied forces, and the opening of channels of discussion between Moscow and Paris. Bullitt returned to Paris enthusiastic about his mission, but he found no ready audience at the Peace Conference for Lenin's proposal. The Big Four (Wilson, Lloyd George, Clemenceau, and Orlando) were in the midst of a crisis over French reparation demands. In addition, Clemenceau disliked the Americans' failure to consult with him before the mission began.

Consequently, the Allied leaders never considered the merits of Lenin's offer and the April 10 deadline passed.

April 17, 1919

The Hoover-Nansen proposal for Russian food relief is approved by the Big Three powers but on conditions the Bolsheviks cannot accept.

Herbert Hoover, who had effectively organized the Belgian Relief Program, proposed on March 28, 1919, a similar relief effort to serve Russia's needs. He and the Norwegian explorer Fridtjof Nansen thought this humanitarian effort was necessary for the Russian people. Because Hoover's proposal came under consideration at the moment when Bullitt's proposal from Lenin was being denied, Colonel House argued that the food relief in exchange for a Russian armistice would be an alternative to simply rejecting Lenin's March offer. The Allied leaders accepted this idea but added other strings to entice Lenin to end the civil war. Food relief would be offered provided that hostilities had stopped, local governments in Russia could distribute the food, and the Food Relief Commission could control transportation in Russia to deliver the goods.

The conditions imposed by the Allies were unacceptable to the Russian government. A Red Army offensive against Admiral Kolchak had turned the war in favor of the Communists. In addition, Lenin would not agree to turn Russia's transportation over to a foreign group. Consequently, on May 20, Foreign Minister Chicherin refused the relief proposal. He informed Nansen that the Russian people appreciated his offer but feared that the Allies' conditions were a trap to overthrow the Bolshevik regime. Later, in 1921, Hoover undertook a less politically conditioned relief program for Russia.

May 4, 1919

The May Fourth Movement begins in China.

This movement united students and Chinese workers against all foreign concessions in China, particularly those of Japan. Although China had only 2 million industrial workers in 1922, Chinese leaders had begun organizing labor groups. In May 1919, these groups joined Chinese students who had long agitated for a modern China that would overthrow the old Confucian authorities of the family and village elders. While traditional Chinese culture continued to thrive, the May Fourth attitudes challenged those ideas by using Sun Yat-sen's Three Peoples' Principles of nationalism, democracy, and livelihood to equalize land rights and modernize China's society.

To obtain support for his revolutionary party, Sun agreed in 1923 to collaborate with the Chinese Communists as part of an arrangement with the Moscow-sponsored Comintern. The Soviet government granted aid and dispatched military advisors.

See January 26, 1923.

June 23, 1919

Facing the alternative of a renewed Allied assualt, Germany's republican government representatives sign the Treaty of Versailles.

The German delegates were presented with the treaty on May 7, but after reading its terms, Count Ulrich von Broskdorf-Rantzau protested that the terms did not accord with conditions laid down by the Allies when the armistice was signed on November 11, 1918. After a new Reichstag coalition was formed, the new Prime Minister Gustav Bauer agreed to sign the Treaty. On July 7, the German government ratified the treaty. France ratified it on October 13, Great Britain and Italy on October 15, and Japan on October 30. The U.S. Senate refused to ratify the treaty.

See March 19, 1920.

June 27, 1919

American forces withdraw from northern Russia.

Immediately after the armistice on November 11, 1918, Secretary of War Baker urged Wilson to withdraw American troops from Archangel. Having learned of the unauthorized use of the troops by the British, Wilson agreed, but the withdrawal became impossible because of the freezing of the rivers and ports near Archangel. As a result, the American soldiers endured a miserably cruel winter in north Russia, huddled in blockhouses and alert against a possible Bolshevik attack.

American troops in Russian port about to leave that country. They are cheering and displaying the stars and stripes as the tender was coming to pick them up. National Archives

One American outpost was attacked, and the U.S. troops withdrew under dangerous conditions. This was the only actual engagement with the Bolsheviks following the August "conquest" of Archangel by the Allies. Nevertheless, the morale of the American troops deteriorated during the winter, and near mutinies took place in some units. Even as the spring thaw began, the U.S. troop removal proceeded slowly.

The Allied difficulties in north Russia had grown over the winter because the British and French commanders argued about which local political factions should be recognized. The British supported the pro-czarist Gregory Chaplain, who had assisted them in the takeover at Archangel, while the French backed a local Social Revolutionary, Nikolai Chaikovsky. The Social Revolutionaries gained control at Archangel, but when Chaikovsky left for Paris in January 1919, the Allies lost all local support. Meanwhile, the Bolsheviks rallied the peasants in the surrounding regions by opposing the "invaders" of the homeland. In this situation, President Wilson delayed the U.S. withdrawal out of deference to British requests to maintain some strength at Archangel.

U.S. Senate action finally stirred Wilson to speed up a program to bring the troops home from Archangel. The soldiers were largely from regiments out of Michigan and Wisconsin, and citizens from those states flooded Congress with petitions. On February 14, Senator Hiram Johnson offered a resolution to withdraw troops from north Russia; this resolution failed to pass the Senate only because Vice President Marshall cast his tie-breaking vote against the resolution. Three days later, Secretary Baker announced that American troops would leave north Russia as soon as weather permitted. Delay continued, however, because of British Minister of War Winston Churchill's attempt to persuade the Allied leaders at Paris to launch an attack south of Archangel, where they might link up with Admiral Kolchak's armies. Wilson opposed this action but did not speed up the U.S. withdrawal in order to placate Lloyd George, who was in political difficulty in Great Britain against Churchill's Conservative Party followers.

After Kolchak's army in Siberia retreated in May 1919, the British command overruled Churchill and began a withdrawal. The last American troops evacuated on June 27; the British and French stayed in Archangel until September 27, and at Murmansk until October 12, 1919. They turned Archangel over to a former czarist officer, General E. Miller, who held out against the Red Army until February 2, 1920.

At Archangel, the British and French lost 327 men; the American casualties were 139 from injuries or accidents.

August 1, 1919

The Communist dictator of Hungary, Béla Kun, flees to Austria when Romanian forces attack Budapest.

Hungary had declared war on Czechoslovakia on March 28 to regain its Slovakian provinces. When Béla Kun's Hungarian army threatened to conquer Transylvania as well, Romania began a preemptive war and invaded Hungary on April 10. While Romania's army invaded successfully, Admiral Miklós Horthy formed a counterrevolutionary movement that replaced Kun, who fled to Vienna on August 1.

After the Romanian armies withdrew from their occupation of Budapest on February 25, 1920, Horthy's followers took control and proclaimed a monarchy on March 23, 1920.

September 2, 1919

The American socialists split into three blocs: the Socialist Party, the Communist Labor Party, and the Communist Party of America.

Although there had been factions in the Socialist Party of the United States before 1914, the Bolshevik victory in Russia and Lenin's formation of the Third International in March 1919 caused the Socialist Party to split into three irreconcilable divisions in 1919. The old leadership of the Socialist Party (SP) retained majority control, espousing an evolutionary style socialism related to American conditions and willing to work with trade unions. When the SP met in Chicago on August 30, 1919, one division developed because the moderates refused to seat John Reed and Benjamin Gitlow, who represented the left-wing faction.

This initial split caused another division when the radical socialists met in Chicago on September 2, 1919. One group, led by Louis Farina, extolled Russia's call to immediate revolution and to break relations with the moderates, the trade unions, and liberal reformers. They formed the Communist Party of America (CP), which, after much competition with other factions, gained the backing of Moscow's Comintern.

The second bloc in Chicago at the September 2 meeting was the Communist Labor Party (CLP), which was led by Reed. The CLP disagreed with the CP because it rejected the possibility of an immediate revolution in America and did not want to isolate itself from appeals to the majority of Americans. The CLP endorsed the direct action of the International Workers of the World (IWW) but condemned the American Federation of Labor as did most socialists. Unlike the CP, the CLP wanted to create an American movement that did not declare the unconditional loyalty to the Third International demanded by the Russian Bolsheviks.

According to historian Theodore Draper, the CP and CLP had approximately 40,000 members after September 2, 1919, with 23,744 paying dues to the CP. He believes that because 75 percent of these were native Russians or East Europeans, they joined out of national sympathy for Russia, not because they were ideologically committed to Bolshevism. The English-speaking members of the CP and CLP became leaders of the organizations, even though they made up only 10 percent of the membership.

November 7, 1919

The "Palmer raids" begin: anti-Communist fears lead to Bureau of Investigation raids against American radicals.

With President Wilson's approval, Attorney General A. Mitchell Palmer ordered the Justice Department's Bureau of Investigation to examine socialist-Communist agitation. On January 21, 1919, the Seattle, Washington, shipyard strike focused attention on alleged Communist influence in America. Organized by the IWW, the Seattle strikers carried red flags and made anticapitalist speeches. On February 6, the IWW called a general strike, a tactic that many Americans believed was Communistic. Although there was no violence by the Seattle workers, Mayor Ole Hanson, who hated the IWW, claimed they plotted to overthrow the government.

Local newspapers took Mayor Hanson's cue and when the strike ended on February 10, the Seattle *Star* headlines read, "Today the Bolshevik-sired Nightmare Is at an End"; the Post-Intelligencer asserted, "Our Flag Is Still There," beneath a cartoon showing the tattered red Bolshevik flag.

Other U.S. strikes and bomb plots plus several European events in 1919 appeared to be part of the Bolshevik world revolution. In February, an assassin unsuccessfully attacked French Premier Clemenceau;

in March, Béla Kun's Communists held temporary control over Hungary, and Moscow announced the formation of the Third Communist International. Bomb plots were disclosed in the United States. On April 28, Mayor Hanson's office workers discovered a bomb, and soon after, the Postal Department found bombs in 36 packages. The most significant bomb attack was on Attorney General Palmer's home in Washington, D.C., on June 2. The fronts of Palmer's and his neighbor's houses were demolished. An anarchist pamphlet was discovered near Palmer's home. The booklet advocated terrorist methods to suppress the capitalist classes.

In July, Palmer prepared an assault on radical groups. He appointed William Flynn, chief of the Bureau of Investigation, to uncover the "red" network. Congress authorized $500,000 for a special General Intelligence Division (GID) of the Bureau, and Palmer named J. Edgar Hoover to head the GID. Hoover and Flynn prepared a file on 200,000 radically oriented individuals and 60,000 radical groups. The GID warned all Americans to beware of the Communist danger to the American way of life. Hoover had found a career that ultimately gave him vast investigative powers, his division later being renamed the Federal Bureau of Investigation.

On November 7, the GID launched raids against radical groups, using deportation provisions of the Alien Law of 1918 (see October 16, 1918). Hoover estimated that 90 percent of all domestic radicals were aliens who infiltrated and corrupted the United States. The November 7 raid hit the Russian Peoples' House in New York City that allegedly attracted "atheists, communists and anarchists." The CID found several truckloads of radical propaganda and seized 200 men and women. According to the *New York Times* some of those arrested were "badly beaten by the police... their heads wrapped in bandages" when they were taken to the GID headquarters.

Simultaneous raids took place on the Union of Russian Workers offices in other cities, where 250 members of that group were arrested. Of the first 450 prisoners taken on November 7, 39 were held for questioning for up to five months; 411 were freed after court hearings with no charges being filed. Additional raids followed throughout November.

The process resulted in deportation orders against 246 aliens. On December 21, 1919, the Army transport ship *Buford*, which reporters christened "*Soviet Ark*," carried the radical aliens back to their European homelands. Most of these deportees had participated in terrorist acts or had a criminal record. Among those sent home were Emma Goldman, who "menaced the public order," and Alex Berkman, who had tried but failed to assassinate Henry C. Frick during the Homestead Steel strike of 1892.

1920

January 2, 1920

The Red Scare in America continues when 2,700 persons are arrested during anti-Communist raids in 33 cities.

To learn better procedures because many of those arrested on November 7, 1919, went free, Attorney General Palmer consulted with officials of the Labor Department and the Immigration Office as he prepared the second raids. The secretary of labor signed 3,000 warrants for the arrest of aliens who belonged to the Communist Party or the Communist Labor Party. In addition, the Immigration Office changed its previous rules governing the arrest of aliens. Aliens no longer had the right to inspect the arrest warrants and be represented by counsel at the beginning of a deportation hearing. The new ruling stated, "Preferably at the beginning of the hearing... or at any rate as soon as such hearing has proceeded sufficiently in the development of the facts to protect the Government's interest" the alien could inspect the warrant and have counsel present.

The government had wide latitude in dealing with aliens because deportations did not involve a criminal proceeding but simply a hearing before an immigration officer. Moreover, the aliens' only appeal was for review by the secretary of labor or a federal writ of *habeas corpus* if the deportation process were manifestly unfair. This was a major reason Palmer used deportation rather than criminal action against the alleged Communists.

Thus, unlike the November raids, the January 2 raids included extensive plans. On one night over 4,000 suspected radicals were rounded up from 33 cities in 23 states. Virtually every Communist or left-wing group in the nation was hit and every leader was affected. Some arrests were with warrants; some were without warrants or any real cause. In Massachusetts 800 aliens were seized, and almost half of them were sent to the Boston Immigration

An example of the "Red Scare" cartoons that found subversives everywhere. *Philadelphia Inquirer*

Station for investigation. In New York, 400 were arrested; in Philadelphia, 100; in Pittsburgh, 115; in New Jersey towns, 500; in Detroit, 800; in Kansas City, 100. In Chicago, raids on January 1 and January 2 netted 425 prisoners. In the Far West, members of radical groups had been arrested during earlier IWW strikes, and only a few such groups remained there in 1920.

Despite his gross violations of the civil rights of some non-aliens as well as all rights of aliens, the American public considered Palmer to be the savior of the nation. The attorney general claimed he had "halted the advance of 'red radicalism' in the United States," and he predicted there would be 2,720 deportations.

Palmer exaggerated both the red threat and the number of radical aliens. By the spring of 1920, the red hysteria of 1919–1920 ended; only 591 aliens were deported.

January 20, 1920

A crisis with Mexico ends when Carranza compromises with the Petroleum Producers Association; Senator Albert Fall charges Bolsheviks behind policy.

A crisis in Mexican-American relations arose in 1919 when Venustiano Carranza's government had neither ended all the social disorders in Mexico nor fulfilled its promise to protect oil holdings obtained before 1917 under the provisions of Article 27 of the constitution of 1917, which gave the Mexican government control over subsoil resources.

By November 1919, a serious issue surfaced. It was a Mexican law that required government permits before new oil wells could be drilled in Mexico. The Mexican army began forcibly to close down oil drilling operations that lacked permits. The oilmen could have purchased the permits, but several mutually agreed not to do so because they feared the purchase of a permit would set a precedent validating Article 27. They appealed to Secretary Lansing for help; consequently, early in December, Lansing and Ambassador Fletcher used the oil permit issue to seek Wilson's approval for a strong policy to convince Carranza to accept concessions on Article 27.

In addition to the oil issue, Lansing's appeal to Wilson cited Senator Albert B. Fall's report that Carranza's government was influenced by Bolsheviks who hoped to undermine the American way of life. Therefore, Lansing suggested to Wilson in his note of January 3 that Ambassador Fletcher should give Carranza one final opportunity to make concessions on the oil issue and provide protection for the "lives, rights, and property of Americans." If Carranza did not comply with Fletcher's request within four weeks, the United States would break diplomatic relations. Lansing believed, however, that such strong inducements would force Carranza to yield to American demands. President Wilson never approved Lansing's proposal. The president had received reports from friends such as Joseph P. Guffey, president of Atlantic Gulf Oil Corporation, which stated that the Mexican situation was less acute than Lansing and Fletcher had indicated.

As soon as the Petroleum Producers Association members realized that Wilson would not exert pressure on Mexico, they appealed directly to President Carranza to obtain provisional oil drilling permits provided that the Mexican government agreed that this acceptance would not "destroy or prejudice such rights as they may have." On January 20, Carranza accepted the oilmen's proposal. This temporary truce ended the crisis and satisfied the U.S. oil interests until a more definitive Mexican policy could be approved.

February 25, 1920

President Wilson appoints Bainbridge Colby as secretary of state.

Colby's appointment surprised many observers who anticipated the nomination of Frank Polk, the Secretary of State *ad interim* following Lansing's resignation. Wilson selected Colby for his loyalty, not for his foreign policy experience, because the president expected to make the important policy decisions. Because of extensive Senate confirmation hearings, Colby did not begin official service as secretary of state until March 23, 1920.

March 19, 1920

A final Senate vote defeats the Treaty of Versailles and U.S. membership in the League.

The final Senate action on the Treaty of Versailles with amendments was 49 to 35. This defeat also meant the United States did not become a member of the League of Nations. Although the United States would gradually participate in League-endorsed undertakings by the mid-1920s and especially in the 1930s, it would never become a full member of the League.

April 1, 1920

American forces evacuate Vladivostok, ending its Siberian episode.

Although Britain and France used the Siberian intervention as an additional effort to assist the White anti-Bolshevik armies to overthrow the Communists, the Allied attempts were neither well-planned nor well-executed programs. Great Britain's plans focused on assistance to Admiral A. V. Kolchak, who established headquarters at Omsk; the Japanese objective was to secure power in Manchuria and eastern Siberia; while the American effort began as a venture to help the Czech Legions escape but ended by preventing Japanese ambitions in East Asia and China from getting out of control.

Thus for U.S. General Graves, his Siberian command became a diplomatic contest against Japan and Britain as well as a series of protests against the Don Cossack generals who spread terror in their attempts to become wealthy by looting Russian and Chinese peasants. By 1919, the British, Japanese, and Cossack generals believed Graves was pro-Communist because his opposition restricted their interference in local political and economic affairs.

The Japanese had initially gained much of their major objective in northern China and Siberia by the end of August 1918. Before Graves arrived, the British and Japanese had waged several minor battles against local Russian Communist forces along the Trans-Siberian Railway. Defeating the Russians easily, the Japanese controlled the railway line as far west as Irkutsk, where the main forces of the Czech army held control. Subsequently, a Japanese-Anglo-American pact on January 9, 1919, established an Inter-Allied Railway Agreement to keep the Trans-Siberian line operating. American forces assisted this railway effort until 1920. During the 18 months of Allied occupation the Japanese tried to consolidate their status in that area but reluctantly withdrew in October 1922, because America insisted. In 1922, the Soviet regional government in eastern Siberia thanked Washington for its friendly interest in forcing Japan to leave.

Great Britain's assistance to Admiral Kolchak's forces at Omsk was a more direct attack against the Russian Communists. A former czarist naval officer, Kolchak moved into central Siberia during the fall of 1918 and became the supreme commander of the White army at Omsk. To protect and supply Kolchak with arms, the British sent 2,000 men under Colonel Ward. Yet the only British forces to fight Communists in the area of the Ural Mountains were an unusual naval gun crew. These sailors dismantled a gun from their cruiser, the *Suffolk*, at Vladivostok. They mounted it on an armored train and moved it 4,000 miles into Asia to aid Kolchak against the Red Army.

Unfortunately, Kolchak's policies were less imaginative than the *Suffolk*'s gun crew; thus, the admiral's anti-Communist campaign failed miserably. A typical counterrevolutionist, Kolchak did not understand the difference between the moderate agrarian socialistic Social Revolutionists (SR) and the radical Bolshevik Communists. The largest revolutionist group in Russia in 1917, the SR advocated peasant land ownership, but their moderate goals had succumbed to the Leninists. The SR preferred to fight the Communists, but the tactics of White leaders such as Kolchak, together with the Allied foreign intervention, caused the moderates to accept the Bolsheviks as the lesser evil. Kolchak tried to suppress the SR but ended by losing the support of the local peasants near Omsk, as well as the Czech Legion at Irkutsk. Eventually, Kolchak had many officers but few soldiers to fight in his army. By the end of April 1919, Kolchak's forces in Central Asia began retreating, and in August Great Britain withdrew all its support from the admiral. Kolchak resigned as supreme ruler of the White armies on January 4, 1920. Local Soviet leaders in Irkutsk arrested him on January 15, and he was executed by firing squad on February 7, 1920.

American troops under General Graves did not directly aid Kolchak. They protected the Trans-Siberian Railway, a duty that resulted in one defensive engagement against the Bolsheviks. The incident occurred at a coal mine in Suchan near Vladivostok, where Americans guarded the coal supply for the railroad line. Because Don Cossack officers had engaged in atrocities against the local populace, trouble spilled over against the Americans as well. The U.S. troops increased their patrols in the area, which resulted in a shooting incident during which several Bolsheviks died. Nevertheless, this conflict was defensive in nature because General Graves ordered no offensive attacks against the Bolsheviks.

In 1919 and early 1920, General Graves became more concerned with limiting the actions of Japanese, British, and Cossack officers. President Wilson had considered withdrawing the Siberian force in November 1918 but agreed with the Allies to wait until the Paris Peace Conference determined the future of Russia. The peace conference had been unable to deal with Russia, and the Senate rejection of the Treaty of Versailles negated any possible U.S. influence on European-Soviet relations.

About the time that the Senate rejected the treaty in November 1919, the Czech Legion arranged its final withdrawal from Siberia. The Czechs had lingered at Omsk and Irkutsk through 1919 to assist Kolchak.

They became disillusioned with the admiral's tactics, however, and in November 1919 completely withdrew assistance from the White armies and dealt with Communist leaders for safe transportation to Vladivostok. Although Japanese-American control of the railway in 1919 had given the Czech Legion the opportunity to leave, it did not begin its mass evacuation from Omsk and Irkutsk until December 1919. The Czechs experienced more difficulty now than they would have in 1918 because they had to convince the Soviets they no longer were aiding Kolchak. By helping the Soviets capture the admiral on January 15, they proved their point, and the day after Kolchak's execution, the Czech trains left Irkutsk. Finally in April 1920, at the same time that the American evacuation began, the Czech Legions boarded ships at Vladivostok. Two years after beginning their trek from Kiev, the Czechs left Siberia. Actually, General Graves had given less attention to the Czechs than to the Japanese. The Japanese stayed on in Siberia, however, and did not leave until October 1922.

The historian George Kennan cites a later incident to illustrate the passive character of the U.S. intervention in Siberia. During the 1933 negotiations in Washington preceding U.S. recognition of the

Soviet Union's Foreign Minister, Maxim Litvinov, raised questions about claims against U.S. destruction in Siberia from 1918 to 1920. The American officials showed Litvinov documents on the Siberian intervention, convincing him to withdraw his indemnity claims arising in Siberia. Litvinov gave President Franklin Roosevelt a public letter in which the Soviet Union waived any and all claims arising from U.S. military action in Siberia after World War I. The main result of American action in Siberia had been to limit Japan's presence.

May 7, 1920

America's Red Scare abates after Louis F. Post effectively explains the injustices of the Palmer raids.

The postwar Red Scare ended almost as abruptly in 1920 as it had begun in 1919. Not only had the Bolshevik threat declined in Europe by 1920, but Americans of both parties began to realize that the threat of Communism had been exaggerated. Congress especially was concerned that Attorney General Palmer's tactics between November 1919 and April 1920 had threatened American civil liberties.

A significant role in ending this Red Scare was played on May 7 by Assistant Secretary of Labor Louis Post, who defended himself against impeachment charges made in the Rules Committee of the House of Representatives. Having been designated by Secretary of Labor Wilson to be the arbiter in the deportation hearings of the arrested aliens, Post soon realized that not only had the aliens' procedural rights been violated but also few of the aliens were Communists or radicals. Therefore, Post ordered the wholesale cancellation of deportation orders and released almost half of those arrested in January. These aliens, Post said, were "wage workers" who committed no offense and were not the aliens Congress "intended to comprehend in its antialien legislation." Post canceled 2,202 deportation orders. Only 556 of the more than 4,000 aliens arrested in January were deported.

Post's action did not go uncontested. Palmer and American anti-Communist groups complained bitterly that Post was "coddling the Reds." In April, Representative Homer Hood of Kansas offered a resolution in Congress to impeach Post if the facts warranted. On May 1, the House Rules Committee, which had investigated Hood's charges, recommended that Post be censured for leniency.

At this point, Post demanded a personal hearing before the House Rules Committee. The committee complied, and on May 7, Post accomplished what few congressional witnesses have ever achieved. He presented testimony so eloquent and precise that the Rules Committee voted to suspend further consideration of his censure. Post offered detailed information to show how newspapers and super-patriots had manufactured a nonexistent Communist threat. During the January raids, he pointed out, only three pistols were found and two of these were .22-caliber guns, not the type suited for a revolution. He provided detailed information from the deportation hearings to demonstrate the Justice Department's high-handed and illegal arrest procedures. Finally, Post explained the exact differences between the disciples of Marx, Tolstoy, Proudhon, and Sorel, the principal philosophers of modern radicalism. He indicated how the ideas of these four men were arranged along the spectrum from democratic liberalism to violent, terrorist radicalism.

Post got his message across. Newsmen and their editors listened carefully enough to realize that the "Red Scare" tactics endangered Americans more than Bolshevism. Post's vindication turned congressional attention to an investigation of Attorney General Palmer's illegal proceedings. Palmer denied the charges, of course, and blamed Post's "perverted sympathy for the criminal anarchists" for his failure to deport the aliens. By this time, however, the nation and Congress became apathetic about the issue as the 1920 presidential campaign began.

The renewed sanity of the public became clear in September 1920, when a terrorist attack took place on Wall Street. At noon on September 6, a large bomb exploded in front of the U.S. Assay Office across the street from the House of Morgan building. The bomb killed 29 persons outright, 4 more died in the hospital, and 200 others were wounded. Although Palmer revived charges of a radical plot, Americans reacted less drastically. While the New York police investigated, public opinion seemed to recognize that bomb attacks were insane plots that could not overthrow the government. The *Rocky Mountain News* ridiculed Palmer's charges. Palmer, the news editorial said, was "subservient to a bureaucracy, a great big secret-service army composed largely of politicians it employed. The usual pinch of salt must be" added to Palmer's claims. The first Red Scare had ended in America.

July 7, 1920

The United States removes its trade restrictions on Russia, but does not recognize Russia's Communist regime.

The Allied governments had restricted trade by their nationals with Russia after the Russian Revolution of November 1917. When the British and French began negotiations to resume commerce with Lenin's government, American business and labor organizations also asked Washington to end its limitations. On June 19, the State Department learned that the British proposed to reopen trade without recognizing the Soviet regime, and Secretary Colby recommended to President Wilson that the United States act similarly.

Wilson agreed, and on July 7, the State Department announced that U.S. trade restrictions would be removed but that the United States could give no official support to its citizens engaging in commerce with Russia. The Wilson administration would not recognize the Soviet regime because, it claimed, it did not represent the will of the people. The United States also continued to restrict travel and mail sent to Russia.

August 10, 1920

The Wilson administration explains it cannot recognize Lenin's government because his regime is "based upon the negation of every principle of honor and good faith."

Composed largely by Secretary of State Colby, the August 10 note detailed why Wilson would not recognize the Soviet government and enunciated attitudes toward Bolshevism that recurred in U.S. politics long after the United States finally recognized the Soviet Union in 1933. The note of August 10 was technically a response to an Italian request for American aid to Poland during the Russo-Polish War.

In this particular case, Colby said the United States was in favor of the territorial integrity of both states and could not accept Polish aggression in seeking land east of its ethnic region (the Curzon Line). The United States hoped the Russo-Polish War would end soon on the basis of national self-determination for both nations. (Polish armies had invaded Russia on April 25 in a vain attempt to conquer the Ukraine.)

Colby then shifted to a detailed explanation of why the United States could not deal with the Russian government until the Russian people were able to surmount their present crisis. Non-recognition was not based on the political structure of Russia but on the fact that the present regime negated "every principle of honor and good faith," which made it impossible to have "harmonious and trustful relations" with the Communists. The ideology of the Bolsheviks prevented their agreement with a non-Bolshevik government with any moral standards. They instigated revolution in other nations and would abuse diplomatic privileges. "Inevitably, therefore, the diplomatic service of the Bolshevik Government would become a channel for intrigues and the propaganda of revolt."

On September 27, Wilson again defended his administration's policy toward Moscow stating that "Bolshevism is a mistake and it must be resisted as all mistakes must be resisted... It cannot survive because it is wrong." This theme, of course, was also the later rationale for the U.S.'s post-World War II containment policy.

April 25, 1920

Events lead to a Russo-Polish War.

The border between Russia and Poland had never been delineated to both parties' satisfaction, even though a boundary line—drawn basically with ethnic considerations in mind—had been proposed by Lord Curzon in 1919. Because of the ambiguity, both Russia and Poland sought to define it at the other's expense. On April 25, 1920, Polish armies invaded Russia in an abortive effort to conquer the Ukraine. Subsequently, Russian forces followed the retreating Polish army and threatened to capture Warsaw until the Russians were turned away in a protracted battle lasting from August 16 to August 25. At this point both sides gave up their territorial ambitions and agreed to an armistice in October. The Treaty of Riga in March 1921 established the Russo-Polish borders until 1939. During World War II Stalin made it clear that he wanted the border adjusted to the Soviet Union's advantage.

Meanwhile, Lenin had written about his hope that the Red army would have been able to carry the Communist revolution to Warsaw and that the

Polish people would have rallied to it. He lamented: "If Poland had become Soviet, if the Warsaw workers received help from Soviet Russia that they expected... the Versailles Treaty would have collapsed." Presumably, Lenin believed Germany would also become a Communist nation. Obviously Lenin failed to recognize the powerful pull of nationalism, for just as Russian nationalists rallied to beat back the perfidious Poles, the Polish nationalists would not welcome Russians as saviors. Indeed, the USSR's experiences of the 1980s and early 1990s revealed just how deep the spirit of nationalism ran as the Soviet empire disintegrated under the impact of nationalism in Eastern European states such as Hungary.

November 2, 1920

Warren G. Harding is elected President as the Republicans also regain control of Congress.

The Democrats nominated James M. Cox, who promised to seek U.S. membership in the League of Nations. The Republican Party platform straddled the issue, favoring an "organization to preserve peace." Because of the Republican divisions on both domestic and foreign issues, they chose the "available" man rather than the "best" man. The Republican candidate was Harding, a man who had no deep convictions about any issue, advocating a "return to normalcy." In the election, Harding won 404 electoral votes to 127 for Cox.

1921

March 4, 1921

Charles Evans Hughes is commissioned as Secretary of State by President Harding.

Soon after his election in November 1920, Harding asked Hughes to serve as his secretary of state. Harding respected Hughes's advice on foreign relations and generally permitted him a free hand in foreign policy decisions. Hughes served as secretary until Harding's death and then for President Coolidge until March 4, 1925.

As secretary of state, Hughes immediately announced the Soviets would have to acknowledge the czar's debts and halt their efforts at fomenting revolutions. Wilson's non-recognition policy remained in place throughout the Harding, Coolidge, and Hoover administrations.

March 16, 1921

Anglo-Russian trade pact signed.

The signing of the Anglo-Russian agreement constituted *de facto* recognition of the Bolshevik regime. As with most of its agreements the Soviet government pledged non-interference in internal relations. The pact stated: "The present treaty is conditioned upon the fulfillment of the following: Both sides will refrain from hostile acts or measures against the other party as well as from introducing into its territory any official, direct, or indirect propaganda against the institutions of the British Empire or the Russian Soviet Republic."

See February 1, 1924.

May 19, 1921

Congress approves the emergency quota act restricting immigration to the United States, hoping to prevent radicals from entering.

Disillusionment with World War I, fears that larger numbers of eastern Europeans with socialist-Communistic beliefs would arrive, and a general xenophobic view held by many conservative Americans caused Congress to pass a law that broadly restricted immigration for the first time in the nation's history. The 1921 law limited the number of aliens admitted to the United States from a given country in one year to about 3 percent of the number of such nation's inhabitants in America in the 1910 census.

July 14, 1921

The Sacco-Vanzetti trial ends with guilty verdict.

Nicola Sacco, a skilled shoemaker and Bartolomeo Vanzetti, a fish peddler, were arrested on May 5, 1920, and charged with a payroll robbery and murder in South Braintree, Massachusetts. When the trial took place, the emotional impact of the first Red Scare was raging. Consequently, the men insisted they were innocent and were being charged only because of their commitment to philosophical anarchism. A jury in this tainted trial, conducted by Judge Webster, found them guilty and they were sentenced to death. The case drew the attention of civil rights advocates who asked an appeals court to review the jury's verdict.

See August 23, 1927.

August 20, 1921

Russia agrees to admit an American Relief Administration (ARA) to provide food for its starving citizens.

The ravages of World War I and the civil war between the Bolsheviks and the various White armies left Russia in a disastrous economic situation, in which lack of food supplies and poor distribution systems combined to cause large-scale famine. In July 1921, the Soviet government called for aid from the workers of the world, and Herbert Hoover's relief organization responded immediately. The Hoover-Nansen offer of food relief in April 1919 had been affected by political problems between the Allied powers and Lenin's regime.

But in 1921 there were direct contacts between Hoover's ARA and Maxim Litvinov, the Soviet's assistant minister of foreign affairs. Hoover promised to deliver food to Russia but insisted that the Soviets must first release any Americans held in Soviet jails. Five days later, on July 15, the Soviets began releasing American prisoners. On August 20, Litvinov and the ARA agreed on terms for relief supplies to be distributed in Russia by ARA members. The ARA insisted on the right to distribute relief to make certain the aid reached those in need. Although granting this authority to foreign representatives was humiliating to Soviet authorities, the need for food was so great that Litvinov had no alternative.

Washington temporarily lifted its ban on Soviet gold and over $12 million worth of it was used to help pay for American grain although it only covered a fraction of the total cost. On December 24, President Harding signed a relief bill that authorized the U.S. Grain Corporation to spend up to $20 million for food stuffs. During the next year, ARA delegates brought food and medicine to distribute in Russia. Most aid went to the Volga River region, where the famine was the most serious. In December 1922, the All-Russian Congress of Soviets formally thanked the ARA for $66 million of assistance, a greater amount than all other sources combined gave to Russia after its July call for help. Good grain harvests for Russia in the fall of 1922 ended the need for additional relief aid as the Russians were now exporting grain.

1922

February 28, 1922

Soviet government forms the All-Union Textile Syndicate (VTS).

Seeking to reconstruct its textile industry, Moscow chartered the All-Union Textile Syndicate (VTS) that combined various companies dealing in the production of cotton, wool, linen, silk, and hemp goods. VTS employed nearly a half-million workers in 342 factories that comprised 95 percent of all textile production in Russia. Later VTS would open branches in Berlin, London, Riga, and Paris. In November 1923, VTS Vice President Viktor Nogin opened an office in New York City. Controlled by Moscow, VTS's American branch, the All-Russian Textile Syndicate (ARTS), purchased 261,600 bales of American cotton during 1924 for the Soviet textile industry.

April 16, 1922

Treaty of Rapallo is signed between Germany and Russia.

Russia and Germany signed a formal treaty establishing normal diplomatic and commercial relations. Both parties renounced previous debts and created consular representation. However, the most significant aspect of the pact was that both nations were no longer isolated and that Russia's campaign to be recognized as a normal nation had succeeded with at least one European nation.

October 11, 1922

The Greco-Turkish War ends; the Bolsheviks aid the army of Mustafa Kemal.

Turkey's Ottoman Empire had been an ally of Germany during World War I. After the war the British, French, Italians, and Greeks disagreed over how to get a peace treaty. Initially, the Ottoman

Empire's Sultan Mohammad VI signed the Treaty of Sevres that ceded the city of Smyrna and other parts of the western shores of Anatolia to the Greeks. In accord with the treaty, the British commander in Istanbul then approved the landing of a Greek army at Smyrna (Izmir to the Turks) on March 15, 1919. The Greek landing was the opening round of a war between the Greeks and the Turkish Ninth Army commanded by Mustafa Kemal Pasha (Ataturk). Initially, the Greek army advanced toward the city of Ankara. In 1920 and 1921, Ataturk's forces drove French and Italian contingents back to Aleppo, forcing them to accept an armistice. Ataturk's forces also captured the cities of Kars, Ardahan, and Mount Ararat in the Armenian Republic where Bolshevik forces were located. In December 1920, Ataturk signed the Treaty of Gumru with the Soviets that gave the USSR control of the Republic of Armenia in exchange for Moscow pledging aid to Ataturk's military forces against the Western imperialists. The Comintern considered Turkey to be the key to their Middle Eastern interests and ambitions. With Bolshevik assistance, Turkey's armed forces went on the offensive against the Greeks, driving them back from Ankara to Izmir and from the entire Anatolian coastline by September 19, 1922. The Greco-Turkish war persisted until the Greeks were routed by Ataturk's army. The previous month Turkish forces led by General Kemal Pasha received valuable assistance from Russia. The Convention of Mudania on October 11, 1922, ended the war and set the stage for the Lausanne Conference where a Treaty was signed July 24, 1923. Turkey's Grand National Assembly in Ankara ratified the Treaty of Lausanne on October 23, 1923, declared Turkey an independent republic, and elected Ataturk as its first president.

October 27, 1922

Fascists march on Rome, and Mussolini gains power.

Fascist efforts to seize power were successful as their paramilitary formations marched on the government in Rome where they persuaded the king to name Benito Mussolini prime minister. Mussolini gradually steered the nation to a one-party state and then to a dictatorship. Mussolini was supported by industrial and financial leaders and, later, by the Catholic Church.

Mussolini's claim that he had saved Italy from a Communist take-over was false as the radical revolutionary tide had crested in 1921.

December 30, 1922

The Union of Soviet Socialistic Republics (USSR) is organized in Moscow.

During 1921, the Red Army under General Leon Trotsky defeated the White army forces trying to restore the czar's Russian Empire. The Red Army's victories permitted the Bolsheviks to consolidate their power in Moscow by organizing the Union of Soviet Socialist Republics. In 1922, the original USSR consisted of four republics: Russia, Ukraine, White Russia, and Transcaucasia. By 1937, eight more republics were added: Armenia, Azerbaijan, Georgia, Kazakistan, Kirgistan, Tadjikistan, Turmenistan, and Uzebekistan.

1923

January 26, 1923

Adolf A. Joffe and Sun Yat-sen release a communiqué; Soviets agree to supply aid.

On New Year's Day 1923, Sun Yat-sen's Kuomintang (KMT) had taken an antiforeign position as well as calling for the abolition of unequal treaties and social and economic reforms. The party, Sun declared, would now focus on revolution and gaining the support of peasants, workers, and women.

Joffe, the Comintern's representative to China, and Sun agreed the KMT would work with the Chinese Communists—the Comintern being satisfied with supporting a bourgeois nationalist revolution—while the Soviet Union offered aid to Sun. In March 1923, Moscow provided two million Mexican dollars and in June sent the first group of military advisors. The KMT's merger with the Soviet Communists never went smoothly because the newcomers were met with suspicion by the Chinese. Sun continued to request additional arms and instructors from the Soviets in order to field a strong army, and in the fall of 1923 he sent Chiang Kai-shek to Moscow to press for action on his request.

On December 4, 1923, the Soviet Commissar of Foreign Affairs, Georgi Chicherin, urged Sun to focus more on China's political needs:

> We think that the fundamental aim of the KMT [Kuomintang] is to build up a great powerful movement of the Chinese people and that therefore propaganda and organization on the biggest scale are its first necessities... The whole Chinese nation must see the difference between the KMT, a popularly organized mass party, and the military dictatorship [warlords] of the various parts of China.

June 15, 1923

Hoover's American relief program in Russia ends.

An American-Soviet liquidation agreement was signed on June 15 that eliminated any implied agreement between the two nations. Herbert Hoover and other Americans had hoped the ARA efforts would undermine the ideological foundations of the Soviet government. Unfortunately, the anti-Communist attitude of some ARA delegates caused them to treat all Russians with disdain and the result was ill will among the Russian people despite their gratitude for the food supplies.

For their part, the Soviets desired to see this cooperative venture lead to a political reconciliation between the two nations that would lead to joint technical and economic undertakings. The U.S. government, for example, restored its ban on Soviet gold and refused to extend official recognition to the USSR. While neither side achieved their political objective, the United States acquired, transported, and distributed some 540,000 tons of food and saved an estimated ten million Russian lives.

See August 20, 1921.

July 24, 1923

After the Treaty of Lausanne is ratified, Turkey becomes an independent republic.

The Comintern supported Turkey during the Greco-Turkish war, 1920–1922, with the hope that a Communist state might rise from chaos of the dissolving Ottoman Empire. (See October 11, 1922.) The Treaty of Lausanne formally demilitarized each shore of the straits that would be regulated by an international convention, restored Turkish territories, and left Asia Minor solely in Turkish hands. Turkey's Grand National Assembly not only ratified the Lausanne Treaty but also declared the independent Republic of Turkey and elected Ataturk as its president. Once in power, however, Ataturk suppressed the Turkish Communist Party while at the same time acknowledging the need for Soviet friendship. Moscow had to be satisfied with the withdrawal of Allied forces from Istanbul on August 23, thus removing a potential threat from the USSR's southern flank.

August 2, 1923

President Harding dies and is succeeded by Vice President Coolidge.

The president died in San Francisco while returning from a trip to Alaska. The cause of his death was listed as an embolism. On August 3, Calvin Coolidge took the oath of office as president.

1924

February 1, 1924

Britain, Italy, and France grant *de jure* recognition to the Soviet Union.

After the Labor Party gained a majority in Britain's Parliament, Ramsey MacDonald became prime minister on January 23, 1924. While an earlier trade agreement had constituted *de facto* recognition (See March 16, 1921), the MacDonald government extended *de jure* or formal recognition on February l. However, this status would soon be in jeopardy. (See October 25, 1924.)

Aligning with British recognition, the Italian government of Benito Mussolini recognized the Soviet government on February 7. Eight months later, the French government led by Raymond Poincare also extended *de jure* recognition to Moscow's government.

May 23, 1924

The Soviet Union abrogates most of the czar's treaties with China.

Knowing that the Chinese revolutionaries had been urging the abolition of the "unequal treaties" forced on the Ch'ing dynasty between 1842 and 1914, Lenin's government announced as early as July 1919 that the Soviet Union would repudiate those treaties. By 1924, however, the Red Army had defeated the White armies in Central Asia. Now, Moscow was less willing to end all the czar's previous arrangements in East Asia. Therefore, while generally ending the czar's tariff and economic concessions with China, the Soviets worked out two exceptions with that country: (1) the Soviets retained control of the Chinese Eastern Railway to restrain Japanese interests in Manchuria; (2) Outer Mongolia continued to be a Soviet protectorate.

This decision required that the Red Army intervene in Outer Mongolia to defeat refugees from Cossack and other White armies who were terrorizing the Mongolians. The Red Army suppressed these military bandits and placed a "friendly" ruler in control of Outer Mongolia under Soviet guidance.

May 27, 1924

The Amtorg Trading Company is incorporated in New York to stimulate U.S.-Russian commercial activities.

The merger of two British based barter companies—Products Exchange (Prodexo) and the All-Russian Cooperative Society (Arcos), Ltd.—resulted in the formation of the Amtorg Trading Company in New York City. Amtorg sought to stimulate commerce between American companies and Russia by providing trade statistics, and operated as an unofficial Soviet consulate. It also oversaw a number of minor Soviet companies operating in the United States.

July 1, 1924

Secretary of State Hughes reaffirms America's refusal to recognize the Union of Soviet Socialist Republics.

Although Hughes, like President Wilson in 1917, said he was sympathetic toward the Russian people, he continued to refuse to grant diplomatic recognition to the USSR, although most European nations had done so. After Great Britain recognized the Soviet government on February 1, 1924, many Americans questioned U.S. policy toward the Soviet Union. Subsequently, on July 1, Hughes issued a statement to clarify America's reasons for nonrecognition.

The secretary's three basic reasons for not granting recognition were (1) the USSR's refusal to accept the debts of the Russian State and its repudiation of all prior Russian debts, including the $187 million loaned to the Kerensky government by the United States; (2) Moscow's attempt to seek the overthrow of the existing social and political order of the United States through the subversive activity of the U.S. Communist Party and the Workers' Party; and (3) the U.S. claim that the new regime had not yet been accepted by the Russian people.

October 25, 1924

The alleged Zinoviev letter causes diplomatic tensions between Great Britain and the Soviet Union.

Within British domestic politics, the issue of recognizing the Soviet government continued to be controversial after Ramsay MacDonald's Labour cabinet extended *de jure* recognition to Moscow on February 1, 1924. The Labour cabinet had signed a commercial treaty on August 8 that gave the Soviets most-favored-nation trading status. Together, these actions by MacDonald provided the election campaign of the fall of 1924 with a major issue that Stanley Baldwin's Conservatives capitalized on due to an unwise letter that Grigory Zinoviev sent on October 25.

On behalf of the Communist Third International, whose headquarters were in Moscow, Zinoviev allegedly wrote a letter to leaders of the British Communist Party urging it to conduct a subversive propaganda program within the British armed services. The uproar over this document, which quite likely was a forgery according Adam Ulam, did manage to create a minor "Red Scare" in Britain. The publicity given to the message supposedly from Zinoviev was largely responsible for Baldwin's victory in the elections of October 29, 1924.

On November 21, 1924, Baldwin's ministry abrogated the August commercial treaties and adopted a hard-line policy toward the Soviet Union. The hostile British policy eventually caused a break in Anglo-Soviet relations on May 26, 1927.

October 28, 1924

France grants *de jure* recognition to the Soviet Union.

1925

March 5, 1925

Frank B. Kellogg becomes secretary of state.

In November 1924, following President Coolidge's reelection, Hughes notified the president that he intended to resign. He recommended Kellogg who had been a senator from Minnesota (1917–1923) and ambassador to Great Britain (1923–1925). Kellogg had been trained as a lawyer and had once served as president of the American Bar Association. Thus, while his foreign experience was limited, he brought impressive credentials to the State Department where he would serve until March 28, 1929. Kellogg was concerned about the possible spread of Communism, which like many others, he often confused with the rising force of nationalism.

December 17, 1925

Turkey and the Soviets agree on a treaty.

Before Turkey gained its independence in 1923, the Turks had been uneasy about its relations regarding Russia or the Soviet Union's interest in controlling or influencing policies regarding the Straits. In 1925 Turkey became more suspicious of Britain's having control of Iraq and turned to the Soviets for a temporary counterbalance. The Turko-Soviet Treaty of 1925 was a non-aggression pact but this was offset in 1926 by Turkey's desire for more cordial relations with the West. In 1926, Turkey signed accords with Great Britain and Greece. As a result of these accords, the Soviet's Comintern abruptly demoted Kemal Ataturk "from a revolutionary hero to a reactionary tyrant." In the fall of 1929, Soviet-Turkish relations made a dramatic improvement stimulated by the continued Turkish leaning toward the West. The upshot of this was a renewal of the 1925 Treaty that was set to expire in December 1929.

See March 7, 1931.

1926

March 26, 1926

Trotsky's report urges a policy of restraint for Chinese Communists.

A special committee headed by Leon Trotsky reported to the Politburo about the incredibly difficult situation in China that was complicated by several competing groups. In Trotsky's remarkable report, Adam Ulam reveals "the subordinate role of China, not to speak of the Chinese Communists, in the Soviet view of the foreign situation." Trotsky viewed the recent Locarno pact as uniting the West against the USSR and seeking to keep it isolated; therefore, he believed the Soviet Union "needs a breathing spell" to let the policies of Western nations become more moderate. In turn, Trotsky believed the Chinese Communists should adopt a policy of moderation. They should avoid any rash action against foreign, especially Japanese, interests in China that might lead to an anti-Soviet coalition. Also, the Kuomintang and the Chinese Communists should not challenge the pro-Japanese warlord Chang Tso-lin, who controlled Manchuria. Above all, Trotsky emphasized, the Soviets did not want a military confrontation with the Japanese.

March 20, 1926

Chiang Kai-shek seizes power from the Communists in Canton.

While the Soviet Politburo debated the Trotsky report, Chiang took matters in his own hands. Although the Comintern believed Chiang was a pliable KMT member because of his military training in Russia, Chiang now arrested many Chinese Communists and confined Soviet advisers to their quarters during the coup. Although he removed many Communists from important positions, Chiang avoided a rupture with Moscow because he needed the Soviet's military and organizational assistance. When Chiang launched a Northern Expedition to expand KMT control, the Chinese Communists pleaded with Moscow for the freedom to challenge Chiang's leadership. The Soviets denied the Communists' request because Chiang remained in the Comintern's good graces.

April 24, 1926

The Treaty of Berlin reaffirms the Russo-German Rapallo pact of 1922.

Germany and the Soviet Union reaffirmed, and extended for five years, their diplomatic and commercial ties that had been established in the Rapallo Treaty of April 16, 1922. Additionally, both parties agreed to remain neutral should either one be attacked by a third party and to abstain from any commercial or financial boycott against either signatory.

June 11, 1926

U.S. business leaders resurrect the moribund American-Soviet Chamber of Commerce.

As American businessmen watched their European counterparts recoup their losses from Russia's czarist era through new business operations with the Soviets, the Americans brought together key financiers, exporters, importers, lawyers, and industrialists to share their business information. The board of directors of the rejuvenated chamber included those who had long engaged in American-Soviet trade and some newcomers such as Averell Harriman who would long be involved in U.S.-Soviet diplomacy. The chamber provided several useful services, including gathering data on Soviet economic conditions—something the U.S. government would not undertake until the end of the decade.

1927

April 12, 1927

In Shanghai, Chiang Kai-shek launches a white terror against China's Communists that gives him full control of the KMT.

Following the formation of the Chinese Communist Party (CCP) in 1921, Moscow directed CCP members to join a united front with the KMT under Sun Yat-sen for the purpose of abolishing foreign control and infiltrating the KMT. After Sun Yat-sen died in 1925, the KMT-CCP alliance became precarious. CCP leaders such as Ch'en Tu-Hsiu suspected the KMT had bourgeois tendencies, while the KMT never fully trusted the Communist extremists. By 1927, the policy divergences in the united front increased as Chiang Kai-shek used Soviet help to create an impressive military force, while the CCP organized workers and peasants to control China. Nevertheless, even after Chiang sent his Soviet advisers home and purged the KMT of influential Communists, Soviet leader Stalin advised the CCP to cooperate with Chiang. Previously, Leon Trotsky, who led a bloc of Bolsheviks against Stalin, had opposed the CCP-KMT front, so Stalin had to prove its practicality to his adversary.

Therefore in 1926, Michael Borodin returned to Canton to represent the Comintern and urge the CCP to work with Chiang in forming a northern expeditionary army to capture Peking. In return for Chiang's promise to restrain the right-wing faction of the KMT, Borodin offered Soviet aid and agreed to restrict CCP opponents of the KMT. With his status secure in Canton, Chiang launched his campaign to control central and northern China. His men "liberated" Nanking on March 24, 1927. When the Nationalists conducted attacks on Westerners in Nanking, Chiang blamed the Communists. Thus, the same day—April 11—that the foreigners protested against the Nanking demonstrations, their representatives in Shanghai were working with Chiang to plot his bloody terrorist raids on the Communists.

On April 12, 1927, with the support of British police and anti-Communist Shanghai merchants, Chiang moved to eliminate the CCP and its worker allies in Shanghai. Beginning at 4:00 A.M., KMT forces attacked working-class headquarters throughout the city. All workers and union organizers in the buildings were either shot on the spot or marched into the streets to be executed. All CCP members were disarmed; over 700 CCP leaders were killed during the day.

The purges and disorders continued for several weeks. Eventually, the KMT forced businessmen to pay them money or be charged with treason. Chiang's dictatorship made the bourgeoisie pay a high price, but he "saved" them from Communism. Similar purges were conducted by Chiang's men at Ningpo, Foochow, Amoy, Swatow, and Canton.

Temporarily, at least, Chiang controlled the strongest political and military bloc in China.

May 12, 1927

The Peace of Tipitapa ends political disputes in Nicaragua. U.S. Marines land to allegedly prevent Bolsheviks from taking over Central America.

During the spring of 1927, President Coolidge sent a personal representative, Henry L. Stimson, to Nicaragua to settle a civil war that had developed and persuaded the president again to dispatch Marines on May 2, 1926, to preserve order. Nicaragua's problems began just three weeks after the U.S. Marines, who had been in Nicaragua since 1912, withdrew on August 4, 1925. After two years of chaos, an uprising began backed by President Calles of Mexico, who supplied the Nicaraguan Liberal insurgents with arms, ammunition, and soldiers.

Mexico's intervention prompted Secretary Kellogg to recommend dispatching U.S. Marines to Managua, and they arrived on January 6, 1927. Marine contingents also landed on February 20 on the west coast of Nicaragua to halt the influx of Mexican arms and to protect Americans who lived there. On January 12, Kellogg sent a memorandum to the Senate Foreign Relations Committee that used nearly hysterical terms to justify the intervention as resulting from Bolshevik plans to take over Central America under Mexican auspices.

Henry Stimson worked out an agreement on May 12, known as the Peace of Tipitapa that provided for a general amnesty and the peaceful election on November 4, 1928, of General Moncada. Augusto C. Sandino, who rejected the Peace of Tipitapa negotiated by "imperialist Yankees," continued to fight. The Sandinistas were suppressed in 1933 and Sandino killed in 1934, but his followers continued sporadic fighting for many years. In the 1980s there would be a group of "Sandinistas" who would confront the Reagan administration.

August 23, 1927

Sacco and Vanzetti are executed.

The *cause célèbre* of the 1920s climaxed on August 23, 1927, when Nicola Sacco and Bartolomeo Vanzetti died in the electric chair at Charlestown, Massachusetts. Convicted in 1921 (see July 14, 1921), many observers believed that the politically charged Red Scare, which dominated the domestic scene during 1919–1920, had unduly influenced the judge and jury. During the following six years, their lawyers argued a series of appeals before Judge Thayer, the Massachusetts supreme court, and the governor's special advisory commission, which consisted of complex motions that included old and new evidence. All was to no avail.

Subsequent scholarly legal assessments have overwhelmingly concluded that the trial, conducted in the

General Sandino (center) and staff *en route* to Mexico, June 1929. National Archives

red-baiting atmosphere of the time, represented a grievous failure of the justice system. In 1977, the governor of Massachusetts issued a proclamation declaring that Sacco and Vanzetti had not been treated fairly.

November 30, 1927

Soviets join the Preparatory Commission to discuss disarmament plans.

The Preparatory Commission began its discussion on disarmament in 1926, but accomplished very little. The major dispute was between France's desire to obtain guarantees of security before disarming and the Anglo-American desire to disarm first and discuss security arrangements later. The Soviet Union finally joined the commission's discussions in November 1927 because there was a Soviet dispute with the Swiss government about the assassination of Vatzlav Vorovsky at Lausanne in 1923. The dispute was resolved with a Swiss apology and the payment of compensation to Vorovsky's family.

Although the Soviets had not been a participant in the League of Nation's earlier disarmament talks, the Soviets had followed the discussions since 1926. In 1921, the Russians claimed they were insulted by not receiving an invitation to the Washington Naval Conference and, in December 1922, they sponsored an abortive disarmament conference in Moscow that was attended by only five neighboring Eastern European countries. When the Soviets arrived at the Preparatory Commission meetings on November 30, 1927, they called for "the complete abolition of all land, navy, and air forces." Not surprising, the other delegates and the Western press considered these proposals as propaganda and summarily dismissed them.

1928

January 11, 1928

The Mexican-American dispute over subsoil rights is resolved. Secretary Kellogg raises the specter of Bolshevism and "world revolution."

Diplomatic relations between America and Mexico reached crisis proportions between 1925 and 1928. Following the election of President Plutarco Elias Calles in 1925, the Mexican legislature passed two laws based on Article 27 of its constitution of 1917. Because Article 27 gave all oil and mineral resources of Mexico to the state, U.S. and other foreign oil companies appealed to their governments to prevent the implementation of the Petroleum Law and the Alien Land Law passed in December 1925, claiming they violated the Bucareli Agreements of 1923.

The oil companies' appeals to Washington ran into two problems: theoretical and personal. The theoretical issue was Mexico's assertion of the Calvo Doctrine that declared corporations doing business in a foreign nation should appeal only to the native government's institutions, not to their home government. President Coolidge upheld American investors' right to appeal to their home government. Mexico's Minister of Foreign Relations, Aaron Saenz, declared the U.S. argument created a double standard. Saenz quoted Chief Justice John Marshall's court ruling: "The jurisdiction of the nation within its own territory is necessarily exclusive and absolute. . . .Any restriction on it, deriving validity from an external source, would imply a diminution of its sovereignty."

The more serious problem of U.S.-Mexican relations was personal, "being based on the conservative Secretary of State Kellogg's belief that all land reforms were Communistic, and on the prejudiced U.S. Ambassador James R. Sheffield's intense and prejudiced disdain for all things Mexican." Kellogg and President Coolidge believed Mexican policy was directed by the Soviet Union's Communist Third International. Kellogg informed the Senate Foreign Relations Committee in January 1926: "The Bolshevist leaders have had very definite ideas with respect to the role which Mexico and Latin Americans are to play in their program of world revolution. They have set up as one of their fundamental tasks the destruction of what they term American imperialism."

Sheffield personified all the worst aspects of America's self-righteous, racist, and closed-minded elite. He complained in a letter to Nicholas Murray Butler: "There is very little white blood in the [Mexican] cabinet—that is it [the blood] is wholly thin." In addition, the Mexicans "recognize no argument but force" for, as Sheffield wrote to former President Taft, Mexico "is one of the only countries where the gun is mightier than the pen."

Following his January 1927 report to the Senate Foreign Relations Committee, explaining his dispatching of Marines to Nicaragua as an anti-Bolshevik measure (see May 12, 1927), Kellogg began a gradual retreat from the hard-line policy. In Congress, strange bedfellows who criticized these policies were Senators Borah, La Follette, Burton K. Wheeler, and George Norris. Religious groups and academic interests also opposed U.S. intervention in Mexico and Nicaragua.

The appointment of Dwight W. Morrow as ambassador to Mexico inaugurated a complete change in U.S.-Mexican relations. On November 8, Morrow suggested to President Calles that the questions of Article 27 and the land laws were not diplomatic but legalistic. Morrow noted that Article 14 of the 1917 constitution stated that no legislation should apply retroactively in Mexico and wondered if Article 14 invalidated any law that affected oil rights contracted before 1925. Calles responded quickly, and on November 17, the Mexican court ruled that the law of 1925 was not constitutional. On December 28, the Mexican legislature passed a new law that applied Article 27 only to future subsoil concessions. The oil issue was not permanently settled because new efforts to nationalize began again in Mexico in 1935.

July 25, 1928

The United States recognizes Chiang Kai-shek's Nationalist government of China.

Between 1926 and 1928, Chiang's Kuomintang broke ties with its Communist allies and, on June 8, completed the pacification of most of central China by capturing Peking. In addition, Chiang's government had negotiated a settlement of the Nanking protests of April 11, 1927, by paying reparations for damages and accepting an American apology for the U.S. naval bombardment of Nanking.

October 20, 1928

China's KMT promulgates organic laws creating the Chinese Nationalist government, and Mao begins organizing Chinese Communist forces.

By the laws of October 20, five administrative divisions of government were established under the jurisdiction of China's president and highest military authority, Chiang Kai-shek. Only the KMT party was legal, and as leader of the KMT's executive council Chiang was both the party and the government head. In brief, Chiang Kai-shek was the military dictator of China. Chiang's government resembled the Soviet Communist system that Sun Yat-sen established in 1924.

China had official political unity under Chiang. Nevertheless, followers of the Chinese Communist Party were actively organizing peasant support in Kiangsi Province under the leadership of Mao Tse-tung.

November 6, 1928

Herbert Hoover is elected president.

On June 14, 1928, the Republican Party nominated Hoover at its convention in Kansas City, Missouri. The party favored the protective tariff and the continuation of Coolidge's foreign policies. The Democratic Convention selected Governor Alfred E. Smith of New York for its candidate and its platform condemned Coolidge's policies in Central America.

Hoover won by 444 electoral votes to Smith's 85. The Republicans also retained control of Congress.

December 20, 1928

Great Britain recognizes Chiang Kai-shek's Nationalist government of China.

In addition to recognition, Britain concluded a treaty with the Chinese that provided a partial release for China from the unequal treaties that the British instituted after the Opium War in 1842.

1929

March 5, 1929

Henry L. Stimson is commissioned as secretary of state by President Hoover.

Stimson was well qualified to serve as secretary of state. Trained as a lawyer, he was a progressive Republican who admired Theodore Roosevelt. He served as secretary of war under President Taft (1911–1913); as a special presidential representative to Nicaragua during a crisis there in 1927; and as governor general of the Philippine Islands from 1927 to 1929. Stimson was secretary throughout Hoover's term of office.

October 1, 1929

Great Britain resumes diplomatic recognition of the Soviet Union.

The Zinoviev letter's alleged interference in Britain's election of October 1924 resulted in generally bad relations with the USSR and a diplomatic break between the two nations on May 26, 1927. The Labour Party's victory in the elections on May 30, 1929, returned Ramsay MacDonald as prime minister, and new British discussions began with the Soviets. On October 1, the MacDonald government renewed diplomatic relations with the Soviet Union on an official basis.

October 29, 1929

The Wall Street stock market plunges—usually ascribed as the beginning of the worldwide Great Depression.

Although there had been signs of trouble in the stock market before October 29, the trading of 16 million shares in one day heralded a four-year period of price declines. By November 13, nearly $30 billion of market value of listed stocks had been lost. As John Kenneth Galbraith notes, the lost sum was greater than all the dollars in circulation in America in 1929. The international financial community of all nations suffered except for the Soviet Union, which was isolated generally from the capitalist financial structure. The low point of the Great Depression was reached in March 1933.

Of course, the decline in agricultural prices not long after the conclusion of World War I caused grave economic hardships, seriously disrupting the economies of many countries during the early 1920s. Consequently, historians have established different dates for the beginning of the Great Depression, although the U.S. stock market crash was the most dramatic episode.

International relations were affected as nations sought different solutions for their economic problems.

December 2, 1929

Secretary Stimson invokes the Kellogg-Briand Pact to prevent a Sino-Soviet war.

On July 10, 1929, Chinese Nationalist troops seized the Chinese Eastern Railway in Manchuria in an attempt to end the Soviet Union's control over the railroad. Chiang Kai-shek proposed to regain the Chinese rights in Manchuria that Russia, later the Soviet Union, and Japan had shared since 1896, with the Soviets controlling the Chinese Eastern Railway. The Soviets opposed the July 10 attack, and in November 1929 Soviet forces invaded Manchuria, where several armed skirmishes resulted with China's army.

Because the Kellogg-Briand Peace Pact, which outlawed war, had gone into effect on July 24, 1929, Secretary of State Stimson tested it by using the pact to avert a Sino-Soviet conflict. On July 25, Stimson called on Great Britain, France, Germany, Italy, and Japan to join America in a six-power commission acting under the Peace Pact to settle the Manchuria dispute. The other nations resented Stimson's interference, largely because he had not consulted them in advance, but also because they believed the request was not consonant with the pact.

On November 26, Stimson tried again. He sent identical notes to the five powers, asking them to publicly urge China and the USSR to observe the Kellogg peace agreement. Although all the powers except Italy ignored Stimson's note, the secretary assumed that silence was consent, and on December 2, he wired notes to the Soviet Union (by way of France since the United States did not recognize the Soviet regime) and China, admonishing them to follow the Peace Pact's obligations because both nations had signed the pact in 1928. Similar notes were sent to the antagonists by 37 other nations, but their efforts were fruitless. China denied it had violated the pact; the USSR told the other nations to mind their own business.

By early December, aside from the Peace Pact, China and the Soviet Union undertook discussions to avert war. The latter was too concerned about its domestic Five-Year Plan to fight a war; China was too weak for a long struggle. On December 22, both nations accepted the status quo in Manchuria by signing the Protocol of Khabarovsk.

1930

July 1, 1930

U.S. Customs temporarily halts imports of Russian pulpwood.

Under the authority of Section 307 of the Hawley-Smoot tariff act, the United States could embargo any imports produced by convict labor. Treasury Secretary Andrew Mellon, who was highly critical of the Soviet's dumping cheap matches on the depressed American economy, allowed his assistant to ban all Soviet pulpwood, with the implication that other products could also be denied entry. (This was a somewhat odd position for Mellon, since he was currently investing millions in Russian art treasures.) Americans who endorsed the ban were motivated because they opposed Communist ideology and assumed imported Soviet goods damaged America's already desperate market, but most of these imports did not compete with American products.

United States exports to the Soviet Union were more important to the American economy. Indeed in 1930, the United States held a 25 percent share of the Soviet market. As the government retained the right to challenge any Soviet import, uncertainty greatly disrupted U.S.-Soviet trade during the next few years. Although the temporary ban on Soviet pulpwood was raised and the Soviet cargo unloaded, the ban was a pivotal event in American-Soviet trade relations.

October 20, 1930

Moscow takes steps against countries interfering with Soviet imports.

The Soviet government retaliated against the U.S. trade restrictions by issuing a decree allowing the People's Commissariat of Foreign Trade to impose sanctions against nations impeding Soviet imports. Thus, Moscow's action would use less, not more trade, to damage the American economy and bring about a change of policy. Obviously, the Soviets wanted the American government to remove trade restrictions and recognize the USSR's legal existence. The results of Moscow's retaliation were dramatic when the American share of the Soviet market dropped from 25 percent in 1930 to 4.5 percent in 1932. At the same time, European nations substantially increased their share of Soviet trade. Not surprising, the American-Soviet Chamber of Commerce together with other business executives began clamoring for Washington to review its policies. Although President Hoover opposed any embargo of Soviet goods, it awaited the arrival of Franklin Roosevelt before fundamental policy changes were achieved.

1931

March 7, 1931

Turko-Soviet naval protocol stabilizes naval forces in the Black Sea.

After uneasy Turko-Soviet diplomatic relations during the 1920s, in 1930 Turkish diplomats were concerned that the naval power balance in the Black Sea might be altered. On March 7, 1931, the Turko-Soviet naval protocol was devised to head-off the race to build more naval vessels and to stabilize the existing naval equilibrium. Since the 1929 Preparatory Commission was unsuccessful in its effort to secure naval reductions, the Soviets were concerned about Italy's growing naval strength in the Mediterranean. Stipulations of the Lausanne Convention governing the Straits allowed any other power to match Soviet naval strength in the Black Sea. Not surprisingly, the Soviets now wanted the Straits to be closed to outside navies and, short of that, cordial relations with Turkey. (See Lausanne Conference, July 24, 1923, and Montreux Convention, July 20, 1936.)

December 2, 1931

In El Salvador, Maximiliano H. Martinez creates a right-wing dictatorship, suppressing Communism and liberal movements.

December 31, 1931

Soviets complete their first Five-Year Plan.

Stalin's first Five-Year Plan had two basic features: collectivization of agriculture and industrial growth. The confiscation of large and middle-sized estates and redistributing them to peasant families shifted the agricultural economy from market production to subsistence farming. While these early programs raised Soviet production to its pre-World-War I level, it created a peasantry that was highly resistant to the large-scale industrial development that Communist leaders envisioned to create socialism in Russia. The forcible merging of 25.6 million individual farms into 250,000 collective farms was costly in terms of lives and personal misery because five million families and perhaps 24 million people disappeared from the countryside. Approximately one-half of these people moved to cities and became employed in construction and factories, while the other half either perished or were sent to labor camps for refusing to give up their land. Although the massive transformation substantially underwrote the financing of industrial projects, collectivized agricultural remained a perennial weakness in the Soviet economy.

Even though central planners made mistakes, industrial activity grew at annual rates of 12 to 14 percent and the Soviet Union rose from fifth place to second place among industrial nations. This was a most remarkable feat, especially during the depression in Western nations. However, the first Five-Year Plan could not have attained its objectives except for the imports and technical assistance provided by the West, especially the United States.

1932

February 2, 1932

A general disarmament conference convenes at Geneva.

Sixty nations met at Geneva to negotiate a general disarmament agreement; however, their prospects for success were dim from the outset. The conference failed to achieve any significant accords.

November 8, 1932

Franklin Delano Roosevelt is elected president.

On June 19 in Chicago, the Republican Party Convention again nominated Herbert Hoover for president. The Democratic Convention selected Governor of New York Franklin D. Roosevelt as its nominee. In the November balloting, Roosevelt secured 472 electoral votes to Hoover's 59. Roosevelt carried 42 of the 48 states.

1933

January 30, 1933

Adolf Hitler, leader of the Nazi Party, becomes head of the German government.

In Germany, the Great Depression posed grave dangers for the fledgling Weimar Republic's government. Both the National Socialist (NAZI) Party and the Communist Party attacked the republic's policies as well as each other. Republican leaders attempted to fulfill the cooperative policies represented by the League of Nations and other international conferences of the 1920s. The radical left and reactionary right groups advocated abandonment of the Treaty of Versailles and blamed all the subsequent shattering consequences on the Allies' unjust punishment of Germany since 1919.

The resulting March 5, 1933, election gave the Nazis 288 seats, the Nationalists 52. The Socialist-Communist seats fell from 222 the previous November to 201. With some Catholic Center votes, the Nazi-Nationalist coalition outlawed the Communist Party and on March 23, 1933, voted dictatorial powers to Hitler until April 1, 1937. A Nazi "legal" revolution occurred during the next two years. The Nazi Party became the only party on July 14, 1933, and Germany became a nation (the Third Reich) rather than a federal state on January 30, 1934. Judicial, racial, religious, economic, and military legislation gave Hitler and his party complete control of Germany.

March 4, 1933

Cordell Hull is commissioned as secretary of state by President Roosevelt.

Hull had the respect of Democratic Party regulars, having served as a Tennessee congressman (1907–1921 and 1923–1931) and senator (1931–1933) for 23 years. Roosevelt chose Hull largely because he was well known as an economic internationalist who opposed protective tariffs and desired reciprocal agreements. Hull guided the State Department until November 30, 1944, longer than any previous secretary of state.

November 17, 1933

President Roosevelt and the Soviet Union's foreign minister sign an agreement to normalize relations between the United States and the USSR.

Following the Bolshevik Revolution of November 1917, the United States refused to recognize the Soviet government. In 1933, however, Roosevelt discerned that American public opinion no longer strongly opposed recognition of the Communist regime. Some

Europe between the Wars

businessmen believed diplomatic relations would stimulate trade with the Soviets, and some internationalists thought U.S.-Soviet diplomacy might restrain Japanese ventures in Manchuria. In April 1933, Roosevelt urged Senator Claude Swanson to promote a national discussion about the benefits of recognition.

Roosevelt's principal concerns in Soviet relations were the opposition of religious groups who disapproved of recognition of the atheist Communist government and American nationalists who disliked the propaganda and possible subversive activity of the Communist Party under the direction of the Third Communist International (Comintern). To forestall criticism, Roosevelt met in October with Father Edmund A. Walsh of Georgetown University, the nation's leading Roman Catholic spokesman against Soviet recognition. Roosevelt persuaded Walsh to trust his ability as "a good horse dealer" to require the Soviets to grant Americans religious rights in the USSR and to obtain guarantees against Communist subversive activity in America. Walsh's backing assisted the president.

Having secured some acceptance from public leaders, Roosevelt arranged through Boris Skvirsky, Moscow's trade representative in New York, to issue an invitation to the Soviet Union to send a representative to discuss American-Soviet relations. Because Soviet leader Joseph Stalin now desired cooperation against the rising threat of fascism, the Soviets responded positively and appointed their foreign minister, Maxim Litvinov, to go to Washington for talks.

Litvinov's negotiations took place from November 8 to 16, 1933. In his formal discussions at the State Department, Litvinov initially showed little interest in meeting American conditions for recognition. On November 10, however, he began direct discussions with the president, and agreements were reached that resulted in the normalization of U.S.-Soviet relations. The Soviets agreed to extend religious freedom to U.S. citizens in the Soviet Union and to negotiate an agreement to provide fair trials for Americans accused of crime there. The Soviet government also agreed not to engage in subversive activities, although the wording of this clause did not include the action of the Communist Party as distinct from the government.

Finally, details regarding Soviet debts and U.S. financial claims were delegated to future discussions, the Soviets agreeing to pay between $75 million and $150 million in claims. The debt issue raised less suspicion than it had previously because most major European nations had defaulted on their U.S. debts after 1931. Although the 1933 agreements restored U.S.-Soviet diplomatic recognition, the trade and international stability that advocates of recognition predicted did not materialize. No immediate consequences may be attributed to recognition; however, it later permitted the "strange alliance" of 1941 to 1945 to proceed without difficulty after Hitler invaded the USSR in June 1941.

1934

February 2, 1934

President Roosevelt establishes the Export-Import Bank to encourage overseas commerce.

Acting under provisions of the Reconstruction Finance Corporation and the National Recovery Act, the president established the Export-Import Bank. It was to finance foreign trade with short-term credits for exporting agricultural commodities; with longer-term credits for U.S. firms exporting industrial manufacturing; and with loans to U.S. exporters where foreign governments did not provide sufficient exchange credit to meet their dollar obligations.

Two banks were originally set up: one for trade credits to the Soviet Union, the other for credit facilities with Cuba and other foreign nations. In 1936, these two banks were merged.

1935

March 23, 1935

Under pressure from Japan, the Soviet Union sells its interests in the Chinese Eastern Railway to Manchukuo.

This railway had been under constant dispute between Japan and the Soviet Union because it gave the Soviets a direct route between Irkutsk and Vladivostok. After the USSR renounced other czarist treaties with China on May 31, 1924, it retained joint management with China of the railroad through Manchuria. By the act of March 23, the Soviets yielded their control to Japan's puppet government in Manchukuo.

May 2, 1935

France and the USSR form an alliance in case of unprovoked aggression.

Following Germany's rearmament decree of March 16, 1935, France and the Soviet Union undertook discussions to develop a defensive alliance by which an attack on one would result in a two-front war for Germany. Stalin was now promoting antifascist, popular-front movements outside the Soviet Union and was eager to sign. In France, however, the political divisions between right-wing and left-wing groups deepened because of this projected alliance. The rightist conservatives in France denounced any form of agreement with the Communists. This division in French politics persistently weakened French foreign policy between 1935 and 1940 as the struggle between proto-fascists and socialists caused the deterioration of the centrist advocates of the Third Republic.

May 16, 1935

The Soviet Union and Czechoslovakia conclude an alliance by which Moscow would aid Prague in case of an attack on the Czechoslovaks provided France also acted.

During the years preceding the Munich crisis of September 1938, the Soviet Union repeatedly sought united action with France and England in opposing Nazi German expansion. The "appeasement" policy followed by London and Paris was anti-Communist, however. Chamberlain, Édouard Daladier, and others considered the Soviets a greater menace than the Germans.

July 13, 1935

The United States and Soviets sign a trade agreement.

American Ambassador William Bullitt and Foreign Affairs Commissar Maksim Litvinov signed a trade

Far East

pact by which the Soviets promised to buy at least $30 million worth of U.S. goods within the following 12 months. In return, the United States would extend the most-favored-nation tariff treatment under the Reciprocal Trade Agreements Act, which could mean up to a 50 percent reduction in tariffs for some Soviet products. This arrangement was accomplished by consciously avoiding discussion of the Soviet debt issue that continued to plague U.S. foreign policy.

The Soviets took advantage of this new arrangement and substantially increased their U.S. imports; however, the types of purchases changed. Moscow was now interested in obtaining products and technologies that would enhance their military capabilities—especially aircraft and petroleum processes. The trade pact was extended annually by both governments until 1942, at which time it was indefinitely renewed. The commercial agreement remained in effect until 1951 when Congress insisted on its termination. The Trade Agreements Extension Act of 1951 prohibited continuing the most-favored-nation tariff treatment to the Soviet Union.

1936

June 5, 1936

In France, the left-wing Popular Front coalition of Léon Blum gains control of the ministry.

The parliamentary elections of May 3 had given the Socialists and Radical Socialists a majority in the Chamber of Deputies. The Communist Party did not join the ministry but cooperated with the Popular Front. The Blum government tried to install an extensive program of economic and social reforms that caused financial difficulties for the government and led many of the French to gravitate to the political right.

July 17, 1936

The Spanish civil war begins as insurgents led by General Francisco Franco and other army chiefs revolt in Spanish Morocco.

Established on December 9, 1931, the Spanish republic experienced difficulties with separatist movements

General Francisco Franco. National Archives

in Catalonia and political disputes between republican and socialist left-wing factions. In addition, the republic's army and the Roman Catholic Church opposed the anticlerical legislation affecting education and the property of the religious orders. During October 1934, the Catholic Popular Action Party won positions in Prime Minister Alejandro Lerroux's cabinet and were able to block his attempts to solve Spanish problems in 1935. To offset the Catholic Party's growth and other right-wing groups, the socialist left united in a Popular Front and forced Lerroux to call new elections. On February 16, 1935, the Popular Front won a decisive victory over the Conservative, Republican, Catholic, and Monarchist Parties.

The Popular Front victory precipitated General Franco's decision to rally the right-wing armies to rebel against the republic. The rebels had no political program but called themselves Nationalists. Instead, the Nationalists claimed to wage a mighty struggle pitting Christian civilization against the Popular Front members who were part of an unholy conspiracy dominated by Bolsheviks. The Nationalists claimed the Popular Front espoused such un-Spanish notions as atheism and materialism and should be called "Reds." At Franco's call, the Catholic Clerics, army, and air force leaders joined the Nationalists who appealed to German and Italian fascists for military aid. The Nationalists' appeal brought German and Italian "volunteer" contingents to join Franco's rebels. Soon after, the Soviet Union sent advisors and military equipment to the government.

See August 9, 1936.

July 20, 1936

The Montreux Convention remilitarized the Straits; a qualified Soviet success.

After Italian forces attacked Ethiopia in 1936, Turkey asked the League of Nations to change the demilitarization of the Straits so that they could erect fortifications in the Straits. When Lausanne signatories met at Montreux, the Turkish delegate offered a draft proposal that the British thought was written by the Soviet Union. The draft called for closing the Straits to non-Black Sea navies, which meant Soviet naval units could pass freely into the Mediterranean. The French supported the Turkish proposal but the British and Japanese delegates opposed the draft. Confronted with these alternatives, the Soviets chose to have it closed to all belligerents. When the final Montreux Convention was prepared on July 20, 1936, Turkey, the USSR, Bulgaria, France, Great Britain, Japan, and Romania signed the Montreux Convention. Only Italy refused to sign it. The convention allowed Turkey to fortify the Straits and to have full sovereignty over the Straits, a notable victory for Ataturk. In 1946, the Soviets would try once again to revise the Straits' convention.

See August 15, 1946.

August 9, 1936

French Premier Léon Blum follows British advice and calls for a meeting of all European nations to adopt nonintervention policies in the Spanish civil war.

As the leader of the French Popular Front government of left-wing liberal and socialist parties in France, Blum's first reaction to the Fascist civil war against the Spanish republic was to aid the loyalist republicans in Madrid. Great Britain's Conservative Party ministry did not support this policy, and Foreign Secretary Anthony Eden warned Blum that if Germany attacked France over the Spanish issue, England would not aid the French.

At Britain's suggestion, Blum called for a general European conference to adopt a nonintervention policy in Spain. Also on August 9, Blum suspended all French war exports to Spain.

See September 11, 1936.

August 11, 1936

Secretary of State Hull announces a "moral embargo" against both belligerents in the Spanish civil war.

Following General Franco's Fascist-inspired attack on the Loyalist Republican government of Spain on July 17, 1936, Britain and France urged general European neutrality in the civil war. Secretary Hull and President Roosevelt found this course of action acceptable, and on August 11, Hull publicly announced the American desire not to assist either side in the war.

Although the Neutrality Act of 1936 did not apply to a civil war, Hull stated he hoped all Americans would apply the spirit of that law to the Spanish conflict. The United States, he said, would "scrupulously refrain from any interference whatsoever in the unfortunate Spanish situation." Despite Hull's statement, many American Roman Catholics favored Franco's effort to overthrow the government.

During the fall of 1936, the Spanish crisis had not yet acquired the ideological dimensions that appeared clearly during the spring of 1937. While some rumors of German and Italian aid to Franco surfaced in August and September, no overt evidence had appeared. Britain and France organized a collective neutrality system in Europe. The policy of neutrality also served Roosevelt well during the presidential campaign of 1936. Although domestic issues predominated in the election, Roosevelt's neutrality in Spain pleased both the isolationists and the European-oriented internationalists during the fall and winter of 1936.

See October 8, 1936.

August 19, 1936

The Moscow trials of old Bolsheviks opens.

In January 1935, Grigori Zinoviev, Lev Kamenev, and several other old Bolsheviks from the 1917 Revolution were tried for treason in secret sessions and sentenced to prison. In reality, these men had sided with Leon Trotsky against Stalin's rise to power during the 1920s. Continuing to be suspicious of anyone who differed with him, Stalin decided to stage public "show-trials" in 1936, beginning with those found guilty in 1935. At the second trials, Zinoviev, Kamenev, and fourteen other old Bolsheviks were accused of plotting with enemy countries against Stalin's regime. The sixteen men were convicted and immediately executed.

Additional show trials were held between August 1936 and May 1938, during which other Soviet political and military leaders who earned Stalin's distrust were executed after being convicted of treason or of trying to restore bourgeois capitalism. The most important old Bolshevik executed in 1938 was Nikolai I. Bukarin, who opposed Stalin's forced collectivization of the Soviet Union's peasant population in 1929. Details of these events are in Robert Conquest's *The Great Terror: A Reassessment* (1990).

October 8, 1936

At the International Non-Intervention Committee meeting, the USSR objects to Fascist violations of the agreements, but Britain and France do not act.

The accusations made by the Soviet delegate at the London nonintervention conference illustrate the duplicity of Germany, Italy, and the Soviet Union in proclaiming nonintervention in Spain while at the same time providing aid to either Franco's Nationalist forces or the Loyalist Republicans. The first meeting of the Non-Intervention Committee that Léon Blum proposed on August 9, 1936, was held in London on September 9. Subsequently, throughout the civil war the Non-Intervention Committee gave the appearance of advocating no aid to either belligerent, although each of the 24 nations working on the Non-Intervention Committee provided varying degrees of aid to either the Fascist or Republican cause. The historian Hugh Thomas describes the committee's existence after September 9 as moving "from equivocation to hypocrisy and humiliation" but enduring until Franco's Fascist forces triumphed.

The Non-Intervention Committee served each nation's interest in different ways. For the British, the Conservative ministry appeared to be acting impartially while following covert practices that aided Franco's forces of "law and order." For France, the Popular Front government placated its liberal and left wings by providing small amounts of secret aid to the republic but appearing to be impartial. For Germany and Italy, their larger amount of aid to Franco was masked sufficiently to greatly assist Franco while the Spanish republicans received little aid, even though they represented the legitimate Spanish government. The Soviet Union provided some help to the Spanish republic but was generally dismayed by the Fascist aid to Franco. The Soviets stayed on the committee to retain the goodwill of the British and French.

On October 15, following its complaint at the committee session about Fascist intervention, the Soviet Union rapidly increased its military aid to the Loyalists. The smaller nations that joined the Non-Intervention Committee simply followed the five larger powers: some aided the Fascists; some aided the Republicans in Spain.

In retrospect, the Non-Intervention Committee's duplicity assisted Franco's forces more than the Loyalists. But it did provide a curious method for avoiding direct confrontations and, thus, a general European war. In this respect, the Anglo-French policy was a progenitor of appeasement. In each European country, the general public feared the Communist revolutionary threat represented by the Spanish republic more than the Nazi-Fascist ideology represented by Franco. The possible continuation of a liberal republican government in Spain was sacrificed to Franco's Fascist dictatorship, determining Spain's authoritarian society for the next 40 years.

See November 18, 1936.

October 25, 1936

The Berlin-Rome anti-Comintern Pact is formed.

Hitler and Count Ciano of Italy signed an agreement to cooperate in seeking revision of the World War I peace treaties. In 1934–1935, Mussolini had often consulted with England and France because Italy's interests in the Danube region had differed from Hitler's. These conflicts were overlooked in 1936, and the two Fascist dictators agreed to work together against both democratic governments and Communism. In November, Japan negotiated with Germany and Italy to join the Axis alliance.

Both Britain and France were deceived by the anti-Comintern rhetoric of the Axis powers. As Italian Foreign Minister Count Galeazzo asserted, the anti-Comintern pact was "unmistakably anti-British" in Europe, the Mediterranean, and the Far East, not anti-Communist. For fascists, of course, anti-Communism included the center liberal republican and democratic parties as well as the Soviet Union. During the 1930s, however, many who favored parliamentary government in England and France held an exaggerated fear of Communism that led them to embrace the "law and order" speeches of the extreme right. Lacking sufficient devotion to the basic concepts of human rights, the centrists were weak apostles of democracy for whom the watchword slogan was "better Hitler than Stalin."

November 3, 1936

Roosevelt wins an overwhelming victory in the presidential contest.

The election campaign was a bitter contest because the Republicans vigorously condemned the New Deal. Roosevelt won the biggest electoral majority since Monroe in 1820: Landon, 8, Roosevelt, 523. The Democratic majority in the Senate was 77-19; in the House, 328-107.

November 18, 1936

Germany and Italy recognize Franco's insurgent government in Spain.

Although they joined the London Non-Intervention Committee on September 9, 1936, Hitler and Mussolini supported General Franco with arms, technical experts, and some troops. On October 1,

Adolph Hitler and Benito Mussolini are seen here in Munich in 1940. National Archives

Franco named himself head of the Spanish state. To aid Franco overtly in blockading the Loyalist supply routes, Germany and Italy formally recognized his regime on November 18.

Although Britain's Conservative government's policy preferred Franco, London withheld recognition to retain the cooperation of French Premiers Léon Blum and Édouard Daladier until their Popular Front governments fell on October 4, 1938.

See January 8, 1937.

November 25, 1936

Germany and Japan sign an anti-Comintern pact.

Ostensibly, the pact between Hitler's Nazi government and Japan's military-dominated government emphasized their agreement to oppose Communism as identified by the Moscow-dominated Comintern. Of course, to these ultranationalists "Communists" included liberal democrats, socialists, and other center and left-of-center groups.

Japan and Italy also negotiated an agreement, completed on November 6, 1937, which joined the three extreme rightist governments as ideological and political allies.

1937

January 8, 1937

President Roosevelt signs legislation that specifically applies an impartial arms embargo to the Spanish civil war.

From August 11 to December 28, America's "moral embargo" against the shipment of arms to either side in Spain had been generally effective. On December 26, however, the first organized group of 26 American volunteers left New York for Spain. Because these and later U.S. volunteers, all of whom fought for the Loyalist Republicans, officially volunteered when they reached France, the U.S. government could not prosecute them. After January 11, 1937, the passport office stamped all passports as "Not Valid for Spain," but after reaching France, passports became unnecessary for the volunteers.

On December 28, the moral embargo was circumvented by Robert Cruse, who applied for a license to ship $2,775,000 worth of aircraft engines to the Spanish government. Cruse received his license because the State Department had no legal means to reject it. Subsequently, Cruse's cargo left New York the day before the congressional embargo was passed on January 8. Carried on board the Spanish ship *Mar*

Cantabrico, the cargo was captured by the Spanish nationalists in the Bay of Biscay and was used by the Fascists rather than the Republican forces in Spain.

Cruse's license application prompted President Roosevelt to urge Congress to make such sales illegal as soon as it reassembled on January 6, 1937. The law as passed on January 6 and signed by the president on January 8 embargoed all sales of arms, ammunition, and implements of war to Spain. Neither belligerent could obtain U.S. arms.

Roosevelt's principal reason for requesting the arms embargo appears to have been his desire to align his policy to what he perceived to be the Anglo-French policy. Whether or not Roosevelt or other Americans understood the role that British Conservatives and France were playing in Europe is not certain. Although the U.S. consul at Seville made frequent reports to the State Department on the large amount of German and Italian matériel and the "volunteers" entering Spain, the president may have been too concerned with domestic problems to have noticed. Whatever the reason for Roosevelt's decision to act "impartially" in Spain, the net result of the U.S. embargo was, as in the case of the Anglo-French embargoes, favorable to the Spanish Fascists.

Realizing this, Franco announced in January that the president acted as a "true gentleman" in approving the Embargo Act. The Germans also praised Roosevelt. Increasingly, however, U.S. liberals, socialists, and Communists condemned the embargo and supplied volunteers to assist the Spanish Republicans.

See March 28, 1939.

January 30, 1937

Stalin's purge of the Communist Party extends into military ranks.

Although the trials and executions of "Old Bolsheviks" whom Stalin distrusted began in 1935, he extended the purges for "treason" to military commanders in 1937. From January 23 to 30, Stalin ordered the execution of 13 more assumed political competitors, the most prominent being Yuri Pyatakov and Karl Radek. Yet in light of their effect on Soviet fortunes in World War II, Stalin's most crucial purges were of military leaders that began on June 11, 1937. As Robert Conquest reports, the arrest of military officers in May came as a surprise when they were announced. To justify their trials, the Communist Party organ *Pravda* reported on June 15 that these commanders had "admitted their treacherousness, wreckings, and espionage."

Among the seven top-ranking military officials executed on June 12, the most prominent were Marshal M. N. Tukhachevsky, the deputy people's commissar of defense, and Yan Gamarnik, the first deputy commissar of defense. As Conquest explains, the "assault on the army" probably derived from a German plot to "betray" Tukhachevsky and cripple the Red Army. The German head of intelligence, Reinhard Heydrich, engineered the plot by forging a "dossier" of 23 documents. Next, a German agent contacted an official of the Soviet embassy, showing him 2 pages of the dossier and asking payment for the other 30 pages. Moscow quickly bought the dossier for one-half million counterfeit marks and between May 20 and 31, Stalin ordered the arrest of the seven military leaders. Additional army purges followed over the next two years.

Although at least one million Soviet citizens were swept away during Stalin's purges of the 1930s, the army executions between May 1937 and September 1938 left the USSR with grave deficiencies in military experience. Conquest indicates that the one military area where the Germans were "immensely superior" in 1941 was the quality of command and staff officers. By 1940, at least 428 of the top-level Soviet officer corps had been executed plus many others, perhaps 43,000, were dismissed. Robert Conquest's *The Great Terror: A Reassessment* (1990) provides an informed discussion of Stalin's purges.

May 28, 1937

Chamberlain becomes British prime minister. He maintains an appeasement policy toward Germany and antipathy toward the Soviet Union.

Since 1934, Stanley Baldwin's Conservative ministry was uncertain about proper policies toward Germany and Italy. When Neville Chamberlain became prime minister on May 28, he followed his prior desire to negotiate peace with Hitler and Mussolini, even if concessions were essential. As F. S. Northedge's *The Troubled Giant* explains, Chamberlain did not invent "appeasement" but carried it to its logical conclusions, showing that in a violent world the assumptions of many British politicians were "out of place." Chamberlain's beliefs did not differ from those of the bulk of British public opinion that thought war was the worst evil and should be avoided at almost any cost. He thought peace depended on understanding between the Great Powers, especially Britain and Germany.

Chamberlain had slight respect for France's unstable government and almost no respect for Italy. He abhorred Soviet Communism and thought its ongoing purges weakened the Soviet state. As for the United States, he thought isolationism meant Britain could "count on nothing from the Americans but words." With Britain and Germany as the effective powers, Chamberlain believed Britain must remove the injustices of the 1919 Versailles Treaty and the mistrust in the minds of English and Germans. He supposed the appeasement policy could build confidence by making concessions to Hitler.

July 7, 1937

An incident between Chinese and Japanese troops at the Macro Polo Bridge develops into an undeclared war.

At the Marco Polo Bridge 13 kilometers outside Peking, Japanese troops fought against Chinese soldiers. Exactly what happened remains a mystery but the Chinese claimed the Japanese were looking for a missing soldier in the city of Wanping and began firing artillery that killed or wounded 200 Chinese in Wanping. The Japanese contend Chinese soldiers fired at Japanese troops without provocation. Whatever occurred, the Japanese army used the incident as an excuse to pour reinforcements into north China. By December attempts to localize the fighting ended. Although it would be four and half years before a formal declaration, the Pacific War had begun and would be fully joined by the United States after Pearl Harbor.

This terrified baby was almost the only human being left alive in Shanghai's South Station after Japanese bombing raid. National Archives

Meanwhile Washington bombarded Tokyo with diplomatic protests and the Soviets continued to send military supplies and advisors to assist the Nationalist Chinese during the early years of fighting.

December 12, 1937

Roosevelt secretly asks the Soviets to exchange military information regarding the Far East.

On December 12, 1937, Japanese aircraft attacked and sank the U.S. gunboat *Panay* and three Standard Oil tanker ships above Nanking on the Yangtze River. Soon after, President Roosevelt asked Ambassador Joseph E. Davies to ask the Kremlin about a mutual exchange of military information related to the military situation in the Far East. The president warned Davies to keep the inquiry in strict confidence and not to mention it to his embassy staff. This caution arose because of the anti-Soviet hostility prevalent in the U.S. Embassy in Moscow. During the past spring, the State Department's Division of East European Affairs had been eliminated because of its strident anti-Soviet attitudes.

Stalin agreed to the military liaison system, but he also insisted that the exchange of information be kept secret. The president's proposal encouraged Stalin to ask about a settlement of the Kerensky debt in order to stimulate closer collaboration. But once again the debt issue blocked an opportunity to improve relations.

As for Japan's sinking of the *Panay*, Japan's Foreign Minister Hirota told the U.S. Ambassador Joseph Grew that Japanese planes following the Chinese army mistakenly hit the *Panay* due to poor visibility in the area. This excuse was soon proven to be false because several eyewitnesses in China agreed there was clear visibility when the four ships were attacked.

1938

May 13, 1938

The Senate Foreign Relations Committee blocks Senator Nye's resolution to extend cash-and-carry provisions for arms to Spain's loyalist government.

The threatened defeat of the Spanish Republicans by Franco's troops and the terrorist attacks by German and Italian aircraft on Spanish cities led many Americans to advocate some action against the Fascist forces in Spain. By 1938 there were many examples of German and Italian military units fighting with Franco's armies. The bombing of Guernica on April 26, 1937, became the most dramatic evidence of the new terror from the sky. Waves of German planes bombed and strafed the city for three hours, killing 1,654 people and wounding 889 in an indiscriminate attack on the civilian population.

Although many Roman Catholic groups in America, led by Cardinal Mundelein of Chicago, supported Franco, many liberal groups pressured Roosevelt to aid the Republicans. Nye's resolution of May 3 authorized the president to end the Spanish arms embargo of January 8, 1937, and permit the Spanish Loyalists to obtain arms on the "cash and carry" basis of the Third Neutrality Act of May 1, 1937.

President Roosevelt wanted to consider ways to aid the anti-Fascist forces, but he agreed with Secretary of State Hull that Nye's resolution was not suitable. Subsequently, Hull sent the Senate Foreign Relations Committee a message on May 12 opposing the Nye Resolution. Hull argued that there was danger in Europe that the Spanish war could become a wider international conflict. Therefore, he said, he feared the complications likely to arise from "a reversal of our policy of strict neutrality." The committee concurred, rejecting Nye's proposal by a vote of 17 to 1.

In November 1938, there were renewed attempts to remove the Spanish embargo in favor of the Republicans in Barcelona. Again, Hull contended that only Congress could repeal the arms legislation, and prospects for such action were nil. By the winter of 1938–1939, the Spanish embargo became part of the larger Roosevelt attempt to change the entire Neutrality Act of 1937.

August 10, 1938

Following nearly four weeks of fighting at Changkufeng Hill, Japanese and Soviet forces arrange a truce that reasserts the status quo.

The fighting took place on the borders of Siberia, Manchukuo, and Korea. This was one of the more serious border incidents between Japan and the Soviet Union that recurred until the signing of the Soviet-Japanese neutrality pact of April 13, 1941. The most significant of these was the Khalkin Gol (Nomonhan) Incident in May–September 1939 that resulted in over 17,000 Japanese casualties and perhaps similar losses for the Soviets. However, the overwhelming Soviet military prowess demonstrated in this clash persuaded Japanese army officers that they did not have the modern weapons to successfully wage a full-scale war against the Soviet Union. Subsequently, the Japanese army focused on its intervention in China and endorsed their navy's subsequent decision to challenge Great Britain and the United States.

September 29, 1938

The Munich Conference solves the Czech crisis because France and England "appease" Hitler: The Appeasement Policy.

After Hitler's September 12 speech demanded self-determination for Germans in Czechoslovakia's Sudetenland, a European war seemed imminent. On September 15, British Prime Minister Chamberlain met Hitler at Berchtesgaden, where Hitler demanded the annexation of the Sudetenland, which had been given to the Czechs by the Treaty of Versailles for security reasons. Hitler said the Germans would risk war if necessary to obtain these "just" demands of self-determination. Although French Premier Daladier and the Soviets wanted to strongly oppose Hitler, Chamberlain convinced the Czechs to accept Hitler's terms.

A Sudeten woman is unable to conceal her tears as she dutifully salutes the triumphant Germans occupying her town. National Archives

Chamberlain's policy of appeasement reached its apogee after he returned from Munich. The British public lauded Chamberlain's statement that he brought "peace in our time." British preparations for war ended. Gas-mask drills stopped in London. The final results of the Munich Conference turned Chamberlain's term "appeasement" into a derogatory expression for diplomacy, whereas Chamberlain saw appeasement as a positive way to peacefully settle disputes. In order to understand appeasement as a diplomatic way to compromise, the particular circumstances of 1938 must be understood. Many people in Europe and America believed that the terms of the Treaty of Versailles should be revised because the Allies had dealt too harshly with Germany in 1919. Chamberlain believed revising these terms would be a just and sufficient way to satisfy Hitler's demands. Like many Europeans and Americans, Chamberlain also thought Soviet Communism was a greater menace than Fascism and that war between Germany and England would be devastating.

The second circumstance influencing Chamberlain was Britain's failure to prepare for war as rapidly as Hitler. As Gaines Post Jr.'s 1993 *Dilemmas of Appeasement* indicates, Chamberlain's diplomatic efforts with Hitler were difficult, if not impossible, because British decisions to rearm fell short. The Stanley Baldwin cabinet in 1934–1935 had opted for a gradual arms buildup because they assumed Germany would not be ready for war until 1942.

October 4, 1938

France's left-wing Popular Front ministry ends.

From June 5, 1936, to October 4, 1938, Léon Blum and Édouard Daladier had kept together a coalition of left-of-center Popular Front parties. The French Senate could not overthrow the ministry, but the conservatives and extreme rightists in the Senate effectively blocked the leftists from making significant economic or social changes.

The Munich Conference broke up the Popular Front. The Socialists disapproved of the agreement with Hitler, and the Communist Party, which voted with but never joined the ministry, now withdrew its support. Daladier obtained center and right-of-center support in the Chamber of Deputies and continued as premier until March 20, 1940.

1939

March 28, 1939

The Spanish civil war ends when Madrid surrenders to General Franco's forces.

The final struggle that began in Spain on July 18, 1938, had been bitter and bloody as Franco's insurgents received considerable assistance from Germany and Italy, who had recognized his government on November 18, 1936. Madrid was under siege from November 6, 1936, to March 28, 1939. The Loyalist Republican government had fled from Madrid to Valencia, and later to Barcelona. Franco's capture of Barcelona on January 26, 1939, effectively ended Loyalist resistance. Madrid held out, however, because General José Miaja sought lenient terms, but Franco demanded unconditional surrender. Following a Communist uprising in Madrid that Miaja defeated in March, the defenders of the city decided to surrender to Franco with no conditions.

March 31, 1939

British and French pledges to aid Poland in the event of aggression end the British appeasement policy.

On March 15, Chamberlain's appeasement of Hitler ended with Germany's conquest of the reduced Czechoslovakia. Now, Hitler demanded that Poland cede the free city of Danzig to Germany and construct a railway and highway across Pomorze (the Polish corridor) to the Baltic Sea. In return, Germany would guarantee Poland's frontiers and sign a nonaggression pact. Warsaw rejected these demands and, on appeal to Paris and London, obtained the British and French pledges of March 31 that expanded into a mutual assistance treaty on April 6.

The British decision meant Chamberlain's appeasement policy fell apart. Chamberlain had taken Hitler's demands at face value, believing his territorial objectives were limited to recovering German land lost through the 1919 Versailles Treaty. Hitler's aim, of course, was to conquer Europe. Chamberlain was not the only mistaken politician in 1939. During the interwar years, Poland never discovered how to unify and strengthen its government.

From 1926 until his death on May 12, 1935, Marshal Józef Pilsudski was a military dictator who could not establish a unified state because of opposition. In 1935, Poland abolished its democratic system, but the military leaders could not effectively end the opposition of the Socialist and Peasant parties or the Ukrainian nationalists. On March 1, 1937, Colonel Adam Koc's Camp of National Unity secured greater support. Koc's program emphasized anti-Communism, army control, land reform, Polanization of minorities such as the Ukrainians, and violent anti-Semitism.

Koc was overthrown on January 11, 1938, by General Stanislaus Skwarczynski, whose policies loosened government control of society. In 1939, the Polish army exaggerated its ability to defend the nation. Poland's nationalists despised the Russians, whom they defeated briefly in 1920 (see August 10, 1920), a war resulting in disputed territory until 1939.

Between March and August 1939, France and Britain promised to protect Poland even though there was no practical way for their armed forces to save Poland's ineffective army.

April 3, 1939

The United States recognizes General Franco's government in Spain.

A final offensive by Franco's forces between December 1938 and February 1939 had devastated the Loyalist armies in Catalonia and central Spain. Following the fall of Madrid on April 3, President Roosevelt recognized Franco's government. He had withdrawn the arms embargo from Spain on April 1 because the Fascist Nationalist victory was certain. France and Great Britain had recognized the Franco regime on February 27, 1939.

Before accepting the fate of the fallen Spanish republic, Roosevelt realized that the democratic powers including America had made a grave mistake in their Spanish policy. He told his cabinet on January 27 that the United States should have simply forbidden the shipping of munitions in U.S. ships. Then Loyalist Spain could have obtained other vessels to carry what was needed "to fight for her life and the lives of some of the rest of us as well, as events will very likely prove." But also, as events proved, neither Congress nor the American public had learned this lesson between 1937 and 1939. The spirit of isolationism refused to die in the United States during the late 1930s. Congress remained reluctant to provide firm backing for the democratic forces in Europe.

August 23, 1939

A Nazi-Soviet pact is signed at Moscow by which each nation agrees not to attack the other and to be neutral if the other is attacked by a third power.

The signing of the Nazi-Soviet pact resulted from six months of a complex negotiating game between Germany and Russia and Russia and England, including France. These talks began after Germany annexed all of Czechoslovakia and began making demands for Poland to turn over territory where Germans lived. The unsuccessful talks between England, France, and Russia began on April 18 when Soviet Foreign Minister Maxim Litvinoff proposed a Three-Power Alliance to counteract Nazi demands. Litvinoff's offer looked good on the surface but Prime Minister Chamberlain backed off because the proposal failed to clarify Russia's relations with Poland and included clauses requiring assurances that if war began none of the three parties would accept peace talks unless all parties agreed.

In July, the new Soviet Foreign Minister Vyacheslav Molotov proposed talks on military assistance and on August 11 the Anglo-French military mission reached Moscow. Their talks got nowhere, stumbling on Poland's refusal to have Soviet troops cross their territory. While his delegates talked with Molotov, Chamberlain held secret discussion about a nonaggression pact with a German official, Helmut Wohlstat. Thus, by early August, all four powers were involved in divergent negotiations when Germany made demands on Romania as well as Poland. At the same time, Chamberlain learned the Soviets had been negotiating with Hitler since July 26.

In the context of these six months of discussions, Chamberlain's main concern was the assurances France and Britain gave to protect Poland from a German attack. The British could find no satisfactory way to employ Russian forces in the defense of Poland whose government insisted Soviet troops could not enter their territory to engage the German army and air force. Poland's Foreign Minister Colonel Joszef Beck opposed any concessions to the Soviet Union and Chamberlain readily agreed. Chamberlain said "I very much agree with him [Beck], for I regard Russia as a very unreliable friend with an enormous irritative power on others." By August, Chamberlain tried to persuade Beck to negotiate with Germany regarding Hitler's demands for the Danzig-Polish corridor along the Vistula River. On August 21, an announcement that a Nazi-Soviet non-aggression pact would be signed ended the possibility of Beck's talking with Hitler.

The final Nazi-Soviet pact was signed on August 23 (actually August 24 at 1:00 A.M.). In addition to a nonaggression pact, a secret Nazi-Soviet protocol partitioned Poland and divided the four Baltic states. Poland was divided along lines defined by the Pisia, Narew, Vistula, and San rivers. In the Baltic, Russia would control Finland, Estonia, and Latvia; Germany would control Lithuania. In southeast Europe, Russia could regain Bessarabia. With a Soviet agreement finalized, Hitler made final preparations to attack Poland.

The pact's impact on Americans, especially its diplomats, was devastating. The State Department's Soviet experts saw Stalin's earlier agreements to curb Germany were readily cast aside and concluded that any agreement with Stalin was essentially worthless. The diplomats complained that there was no limit on what Stalin would do to further the Soviet Union's interests, an assessment boding ill for future Soviet-American relations. There appeared to be "little future for Russian-American relations," George Kennan recorded in his memoirs, "other than a long series of misunderstandings and disappointments and recriminations on both sides." This was a most perceptive forecast.

September 1, 1939

Germany invades Poland; on September 3 Britain and France declare war and World War II is under way.

The alleged reason for Germany's invasion was that Poland had not fulfilled Hitler's March demands to have Danzig unite with Germany's East Prussia and allow the Germans to build a railway and highway across the Polish corridor. The Germans did not believe that England and France would intervene.

Soviet Foreign Minister Molotov signs the German-Soviet nonaggression pact; Joachim von Ribbentrop and Josef Stalin stand behind him. National Archives

Although Ian Colvin's *The Chamberlain Cabinet* explains Chamberlain's attempts until August 31 to resolve the Polish issues, it was not possible to meet Hitler's many demands. As some of Chamberlain's cabinet suspected, Hitler was probably stalling to complete Germany's preparations to launch the attack on Poland. The British and French finally concluded that Hitler's ambitions exceeded the revision of Versailles and they must resort to "balance-of-power" politics to maintain their own security.

World War II began in Europe when the German armies made their blitzkrieg attack on September 1.

September 5, 1939

President Roosevelt announces U.S. neutrality in the European war, applying the Neutrality Acts, which embargoed arms to all belligerents.

The declaration of war by France and England left Roosevelt no choice but to issue a neutrality decree.

Soviet Union, 1929–1953

Roosevelt did not, however, ask Americans to be neutral in thought as well as deed as Woodrow Wilson had in 1914. In addition, the president began preparations to call a special session of Congress to revise the U.S. neutrality legislation.

September 17, 1939

Soviet forces invade eastern Poland, occupying areas Hitler had designated for the USSR in the secret protocol of the August 23 Nazi-Soviet Pact.

Soon after occupying eastern Poland, Stalin forced the Baltic states of Estonia, Latvia, and Lithuania to permit the Red Army to establish military bases on their territory. Soon after, 20,000 Soviet soldiers entered these states and the USSR absorbed these small countries in June 1940.

Although the original Nazi-Soviet Pact gave Lithuania to Germany, a new agreement was concluded on September 28. Stalin proposed to give Germany additional Polish territory as far east as the Bug River (east from the Narew River). In return, the Soviet Union occupied Lithuania.

October 11, 1939

Albert Einstein and other scientists inform President Roosevelt that an atomic bomb could possibly be developed.

Einstein's letter was inspired by atomic scientist Leo Szilard, who, unlike Einstein, was involved in nuclear fission research. Einstein's letter warned that Germany seemed to be moving to control uranium supplies that were used in nuclear fission. From the suggestion of this message, Roosevelt eventually organized the top-secret Manhattan Project, which produced the world's first atomic weapon in 1945.

November 4, 1939

Roosevelt ends the arms embargo and permits cash and carry sales of arms.

On September 13, the president called a special session of Congress to revise U.S. neutrality legislation. During the period of debate, Roosevelt's theme was that a cash and carry program would allow France and England to purchase arms in the United States

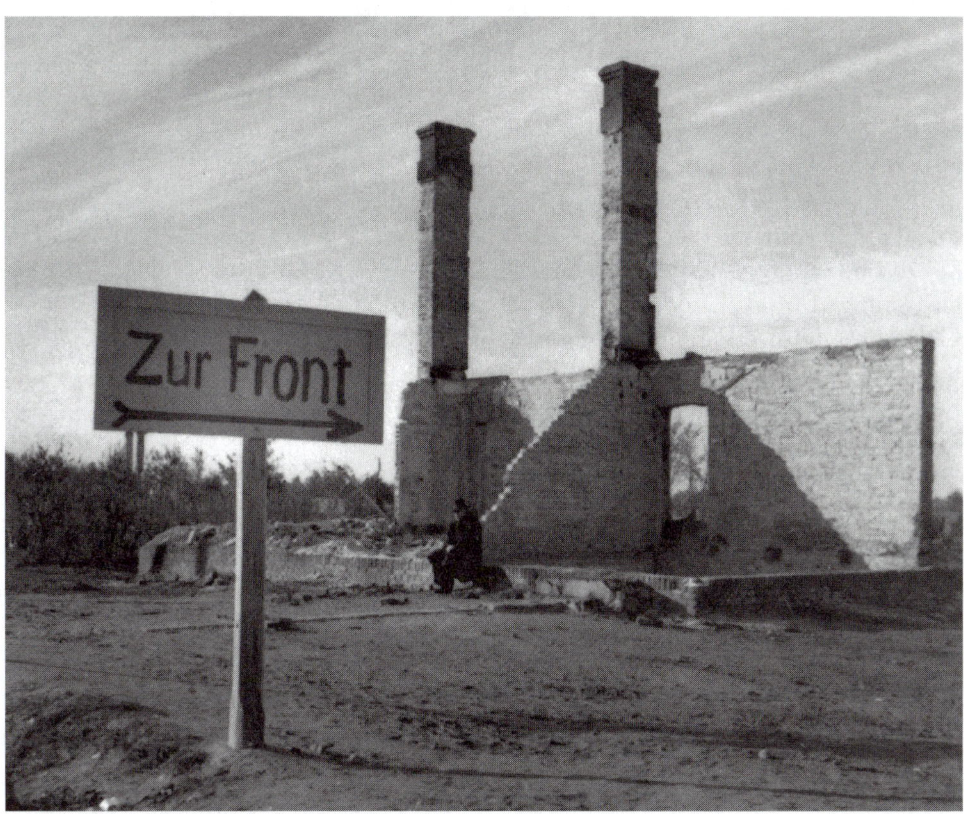

Sign directs German forces in the field toward Warsaw. National Archives

and keep America out of war by preventing the German conquest of those two Western European democracies. The president argued that the United States would not be severely threatened unless Germany defeated England and France.

On November 4, Roosevelt signed the new bill, issued a proclamation lifting the arms embargo, and defined the combat areas from which U.S. ships and citizens were excluded. The combat zone included only the waters adjacent to the British Isles and France and the North and Baltic Seas. A major handicap of this revision was to prohibit U.S. ships with cargo other than arms from entering British and French ports. All purchases by the Europeans would be cash and carry.

In addition, the act of November 4 continued all the provisions of the Neutrality Act of 1937 except the change of the arms embargo that permitted arms to be sold on a cash and carry basis. The United States did not return to the defense of its neutral rights, which it had followed from 1914 to 1917 and prior to 1935. U.S. ships could not carry freight or passengers to belligerent ports; U.S. ships could not be armed; American citizens could not travel on belligerent ships; loans to belligerents were prohibited except for short-term, 90-day credits.

These provisions of the 1939 Neutrality Act restricted aid that America might have given to the European democracies.

November 29, 1939

Roosevelt's attempt to mediate between the USSR and Finland fails. Soviet planes and troops attack Finland.

Early in October 1939, Moscow demanded military bases in Finland similar to agreements given by the governments of Estonia, Latvia, and Lithuania on September 28. But Finland refused and asked Washington to assist in persuading the Soviets to withdraw their unreasonable requirements. On October 11, Roosevelt sent a telegram to Mikhail Kalinin, president of the Soviet Union, asking that country to limit its demands on Finnish independence. The October 11 message, as well as a similar appeal by Roosevelt on November 29, was rebuffed by the

USSR. On November 29, the Soviet army invaded Finland to impose the USSR's demands but met stiff resistance from Finnish forces.

Because the Soviet Union did not officially declare war on Finland, Roosevelt and Hull acted as they had in the Sino-Japanese conflict of 1937. They called for a "moral embargo" on airplane sales to the Soviets but did not apply the Neutrality Acts. Finland would have suffered from the neutrality laws more than the USSR. In addition, diplomatic relations were maintained in Moscow because the Roosevelt administration believed that sooner or later the Soviets would forsake their Nazi pact and join the Western Allies.

During the winter of 1939–1940, the restrictions of neutrality prevented Roosevelt from aiding Finland, as much as he desired. Although the president arranged an Export-Import Bank loan of $10 million, the funds could not be used for arms. Finnish Ambassador Hjalmar Procopé desired $60 million that could be used to buy arms and planes. In January 1940, Senator Prentiss M. Brown of Michigan presented a Senate bill to provide Finland an unrestricted loan that failed because isolationists in the American First Committee opposed the measure as an example of what they called Roosevelt's desire for "dictatorial power."

1940

March 12, 1940

Finland accepts Soviet peace terms, retaining independence but surrendering territory and making economic and military concessions to Moscow.

Support for "little" Finland's ill-fated efforts to defend itself from Russia's large forces was high in the United States. Public opinion ran strongly in favor of aiding Finland because that small country had been the only nation to pay fully its World War I debts but this sentiment was not sufficient to call for the discarding of the restrictive neutrality laws or run the risk of war.

April 9, 1940

Germany invades Norway and occupies Denmark.

Although Norway offered some resistance and Anglo-French forces landed in southern Norway on April 16, Hitler rapidly reinforced the German army, and by April 30, effective Allied resistance ended. The English and French withdrew, and after June 10 only underground activity against Germany remained in Norway.

May 10, 1940

Germany attacks the Netherlands, Belgium, and Luxembourg.

Without warning, Nazi armies seized the Netherlands, Belgium, and Luxembourg without a great deal of effort on their way to circle behind France's Maginot Line.

May 10, 1940

Winston Churchill becomes Britain's prime minister.

Churchill established a coalition cabinet that included both Conservative and Labour Party members. Churchill's rhetoric and dogged persistence rallied the British to resist the Fascist forces and symbolized his nation's determination to defeat its enemies. He had previously established correspondence with President Roosevelt, and the two leaders generally cooperated well throughout the war years.

The new prime minister made no secret of his personal hatred of Communism because he found in Marxist-Leninist philosophy an antipathy to his basic values of monarchy, parliamentary democracy, and private property. He had supported British intervention in the Russian civil war and had been suspicious of Soviet activities during the 1920s and 1930s.

June 17, 1940

France surrenders, asking Germany for an armistice.

The Nazi blitzkrieg moved swiftly through the Low Countries and deep into northern France by May 21, outflanking France's defensive works, the Maginot Line. The Belgian armies surrendered on May 26 and, left in an exposed condition, the British expeditionary force of 250,000 men staged a hasty and gallant retreat by sea at Dunkirk on May 28, leaving most of their equipment behind. On June 20, Italy declared war against France and Great Britain and invaded southern France. On June 13, Premier Paul Reynaud resigned. Marshal Philippe Pétain assumed

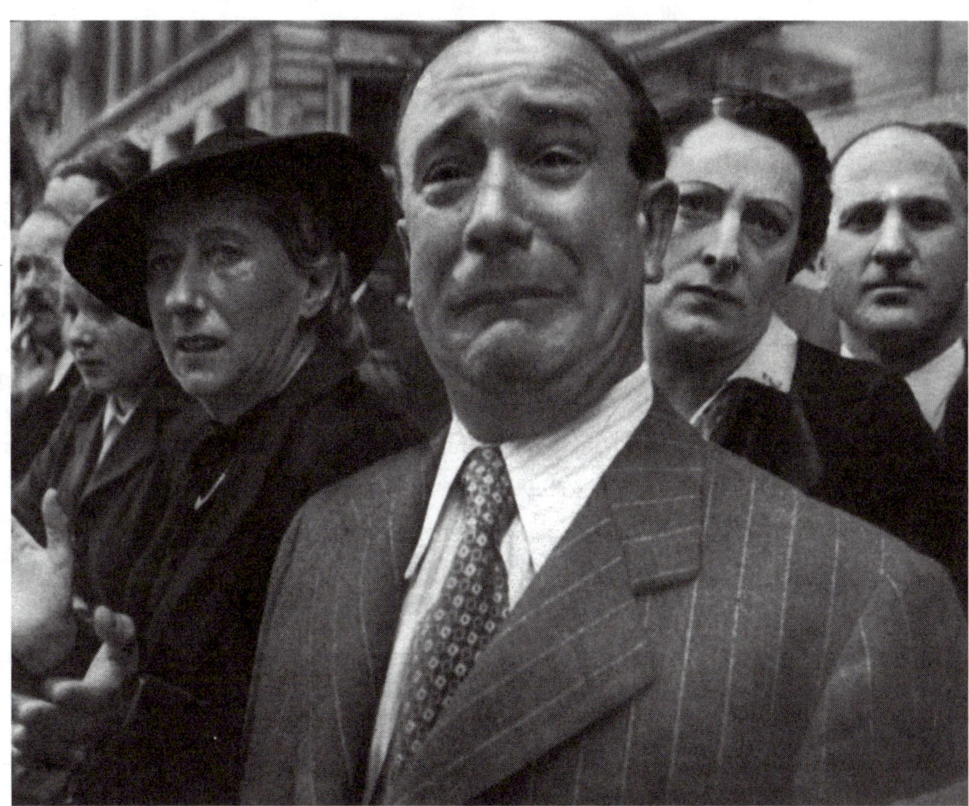

A Frenchman weeps as German soldiers march into Paris on June 14, 1940. National Archives

the office and asked the Germans for an armistice on June 17. The French signed the German armistice demands at Compiègne on June 22. On June 24, Petain's government signed an armistice with Italy who had declared war on France on June 20. The French government set up headquarters at Vichy on July 2. In London on June 2, General Charles de Gaulle formed the French National Committee and pledged to continue French resistence to Germany.

June 27, 1940

Romania cedes northern Bessarabia and northern Bukovina to Soviets.

Stalin forced Romania to cede the territory to the USSR.

June 28, 1940

The Alien Registration Act (Smith Act) attempts to check subversive activity in the United States.

This act governed the admission and deportation of aliens, and required all aliens to be fingerprinted. The act made it unlawful to teach or advocate the overthrow of the U.S. government by force or violence or to organize or become a member of any group advancing such doctrines.

After 1945, this law was employed in the government's efforts to dismantle the American Communist Party. Eleven U.S. Communist Party members were convicted and imprisoned under the Smith Act. In the 1957 *Yates v. U.S.* decision, the Supreme Court reversed the conviction because the eleven people were tried for their ideas, not for using force or violence.

September 27, 1940

Japan signs a tripartite pact with Italy and Germany, making the Anti-Comintern Pact a political and military alliance.

Japan had been uncertain about its alliance with Rome and Berlin because it could not comprehend the Nazi-Soviet Pact of August 23, 1939, as reflecting only Hitler's temporary policy. But by July 27, 1940, the Konoye government pledged itself to take stronger measures to assure Japan's dominance in East Asia. In August and September, the British withdrew from Shanghai, having previously agreed to close the Burma Road as a supply route for Chiang Kai-shek's Chinese government. In addition, France agreed to recognize Japan's predominant rights in Indochina, while the Dutch undertook negotiations to supply Japan with oil for five years.

In the context of these policies, Japan wanted German and Italian assistance against possible United States' intervention. Thus, the major part of the Axis military pact of September 27 was the three-power agreement to help one another if any were attacked by a power not currently involved in either the European or Sino-Japanese fighting.

Obviously, this other power was the United States, which strongly objected to Japan's aggressive action in south and southeast Asia. The Soviet Union and Communism did not play a major role in the tripartite pact.

October 8, 1940

German troops begin a Balkan campaign. Italy invades Greece on October 28.

In the Balkans, only Greece offered stiff resistance to the Italian and German armies, holding out with British aid until April 23, 1941. Hungary joined the Axis alliance on November 20, Romania on November 23, Bulgaria on March 1, 1941, and Yugoslavia on March 25. Yet in Yugoslavia, a political coup on March 28 denied the Axis alliance and announced a neutral policy. As a result, German troops moved into Yugoslavia, and the opposition resorted to guerrilla warfare.

November 5, 1940

Roosevelt wins the presidential election with a decisive margin over Willkie.

Although Willkie won 5 million more votes than Landon had in 1936, he won in only 10 states. The electoral count in 1940 was Roosevelt, 449; Willkie, 82.

December 29, 1940

President Roosevelt's "Fireside Chat" over national radio networks emphasizes the Axis powers' threat to America and urges an American production buildup to be the "great arsenal of democracy."

During the fall of 1940, Great Britain experienced financial problems in attempting to continue its purchases of war supplies in America. On December 9, Winston Churchill sent a personal appeal to Roosevelt, outlining Britain's need for more war matériel and ships, as well as requesting elimination of the cash requirements to pay for these materials. Although the potential for a German invasion of the British Isles had diminished, England needed funds and arms to continue the struggle and had asked Roosevelt to find "ways and means" to continue the flow of supplies to Britain.

By December 12, Roosevelt had conceived the lend-lease program to aid Britain, but he decided to prepare the way for the favorable U.S. reception of this program. After Roosevelt mentioned lend-lease during a December 17 press conference, he explained to reporters: "Suppose my neighbor's home catches fire, and I have a length of hose four or five hundred feet away. If he can take my garden hose and connect it up with his hydrant, I may help him to put out his fire." The president added, "I don't say to him before that operation,'Neighbor, my garden hose cost me $15; you have to pay me $15 for it.' What is the transaction that goes on? I don't want $15—I want my garden hose back after the fire is over." On December 20, the president began the lend-lease program by establishing the Office of Production Management under William D. Knudsen to coordinate defense production and to speed all aid "short of war" to Great Britain and other anti-Axis nations including the Soviet Union.

In this context, Roosevelt's speech of December 29 further stimulated American opinion to provide aid to the democracies. The United States would send all possible aid to opponents of aggression. While any course of action was risky, providing aid to the people of Europe fighting aggression would save America from the agony of war. "We," he said, "must be the great arsenal of democracy. For us this is an emergency as serious as war itself." Roosevelt's speech proved one of his most popular and effective. Of those who heard the speech, a Gallup poll showed that 80 percent supported and only 12 percent opposed aid to Britain. Moreover, the same poll found that 76 percent of the public heard the speech, the largest number recorded for a presidential speech since 1933.

II. THE ''STRANGE ALLIANCE,'' 1940–1945

During the dark days of 1941, the Nazi invasion of the Soviet Union consummated an unusual alliance that would eventually lead to the defeat of the Axis powers. Prime Minister Churchill immediately offered Stalin what help Britain could provide and, as an aside, told his secretary, "If Hitler invaded Hell, I would at least make a favorable reference to the Devil in the House of Commons." In America, however, the State Department did not want any assistance provided without Soviet political concessions, and the War Department felt any military aid would be wasted because the Red army would collapse in three months. President Roosevelt ignored his advisers and gradually increased U.S. assistance to the embattled Russians.

The wartime alliance was, in many ways, a strange arrangement. After approving lend-lease aid for the Soviet Union, Roosevelt treated Russia differently from other Allies because he did not expect to evaluate the Soviets' needs or their use of the military equipment they received. Despite this special treatment, Stalin did not respond in kind. Rather, Stalin constantly berated his Allies for not opening a second front in France in 1942 or 1943. Stalin also annoyed the Pentagon because he refused to provide military medical information, answer requests for intelligence regarding Germany war plans, allow Allied planes to fly over Soviet territory, or use landing strips for Allied planes that were bombing Nazi territory. (See entry for August 21, 1945, on the termination of lend lease.)

The Soviets appeared to be suspicious of Allied wartime and postwar intentions, and their suspicions were fostered by wartime disagreements. Even as the alliance was being formed, Stalin pressed Churchill and Roosevelt to formally guarantee the Soviet Union's territorial gains from the Nazi-Soviet pact—an acknowledgment that Churchill favored but Roosevelt finally insisted should be decided after the war. As the Russians were trying to stem German military advances in 1941, Stalin urged the Allies to launch a "second front" to cause Hitler to withdraw a significant number of divisions from the eastern front—but the best the Allies could do was to invade North Africa. Stalin also was upset when the Allies suspended the northern convoys carrying much needed lend-lease supplies because German aircraft operating from Norwegian bases used the long hours of daylight to locate and sink many of the ships attempting to reach Murmansk. Consequently, during these early desperate months Stalin wondered if the Allies intended to let the Soviet Union carry the burden of the European war.

As Allied armies advanced, it was unclear who would set policy in occupied enemy countries and liberated nations. In early 1945, Stalin objected to the United States and Britain engaging in negotiations for the surrender of German forces in Italy because he feared the Western Allies might be allowed to occupy Germany while the Nazis shifted their divisions to the eastern front. More significantly, when Roosevelt and Churchill virtually excluded Soviet influence in the Italian occupation government, this decision was interpreted by Stalin to mean that Moscow could establish the occupation policies in the areas seized by the Red army—especially Eastern Europe. This arrangement allowed the Soviets to gain the secure frontiers they had sought since the early 1920s. In this same context, Truman insisted on American control of the occupation of Japan.

Another area of disagreement and misunderstandings occurred in the abrupt termination of the lend-lease program, in the U.S.'s refusal to grant postwar loans to the USSR, and in disputes over the amount of reparations enemy states should pay. The Soviets believed that since they had suffered the most deaths and destruction during the war, the Allies should be more considerate of the postwar economic needs.

The Yalta and Potsdam conferences in 1945 identified the major outstanding issues confronting the Allies including the question of Axis reparations, the termination of lend lease, the makeup of the Polish government, the removal of Allied troops from Iran, revision of the Montreux Convention, and the status of governments in the liberated and occupied nations. The failure to resolve these and other issues signaled the beginning of what would become known as the Cold War.

1941

January 6, 1941

The president's State-of-the-Union message informs the nation of his proposal for a lend-lease program and enunciates the "four freedoms."

Having prepared the way for a lend-lease bill during his December 29, 1940, speech, the president in his annual message to Congress indicated his intention to send Congress a bill to support peoples resisting aggression. This, he said, was the best means to keep "war from our Hemisphere" and to oppose aggressors.

Indicating the common objectives of the democratic powers in their fight against totalitarian Fascism, Roosevelt declared that victory over the aggressors would mean a world "founded upon four essential human freedoms"—the freedom of speech, of religion, from want, and from fear.

March 11, 1941

Congress approves the Lend-Lease Act.

On January 10, Democratic leaders introduced H.R. 1776 as the Lend-Lease Bill, entitled "An Act to Further Promote the Defense of the United States, and for Other Purposes." The legislation authorized the president to "sell, transfer title to, exchange, lease, lend, or otherwise dispose of ... any defense article" to countries whose defense was deemed "vital to the defense of the United States." The president would decide if repayment would be "in kind or property, or any other direct or indirect benefit" he thought satisfactory.

Although the Lend-Lease Bill had safe majorities in both houses of Congress, isolationists attacked the measure and required several amendments, none of which seriously hurt the measure. The most extreme isolationist assertion about the proposal was a remark by Senator Burton Wheeler, who called the act the "New Deal's Triple A foreign policy; it will plow under every fourth American boy." The amendments that Roosevelt agreed to placed a time limit on his authority, required periodic reports and consultation with the army and navy on defense equipment, and prevented use of the U.S. navy to transfer lend-lease goods.

On March 11, the amended bill passed the Senate by a vote of 60 to 31; the House by 317 to 17. The initial Lend-Lease Bill authorized expenditures of $7 billion. From 1941 to 1945, lend-lease aid amounted to $50,226,845,387 and played a significant role in strengthening opposition to the Axis powers.

April 13, 1941

Japan and the Soviet Union sign a mutual nonaggression pact.

Until the conclusion of this neutrality pact between Tokyo and the USSR, Roosevelt and Hull considered the possibility that Japan would move north against the Soviets rather than south against Singapore and the Dutch East Indies. Hitler, however, encouraged Tokyo to move to attack Singapore. By obtaining Soviet neutrality in the north, the Japanese could begin action in Indochina during June and July 1941.

May 6, 1941

President Roosevelt indicates that China is eligible for lend-lease assistance.

This executive action inaugurated a direct U.S. aid program to the Chinese Nationalist government of Chiang Kai-shek. Over the next five years, Chiang's government received $1.5 billion from America.

China received only about 3 percent of the total lend-lease aid given during World War II, because Anglo-American war plans gave China a low military priority and because Japan's occupation of China's coastline required all goods to be airlifted to China's interior from India or Burma. Most lend-lease aid went to Great Britain and the Soviet Union to fight against Germany. U.S. forces did the largest share of the fighting that defeated Japan in the Pacific theater of war.

May 27, 1941

President Roosevelt announces an unlimited national emergency.

In proclaiming this emergency, Roosevelt made an address to Congress that described the threat to the

Western Hemisphere resulting from the German occupation of French possessions in Africa, which reached to Dakar on the western extremity of Africa across from Brazil. The Battle of the Atlantic, he said, required a victory for the British fleet. To assist, the United States needed to build more ships and to help Britain cut its losses from German submarine attacks.

Roosevelt's speech did not outline specific measures to meet the emergency. Yet the positive public reaction to the speech enabled the president to take some action in June. On June 14, he froze all German and Italian assets in the United States, and on June 16 he ordered all German and Italian consulates to be closed.

June 22, 1941

Germany launches an invasion of the Soviet Union.

The German attack did not surprise Washington. Earlier, England and the United States had learned about the German preparations and warned Soviet leader Stalin of the Nazi German plans. As soon as the war began on the eastern front, Winston Churchill, who had since 1917 been an ardent anti-Communist, welcomed the Soviets as a British ally. In Churchill's view, "any man or state who fights on against Nazidom will have our aid." Within two days, Roosevelt agreed.

The German invasion of the USSR took place along a 2,000-mile front from Finland (which had allied with the Axis) to Romania. The Germans overran the Ukraine and reached Leningrad by early September. Nazi armies reached the outskirts of Moscow before the Soviets undertook a counteroffensive in December 1941.

German troops in Russia, 1941. National Archives

June 22, 1941

Churchill declares British support for the Soviet Union.

On the very day of the Nazi invasion, Churchill, the former archenemy of the Soviet system, offered Stalin his unconditional support. "We shall give whatever help we can to Russia and the Russian people. We shall appeal to all our friends and allies in every part of the world to take the same course and pursue it, as we shall, steadfastly to the end."

Given Britain's desperate situation in 1940–1941, Churchill immediately accepted the necessity of a wartime partnership with Stalin. Churchill said he would make a pact with the devil himself to defeat Hitler, and perhaps at times he felt he had. Throughout the war years Churchill tried to limit Soviet expansion, for which opportunities would certainly arise during the Moscow Conference of 1944 and when Germany and its allies were defeated.

See October 18, 1944.

June 23, 1941

President Roosevelt announces the United States will aid the Soviet Union's war against Germany.

Following the announcement of the 1939 Nazi-Soviet Pact, U.S. relations with the Soviet Union cooled considerably. When the Soviets attacked Poland and Finland, the United States requested a moral embargo on airplane and aviation supplies to the aggressor and tried to prevent all war exports to the USSR. The Neutrality Act had not been invoked, because Roosevelt wished to aid Finland and not push the Soviets further into Germany's alliance. Friendlier American overtures to the Soviet Union began after Japan signed the Tripartite Pact with the Axis on September 27, 1940. Undersecretary of State Welles began regular conversations with Soviet Ambassador Constantin Oumansky between September 1940 and the spring of 1941, but he had no success in wooing the Soviets from the German alliance.

Prior to the German attack on June 22, 1941, the State Department was reluctant to assist the Soviets against the Nazis. But the German attack on Russia quickly changed Secretary of State Cordell Hull's opinions. He immediately told Roosevelt and Welles "We must give Russia all aid to the hilt." Subsequently, Welles told a press conference on June 23 that aid to the USSR in some form would be vital to the defense of America. According to Welles, the president said, "Hitler's armies are today the chief dangers of the Americas."

Between July and November, U.S. aid to the Soviet Union was minimal. The president was seeking additional lend-lease aid for Britain and did not wish to bring the Soviet situation into the political arena in Congress. The additional lend-lease funds passed Congress on October 28, 1941, and on November 6, Roosevelt ordered a credit of $1 billion for Soviet aid, informing the lend-lease administrator that the USSR's defense was "vital to the defense of the United States." The United States and the Soviet Union signed a master lend-lease agreement on June 11, 1942.

July 18, 1941

Stalin's reply to Churchill and Roosevelt is that the Soviets want a "Second Front."

In his reply, Stalin also made his only attempt to justify his signing of the Nazi-Soviet Pact. The main thrust of Stalin's note was the first of many requests for the British and Americans to immediately launch a "second front" in France to force Hitler to reallocate German forces. Stalin also stated it also would be helpful if the Allies deployed their naval and air forces to join with Russian ground forces in establishing a northern front in Finland and Norway to relieve Nazi pressure on Leningrad.

Roosevelt and Welles, seen here together, led the planning of aid for Russia. Franklin D. Roosevelt Library

Later, Churchill responded that an Allied invasion was impossible due to Britain's depleted manpower and military material. Churchill added that any thoughts of Britain invading, either in the north or across the channel to France, bordered on fantasy. That the Soviets never acknowledged Churchill's response reflected the current reality, and they continued to be suspicious of British and later American motives in not launching an immediate attack through France.

The Soviets continued to demand a "second front" and its delay would often be seen in Moscow as guided by ulterior motives toward his alleged allies.

August 12, 1941

Secret meetings take place between Roosevelt and Churchill, during which the Atlantic Charter is prepared.

Since December 1940, Roosevelt had sought an occasion to meet with Prime Minister Churchill to dramatize for world opinion what was at stake in fighting the Nazis. Arrangements were made in July, and on August 9, 1941, British naval ships brought Churchill to Placentia Bay off Newfoundland, where the two leaders held their first meeting on board the president's ship, *Augusta*, a heavy cruiser.

The Atlantic Charter was the historic document formulated by Roosevelt and Churchill between August 9 and 12. The charter was a joint declaration of principles, issued by Washington and London on August 14, that became the basis for Allied war objectives after December 7, 1941. The important points in the charter are listed here:

1. Both nations renounced the desire for territorial or other aggrandizement at the expense of other peoples.
2. The people concerned must decide territorial changes for themselves.
3. People have a right to choose their own government.
4. With due respect to existing obligations (i.e., Britain's Commonwealth preference duties), trade restrictions would be eased and equal access given to raw materials.

President Roosevelt and British Prime Minister Winston Churchill meet at sea. The Atlantic Charter is formulated. National Archives

5. Cooperation would aid the economic security of all peoples of the world.
6. There must be freedom from want and fear.
7. There must be freedom of the seas.
8. There would be disarmament of aggressors after the war, pending creation of a permanent peace structure.

By September 15, 1941, the Soviet Union and 14 other non-Axis nations had endorsed the Atlantic Charter.

August 25, 1941

British and Soviet forces begin the occupation of Iran.

In a fashion similar to the Anglo-Russian agreement before World War I, Soviet forces took over Azerbaijan and provinces in the north of Iran; the British occupied the southern region and protected the Persian Gulf.

October 4, 1941

Freedom of worship is guaranteed in Soviet Union.

People who opposed Roosevelt's desire to include the Soviet Union in the lend-lease program quickly pointed out that Stalin had agreed to the "Four Freedoms" contained in the Atlantic charter but there was no mention of freedom of religion. To remedy this oversight, Roosevelt suggested to the Soviet ambassador in Washington that Moscow should improve its public image regarding "the freedom of religion in Russia" before Congress considered the next lend-lease funding legislation. Much to Roosevelt's relief, on October 4 Moscow officially guaranteed the right to worship in the Soviet Union provided such activity did not challenge government policies.

November 6, 1941

Roosevelt identifies the Soviet Union as being eligible for lend lease.

On June 23, when the president announced that the United States would aid the Soviet Union in its war with Nazi Germany, he did not indicate what that aid would be and hesitated to apply the Lend-Lease Act. On June 24, he released $39 million of frozen Russian assets and the next day decided not to invoke the Neutrality Act, which would have prohibited U.S. ships from carrying supplies to the Soviet Union. Then on July 23, he sent $22 million of war matériel to the USSR.

The president's most significant decision in July was to send his close adviser Harry Hopkins to Moscow. Hopkins talked with Stalin late in July and returned to report to Roosevelt just before the Atlantic Conference of August 9. Hopkins said Stalin was confident that the Soviet armies would eventually triumph, although a long war was expected. Stalin wanted the United States to send antiaircraft guns, aluminum for planes, 50-caliber machine guns, and 30-caliber rifles. Both Roosevelt and Churchill agreed that they should provide all possible aid to the Soviets.

Washington planners worked on a Victory Program during the summer of 1941 to increase U.S. production that would supply Britain, the Soviets, and the U.S. armed forces. In September, Lend-Lease Administrator Harriman visited Moscow with Britain's Lord Beaverbrook to discuss Stalin's military needs. Because the Soviets had 280 army divisions (2 million men) engaging German and other Axis-power troops, the eastern front was crucial to the Allied effort.

Prior to the announcement of lend-lease aid to the Soviet Union, Roosevelt undertook methods to convince possible American opponents of the Soviets to accept such aid. He encouraged American Catholics to accept Soviet aid as a necessity and obtained a petition of 100 Protestants who supported help for the USSR. Nevertheless, little opposition appeared to the idea of providing lend lease to the Soviet ally. After Congress approved $6 billion additional lend-lease funding on October 24—which did not mention, but did not exclude the USSR—the president allocated part of it for the Soviets.

His decision was formalized on November 6, when he declared that assistance for the Soviet Union under the Lend-Lease Act was approved because its fight was "vital to the defense of the United States."

Harry Hopkins, President Roosevelt's special envoy, visits Moscow regarding lend-lease aid. Franklin D. Roosevelt Library

November 19, 1941

The United States and Mexico announce the settlement of an oil and agrarian expropriation compensation agreement.

Following Mexico's decision on March 18, 1938, to expropriate American and British oil companies' property, President Cárdenas asserted his desire to compensate the oil companies. Until 1941, however, the oil companies avoided serious negotiations of the settlement because they hoped to pressure Mexico into abrogating the expropriation act. The companies' attempts failed in part because of the desire of President Roosevelt and U.S. Ambassador to Mexico Josephus Daniels to deal sympathetically with Mexico and to make the Good Neighbor Policy work. Consequently, Daniels took a strong stand against State Department bureaucrats who supported the oil companies' viewpoint and knew little of the Mexican populace's backing for Cárdenas' policies. Even Secretary of State Hull succumbed to the oil lobbyist contention that Cárdenas was a Communist who wished to create a Mexican Soviet as part of Moscow's world revolution.

Daniels ignored the oil lobbyists' propaganda and backed Mexican leaders seeking a legal but Mexican solution to the issue. The oilmen's hope that the conservative candidate, General Juan Andreu Almazan, for Mexico's presidency would win the election of 1940 or stage a counterrevolution such as General Franco had done in Spain did not materialize.

The November 19 agreement with the new Camacho government finalized both the oil and the agrarian claims of the United States.

December 7, 1941

Japanese planes attack Pearl Harbor.

Not only did the attack not cripple the fleet because U.S. aircraft carriers were at sea that morning, but the attack rallied the U.S. populace to become nearly unanimous in its determination to win the war. At Pearl Harbor, the Japanese attack lasted from 7:55 A.M. to 9:45 A.M. All eight U.S. battleships in

U.S. aircraft are surprised on the ground at the Naval Air Station at Pearl Harbor. National Archives

port were either sunk (the *Arizona*, *California*, and *Utah*); grounded (*Nevada*); capsized (*Oklahoma*); or damaged (*Pennsylvania*, *West Virginia*, and *Tennessee*). A total of 19 U.S. ships were sunk or disabled. In addition, 177 U.S. planes were destroyed and 2,335 soldiers and sailors and 68 civilians were killed.

Americans often overlook Japan's simultaneous attacks on December 7–8 in the Philippines and against British forces in Hong Kong and Malaya.

December 8, 1941

Congress formally declares war on Japan.

President Roosevelt's message to Congress asking for war on December 8 emphasized Japan's treachery in the way in which it launched the war. His famous opening words were: "Yesterday, December 7, 1941—a day which will live in infamy—the United States was suddenly and deliberately attacked by naval and air forces of the Empire of Japan." Congress promptly voted for war with only one dissenting vote—that of Jeannette Rankin, who had also voted against war in 1917. Japan's attack had united U.S. politicians.

December 11, 1941

Germany and Italy declare war on the United States.

Acting under their agreements as Axis allies of Japan, Rome and Berlin declared war. In response the same day, the U.S. Congress issued a declaration of war against Germany and Italy.

Once at war, the United States, Great Britain, and the Soviet Union sought to unite their efforts and energies against Nazi Germany. The resulting alliance proved to be an uneasy one for all parties, especially because Stalin was suspicious of his allies and his allies were uncertain about Russia's postwar ambitions. Thus began the so-called "Strange Alliance."

1942

January 1, 1942

The United Nations declaration is signed at Washington by 26 nations fighting the Axis powers.

By this declaration the 26 nations affirmed the Atlantic Charter, pledged not to make a separate peace with their common enemies, and agreed to use all of their military and economic resources to defeat the Axis powers. The four major powers signing were Great Britain, the Soviet Union, China, and the United States. By the spring of 1945, 47 nations had signed the Declaration of the United Nations.

Unlike its position in World War I, when the United States was an "associated power" rather than an ally, this declaration was a virtual alliance made without Senate approval. Roosevelt's legal advisers checked the documents to be certain the language was a declaration and not a treaty.

January 14, 1942

Washington (Arcadia) Conference takes place.

Winston Churchill concluded his visit to Washington where, since December 22, he and Roosevelt had been planning cooperative Anglo-American efforts to fight the war. During a series of meetings, President Roosevelt and Prime Minister Churchill set up an Anglo-American Combined Chiefs of Staff to conduct the war. Then, soon after, they established the Combined Boards for Raw Materials, Munitions Assignments, Shipping Adjustments, Production and Resources, and Food. Together these boards and the Combined Chiefs formed a Supreme War Council, but they did not include representatives of China or the Soviet Union. The latter two had been considered for membership, but Roosevelt and Churchill decided that their inclusion caused too many problems.

February 4, 1942

Secretary of State Hull and Roosevelt reject Soviet demands for recognition of the USSR's western boundary as being that which the Soviets occupied when Hitler attacked them in June 1941.

The Soviets told Britain's foreign secretary, Anthony Eden, during a visit late in December 1941 that they wanted their legitimate western boundary line to be that of June 1941—the gains outlined in the Nazi-Soviet pact. The Soviets considered Estonia, Latvia, Lithuania, part of eastern Poland, and province of Bessarabia as "lost" territories since they belonged to the pre-1914 Russian empire. During later border discussions with Britain's Anthony Eden, Stalin claimed these areas would create friendly border states, which would enhance Soviet security. Eden referred this issue to Churchill and Roosevelt in January 1942, but the Anglo-American leaders rejected Stalin's request as violating the Atlantic Charter.

Because Stalin continued to pursue his request to Eden and to the U.S. ambassador at London, John G. Winant, Hull sent the president an extended memorandum dealing with this issue on February 4, 1942. Hull indicated that Stalin's demand for a boundary settlement generated mutual suspicions because the small nations that signed the United Nations Declaration would be alarmed. He told Roosevelt that Stalin's test of our "good faith" should not be an agreement to accept new boundaries but to provide the promised military supplies to the Soviet Union.

Roosevelt agreed with Hull and inaugurated a general "boundary policy" for the United States—all boundary questions should wait until the war ended. During the next several months, Churchill nearly agreed to give in to Stalin, but Roosevelt and Hull prevented this.

February 9, 1942

President Roosevelt attempts to bolster China's importance.

During the January meetings between Churchill and Roosevelt, the Allied leaders endeavored to agree on China's precise role in the war effort against Japan. The president sought to promote the American public's favorable view of China because a 1942 opinion poll showed 80 percent to 86 percent of Americans believed China would cooperate with the United States during and after the war.

On February 9, Roosevelt met with General Joseph W. Stilwell, who had been selected to go to Chungking to serve as chief of staff to Generalissimo Chiang Kai-shek. The basic problem was that Chiang Kai-shek held unrealistic visions of China and Chiang's importance to the Allied war effort, while the president and Churchill gave the China theater a low priority in terms of men, matériel, and war equipment. Roosevelt chose to emphasize China's status as one of the Big Four powers and the long-term gains China would receive by continuing to fight Japan. Although Churchill found these views of the president "strangely out of proportion," Roosevelt substituted the rhetoric about Chiang Kai-shek's importance for the practical assistance Chiang desired. Neither Churchill nor General Stilwell agreed with this assessment.

February 23, 1942

Stalin hints at a separate peace accord with Germany and wants Russia's pre-1941 border recognized.

Once the German assault on Moscow was halted in December 1941, Stalin requested an Allied agreement on the Soviet Union's eastern borders that included territories mentioned in the 1939 Nazi-Soviet pact. After Anthony Eden had rejected Stalin's request during an early February meeting, Stalin's speech on February 23 intimated that a separate peace agreement might be possible with the Germans.

March 7, 1942

Churchill is desperate to keep Russia in the war and considers recognition of pre-1941 Soviet borders.

Because Stalin's speech on February 27 captured his attention, Churchill asked Roosevelt to accept Stalin's request for regaining Russia's pre-1941 borders. Churchill feared that Soviet withdrawal from the war would damage Britain's chances of survival against the Germans; consequently, Churchill was willing to accede to Stalin's demand for all territories except eastern Poland.

Roosevelt appeared willing to agree with Churchill but was forced to reconsider by Secretary Hull and the State Department's strong opposition. To move away from territorial concessions, FDR suggested that Molotov visit Washington to discuss a second front this year.

May 26, 1942

England and the Soviet Union sign a 20-year alliance treaty that does not mention the Soviets' western boundary, an omission due to U.S. opposition.

On May 8, 1942, Soviet Commissar for Foreign Affairs Vyacheslav Molotov flew to England to seek a formal treaty of alliance. Molotov had instructions from Stalin to gain England's recognition of the USSR's western borders as of June 22, 1941. This was a matter that Stalin had brought up before, only to have Secretary of State Hull and President Roosevelt object strongly to the Soviet demand, and the result was a long-term dispute between the Big Three allies.

On March 7, 1942, Churchill cabled Roosevelt that he wanted to accept the Soviets' border request. In the "deadly struggle" with the Germans, Churchill said, we cannot "deny Russia the frontiers she occupied when Germany attacked her." Although Roosevelt searched for a compromise, Hull opposed the Soviet position and Roosevelt eventually agreed with the secretary. The United States informed the British that any boundary agreement would be a "terrible blow" to the "whole cause of the United Nations." In addition, Roosevelt asked the Soviets to send Molotov to Washington to discuss a second front.

Consequently, Anthony Eden proposed that Molotov accept an alliance with England that did not mention boundaries. Molotov immediately reported to Stalin that he had informed Eden, "We consider the treaty to be unacceptable... an empty declaration." However, Stalin responded changing his instructions: "1. We don't consider it an empty declaration but regard it as important... Not bad perhaps. It gives us a free hand. The question of borders will be decided by force. 2. It is desirable to sign the treaty as soon as possible and fly to America." (Simon Sebag Montefiore, *Stalin: The Court of the Red Tsar* [New York: Knopf, 2004], p. 409)

The Anglo-Soviet treaty of May 26 was signed on the basis that neither nation sought "territorial aggrandizement" from the war. From the Soviet view, of course, the boundary of June 22, 1941, did not mean "territorial aggrandizement" since the territory the Soviets annexed between 1939 and 1941 had belonged to the pre-1914 Imperial Russian Empire.

June 1, 1942

Roosevelt promises the Soviet Union there will be a second front in Europe by the end of 1942.

During April 1942, when Britain and the Soviet Union discussed an alliance and the Soviets' future boundaries, Roosevelt heard about and accepted a U.S. army plan to make coastal raids on Europe by August 1942, preceding a major assault in France by April 1, 1943. To entice the Soviets to forgo their boundary issues in favor of the advantages of a second front against Germany, Roosevelt asked Stalin on April 20 to send Foreign Minister Molotov to America to discuss a second front. Although Churchill and British officers opposed the plan to invade France in 1942, they permitted Roosevelt to explore the possibility of a second front with the USSR.

On May 29, Molotov arrived in Washington to discuss with the president and U.S. military leaders future supplies to the Soviet Union and a second front. Stalin greatly desired the new front as the best means to relieve German military activity on the eastern front. On June 1, Roosevelt, Hopkins, Marshall, and the new CNO, Admiral Ernest S. King, met with Molotov to discuss a second front. Marshall and his aide, General Dwight D. Eisenhower, had, in April 1942, planned attacks on Western Europe. They calculated that the Western allies could begin diversionary air and coastal raids on Europe beginning in August 1942, so that by April 1, 1943, 48 divisions and 5,800 planes would be ready to invade the Continent. On this basis, the president told Molotov to inform Stalin "that we expect the formation of a second front this year." Marshall told the president to qualify this statement because there were many difficulties to overcome.

Therefore, the president said the attack would be "sometime in 1942." Nevertheless, Churchill and the British continued to oppose a cross-channel invasion in 1942 because they feared it might fail. To assuage Roosevelt, the prime minister decided to emphasize the significance of a North African attack as a better preliminary attack on German troops. Molotov was not pleased to learn about the North African front and was less pleased when President Roosevelt informed him that American shipping requirements for the African front would mean that Russia would find its lend-lease tonnage reduced from 4.1 to 2.5 million in the coming year.

Molotov returned to Moscow with a vague commitment of a second front and a lend-lease accord with the United States as well as an alliance with Britain. "My journey," he reported, "and its results were a great victory for us."

June 6, 1942

Battle of Midway ends Japan's advance in the central Pacific Ocean with a major naval defeat.

This naval and air battle prevented Japan from seizing Midway Island and eliminated the threat to Hawaii. Japan lost four aircraft carriers and 275 planes and

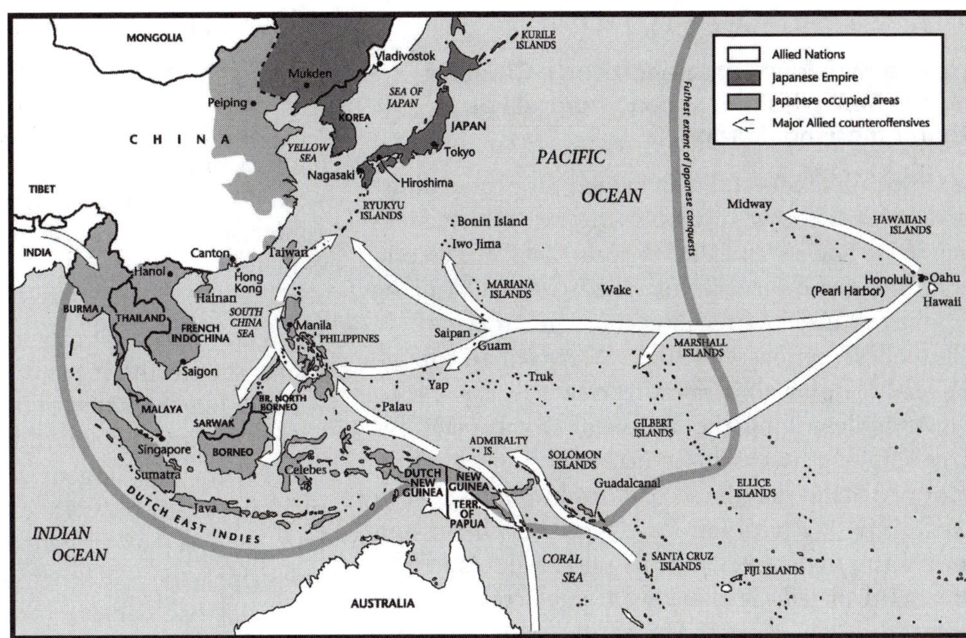

WWII: Pacific Theater

their trained air crews, shifting the balance of naval power in the Pacific to the United States. The U.S. navy lost one carrier and one destroyer in the battle.

This battle is considered the "turning point" in the Pacific war, assuring that Japan could not prevail.

June 13, 1942

The Office of Strategic Services (OSS) is established.

By executive order, President Roosevelt created the OSS for intelligence operations abroad and the analysis of strategic information. William J. Donovan became the director of the OSS. This organization would be the forerunner of the postwar Central Intelligence Agency.

July 1, 1942

A formal lend-lease agreement between the Soviet Union and the United States goes into effect.

This agreement was formally approved when Molotov visited Washington on May 29–June 1, 1942. The pact provided that materials received from the United States would not be transferred by the Soviets to other parties and that at the end of the war any serviceable materials could be returned to the United States.

July 27, 1942

An Anglo-American invasion of North Africa in the fall of 1942 (Torch) is set.

Since April 1942, American and British leaders had discussed the question of where a second-front attack on German forces could best be implemented in 1942. Initially, General Marshall and U.S. army leaders preferred to work immediately for a cross-channel invasion of France in 1943. Churchill and his advisers recommended action against either Norway or North Africa, preferring to delay the attack on France to make certain that once begun, the cross-channel landings would be followed through to the defeat of Germany.

On July 18, the British convinced General Marshall that an attack on France (coded "Sledgehammer") could not succeed. Marshall referred the issue to Roosevelt for a decision. Because the president wanted some type of ground operations against Germany in 1942, he opted for an invasion of North Africa as soon as possible. The British concurred, and as preparations began, Roosevelt cabled Churchill that he believed Torch would be a "turning point" in defeating the Axis powers, for "we are on our way shoulder to shoulder." Of course, Stalin (and most historians) believed the turning point of the war in Europe took place when Soviet forces turned back the Germans at Stalingrad on February 2, 1943.

See November 19, 1942.

August 15, 1942

The First Moscow Conference ends: Churchill informs Stalin that the second front will be in North Africa, not Europe.

At Churchill's request, Stalin invited the prime minister to visit Moscow to discuss the two major issues facing the Soviets and the Western Allies: the second front and the difficulties of Allied convoys bringing supplies to the Soviet Union through Archangel. At Churchill's meetings with Stalin, W. Averell Harriman, the lend-lease administrator, represented Roosevelt.

After describing the British air force plans for large bombing attacks on Germany, the prime minister informed Stalin that the second front would be North Africa, not Western Europe. Using his charm and enthusiasm on Stalin, Churchill said Anglo-American strategy depicted Germany as a giant crocodile. By going through North Africa and into southern Europe, Churchill said, the Allies would attack both the "soft underbelly" and the hard snoot of Hitler's empire. Stalin was intrigued at first but later turned surly when he realized that few German divisions would be diverted by the North African campaign. Hitler would shift large numbers of his forces from the eastern front only if France were attacked directly. Thus, the second-front dispute with Stalin continued.

Regarding the supply routes to the Soviet Union, Stalin showed greater concern about his country's need for more war matériel. In mid-July, German submarines sank 23 out of 34 merchant ships being convoyed to Archangel. The Allied losses in the North Atlantic reached 400,000 tons in one week, more than twice the Allies' weekly construction ability. As a result, the northern convoys to the USSR were suspended for the summer because the long daylight hours in the area of the North Cape of Norway made them easy targets. To supplement the convoy, the Allies made plans for a trans-Caucasian air transport service that they hoped to begin in October. Following the Moscow sessions, Roosevelt and Churchill also decided to try some smaller convoys, and 10 ships were sent to Archangel in October.

Meanwhile, German army attacks were penetrating deep into southern Russia. Stalin needed planes in particular to help launch his counteroffensive against the Germans, which would begin in November 1942.

Stalin and Molotov discuss possible second front. National Archives

November 8, 1942

General Dwight D. Eisenhower the invasion of North Africa by an Anglo-American force.

The Allied troops made amphibious landings in French Morocco and Algeria. Aided by Admiral Jean-François Darlan of the French Vichy government, Allied forces overran the French garrison and an armistice was signed on November 11.

November 19, 1942

The Soviet counteroffensive against Germany begins at Stalingrad.

German armies drove deeply into the southern part of the Soviet Union during the summer of 1942, capturing Sevastopol on July 1, Rostov on July 24, and beginning the siege of Stalingrad on September 13. On September 21, the Soviets began thrusts against the German lines, first to the northeast, later to the southeast of Stalingrad. On November 19, a full-scale offensive began against Germany. The Soviets' successes temporarily ended Germany's offensive activity on the southern front. At Stalingrad, the Soviet pincer movements surrounded and cut off 22 German army divisions, and some 80,000 Germans capitulated on

February 2, 1943. The Soviet victory at Stalingrad—if not the Battle of Kurst—is considered the turning point of the war against Germany in the European theater of war.

For Churchill's turning point see July 27, 1942.

1943

January 24, 1943

The Casablanca Conference results in two significant decisions: the plan to invade Sicily and Italy and an agreement on requiring the Axis powers to surrender unconditionally.

Roosevelt and Churchill began plans for their meeting at Casablanca in December, even though Stalin said he could not attend. Roosevelt wanted to plan campaigns for 1943 and to get Churchill's agreement for unconditional surrender. Marshall went to Casablanca to obtain Britain's commitment to build up the Allied base in England for a 1944 assault on western France. Marshall received these commitments at Casablanca and the British also accepted a combined planning staff for the 1944 assault. In 1943, however, the Allied attacks would be on Sicily and Italy.

Regarding unconditional surrender, Roosevelt had begun to discuss such a policy as early as May 1942. Roosevelt wanted not only to disarm the Axis nations but also to compel them to abandon their Fascist philosophy. Roosevelt did not present this policy with the Joint Chiefs of Staff, but he discussed it with Secretary of State Hull, who opposed announcement of such a policy for fear of ending any

Roosevelt and Churchill talk with reporters at Casablanca Conference. National Archives

flexibility in later surrender situations. On this issue, however, Roosevelt had a closed mind and did not permit Hull to come to Casablanca.

At Casablanca the unconditional surrender decision was discussed but not made part of the final official communiqué by Churchill and Roosevelt. Later, on January 24, Roosevelt made an oral declaration to newsmen that he and the prime minister had agreed to demand the unconditional surrender of Germany, Italy, and Japan as the only way to assure future peace in the world.

March 8, 1943

Roosevelt again appears to yield to Chiang Kai-shek.

During the winter of 1942–1943, Britain, China, and the United States argued over a campaign in Burma and General Chennault's plan for a strong air offensive against Japan. Although Generals Marshall and Stilwell believed that effective aid to building up ground forces against Japan could be obtained by opening the Burma Road, the British and Chiang—if for different reasons—were reluctant to pursue a war in the jungles of Burma and supported the air attacks advocated by Chennault.

Although Roosevelt seems to have realized that Chiang's forces were corrupt and inefficient because on this point U.S. and British estimates agreed, he told Churchill that he had to placate Chiang for political reasons. Churchill could not fathom this mysterious American attraction for Madame Chiang and the Chinese, but after witnessing the emotional attachment of pro-Chinese U.S. politicians and the pro-Chiang publicity of the Time-Life magazine chain of Henry Luce, the prime minister was politically astute enough to appreciate the president's problem.

Roosevelt's endorsement aided Madame Chiang and the China lobby in creating an unrealistic evaluation of the Chinese Nationalists that would later cause vast problems for General Marshall and President Truman in 1945. One part of Roosevelt's rationale for supporting Chiang lay in the hope that a strong postwar China would become a counterweight to the Soviet Union's aspirations in Asia. This was a geopolitically astute perception, but Roosevelt refused to force Chiang to adopt measures that would strengthen his army and gain the support of the Chinese people. Meanwhile, the Chinese Communists were gaining strength because of their identity with the common people and the Soviet Union.

April 27, 1943

The Soviet Union suspends relations with Poland's government-in-exile; dispute over Katyn massacres.

On April 13, 1943, Germany announced it had discovered a mass grave containing at least 10,000 Polish officers in the Katyn Forest, near the Soviet city of Smolensk. The Germans claimed Soviet forces had massacred these officers in the spring of 1940. Although Winston Churchill cautioned the leader of the Polish government-in-exile in London, General Wladyslaw Sikorski, to beware of German attempts to sow discord among the allies, Sikorski asked the International Red Cross to investigate the incident. Stalin denied that request on April 18.

Poland's request for an investigation became the official reason Stalin broke relations with the government-in-exile in London that the Soviets had recognized in June 1941. Probably, Stalin was looking for an excuse to break with Sikorski because the USSR was sponsoring the Communists in the Union of Polish Patriots, who were exiled in the USSR. The 1943 Allied split over Poland continued in determining Poland's postwar status.

Regarding the massacres, post-Cold War documents confirmed Germany's allegations that Soviet soldiers killed the Polish officers. Soviet documents declassified in 1992 revealed that Stalin ordered the massacre of about 20,000 Poles in the Katyn Forest. On October 14, 1992, Soviet Politburo records and other documents from March 1940 showed Stalin was directly responsible for the massacres. For these reports, see the *New York Times* for October 15 and 16, 1992.

May 13, 1943

The North Africa campaign ends when 250,000 Axis troops surrender in Cape Bon, Tunisia.

As U.S. forces under General Eisenhower moved into Morocco, Algiers, and Oran after November 8, 1942, British troops in the east forced General Erwin Rommel's armies to retreat from Egypt. British forces under General Bernard L. Montgomery launched an offensive from El Alamein on October 23, expelling the German armies from Egypt by November 12. As Rommel's armies retreated, the British regained Tobruk on November 13 and advanced across Libya to occupy Tripoli on January 24, 1943. On March 19, U.S. forces captured El Guettar and joined with British forces in Tunisia on April 7 near Gafsa. The final U.S.-British action in Tunisia defeated German troops at Tunis and Bizerte before the Axis forces, mostly Italian, surrendered at Cape Bon on May 13.

May 22, 1943

Moscow announces the dissolution of the Third Communist International (Comintern).

Since 1933, the United States had repeatedly asked the Soviet Union to abandon the subversive activity of the Comintern. Stalin officially did so on May 22. Although this was a gesture of friendship to the United States, the Soviets did not end their attempts to influence the activity of Communist parties throughout the world, including the Communist Party of the United States, which Earl Browder led in 1943.

May 25, 1943

The Trident Conference ends: Roosevelt, Churchill, and their advisers conclude a series of strategic meetings in Washington.

In addition to decisions about the China-Burma theater, the Trident Conference worked out further plans for an Allied attack on Sicily and a buildup of forces for the 1944 cross-channel attack. Although British military leaders continued to push for greater efforts in the Mediterranean, General Marshall secured further commitments for the Allies to prepare for the cross-channel attack. The invasion of Sicily in 1943 and perhaps of Italy would be designed as preludes to the major attack on western France. It was also agreed that the full-scale attack on France (Roundup) would be ready by May 1, 1944. A final decision approved an Italian invasion after the Sicilian attack ended.

July 10, 1943

Anglo-American forces launch an invasion of Sicily—Operation Husky.

British, Canadian, and U.S. forces invaded Sicily under the command of General Dwight D. Eisenhower. Over 2,000 vessels conveyed 160,000 men to land along Sicily's southern coast. The allied forces occupied half of Sicily when Palermo fell on July 24. The capture of Sicily, which provided the necessary springboard to the invasion of Italy, was completed by August 17.

July 12, 1943

The Russians prevail at the Battle of Kursk.

On July 5, the Germans initiated the greatest tank battle of World War II with 900,000 troops and 2,700 tanks. When the German assault faltered, the Soviets led by General Zhukov counterattacked with nearly a million men and 6,000 tanks. The result has been likened to the "mechanized equivalent of hand-to-hand combat," resulting in the destruction of 700 tanks and tens of thousands of troops. After this defeat—and the defeat at Stalingrad—Hitler had no chance of prevailing.

July 25, 1943

The resignation of Premier Mussolini and his cabinet is announced by King Victor Emmanuel III of Italy.

Mussolini was replaced by Marshal Pietro Badoglio, who dissolved the Fascist Party on July 28. After German troops rescued him from a prison in Rome on September 12, Mussolini proclaimed a Fascist Republic in Italian areas under German control.

August 24, 1943

The First Quebec Conference (Quadrant) of Roosevelt, Churchill, and their military advisers concludes.

These meetings from August 11 to 24 confirmed and finalized military decisions made or begun at the Trident Conference, which ended on May 25. The Normandy invasion (Overlord) was reaffirmed for May 1, 1944, and supplemental landings in southern France were added (Anvia, later Draoon). An attempt to step up military operations in Burma was agreed to, and Lord Louis Mountbatten was named supreme commander in Southeast Asia.

A decision was also made at Trident to drop the British plans for an Allied attack through the Balkans into central Europe. Although Churchill argued that a Balkan attack would have postwar political

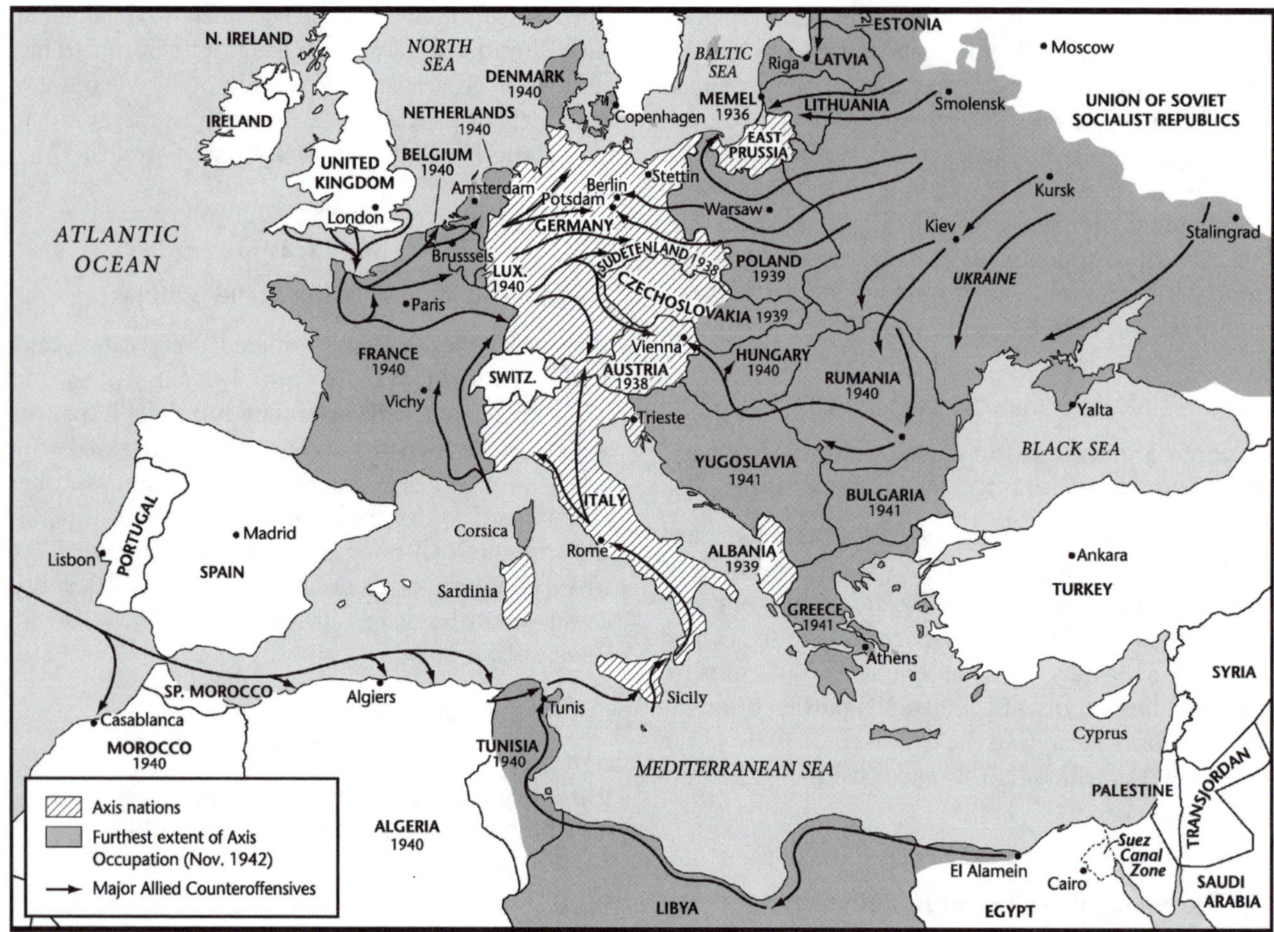

WWII: Europe and North Africa

advantages against the Soviet Union, General Marshall believed that if the Allied forces became bogged down in the mountainous areas of southeastern Europe, the Soviet armies would capture all of Germany and the Rhineland. Thus, with the president's support, the invasion of the Balkans was not undertaken.

September 3–9, 1943

The Italian campaign begins.

The day before the major Allied operations against Italy began (September 8), the surrender of the Italian government (on September 3) under General Badoglio to Eisenhower was announced. Although there was some German resistance in the southern part of Italy, the initial Allied landings were comparatively easy. Salerno was captured by September 18, and by October 14, the Allies crossed the Volturno River north of Naples. On September 10, German forces took Rome.

After Mussolini escaped on September 12 and proclaimed a Fascist republic, German forces made the central and northern Italian campaign very difficult for the Allies.

September 10, 1943

The Allies establish a military-political commission for negotiating with German allies because Stalin dislikes the Anglo-American settlement with Italy that had no Soviet involvement.

When British and U.S. authorities began talks with the new Italian ministry of Badoglio in July 1943, Stalin complained that the Soviet Union was not represented on the negotiating team. The Western powers agreed to keep Stalin informed of their discussions, but in August Stalin insisted on forming a special commission to negotiate with "Governments disassociating themselves from Germany."

On September 10, Churchill and Roosevelt agreed to establish a commission at Algiers to deal with Axis negotiations except those with Germany and Japan. But Roosevelt instructed General Eisenhower that the commission was subordinate to the Allied commander in chief. Although Stalin protested, Roosevelt stood firm. The president understood at this time that the occupation of Italy would set a precedent because it was the first "liberated" European state. He realized the Italian decision would justify Stalin's unilateral action in the Eastern European nations that would be liberated by the Soviet armies.

In Italy, however, Roosevelt preferred to minimize the Soviet role, and this set that precedent. When the Red Army took over Romania in early 1944, both Secretary of State Hull and the Joint Chiefs of Staff assumed the Soviets would insist on prime responsibility there. To reach agreement on a policy of liberation, the foreign ministers of the United States, Britain, and the Soviet Union met in Moscow.

October 13, 1943

Britain and the United States recognize Badoglio's government in Italy.

General Badoglio replaced Mussolini as premier of Italy on July 25 and soon contacted the Western Allies about surrender terms. Although the British favored recognizing a monarchy under King Victor Emmanuel III, the Americans hesitated to do this, preferring a more liberal government in Italy. The issue was not yet settled on September 3 when Badoglio agreed to the military terms of Italy's surrender.

Somewhat reluctantly, and because Churchill said the only alternatives in Italy were a monarchy, fascism, or Communism, Roosevelt agreed to accept Badoglio's regime if he declared war on Germany and expressed his interest in holding democratic elections in the future. On October 13, Badoglio fulfilled these conditions and Roosevelt and Churchill recognized the Italian government.

October 30, 1943

The Moscow Conference of Foreign Ministers ends.

Sessions in Moscow between October 19 and 30 were the first three-power meetings of the war. The participants were Secretary of State Hull, Foreign Minister Anthony Eden, and Foreign Minister V. M. Molotov, with their military advisers. The important decisions at this conference were as follows:

1. The Soviet Union was assured that plans for a second front in Western Europe were under way.
2. Stalin refused to renew Soviet relations with the Polish government-in-exile in London, which he had ended on April 27, 1943.
3. A European Advisory Commission was created to formulate a postwar policy for Germany. An Advisory Council for Italy was also set up.
4. Stalin promised to enter the war against Japan as soon as Germany was defeated. This was an informal oral commitment made to Secretary Hull.
5. The Four-Nation Declaration stated that a general international organization to maintain peace and security was a necessity. The Four-Nation Declaration was signed for China by the Chinese ambassador to Moscow, Foo Ping-sheung.
6. The Declaration of German Atrocities stated that German war criminals would be apprehended and sent for trial to countries where their crimes had been committed. The Allied governments would jointly punish the "major criminals."
7. Not approved was Secretary Hull's proposal of a "declaration against colonialism." Molotov approved this idea but the British prevented its passage.
8. Austria's annexation by Germany on March 15, 1938, was declared null and void. Although Austria held responsibility for participating in the war on the side of Germany, the final war settlement would consider Austria's contribution to its own liberation.

November 5, 1943

The Senate approves the Connally resolution, which favors an international peace organization after World War II; previously (September 21) the house had approved a similar resolution of J. William Fulbright.

Early in 1943 a group of senators began a bipartisan movement to commit the United States to a postwar international peacekeeping organization. On September 21, the House adopted the Fulbright Resolution to create international machinery with power adequate to establish and maintain a just and lasting peace. The resolution of Senator Tom Connally was worded similarly and approved by the Senate. The

Connally Resolution said any treaty to carry out the bill would require a two-thirds Senate vote. It passed the Senate by 85-5.

November 7, 1943

Soviet forces recapture Kiev in the Ukraine.

Following Soviet successes at Stalingrad on February 2, 1943, the Germans launched a counterattack on July 5, but they made few advances. The Soviet armies repelled them and undertook a new offensive in August that recaptured Smolensk on September 25 and won Kiev by November 7.

The capture of Kiev opened the way to Polish territory, which the Red Army entered on January 3, 1944.

November 9, 1943

The United Nations Relief and Rehabilitation Administration (UNRRA) is established by a meeting of 44 nations in Washington.

UNRRA would provide aid to liberated populations of Europe and the Far East. Former New York Governor Herbert H. Lehman was named as the first director general of UNRRA.

November 26, 1943

The First Cairo Conference results in British and American agreements on China and the Far East.

At Roosevelt's insistence American and British military advisers met with Churchill, Chiang Kai-shek, and China's military leaders. The delegates considered East Asia's future. Roosevelt particularly pleased Madame and Generalissimo Chiang by agreeing to strip Japan of all its Pacific possessions. Formosa, Manchuria, and all areas taken from China would be returned.

In turn, Chiang agreed that the Soviets would receive all of Sakhalin and the Kurile Islands, as well as the use of Darien as a free port. The USSR would cooperate with Chiang in China and agree not to impair China's territorial integrity.

In addition, Roosevelt promoted the idea that China was one of the Big Four powers that would have a vital role in Asia after the war. The three powers also made a final agreement that Korea should "in due course become free and independent," a statement Korean exiles denounced for including "in due course" and not "immediately."

After the sessions ended in Cairo on November 26, Roosevelt and Churchill went to Tehran for discussions with Stalin and Soviet military experts. During informal sessions at Tehran, Roosevelt and Churchill obtained Stalin's oral affirmation of the territorial changes agreed to with Chiang Kai-shek at Cairo.

December 1, 1943

The Big Three Conference ends at Tehran, Iran.

For the first time, Roosevelt, Churchill, and Stalin met for the purpose of discussing a variety of strategic war issues and postwar plans. Because of security concerns, Stalin invited Roosevelt to stay with him in quarters at the Russian embassy compound. Roosevelt readily accepted the invitation because he desired some private time with Stalin to dispel any notion that the Anglo-Americans planned to gang up on him. FDR assumed his room would be "bugged", which it was, and hoped the eavesdropping would reinforce Stalin's belief in his honest desire to cooperate with the Soviets.

Regarding the military situation, the three leaders discussed the coordination of Soviet attacks on Germany with the D-day landings in France in 1944. Once again, Stalin agreed to enter the war against Japan as soon as Germany was defeated. Three key postwar matters were discussed but not finalized at Tehran. First, Roosevelt tried to convince Stalin to use American methods to ensure the future security of the Soviet Union in Eastern Europe. Rather than simply annexing the Baltic states or Poland, Roosevelt urged Stalin to use "referendums" and to allow for "self-determination." Churchill indicated that since England had gone to war in 1939 to protect Poland, the British were particularly concerned about the future of Poland. Churchill wanted Stalin to recognize the Polish government-in-exile in London or to give it a vital role in Poland's future government. Neither Roosevelt nor Churchill was concerned about the exact borders of Poland, for these could be adjusted. They desired, however, that some semblance of self-determination be used in all areas liberated by the Big Four powers. Regarding Poland's government, Stalin expressed his willingness to grant some representation to the London exiles. He wanted them first to accept the Curzon Line as Poland's eastern border, to renounce Nazism, and to sever all connections with German agents in Poland. They should also give support to the Communist partisans fighting underground in Poland. No final decisions on Poland were made, however. A variety of ideas were considered by the Big Three concerning postwar Germany. Roosevelt suggested dividing Germany into three parts for political purposes.

Finally, Roosevelt requested that the other two leaders join the United States and China in sponsoring an international peace organization after the war. Although Churchill and Stalin both preferred regional peace blocs, the president argued that these seemed to be too much like spheres-of-influence pacts. Stalin eventually agreed that some sort of world organization should be established after the war.

December 6, 1943

The Second Cairo Conference concludes.

Following the Tehran Conference, Roosevelt and Churchill returned to Cairo for further discussions between their military chiefs and with Ismet Inönü, president of Turkey. Great Britain reaffirmed its alliance with Turkey, and the "firm friendship" between Turkey, the United States, and the Soviet Union was recognized.

In personal conversations with Churchill at Cairo, the president indicated his suspicions about Stalin's keeping his word regarding intervention in China or in the postwar peace organization. The president also believed that realistic solutions to European problems would be difficult because of the American public's insistence on idealistic standards with other nations.

December 21, 1943

General Stilwell begins a campaign to open a road from Ledo through northern Burma to China.

At the Cairo Conference, the south Burma campaign was canceled. Nevertheless, General Stilwell opened the campaign from Ledo, India, because he wanted a supply road to China's Yunnan Province, and he wished to demonstrate that the Chinese soldiers he trained in India were good fighters. In addition to assistance from the Chinese under Stilwell, the Ledo Campaign was aided by American airborne troops known as Merrill's Marauders, named after General Frank Merrill, and British airborne troops under General Orde Wingate.

Throughout the winter of 1943–1944, Stilwell tried to persuade Chiang Kai-shek to use the Chinese forces in Yunnan to attack from the east toward Ledo,

Generalissimo and Madame Chiang Kai-shek with General Joseph W. Stilwell. National Archives

but Chiang refused. Finally, on April 3, 1944, President Roosevelt made a strong appeal to Chiang to use the Yunnan forces that the United States had armed and trained. Chiang finally yielded, and on May 10 the Yunnan Chinese army of 40,000 began an attack across the Salween River into northern Burma.

Nevertheless, the 1944 Burma campaign to open the Ledo Road was extremely long and difficult. The Japanese brought in reinforcements and fought fiercely. The monsoon rains from May to October complicated the struggle and brought disease to Merrill's Marauders. U.S. supplies through Ledo had a 15,000-mile journey to reach the 31,000 U.S. forces along the route. Finally, the Japanese in China began an offensive toward Chungking during the spring of 1944 and frightened Chiang into reducing aid to the Yunnan forces in Burma. The Ledo Road was not opened until January 26, 1945, when the Yunnan forces linked up with Stilwell's forces from India.

1944

January 22, 1944

In Italy, landings at Anzio beachhead near Rome begin an assault against fortified German positions in central Italy.

The Italian fighting was difficult because of the mountainous terrain and the key German defenses at the Gustave Line. Cassino was overrun on May 18 and, on June 4, Rome was liberated by the U.S. Fifth Army. The Italian campaign did have a salutary effect on preparations for the June attack on Normandy. The Germans committed nearly 39 divisions to Italy, which subtracted from Hitler's strength in France and Eastern Europe.

March 26, 1944

As Soviet troops begin to invade Romania, Churchill obtains Stalin's assent to give Britain primary responsibility for Greece.

The Soviet Union's successful drive through the Ukraine after the capture of Kiev brought the Soviet army to the borders of Romania by late March. In Greece, Communist-inspired uprisings began, causing Great Britain to be concerned about its traditional control in the Aegean and Mediterranean Seas. As a result, Churchill proposed and Stalin agreed that while the Soviets would have responsibility in Romania, Britain could have the same in Greece.

When Churchill asked Roosevelt to accept this, the president hesitated to give approval because he feared that Americans would understand such an arrangement as a "sphere of influence." Nevertheless, Roosevelt agreed to try it for three months, after which the matter could be reviewed. The Stalin-Churchill agreement became the first of several attempts to reach a settlement on Eastern Europe's future.

June 2, 1944

The French provisional government-in-exile is formed in French Algiers.

This government developed as a joint venture of Giraud and Charles de Gaulle, who had resolved their differences on May 31, 1943, by forming the French Committee of National Liberation. On June 2, the French provisional government proposed its full support in the war against the Axis powers.

On October 23, 1944, the United States, Great Britain, and the Soviet Union recognized this government.

June 6, 1944

D-Day: Operation Overlord begins an Allied invasion 60 miles wide along the Normandy coast of western France.

As Stephen E. Ambrose's *D-Day June 6, 1944* (1994) explains, the first day of the Overlord Invasion Plan launched 1,000 invasion craft, 600 warships, and 11,000 airplanes to transport Allied forces to invade France. The large-scale landings succeeded, and by June 27 Cherbourg was captured. By July 2, the Allies had landed 1 million troops plus 566,648 tons of supplies and 171,532 vehicles. By August 10, Normandy was secured and the Allied armies advanced into France, liberating Paris on August 25, Belgium on September 4, and Luxembourg on September 11.

June 21, 1944

Vice President Wallace visits China to assist the formation of a coalition Chinese government of Communists and Nationalists.

Throughout the war against Japan, Chiang Kai-shek had preserved his armies by avoiding conflict with the

Vice President Henry Wallace visits China on behalf of Roosevelt. Wallace would later contest Truman for the White House. National Archives

Japanese in order to blockade the Chinese Communist forces in northern China and to have troops to fight the Communists after the United States and Great Britain defeated Japan. Nearly 500,000 Nationalist forces were in constant deployment to block any Communist advances.

In 1944, Roosevelt and his advisers decided to strive for a Nationalist-Communist Party coalition government so that all China's efforts could be directed against the Japanese enemy. When neither Stilwell nor U.S. Ambassador Clarence Gauss could persuade Chiang to talk with the Communists, Roosevelt sent Vice President Henry Wallace to China to obtain Chiang's cooperation. Wallace received only a few small concessions from Chiang. He allowed U.S. observers to visit Communist-controlled areas and accepted Roosevelt's offer to attempt mediation with Moscow. Chiang would not open discussions with Communist leader Mao Tse-tung and strongly opposed cooperation with the Chinese Communists.

According to Chiang, Mao was both subject to the "orders of the Third International" and "more communistic than the Russian Communists." Too many Americans, he said, were fooled by the Communists. The United States could best remain aloof and cool toward Mao's bandits. Chiang told Wallace he agreed with Roosevelt's efforts to gain better relations for the Nationalists with Moscow. He wanted to reach an understanding with the Soviet Union that would cut off aid to Mao. He also asked the vice president to get rid of Ambassador Gauss and General Stilwell and asked the president to appoint a personal representative so that Chiang could deal directly with Roosevelt.

July 22, 1944

The United Nations Monetary and Financial Conference ends at Bretton Woods, New Hampshire.

The Bretton Woods Conference achieved cooperative agreements by 44 nations to stabilize their national currencies and stimulate world trade. The principal results of the conference were as follows: (1) Establishment of the International Monetary Fund (IMF) of $8.8 billion to be used to stabilize national currency exchanges. The United States contributed about 25 percent of this fund; (2) Creation of the International Bank for Reconstruction and Development. Capitalized at $9.1 billion, this bank made loans to nations for postwar economic reconstruction. The United States supplied 35 percent of these funds.

Significantly, the Soviets refused to be part of these financial arrangements by which, they believed, capitalists sought to continue to control the world economy.

August 1, 1944

The Polish Home Army in Warsaw attacks the German occupation troops while the Soviets refuse assistance.

The Warsaw uprising broke out on orders from the Polish Home Army headquarters. The Home Army (Armia Krajowa) was an underground organization operating in German-occupied territory and a legal successor of the Polish Army. In association with the Polish government-in-exile based in London, the Home Army's commander-in-chief was General Tadeusz Komorwski. When the Home Army was established, its military goal was to liberate Warsaw, save the city from destruction, and protect its inhabitants from mass extermination by the Germans. It also hoped to demonstrate its power by assisting the Soviet Army, whose advance patrols were only six miles from Warsaw on August 1. In addition, on July 29 the Lublin Committee for National Liberation, whose Polish Communist leaders were in Moscow, broadcast a signal for the underground to begin an insurrection to aid the Red Army's liberation of Warsaw.

But when the German army halted the Soviet army on the east bank of the Vistula River, the Red Army did not advance toward Warsaw. While the Red Army stalled, Stalin condemned the uprising and prevented American and British air forces from trying to help the Home Army. The Polish Home Army had to fight against at least 20,000 well-armed German soldiers whose ranks increased to 50,000 after the insurrection began. In Moscow, Stalin told Mikolajczyk the Soviets would aid the insurgents, but later he refused to help the Home Army. Stalin wanted to abolish the Home Army because of its affiliation with the anti-Communist Polish government-in-exile in London.

The Poles, Churchill, and Roosevelt pleaded with Stalin to airlift armaments and supplies to the Home Army, but Stalin refused, saying the insurgents acted recklessly and without his authorization. After repeated requests for aid to the Home Army, Stalin permitted one flight of 104 U.S. airplanes to drop supplies to Warsaw. When these supplies ran out, Stalin refused to allow another airlift of supplies requested by the British and Americans.

By October 4, 1944, the Germans had suppressed the Warsaw uprising. During the uprising, 20,000 insurgents and 150,000 civilians were killed and 25,000 injured. About 16,000 were taken as prisoners-of-war and, despite Soviet protests, were granted the full status of regular soldiers of the Allied forces. As for the Germans, 10,000 were killed and about 9,000 severely wounded.

The Soviet army liberated a ruined Warsaw on January 17, 1945. As a result of the uprising, any hope of creating an anti-Soviet regime in Poland vanished in the immediate post-war years; however, a lingering animosity would ultimately spark later uprisings against domination by the Soviet Union

August 15, 1944

Allied forces land in southern France.

This attack, Operation Dragoon, was made on the coast between Nice and Marseilles. After securing a beachhead, the U.S. Seventh Army and French First Army continued an offensive up the Rhône River valley.

August 25, 1944

Romania leaves Axis and becomes an ally of the Soviet Union.

As the Red army moved into the Balkans, Romania deserted the Axis powers.

September 10, 1944

Ambassador Averell Harriman reports that Moscow has become uncooperative in the past two months.

Harriman sent a message to President Roosevelt through Harry Hopkins, indicating his concern that U.S. relations with the Soviets "have taken a startling turn" since July. The Soviets had become indifferent to U.S. requests and to discussion of vital problems. Specific American requests had been ignored, such as those for air shuttles by U.S. aircraft between Britain and the USSR to bomb or make air reconnaissance of Germany; for the transport of trucks through the Soviet Union to China; to allow U.S. air officers to appraise their bombing raids on Ploesti in Romania; and to plan for later aid against Japan. The Soviets, Harriman contended, were now "unbending" toward Poland and acted as a "bully" where their interests were involved.

Harriman told Roosevelt he would like to return home to report more precisely on these matters. The United States, he said, must be "firm but friendly" and should use a "quid pro quo attitude" in discussions with the Soviets.

September 9, 1944

Bulgaria deserts the Axis powers and sides with Soviets.

Just as Romania previously deserted the German Axis, Bulgaria is now allied with the Soviet Union.

September 12, 1944

U.S. forces begin the invasion of Germany near Trier.

This advance force was the first to reach German territory. The first large German city captured by the Allies was Aachen on October 21. The Germans had built secure defenses, known as Westwall, which offered strong resistance to the Allies.

September 16, 1944

At the Second Quebec Conference, Roosevelt and Churchill make final plans for victory over Germany and Japan.

The chief topic of the conference was the German issue. The British and American leaders decided to create occupation zones in Germany. The president still wanted to be "tough with Germany," yet later, at the Yalta Conference of February 1945, the president took a firm stand against the Soviets in trying to limit German reparations for the war. U.S. officials needed some time to determine whether they preferred to repress or rehabilitate postwar Germany.

October 7, 1944

The Dumbarton Oaks Conference prepares a basic draft for the United Nations organization.

Representatives of the United States, Great Britain, the Soviet Union, and China met to draw up plans for the postwar international organization that had been agreed on at the Moscow and Tehran Conference of 1943. Held in a suburban area of Washington, D.C., the conference agreed on the form of a General Assembly and a Secretariat for the United Nations. It could not decide on the veto issue for the Security Council.

This and other questions were reviewed by the Big Three in February 1945 at the Yalta conference. The Dumbarton Oaks draft was finalized at the San Francisco Conference, which convened on April 25, 1945.

October 15, 1944

Soviet Army liberates Belgrade, Yugoslavia.

Yugoslavia followed the Soviet path through Romania and Bulgaria when Yugoslavia became an ally of the Soviet Union.

October 18, 1944

At the Second Moscow Conference, Churchill and Stalin decide on east European "spheres of influence" with which Roosevelt later concurs.

With Ambassador Averell Harriman representing President Roosevelt, Churchill and Stalin finalized details regarding postwar Eastern Europe as the Red Army had liberated the Balkans. During the first conference session on October 9, Churchill and Stalin agreed on spheres of influence, with the Soviets having 90 percent influence in Romania, 75 percent in Bulgaria, and equal influence with Britain in Yugoslavia and Hungary. The British and Americans would have 90 percent influence in Greece.

Churchill was especially concerned about the civil war in Yugoslavia, where Chetnik guerrillas loyal to King Peter II of Yugoslavia vied for control with the Communist Partisans led by Tito (Josip Broz). Britain had backed the Chetniks until February 1944, when Churchill realized the Chetniks' General Dragoljub Mihailovič collaborated with the Germans. Churchill shifted support to Tito but his decision came too late to receive Tito's blessing.

Tito gained widespread popular backing and triumphed against both the Germans and the Chetniks with little outside military support from Moscow or the Western powers. Tito solidified his authority in September 1944, when he received Stalin's promise to withdraw the Red Army from Yugoslavia as soon as it helped the Partisans liberate Belgrade from the Germans. On October 20, three weeks after liberating Belgrade, Soviet forces left Yugoslavia. Tito's guerrillas could concentrate on eliminating the remaining Germans, the Chetnik collaborators, and the Nazi-backed Croatian Ustasa, whose members had committed many atrocities against other South Slavs, Jews, and Muslims from

1941 to 1944. By May 15, 1945, Tito controlled Yugoslavia. Mihailovič was captured, convicted of collaboration, and executed in July 1946.

October 20, 1944

The Philippine campaign begins as General Douglas MacArthur's forces invade Leyte.

Throughout 1943 and early 1944, preparations leading to the return to the Philippines required a series of Allied campaigns such as landings at the islands of Arawe and New Britain in the Solomon Islands in December 1943, and the Admiralty Islands and Dutch New Guinea during the spring of 1944. The naval and air battle of the Philippine Sea on June 19–20 sank three Japanese carriers and 200 planes, as well as crippling several battleships and cruisers. Later, on October 23–25, the Battle of Leyte Gulf was the last great naval action of the war. It decisively destroyed Japan's sea power and gave the United States control of the Philippine waters. The land battle for the Philippines continued for four months.

October 21, 1944

General Stilwell leaves China after being recalled at Chiang Kai-shek's insistence.

Chiang successfully resisted Roosevelt's attempt to get Chinese Nationalist and Communist forces to unite in a campaign against the Japanese. As a result of Vice President Wallace's visit with Chiang, President Roosevelt decided in July to make a strong demand that Chiang undertake a vigorous campaign against Japan, which he had delayed since 1941. Roosevelt lost the struggle, however. By October 21, Chiang's ability to avoid Roosevelt's demands that China engage Japanese troops demonstrated how a military ruler of a lesser, dependent nation can ignore with impunity the requests of a greater power. One outcome of Chiang's persistent refusal to engage Japanese forces in China is that military historians will never know how the Pacific war would have ended if the Chinese had fought against Japan with the determination that the Americans did in their Pacific campaigns.

In July 1944, Roosevelt initially tried to pressure Chiang into accepting conditions that might have resulted in an effective Chinese offensive against Japan. Telling Chiang that the "future of Asia is at stake," Roosevelt proposed drastic measures to stem Japanese advances in China and to save both American and Chinese interests. Roosevelt reversed his earlier policy of placating Chiang by avoiding any strings on U.S. aid to obtain a more effective Chinese military effort. Although in theory Roosevelt held the power to make Chiang comply with his demands to actively engage Japanese forces, the Chinese Nationalist leader would not engage the Japanese. From the early 1930s, Chiang Kai-shek considered the Chinese Communists to be his most serious threat, more than the Japanese. Chiang had survived against great odds since 1927 and he would survive again until 1949.

Initially Chiang wrote Roosevelt that he agreed in principle with all his requests. However, it would take "preparatory time" to effect a change of command to General Stilwell. On July 13, the president walked into Chiang's "time trap." Seeing only a difference in timing between immediate and "preparatory," Roosevelt urged "speed" on Chiang and in August accepted Chiang's request to send a personal representative to China. The president sent Patrick Hurley and Donald Nelson to persuade Chiang to comply. Before Hurley and Nelson arrived at Chungking on September 7, Chiang informed Roosevelt that certain limits would have to be placed on changes the president proposed on July 13. These limits, if accepted, would have the practical effects of nullifying Roosevelt's intentions.

Chiang's requests were that (1) the Communist forces must accept the Nationalist government of Chiang; (2) clearer relations must be defined between Chiang and Stilwell; (3) the Chinese Nationalists must control all lend-lease aid; (4) Stilwell would command only those Chinese forces already fighting Japan. In particular, the first and fourth of these demands would preclude both a settlement with the Communists and Stilwell's effective uniting of all Chinese troops to fight the foreign enemy.

For Chiang, Mao was still his major enemy. As Stilwell wrote to General Marshall, Chiang simply did not want to risk a fight with Japan. He wanted the United States to defeat the Japanese so he could retain all his strength to fight the Chinese Communist Party. Ironically, Henry Luce's *Time* and *Life* magazines edited out Theodore White's accurate reporting on Chiang's unwillingness to fight Japan, so Americans who read these popular magazines believed that Chiang had been a vigorous democratic freedom fighter since 1937.

On September 16, Roosevelt made one final effort to convince Chiang to take stronger action against Japan. Roosevelt told Chiang he feared that China would be lost if Chiang did not act immediately. He concluded that it appeared evident that all "our efforts to save China are to be lost by further delays." Chiang did not accept Roosevelt's analysis or demands for action. Smugly content to compromise with Japan by living in Chungking while the Japanese controlled all China's major cities and strategic areas, Chiang could wait for the United States to defeat Japan with American lives. Then Chiang could control China. The Chinese leader won the battle with Roosevelt. However, he lost the long-term struggle with Mao because he failed to deal with the corruption and moral decay that rotted his armies as they remained at ease for almost 10 years. Moreover, Chiang had lost his claim to being a "Nationalist" and appeared to be just another warlord.

Rather than respond directly to the president's September 16 message, Chiang demanded Stilwell's recall. Chiang told Roosevelt that the only way the centralized command Roosevelt desired could be effective would be if the American commander was acceptable to Chiang; Stilwell was not. Roosevelt gave in. Having learned from the Soviet Union in September and October that it planned to invade Manchuria to fight Japan as soon as the war in Europe ended, Roosevelt decided that a campaign by the Chinese would be unnecessary. This decision meant Roosevelt would not have to face the domestic political risk of attempting Chiang Kai-shek's overthrow.

On October 28, Major General Albert L. Wedemeyer replaced Stilwell as commander of U.S. forces in China. Henceforth, Roosevelt did not expect to have any effective Nationalist army operations against Japan. The president's policy in China shifted toward finding a method to have Moscow cooperate in preventing a civil war in China between Mao and Chiang.

November 7, 1944

Roosevelt is elected president for a fourth term.

The Republican National Convention nominated Thomas E. Dewey, governor of New York, on June 27. Roosevelt's age (62) and ability to survive another four years became a major campaign issue. Roosevelt frequently looked gaunt during the campaign, but he also made some notable campaign speeches recalling the fighting, reformist days of the 1936 campaign.

While the popular vote results were the closest since the Wilson-Hughes campaign of 1916, Roosevelt won a huge electoral victory, 432 to 99. In the popular vote, he won by 3.6 million votes.

November 30, 1944

Edward R. Stettinius Jr. replaces Cordell Hull as Secretary of State.

Secretary Hull had held the post as Secretary of State longer than any other person, having served since March 1933, but his illness made it increasingly difficult for him to continue to serve, so he resigned.

Roosevelt selected Stettinius as secretary because he had served usefully as undersecretary of state. The president wanted an uncontroversial person who would encourage bipartisan support for a sound postwar foreign policy. Stettinius agreed later to serve President Truman until the end of the San Francisco Conference, resigning on July 2, 1945, to become a representative to the United Nations Organization.

1945

January 1, 1945

Stalin recognizes Soviet-sponsored Polish government.

Despite a plea from President Roosevelt to withhold formal recognition of the Poland Communist government, Moscow endorsed the Communist-dominated Polish Committee of National Liberation. Later at Yalta, Stalin softened his stance a bit by promising that the Polish government would hold elections.

January 3, 1945

Molotov requests a $6 billion line of credit.

The Soviet Union formally requested a $6 billion line of credit to assist in rebuilding their devastated countryside. The credit would run for 30 years at 2.25 percent interest. While the Soviets tended to exaggerate their losses, their estimate that they suffered about one-half of Europe's war-related destruction seems reasonable between the Red army's wartime scorched-earth policy when withdrawing toward Moscow in 1941 and the Nazi's use of the same tactic as they retreated from Stalingrad and Moscow. Thus, the war had destroyed some 70,000 towns and villages involving some 6,000,000 buildings, 84,000 schools, 43,000 libraries, 31,000 factories, and 1,300 bridges. The agricultural sector's losses included 137,000 tractors, 49,000 harvesters, 7,000,000 horses, 17,000,000 cattle, 20,000,000 hogs, and 27,000,000 sheep and goats.

When the Soviet Foreign Affairs Commissar Molotov handed the request to Ambassador Harriman, the Soviets believed America's wartime build-up of factories would lead to peacetime overproduction and, thus, their request would benefit the United States. Consequently, Molotov suggested the Soviet purchases would prevent a serious disruption of the American economy. Ultimately, the loan request fell victim to the emerging Cold War between the two countries.

See August 28, 1945.

January 21, 1945

Western front: Allied armies restore their battle lines after the Battle of the Bulge.

Between December 16 and 26, 1944, a German counteroffensive dislodged Allied armies near the Ardennes Forest. A portion of the Allied lines gave way as German tanks tried to strike toward Antwerp. Although the German offensive was checked on December 26, the Allies required nearly four weeks to regain the territory they had lost. The Battle of the Bulge cost 77,000 U.S. casualties with 8,000 deaths. In addition, 21,000 men were captured. The Germans sacrificed 600 tanks and over 100,000 men in the offensive.

January 23, 1945

Eastern front: A Soviet offensive completes the "liberation" of Poland.

Beginning on January 12 from the eastern outskirts of Warsaw, the Red Army captured Warsaw on January 17 and carried forward to the Oder River by January 23. There the Soviets regrouped preparatory to an assault on Germany and Berlin.

February 5, 1945

U.S. forces begin the invasion of Luzon.

On this day, General MacArthur achieved his promise to return to the Philippines, from which he had fled in 1942. Manila was liberated on February 23, 1945.

February 11, 1945

Yalta conference concludes.

This summit conference of the Big Three—Winston Churchill, Joseph Stalin, and Franklin D. Roosevelt—planned for the postwar status of Europe and for establishing the United Nations. The important conference decisions are listed below:

1. *Eastern Europe:* The spheres of influence of the USSR and Great Britain remained as agreed to at the Moscow Conference of October 18, 1944. However, critics would later see this understanding as conflicting with Yalta's Declaration on Liberated Europe that asserted the "right of all peoples to choose the form of government under which they will live."
2. *Poland:* The Soviet-backed Polish provisional government (Lublin Government) was accepted, but Stalin agreed to expand its personnel to include "democratic leaders" both from Poland itself and from the Polish government-in-exile in London. It was agreed that, with a few digressions, the Curzon Line of 1919 would be Poland's eastern boundary. This line gave the Soviet Union Vilna and other territory gained by Poland in the Treaty of Riga (March 18, 1921) ending the Russo-Polish War of 1920. To compensate Poland, the western Polish border was extended to the Oder-Neisse line at the expense of Germany.
3. *Germany:* To give "future peace and security" in Europe, Germany would be required to disarm, be demilitarized, and be dismembered. Germany would be divided into three zones for occupation purposes, with a fourth zone given to France from portions of the British and American zones. Stalin did not recognize France as a fourth "big power," but Churchill and Roosevelt wished to reward the French. The Big Three also agreed that Germany should pay reparations, a proposal strongly advocated by Stalin. Specific details on reparations would be prepared by an Allied Reparations Commission consisting of representatives of each of the Big Three powers. Although Churchill objected, a special clause of

Churchill, Roosevelt, and Stalin at the Yalta Conference making plans for end of war. National Archives

the Yalta agreements stated that the commission should consider as one proposal that reparations would be $20 billion, with 50 percent to go to the Soviet Union.

4. *The Far East:* The Soviet Union agreed to declare war on Japan within two or three months after Germany surrendered. In return for fighting Japan, Moscow would "regain rights" lost in the 1904–1905 Russo-Japanese War: rights to the southern part of Sakhalin Island, Port Darien and Port Arthur in China, the Manchurian Railway, and the Kurile Islands. To confirm these Soviet rights, Stalin would make a Treaty of Friendship and Alliance with Chiang Kai-shek's Nationalist government and gain Chiang's concurrent approval of the Yalta agreements.
5. *The Straits:* Stalin wanted to revise the Montreux Convention, under which Turkey had the right to close the Dardanelles and Bosporus straits to foreign warships. Now Stalin wanted the Soviet Union to have some voice in the decision about closing the straits. Both Churchill and Roosevelt acknowledged some revision could be considered at a later foreign ministers' conference.
6. *Iran:* U.S., British, and Soviet forces had occupied Iran during the war to assist in moving lend-lease supplies to Russia. Both Roosevelt and Churchill again pledged to withdraw their troops as soon as the war ended and sought to get Stalin's pledge to do likewise. The Soviets however, refused to withdraw their forces until they obtained oil concessions from the Iranian government similar to ones held by Western nations—thus, setting the stage for a subsequent East-West confrontation.
7. *United Nations:* Stalin's wish to give separate membership in the United Nations to the Soviet republics of Byelorussia and the Ukraine was approved; the argument used was that this was similar to separate membership for nations in the British Commonwealth. The veto power of the Big Five (Britain, China, France, the Soviet Union, and the United States) in the Security Council was also discussed. The agreement was that substantive action could be vetoed but that discussion of a topic could not be prevented by veto. Thus, topics involving the Big Five could be discussed and might assist the peaceful settlement of a dispute.

James F. Byrnes, who attended the conference, was the first senior official to return to Washington and later became the Truman administration's spokesman and the "authority" on what took place at Yalta. What Truman, the media, and the public did not know was that Roosevelt had kept Byrnes out of the most sensitive negotiations, and thus he was ignorant of most of the crucial decisions reached at Yalta.

February 14, 1945

U.S. and British air forces bomb Dresden: A review of Allied bombing strategies.

The bombing of Dresden on the night of February 14 caused widespread damage that led to exaggerated reports of the bombing of culturally important cities. The bombing raid of February 14 plus two later raids in March killed some 35,000 persons, according to research by David Irving in 1966. In 1945, exaggerated reports estimated deaths at between 135,000 and 250,000. Dresden's notoriety arose because of a briefing officer's statement at Eisenhower's headquarters, which was reported by the AP, that "Allied air commanders have made the long-awaited decision to adopt deliberate terror bombing of the great German population centers as a ruthless expedient to hasten Hitler's doom." Army Air Force headquarters in Washington immediately warned Eisenhower's air staff "of the nation-wide serious effect on the Air Forces as we have steadily preached the gospel of precision bombing against military and industrial targets." SHAEF (Supreme Headquarters, Allied Expeditionary Forces) officers responded with a statement that there had been "no change in the American policy of precision bombing directed at military targets." The RAF had been long engaged in area bombing directed at civilian populations, but the U.S. official directive had remained anchored to precision bombing. For the policy to be effective, the bombardier had to see the target to engage in precision bombing; but weather conditions over Germany largely precluded visual sightings. Consequently, the American bombers had been engaged in radar-directed bombing, or "blind bombing," on roughly three-fourths of their missions by the end of 1944—actions that differed only semantically from the RAF's area bombing strategy. See Michael S. Sherry, *The Rise of American Air Power: The Creation of Armageddon* (1987) and for the British side, Noble Franklin, *The Bombing Offensive Against Germany* (1965).

The civilian death toll from aerial bombing in World War II is difficult to ascertain. British losses have been estimated at about 60,000, German losses at approximately 500,000, and Japanese losses at about 325,000. One should be forewarned, however, that actual figures of deaths and injuries as a result of aerial attacks are impossible to reconstruct, given the resulting chaos—under such circumstances survival became the highest priority and record keeping a much lower one.

March 9–10, 1945

A firebomb air raid on Tokyo by 334 Army Air Force B-29s based in the Marianas.

After U.S. forces captured Saipan on June 15, 1944, the island's air fields became the main location for the U.S. 20th Air Force's B-29s to stage raids on Japan after October 24 because the Saipan-Tokyo route was a dangerous 14-hour mission flown in daylight precision-bombing at 32,000 feet. Because the B-29s that passed through Japan's and Iwo Jima's antiaircraft fire, U.S. pilots experienced a heavy casualty rate. Despite the heavy casualties, the B-29 missions destroyed over one-fourth of Tokyo's buildings and over 1 million persons became homeless from a firestorm that consumed 15.8 square miles. Though figures on casualties vary greatly, 90,000 to 100,000 killed are generally accepted estimates. See Richard B. Frank. *Downfall: The End of the Imperial Japanese Empire* (1999), p. 18. Frequent air raids continued and by June, more than 3,100,000 Japanese were homeless in Tokyo. The frequently cited estimates of some 325,000 civilians killed in Japan as a result of Allied air raids—including Hiroshima and Nagasaki—are probably quite low. Moreover, these figures probably do not include other nationals residing in Japan, especially Korean laborers.

March 17, 1945

U.S. Marines complete the Conquest of Iwo Jima *en route* to Okinawa.

After bitter fighting that began on February 19, U.S. Marines raised the flag on Mount Suribachi on February 23 before completing the conquest of the island on March 17. After Iwo Jima's capture, Air Force General Curtis LeMay adopted his new B-29 tactics using low-level flights at 5,000 feet with planes carrying more bombs after removing the plane's rear turret guns and ammunition. Following victory at Iwo Jima, U.S. forces began an attack on Okinawa that lasted until June 21. Okinawa's capture brought U.S. Air Force bases within 325 miles of Japanese cities. This gave LeMay's air force complete dominance over Japan's air space in July 1945.

March 24, 1945

Controversy erupts over treatment of downed Allied flyers behind Red Army lines and prisoners of war (POWs) released by Soviet forces.

Averell Harriman, the American ambassador at Moscow, complained bitterly to President Roosevelt about the treatment of Allied POWs who had been freed as the Red Army advanced into Poland. Between November 1944 and April 1945, some 300 U.S. and British airmen either bailed out or crashed behind Soviet lines; in addition, between late January and early February 1945, the Soviet forces liberated some 7,000 U.S. and Soviet POWs. Since the Soviets did not provide transportation behind the lines for their own personnel, the POWs walked or hitchhiked eastward to central Poland and boarded boxcars destined for Odessa where by late March most of them had boarded British ships.

The trip to the railroad was often a frightening experience for many POWs. "What with the Ukrainian partisans, the Communist Lublin Poles, the London Poles, the Soviet forces and deserters from the Soviets," Harriman's private secretary Robert Meiklejohn noted, "things got quite complicated, with our men likely to be shot at by most anybody." While some POWs fared rather well at the hands of Soviet officers who gave them food, a truck ride, and medical attention, others had Soviet troops shoot at them, ignore them, or steal their watches and jewelry.

Ignoring the varying POW experiences, on March 24 Harriman cabled Roosevelt to protest to Stalin about the unacceptable treatment and miserable conditions extended to these men. "Stalin's statement that our liberated prisoners are in Soviet camps under good conditions is far from the truth. The hardships undergone [by POWs] have been inexcusable." Harriman wanted Roosevelt to retaliate by restricting the activities of Soviet officers repatriating their POWs from Western Europe; however, while the president did complain to Stalin, Roosevelt did not choose to retaliate. In retrospect, Harriman's complaint was oversimplified because of the fluidity of the front and the extremely diverse experiences of the individual POWs. See Frank Costigliola, "Like Animals or Worse": Narratives of Culture and Emotion by U.S. and British POWs and Airmen behind Soviet Lines, 1944-1945," *Diplomatic History* 28:5 (2004).

April 4, 1945

The Berne incident: The United States and Britain exclude the Soviets from discussions about the German surrender of northern Italy.

As in the case of the Anglo-American talks with Badoglio's representatives (see September 10, 1943) the United States and Britain had undertaken discussion with Germany's General Karl Wolff to surrender his Italian forces. Wolff came to Berne, Switzerland, early in March 1945 to discuss surrender terms, and Roosevelt told the Joint Chiefs of Staff to handle the meeting as a military matter even though it contained political implications.

When Stalin protested on March 15, Ambassador Harriman told him that his delegates could sit as observers during the formal negotiations but that the Berne talks with Wolff were only preliminary discussions. On March 29, Stalin again protested, claiming that the Germans had shifted three divisions from Italy to the Soviet front. He believed the British and Americans were plotting with Germany to let the Western Allies take over Germany while the Germans increased their fight against the USSR. On April 4, Roosevelt responded to Stalin's accusations by saying that they were "vile misrepresentations of my actions" and were bitterly resented.

The increased antagonism between the Soviets and the Western powers indicated that the "strange alliance" of World War II had rapidly deteriorated between September 1944 and April 1945. The Berne incident ended because the German surrender in Italy became part of the Anglo-American effort to cooperate with Stalin in the German surrender during April–May 1945. The Western powers desired to work with Moscow in defeating Germany and assuring four-power Allied control in Germany and Berlin as agreed to at Yalta. In accordance with Eisenhower's decision, U.S. forces reached the Elbe River on April 11, and Soviet forces began fighting their way into

Berlin on April 20, where they met strong German resistance until May 1. U.S. and Soviet armies joined at Torgau on the Elbe on April 25, 1945.

April 7, 1945

Eisenhower believes a race to Berlin is militarily unsound.

During the early months of 1945, U.S. and British officials disagreed about a "race to Berlin" to prevent the Soviets from "liberating" the city. General Eisenhower informed General Marshall that while he thought it militarily unsound to "make Berlin a major objective," he would adjust plans if the combined Chiefs of Staff gave him a directive to place political considerations first.

Although Churchill thought there was a psychological value in capturing Berlin, President Roosevelt and the U.S. Joint Chiefs of Staff claimed psychological values should not override military considerations in destroying Germany's army. Britain's General Montgomery wanted his army of British and Canadian forces to move across the Rhine River and to "race" across northern Germany to Berlin. Montgomery's armies, however, were slow to cross the Rhine, not arriving until March 24, while American forces crossed the Rhine at Remagen on March 8.

Meanwhile, the Soviet Union's mechanized forces spearheading the Red Army were 35 miles from Berlin on February 20. Because Generals Eisenhower and Marshall had opposed a race to Berlin, their decision to move toward the Elbe River through Leipzig and Dresden was mandated by Montgomery's delay. Eisenhower wanted a demarcation line to join the Red Army and to avoid exposing his flanks to attacks by German troops. Thus, Eisenhower and Stalin agreed to make the dividing line at the Elbe-Mulde Rivers.

April 12, 1945

President Franklin D. Roosevelt dies and Harry S. Truman is sworn in as the 32nd president.

Roosevelt died of a cerebral hemorrhage at Warm Springs, Georgia. President Truman was seldom

Marshal Zhukov decorates Field Marshal Montgomery with the Russian Order of Victory. Allied chiefs attend ceremony at General Eisenhower's Headquarters at Frankfurt. National Archives

consulted by Roosevelt about foreign policy decisions. Although there were indications shortly before his death that Roosevelt had become convinced of the need for a stronger stand toward Stalin, Truman came to symbolize the idea of "standing up" to the Soviet Union.

Historians differ about whether or not Truman's tough actions toward the Soviet Union stimulated the Cold War or whether other policies might have prevented the protracted conflict. For an author who blames Truman, see Arnold A. Offner, *Another Such Victory: President Truman and the Cold War, 1945–1953* (2002). For other views see Gabriel Kolko, *The Politics of War* (1968) or Martin J. Sherwin, *A World Destroyed, The Atomic Bomb and the Grand Alliance* (1973), or Melvyn P. Leffler, *A Preponderance of Power: National Security, the Truman Administration, and the Cold War* (1992).

April 21, 1945

The Soviet Union and Poland sign a 20-year mutual assistance pact.

Stalin signed this treaty with the Polish provisional government that the Soviets had established under the Lublin Polish leaders. They had not enlarged the government to include members of the government-in-exile in London, as Stalin had promised at Yalta. Later, at the San Francisco Conference, which opened on April 25, the Soviets nearly destroyed the conference's work by attempting to have their Polish government represented.

April 25, 1945

The San Francisco Conference on the United Nations convenes.

During the early weeks of the conference, the seating of the Polish delegation and the veto procedure in the Security Council caused much debate.

May 1, 1945

Adolf Hitler dies in a Berlin bunker.

Hitler's death by suicide on April 30 was announced in Berlin by Admiral Karl Doenitz on May 1. On April 28, Benito Mussolini had been captured and executed by Italian anti-Fascists in a village near Lake Como, Italy.

May 7, 1945

Germany's unconditional surrender is signed by Field Marshal Alfred Jodl at 2:41 A.M. French time.

President Truman and Winston Churchill announced the end of the war in Europe on May 8.

May 11, 1945

President Truman orders an end to unconditional aid to the Soviet Union and cuts back the Soviets' lend-lease aid, limiting such aid to their military needs for war against Japan.

Truman's orders resulted from the knowledge that some leading congressmen proposed to stop lend lease early so the aid would not be for postwar Soviet reconstruction. Leo Crowley, the head of the Foreign Economic Administration, interpreted Truman's orders strictly so that ships bound for the USSR were recalled and immediately halted before orders were completed for the Soviet Union. Although the Soviets expected some cutbacks after Germany surrendered, Truman seemed to be employing "economic diplomacy" to persuade Moscow to change its Eastern European policies in order to obtain a loan or grant. Consequently, the Soviet Union complained about Truman's unilateral action.

Actually, Truman's policy on cutbacks in lend lease as soon as the war ended hurt the British and French more than the Soviets. When he discovered Crowley's policies, Truman rescinded his action on May 12.

May 14, 1945

The Democratic Republic of Austria is established with socialist Karl Renner as chancellor.

Austria was still occupied and divided into four zones, but the Four Powers agreed to recognize the republic within its 1937 frontiers. Attempts by the Big Four to make a final peace treaty with Austria were unsuccessful until 1955 when the formal occupation ended.

Field Marshall Wilhelm Keitel signing the surrender terms at Russian headquarters in Berlin. National Archives

June 5, 1945

The European Advisory Commission decides on the division of Germany and Berlin.

Consisting of representatives of Britain, France, the USSR, and the United States, the European Advisory Commission had been studying the best means of dividing Germany for postwar occupation. Because of decisions by the Big Three at the Tehran and Yalta Conferences, France received a portion of the U.S. and British zones but none of the Soviet zone. As agreed on June 5, the Soviets controlled the east zone, Great Britain the north, and the United States and France divided the southern zone of Germany. Berlin was also divided into four parts under the administration of a four-power military command. Berlin was surrounded entirely by the Soviet eastern zone.

June 6, 1945

Harry Hopkins reports that Stalin has compromised on the U.N. veto and Polish questions.

President Truman sent Hopkins to Moscow to confer on issues that were handicapping decisions at the San Francisco Conference. Truman selected Hopkins for this job because, as Roosevelt's former confidant, Hopkins wanted to obtain Soviet cooperation. Regarding Poland, Hopkins stated the U.S. viewpoint, which accepted the concept of having a government in Poland friendly to the Soviets. The U.S. public had been outraged by Stalin's unilateral recognition of Poland's provisional government. Some of the London Polish government members, Hopkins said, should be accommodated by the Soviets as Polish officials.

After explaining that Soviet security required a non-hostile government in Poland, Stalin agreed that four or five members of other friendly Polish groups might be added to the 18- or 20-member present Warsaw cabinet. Although the London exiles did not like this compromise, Hopkins accepted it and Truman concurred. Truman hoped Stalin would later agree to "free" elections in Poland.

Stalin also agreed to the U.N. Security Council proposal that any member of the Big Five powers could veto substantive issues but could not veto discussion of any item to be put on the agenda of the council.

June 21, 1945

U.S. forces withdraw from parts of East Germany in the Soviet zone, parts of Czechoslovakia, and most of Austria.

Truman ordered the withdrawal in compliance with the Yalta agreement. The Soviet Union also followed the Yalta pact by permitting American and British troops to move into their Berlin zones on July 4, 1945, and French troops to enter their Berlin zone on August 12, 1945. Winston Churchill had, since April, urged Truman not to withdraw unless the Soviets met certain requirements regarding Allied aims in Eastern Europe. Truman rejected this advice, although he delayed the withdrawal by about six weeks.

June 26, 1945

The United Nations charter is signed in San Francisco.

The charter had been unanimously approved on June 25 and was signed by delegates of 50 nations the next day. During the convention, the principal disputes were about Polish representation; the admission of Argentina's delegation because Argentina had not declared war on Germany and Japan until March 27, 1945; and voting procedures in the Security Council. The United Nations organization consisted of four groups: (1) a General Assembly in which all member nations were represented and had one vote; (2) a Security Council to supervise military and political matters and to approve any substantive action by the United Nations, with veto power for the Big Five (China, France, Great Britain, the United States, and the USSR); (3) an Economic and Social Council; and (4) an International Court of Justice. The United Nations would be administered by a secretary-general elected by the General Assembly. On July 28, the U.S. Senate ratified the United Nations Charter by a vote of 89 to 2 after six days of debate.

July 3, 1945

James F. Byrnes becomes Secretary of State.

Although Byrnes had little diplomatic experience, he had served in both houses of Congress, on the Supreme Court, and as director of the Office of War Mobilization and Reconversion. However, he had been close to Roosevelt on certain foreign policy issues as early as 1940, when he managed such legislation as the repeal of the arms embargo, the draft, and lend lease for the administration.

According to historian Robert Messer, the Yalta conference "marked Byrne's first direct involvement in high-level international politics." That meeting "was a formative experience in Byrnes's approach to the conduct of summit diplomacy. It also provided him with a new public image as an expert on wartime foreign policy and a new unofficial role as Roosevelt's 'elder statesman.'" Although Truman chose him to be secretary of state because Byrnes "knew what went on at Yalta," in actuality, Byrnes had been absent when most of the crucial decisions were made. Only much later was this evident to Truman.

July 16, 1945

Truman, Churchill, and Stalin begin discussions at Potsdam, near Berlin.

The Potsdam Conference lasted until August 2, having been interrupted for two days because of British elections, during which Clement Attlee's Labour Party won control of Parliament from Churchill's Conservative Party, with Attlee replacing Churchill at Potsdam on July 28. Although the principal concern of the conference was to implement decisions made at the Yalta Conference of February 1945, Truman also dealt with the July 16 news he received about the successful U.S. test of an atomic bomb. On July 21, Truman received a full report of the test, showing the bomb's destructive power equaled that of 10,000 to 20,000 tons of TNT. He shared the information with Churchill, Attlee, and Stalin. Because of the successful test, Truman decided to use or threaten to use the bomb against Japan in order to shorten the war in the Far East and, perhaps, prevent Stalin's army from occupying Manchuria and making contact with the Chinese Communists.

July 16, 1945

An atomic bomb is successfully exploded at Alamagordo, New Mexico.

Until this experiment, scientists working on the Manhattan Project did not know for certain that

Stalin and Truman meet at Potsdam Conference. National Archives

their efforts would succeed. Anticipating the success of the A-bomb, discussions about using it had begun on May 9, 1945, when an Interim Committee was charged with advising the president on the use of the atomic weapon. The committee consisted of men who wanted the bomb to be used to end the war: Secretary of War Henry Stimson (chairman); George L. Harrison, deputy secretary of war; Vannevar Bush, director of the Office of Scientific Research and Development; Karl T. Compton of the Manhattan Project; Navy Undersecretary Ralph Bard; Assistant Secretary of State Will Clayton; and James Byrnes, who would formally replace Stettinius after the end of the San Francisco Conference.

On June 16, the Interim Committee reported that there was no "acceptable alternative to direct military use of the bomb." The bomb should be used against Japan as soon as it was operational. A war plant or military installation in Japan should be the target, but Japan should not be warned in advance of the A-bomb. Some of the scientists involved in the Manhattan Project disagreed with the Interim Committee. Seven members of the University of Chicago group, headed by James O. Franck, proposed holding a public demonstration of the bomb in a deserted place, followed by a warning to Japan to surrender or suffer the consequences of an A-bomb attack. The Interim Committee opposed such a test because if the bomb failed it would render future threats meaningless. On June 18, Truman met with his War Council (the Joint Chiefs of Staff and the secretaries of war and the navy) to consider future actions against Japan. The A-bomb was mentioned but only briefly, because the test had not yet been made in New Mexico.

The Joint Chiefs presented plans for Operation Olympic, an invasion of the Japanese island of Kyushu on November 1, 1945, and for Operation Coronet, an invasion of Honshu, on or about March 1, 1946. General Marshall believed the invasion would cause at least 250,000 U.S. deaths plus a million Japanese deaths. This invasion was preferred, however, to an offensive against Japan in China and Manchuria. Truman ordered plans for the invasion of Kyushu to proceed but delayed a decision on the Honshu invasion. These plans were again reviewed on July 16, when Truman had to consider the use of the A-bomb against Japan.

July 24, 1945

Truman orders use of the atomic bomb on any of four possible military targets in Japan.

The identified targets were in the cities of Hiroshima, Kokura, Niigata, and Nagasaki. The precise target would be determined by weather conditions permitting a daylight visual-bombing attack.

July 26, 1945

The United States and Great Britain issue an ultimatum to Japan, asking for an unconditional surrender and warning that rejection will lead to the use of vast, destructive force against Japan.

While at Potsdam, President Truman agreed with Churchill to send Japan an ultimatum to surrender. After obtaining the concurrence of Chiang Kai-shek, the so-called Potsdam Proclamation was released to newspaper and radio reporters. It called on the "Government of Japan to proclaim now the unconditional surrender of all the Japanese armed forces," with the alternative being Japan's "prompt and utter destruction." The proclamation did not mention the existence of the atomic weapon or the possibility of a compromise by which the emperor might remain as Japan's ruler. Truman and Churchill signed the proclamation with the notation that Chiang Kai-shek approved by radio. Stalin did not sign because the Soviets had not yet declared war on Japan.

On July 27, Japanese officials received the proclamation's message by radio, not through diplomatic sources or a neutral country. Prime Minister Susuki told a Tokyo press conference that the proclamation was of no importance and should be "ignored" (*mokusatsu*). While the prime minister was holding the press conference, American airplanes were dropping 27 million leaflets over Japanese cities that explained the ultimatum and listed 11 Japanese cities of which four might be destroyed from the air if Japan failed to surrender. During July 25 to 28, Japan's ambassador to Moscow asked the Soviet Union to mediate with the Allies to end the war if the Allies would approve concessions to an unconditional surrender such as allowing Japan's emperor to remain in power. Soviet Foreign Minister Molotov delayed his country's response by asking the ambassador to put his ideas in writing. Although the Japanese terms for mediation were neither precise nor clearly known to Japan's ambassador to Moscow, Molotov's delay allowed Soviet troops to move toward Manchuria before declaring war on Japan. Details about these activities are in Charles L. Mee Jr.'s *Meeting at Potsdam* (1975) and Herbert Bix's *Hirohito and the Making of Modern Japan* (2000).

August 2, 1945

The Potsdam Conference adjourns.

Truman apparently believed, according to Robert Messer's *The End of an Alliance*,

> that Stalin was an honest man with whom he could deal and who like 'any smart political boss' would keep his word and deliver what he had promised to those other politicians who depended upon that promise.

The Big Three talks considered the details of the German occupation and other European problems. The principal decisions were as follows:

1. German reparations—The Soviet Union dropped the $20 billion proposal made at Yalta, agreeing to base reparations on useful materials in the eastern zone and capital equipment available in the three western zones of Germany.
2. Transfer of Germans—More than 6.5 million Germans would be transferred to Germany from previously disputed territory in Hungary, Czechoslovakia, and Poland.
3. War crimes—It was agreed to try leading Nazis for war crimes; an International Military Tribunal was to be set up soon after the conference ended.
4. German economy—Proposals accepted would convert the German economy to a principally agricultural one. Powerful industrial cartels would be abolished, and only nonmilitary products would be manufactured by German industry.
5. Other peace treaties—A Council of Foreign Ministers representing each of the Big Five powers was directed to prepare peace treaties for Austria, Hungary, Bulgaria, Romania, and Finland. Once Germany regained a central government, the council would draft a peace treaty for Germany.

Truman was reluctant to discuss Stalin's previously pledged willingness to declare war on Japan. According to Messer, "the impact of the successful

WWII: Occupation Zones

atomic test the day before the Potsdam conference began makes clear that... Truman and Byrnes were anxious to keep the Russians out of the war with Japan as much as possible."

August 6, 1945

The first atomic bomb used in the war is dropped on Hiroshima, Japan.

Flying from an airfield on Tinian Island, a U.S. air force plane, named *Enola Gay* for pilot Paul Tibbets's mother, dropped a uranium nuclear bomb code-named "Little Boy" at 8:16 A.M. Some of the initial consequences for Hiroshima, a city with 320,000 inhabitants at the time, were 130,000 killed or seriously injured; 64,521 buildings destroyed; 70,000 water-main breaks; 52 of 55 hospitals and clinics destroyed; 180 of 200 doctors and 1,654 of 1,780 nurses killed or injured. In addition, 12 U.S. navy pilots were killed while in Hiroshima's prison, although the U.S. government has never admitted this. See Committee for the Compilation of Materials on Damage Caused by the Atomic Bombs in Hiroshima and Nagasaki, *Hiroshima and Nagasaki: The Physical, Medical, and Social Effects of the Atomic Bombings* (1981). The bomb had a yield of 13 kilotons, equal to the explosive power of 13,000 tons of TNT. The largest conventional bomb used in World War II yielded the power of 10 tons of TNT.

August 8, 1945

The Soviet Union declares war on Japan; Soviet armies invade Manchuria.

In keeping with its pledge made at Yalta, the Soviet Union declared war on Japan 30 days after the war ended in Europe. Before the war ended, the Soviets prepared for a military attack on Manchuria and into northern China to align with its Communist forces. On April 10, Mao Tse-Tung ordered his Communist armies to find a way to obtain the surrender of Japanese troops in China. After Japan surrendered on

August 15, Stalin made sure that Mao's Communist army took over all of Manchuria from Japan. Yet, Stalin fulfilled his Yalta agreement to make a "friendship treaty" with Chiang Kai-shek.

See August 14, 1945.

August 9, 1945

The second atomic bomb is dropped on Nagasaki bringing about a Cold War charge of "Atomic Diplomacy."

Although originally scheduled to be dropped on August 11 if Japan had not surrendered, "Fat Boy," a plutonium bomb, was dropped within 75 hours of the first bomb apparently because of predictions of bad weather over Japan on August 10 and 11. Although the plutonium bomb was more powerful than "Little Boy," damage and casualties were less extensive because of Nagasaki's terrain; approximately 100,000 were killed or seriously wounded. After World War II ended, Truman's decision to drop atomic bombs on Japan was controversial; it is unclear if the A-bombs were intended to influence the Soviet Union or if the atomic bomb was essential to obtain Japan's surrender.

In 1995, for example, on the fiftieth anniversary of the end of the war, an extensive dispute arose regarding the Smithsonian Institution's exhibition regarding the decision to use the bomb. One faction approved Truman's decision as preventing the deaths of many American soldiers who might have had to invade Japan's home islands; the opponents of the decision cited various counterfactual methods Truman could have used to force Japan's surrender.

A dense column of smoke rises over Nagasaki after the second A-bomb was dropped. National Archives

August 14, 1945

China and the USSR sign a treaty of friendship and alliance.

Stalin recognized Chiang Kai-shek's Nationalist regime as the central government of China. Chiang accepted the Yalta Conference decisions that gave the Soviets the 30-year control of the Manchurian Railway, the use of Darien, and the right to join with China in the exclusive use of Port Arthur as a naval base. This relationship would last, as the Soviets would support the Chinese Communists' bid for power.

August 15, 1945

Japan surrenders.

After ignoring the Allies' ultimatum of July 26, Japan's leaders did not meet again until August 9, after the United States dropped the second atomic bomb, on Nagasaki. Even at this late date, Japan's military officers wanted to fight on, despite reports that their defense installations were not prepared to defend against an Allied invasion of their home islands. Prime Minister Susuki Kantaro on August 10 requested that the emperor retain his throne and the United States granted this concession.

U.S. occupation forces began to land in Japan on August 26. On September 2, 1945, Japanese delegates signed the formal surrender terms with General Douglas MacArthur on board the USS *Missouri* in Tokyo Bay.

August 15, 1945

General MacArthur orders certain Japanese forces to surrender to Soviets. Stalin wants to join the occupation of Japan.

MacArthur's General Order No. 1 instructs the Japanese armies in Sakhalin, Manchuria, and Korea north of the 38th Parallel to surrender to the Russians. Stalin promptly asked that the Japanese forces on the Kurile Islands be added to this list. (This request followed the decisions made at Yalta that called for the islands to go to the Soviets.)

Stalin also desired to participate in the occupation of Japan, at least the northern half of the northern most island of Hokkaido. Stalin informed Truman that Russian public opinion would be insulted if Russian armies did not occupy some part of Japan proper and he hoped Truman would not oppose his modest wishes.

Truman refused Stalin's "modest request" for an occupation zone in Japan but asked Stalin if the U.S. could have a landing base in the Kurile Islands in exchange for Soviet landing rights in Alaska's Aleutian Islands. Stalin refused Truman's proposed basing rights in a region where the two countries nearly touched each other. Thus, nothing came from these exchanges.

August 21, 1945

Lend-lease aid is terminated by the United States, but problems remain.

From its beginning on March 11, 1941, until its final orders were filled in September 1946, lend-lease aid approximated $11.3 billion ($90 billion in terms of 1998 dollars) minus reverse lend lease of $7.8 billion received by the United States from Great Britain. After President Roosevelt decided to give unlimited amounts of lend lease to the Soviet Union, Moscow received the largest share of lend lease especially after early problems of transportation were resolved in mid-1943. Initially, the United States sent light-type Sherman tanks to Russia that proved to be inferior to the Soviets' heavy T-34 tanks in combating heavy-type German tanks. The most important American and British aid to Russia consisted of 50 percent of Russia's aviation fuels; 53 percent of its explosives; 50 percent of its copper, aluminum, and tire requirements; and 57 percent of its railway needs. More specifically, America's lend lease provided Russia with 20,000 military aircraft; 1,900 locomotives; 11,075 railroad cars; and 425,000 trucks, jeeps, and motorcycles.

Indicative of the growing tension between the United States and USSR in 1945, however, American aid officials suspended lend lease supplies to the Soviet Union three days before ending assistance to other recipients. Once again the American allies complained about the United States cutting off the aid, and the humanitarian aid shipments were resumed until the aid program officially ended on September 3, 1945. At the same time, Washington gave all the recipients the opportunity to purchase lend-lease materials that were ordered or manufactured by September 3 but not yet shipped.

Japanese dignitaries arrive aboard the USS *Missouri* in Tokyo Bay to sign the surrender documents. National Archives

On October 15, the Soviets agreed to buy $400 million worth of goods in the pipeline under terms that gave them nine years to begin the first of 22 annual payments at 2.38 percent interest. Most of the goods were sent to Russia during the following fourteen months. Because the United States had built these goods to Soviet specifications, Washington was delighted to sell them. Due to legislation passed in 1946, the United States ruled that pipeline deliveries must be completed by December 31, 1946. By employing such technicalities, most of the supplies were delivered to Russia on time even though the premature termination of the agreement was an American violation of a contract with the Soviet government. These terms complicated the final settlement of America's lend-lease program.

Although Washington did not expect to be reimbursed for supplies consumed during the war, it did expect to be paid for civilian goods, such as locomotives and industrial machinery, which was still in use after the war. Because the Soviets would not allow a post-Japanese war "V-J day" audit of usable lend-lease equipment, the United States set the total value at $2.6 billion but in 1948 Washington reduced the Soviet debt by half. For their part, the Soviets thought their debt should be forgiven because their people had suffered the most casualties and destruction. Discussions over this issue and the one dealing with the disposition of 711 U.S. ships, mostly small craft, dragged on for years.

From its beginning in March 1941 until September 1946, lend lease amounted to $50.6 billion, minus reverse lend lease of $7.8 billion received by the United States from its allies.

August 28, 1945

The Soviet Purchasing Commission requests a $1 billion loan, but the request is "lost."

General Leonid Rudenko, head of the Soviet Purchasing Commission, submitted a request for a $1 billion loan to the U.S. Foreign Economic Administration (FEA) on August 28. The FEA, who coordinated lend lease and 19 other wartime agencies, gave Rudenko's request to State Department officials who had final approval on foreign aid. But the State Department officers gave a low priority to the loan and Moscow failed to pursue its request. Finally in January 1946, the Truman administration admitted Rudenko's request had been "lost."

See April 20, 1946.

September 2, 1945

In Hanoi, Ho Chi Minh proclaims Vietnam's independence.

Following Japan's surrender, Ho Chi Minh and his Vietminh forces entered Hanoi to replace the Japanese and proclaim Vietnam's independence from France as well as Japan. The Vietminh (Vietnamese Independence League) was a national coalition organization formed in May 1941 to attract all Vietnamese patriots to fight the occupation by Japan as well as the French. It was based on the Indochinese Communist Party because the French had suppressed all moderate nationalist groups during the 1930s and the small Communist group went underground. By 1945, however, the Vietminh included nationalists from many political groups who united against France and Japan. During World War II, the Vietminh aided Americans on missions against the Japanese in Indochina. They rescued downed pilots, committed sabotage at Japanese military bases, and gave intelligence information to the U.S. Office of Strategic Services (OSS). Many OSS officers admired the Vietminh's and urged them to seek U.S. support in an independence struggle.

Perhaps it is not surprising that when Ho Chi Minh declared Vietnam's independence in 1945, his decree began: "All men are created equal. They are endowed by their creator with certain inalienable rights, among these are life, liberty, and the pursuit of happiness." Within four weeks, however, the Vietminh's hopes turned sour. Although President Roosevelt once spoke about the end of French colonial power in Indochina, British forces "liberated" that area and brought French colonial officials with them but President Truman ignored Ho's appeal for help. The French regained Saigon in September and moved to end Vietnamese independence. In Paris and Moscow, exiled Vietnamese Communist leaders told Ho to compromise with France but he refused to do so.

See November 23, 1946.

September 9, 1945

Japan signs capitulation terms with China's Nationalist government at Nanking and with the British at Singapore (September 12).

China regained control of Inner Mongolia, Manchuria, Formosa, and Hainan Island. The British reoccupied Hong Kong as agreed at Potsdam in July 1945.

October 20, 1945

The Council of Foreign Ministers adjourns its first meeting in London.

Meeting in London, Council meetings began in mid-September but talks scheduled to draft a peace treaty for Italy never materialized. When the sessions convened, Soviet Foreign Minister Molotov, who was being closely monitored by Stalin, diverted the agenda to discuss Romania, Bulgaria, and Japan. Molotov's first question to U.S. Secretary of State Byrnes and British Foreign Minister Bevin was why they would not recognize the Romanian government of Petru Groza. Romania's King Michael had been forced by the Soviets to install Groza on March 2. King Michael headed Romania's government after the Soviet army occupied Bucharest in August 1944, but in 1945 the Soviets wanted Groza, a Communist, to be premier. Secretary Byrnes told Molotov the United States and

Britain refused to recognize Romania's new government because Groza was not democratically elected under terms of the Yalta agreement's Declaration of Liberated Europe. Molotov rejected Byrnes's explanation, claiming Groza's government was a "friendly" neighbor while the former premier was hostile to the Soviet Union. Similarly, Byrnes and Molotov disagreed about Bulgaria's new government, installed by Soviet officials but not recognized by Britain and the United States.

Finally, on September 23, Molotov wanted to discuss a Control Council for Japan. In his memoirs, Byrnes believes Molotov's proposal on Japan "broke the back of the London Conference" because he wanted to devise a new method to replace General MacArthur's authority in Japan. In November 1945, Ambassador Harriman and Molotov discussed Japan and Molotov accepted Harriman's proposed U.S. veto rights on Molotov's proposed Far Eastern Control Commission for Japan. Stalin rebuked Molotov because he said Americans were devious and sought to isolate the USSR. Stalin said "Molotov's behavior in detaching himself from the government and in presenting himself as more liberal and more compliant than the government," will get us nowhere. See Y. Gorlizki and O. Khlevniuk, *Cold Peace: Stalin and the Soviet Ruling Circle, 1945–1953* (2004).

On Stalin's orders, Molotov insisted on excluding China and France from discussions on the peace treaties. Stalin's tactics delayed and disrupted completion of final peace treaties while the Soviets created puppet governments in territory occupied by the Red Army after World War II. Although the London sessions continued until October 20, Byrnes called for a December meeting in Moscow because he thought Stalin would make compromises Molotov rejected.

October 21, 1945

Left-wing parties win the French elections for a constituent assembly.

In the elections for 441 seats, the Communists won 152 seats, the Socialists 151, and the Moderates (Mouvement Républicain Populaire—MRP) 138. Nevertheless, on November 16, 1945, General Charles de Gaulle was elected president of the provisional government.

November 15, 1945

The United States, Canada, and Britain agree on an atomic energy control plan supported by the United Nations.

As Truman remarked in the fall of 1945, the control of atomic weapons would become humankind's major problem. Neither he, Secretary Byrnes, nor others had any precedent on which to proceed. Therefore, a variety of proposals had appeared from advocates of ideas ranging from the free exchange of all secrets with the Soviet Union to the United States' use of the bomb to compel all nations to adopt American policies. Neither of these extremes held the serious attention of American leaders who searched for a means to prevent a nuclear arms race and promote peaceful uses of atomic power. On November 15, President Truman, British Prime Minister Clement Attlee, and Canadian Prime Minister MacKenzie King agreed on a basic step-by-step proposal to be established under the auspices of a United Nations Atomic Energy Commission.

Vannevar Bush of the Office of Scientific Research had suggested the steps in the proposal:

1. Extending the international exchange of all scientific information as a first test of the USSR's good intentions;
2. Establishing a U.N. Committee of Inspection to inspect science laboratories of all nations engaged in atomic research. This would be done on a gradual basis so that the United States would not have to disclose any "secrets" immediately;
3. Stockpiling by all nations capable of atomic fission of such materials, which would be used only for peaceful purposes; the Committee of Inspection would oversee their use.

The U.N. commission would also work to eliminate atomic weapons and to provide safeguards for nations that cooperated with the U.N. commission. Each stage of the commission's work would be completed only when the confidence of the world had been secured to proceed to the next step.

Once this plan was announced in November 1945, its supporters and critics began to analyze it. Washington's interest in establishing international control, however, decreased as suspicions between the Western nations and the Soviet Union grew after August 1945.

November 27, 1945

Patrick J. Hurley resigns as U.S. Ambassador to China. His efforts to mediate between Chiang Kai-shek and Mao Tse-tung fail.

In announcing his resignation, Hurley leveled charges against State Department officers and Truman's China policy, which provided ammunition for attacks during the next decade on Truman, the Democratic Party, the U.S. Foreign Service, and the State Department. Hurley blamed the failure of his efforts and Chiang's difficulties on "career diplomats in the Embassy at Chungking and Far Eastern Division of the State Department." These officials, he asserted, did not implement the "principles of the Atlantic Charter" but supported both Chinese Communists and "British imperialists" against Chiang Kai-shek.

President Roosevelt had sent Hurley to China on August 18, 1944. As the president's special representative, Hurley was charged with resolving the lengthy dispute between U.S. General Stilwell and Chiang Kai-shek and establishing unity between the Chinese Nationalist and Communist forces so that they would fight the Japanese. Hurley interpreted his mission as maintaining the Nationalist government by supporting Chiang. Hurley's year in China caused much controversy. He oversaw the removal of General Stilwell; replaced Clarence Gauss as ambassador to China on December 12, 1944; demanded the removal of two career Foreign Service China experts, George Atcheson and John Service, because they disputed his analysis of Chinese developments; and became a friend and admirer of Chiang Kai-shek. In addition, while visiting Moscow on his way to China in August 1944, he became convinced that the Soviet Union differed with Mao Tse-tung's regime and would cooperate with the Nationalist government.

Finally, as an old-time Irish Anglophobe, Hurley was equally convinced that Winston Churchill had usurped Roosevelt's anticolonial policy because he wanted Hong Kong returned and planned to restore Anglo-French control in East Asia. Thus, he blamed U.S. diplomats both for aiding Mao's Communist growth and for supporting British attempts to renew their imperial regime in Asia. Because he accepted Moscow's good faith and Chiang's power, Hurley lauded the August 1945 pact between China and the Soviet Union. He also was pleased that Truman extended lend-lease aid to Chiang for six months after the war's end and that the U.S. navy aided Chiang by carrying Nationalist troops to northern China.

Chou En-lai, Mao Tse-tung, and Patrick Hurley meet to discuss political situation in China. National Archives

Thus, on September 26, 1945, Hurley returned home ready to resign because he believed everything was calm in China. During the next month, the State Department kept Hurley informed of the deteriorating relations between the two Chinese factions. Truman and Secretary Byrnes urged him to return to Chungking. Contrary to Hurley's expectation, the Soviet Union did not keep its promises to cooperate with Chiang. The Soviets helped the Communists gain control in Manchuria and refused to allow Nationalist troops to disembark from U.S. ships at Dairen or other ports near Manchuria. Hurley also learned that the truce arrangements between Mao and Chiang had been postponed, and the two sides were as far apart as ever by November 1945. Finally, Hurley was dismayed to discover that against his advice, both George Atcheson and John Service had been posted to Tokyo as consultants on General MacArthur's staff.

Russell Buhite, Hurley's biographer, is not certain what prompted Hurley's actions in November 1945. First, he agreed to return to China but later surprised both Byrnes and Truman by calling a press conference to announce his resignation. Moreover, Buhite cannot explain why Hurley, in his resignation and his testimony to the Senate Foreign Relations Committee, blamed China's problems on the Foreign Service and the State Department rather than on the Soviet Union's failure to cooperate and the intransigent policies of both Mao and Chiang. Hurley's Senate testimony exaggerated the blame of career officers who disagreed with him or "favored" the British and Chinese Communists. Subsequent to Hurley's charges, Secretary of State Byrnes defended Service and Atcheson, stating that these experts had to be free to give their honest judgments on policy. They were not, Byrnes said, disloyal to Hurley, but their long years of experience in China gave them different perspectives. Byrnes's support for the Foreign Service officers in 1946 contrasts with the treatment accorded to these experts during the McCarthy era from 1950 to 1954.

November 27, 1945

The Marshall mission to China begins after he receives instructions from Truman.

Immediately after learning of Patrick Hurley's resignation, President Truman called General George Marshall, asking him to act as the president's personal representative to China. Truman, Marshall, and Secretary of State Byrnes agreed on December 9, 1945, that U.S. policy was (1) to seek a cease-fire; (2) to seek a united and democratic China; and (3) to retain Chinese sovereignty over Manchuria. To do this, Marshall would seek a truce between Mao and Chiang in north China and assist the Nationalist government in replacing the Japanese and Soviet troops that had evacuated northern China. Marshall's most perplexing problem was how to mediate between the two Chinese groups while the United States continued to support Chiang Kai-shek. He was told that he should pressure Chiang as much as possible, but that the United States would not cease support of the Nationalists.

This, of course, made real pressure impossible and, as under Stilwell, Chiang thought he could do as he wished by appealing either to the White House or to the friends of the China-Chiang lobby in Congress. Although Marshall secured a temporary truce on January 10, 1946, by April 14, 1946, he realized that neither Mao nor Chiang wanted a genuine truce. Chiang wanted to control all Manchuria and seemed successful in June 1946. A new truce from June 7 to 30 was broken by the Communists, and by July 1, 1946, all-out civil war began.

See April 14, 1946.

December 3, 1945

General Groves claims the "real atomic secret" is the U.S. monopoly of uranium.

In 1945, most Americans believed the Manhattan Project's "secret" in developing the atomic bomb was the scientific and technological knowledge of U.S. scientists that the Soviet Union lacked. On December 3, General Leslie Groves told the Combined Policy Committee and representatives of the Truman administration that the "real secret" of the U.S. success was obtaining a monopoly of high-grade uranium—Groves did not make this alleged "secret" public until 1954. Because Groves knew Soviet scientists had the ability to build an atomic weapon, he decided in 1943 to secure U.S. control of the supply of fissionable materials, uranium and thorium. At the 1943 Quebec Conference, the Combined Policy Committee was established to obtain British and Canadian cooperation and enlist aid from the Belgian government-in-exile in London because the Belgian Congo had large deposits of uranium. On December 3, 1945, Groves reported that the United States and its allies controlled 97 percent of the world's high-grade uranium and 35 percent of low-grade deposits, which were more expensive to use for a nuclear weapon. Most of the other 65 percent was in neutral Sweden and the British dominions, although the USSR and South American nations had some low-grade material. According to his calculations on uranium supplies, Groves believed the Soviets would need at least 20 years to build an atomic weapon.

Unfortunately, Groves's calculation was mistaken about a monopoly of uranium. If he had told his "secret" to U.S. scientists such as James Conant or Vannevar Bush, Groves could have learned controlling uranium would not prohibit the Soviets from making an atomic bomb. In 1944, Conant had told Secretary of War Henry Stimson that a monopoly of materials was impractical because the supply of heavy hydrogen is "essentially unlimited." In addition, U.S. scientists knew the Soviets could obtain high-grade uranium in East Germany's province of Saxony, liberated by Soviet troops in early 1945; later they would learn of the huge newly discovered deposits in the Urals.

In contrast to Groves, Conant and other U.S. scientists predicted the Soviets would have an atomic bomb in four or five years. As Gregg Herken's *The Winning Weapon: The Atomic Bomb in the Cold War, 1945–1950* (1980) explains, Groves' "secret" created a myth about the U.S. monopoly of scientific and technological superiority that presumed the Soviet Union could not make atomic weapons without Western spies providing all the information. This myth of U.S. scientific superiority promoted Senator Joseph McCarthy's spy allegations in 1950. Soviet documents declassified during the 1990s reveal that by 1945 spies Klaus Fuchs and Theodore Hall provided data from the Manhattan Project to help Soviet scientists build a bomb by 1949, the time predicted by Conant and Bush.

December 20, 1945

The Truman administration backs legislation for civilian control of America's atomic energy.

Although General Leslie Groves and others desired military control of atomic developments, Senator Brien McMahon's bill provided for civilian control. The McMahon Bill passed Congress and became law on August 1, 1946. This law also limited Anglo-American nuclear cooperation, which became an issue between the two nations.

December 26, 1945

At Moscow, Byrnes and Stalin agree on Eastern Europe and Japan.

Following the breakdown of the London Conference of October 20, 1945, Secretary of State Byrnes called for a second foreign ministers' meeting in Moscow, where he hoped Stalin would be easier to deal with than Molotov regarding the status of Romania and Bulgaria. Byrnes persuaded Britain's Foreign Minister Ernest Bevin to attend the Moscow session that began on December 16. Byrnes met with Bevin and Molotov for several days before obtaining the compromises he sought in a session with Stalin on December 23. Regarding Eastern Europe, Stalin agreed to have Bulgaria add opposition leaders to its government and to send a three-power commission to Romania and advise Romanian leaders to add two opposition members to their cabinet. Stalin's concessions did not weaken Soviet control of those two countries, but the agreement justified U.S. diplomatic recognition in order to conclude peace treaties with Bulgaria and Romania.

In other Moscow agreements, Stalin accepted a Western Allies proposal for creating a U.N. Atomic Energy Commission, while Byrnes approved the formation of an Allied Council to consult with General MacArthur about Japan's occupation, although MacArthur did not have to take the Council's advice. Each of these agreements proved to be irrelevant: the Soviets kept control of Eastern Europe and the United States controlled developments in Japan.

III. CONTAINMENT AND DÉTENTE, 1946–1976

Political and territorial disputes that arose during World War II, blended with prewar suspicions and ideological differences, led in 1946 to mutual distrust and the emergence of the "Cold War"—a term attributed to Walter Lippmann. Europe was the initial focus of the differences. Premier Stalin sought to reclaim Russian territories "lost" during World War I and to install Communist governments in the East European nations occupied by the Red Army in order to provide the Soviet Union with a protective corridor of friendly nations along its border. The Americans and British wanted a return to 1939 Europe and viewed Soviet activities as unwarranted expansionism and only the beginning of Moscow's efforts at world domination.

As tensions mounted, most Americans agreed with Winston Churchill that an "Iron Curtain" had fallen across Europe, separating East and West into Communist and non-Communist regions. The Truman administration adopted a policy of containment that included the Truman Doctrine, Marshall Plan, economic sanctions, and later the North Atlantic-Treaty Organization (NATO). Meanwhile, Stalin urged his people to bear the sacrifices required to rebuild their shattered countryside and insisted upon reparations from the defeated Axis states to aid the rebuilding of their heavy industrial sector. To offset the U.S.'s atomic weapons, the Kremlin maintained a large contingent of conventional military forces in the Eastern European satellites that, to balance NATO, formed the Warsaw Pact.

The Cold War soon expanded to Asia and later into the Caribbean. Despite the unsuccessful efforts of General Marshall to create a coalition government in China, Mao's Chinese Communist forces forced Chiang Kai-shek to flee to Taiwan. As the Japanese withdrew from Korea, that country became divided into the non-Communist South and Communist North. In 1950, the United States found itself engaged in a full-scale war to prevent the North from reuniting Korea as a Communist nation. Meanwhile in Southeast Asia, Ho Chi Minh, a dedicated Communist, was rallying Vietnamese nationalists to gain their independence from the French. During the First Indochina War, the United States provided the French with arms and other supplies.

After the French were forced to withdraw, the United States undertook the defense of South Vietnam during the 1960s and 1970s against the efforts of the North—led by Ho Chi Minh—to reunite the country. This protracted struggle found the United States and its allies engaged in a war that also involved Thailand, Cambodia, and Laos and resulted in a great loss of life and destruction of the environment. American politics were shaken by the failure of military actions to force the North to end the war and by opponents to the war who could not find the U.S. national interests at stake. The Nixon Doctrine, by which the United States supplied the arms and the locals the manpower, provided the way for the United States to temporarily end the fighting and withdraw. Several months later the North would forcibly establish a united Communist Vietnam.

In the late 1950s, Fidel Castro led a successful struggle to seize power in Cuba. Eventually declaring himself a Communist, Castro became a significant factor in the Cold War prompting U.S. countermeasures as Kennedy's Alliance for Progress. The ill-fated U.S.-sponsored Bay of Pigs intervention in 1961 provided the impulsive Nikita Khrushchev with an opportunity to support Cuban security and improve the Soviet Union's strategic military position by sending Soviet forces to secretly build missiles bases in Cuba. Upon discovery of the construction in 1962, President John F. Kennedy's demand for their withdrawal created a crisis that found the superpowers dangerously close to a military confrontation. The successful resolution of the Cuban missile crisis led to a new appreciation of the dangers of the nuclear environment.

The Cold War found its way into the Middle East and Africa during those years. The Israeli-Arab conflicts and subsequent deadlock over territorial and recognition issues soon saw the superpowers supporting different sides in a constantly evolving political environment. While Washington's support of Israel and Jordan was fairly constant, Moscow supplied arms for various Arab nations, principally Egypt, Syria, and Iraq. The Suez crisis of 1956, however, found the United States and the Soviet Union briefly allied against Israel, Britain, and France over usage of the canal. The basic disputed issues of the early Arab-Israel conflicts have continued unresolved into the twenty-first century.

Civil wars drew the superpowers into African conflicts, often where it was difficult to find their national interests threatened and frequently where local factions played Washington and Moscow against each other. In the Congo and Angola, the superpowers (and occasionally China) found themselves supporting different factions seeking to seize power. Angola's drawn out struggle drew the most attention and sharpest exchanges between Moscow and Washington. Later they were at odds over the Horn of Africa where the conflict between Ethiopia and Somali was viewed in a Cold War context—which superpower would control the entrance to the Red Sea.

Efforts to control atomic weapons began early when the United States presented the Baruch Plan to the U.N. Atomic Energy Committee in 1946; however, Moscow rejected the plan because it perpetuated the American monopoly and because they viewed the inspection plan as espionage. Three years later the Soviet would detonate their A-bomb. After the Cuban missile crisis, the superpowers began an almost continuous effort to find means of controlling the dangers of nuclear weaponry, first with the Limited Test Ban, then with the Non-Proliferation Treaty and Anti-Ballistic Missile Treaty of 1972. Subsequently, there was a continuing arms control effort to limit strategic nuclear weaponry—the SALT negotiations—and other less dramatic undertakings to reduce tensions or to avoid possible conflict.

President Nixon, assisted by Henry Kissinger, took control of U.S. foreign policy and established the climate for an American-Soviet détente. Together with a Kremlin that was also interested in reducing tensions between superpowers, led by Leonid Brezhnev, the two sides engaged in the first extended period of serious, wide-ranging negotiations. These discussions between Moscow and Washington resulted in compromises by both sides—the strategic arms limitation negotiations being a primary example—and agreements that temporarily eased Cold War tensions, but frequently did not satisfy hard-line critics at home.

1946

January 1, 1946

Japan's Emperor Hirohito appears to disclaim his divinity.

Although the Tokyo International Military Tribunal granted immunity to Emperor Hirohito from a trial or testifying in cases on Japanese war criminals, General MacArthur's staff suggested the emperor should issue a statement to disclaim his divinity. John Dower's *Embracing Defeat* (1999) notes that Hirohito descended only "partway from heaven," because in Japanese eyes the emperor's words were not a renunciation of divinity. At best, Hirohito desired "imperial democracy." In November 1946, Japan adopted a constitution prepared by the Americans. MacArthur also issued decrees for other reforms such as restoring civil liberties, dissolving the secret police, prohibiting military forces, and liberalizing education. Although Japan's leaders praised MacArthur's administration, Japan's prewar conservatives retained a strong hold on the government. As a result of the U.S. reforms, Japan would remain within the Western bloc during the Cold War.

January 10, 1946

First session of the United Nations opens in London.

During its first session, the U.N. General Assembly unanimously passed a resolution on January 24 that created the U.N. Atomic Energy Commission (AEC). The commission included all of the Security Council members from China, France, the Soviet Union, the United Kingdom, and the United States, plus Canada, Australia, Brazil, Egypt, Mexico, the Netherlands, and Poland. The other commission members concurred with a Soviet suggestion that the commission would be accountable to the five permanent members of the Security Council who had veto powers.

President Truman sends General Marshall to China in an effort to arrange a cease fire between the Nationalists and Communists. National Archives

January 10, 1946

George Marshall brokers a truce between Chinese Nationalists and Communists.

Truman's special envoy General George Marshall arrived in China on December 20, 1945, where he hoped to get a cease-fire between the Nationals and the Communists as well as getting their approval to form a government of National Unity. After meeting with Chiang Kai-shek on December 21, Marshall met with the Communist's Chou En-lai two days later. While Chiang told Marshall he was suspicious of all Communist activity and was reluctant to form a coalition government, Chou En-lai favored a united China as long as all parties were represented in a National Assembly. Chou also said Mao wanted Moscow to abolish the Friendship Treaty that Stalin made with Chiang's Nationalists in August 1945. (See August 14, 1945.)

Beginning on December 30, Marshall held extensive negotiations with both sides. On January 9, Chiang Kai-shek compromised regarding the joint control of key railroad centers in Jahol and Chaha. The compromise resulted in the Communists accepting a cease-fire on January 10, 1946. The cease-fire would be supervised by an Executive Headquarters established in Peking (Beijing). At headquarters, representatives from the United States, the Communist Party, and the Nationalist Party would oversee the cease-fire and create a government of National Unity, although Chiang Kai-shek had misgivings because of Soviet forces in Manchuria.

As it turned out, Marshall made a mistake by returning to Washington in March 1946, while Lt. General Alvan C. Gillem acted as the U.S. representative in China. After Marshall left, Chou En-lai left for Yenan to consult with Mao Tse-tung but never came back. The cease-fire deteriorated. In early April, Chou blamed Gillem for his concessions to Chiang while Nationalist forces violated the cease-fire by attacking Communists in Southern Manchuria, resulting in another civil war. The truce did not last. (See April 14, 1946.) For details of Marshall's mission see Forrest C. Pogue, *George C. Marshall: Statesman, 1945–1959* (1987).

January 19, 1946

U.N. Security Council hears its first complaint.

Soon after the United Nations held its first meeting on January 10, the U.N. Security Council received a complaint from Iran. During World War II, Britain and the Soviet Union agreed to protect Tehran from the Germans by occupying Iran, with British forces in the south and Soviet troops in the north. After Germany surrendered, Britain and the United States agreed to withdraw from Iran by early 1946.

The British withdrew at the end of 1945 while Soviet forces were helping Azerbaijan rebels seize power to establish the Autonomous Republic of Azerbaijan. The Soviets also helped Kurdistan rebels establish an independent Kurdish People's Republic. On November 28, Tehran sent two Iran army battalions and tried to regain Azerbaijan but Soviet troops blocked the Iranians. At the same time, Moscow sought Iran's oil concessions similar to those Britain had in southern Iran. The Iranian government contended that the Soviet Union interfered in its internal affairs by refusing to leave territory it occupied in northern Iran during World War II. The Security Council urged the Iranians and Soviets to settle their differences; however, as the negotiations dragged on the United States condemned Moscow's refusal to withdraw its force.

See April 3, 1946.

January 27, 1946

In the U.S. zone of Germany, local elections are held.

The Christian Democratic Party won the greatest number of local offices; the Social Democrats ranked second. Soon after, the Christian Democrats also won similar elections in the British and French zones. The Christian Democrats were a middle-of-the-road party whose principal strength was with business interests and Roman Catholics. The Social Democrats were a slightly left-of-center, evolutionary Socialist party.

The Soviet Union conducted elections in its zone on April 21, 1946. In East Germany, the Social Democrats merged with the Communist Party to form the Socialist Unity Party (SED), the party that dominated subsequent elections in East Germany.

February 3, 1946

Soviet spy ring in Canada is disclosed on Drew Pearson's radio program.

On February, 3 Canada arrested 22 men accused of spying. According to Prime Minister MacKenzie King, the Canadian authorities moved earlier than their investigation of the spies required, because of Pearson's report. A wave of spy scandals and accusations began in the United States as a result of these actions. Soon after, Washington columnist Frank McNaughton said a "confidential source" claimed that the Canadian spies sought data on U.S. atomic secrets and that a Soviet spy ring also operated in the United States. This second ring, McNaughton reported, had not been broken by the FBI because certain "State Department men" believed it "would upset our relations with Russia." McNaughton's source was later found to be General Leslie Groves, head of the Manhattan Project. Groves and the army were then involved in a dispute with Senator Brien McMahon over the issue of civilian or military control of U.S. atomic energy policy. Thus, the spy accusations led Congress to amend prior McMahon legislation so that the military could defend against "spies."

At this time most Americans believed there existed some single secret to the construction of an atomic bomb that the Soviets could only gain through the employment of spies. Atomic scientists and experts such as Groves, however, knew this was not the case—the necessary basic scientific information had appeared in scientific journals during the 1920s and 1930s. The only "secrets" were who had supplies of uranium and what were the precise technological methods used in the United States to efficiently enrich uranium as the source of atomic power. Groves incorrectly believed he had secured a monopoly of uranium supplies for America.

When the Canadian government issued its report on the spy cases in the summer of 1946, it indicated the Soviets obtained little from their spy ring. The alleged master spy, British physicist Alan Nunn May, gave them samples of enriched uranium ore that General Groves had presented to Canadian scientists in 1944. As Groves later admitted, May had only general knowledge about the atomic bomb and the Soviets did not gain details about building this bomb. Nevertheless, Soviet spy stories and allegations became recurrent in America after February 1946. This "scare" influenced Congress and the public to refuse to share nuclear "secrets" with allies, as well as to accept a larger degree of military control over atomic energy.

February 9, 1946

A speech by Joseph Stalin is "the declaration of World War III," in the words of Supreme Court Justice William Douglas.

Douglas's words about "World War III" to Secretary of the Navy James D. Forrestal reflected concerns among Washington officials about Russia's refusal to move Red Army units out of Iran and Manchuria. In this context, Stalin's assertion that there was an inevitable clash between Communism and capitalism led Douglas, Forrestal, and other American leaders to fear Stalin's call for the Soviet people to prepare to sacrifice again, as they had during the 1930s, to rebuild the USSR Stalin said

> Our Marxists declare that the capitalist system of world economy conceals elements of crisis and war, that the development of world capitalism does not follow a steady and even course, but proceeds through crisis and catastrophe. The uneven development of the capitalist countries leads in time to sharp disturbances in their relations and the group of countries which consider themselves inadequately provided with raw materials and export markets try usually to change the situation and to change the position in the favor by means of war. As a result of these factors, the capitalist world is into two hostile camps and war follows.

After praising the Russian people and the Red Army for its success in defeating the German armies, Stalin turned to the Soviets' need for a new set of five-year plans to restore "the areas of the country which have suffered, restoring the pre-war levels in industry and agriculture, and then exceeding this level by more or less considerable amounts." Once this was achieved, he declared, the Red Army would also have sufficient military equipment to defend the motherland.

February 22, 1946

Kennan's "Long Telegram": an analysis of Soviet foreign policy and proposal for "containment" policy.

In response to a State Department query of February 3 requesting information regarding the nature of Soviet foreign policy and the implications it held for U.S. policy, George F. Kennan offered a lengthy telegram from the U.S. embassy in Moscow that presented a concise survey of the issues. His views, which dovetailed neatly with the opinions forming in the minds of many administration officials and provided them with a tidy pedagogical underpinning, had a sensational impact on Washington. "My reputation was made. My voice now carried," he noted in his memoirs.

The following are extracts from his telegram:

> At bottom of Kremlin's neurotic view of world affairs is traditional and instinctive Russian sense of insecurity. Originally, this was insecurity of a peaceful agricultural people trying to live on vast exposed plain in neighborhood of fierce nomadic peoples. To this was added, as Russia came into contact with economically advanced West, fear of more competent, more powerful, more highly organized societies in that area. But this latter type of insecurity was one which afflicted Russian rulers rather than Russian people; for Russian rulers have invariably sensed that their rule was relatively archaic in form, fragile and artificial in its psychological foundations, unable to stand comparison or contact with political systems of Western countries. For this reason they have always feared foreign penetration, feared direct contact between Western world and their own, feared what would happen if Russians learned truth about world without or if foreigners learned truth about world within. And they have learned to seek security only in patient but deadly struggle for total destruction of rival power, never in compacts and compromises with it.
>
> It was no coincidence that Marxism, which had smoldered ineffectively for half a century in Western Europe, caught hold and blazed for the first time in Russia. Only in this land which had never known a friendly neighbor or indeed any tolerant equilibrium of separate powers, either internal or international, could a doctrine thrive which viewed economic conflicts of society as insoluble by peaceful means. After establishment of Bolshevist regime, Marxist dogma, rendered even more truculent and intolerant by Lenin's interpretation, became a perfect

vehicle for sense of insecurity with which Bolsheviks, even more than previous Russian rulers, were afflicted.... This is why Soviet purposes must always be solemnly clothed in trappings of Marxism, and why no one should underrate importance of dogma in Soviet affairs.

Kennan concluded,

In summary, we have here a political force committed fanatically to the belief that with U.S. there can be no permanent *modus vivendi*, that it is desirable and necessary that the internal harmony of our society be disrupted, our traditional way of life be destroyed, the international authority of our state be broken, if Soviet power is to be secure.... Problem of how to cope with this force [is] undoubtedly greatest task our diplomacy has ever faced and probably greatest it will ever have to face. It should be point of departure from which our political general staff work at present juncture should proceed. It should be approached with same thoroughness and care as solution of major strategic problem in war and, if necessary, with no smaller outlay in planning effort. I cannot attempt to suggest all answers here. But I would like to record my conviction that problem is within our power to solve—and that without recourse to any general military conflict. And in support of this conviction there are certain observations of a more encouraging nature I should like to make:

1. Soviet power, unlike that of Hitlerite Germany, is neither schematic nor adventuristic. It does not work by fixed plans. It does not take unnecessary risks. Impervious to logic of reason, and it is highly sensitive to logic of force. For this reason it can easily withdraw—and usually does—when strong resistance is encountered at any point. Thus, if the adversary has sufficient force and makes clear his readiness to use it, he rarely has to do so. If situations are properly handled there need be no prestige-engaging showdowns.
2. Gauged against Western world as a whole, Soviets are still by far the weaker force. Thus, their success will really depend on degree of cohesion, firmness and vigor which Western world can muster. And this is a factor which it is within our power to influence.
3. Success of Soviet system, as form of internal power, is not yet finally proven. It has yet to be demonstrated that it can survive supreme test of successive transfer of power from one individual or group to another. Lenin's death was first such transfer, and its effects racked Soviet state for 15 years. After Stalin's death or retirement will be second. But even this will not be final test. Soviet internal system will now be subjected, by virtue of recent territorial expansions, to series of additional strains which once proved severe tax on Tsardom. We here are convinced that never since termination of civil war have mass of Russian people been emotionally farther removed from doctrines of Communist Party than they are today. In Russia, party has now become a great and—for the moment—highly successful apparatus of dictatorial administration, but it has ceased to be a source of emotional inspiration. Thus, internal soundness and permanence of movement need not yet be regarded as assured.
4. All Soviet propaganda beyond Soviet security sphere is basically negative and destructive. It should therefore be relatively easy to combat it by any intelligent and really constructive program.

For these reasons I think we may approach calmly and with good heart the problem of how to deal with Russia. As to how this approach should be made, I only wish to advance, by way of conclusion, following comments:

1. Our first step must be to apprehend, and recognize for what it is, the nature of the movement with which we are dealing. We must study it with the same courage, detachment, objectivity, and same the determination not to be emotionally provoked or unseated by it, with which a doctor studies unruly and unreasonable individual.
2. We must see that our public is educated to realities of Russian situation. I cannot overemphasize importance of this. Press cannot do this alone. It must be done mainly by Government, which is necessarily more experienced and better informed on practical problems involved.... I am convinced we have better chance of realizing those hopes if our public is enlightened and if our dealings with Russians

are placed entirely on realistic and matter-of-fact basis.

3. Much depends on health and vigor of our own society. World communism is like malignant parasite which feeds only on diseased tissue. This is point at which domestic and foreign policies meet. Every courageous and incisive measure to solve internal problems of our own society, to improve self-confidence, discipline, morale and community spirit of our own people, is a diplomatic victory over Moscow worth a thousand diplomatic notes and joint communiqués. . . .
4. We must formulate and put forward for other nations a much more positive and constructive picture of sort of world we would like to see than we have put forward in past. It is not enough to urge people to develop political processes similar to our own. Many foreign peoples, in Europe at least, are tired and frightened by experiences of past, and are less interested in abstract freedom than in security. They are seeking guidance rather than responsibilities. We should be better able than Russians to give them this. . . .
5. Finally we must have courage and self-confidence to cling to our own methods and conceptions of human society. After all, the greatest danger that can befall us in coping with this problem of Soviet communism is that we shall allow ourselves to become like those with whom we are coping.

Historians have compared Kennan's long telegram with the communiqué of his British counterpart at Moscow, Frank Roberts, which contained similar assessments and recommendations. (Joseph M. Siracusa's, "The Author of Containment: The Strange Case of George F. Kennan & Frank Roberts," in his *Into the Dark House: American Diplomacy and the Ideological Origins of the Cold War* [Claremont, CA: Regina Books, 1998] contains the full text.)

See March 17, 1946.

February 24, 1946

Colonel Juan D. Perón is elected president of Argentina.

As the leading military official in Argentina, Juan Perón had effective control of Argentina during most of World War II, when Argentina remained neutral, and, later, when it became a haven for Fascist and Nazi sympathizers and war criminals. When Perón decided to run for the presidency, the U.S. State Department issued a "Blue Book," based on captured German documents, which accused Perón of collaboration. Sprulle Braden, who intensely disliked Perón and often criticized him while Braden was ambassador in Buenos Aires, inspired the report. The United States was accused of intervention in Argentina's internal affairs; consequently, Perón won the election with no difficulty.

March 4, 1946

The United States, Britain, and France issue an unusual appeal, asking the Spanish people to overthrow Franco's Fascist regime.

Partly because of President Truman's intense dislike for General Franco's government, the United States joined Paris and London in this search for some means to give Spain a democratic, anti-Communist administration. Spain had been excluded from the United Nations at the San Francisco Conference. Later, on December 11, 1946, the U.N. General Assembly voted to prohibit Spain from participation in any U.N. activities and urged its members to sever diplomatic relations with Madrid. The appeal of March 4 did not succeed. Franco's hold on the Spanish government was far too great for outsiders to overthrow him by verbal appeals.

March 5, 1946

Winston Churchill delivers his "Iron Curtain" speech at Fulton, Missouri.

Churchill's speech delineated the growing chasm between the Soviet regions of Eastern Europe and the Western "free states." President Truman evidently knew in advance of Churchill's intent. Not only did Churchill contend that "police states" ruled Eastern Europe, he also emphasized that the Soviets desired "the indefinite expansion of their power and doctrines." The British and Americans, he said, must work with the aid of atomic weapons to create unity in Europe to protect the free nations.

> The United States, Churchill said, stands at this time at the pinnacle of world power. It is a solemn moment for the American democracy. With

> primacy in power is also joined an awe-inspiring accountability to the future.... To reject it or ignore it or fritter it away will bring upon us all the long reproaches of the aftertime. It is necessary that constancy of mind, persistency of purpose and the grand simplicity of decision shall guide and rule the conduct of the English-speaking peoples in peace as they did in war. We must, and I believe we shall prove ourselves equal to this severe requirement.

Most significant of all, Churchill said "A shadow has fallen upon the scenes so lately lighted by the Allied victory. Nobody knows what Soviet Russia and the Communist international organization intends to do in the immediate future, or what are the limit, if any, to their expansive and proselytizing tendencies." Although he welcomed Russia's rightful place in the world, Churchill said: "It is my duty, however, to place before you certain facts about the present position in Europe." Thus, Churchill stated

> From Stettin in the Baltic to Triest in the Adriatic, an iron curtain has descended across the Continent. Behind that line lie all the capitals of the ancient states of Central and Eastern Europe. Warsaw, Berlin, Prague, Vienna, Budapest, Belgrade, Bucharest and Sofia, all these famous cities and the populations around them lie in the Soviet sphere and all are subject in one form or other, not only to Soviet influence but to a very high and increasing measure of control from Moscow.

Churchill feared the current situation was not the liberated Europe envisioned by the Allied forces in 1945. "The safety of the world, ladies and gentlemen," he said, "requires a new unity in Europe from which no nation should be permanently outcast." He concluded that "Great States and small States must worktogether to build a friendlier and happier world. If we fail to work together there can be no peace, no comfort and little hope for any of us." Churchill's "Iron Curtain" speech would be remembered until the "curtain" fell between 1989 and December 1991.

March 6, 1946

The French foreign office seeks peace in Indochina by the accords of March 6.

Vietnam, Laos, and Cambodia were recognized as "free," but not independent, states in the French Union. These accords proved to be only a temporary armistice because they only reflected the basic interests of the French.

March 17, 1946

The Roberts Dispatches: a British assessment of Soviet policies.

A British diplomat at Moscow sent a series of communiqués to the Foreign Office that paralleled George F. Kennan's, "Long Telegram." Several historians have noted similarities between the two reports. Joseph M. Siracusa's, "The Author of Containment: The Strange Case of George F. Kennan & Frank Roberts," in his *Into the Dark House: American Diplomacy and the Ideological Origins of the Cold War* (1998) contains the full texts of both.

Below are excerpts from Roberts's dispatches:

> There is one fundamental factor affecting Soviet policy dating back to the small beginnings of the Muscovite State. This is the constant striving for security of a State with no natural frontiers and surrounded by enemies. In this all-important respect the rulers and people of Russia are united by a common fear, deeply rooted in Russian history. National security is, in fact, at the bottom of Soviet, as of Imperial Russian, policy, and explains much of the high-handed behaviour of the Kremlin and many of the suspicions genuinely held there concerning the outside world.... The frontiers of Russia have never been fixed and have gone backwards and forwards with defeats or victories in war. But even after her greatest victories in the past Russia has somehow found herself deprived of many of the fruits of those victories, and has never achieved the security which she thought her due reward....
>
> We have tried many methods in the recent past. After a brief attempt at the beginning of the Revolution to work with the new regime in order to keep Russia in the war, we tried armed intervention and the support of separatist movements throughout the Russian Empire in order to break down the Soviet regime and ensure its replacement by some government more akin to other European governments. This failed lamentably, and not even the most stubborn and shortsighted reactionaries would

advocate another attempt at foreign intervention today.... During [World War II] Anglo-Soviet cooperation and relative confidence was built up slowly and painfully, with many setbacks, and by last summer a solid foundation appeared to have been achieved and there seemed reason to hope that the Soviet Union might settle down into a more or less normal member of international society, and that Anglo-Soviet relations could become progressively more intimate and more trusting. But unfortunately this last period was in no sense typical. Apart from the fact that we were both fighting for our lives and were therefore compelled to cooperate, all the concessions, approaches and even gestures came from our side, and the Kremlin must have found the course of Anglo-Soviet relations a very pleasant and convenient arrangement under which they received big gains, though it must be remembered that in Russian eyes at least the Soviet Union had borne the main burden of the war....

How to deal with other countries in this democratic age. In these respects the old should be mixed with the new diplomacy in the conduct of our relations with the Soviet Union, both in regard to secrecy and also to outward forms. When there are deadlocks, as there will often be, we should cultivate the same patience as is shown by our Soviet allies, and cease to feel that it is always our task to make an early gesture to break the deadlock. Such gestures are interpreted here as a sign of weakness and do harm rather than good to our relations. However unpromising the prospects may be, we should, however, continue to take the initiative in fostering closer contacts between the two peoples, e.g., cultural and other exchanges and visits by representative persons and delegations....

See February 22, 1946.

April 3, 1946

Iran's crisis is resolved when the Soviet Union agrees to withdraw its armed forces.

The Soviet Union had delayed the withdrawal of its troops that were scheduled to leave Iran by March 2, 1946. During World War II, Britain and the Soviet Union agreed to protect Tehran from the Germans by occupying Iran, with British forces in the south and Soviet troops in the north. After Germany surrendered, Britain and the Soviets agreed to withdraw from Iran by early 1946. The British withdrew before the end of 1945, but in November 1945 Soviet forces helped rebels in Azerbaijan seize power to establish the Autonomous Republic of Azerbaijan.

Secretary of State James F. Byrnes. National Archives

The Soviets also helped Kurdistan rebels establish an independent Kurdish People's Republic. On November 28, Tehran sent two army battalions to regain control of Azerbaijan, but Soviet troops blocked the army from gaining control over the province. At the same time, Moscow sought oil concessions from Iran similar to those Britain held in southern Iran. In response to these Soviet actions, the United States and Britain supported Iran's January 19 appeal to the U.N. Security Council to investigate Soviet interference in Iran's northwestern provinces.

The Council directed Iran to negotiate and in February Iran's Prime Minister Ahmad Quavam went to Moscow to discuss the situation with Stalin and Foreign Minister Molotov. The Soviet Union again refused to withdraw its troops on the established deadline of March 2, 1946. On March 5, U.S. Secretary of State Byrnes sent a telegram to Moscow calling for the Soviets' immediate withdrawal from Iran. Although Quavam continued negotiating in Moscow, the United States now received reports from its Azerbaijan consulate that the Red Army was moving forces toward Turkey, Iraq, and Tehran. The Soviets had not replied to his March 5 note, but Byrnes dispatched a second note asking about Soviet troop maneuvers. The Soviet leaders continued their silence until March 15, when the Soviet news agency Tass absolutely denied the allegation that the troops were moving toward Tehran, Turkey, or Iraq.

Byrnes advised Iran to request another Security Council investigation that Tehran submitted on March 25. After Tass announced on April 3 that Soviet forces would leave Iran in six weeks, the Soviet Security Council delegate, Andrei Gromyko, argued that the Council should not consider Iran's problem, but the Council voted to keep the matter on the agenda. One week later, Iran and the Soviets agreed on an oil concession and on the Soviet troop withdrawal in May. Under the oil agreement, the Soviets would receive a 51 percent share of an Iranian-Soviet Oil Company, but Iran's parliament rejected the oil treaty and the Soviets received no oil concession.

In terms of U.S. policy, Byrnes's relatively tough stance against the Soviets signaled that the Truman administration would be less conciliatory toward the Soviet Union.

April 14, 1946

Chinese civil war is renewed only three months after General Marshall thought a truce had been reached.

The conflict arose in Manchuria because the Soviet troop withdrawal was timed to benefit a takeover by the Chinese Communists. Chiang Kai-shek objected to this procedure and fighting broke out between the Nationalists and Mao's forces. Marshall reestablished a truce from May 12 to June 30, but all-out civil war began again in July.

April 15, 1946

Afghans get U.S. Economic Aid but turn to Russia for military aid.

On April 25, 1946, King Zahir sought economic aid from the U.S. government. The Truman administration refused his request because Zahir's five-year economic plan was vague in its concepts. Soon after, Zahir signed a $17 million contract with the Morrison-Knudsen Company of Boise, Idaho, to build gravel roads to replace rough tracks from Kabul to Kandahar and east to the Durand Line's crossing point near Pakistan. The Idaho company also repaired irrigation ditches and dug new canals in the Helmand River valley. Zahir's plan was for the Helmand Valley to grow valuable agricultural products but the Afghan peasant farmers did not realize the river valley water contained too much salt and its thin layer of fertile earth would become water logged. Although Zahir blamed the Morrison-Knudsen Company for the Helmand Valley's failure, the problems were largely due to the illiterate, previously isolated peasant farmer who could not adopt modern farming techniques.

Although the Truman administration refused to help the Afghans in 1946, the arrival of the Cold War after 1947 and the fear of possible Soviet influence in Afghanistan prompted the United States to help Afghanistan. In 1949, the U.S. Export-Import Bank approved $21 million of credits for the Morrison-Knudsen Company to continue work in the Helmund Valley where they taught Afghans to grow cotton for their cotton textile plants as well as a type of wheat suitable for Afghan conditions. Between 1949 and 1979 when U.S. aid was halted, the United States provided Afghanistan with $532.87 million of aid in terms of grants and loans.

During the same period from 1949 to 1979, the Afghan government sought military and police aid to help secure Kabul's government from rival tribesmen such as those who had burned down an Afghan army base in Jalalabad in 1949. The United States was reluctant to send military aid to the Afghans. In 1949, a report from the office of the U.S. Joint Chiefs of Staff stated that "Afghanistan is of little or no strategic importance to the United States...Its geographic location coupled with the realization by Afghan leaders of Soviet capabilities presages Soviet control of the country whenever the situation so dictates." The report recommended that Afghanistan should remain neutral if there was a war between the USSR and the Western powers or the Soviets would immediately occupy Afghanistan. After the Eisenhower administration took office, Secretary of State John Foster Dulles made a similar assessment of Afghanistan's lack of importance to the United States. In 1954, Dulles responded to Afghan Foreign Minister Sardar

Mohammed Naim's request for military aid by saying America has no "security interest" in Afghanistan. "After careful consideration," Dulles said, "extending military aid to Afghanistan would create problems not offset by the strength it would generate."

Because Washington refused military aid to Afghanistan, Afghan's Premier Daoud Khan turned to Moscow. In 1955, Nikita Khrushchev and Nickolai Bulganin visited Kabul for four days on their way home from India. During their visit, Khrushchev offered to provide King Zahir with a grant of $100 million. The grant would not only provide military equipment to Afghanistan but would also build a highway and tunnel through the Hindu Kush Mountains linking Kabul to the Oxus Valley. The highway would give Afghanistan businessmen the use of trucks to move their cotton textiles and other products to Russia and other European nations. This outlet was essential because Pakistan no longer allowed Afghans to use their port at Karachi. Khrushchev also informed Zahir that Russia had found large deposits of oil and gas near the Afghan border. After Khrushchev retired from office in 1964, Leonid Brezhnev and King Zahir agreed in 1969 that the Soviets could build a gas pipeline in Afghanistan.

In 1964, King Zahir also decided to have Afghan's legal expert Mohammad Moosa Shafiq Kamawi write a constitution that provided for a Constitutional Monarch with an elected National Assembly. Thus, with military help from the Soviet Union and economic help from the United States, King Zahir began to establish a modernized Afghanistan. Unfortunately, between 1969 and the winter of 1971 little rain fell in many parts of Afghanistan The Afghan relief efforts were inefficient and plagued with corruption causing the estimated deaths of at least 80,000 people. Hoping to correct the political effects of this catastrophe, Zahir appointed Moosa Shafiq to be prime minister. Moosa Shafiq launched an anticorruption drive, promoted advances in literacy, and revived economic development.

His efforts ended on July 17, 1973, when Daoud Khan led a small group of Afghan army officers with several hundred troops to seize the king's Kabul palace, the radio station, the airport, and other key locations. They arrested the king's first cousin Abbdul Wai and other key members of the royal family. King Zahir was not in Kabul because he was in Italy for eye treatment and medicinal mud baths. Despite Daoud's victory in 1973, he would be ousted five years later. (See April 27, 1978.) For details see Henry S. Bradsher, *Afghanistan and the Soviet Union* (1983); M. Hassan Kakar, *Afghanistan: The Soviet Invasion and the Afghan Response* (1995); and Nikita Khrushchev, *Khrushchev Remembers: The Last Testament* (1974).

April 20, 1946

U.S.-Soviet discussions regarding the USSR's 1945 request for a loan conclude with no positive results.

Because the United States admitted in January 1946 that it had "lost" the Soviet loan proposal of August 28, 1945, Stalin held new discussions with Ambassador Harriman on January 23 regarding a possible U.S. loan. In these discussions, Stalin intimated that Russia might be interested in a possible U.S. loan. He alluded to the recent British loan and wondered if the United States would consider such a Soviet request. After the Iranian crisis abated in April 1946, the United States agreed on discussions with the Soviets about a loan. The negotiations collapsed, however, because Stalin rejected the Americans' desire to link talks about the loan with agreements on trade with the Balkans and various peace treaties.

The U.S. refusal to negotiate a loan for the Soviets was one of many factors indicating less cooperative policies between the two governments after April 1946.

May 3, 1946

U.S. military government in Germany halts Soviet reparations.

The head of the American military government in Germany, General Lucius D. Clay, announced that the Soviet Union could no longer remove material—such as machinery, rolling stock, etc.—as payment of reparations from the three western occupied zones of Germany.

Disagreement on German issues increased in 1946 after the Soviet Union refused Secretary of State Byrnes's offer to permit German reunification if it agreed to be demilitarized. In March, the Soviets changed their reparations policy in East Germany. Rather than continue to remove machinery to the USSR, the Communists decided to use East German labor and resources to produce goods for shipment to the Soviet Union. Coupled with Clay's announcement of May 3,

Soviet-American decisions prevented a treaty for a united Germany.

May 25, 1946

The Kingdom of Transjordan is proclaimed under King Emir Abdullah.

Great Britain relinquished its protectorship and recognized the independence of Transjordan on May 25, 1946. The nation was renamed Hashemite Kingdom of Jordan on June 2, 1949.

June 2, 1946

In a plebiscite, Italians vote for a republic, rejecting the restoration of a monarchy.

June 3, 1946

Japanese war crime trials begin in Tokyo under American jurisdiction.

The Potsdam Proclamation said "stern justice shall be meted out to all war criminals, including those who have visited cruelties upon our prisoners." (See July 26, 1945.) Accordingly, when the war ended thousands of Japanese ranging from former Prime Minister Hideki Tojo to POW guards were tried for war crimes. In Tokyo's lengthy trials, from May 3, 1946, to November 12, 1948, an 11-judge International Military Tribunal chaired by Australia's Sir William Webb tried 28 high-ranking Japanese accused of crimes against humanity or crimes against peace referred to as "Class A crimes." In particular, the 28 men were held responsible for planning and carrying out Japan's war in the Far East from 1937 to 1945. During the Tokyo trials, the judges dropped 45 of the 55 counts of the indictments against the accused Japanese. When the trials ended in November 1948, a majority of the judges sentenced seven of the accused to be executed, 16 to life in prison, one to 20 years in prison, and one to seven years. Two Japanese died during the trial, while one was excused for mental incompetence. Nineteen other Japanese wartime leaders remained in Tokyo's Sugamo prison but were never tried, being released in December 1948 for alleged "lack of evidence."

In part, their release was because by 1948, the United States and its allies preferred to make Japan an ally against the threat of expansion in Asia attempted by the Soviet Union and Chinese Communists. Although critics called the Tokyo trials "victors' justice" or "racism," Tim Maga's *Judgment at Tokyo* (2001) argues that "evil should never go unpunished" and both prosecutors and defense teams acted properly. In addition to the Tokyo trials, the United States, Australia, Britain, France, the Netherlands, India, China, and the Soviet Union established 50 local tribunals.

Of four U.S. tribunals the most controversial ended in the convictions of Japanese General Masaharu Homma and General Tomoyuki Yamashita. The seven other allied nations set up tribunals in various Far East and Pacific Island locations. Excepting the Soviet Union, these tribunals tried 5,700 individuals including 173 Taiwanese and 148 Koreans. During these trials 948 received death sentences, of which 50 were commuted after appeals; 1,018 were acquitted; 2,944 received prison sentences; and 279 were never brought to trial for various reasons.

Regarding the Soviet Union, the Red Army held secret trials in Manchuria and Korea. It is estimated that 3,000 were summarily executed including 12 Japanese doctors from Manchuria's Unit 731 that conducted lethal medical experiments on prisoners of war. Details about these Japanese trials are in John Dower's *Embracing Defeat* (1999).

June 14, 1946

Bernard Baruch presents to the United Nations the American plan (Baruch Plan) for the international control of atomic energy.

In accepting this plan, President Truman opted for a "hard-line" policy on international control. The United States would agree to disclose its atomic program and disarm only after safeguard and inspection procedures had been adopted that would protect U.S. national security. The Baruch Plan was based on the Dean Acheson-David Lilienthal Report that emphasized the technical characteristics of atomic energy that would determine the design of an international control system. The proposal called for "the creation of an International Atomic Energy Development Authority, to which should be entrusted all phases of the development and use of atomic energy, starting with the raw material." The Authority would have direct control of all potentially dangerous atomic activities

Bernard Baruch presents U.S. plan for international control of atomic weapons. National Archives

and would regulate the licensing of all other atomic projects.

The verification portion of the plan called for the Authority to be empowered to send officials to any nation to conduct comprehensive inspections of their atomic facilities seeking any treaty violations. (The Acheson-Lilienthal Report would permit partial disclosure of information as a good faith gesture prior to acceptance by all nations, including the Soviet Union, of inspection agreements.) Baruch added provisions calling for sanctions for violating the control agreements to be made in the U.N. Security Council by action that would allow no veto by one of the Big Five powers.

The public response to Baruch's plan was mixed. Some viewed the proposal as imaginative and courageous for seeking a solution to a vexing menace, while others called it imbecilic because it surrendered America's secret to the making of an atomic bomb. One survey in September 1946 found 78 percent of Americans favored the plan.

June 19, 1946

Soviet Union presents plan for controlling atomic weapons.

During the second meeting of the U.N. AEC, Soviet Deputy Foreign Minister Andrei Gromyko responded to the U.S. proposal by offering two resolutions designed to deal with atomic weapons. First, he urged that the initial step in controlling atomic energy be an agreement outlawing the production and the use of atomic weapons, and destroying existing atomic weapons within three months. Additionally, Gromyko called for an agreement to pass laws within their own countries to punish violators. Second, he asked for the formation of two committees: one for exchanging scientific information and the second to determine methods of ensuring compliance with the first step.

As a rebuke to the U.S. plan, he argued that the elimination of the veto "attempts to undermine the principles, as established by the Charter of the Security Council, including unanimity of the members of the Security Council in deciding questions of substance, are incompatible with the interests of the United Nations.... Such attempts must be rejected." Later on June 24, *Pravda* simply labeled the Baruch Plan "a product of atomic diplomacy."

July 1, 1946

The United States tests atomic bombs near Bikini Atoll in the South Pacific.

These July tests used an advanced Nagasaki-type implosion device. Their purpose was to demonstrate the bomb's use in naval warfare, an experiment advocated by the Navy Department. Directed by Vice Admiral William H. Blandy, two tests resulted from the project, code-named Crossroads. On July 1, bomb "Able" was dropped from an airplane and landed two miles from its target, a flotilla of 75 obsolete (mothballed) or captured enemy ships of World War II vintage. The results were unimpressive. The bomb exploded in shallow water, sinking few of the ships but making most of them radioactive. On July 25, the second bomb, "Baker," was suspended in 90 feet of water and exploded electrically. It caused spectacular damage in destroying the naval vessels and reinforcing the U.S. navy's desire to have a larger role in nuclear development.

July 4, 1946

The Philippine Islands receive independence and are embroiled in domestic conflict with the "communist" Huks.

The Philippines created a republic, having elected Manuel A. Roxas, head of the Liberal Party, as president on April 23. The U.S. Congress also passed the Rehabilitation Act and the Bell Act to assist in the economic recovery of the islands. In return for this aid, a national referendum in the Philippines on March 11, 1947, passed a constitutional amendment to allow U.S. citizens to exploit the island's national resources on a basis of equality with the Filipinos.

In 1946 a domestic dispute broke out between peasant farmers and landlords who had fled to urban areas during the war. In late 1945, the landlords returned to the villages and demanded that the peasants pay back rent for the three years of the Japanese occupation, enforcing their demands by using local police or mercenary soldiers. Many of the peasants had joined guerrilla forces as part of the resistance movement against the Japanese occupation. Having retained their weapons, many of the peasants decided to use them to resist the landlords and organize a National Peasant Union (PMK—*Pambansang Kaisahan ng mga Magbubukid*). They also joined a Democratic Alliance Party in cooperation with labor unions, an alliance that elected six members to the Philippine Parliament in 1946. In the parliament, the majority party refused to seat the six Democratic Alliance members on charges they used terrorist methods during the election campaign. This legislative action incited PMK members to organize a rebellion and to change its name to the People's Liberation Army (Huk—*Hukbong Mapagpalata ng Bayan*). In 1950, the Philippine Communist Party (PKP) joined the Huks, calling themselves the military army of the revolutionary movement. Although most Huks knew nothing about Communism but simply wanted to own their farmland, the Philippine government referred to all Huks as Communists.

The conflict between the government and the Huks took place primarily in Central Luzon with the warfare peaking between 1949 and 1951 before subsiding. By the time President Elpidio Quirino adopted a reform program in 1951, emphasizing agricultural policy to conciliate the peasants, many peasants had abandoned the rebellion or had been imprisoned by Philippine forces trained by the U.S. military. Some Huk and PKP organizations degenerated into individuals who committed murder or robbed banks, but the Huk rebellion was over by 1952.

July 15, 1946

Truman signs legislation granting Great Britain credits of $3.75 billion.

After the cutoff of lend-lease aid in August 1945, the British government experienced increased difficulty in financing the rebuilding of its economy. At Truman's request, Congress approved credits to the British to assist them in purchasing American goods.

July 24, 1946

Soviet Plan for Control of Atomic Energy is rejected.

The plan submitted to the U.N. by Foreign Minister Andrei Gromyko had been rejected on July 24.

August 1, 1946

The McMahon Bill on atomic energy is signed into law by President Truman.

Against McMahon's wishes, the committee's bill had transformed his desire for civilian control into a U.S. military veto on decisions by civilians on the AEC. In addition, the bill emphasized restrictions on atomic energy information. The bill even restricted information that the United States could share with Britain and Canada as it had done during World War II. Finally, the War Department retained control of two essential duties: responsibility for stockpiling uranium and thorium and for monitoring foreign progress on the atomic bomb. The revised McMahon Bill gave the military a large measure of control over the AEC and fit the "hard-line" nature of the Baruch Plan for control of atomic energy.

August 1, 1946

The Fulbright Act to finance foreign study becomes law.

By act of Congress, U.S. surplus property in foreign countries would be sold and the funds used in that nation to finance scholarships for research and academic exchanges of faculty members.

August 15, 1946

A dispute between the Soviet Union and Turkey prompts President Truman to approve a memo stating that the United States would resist any Soviet aggression against Turkey.

The Soviet Union raised once again a long-held Russian desire to share control of the Straits of the Dardanelles and to establish a naval base in Turkey. The Turkish government and the United States opposed both of these objectives. In the Treaty of Unkiar-Iskelessi (1833), the czar succeeded in forcing the Turks to close the straits to non-Russian warships, thereby rendering the Black Sea a virtual *mare clausum*, a closed sea. This was highly unpopular with the Western powers, especially Britain, who were concerned with control of the Mediterranean Sea. The Treaty of Lausanne (1923) demilitarized the straits; however, it was the Montreux Convention (1936) which gave Turkey the right to fortify the Straits and to monitor the passage of warships. As signatories to the Montreux Convention, which expired in 1946, the Soviets were within their rights to seek modification of that agreement.

The British and Americans resisted the Soviet demands that would give them access to the Mediterranean and the Black Sea. At the same time, the British and Americans maintained their right to send naval vessels into the Black Sea.

September 1, 1946

A Greek plebiscite amidst a civil war favors restoring the monarchy.

After British forces liberated Greece on October 13, 1944, a civil war broke out between leftist factions (including the EAM Communists) and the Royalist Popular Party. The British arranged a truce on January 11, 1945, with a regency government under Archbishop Damaskinos. Political instability continued, however, and no leader appeared who could mediate between republicans, royalists, and left-wing parties. The civil war resumed in 1946, with the EAM gaining covert aid from Albania, Yugoslavia, and Bulgaria.

The September plebiscite, which favored (by 69 percent) restoring George II as king, took place during the guerrilla struggle, with the left-wing parties boycotting the election.

September 20, 1946

Wallace resigns after Truman objects to his critical Madison Square Garden speech.

In a September 12 speech, Secretary of Commerce and former Vice President Henry A. Wallace sharply criticized the president's "hard-line" against the Soviets and called instead for cooperation with the former ally. This incident disclosed disagreement within Franklin Roosevelt's New Deal coalition about Truman's postwar policies.

Harold Ickes and Henry Morgenthau, Jr., two of Roosevelt's stalwarts, joined Wallace, who had been Roosevelt's vice president from 1941 to 1945, in opposition to Truman's unwillingness to emphasize international cooperation as the means to peace.

October 1, 1946

The Nuremberg War Crimes tribunal announces its decisions.

The first trials of the International Military Tribunal at Nuremberg were held for the leading Nazi German war criminals between November 14, 1945, and September 30, 1946. During the trial, four judges and four alternates, with one of each from the United States, Britain, France, and the Soviet Union, heard the evidence from American prosecutors Robert Jackson and Telford Taylor. Only 21 major Nazi leaders were tried at Nuremberg because Gustav Krupp's trial was suspended due to his senility, while Adolf Hitler, Heinrich Himmler, Joseph Goebbels, and Robert Ley had committed suicide. Of the 21 standing trial, three were acquitted and seven received prison sentences for 10 years or more, including Rudolf Hess, who was sentenced for life and incarcerated in Berlin's Spandau prison. Ten defendants were sentenced to execution but Hermann Goering committed suicide while in prison awaiting execution.

In addition to these trials, war crime trials were held in each of the four zones of Germany by the United Nations War Crimes Commission (UNWCC) and by individual nations where such crimes were

Nuremberg Trials. Defendants in their dock: Goering, Hess, von Ribbentrop, and Keitel in front row. National Archives

committed, including those by new governments of former enemy countries in Eastern and Central Europe. Tribunals of the Western allies pronounced a total of 1,800 death sentences of which only 500 were carried out. In the Soviet zone, Moscow reported on January 1, 1947, that 14,240 suspects were tried for war crimes with 142 acquitted and 138 sentenced to death; critics claimed that the Soviet data were unreliable. Details about the European trials are in Telford Taylor's *The Anatomy of the Nuremberg Trials* (1992) and in Arieh J. Kochavi's *Prelude to Nuremberg* (1998).

Regarding the trials of war criminals, evidence shows that British and American military officials and intelligence agencies allowed some alleged war criminals to escape through secret "ratlines" to obtain information about the Soviet Union or to recruit spies and create anti-Communist "guerrilla" groups to destabilize Communist governments. Launched with enthusiasm, these activities were strikingly unsuccessful. Under the U.S. Freedom of Information Act, considerable data were declassified during the 1980s, much of which is described in Christopher Simpson's *Blowback* (1988); also see Stephen Dorril, *MI6: Inside the Covert World of Her Majesty's Secret Intelligence Service* (2000).

October 10, 1946

Ambassador George Marshall's mission to China reaches an impasse.

Marshall instructed Chiang not to continue his offensive by capturing Kalgan because the Chinese Communists had agreed to negotiations if the Nationalist army stopped its offensive. In addition, Marshall warned Chiang that the front lines of his armies had been overextended, giving the Communist armies a tactical advantage of supply and attack if the civil war continued.

To strengthen his warning, Marshall told Chiang that the United States would cut its economic aid and withdraw the U.S. Marines stationed in China unless Chiang stopped outside Kalgan and accepted peace talks with Mao. Kalgan was the most important city under Communist control south of the Great Wall of China. Therefore, Mao claimed the Nationalists' conquest of Kalgan would end the possibility of a peaceful solution to the conflict.

Since the renewal of fighting in June 1946, Marshall had continued efforts to secure negotiations between the Nationalist and Communist leaders. Meanwhile, Chiang's armies had been well supplied by the United States, and the U.S. navy had moved Nationalist troops to strategic places. As a result, the Nationalist offensive had great success between July and October. Although he originally promised Marshall he would stop his offensive and not capture Kalgan, Chiang changed his mind early in October and announced an offensive against Kalgan.

Consequently, Marshall believed his mission's attempt to end the civil war through mediation was no longer possible. He wrote to President Truman that his recall would be appropriate. Both Marshall and the U.S. ambassador to China, J. Leighton Stuart, believed that Marshall could no longer be impartial between the two warring factions in China. Despite Marshall's forebodings in October, he remained in China because other methods to achieve a truce seemed possible. Not until December 28 did President Truman and Marshall finally agree that the peace mission was doomed to failure. On January 3, Truman formally recalled Marshall to Washington.

November 3, 1946

The draft of a new Constitution has Japan renouncing war.

The draft of the Japanese constitution, prepared by American advisers to the occupation headquarters, hoped that the nation would not again see "the horrors of war through the action of government." Article 9 stated "the Japanese people forever renounce war as a sovereign right of the nation and the threat or use of force as means of settling international disputes." To accomplish this objective "land, sea, and air forces, as well as other war potential, will never be maintained. The right of belligerency of the state will not be recognized."

After the outbreak of the Korean War in 1950, the United States had second thoughts about Japan's unilateral disarmament and began urging Tokyo to rearm and join Washington in an effort to contain the Soviet Union. General MacArthur instructed Prime Minister Yoshida to establish a 75,000-man national police reserve. Subsequently, Yoshida recalled many former low-ranking officers of the Imperial army to organize the police reserve. During the 1951 negotiations for a bilateral mutual security treaty, the U.S. chief delegate John Foster Dulles unsuccessfully sought to gain Yoshida's approval to create a 350,000-man army to defend Japan against a Soviet invasion. Not until 1957 did Tokyo authorities adopt the "Basic Policies for National Defense," which called for the establishment of "effective defense capabilities necessary for self defense, with due regard to the nation's resources and the prevailing domestic situation."

Gradually the new self-defense forces acquired modern military equipment, including new fighter planes, antiaircraft missiles, and antisubmarine capabilities. By 1969, the number of uniformed personnel reached 235,000, but the actual percentage of gross national product devoted to defense expenditures actually decreased from 1.78 percent in 1955 to 0.72 percent by 1971. This latter factor prompted Washington, with only partial success, to pressure Tokyo to devote more resources to defense. Under the 1969 Nixon Doctrine, each nation that could afford to do so was to increase its spending and so reduce the burden on the United States.

November 5, 1946

The Republican Party gains control of both houses of Congress in national elections.

This was the first national Republican Party victory since 1930. Although President Truman had previously sought bipartisan support for his international policies, the results of this election necessitated even closer cooperation between the president and the opposing party for the next two years.

November 10, 1946

France's Fourth Republic begins with elections for the National Assembly.

After a referendum on May 5 rejected the first draft constitution, a second constituent assembly revised the document and the electorate adopted it on October 13. The new constitution closely resembled that of the Third Republic. The Assembly election resulted in a deadlock between the Communists, with 186 seats, and the *Mouvement Républicain Populaire* (MRP), with 166 delegates. Consequently, the Socialists, with 103 seats, formed a coalition cabinet under Leon Blum. As in the Third Republic, the coalition government in France found it difficult to formulate stable policy, and French political divisions continued to plague the nation.

November 19, 1946

Romanian elections confirm the government set up by the Soviet Union.

After Soviet forces occupied Bucharest on August 31, 1944, they gave the Communist's National Democratic Front (NDF) control of the government. On January 7, 1946, the three-power commission established by the Foreign Ministers Council persuaded the NDF to give several opposition party members cabinet posts. Despite this change, the NDF restricted the publicity of opposition groups during the general election campaign and non-communists experienced violent attacks and threats before the November voting.

Although the United States and Britain protested the lack of "free" elections in Romania, they could do little but object to Communist tactics in Eastern Europe. On July 28, 1947, the NDF forced opposition members to resign from the cabinet and officially dissolved the largest opposition party, the National Peasants Party.

November 23, 1946

French forces bombard the port of Haiphong in Vietnam, leading to renewal of Vietnam's war of independence.

The March 6, 1946, accords had led to further discussions between Ho Chi Minh, an avowed Marxist, and the French Colonial Office, but an agreement was never reached that would provide a permanent basis for Vietnam as part of the French Union. The French attack on Haiphong resulted from disagreements between French customs officers and the Vietminh commanders. On December 19, 1946, Vietnamese guerrillas attacked French troops in Hanoi and war began again. The French were determined to retain their position in Indochina.

December 2, 1946

The United States and Great Britain agree to provide an economic fusion of their German zones.

It was hoped that this fusion, known as Bizonia, would strengthen West Germany's economy. The British and American governments invited France and the Soviet Union to join them, but they refused. As early as September 6, Secretary of State James Byrnes had announced in Stuttgart that the United States would follow a more lenient policy toward Germany and desired to unify the German economy.

December 12, 1946

Peace treaties are completed with the smaller Axis allies of World War II.

Beginning in Paris on April 25, 1946, a series of conferences among foreign ministers of 21 nations that fought the Axis prepared drafts of these treaties. On December 12, at a meeting in New York City, the treaties were finalized for Italy, Romania, Hungary, Bulgaria, and Finland. The treaties were signed on February 10, 1947.

The United States played a major role in obtaining a relatively lenient peace treaty for Italy due to the hardening lines of the Cold War. Discussions on the terms of the Italian treaty had begun during the Council of Foreign Ministers meeting in April 1946. By that time, Italy was treated by the United States and Britain more as a friendly power than a former enemy. Therefore, the British and Americans persuaded the USSR to cut its reparations demands from $300 million to $100 million, which could be paid from Italian assets in the Balkans or Italian goods over a period of years. Together with the claims of small countries against Italy, the total Italian reparations payment was $360 million in the treaty of December 12.

On the issues of Italian colonies and the Italy-Yugoslav border there was greater disagreement. According to Foreign Minister Molotov, the Soviets held rights to Italian colonies in Africa because the Soviet navy needed bases in the area. The British and Americans opposed this claim, and it was decided to leave the colonial issue until after a peace treaty was made. On the border issue, the old problem of Trieste and Dalmatia appeared once again. In April the Soviets agreed to accept less territory for Yugoslavia, but Marshal Tito objected and, during the December sessions in Paris, Molotov insisted on changes in the Italian border. Finally, the delegates agreed that the April 1946 territorial border favoring Italy would stand but Italy would pay another $35 million of reparations to Yugoslavia. The peace treaty with Italy was signed leaving only the colonial issue to be settled.

See February 22, 1946.

December 31, 1946

The U.N. Security Council accepts the Baruch Plan for control of atomic energy.

The U.N. AEC had debated the Baruch proposal since July. (See June 14, 1946.) Since the Soviet plan offered by Foreign Minister Andrei Gromyko had been rejected on July 24, Baruch believed that with effort the committee's approval could overcome Soviet efforts to delay his plan. Despite criticism from such opponents as Henry Wallace, Baruch refused to compromise on his plan's basic terms. By mid-December, Truman, Secretary Byrnes, and Baruch decided to force a U.N. vote by the year's end. Thus, on December 31, Baruch called for a vote. Ten nations approved; the Soviet Union and Poland abstained.

In effect, the Baruch Plan left the United States insisting on an exclusive monopoly of atomic power until its terms were met. Given the earlier serious post–World War II disagreements, the failure to achieve an East-West agreement on atomic weapons is understandable. At this time neither the United States nor the USSR as prepared to make the compromises necessary to reach an accord on strategic atomic weapons. In December 1946, Baruch summarized the attitude of many in Washington: "American can get what she wants if she insists on it. After all, we've got it and they haven't, and won't for a long time to come." The Soviets, however, would break the monopoly in four years.

1947

January 8, 1947

George C. Marshall becomes Secretary of State.

Secretary Byrnes resigned from office because he was tired and in poor health; moreover, his relationship with Truman had deteriorated. The president had decided in January 1946, that he was going to assume more direction of U.S. foreign policy and that the old Truman-Byrnes partnership was going to change. General Marshall had just returned from China, and the president had long desired to appoint him as secretary. Although he was a military man, Marshall's aura of integrity made him a readily acceptable choice. Marshall served as secretary until January 20, 1949.

Secretary of State George Marshall. National Archives

January 19, 1947

Elections are held in Poland.

Socialist Premier Eduard Osobka-Morawski's party won 394 seats compared with 28 seats for the Peasant Party of Deputy Premier Stanislaw Mikolajczyk of London's government-in-exile. The victorious Socialist Party replaced the Lublin goverment formed by Moscow after the war. The opposition Peasant Party's activities were hindered by repressive measures sanctioned by the Lublin government. Subsequently Mikolajczyk was subject to intense criticism before fleeing to London on October 24, 1947.

Both Great Britain and the United States charged that the January 19 elections violated the Yalta agreement for "free and honest" elections; however, their protests were ignored as the Communists, with Soviet backing, gained control of Poland's government.

January 29, 1947

The United States abandons mediation efforts in China.

In his final report on the Chinese mission, George Marshall acknowledged that efforts to achieve a compromise failed because reactionaries in the Kuomintang of Chiang Kai-shek as well as extremists in the Communist Party of China were determined to seek victory. U.S. aid continued to Chiang, reaching over $2 billion between August 1945 and December 31, 1947. Despite U.S. assistance, Chiang's Nationalist forces would not prevail.

February 10, 1947

Peace treaties are signed in Paris with states associated with Germany in World War II.

Italy lost four border areas to France, its Adriatic islands and Venezia Giulia to Yugoslavia, and the Dodecanese Islands to Greece. Trieste became a Free Territory, although boundary disputes continued between Italy and Yugoslavia. Italy and Austria also had persistent boundary disputes in the Tyrol. In a 1946 agreement between the two countries, the Italians regained South Tyrol as the autonomous province of Trentino-Alto-Adige (formerly Bolzano). Italy agreed to adopt both German and Italian as official languages in the region. Problems continued, however, between the German and Italian population.

In Eastern Europe, Romania lost Bessarabia and northern Bukovina to the USSR but regained Transylvania as consolation. Hungary regained its 1930 borders except for a few minor changes favoring Czechoslovakia. Bulgaria retained South Dobruja; meanwhile, Finland lost the port of Petsamo to the Soviet Union.

March 10–April 24, 1947

The Big Four foreign ministers continue to disagree on Germany.

The Soviets demanded $10 billion in reparations from Germany, which would greatly impair British and American efforts to make West Germany self-supporting. The Council of Foreign Ministers met in London later in 1947 (November 25–December 15) to consider the German treaty but, again, could not resolve their differences.

March 12, 1947

The Truman Doctrine is stated in a speech to Congress.

The immediate occasion for President Harry Truman's pronouncement was a request to Congress for $400 million in assistance to Greece and Turkey. Both countries were experiencing either internal or external Communist threats, which the Truman administration believed constituted evidence of a plot to expand Soviet control or influence. During 1946, the U.S. navy had gradually enlarged its Mediterranean fleet by adding the battleship *Missouri* and the aircraft carrier *Franklin D. Roosevelt.* During the winter of 1946–1947, economic problems in Great Britain caused Prime Minister Attlee's government to decide that the expenses of British naval power in the Mediterranean and economic aid for the Greek government could no longer be met by London. In January 1947, the British government informed the White House that it had no choice but to withdraw from the Aegean-Mediterranean region and appealed to the United States to take over in its place.

Truman, Marshall, and Dean Acheson, then undersecretary of state, consulted with congressional leaders including Senator Arthur Vandenberg, the ranking Republican on the Foreign Relations Committee. With bipartisan political support, the president proposed to seek congressional aid for Greece and Turkey. Acting on suggestions by some advisers to "scare the hell out of the American people," Truman undertook to do so in this speech. To justify economic and military aid to Greece and Turkey, the president envisioned a struggle between the "free world" and the tyrannical world of Communism. Only America, he said, could defend the free world against "attempted subjugation by armed minorities or by outside pressure." Employing a version of an old ploy used to circumvent close scrutiny—the "domino theory"—first suggested by Undersecretary of State Acheson during a White House session with congressmen, Truman claimed that if Greece fell, Turkey would fall, and "confusion and disorder might well spread throughout the entire Middle East." Truman's rhetoric won the support of Congress, and his doctrine became the guideline for U.S. subsequent global commitments.

Although the doctrine was originally planned only for Europe and the Mediterranean, Truman's critics used the implications of his speech to charge him with failure to apply his beliefs in Asia and other parts of the world when Communists appeared to threaten. On May 27, Truman signed the congressional bill providing economic and military aid to Greece and Turkey.

April 2, 1947

The U.N. Security Council awards former Japanese islands in the Pacific to the United States under a trusteeship.

The United States had occupied these islands during World War II and President Truman had bluntly said the United States would retain them regardless of the U.N. action. These small but strategic islands were the Marianas, Marshalls, and Carolines.

May 3, 1947

Japan's new constitution goes into effect.

The constitution, written largely by U.S. occupation personnel and sounding much like an American political statement, recognized the sovereignty of the people, making the emperor only a symbolic figure. It also protected individual rights and provided large measures of local self-government. The central government would consist of a two-house parliament (Diet) and a ministry whose term of office required majority approval of the Diet.

Article 9 was designed to prevent a renewal of Japanese militarism. It stated, in part:

> Aspiring sincerely to an international peace based on justice and order, the Japanese people forever renounce war as a sovereign right of the nation and the threat or use of force as means of settling international disputes. In order to accomplish the aim of the preceding.... land, sea, and air forces, as well as other war potential, will never be maintained.

In the April 1947 elections a right-wing majority gained control of the upper house of councilors, while the Social Democratic Party won the greatest plurality of seats in the House of Representatives. On May 23, the Socialist leader Tetsu Katayama formed a coalition government approved by the Diet.

May 5, 1947

The State Department policy-planning staff is established with George Kennan as director.

The planning group's purpose was to assure long-range policy planning, to provide a framework for planning, and to guide current policy decisions and operations. George Kennan was the logical candidate to head this post, having served the State Department as a Soviet expert since 1929 and heading the Soviet desk at the State Department in 1937. In 1944, he was the minister-counselor in Moscow and became acquainted with U.S. Ambassador Averell Harriman. In this position, he sent the "Long Telegram," inspired in part by his British counterpart Frank Roberts, to Washington describing the Soviet Union's desire to expand Communism throughout the world by subverting local governments. (See February 22 and March 17, 1946.) In line with his detailed telegram regarding Soviet policy, the State Department brought Kennan to Washington in April 1947, to promote Soviet containment by assisting other nations in solving their economic problems, beginning with the Truman Doctrine for Greece and Turkey and the Marshall Plan for Europe. Kennan's ideas regarding U.S. policy gained popular attention through his "Mr. X" article, "The Sources of Soviet Conduct," in the July 1947 issue of *Foreign Affairs*.

June 5, 1947

Secretary of State Marshall proposes economic aid to rehabilitate the economies of European nations and to lessen the appeal of Communist parties.

Two years after the German surrender, the nations of Western Europe continued to suffer from the destruction of their industry and the economic dislocation of war. Although the United States had provided refugee relief and some loans to Britain and France since 1945, the standard of living of these and other European nations had not recovered from the war. As a result, the local communist and left-wing political parties were gaining parliamentary seats, especially in France and Italy. At the time when Truman offered aid to Greece and Turkey in March 1947, a committee of the State-War-Navy Coordinating Committee prepared estimates of European needs and presented a report to Marshall and Undersecretary of State Dean Acheson in the middle of April.

It was soon decided that Marshall should propose an aid program for Europe in a Harvard University commencement address on June 5. Marshall told the Harvard audience that the United States would do whatever was necessary to assist in "the return of normal economic health...without which there could be no political stability." The United States wished to fight "hunger, poverty, desperation and chaos." Although cloaked in humanitarian terms, it was obvious that the United States sought to lessen the appeal of local left-wing and Communist parties by improving living standards and providing economic stability.

Marshall asked the Europeans to indicate their desire to cooperate with America. If they would draft a program of their needs (see June 27, 1947), the United States would help them.

June 25, 1947

The Soviets veto a U.N. report that foreign neighbors are interfering in the Greek civil war.

Responding to a request of the Greek government, a U.N. Commission investigated the charges of foreign intervention in the Greek civil war. The Greek Communist rebels, the report said, received aid from Soviet allies—Albania, Bulgaria, and Yugoslavia. In a vote on the report, the Security Council rejected the commission's action because of a Soviet veto. The official vote had been nine for and two against.

June 27, 1947

British, French, and Soviet Foreign Ministers consider Secretary Marshall's aid proposal.

Immediately after Marshall's Harvard University speech, British Foreign Minister Ernest Bevin rushed to arrange a British-French-Soviet meeting in Paris and began talks with Georges Bidault of France. Although Bevin and Bidault hoped the Soviets would not attend, they did. Foreign Minister Molotov arrived in Paris on June 27, with 140 "technical advisers." During the formal talks, Bevin and Bidault united in preventing Molotov from using delay tactics or seeking a "blank check" from America. Moscow was concerned that the United States would employ "economic diplomacy" to push for the Soviet withdrawal from Eastern Europe.

Following a session on July 2, there was a clear break with the Soviets. (See October 5, 1947.) Molotov would not budge from his views; Bevin and Bidault told him they would proceed without him. On July 3, the British and French governments invited all European states to meet in Paris on July 12 to draw up a coordinated plan that described their economic needs to the U.S. government. The Soviets still could have attended but did not. Because the United States told Moscow it would have to share information regarding its financial condition, as did all other parties, Stalin refused to participate. If Stalin had joined, Truman and Marshall would have had greater problems in getting Congress to accept the Marshall Plan. However, if the Soviets and Americans had worked out an agreement, Europe might not have been divided into East-West blocs.

July 15, 1947

Congress passes the Second Decontrol Act, and U.S.-Soviet trade is affected.

President Truman, who had urged its passage, signed the Second Decontrol Act on July 15. Although this legislation was not directed specifically at the Soviet Union, its procedures for controlling exports provided the basis for future Cold War economic sanctions. (See December 17, 1947.)

Nonetheless, the act had an immediate detrimental impact on American-Soviet trade because the importing nation was required to report current consumption, imports, production, and reserve stocks of the goods sought from American exporters. Since the Soviets restricted such information, the list of American products unavailable to them grew—by the end of 1947, the Soviets no longer were able to import American steel, railroad equipment, or petroleum products.

Feeling that they were being discriminated against, the Soviets sought to retaliate by insisting that future agreements between American firms and Soviet import agencies include an assurance that the Commerce Department would issue an export license. This tactic failed because American businessmen were caught up in the anti-Communist sentiment and willing to forego Soviet orders. In February 1947, the Moscow-backed Czechoslovakian coup following the Berlin blockade prompted severe restrictions on the export of U.S. products to the Soviet Union. Between 1947 and 1948, American-Soviet trade fell almost by half, from $226.1 million to $114.7 million.

See February 26, 1949.

July 26, 1947

National Security Act creates a unified organization of the U.S. armed forces.

Although suggestions for a united organization of the nation's defense program had recurred since the 1920s, the serious study of such a plan did not begin until April 1944, when a House Select Committee on Postwar Military Policy held hearings on a War Department unification plan. Additional studies continued throughout 1945, with the War Department generally favoring consolidation of the armed forces and the Navy Department generally preferring closer interservice coordination. General J. Lawton Collins prepared the army plan; the navy plan appeared in the Eberstadt Committee Report of September 1945.

Eventually, on December 19, 1945, President Truman sent a message to Congress on military reorganization, indicating that he favored consolidation of the armed forces. As a result, throughout 1946 there was extensive debate and a number of congressional hearings on military organization. Truman's consolidation view prevailed, however, and the 1947 legislation reflected his ideas, as modified to secure the support of army, navy, and air force leaders. The 1947 act established the army, navy, and air force as equal departments with civilian administrators, supervised by a single, civilian Secretary of Defense.

The act also reorganized the various agencies and departments of government concerned with national security. Three groups separated from the military were established by Title I of the 1947 act: the National Security Council, Central Intelligence Agency, and National Security Resources Board. The National Security Council (NSC) would coordinate the foreign and military policies of the nation and advise the president on integrating those policies. Its members were the president; the secretaries of defense, state, army, navy, and air force; the chairman of the Resources Board; and other government officers the president might designate. The Central Intelligence Agency (CIA) was under the NSC. It would coordinate the intelligence-gathering activities of all government departments, evaluate the data obtained, and report its findings to officials with a "need to know."

The National Security Resources Board (NSRB) would coordinate all military, civilian, and industrial capacities of the nation needed for an emergency mobilization. Chaired by a civilian, the board drew its members from government departments and agencies designated by the president. Title II of the 1947 act established the National Military Establishment (NME), led by a civilian Secretary of Defense with cabinet status. The NME, which on August 10, 1949, was renamed Department of Defense, consisted of the Departments of the Army, Navy, and Air Force; the Joint Chiefs of Staff; the War Council; the Munitions Board; and the Research and Development Board.

The secretary of defense had authority over all parts of the NME. He was directed to eliminate unnecessary duplication or overlapping in defense procurement, supply, transport, health, research, and storage, and to coordinate the budget preparation of parts of the NME. Within the NME (Defense Department) the Joint Chiefs held a prominent role. They formulated strategy, issued military directives, and recommended defense policy to the NSC and president. Former Secretary of the Navy and strident anti-Communist, James Forrestal became the secretary of defense on September 17, 1947.

August 15, 1947

India and Pakistan gain independence from Great Britain.

After Britain decided to give India self-government, religious differences in the subcontinent had to be resolved. This was accomplished in 1947 by partitioning the country between Hindus and Muslims. As a result, the British Parliament approved an Indian Independence Bill on July 5, 1947. The legislation left India in a large middle section of the subcontinent, and parts of Pakistan separated by some 1,000 miles. On August 15, the Dominion of Pakistan established a government under Prime Minister Liaqat Ali Khan and Governor-General Mohammed Ali Jinnah. India was led by Prime Minister Motilal Nehru and Governor-General Lord Mountbatten. Both Pakistan and India became subject to Cold War pressures. India became a leader of the nonaligned neutral bloc, while Pakistan was a sometime American ally.

September 2, 1947

Nations of the Western hemisphere sign an inter-American Mutual Assistance Treaty.

Known as the Rio Pact, the Mutual Assistance Treaty was designed to counteract any aggressor's attack in a defense zone extending from Greenland to Argentina. The treaty became the forerunner of the Organization of American States and was sanctioned by the U.N. charter that provided for regional security agreements.

The Rio Pact appeared to anticipate Chile's problems with Communists. On October 21, 1947, Chile broke diplomatic relations with the Soviet Union following the arrest of 200 Communists who had led a series of labor strikes in Chile.

September 19, 1947

General Albert Wedemeyer reports to Truman on his visit to China.

On July 9, the president sent General Wedemeyer to China on a fact-finding mission to survey what had taken place since Marshall's mission ended in December 1946. Truman wanted to know if Chiang Kai-shek had instituted any of the reforms Marshall recommended. Since 1946, the United States had withdrawn its Marines and had instituted a limited arms embargo in an attempt to pressure Chiang to accept the proposed changes. Meanwhile, the marines left 6,000 tons of ammunition for Chiang as they departed.

President Truman wanted up-to-date information because the "China lobby" and Chiang's friends in Congress had become vocal critics of Truman's China policy. They demanded that the Nationalist Chinese be given whatever Chiang wanted. Wedemeyer's visit ended on August 24, and he took several weeks to write his analysis. Much like Marshall, Wedemeyer believed both sides in the civil war shared blame for the disunity. Nevertheless, he recommended that the United States provide greater military aid if Chiang agreed to "sweeping changes" in his administration and army.

Truman and Marshall disagreed with Wedemeyer's emphasis on greater aid because Chiang had had 20 years to reform the government and revitalize the army, but had continually failed to do so. Because of their dissatisfaction, Truman sought to keep Wedemeyer's report secret. In doing so, however, he caused greater suspicion among his critics and the general public. Only after the China lobby had successfully depicted Chiang as a loyal warrior whose aid was unceremoniously cut by Truman did the administration, in August 1949, issue a full explanation of all reports on China.

Truman was widely condemned by members of the China Lobby who claimed he "lost China." Later, these partisan charges influenced U.S. policy. In Vietnam, for example, American presidents did not wish to leave themselves open to a similar charge.

September 22, 1947

Sixteen European nations report to the United States on their needs under the Marshall Plan.

The delegates who convened at Paris on July 12 set up an interim Committee of European Economic Cooperation (CEEC) to prepare a report for the United States. The CEEC estimated that the 16 European nations would need between $16.4 and $22.4 billion over the next four years. Truman presented his request to Congress for funding the CEEC program on December 17, 1947.

October 5, 1947

Molotov Plan is Soviet version of the Marshall Plan and basis for Comecon.

The two economic plans reinforced the military division of Europe. After rejecting participation in the Marshall Plan, Foreign Minister Molotov extended to Moscow's Eastern European satellites his version of an economic assistance program. When Czechoslovakia and Poland showed interest in the Marshall Plan, Stalin prohibited participation by any member of the Eastern bloc. To offset criticism, the Soviets extended credits to the liberated countries of Bulgaria, Czechoslovakia, and Yugoslavia, and forgave 50 percent of the reparations previously demanded of the former Axis members Hungary and Romania. This program would give way to the Council for Mutual Economic Assistance (Comecon) in 1949. The economic division of Europe was followed by Soviet repression of political dissent in the Eastern bloc because Stalin no longer saw reason to placate his former allies.

See April 26, 1949.

October 5, 1947

The Communist Information Bureau (COMINFORM) is created in a conference at Warsaw.

The COMINFORM was founded at Wilcza Gora, Poland under the auspices of the Soviet Union. It began with the nine Communist parties of the USSR, Bulgaria, Czechoslovakia, Hungary, Poland, Yugoslavia, Romania, France, and Italy. While officially designed to coordinate the activities of Europe's Communist parties, Western observers believed the COMINFORM replaced the Comintern as the mechanism for the Kremlin's control of all local Communist organizations around the world. The COMINFORM's first headquarters was in Belgrade, Yugoslavia, but in 1948 it moved its headquarters to Bucharest, Romania. As a tool of the Soviet Union, the COMINFORM failed to obstruct the Marshall Plan in France and Italy.

While officially designed to coordinate the activities of Eastern Europe's Communist parties, Western observers believed COMINFORM replaced the Comintern—which had been disbanded during World War II as a gesture to the allies—as the mechanism for Kremlin control of all local Communist organizations around the world. The COMINFORM's creation quickly raised the ire of Tito's Communist Party of Yugoslavia, which questioned Moscow's motives. Tito felt that the purpose of the organization was to place Eastern Europe in a subservient role to the Soviet Union and, therefore, he refused to participate in Moscow's plans for joint economic ventures and created Yugoslavia's own ambitious industrialization program. In 1948, Yugoslavia's Communist Party would be expelled from COMINFORM, and Soviet trade was embargoed until after the death of Stalin in 1953. COMINFORM disbanded on April 17, 1956, because Khrushchev wanted to be reconciled with Yugoslavia.

October 30, 1947

The General Agreement on Tariffs and Trade (GATT) is signed.

Following six months of negotiations in Geneva, 23 nations approved an effort to lower trade barriers. The GATT had three essential features: a multilateral schedule of tariff concessions; a code of principles governing imports and exports; and periodic meetings that provided an international forum for discussing trade problems. Tariffs were first negotiated on a bilateral basis before there were multinational discussions to form a schedule of tariff concessions. The commerce of these 23 nations comprised three-fourths of the world's trade. The countries were Australia, Belgium, Brazil, the Netherlands, Luxembourg, Canada, Chile, Republic of China, Cuba, Czechoslovakia, France, India, Pakistan, Ceylon, Burma, Lebanon, Syria, New Zealand, Norway, South Africa, the United Kingdom, Southern Rhodesia, and the United States.

The 1947 Geneva Conference resulted in significant lowering of tariff barriers among the participating nations. About 54 percent of U.S. dutiable imports were affected by the Geneva reductions. The average of reductions was 18.9 percent, a sum that was calculated on the lower levels that the United States had previously negotiated in bilateral agreements under the Reciprocity Act of 1934.

November 14, 1947

The U.N. General Assembly votes to recognize Korea's independence.

In September 1945, the United States and the Soviet Union agreed to divide their occupation forces in Korea at the 38th parallel. Later, at the December 1945 Moscow Conference, delegates of the Soviet Union and the United States agreed to form a provisional government for Korea, but this agreement was never enforced. Thus, in September, the United States had referred the issue of the future status of Korea to the United Nations because it could not agree with the Soviet Union on the establishment of a provisional government for all Korea.

A U.N. study recommended plans for the withdrawal of both U.S. and Soviet forces and the creation of a Korean government, a proposal approved on November 14, 1947.

November 29, 1947

The U.N. General Assembly approves a partition plan to divide Palestine between Arabs and Jews.

During World War II (May 1942), the Conference of American Zionists had rejected the British plan of 1939 to give Palestine independence under joint administration. In August 1945, President Truman asked Britain to allow at least 100,000 displaced Jews into Palestine after the World Zionist Congress demanded

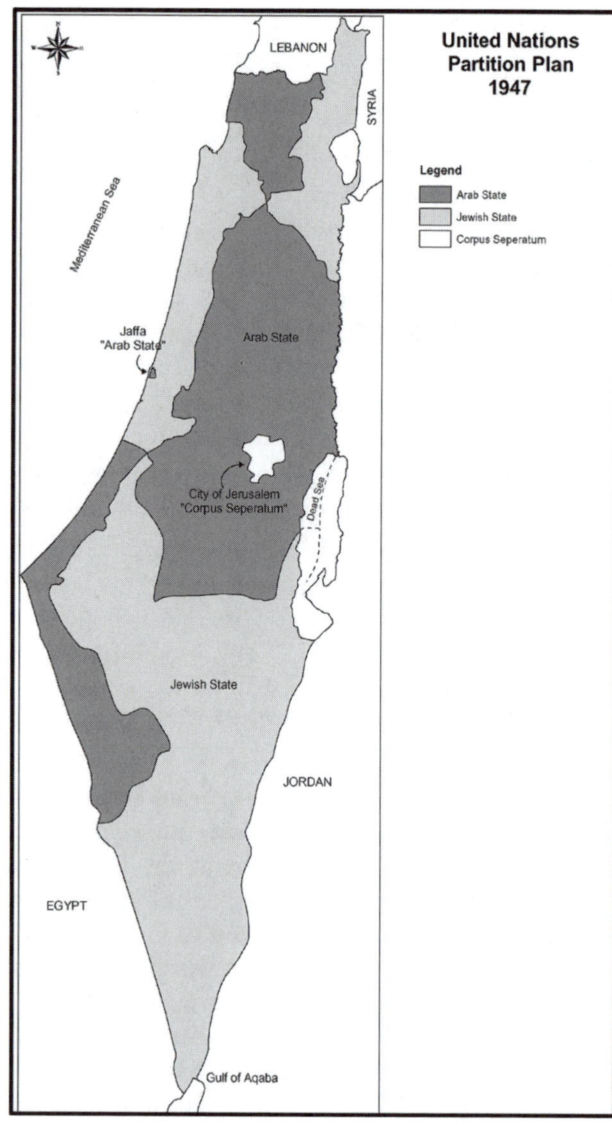

that 1 million Jews be admitted. Although an Anglo-American committee on August 29, 1946, advised against the partition of Palestine, Zionists rejected any state without full Jewish autonomy. By early 1947, the British announced they would withdraw from Palestine as they had from Greece. On April 2, the British referred the Palestinian problem to the United Nations. A U.N. commission studied the issue and on November 29 recommended that Palestine be divided into Arab and Jewish states. Jerusalem would be under a U.N. Trusteeship. The Jews accepted the U.N. plan but the Arab League rejected it. On December 17, the Council of the Arab League announced it would use force to stop partition and began raids on Jewish communities in Palestine. A Jewish terrorist group, Irgun (Stern Gang), retaliated with guerrilla attacks on Arabs.

December 17, 1947

Congress passes the Foreign Aid Act of 1947.

This act provided $540 million of interim relief to France, Italy, Austria, and China. The legislation was designed to carry the European nations through the winter, pending final enactment of Marshall Plan aid in 1948. China was added to the list of those receiving aid because of the pro-China views of such leading Republicans as Senators Vandenberg and Styles Bridges. While Marshall, the Joint Chiefs of Staff, and Truman believed aid to China was a poor risk expense, the China lobby vociferously complained that Chiang Kai-shek should be aided as well as Europe.

President Truman also requested funds for the European Recovery Program (Marshall Plan). On March 31, 1948, Congress authorized $5.3 billion for this program. Truman appointed Paul G. Hoffman as chief of the European Cooperation Administration on April 6.

December 17, 1947

The Truman administration plans to control exports to Communist states: NSC-17.

The National Security Council (NSC) prepared a report titled "Control of Exports to the USSR and Eastern Europe" that described one means of conducting the Cold War by economic action. NSC-17 recommended limited shipment of all goods that were "critically short" in America or would "contribute to Soviet military potential." This policy was based on a recommendation of the Commerce Department, approved by the State Department.

To operate as quietly as possible and avoid breaking existing commercial treaties with Eastern European nations, Secretary of Commerce Averell Harriman suggested an "R" export-control procedure. The "R" procedure named all Europe as a "recovery area." To assist economic recovery, America would issue export licenses for commodities to Europe, granting a license to an area found to have the "greatest need." This "R" policy, but not its purpose, was announced by the Commerce Department in a press release of January 15, 1948. As described publicly, goods were not embargoed to any nation; they were simply sent where they were most needed. The Department of Commerce, of course, would decide what nation had the "greatest need."

the people of the United States and other peoples of the world.

1948

January 21, 1948

The State Department publishes captured German documents on the 1939 Nazi-Soviet pact.

These documents on the temporary alliance of Hitler's Germany with Stalin's USSR seemed to reinforce the growing U.S. belief that German Nazi totalitarianism and Soviet Communist totalitarianism were synonymous. Although Secretary of State Marshall denied it, some American reporters believed the publication of these documents in 1948 supported the U.S. desire to implicate Stalin in using the same tactics that Hitler employed in seeking world domination. Because the documents showed only the Berlin events and Soviet dispatches to Germany, the impression grew that Stalin sought the alliance with Germany in 1939 because Germany and the USSR shared political goals. Therefore, Americans such as President Truman could assert that there was no difference between the totalitarianism of Nazi Germany and the Communist Soviet Union.

Although this analysis had some validity in terms of the Soviet Union's methods of deceit and ruthlessness during the purges of the 1930s, it blurred the ideological distinctions between Communism and Fascism. Marxian theory adhered to humanistic goals that the Soviet Union failed to implement; the Nazis' antihumanistic and destructive ideology had been vigorously carried out by Hitler by aggression and an attempt to exterminate the Jewish and other peoples. In addition, this analysis considered Soviet armies in Eastern Europe as aggressors, whereas, in fact, they had liberated Eastern European nations from Nazi conquest, just as the Anglo-American offensive had liberated Western Europe.

January 27, 1948

Truman signs legislation finalizing the U.S. Information and Education Exchange Act of 1948.

Under the law, America would prepare and distribute information to promote understanding between

February 2, 1948

The United States and Italy sign a Treaty of Friendship, Commerce, and Navigation.

Designed to replace a previous treaty that Washington abrogated in 1937, when Italy joined an Axis of Powers with Germany and Japan, this treaty was signed by Italian Foreign Minister Carlo Sforza and U.S. Ambassador to Italy James C. Dunn. The treaty granted reciprocal use of seaports and equal treatment of each other's citizens abroad, but each country reserved control of its arms and munitions shipments, including atomic materials. A separate U.S.-Italian civil aviation treaty on February 6 formalized an agreement for America's Trans-World Airlines (TWA) to use Italian airports.

The U.S.-Italian friendship treaty assisted Italy's pro-Western political parties to win a majority of votes in Italy's elections on April 18–19, 1947. In the election, Premier Alcide de Gasperi's Christian Democrats Catholic Party won 49 percent of the vote and a 53.5 percent of the vote in the Chamber of Deputies. The Popular Front party of Communists and Socialists won only 31 percent of the popular vote and 30 percent in the Chamber of Deputies. Another factor in Italy's pro-Western vote took place on March 20, 1947, when the United States, Britain, and France announced that Trieste should be returned to Italy rather than being administered as a U.N. Free Territory that was imperiled by being controlled by Yugoslavia's Communists.

February 25, 1948

A Communist coup is carried out in Czechoslovakia.

In the 1946 elections for a constituent assembly, the Communists won 114 of 300 seats, gaining a plurality that permitted the Communist Klement Gottwald to form a coalition government. Next, Gottwald threatened a coup unless President Edvard Beneš agreed to a predominantly Communist ministry. The Communists then proceeded to purge the country of anti-Communist groups; one instance of this plan included the mysterious death of Foreign Minister Jan Masaryk, who reportedly committed suicide by falling from his office window.

Foreign Minister Jan Masaryk in happier times. National Archives

New elections on May 30 had only a single list of Communist candidates, which assured that party's victory. On June 7, President Beneš resigned and Gottwald became president of the Communist government.

It also indicated that both Great Britain under the Labour Party government and France, whose centrist parties had placated the French Communists previously, had become alarmed at Stalin's policies in Europe. France and Britain therefore began a united Western European action to indicate their willingness to confront the Soviet Union if necessary.

March 17, 1948

The Brussels Treaty is signed as a step toward European cooperation.

The 50-year defensive alliance was approved by delegates of Great Britain, France, Belgium, the Netherlands, and Luxembourg. They also pledged cooperation in economic, social, and military affairs. The Brussels Treaty broadened a previous French-British defensive alliance against Germany into a pact to coordinate military policies of the five nations against any power that might attack one of them. It was clearly directed against the Soviet Union and ended the traditional neutrality policy of the Benelux nations.

March 20, 1948

The Soviet delegate walks out of the Allied Control Council, charging that the three Western powers seek to undermine the four-power control of Berlin.

Previous rifts between the Soviet delegate to the Four-Power Control Council for Germany, Vasily D. Sokolovsky, and the three Western delegates escalated early in 1948 because Sokolovsky vigorously denounced the Allied moves to unify their three zones of West Germany. The Soviet Union hoped to use its veto power in the Control Council to block the Allies' actions, but the three Allied nations were determined that their plan not be sidetracked by the Soviets.

Subsequently, the conflicts at the Four-Power Control Council meetings became what historian Herbert Feis called "brawls." The Western delegates, led by General Lucius Clay of the United States, challenged Sokolovsky and protested Soviet actions in East Germany that violated the Control Council decisions. On March 20, the final split took place when the Soviets asked the council to consider challenges by Poland and Yugoslavia to Western occupation policies in Germany. Clay refused, saying those complaints contained false and distorted information. Sokolovsky read a long statement that repeated all of the USSR's previous charges against the Western powers' activities in Germany. Then the Soviet who was the council chairman for the month of March adjourned the meeting and left. No new meeting date was set and General Clay decided not to ask the Soviets for another session.

March 28, 1948

The charter of the International Trade Organization (ITO) is finalized at the Havana World Conference on Trade and Employment.

Sixty nations participated in this conference, which was sponsored by the United Nations and convened on November 21, 1947. The ITO developed from a suggestion made by the United States in December 1945. Its purpose was to create an organization for consultation on trade issues and to formulate a fair practices code for international commerce.

April 6, 1948

Finland and the Soviet Union sign a Treaty of Friendship, Cooperation, and Mutual Assistance.

Washington's early negative view of the Finnish-Soviet relationship was popularized by Walter Laqueur's *Commentary* article (December 1977) termed "Finlandization." He claimed Finland set a bad example by turning control over foreign and domestic affairs to Moscow by retaining an illusion of sovereignty. This simplistic view saw Finnish-Soviet relations in the context of the superpower conflict and ignored assessments that Finland successfully handled a unique situation.

Despite the devastating effects of World War II and the harsh 1944 armistice terms leading to Finland's loss of territory, Finnish-Soviet relations were stable during the Cold War. According to Keith W. Olson, three Finnish presidents from 1944 to 1981 maintained Finland's neutrality and enjoyed "friendly relations with its giant eastern neighbor; a western market economy; a Protestant national church; and a constitutional democratic political system." For recent views and bibliography, see T. Michael Ruddy, ed. *Charting an Independent Course: Finland's Place in the Cold War and in U.S. Foreign Policy* (1998).

April 16, 1948

Sixteen European nations form the Organization for European Economic Cooperation (OEEC).

This agreement provided for the non-Communist European nations to work together in using U.S. aid under the European Recovery Program (the Marshall Plan).

May 2, 1948

The Organization of American States (OAS) is established at Bogotá, Colombia.

Following up on the Rio Pact of August 1947, the Ninth International Conference of American Republics formed the OAS as an anti-Communist pact for the Western Hemisphere. During the conference deliberations at Bogotá, the meetings had to be suspended for several days because of a local Communist-led riot that severely damaged the city and took hundreds of lives. The OAS formed a hemispheric defense council and established a process by which sessions of the defense council would be called in case of aggression against any member nation. It also adopted an anti-Communist resolution at Bogotá. Not all was harmonious in the Western Hemisphere, however. Many of the Latin American delegates wanted the United States to provide a "little Marshall Plan" to solve their economic problems. President Truman disappointed them by offering only half a billion dollars of Export-Import Bank funds.

May 7, 1948

The Congress of Europe meets at the Hague to discuss plans for establishing a European union.

The honorary chairman was Winston Churchill. This meeting brought to life the dreams of European statesmen, such as the Frenchman Jean Monnet, who had urged a political program for the gradual unification of Europe.

May 14, 1948

The state of Israel is proclaimed under a provisional government headed by David Ben-Gurion.

After the British mandate ended and British troops withdrew, the U.N.'s partition plan—initially supported by both the United States and Soviet Union—was supposed to resolve the internal conflict between the Jews and the Palestinian Arabs. However, civil strife between Arabs and Jews raged between November 1947 and May 1948, as neither the Jews nor the Arabs were satisfied with the partition arrangement.

Both the United States and the Soviet Union recognized Israel by May 16, 1948; however, this did not deter the immediate outbreak of the first Arab-Israeli war. Washington's acquiescence to Israeli territorial aggrandizement and diplomatic maneuvering during and after the war helped to ensure an outcome that would greatly disturb Arab leaders. While during World War II Franklin Roosevelt had indicated support for the Arab states, now the strategic balance of the Middle East was becoming precarious and American interests were being endangered.

Moscow's behavior throughout the war was shrewd. Beginning with assistance to Soviet Jews emigrating to Palestine, Moscow continued to support Israel through the provision of armaments throughout the war as the Soviets sought to counter American influence in the region. As it became apparent that the Truman administration was siding with Israel, Moscow began to align itself with the Arab world as Israel's military success created a sense of Arab desperation that would make them increasingly susceptible to Soviet offers. While political support of Israeli took pressure off Truman, the one-sided nature of the victories ensured that instability would continue to beset the region. As Israel aligned itself with the West, the Cold War was extended into the Middle East.

See May 25, 1950.

June 1, 1948

Six-Power agreement defines West Germany's status.

By 1948, the Western Allies believed Germany would be divided for the foreseeable future and decided the Western section's status should be determined. Following extensive discussions, the United States, Britain, France, Belgium, Luxembourg, and the Netherlands signed a Six-Power agreement. The agreement's main points were that (1) the Ruhr would be under international control; (2) West Germany could join the European Recovery Program; (3) the three Western zones of Germany would be integrated; (4) a constitution would be drafted for a Federal Republic of West Germany.

June 11, 1948

The Vandenberg Resolution is approved by the U.S. Senate.

Sponsored by Republican Senator Arthur H. Vandenberg, this resolution affirmed U.S. support for regional security pacts such as the Brussels Pact. This resolution was meant to support the State Department's efforts to negotiate U.S. membership in a European defense pact. Senate approval of the Vandenberg Resolution marked a significant point in the final shifting of U.S. foreign policy from earlier isolationism to international involvement. As Herbert Feis remarked, Hitler did not change the Republican Party's isolationism; Stalin did.

Beginning on April 11, Senator Vandenberg worked with Undersecretary of State Robert Lovett in drafting a resolution that would commit America to the collective defense of Western Europe against any acts of aggression. On May 19, Vandenberg introduced his resolution as recommended by the Senate Foreign Relations Committee. As approved by the Senate on June 11, the resolution gave Senate favor to any "regional and other collective security arrangements for individual and collective self-defense." The Senate approved the resolution by a vote of 64 to 4.

June 24, 1948

The Soviets begin the Berlin Blockade. The United States launches an airlift.

Dismayed by the success of the French, British, and Americans in uniting their zones of Germany, the Soviets retaliated by shutting down all land, rail, and water traffic through their zone to Berlin. Apparently they hoped the Western Allies would abandon Berlin and permit it to become the capital city to rally Germans to Communism. After the Soviets sidetracked two trains sent from West Germany to test the blockade, President Truman determined, with British support, to stay in West Berlin and to employ an airlift to supply the 2.5 million Berliners in their respective zones. The Western Allies also hurt the Soviet–East German economy by a counterblockade of their zone.

The airlift, code-named Operation Vittles, continued to supply West Berlin for over a year. Up to 4,500 tons of supplies, including coal, were flown in each day. Although at times these planes encountered Soviet fighter planes, no incident took place. The Soviets did not want a war and finally agreed in 1949 to end the blockade. Truman's response to Moscow's challenge found the United States and its allies gaining popular support in Europe; thus, the blockade backfired against the Soviets. To the American public, the successful conclusion of the Berlin blockade seemed to demonstrate the validity of the president's "get tough" policy toward the Soviet Union.

June 28, 1948

Truman orders 60 B-29 bombers sent to British bases and a smaller number to German bases.

Although this action had been under consideration for some time, the Berlin blockade underscored the need for U.S. bombers at advance European bases as

Operation Vittles included milk for children. National Archives

part of the Forward Strategy of defending Europe. Some news sources implied that these bombers were "atomic-capable," but, in fact, the B-29s sent to Europe had not been modified to carry the atomic bombs available at the time.

June 28, 1948

Stalin expels Yugoslavia from the COMINFORM for ideological errors and hostility to the Soviet Union.

Stalin felt the Yugoslav Communist Party was too independent after Marshal Tito (Josip Broz) questioned Soviet plans for the Eastern European satellite nations and rejected Yugoslavia's role second to Stalin. As the Yugoslav leader during World War II, Tito led Communist resistance and was elected to rule Yugoslavia on November 11, 1945. Now, he rejected Stalin's offer to create joint companies that would develop an autonomous industrialization plan. Desiring to teach Tito a lesson, Stalin had the COMINFORM expel the Yugoslav Communist Party and terminated its trade arrangements with Belgrade.

Stalin failed to bring Tito in line in part because the United States filled Yugoslavia's economic void. The breach between Moscow and Belgrade continued until Stalin's death, after which Moscow reopened trade relations but the basic disagreements between the two parties were never fully resolved. Tito would remain neutral in superpower Cold War disputes.

July 23, 1948

Chinese Communists in Malaya begin a guerrilla war against the British.

After Japan surrendered to the British in Malaya in September 1945, armed groups from the Malaya Communist Party (MCP) captured large numbers of armed weapons discarded by the Japanese troops. The MCP did not immediately take actions against the British. The British had promised to make Malaya an independent nation, just as London did for India and Burma after World War II, as soon as details for a power transfer were worked out. In Malaya, the MCP's main problem was that its Chinese emigrant members were outnumbered by the native Malaya population whose United Malaya Organization supported Britain's offer of future independence.

After attending the Communist Asian Youth Congress in Calcutta in February 1948, the MCP General Secretary Chen Peng and other MCP members were inspired to begin their rebellion against the British as soon as possible. Although Malayan independence was pending in 1948, Communist leaders in Moscow and Peking (Beijing) persuaded Chen Peng to prepare to attack the British even though they offered him little military aid because the British Navy dominated the water in the strait of Malaya. Chen Peng renamed the MCP the Malayan Races Liberation Army (MRLA). On June

16, MRLA members raided and destroyed three rubber plantations before killing their British landlords in Perek and Jahore provinces of northern Malaya. A month later on July 23, 1948, MRLA rebels began a series of major attacks that enabled them to gain control of many jungle and rural regions in northern Malaya.

Following these initial attacks, Britain's Lt. General Sir Harold Briggs declared a State of Emergency throughout Malaya, declared the MRLA to be an unlawful society and laid out plans to defeat the MRLA insurgents. Using Briggs's plan, British troops and Malaya's police first secured population centers where many Chinese businessmen and their families lived. Briggs now realized there was no way to win the war against insurgents and establish an independent Malaya. In February 1952, the British government replaced Briggs with General Sir Gerald Templer. It was obvious that more fighting would be necessary before the British could successfully defeat the MRLA. (See July 12, 1960.) For complete details see Edgar O'Balance, *Malaya: The Communist Insurgent War, 1948–60* (1966). For brief summation of events see David Stone, *Wars of the Cold War, Campaigns and Conflicts, 1945–1990* (2004).

July 30, 1948

Whittaker Chambers and Elizabeth Bentley tell the House Un-American Activities Committee (HUAC) that Communists infiltrated the State Department in the 1930s.

Chambers and Bentley were self-confessed former Communist Party members whose testimony became the highlight of the HUAC hearings in the late 1940s. Bentley, labeled the "Red Queen" by the press, told the FBI of some 14 Americans who had spied or were spying for the Soviets, including Assistant Secretary of the Treasury Harry Dexter White, OSS Executive Assistant Duncan C. Lee, and Roosevelt's former aide Lauchlin Currie.

Chambers soon identified Alger Hiss, who had worked in several executive departments after 1933, including the State Department in 1944, as a Communist Party agent. Hiss denied Chambers's testimony, and the long-lived Hiss-Chambers Affair began, an affair that would, among other things, propel Richard Nixon into the national limelight when Nixon backed Chambers.

August 18, 1948

A Communist-dominated conference on navigation of the Danube River ends when the Danube Convention is signed by seven Communist nations who outvote the U.S., France and Britian.

The Conference on the Danube opened on July 30, 1948, at Belgrade, after Moscow's refusal to delay the sessions until December. The three Western powers reluctantly attended, arguing Austria could have no official role because the Austrian peace treaty was pending. The seven Communist states represented were the USSR, Bulgaria, Czechoslovakia, Hungary, Romania, Yugoslavia, and the Ukraine. Rather than negotiate a new treaty to supersede the Convention of 1921, the Soviets insisted, and their allies agreed, on using the Soviet draft treaty as the basis for debate and voting.

The three Western powers claimed the Soviet draft violated the free navigation of the river by giving the Soviets a "monopoly control" of the Danube. The Western powers offered amendments to the draft but were consistently outvoted by 7 to 3. The agreement signed on August 18 was essentially a Soviet convention. It passed 7 to 1, with the United States voting no. France and Britain believed that abstaining was the best method for objecting to the "railroading" tactics used by the USSR's Andrey Vishinsky. At the final session, the French delegation spoke harshly of the convention, which "one power issued and a docile majority" accepted. Following the sessions, France, Great Britain, and the United States issued statements that rejected the document as "Soviet imperialism," and claimed that the nonriparian nations that used the Danube but were not invited to the meeting retained the rights of the 1921 Convention. Austria's delegate stated he could not accept the convention because Austria had not had a vote at the conference.

October 29, 1948

In a military coup in Peru, General Manuel Odrıá overthrows President José Luis Bustamente's government.

The new government outlawed both Peru's Communist Party and the peasant-worker–supported APRA party.

November 2, 1948

Harry S. Truman is reelected president, winning a surprise victory over Thomas E. Dewey.

Truman received 303 electoral votes to Dewey's 189. The Democrats also gained control of both houses of Congress. The election campaign included a bitter foreign policy struggle between the Democrats and Henry Wallace's Progressive Party. Wallace blamed Truman for the Cold War against the USSR because he stopped Roosevelt's cooperative policies with the Soviet Union.

November 12, 1948

The Japanese War Crime trials end.

The Military Tribunal sentenced General Hideki Tojo and six other Japanese leaders to death for major war crimes; 16 others received sentences of life imprisonment.

November 20, 1948

The U.S. Consul General and staff at Mukden, China, are confined to the consulate by the Chinese Communists.

Mukden, Manchuria, became the first urban center with foreign diplomatic representation to be captured by Mao Tse-tung's Communist armies. The Communists gained control of the city on October 31 and initially seemed willing to discuss trade agreements with the American, English, and French consuls in Mukden. On November 14, a problem arose because the three foreign consuls were requested to turn their radio transmitters over to the government within 48 hours. The French and British had no independent transmitters and the U.S. consul, Angus J. Ward, refused to do so until he could receive permission from Washington. He offered, however, to stop transmitting radio messages. Ward's offer was rejected by the Communists.

On November 20, Communist soldiers cordoned off the office and residence compounds of the U.S. consulate. The Chinese officials informed Ward that no one could leave the compound or communicate with the outside. The troops cut the consulate's telephone and electrical lines and shut off the water supply. Ward's radio transmitters and generators were also seized. During the next 30 hours, the guards gave the 22 persons only one bucket of water and no food. Although the consulate's electricity was restored in December, Ward did not get to communicate with the outside world until June 7, 1949. The plight of the 22 "hostages" continued for more than a year, causing President Truman to consider military measures to free the "prisoners."

December 9–10, 1948

The U.N. General Assembly adopts a human rights declaration and a genocide convention.

The Universal Declaration of Human Rights was approved at a U.N. General Assembly meeting in Paris. A U.N. commission headed by Eleanor Roosevelt, wife of President Franklin D. Roosevelt, prepared the declaration. The December 10 declaration was a nonbinding statement of principles that would be supplemented by an International Covenant on Human Rights to be drafted by Mrs. Roosevelt's commission.

Because the commission members disagreed about its contents, it adjourned in 1953 without an agreement. A second human rights committee was formed and in 1966 presented a covenant divided into two parts; one, an International Covenant of Civil and Political Rights, the other a Covenant on Economic, Social, and Cultural Rights. Although Mrs. Roosevelt traveled the world until her death to promote peace and human rights, as of 2000 the U.S. Senate had ratified only the Covenant on Civil and Political Rights. Conservative congressional leaders claim the Covenant on Economic, Social, and Cultural rights conflicts with the U.S. Constitution.

The Convention on the Prevention and Punishment of Genocide approved by the General Assembly was an international response to the Holocaust committed by the Germans during World War II. Although President Truman sought ratification of the Genocide Convention, the U.S. Senate delayed ratification using constitutional arguments, although a majority of the Senate wanted to protect racial and segregation laws and avoid the scrutiny of U.N. officials. The 1940s were an era in the United States when African Americans often were not allowed to vote and when lynchings were not uncommon in some Southern states. Consequently, the Senate did not ratify the Genocide Convention until 1986, after adding several reservations such as giving the U.S. Constitution precedence over the International Court of Justice. On October 10, 1988, Congress finally passed legislation making genocide a crime and levied fines and imprisonment for anyone convicted of such crimes.

For details on human rights, see Natalie H. Kaufman's *Human Rights Treaties and the Senate: A History of Opposition* (1990) and the excellent philosophical analysis of human rights by eminent scholars from around the world in United Nations Educational, Scientific and Cultural Organization's (UNESCO) volume *Human Rights* (1949). On the Genocide Convention, see Lawrence Leblanc's *The United States and the Genocide Convention* (1991).

1949

January 20, 1949

President Truman's second inaugural address proposes the Point Four program.

The Point Four program would provide technical assistance to economically underdeveloped areas in the hope of combating the spread of Communism in the Third World. The focus of the technical aid was on agriculture, health care, transportation, finance, irrigation, and vocational training. Congress authorized $34.5 million for Point Four in May 1950—well below the formulas used in the Marshall Plan—but increased funding in 1953 to $155.6 million. At this time dozens of countries joined the program, including India, Iran, Paraguay, and Liberia and were hosting American technical experts. American businesses were encouraged to invest in these areas with an eye toward developing markets and sources of raw materials.

During Truman's address to Congress, his previously mentioned three points were to encourage European recovery, to support the United Nations, and to aid nations from Communism. Point Four was injected into Truman's speech for dramatic effect.

January 21, 1949

Dean Acheson replaces George Marshall as Secretary of State.

Acheson had been undersecretary of state from 1945 to 1947, resigning in the spring of 1947 to return to private legal practice. Nevertheless, Marshall resigned in December 1948 due to poor health.

Truman immediately asked Acheson to become secretary of state, and the appointment was announced on January 7, 1949. False charges were raised in the Senate confirmation hearings regarding Acheson's conduct. The unproven allegations came from former U.S. Ambassador to Poland, Arthur Lane Bliss, and a former State Department associate, Adolf Berle. Bliss charged in his book *I Saw Poland Betrayed* (1948) that Acheson appeased the Soviet Union by giving loans and credits to the Polish government from 1945 to 1947. Berle had told the House Un-American Affairs Committee in August 1948 that Alger Hiss was one of the "Acheson-group" in the State Department that had a "pro-Russian point of view."

This latter charge was disproved during the Senate hearings in January 1949, when it was learned that it was Donald Hiss, Alger Hiss's brother, who had worked with Acheson. This testimony did not, however, receive the widespread attention that Berle's charges had in 1948. Later Senator Joseph McCarthy rehashed these same false accusations. Acheson's nomination was endorsed by a wide variety of people, including Herbert Hoover and John Foster Dulles. Senator Arthur Vandenberg, the leading Republican on the Senate Foreign Relations Committee, also supported Acheson, knowing that far from being "soft" on Communism, Acheson had strongly urged measures to combat the Soviet Union between 1945 and 1947.

Secretary of State Dean Acheson. National Archives

February 26, 1949

The U.S. Export Control Act of 1949 seeks to weaken Communist states.

Soviet-American economic relations were caught up in Cold War measures and countermeasures. The USSR's decision in December 1948 to restrict the export of such items as manganese and platinum—in retaliation for earlier U.S. economic sanctions (see July 15, 1947)—prompted, in part, the 1949 export controls. The Export Control Act of 1949 was designed to control items in short supply, to further U.S. foreign policy goals, and to restrict exports to Communist countries that might have military application. This legislation created an elaborate licensing system for all exports under the Department of Commerce. It also established commodities lists designed to limit or prevent the sale or transfer of designated items or technologies with the potential to strengthen any adversary. Following the Berlin blockade crisis, the administration viewed virtually all U.S. exports to the Soviet Union as possessing military value—thus by 1950 U.S. exports comprised less than a million dollars.

The 1949 Act, amended and extended, remained in effect for 20 years until replaced by the Export Administration Act (EAA) of 1969, which in turn was replaced by the EAA of 1979. The 1979 EAA was reauthorized with amendments both in 1985 and in 1988, but expired on September 30, 1990, when Congress was unable to agree on the provisions for a new EAA. Following this expiration in 1990, the president was forced to step into the legal vacuum and maintain the existing export control regime by invoking authority under the International Economic Emergency Powers Act (IEEPA).

April 4, 1949

The North Atlantic Treaty Organization (NATO) is chartered by 12 nations, including the United States.

NATO evolved from the 1948 Brussels Treaty, in which Britain, France, Belgium, the Netherlands, and Luxembourg pledged economic and military cooperation. (See March 17, 1948.) NATO's charter members included the five members of the Brussels pact plus the United States, Canada, Italy, Portugal, Denmark, Iceland, and Norway. The ratification of the North Atlantic Treaty by the U.S. Senate on July 21, 1949 (a vote of 82 to 13) committed the United States to a peacetime political-military alliance with Europe for the first time since the abrogation of the French Alliance in 1800.

The treaty signatories agreed to consult together if anyone's security were threatened. Article 5 was a key clause, because it stated: "an armed attack against one or more of them . . . shall be considered an attack against them all." Thus, they would join together with whatever action was necessary, "including the use of armed force," to restore the security of the North Atlantic area. The clause "such action as it deems necessary" limited the pledges of each nation and made the alliance uncertain. The United States believed that the clause was essential because the U.S. Constitution required congressional approval to go to war. But other signatories could also use this clause to limit their military commitment.

The NATO charter was more than a military alliance because it permitted continuous cooperation in political, economic, and other nonmilitary fields. Cooperation among the NATO allies was through the treaty organization. Each member sent delegates to the NATO Council, which could "meet promptly at any time." The Council appointed a secretary-general and various committees to assist in its work. Committees included such groups as Defense Planning Committee, Nuclear Defense Affairs Committee, Economic Affairs Committee, and others. A Military Committee had special responsibilities for guidance and recommendations on military matters.

All members ratified the NATO charter, which became effective on August 24, 1949. On September 28, the U.S. Congress approved the Mutual Defense Assistance Program, providing military aid to NATO.

April 26, 1949

First Comecon Session meets in Moscow.

The Council for Mutual Economic Assistance (Comecon) had its origins in the Molotov plan offered to Eastern bloc members on October 5, 1947, as an alternative to the Marshall plan. Also announced on October 5, 1947, was the Communist Information Bureau (COMINFORM) formed to unite the Eastern bloc Communist parties; however, Moscow soon found the COMINFORM—as indicated by the dispute with Yugoslavia—to be an unsatisfactory device to integrate the economies of the satellite states with the Soviet Union. Thus delegates from Bulgaria,

Czechoslovakia, Hungary, Poland, and Romania met in January 1949 to organize Comecon; they were later joined by East Germany and Albania—which withdrew following a 1961 break with Moscow.

Comecon sought a strategy to improve the reciprocal economic relations of the member nations, through coordination of each state's national plans aligned with their existing specializations. As James Libbey has noted in *American-Russian Economic Relations* (1989): "Theoretically, this meant realigning foreign trade, perfecting exchange rates, and forming clearinghouses for the smooth transfer of products." Other objectives of Comecon were to provide mutual aid, as needed, to member states and to share scientific and technical data aimed at improving the bloc's economic base. Political circumstances, such as mounting Cold War tensions and regional unrest, led the satellites to place more emphasis on producing armaments than developing a multinational socialist economy. By Comecon's Third Session in 1950 it had become evident delegates could not devise a satisfactory method of coordinating the members' centrally planned economies. Moscow's inability to focus on either a bilateralist or multilateralist economic policy furthered the decline of Comecon. Although later revived, the program never lived up to its original goal of integrated socialist economies.

May 8, 1949

The Federal Republic of Germany (FRG) is formed at Bonn.

The Germans adopted the Basic Laws of the Federal Republic in meetings at Bonn. On August 14, 1949, elections to the Bundestag (parliament) resulted in a victory for Konrad Adenauer's Christian Democratic Party, which won a plurality of 31 percent of the vote, compared with the Social Democrats' 29.2 percent. Theodore Heuss became president of the republic and Adenauer became Chancellor.

May 11, 1949

The Berlin blockade ends with a four-power accord on the city.

As early as January 30, 1949, Stalin told an American journalist, Kingsbury Smith, that he would be willing to end the blockade. Yet serious discussions on an agreement to end the crisis did not begin until April. Moscow realized the blockade had not been successful—it had drawn the Western powers closer together rather than dividing them. Finally, Western countermeasures had inflicted considerable damage on the economic life of East Germany and the other Soviet satellites of Eastern Europe.

A few of the planes that participated in the Berlin airlift. National Archives

On May 5, the four powers announced in Berlin that accords had been achieved to end the Soviet blockade as well as the Western nations' countermeasures that had been in place since the summer of 1948. The U.S. airlift continued to send supplies to West Berlin until September 30. During the airlift—from July 24, 1948, to September 30, 1949—the Western allies flew 277,264 flights to Berlin. When the airlift reached its peak between February and June 1949, an average of one plane landed in Berlin every two minutes; 7,000 to 8,000 tons of food and fuel were carried each day.

May 12, 1949

The Far Eastern commission announces the termination of reparations to aid Japan's economic recovery.

The 11-nation Far Eastern Commission had been established in Washington in 1945 to oversee the Allied Control Council in Tokyo. By 1947, the commission began to change its policy from punishing the Japanese to strengthening them as much as possible. The initial change in policy took place in 1948 when the Allies stopped dissolving the *zaibatsu*—the economic empires of 10 Japanese families that controlled 75 percent of Japan's financial, industrial, and commercial business. In March 1948, George Kennan visited with General MacArthur in Tokyo to explain the necessity for promoting the interests of those upper-class Japanese who were friends of America. This required not economic reform but recovery. American business and banking officials also visited Tokyo to emphasize the same thing to MacArthur.

MacArthur quickly got the message. Previous decrees for the dissolution of 325 Japanese corporations under *zaibatsu* control ended after only nine had been broken up. MacArthur also had the Japanese government alter its labor laws to deny government workers the right to strike or to engage in collective bargaining. In June 1950, MacArthur purged 23 leaders of the Japanese Communist Party and other radical leaders. The May 12, 1949, order to end the removal of Japanese goods as reparations effectively ended all reparations for Japan. Reparations based on industrial equipment had stopped in 1948.

The Cold War dictated policy after 1948, as Washington deemed it desirable to build a strong Japan as a U.S. ally in Asia. By early 1949, most observers believed that Nationalist China's collapse appeared certain.

May 15, 1949

Communists gain control of the Hungarian government.

In the first postwar elections on November 3, 1945, the anti-Communist Smallholders Party won an absolute majority and Ferenc Nagy became premier. With Soviet backing, however, the Communists began a gradual purge of the Smallholders' leaders, accusing them of conspiracy. By early 1949, the Communists' National Independence front had purged Nagy and other Smallholders. Jószef Cardinal Mindszenty had been sentenced to life in prison but fled to asylum in the U.S. embassy, where he became a symbol of anti-Communist resistance. On May 15, 1949, a general election resulted in a complete Communist victory, with Istvan Dobi as premier and the real Communist boss, Mátyás Rákosi, as deputy premier.

June 14, 1949

The French government returns the Emperor Bao Dai to rule Vietnam.

In the Élysée Agreement of March 8, 1949, French President Vincent Auriol and Bao Dai agreed on the establishment of the independent State of Vietnam within the French Union. Paris continued to control matters of finance, trade, defense, foreign affairs, and internal security in Vietnam but agreed to recognize the southern province of Cochin China as part of a United Vietnam. Because Ho Chi Minh's forces continued to fight French forces, Paris hoped Bao Dai would provide a political solution to the war by symbolizing Vietnamese independence under French authority. Bao had few followers in Vietnam and further alienated himself by taking the title emperor as well as chief of state. Bao said the people could prepare a constitution in the future, after order was restored.

July 16, 1949

Chiang Kai-shek prepares retreat to Formosa.

Chiang formed a reorganized supreme council of the Nationalists. When the civil war renewed in 1946, Chiang's forces seemed to make notable advances, but throughout 1948, his corrupt and ineffective officers were not able to gain popular support, which was rallying to the Communists. On January 21, 1949, Chiang resigned as president and retreated to the southwest while Vice President Li Tsung-jen tried to persuade Mao to negotiate a truce. By July, Communist victory appeared certain. Thus, Chiang prepared to move to Formosa, claiming his followers would reconquer the mainland of China in the future.

August 5, 1949

To explain U.S. policy relating to Chiang Kai-shek's "loss of China," the State Department issues a white paper.

Consisting of 1,054 pages of documents and a lengthy introduction by Secretary of State Acheson, the volume's thesis was that the "loss of China...was beyond the control of the government of the United States." The consequences of the Chinese civil war resulted from "internal Chinese forces" and the inadequate policies of Chiang Kai-shek. The white paper marked a break in the bipartisan foreign policy fostered by Senator Vandenberg and the Roosevelt-Truman administrations.

Many conservative Republicans followed an "Asia-first" policy based strongly on support of Chiang Kai-shek's policies as rationalized by the so-called China lobby, whose leading proponent was the charming Madame Chiang. The Republican China bloc claimed the white paper was a "whitewash of a wishful, do-nothing policy" that placed all of Asia in danger of Soviet conquest. Their emphasis was on Moscow's monolithic control of all Communists and envisioned Mao's victory as a Soviet triumph. This limited vision ignored what should have been obvious—that all nationalists, including Mao, would object to domination by another outside power.

What was little understood at the time was that Mao was strongly suspicious of all Soviet moves. Others reacted differently to the white paper. Walter Lippmann, a well-known columnist, said the white paper failed to explain "Chiang's stronghold in American policy" for so long. John K. Fairbank, an expert on Chinese history who taught at Harvard, declared the volume was a frank admission that the United States "made the wrong approach to the problem of revolution in Asia." Nevertheless, the strongly partisan debate over the "loss of China" stimulated the rise of McCarthyism and rabid anti-Communism throughout the 1950s and, for some Americans, for the rest of the century.

August 10, 1949

The Department of Defense is established.

President Truman signed congressional legislation that renamed the national military establishment the Department of Defense. This act gave broader and more definite powers to the secretary of defense to coordinate the various branches of military service.

August 22, 1949

The "first use" of atomic weapons by U.S. forces is sanctioned in a recommendation of the Joint Chiefs of Staff (JCS).

Approved two weeks later by the National Security Council (NSC-57), the "first use" principle became part of a NATO defense plan integrating the use of atomic weapons into the war plan. Although the contingency war plan hoped the American nuclear umbrella would deter a Soviet attack on Western Europe, the plan permitted use of the atomic bomb if the Soviets invaded.

This JCS plan both promoted and required the May 1949 JCS request for additional funds to expand the production of atomic bombs. From a strategic viewpoint, the JCS action backed the air force's airborne delivery of atomic weapons, and rejected the navy's carrier plane attack method. The Air Force plan code-named OFF TACKLE was prepared during the summer of 1949. It proposed that aircraft, particularly the new B-36, would carry atomic bombs against the Soviet Union, the bomber being the nation's primary weapon. The U.S. navy advocated that "super-carriers" capable of launching planes with atomic bombs should be the first line of U.S. defense. During the fall of 1949, the navy was losing the status it had enjoyed before 1941. The JCS war plan denigrated the navy carrier-attack program, and Secretary of Defense Louis Johnson stopped construction of the super-carrier, the USS *United States*, claiming it was too costly.

In October 1949, U.S. navy officers, led by Chief of Naval Operations Admiral Louis Denfeld, staged a last-ditch "admirals' revolt" to protest against Johnson and the JCS plan. Taking their case to Congress, high-ranking naval leaders testified in opposition to the "air-atomic" strategy at hearings of the House

Armed Services Committee. The navy claimed air force bombers would not be able to sufficiently penetrate Soviet defenses. They also pointed out that if the bombers got through, the air force doctrine of saturation bombing with heavy civilian casualties would, as in World War II, not only fail to cause the enemy to surrender but would increase their "will to survive and resist." By using carrier-based bombers, the navy proposed defeating the enemy by hitting only military targets and Soviet forces. The October "admirals' revolt" lost.

Both Truman and Secretary of Defense Johnson favored the air-atomic strategy, and the coming of the H-bomb between 1950 and 1952 seemed to them to confirm that view. Soon after the conclusion of the October hearings, Truman removed Denfeld and other participants in the revolt from their high-level positions. However, with the subsequent development of nuclear-powered submarines capable of launching nuclear-tipped Polaris ballistic missiles, the navy played a significant role in deterrent strategy.

August 29, 1949

Soviet Union tests first atomic bomb.

This test was conducted in complete secrecy and the Soviets did not announce it had taken place. They were quite upset when President Truman announced that it had taken place.

See September 23, 1949.

September 2, 1949

The United Nations Commission on Korea announces that mediation has failed.

Since the United States had referred the Korean problem to the United Nations in September 1947, the commission had sought some means to unify the country and hold national elections. The commission was not, however, permitted by the Communists to operate north of 38th parallel. In 1948, the Republic of Korea was set up in South Korea (August 15), and the Korean People's Democratic Republic in North Korea (September 9). In respect of the U.N. Commission findings, both the Soviet Union (by December 25, 1948) and the United States (by June 29, 1949) withdrew their occupation forces. Nevertheless, the U.N. Commission could not persuade Kim Il Sung, the North's leader, and Syngman Rhee, the South's president, to work together to try to reach a satisfactory compromise.

September 15, 1949

The Reciprocal Trade Agreements Act is extended for two years.

This act renewed the Hull program of 1934, although Hull's original hope of lowering tariffs had been damaged since 1945 because the Republican Congress inserted "escape" clauses to allow certain American producers to get higher tariffs and to set an export control program designed to discriminate against the Communist bloc but that could also be used in trade with the "free" world.

September 23, 1949

A White House press release announces that the Soviet Union has detonated an atomic bomb.

The Soviets' successful explosion occurred on August 29, 1949. On September 9, AEC monitors detected excessive radioactivity coming from central Asia, and on September 14, samples of rainwater clouds confirmed this. U.S. intelligence estimated the samples were one month old and that the Soviets used a Nagasaki-type plutonium bomb. President Truman learned of this success on September 12. He and General Groves doubted the accuracy of the data; however, Groves believed that there was a nuclear accident in the Soviet Union. The intelligence data was certain and Truman released the information on August 23.

Soviet documents declassified in the 1990s disclose that the Soviets' 1949 bomb was an exact copy of the U.S. bomb tested in July 1945. For information on data given the Soviet Union by Klaus Fuchs and Theodore Hall, see Christopher Andrews *The Sword and the Shield: The Mitrokhin Archive* (1999).

September 27, 1949

The USSR repudiates its 1945 Treaty of Friendship with Yugoslavia.

This announcement from Moscow came following a lengthy dispute with Yugoslavia's ruler, Marshal Tito. While Tito claimed to follow Communist doctrine, he was a Yugoslav nationalist who rejected Moscow's attempt to control all Communist parties. This intraparty split persisted and "Titoism" became synonymous with the independence shown by some nationalistic Communists who followed policies in the best interests of their own nations and were often anti-Soviet.

October 1, 1949

Mao Tse-tung proclaims the creation of the People's Republic of China.

Mao became head of the Central People's Administrative Council. Chiang Kai-shek continued to claim to be the legitimate head of the Chinese government as he and his Nationalist followers moved their government to the island of Formosa.

Mao Tse-Tung. National Archives

October 7, 1949

The Soviet zone of Germany is established as the German Democratic Republic (GDR).

The Communist Party dominated the new government, with Wilhelm Pieck as president and Otto Grotewohl as minister president.

November 18, 1949

The Soviet Union and other Communist delegates challenge the right of China's Nationalist government to represent China in the United Nations and on the Security Council.

The issue of China's status was first considered by the Security Council in September 1949, when the Nationalist government charged that the USSR had interfered in Chinese affairs, and asked the United Nations to condemn Communist China and recommend that no U.N. member assist Mao's regime in Peking.

This caused the People's Republic to inform the secretary-general that the Nationalists had no right to continue to represent the Chinese people in the United Nations. The Nationalist Chinese retained their U.N. membership until October 25, 1971. France, Great Britain, and other nations had recognized the new Chinese government, but the United States had not. America continued to recognize the Chinese government on Formosa until, as Acheson stated on October 12, the new Peking government "met traditional American conditions." The United States did not finally recognize the People's Republic of China until 1979.

November 22, 1949

The Consultative Group and CoCom are created to enforce trade restrictions with Communist countries.

The Consultative Group and the Coordinating Committee for Multilateral Export Controls (CoCom) were created on November 22, 1949, and CoCom started operating on January 1, 1950. Although CoCom was a "gentlemen's agreement," in reality it functioned as an international treaty with binding effects on the participating nations. The origin of CoCom was veiled in secrecy, as was much of its operation. It was not really even an organization in the sense of a body or institution separate from its member governments; however, it maintained a small permanent staff in Paris where member nations coordinated policy regarding controlled or potentially controlled goods and technologies.

CoCom's committee consisted of delegates from all NATO countries (except Iceland) and was charged with coordinating policies restricting exports of potential strategic value to the Soviet Union, its Eastern bloc satellites, and the People's Republic of China between 1949 and 1994. Created in 1949, the committee not only reviewed military technology transfer for potential embargo but also tried to anticipate the end use of products manufactured for civilian purposes, such as computers and transistors. Unless

CoCom approval of a license request was granted, the export was prohibited. But the CoCom process did not include a mechanism for monitoring compliance by member nations or sanctions should a member nation appear to be acting in bad faith. The United States concluded bilateral accords with more than 50 nations concerning restrictions on trade with Communist nations.

For reasons including the disintegration of the Soviet Union and the goal of assisting economic and political reform in Russia and the newly independent states, the CoCom partners agreed in 1993 to end the Cold War regime effective March 31, 1994, and to work toward a new arrangement to enhance transparency and restraint in exporting conventional weapons and sophisticated technologies to countries whose behavior is cause for serious concern and to regions of potential instability. The successor regime to CoCom is the Wassenaar Arrangement on Export Controls for Conventional Arms and Dual-Use Goods and Technologies, which began operations in September 1996 and is headquartered in Vienna, Austria.

November 24, 1949

The U.S. consul at Mukden and 21 others are released after a year's confinement.

Angus Ward, the U.S. consul at Mukden, Manchuria, had been held incommunicado by the Chinese Communists since November 20, 1948. During that time, the U.S. State Department possessed little knowledge of the exact situation at Mukden, although U.S. diplomats in other Chinese cities hoped the problem would be resolved as soon as the civil war ended in China. Mukden had been the first city with foreign consulates captured by the Communists. The advances of Mao's armies had proceeded rapidly during the next nine months, and on October 1, they controlled all China. During this time, the U.S. State Department and President Truman considered a variety of measures to free Ward and the other 21 persons held at the Mukden consulate. On April 26, Secretary Acheson instructed Oliver Clubb, the U.S. consul general in Peking, to inform the Communist government that unless it removed the arbitrary restrictions on the Mukden consulate, the United States would close the Mukden office and withdraw its staff. Mao's government did not respond, and on May 17, Acheson notified Clubb that the Mukden consulate should be closed.

Somehow, Acheson's May 17 order to close the Mukden consulate was delivered to Ward on June 7. On June 10, Ward sent a telegram to Clubb in Peking, saying he was trying to evacuate his staff. Ward's hopes proved to be premature. On June 19, the Chinese Communist press reported that its Mukden consulate had been discovered to contain a major U.S. spy operation against the Chinese people. Both Ward in Mukden and the U.S. embassy in Nanking refuted the spy charges. Nevertheless, Ward's plan to evacuate the consulate at Mukden was delayed by the Communist authorities. Ward's continued detention led President Truman to consider harsher measures in October 1949, when two events raised questions in Washington.

First, on October 1, China's Foreign Office asked all foreign representatives in China to recognize the Communist government. Concerned about the status of its crown colony of Hong Kong, Great Britain wanted to recognize the new regime as soon as possible. Concerned about its war in Indochina, France preferred to delay recognition. The United States believed it could not establish relations with Mao's regime until the Ward affair was settled. These considerations prompted the U.S. State Department to begin a diplomatic "offensive," asking all foreign representatives to withhold recognition until Ward was released. China, Acheson said, must demonstrate it could protect diplomatic officials.

The second event in October seemed to be the more serious. On October 24, Ward and four members of his staff were arrested by the Communists for allegedly directing a mob that attacked a Chinese worker. As Ward later explained, the trumped-up assault charges resulted from his attempt to escort from the consulate a Chinese messenger, Ji Yutteng, who had been fired from the consulate staff. Because Ji refused to leave, there was a scuffle in which Ji and his brother were injured. Ward's arrest caused an angry reaction in America, where Truman's administration was already under attack for not adequately supporting Chiang Kai-shek.

As a result, between October 31 and November 18, Truman explored the possibility of either a blockade of China or military action to liberate Ward and his staff. The Joint Chiefs of Staff and General Omar Bradley, its chairman, advised Truman that military action would be difficult and might lead to a global war. A blockade, they advised, would not be effective. Secretary Acheson's diplomatic offensive seemed to be the best option. At a news conference on November

16, Acheson stated that the United States could not consider recognition until the Americans at Mukden were released. China's desire for diplomatic recognition by foreign governments may have been the reason that the Mukden affair suddenly ended on November 24. The precise reasons for China's action on November 20, 1948, and on November 24, 1949, are unclear. On the latter date, Ward called Clubb in Peking, reporting that he and his four codefendants had been found guilty of the charges against them. They were to be deported, however, in lieu of imprisonment. Within a month, on December 12, Ward and the others who had been confined at Mukden left China on the liner *Lakeland Victory.*

Why the Mukden incident arose is not certain. The best evaluation seems to be that of William N. Stokes, who, as the vice consul at Mukden, had been confined with Ward. Stokes believed that because Mao's civil-war propaganda had denounced the United States and other Western powers for aiding Chiang Kai-shek, and because Mukden was the first contact that Communist authorities and troops had with Western representatives, the hostility of Mao's armies to the West caused the Mukden affair. A year later, the Chinese Communists desired Western recognition; hence the change in China's attitude at Mukden on November 24, 1949. One consequence of the Mukden affair may have been the U.S. nonrecognition of the People's Republic of China for the next 30 years. Indications are that in 1948–1949, the United States was ready to join the British in accepting the new Chinese government. The Mukden crisis delayed recognition by Washington. Furthermore, the arrest of Ward in October 1949 further inflamed U.S. feelings against China, making it difficult for Truman to grant recognition.

December 1, 1949

The U.N. General Assembly adopts a U.S.-British-sponsored "Essentials of Peace" resolution.

The "Essentials of Peace" proposal was the U.S.-British answer to a Soviet-sponsored U.N. resolution against the North Atlantic Treaty Alliance. On September 29, the General Assembly agreed to consider a USSR resolution titled "Condemnation of the preparations for a new war and conclusion of a five-power pact for the strengthening of peace." Without specifically citing the Atlantic pact, the Soviets claimed that the Anglo-American bloc followed an aggressive policy to isolate the Soviets from European politics. They stated this was contrary to the U.N. Charter and that the Big Five powers should handle basic issues of world peace.

The U.S. delegation decided to submit the "Essentials of Peace" resolution as a substitute motion that eventually passed the General Assembly on December 1 by a vote of 53 to 5. The "peace" resolution affirmed the principles of the U.N. Charter and asked all members to cooperate to ease world tensions. The key clause stated the U.S.-British contention that peace was endangered by the Soviet Union's frequent use of the veto power in the Security Council. This clause called on the five powers to show cooperation and "to exercise restraint in the use of the veto" so that the Security Council could act effectively to maintain peace.

December 27, 1949

Indonesia is granted sovereignty by the Netherlands.

Following the Japanese evacuation of the East Indies in 1945, the Republic of Indonesia, which declared independence on August 17, and the Netherlands, which desired to reclaim its colonial ownership, had clashed in war and endeavored to negotiate. After intermittent periods of fighting, the Netherlands, on the urging of the United States, agreed to a settlement concluded with the aid of the United Nations Good Offices Committee. The Indonesian leader in the independence movement was Achmed Sukarno.

During the Cold War, Indonesia would initially avoid a direct alliance with either superpower, but would identify with the neutralist nations.

December 28, 1949

National Security Council document NSC 48/1 indicates Southeast Asia is a vital area for the United States.

This document, which was classified secret until the Pentagon Papers were published in 1971, indicates that important personnel of the State and Defense Departments, probably Paul Nitze and Dean Acheson, believed even before the Korean War that U.S. interests in Indochina needed to be protected from Communism. NSC 48/1 read in part: "The extension of communist authority in China represents a grievous political defeat for us. If southeast Asia also is swept by communism we shall have suffered a major political rout the repercussions of which will be felt throughout the rest of the world."

Thus, Mao's victory in China caused the NSC to believe Indochina was the next objective of Communism. Notably, no one in the NSC seems to have realized the historic tradition of fierce antagonism between China and Vietnam, a fact on which all scholars of Vietnamese history and politics agreed.

1950

January 12, 1950

Secretary of State Acheson describes a "perimeter strategy" for east Asia.

Speaking at the National Press Club, Secretary of State Dean Acheson explained how the U.S. Asian strategy was to control large land areas, such as China, by controlling the surrounding sea perimeter extending in a crescent shape from India to Japan. Acheson described this strategy to persuade Congress to pass the Korean Aid Bill for 1949–1950, to answer Republican complaints that Truman did not do enough to help the Chinese Nationalists, and, above all, to sow seeds of distrust between Mao and Stalin.

Acheson said he did not expect a Chinese-Soviet alliance to last long because Mao did not want Moscow to dominate China. Unlike Eastern Europe, Soviet troops did not occupy China after World War II. Knowing that Mao was in the Moscow meetings with Stalin, Acheson argued that China would find the United States its best friend in keeping the country independent. Acheson's remarks sought to divide Mao and Stalin, declaring that the Soviets were acting to annex parts of China by a "process that is complete in outer Mongolia... [and] nearly complete in Manchuria," as well as repeating the U.S. hands-off policy for Taiwan. The secretary also recognized U.S. responsibility for economic aid to Korea, Taiwan, and Japan but believed the greatest U.S. threat was a Chinese attack west of the perimeter. (Congress passed the aid bill on February 10.) He also indicated the Communists would use "subversion and penetration" to influence Asia, tactics that would be difficult for the Western Powers to deal with because of anticolonial movements in Asia.

Although January 1950 news reports hardly mentioned the Korean parts of Acheson's speech, after the Korean War began on June 27, Republican opponents such as Senator Joseph McCarthy claimed Acheson's speech gave the Communists a "green light" to attack South Korea. In contrast to McCarthy's claim, Bruce Cummins's analysis in *The Origins of the Korean War* (1990) demonstrates Acheson assumed the United States must defend both Korea and Japan but hoped to disrupt Chinese-Soviet relations. Those interested in the consequences of Acheson's speech should also consult *Uncertain Partners: Stalin, Mao and the Korean War* (1993), by Sergei N. Goncharov, John W. Lewis, and Xue Litai, especially the translation of the Chinese Xinhua Agency dispatch of January 20 criticizing Acheson's speech as "shameless slander."

January 13, 1950

Soviet delegate Jacob Malik walks out of a Security Council session, beginning a seven-month Soviet boycott of U.N. meetings.

Moscow's decision to walk out of the Security Council followed the failure of a motion to expel the Chinese Nationalists from the United Nations. The vote was 6 to 3 against the motion (Great Britain and Norway abstained). Although the Soviets appeared adamantly in favor of the Peking government, U.N. observers such as British delegate Sir Alexander Colgan believed the Soviet Union preferred to impede admission of Mao's government to the United Nations to more effectively dominate the People's Republic. By preventing further debate on the China issue after the first vote, Moscow's boycott kept China out of the United Nations. The boycott continued until August 1, 1950.

January 21, 1950

Alger Hiss is convicted of perjury on two counts of false testimony before a grand jury of New York state.

Hiss was convicted for two statements he made to the grand jury: (1) he had not turned over any secret, confidential, or restricted documents to Whittaker Chambers in 1938, and (2) he definitely said he had not seen Chambers after January 1, 1937, whereas he had seen and conversed with Chambers in February and March 1938. Hiss had been an active New Dealer who worked for the Nye Investigation Committee in the early 1930s and for the State Department. During

World War II, he helped plan the foundation of the United Nations and in this capacity was present at the Yalta Conference of February 1945.

Chambers first called attention to Hiss in 1948, during hearings of the House Un-American Activities Committee (HUAC), where, as an ex-Communist, Chambers became a star witness. Chambers claimed he had known Hiss from 1934 to 1938 as a member of a special underground group in the U.S. Communist Party. Before HUAC, the House Un-American Activities Committee, and later the grand jury, Hiss denied having been a member of such a Communist group. He also denied having given Chambers any confidential State Department data. The chief interrogator of Hiss during the HUAC hearings was Congressman Richard Nixon. Two trials became necessary to convict Hiss. In the first trial, the jury could not reach a verdict (July 8, 1949). The second trial began on November 17, 1949; the jury found him guilty on both counts on January 21.

The precise nature of Hiss's trial and conviction was generally lost on the public, who conceived of Hiss as a Communist spy whose influence aided the Soviet Union during and after World War II. When friends of Hiss, such as Dean Acheson, refused to believe Chambers's testimony and accepted evidence that contradicted Chambers, the critics of Truman and Acheson alleged that this was further evidence of Communist infiltration of the State Department. The U.S. Supreme Court rejected Hiss's petition to review the conviction, and he went to prison from March 22, 1950, until November 1954.

Hiss continued to profess his innocence, but post–Cold War revelations from Soviet archives of its military intelligence group, the GRU, confirm that Hiss spied for the Soviets at various times after 1934. Details about his espionage are given in six books reviewed by Thomas Powers in the May 11, 2000, issue of the *New York Review of Books.*

January 24, 1950

British atomic physicist Klaus Fuchs confesses to being a Soviet spy.

Fuchs was a division chief of theoretical physics in the British atomic program at Harwell. He confessed to giving the Soviets data about American activity at Oak Ridge, Tennessee, and Los Alamos, New Mexico. On March 1, 1950, English courts convicted him of espionage, sentencing him to 14 years in prison. Fuchs's confession led to charges against Harry Gold and, subsequently, Julius and Ethel Rosenberg.

January 31, 1950

President Truman announces the decision to hasten development of the hydrogen bomb.

This decision ended intensive debate within the administration about building the superbomb, which offered far more destructive capability than the A-bomb. David Lilienthal and George Kennan wanted the United States to renounce the first use of any atomic bomb and to actively seek international control. Advocates of the H-bomb included General Omar Bradley, the chairman of the Joint Chiefs, and the physicist Edward Teller. Surprised by news of the Soviet atomic test in 1949 and convinced of the Soviets' desire to expand its empire, President Truman gave little thought to abandoning the development of the H-bomb. Clearly, by 1950 the H-bomb had come to be seen as a winning, therefore necessary, weapon for America to possess.

February 7, 1950

The United States recognizes Bao Dai's government of Vietnam.

At the same time, the United States recognized the governments of Vietnam, Laos, and Cambodia as "associated states within the French union." Laos had been made a free state in the French Union in 1946 under King Norodom Sihanouk. In the fall of 1949, France gave *de jure* independence to Cambodia but, as in the case of Vietnam, controlled its defense, foreign affairs, and internal security. Bao Dai's government had been established with French help in 1949, in the hope that Bao could gain a following to counteract Vietminh influence in Vietnam. Bao, who had spent much of his life in France and obviously preferred Paris to Saigon, was an unfortunate and unsuccessful choice.

February 9, 1950

Senator Joseph McCarthy charges that many Communist spies have infiltrated the State Department.

McCarthy's first accusations came during a speech at Wheeling, West Virginia, when he said 205 Communists held high, influential positions in the State

Senator Joseph McCarthy. Harry S. Truman Library

Department. He continued to make similar charges in other speeches, giving the number of spies variously as 57, 81, 205, or 11. Apparently McCarthy's charges were intended to help his 1950 senatorial campaign in Wisconsin, but they also became a simple way for friends of Chiang Kai-shek's government to blame the Chinese Nationalist loss on "reds" in the State Department who had allegedly "sold China down the river." Regardless of how vague, incorrect, or false, McCarthy's charges found a receptive audience—an audience conceived in Truman's March 1947 "scare the hell out of them" speech and nourished with the evidence of Soviet expansion in "East Europe and China," and the Soviet explosion of an atomic bomb in 1949.

The years from 1950 to 1954 may be called the "Era of McCarthyism" to denote the near-hysterical anti-Communist emotions affecting large segments of U.S. society and, ultimately, its foreign policy. Politicians feared to deny or denounce the Wisconsin senator, lest they be accused of being "soft" on Communism. Even President Truman and Dean Acheson, in spite of their efforts to initiate America's anti-Communist containment program, fell victim to McCarthyism. Their denials of McCarthy's charges were often not accepted by many Americans.

February 14, 1950

Stalin-Mao talks end with an alliance and the Soviets recognizing Ho Chi Minh's regime.

The day after Mao Tse-tung (Mao Zedong) created the People's Republic of China on October 1, 1949, the Soviet Union was the first state to recognize the People's Republic. Nevertheless, Stalin refused Mao's request to abolish the Soviet Union's 1945 Friendship treaty by which the Stalin recognized Chiang Kai-shek's regime. (See August 14, 1945.)

After Stalin's refusal, Mao's first order of business with the Soviet Union was to obtain a new treaty with the Soviet Union to replace the 1945 treaty. On October 20, Mao appointed Wang Jiaxian as Ambassador to the Soviet Union and began meeting with Chou En-lai to plan a summit meeting with Stalin that could replace the 1945 treaty and promote the recognition of Ho Chi Minh's Vietnamese government. In early November, Mao met with Politburo members of China's Communist Party (CCP) and they agreed on three main points for dealing with Stalin. First, negotiations in Moscow would obtain a new treaty to replace the "humiliating" Sino-Soviet treaty of 1945. Second as Premier of China and Foreign Minster, Chou En-lai would negotiate the details of the new treaty. Third, Mao would visit Moscow in December to celebrate Stalin's birthday and to obtain Stalin's consent for a treaty while Chou would not go to Moscow unless Stalin agreed with Mao, a tactic designed to prevent a split in Chinese-Soviet relations. In line with this decision, the CCP Central Committee sent a cable to Ambassador Wang, instructing him to tell Stalin that Mao planned to visit Moscow in December 1949.

On December 6, Mao boarded a train in Beijing that reached Moscow on December 16. When Mao arrived at Moscow's train station, Foreign Minister Molotov and General Bulganin met him to hold an arrival ceremony before driving him to a dacha in the suburbs of Moscow. The next day, Mao met with Stalin at his Kremlin office where he informed Stalin that his main item of business was to negotiate a treaty to replace the obsolete 1945 friendship treaty. Initially, Stalin rejected Mao's request, saying a new treaty would jeopardize the 1945 Yalta agreement with Roosevelt and Churchill. (See February 11, 1945.)

During the next four days, Mao's only meetings were with Soviet Ambassador to China R.V. Roshchin regarding Japan's Communist Party and with Stalin's Proconsul Ivan Vladimirovich Kovalev regarding future talks with Stalin on a friendship treaty. Mao bluntly told Kovalev that Stalin must either accept quality discussions on a new treaty with details worked out by Chou En-lai or inform Mao there would be no new treaty, in which case Chou would not need to come to Moscow. Instead, Mao and Stalin could simply discuss the status of Burma, Vietnam, and other areas of Southeast Asia. Either way, Mao said he wanted to meet with Stalin on December 23 or 24.

On December 21, Mao attended Stalin's birthday celebration but there were no discussions about treaties or other official business. At the birthday party, Stalin honored Mao by setting next to him and the event went well. Next Stalin met with Mao on December 23, 25, and 30 but Stalin would only discuss minor issues such as agreeing that Soviet professors would visit Beijing as instructors at the People's University. In part, Kovalev was responsible for Stalin's reluctance. On December 24, Kovalev gave Stalin a report that was highly critical of CCP policies on trade and relations with Western European countries, implying that Mao could not be trusted. During this time, the Western press had spread rumors that Mao was being mistreated in Moscow and might even be under house arrest. To correct this image on January 2, 1950, Stalin agreed Mao could have an interview with the Soviets' Tass, to dispel the rumors. On January 2, Mao told the Tass reporter that the problems he faced with were the Sino-Soviet Treaty (of 1945), a trade treaty, and a Soviet loan to the People's Republic. When asked how long he would be in Moscow, Mao replied that depended upon having meaningful discussions about the pending issues with the Soviet Union.

Mao's interview brought a quick response from Stalin who had Molotov visit to ask about his concerns. Mao replied by saying, as he did previously to Kovalev, that Stalin must either begin substantial discussions on a new treaty in which case Chou would come to Moscow to work out details or agree there would be no new treaty while simply discussing issues about Southeast Asia. The next day, Mao was informed new treaty negotiations could begin as soon as Chou En-lai arrived in Moscow. Chou arrived in Moscow on January 20 and the treaty was signed on February 14, 1950. Formally, the document was called the Treaty of Friendship, Alliance and Mutual Assistance. The 30-year treaty included provisions for a $300 million Soviet loan to the People's Republic that would enhance China's military capabilities.

Meanwhile, Mao was concerned about Stalin's willingness to recognize the new Vietnamese government of Ho Chi Minh. On January 18, Mao officially granted recognition to Ho's government. Mao also had China's Ministry of Foreign Affairs tell Moscow about Vietnam's request for recognition. Stalin agreed and on January 31 the Soviet Union granted recognition to Ho Chi Minh's government. These and other details of the negotiations are in the 1993 book *Uncertain Partners* by Sergei Goncharov, John W. Lewis, and Xue Litai, published by Stanford University Press.

NSC-68 is presented to the National Security Council.

Drafted by Paul H. Nitze, director of the State Department's Planning Staff, NSC-68 was a secret document depicting the Soviets as aggressively seeking to conquer the world. It declared that America's "fundamental purpose is to assure the integrity and vitality of our free society, which is founded upon the dignity and worth of the individual." However, the

> design of those who control the Soviet Union and the international communist movement is to retain and solidify their absolute power, first in the Soviet Union and second in the areas now under their control. In the minds of the Soviet leaders, however, achievement of this design requires the dynamic extension of their authority and the ultimate elimination of any effective opposition to their authority.... The Kremlin regards the United States as the only major threat to the achievement of its fundamental design. There is a basic conflict between the idea of freedom under a government of laws, and the idea of slavery under the grim oligarchy of the Kremlin, which has come to a crisis with the polarization of power...and the exclusive possession of atomic weapons by the two protagonists. The idea of freedom, moreover, is peculiarly and intolerably subversive of the idea of slavery. But the converse is not true. The implacable purpose of the slave state to eliminate the challenge of freedom has placed the two great powers at opposite poles. It is this

fact which gives the present polarization of power the quality of crisis.

To counteract the Communists, NSC-68 advocated a greatly enlarged U.S. and European military force, as well as a diplomatic and psychological offensive, to roll back previous Soviet expansion.

> For us the role of military power is to serve the national purpose by deterring an attack upon us while we seek by other means to create an environment in which our free society can flourish, and by fighting, if necessary, to defend the integrity and vitality of our free society and to defeat any aggressor. The Kremlin uses Soviet military power to back up and serve the Kremlin design. It does not hesitate to use military force aggressively if that course is expedient in the achievement of its design. The differences between our fundamental purpose and the Kremlin design, therefore, are reflected in our respective attitudes toward and use of military force.

Consequently, NSC-68 sought to define the ramifications of the "containment" policy:

> it is one which seeks by all means short of war to (1) block further expansion of Soviet power, (2) expose the falsities of Soviet pretensions, (3) induce a retraction of the Kremlin's control and influence, and (4) in general, so foster the seeds of destruction within the Soviet system that the Kremlin is brought at least to the point of modifying its behavior to conform to generally accepted international standards.
>
> It was and continues to be cardinal in this policy that we possess superior overall power in ourselves or in dependable combination with other like-minded nations. One of the most important ingredients of power is military strength. In the concept of "containment", the maintenance of a strong military posture is deemed to be essential for two reasons: (1) as an ultimate guarantee of our national security and (2) as an indispensable backdrop to the conduct of the policy of "containment." Without superior aggregate military strength, in being and readily mobilizable, a policy of "containment"—which is in effect a policy of calculated and gradual coercion—is no more than a policy of bluff.

Nitze's document argued that the United States could afford a large buildup of conventional forces without new taxes or crippling inflation if it shifted some production to nonconsumer goods. Conventional forces would make the United States less dependent on nuclear forces if the Soviets attacked, as NSC-68 predicted they might be prepared to do in 1954. In addition, while a U.S. nuclear arsenal would deter the Soviets from using nuclear weapons, the large conventional forces would be more available against Soviet "piecemeal aggression" and limited wars with other countries.

When the Korean War broke out in June 1950, President Truman had reviewed but not approved the defense costs envisioned by NSC-68. Whether or not Congress would have agreed to such a huge defense buildup became an academic question because the war required a defense increase for all branches of the armed forces. Both before and after NSC-68 was declassified on February 27, 1975, the document has been criticized by many U.S. policy analysts for militarizing foreign policy, upsetting the economy, and being developed for one moment in history. Instead it influenced more than 30 years of U.S. policy.

May 25, 1950

Tripartite Arms Declaration seeks to regulate arms traffic in Middle East.

Great Britain, France, and the United States, the three dominant powers in the Middle East immediately after World War II, sought to regulate the amount of armaments being transferred into the Middle East. Their declaration was built on the temporary U.N. arms embargo during the first Arab-Israeli war from May 29, 1947 to August 11, 1949. Since they were the primary arms suppliers to the region, they established the Near Eastern Arms Coordinating Committee to regulate their weapons deliveries in an effort to prevent an arms race between Israel and the Arab states.

There were two major flaws in the program: their regulating of the amount of arms drew severe criticism from the Arab countries; and it excluded one major possible arms merchant. These flaws meant that when the Soviet Union, using Czechoslovakia as its middleman, brokered an arms deal with Egypt in 1955, the informal agreement dissolved. Shortly, the Soviet Union's clients included Syria, Iraq, and Egypt and a regional arms race was underway. Between 1956

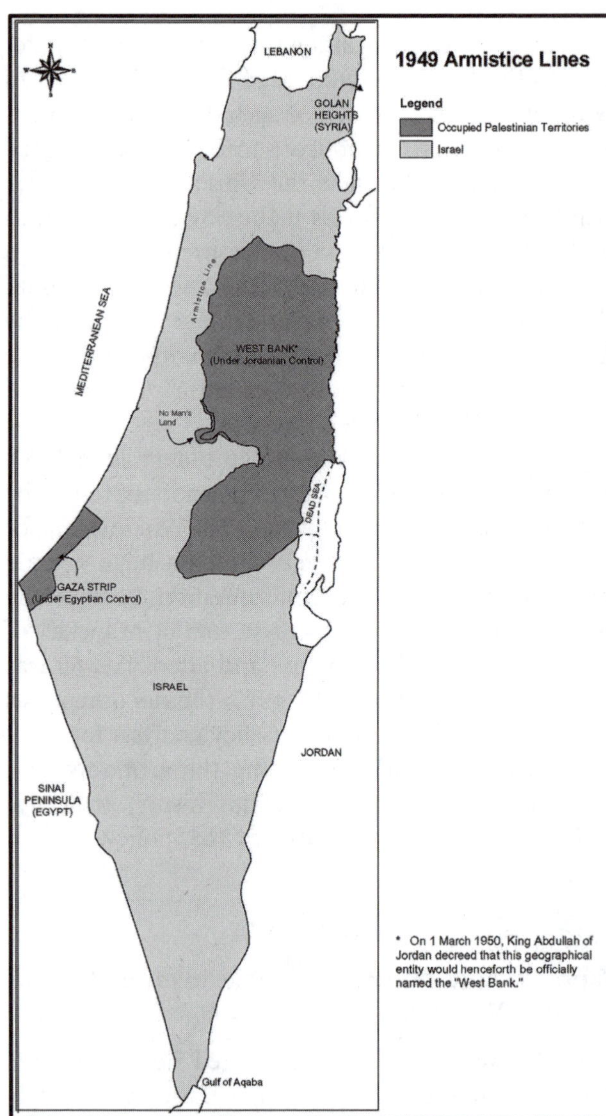

and 1958, Moscow did on one occasion suggest that the four powers stop shipping arms to the region; but the proposal was rejected by the Western nations.

June 5, 1950

President Truman signs his third foreign aid bill, granting nearly $3 billion for the European Recovery Plan and the Point Four Program.

Following Secretary of State George Marshall's June 1947 call for the United States to assist Europe's economic recovery, President Truman asked Congress for several types of foreign aid programs. In December 1947, Congress approved funds for interim aid to European countries. Next, on March 31, 1948, Congress approved the basic economic aid for the European Recovery Program known as the Marshall Plan. Truman's third request for foreign economic aid was passed by Congress on June 5, 1950, allowing $3 billion to be used for the Marshall Plan as well as the Point Four Program. Further economic aid for Europe continued until 1952. Michael L. Hogan's *The Marshall Plan* (1987) provides complete details for the U.S. financial aid programs.

June 25, 1950

North Korean forces attack South Korea.

Because a U.N. commission was present in South Korea, North Korea was readily identified as the aggressor in crossing the 38th parallel. In the Security Council, the Soviet boycott facilitated action because the USSR could not veto council measures. Consequently, after North Korea rejected a Security Council order to withdraw, President Truman ordered U.S. forces in Japan to support South Korean forces (June 26). The next day, the Security Council asked U.N. members to assist South Korea in defeating the aggressor (June 27).

On June 30, Truman ordered U.S. ground troops into the fighting in South Korea, and on July 7, the Security Council agreed that U.N. troops would fight under a commander designated by the United States. President Truman appointed General Douglas MacArthur as the commanding general of U.N. forces in Korea. Despite his U.N. designation, MacArthur took orders from Washington, not from the United Nations. Truman and the State Department favored the concept of a unified war effort, but they acted unilaterally in directing military and diplomatic policies in Korea. Sixteen nations sent troops to assist in Korea, with the United States providing 50 percent of the ground force (South Korea provided most of the other 50 percent), 86 percent of the naval power, and 93 percent of the air power.

After 1980, documents from Soviet and Chinese Communist files revealed more about North Korea's decision to invade South Korea. Although in 1950 President Truman asserted the invasion was part of Stalin's expansion of Communism, recent documents show that Kim Il Sung initiated plans to unify Korea while Stalin and Mao Tse-tung were finally persuaded to help North Korea. Kim told Stalin that Communist guerrillas would rise up in South Korea and enable Kim's forces to unify Korea before the United States

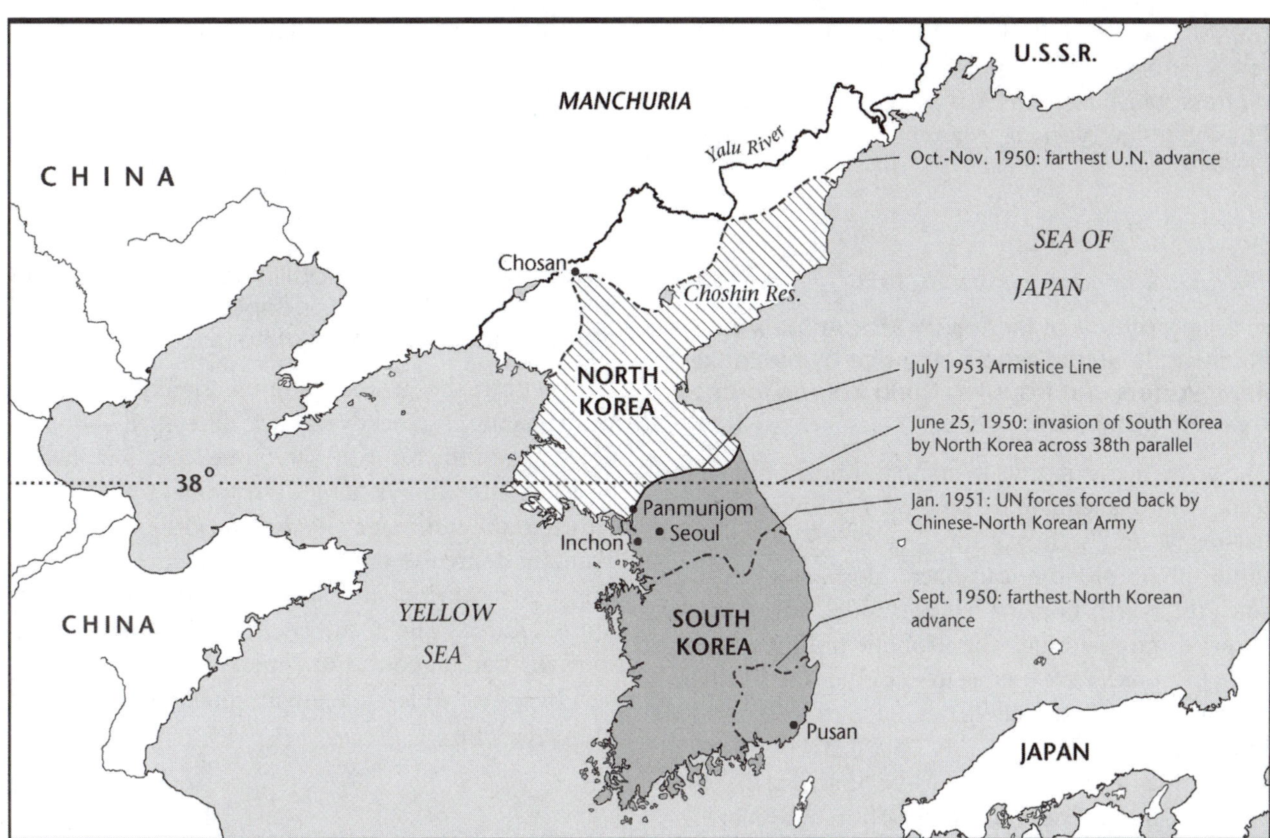

Korea: Early 1950s

could respond. Although there were guerrilla actions, these failed to turn the tide.

Not only was Moscow caught off-guard because it was boycotting sessions of the United Nations and had no delegate to veto U.N. Security Council action but by mid-July, Kim's forces were stalled at Pusan by U.S. soldiers who arrived to help South Korea.

In brief, Stalin was not attempting to expand in East Asia; his main concern was Europe, where in 1948 the Soviet Union lost control of Yugoslavia while NATO was organized to defend Western Europe from any Moscow-inspired aggression.

July 20, 1950

Senator McCarthy's charges that Communists have infiltrated the State Department are found to be untrue by a special Senate subcommittee chaired by Senator Millard Tydings.

McCarthy did not stop his speeches, however, but continued to level accusations against the Truman administration. Soon after the committee report, McCarthy named Owen Lattimore as the "top Russian espionage agent" in the United States. Lattimore was a professor at Johns Hopkins University who frequently served as a consultant to the State Department on affairs of China and Mongolia. When asked to verify his charges against Lattimore, McCarthy said President Truman kept his evidence locked up in the loyalty files. The Tydings Committee then conducted an investigation that cleared Lattimore of McCarthy's charges.

Nevertheless, the Tydings Committee received less attention than Senator McCarthy. Fear and suspicion came to infect many avenues of American life, an emotional atmosphere suited to the irrational accusations of the senator, not to reasoned efforts at response from his critics.

August 30, 1950

The United States and the Philippines sign a mutual assistance pact.

This treaty extended and implemented legislation of 1946. Its three major clauses were (1) a Trading Act to continue free trade until 1954 before a gradual imposition of U.S. tariffs; (2) a Rehabilitation Act to give economic aid to the Philippines; and (3) a military assistance act, which included U.S. bases in the Philippines as well as equipment for the Filipino armed forces.

September 15, 1950

A daring attack at Inchon by MacArthur's forces finally halts North Korea's offensive by outflanking the invaders and trapping North Korean forces in a pincer movement.

The first American units to arrive in Korea from Japan were lacking adequate firepower, were far from combat-ready, and were far too few. Consequently, the initial phase of American operations was disastrous since the North Koreans had the added advantage of surprise and planning. The Republic of Korea (ROK) and U.S. forces were unable to stem the North's offensive and were ultimately driven back to the so-called Pusan perimeter. The U.N. September offensive soon drove the North Koreans back across the 38th parallel—the border between South and North—raising serious political questions: (1) Should North Korea be liberated from Communist control? (2) Should the U.N. objective be only to contain North Korea at the 38th parallel?

September 23, 1950

Congress adopts the McCarran Internal Security Bill over President Truman's veto.

This law required members of the Communist Party and Communist front organizations to register with the attorney general. Indirectly, such registration would self-incriminate a person because the Smith Act of 1940 made it a crime to belong to any group advocating the violent overthrow of the government. The McCarran Act also allowed deportation of aliens who were Communists and gave the government broad jurisdiction to detain persons in time of war.

Truman vetoed the bill on September 20, arguing that it was a confused measure and would not work properly. But the nation's hysterical anti-Communist mood persuaded most politicians to support the bill. In the House, whose members faced an election in November, the president's veto was overridden after only one hour of discussion. In the Senate, Hubert Humphrey and Paul Douglas conducted a 22-hour filibuster but failed to convince their colleagues to uphold Truman's veto.

October 7, 1950

A U.N. General Assembly resolution desires to "ensure conditions of stability throughout Korea," and calls for a "unified, independent and democratic government of Korea."

Both within the Truman administration and at the United Nations, controversy had developed about the objectives of the Korean War. Some leaders wished to be lenient to Kim Il Sung's government and simply return to the *status quo ante bellum.* Others, including Truman, desired to cross the 38th parallel, overthrow Kim's government, and stage "free elections" for a united Korea. The October 7 U.N. resolution was somewhat ambiguous, but appeared to favor unification of Korea. At least, Truman initially interpreted it in this fashion.

October 15, 1950

President Truman and General MacArthur meet at Wake Island.

Since July 1950, Truman and MacArthur had disagreed about using Chiang Kai-shek's forces against either North Korea or mainland China. MacArthur especially irritated the president by sending a message to the Veterans of Foreign Wars convention, in which he called the efforts to restrain Chiang's forces an "appeasement" of Communism.

At Wake Island, Truman reviewed U.S. policy for MacArthur, including the desire to protect Formosa but not to use Nationalist armed forces against the People's Republic of China.

November 3, 1950

A "uniting for peace" resolution is passed by the U.N. General Assembly.

This action gave the assembly the right to recommend collective security measures to U.N. members if the use of the veto in the Security Council prevented U.N. action. In effect, this resolution weakened the Big Powers' veto, not only for the Soviets but also for the United States. At the time, however, the U.S.

General Douglas MacArthur. National Archives

delegation believed it had sufficient influence to control the votes of the assembly and that some method for collective action was needed to bypass the USSR's frequent use of the veto power.

November 4, 1950

The United Nations rescinds a 1946 resolution condemning Spain's Fascist government—Franco joins the West's anti-Communist coalition.

This action reversed not only past U.N. policy but also U.S. policy. In 1945, the United States, Britain, and France opposed Spain's membership in the United Nations, and in 1946 they appealed to the Spanish people to end Francisco Franco's dictatorship. By 1950, U.S. efforts to unite all non-Communists against the Soviet Union caused a shift in policy. This first became evident when Congress approved $62.5 million in Marshall Plan loans to Spain on September 6, 1950.

The U.N. action on November 4, 1950, prepared the way for Spain's admission to the Western anti-Communist camp. It removed a U.N. resolution of December 11, 1946, that had excluded Spain from all U.N. activity. Several Latin American countries sponsored the resolution to rescind previous action against Spain. The action permitted Spain to participate in special agencies of the United Nations; full U.N. membership for Spain was approved on October 14, 1955.

November 7, 1950

Congressional elections reduce the Democratic majority in both houses of Congress.

Senator McCarthy's activity played a role in this election, with his proponents helping Republicans to win at least three Senate seats: John M. Butler defeated McCarthy's nemesis, Millard Tydings of Maryland; Everett Dirksen won over Majority Leader Scott Lucas of Illinois; and Richard Nixon defeated Helen Gahagan Douglas in California. Altogether, the Democrats lost 5 Senate seats and 28 House seats. The issue of Communism and how to contain the Soviet Union had become significant issues in U.S. politics.

November 26, 1950

Chinese Communist forces launch a massive counteroffensive against U.N. troops in the Yalu river valley.

After the United Nations passed a resolution on October 7 supporting the unification of Korea, China denounced the U.N. decision. As Chen Jian's research in the 1990s disclosed, China began preparing to help North Korea in July 1950 because Mao Tse-tung wanted to drive all U.S. forces out of the Korean peninsula to expand the Communist revolution in East Asia.

By early September, North Korea's armies had nearly achieved this objective, but on September 15 U.S. forces launched an invasion at Inchon and captured Seoul. In October, U.N. forces crossed the 38th parallel and some reached the Yalu River on China's border before Chinese "volunteers" joined North Korea in a counteroffensive. On November 24, General MacArthur ordered an "end-the-war by Christmas" offensive that failed because it inspired an offensive by massive numbers of Chinese troops. The "surprise" Chinese winter intervention

Astonished Marines, who have pushed back a surprise Chinese Communist attack, hear they are to withdraw. National Archives

shattered U.N. forces and forced them to retreat below the 38th parallel. The Communist armies again captured Seoul on January 4, 1951. U.S. and South Korean forces did not reoccupy Seoul until March 14, 1951.

December 18, 1950

Brussels conference of NATO's foreign ministers approves plans for the defense of Western Europe.

The next day, the ministers named General Dwight D. Eisenhower as supreme commander of the North Atlantic forces. The foreign ministers' action finalized NATO plans that had been under preparation since October 1949. The military plan's important sections were as follows: (1) the United States had responsibility to use atomic weapons if necessary to defend NATO nations; (2) a "Forward Strategy" provided for the defense of Germany as far east as possible; (3) sea control would be the duty of the U.S., British, and French fleets; and (4) Western European aircraft would have defensive and short-range bombing responsibilities.

To increase NATO's forces, the United States proposed forming 10 divisions of German troops as part of the defense effort. Adoption of the plan raised two vital questions: (1) How would the NATO ground forces be increased? and (2) How would Germany be rearmed? The first question caused problems in America because congressional critics opposed Truman's plan to send from four to six U.S. divisions to augment NATO forces. The second question raised problems in France because French opinion opposed the rearmament of Germany. On September 9, 1950, Truman had announced that America would send four new divisions to Europe.

In Congress, opponents of this Europe plan challenged Truman's decision. Such spokesmen as former President Herbert Hoover, Senator Robert Taft, and Senator Kenneth Wherry disliked the European orientation of this policy. Generally, they desired greater American activity in the Pacific region, arguing that Europe could defend itself. Other Republicans backed Truman, however. After New York's Republican Governor Thomas Dewey and General Eisenhower defended Truman's program, the Senate passed a series of resolutions on April 4, 1951, which accepted Truman's NATO policy. The Senate agreed that the four U.S. army divisions could go to Europe but requested that the president consult with Congress before sending additional troops.

In contrast to the American difficulty, the German rearmament question caused a lengthier dispute because of French opposition. In October, the French National Assembly adopted Prime Minister René Pleven's plan to include German troops in NATO only at the lowest (regiment) level, under a European political authority. Generally, however, the NATO foreign ministers disliked the Pleven Plan. At the December 1950 meeting no satisfactory solution could be found. The foreign ministers finally accepted German troop participation, in principle, but left the details of the plan for later discussion.

December 23, 1950

The United States, France, and the associated states of Indochina (Vietnam, Laos, and Cambodia) sign a mutual defense agreement for military aid in combating Communist forces under Ho Chi Minh.

This agreement finalized prior American agreements on May 8, 1950, to give aid to France for use in Indochina and to send 35 U.S. military advisers there. Although Washington wanted the funds for Indochina to go directly to Saigon, the French insisted that all aid go through the Paris office of the French Union. By December 1950, the United States committed $50 million for arms, ammunition, naval vessels, military vehicles, and aircraft.

December 28, 1950

O. Edward Clubb, a high-ranking U.S. foreign service officer and expert on China, is ordered to answer allegations before the State Department's Loyalty Security Board (LSB).

A foreign service officer since 1928, Clubb served principally as a consul in China. He had closed the U.S. consular office in Peking on April 12, 1950, when he returned to Washington to become director of the Office of Chinese Affairs of the State Department. The allegations made against Clubb on December 28 were anonymous and largely indefinite. Such charges as "viewed some aspects of Communism favorably, 1932–1934" or "friendly toward the USSR and Communism, 1935–1937" made up all but one of the charges.

The one specific allegation was that he "delivered a sealed envelope to the office of the editor of the *New Masses*. . .for transmittal to Grace Hutchins," a reputed Communist. This event took place in 1932. Later, Clubb learned that Whittaker Chambers, an editor of *New Masses* in 1933, was the accuser and that the "sealed envelope" was his letter of introduction to Walt Cameron, the 1932 editor of *New Masses*. Following many lengthy interrogations, Clubb received clearance from the LSB on February 8, 1952. He decided, however, to retire from the Foreign Service, dismayed at the shabby treatment accorded someone who had worked for the government for over 20 years. Clubb's experience was repeated frequently enough to demoralize the professional, objective foreign service officers. Clubb and others had committed the offense of expertly analyzing the events where they served even when their superiors and political appointees in Washington wanted to hear reports that confirmed their prejudices in favor of Chiang Kai-shek.

In addition to Clubb, other State Department experts on China who suffered similar rebuffs were John Carter Vincent, John S. Service, and John Paton Davies. The demoralizing conditions within the diplomatic corps were examined by a special State Department Committee on Personnel. In 1954, this committee reported to Secretary of State John Foster Dulles: "The morale of the [Foreign] Service today stands in need of repair."

1951

January 5, 1951

A "great debate" begins on Truman's policies in Europe and Korea.

When the Senate convened in January, Republican Senator Robert A. Taft (Ohio) presented a speech that revived a policy of isolationism opposing Truman's commitment to NATO and his limit on the war in Korea to regain the 38th parallel for South Korea. Rather than having America cooperate with NATO or the United Nations, Taft wanted to return to policies some politicians preferred before the Pearl Harbor attack of 1941; that is, a policy under which the United States would unilaterally decide when and how to intervene abroad. Taft claimed "Truman's War" in Korea was unconstitutional because Congress did not declare war and that Truman made a serious mistake in December 1951 by appointing Dwight D. Eisenhower as commander of NATO forces in Europe, a decision that entangled America in Europe's quarrels.

Taft's ideas were strongly endorsed by former President Herbert Hoover and Republican Senator Kenneth Wherry (Nebraska) among others. Taft's January 5 speech opened a series of Senate debates and congressional hearings that culminated in a Senate hearing on Truman's dismissal of General Douglas MacArthur as commander of U.N. forces in Korea.

April 5, 1951

Julius and Ethel Rosenberg are sentenced to death, having been convicted of conspiring with others to transmit secret information on atomic fission to the Soviet Union.

The Rosenbergs had been arrested in July 1950 as a result of the confession of British spy Klaus Fuchs. His testimony led first to the arrest of Harry Gold and David Greenglass, who implicated the Rosenbergs and Morton Sobell. The Rosenbergs were allegedly the Soviet contacts for Greenglass, who worked at the Los Alamos project. The Rosenbergs persistently claimed their innocence. They were not accused of any specific overt act of espionage but of conspiracy to transfer secret materials.

The U.S. press as well as the court treated the conspirators as traitors. The trial judge, Irving Kaufman, declared: "All our democratic institutions are...involved in this great conflict.... The punishment to be meted out in this case must therefore serve the maximum interest for the preservation of our society against these traitors in our midst." The government's case depended largely on the confessions of David Greenglass and Harry Gold. Judge Kaufman also allowed wide latitude for the prosecutor to question the Rosenbergs about their political beliefs. This enabled the government to convince the jury that their motivation to spy depended on their Communist sympathies.

After their conviction, the Rosenberg case followed normal appeal procedures for the next two years. After the Supreme Court rejected a further review, the possibility arose that President Eisenhower would commute the death sentence, provided the Rosenbergs confessed. They did not because they said they were innocent and they could not confess a lie. Consequently, they were electrocuted at Sing Sing Prison, New York, on June 19, 1953. Subsequent evidence from the files of the KGB (Soviet secret police) supported the government's charges. The co-conspirators in the Rosenberg case received prison terms. Morton Sobell and Harry Gold each were given 30-year sentences; David Greenglass was sentenced to 15 years.

The political overtones and uncertain evidence in the Rosenberg case and execution led later to a number of dramatizations. These included a documentary film, *The Unquiet Death of Julius and Ethel Rosenberg* (1975); a play, Donald Freed's *Inquest* (1930); and three novels: Robert Coover's *The Public Burning* (1977); E.L. Doctorow's *The Book of Daniel* (1971); and Helen Yglesias's *How She Died* (1972).

April 10–11, 1951

President Truman dismisses General MacArthur from all his command positions.

Truman signed the order late in the evening of April 10 to relieve the general for insubordination, announcing the decision in a White House press release at 1:00 A.M. on April 11, 1951. Although Truman's "firing" of the popular general brought criticism from conservatives, Republicans, and Asia-firsters, the president had the unanimous backing of the Joint Chiefs of Staff, who realized that MacArthur had frequently undermined Truman's policy and had failed to follow proper procedures in the past six months.

The dispute between the general and the president centered on the administration's decision to limit the objectives of the Korean War, short of unification, in order to seek a negotiated settlement to the conflict. MacArthur preferred to continue the traditional American military policies of permitting the armed forces to take whatever action was necessary to achieve a "total victory." Thus, the Truman-MacArthur controversy represented a major conflict in policy

General MacArthur addresses an audience at Chicago after being removed from his command by President Truman. National Archives

perceptions prevalent in America during the last half of the twentieth century. One policy recognized that wars in the Third World were, at best, fought for limited political objectives and that containment of Communist expansion was a major goal of U.S. policy. The second approach attempted to attain a total triumph not just over a political foe but also over an ideologically different way of life that appeared to threaten capitalist democracy.

Specifically, in 1950–1951 the Truman-MacArthur conflict translated into the methods for fighting in Korea after the Chinese intervened in November 1950. MacArthur claimed military restrictions had prevented him from responding effectively to the Chinese attack. He had been directed to use only Korean forces north of the 38th parallel and, even worse, was instructed not to conduct air raids along the Manchurian border to avoid a direct confrontation with China and Russia. In December, MacArthur publicly objected to these restrictions, telling newsmen that the limits imposed from Washington were "an enormous handicap, without precedent in military history." He could not retaliate effectively against the Chinese. Initially, Truman sought to silence MacArthur by issuing directives that required that all public statements first be cleared with the White House. MacArthur remained quiet only until February 1951. By that time the opposing Korean forces had fought to stabilized positions near the 38th parallel.

Then, on February 6, a news "leak" from MacArthur's headquarters disclosed the general's impatience with the restrictions on his activities. He wanted to bomb the Manchurian sanctuaries across the Yalu River that contained Chinese supplies and to defeat Communism not just in Korea but throughout the Orient—a total victory over Communism. In contrast, Truman, in consultation with allies from the United Nations, decided after the Chinese intervention that neither an atomic war nor a Soviet attack in Western Europe should be risked over Korea. The prevailing decision was to contain the Communists in Asia at the 38th parallel.

MacArthur opposed this policy, claiming it was an "appeasement" of Communism. Until March, Truman continued to be patient with the general. On March 20, he and the Joint Chiefs agreed to approach North Korea and China to seek a truce in Korea that would restore the 38th parallel. MacArthur responded to this effort by issuing a statement on March 24 in which he offered a military settlement to the Communist commanders. He added a thinly veiled threat, however, that if they refused a truce, the United Nations might extend military operations to coastal areas and interior bases of China. MacArthur's uncalled for statement convinced Truman to find the right time to dismiss the general. The general's statement undermined the negotiating proposals being laid out. Later, the general went further, sending a letter to the House minority leader and a MacArthur favorite, Republican Joseph W. Martin. The letter of April 5, which Martin read to Congress, reiterated the general's former proposals: to end limits on military operations, to use Chiang Kai-shek's forces in Korea, and to recognize that Asia, not Europe, was the place to defeat the Communist threat. The letter to Martin was not the cause but the occasion for Truman to remove MacArthur.

After consulting with the State Department and the Joint Chiefs of Staff and receiving their unanimous agreement that the general should be dismissed, Truman signed the orders on April 10, appointing General Matthew Ridgeway to replace MacArthur. The large public outpouring of sympathy for MacArthur on his return to the United States and his speech to a joint session of Congress on April 19 symbolized the split in American understanding of the differences between limited and total war in the nuclear age. Unable to comprehend or uncaring about the implications of a total war against Communist China and, perhaps, the USSR, American demonstrators and many news editors issued startling accusations against the president. The state legislatures of Illinois, Michigan, Florida, and California passed resolutions condemning Truman. Senator Richard Nixon called the dismissal "rank appeasement," asking the Senate to insist on MacArthur's reinstatement and to censure the president. The most extreme criticism came, of course, from Senator McCarthy, who said the president was a "son of a bitch who ought to be impeached."

On May 3, a Senate investigating committee began hearings on the reasons for MacArthur's dismissal, hearing 13 witnesses and recording 3,691 pages of testimony in 42 days. At its finish, the report generally concurred with Truman. General Marshall's statement to the committee summarizes the essence of the group's conclusions. According to Marshall, it was not new for a military commander to be required to follow stipulated policies, despite disagreeing with them. "What is new and what has brought about the necessity for General MacArthur's removal," he stated, "is the wholly unprecedented situation of a local theater commander *publicly expressing* his displeasure and his disagreement with the foreign and military policy of the United States" (italics added). In such a case, Marshall concluded, "there was no other recourse but to relieve him." For Truman, not just policy but principle was involved: that principle was that the U.S. Constitution guaranteed the superiority of the president, a civil and elected official, over military officers. In 1951, MacArthur was replaced and, after a brief effort to seek the Republican presidential nomination in 1952, he "faded away." The Senate did not seek to impeach, censure, or override the president. A truce with North Korea was delayed for over two years.

The political objective of a limited conflict to contain North Korea at the 38th parallel was sustained over the concept of total war. Yet the supporters of MacArthur and his views continued on into future decades to have an impact on U.S. policies.

May 2, 1951

The West German Federal Republic becomes a full member of the Council of Europe.

This was one step toward the American objective of rearming the Germans and integrating them into the NATO forces, a process that France remained reluctant to approve.

May 2, 1951

Iran's Majlis (parliament) and senate vote to nationalize Iran's oil industry.

This action followed an Iranian effort in 1950 to secure a larger share of the oil profits from the British-controlled Anglo-Iranian Oil Company. On April 29, a nationalist leader, Mohammed Mossadegh, was named premier, and he quickly pushed the oil nationalization decree through both legislative bodies. The British objected to the decree, appealing to the International Court of Justice to require Iran to arbitrate the dispute. Mossadegh refused to recognize the court's jurisdiction and an impasse ensued.

May 4, 1951

The United States and Iceland agree on a treaty to use Iceland's defense facilities for NATO forces.

May 18, 1951

The U.N. General Assembly approves an arms embargo against Communist China.

The General Assembly approved the arms embargo on China on February 1, 1950, after a long-delayed response to China's military intervention in Korea. The Assembly vote was 47-7 with 9 abstentions. It condemned China's participation in North Korea's aggression against South Korea and established the U.N. Advanced Measures Committee to consider how to deal with the situation. While some members of the Advanced Measures Committee such as Great Britain wanted to delay any political sanctions on China, the Chinese army's Spring Offensive in April convinced Britain and other committee members to act. On May 14, the Advanced Measures Committee referred their proposal for the economic arms embargo on China to the U.N. Political Committee. Three days later, the Political Committee voted for an embargo by 47-0, the Soviet Union abstaining. Finally, on May 18, the U.N. General Assembly approved the Resolution and asked all U.N. members to embargo exports to the People's Republic of China and the Democratic People's Republic of North Korea. The resolution defined the exports as "arms, ammunition and implements of war, atomic energy, materials, petroleum, transportation materials of strategic importance, and items useful in the production of arms, ammunition and implements of war." Information on these and other U.N. resolutions are in James I. Matray, editor, *Historical Dictionary of the Korean War* (1991).

June 19, 1951

The U.S. draft of men for military service is extended to July 1, 1955—and universal military training is authorized.

President Truman signed legislation lowering the draft age to 18 years and authorized universal military training (UMT) for all American young men at some unspecified future date. For several years Truman had requested UMT but Congress opposed it. Although this bill approved UMT in principle, Congress did not provide the necessary funds to make it effective.

July 8, 1951

Truce negotiations begin in Korea.

Arrangements for the talks originated on June 23, 1951, when Soviet Ambassador to the U.N. Jacob A. Malik called for cease-fire and armistice talks. Truman announced that the United States was ready for such discussions, and by July 8 talks began at Kaesong. In August, the negotiations stopped, first over U.S. objections to Communist violation of agreed regulations and later because the Communists claimed U.N. planes bombed Kaesong. On October 8, talks began again at Panmunjom near the 38th parallel, where they continued over the next two years.

During this time, heavy fighting by both sides frequently interrupted the discussions. Each time, however, the talks began again. During 1952, the principal issue became the repatriation of prisoners of war. After reports that nearly half of the 130,000 prisoners held by the United Nations did not wish to return to their homeland, the North Koreans and Chinese refused to accept such claims and insisted on the full exchange of all prisoners.

During the 1952 election campaign Eisenhower declared if elected president he would go to Korea, implying that somehow such action would bring the negotiations to a conclusion. He did visit the troops on the Korean battlefield, but there is no evidence that this action influenced the Communist side. Meanwhile, a stalemate continued during which negotiating and fighting occurred at different times as the truce negotiations moved slowly toward a successful cease-fire in Korea.

August 30, 1951

The United States and the Philippines sign a treaty of mutual defense.

An armed attack on either of the parties in the Pacific would be dangerous "to its own peace and safety," and each party would act against the common danger "in accordance with its own constitutional processes."

September 1, 1951

The ANZUS Tripartite Security Treaty is signed.

This was a mutual assistance agreement between Australia, New Zealand, and the United States. It was the product of persistent Australian efforts, according to historian Joseph Siracusa, "despite the misgivings of the State Department and with the firm resolve of the Joint Chiefs to keep contacts with the Australians and New Zealanders on defense matters as superficial as possible." See his *America's Australia, Australia's America* (1997).

Panmunjom, Korea, site of military armistice talks. National Archives

September 6, 1951

A U.S.-Portuguese pact integrates the militarily strategic Azores into NATO's defense structure.

September 8, 1951

United States and Japan sign a peace treaty at San Francisco, USSR objects.

The treaty, stimulated by the ongoing Korean War, had been negotiated between John Foster Dulles, a special consultant to U.S. Secretary of State Acheson, and Premier Shigeru Yoshida of Japan. At the treaty conference, the Soviet Union objected to the proceedings and its delegate boycotted the final session, refusing to sign the treaty. Because of the relative leniency of the final treaty and the Anglo-American desire to make Japan a strong ally in East Asia, the treaty is referred to as "the Treaty of Reconciliation." Japan's Diet ratified the treaty on November 18, 1951, the U.S. Senate on March 20, 1952.

September 8, 1951

Japan and the United States sign a mutual security treaty.

At the same time as the peace treaty was negotiated, a Mutual Security Treaty was also developed guaranteeing a continued U.S. military presence in Japan. Under the terms of the treaty, U.S. troops and naval and air bases would remain in Japan indefinitely. Japan would not permit any other nation to have bases or military authority within its boundaries without American consent. While the agreement was popular with conservative Japanese political leaders, it was vigorously denounced by leftist groups of Communists and socialists.

Premier Shigeru Yoshida of Japan signs peace treaty, John Foster Dulles is directly behind him and Secretary of State Acheson is to the right. National Archives

September 20, 1951

Greece and Turkey become NATO members.

The NATO Council, meeting in Ottawa, Canada, recommended the admission of these two states. The formal admission took place in Lisbon on February 20, 1952.

October 19, 1951

The war between Germany and the United States formally ends.

President Truman signed a joint congressional resolution declaring an end to the conflict of 1941–1945. Earlier, on July 9, 1951, Great Britain and France signed a formal agreement with Germany that ended the war for them. On September 10, the foreign ministers of Great Britain, France, and the United States agreed to replace the West German occupation statute and to use West German troops in a European army.

October 25, 1951

Winston Churchill and the Conservative Party win the British elections.

Churchill replaced Attlee's Labour government, which had been in power since July 1945. Anthony Eden became minister of foreign affairs.

October 26, 1951

Congress passes the Mutual Defense Assistance Control (Battle) Act of 1951.

Congress pulled together several strands that comprised an economic embargo of Communist states and placed them in the Mutual Defense Assistance Control Act of 1951. On February 28, 1949, the United States had created a new Export Control Act and on August 12 the Department of Commerce issued a master list of all goods requiring an export license. On November 22, 1949, delegates from NATO countries formed the Coordinating Committee for Multilateral Export Controls (CoCom) that was to oversee export licensing of potentially strategic goods. (See November 22, 1949.)

The so called "Battle Act" was designed to back up the informal CoCom process with unilateral sanctions. Any country that allowed strategic materials to be shipped to a Communist country was denied all U.S. aid. Given the Marshall Plan and other massive U.S. aid programs, the economic hegemony of the United States over the free world was sufficient to make this provision effective for a number of years. During the 1960s, especially late in that decade, export control policy underwent a significant moderation as closer relations developed with Soviet bloc countries. More importantly, recognition of the growing importance of trade to the U.S. economy led to a significant new emphasis on promoting exports.

At the same time, the United States had lost much of the economic leverage that was essential for the Battle Act's comprehensive controls to be effective. The resurgent economies of Japan and the Western European allies were beginning to rival the United States in product development and export markets. Because of geographic proximity, the natural tendency of these nations was to engage in trade with the East. This increased the strain on the international system of comprehensive restrictions. Moreover, a growing number U.S. firms were clamoring for relaxation of the barriers to export trading. Reacting to these new circumstances, the Congress moved in 1969 to revise U.S. export control policy.

October 27, 1951

Egypt unilaterally abrogates the Anglo-Egyptian Treaty of 1936.

The 1936 treaty provided for a 20-year military alliance between Britain and an independent Egypt that permitted British troops to be stationed in Egypt. After World War II, Egypt became a charter member of the United Nations but problems arose in 1948. After a U.N. partition plan established the State of Israel, neighboring Arab states engaged in a war against Israel with Egypt bearing the brunt of the conflict before an armistice was signed in 1949. Because the British did not assist Egypt's troops, popular nationalistic demonstrations in Egypt called for the eviction of British forces. With the approval of Egypt's parliament, Prime Minister Mustafa al-Nahhas Pasha announced Egypt was abrogating the 1936 Anglo-Egyptian Treaty. Britain refused to accept the unilateral abrogation of the treaty, leading to clashes between British and Egyptian forces. In Cairo, riots and demonstrations against the British and other foreign officials finally led to an army coup to overthrow King Farouk in 1952.

See July 23, 1952.

November 14, 1951

An aid agreement is signed by the United States and Yugoslavia.

After Tito split with Stalin in 1948 (see June 28, 1948), the Truman administration considered ways to assist Yugoslavia because its geographical location was of strategic importance to the NATO allies. In February 1949, Truman relaxed export controls of goods shipped to Yugoslavia and in September 1949 the Export-Import Bank gave Tito's government a $20 million loan to purchase mining machinery. In order to make things easier for Truman in 1949, Tito changed some of his foreign policies, especially by withdrawing assistance to rebel Greek Communists and closing the border between Yugoslavia and Greece. As a result, on October 20, 1950, Yugoslav Ambassador to the United States Vladimir Popovic asked for, and Truman approved, a grant of $105 million to finance food imports because Yugoslav farmers had suffered recent droughts. In light of Tito's policy changes, Truman was able to have Congress approve the Yugoslav Emergency Relief Act of 1950. The legislation authorized $50 million for the Economic Cooperation Administration (ECA) to provide food aid for Yugoslavia. In November 1950, Truman modified the ban on shipments of "war potential" materials by secretly shipping some old weapons and in March 1951, Truman relaxed military export rules to permit the shipping of material for military use. The U.S. offer of military aid was finalized on November 14, 1951, when the Mutual Assistance Pact was signed. By this pact, the United States supplied military equipment, materials, and services to the armed forces of Tito's Communist government. The pact was designed to sustain the breach between Tito and Stalin. Further details are in an article by Robert M. Hathaway in William F. Levantrosser, ed., *Harry S. Truman: The Man From Independence* (1986).

December 31, 1951

Marshall Plan aid ends; the Mutual Security Agency replaces the OEEC.

While the Marshall Plan had not solved all of Western Europe's economic problems, most nations had recovered sufficiently from World War II to permit the restoration of an economic pattern resembling that of the prewar era. The new Mutual Security Program provided $7.428 billion for economic, military, and technical aid to Europe.

1952

January 5, 1952

India and the United States sign a five-year "Point Four" agreement.

Each country would contribute equal funds to develop the Indian economy. Later, on March 1, 1952, Prime Minister Jawaharlal Nehru's Congress Party won India's first national elections under the federal republican constitution adopted on November 26, 1949. Although Nehru agreed to this program of economic aid, he refused to accept any political agreements tied to it because he desired to follow a strictly neutral policy between the United States and the Soviet Union.

January 11, 1952

The U.N. General Assembly creates a 12-nation disarmament commission to achieve a "balanced reduction" of armed forces and armaments.

The commission consisted of the 11 Security Council members and Canada. Frequent disarmament discussion resulted from this commission, but no significant agreements resulted from its work during the next 10 years. U.S. policy, as stated early in the commission discussions, was not to accept any disarmament or other limitations on military affairs without strict international control and inspection mechanisms to prevent cheating. The Soviet Union saw the systems of inspection as nothing more than a thinly disguised attempt to spy on its defenses.

This position was so staunchly advocated that many observers believed Washington's cold warriors counted on the Soviets' refusal to accept inspections as a way of preventing significant arms control or disarmament agreements. It should also be noted that the Americans took this position without extensive examination of its implications. When the USSR did agree to the U.S. demand for strict inspection during the 1988 INF negotiations, Frances Fitzgerald, *Way Out There in the Blue* (2000) reports that a quandary resulted in Washington: On the one hand, the hard-liners—this time in the Congress—insisted on intrusive inspections; on the other hand, the [Joint] Chiefs [of Staff] and the U.S. intelligence agencies did not want the Soviets snooping around U.S. defense plants. "Verification," Secretary of Defense Carlucci said, "has proved to be more complex than we thought it would be. The flip side of the coin is its application to us. The more we think about it, the more difficult it becomes."

February 2, 1952

Great Britain joins the nuclear club.

London announces it has successfully exploded an atomic bomb at tests in the Monte Bello islands near Australia.

March 10, 1952

In Cuba General Fulgencio Batista overthrows President Prio Socarras and makes himself Chief of State and Premier.

Batista had been military ruler of Cuba from 1933 to 1944; however, just before elections were to be held in 1952, he again took control allegedly to save Cuba from economic chaos and left-wing radicals who opposed the existing regime. The radicals would ultimately rally around Fidel Castro and create the first Communist state in the Americas.

May 26, 1952

Britain, France, and America grant West Germany internal independence.

In four so-called peace conventions signed at Bonn, West Germany, the three Allies ended their occupation of Germany and extend West Germany virtually complete sovereignty.

May 27, 1952

The European Defense Community (EDC) is created to unify Western European defense plans and to bind West Germany to this defense.

In meetings at Paris, a series of documents were signed: (1) the EDC charter signed by France, West Germany, Italy, Belgium, the Netherlands, and Luxembourg; (2) an EDC treaty with Britain to join together if any nation were attacked; (3) a NATO protocol with West Germany to extend NATO guarantees to that nation; and (4) a declaration in which Britain and the United States agreed to regard a threat to the EDC as a threat to their own security. The U.S. Senate ratified the NATO protocol on July 1, 1952.

June 26, 1952

The McCarran-Walter Immigration and Nationality Act is passed by Congress over President Truman's veto.

This act permitted naturalization of Asians and set a quota for their further admission. Truman objected, however, to the clauses that provided for the exclusion and deportation of aliens and the control of U.S. citizens abroad.

President Harry S. Truman. National Archives

July 1, 1952

The Schuman Plan for integrating Western Europe's coal and steel industries goes into effect.

This plan was proposed on May 9, 1950, by French Foreign Minister Robert Schuman. On April 18, 1951, six nations agreed to establish a single market for coal and steel, an agreement that now became effective. The six nations were France, West Germany, Italy, Belgium, the Netherlands, and Luxembourg. The Schuman Plan became known as the European Coal and Steel Community (ECSC).

November 1, 1952

The United States announces the success of the first thermonuclear (hydrogen) bomb.

After hearing recommendations from the Chairman of the Joint Chiefs General Omar N. Bradley and scientist Edward Teller, Truman agreed to have work proceed on a thermonuclear bomb. (See January 31, 1950) Thus, on November 1, 1953, the test of the H-bomb yielded a force of 14 megatons (14 million tons of TNT). The test was held on the Pacific Ocean's atoll of Eniwetok (later Bikini) in the Marshall Islands.

November 5, 1952

Dwight D. Eisenhower is elected president, defeating the Democratic Party nominee, Adlai Stevenson.

The Republican Party also gained a slight majority in both houses of Congress. General Eisenhower's nomination was a victory for the liberal and progressive wing of the party, which hoped that Eisenhower would firmly establish control of the party for the "modern" progressive faction. The conservative Old Guard Republicans, who had considerable strength in the Senate and House, were bitter because of Eisenhower's nomination. The philosophical differences between the liberal and conservative Republicans were not healed by the 1952 presidential victory. In foreign affairs, the Old Guard preferred an Asia-first policy and a neo-isolationist, go-it-alone international policy; in contrast, Eisenhower believed Europe deserved first priority in U.S. national security and realized the value of NATO and other U.S. allies in world affairs.

1953

January 20, 1953

President Dwight D. Eisenhower is inaugurated as the 34th president of the United States.

He appointed John Foster Dulles as secretary of state and Charles Wilson, former president of General Motors Corporation, as secretary of defense. Dulles was eminently qualified to serve as secretary of state. He had been an adviser to President Wilson during the Paris Peace Conference and a member of the Reparations Commission in 1919. During World War II, he became an internationalist interested in urging Republicans to act in a bipartisan fashion in foreign policy. He had been a delegate to the San Francisco Conference on the United Nations in 1945 and served as a special representative of President Truman to negotiate the Japanese Peace Treaty of 1951. He served as secretary until illness forced him to resign on April 22, 1959.

President Dwight D. Eisenhower and John Foster Dulles. Dwight D. Eisenhower Library

March 5, 1953

Joseph Stalin dies and is interred in the Lenin Mausoleum on Red Square.

Outside the USSR, two related questions arose after his death. Did Stalin die a natural death? Would his successors adopt new policies? The latter was the more important. In the six months prior to his death, Stalin had taken steps to assure a continued hard-line policy. At the 19th Communist Party Congress in October 1953, he declared that Soviet economic programs must stress heavy industry and agricultural collectivization. He also asserted that tight party controls should be adopted against capitalist aggression, which could be expected at any time.

However, Stalin's continued hard line contrasted with recent statements of some Politburo members. Georgy Malenkov had urged stress on consumer products and cooperation with Western powers. Stalin seemed to disagree and appeared to be ready for another party purge. In October, he added 14 members to the Politburo and renamed it the Presidium of the Central Committee. More threateningly, on January 13, 1953, *Pravda* newspaper reported a "Doctor's Plot," and a group of nine doctors serving in the Kremlin was arrested, accused of assassinating the Soviet Union's chief propagandist, Andrey Zhadanov, in 1948 and of trying to kill several Red Army generals. By February, rumors in Moscow threatened party members such as Malenkov, M. Vyacheslav Molotov, and Anastas Mikoyan.

Soviet historian Dmitri Volkogonov's *Stalin: Triumph and Tragedy* (1991) provides a detailed account of Stalin's last days. Volkogonov begins with the dictator's signs of weakness "almost beyond his strength" during his October 1953 speech to the 19th Congress of the Communist Party of the Soviet Union. Soon after, Stalin suffered a number of falling spells, twice falling down stairs. Although he had stopped smoking because of high blood pressure, Stalin continued drinking wine and, despite his doctor's advice, took hot steam baths. On March 1, Stalin's close comrades left his dacha at 4:00 A.M. after a night of feasting. During the day, Stalin never left his bedroom after noon as was usual. By 11:00 P.M. on March 1, his bodyguard and housekeeper entered his room and found him unconscious. At 7:00 A.M. March 2, Lavrenty Beria, head of the secret police, brought a physician who found Stalin in a coma, breathing irregularly, and having damage to his cerebral blood vessels. The doctor kept a log of Stalin's symptoms until his death at 9:50 A.M. on March 5.

By that time, the Soviet Presidium of the Central Committee met to select Malenkov as chairman of the council and General Secretary of the Communist Party. On the Presidium with Malenkov were Beria, Molotov, Nikolay Bulganin, and Lazar Kaganovich as first deputy chairmen. During the next year, there was a power struggle in the Soviet hierarchy. On March 20, 1953, Nikita Khrushchev succeeded Malenkov as first secretary of the Party. Beria, who was feared by the others, was expelled from his government and party posts on July 10 and executed on December 23, 1953. The power struggle did not end until February 8, 1955, when Malenkov was forced to resign, making Khrushchev the general secretary of the Communist Party and Bulganin chairman of the Presidium.

Both Bulganin and Khrushchev spoke of "collective leadership." They also relaxed the tight controls Stalin had imposed both at home and abroad. In economics, they placed more investment in consumer goods such as textiles and housing, and allowed farmers to grow vegetables in private plots and sell them in the market. Internationally, they mixed claims of military buildups with speeches on "peaceful coexistence." This period, which came to be known as the thaw in Cold War relations, lasted from 1954 to 1960.

March 27, 1953

The U.S. Senate confirms Charles Bohlen as ambassador to the Soviet Union in spite of Senator McCarthy's attempts to prevent it.

This incident was the first effort of the Eisenhower administration to stand firm against McCarthy's intemperate charges against a government official. Bohlen's appointment as ambassador had been supported because of his excellent qualifications and Eisenhower's personal acquaintance with him in Paris. McCarthy and his followers charged that Bohlen was a security risk. They claimed that as an assistant secretary of state and interpreter at the 1945 Yalta Conference, he had a role in those decisions. McCarthyites claimed that Roosevelt sold out Chiang Kai-shek at Yalta. The Senate hearings gave Bohlen an opportunity to clarify the record on the Yalta agreements. He pointed out that Chiang in 1945 greatly appreciated being able to have a pact signed with Stalin to accept his regime. Only the later violations of the Yalta agreements by Stalin caused difficulty, not the Yalta agreements themselves.

During the Senate debate on Bohlen, McCarthy went too far in his charges. After reviewing Bohlen's personnel and FBI files, both Senator Robert Taft and Senator William Knowland, two Republican conservatives who had previously backed McCarthy, reported that they accepted Bohlen's nomination. McCarthy sought to challenge the report of Taft and Knowland and was rebuked. Secretary of State Dulles and President Eisenhower expressed support for Bohlen and the Senate registered its approval, 74 to 13. Senator McCarthy's fanatic efforts continued for another 18 months before the Senate voted to condemn his methods.

April 16, 1953

President Eisenhower is cautious in reacting to the new Soviet leadership's desire for relaxation of the Cold War.

Eisenhower declared that better relations with the United States would be possible if Moscow first demonstrated its policy by actions such as "free elections in Korea"; approving U.N. control and inspection of "disarmament agreements"; restoring "free choice" in Eastern European nations; and giving similar evidence of policy changes.

In contrast, Winston Churchill on May 11 showed more appreciation of the new Soviet rulers. He suggested a summit conference "on the highest level" to prepare an agenda of problems to resolve. He indicated that President Eisenhower should not, perhaps, expect too much at one time. Generally, the continued strong anti-Communist feelings in America prevented Washington from responding more positively to Soviet overtures for an easing of tension.

June 16, 1953

Soviet tanks and troops are sent in to quell an uprising of workers in East Germany.

In May, the Soviet Union had abolished its control commission in East Germany and relaxed controls on protests. But it demanded an increase in production for the same wages. Marching in Stalinallee on June 16, workers protested the low wages. Strikes soon spread throughout East Germany until Soviet tanks rolled into Berlin, Dresden, Leipzig, and other cities to smash the demonstrations. The Soviet assault killed 125 people and a thousand more were arrested. To placate the workers, the Communist government instituted a 10-point reform plan on June 22. This plan increased wages, improved living conditions, ended travel restrictions between East and West Berlin, and announced that martial law would end on July 11.

The United States and its Western allies avoided military intervention in East Germany but employed psychological methods in an attempt to weaken the Communist government and demonstrate that West Germans benefited by cooperating with the Western powers. In addition to using the Radio in the American Sector (RAIS) of Berlin to inform Germans of the many strikes, riots, and protest movements in the socialist state, the Eisenhower administration devised a program to help feed East Germans. Between July and September 1953, over 75 percent of the East German population went to West Berlin to get U.S. food packages. By the end of 1953, the East German government had tightened its controls over East Germans to prevent them from obtaining food packages in West Berlin. The U.S. program also solidified support among West Germans for the Federal Republic and its chancellor, Konrad Adenauer.

July 10–14, 1953

The U.S. Secretary of State confers in Washington with the French and British foreign ministers.

Their final communiqué invited the Soviets to meet and discuss German unity and an Austrian peace treaty. They also warned the Soviet and North Korean Communists that the Korean War would be reopened if there were truce violations or other Communist aggression in Asia.

July 26–27, 1953

An armistice agreement is signed and becomes effective in Korea.

The armistice agreement came slowly despite Eisenhower's visit to Korea on December 14 to fulfill his campaign pledge. Not until March 30, when the Chinese suggested letting the prisoner-of-war issue be decided by an international authority, was progress made. An important historical question regarding the armistice was whether or not the Eisenhower administration issued an ultimatum on May 22 demanding that Chinese officials make concessions to complete the armistice or risk the United States dropping an atomic bomb on China. In 1956, Secretary of State Dulles claimed an ultimatum was delivered to China, but documents declassified 30 years later gave no evidence to support his claim. Perhaps Dulles exaggerated the events of 1953 to explain why U.S. policies of "massive retaliation" and "brinkmanship" could be valuable.

On June 18, Syngman Rhee, president of South Korea, opposed the agreement because it kept Korea divided into two segments and tried to sabotage the negotiations by releasing 27,000 Chinese and North Korean prisoners. Rhee's attempt to stop the talks failed and an armistice was reached in July. Yet the armistice did not result in a peace treaty or Korean unity. Further negotiations continued on a sporadic basis but without success. The United States assisted South Korea by giving Seoul over $6 billion in the next decade and stationing American troops south of the 38th parallel. But the negotiations for permanent peace would become stalemated, lasting into the twenty-first century.

August 8, 1953

The Union of Soviet Socialist Republics successfully explodes a hydrogen thermonuclear device.

The Soviets' concept of a thermonuclear weapon was first suggested in a 1946 article, "The Use of Atomic Energy of Light Elements," by Ya B. Zeldovich, I. Tu Pomeranchuck, and Yu B. Khariton. On June 10, 1948, the Soviet Council of Ministers established a working group to study the feasibility of an H-bomb. The group that came up with a feasibility plan was headed by I.E. Tamm and the other members were A.D. Sakarov, S.Z. Belen'kiy, V.L. Ginsberg, and Yu A. Romanov. After their first proposal failed to generate sufficient temperatures to obtain a thermonuclear reaction, Sakarov and Ginsberg proposed modifications to surround the thermonuclear fuel with uranium-238. Based on these changes, the weapons test in August 1953 produced a yield of 400 kilotons.

Premier Malenkov announced the successful test in a speech to the Supreme Soviet in which he emphasized that the Soviet Union was ready to ease tension and seek peace if Western Europe would agree. But he emphasized that the USSR now also had the power to prevent aggressive war by the capitalists. While the Soviets' initial atomic bomb had been a copy, the hydrogen device was from an original design. For more, see David Holloway, *Stalin and the Bomb: The Soviet Union and Atomic Energy, 1939–1956* (1994).

August 19, 1953

Premier Mossadegh's government is overthrown by a coup in Iran. Mohammad Reza Pahlavi regains control as shah.

Mossadegh was elected Iran's prime minister on April 19, 1951, having become Iran's most outspoken politician seeking more oil profits for Iran than the 20 percent the British had provided in the 1930s. In 1948, Iranian officials began negotiating with the Anglo-Iranian Oil officers to obtain a 50-50 split in the profits, but British officials refused. Owing to Britain's intransigence, Mossadegh's National Front Party gained a majority in parliament and passed legislation to nationalize the oil wells and take 100 percent of the profits. As Iran's prime minister, Mossadegh offered to negotiate with the British while shutting down the oil production in Iran in the summer of 1951.

Rather than allow Iran to nationalize its oil production, the British government planned clandestine operations to overthrow Mossadegh, obtaining assistance from the U.S. Central Intelligence Agency (CIA). Although President Truman had rejected the British request for CIA help, President Eisenhower approved CIA assistance in early 1953. Secretary of State John Foster Dulles believed the Tudeh Communist Party was at work in Iran, although Mossadegh's National Front Party primarily enrolled middle-class Iranians who sought more money to modernize Iran's economy. Iran's Tudeh Communist Party had been damaged after Stalin backed down and left northern Iran in 1946.

Initially in 1952, the British saw little chance to overthrow Mossadegh because of his popularity, but in March 1953 Iran's Army General Fazollah Zahedi asked CIA agents in Tehran's embassy to support the army's efforts to topple Mossadegh. The CIA approved $1 million to bring down the prime minister, sending both Donald Wilber and Kermit Roosevelt to

Shah of Iran. National Archives

plan and direct operations. In addition, U.S. General H. Norman Schwarzkopf, father of the general who led U.N. forces in the Gulf War (1990–1991), went to Iran because he had become a friend of Mohammad Reza Pahlavi, the Shah of Iran, during a tour of duty in Tehran during World War II. To overthrow Mossadegh, the CIA and British intelligence agents spread propaganda opposing the prime minister and paid Iranians to stage protests against the National Front Party. In part, these efforts succeeded because Iran's lack of any oil income since 1951 had impoverished many Iranians and caused disputes among National Front Party members. Mossadegh tried to solidify his power by dissolving parliament and holding a referendum to approve his action. Although on August 4 Mossadegh announced that 99 percent of the voters approved, many moderates in Mossadegh's party had boycotted the referendum.

Finally, on August 13, Roosevelt and Schwarzkopf persuaded the shah to dismiss Mossadegh and make General Zahedi prime minister. On August 19, General Zahedi's troops arrested Mossadegh and Zahedi took office. Details about the CIA's role in Iran can be found in a *New York Times* article on April 16, 2000, that is based on a CIA history of the "Overthrow of Mossadegh of Iran," written in 1954 by Donald N. Wilber, who had planned CIA Operation TP-Ajax.

September 15, 1953

Communist China announces that the Soviet Union has agreed to provide massive economic aid to help it build its heavy industry.

When Malenkov replaced Stalin after his death in March 1953, he hoped to foster good will with the People's Republic of China by agreeing to help China carry out its Five-Year Plan begun in January 1953. Malenkov provided China with a $300 million, five-year loan and a grant for China's long-term economic advancement. In 1954, the Soviet Central Committee and Council of Ministers asked Nikita Khrushchev to lead a five-member delegation to China that included Nikolai A. Bulganin as Chairman of the Council of Ministers. During their visit, the Soviet delegates encountered many unusual Chinese customs. Khrushchev thought the custom of the Chinese serving them green tea every time they sat down soon became outrageous. Initially, he drank the tea out of respect for the customs but after several days he refused their offer of tea, saying, "I can't take that much liquid." Khrushchev's memoir also notes that Bulganin drank so much tea that he got insomnia.

More seriously, Khrushchev arranged to provide China with another loan of $130 million to assist the reconstruct their war-torn country. The Soviet delegates also agreed to help China increase their military defenses against non-Communist countries such as Japan by sending them Soviet military experts, artillery, machine guns, and ammunition. Finally, Khrushchev approved Mao Tse-tung's request to return Port Arthur to China. Under the 1950 Sino-Soviet Friendship Treaty, the USSR obtained Port Arthur as a Soviet naval base but Mao believed Port Arthur was part of China's territory. Although Khrushchev agreed to return Port Arthur to China, he was concerned about the expensive shore batteries the Soviets had recently built at Port Arthur. After Mao indicated China would repay the Soviets for the fortifications, Khrushchev agreed the Port could be taken over in May 1955. For other details see *Khrushchev Remembers: The Last Testament.*

September 21, 1953

Andrey Vishinsky, the Soviet delegate to the United Nations, offers the General Assembly a proposal to reduce all great powers' armed forces by one-third and to ban the use of atomic weapons.

The proposal became the basis for the U.N. Disarmament Commission to ask a five-power subcommittee (United States, USSR, Great Britain, France, Canada) to consider the question of an inspection system, a means to prevent surprise attacks, and a nuclear test ban. The subcommittee met from May 13 to June 22, 1954, but achieved no results.

September 26, 1953

The United States and Spain agree that the United States may establish air and naval bases in Spain.

This action culminated more than four years of effort by conservative Senators Pat McCarran, Robert Taft, and Owen Brewster working with Spanish head of State Francisco Franco to involve Spain in the free world's battle against Communism. On August 25, 1953, Spain awarded McCarran the Special Medal of the Grand Cross for his devotion to the country. Truman despised Franco but allowed negotiations because U.S. military officers advised him that forward bomber bases were essential to deter the Soviet Union. The agreement was not made, however, until Eisenhower and Dulles accepted the idea of "working with a Fascist." There was a price tag attached to the deal—$250 million of economic and military aid.

October 30, 1953

President Eisenhower's "new look" policy is described in NSC-162.

The Eisenhower administration wanted to continue Truman's Containment Policy but developed a new national security plan to replace NSC-68 and its revised defense plan of 1952 (NSC-141). Eisenhower believed the Truman methods failed to provide for a balanced federal budget and were not adaptable to a "long-haul" defense program designed to outlast Communism and demonstrate capitalism's superiority. Showing his concern for budgetary matters, Eisenhower appointed Secretary of the Treasury George Humphrey to the NSC, where he could comment on the fiscal significance of defense plans.

To relate fiscal, foreign, and defense policies, Eisenhower's plan emphasized the primary U.S. effort in maintaining a sufficient nuclear strike force to hit the Soviet Union if a crisis necessitated a nuclear attack. Although in 1953 news reports of Eisenhower's "new look" emphasized "massive retaliation," the president intended to combine a retaliatory air force capability with negotiations with the Soviet Union to reduce the risk of a nuclear war that he felt no one could win. In line with the Joint Chiefs of Staffs' desire for a clear decision to use nuclear weapons if needed, Eisenhower opted to build a strong strategic air force while offering to meet with Soviet leaders. To seek diplomatic discussions, Eisenhower proposed an "atoms for peace" plan in December 1953 and an "open skies" plan in 1955. (See December 18, 1953, and July 18, 1955.) To reduce expenditures on U.S. conventional forces, Eisenhower wanted the various U.S. allies to provide armed forces for their own defense. Overall, Eisenhower's new look policy would reduce the $74 billion envisioned in the 1952 fiscal year budget and stabilize defense expenses at between $38 and $40 billion per year.

The particular cuts in the army and navy budgets became clear in February 1954, when Secretary of Defense Wilson told a congressional committee that the army would be decreased from 20 to 17 divisions; the navy would modestly reduce its ships; and the air force would seek 137 wings, not 143. The major defense increase would be $1 billion over 1954 "for continental air defense." The following tables indicate the shift in defense emphasis involved in the new look policy. They also explain why the army and navy eventually sought aid from Congress and the public to oppose Eisenhower's program, which met its fiscal and military priority goals by cuts in army and navy budgets and personnel. Over the years the growth of the "military-industrial" complex that worried Eisenhower made it increasingly difficult to rein-in or reduce military budgets.

October 30, 1953

The United States and Japan agree that Japan may enlarge its self-defense forces to protect itself from aggression.

Beginning on October 5, 1953, America's Assistant Secretary of State for Far Eastern Affairs Walter S. Robertson and Hayato Ikeda, the personal representative of Japan's Prime Minister, began negotiations that were completed on October 30. The two representatives agreed on the need to improve Japan's defensive capabilities and for the United States to provide about $50 million of economic aid to Japan. Despite Japan's limited resources due to constitutional budgeting, Japan would expedite the military build-up as quickly as possible. The United States would also supply Japan's self-defense forces with major items of military equipment for the land, sea, and air forces.

December 8, 1953

President Eisenhower proposes an atoms-for-peace plan to the United Nations.

Speaking before the U.N. General Assembly, Eisenhower suggested that all nations should pool their fissionable nuclear material to use for peaceful industrial purposes. The underlying idea behind the plan was that by promoting regulated transfers, it would be possible to provide the benefits of nuclear energy yet inhibit various nations from developing nuclear weapons programs. The U.S. delegation presented the U.S. atoms-for-peace plan to the United Nations on September 23, 1954. Specifically, the

United States suggested that an agency be established for promoting the beneficial uses of atomic energy. The General Assembly unanimously endorsed this plan on December 4, 1954.

Before and after Eisenhower presented the U.N. speech, there were critics of his proposal both inside and outside the administration, especially in Congress. Secretary of State John Foster Dulles and AEC Director Admiral Lewis Strass thought the atoms-for-peace idea was unrealistic and would make the United States look weak in the eyes of Soviet leaders. In Congress, the atoms-for-peace program was criticized by Old Guard Republicans such as John W. Bricker of Ohio and other conservative followers of Senator Robert Taft who had died on July 31, 1953. Despite such opposition, the Senate approved the Atoms-for-Peace Treaty in 1957.

By the mid-1970s, the United States had reached agreements on nuclear cooperation with nearly thirty countries that initially involved the United States providing small research reactors and fuel. As various programs matured, the basic agreements were modified to provide for the sale of commercial nuclear-power reactors and long-term fuel supplies. Canada, France, Great Britain, and the Soviet Union were soon engaged in exporting significant nuclear technology and supplies; later West Germany also became a leading exporter. In 1957, the United States and the Soviet Union joined in supporting the creation of the International Atomic Energy Agency (IAEA) that was charged with promoting the peaceful uses of nuclear energy and with providing certain safeguards or accountability among member states.

Unfortunately, some nations abused the program and later aroused concern about their employing this knowledge and equipment to produce nuclear weaponry.

1954

January 12, 1954

Secretary of State John Foster Dulles delivers a speech outlining the "massive retaliation" defense policy of Eisenhower's "new look" program.

Dulles emphasized that the United States would respond to Communist aggression by building "a great capacity to retaliate" instantly "by means and at places of our choosing." Although Dulles's speech cited the "new look's" desire to have local defense forces and to prefer to stress the deterrent aspects of the policy, news accounts and critics oversimplified the complex purposes of Eisenhower's concepts and emphasized "massive retaliation" as the whole focus of the new look.

January 25, 1954

A big-four foreign ministers conference results in an invitation to Communist China to discuss Far Eastern problems.

The foreign ministers conference at Berlin failed to agree on treaties for Germany and Austria, but did manage an agreement to hold a conference at Geneva on Far Eastern problems of Korea and Indochina. More significantly, it was agreed to invite Communist China to attend. Secretary of State Dulles reluctantly accepted a Chinese presence at Geneva. He did so after Anthony Eden offered a compromise by which all countries representing the U.N. command in Korea would be present on one side, with the delegates of the Soviet Union, Communist China, and North Korea on the other side. But Dulles made it clear that this did not mean U.S. diplomatic recognition of the Peking government.

January 26, 1954

The U.S. Senate ratifies a mutual security treaty with South Korea.

The United States agreed to assist South Korea if it were attacked but would not assist any attempt by Seoul to unite Korea by force.

February 25–26, 1954

The Senate rejects various versions of the Bricker Amendment as well as other proposals to limit the treaty-making powers of the president.

Senator John Bricker of Ohio, one of a group of conservative Republicans who claimed that the presidential decisions of Franklin Roosevelt and Harry Truman had caused problems for the nation, proposed that all future presidential executive agreements, as well as all treaties, must be ratified by both houses of congress and every state. If ratified as a constitutional amendment, Bricker's proposal would have drastically curtailed the executive conduct of foreign affairs; consequently, both Eisenhower and Dulles opposed it. Yet in the Senate, the amendment lost by only one vote.

March 1, 1954

The United States successfully tests a hydrogen bomb dropped from an airplane at Bikini Atoll in the Pacific.

The 15-megaton (15 million tons of TNT) bomb unleashed a heavy amount of radioactive debris. Radioactive particles drifting for over 100 miles landed on and caused illness for the crew of a Japanese fishing boat, *Lucky Dragon* (*Fukuryu Maru*). This incident revived anti-American feeling in Japan, especially after the boat's radio operator, Aikichi Nagakubo, died of radiation sickness on September 23, 1954.

March 14, 1954

Vietminh forces attack 10,000 French soldiers at Dien Bien Phu.

The Vietminh attack was exactly what French General Henri Navarre had hoped for in November 1953, when he concentrated his forces at the small northern, rural outpost of Dien Bien Phu. The "Navarre plan" wanted to entice the Vietminh's General Vo Nguyen Giap away from his guerrilla tactics so that he would engage the French in a conventional battle where Navarre's crack legionnaires could decisively beat the Communists. Navarre's plan backfired because like many French and, later, American military officers, he underestimated the Vietnamese. The Vietminh fought aggressively and Giap used his artillery in superior fashion to besiege Dien Bien Phu. Monsoon rains also handicapped the French, because they could not adequately resupply their forces.

By March 22, a decisive Communist victory appeared possible, causing Paris to appeal for help to Washington. General Paul Ely came to Washington to seek U.S. air support. The French wanted aircraft from the USS *Boxer* and USS *Essex* to help their besieged forces. In Washington, Ely's request precipitated a lengthy consideration of whether the United States should intervene in this French colonial war.

April 4–5, 1954

President Eisenhower decides not to intervene to assist the French besieged at Dien Bien Phu.

When General Ely first arrived in Washington, rumors in the press suggested that the United States would intervene. On March 24, the president stated that the defeat of Communism in Southeast Asia was critical to U.S. interests. He and Dulles agreed, however, with a military study (the Erskine Report) prepared in March 1954 that recommended the United States act only in coordination with Great Britain and France. Neither Britain nor France wanted a joint action with the United States. The British were unwilling to aid French colonialism; the French did not want to internationalize the war because Paris wished to retain control over the solution to Indochina's rebellion.

Eisenhower also asked Dulles to consult with congressional leaders to gain their support. When Secretary of State Dulles and Admiral Arthur D. Radford, chairman of the Joint Chiefs of Staff, met with congressional leaders, the congressmen learned that only Radford of the Joint Chiefs of Staff supported intervention. General Matthew Ridgeway and the others opposed such action. Consequently, the congressmen suggested that a multinational force to assist France would be best. Although Vice President Richard Nixon urged action despite the lack of support, Eisenhower preferred a united approach and the backing of Congress. Therefore, on April 5, he refused U.S. action on the terms sought by General Ely.

From early April to June 17, Dulles and Eisenhower searched for some formula to achieve "united action" with allies to help the French. The president wrote to Churchill, who rejected his request for British action. Later, Dulles flew to London to try to convince Churchill and Anthony Eden that the Communists should not be permitted to win Indochina but he could not convince them that Vietnam was a critical world region. Yet until June 17, when a new French premier, who was committed to secure "peace" in Indochina, took office, Dulles continued to believe that there should be some means to sustain French control in Indochina.

April 26, 1954

The Geneva Conference on Korea and Indochina begins.

As agreed at the Berlin foreign minister's conference (January–February 1954), the delegations included the Soviet Union, North Korea, Communist China, France, Great Britain, the United States, and 13 other non-Communist nations that had contributed to the U.N. forces in the Korean War. During the first month, the delegates argued the question of Korea. By June 15, no solution was in sight and the 16 non-Communist delegates issued a statement that further talks "would serve no useful purpose." They blamed the three Communist states for rejecting the principle of Korean independence and unity through free elections.

May 19, 1954

The United States and Pakistan sign a mutual defense pact by which Washington helps to arm Pakistan against Communism.

Secretary of State John Foster Dulles was willing to provide a similar pact for India but Prime Minister Nehru preferred to remain neutral in the Cold War. India bitterly opposed U.S. aid to Pakistan because of the frequent threats of war between these neighboring nations. Nehru believed Pakistan's arms would be used against India, not the Soviet Union. Although the Pakistan alliance became part of the Baghdad Pact, the Eisenhower administration never shipped any armaments to Pakistan because of a military coup abolishing Pakistan's republic. But subsequent administrations did send arms to the Pakistanis.

June 1, 1954

The Personal Security Board of the AEC unanimously finds Dr. J. Robert Oppenheimer is "loyal" in handling atomic secrets. Nevertheless, it votes 2 to 1 not to reinstate him as a government consultant on atomic energy.

Although Oppenheimer was one of America's most renowned physicists and had directed the Los Alamos laboratory in its production of the atomic bomb in 1945, he had been criticized for opposing the H-bomb development in 1949. He had joined many scientists who desired international controls on nuclear weapons and who feared the consequences of an unbridled nuclear arms race.

The Oppenheimer case of 1954 indicated Senator McCarthy's influence on American life. Later, Thomas E. Murray, an AEC member who voted not to reinstate Oppenheimer, admitted his vote was cast in the "exigencies of the moment," the "moment" being McCarthyism. According to John E. Haynes and Harvey Klehr's *Venona* (1999), the secret Venona files released in 1995 indicate that although Oppenheimer was not "an active Soviet source," he had strong ties to the U.S. Communist Party until 1941. After becoming head of the Manhattan project in 1943, he only gave "security officials enough information to bring about a neutralization of the [spy] problem but not enough to expose associates to retribution for what they might have already done" (page 330).

June 9, 1954

A left-wing government in Guatemala is overthrown with assistance of the U.S. Central Intelligence Agency (CIA).

Since 1944, Guatemala's political leaders had talked about land reform as a means of resolving social unrest in rural areas; however, until the 1951 election of Colonel Jacobo Arbenz Guzmán, the reformers had accomplished little. Arbenz decided that real reform required the takeover of the United Fruit Company's holdings, an American company that profited from Guatemala's banana plantations. In 1953, Arbenz's government confiscated 225,000 acres of United Fruit's 300,000 acres of land. The U.S. State Department protested on behalf of United Fruit, demanding compensation for the property. Arbenz claimed Guatemala could not afford the payment expected by United Fruit and argued that Guatemala's land belonged to its people.

Secretary of State Dulles believed Arbenz was a Communist and should be removed. In March 1954, Dulles took the issue to the Tenth Inter-American Conference session at Caracas, Venezuela. Without specifying Guatemala, Dulles persuaded the conferees to adopt a declaration that Communism was "incompatible with the concept of American freedom," and nations should act to "eradicate and prevent subversive activities." The vote was 17 to 1: Guatemala voted no; Mexico and Argentina abstained; Costa Rica was absent.

In January 1954, Arbenz told reporters the military aid the CIA gave to dictators in Nicaragua, Honduras, and El Salvador amounted to an "international plot" to overthrow Guatemala's government. Arbenz's remarks appear to have been correct. On January 29 rebels led by Colonel Carlos Castillo Armas launched an attack that reached Guatemala's capital city on June 18. Although Arbenz received armaments from Czechoslovakia, his army was no match for the rebels. To oversee Arbenz's ouster in June, Secretary of State Dulles sent John Peurifoy as ambassador to Guatemala. At Peurifoy's direction, Armas headed the military junta that took over Guatemala.

Based on declassified documents, Nick Cullather's 1999 book *Secret History: The CIA's Classified Account of Its Operations in Guatemala 1952–1954* provides an account of the CIA's role in the overthrow of Arbenz.

June 12, 1954

The French National Assembly votes no confidence in George Bidault's ministry; on June 17, the assembly approves Pierre Mendès-France as head of a new ministerial coalition.

Bidault's government fell as a result of criticism of his Indochinese policies. Mendès-France promised to solve the problem and vowed to resign if an "honorable peace" had not been concluded in Indochina by July 20, 1954.

June 15, 1954

Ngo Dinh Diem replaces Buu Loc as Premier of the French-recognized Vietnamese government.

Diem, whose rule greatly influenced both Vietnam and the United States from 1954 until his assassination in November 1963, was born in Vietnam of a Mandarin family. During the 1930s, he favored moderate reform to obtain some local government from the French, but by 1933 he abandoned the possibility of cooperating with the French and retired from active politics. In 1948, Diem refused to accept the French terms that Bao Dai had agreed to when he became head of state.

Diem spent the early years of the 1950s in the United States at Maryknoll seminaries. There he gained many influential friends including Supreme Court Justice William O. Douglas, Francis Cardinal Spellman, and Senators Mike Mansfield and John F. Kennedy. Thus, when Bao Dai selected Diem as premier in 1954, he chose someone acceptable to the United States. Although Bao Dai appointed Diem on June 15, he did not announce the new ministry until July 5, 1954.

July 20, 1954

The Geneva Conference approves a settlement of the Indochinese war.

In May, the conferees had become deadlocked on the status of the governments of Laos and Cambodia. On May 31, the delegates approved a British proposal to invite both sides in each Indochinese state to hold cease-fire talks at Geneva. The United States opposed negotiating with the Communists and, while never completely abandoning the conference, became generally less active in cooperating in or leading the decision-making process. After the opening session, Dulles never returned to the conference, sending Walter Bedell Smith as the U.S. representative.

The final Geneva agreements provided for the cessation of hostilities in each of the three Indochinese states (July 20) and for a Final Declaration of the Geneva delegations (July 21). Together, the agreements recognized Laos and Cambodia as independent nations and temporarily divided Vietnam into two parts separated by a demilitarized zone (DMZ) at the 17th parallel. An election in 1956 would unify and decide on a future government of Vietnam. In Vietnam, each side's forces would regroup on its side of the DMZ. The Vietminh government of Ho Chi Minh controlled the north with its capital at Hanoi; the Vietnamese Nationalist government of Bao Dai controlled the south from Saigon. French forces could remain in the south but no new forces were to be introduced or rotated by either side. No new military equipment could be added, but replacement of destroyed, damaged, or worn equipment was allowed. Refugees from either side would be able to move freely to the north or south, according to their wishes. Finally, an International Control Commission with representatives from India, Poland, and Canada would supervise the cease-fire accords and the election procedures.

The United States announced it could not accept the conference declaration, but it agreed not to use force or threats to disturb the accords. Furthermore, the United States would view a violation of the accords as a threat to international peace. Speaking for the Nationalist Vietnamese government at Saigon, Tran Van Do informed the final conference session that his government had reservations about the Geneva accords but would not use force or threats to resist the cease-fire. He said his government would support "every effort to reestablish a real and lasting peace in Vietnam." To obtain a final settlement of the Indochina issues, the United States had to compromise on such issues as dividing Vietnam at the 17th parallel, and France withdrawing all of its troops from Vietnam.

July 23, 1954

Chinese Communist fighter pilots shoot down a Cathay-Pacific Airways commercial airliner.

Later, the Chinese government apologized to Great Britain, owner of the airline, and agreed to pay compensation. Ten passengers died in the crash; eight survived. The Cathay-Pacific plane was shot down in the South China Sea near Hainan Island. Following a strong protest by Prime Minister Churchill, the Chinese government admitted its pilots had mistaken the plane for a Chinese Nationalist airplane. Mao's government apologized and offered to compensate the victims' families and the British airline.

August 30, 1954

The French National Assembly rejects the European Defense Community (EDC) treaty.

The EDC plan had been agreed to on May 27, 1952, but disputes over French foreign policy in Indochina and Europe prevented the French assembly from voting on the EDC until 1954. The French veto compelled the NATO allies to seek another method for attaining a united European defense plan. U.S. Secretary of State John Foster Dulles was determined to have German troops in the NATO defense structure. French intransigence was the only factor preventing this.

September 8, 1954

The Southeast Asia Treaty Organization (SEATO) is formed at Manila to protect the region from outside attack or "any state or territory hereafter designated."

The designated states were Cambodia, Laos, and Vietnam. If any state were threatened by subversion or aggression, the signatory states would consult on appropriate action. The members of SEATO were the United States, France, Great Britain, Australia, New Zealand, Thailand, Pakistan, and the Philippines. In hearings on the SEATO treaty, Senator Alexander Wiley asked Secretary Dulles if agreeing "to counter subversive activity" is not different from agreeing to resist armed attack. Dulles acknowledged that it was different because it involved a Communist threat within a foreign country. Significantly, Dulles added: "We are confronted by an unfortunate fact—most of the countries of the world do not share our view that Communist control of any government anywhere is in itself a danger and a threat."

In fact, France, Britain, and most U.S. allies would not accept the unusual U.S. concept expressed by Dulles, that America must fear any nation with a Communist government. This reflected America's myth that all Communists received orders from Moscow as part of the universal Communist threat to capitalism. It also reflected the "globalization" of containment that American critics denounced.

October 21, 1954

American oil companies secure a share in Iran's oil concessions as a result of a State Department deal with Britain and the Iranian government.

On August 19, 1953, the Iranian nationalist leader Mossadegh was ousted with U.S. aid on behalf of Shah Mohammad Reza Pahlavi. Because the shah did not desire exclusive British ownership of Iranian oil, President Eisenhower's adviser on petroleum, Herbert Hoover Jr., undertook negotiations to form an international consortium to take over the Anglo-Iranian oil concessions. Basically, Hoover and the Eisenhower administration conceived of this as a Cold War measure necessary to keep Soviet interests out of Iran. The National Iranian Oil Company was set up. For this company, Iranian oil would be extracted, refined, and marketed by the international oil consortium. Iran received 50 percent of the profits, and the other 50 percent were divided by the consortium members as follows: Anglo-Iranian Company, 40 percent; Royal Dutch Shell, 14 percent; French Petroleum Company, 6 percent; and each of the five American companies, 5 percent for a total 40 percent U.S. shares.

October 23, 1954

A letter from President Eisenhower offers aid to Ngo Dinh Diem.

This letter and the SEATO alliance formed the basic "commitment" for U.S. aid to South Vietnam, the region of Vietnam below the 17th parallel established by the Geneva cease-fire agreement. In his letter, Eisenhower limited aid in accordance with the "new look," which expected Diem to establish satisfactory local defense capabilities. In sum, Eisenhower agreed to: 1. provide a "humanitarian effort" for assisting refugees from the north; 2. give aid for the "welfare and stability of Diem's government," provided Diem

USS *Montague* helps French evacuate Vietnam refugees from Haiphong, August 1954. National Archives

gave "assurances as to the standards of performance" his government would maintain; 3. provide aid to help Vietnam develop and maintain "a strong, viable state, capable of resisting attempted subversion or aggression through military means"; and, 4. expect Diem's government to begin "needed reforms" that would establish an independent Vietnam "with a strong government" that would be respected "at home and abroad."

Eisenhower's letter had one other significant consequence: U.S. economic aid began to go directly to Diem's government in Saigon, not through French officials in Paris, as it had since 1950. French Premier Mendès-France thought Washington had agreed to continue sending aid through Paris, a belief that resulted in increased friction between the French and U.S. governments in 1954 and 1955.

November 2, 1954

Congressional elections return control of both houses to the Democratic Party by a majority of one in the Senate and 29 in the House.

This change did not affect Eisenhower's foreign policy at first because the Democratic congressmen held positions closer to the president than many Republicans, such as Senator William Knowland of California. After 1957, however, Senate Democratic leader Lyndon Johnson attacked Eisenhower's "new look" reduction in conventional forces and his "peaceful coexistence" discussions with Premier Khrushchev.

November 23, 1954

A Communist Chinese military court convicts 13 American airmen of spying and sentences them to long prison terms.

The airmen had disappeared while flying missions during the Korean War. In response to the court's action, the United States protested both to Peking through the British embassy and to the United Nations. On December 10, the U.N. General Assembly voted 47-5 to condemn China's treatment of the airmen and instructed U.N. Secretary-General Dag Hammarskjöld to confer with the Chinese. On December 17, after meeting with Hammarskjöld, China's Premier Chou En-lai agreed to release the airmen.

December 1, 1954

The United States and Nationalist China sign a mutual defense pact.

This treaty authorized the United States to disperse its naval forces around Formosa and the Pescadores to protect those island groups. Notably, U.S. protection did not include offshore islands such as Quemoy and Matsu. In addition, the Nationalists stipulated that they would not use their armed forces except in a joint agreement with the United States, a clause to prevent Chiang Kai-shek from unilaterally invading China's mainland. Yet, Dulles feared Chiang did not take the stipulation seriously because he constantly talked about invading China as a "supreme" Nationalist mission.

The U.S.-Nationalist treaty was negotiated following an August 11 declaration by Chinese Foreign Minister Chou En-lai that "the liberation of Taiwan is a glorious, historic mission of the Chinese people." Taiwan, he said, must be freed from the "traitorous Chiang Kai-shek group." When a journalist asked Eisenhower about Chou's statement, the president said "an invasion would have to run over the Seventh Fleet," which had been stationed in the Formosa Straits since 1950. When China began intermittently to bombard the offshore islands in August 1954, the United States had begun negotiating the security treaty that was finalized on December 2.

December 2, 1954

A U.S. Senate resolution condemns the conduct of Senator Joseph McCarthy by a vote of 67-22.

This action, together with the Democrats regaining a majority in Congress and removing McCarthy from his chairmanship of a Senate Operations subcommittee, ended the worst aspect of McCarthyism. The vote followed an extensive public hearing that was one of the first congressional actions to be televised nationwide. Nevertheless, the fears, suspicions, and myths concerning Soviet spies continued to influence attitudes of intense anti-Communism among Americans, even those who disliked McCarthy's extreme methods.

1955

January 25, 1955

Congress authorizes Eisenhower to use American armed forces to defend Formosa and the Pescadores.

The congressional resolution to defend Formosa resulted from a crisis that developed between 1953 and 1955. While Truman had provided Formosa with U.S. navy support, the Nationalist Chinese limited their activities to hit-and-run attacks and bombing raids against the Chinese mainland. Eisenhower said in a February 2, 1953, speech to Congress that the Korean War made it illogical to protect China's mainland from Nationalist Chinese attacks. Eisenhower declared the United States had no aggressive designs on the People's Republic of China, but critics claimed Eisenhower "unleashed" the Nationalists to attack China's mainland in any way they desired. Following the president's 1953 speech, the Nationalist government began persistent raids on China's coastline and built up its armed forces on Quemoy, Matsu, and Tachen—islands located a few miles from China's mainland.

As a result of these Nationalist provocations, the Chinese Communists began bombarding the offshore islands in 1954. On January 1, 1955, the People's Republic of China escalated its attacks on the offshore islands by intensifying its shelling and constructing jet airfields along the coastline opposite Formosa. On January 10, about 100 mainland planes raided Tachen, located 200 miles from Formosa, while 40,000 Chinese troops seized Ichiang, an island seven miles from Tachen. These Chinese attacks led Eisenhower to order U.S. navy ships to prepare to convoy Nationalists from Tachen and to draw up a January 24 message to Congress giving the president permission to fight the Chinese Communists if necessary. The president told Congress the United Nations would ultimately decide Formosa's status, but the critical situation required congressional authority for using U.S. armed forces to protect Formosa and "such related positions and territories required to assure the defense of Formosa." As Stephen E. Ambrose's *Eisenhower the President* (1984) indicates, Eisenhower did not specify Quemoy and Matsu as part of the defense area. Chiang Kai-shek wanted assurances to protect those two islands, but Eisenhower preferred to "confuse" the situation on Quemoy and Matsu, making any decision dependent on circumstances if the Chinese Communists tried to seize those islands.

On January 28, Congress approved the resolution Eisenhower requested. The House approved it on January 24 by a vote of 410 to 3; the Senate held hearings on the resolution before approving it on January 28 by 83 to 3. The Senate gave further support to the president by ratifying the SEATO treaty on February 1 and the Mutual Security Treaty with Nationalist China on February 9. In February, the U.N. Security Council discussed Formosa but abandoned its efforts to get a cease-fire in the Formosa Straits because China's Foreign Minister Chou En-lai rejected an invitation to attend the U.N. Security Council meeting. In light of China's continued bombardment of the offshore islands, Eisenhower and his staff considered having U.S. forces occupy Quemoy and Matsu or using tactical nuclear weapons against the Chinese forces located opposite Formosa.

Eisenhower delayed making either choice, and his caution was rewarded when Chou En-lai offered a conciliatory proposal in April. Speaking to an African-Asian Conference in Bandung, Indonesia, Chou said he was willing to negotiate with the United States because "the Chinese people are friendly to the American people" and do not want a war. Chou wanted to "relax tensions in the Far East" and especially "relaxing tensions in Taiwan"—the name China preferred to Formosa. In response to Chou's offer, Secretary of State John Foster Dulles finally agreed to negotiate if there were a cease-fire in the Formosa

Straits. Chou agreed and in May 1955, China not only ended the bombardment, but released 11 U.S. airmen captured during the Korean War who had been convicted of espionage and given prison terms by a Chinese court on November 22, 1954.

In August 1955 negotiations began in Warsaw, Poland, between the Chinese ambassador to Poland and the U.S. ambassador to Czechoslovakia. The negotiations were unsuccessful because China regarded the issue of Formosa as an internal Chinese affair not subject to international or United Nations interference. By 1956, the Formosa issue was calmed before heating up again in 1958.

February 5, 1955

The French National Assembly votes "no confidence" in the ministry of Mendès-France.

This ministry had arranged the Geneva declarations of July 1954 but ran into difficulty by seeking a compromise with the rebellion in Algeria. The overthrow of Mendès-France's cabinet resulted in two years of political instability that eventually led to General de Gaulle's return to power in 1958.

February 12, 1955

The U.S. army agrees with France to assume training the Vietnamese national army.

Under this arrangement, General Paul Ely announced that French forces would cease training operations but would continue defensive activity in the northern provinces near the DMZ prior to their final withdrawal in 1956. American General John O'Daniel commanded the training mission in Vietnam after February 12. This agreement was instrumental toward the United States replacing France as the Western power in Vietnam. U.S. military experts believed that the French had not allowed sufficient independence for Vietnam's officers and that the Americans could more ably prepare Diem's army to fight Communism. It was the first step in a series that led to the Second Indochina War.

February 18, 1955

The Baghdad Pact creates a defensive alliance between Turkey and Iraq.

Soon after, Great Britain, Iran, and Pakistan joined the alliance. The United States gave wholehearted support to the pact but never joined it. After 1956, the United States provided economic aid for the pact's members. In 1957, following the Suez crisis with Egypt, the United States met with the Military Committee of the Baghdad Pact and provided weapons for the pact's members.

March 19, 1955

Harold Stassen appointed special assistant for disarmament.

President Eisenhower created the post of special assistant to the president for disarmament and appointed Harold Stassen to the position. While he viewed the prospects of arms control negotiations with the Soviets more optimistically than Secretary Dulles, Stassen never had much impact on policy decisions.

March 23, 1955

Eisenhower seeks to clarify Dulles's "massive retaliation" assertions by declaring that the United States would not use nuclear weapons in a "police action."

Actually, Eisenhower's comments at a news conference on March 23 were not intended to "clarify" but to confuse the journalists. The question that had been asked was whether or not the president would use atomic weapons to defend Chinese offshore islands under Chiang Kai-shek's control. On March 12 and 15, Secretary of State Dulles had spoken of the United States using tactical nuclear weapons against Chinese airfields and troops near Quemoy and Matsu. On March 16, Eisenhower told a reporter that the tactical weapons Dulles referred to could be used for "strictly military targets and for strictly military purposes." The president hoped this statement would warn Peking of the dangers of the Quemoy-Matsu crisis. In the context of these statements, a minor war scare developed in America. Cold war hawks urged war on mainland China; but critics feared that an attack on China might result in all-out nuclear war with the Soviet Union.

Thus on March 23, the president withdrew slightly from his March 16 remarks. He told the press that he could not predict how war would occur or what would result. Eisenhower said it would depend on the circumstances at the time the decision was made.

There would be no automatic nuclear attack by the United States in the manner that some Americans interpreted as "massive retaliation."

April 18–24, 1955

Bandung Conference of Asian-African nations agrees to promote the self-determination of all nations.

Twenty-nine Asian and African nations attended. This conference was a milestone along the way to the liberation of many former colonial nations from Western European control between 1955 and 1960. Because anticolonialists often used Marxian terminology to explain "the imperialist-capitalist" use of colonies to exploit nations of Asia and Africa, many Americans associated these statements with Moscow's rhetoric, assuming that such conferences as that at Bandung were in fact Communist fronts for "national liberation."

Such analysis disclosed how far away some Americans had moved from their anticolonial heritage of 1776, as renewed by Woodrow Wilson and Franklin D. Roosevelt in the twentieth century. Prior to the Cold War, America had been a champion of self-determination and the end of European colonial empires.

May 2, 1955

Diem centralizes his political power in Saigon by defeating local sects with whom French officials had compromised by bribery.

Three large non-Communist sects in the Saigon area had gained much local influence from 1946 to 1954, because France paid them to fight the Vietminh and gave them much local control. These three were Cao Dai, Hoa Hao, and Binh Xuyen. Using tactics of divide-and-conquer, Diem gained control over these sects and other smaller ones by the summer of 1955. Between March 21 and May 2, virtual civil war took place in Saigon, as Diem fought the Binh Xuyen and drove them from the city. Diem's success against the sects increased his prestige. On May 1, he gained control of Vietnam's army from Bao Dai, and on May 5, a political congress in Saigon urged that all Bao Dai's powers be given to Premier Diem, pending the formation of a new government.

May 7, 1955

The Western European Union (WEU) is organized to provide a defensive alliance that would include West German forces.

After the French National Assembly rejected the EDC in August 1954, British Foreign Secretary Anthony Eden proposed that a Western European Union, including German forces, four divisions of British troops, and U.S. forces in Europe, be coordinated into a Western European defense program. German Chancellor Konrad Adenauer cooperated by agreeing that West Germany would not "have recourse to force" as a means of uniting Germany. Eden's plan was officially drawn up and signed by the foreign ministers of Belgium, Britain, France, West Germany, Italy, Luxembourg, and the Netherlands on October 23, 1954.

The plan provided for ending the occupation of West Germany and admitting West Germany to NATO. Under French Premier Mendès-France's guidance, the WEU pact was approved by the French National Assembly on December 24, 1954. Thus, on May 7, concluding formalities organized the WEU, whose members were France, Great Britain, West Germany, Italy, Belgium, Luxembourg, and the Netherlands. The West German Federal Republic joined NATO on May 9, 1955, just two days after gaining sovereign status with the implementation of the Paris treaties (WEU) of October 23, 1954.

May 10, 1955

Soviet proposal designed to reduce tensions and move arms limitation discussions.

The Soviet representative to the U.N. Disarmament Subcommittee, Yakov Malik, presented a proposal that consisted of three parts. It call for the reduction of tensions through the dismantling of overseas bases and the numerical reduction and eventual elimination of the armed forces of the major world powers, the reduction and eventual elimination of nuclear weapons, and the establishment of an international control organ. Malik suggested that this plan offered "all the most important and fundamental wishes of the Western Powers."

It did incorporate several of the ideas put forward in the 1954 Anglo-French proposal. Jules Moch, the French delegate, declared that the Soviet proposal "looks too good to be true," while the British representative, Anthony Nutting, believed the plan to be "an encouraging development and a significant advance." The offer marked a significant shift in Moscow's policy on four accounts: 1) it suggested that the new Soviet leadership understood the devastation that nuclear weapons could bring to all societies; 2) the proposal indicated that with the number of stockpiles of nuclear weapons grade material available throughout the world, some kind of verification procedures were necessary to prevent hidden stores; 3) it indicated that the Soviets were concerned about the possibility of a surprise attack and wanted to alleviate the prospect; and 4) it presented the first indication that the Soviets were prepared to discuss partial arms limitation measures instead of the comprehensive proposals for general and complete disarmament as previously offered.

Although the Soviet proposal suggested several avenues for negotiation, the Eisenhower administration did not formally respond to it. Harold Stassen, the newly appointed special assistant to the president for disarmament, and Eisenhower were preoccupied with a complete review of previous U.S. proposals and may not have understood the significance of Moscow's new offer. Also there was internal disagreement, as Secretary Dulles, the Joint Chiefs of Staff and the AEC steadfastly opposed serious arms control negotiations with the Soviets. Whether or not a "moment of hope" was missed, as some critics charged, is not evident.

May 14, 1955

The Warsaw Pact Defense Alliance is formed by European Communist nations.

The Warsaw Pact was the Soviet Union's answer to U.S. integration of West German troops into NATO. Eight Eastern European nations signed the pact. Early in January 1956, the East German army became part

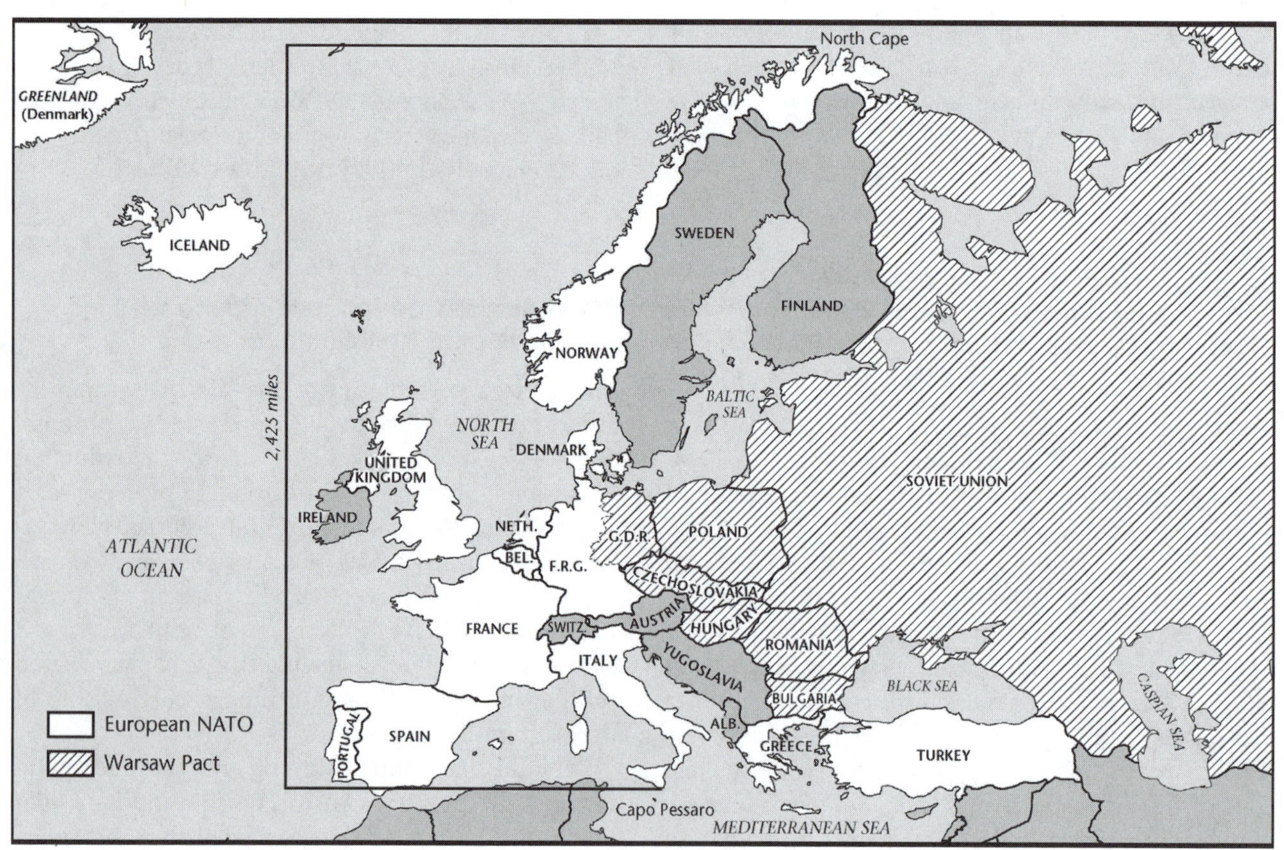

NATO and the Warsaw Pact

of the Warsaw Pact forces under Soviet Marshal Ivan S. Konev.

May 15, 1955

The big four powers agree to an Austrian peace treaty.

Although the Austrian State Treaty had been under discussion over 370 times since 1947, serious negotiations began in February 1954. The Austrians initially proposed a declaration of neutrality to the Soviets who introduced the idea, but the Americans were uneasy about a weak, neutral nation in the center of Europe. The State Department was willing to accept neutralization, but the Pentagon wanted an Austria with armed forces sufficient to guarantee its independence. Foreign Minister Molotov opposed the idea of Soviet armed forces withdrawing from Central Europe and giving up territory won during the war; however, he was overruled. The foreign ministers of Britain, France, the Soviet Union, and the United States accepted peace terms, agreeing to withdraw all foreign forces from Austria by December 31, 1955. Unlike Germany, Austria would be a neutral nation much like Switzerland, with severe limits on the types of weapons its armed forces could possess. Following the Austrian agreement, Eisenhower announced he would participate in the July 1955 summit conference at Geneva.

June 25, 1955

Soviet foreign minister Molotov apologizes to the United States for the Soviets' shooting down a U.S. navy plane on June 24, offering to pay part of the damages.

The Soviet apology for this incident was unusual because it was contrary to Soviet practice. Both in 1953 and in 1954, the Soviets rejected U.S. protests and claims for damage. On July 29, 1953, the Soviets shot down a B-50 flying near the Siberian coast. On September 6, 1954, a U.S. navy P2V-5 was downed near Siberia. In neither instance did the Soviets respond to U.S. protests, except to claim that the planes had violated Soviet air space.

On June 24, another P2V-5 on patrol in the Bering Sea was shot down by Soviet jet fighter pilots. The plane crash-landed on St. Lawrence Island, injuring seven members of the crew. The next day, Molotov wrote to the United States, expressing the USSR's regrets for the incident and offering to pay 50 percent of the damages. Molotov insisted that the American plane was over Soviet air space. He stated, however, that the cloudy sky made errors possible on both sides. Later, on July 18, the USSR proposed that some method be found to prevent such incidents in the future. In Washington, President Eisenhower was willing to accept the Soviet response. Secretary Dulles believed that the Soviets should be made to pay a greater compensation, but the State Department did not pursue this matter. For an understanding of U.S. aerial surveillance policies, see William E. Burrows, *By Any Means Necessary: America's Secret Air War in the Cold War* (2001).

July 18–23, 1955

President Dwight Eisenhower, British Prime Minister Anthony Eden, French Premier Edgar Faure, and Soviet Premier Nikolay Bulganin attend the big four summit conference at Geneva.

The conference discussed the reunification of Germany, European security, and disarmament. The talks stalled, however, on the German issue. The United States wanted a united Germany that would be free to join NATO if it wished; Moscow wanted all foreign forces out of Germany and it to be a neutral country.

During the conference, Eisenhower gained favorable world reaction with his "open skies" proposal. This plan would permit U.S. and Soviet reconnaissance aircraft to photograph each nation's territory to ensure against a surprise attack. In addition, each nation would exchange plans on military facilities. To Khrushchev, however, the open skies proposal was nothing more than legalized espionage. Although the U.N. General Assembly eventually supported this plan, the Soviet Union refused to permit such verification tactics.

Eisenhower took considerable pains to emphasize the destructive nature of nuclear weapons and to convince the Soviet delegation that the United States had no intention of attacking Russia. He succeeded better than he knew: Khrushchev left the conference apparently convinced that he could "practice nuclear bluster and bluff" and "play on American fears." (See William Taubman, *Khrushchev: the Man and His Era* [2003].)

The first summit meeting since World War II. Dwight D. Eisenhower Library

July 22, 1955

A rearmament bill is enacted by the West German parliament.

The bill authorized the enlistment of 6,000 officers as the nucleus of a 500,000-man army. Compulsory military service was enacted, to become effective July 25, 1956.

July 27, 1955

Bulgarian fighter planes shoot down an El Al (Israeli) airliner; 58 passengers are killed.

The El Al Constellation airliner was en route from London to Israel and strayed off course, flying over Bulgarian territory. Bulgaria admitted on August 3, following its investigation of the incident, that its fighter pilots were "too hasty" in shooting down the aircraft. They pledged to punish the pilots and take steps to prevent a recurrence of the incident. They also agreed to pay compensation to families of the victims and to share in paying for the destroyed plane. During the fall session of the U.N. General Assembly, member nations approved a resolution on December 6 that asked all governments to avoid attacks on civilian aircraft that violated their international borders.

September 13, 1955

The Soviet Union establishes diplomatic relations with West Germany.

Soviet recognition of West Germany came one week before the USSR conferred sovereignty on a separate East Germany on September 20. The Soviets also gave East Germany the control of civilian traffic between West Germany and West Berlin.

October 11, 1955

Canada signs an agreement with the Soviet Union granting most-favored-nation trade privileges and cooperation in Arctic research.

Canada's Minister for External Affairs, Lester Pearson, negotiated the treaty for Canada.

October 26, 1955

Ngo Dinh Diem gains complete control of the South Vietnamese government, proclaiming a republic with himself as the first president.

With U.S. support, Diem rejected French plans to reorganize the government under Bao, and on October 18 he refused to resign as premier when ordered to by Bao Dai. To gain power, Diem organized a referendum on October 23 that overwhelmingly voted for Diem against Bao Dai. This "election" permitted Diem to proclaim a republic, end Bao Dai's emperorship, and announce that elections for a national legislature would follow in the near future.

November 8, 1955

President Eisenhower and Secretary of Defense Wilson give intermediate range ballistic missiles (IRBM) equal priority with intercontinental ballistic (ICBM) missiles.

Within the U.S. air force during the early 1950s, internal disputes had slowed the development of both ICBMs and IRBMs. On September 8, 1954, a new ICBM organizational arrangement gave this missile the highest priority for development, ending the air force's inclination to emphasize bomber delivery systems. In the fall of 1954, the president appointed James Killian to head a committee to review the entire missile program. In February 1955, Killian's group recommended that the IRBMs were "of utmost importance to national security" and should be made operational as early as possible.

To effect the IRBM development, Secretary Wilson established a Ballistic Missiles Committee to oversee missile advances. A separate directive by Wilson told the committee to assign the IRBMs equal priority with the procurement of ICBMs. The IRBM would have a range of 1,500 to 2,000 miles. Although the air force first interpreted the November directive as making the IRBM "second" to the ICBM, this decision was corrected in January 1956. Intermediate range ballistic missiles required bases in Europe from which they could hit Soviet targets.

November 18, 1955

Soviet Premier Bulganin and Khrushchev, First Secretary of the Communist Party's Central Committee, visit India, Burma, and Afghanistan to promote friendship for the Soviet Union among Third World nations.

For nearly two months, Bulganin and Khrushchev toured thousands of miles to visit nations that were emerging from colonialism in an effort to aid national liberation movements. As they visited cultural sites and industrial plants, Khrushchev became the chief spokesman in what he considered "a new active diplomacy between us and the capitalists."

See April 15, 1946.

November 22, 1955

First "true" Soviet superbomb test.

The Soviet Union tested their RDS-3—a thermonuclear device that has a yield of 1.6 megatons—at the Semipalatinsk test site in Kazakhstan. It was also the world's first air dropped H-bomb test.

December 14, 1955

Sixteen nations are admitted to the United Nations.

They were Albania, Austria, Bulgaria, Cambodia, Ceylon, Finland, Hungary, Ireland, Italy, Jordan, Laos, Libya, Nepal, Portugal, Romania, and Spain.

December 16, 1955

Eisenhower's "open skies" plan is approved by the U.N. General Assembly.

The U.N. action scored some public opinion points for the United States, but the Soviet Union opposed this or any other means for intrusive verification of its military installations.

1956

January 19, 1956

The U.N. Security Council unanimously votes to censure Israel for a December 11, 1955 attack on Syria.

This attack was the most serious of several border engagements between Israeli and Egyptian-Syrian forces during 1955. The 1955 raids occurred in the Gaza Strip near the Sinai Desert and in the Lake Galilee region of the Israeli-Syrian border. Following the U.N. vote, the United States asserted on February 17 that it would suspend all arms shipments to both Israel and the Arab nations. An Israeli-Egyptian cease-fire, arranged by U.N. Secretary-General Hammarskjöld, became effective in April. In Washington, administration officials were concerned that the continuing Israeli-Arab conflict would result in the Soviet Union siding with the Arabs.

January 28, 1956

President Eisenhower rejects a friendship proposal by Soviet Premier Bulganin.

As part of a so-called peace offensive, Premier Bulganin wrote to Eisenhower early in January to propose a 20-year treaty of friendship and economic, cultural, and scientific cooperation. He called the president an outstanding leader and recalled that only during the Russian Civil War of 1918–1920 had the two nations clashed. The two nations had no territorial or interest conflicts. Therefore, Soviet-U.S. cooperation would be based on "vital and long-term interests of both parties." Because Washington was astounded and uncertain how to receive Bulganin's note and the accompanying treaty draft, Eisenhower replied in polite but evasive terms. He thought Moscow should first cooperate on German unity or aerial inspection. Consequently, correspondence between Bulganin and the president continued until the Suez and Hungarian crises of October 1956.

Exactly why the Soviets made this suggestion is not known. Adam Ulam, a U.S. Sovietologist, believes the Soviets either wished to frighten China into compliance with Soviet terms or Moscow was trying to interest Washington in a treaty against mainland China. These were the early days of the Sino-Soviet split, during which Peking demanded nuclear capabilities and additional heavy industry from their wary Soviet allies.

February 14, 1956

Speaking before the 20th Communist Party Congress, Khrushchev criticizes Stalin's crimes against the party and the nation.

This de-Stalinization speech blamed Stalin for unnecessary party purges and terrorist tactics. Clearly, however, Khrushchev blamed Stalin, not the Communist system, for the faults in Soviet policy since 1928. He justified the central party controls and overall objectives of the Soviet government in domestic affairs. Khrushchev's speech enhanced his power and assisted his shift of emphasis to consumer goods and worker incentives as a means to bolster the Soviet economy. The speech's greatest effects, however, were in the Eastern European satellite nations, where Khrushchev's message implied that Communist leaders could use a variety of methods of Communism, not just Stalin's. Khrushchev also recognized this change by seeking to heal the breach with Yugoslavia's Tito, whom, he said, Stalin had mistreated. (See September 27, 1949.) In international affairs, he proposed a policy of "peaceful coexistence" with capitalist nations while the Soviet Union enhanced its consumer economy.

April 17, 1956

The Soviet Union announces it has dissolved the Cominform.

Since its inception in 1947 as a replacement for the Comintern, the single achievement of the Cominform was the expulsion of Tito and Yugoslavia from the world Communist movement. For this reason, Khrushchev hoped to reconcile Tito to renew his world socialist affiliation by abolishing the Cominform. Tito was not seduced by Khrushchev's ploy. Although the Yugoslav leader conducted negotiations with Moscow, Tito retained and strengthened his role as a neutralist between the two superpowers.

April 23, 1956

Khrushchev visits England and issues threats.

He announced the Soviet Union would arm guided missiles with H-bombs and claimed Soviet leadership in nuclear weapons. The Soviet visit accomplished little and it turned out to be little more than a public relations event, even if Khrushchev found himself loudly challenged by British leftists.

May 9, 1956

Dulles refuses to supply arms to Israel, claiming that this could lead to a Mideast arms competition with the USSR because the Arab states sought military aid from the Soviets.

As a crisis seemed imminent in the Middle East because of the demands of Nasser of Egypt and incidents along the Arab-Israeli borders, Dulles hoped to avoid providing U.S. arms for Arabs or Israelis. He denied export licenses for arms to Israel and all Arab states except Iraq and Saudi Arabia. At the same time, however, Dulles encouraged Canada and France to sell F-86 aircraft and French Mysères to Israel. Although the Israeli leaders accepted this tactic, they had already begun preparations with France to undertake preemptive action in the Sinai-Suez area.

May 14, 1956

Soviets protest continued U.S. penetration of their airspace.

The American Strategic Air Command's Project Home Run had undertaken extensive over-flights of northern portions of the Soviet Union using 16 American RB-47Es photo-reconnaissance aircraft and five RB-47H electronic reconnaissance planes, supported by 28 KC-97 tanker aircraft for in-flight refueling. Based at the U.S. airbase at Tule, Greenland, these reconnaissance aircraft flew 156 missions between March 21 to May 10, 1956, collecting photos, radar intelligence, and communications data from a 3,500-mile-wide strip ranging from Murmansk on the Kola Peninsula to Provideniya on the Bering Strait. On May 6–7, six RB-47Es flying abreast in daylight crossed over Soviet territory at Ambarchik and photomapped all the way to Anadyr in the Bering Strait where Soviet fighter planes tried but failed to intercept them in three or four attacks. This episode revealed how poorly defended this region was—something Soviet leaders knew, but they could not but be irritated at its exposure.

On May 14, the Kremlin finally registered a formal protest after this rather blatant episode. The Eisenhower administration responded on May 29 with its regrets that "navigational difficulties" had caused the unintentional violation of Soviet airspace. See William E. Burrows, *By Any Means Necessary: America's Secret Air War in the Cold War* (2001).

May 21, 1956

A U.S. H-bomb dropped from an airplane is detonated at Bikini Atoll.

In a series of nuclear tests code-named Redwing, a B-52 dropped the bomb that exploded at a height of from 10,000 to 15,000 feet. Although Japan complained about the nuclear fallout, U.S. experts said the radioactive debris was slight compared with the 1954 tests.

June 20, 1956

Yugoslavia's President (or Marshal?) Tito concludes a three-week visit to Moscow.

This visit symbolized Khrushchev's promise to improve relations with Tito. Later in the year (September 19), Khrushchev visited Belgrade. The talks did not go well, however, and on February 19, 1957, Khrushchev said that because Tito rejected the Soviet proposals, Yugoslavia would not get further economic aid from the USSR. In subsequent years, relations between Khrushchev and Tito varied widely as each leader was suspicious of the other's intentions.

June 28, 1956

Riots break out in Poznan, Poland, as workers demonstrate for better economic and social conditions.

This was the initial Polish reaction to Khrushchev's de-Stalinization speech. Tensions continued in the USSR throughout 1956, but Wladyslaw Gomulka, who became first Secretary of the Polish Communist Party on October 21, carefully steered Warsaw's policy to gain concessions from Khrushchev without antagonizing the Soviet leader.

See November 18, 1956.

July 1, 1956

The first three West German divisions join the NATO command.

Germany was committed eventually to provide 12 divisions to NATO.

July 4, 1956

First U-2 flight is over Moscow and Leningrad.

Described as "a manned, high-flying jet-propelled glider," the U-2 was designed to fly over the Soviet Union at altitudes beyond the reach of Soviet fighter planes. Its mission was aerial reconnaissance, but electronic intelligence gathering continued to be collected by "ferrets," lower flying aircraft that were frequently in harm's way. (See August 22, 1956.) Also on July 4, Khrushchev and his entourage visited the U.S. embassy to join in the Independence Day party. Although the Eisenhower administration thought Soviet radar could not "see" the U-2, they were wrong. On July 10, Moscow filed a formal diplomatic protest of the over-flight.

July 17, 1956

Soviet Premier Bulganin and East German Premier Otto Grotewohl meet.

The two leaders declare that unification of Germany should be worked out by East-West German governments, not by the four powers that occupied Germany in 1945.

July 19, 1956

Dulles cancels the U.S. offer to aid Egypt in constructing the Aswân High dam.

Although in December 1955, the United States, Great Britain, and the World Bank jointly offered funds to Egypt for its dam project on the Nile, President Nasser persistently refused to discuss details of the loan with Washington. Instead, Nasser undertook policies to upset the calm in Ethiopia, Uganda, and the Sudan. He also arranged arms purchases with Communist countries and held talks with the Soviets and Communist Chinese. On July 19, Egyptian Ambassador to the United States Ahmed Hussein arrived back from Cairo and immediately told Dulles he wanted to finalize the Aswân Dam loan. Negotiations were unnecessary, he said, for if the United States did not guarantee the loan, "the Soviet Union would do so."

Dulles rejected Hussein's abrupt "blackmail" demand. The United States, the secretary said, had assumed Egypt did not want the loan because it had rejected offers to negotiate the arrangement. Conditions in the Middle East needed to improve, Dulles observed, before a loan could be concluded. Commentators in July 1956 showed surprise that Dulles had abruptly withdrawn the loan. Actually, Dulles had previously discussed the loan with the British and tentatively agreed to withdraw or not renew the offer to Egypt. In addition, Dulles indicated to Hussein that if Egypt desired, further talks on the loan could be undertaken. Nasser chose to accept a Soviet loan.

July 26, 1956

Egypt nationalizes the Suez Canal Company.

This action was in response to Secretary of State Dulles's refusal to fund the Aswân High Dam and because Egypt received only about $2 million as its share of the canal's annual $31 million in profits. President Gamal Abdel Nasser announced that while Egypt would repay investors for their loss, his government would henceforth control and operate the Suez Canal. The British had withdrawn the last of their troops from Suez on June 13, 1956, making it difficult for them to protest as effectively as previously.

Nasser was especially chagrined at the U.S. withdrawal of financial support to construct the Aswân Dam, a project Egypt believed would benefit its economy and help modernize the nation. Dulles and British Prime Minister Anthony Eden had promised to back the Aswân project in December 1955. In February 1956, Eugene Black, president of the World Bank, agreed to provide $200 million for the dam; however, between February and July, Dulles and Eisenhower changed their minds. Owing largely to criticism from Congress, Dulles decided Nasser was too close to his Communist friends to deserve a loan. Dulles underestimated Moscow, because he believed the Soviets would not aid Egypt's costly project. More important, during this presidential election year, Dulles feared opposition from pro-Israeli groups; China lobbyists who disliked Nasser's recognition of mainland China in May 1956; and ardent anti-Communists who objected to Egypt's purchase of arms from Eastern European countries. Therefore, in spite of prior promises, Dulles announced the withdrawal of U.S. aid for the dam on July 19, 1956, at the very time when Egypt's ambassador returned to Washington to notify Dulles that Nasser was prepared to accept the terms of the loan. Within a week, Nasser declared Egypt would take over the Universal Suez Canal Company. Profits from the canal, he claimed, would help build the dam. Nasser's action caused extreme concern in London and Paris, giving rise to the Suez crisis.

August 22, 1956

Chinese Communists shoot down U.S. naval reconnaissance plane; they are angry at Nationalist Chinese planes violating mainland airspace.

A Martin P4M-1Q Mercator, based at Iwakuni Air Base in Japan, was shot down by Chinese Communist MIGs some 30 miles over the shore near Shanghai shortly after midnight. The following morning Chinese officials broadcast that its fighters had damaged a "Chiang Kai-shek" aircraft near the Chushan Islands but that it had disappeared. United States search planes and naval craft recovered parts of the Mercator and bodies of two crewmen.

The State Department requested the British to act as diplomatic intermediaries, since the United States did not recognize the Beijing government, in delivering a letter that stressed that the U.S. plane had been on a routine flight. Chang Han-fu, the Chinese Communist vice-minister for foreign affairs, insisted he knew nothing about the downed U.S. naval aircraft. However, he angrily denounced the "war acts of harassment and destruction carried out by the military planes" of the "Chiang Kai-shek clique" that had become more frequent this year, and emphasized that they had been intercepted and frequently shot down. After declaring that "this Chiang plane which intruded over the Ma An Islands" had been intercepted and damaged, he pointed out that all of Chiang's planes were "of the American type." Two additional bodies were turned over to the British in Shanghai.

A week after the incident Eisenhower rebuked the National Security Council for not having prepared a cover story in advance, but he did see the situation for the mainland Chinese stand point. He stated that "if planes were flying twenty to fifty miles from our shores, we would be very likely to shoot them down if they came in closer, whether through error or not." Soviet reconnaissance planes that later came in close to the U.S. coasts were carefully escorted, but none were shot down. See William E. Burrows, *By Any Means Necessary* (2001).

October 19, 1956

The Soviet Union and Japan issue a declaration ending their 11-year state of war.

Because the two nations could not settle the issue of the Kurile Islands, it went unresolved.

October 23, 1956

The Hungarian uprising begins; Soviet forces gain control by November 4.

Hungarians staged an uprising against Moscow's control that had been established after World War II. In Hungary, dissenters urged government reforms similar to those advocated by Soviet leader Nikita Khrushchev in denouncing Stalinism. (See February 14, 1956.) As disclosed by declassified Soviet records after 1985, Moscow detected unrest in Budapest in July 1956. Khrushchev expected to end these disputes among Hungary's Communist leaders by having Ernö Gerö replace the notorious Mátyás Rákosi as prime minister on July 18.

Khrushchev miscalculated because the real sources of Hungarian opposition to Stalinism were young unskilled workers, university students, and Hungary's soldiers, including a few military officers. These factions agreed on rejecting the economic and political system imposed by Stalin in 1945. On October 23, the initial rebellion was sparked at the local police station in the village of Drebecen. Although János Kádár, Hungary's Communist Party leader, claimed uprisings were confined to Budapest and other large cities, Hungary's rural areas staged protests prepared by 2,100 workers councils having 28,000 members. Between October 23 and November 4, several hundred thousands of rural inhabitants participated in demonstrations against the regime. In fact, the last rebel stronghold was on the small island of Csepel in Budapest, where Soviet troops did not get control until November 14, 1956.

In Budapest on October 23, the demonstrations drew larger crowds in the afternoon before Gerö asked the Soviets to deploy armed forces to suppress the protestors. Moscow responded by sending 1,130 tanks, 380 armored personnel carriers, and 185 air defense weapons to Budapest on October 24. Their arrival proved counterproductive because without infantry units the tanks and armored vehicles were easy targets to be blown apart by the grenades and

Molotov cocktails used by the protestors. Moreover, Hungary's state security police and army refused to support the Soviet forces, some soldiers joining the rebels during the next four days. In addition to sending Soviet tanks and armored vehicles, Khrushchev again sought to satisfy the rebels by changing Hungary's political leaders. Gerö was replaced as prime minister by Imre Nagy, a Hungarian Communist known to advocate reforms similar to Khrushchev's. Moscow officials also agreed to let Nagy appoint members of opposition parties to government ministries, creating a multiparty coalition government. On October 28, Nagy agreed with two Soviet representatives in Budapest, Mikhail Suslov and Anastas Mikoyan, to call a cease-fire and remove all Soviet army units from Budapest. The truce calmed the demonstrations in Hungary, but on October 30 Khrushchev became enraged when he learned that Nagy had appointed enough non-socialists to the multiparty coalition to threaten Communist control of Hungary. Fearing Nagy's action would upset not only Soviet control in Hungary but also in Poland, where de-Stalinization was being debated, Khrushchev decided to send Soviet infantry, tanks, and armored vehicles to put down Hungary's rebellion.

On November 1, the Soviet army began deploying throughout Hungary, and on November 4, 60,000 Soviet soldiers entered Budapest to quash the rebellion. The same day, János Kádár, Hungary's Communist Party Chief, replaced Nagy. Soviet power was quickly restored. After Kádár took charge, Nagy took refuge in the Yugoslav embassy, but later, while on a bus leaving Budapest, he was arrested by Soviet troops under Kádár's orders. Following a show trial in 1958, Nagy was executed. For many Hungarians, Nagy became a national hero, although Soviet documents declassified in 1989 indicate Nagy was an informer for Stalin's secret service during the 1930s and 1940s. In June 1989, Hungarians celebrated the careers of Nagy and other leaders in Budapest's Hero's Square.

Details of the declassified Soviet records on 1956 are in the Spring 1995 *Bulletin of the Cold War International History Project*; while William Taubman reveals that Soviet leadership, including Khrushchev, was initially quite indecisive about what action to take, *Khrushchev: The Man and His Era* (2003).

October 26, 1956

Diem promulgates a new constitution for South Vietnam.

Early in 1956, Diem's cabinet approved the appointment of an assembly to draw up a constitution. The assembly's recommendation was completed and signed by Diem on October 26. Establishment of the new government occurred during the period when, according to the Geneva agreements, an election was to take place to unite Vietnam and choose a government that would end the division of the nation. Diem refused to work with the International Control Commission regarding elections, and, despite Hanoi's protests, elections never took place.

The United States approved Diem's decision because it was obvious from American intelligence reports that in a "free election," Ho Chi Minh and the Vietminh would win. In this manner, Diem and the United States bypassed the Geneva Conference's attempt to provide self-determination for all Vietnamese to decide on their future government and national unity.

October 29–November 6, 1956

The Suez crisis erupts when Israeli, British, and French forces attack Egypt.

The attack on Suez was one of several Israeli-Egyptian engagements during the years since Israel became a nation in 1948. Britain and France joined in this attack in an attempt to regain some control of the Suez Canal following Egypt's nationalization decree of July 26, 1956. Israel had an interest in the canal's status because Egypt had denied Israeli ships the use of the canal, a situation Israel wished to abolish. London and Paris wanted to be certain Cairo never denied them use of the canal because Western European nations depended on oil supplies going through Suez. After Nasser's nationalization decree, England and France rushed naval units and paratroopers into the region between Cyprus and Suez, threatening to use force if Nasser did not accept joint control plans for the canal. Compromise efforts had failed between July and October.

Secretary of State Dulles proposed the formation of a Suez Canal User's Association (SCUA) to operate the canal, but Nasser refused. Next, the U.N. Security Council worked out a compromise for an international canal agency. On October 13, the Soviet Union vetoed the plan, even though it appeared Egypt would accept it. As compromise talks went on, French, British, and Israeli representatives held secret military talks.

On October 24, at Sèvres, near Paris, the three nations agreed to a secret joint attack on Suez. As planned at Sèvres, Israeli troops first launched a raid in the Sinai Desert on October 29. London and Paris sent cease-fire requests to Cairo and Tel Aviv that, as expected, Nasser rejected. On October 31, Anglo-French planes bombed Cairo, Egyptian air bases, and the canal. On November 2, British naval forces and paratroopers occupied Port Said, making Egyptian forces retreat to west of the Canal Zone. United Nations action to halt the crisis was initially ineffective. The British and French vetoed an October 31 Security Council resolution to "refrain from the use of force." On November 2, a U.N. General Assembly resolution called for a cease-fire and mutual troop withdrawal, but included no method of implementation. Therefore, on November 4, Lester Pearson of Canada proposed that a U.N. emergency force supervise the cease-fire. Pearson's proposal passed the General Assembly by a vote of 57-0 with 19 abstentions. At 12:15 A.M. on November 5, the assembly authorized General E. L. M. Burns of Canada to recruit and lead an international force to Suez, with the force to exclude troops from any permanent Security Council members. On November 6, the Soviet Union supported Egypt when Khrushchev threatened to send Soviet forces to stop the aggressors if a cease-fire did not occur immediately.

Eisenhower and Dulles (who had emergency cancer surgery on November 3) opposed the British-French-Israeli attacks from the outset. They sought to use the United Nations and backed Pearson's attempt to intervene through the assembly. On November 6, Eisenhower decided to apply greater pressure on Britain and France. The United States applied financial pressure by selling British pounds on the currency exchange to damage British currency rates and cutting off oil supplies from Latin America to Europe. Before the end of the day, the fighting in Suez had stopped because the British, French, and Israelis accepted the cease-fire and the intervention of the U.N. supervisory force. The U.N. supervisory force still had to overcome obstacles before the Suez situation reached peaceful terms.

November 6, 1956

The Republican ticket of Eisenhower and Nixon wins the presidential election.

Eisenhower received 57 percent of the vote, but the Democrats retained control of both houses of Congress. Regarding foreign policy, commentators thought Eisenhower best expressed two major points about which most liberals and conservatives agreed in 1956: (1) the underdeveloped nations, not Europe, were becoming the central area of conflict in the Cold War; and (2) the United States must find a means to keep the "neutrals" and new developing nations tied to U.S. interests or they would become "virtual allies" of the Soviet Union.

November 18, 1956

Poland and the Soviet Union agree to compromise and avoid violence.

In order to avoid the violence taking place in Hungary, Nikita Khrushchev and Poland's Wladyslaw Gomulka reached a *modus vivendi* whereby Poland received greater leeway in following its own road to a socialist economic system. Gomulka agreed to maintain Poland's membership in the Warsaw Pact and be a loyal ally of the Soviet government. Informally, this agreement was made on November 18, ending years of problems between Poland and the Soviet Union. (Notably, Stalin had imprisoned Gomulka in 1951 because he advocated "Titoist" policies that permitted Yugoslavia to have its own form of socialist system.)

The Polish-Soviet problems had intensified in June 1956 when Poznan protesters demonstrated against an increase in food prices and hard-line practices of Polish Stalinists. During the demonstrations, Soviet troops fired on demonstators and killed 53 people and wounded hundreds more. To rectify these problems in Poznan and elsewhere, Communist leaders of the Polish Worker's Party (PUWP) debated whether they should retain Stalinist policies or accept proposals of Gomulka to introduce reforms in line with Khrushchev's February speech that de-Stalinized the Soviet Union. Although Gomulka's program called for the eviction of Soviet officers in command of the Polish army, Khrushchev accepted the request to return those Russian officers to the Soviet Union. Members of the PUWP Plenum at its eighth official meeting on October 19 agreed to remove Soviet General Konstantin K. Rokossovsky, the Soviet commander of the Polish army, from PUWP membership and his seat on the Politburo. The Plenum took this action despite Rokossovsky's threat to use violence against Gomulka and his followers. Amid this crisis, Khrushchev and a delegation of Soviet officials visited Warsaw to clarify the situation. The Soviet leaders talked with Gomulka and the PUWP's current leader, Edward Ochab, about their ideas on the crisis and then flew back to Moscow.

Khrushchev met with the Soviet Presidium on October 24, persuading them to accept Gomulka as the first secretary of the PUWP and bring home Rokossovsky and most other Soviet generals in charge of the Polish army. Later in the day of October 24, Gomulka gave a "victory" speech during a Warsaw rally of at least 300,000 Poles. He said he would lead the Polish way to socialism but also called for an end to all anti-Soviet demonstrations because, he said, Poland needed friendly ties with its Soviet neighbor and the Warsaw Treaty alliance. After Gomulka released Polish Primate Stefan Cardinal Wyszynski from army custody on October 29, he proceeded to finalize the agreement with the Soviet Union signed on November 18. New details about Polish-Soviet relations in 1956 may be found in documents declassified from Russian and Eastern European Archives and appearing in the *Bulletin of the Cold War International History Project* (Spring 1995).

1957

January 5, 1957

The Eisenhower Doctrine is presented in an address to Congress.

The President asked Congress to authorize the use of U.S. armed forces if there were Communist aggression in the Middle East. Congress approved the resolution on March 5, 1957. The congressional resolution stated that a nation must request assistance from the United States. The doctrine was seldom used, however, because U.S. forces could not check the growth of Soviet diplomatic influence in the Middle East, and Arab nations hesitated to request aid because the United States supported Israel.

February 8, 1957

Saudi Arabia renews the U.S. lease on the Dhahran air base in exchange for American arms.

The agreement was announced after King Saud visited Washington for 10 days.

March 13, 1957

Jordan gains independence when Great Britain terminates the 1948 alliance and agrees to withdraw its armed forces within six months.

King Hussein I, who became monarch of Jordan on May 2, 1953, also acted vigorously to purge his national army of Egyptian and Syrian sympathizers. Although the United States sympathized with Hussein's actions and later sent arms to aid him, Hussein refused to make any commitments to America and claimed to seek a neutral policy in the Cold War.

March 24, 1957

British and U.S. leaders meet at Bermuda to repair strained relations resulting from the Suez crisis.

Prime Minister Harold Macmillan represented Great Britain, who had replaced Eden following the failure of the latter's Suez policy in 1956. President Eisenhower and Macmillan discussed the improvement of British defenses. The British explained their need to cut the number of their troops in NATO from 75,000 to 50,000 (accepted by the WEU on March 19), and Eisenhower agreed to supply Britain with intermediate-range guided missiles.

March 25, 1957

The European Common Market is agreed to in the Treaty of Rome.

France, West Germany, Italy, Belgium, Luxembourg, and the Netherlands were the charter members.

April 25, 1957

The Eisenhower Doctrine is applied to help King Hussein of Jordan against the threat of "international Communism."

Although historians disagree on whether or not the Eisenhower Doctrine applied to the Jordanian crisis, the president ordered the U.S. Sixth Fleet to the eastern Mediterranean, and Secretary Dulles advised that this action was designed to protect Jordan from Syrian and Egyptian pressure. Both Syria and Egypt received Soviet aid, causing Dulles to link them with Moscow's supposedly clandestine activity to promote Communism.

On March 13, 1957, Hussein also lost Britain's financial subsidies and, although Saudi Arabia helped to replace those funds, Hussein had financial problems that Egypt's President Nasser hoped to exploit by forcing Jordan to join Syria and Egypt in forming a United Arab Republic. Hussein opposed the efforts of Syria and Egypt, and President Chamoun of Lebanon asked the United States to act on behalf of Jordan. Partly because of Eisenhower's show of force in the Mediterranean, Hussein maintained power in Jordan and the United States offered him a grant of $10 million.

May 1, 1957

The United States agrees to provide aid to Poland in the form of $95 million worth of commodities and mining machinery.

The Eisenhower administration began considering possible economic aid to Poland on April 12, 1957, when Secretary of State Christian Herter told a Cabinet meeting that Poland had requested financial assistance. Herter indicated that the State Department believed Poland's Premier Gomulka wanted to avoid becoming a "Moscow tool." In addition, Eisenhower reported a meeting he had with Polish exile leaders in America who favored American assistance to Poland. All cabinet members agreed and legislation was prepared for Congress to approve on June 7, 1957.

Eisenhower signed legislation that approved loans and other financial aid to Poland. Using Public Law 480 of July 10, 1954, the United States sent surplus American food products to be sold for Polish currency in addition to $48.9 million loans for other American commodities and mining machinery.

May 15, 1957

Great Britain successfully explodes a hydrogen bomb at Christmas Island.

May 30, 1957

President Batista of Cuba orders the army to intensify its fight against Fidel Castro's rebels in Oriente Province.

After gaining power in "rigged election" to defeat President Sacarras (see March 10, 1952), Fulgencio Batista established a dictatorship characterized by corruption, repression, and internal dissent. To overthrow Batista, Fidel Castro organized a rebellion by promising free elections, social reform, new schools, and economic justice. The Eisenhower administration's response was to deny armaments to both sides, despite the fact that Castro's promises made him popular among many Americans. Although Castro claimed the United States continued arming Batista, the White House denied Castro's claim, saying the United States did not send arms to either side.

During the next 20 months, Castro's rebels in the July 26th movement steadily drove Batista's forces back toward Havana. In the United States, the main issue was whether or not Castro was a Communist. Probably, no one knew or could predict whose side Castro favored until he accepted aid from the Soviet Union and announced he was a Communist in December 1961.

June 12, 1957

The Chinese Communists indicate they are relaxing their severe restrictions on the populace.

Despite the U.S.-Chinese impasse over Formosa, China's leaders appeared ready to seek friendly relations between the people of China and the people of the United States. During the Bandung Conference (see April 18–24, 1955), China's Foreign Minister, Chou En-lai, announced that his government did not want war with the United States and that China was willing to "discuss the question of relaxing tensions in the Far East." Also, in domestic affairs, China's leaders undertook a greater liberalization; perhaps to follow the lead of the Soviet Union's First Secretary Khrushchev's "de-Stalinization" movement.

In accordance with the apparent relaxation, the Chinese Communist press reported on two of Mao Tse-tung's recent speeches in which Mao explained that the government had to liquidate 800,000 Chinese between 1949 and 1954 because of the "contradictions" between these deviationists and the government. Mao hoped there would be freer expression in the future, declaring "Let a hundred flowers bloom, let a hundred schools of thought contend." Although China's leaders offered conciliatory moves toward the United States, Secretary of State John Foster Dulles rejected their overtures. Some members of Congress and some editorial writers urged the Eisenhower administration to change U.S. policy toward China, but Dulles and Eisenhower stood firm.

When 15 American news reporters were offered visas to visit China, Dulles said that he believed China's talk of greater democracy was an aberration and that the U.S. travel ban levied during the Korean War remained in place. The State Department would not validate passports for the newsmen to visit the People's Republic of China. Although some newsmen visited China without valid passports, Dulles' views proved correct. China's experiment with "more democracy" brought internal problems and Mao restored his dictatorial power.

June 13, 1957

The aftereffects of the Suez crisis of October 1956 are finally resolved when Egypt approves terms for all nations to use the canal.

After the November 6 cease-fire, Britain and France delayed withdrawing their forces until December 22, 1956, to assume negotiations for use of the canal. Israel refused to withdraw from the Gaza Strip and Aquaba until Washington agreed to support Israel's free passage through the Gulf of Aquaba (February 11, 1957), and U.N. forces agreed to build a mined fence and to patrol the Gaza border (March 29, 1957). Finally, Israel demanded that terms for the use of the Suez Canal include permission for its ships to navigate the canal. Terms satisfying France and England were approved by Egypt on June 13.

June 18, 1957

The U.S. Senate approves the International Atomic Energy Agency (IAEA).

This treaty evolved from President Eisenhower's December 1953 proposal through the United Nations where 80 nations had joined in forming the International Atomic Energy Agency, a group including the Soviet Union. The treaty provided for the sharing of fissionable materials for peaceful uses. (For development of the agreement, see July 29, 1957.)

July 29, 1957

The International Atomic Energy Agency's statute goes into effect after necessary ratification papers are deposited.

After President Eisenhower's "Atoms for Peace" speech was delivered to the U.N. General Assembly in December 1953. The U.S. State Department gave a copy of a proposed IAEA Statute to Soviet Ambassador Georgy Zaroubin on March 10, 1954. In response, the Soviet Union expressed doubts about the Eisenhower plan, preferring to gain support for their proposal to have all nations renounce their nuclear weapons, a proposition that the United States and its NATO allies previously rejected. Thus, on May 1, 1954, the State Department told Zaroubin that Eisenhower would go ahead with his own creation whether or not the Soviets participated. In early 1955, the United States invited eight other states with uranium resources to visit Washington to consider a United States–United Kingdom proposal for an international atomic energy agency. In addition to the United States and United Kingdom, the delegates were from France, Belgium, South Africa, Australia, Canada, and Portugal.

President Eisenhower signs International Atomic Energy Agency agreement. Herbert Hoover Library

Surprising everyone, the Soviet Union agreed to join the other eight members on July 18, 1955, expanding the group to nine members. Delegates from these nine states accepted an IAEA Statute, the contents of which were very close to the final wording of the IAEA Statute agreed on in 1957.

For the next step in the process, the United Nations called for what became known as the "First Geneva Conference" that met from August 8 to 20, 1955. More than 1,500 people attended the conference including 1,000 scientists whose papers illuminated progress on various peaceful uses of nuclear technologies. For example, a French scientist presented a report on how to reprocess spent nuclear fuel to recover plutonium, a process that previously was a well-kept secret. Other scientific reports covered diverse peaceful atomic uses, especially on methods to generate electricity. The only item *not* presented regarded methods to enrich uranium-235 in making nuclear bombs.

On September 20, 1956, representatives from 82 states attended a conference regarding a final IAEA Statute at the United Nations headquarters in New York City. The main purpose of the conference was to allocate seats on the future Board of Governors and the division of powers between the Board and the U.N. General Conference. After agreeing that Vienna, Austria, would be the seat of the IAEA Board, the only matters raised regarded Chinese membership in the IAEA and the proper safeguard methods for member states who joined the IAEA. Despite Soviet insistence that the People's Republic of China should be represented, the United States' objected because it favored the Republic of China on Formosa (Taiwan). Consequently, China had no IAEA representative until the People's Republic was accepted by the United Nations in 1982. Regarding safeguards for member states, the delegates agreed that the IAEA would apply safeguards in its projects at the "request of the parties to any bilateral or multilateral arrangement" of the member states.

The U.N. Conference members approved the completed IAEA Statute on October 23, 1956, and the 81 members signed the Statute. The Statute became effective on July 29, 1957, when the necessary 26 states deposited instruments of their ratification of the Statute. Further details are in David Fischer, *History of the International Atomic Energy Agency: The First Forty Years* (1997) and available on the IAEA website.

August 26, 1957

The Soviet Union announces it successfully test-fired the first intercontinental ballistic missile.

The Soviets now had a weapon capable of carrying a nuclear warhead to targets in the United States.

September 5, 1957

President Eisenhower announces plans to airlift arms to Jordan and to assist Lebanon, Turkey, and Iraq against Communist plots from Syria: The Syrian crisis of 1957.

Tensions increased between Washington and Damascus during the summer of 1957, and the United States concluded that a "takeover by the Communists would soon be completed" in Damascus. A Syrian agreement with the Soviets provided Damascus with $500 million of assistance and military aid. On August 13, Syria charged three American embassy officials with plotting to overthrow President Shukuri al-Kuwatly and forced them to leave the country. Joined by diplomats from Turkey, Lebanon, Iraq, Israel, Jordan, and Saudi Arabia, the Eisenhower administration became convinced that Moscow wanted Communists to take power in Syria. Eisenhower reaffirmed his Middle East doctrine and took action to prevent Soviet subversion. With assurances of help from the United States, forces of Turkey, Iraq, Jordan, and Lebanon massed around Syria's borders. U.S. air forces were sent to a base in Adana, Turkey, and the Strategic Air Command was placed on alert. The U.S. Sixth Fleet proceeded to the eastern Mediterranean.

Whether or not Eisenhower overreacted to the Syrian situation is not certain. Following the preparations in territory surrounding Syria, the United Nations undertook to calm the affair. Of the nations that sent forces to Syria's borders, only Turkey desired to intervene. Arguments in the United Nations thoroughly aired charges and countercharges, but mediation efforts were rejected. Finally, King Saud informed Washington that the crisis was not serious. By October 31, the dispute faded. Moscow had gained influence in Syria but no Communist takeover was attempted in Damascus.

October 2, 1957

Poland submits plan for a denuclearized Central Europe.

In the U.N. General Assembly, Poland's Foreign Minister Adam Rapacki proposed the creation of a nuclear-free zone covering Poland, Czechoslovakia, and the two Germanys.

See December 19, 1957.

October 5, 1957

Sputnik becomes the first artificial earth satellite.

The Soviet Union fired Sputnik into an earth orbit by which it circled the world at 18,000 miles per hour. A second satellite, Sputnik II, was launched on November 3, carrying a live dog aboard for experimental purposes.

October 23–25, 1957

British Prime Minister Macmillan visits Washington to discuss the consequences of the USSR's Sputnik launching.

Following the October 17–20 visit of Queen Elizabeth II to Washington, this session helped to reestablish the "special relationship" between England and America that had become part of U.S. policy since 1941.

October 26, 1957

Political troubles in Guatemala follow the assassination of President Castillo Armas (July 26) and the election (October 20) of Miguel Ortiz Passarelli.

On October 26, a military junta annulled the election and installed Guillermo Flores Avendano as interim president. On March 2, 1958, General Miguel Ydiguras Fuentes was elected and installed as president for six years.

November 7, 1957

The Gaither Report is presented to the National Security Council.

In the summer of 1957, President Eisenhower asked a group of private citizens chaired by H. Rowen Gaither to study U.S. defense security for the country's survival in the atomic age. The final Gaither report went beyond the president's original intent to report on the possibility of bomb shelters for civil defense. Instead, the committee reported on the entire U.S. defense posture. The Gaither Committee claimed the U.S. strategic air force was highly vulnerable to Soviet intercontinental ballistic missiles (ICBMs), leaving the American population critically at risk. It advocated a buildup of U.S. strategic offensive weapons by diversifying missile bases and increasing U.S. forces for conventional war.

The Gaither report also advocated a program to build fallout shelters to protect Americans from nuclear attack, although Eisenhower rejected shelters as wasteful unless they were blast proof. Democratic Party candidates publicized the need for fallout shelters during the 1958 election, a proposal inspiring some Americans to build backyard shelters during the next decade. The concept of shelters was revived under the Reagan administration.

November 7, 1957

Eisenhower begins a series of "confidence" speeches to reassure the nation that U.S. defenses are excellent and capable of countering any Soviet threat.

The launching of Sputnik by the Soviets in October and the rise of critics of the "new look" policies in Congress, the army, and the navy caused Eisenhower to better inform the public about U.S. force capabilities and the value of his "long-haul" defense policy related to sustaining a prosperous U.S. economy.

Between October 1957 and the end of his second term of office, Eisenhower's massive-retaliation policy with a cost-effective defense program was disputed by former Army Chief of Staff Maxwell Taylor; Senators Lyndon Johnson, John F. Kennedy, and Stuart Symington; and academic commentators Henry Kissinger and Herman Kahn. These and others argued that the United States needed "flexible response" forces, which required a large army and navy as well as strategic and tactical nuclear forces and would necessitate a huge defense budget, far beyond the budget needs Eisenhower believed necessary.

By 1960, the "new look" critics also raised the issue of a "missile gap," which asserted that the Soviet Union would soon gain superiority over America in missiles. Eisenhower denied the missile gap theory, but the accusation continued to be pressed by John F.

Kennedy and his supporters through the election of 1960. Later, early in 1961, Kennedy's secretary of defense would admit that Eisenhower had been correct; there was no missile gap. Nevertheless, in Congress and among many persons concerned about U.S. defense, both the "flexible response" policy and the "missile gap" were concepts that opposed Eisenhower's "long-haul," economy concerned "new look" program.

November 7, 1957

Speaking on the 40th anniversary of the 1917 revolution in Moscow, Mao Tse-tung provides an overt indication of the divisions between Peking and Moscow that eventually lead to the Sino-Soviet split.

Mao stated that the international situation was at a turning point because "There are two winds in the world today: the East wind and the West wind." And, he added: "I think the characteristic of the situation today is the East wind prevailing over the West wind." Additionally, Mao commented, "If worse came to worst [in a nuclear war] and half of mankind died, the other half would remain, while imperialism would be razed to the ground and the world would become socialist."

Mao was urging strong, committed Communist backing for revolution in the former Asian and African colonies as they struggled to free themselves from Western control. He believed the Chinese victory in 1949 demonstrated the proper tactics to use in the emerging nations and criticized Soviet leader Khrushchev for his program of "peaceful coexistence" with capitalism. Four months earlier on July 22, Mao showed anger in a conversation with Soviet Ambassador Pavel Judin, complaining about the Soviet Union's "unequal" treatment of China. The Soviets' attitude toward China, Mao said, "can be described as father and son or between cats and mice," rather than as brotherly relations. Mao, of course, wanted China to be the leader of international Communism. On July 31, 1958, Khrushchev flew to Beijing to resolve his differences with Mao, who rejected Khrushchev's overtures for better relations. As a result, Chinese-Soviet differences increased during and after 1958.

Mao introduced the policy known as the Great Leap Forward to collectivize Chinese landholdings and extend China's influence in Third World countries, while Khrushchev continued the Soviet emphasis on heavy industry to improve the Soviet economy, giving little attention to the Third World until 1960. Details regarding the Chinese-Soviet split became available in 1997 when declassified materials from Russia and China revealed new information on the years after 1953. (Articles by Vladislav Zubok and Chen Jian summarize the new data in the *Cold War International History Project's Bulletin* for March 1998.)

During 1958, the differences became more emphatic. Mao began the Great Leap Forward in China, a program forcing collectivization of land into communes and indoctrinating peasants with Communist ideas. The Soviets insisted on heavy industry first, and preferred to seek mass support from the people as only a secondary part of their branch of Communism. Mao was also striving to devise Communist programs for China that would be aided but not controlled by the Soviet Union.

November 14, 1957

East and West Germany sign a $260 million trade agreement for 1958.

November 15, 1957

Portugal extends the U.S.-Azores Island defense pact to 1962.

The original pact was made in 1951.

December 5, 1957

President Sukarno of Indonesia expels all Dutch nationals.

During the previous three years, Sukarno's government had had political problems with the Netherlands; with rebels in parts of his country such as Sulawesi (the Celebes) and Borneo; and with competing political groups in Jakarta. To help resolve the economic costs of these continuing problems, Sukarno had repudiated $1 billion of debts to the Netherlands (August 4, 1956) and received a loan from the Soviet Union of $100 million (September 15, 1956). As Indonesia's problems continued, the United States was concerned about the Soviet Union gaining control in Indonesia through its loans to Sukarno and the influence of Indonesia's Communist Party as part of Sukarno's ministry.

December 17, 1957

The first successful test of America's Atlas intercontinental ballistic missile.

The Air Force program for the ICBM began on July 27, 1955. On November 28, 1958, the Series B-ATLAS missile performed a full-range test of 5,506 nautical miles. The American intermediate range missile, Thor, had its first successful flight on September 20, 1957.

December 19, 1957

NATO members conclude their Paris meeting.

The session indicated the European concern about recent Soviet technological developments. A major issue among the delegates centered on the American desire for missile bases in Europe and the Europeans' desire for the United States to pursue disarmament talks. The issue resulted in compromise; the Europeans agreed to accept U.S. IRBM bases, and the United States said it would discuss any "reasonable proposal" for "comprehensive and controlled disarmament." This dual-related issue constantly reappeared at NATO meetings during future sessions.

In 1957, NATO described the deployment of IRBMs as a temporary measure to deter the Soviets until American ICBMs became operational from U.S. bases. NATO also indicated that missile deployment was subject to American agreement with the countries where missiles were based. Only Great Britain, Italy, and Turkey accepted the U.S. offer to permit missile bases on their soil. A large part of the difficulty in persuading NATO allies to accept U.S. missile bases was the American desire to keep monopoly control of atomic weapons. As an anonymous French general told a reporter in November 1957, the risk of the absolute weapon was too grave to allow "a single one of the allies the monopoly of a retaliation which in the hour of danger, could be neutralized by the enemy or by the opposition of its own press or public opinion."

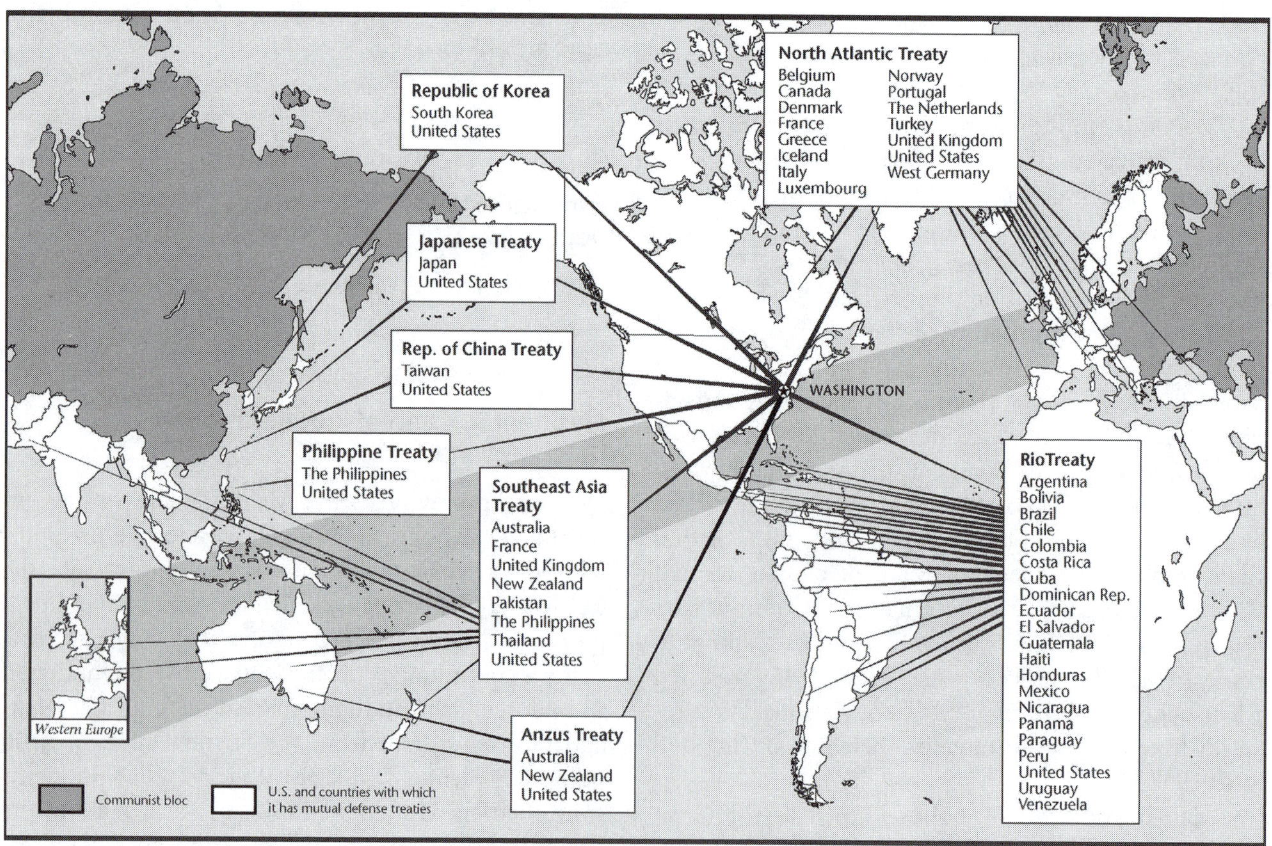

U.S. Collective Security Pacts

Although Eisenhower wanted to cooperate further with the allies in nuclear plans and control, Congress and the Joint Committee on Atomic Energy would not permit him to share U.S. "secrets." The U.S. distrust of Europeans as indicated by this unwillingness to share responsibility for nuclear decisions became a persistent point of dispute in NATO. Eventually under the December 1957 NATO agreement, the United States placed IRBMs in England, Italy, and Turkey—60 Thor missiles in England, 30 Jupiters in Italy, and 15 Jupiters in Turkey. The Turkish Jupiters became a significant problem during the 1962 October missile crisis.

Warsaw Pact members were also concerned about NATO's missile plans. Late in 1957, Poland's Foreign Minister Adam Rapacki had proposed the creation of a nuclear-free zone covering Poland, Czechoslovakia, and the two Germanys. In the zone, atomic, hydrogen, and rocket weapons would be neither manufactured nor deployed. As Adam Ulam's *The Rivals* (1971) suggests, the Rapacki plan was probably written in Moscow, enabling Khrushchev to approve it on March 3, 1958. The United States and NATO rejected the plan because it had "no methods for balanced and equitable limitations of military capabilities" in central Europe. This meant that Warsaw Pact members could assemble larger conventional armed forces in Central Europe. In contrast to the potential large Communist forces, NATO faced opposition in West Germany regarding the conscription of a large German army.

1958

January 27, 1958

The United States and the Soviet Union sign a cultural exchange agreement.

On June 2, 1957, Khrushchev had appeared on the American television program "Face the Nation" and urged the removal of trade barriers and increased use of cultural exchanges. Within a week, the Soviets presented the administration a wide-ranging proposal that Washington official ignored as a propaganda stunt. To the administration's surprise, the initiative stirred the interest of many Americans, prompting Senators Lyndon Johnson and J. William Fulbright to persuade an unenthusiastic State Department to explore its possibilities. The outgrowth of the initiative was the January 1962 pact that provided for visits by educators, technicians, sports teams, and musicians on a mutual interchange basis.

January 31, 1958

The first U.S. earth satellite, Explorer I, is placed in orbit by a modified Jupiter-C rocket.

This began a series of experiments in the next two years with U.S. earth satellites known as Explorer, Vanguard, Discoverer, Tiros, Nimbus, and Essa.

U.S. launch continues space exploration. Brune photo

February 22, 1958

The United States agrees to supply England with 60 Thor IRBMs capable of carrying atomic warheads.

This was an essential follow-up to the October 1957 meeting between Macmillan and Eisenhower, which reviewed the effect of Sputnik on Western defense capabilities.

March 27, 1958

The United States announces a space flight program is headed for the moon—to beat the Soviets.

Secretary of Defense Neil McElroy reported the president's approval for a program to explore space to "obtain useful data concerning the moon, and to provide a close look at the moon." Officially, the exploratory Pioneer-Ranger programs would be part of the U.S. contribution to the International Geophysical Year. Although John F. Kennedy later publicized the "race to the moon" featuring a human landing, the Pioneer-Ranger program, which started in 1958, provided essential data on moon-landing sites. It also was intended to counter the Soviet Sputnik feat of October 1957 and promote U.S. space technology.

Unfortunately, the Pioneer program's initial rocket launchings failed on August 17, October 11, November 8, and December 6, 1958. Pioneer 4 made a successful fly by of the moon on March 3, 1959. On January 2, 1959, the Soviets beat the United States by successfully flying Luna 1 by the moon; and on September 12, 1959, the Soviets' Luna 2 impacted on the moon. Not until July 28, 1964, did a U.S. moon shot begin to surpass the Soviets' achievements.

Ranger 7, using television, returned the first high-resolution pictures of lunar mares, which was the basic objective of the Ranger program as a prelude to the manned Apollo flights. The first clear Soviet pictures were transmitted from the moon on July 18, 1965, with the flight of Zond 7.

March 27, 1958

Nikita Khrushchev becomes premier as well as head of the Party in the Soviet Union.

In replacing Bulganin as premier, Khrushchev had gained firm control of the central party organization. According to Western Soviet watchers, Khrushchev had nearly lost his position as General Secretary in June 1957 when the Communist Party Presidium sought to dismiss him in favor of Bulganin and old Stalinists such as Molotov, Malenkov, and Kaganovich. By appealing to the whole Central Committee, Khrushchev retained his position because the Central Committee reversed the Presidium decision. This enabled Khrushchev to remove Molotov and his other opponents and, in March 1958, to get rid of Bulganin as well.

Having achieved complete power, Khrushchev began to change. According to those who knew him, this change was for the worse—becoming arbitrary, arrogant, and insistent on his own infallibility. For these observers, the Khrushchev era falls into two periods: before and after 1958. After 1958, he ignored advice, relied on "yes" men, and seemed to give in to his own weaknesses. He now would issue major policies on impulse rather than consideration, a failing that would result in his removal from office in 1964. (See William Taubman, *Khrushchev: the Man and His Era* [2003].)

April 28–May 14, 1958

Vice President Nixon encounters intense anti-American feelings while touring Latin America.

In some cities, mobs hurled eggs and stones at Nixon. On May 13 in Caracas, mobs attacked his limousine, nearly overturning the car before the vice president escaped. These events awakened some Americans to the fact that U.S. assistance went to other parts of the world but neglected its neighbors' economic problems. Between 1945 and 1960, for example, the United States gave three times more aid to the Benelux countries than to all 20 Latin American countries combined. U.S. private capital investment continued, but these funds increased the imbalance of the Latin American economies because they were seen as unduly profiting citizens of the United States.

Nixon's experience led the Eisenhower administration to reconsider its Latin American policy in an effort to reduce the influence of left-wing groups. In December 1959, the Inter-American Development Bank was established with $1 billion to channel low-interest development loans to Latin American nations. In September 1960, a meeting at Bogotá made long-range economic aid plans designed to benefit Latin America's economic growth.

May 31, 1958

De Gaulle heads an emergency government and begins to organize a new French constitution.

Since the National Assembly's "no confidence" vote overturned Mendès-France's cabinet in February 1955, France had experienced a succession of coalition governments that failed to resolve the nation's economic problems or the rebellion in Algeria, and full-scale civil war seemed likely. On May 31, 1958, President René Coty named de Gaulle as premier, and on June 1, the assembly voted him emergency powers by 329-244.

On September 28, 1958, the Constitution of the Fifth Republic was approved, and following elections (November 23 and 30), de Gaulle became president of the Fifth Republic.

June 13, 1958

Six nations agree to discuss technical problems of nuclear test detection at Geneva.

The participants at Geneva were the United States, Great Britain, the Soviet Union, France, Poland, and Czechoslovakia. Two months later a panel of scientific experts concurred in a report that it was technically feasible to build a system to detect violations of a nuclear test ban.

See October 31, 1958.

July 10, 1958

Cambodian Prince Norodom Sihanouk grants recognition to the Chinese Communist regime.

Sihanouk's *de facto* recognition indicated his determination to remain neutral in the Cold War between Communism and capitalism and followed the actions of other neutralists who recognized Mao Tse-tung's government. The recognition of China was one of Prince Sihanouk's earliest acts after gaining control of the Cambodian government. On March 23, 1958, his Communist-Socialist Party won all 61 seats in the National Assembly. While the prince now ruled as prime minister, his father, Norodom Suramarit, was king. On June 5, 1960, on the death of his father, Prince Sihanouk became chief of state after a

Premier Prince Norodom Sihanouk. National Archives

nationwide referendum voted approval. Prince Sihanouk was not a Communist, although his party's name confused most Americans. His main goal was to keep Cambodia independent by following a neutralist foreign policy.

July 15, 1958

American forces intervene in Lebanon as 1,400 U.S. Marines land on the beaches near Beirut.

Lebanon's President Camille Chamoun requested U.S. help because he feared possible intervention by President Nasser's United Arab Republic (Egypt and Syria). Lebanon's political system had for some time hinged on cooperation of the three competing religious factions—Christians, Muslims, and Druze. This precarious triad was disrupted in 1958 as street fights and riots advocated a new political alignment. President Chamoun asked Eisenhower for assistance and Washington responded quickly. On July 15, U.S. forces landed but met no resistance. They remained until October 25, after a political compromise was again renewed in Beirut. Eisenhower had demonstrated that the United States could intervene in the Middle East with its Sixth Naval Fleet if necessary.

Critics charged that the president acted in haste and that Dulles incorrectly blamed the Communists for difficulties in Lebanon and the Middle East in general.

July 22, 1958

Mao rejects Soviet requests for a radio station based on China's coast and a joint Sino-Soviet submarine fleet.

Just as Mao was expressing a desire for more Chinese "self-reliance" (the Great Leap Forward program), Khrushchev proposed a joint Sino-Soviet submarine fleet for the Pacific that would to use a long-range radio station based on the China coast for communications. According to his memoirs—*Khruschev Remembers: The Last Testament* (1974)—the Soviet leader "fully expected the Chinese to cooperate with us when we asked for a radio station on their territory."

However, when Soviet Ambassador Pavel Yudin met with Mao on July 22, 1958, he was informed that a joint force was a substitute for assisting the Chinese to build their own submarines and that the request for a base on Chinese soil was degrading. After concluding that the ambassador did not understand his position, Mao demanded that Khrushchev come to Beijing. Khrushchev immediately flew to Beijing and soon was embroiled in a series of heated, often insulting, arguments with Mao. When the Soviets left for Moscow, they thought that the confrontation had eased, but shortly thereafter Mao ordered the shelling of the Nationalist Chinese-occupied offshore islands without warning them in advance. Consequently, when Khrushchev supported Mao's actions, many Americans assumed that the Soviets were behind the incident. The entire episode with Mao, and the prospect that had fighting occurred in the Taiwan Straits they would have been pulled into it, gave the Soviets pause to consider their earlier pledge to assist the Chinese in developing atomic weaponry.

See August 20, 1959.

July 26, 1958

Romania announces the withdrawal of all Soviet occupation forces.

This did not end Soviet influence in Bucharest, but it gave the Romanians more political latitude without the disrupting riots that occurred in Hungary and Poland.

August 3, 1958

The USS *Nautilus*, America's first nuclear-powered submarine, completes an undersea crossing of the North Pole.

August 13, 1958

President Eisenhower outlines a new U.S. policy toward the Middle East that recognizes Arab nationalism and ends the tendency to view the area in Cold War terms.

On August 13, Eisenhower's speech at the United Nations suggested a new attitude toward the Middle East. Rather than simply to link aid to the Arab states in return for a commitment to anti-Communism as the Eisenhower Doctrine implied, the president recognized "positive neutralism" as a factor in the Middle East. As a consequence of his new approach, Eisenhower agreed to send wheat to Egypt in 1959 and to deal evenhandedly with Arabs and Israelis. Some historians discount the concept that Eisenhower began this new approach, attributing it instead to President Kennedy.

August 23, 1958

Chinese Communists again bombard the offshore islands of Quemoy and Matsu.

A crisis in the Formosa Straits that ended in 1955 (see January 28, 1955) was renewed when the Chinese Communists renewed their bombardment of Quemoy and Matsu on August 23. The Eisenhower administration had believed tensions in the Formosa Straits had ended on February 5, 1958, when the U.S. navy's Seventh Fleet evacuated the Nationalist Chinese from Tachen Island. When the bombardment began again, American commentators assumed Mao Tse-tung had returned to a hard-line policy, enlisting a threat against Formosa to force the United States to threaten or bomb China so Moscow would have to aid China's Communists.

Such speculation influenced Eisenhower's advisers, although post-Cold War documents from China and the Soviet Union reveal this speculation was not correct. According to declassified documents, Mao sought to demonstrate China's support for anti-imperialist uprisings in the Middle East, where the United States sent forces to Lebanon and Iraqi rebels assassinated King Faisal II, whom British "imperialists" previously controlled. Because Mao also wanted to avoid war with the United States, he ordered the Chinese military to do everything possible to avoid hitting American ships. Whatever China's rationale, Eisenhower ordered the Seventh Fleet to escort Nationalist troops and supplies to Quemoy and Matsu. He also reinforced the fleet by sending an aircraft carrier and four destroyers to the Formosa Straits. In addition, Secretary Dulles announced U.S. forces would aid the Nationalist Chinese in defending Quemoy and Matsu.

On September 15, ambassadors from the United States and the People's Republic of China renewed negotiations in Warsaw, Poland. While these talks continued, the Chinese reduced their bombardment of Quemoy and Matsu.

August 26, 1958

President Eisenhower begins a 12-day visit to Germany, France, and Britain.

The goodwill visit was designed to reassure American allies of the U.S. desire and ability to protect Western Europe. Since the Geneva Conference of 1955, Britain and France complained that Washington did not understand their economic and defense problems. Dulles often employed little tact in his dealings with the Europeans; Eisenhower, it was hoped, would be more capable of gaining continued support and goodwill in the NATO organization and its member nations.

September 2, 1958

Eisenhower signs the National Defense Education Act.

Enacted largely in reaction to the fear of Soviet leadership in science and technology, this bill provided loans to college students, grants for science and foreign-language instruction, and graduate school fellowships for students preparing to teach.

October 23, 1958

The Soviet Union agrees to loan Egypt $100 million toward building the Aswân High Dam.

Construction was scheduled to start on January 1, 1959.

October 23, 1958

Quemoy-Matsu crisis ends after Chiang renounces use of force against mainland China.

The U.S. negotiations with China were stalemated in Warsaw, Poland, because Chinese Nationalists persisted in staging raids on the mainland. To end the crisis, Secretary of State Dulles visited Chiang Kai-shek from October 20 to 22 and persuaded him to change his policy of trying to regain control of China's mainland. Dulles claimed that it perpetuated a potential crisis that, if resulting in war, would be a disaster for the United States and the entire world. Dulles often talked about a "two-China" policy as the way to permit Chiang to govern Formosa without threatening to retake China's mainland.

On October 23, Dulles and Chiang agreed to neutralize Quemoy and Matsu with a reduced number of Nationalist troops and stop commando raids along China's coastline. Dulles announced the United States would continue to recognize Chiang's government and Chiang said the Nationalists would not use force to recapture control of the mainland. The Dulles-Chiang announcements ended the 1958 crisis and Mao stopped shelling the offshore islands. The cease-fire ended the crisis but did not settle all problems in the Formosan Straits. On October 31, the U.S. State Department revealed that the Nationalists could attack China if there were a large-scale uprising on the mainland. On October 7, 1959, Undersecretary of State Douglas Dillon stated Mao would risk "total" war if China attacked the offshore islands.

October 31, 1958

Conference on a nuclear test ban opens at Geneva between delegates of the United States, Britain, and the Soviet Union.

During the 1950s, the testing of nuclear weapons caused radioactive particles to travel about the world's atmosphere, and some scientists warned of present and future hazards, such as radioactive rain that could find its way into the food supply. In March after completing their tests, the USSR, Britain, and the United States each announced, unilaterally, that it would suspend nuclear tests, reserving the right to renew tests if other nations did so.

The October 1958 sessions opened with optimism, but there were technical problems to deal with, particularly establishing a control system. The difficulty here lay primarily in distinguishing between seismic signals of underground tests and earthquakes. Earlier, on July 1, a Conference of Experts—four from the East and four from the West—had convened in Geneva to study the problems. Their conclusion announced in late August suggested that there was a "good probability" of resolving the issue by detecting explosions in the atmosphere as little as one kiloton and as little as five kilotons underground employing ten ships and 160-178 land-based instrumented control posts. (In late 1958, U.S. tests indicated the Conference of Experts overestimated the ability of their proposed control system.) No agreements were reached during the next two years because the United States insisted there must be on-site inspections, which the Soviets considered a pretext for Western intelligence gathering. The discussions, however, did provide a foundation for more successful talks in the 1960s.

November 10, 1958

Khrushchev demands Western forces leave West Berlin, making it a "free city."

On November 10, First Secretary Nikita Khrushchev during a Soviet-Polish friendship dinner in Moscow demanded that the Western allies leave Berlin. He claimed the Western powers used West Berlin to launch aggressive maneuvers against the German Democratic Republic and other socialist countries including Poland. He also said the impending atomic armament of West Germany by NATO would make the Berlin situation worse if it were not corrected. On November 27, Khrushchev gave the Western nations details of his demands based on the argument that previous Berlin agreements were nullified by NATO's rearming West Germany. He gave the Western powers six months to negotiate a final peace treaty for Germany that would make West Berlin a free, demilitarized city.

Immediately, the United States and its Western allies denounced Khrushchev's ultimatum. On December 14, the Western allies met to assert their rights and duties in Berlin. The allies agreed that negotiations on Berlin must be made in the broader context of German unity and European security. Eventually, Khrushchev agreed to negotiate on Germany. The details of Khrushchev's personal role on sending the 1958 ultimatum is explained in Hope Harrison's article in the *Cold War International History Bulletin* (Fall 1994).

December 14, 1958

The U.S., British, and French foreign ministers reassert their rights and duties in Berlin.

On November 27, Soviet Premier Khrushchev asserted that the four-power occupation of Berlin should end and the city should be demilitarized. The foreign ministers of the three Western powers rejected the Soviet demand but requested talks with the USSR on Berlin in the context of German unity and European security.

See May 11, 1959.

December 28, 1958

A State Department memo on Cuba outlines the need to remove Batista for a centrist party proponent.

In 1958, the struggle with Fidel Castro's rebels in Cuba began to cause difficulties for the Batista government. Batista's repression and corruption led the State Department to prefer that he resign in favor of a moderate leader, but no method to achieve this could be found. Although some U.S. writers such as Jules Dubois of the *Chicago Tribune* liked Castro's reform proposals, U.S. diplomats disliked his anti-Americanism and left-wing associates. The report of December 28 indicated that there were Communists in Castro's camp but that the rebels did not appear to be dominated by them. Thus, the report principally outlined the U.S. dilemma: how to get a moderate reform leader in Cuba. Some Latin American nations assisted in the search for a moderate to replace Batista, but no solution was found. By early January, Castro gained power.

1959

January 1, 1959

Cuban President Batista resigns after Fidel Castro's forces capture Santa Clara on December 31, 1958.

Castro's forces marched on Santiago and Havana, giving him control of all Cuba by January 3.

January 19, 1959

The United States rejects a Soviet request to lower U.S.-Soviet trade barriers.

This request came during a two-week Washington visit by Soviet First Deputy Premier Anastas I. Mikoyan.

January 27–February 5, 1959

At the 21st Communist Party Congress, Khrushchev clarifies several ideas on "peaceful coexistence."

The two basic parts of Khrushchev's strategy for "peaceful coexistence" with capitalism were (1) a declaration that war between socialist and capitalist states was not inevitable. In Khrushchev's view, the Soviets were young and would grow in strength; the Western capitalists were old, becoming weaker, and would collapse as wars of national liberation damaged their imperial-based economies; and (2) A proposal to construct an atom-free zone in the Far East and the entire Pacific Ocean. This would preserve the continuance of two real superpowers, preventing China and Japan from developing nuclear weapons. The Soviet premier warned that without such an agreement, his country would continue to mass-produce ICBMs, which gave it the lead in nuclear weapons.

After China's Foreign Minister Chou En-lai gave a message to the 21st Congress from Mao to emphasize the "unshakable unity of the socialist camp," the Soviets offered an aid package to China. On February 9, 1959, a Sino-Soviet announcement described a five billion ruble economic and technological assistance pact in addition to having Soviet technicians provide China information to build their heavy industry. Yet, these signs of unity were soon imperiled by China's desire to be a nuclear power, independent of Soviet influence. (See August 20, 1959).

The Soviets' 21st Congress also disclosed rifts in Moscow's relations with Tito's Yugoslavia. Although Khrushchev had recently expended much political capital on Yugoslavia to bring Tito into alignment with Moscow's views, Tito continually rejected Khrushchev's overtures. Now, the Soviets again declared opposition to Tito's revisionist socialist methods.

March 5, 1959

The United States signs bilateral defense pacts with Iran, Pakistan, and Turkey.

The military coup that brought General Abdul Karin al-Kassem to power led to Iraq's withdrawal from the Baghdad Pact, which was formalized on March 24, 1959. To replace the Iraq alliance, the United States signed separate treaties with the states along the southern border of the Soviet Union. Soon after forming the alliance with Turkey, the United States obtained permission to establish IRBM bases in Turkey. After the Baghdad Pact ended, the alliance, without Iraq, was recreated as the Central Treaty Organization (CENTO). The United States did not join the pact but supported its objectives.

March 31, 1959

Communist China completes its occupation of Tibet.

Fighting between Communists and Tibetans began on March 13, 1959, following Chinese infiltration of this small Himalayan country. The Chinese had always claimed sovereignty over Tibet and began actively to seek control in 1956, when they concluded a treaty with Nepal (September 24, 1956), which surrendered Nepalese rights to the area in recognition of Chinese sovereignty. The Tibetans stood little chance against Chinese forces, and on March 28, 1959, China's Premier Chou En-lai declared the Tibetan government of the Dalai Lama dissolved, so that a new government for the Tibetan autonomous region could be organized. The Communists gained full control when the Dalai Lama fled to India on March 31.

April 15, 1959

Fidel Castro visits Washington, where he declares his regime is "humanistic," not Communist.

Nevertheless, talks with the Americans about his desired reforms soon prompted U.S. opposition. Castro wanted national control over the Cuban economy, which heretofore was largely manipulated by Americans who owned 80 percent of Cuba's utilities, 40 percent of its sugar, and 90 percent of the mining wealth. Washington also controlled how much Cuban sugar could enter the U.S. market. Although

Castro's arbitrary arrests and executions of his opponents in January and February alarmed some of his U.S. supporters, his April visit generally left many believing he was a moderate. During a three-week period, Castro had executed 250 Cubans and many others had been threatened with imprisonment. The United States, however, had sent a new ambassador to Havana, Philip Bonsal, on January 19 and recognized Castro's government. In addition, Castro's demand for the United States to retain its economic and sugar quotas, as well as his promise to pay for any expropriated property in Cuba, again projected a moderate image during April 1959.

April 22, 1959

Christian A. Herter replaces John Foster Dulles as Secretary of State.

Dulles had been suffering from cancer for several years, having had emergency surgery in November 1956, during the height of the Suez crisis. Dulles died on May 24, 1959. Herter was highly qualified to be secretary of state. He had served on the U.S. Peace Commission at Paris in 1918–1919 and as Herbert Hoover's personal assistant in the Commerce Department to 1924. Prior to becoming secretary, he served as undersecretary of state from 1957 to 1959. He served as secretary until January 20, 1961.

May 11, 1959

Western foreign ministers fail to solve the Berlin problems with the Soviet Union.

After Khrushchev issued an ultimatum on Berlin, the Western foreign ministers rejected Khrushchev's demands as a violation of the 1945 Potsdam Agreement but wanted to avoid a confrontation with the Soviet leader. In March 1959, British Foreign Minister Harold Macmillan visited Moscow, where Khrushchev agreed to cancel the ultimatum provided a summit meeting would discuss the German situation. President Eisenhower agreed a summit could be held provided preliminary talks by foreign ministers showed positive results. Foreign ministers talks began in Geneva on May 11 but in three months achieved no beneficial results. Because of the deadlock on Germany, Eisenhower invited Khrushchev to visit the United States to discuss the German problem.

May 24, 1959

A five-year Anglo-Soviet trade agreement is signed in Moscow.

Unlike the United States, Great Britain and most Western European governments welcomed Khrushchev's détente and peaceful coexistence overtures, especially hoping to get new markets for their products. Thus, while Washington rejected trade agreements, European nations pursued negotiations with Moscow.

June 4, 1959

Castro's agrarian reform decree is a sign of his more radical intentions.

The new Cuban government had approved land reform legislation on May 17 that Castro put into operation on June 4. The law abolished all large sugar plantations and decreed that sugar mill operators could not own sugar-growing operations. Both foreign and Cuban landowners were affected. They would be paid by Cuban bonds over a 20-year period at 4 percent interest. Proceeds from the bonds had to be reinvested in Cuba and could not be converted into dollars. Finally, Castro asserted that the property value would be based on the most recent tax assessment values of the property. Obviously, property owners protested.

On July 12, the U.S. State Department objected to the method of valuation and bond payment and said the action amounted to confiscation, not expropriation, of property. Castro rejected all protests and told television audiences in Cuba that anyone opposing land reform was a traitor. By August 1959, many of Castro's moderate backers began to flee to the United States.

July 8, 1959

The United States announces that 200 U.S. planes will be moved from France to West Germany and Great Britain.

French President Charles de Gaulle disagreed with Washington's European defense plans and advocated France's "separate" role in NATO defenses, in preference to an integrated role. On March 14, U.S.-French defense talks ended in dispute because de Gaulle refused to place one-third of France's Mediterranean fleet under NATO, as previously arranged. De Gaulle believed French "grandeur" required a separate French nuclear force. He also argued that the United States would not use its nuclear forces to defend Europe and, therefore, France needed its own nuclear weapons to deter the Soviet Union.

July 24, 1959

"Kitchen debate" between Vice President Nixon and Premier Khrushchev takes place.

Nixon made a goodwill visit to the Soviet Union at the time that an American national exhibit opened in Moscow. He and the Soviet premier attended the opening together and visited a model of an American home on display. As they surveyed the technology of a U.S. kitchen, they began an impromptu argument on the virtues of Communism and capitalism that the news media highlighted.

August 19, 1959

The Central Treaty Organization (CENTO) replaces the Baghdad Pact.

Because Iraq withdrew from the Baghdad Pact on March 24, CENTO was formed to continue the defensive alliance of Turkey, Iran, Pakistan, and Great Britain. As in the case of the Baghdad Pact, the United States supported but did not join the alliance. America's bilateral defense pacts served the same purpose in the Middle East.

August 20, 1959

The Soviets refuse to give China a prototype atomic bomb.

During the fall of 1957, Sino-Soviet relations appeared to improve after Mao supported the Soviet Union's position at a meeting of Communist leaders in Moscow. In return for this support, Khrushchev promised to give the Chinese a prototype nuclear weapon and assist them in developing ballistic missiles. The situation changed by mid-1958 when Mao began to stress China's independence even though there were signs of Communist unity during Moscow's 21st Congress in January 1959.

See July 22, 1958 and January 27, 1959.

September 15, 1959

Khrushchev tours the United States and meets with Eisenhower at Camp David.

The Soviet leader visited Washington, the United Nations, Iowa, Los Angeles, and Hollywood's 20th Century-Fox movie studio for the filming of *Can-Can*. His request to visit Disneyland was turned down because his security could not be guaranteed. During his Iowa visit, Khrushchev went to the farm of Roswell Garst, who had visited the USSR earlier to acquaint the Soviets with U.S. seed corn growing and pig-raising techniques. On Garst's farm in Coon

Premier Nikita Khrushchev visits Iowa farm. National Archives

Rapids, as elsewhere during his visit, Khrushchev was a hit with many Americans because of his humor and display of common sense.

On the final three days of his visit, Khrushchev met with President Eisenhower at his Camp David retreat. Their meeting appeared to end cordially and the two leaders agreed to discuss further such pending issues as Germany, Berlin's status, and a nuclear test ban. Over the winter, reporters talked about "the spirit of Camp David" as defining better relations between Moscow and Washington. The Camp David meetings did not accomplish anything specific but served to temporarily diffuse the tensions over Germany. Khrushchev dropped his previous time limit on negotiations regarding Germany, and Eisenhower agreed to a summit meeting in 1960 without the necessity for successful lower-level agreements preceding the summit.

December 1, 1959

The United States, the USSR, and 10 other nations approve a treaty to reserve the Antarctic for scientific and peaceful purposes.

Soviet activity in the Antarctic during the 1950s caused concern in the Eisenhower administration regarding Moscow's interests. Because the Antarctic already had conflicting claims about sovereignty, Eisenhower hoped to use diplomacy and formulate a treaty to avoid Cold War rivalry in the region. The December 1 agreement was arranged to regulate the extraction of minerals and protect the environment; the accord's essential theme was the peaceful use of the Antarctic's resources with the agreement to disarm the continent. An environmental agreement on the Antarctic was not approved until June 2, 1988.

December 19, 1959

Eisenhower's goodwill tour begins with a Paris meeting of NATO leaders.

The first stop on President Eisenhower's 22,370-mile journey to three continents was Paris for a meeting with French President de Gaulle, British Prime Minister Macmillan, and West German Chancellor Adenauer. Their most important decision was to invite Soviet Premier Khrushchev to a summit meeting in Paris. After Khrushchev accepted the invitation, the meeting was set for May 16, 1960. On December 22, following the Paris meeting, Eisenhower's goodwill trip took him to Italy, Turkey, Pakistan, Afghanistan, India, Iran, Greece, Tunisia, Spain, and Morocco. Throughout the long, tiring journey, millions of people turned out to welcome Eisenhower as the world's most respected and beloved leader and peacemaker.

1960

January 19, 1960

The U.S.-Japanese Treaty of Mutual Security (1951) is renewed.

The treaty renewal caused leftist riots in Japan in an effort to prevent the treaty's ratification by the Japanese House of Representatives. Japan's Premier Nobusuke Kishi and his Liberal Democratic cabinet held firm, however, and the treaty was ratified on June 19, 1960. The accord continued to permit American military bases on Japanese soil, which was the principal clause detested by the critics of Kishi's government.

January 28, 1960

Burma and the People's Republic of China sign a 10-year nonaggression treaty.

February 13, 1960

Cuba and the USSR sign an economic pact.

The Soviets agreed to buy 5 million tons of Cuban sugar and to give Castro $100 million of Soviet trade credits. The Soviet-Cuban agreement was offered by Anastas Mikoyan, deputy premier of the Soviet Union, who visited Cuba in February. In addition to the credits and sugar purchase, the Soviets would provide technical assistance to build factories in Cuba.

February 13, 1960

France explodes its first atomic bomb in the Sahara region of Algeria.

This successful test fulfilled President de Gaulle's desire to create an independent French nuclear capability.

March 7, 1960

The United States renews diplomatic relations with Bulgaria after a nine-year disruption.

U.S. Minister Edward Page Jr. arrived in Sofia on March 7.

April 25, 1960

Khrushchev again raises the Berlin issue, asserting that a separate peace treaty with East Germany would end Allied rights in Berlin.

Eisenhower replies that Western troops would not evacuate West Berlin. Throughout 1959, several attempts to resolve the Berlin issue failed. Most notable was the foreign ministers conference at Geneva between May 11 and August 5, 1959, which discussed the issues of Berlin, German reunification, and the guarantee of free elections. In October at Camp David, there was hope that the Khrushchev-Eisenhower sessions had established a timetable to resolve the Berlin issue. Now, on the eve of the Geneva conference of May 1960, Khrushchev again threatened to settle the question unilaterally.

April 27, 1960

South Korean President Syngman Rhee's resignation leads to a military junta.

On March 15, 1960, Rhee won an unopposed reelection for a fourth term of office. During the elections, protestors criticized Rhee's repressive measures, and in March demonstrators claimed Rhee's Liberal Party rigged elections to the National Assembly. On April 27, Rhee resigned from office and on July 29, new assembly elections resulted in a victory for Chang Myron's Democratic Party. Because many of South Korea's military leaders opposed Chang's attempts to negotiate a unity proposal with North Korea's Kim Il Sung, a junta led by Major Park Chung Hee overthrew the Second Republic on May 16, 1961.

The United States opposed the military regime and urged Park to restore civilian government. To comply, Park arranged elections for October 15, 1961. After designating himself a civilian, Park restricted campaigns by opponents and won a plurality of the votes before declaring himself president of South Korea. Park's program for South Korea was to build the country's economy and eventually "win a victory over Communism" by taking control of North Korea. He did not change this policy until 1971, when President Nixon announced he would visit China. For details of Korea's governments and unification efforts, see In K. Hwang's essay, "Korea's Unification Struggle" in Lester H. Brune, ed., *The Korean War* (1996).

May 5, 1960

Khrushchev announces a U.S. spy plane has been shot down over the Soviet Union.

The Soviet downing of the U-2, a high-flying reconnaissance aircraft, resulted in a controversy between Moscow and Washington on the eve of the Paris summit. Following Khrushchev's announcement, the U.S. Department of State issued a "cover story" denying it was a spy plane, saying a weather plane flew off course from its base in Turkey or Iran. To rebut the States Department, Khrushchev produced films from the U-2, saying its pilot, Gary Francis Powers, was captured after parachuting to safety. Powers failed to push the destruct mechanism designed to demolish the U-2. After Khrushchev's disclosure, President Eisenhower told reporters he accepted responsibility for the incident, but hoped Khrushchev would not use the affair to disrupt the positive results expected at the forthcoming Paris summit.

Later, the United States disclosed that the U-2 flights began in 1956 when aviation and photo technology made them feasible. These flights provided Eisenhower with specific data on Soviet military technology and showed that some so-called missile experts were mistaken in claiming that a "missile gap" had made for an inferior American defense. Eisenhower kept the U-2 reports secret to prevent the Soviets from learning about new U.S. intelligence breakthroughs. Declassified U-2 photos were released in 1975.

From 1957 to 1960, Eisenhower's critics, including John F. Kennedy and Lyndon B. Johnson, created an atmosphere of distrust about the U.S. defense system. Although Eisenhower frequently denied that there was a missile gap, reputable journalists rebuked the president and accepted the Gaither Report or the claims of U.S. General Maxwell Taylor, who opposed Eisenhower's "new look" policy, or of Henry Kissinger, a political scientist at the time. If the president had released the U-2 data, he would have proven there was no missile gap.

From its inaugural flight (see July 4, 1956) to April 9, 1960, there were 23 U-2 flights over the Soviet Union, each having received Eisenhower's reluctant approval. The flights covered 15 percent of Soviet territory and produced 250 miles of photo strips to provide an extraordinary amount of information. In addition, the U-2s gave assistance during the Suez and Cuban crises. The U-2s were given to Nationalist Chinese on Formosa who used them with good effect.

May 16, 1960

The Paris Summit Conference is aborted after Eisenhower refuses to apologize to Khrushchev for the U-2 flights.

Eisenhower was willing to cancel future flights but refused to apologize. Khrushchev walked out of the conference, blaming the United States for preventing peaceful solutions to world problems. Although British Prime Minister Harold Macmillan tried to heal the differences between Eisenhower and Khrushchev, he could not persuade the Soviet leader to accept the president's pledge of no future over-flights. Apparently Khrushchev overplayed his hand. He had permission from the Politburo to criticize American policies but it was his own idea to demand a personal apology from Eisenhower. He believed that the president would give in, but instead Khrushchev wrecked the conference.

After the Geneva Conference of 1955, summit sessions were widely publicized and open to television cameras and newsmen. As a result, the Great Power leaders could not negotiate on the give-and-take basis that was possible behind closed doors. At the 1960 Paris session, Khrushchev used the news media to berate the president but he was unable to resolve any outstanding issues. Diplomatic maneuvering became difficult or impossible in the public glare of the media. Consequently, summits of world leaders became sessions to ratify previously accepted treaties, not to engage in negotiations—a matter not often understood by journalists and their public.

May 27, 1960

A Turkish military coup ousts Premier Adnan Menderes.

The overthrow was led by Lieutenant General Jemal Gursel, who established a junta known as the Turkish National Union. The new regime announced continued support for NATO and Turkey's U.S. treaties.

June 5, 1960

Prince Norodom Sihanouk wins control of Cambodia in a national referendum.

Prince Sihanouk had been elected premier of Cambodia on April 7, 1957, as a member of the People's Socialist Communist Party. Following the death of King Norodom Sumarit on April 3, the prince resigned his office and appealed to the nation for acceptance of his control of the country without a new monarch. The referendum of June 5 provided Sihanouk with this authority. Sihanouk wanted his country to be neutral in the U.S.-Communist dispute in Southeast Asia, which disturbed many Americans who disliked Sihanouk's having some Communist Party members in his government.

June 12–21, 1960

President Eisenhower makes a goodwill tour of the Far East, visiting the Philippines, Formosa (Taiwan), Okinawa, and Korea.

The Far East tour caused difficulty regarding relations with Japan. Eisenhower had scheduled a visit to Tokyo, but anti-American riots escalated to such a degree that he canceled his Japanese visit. The rioting focused on the January 1960 renewal of the U.S.-Japanese alliance in terms that left-wing critics in Japan claimed were not favorable to their nation. Eisenhower's visit was planned for the week the treaty ratification was being debated in Japan's House of Representatives, a time when the left-wing parties staged their most violent demonstrations. As a result, Premier Kishi recommended that the president not visit Tokyo at that time.

June 18, 1960

Khrushchev announces he will attend the Romanian Communist Congress where he denounces Mao and withdraws Soviet advisers from China.

After Khrushchev's initial address at the Congress defends the policy of peaceful coexistence, China's sharp criticism of peaceful coexistence provokes

Khrushchev into an outburst of invectives against Mao, who was not at the congress. Following Khrushchev's criticism, the head of China's delegation Peng Zhen declared Khrushchev only acted and reacted impulsively toward the West rather than deal with it as Communists should.

After Peng Zhen's charges against him, Khrushchev, without thinking, announced the withdrawal of Soviet advisers and economic support from China. This action involved the withdrawal of 1,390 technicians, ending 343 contracts and withdrawing from 257 cooperative science and technology projects. Although Khrushchev's action damaged China's economy, it also reduced the China market that purchased Soviet exports.

June 27, 1960

Communist bloc countries withdraw from talks by the 10-power Committee on Disarmament meetings in Geneva.

The meeting had begun optimistically on March 15, 1960, but Khrushchev stopped Soviet participation after the U-2 incident weakened his "peaceful coexistence" concepts and indicated the United States knew of the Soviet weakness in ICBMs despite the premier's public claims of superiority.

June 30, 1960

Belgium grants the Congo Republic full independence under President Joseph Kasavubu and Premier Patrice Lumumba.

The Belgians decided in 1959 to give their colony freedom as soon as possible; consequently, elections took place in the Congo on December 20, 1959, and the elected Congo assembly demanded immediate, unconditional independence. Within two weeks of the separation, the new Congo government faced dissident groups that wanted tribal or provincial separation from the central government. The most serious uprising occurred in Katanga Province, where dissidents led by Moise Tshombe proclaimed independence for the province. Tshombe was backed by European copper and cobalt mining interests who desired to keep control of these vital resources and their investments.

Because of these problems, Lumumba asked for U.N. help, and on July 14 the Security Council voted to send a U.N. force to replace Belgian troops and attempt to secure peace among the contending factions. U.N. forces and negotiators led by Secretary-General Dag Hammarskjöld began a four-year effort to mediate amid the contending Congolese factions and to secure an orderly government. While working at this effort, Hammarskjöld perished in an airplane crash in the Congo on September 18, 1961. This made the Congo a Cold War arena.

See August 17, 1960.

July 1, 1960

The Soviets shoot down an American plane over the Barents Sea, claiming it violated Soviet borders.

The plane was a reconnaissance bomber (RB-47) that the United States contended was on an International Geophysical Year (IGY) mission to collect data on electromagnetic activity in Arctic waters. NATO ships and planes had searched the area for two days, giving it up for lost on June 3. Finally, on July 11, Moscow announced that a Soviet fighter plane shot down the RB-47 as it flew over Soviet territorial waters, heading for Archangel. The Soviets captured the two American airmen who survived out of a crew of six. Moscow said the two rescued men confessed to being on a spy mission. The United States reported that when it last radioed to a Norwegian air force base, the RB-47 was 300 miles outside Soviet territory. The wreckage was recovered about 60 to 70 miles from the USSR's coastline. For details see William E. Burrows, *By Any Means Necessary* (2001).

Washington requested an impartial U.N. investigation of the incident and the return of the rescued pilots. On July 26, the Soviets vetoed a U.N. Security Council resolution for an inquiry and later vetoed a proposal to let Red Cross workers see the two rescued airmen. On January 23, 1961, both men were turned over to the American embassy in Moscow.

July 6, 1960

Congress approves and Eisenhower levies cuts in Cuba's sugar quota. Castro retaliates by nationalizing all U.S. property in Cuba.

On March 15, 1960, President Eisenhower asked Congress to renew the Cuban sugar quota, which had given special prices to Cuba since 1934. He also asked Congress to include authority for the president to change the quota if it was in the national interest. Congress passed this quota law, which Eisenhower signed on July 6, 1960. The only change Congress made in Eisenhower's March request was to permit the president to fix but not increase the sugar quota until April 1, 1961.

After signing the law, the president immediately cut Cuba's 1960 quota by 95 percent, from 700,000 tons to 39,752 tons. While this action constituted economic intervention in Cuba, Congress approved the law because Castro's connections with the USSR had become apparent since February 13, 1960. As soon as Eisenhower announced the sugar cut, Castro retaliated by issuing the Nationalization Law, which applied exclusively to Americans. This law ordered the seizure of all U.S. property without compensation. The United States protested this law on July 16, but there was no response from Havana. As tensions increased between the United States and Cuba, Khrushchev added to the difficulties. On July 9, the Soviet leader pledged Russia's fullest support of Cuba. Soviet rockets, Khrushchev said, could "figuratively speaking support the Cubans in case of Pentagon aggression."

July 12, 1960

Malaya becomes independent; Britain's counterinsurgency succeeds.

After General Gerald Templer became the British High Commissioner and Director of Military Operations in February 1952, he continued Brigg's counterinsurgency plans but he also adopted political programs designed to win the "hearts and minds" of Malaya's populace. When he arrived in Malaya, Templer had about 60,000 Malaya Police and 20,000 military personnel to use against an estimated 10,000 guerrillas. Templer's typical joint police-army operation, Operation Hive, was conducted late in 1952. Operation Hive included operations by two battalions of Gurkas riflemen, two British Special Forces groups, and a regiment of Fijian infantry from the Commonwealth. Operation Hive successfully countered the insurgents by finding and destroying ambush tracks used by insurgents in jungle areas. To speed the process of counterinsurgency, Royal Air Force dropped bombs on jungle areas as a prelude to British volunteer Special Forces making a risky parachute drop in a tactic called "tree jumping." Using these methods, the British forced the MRLA to retreat deeper into the jungle where it was split into smaller groups of five to 15 men and women. Most of the remaining insurgents had to go underground.

Thus, Templer reported in May 1954 that in many designated areas all emergency restrictions were lifted because they were free from insurgents. These areas included the coastal areas of Malacca and Trengganu and the provinces of Perlis, Kedah, and Nrgri Sembilan. At the same time, Templer won the hearts and minds of the populace by raising morale in these areas and especially, giving the people of Malaya a sense of how and why they must defeat the Communist insurgents. When Templer left, local councils had been elected, new villages had been consolidated, and even the Chinese in Malaya had formed their own Home Guard against the insurgents.

On May 30, 1954, he handed over his office to his Deputy Sir Donald MacGillivray as high commissioner and Lt. General G.K. Bourne as director of military operations. Bourne's forces had only to deal with a declining Communist group of insurgents, mostly along the northern border with Thailand. Thai intelligence officers cooperated with the British in exposing areas were insurgents were located. Eventually in August 1957, Malaya became a sovereign independent state with Tunku Abdul Rahman as prime minister and leader of the Alliance government. The emergency measures for all of Malaya were completed in July 1960. (For sources see July 28, 1948)

July 20, 1960

A Polaris missile is launched from a submerged submarine.

This success gave the U.S. navy a new role in nuclear weapons. The United States gained a new form of deterrent power because the submarines were mobile and difficult to detect by the Soviet Union.

August 9, 1960

In Laos, a coup led by Kong Le returns Souvanna Phouma to power and results in U.S.-Soviet tensions.

After the Geneva Accords of 1954 gave Laos independence, international conflict increased over the failure of this state to achieve political order. The Geneva agreements called for the regrouping of all Communist Pathet Lao (left-wing nationalists) in the two northern provinces of Laos. In 1957, the neutralist Premier Souvanna Phouma compromised with the

Polaris missile test launched from submarine. Brune photo

Communists and brought his half-brother, who was a Communist, into the cabinet. The compromise failed because Communist election gains in 1958 threatened a left-wing takeover. As a result, civil war began as the extreme right- and left-wing groups fought. Disliking the turn of events, Premier Souvanna resigned on July 23, 1958.

In October 1958, pro-Western ruler Phoui Sanaikone promised to bring economic and political reforms to Laos, and the United States provided about $25 million of aid to Laos for 1959. During 1959, Phoui complained that Communist guerrilla war had begun in Laos and appealed to the United Nations to stop the invasion of the North Vietnamese. On September 7, the U.N. Security Council sent a subcommittee to make an "inquiry" in Laos, and in October the subcommittee reported that the North Vietnamese had sent arms and supplies to Laos but that it could not clearly establish whether North Vietnamese troops crossed the border. The U.N. report led to the resignation of Phoui in December 1959; Kou Abhay then became provisional head of the government. Elections were conducted in April 1960, but they were rigged to favor the government, and the Pathet Lao protested. As a result, guerrilla war increased, and on August 9 a coup overthrew Abhay, installing Tiao Somsanith as head of the new regime.

The power behind Tiao was a young army captain, Kong Le. After Tiao's government ended its fight against the Communists and brought the neutralist Souvanna Phouma back to office, the coup presented a dilemma for the United States because there were now three factors in Laos: the neutral Souvanna Phouma controlled the government but lost control of the army because the pro-Western Phoumi Nosavan headed a conservative group that refused to cooperate with Souvanna. The third faction was the Soviet-supported Pathet Lao. By the end of Eisenhower's term of office in January 1961, no solution to the Laos imbroglio had been reached.

August 12, 1960

The Cold War in the Congo: Eisenhower ultimately decides Lumumba must go.

Following anti-European riots in Léopoldville, the capital of the Belgian Congo, the Belgium government allowed Congolese nationals to hold elections in May 1960. The elections made Joseph Kasavubu president of the Congo and Patrice Lumumba Prime Minister of the Central government. Subsequently, on June 30, 1960, the Belgium Congo became the independent Congo Republic, later named the Republic of Zaire. Independence Day was barely celebrated before soldiers in the Congo army, known as the Force Publique, mutinied against their Belgian officers. About the same time, Moise Tshombe, who in May 1960 was elected governor of Katanga, declared independence for Katanga as a separate state. Tshombe was assisted by the Belgian government, with whom he made a deal to continue mining Katanga's natural resources for sale to Belgian and other Western merchants.

In late July, Prime Minister Lumumba requested armaments and financial aid from the United States to help his government regain control of

Katanga. When the United States rejected his request, Lumumba turned to the Soviet Union, which quickly airlifted food and weapons to the Léopoldville government. In addition, the United Nations Security Council (U.N. Security Council) agreed to send U.N. peacekeepers to help maintain the unity of the Congo. The Eisenhower administration favored the U.N. Security Council action, concerned that Katanga's uranium, a substance needed to make nuclear weapons, might be sold to the Soviet Union. On August 18, Undersecretary of State C. Douglas Dillon told the National Security Council (NSC) that the Soviet Union and Lumumba demanded the U.N. peacekeepers leave the Congo. As Stephen E. Ambrose's *Eisenhower: The President* (1984) explains, Eisenhower decided that rather than have U.N. peacekeepers leave, someone must "get rid of that man [Lumumba]."

On August 25, the CIA's watchdog Committee 5412 met to discuss what action should be taken against Lumumba. The next day, CIA Director Allen Dulles cabled the CIA agent in Léopoldville that the removal of Lumumba was an "urgent" matter. On September 5, Congo's President Kasavubu dismissed Lumumba as premier. Lumumba was captured—perhaps with CIA help—and placed in the custody of the U.N. peacekeepers. On September 12, the Congo's army led by Colonel Joseph Mobutu arrested Lumumba, who was executed either by the army or by "hostile tribesmen."

August 28, 1960

The San José declaration of the OAS condemns intervention "by any extracontinental power," an indirect warning against Soviet interference in Cuba.

The United States asked for a special OAS meeting in July 1960, following Soviet Premier Khrushchev's threat to support Cuba with rockets. Khrushchev also told the State Department that the Monroe Doctrine had "outlived its time." During the conference sessions, Secretary of State Herter wanted the group to condemn Castro for violating principles of the inter-American system. The other delegates refused to specify Cuba as a guilty party, preferring to issue a declaration that reaffirmed American "solidarity and security" and opposed intervention by an outside power.

September 8, 1960

East Germany institutes a permanent restriction on travel by West Germans to East Berlin.

West Germans would be required to obtain a police pass to enter East Berlin. The Allies protested this violation of the Four-Power Pact on Berlin.

September 10, 1960

The Organization of Petroleum Exporting Countries (OPEC) is formed in Baghdad.

The original members were Iraq, Iran, Kuwait, Saudi Arabia, and Venezuela. These nations agreed to demand stable oil prices from oil companies. The impetus to form OPEC occurred when Standard Oil of New Jersey unilaterally cut posted oil prices in 1960, drastically reducing Saudi Arabia's oil revenues.

September 20, 1960

At the 1960 U.N. General Assembly session, Khrushchev, Tito, and Fidel Castro head their nations' delegations.

Before the U.N. session concludes, the Soviet premier displayed amazing methods of debate. Khrushchev used the United Nations as a forum to woo the support of Third World nations for Soviet policy. Sixteen nations, mostly from Asia and Africa, joined the United Nations during this 15th session of the General Assembly. U.N. membership by October 1960 totaled 98 nations, of which the Asian-African bloc numbered 44. Khrushchev's September 24 speech at the United Nations attacked Secretary-General Dag Hammarskjöld's policy in the Congo as pro-colonial. He demanded Hammarskjöld's ouster and replacing the secretary-general with a three-man (troika) executive. Both proposals were defeated by the assembly.

On October 12, the chairman of the General Assembly, Frederick H. Boland of Ireland, had to suspend the assembly's session because of Khrushchev's outburst. Khrushchev had argued strongly for a resolution to end all colonialism. The Philippine delegate, Lorenzo Sumulong, responded by contending that the resolution should include Soviet imperial control of Eastern Europe. Khrushchev interrupted Sumulong, calling him a U.S. "lackey." As Boland tried to bring order, breaking his gavel in the process, Khrushchev remarked, laughingly, on the weakness of the United

Nations. The Soviet premier then took off his shoe and banged it on his desk to protest Sumulong's speech. Chaos erupted before Boland finally adjourned the meeting.

October 1, 1960

For the first time since 1903, the U.S. and Panamanian flags are flown together over the Canal Zone.

Although the Panamanian flag issue was not the only question about which Panamanians had complained, it symbolized Panama's desire for national respect. Thus, President Eisenhower's decision on September 17 to permit both flags to fly together also indicated Eisenhower's attempt to relieve some of the difficulties between the United States and Panama.

October 19, 1960

The United States embargoes all Cuban exports except medicines and certain food products.

The embargo was intended to put further pressure on Fidel Castro to moderate his anti-American policies. The next day, Eisenhower recalled the U.S. ambassador to Cuba, Philip Bonsal. Castro had refused to talk with the ambassador since a brief conversation on September 3, 1959. Since January 1, 1959, the United States had requested negotiations with Cuba on nine formal and 16 informal occasions. Only once, on February 22, 1960, did the Cuban government respond, and then it offered absurd conditions for undertaking negotiations.

November 8, 1960

John F. Kennedy defeats Richard M. Nixon in the presidential race.

Although the election was close, the Democratic Party enlarged its majority in both the House (260 to 172) and the Senate (65 to 35). Kennedy's victory margin was 114,000 votes out of 68.3 million ballots. During the campaign, neither candidate offered unique foreign policy programs. Both emphasized the importance of the newly developing nations. On defense policy, Kennedy continued to be critical of Eisenhower's alleged complacency toward the USSR and the "loss" of Cuba, and advocated Maxwell Taylor's "flexible response" program for a vigorous defense budget increase. Nixon never provided a firm response to the criticisms of Eisenhower's program.

President John F. Kennedy. National Archives

November 11–12, 1960

In Saigon, President Diem regains power after an army paratroop brigade temporarily ousts him from office.

The paratroop uprising reflected opposition to Diem's policies in the military and among other non-Communist politicians in South Vietnam. In addition to the unsuccessful plot of the paratroopers, 18 old-time non-Communist politicians showed their displeasure with Diem in August 1960 by issuing the so-called Caravelle Manifesto.

The Caravelle group urged Diem to reevaluate his policies by recognizing that not all his critics were

Communists. They asked that he hold free elections, end censorship, and stop political repression by releasing political prisoners who filled the jails "to the rafters." They asked Diem to secure dedicated civil servants, end army factionalism, and stop exploiting farmers and workers. Diem claimed he saw no difference between the Caravelle group and Communists; therefore, he arrested and imprisoned the 18 signatories of the petition.

By 1960, Diem's publicity had made him as popular in America as he was disliked in South Vietnam. The American Friends of Vietnam had been formed in 1955, and its letterhead cited Senator John F. Kennedy as a founding member. By 1960, the U.S. media called Diem the "tough little miracle man," and *Newsweek's* Ernest Lindley exclaimed that he was "one of the ablest free Asian leaders." In 1960, both Diem and Chiang Kai-shek won Freedom Foundation awards from a Valley Forge–based organization.

November 19, 1960

The United States and Canada join 18 members of the OEEC to form the Organization for Economic Co-operation and Development (OECD).

The purpose of the OECD was to expand trade and economic cooperation and to aid underdeveloped states to expand their economies.

December 5, 1960

The U.S. Ambassador to South Vietnam, Elbridge Durbrow, issues a final critical report on Diem's policies.

After serving four years in Saigon, Ambassador Durbrow had grown increasingly disillusioned with Diem. He said there was only weak domestic support for Diem and blamed many of the problems on corruption in the officer class and the influence of Diem's family members who held high office, especially Ngo Dinh Nhu, Diem's brother, and Madame Nhu. Durbrow wanted Diem replaced if he did not initiate economic reform, broaden the non-Communist base of his cabinet, and eliminate corrupt army and government leaders; however, the report was not acted on because Kennedy replaced Durbrow with a European expert, Frederick E. Nolting Jr.

December 5, 1960

Clearer signs of Sino-Soviet split are evident at a Moscow meeting of world Communist Parties.

At the end of the meeting (November 7–December 5, 1960) 81 parties signed a Communist Manifesto that pledged Communist victory by peaceful means and affirmed the Soviet leadership of all Communist parties. The Chinese Communists' objections to these views reflected the prevailing arguments on policy between Peking and Moscow, which had increased during 1960. On May 14, 1960, Mao Tse-tung published an interview in which he taunted the Soviets for permitting U-2s to spy on them and for believing they could work cooperatively with Western imperialists. In June, Khrushchev sent letters to a Communist meeting in Romania. The letters attacked Chinese views on Communist policy and blamed Mao for being a revisionist. Khrushchev said the Chinese were madmen and "left adventurists" desiring to unleash a nuclear war. (See June 18, 1960.) The November-December sessions in Moscow failed to heal the division between China and the Soviet Union. Albania was the only country joining China in criticizing Khrushchev.

December 20, 1960

The National Liberation Front (NLF) is created in South Vietnam.

The NLF said it represented all Vietnamese peoples south of the 17th parallel in their fight against Diem's tyranny. The formation of the NLF indicated attempts by the South Vietnamese to overthrow Diem's government. After securing control of Saigon in 1955, Diem did not display equal skill in bringing economic reform and political prestige to his government. He failed to carry out land reform for the peasants and increasingly suppressed all who dissented from his policies. In 1958, the first anti-Diem organizations appeared in the south. The rural groups used sabotage and attacks on village chiefs or informers who were loyal to Diem. As resistance grew in the country, Diem used greater repression, until by 1960 those opposing him decided to organize as the NLF to coordinate their attacks on Saigon and Diem's officials.

1961

January 3, 1961

The United States severs diplomatic relations with Cuba.

While the United States recalled Ambassador Bonsal from Havana on October 20, 1960, Castro had assigned no ambassador to Washington since he took office in 1959. On January 2, 1961, Castro charged that the U.S. embassy in Havana was a center for counterrevolutionaries. He ordered that the embassy staff be reduced from 36 to 11 persons in 48 hours. This convinced President Eisenhower to break diplomatic relations with Cuba.

January 4, 1961

Castro's claim that the United States is preparing an invasion is ignored by the U.N. Security Council.

On October 18, 1960, Cuba first asked the U.N. General Assembly to investigate U.S. plans to invade it. The assembly refused to act. Later, on January 4, 1961, Castro petitioned the U.N. Security Council to prevent U.S. intervention in Cuba. Again, Castro's charges were rebuffed. On March 17, 1960, President Eisenhower had secretly ordered the CIA to train Cuban exiles for possible guerrilla operations against Castro. By the end of 1960, nearly 1,200 men were being trained by the CIA, most of them in Guatemala. While very few Americans knew about this force, it was an "open" secret elsewhere.

January 6, 1961

Soviet Premier Khrushchev asserts that his government will support wars of national liberation.

Addressing a Communist Party meeting in Moscow, the Soviet leader reiterated his desire for peaceful coexistence with the Western world. The only exception, he stated, was Soviet backing for "just" wars of liberation from capitalist imperialism. Khrushchev's speech reflected the end of the era of Western colonialism; the end of colonialism had accelerated after Ghana gained independence in 1957. National uprisings against foreign control had become one of the major causes of conflict throughout the world. This had the greatest impact on British, French, and U.S. policies because they were the powers whose trade and financial policies had become global since the eighteenth century. When Khrushchev spoke of national liberation, he did not include the many national minorities in the Soviet Union.

January 17, 1961

Eisenhower's "farewell address" warns Americans of the dangerous power of the American military-industrial complex.

During debate on Eisenhower's "new look" policy, the president had become acutely frustrated with the "conjunction of an immense military establishment and a large arms industry" whose "total influence" was felt throughout the nation. Americans, Eisenhower warned, "must guard against the acquisition of unwarranted influence, whether sought or unsought, by the military-industrial complex." Because of this connection, "the potential for the disastrous use of misplaced power exists and will persist."

January 19, 1961

The Laotian problem is reviewed for President-elect Kennedy and his incoming cabinet members.

Following the return to power of Laotian General Kong Le, the Eisenhower administration opposed Premier Souvanna Phouma's neutralist coalition government that included members of the Pathet Lao Communists. In October 1960, Eisenhower sent Assistant Secretary of State J. Graham Parsons to Vientiane, the capital of Laos, to demand that Souvanna Phouma renounce the Pathet Lao and abandon his neutralist coalition. Eisenhower believed such a coalition would come under the complete control of Communists, after Souvanna refused.

Eisenhower decided to divert U.S. economic and military assistance through the CIA to Phoumi Nosavan, who denounced neutralism and had resigned as minister of defense in the coalition. This action persuaded the genuine neutralists in Souvanna's cabinet to cooperate with the Pathet Lao. By December 1960, the Kong Le-Pathet Lao forces defeated Phoumi Nosavan's forces, driving them out of the region surrounding Vientiane. On December 4, the Soviet Union airlifted military supplies to the Pathet Lao troops, who began an offensive against Phoumi Nosavan's army. As a result, President Eisenhower and Secretary of State Herter's review of the Laos situation was that the United States was in dangerous trouble in Laos.

The new Kennedy administration inherited support for a pro-Western but weak government of Phoumi Nosavan and members of clans who recognized Prince Boun Oum as monarch of Laos. In addition, on January 2, 1961, U.S. delegates to a SEATO meeting requested that the group intervene with a military force to support the pro-Western government, but neither Britain nor France would approve a Laotian intervention. Eisenhower did not want to intervene unilaterally or negotiate with neutralists in Laos, but he sent six U.S. fighter-bombers to assist Phoumi Nosavan's forces. Although Eisenhower thought that saving a pro-Western Laos was the key to the entire region of Southeast Asia, he offered no satisfactory solution to Kennedy and Rusk.

January 20, 1961

President John F. Kennedy's inaugural address calls on the nation to renew its commitment to extend freedom throughout the world.

In his inaugural address, the president called on the American people to defend freedom in this hour of need. He asserted: "Let every nation know, whether it wishes us well or ill, that we shall pay any price, bear any burden, meet any hardship, support any friend, oppose any foe, in order to assure the survival and success of liberty. This much we pledge, and more."

January 21, 1961

Dean Rusk is commissioned as Secretary of State under President John F. Kennedy.

Although Rusk was well qualified to be secretary, President Kennedy desired his to be the dominant voice in foreign affairs. In selecting Rusk, he had a person who would be loyal and hardworking but not try to capture the headlines. During World War II, Rusk served as a deputy chief of staff in the China-Burma-India theater. Between 1945 and 1952, he held several positions in the State Department, achieving the post of assistant secretary for Far Eastern Affairs in 1950– 1951. From 1952 to 1961 he was president of the Rockefeller Foundation. Rusk was secretary throughout the administrations of Kennedy and Johnson, leaving office on January 20, 1969.

February 6, 1961

The missile gap is a myth. Secretary of Defense McNamara tells journalists that the "missile-gap" criticism levied against the Eisenhower administration has no foundation in fact.

Between 1957 and 1961, the widespread criticism of Eisenhower's "new look" policy had been based partly on the incorrect claim that Eisenhower's nuclear sufficiency program to build 200 ICBMs would allow the Soviets the opportunity to achieve a superiority in nuclear weapons during the early 1960s. Eisenhower insisted that there was no missile gap, but this notion became so popular that both Republican and Democratic politicians assumed its validity. It was used effectively by Kennedy to assert that Eisenhower's foreign programs had been weak and ineffective. It also was part of Maxwell Taylor's plan to build up the army's counterinsurgency forces to win brushfire wars under the protection of a superior nuclear force umbrella.

Soon after McNamara took over the Defense Department, he saw evidence that Eisenhower's denials of a missile gap were based in fact. In a background briefing, McNamara admitted that there was no missile gap. Nevertheless, neither the Kennedy administration nor the news media played up the fact that the claims of a missile gap had been false. McNamara and Kennedy wanted to build a superior nuclear force whether or not there was a missile gap. As Richard Aliano has noted, Kennedy wanted a missile gap in reverse, with the gap being on the Soviet side. Therefore the rapid buildup of ICBMs became one part of the large defense expenditures Kennedy promoted for all branches of the armed forces after 1961.

On October 21, 1961, Deputy Secretary of Defense Roswell Gilpatric stated that the United States had a nuclear second-strike force at least as large as the Soviets' first strike capability. In February 1962, McNamara told the Senate Foreign Relations Committee that America's nuclear forces would be superior in any military conflict. In March, Kennedy renounced the no-first-strike doctrine, informing Khrushchev that the United States would strike first if its interests were threatened.

The U.S. announcement that it, in fact, had more ICBMs than the Soviets embarrassed Khrushchev, who had boasted about the Soviets' nuclear superiority. The Soviets had decided not to build more liquid fuel missiles, but to wait until the solid fuel models were ready. Meanwhile Khrushchev had resorted to bluff with claims of the Soviets' missile prowess, but in doing this he had fostered the American myth of a "missile gap."

By 1967 the United States had increased the number of nuclear weapons with ICBMs from 200 to 1,000. The United States also had 41 Polaris submarines with 656 missile launchers and 600 long-range bombers for nuclear attack. The Soviets responded by matching the U.S. nuclear arsenal. Kennedy had stimulated a nuclear arms race.

See June 25, 1967.

February 28, 1961

Secretary Rusk informs the Senate Foreign Relations Committee that Kennedy, like Eisenhower, supports U.N. action in the Congo.

Since the Congo dispute first went to the U.N. Security Council on June 30, 1960, the United States had voted with most nations in backing the U.N. peacekeeping mission there. Also, Washington supported U.N. Secretary-General Dag Hammarskjöld's policy, which recognized the Léopoldville government against both the pro-Belgian faction in Katanga and the Soviet-backed forces led by Antonio Gizenga, who had replaced Patrice Lumumba after his execution. The only problem for the United States was the support given to Tshombe and the rebels in Katanga, whose independence was urged by such conservatives as Senator Barry Goldwater and news editor William F. Buckley. The American opponents of the U.N. policy were more vocal in the summer of 1961 when the United Nations attempted to use force to defeat Katanga.

March 1, 1961

President Kennedy issues an executive order creating the Peace Corps.

The Peace Corps was set up to train Americans to go to underdeveloped nations that requested U.S. assistance and to provide teaching and technical services.

John F. Kennedy with early Peace Corps volunteers. John F. Kennedy Library

The idea had been suggested by Hubert Humphrey during the Democratic primaries and was seized upon by Kennedy. Ideally, the corps would allow Americans and citizens of other nations to work side by side to promote both economic development and the democratic way of life. Kennedy believed the Cold War could be won in Third World nations by demonstrating U.S. virtues on a person-to-person basis. Kennedy saw the Peace Corps as an important Cold War weapon. He argued that many technicians from the Soviet Union and China "spend their lives abroad in the service of world communism." Young Americans dedicated to freedom, he said, "are fully capable of overcoming the efforts of Mr. Khrushchev's missionaries who are dedicated to undermining that freedom."

March 13, 1961

President Kennedy announces the Alliance for Progress to aid Latin America.

This program, Kennedy said, would extend previous aid of the Eisenhower administration by committing the United States to a 10-year program of $20 billion. Details of the program would be finalized at an Inter-American Conference in Punta del Este, Uruguay, in August.

April 12, 1961

Soviets send first man into space.

Major Yuri A. Gagarin in spaceship Vostok I circled the earth for 108 minutes at a maximum altitude of 203 miles.

April 17, 1961

In the U.S.-backed Bay of Pigs invasion, Cuban rebels fail to topple Castro's regime.

The Eisenhower administration began plans for guerrilla operations in Cuba on March 17, 1960. After the 1960 presidential election, the CIA apprised Kennedy of these plans. Although Secretary Rusk opposed the guerrilla operations, CIA Director Allen Dulles and U.S. Chairman of the Joint Chiefs of Staff General Lyman Lemnitzer assured Kennedy the plans would succeed even though a March 3 CIA report indicated only 25 percent of the Cuban population opposed Castro. Kennedy agreed that planning should continue, but by April 5, the Cuban operation changed from a guerrilla infiltration to an invasion, with Cuban exiles landing near the Zapata swamps at the Bay of Pigs to join Cuban rebels in the mountain area.

From its first hours on April 15, the CIA plans became a fiasco. Of eight B-26 bombers supposed to destroy Cuba's air force, one crashed in the ocean, a second unexpectedly landed in Key West, Florida, and air raids by six B-26s failed to knock out all of Cuba's planes. Castro's remaining two bombers, four fighter planes and several T-33 trainer aircraft, supported 20,000 Cuban troops with tanks and artillery that quickly surrounded the 1,200 exile rebels who landed at the Zapata swamps on April 17. Although President Kennedy canceled a second B-26 bombing raid on April 26, he acted too late to stop the exiles' invasion effort. In addition to embarrassing the Kennedy administration, the Bay of Pigs incident damaged U.S. relations with the U.N. Security Council and the OAS. At the United Nations, Ambassador Adlai Stevenson had unknowingly denied the story of U.S. involvement in the rebels' invasion because he had not been fully briefed on the secret operation.

America's unilateral operation reaped a harvest of ill will around the world and probably influenced Kennedy's decision to undertake future attempts to overthrow Castro. Nearly 40 years later, on April 26, 2000, Maxwell Taylor's secret report on the Bay of Pigs operation was declassified. Taylor disclosed that the CIA learned on April 9 that the Soviet Union knew the exact time and day of the amphibious landing but the agency still carried out the planned invasion. As a result, Castro's soldiers repelled the attack in fewer than 72 hours, killing 200 rebels and capturing 1,197 others. The Taylor report did not say who the spy was, but in *Cassidy's Run* author David Wise believes a Mexican, Gilbert López y Rivas, was involved. The Taylor report was declassified after Peter Kornbluh of the National Security Archives obtained it through the Freedom of Information Act. Kornbluh also requested the release of a four-volume history of the Bay of Pigs operation written by CIA historian Jack B. Pfeiffer, but the CIA continued to withhold that classified study, saying it was still under review.

May 3, 1961

A cease-fire takes effect in Laos soon after the United States threatens military intervention.

Less noticed than the Cuban Bay of Pigs incident of April 1961 was the fact that the United States seriously considered war in Laos if the Communist advances continued in that state. U.S. support for the rightist Phoumi and Oum in Laos increased the regime's unpopularity and the strengthened Communist and neutralist unity. By March 1961, the Communist drive in Laos left Phoumi's forces in disarray, causing Kennedy and Rusk to seek some means to obtain a neutral, non-Communist state in Laos. On March 23, Kennedy ordered U.S. forces to move to areas near Laos. The aircraft carrier Midway was sent to the Gulf of Siam, a marine unit to Thailand, and forces on Okinawa were placed on alert. At the same time, Secretary Rusk attended a SEATO meeting in Bangkok to obtain support for U.S. military action if necessary.

At Bangkok, Rusk added a clear global dimension to the Truman Doctrine, telling the SEATO delegates that U.S. assistance to "freedom-loving nations" had "no geographical barriers." The French and British, however, did not desire military action in Laos; they did not consider the area to be of vital interest. Nevertheless, Rusk persuaded SEATO delegates to endorse a resolution declaring SEATO's resolve not to "acquiesce" in any takeover of Laos or Vietnam and to keep developments in those countries under review. While Rusk and Kennedy prepared for possible unilateral military intervention in Laos, British Prime Minister Harold Macmillan arranged for a cease-fire in Laos and a conference at Geneva. Soviet Premier Khrushchev also favored a conference, and on May 3 a cease-fire was announced in Laos. The Geneva meetings began on May 16 but did not reach agreement until 1962.

May 5, 1961

A NATO council meeting at Oslo discloses European concern for a greater role in NATO defense operations.

Europeans did not look favorably on Kennedy's shift from the Eisenhower-Dulles "massive retaliation" to a "flexible response" strategy. The Kennedy program to use conventional forces wherever necessary, and to build a superior nuclear force that might or might not be used, seemed to French President de Gaulle and other European leaders to be a design to keep America aloof from the interests of European powers. In addition, the Europeans had grown less dependent on the United States and asked for some degree of control over nuclear weapons and the NATO forces in Europe.

At the Oslo meeting, Secretary Rusk indicated America would steadfastly support Europe. He could not, however, offer an end to the U.S. monopoly of the alliance's strategic nuclear weapons. In addition, by asserting that all areas of the world were important and would be defended, Rusk by definition lowered Europe's former rating as the first U.S. priority. Rusk offered the Europeans five Polaris submarines as part of the NATO command. But he insisted that Americans must command the subs and control nuclear missiles. The Europeans wanted more. They wanted a respected position in the NATO command and spoke of a multilateral defense force (MDF) that would include nuclear weapons under European control. The United States was not willing to relinquish its control of the NATO forces, especially nuclear forces.

May 25, 1961

President Kennedy launches a "moon race" to beat the Soviet Union in landing the first man on the moon.

Kennedy had asked Vice President Johnson on April 20 to study U.S. space capabilities and determine if the United States had a chance of beating the Soviet Union in the moon race or some other dramatic space program. This feat, Kennedy believed, would reassert U.S. technical superiority over the Soviets. Johnson, as chairman of the Space Council, conducted a study and reported that the Soviets had larger boosters for a possible moon flight. With a strong U.S. effort, however, the Space Council believed the United States could accomplish a moon mission by 1966 or 1967.

On May 25, Kennedy told Congress that it was time for the United States to organize a "great new American enterprise" and "take a clearly leading role in space achievement." He committed the nation to achieve the goal, "before the decade is out, of landing a man on the moon and returning him safely to earth." The "space race" was on. This launched the Apollo program, which was successful on July 20, 1969.

June 3–4, 1961

Kennedy and Khrushchev hold a summit in Vienna.

It was hoped this meeting would resolve the Berlin issue. On February 17, Premier Khrushchev informed the West German government that West

President Kennedy and Premier Khrushchev leaving meeting at Vienna. John F. Kennedy Library

Berlin should become a "free city." In addition, he wished to conclude a final German peace treaty. If not, Khrushchev said, he would sign a separate pact with East Germany. The Vienna meetings did not settle either the German or the pending Laotian problem. Khrushchev stated he would act unilaterally with East Germany on a German peace treaty if none were achieved by December 1961. If the West interfered, there would be war. Kennedy countered by warning Khrushchev the United States would fight to keep access routes to Berlin and the Soviets must not act unilaterally.

Regarding Laos, both leaders desired a neutral Laos. Khrushchev said, however, the Pathet Lao would eventually win while Kennedy stated that America was determined to protect Laos. Thus, the two leaders defended a strong position to maintain their status in Laos and Germany. On his return home, Kennedy told Americans the Vienna visit was "a very sober two days."

July 25, 1961

President Kennedy delivers a speech strongly backing the importance of Berlin as vital to America.

After Khrushchev indicated at Vienna that the Soviets would act unilaterally in Berlin and East Germany by December 1961, Kennedy decided to assert American rights and duties in Berlin. He refused to negotiate access to Berlin or the U.S. military presence in that city. The president also placed National Reserve troops on duty and announced a 25 percent increase in U.S. military power. Kennedy declared the U.S. position on Berlin without prior consultation with American allies, as recommended by Rusk. Kennedy's attitude toward U.S. allies was to avoid reliance on them. Unlike Eisenhower, who emphasized close cooperation with NATO, Kennedy and Johnson believed the United States must act unilaterally if necessary. In July 1961, Prime Minister Macmillan approved Kennedy's action; President de Gaulle and Chancellor Adenauer were troubled by his bellicose overtones.

August 13, 1961

The Soviets begin construction of the Berlin wall, dividing East and West Berlin.

One of the Soviets' principal concerns regarding Berlin was the drain of East Germany's educated and technical elite to West Germany through the city. After the Vienna Conference of June 1961, this flow increased to 30,000 in July and 4,000 on August 12. On August 13, East German police erected barriers to separate East and West Berlin. Because Kennedy had never argued for direct access to East Berlin, he and Secretary Rusk protested the barriers but did not take military action to stop the wall's construction, although some critics argued that Kennedy should have challenged the Soviets with U.S. soldiers. But Kennedy emphasized the wall as a symbol of the Communists' failure to provide adequately for their own people. During the next year, East Germany replaced the original barbed wire barricade with a more elaborate concrete wall and machine-gun nests to prevent East Germans from fleeing to the West.

The Berlin Wall with East German soldiers on patrol. Brune photo

August 17, 1961

The Alliance for Progress charter is signed at the Inter-American Conference in Punta del Este.

This meeting finalized a U.S. agreement that all Latin American nations except Cuba had signed. Over 10 years the United States would provide $20 billion for a public and private investment program in Latin America. There would also be another $300 million annual investment from private capital in the United States. The Latin American governments pledged $80 billion of investments over 10 years. In addition, they pledged to enact land, tax, and other socioeconomic reforms in their nations.

Unfortunately, the Alliance for Progress did not function as well as expected. Brazil, Argentina, and Mexico did not want close scrutiny of their programs. Thus, many Latin American governments did not enact the necessary reforms. Although some benefits resulted from the program, the hoped for orderly, stable, and improved political and economic conditions did not occur in Latin America in the next decade.

August 31, 1961

Moscow announces the Soviets are renewing nuclear tests.

By this action, the Soviets canceled an informal 1958 agreement between Khrushchev and Eisenhower that temporarily halted tests. Soon after August 31, the USSR began a series of nuclear tests.

See October 30, 1961.

September 18, 1961

U.N. Secretary-General Hammarskjöld is killed in a plane crash while seeking a truce in the Congo.

At the time of Hammarskjöld's death, he and Secretary of State Rusk disagreed about the use of U.N. forces against Tshombe's regime in Katanga. The Congo dispute had narrowed to a struggle between Cyrille Adoula, who was elected premier of the Léopoldville government backed by the United Nations, and Tshombe's state, backed by some European nations, South Africa, and Southern Rhodesia, as well as many U.S. conservatives. Rusk backed U.N. support for Adoula as the moderate candidate in the

Congo but objected to Hammarskjöld's use of U.N. forces against Tshombe. Rusk desired negotiations between Tshombe and Adoula to solve their dispute. On September 20, two days after Hammarskjöld died in a plane crash in the Congo, the opposing Congolese leaders agreed to a cease-fire. The truce did not end successfully, however. By November 11, Kennedy agreed to Rusk's recommendation to allow the United Nations to use force if necessary against Katanga.

September 21, 1961

Soviet Foreign Minister Andrei Gromyko agrees to delay the USSR's December deadline for settlement of the German issue.

The administration was greatly disturbed by Khrushchev's threat on June 3, 1961, to act unilaterally on a German peace treaty. Therefore, in September, Secretary Rusk and Gromyko discussed the dangerous implications of the situation. During a series of three discussions, Gromyko indicated that the Soviet deadline could be delayed if negotiations began. Rusk agreed to talk, suggesting that a four-power agreement could guarantee Western access to Berlin. In addition, Rusk said that if the German problem were settled, arms limitations in Central Europe might be discussed. The September talks did relieve East-West tensions over Germany. Although French President de Gaulle and some U.S. critics, such as Harvard Professor Henry Kissinger, believed Rusk's "weakness" bordered on "appeasement," it had not. Rusk had not committed any nation to arms limits but had obtained a delay in the Soviet deadline on Germany. Rusk's talks, combined with Kennedy's frequent assertions of U.S. support for West Berlin, ended the Berlin crisis of 1961. Further talks on Berlin and Germany continued, but Khrushchev's ultimatum no longer added to the tense atmosphere.

October 28, 1961

The Berlin crisis ends after the Soviets agree West Berlin military need not show identification.

When East Berlin officials began building the wall in August, President Kennedy took a cautious approach to determine what action to follow. His caution became a compromise two months later. On October 22, Allen Lightner and his wife drove their Volkswagen bearing U.S. license plates to the Friedrichstrasse crossing point—later called Checkpoint Charlie—but East German border guards stopped them from entering. Lightner called General Lucius Clay, the U.S. military authority in Berlin, who sent a jeep with armed soldiers to escort Lightner's car into East Berlin to see a theater performance. For the next five days, more U.S. soldiers in uniform went through the checkpoint without identifying themselves. On October 27, the crisis escalated with U.S. and Soviet tanks facing each other at Checkpoint Charlie. The next day, the crisis ended after Kennedy and Khrushchev agreed Western civilians would not cross the border but American, British, and French soldiers in uniform would not be stopped from entering East Berlin. Of course, East Germans continued building the wall separating East and West Berlin.

October 30, 1961

Soviets test a fifty-ton megaton bomb.

The USSR's newest bomb had ten times the power of all weapons used during World War II, including America's A-bombs dropped on Japan.

November 22, 1961

President Kennedy approves the "first phase of Vietnam program," which broadens the U.S. commitment to Vietnam by adding U.S. "combat support" troops.

Although in April 1961 President Kennedy had added 100 advisers to the U.S. contingent and thereby exceeded the number permitted by the Geneva Accords of 1954, his first critical decision on Vietnam was made on November 22. Kennedy based the decision on a report by General Maxwell Taylor and Walter W. Rostow, who visited Saigon in October 1961. (Taylor, who had been the leading critic of Eisenhower's "new look" policy in the late 1950s, became Kennedy's principal military adviser. Rostow was a White House adviser to the president.) These two men discounted the 1960 report of Ambassador to Saigon Elbridge Durbrow, which severely criticized Premier Diem of South Vietnam. Taylor and Rostow thought Diem had "extraordinary stability, stubbornness and guts." They recommended a "limited partnership" with Diem. The November 22 "First Phase..." was based on the Taylor-Rostow recommendations and, subsequently, Kennedy ordered a gradually increased number of "combat support" troops to Vietnam. General Taylor, who expected a few highly qualified "Green Berets" to deal easily with "brushfire wars," did not believe many troops would be needed, but he was uncertain just how many because estimates varied from 8,000 to 25,000.

In December 1961, 400 men in two helicopter companies with 33 H-21 aircraft reached Saigon. By November 1963, Kennedy had ordered 16,263 "combat support" troops to Vietnam; combat support, according to the White House, meant they would not fire until fired on but would accompany South Vietnamese army patrols. In addition to these forces, the November 22 plan called for a Strategic Hamlet Program. Based on British counterinsurgency plans used in Malaya, the "Hamlets" were fortified villages for the rural populace to occupy while the Communists were driven out of their home region. Then the peasants could return home in peace. In South Vietnam, unfortunately, the program was a disaster in part due to its management by Diem's unpopular and corrupt brother and sister-in-law, Ngo Dinh Nhu and Madame Nhu.

December 2, 1961

Fidel Castro announces that he is a Marxist-Leninist.

Although conservative Americans had suspected throughout the 1950s that Castro was a Communist, the Cuban leader had previously shaded his reform efforts in Cuba with promises of election and compensation for nationalized property. Now, Castro had become dependent on the Soviet Union for economic aid. On December 2, he called for the formation of a united Cuban party to bring Communism to Cuba.

1962

January 18, 1962

Secretary Rusk believes that the United States must support Cyrille Adoula and the United Nations in the Congo as the best anti-Communist measure.

Following Secretary-General Hammarskjöld's death on September 18, 1961, a truce was arranged between Tshombe of Katanga and Adoula of the central Congolese government. The truce was not sustained, however, and by November 11, Rusk and Kennedy agreed to allow the United Nations to use whatever force was necessary to pressure Tshombe to negotiate. Tshombe and Adoula agreed on December 21 to end Katanga's secession. Tshombe was slated to have a role in the Léopoldville government.

On January 18, Rusk told the Senate Foreign Relations Committee that the United States would continue to back the U.N. program as the best solution to keep the integrity of the Congo and to defeat Communist efforts. Those who backed Tshombe, Rusk said, followed a policy that would weaken Adoula's government and allow the Soviets to defeat both the moderate Adoula and the conservative Tshombe. In a meeting at the abandoned Belgian airbase at Kitonia, Tshombe violated the December 21 Kitonia agreement. Therefore, the United Nations was required to apply force to restore Katanga to the control of the Léopoldville government.

January 31, 1962

Cuba is excluded from the Inter-American system.

At the end of a 10-day meeting at Punta del Este, Uruguay, the American foreign ministers approved by a two-thirds vote a resolution excluding Cuba from the Inter-American system. Brazil, Argentina, Chile, Ecuador, and Mexico abstained in the vote.

February 10, 1962

The USSR and the United States exchange "spies."

Gary Francis Powers, who piloted the U-2 that crashed in the Soviet Union in 1960, was released in exchange for the U.S. release of Colonel Rudolf Abel, a Soviet spy who had been convicted of espionage in 1957.

February 20, 1962

Lieutenant Colonel John H. Glenn Jr. is the first U.S. astronaut to orbit the earth.

On his flight Glenn circled the earth three times before landing in the Pacific Ocean, where U.S. naval vessels picked him up. A Soviet citizen had been the first to orbit the earth.

See April 12, 1961.

April 25, 1962

By exploding a nuclear device at Christmas Island, the U.S. responds to the Soviets' resumption of nuclear tests in 1961.

Moscow's August 31, 1961 announcement that they were renewing nuclear testing, ending the informal

1958 agreements of Khrushchev and Eisenhower that had temporarily terminated such tests, was followed shortly by a series of tests. Following a thorough review of the situation, President Kennedy announced on March 2, 1962, that the United States would resume its tests in April unless an effective test ban agreement was reached with the Soviet Union during the interim. In announcing his decision, Kennedy stated that the United States needed to check the effectiveness of high-altitude explosions to counter gains made by the Soviet Union during its 1961 test series. He said no "superbombs" would be detonated and that radiation fallout would be minimized.

The president's decision divided public opinion in America and in other "free world" nations. At home, the White House admitted that the telegrams it received were divided evenly between those in favor and those opposed to the tests. There were large peace and antinuclear demonstrations in New York and other American cities as well as in London and, especially, Japan. The Japanese government warned Washington that it would seek compensation for any damages to its citizens.

Nevertheless, after Khrushchev spurned a special message from Kennedy and British Prime Minister Macmillan that urged him to accept an effective test ban, Kennedy authorized the tests to begin on April 24. The tests in the region of Christmas Island and, later, Johnson Island and Nevada were conducted between April 25 and November 4, 1963. The tests' time schedule was extended from July to November because the explosions of high-altitude bombs failed on several occasions. Eventually, a total of 36 bombs were exploded by the United States during 1962. On September 2, the AEC and the Defense Department admitted that the high-altitude test of July 9 had increased space radiation more than anticipated. In particular, the radiation in the earth's Van Allen belt was extended lower in the atmosphere, where it would remain for at least five years.

U.S. scientists disagreed on the effect of radiation in food on Americans. Increased levels of iodine were found in milk taken from cows in parts of the midwest. Some scientists thought the dosage was approaching dangerous levels. There was no agreement on exactly what level was "dangerous." On February 2, 1963, Kennedy threatened another series of U.S. nuclear tests if the USSR did not agree to an effective test ban treaty. Discussions had been held between diplomats in London, Moscow, and Washington during the fall and winter of 1962–1963. These talks eventually succeeded.

May 26, 1962

The Netherlands accepts a U.S. plan to settle the West New Guinea dispute with Indonesia.

A dispute over the possession of West New Guinea had resulted in war between the Netherlands and Indonesia. The United States—in large part to keep Indonesian President Sukarno from appealing to the Soviet Union for aid—proposed to end the struggle by mediation on ownership while the United Nations administered the territory and arranged a plebiscite to permit the Papuan inhabitants to decide their future. Subsequently, on July 31, Indonesia and the Netherlands agreed to transfer West New Guinea (renamed West Irian) to the United Nations on October 1, with the United Nations to transfer it to Indonesia on May 1, 1963. Within six years, Indonesia was to hold a plebiscite of self-determination for the Papuan natives of the area.

May 24, 1962

USSR agrees to a plan for installing missiles in Cuba.

For some time, Khrushchev had discussed the idea of Cuban missiles to balance America's missile superiority, because the Soviets' liquid fueled R-16 ICBMs (U.S. designation SS-6) were no match for America's Minuteman missiles and the U.S. Jupiter missiles to Turkey were operational. After getting mixed opinions about locating nuclear-tipped Soviet IRBMs in Cuba, Khrushchev submitted a plan to a session of the combined Soviet Defense Council-Presidium on May 24. Three days later envoys from the Presidium visited Cuba to get Castro's approval. Rejecting reservations about Cuban missiles, Khrushchev proposed a small task force that became a larger operation. On October 26, 1962, U.S. intelligence estimated that the Soviets had 10,000 Soviet troops in Cuba; in fact there were 41,902.

Khrushchev had been surprised when Kennedy only used Cuban exiles in the Bay of Pigs, and he was convinced the United States would have its troops launch another invasion that, according to an adviser, would be accomplished in three or four days. Thus, Khrushchev thought that Cuba's defense was a factor supporting his decision to install missiles. Finally,

Soviets decide to build a missile site in Cuba. U.S. photograph of nearly completed site. John F. Kennedy Library

Khrushchev was under pressure at home because negotiations between Washington and Moscow produced nothing on Berlin and other issues. Unfortunately, Khrushchev counted on the missile deployment to be a surprise to spring on Kennedy at a November meeting. Although he did not want to start a nuclear war, Khrushchev had no back-up plan if things went awry in Cuba.

See October 14, 1962.

June 1, 1962

Rising consumer prices cause strikes and protests in Soviet cities.

The Presidium approved a decree, set to take effect on June 1, raising retail prices on meat and poultry products as much as 35 percent and on butter and milk as much as 25 percent. While logical in economic terms, the lower prices failed to meet the costs of production and contradicted the public's expectations that consumer prices would decrease as during Stalin's times. Making matters worse was a price increase following Moscow's effort to improve factory production by demanding longer hours of work for equal or less pay.

Widespread protests in response to these policies erupted in Moscow, Kiev, Leningrad, and other cities. The worst episode was at the large Budenny Electric Locomotive factory outside the northern Caucasus city of Novocherkassk, where on June 2 several thousand workers marched to protest at the city's center. When the crowd refused to leave, local police fired shots that killed 23 people and wounded 87. Force was used to put down protests in other areas, and several other people died. For details see William Taubman, *Khrushchev: the Man and His Era* (2003).

June 25, 1962

In Accra, Ghana, a "world without the bomb" conference begins.

More than 100 delegates, including those from the United States and the Soviet Union, attended this meeting. During the seven-day conference, the delegates recommended that the United Nations train disarmament inspection teams and called on African states to disarm throughout their continent. The group also recommended the admission of Communist China to the United Nations.

July 4, 1962

Kennedy informs the European allies that they can have nuclear weapons when they achieve political unity.

Kennedy's message of July 4 responded to the European desire for a multilateral nuclear defense force for NATO. It did not, however, provide the answer French President de Gaulle and other Europeans desired. Kennedy's speech was a plan by Undersecretary of State George Ball to whom Rusk delegated European problems. Ball's dream was an integrated Europe, allied with America and conducive to U.S. leadership. Because European unity was, at best, in the future, Kennedy's agreement to give Europeans a greater role in a European defense force had no immediate impact and did not satisfy President de Gaulle or other Europeans.

July 19, 1962

Kennedy suspends diplomatic relations with, and economic aid to, Peru following a military coup on July 18; military leaders play the Cold War game.

The military junta displeased the United States by suspending all constitutional rights. To act quickly against the regime, Kennedy immediately cut off U.S. benefits to Peru. Only after the junta agreed to return to constitutional practices did Kennedy renew assistance to Peru on August 17, 1962. In 1963, the Kennedy administration made similar agreements with right-wing military groups that had usurped the governments of Argentina, Guatemala, and the Dominican Republic. The military leaders in these states played the Cold War game by claiming to support anti-Communist positions. The Alliance for Progress of 1961 had not brought democratic regimes to power in Latin America as planned.

July 23, 1962

The Geneva conference on Laos agrees to guarantee the independence and neutrality of that state.

The Geneva Conference had convened on May 16, 1961, as a means of avoiding large-scale U.S. intervention in Laos. Over the next 14 months, the delegates met to gain an effective cease-fire and to form a neutral government acceptable to the three competing factions in Laos. Throughout the year, full-scale war threatened to disrupt the conference, but eventually the three rival princes of Laos reached a settlement. The three rivals were the neutralist Souvanna Phouma, the U.S.-backed rightist Boun Oum, and the leftist Communist-supported Souphanouvong. By May 1962, Pathet Lao military actions in Laos had advanced over 100 miles. President Kennedy protested these movements and, on May 12, again ordered U.S. naval ships and Marines to the Gulf of Siam, and 2,000 U.S. soldiers to Thailand. As a result, the Communist advances stopped and the three Laotian princes again met to negotiate. In June, the Laotian leaders announced that a 19- member coalition government had been formed under the neutralist Souvanna Phouma. King Savang Vathana installed this ministry on June 22, and political calm returned to Laos. On July 23, delegates at the 14-nation conference in Geneva recognized the Souvanna coalition government. They also signed an agreement to withdraw all foreign troops and guarantee the neutrality of Laos.

October 11, 1962

The Trade Expansion Act of 1962 becomes law—the Kennedy round in American trade policy.

By 1961, many U.S. international financial experts realized that the United States needed new legislation to give the president greater authority in dealing with foreign tariff and trade policy. The success of the European Common Market after 1957 required special attention. In addition, the U.S. balance of international payments had turned adverse since 1958. During the three-year period 1958–1960, the United States lost $4.7 billion in gold to foreign payments. In contrast, the European Economic Community (EEC) had collectively increased its gold reserves by over $6.5 billion. Because of these conditions, the United States hoped to regain an increase in its exports by obtaining lower trade barriers with Europe and other parts of the world. The 1962 Trade Expansion Act was designed to gain multilateral reductions for U.S. exports to Europe and Japan. After four years of negotiation among the major GATT members, a protocol signed on June 30, 1967, provided for significant tariff reductions. The United States gained a 35 percent reduction in nonagricultural exports. While the agricultural agreement varied, the new tariffs favored U.S. exports in all cases except Denmark. The United States gained especially favorable reduction from Japan and the United Kingdom.

October 14, 1962

U-2 reconnaissance plane flying over Cuba discovers Soviet missiles.

The aircraft returned with 65,000 to 70,000 feet of film that was immediately sent to the CIA's National Photographic Interpretation Center in Washington where it showed that the Soviet Union was constructing launch sites for ballistic missiles. Since President Kennedy was out of town, he was not shown the photographs until the morning of October 16. It was evident that he was stunned by the information and could not comprehend why Khrushchev would undertake such drastic action.

See October 22, 1962.

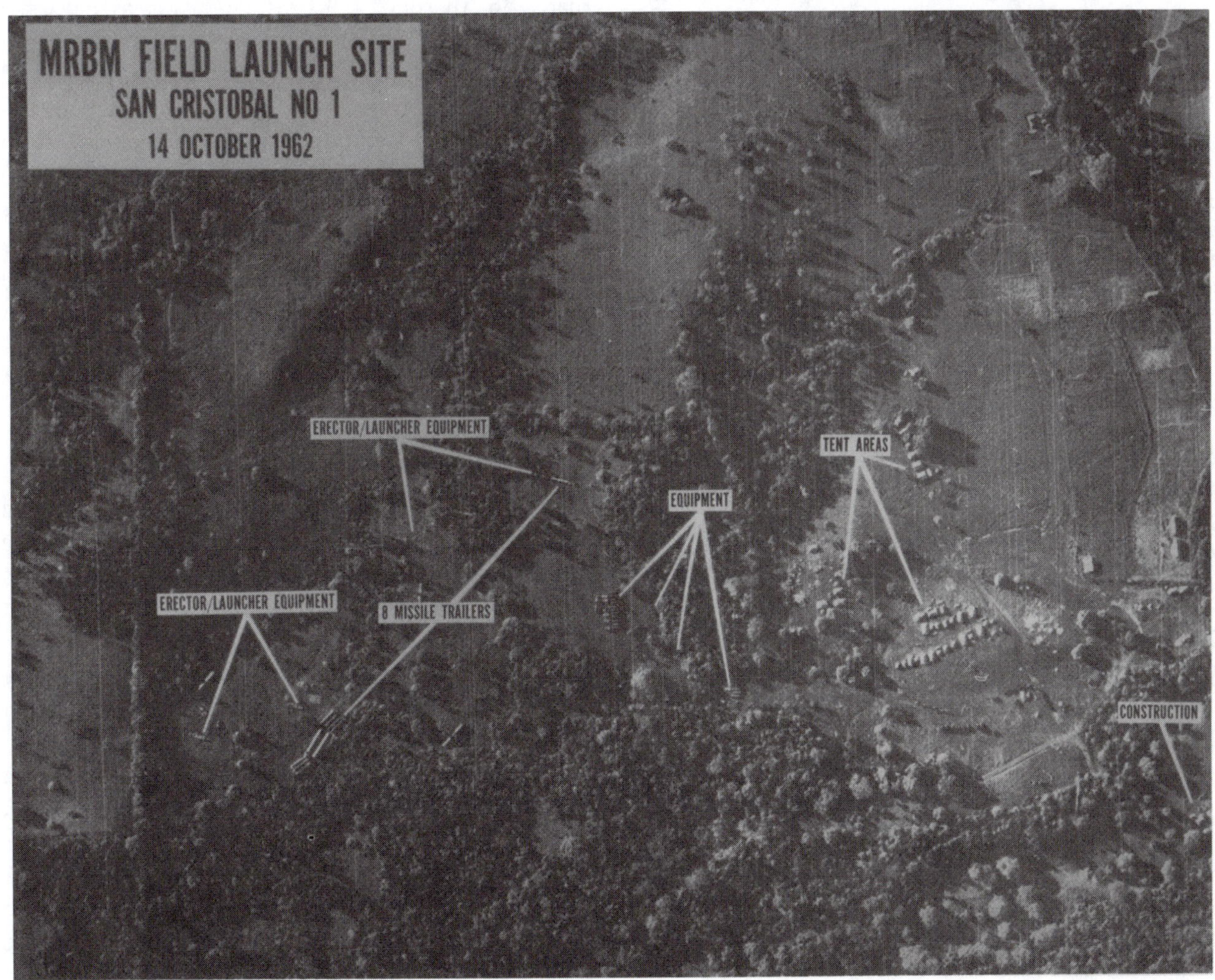

U.S. aerial photo of Soviet missile site in Cuba. John F. Kennedy Library

October 20, 1962

China and India begin large-scale fighting in a disputed border area; Kennedy fails to recognize signs of Sino-Soviet split.

Although Indian border police and Chinese forces had clashed on October 26, 1960, the Chinese-India issue had confined itself to skirmishes before October 1962. India claimed that China unlawfully occupied 12,000 square miles of its territory and demanded its return. During the three weeks after October 20, Chinese forces made successful incursions into Indian territory. On October 31, India's Premier Nehru asked the United States for aid, and in November, Kennedy sent transport planes and crews to transport Indian troops. The U.S. aid was not necessary. On November 21, Beijing announced that the Chinese would withdraw to their 1957 borders and the fighting ended.

In the United States, the India-China war affected U.S. evaluations of the Sino-Soviet split and China's relations with the West. Although Dean Rusk, Undersecretary of State Chester Bowles, and other U.S. leaders wanted to negotiate with China to take advantage of its poor relations with Moscow, President Kennedy disagreed. He had, in fact, made an agreement with Chiang Kai-shek in 1961 to continue U.S. support in the United Nations for the Formosan government. Kennedy's Cold War perceptions of Asian affairs prevented him from comprehending the potential significance of the Sino-Soviet split.

October 22, 1962

Kennedy informs the nation that there are Soviet-built missile sites in Cuba and calls on Soviet Premier Khrushchev to remove these weapons.

During the "Cuban missile crisis," the Executive Committee of the National Security Council (NSC), which President Kennedy ordered to examine alternative responses to the presence of Soviet missile sites in Cuba, had met regularly in secret sessions from October 16 to October 21. The committee included McGeorge Bundy and Secretary Rusk from the State Department, Secretary of Defense McNamara, CIA Director John McCone, Attorney General Robert Kennedy, and others. In addition, Vice President Johnson, U.N. Ambassador Adlai Stevenson, and the president met with the committee on occasion.

After considering a variety of alternative responses to the Soviets, the Executive Committee, the full NSC, and the president agreed to begin action against the Soviets with a naval blockade of Cuba, escalating subsequent actions only if necessary. Other alternatives considered included such suggestions as an invasion or air strike of Cuba, secret negotiations with Cuba, appeals to the United Nations, and doing nothing. By October 19, the consensus favored a blockade because it could be effective but would leave the decision up to Khrushchev as to whether or not to break the blockade. It also left later alternatives for U.S. action if the naval response failed.

On Sunday, October 21, the full NSC decided to act as follows: 1. The president was to inform the public of the Soviet missiles on October 22 over national television. 2. The naval quarantine was to be announced on television. 3. An appeal for support from the OAS and the United Nations was to be made on Tuesday. 4. Khrushchev was to be asked to remove all missiles from Cuba. 5. Dean Acheson and David Bruce would be sent to tell de Gaulle and Macmillan, respectively, of Kennedy's speech in advance. On Monday, these plans went into operation beginning with Acheson's early-morning flight to London to inform Ambassador Bruce and to Paris to visit de Gaulle. At 5:00 P.M., Kennedy met with congressional leaders to explain his decision.

At 7:00 P.M., the president outlined his "quarantine" plans to the U.S. public, explaining that the United States found definite evidence of missile sites in Cuba, although there were no nuclear warheads as yet. Finally, he told the audience that his plan was a difficult and dangerous effort, "but the greatest danger of all would be to do nothing." Kennedy explained that the course chosen was most in keeping with the American character, to seek to avoid war but not to submit or surrender. He concluded: "Our goal is not the victory of might, but the vindication of right—not peace at the expense of freedom, but both peace and freedom, here in this hemisphere, and, we hope, around the world."

The next day, Secretary Rusk obtained approval from the OAS to blockade Cuba and take measures, including force if necessary, to end the crisis. All OAS members but Uruguay approved the blockade decision. Brazil, Mexico, and Bolivia abstained from the section authorizing the use of force. At the same time, Adlai Stevenson indicted the Soviet Union for its aggressive action in Cuba. Because of the Soviet veto power, no action was sought in the U.N. Security Council. The U.S. blockade went into effect on October 24. A naval task force of 19 ships set up a picket line in the Atlantic, 500 miles from Cuba.

October 23, 1962

President Kennedy signs a $3.9 billion foreign aid bill.

This bill included clauses that forbade aid to 18 Communist nations and to any nation that shipped arms to Cuba.

October 28, 1962

An exchange of personal letters between President Kennedy and Premier Khrushchev ends the Cuban missile crisis.

The days from October 24 to 27 were especially critical as Kennedy and his advisers waited to learn what the Soviet ships *en route* to Cuba would do once they reached the U.S. naval blockade. On October 23, U.S. reconnaissance planes spotted 25 Soviet ships in the Atlantic, most of which seemed to be headed for Cuba. Early on the morning of October 24, the first Soviet vessels approached the blockade line but, until the last moment, the Americans did not know what to expect. On October 23, Khrushchev sent two divergent messages about his intentions. In a formal letter to President Kennedy the Soviet leader denounced the blockade as an act of piracy, bringing the world to the brink of nuclear war. He declared that Soviet ships on their way to Cuba would defy the U.S. blockade. At about the same time, he wrote a note to Bertrand Russell, the British philosopher and pacifist, who had appealed to Khrushchev to avoid war. The Soviet Premier told Russell that he was not reckless, it was the Americans who had acted aggressively. Khrushchev understood the disaster that nuclear war would bring. Therefore, he said, he was ready to make a special effort to avoid war. If the United States agreed, he would consider a top-level meeting to settle the Cuban crisis.

Consequently, as Soviet ships neared the U.S. blockade on October 24, the Americans did not know which orders Khrushchev had given to them, the peaceful or the bellicose one. About 10:00 A.M. two Soviet ships neared the blockade point. Then the U.S. naval observers radioed that a Soviet submarine was between the Soviet ships and the American ships. The captain of the U.S. carrier *Essex* was ordered to signal the sub to surface. More tension built at the White House. Then, at 10:25 a preliminary message

Meeting of the Executive Committee (Ex Com) of the National Security Council during the missile crisis. John F. Kennedy Library

President Kennedy's quarantine policy in operation. National Archives

arrived: the Soviet ships appeared to be stopping. By 10:32, navy reports confirmed that 20 Soviet ships in the area of the blockade line had stopped or were turning to head back to Europe. The blockade had not been challenged.

Kennedy now sought to arrange the removal of the Soviet missile sites from Cuba. To achieve this goal, two steps were taken on October 25 and 27. First, the navy was told to let the Soviet ship *Bucharest* pass the blockade because visual sighting indicated it carried no cargo connected with missiles. The ship *Marcula*, however, was stopped and searched. After a two-hour search found no missile equipment, the *Marcula* was allowed to proceed to Cuba. This process was followed with all Soviet ships that had not turned away from their sea route to Cuba.

Second, Kennedy considered the two recent notes from Premier Khrushchev, each of which suggested a settlement. The first, received on October 26, was a personal letter to Kennedy in which the Soviet leader offered to remove the missiles from Cuba if Kennedy gave assurances that the United States would not invade the island. The second, received on October 27, was a more formal message in which Khrushchev offered to dismantle the Soviet missiles in Cuba if the United States dismantled missile bases in Turkey. Although the Turkish bases were obsolete, Kennedy did not want to swap them under pressure from Moscow. In light of the second note, the Joint Chiefs of Staff recommended that an air strike or an invasion of Cuba would be necessary. Kennedy opposed this step for the moment.

Important information about the October 27 meeting was disclosed during the 1989 Moscow conference of participants in the 1962 missile crisis. During the Moscow conference, Theodore Sorenson confessed he edited Robert Kennedy's diary of the crisis published as *Thirteen Days* by deleting the section showing the president's brother had told Soviet Ambassador Dobrynin the United States would remove its missiles from Turkey as Khrushchev had requested. Dobrynin agreed the Soviets would keep the Turkish missile removal secret because NATO members had not been told about this decision. Of course, the secrecy about Kennedy's concession favored the U.S. president's image of "his finest hour," but it helped avoid a nuclear confrontation. On the basis of Kennedy's pledge not to invade Cuba but to remove the Turkish missiles, Khrushchev accepted the concessions, and on October 28 at 9:00 P.M., Moscow radio broadcast Khrushchev's willingness to remove the Cuban missiles.

Fidel Castro was angry with Khrushchev because he thought Moscow would be justified in initiating a nuclear attack on the United States. Thus, Castro refused to let U.N. inspectors observe the dismantling of the Soviet missiles. Moscow agreed to let U.S. naval officers visually inspect the removal, with Soviet crews pulling back the tarpaulins to show the missiles aboard Soviet ships on the way home. Because Castro refused to have on-site U.N. inspections, Kennedy weakened his no-invasion pledge. In a December 14 letter to Khrushchev, Kennedy stated Cuba would not be invaded "while matters take their present favorable course." As Raymond Garthoff explains, in 1970 President Richard Nixon made a definite pledge not to invade Cuba.

November 25, 1962

Kennedy administration seeks to withhold materials for Soviet-European pipeline.

The administrations of Eisenhower and Kennedy were alarmed at the increasing Soviet petroleum sales to Western Europe, fearing their allies might became dependent on this oil supply and support Soviet Cold War positions. American oil companies were concerned about increasing competition for oil sales. Both interests found common ground early in the 1960s with a projected Druzhba (Friendship) Oil Pipeline going from the Soviet Union to Eastern Europe. Its completion would compete with Western oil suppliers but Washington worried it would expand fuel reserves of the Warsaw Pact's armed forces.

After the Soviets could not provide a sufficient supply of wide-diameter steel pipes for the Druzhba project, they inquired about buying steel pipes from West Germany. In response, the Kennedy administration prevailed upon the NATO Council to urge members to withhold steel pipe sales from Moscow. This posed a serious problem for West Germany's government of Konrad Adenauer. It also prompted Britain to buy a large amount of Russian oil. With construction continuing on the Druzhba pipeline and the dissension among members, NATO withdrew its ban.

December 17, 1962

Kennedy and the National Security Council agree to give military aid to the United Nations to fight Katanga.

During the summer of 1962, Moishe Tshombe violated the Kitonia agreement with Cyrille Adoula's Congo government by refusing to forward tax funds from the secessionist province of Katanga and continued to act independently. Tshombe was supported by the Belgian mining company that paid for his mercenary soldiers. In October 1962, U.N. Secretary-General U. Thant wanted to place an economic boycott on Katanga. He agreed, however, to try to negotiate again so that the U.S. November elections would end before forceful action began against Tshombe. By December, fighting began between Tshombe and Adoula's forces, and U. Thant decided the United Nations had to take action. Although American opponents of Adoula opposed U.S. military assistance against Tshombe, the National Security Council and President Kennedy agreed on December 17 to provide airlift operations and military equipment to aid the U.N. forces when they invaded Katanga. U.N. troops attacked in January, and on January 15 Tshombe again ended his secession. On June 14, Tshombe fled to exile and the immediate crisis in the Congo finally ended. This was a victory for the Léopoldville government with U.S. and U.N. backing.

December 20, 1962

Juan D. Bosch is elected president of the Dominican Republic.

On December 20, Bosch won the election, taking office on February 27, 1963. His rule lasted only seven months. On September 25, 1963, a group of military leaders overthrew him. He would later return to office, only to be dislodged by U.S. forces that feared his leftist tendencies.

December 21, 1962

President Kennedy agrees to replace the British Skybolt project with U.S. Polaris missiles.

The U.S. military supported by Secretary of Defense Robert McNamara objected to giving the Europeans independent nuclear capabilities and did not want to let them share control of U.S. nuclear weapons in Europe. Consequently, in the fall of 1962, McNamara unilaterally canceled the Skybolt missile program, which would have given Great Britain independent intermediate-range missiles. Secretary Rusk warned McNamara that the cancellation would provide problems for the British government, but McNamara agreed to settle it with Britain's defense minister, Peter Thorneycroft. This issue arose, however, at the Nassau meeting between Kennedy and Macmillan, because McNamara had not been direct with the British regarding his decision to cancel the Skybolt program.

As a result, Macmillan was unwilling to accept the cancellation and strongly objected. Therefore, Kennedy offered to give Britain Polaris missiles without nuclear warheads and also agreed to do the same for France. If Britain and France built submarines and warheads for the missiles, they would have to assign the vessels to the NATO forces and not be independent. Macmillan did not like these restrictions but accepted them because he at least had something to soften the blow to British pride. But U.S.-British relations did not improve as the British felt Americans did not trust them as an ally.

December 24, 1962

Cuba returns 1,113 Cuban rebels captured in April 1961.

Castro agreed to exchange his Bay of Pigs captives for $53 million worth of food and medicine.

1963

January 29, 1963

France vetoes Great Britain's application to join the European Economic Community (Common Market); Kennedy alters trade program.

Urged by the United States, England reluctantly began discussions in 1962 with France and other EEC members for admission to the Common Market. President de Gaulle opposed Britain's entry into the European economic partnership. In 1961, the United States expected Britain's application to be approved and the Kennedy administration decided to alter the U.S. Reciprocal Trade Act rather than simply extend it. Thus, Kennedy persuaded Congress to approve a new trade act giving the president more power to bargain with the EEC and help reduce the U.S. trade deficit. The French veto of British membership made the Kennedy Round of tariff negotiations more difficult to complete and continued America's unfavorable trade balance. Details of Kennedy's trade policy are in William S. Borden's article in Thomas Paterson, ed., *Kennedy's Quest for Victory* (1989).

May 8, 1963

Buddhist leaders in South Vietnam organize demonstrations protesting Diem's repressive policies.

Between 1961 and 1963, Diem had not enacted any significant reforms but had increased his repressive measures because he envisioned every opponent as a "Communist" enemy. Until 1963, the Buddhists had patiently avoided public demonstrations of their dislike for Diem's terrorization of peasants and discrimination against Buddhists. Diem's methods against the Buddhists reached the breaking point in May 1963, when he forbade them to fly their religious banners in celebrating the Buddha's birthday on May 8. Buddhist leaders at the religious center in Hue defied Diem by carrying their banners and rallying the people to demonstrate against him. Diem moved to stop the Buddhists.

South Vietnamese army units used armored vehicles to break up the crowds. The soldiers opened fire and nine people were killed and 14 wounded. Buddhist leaders endeavored to negotiate a solution with Diem but he refused. As a result, U.S. news reports of Buddhist opposition showed clearly for the first time that Diem's problem was not simply the threat of Communism but his failure to gain the support of his own people. Buddhist protests continued throughout 1963 and were widely reported on American television. One photograph that became famous for its dramatic effect showed a young Buddhist monk aflame on a busy Saigon street. The monk had poured gasoline over himself and lit a match to his yellow saffron robes to show his disdain for Diem. When Diem's sister-in-law, Madame Nhu, ridiculed these events as "barbecues," her support in the United States dropped drastically.

May 12, 1963

Pakistan and China sign a territorial agreement and an air service agreement.

By this treaty, China ceded 750 square miles of land to Pakistan. This treaty fostered good relations between the two countries, both of which had disputes with India. On August 29, Pakistan signed an agreement with China to provide scheduled air service to Beijing. This was the first Western agreement for air service to the People's Republic of China.

May 22, 1963

NATO's Foreign Ministers Council forms a 10-nation multilateral nuclear strike force.

The United States had urged the creation of this multinational force as a symbol of its willingness to cooperate with European defense plans. French President de Gaulle did not approve the plan and on June 21 began withdrawing many French naval ships from the NATO Fleet Command.

May 25, 1963

The Organization of African Unity is chartered.

At Addis Ababa, Ethiopia, 30 leaders of African states formed a regional bloc to work together for their economic well-being. On August 5, delegates of 32 African countries formed an African development bank with a capitalization of $250 million.

June 14, 1963

The Chinese Communist Party indicts Moscow for "revisionist" domestic policies and says it plans to split with any Communist Party supporting the Soviet Union.

Since the Communist Party meetings in Moscow on December 5, 1960, signs of Sino-Soviet division had appeared more frequently. Each side urged other national Communist groups to back its views on foreign and domestic policy. The Beijing declaration of June 14 was a bellicose statement demonstrating the split between Mao and the Soviet leadership. In foreign policy, the Chinese rejected the idea of "peaceful coexistence" and seemed more willing to risk nuclear war. By early 1964, Beijing began recognizing pro-Chinese factions in various nations as the legitimate Communist party in opposition to the Soviet faction.

June 20, 1963

The United States and the Soviet Union agree to create a communications "hot line" to reduce the risk of accidental war.

Following the 1962 Cuban missile crisis, the White House proposed a direct emergency communication with the Kremlin as a method of averting any misunderstanding that might lead to war. The Soviet Union accepted this idea on April 5 and on June 20, 1963, formal arrangements were agreed to establish this instant teletype communication system. This agreement was enhanced by several upgrades, beginning in 1971.

June 26, 1963

President Kennedy visits West Berlin, promising to defend free Berlin from Communist encroachment.

Kennedy's speech in Berlin enthralled West Germans as he concluded his defense of freedom with the words, "Ich bin ein Berliner!" While a "Berliner" had its colloquial meaning (which could be translated as "I am a jelly-filled donut!"), the German audience appreciated Kennedy's sentiment.

July 31, 1963

Although the CIA estimates that China's policies are not aggressive, President Kennedy and Secretary Rusk believe otherwise as a result of a National Security Council meeting.

Following the Cuban missile crisis of 1962, the president and Rusk spoke about the Soviets' compliant policies and China's "blatant aggression" in India and elsewhere. Their concern led to a special NSC session on July 31, 1963. At the meeting, the CIA presented a special estimate of the Chinese situation that discounted Chinese military ambition against India, indicating as others had before that India, not China, had been the aggressor in October 1962. The CIA also dismissed the view that China was acting aggressively in Southeast Asia or elsewhere. The Beijing government spoke often of support for anti-imperial wars but showed respect for U.S. power and still feared the Soviet Union.

Nevertheless, Kennedy, who had always disliked Communist China, continued to back Chiang

Kai-shek and deplored Mao's aggressive talk against America. Although Rusk was less opposed to Beijing than Kennedy, he accepted the president's views. Later attempts by Kennedy's apologists to argue that the president was planning to change his China policy have not been well documented.

July 31, 1963

The United States abstains in a U.N. Security Council vote on a Soviet resolution to halt arms shipments to Portugal's colonial government of Angola.

Native uprisings against Portuguese rule began in Angola in 1961. As a result, on January 30, 1962, the U.N. General Assembly voted 99-2 to urge Portugal to stop its repressive measures against the "people of Angola." Because the Angola rebel leader Holden Roberts had become "friendly" in accepting aid from the Soviet Union and later (January 3, 1964) from China, the United States, Britain, and France faced a dilemma. They wanted Portugal to grant independence to Angola but did not like Roberts's policies.

As a result, the three Western powers abstained on a Soviet-sponsored resolution to stop all arms going to Portugal's colonial government. This began Cold War tensions over Angola.

August 5, 1963

A limited nuclear test ban treaty is signed by Britain, the Soviet Union, and the United States.

Three-power talks on a test ban began in Moscow on July 15. The representatives were Soviet Foreign Minister Gromyko, U.S. Undersecretary of State Harriman, and British Minister for Science Viscount Quintin Hailsham. The three powers signed the treaty on August 5. When it became effective on October 10, over 100 nations had agreed to it. The treaty prohibited tests in space, the atmosphere, and underwater. It did not, however, eliminate underground tests. Negotiations seeking to prohibit underground tests continued to be pursued, usually not enthusiastically by the United States, which argued that they could not always be detected. A U.S.-USSR Threshold Test Ban was agreed to in 1974, but a comprehensive test ban would not be achieved.

September 25, 1963

Dominican President Juan Bosch is overthrown by a right-wing group headed by General Elias Wessin y Wessin and Donald Reid Cabral.

Bosch's election as president of the liberal reform government had been personally approved by President Kennedy in 1962. Therefore, Kennedy cut off aid to the new military junta and tried to pressure it to conduct new elections. In December 1963, President Johnson agreed to recognize Reid's government and renewed its economic assistance.

October 19, 1963

Sir Alec Douglas-Home becomes Prime Minister of England following the retirement of Harold Macmillan.

November 1–2, 1963

A military coup in Saigon overthrows and kills Ngo Dinh Diem.

The increased domestic pressure against Diem that corresponded to the Buddhist protests resulted in several plots by South Vietnamese military generals against Diem. As early as August, U.S. Ambassador to Saigon Henry Cabot Lodge heard of these plots and asked Secretary of State Rusk how to react. Lodge recommended that he give assurances to any anti-Communist groups who opposed Diem. The White House was not certain how to respond because President Kennedy had to deal with conflicting opinions. General Maxwell Taylor and Walt Rostow of the National Security Council clung to their 1961 plan, urging that the U.S. strategic hamlet and combat-support missions be continued, claiming they would succeed by 1964 or 1965. They blamed Diem's younger brother and chief political adviser, Ngo Dinh Nhu, along with Nhu's wife, not Diem, for Saigon's problems.

Two senior U.S. diplomats who had spent much time in Vietnam disagreed. Joseph Mendenhall and Rufus Phillips, who headed the hamlet-assistance program, reported that Diem seldom followed U.S. advice and that the Nhus had corrupted the purposes of the hamlet program. In addition, Phillips said, the Nhus gave Taylor and Rostow falsified reports of the pacification program, which made their military evaluations incorrect. Marine General Victor Krulak was enraged by Phillips's charges but neither he nor Taylor would investigate Phillips's data. Phillips's reports showed that the Vietcong (South Vietnamese Communists) had captured 50 hamlets in recent weeks in the southern delta region near Saigon. The Vietcong controlled 80 percent of Long An province in the south. Krulak and Taylor preferred to base their reports on the northern provinces because they argued that Diem's problem was the invasion of North Vietnam along the 17th parallel. Phillips told them they should look at the heavily populated southern delta area, where local Communists as well as non-Communists opposed Diem.

The dispute, which became a classic between U.S. military and civilian advisers, had begun. The U.S. military saw the war as a Communist invasion from the north; most U.S. civilian advisers saw the domestic economic problems of South Vietnam as the basic threat to the Saigon regime. Kennedy preferred the military viewpoint. As he told Chet Huntley during an NBC interview on September 9, China instigated the problems in Vietnam and if South Vietnam fell, the Chinese could capture all Indochina and Malaya. He told Huntley, "the war in the future in Southeast Asia was China and the communists." Neither Kennedy nor Johnson wanted to be accused of another "China cop-out," as Truman had been in 1949. As David Halberstam observes in his ironically titled *The Best and the Brightest* (1972), seldom has so much Washington talent been so misguided by its incorrect assessment of circumstances.

Nevertheless, in the fall of 1963 the White House estimates shifted enough to enable Ambassador Lodge to inform the plotters in Saigon that the United States would accept a new government. McNamara and Taylor visited Saigon in September and on their return indicated that while there was "great progress" in U.S. military action, Diem was not popular. The United States, they told Kennedy, should "work with the Diem regime but not support it." This curious recommendation enabled Secretary Rusk to inform Lodge on October 6 that the United States would accept a new government led by General Duong Van Minh (Big Minh). Subsequently, on the night of November 1–2, 1963, General Minh and his allies staged an attack on the presidential palace, where they captured Diem and the Nhus. Diem tried to rally his loyal troops in Saigon, but outside of his personal guards he had no loyal troops. The assassination of Diem and his brother and sister-in-law does not appear to have been planned by Big Minh. The United States expected they would be exiled. Allegedly, a long-time enemy of Diem led the armored unit that captured the three family leaders. He had them shot before they reached Big Minh's headquarters.

November 22, 1963

President Kennedy is assassinated in Dallas, Texas, and Vice President Lyndon B. Johnson is sworn in as president.

Rumors persist of Soviet or Cuban involvement in the assassination but such claims have never been substantiated.

December 26, 1963

Secretary McNamara informs President Johnson that political conditions in Saigon are unstable.

The coup against Diem on November 1, 1963, did not solve South Vietnam's political problems. Big Minh's new regime soon came under attack from opposing military groups. Following a visit to Vietnam in December, the secretary of defense presented a gloomy report to Johnson. Present trends, he wrote, "will lead to neutralization at best and more likely to a Communist controlled state." The new government was "indecisive and drifting." The internal reform program lacked leadership. Vietcong progress had been great. McNamara's recommendation was ominous. The United States must watch the situation but prepare "for more forceful moves if the situation does not show early signs of improving."

1964

January 27, 1964

France grants recognition to the People's Republic of China.

February 21, 1964

A crisis with Cuba ends when Castro again turns on the water supply to Guantánamo naval base.

This crisis began on February 2 when the U.S. Coast Guard arrested four Cuban fishing boats in U.S. waters

Vice President Lyndon B. Johnson, Mrs. Kennedy, and President Kennedy at breakfast on the morning of the assassination. John F. Kennedy Library

off the Florida Keys. Thirty-six fishermen were turned over to Florida authorities for legal disposition; two fishermen requested political asylum in the United States. Two of the Cuban captains admitted that they had been selected for this "historic venture" as a means of testing "U.S. reactions." Cuba protested to the United States through Swiss Ambassador Emil Stadelhofer and also complained to the U.N. Security Council. On February 6, Cuba's foreign minister, Raul Roa, sent word that Cuba was cutting off the water to the U.S. naval base at Guantánamo. It would be turned on only when the fishermen were released.

The U.S. navy had contingency plans to supply water at the base on a limited basis, and these were put into effect. In addition, Johnson and the navy agreed immediately to take steps to make Guantánamo self-sufficient by obtaining a permanent water supply and ending the employment of Cubans on the base. On February 21, the Florida court dropped charges against the Cuban crews but fined the four captains $500 each. All the men were released and Cuba immediately turned on the water to Guantánamo. Johnson proceeded to carry out the plan to make the base self-sufficient. The 2,000 Cuban employees at the base were released from work, and on April 1 construction of a desalination plant began at Guantánamo. This water processor was completed in December 1964, and the U.S. base was then self-sufficient.

April 3, 1964

A crisis with Panama ends when President Johnson agrees to "review every issue" with Panama, and diplomatic relations resume.

Growing discontent led to large-scale riots in Panama beginning on January 7, 1964, resulting in Panama breaking relations with the United States and demanding a new canal treaty. President Johnson agreed to review all issues in the treaty relations. With this understanding, President Roberto F. Chiari agreed to renew diplomatic relations with the United States. A new treaty was formalized in 1965.

April 20, 1964

President Johnson announces that he and Soviet Premier Khrushchev have agreed to reduce the production of U-235 for nuclear weapons.

President Johnson had sought some means to curb the arms race, and in his January 8 state-of-the-union message he announced that the United States was cutting its production of enriched uranium 235 by 25 percent and was closing several nonessential nuclear military installations. Between February 22 and April 20, Johnson corresponded with Premier Khrushchev to determine if he would take parallel action in further reducing the Soviet output of U-235, which was used to produce hydrogen bombs. Just as Johnson reached New York to deliver his address of April 20 to the annual Associated Press luncheon, he received a message from Moscow that Khrushchev had agreed on parallel action to reduce U-235 production and to allocate more fissionable material for peaceful uses. Johnson imparted this information to the public in his speech of April 20. He believed that small steps such as this would lead to limits on nuclear weapons and to the decline of the threat of a nuclear holocaust.

April 22, 1964

Romania's Communist Party insists on independence for all Communist nations and parties.

The Romanians desired greater freedom from Moscow's interference and began economic negotiations with the United States, France, and other nations. The Romanian Communist Party agreed, however, to support Moscow in its ideological dispute with China.

April 28, 1964

President de Gaulle announces that French naval staff officers will no longer serve under NATO commands.

Since 1962, de Gaulle had begun to disassociate his nation from NATO organizations. President Kennedy had rejected his suggestion of a pact by which Paris, London, and Washington would jointly oversee Western affairs. Thereafter, de Gaulle began an independent foreign policy program. On January 14, 1963, he rejected a NATO proposal for a multilateral defense force. On January 28, 1964, he signed a five-year trade agreement with the Soviet Union.

July 10, 1964

The former Katanga secessionist, Moise Tshombe, becomes premier of the Congo, and the United States assists the Congo in ending the rebellion.

In March 1964, Undersecretary of State for Political Affairs Averell Harriman recommended that President Johnson provide planes and pilots to assist the Congolese in putting down rebels, some of whom were aided by the Chinese Communists. Harriman wanted to support the Government of National Reconciliation groups headed by Cyrille Adoula. Therefore, Johnson sent planes to "train" the Congolese. Soon after, exiled Cubans recruited by the CIA were flying U.S. aircraft against the Congolese rebels. Adoula resigned on June 30, and on July 10, Tshombe—who had fled the region on June 14, 1963—took over as prime minister. Because Tshombe's former secessionist plots made him unacceptable to other black African leaders, only the United States and Belgium helped him against the rebels.

August 7, 1964

Congress passes the Tonkin Gulf Resolution authorizing the president to take "all necessary measures to repel any armed attack" in Southeast Asia.

Although the congressional Tonkin Gulf Resolution resulted from North Vietnamese gunboat attacks on U.S. destroyers off the coast of Vietnam, Congress did not investigate nor did President Johnson accurately report the developments in the United States of secret plans during 1964 that led to the North Vietnamese attack. (Later, in 1966, the Senate did investigate the Tonkin Gulf incident.) On February 1, 1964, Johnson authorized the use of military Plan 34a for covert action against North Vietnam designed to pressure Hanoi to withdraw from South Vietnamese territory. Plan 34a provided a variety of sabotage and psychological and intelligence-gathering operations against North Vietnam. These included U-2 flights to gather intelligence on targets; assisting South Vietnamese commando raids on North Vietnam to

A contingent of the Royal Australian Air Force arrives at Tan Son Nhut Airport, Saigon, to assist South Vietnamese with transporting soldiers and supplies to combat areas. National Archives

destroy railways, bridges, and coastal defense installations; air raids by U.S. fighter-bombers disguised as Laotian air force planes; and destroyer patrols in the Gulf of Tonkin to collect data on Communist radar and coast defenses. Although the Pentagon later claimed the destroyer patrols and commando raids just happened to occur on the nights when the North Vietnamese attacked the American destroyers, Hanoi could not be expected to disassociate the two types of U.S. interference on its coastline and assumed the commandos and the destroyers worked together.

These covert operations are the only explanation for the small North Vietnamese PT boat attacks on the larger destroyers. On August 2, the commander of the USS *Maddox* fired on a group of torpedo boats that, he said, launched their missiles at his ship. Whatever torpedoes were fired were off target, but the U.S. ships and planes from the carrier *Ticonderoga* damaged two PT boats and destroyed a third. On August 4, sonar on U.S. destroyers detected a "sea ablaze with hostile torpedoes" and the U.S. destroyers *Maddox* and *Turner Joy* fired against the "hostile torpedoes." This alleged second attack was mistakenly reported to Washington. Defense Secretary McNamara asked destroyer officers if there was a second attack but received the reply there was a "slight possibility" it had not taken place. By that time on August 5, Senate hearings on the Tonkin Gulf Resolution were underway on the assumption that there was an August 4 incident. Later, U.S. navy pilot James B. Stockdale stated that on August 4 there were "no boats, no boat wakes, no ricochets off boats, no boat impacts, no torpedo wakes—nothing but the black sea and American firepower." This information is from Marilyn B. Young's *The Vietnam Wars* (1991). President Johnson saw the naval incidents on August 2 and 4 as the opportunity to change U.S. Indochina strategy. At 11:30 P.M. on August 4, Johnson went before a nationwide television audience, interrupting all programs to announce the "unprovoked" attack by Communist boats on the U.S. destroyers in the Tonkin Gulf. Communist subversion in South Vietnam "has now been joined by open aggression on the high seas against the United States of America." The president announced he would act with restraint with a simple reprisal raid on North Vietnam, but he urged Congress to give him greater authority to repel future attacks.

Earlier on May 23, McGeorge Bundy, Special Assistant to the President for National Security, had prepared a resolution for Johnson to obtain such authority from Congress. The president provided this draft to the House and Senate for action. Congress acted quickly. Although Senator Wayne Morse wanted an extended investigation before voting, Senator J. William Fulbright, chairman of the Senate Foreign Relations Committee, refused. The committee supported Fulbright, and with little debate Congress passed the resolution. The House vote was 416 to 0; the Senate vote, 88 to 2.

The Tonkin Gulf Resolution was the closest Congress ever came to a declaration of war in Vietnam. The resolution declared that Southeast Asia was "vital to the national interest and world peace"; therefore, it gave the president the right to "take all necessary steps, including the use of armed forces" to aid any member or protocol state (South Vietnam) of SEATO to defend the region from Communism. Only the impending presidential campaign of 1964 prevented Johnson from immediately taking steps to escalate the war in 1964. Johnson did, however, authorize reprisal raids against North Vietnam. On August 4, within six hours of the reported Tonkin Gulf incident, the Joint Chiefs selected targets and the National Security Council supported the reprisal raids on North Vietnam. Two and a half hours later, planes from the carriers *Ticonderoga* and *Constellation* attacked North Vietnam. Their targets were four torpedo boat bases and an oil storage depot that held 10 percent of Hanoi's petroleum supply. Following this attack, Johnson ordered U.S. bombers to be deployed in the southwest Pacific pending orders for future raids on Vietnam.

October 14, 1964

China enters the atomic era.

China's first atomic test was monitored by U.S. aircraft. The Kennedy-Johnson administrations were alarmed at this prospect and considered drastic countermeasures but did not institute them.

October 14, 1964

Soviet Premier Khrushchev is ousted by Kosygin and Brezhnev.

There was as intraparty struggle in Moscow between 1962 and 1964. To counter the opposition, Khrushchev tried open deliberations of the Central Committee before hundreds of "plain folk." The attempt to silence the opposition failed because it threatened to undermine the power of the Presidium (formerly the Politburo) and the Central Committee of the Communist Party. After the Presidium members Leonid Brezhnev and Alexei Kosygin persuaded all members of the Presidium to remove Khrushchev as chairman, the Central Party Committee joined the antireform members who opposed Khrushchev. Khushchev then retired to his dacha near Moscow and wrote his memoirs, the first of which was published in the West as *Khrushchev Remembers* (1970).

Having worked in government but not having been involved in party apparatus, Kosygin became prime minister to avoid a power struggle. He was an enigma to Westerners but according to the Soviet Ambassador to the U.S. Anatoly Dobrynin, Kosygin

> was an honest, intelligent, and extremely knowledgeable man, highly competent in handling government business. He was not an expert in foreign affairs, but thanks to his common sense, he could handle discussions and negotiations with foreign partners better than any other member of the Politburo except Gromykoy, and certainly better than Brezhnev.

However, it was Brezhnev who had the greater share of power.

Leonid Brezhnev, who took over Khrushchev's role as first secretary of the Communist Party, was an experienced politician and a team player who Dobrynin described as "cautious and unhurried and... used to listening to his colleagues. He was neither as gifted by nature nor such an impulsive innovator as Khruschev.... One cannot call him a great man, or a strong character, or even a strong personality." Earlier, Brezhnev had supervised military-industrial facilities, including weapons production and Soviet efforts to achieve strategic arms parity with the United States. According to Dobrynin, Brezhnev "did not care much for the problems of ideology, yet he firmly adhered to the dogmas of

Marxism-Leninism.... He also knew little about foreign policy.... but basically, he stood for better relations with America, and that was what mattered." Brezhnev depended on Foreign Minister Gromyko to deal with foreign policy, except for strategic arms limits where he had expertise. See Anatoly Dobrynin, *In Confidence* (1995).

October 15, 1964

James Harold Wilson becomes British Prime Minister following a Labour Party victory.

November 3, 1964

Lyndon Johnson wins a landslide victory over Barry Goldwater.

The election of 1964 was the first in which the Republican candidate directly challenged the Cold War consensus policies of containment. He wanted "total victory" over Communism, not containment, and made many Americans fear he might launch a nuclear war. Whether or not he actually said, as alleged, that the United States should "lob a nuclear bomb into the men's room at the Kremlin," both his avid followers and his opponents believed he did.

Against Goldwater, Johnson became a symbol of restraint and progress. Even during the Tonkin Gulf crisis, Johnson's single reprisal raid did not accurately indicate the more bellicose secret plans that he had prepared for use in 1965 if necessary. Therefore, Johnson said as little as possible about Vietnam or other foreign issues. The 1964 election was the apogee of Johnson's political career.

1965

January 27, 1965

The U.S. Defense Department reports on South Vietnam's continued political deterioration.

When interfering in Third World conflicts, American political leaders had consistently failed to develop realistic policies to deal with the governments they supported and with the more vigorous and focused leadership of left-wing rebels and Communists. In most cases, the United States found itself supporting a wealthy, entrenched governing elite who adamantly opposed land reform and other badly needed socioeconomic reforms in such areas as corruption, education, public health, and economic opportunities. American "aid" often never reached the people it was supposed to help. The "rebels" had little difficulty in finding issues that appealed to the exploited and oppressed and that provided them with a strong popular base. The U.S. fear of "Communism" had little meaning to those being exploited by corrupt, often brutal, authoritarian governments.

By the end of 1964, Maxwell Taylor, who became the U.S. ambassador to South Vietnam in June 1964, discovered that the South Vietnamese did not want Americans to interfere in their domestic affairs; they only wanted the United States to fight for them. Reports by Taylor and on January 27, 1965, a summary analysis of the Vietnamese situation by John T. McNaughton (an assistant to McNamara) described the difficulties of the internal political conflicts of 1964 during which Taylor's advice was seldom heeded by the Vietnamese. In January 1964, Big Minh was overthrown by General Nguyen Khanh. In August, a coup against Khanh by General Lan Van Phat aborted and gave power to a triumvirate of Nguyen Cao Ky, Nguyen Chanh Thi, and Nguyen Van Thieu. These three younger officers tried to please Taylor by forming a High National Council.

On December 20, however, General Khanh eliminated the National Council and joined Thi and Ky in a new military junta. With the military, religious, and social factions creating chaos in Saigon, the South Vietnamese army could not function effectively. Because a new government seemed incapable of improvement, Taylor and McNaughton said the war would be won only if the United States controlled it. A vital step to Americanize the war was taken in 1965.

February 6–7, 1965

Johnson orders reprisal air raids after Communists attack U.S. troops at Pleiku.

Plans to escalate the U.S. role in Vietnam began on September 9, 1964, when President Johnson told the principal advisers in the National Security Council to prepare to improve the defenses of South Vietnam. As a result, the NSC principals held lengthy reviews before recommending two options for Johnson, after dropping a third Option C to steadily escalate air raids on North Vietnam. On December 1, Johnson approved Option A to increase counterinsurgency operations against the Vietcong and prepare for reprisal air raids if there were further Communist provocations such as the raid on Bien Hoa on November 1, 1964. The December 1 decisions were critical but often misunderstood because they were based on a theory of war for limited political objectives. The U.S. Joint Chiefs of Staff urged Johnson to permit the military to use all necessary action short of nuclear war to "save" South Vietnam from Communism. Johnson's aim was to fight the war for the political purpose of containing Communism at the 17th parallel and thus protect South Vietnam and other Southeast Asian non-Communist nations.

Thus political objectives shaped military operations, a strategy not traditionally used by the U.S. military until the 1950–1953 Korean War, when President Truman and General MacArthur disagreed on the political objectives of limited war. The Pleiku attack of February 6 launched Option A reprisal air attacks. At Pleiku, the Vietcong killed nine U.S. soldiers and severely wounded 76 more. They also destroyed six airplanes and 16 helicopters. Following a brief session of the NSC, Johnson ordered Option A reprisals, code named Fleming Dart II. Two air raids by jets from a navy aircraft carrier hit North Vietnamese barracks at Dong Hui and a communications center at Vinh Linh. The White House announced the reprisals as a response to Vietcong raids at Pleiku and two other southern villages, thereby linking "their" war with "our" war—an attack on U.S. facilities in South Vietnam.

Johnson also told General Westmoreland, the U.S commander in Vietnam, that the reprisals were not the same as the Option C attacks on North Vietnam. Nevertheless, Option C gradually escalated air raids on North Vietnam combined with peace negotiations in March. More details on U.S. planning are in the *Gravel Edition of the Pentagon Papers* (1971–1972).

U.S. Air Force F-105s drop bombs on Vietnam targets. National Archives

March 19, 1965

"Rolling Thunder," sustained U.S. bomber attacks, begin against North Vietnam.

President Johnson ordered Option C of his "slow squeeze" tactics to begin against North Vietnam on March 19. Except for specific periods when the president halted these raids to consider possible ceasefire agreements, the Rolling Thunder air attacks continued from March 19, 1965 to March 31, 1968. The first bombing pause came between May 10 and 18, soon after the initial attacks inspired many international leaders to seek negotiations that would alleviate the conflict in Vietnam. Great Britain and the Soviet Union proposed to reconvene the 1965 Geneva Conference. Neither this effort nor others were successful during the next three years. In operation, the Rolling Thunder attacks took place at least two or three times each week. Johnson and McNamara controlled the dates and target selection for the raids. Although this control dismayed the U.S. military, Johnson wanted to retain political authority in deciding whether to increase or decrease targets as well as when attacks took place.

Nevertheless, the quantity of Rolling Thunder attacks against North Vietnam was astonishing. During a three-year period, 309,996 U.S. bombing raids dropped 408,599 tons of bombs on North Vietnam, most of these in the area between Hanoi and the 17th parallel. Generally, the area around Hanoi, the port of Haiphong, and the Chinese border were avoided.

By 1967, Johnson gradually eased this restriction, enumerating new targets such as rail yards or oil installations near Hanoi and Haiphong. On April 6, 1965, Johnson also sent combat troops to Vietnam, although this was not announced to the public until July 1965.

March 24, 1965

American objectives in Vietnam are given a quantitative formulation by John T. McNaughton.

The assistant secretary of international affairs in the Defense Department, McNaughton prepared a memo that justified the U.S. bombing campaign against North Vietnam. This memo stated that U.S. aims in Vietnam were: 70 percent—to avoid a humiliating defeat (to our reputation as guarantor); 20 percent—to keep Vietnamese (and adjacent) territory from Chinese hands; 10 percent—to permit the people of South Vietnam a better, freer way of life, and also to emerge from the crisis without an unacceptable taint from methods used. Not to "help a friend," although it would be hard to stay if South Vietnamese leaders asked them to leave. Except for the statement of percentages, the speeches of President Johnson, Rusk, and McNamara from 1965 to 1968 appeared to verify McNaughton's listing. McNaughton's memo was secret and confidential, not reaching the U.S. public until the publication of the *Pentagon Papers* in 1971.

March 24, 1965

Protests against the Vietnam War are made during a "teach-in" at the University of Michigan, beginning a new method of dissent.

Although there were a few war dissenters before March 1965, the criticism against the Johnson administration's White Paper of January 1965 that explained North Vietnam's aggression, the Pleiku reprisal raids of February, and the first Rolling Thunder bombings of March, inspired the start of a slow but growing public opposition to the Vietnam War. Significant dissent arose on college campuses where professors trained in international studies, foreign policy, and Asian or Vietnamese culture opposed the administration's methods. The teach-ins, lasting from two hours to all day and night, became a means to disseminate information about an area of the world that few Americans knew and about which there were misconceptions based on myth or misinformation. Some were conducted as debates for and against Johnson's policies; others were informative or were held to explain why U.S. policies erred. Some presented arguments by moderate dissenters who wanted better U.S. global strategy; others, by radical opponents who described the horrific results of napalm bombs and B-52 raids on helpless South Vietnamese.

The dissenters were aided because Johnson talked about paying for "guns and butter" programs, but the war on poverty was the only low-budget war in American history. In 1965, the Great Society's Office of Economic Opportunity (OEO) received $800 million; the Defense Department obtained $56.6 billion including $5.8 billion for the Vietnam War. In 1966, the OEO received an increase to $1.5 billion; the Defense Department jumped to $72 billion. Antiwar demonstrations spread across the nation.

In 1966 and 1967, Los Angeles, Chicago, Newark, and Detroit had antiwar demonstrations that turned into major riots because Johnson failed to win either the Vietnam War or the War on Poverty. Details on the economic and social consequences of the war are in Anthony Campagna's *The Economic Consequences of the Vietnam War* (1990). The growth of dissent was indicated in public opinion polls. When Rolling Thunder began in 1965, 50 percent of the public supported Johnson's Vietnam policy; by December 1965, this had risen to 65 percent. During 1965, the president's acceptance rate by the public stabilized at 54 percent. In 1967, his popularity steadily declined. Only 44 percent agreed with the war program, and a smaller percentage, 23 percent, thought he was doing a good job as president. By early 1968, Johnson, a devotee of opinion polls, watched the support for the war effort collapse even more.

April 7, 1965

President Johnson emphasizes that America must protect the freedom of the Vietnamese.

In a speech at Johns Hopkins University, President Johnson sought to counteract the first signs of dissent on his Vietnam policy by describing America's idealistic role in fighting in Vietnam. The United States had a "promise" to keep in Vietnam and must show our allies they can depend on us. In addition, China and North Vietnam were allegedly stepping up their attacks on the "brave people of South Vietnam," and only America could slow this Communist aggression. Johnson ended his speech with dramatic but ironic words—ironic because he had just introduced the Rolling Thunder bombing campaign in Vietnam. Johnson said at Johns Hopkins that the American people have a very old dream "of a world where disputes are settled by law and reason." They also have a dream "of an end to war."

We must make these so, he said, concluding:

> Every night before I turn out my lights to sleep, I ask myself this question: Have I done everything that I can do to unite this country? Have I done everything I can do to help unite the world, to try to bring hope to all the peoples of the world? This generation of the world must choose: destroy or build, kill or aid, hate or understand. We can do all these on a scale never dreamed of before. We will choose life. And so doing will prevail over the enemies within man, and over the natural enemies of all mankind.

April 28, 1965

In violation of the OAS charter, President Johnson sends U.S. Marines to intervene in the Dominican Republic, claiming there is a threat of Communism.

Dominican politics had been in flux since May 30, 1961, when Trujillo was assassinated. Juan Bosch had been elected president in 1962 but was overthrown in a coup on September 25, 1963. During 1964, there was frequent unrest in the Dominican Republic when the possibility of another military coup appeared possible. President Reid was not popular. U.S. Ambassador W. Tapley Bennett backed Reid, but a CIA poll showed that only 5 percent of the people favored Reid. A revolt began on April 24, led by officers who favored the return of Bosch. Secretary of State Rusk disliked Bosch and wanted to prevent his accession to power. Rusk thought Bosch had been ineffective in 1962 and that he was under Communist influence. Neither Rusk nor Johnson wanted another Cuba in

Honduran troops, first troops of Inter-American peace force, arrive in the Dominican Republic to replace U.S. Marines. National Archives

the Caribbean. When a CIA-sponsored poll said the Communists supported Bosch, Rusk became convinced that he should not gain control.

As a result, when General Wessin counterattacked against Bosch supporters on April 26, Johnson encouraged the general, asking him only to act moderately against the rebels. Wessin failed, however, and when the U.S. embassy called for Marines to save the country from Communism, Johnson responded quickly to Wessin's request for aid because the government could not protect U.S. lives. On April 28, 500 Marines landed; soon after 20,000 more soldiers arrived. Johnson gave the U.S. public lurid details of the Communist threat, saying the United States acted on behalf of humanity. His action saved Wessin's counterrevolution from the victory of Bosch's rebels. The United States never proved that there was a Communist threat in the Dominican Republic. There was danger to Americans in the country because of conflict, but until U.S. forces arrived, Bosch had hoped to get U.S. support because Kennedy had helped him in 1962.

In early May, Johnson sent John Barlow Martin to Dominica to check on Communist influence. Martin reported that one rebel, Colonel Francisco Caamano Deno, was a potential Castro because he had a Communist adviser. This inspired Rusk and Johnson to further action to back the loyalists in the island republic. Somewhat ironically, by May 21, Rusk told the Senate Foreign Relations Committee that the danger of Communism had vanished. The administration, he said, could accept either Bosch or his leading opponent, Joaquin Balaguer. Also by mid-May, Rusk had referred the intervention to the OAS Council. The OAS agreed to send a multinational force to oversee the return of stability to the Dominican Republic. Later, in June 1966, the OAS held elections and Balaguer won. The fear of Castro and Communism had led Johnson to overreact in April 1965.

June 12, 1965

General Thieu and Marshal Ky gain control of the South Vietnamese government, appearing to give unity to South Vietnam.

Following the political chaos in Saigon from December 1964 to June 12, 1965, the government achieved a semblance of order after Thieu and Ky replaced Prime Minister Phan Huy Quat. Thieu became chief of state; Ky became prime minister. In reality, the Ky-Thieu government created a decentralized order by dividing up the political spoils of South Vietnam with four other generals. The so-called National Leadership Committee that made up the six-man junta set up four corps areas. General Thi held the First Corps area, Vinh Loc the Second, Bao Tri the Third, and Dang Van Quang the Fourth. Each general was in complete charge of his corps area, awarding military and civilian posts to the highest bidder, friends, or relatives. These posts were profitable for the generals—reports were that a province chief's job cost three million piatres plus a 10 percent kickback each month. Ky was the head of the baronies because his charismatic personality suited the U.S. newsmen, television cameras, and visiting politicians. Thieu was in the shadows but was the brains behind the junta, and he eventually gained complete power. As David Halberstam and other reporters have documented, in their corps areas the generals' basic motives were personal power and profit. They conserved their troops for personal use, letting the Americans do the fighting as much as possible. Outwardly, however, Ky and Thieu created an image of government in charge that looked good compared with the era of frequent political changes between November 1963 and June 1965.

July 28, 1965

President Johnson announces he is sending more American forces to Vietnam but tries to explain this as a "restrained" response.

Because of recent "leaks" to the press in Washington about the number of American troops going to South Vietnam, President Johnson held a press conference to explain his decisions. On June 8, Robert McClosky of the State Department told reporters that U.S. forces would "fight alongside Viet forces when and if necessary." Although the State Department clarified McClosky's statement on June 9 by saying there had been "no recent change in mission" of U.S. forces, Secretary McNamara on June 16 acknowledged that U.S. combat troops would "act as was necessary" to cope with the enemy.

President Johnson was enraged by the news headlines of June 9 and 17 generated by McClosky's and McNamara's statements. As the *Pentagon Papers* of 1971 indicated, Johnson had specifically instructed everyone on April 1 that the role of U.S. troops should not be reported as a "sudden change in policy." On April 1, the Third Stage of the slow squeeze had been

Cabinet Room, White House. L-R: Lyndon B. Johnson, Robert McNamara, Henry Fowler, McGeorge Bundy, Dean Acheson, John Cowles, Arthur Dean, Gen. Bradley, John J. McCloy, Robert Lovett (?), Bill Bundy (?), George Ball, Dean Rusk. Lyndon B. Johnson Library

secretly approved. By this decision, 20,000 American troops were ordered to Vietnam, and there was a policy change in the role of U.S. forces. Kennedy's "combat support" role ended. American officers and their troops would assume direct control over actions against the Vietcong and North Vietnamese forces south of the 17th parallel. Johnson wanted this decision to appear not as a change but as action consistent with Kennedy's commitments. Thus, NSAM-328 of April 6 (whose contents had been approved on April 1) stated: "The President desires that . . . premature publicity be avoided by all possible precautions. . . . The President's desire is that these movements and changes should be understood as being gradual and wholly consistent with existing policy."

American troop increases had been in limited increments before July 28. Two Marine Battalion Landing Teams of 3,500 men each arrived at Danang on March 8, and by mid-June 75,000 U.S. troops were in South Vietnam. Moreover, the April 1 policy called for forces to come from Australia, South Korea, New Zealand, and the Philippines. At Ambassador Taylor's request, the government of South Vietnam asked other nations for assistance. One Australian battalion arrived in June 1965. Because Britain and France opposed the U.S. operations, SEATO never sanctioned Johnson's "war" in Vietnam.

U.S. air operations south of the 17th parallel were also ordered on April 1. These included both tactical and strategic aircraft operations. General Westmoreland had charge of the fighter and bomber planes assigned to South Vietnam. These planes substituted for ground artillery by bombing and strafing enemy-held areas. They also dropped napalm firebombs and chemical defoliants to burn out or kill vegetation in jungle areas under Communist control. These attacks caused civilian protests both in South Vietnam and the United States because they indiscriminately damaged combatant and noncombatant areas, but the U.S. air force claimed they served a useful purpose. By the end of 1965, the air force had stationed 500 aircraft and 21,000 men at eight major air bases in South Vietnam. The air force's saturation bombing by B-52s in the south was code-named Arc Light. Beginning in June 1965, B-52s flew area bombing missions from Guam. These area destructive capabilities coming from high-altitude flights gave an extra dimension of fear to both Vietcong and others in the south because the people seldom saw the high-flying planes.

Although the April 1–6 decisions involved the Americanization of the war in South Vietnam, Johnson and his advisers were not certain what terms to use in news releases to the U.S. public. When the Marines landed in March, their mission was described as a "security force" for the U.S. bases at Danang. General Westmoreland's reports called these operations "active counterinsurgency" to give ambiguity to the missions. McClosky on June 8 used the term "fight alongside." On July 28, the president announced that another 50,000 U.S. troops would be sent to South Vietnam (the Pentagon Papers showed the figures approved by July 1965 to be 125,000). This increase, the president said, was minimal and non-provocative because of the large number of North Vietnamese units fighting in the south. The Communists' spring offensive had made large advances during June 1965, and South Vietnam needed greater assistance. When a reporter asked the president if the troop increase implied less reliance on South Vietnam's troops, Johnson assured him: "It does not imply any change in policy whatsoever."

Johnson's attempt to deceive the newsmen failed. Too many reports of the U.S. "search and destroy" missions in South Vietnam contradicted the president's words. The July 28 press conference caused many reporters to realize that the president had purposely misled them. A "credibility gap" grew larger and larger between the president and the Washington press corps after 1965, further serving the groundswell of popular dissent between 1965 and 1968. At various times after July 1965, the number of U.S. ground troops increased in South Vietnam as the war became Americanized. By December 1965, there were 267,500 U.S. ground combat troops in South Vietnam; in December 1966, 385,300; in December 1967, 449,800. The peak number of U.S. ground troops in Vietnam occurred in April 1969, when there were 543,400 U.S. military forces in Vietnam.

September 24, 1965

The United States and Panama sign a new canal agreement.

Negotiations to change the U.S. treaty with Panama began in 1964 following a series of riots in Panama. (See April 3, 1964.) During the next year, the United States and Panama agreed to a treaty that granted Panama sovereignty over the Canal Zone, provided economic aid to Panama, and allowed U.S. bases to protect the canal.

October 14, 1965

The Department of Defense announces the largest draft call since the Korean War.

One consequence of the escalation of U.S. ground forces in Vietnam was the call for more draftees aged 18 to 35. Although the Defense Department preferred to call up trained military reserves or the National Guard, Johnson opposed this method of enlarging the armed forces. The president believed calling reserves and the National Guard was tantamount to a national crisis that would require a declaration of war. He did not want to engage Congress in that debate, preferring to act under the Gulf of Tonkin Resolution permitting him to "take all necessary measures to repel any armed attack against the forces of the United States and to prevent further aggression."

The call-up of more young men from college or their first job opportunity was not popular. During the two days after the Defense Department's October 14 draft call, antidraft demonstrations broke out on college campuses and in all major U.S. cities. Some young men burned their draft cards to symbolize their determination not to go to Vietnam. The "burn your draft card" campaign became so extensive that Congress passed legislation in 1966 to punish such acts with a $5,000 fine and up to five years in prison. Antidraft tactics varied during the next decade. Counseling centers were set up to advise young men on how to fake physical and mental tests in order to fail the army's physical examination. Two Roman Catholic priests, Daniel and Phillip Berrigan, led a group of draft resisters in a raid on the Baltimore Selective Service offices to destroy draft files by pouring ox blood on the records. Some young men avoided the draft by going into exile in Canada or Europe. Nearly 40,000 men deserted from the U.S. army in 1968. Returning war veterans also questioned the war and the draft.

On May 8, 1966, the author Lloyd Shearer published an article in *Parade* magazine based on interviews with 88 wounded soldiers at U.S. hospitals. Eighty of the soldiers "declared flatly" that the "South Vietnamese could not be trusted." One said, "maybe the Vietnamese like us, but after spending 10 months there, I can tell you—they sure do a great job hiding it." These men, said Shearer, fought because the president said they should but they were confused about U.S. war objectives and could not understand why most Vietnamese disliked Americans. *Parade* was a widely read Sunday supplement magazine, and these reports could not help raising questions about Johnson's policy in Vietnam.

November 25, 1965

Two years of political difficulties end in the Congo as General Mobutu becomes President.

Maneuvering in the Congo between Moise Tshombe on the right and a left-wing rebel group that took over Stanleyville on August 5, 1964, placed the Congo in political disorder again. The Stanleyville group was put down, and on October 13, 1965, General Kasabuvu removed Tshombe as prime minister of the Léopoldville government. Finally, on November 25, Mobutu overthrew Kasabuvu and order came to the Congo for the first time since June 1960. On June 30, 1966, Léopoldville was renamed Kinshasa.

December 7, 1965

The United States and India sign an agricultural aid treaty in which India also agrees to give agricultural modernization more attention.

India had experienced severe food shortages in 1964–1965. President Johnson was willing to help but urged Secretary of Agriculture Orville Freeman to link future U.S. food shipments to India's readiness to emphasize food progress as well as industrial advance. Meeting in Rome with India's minister of food and agriculture, Chidambaro Subramaniam, Freeman worked out an agreement based on Johnson's position. In its next Five-Year Plan, India agreed to give greater attention to supplying more food for itself. In turn, the United States agreed to make necessary wheat shipments to meet India's requirements. The India Treaty became the basis for Johnson's Food for Peace program. In spite of India's new efforts, the United States had once again to provide India with food in April and December 1966. Johnson limited this aid because he claimed other nations should also respond to India's needs.

December 27, 1965

President Johnson agrees to make the Christmas bombing pause longer in the Rolling Thunder attacks with a widespread diplomatic attempt to achieve peace.

Since early November, Secretary of Defense McNamara had favored a bombing pause to permit North Vietnam a chance to react positively to the escalated U.S. air and ground action in Vietnam during the past nine months. Both the Joint Chiefs of Staff and Secretary Rusk opposed McNamara's request. In early December, however, Soviet Ambassador Anatoly Dobrynin indicated that the USSR would help obtain an agreement if there was a bombing pause. This convinced Rusk that a bombing pause would succeed or, at least, demonstrate to the American public that Johnson had tried everything possible to seek peace. With the backing of both the secretary of state and the secretary of defense, Johnson concurred.

On December 24, the United States and South Vietnam had agreed to call a Christmas halt to aggressive action. Therefore, on December 27, Johnson simply extended this pause to permit the State Department to examine a peaceful solution. In spite of a large-scale and much publicized U.S. diplomatic effort to use the pause to gain negotiations on Vietnam, the pause failed. Between December 27 and January 31, 1966, U.S. diplomats visited Rome, Belgrade, Warsaw, Paris, and London to seek aid in gaining a settlement. Rusk believed the most hopeful effort was a mission from Hungary, Poland, and the Soviet Union that visited Hanoi to try and convince Ho Chi Minh to seek a settlement. This mission failed. On January 28, Radio Hanoi broadcast Ho Chi Minh's message that America's "so-called search for peace" was "deceitful" and "hypocritical." He insisted that the United States first pull out of Vietnam and recognize the Communist National Liberation Front as the legitimate representative of the people of South Vietnam. On January 31, Johnson ordered the resumption of Rolling Thunder's bombing raids on North Vietnam.

1966

January 17, 1966

The United States loses a hydrogen bomb in an air collision over Spain.

A U.S. plane carrying four unarmed H-bombs crashed near Palomares, Spain. The consequences were less harmful than expected, although several bombs ruptured sufficiently to poison nearby farmland.

January 28, 1966

The Senate Fulbright Committee hearings on Vietnam open in Washington.

Senator J. William Fulbright had been a close friend of President Johnson and had led Senate action in quickly passing the Tonkin Gulf Resolution in August 1964. Fulbright had believed Johnson when the president told him that the resolution was limited and was designed only to steal ground from Senator Goldwater's criticism. During 1965, Fulbright realized that the president had misled him. Gradually, the senator turned against Johnson and the escalation of the war. Joining with other Democratic Party members on the Senate Foreign Relations Committee, Fulbright began hearings on the Vietnam War on January 28, 1966, during which they would hear both sides of the question.

But the hearings provided the television audience and news media with the opportunity to hear and propagate the views of the conflict's major opponents such as George Kennan and Lieutenant General James Gavin. In doing so, Fulbright's hearings added to the growing dissent against Johnson's policies in Vietnam. During the Senate hearings between January 28 and February 18, 1966, Secretary Rusk explained how the war resulted from North Vietnam's "invasion" of South Vietnam and contended that the United States had to keep its pledge to help Saigon. Maxwell Taylor and others also defended Johnson's policy, but their version of the war had already been frequently aired on national television. More significant was the opportunity for the ideas of Kennan and Gavin to reach a large audience. Kennan believed the war was foolish and not vital to the United States. Gavin argued that different tactics were required to minimize the U.S. role and maximize the role of South Vietnam. Finally, Robert Kennedy testified in favor of new policies in Vietnam. Kennedy thought a coalition with the Communists might be better than with the corrupt regime in Saigon. The Senate hearings helped to turn the liberal "egghead" wing of the Democratic Party against the war.

February 6, 1966

France withdraws its troops from NATO and requests NATO to move its headquarters from French soil.

French President de Gaulle had been hostile toward the United States since 1962 because Washington refused to grant the French a more equitable position in their partnership. In particular de Gaulle disliked the multilateral (MLF) NATO force proposed by George Ball and urged by the United States on its European allies from 1963 to 1966. Having previously withdrawn French naval forces from NATO, de Gaulle now extended French independence by withdrawing all French forces from the organization. In addition, at France's request, NATO headquarters were moved from Paris to Brussels. Soon after, the idea of the MLF was dropped by the United States.

February 8, 1966

President Johnson is optimistic at the conclusion of meetings in Hawaii with South Vietnamese leaders Ky and Thieu.

Between June 12, 1965 and early 1966, the political alliance Ky and Thieu established on June 12, 1965, seemed to keep political order. Johnson was pleased and on January 31, 1966, invited the two leaders to meet with him in Honolulu. Ky knew all the right words to satisfy Johnson. Their regime was defeating the enemy, pacifying the countryside, stabilizing the economy, and building democracy. Ky told Johnson that any government may launch a program for a better society, "but such a program cannot be carried forward for long if it is not administered by a really democratic government, one which is put into office by the people themselves and which has the confidence of the people."

At the conclusion of the Honolulu meeting on February 8, the Declaration of Honolulu was issued. In the first part of the decree, the Vietnamese government stated its goals, which included: (1) defeating the Vietcong and those "illegally fighting with them"; (2) eradicating social injustice among our people; (3) maintaining a viable economy to build a "better material life for our people"; and (4) building "true democracy for our land and for our people," including a constitution in a "few months." The United States promised to support the goals and programs stated by the Vietnamese.

February 24, 1966

Kwame Nkrumah, the Ghanaian dictator who had aligned with the USSR, is overthrown in an army coup led by General J. A. Ankrah.

May 14, 1966

The Ky government attacks Danang and Hue following recent outbreaks of Buddhist-led uprisings.

The Buddhist riots of 1966, which in many respects reenacted those of 1963, had been precipitated by

Prime Minister Ky's attempt to remove General Thi as commander of the First Corps area. With strong support from the Buddhists and the Dai Viet organization of Southern Vietnamese Nationalists, Thi had become independent of Saigon's control. When Ky sought to remove Thi, Buddhists led by Thich Tri Quang, a Buddhist monk, began protests on March 10, 1966. Students, trade unionists, and the Dai Viet aided the Buddhists. A nun and eight young Buddhist bonzes set themselves aflame to protest against Ky's government. The U.S. consulate at Hue was burned. On May 14, Ky ordered South Vietnamese troops to quell the uprising. Paratroopers landed at Danang airport but were repelled. Next, loyal Vietnamese marines and infantry besieged Hue, provoking Buddhist hunger strikes throughout South Vietnam in sympathy with Hue. By June 8, however, Ky's forces occupied Hue and Danang. Ky alienated the Buddhist leaders by banning their religious processions and all political acts. Many of the leaders in Hue and Danang were imprisoned or exiled.

In his memoirs, President Johnson said he "always believed" Thi Quang and his followers were either pro-Communist or their movement was "deeply penetrated" by Hanoi's agents.

June 29, 1966

Rolling Thunder's first attack on "POL" targets begins although Secretary McNamara and others had opposed them.

Since September 2, 1965, the air force and Joint Chiefs had urged Johnson to permit the bombing of POL (petroleum, oil, lubricants) targets near Hanoi as well as the aerial mining of North Vietnam's seaports. Secretary McNamara opposed these targets because of the increased risk of war with China or the Soviet Union. Moreover, he claimed, the POL storage areas contained only 10 percent of North Vietnam's needs and their loss would not seriously damage the economy. The JCS favored all efforts to remove the president's restraints on their targets and strongly believed the POL and seaport mines would help the war effort.

Johnson decided in May 1966 not to mine the seaports but to permit the attacks on POL targets. His final orders were delayed, however; first, because British Prime Minister Harold Wilson asked Johnson to reconsider, and later, in June, because Canada sent an official representative to Hanoi to discuss possible peace terms with Ho Chi Minh. After Ambassador Chester Ronning's mission failed, Johnson ordered the POL attacks, which began on June 29.

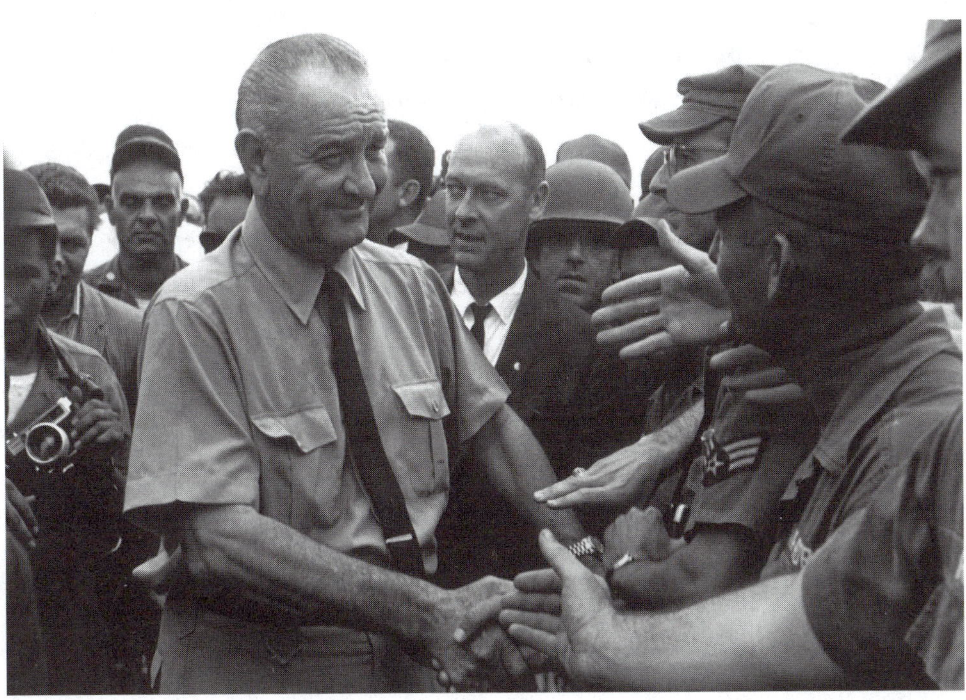

President Johnson greets American troops in Vietnam. National Archives

August 18, 1966

The cultural revolution begins in China.

The complete Chinese title of Mao's policy from 1966 to the early 1970s was the "great revolution to establish a property-less class culture." Edgar Snow described Mao's version of this in his book *The Long Revolution* (1972), which was based on interviews with the chairman of the Chinese Communist Party. According to Snow, Mao realized by the mid-1960s that the Beijing Party Committee led by Liu Shao-chi was making Mao a cult figure to decrease his power. This group had been strongly influenced by the Soviet apparatus of party controls and bureaucratic prerogatives.

As a result, Mao secured supporters in Shanghai as well as the backing of the army under Lin Piao. They organized the masses and the Red Guards to overthrow Liu Shao-chi. In practice, the cultural revolution emphasized agriculture and the village tradition. It sought to train village youths at the university so they could return to their homes and boost village production and culture. In this sense, it was a conflict between the modernization tendencies of the city, technology, and expertise versus the traditional Chinese village and communal life around which Mao had rallied the Communist Party from 1930 to 1949.

September 11, 1966

Elections in South Vietnam select delegates for a constituent assembly.

These elections were set up by the Ky-Thieu government to fulfill a long-sought desire of U.S. advisers to have a "free" election to prepare a constitution for South Vietnam. The election went well; more than two-thirds of the South's adults registered to vote and 81 percent of those registered voted, electing 117 delegates who represented all political factions except the Buddhists, who boycotted the election. Neither U.S. reporters nor European observers found any significant fraud at the ballot box. Between October 1966 and March 1967, the assembly delegates met to prepare a constitution. There was much dissension over the type of government to be established. A document was finally drawn up on March 19, 1967, the day before Ky and Thieu met with President Johnson at Guam.

October 25, 1966

The Manila Conference is attended by President Johnson and representatives of nations contributing troops to the Vietnam War.

At the invitation of President Marcos of the Philippines, President Johnson met in Manila with General Thieu and Prime Minister Ky of South Vietnam; President Park Chung Hee of South Korea; and Prime Ministers Harold Holt of Australia, Keith Holyoake of New Zealand, and Thanom Kittikachorn of Thailand. Following a two-day review of the military and nonmilitary situation in Vietnam, the delegates issued three statements: (1) Goal of freedom. The seven nations at Manila declared their unity in seeking freedom for Vietnam and other Asian Pacific areas. (2) Allies seek no permanent bases in Vietnam. In this statement, South Vietnam asserted it would ask the seven nations to leave Vietnam when peace was restored. The seven allies declared they were in Vietnam only to aid the victim of aggression. They would withdraw within six months after peace was restored. (Soviet Foreign Minister Andrei Gromyko told Johnson on October 10 that a specific statement on withdrawal would aid peace arrangements. Therefore, Johnson said, the second statement of the Manila Conference clarified Gromyko's suggestion.) (3) Declaration of peace and progress in Asia and the Pacific. The seven allies said their objectives were to oppose aggression, poverty, illiteracy, and disease. They would search for peace, reconciliation, and economic, social, and cultural cooperation in Asia.

November 1, 1966

Albania's Communist Party breaks with Moscow and allies with China as the "true" Communist Party.

The Albanians believed their independence might be threatened by a Soviet-Yugoslavia accord. To avert this, Albania's Communist party leader Enver Hoxha threw his lot to the Chinese.

November 11, 1966

President Johnson compromises between proposals of Secretary McNamara and the JCS on activity in Vietnam.

Following the inauguration of POL bombing raids on June 29, Secretary McNamara's aides watched the results closely while a group of leading scientists prepared a report, code-named JASON, that suggested new tactics to be used against North Vietnam. Between August 29 and October 15, 1966, the stream of reports from JASON, the CIA, and the Defense Intelligence Agency all concluded that the POL bombings had no critical effect on North Vietnam.

On September 4, 1966, the commander in chief for the Pacific had redirected the Air Force from a POL emphasis to targets causing "attrition on men, supplies and equipment" in North Vietnam. The conflict over war priorities between Secretary McNamara and the Joint Chiefs focused on new recommendations in October 1966. McNamara's JASON group recommended the construction of an electronic anti-infiltration barrier across the 17th parallel of Vietnam. In addition, McNamara recommended stabilization of the air war or a bombing pause, and the addition of 40,000 combat troops. The JCS disagreed with the secretary, urging an escalation of attacks against the North and requesting an added 150,000 men with the call-up of military reserve units.

Johnson's orders of November 11 sought a middle ground between McNamara and the JCS. He agreed to add 70,000 troops but rejected the call-up of military reserves. At the same time, he rejected the electronic barrier, agreeing with the JCS that it could not work. Finally, Johnson agreed to stabilize the Rolling Thunder attacks. The bombing stabilization was coordinated with an effort by Prime Minister Harold Wilson to persuade Moscow and Hanoi to reconvene the 1954 Geneva talks on Vietnam.

November 12, 1966

President Johnson signs the Food for Peace Act of 1966.

On December 7, 1965, the United States and India signed an agreement to encourage India to modernize its agriculture. President Johnson liked this concept and on February 10, 1966, recommended that Congress approve a program for the United States to assist other nations in agricultural progress by offering U.S. know-how on irrigation, pesticides, and farm equipment to less developed nations. Congress adopted this program and the president signed the bill into law on November 12.

November 13, 1966

Israel launches a large-scale reprisal attack on Jordan. The United States later votes to censure Israel in the United Nations.

During 1965–1966, tensions increased on the Syrian-Israeli border as Syria's new radical government under Premier Salah el-Bitar sent Arab guerrillas across the border, causing the Israelis to retaliate. In addition, a Palestinian group, al-Fatah, operated from bases in Lebanon and Jordan to raid Israel. On August 15, Syria and Israel had a serious conflict at Lake Tiberias using planes, tanks, and patrol boats. On November 13, Israel launched extensive reprisal attacks on the Jordanian towns of al-Samu, Jimba, and Khirbet Karkoy. Jordan appealed to the United Nations, where the Security Council voted to censure Israel. President Johnson also sent military aid to bolster the army of Jordan's King Hussein.

Jordan had generally been pro-Western in its policies, but the increase of Palestinian refugees and the al-Fatah Party made it difficult for Hussein to restrain guerrilla raids on Israel.

1967

January 13, 1967

The Soviet Foreign Ministry presents a detailed analysis as the basis for future policy.

As requested by Brezhnev, Gromyko gave the Politburo a detailed assessment of Soviet-American relations in which he refuted the idea that Moscow directed a push for world domination. As Ambassador Dobrynin notes, the document would have disappointed individuals who "sought evidence of war plans by the Soviet Union to advance its system or even its national interests."

Gromyko's document began: "On the whole, international tension does not suit the state interests of the Soviet Union and its friends. The construction of socialism and the development of the economy call for the maintenance of peace. In the conditions of détente it is easier to consolidate and broaden the positions of the Soviet Union in the world." The report's ideological tone stressed the USSR's desire to support socialist ideas in the "struggle with imperialism" and placed importance on Soviet-American relations, declaring this relationship was directly related to possible nuclear war.

The report deplored "adventurous schemes" from Beijing because it was China, not the Soviets, who believed the United States wanted a major war. Regarding Vietnam, Moscow felt it must "go on rendering comprehensive assistance" to improve North Vietnam's "defensive capacity to repulse" U.S. aggression. The "further escalation" of military actions "will compel the Soviet Union to render its assistance... on an ever-growing scale." The solution to Southeast Asian problems lay "in reaching a political solution on the basis of respecting the legitimate rights of the Vietnamese people.... Needless to say, we should avoid a situation where we have to fight on two fronts—that is, against China and the United States."

January 15, 1967

President Johnson sends Eugene Rostow on a world mission to persuade other nations to help alleviate India's food problems.

Although the United States had supplied wheat shipments to India on various occasions after 1947, including the U.S.-India agreement of December 7, 1965, Johnson believed nations other than the United States should accept the responsibility to assist India. When India appealed to the president for wheat in March 1966, he sent a small amount but decided to restrict the shipments to the "must" requirements, while encouraging India to ask other nations for aid. To emphasize his point, Johnson held up some shipments of wheat between August and December 1966. By mid-December, Australia and Canada each provided 150,000 tons of wheat for India; other nations did not. The French, in particular, irritated Johnson because they offered only to sell 200,000 tons at the "usual commercial terms."

On January 15, he sent Eugene Rostow, the undersecretary of state, on a round-the-world mission to solicit greater assistance. Eventually in 1967, other governments helped India including Canada, Australia, the Soviet Union, Britain, France, West Germany, Japan, Belgium, Austria, and the Scandinavian countries. With this additional aid India obtained nearly 10 million tons of wheat in 1967. During 1965 and 1966, the United States alone had sent 8 million tons and 6 million tons, respectively. This aid from 1965 to 1967 and India's new agricultural program—the "green revolution"—increased food supplies considerably after 1967. Unfortunately, India's subsequent large population increase outran its food increase in Malthusian fashion.

January 21, 1967

President Johnson asks if Soviet leaders desire to curb strategic arms race; this begins discussions on limiting missile defense systems.

President Johnson asked Premier Aleksei Kosygin if the Soviets would consider the possibility of reaching "an understanding... that would curb the strategic arms race." Johnson warned that the current antimissile race would require a "colossal cost" without "enhancing the security of our own peoples or contributing to the prospects for a stable peace in the world." In reply, Kosygin offered little hope that talks to limit missile defenses would take place. At a London press conference on February 9, 1967, Kosygin was asked about possible negotiations to limit antiballistic missiles. He responded that "a defensive system is more expensive than an offensive system, but it is not the cause of the arms race but designed instead to [prevent] the death of people." Kosygin suggested it would be better to abolish all nuclear weapons. Johnson and Kosygin would soon discuss this and other issues at Glassboro.

See June 25, 1967.

January 26, 1967

Secretary of Defense McNamara informs a Senate committee of U.S. nuclear strategy: the concept of mutual assured destruction (MAD) is evolved.

On January 26, McNamara's testimony before the Senate Armed Services Committee was made public. He indicated that the Soviets had built up their ICBM force "faster-than-expected"and deployed an antiballistic-missile defense (ABM) around Moscow. Although the secretary stated that the United States would presently have superiority by three times in the number of ICBMs until the early 1970s, the Soviets were catching up and their ABM program represented a new menace the United States should meet.

McNamara said the U.S. nuclear strategy needed two basic capabilities: (1) 'Assured destruction' as a deterrent. It needed the capability to absorb a surprise first strike and be able to inflict an "unacceptable degree of damage" on any combination of aggressors;

(2) 'Damage limitation' ability to restrict destruction of the U.S. population and industry. This required a build up of America's ABM missiles—the Nike-X program. Together these strategic goals would achieve a state of mutual assured destruction (MAD) that would be a strong deterrent against the use of nuclear weapons. "U.S. fatalities from a Soviet first strike could total about 120 million; even after absorbing that attack, we could inflict on the Soviet Union more than 120 million fatalities." With an American ABM system, the increase in the Soviet ICBM system would give it a second-strike ability to kill some 120 million Americans.

Because both sides would spend money—the United States on ABMs; the Soviets on ICBMs—it seemed in both nations' interests that negotiation should permit each to save money. Thus, McNamara wanted to talk with Moscow about an ABM limitation. Meanwhile, he urged that the Nike-X program be continued until an agreement was reached.

January 27, 1967

The United States, the Soviet Union, and 58 other countries sign the Outer Space Treaty.

This treaty embodies potential outer space contingencies that the signatories agreed to follow including the following: no nation can claim sovereignty over a celestial body such as the moon or planets; outer space will not be used for military purposes; astronauts or equipment forced to land on foreign territory will be returned; the launching country is liable for damage by its rockets, satellites, or space vehicles. The most notable of the clauses in this treaty was the agreement to prohibit weapons of war in outer space. This treaty formalized a resolution of October 1963 in which the U.N. General Assembly called on all nations to avoid placing nuclear weapons in orbit around the earth. At that time, both the United States and the USSR independently declared that they would abide by the U.N. resolution. On April 25, 1967, the U.S. Senate ratified the treaty unanimously.

February 14, 1967

In Mexico City, 14 Latin American nations sign the Treaty of Tlatelolco: a treaty calling for denuclearization.

The Cuban missile crisis of October 1962 provided the catalyst for the Latin American Nuclear-Free Zone (NFZ) initiative designed to keep the nuclear forces of the superpowers out of the region. Costa Rica had presented the idea of a NFZ to the Council of the Organization of American States in 1958 and Brazil joined Bolivia, Chile, and Ecuador in introducing a similar proposal to the U.N. General Assembly in November 1962. Mexico, however, took the lead in the subsequent protracted negotiations between 1964 and 1967. By 1969, 11 nations had ratified the treaty, and by 1992 there were 23 full parties to the agreement.

February 14, 1967

British Prime Minister Wilson's attempt to reconvene the Geneva Conference on Vietnam is not successful.

During the fall and winter of 1966–1967, Wilson and U.S. President Johnson agreed that Washington would stabilize its bombing activity while the prime minister persuaded Soviet Premier Alexsei Kosygin to invite participants in the 1954 Geneva talks to reconvene and resolve the Vietnam War. In addition, other tactics were used to seek negotiations with Hanoi. Initially, in October and November, Ambassador Lodge and Janusz Lewandowski, the Polish delegate on the International Control Commission, conducted talks to arrange meetings in Warsaw between U.S. and North Vietnamese delegates. On December 6, 1966, U.S. delegates waited in Warsaw but the North Vietnamese never showed up, saying they refused because the United States had bombed targets near Hanoi on December 4. On February 8, 1967, Johnson wrote a personal letter to Ho Chi Minh and also ordered a halt to the bombing as part of a Tet holidays general truce arrangement. The North Vietnamese never responded to Johnson's request for direct talks with Ho Chi Minh.

Throughout this period, Harold Wilson contacted Kosygin, inviting him to London for discussion of various matters including Vietnam. The Soviet premier agreed and visited London early in February 1967. Wilson's plans did not succeed. Johnson wanted Hanoi to stop sending supplies to the South before a bombing halt; Ho Chi Minh demanded that the bombing stop while there was only a partial cessation of supplies reaching the South. Wilson blamed Johnson for requiring too much in order to achieve peace, growing dismayed by the president's intransigence. Subsequently, there was a diplomatic misunderstanding between London and Washington about Johnson's minimum requirements. Johnson extended the Tet truce until February 13, but Wilson and Kosygin could find no grounds for an agreement between Hanoi and Washington. On February 14, Johnson ordered the renewal of the bombing of North Vietnam.

February 22, 1967

President Johnson escalates the Vietnamese air war, after the Tet truce failed on February 14, 1967.

Johnson decided to take more vigorous action against North Vietnam. Thus, on February 22, he approved the JCS plan for the aerial mining of North Vietnam's waterways (except Haiphong Harbor) and authorized Rolling Thunder attacks on the Thai Nguyen Iron and Steel Works near Hanoi. The aerial mining began on February 27, 1967; the attack on the iron-steel complex was made on March 10, 1967.

March 20, 1967

At Guam, President Johnson learns about South Vietnam's new constitution and discusses nonmilitary problems with Ky and Thieu.

At their first meeting on March 20, Johnson received a copy of the Vietnamese constitution that had been finalized by the constituent assembly the night before in Saigon. The document was patterned on the U.S. government, having a president, Senate, and House of Representatives. Ky told Johnson there would be a "popularly chosen government" selected later in the year.

The only military matter discussed was the need for regular South Vietnamese army units to make a greater effort to provide security for the hamlets and villages that U.S.-directed pacification teams helped to rid of Communist guerrilla units. Whether President Johnson and his advisers realized the full implication of this shortcoming is not clear. This involved the relationship between South Vietnamese army leaders and the local populace. The generals of the four corps areas elected to use, or not use, the army forces at their command. This is where corruption thrived and the local populace suffered. As General Westmoreland told President Johnson in 1967, the Communists continued successfully to recruit southerners to their ranks, enabling the Vietcong to replace their losses faster than the U.S. attrition tactics killed them.

May 19, 1967

McNamara recommends that military escalation of the Vietnam War cease and greater attention be given to the political and economic problems of South Vietnam.

McNamara's lengthy memo of May 19 reflected the growing division between the JCS and the Defense Department. The split between the civilian and military groups in the U.S. defense establishment was an argument not between hawks and doves but about the proper strategic goods and methods to be used in Vietnam. Both groups wanted to defeat the insurgents, however, they were divided on the war's limitations. In 1967, McNamara believed the air attacks on the North had not been effective, however, America had prevented the fall of South Vietnam to Communism.

Now, McNamara contended, the United States should continue to protect the South militarily, but give attention to developing a strong, viable government in Saigon that could win the "hearts and minds" of the South Vietnamese. Until this objective was achieved that nation would always be threatened. Military solutions could not achieve this goal because political problems required different methods. The JCS solidly opposed McNamara, never fully understanding the war's political ends. The U.S. armed forces wanted more planes, troops, and military authority to force North Vietnam to permit an independent non-Communist South Vietnam. The military wanted more bombing targets and another 100,000 men during the spring of 1967. Thus by May 1967, the conflicting objectives and methods in South Vietnam intensified friction between McNamara and the JCS. Although McGeorge Bundy, William Bundy, the CIA's senior analysts, and the Pentagon's Systems Analysis Team supported McNamara's analysis, the president deferred to the military.

McNamara's May 19 memo provided a detailed argument using data prepared by Alain Enthoven's computer systems office that showed each troop escalation yielded fewer results. Assuming the "body-kill" counts were accurate, 100,000 added soldiers would kill 431 enemies each week, a rate that would require 10 years to gain complete surrender. Errors of

Nguyen Van Thieu, President Johnson, and Prime Minister Nguyen Cao Ky salute during the playing of the U.S. and Vietnamese national anthems. National Archives

assumption in the system would, the report said, make the time longer. Computer data also showed that the Rolling Thunder attacks achieved few results. The air raids on POL targets, Hanoi, and communication links to China had cost heavy losses of men and matériel but yielded no long-term results. In addition, the North Vietnamese will to survive increased as bombing attacks increased. Thus, more bombs would be counterproductive in forcing Hanoi to surrender.

On the positive side, McNamara wanted to step up the pacification program in South Vietnam. Counterinsurgency, he said, meant building a viable economy and government, not laying waste to the country. The army's attrition tactics were exactly those that could not win in the South. If there were a ceiling on U.S. troop additions, Westmoreland and the U.S. military would have to use forces more efficiently as well as strive to pacify South Vietnam. If American troops were used passively, the government and army of South Vietnam could have a greater role in maintaining their own security. Perhaps the South Vietnamese army could learn to be as effective as the South Korean forces, which had been known for their fighting ability since 1953.

Finally, McNamara argued that stabilizing U.S. troop levels would bring an economic benefit to South Vietnam. Inflation in South Vietnam was 20 percent during the first quarter of 1967, and those figures seemed ready to increase. The unstable economy handicapped Thieu's government, the secretary said. Therefore, for economic, political, and military reasons, the May 19 program proposed new approaches to this war. First, it asked for 30,000 more troops that would become the maximum for U.S. combat forces. Second, it proposed concentrating all air attacks between the 17th and 20th parallels to interdict troops and supplies entering the South. Finally, and crucially, McNamara wanted a broadly based representative government set up in Saigon, committed to economic and social reforms to win the people's loyalty. This political phase of the war had to be won while the limited U.S. troops prevented a Communist victory. These methods would secure South Vietnam's peace and contain Communism north of the 17th parallel.

McNamara's memo of May 19 was considered a bureaucratic declaration of war by the JCS and Westmoreland. To counterattack the civilians, the JCS turned to their main supporters: the president,

Congress, and especially the Preparedness Subcommittee of the Senate Armed Forces Committee.

May 23, 1967

President Johnson charges that Egypt's blockade of the Gulf of Aqaba violates international law; he reaffirms Eisenhower's 1957 commitment to keep the Strait of Tiran open to Aqaba.

A Middle East crisis had been brewing for nearly a year. On November 13, 1966, the Israelis made a large reprisal raid on Jordan. On April 7, 1967, the Syrians and Israelis had a border skirmish. Subsequently, Damascus urged Egypt's Nasser to assist it against their common enemy. To show his solidarity with Syria, Nasser asked the U.N. forces to leave Sharm el Sheikh at the mouth of the Gulf of Aqaba. The multinational U.N. force had been in the Sinai area since 1956 as part of the agreement that ended the Suez crisis. U.N. Secretary-General U. Thant decided to withdraw and Egyptian troops entered the area.

At the same time Nasser warned Israel that if it attacked Syria, Egypt would enter the conflict. To further pressure Israel, Nasser announced on May 22 that Israeli ships could no longer pass through the Strait of Tiran leading to the Israeli port of Aqaba. In Washington on May 22, Johnson asked both Israel and Egypt to maintain the peace. To emphasize the U.S. concern, Johnson received a message from Eisenhower on his commitment to Israel regarding the Gulf of Aqaba. After this meeting, Johnson declared that the United States had been pledged to keep the port of Aqaba open. Egypt, he said, must cease its illegal blockade. Johnson took two other steps to avert a conflict. On May 31, the United States asked the U.N. Security Council to appeal to all parties in the Middle East to use diplomacy to resolve the dispute.

Both the Arabs and the Soviet Union opposed this resolution. When the United Nations could not act, Johnson accepted the British suggestion that a multilateral naval force assemble and move through the Strait of Tiran. When other nations doubted the value of this tactic, the United States and Britain sought to obtain a pledge from Egypt to permit all neutral flags to carry goods to Israel at Aqaba. Egypt refused, but so did Israel. Tel Aviv's government wanted its right to free passage without strings. Israel agreed, however, to give the United States two weeks to work out a settlement. War seemed imminent, sooner or later.

June 5, 1967

Israeli forces launch air attacks on airfields in Egypt, Iraq, Syria, and Jordan; then Israeli infantry attacks on three fronts: the Six-Day War.

Although President Johnson was still attempting to organize a multinational naval force to keep the port of Aqaba open and to persuade the United Nations to approve a resolution on the right of innocent passage in the Strait of Tiran, the Israeli cabinet on June 3 secretly voted for war and launched its attack on June 5. The Israeli campaign was highly successful. In three days, the Israelis overran the Gaza Strip and most of the Sinai Peninsula, including Sharm el Sheik. In the east, they captured the west bank of the Jordan River and the part of Jerusalem that Israel had not taken over in the 1949 war. In the northeast, they occupied the strategic Golan Heights on the Syrian border. Having accomplished its objectives, Israel agreed to a cease-fire on June 11.

June 5, 1967

Soviet Premier Alexsei Kosygin calls President Johnson regarding the Middle East War: The first use of the hot line in a crisis.

At 7:57 A.M., Secretary of Defense Robert McNamara called Johnson to inform him that the hot line was being activated for a call from Moscow. This special line had been installed on August 30, 1963, but was previously used only for tests and to exchange New Year's greetings. On June 5, trouble arose because the communications line from the Pentagon to the Situation Room of the White House failed to operate. McNamara had to find a technician to repair this defect while Chairman Kosygin waited on the Kremlin end. Fortunately, the line was repaired so that Kosygin and Johnson could agree to work for a cease-fire. Johnson was to exert influence on Israel; Kosygin, on Syria and Egypt. Thus, both leaders agreed on the necessity to settle the dispute. In addition, Johnson informed Kosygin that the Egyptian charge that a U.S. carrier aircraft helped Israel was not true. Because the Soviet navy had intelligence-gathering ships in the eastern Mediterranean, Kosygin knew that Egypt's claims were false. Johnson asked the Soviet chairman to explain this to Cairo.

June 6, 1967

The U.N. Security Council passes Resolution 234, demanding a cease-fire in the Middle Eastern War.

Although Egypt and Jordan agreed immediately to the cease-fire, Syria and Israel did not. Finally, on June 9, Syria accepted a cease-fire and the United States had to pressure Israel to do likewise. Tel Aviv agreed to do so on June 11, and the Six-Day War ended in victories for Israel. The postwar details now had to be dealt with in the United Nations because Resolution 234 did not state what the boundaries would be following the cease-fire.

During the final efforts to get Israel and Syria to accept a cease-fire on June 9–11, Johnson and Kosygin again used the hot line to keep one another appraised of developments. Both Israel and Syria were prepared to accept the cease-fire, but their mutual mistrust prevented either from quickly agreeing to an effective halt in the fighting. At 3:00 A.M. on June 10, the cease-fire seemed to have been accepted. It was not fully implemented, however, until June 11.

June 8, 1967

Israeli fighter-bombers mistakenly attack an American naval communications ship, the *Liberty*. Using the Moscow "hot line," Johnson tells Kosygin that U.S. carrier planes were flying only to investigate the incident.

The *Liberty* was in international waters when it was attacked by Israeli fighter-bombers. Following the air attack, Israeli torpedo boats launched five torpedos at the *Liberty*, one striking amidships instantly killing 25 crewmembers. This occurred early in the morning, but not until 11:00 A.M. did the Israelis report that their aircraft and boats had attacked in error and offer their apologies. Two U.S. aircraft carriers in the region responded to the *Liberty's* call for assistance by launching fighter-interceptors; however, the White House ordered the fighters to return. A short time later, President Johnson went on television to announce that 10 crewmembers had been killed in a "six-minute accidental" attack; however, 34 American sailors died as a result of the twin attacks. The surviving crew was ordered not to discuss the event, under threat of court-martial, and many believe the Navy's investigation failed to get at the reason for the assault.

To avoid confusion when the incident was first announced, Johnson phoned Kosygin to tell him why U.S. carrier planes were present off the Sinai coast. Earlier, on June 5, Egypt had falsely charged that U.S. carrier planes had participated in the attacks on Arab airfields. Johnson wanted the Soviets to know exactly what U.S. aircraft were doing on June 8.

June 9, 1967

Arab oil ministers declare an oil embargo against Britain and France for assisting Israel in the Six-Day War.

This was the first political oil boycott by the Arab oil states. The boycott was short-lived, ending immediately after Israel defeated Egypt, Syria, and Jordan between June 5 and 11, 1967. But it indicated a possible future boycott of more serious consequences in case of political problems in the Middle East. Western Europe was dependent on the Middle East for 20 percent of its oil needs.

June 10, 1967

Soviet Union breaks diplomatic relations with Israel.

According to Ambassador Dobrynin, Moscow's break was "an emotional step" which "in the long-term proved to be a grave miscalculation because it practically excluded the Soviet Union from any serious role in a Middle East settlement." He concludes the Six-Day War "was the decisive event" in Soviet Middle Eastern policy because tensions were high but did not rupture United States' relations. Subsequently, the United States and the Soviets did not discuss Middle Eastern affairs and the region had no priority on their agenda.

See June 25, 1967.

June 17, 1967

China explodes its first hydrogen bomb.

After successfully testing an atomic bomb on October 16, 1964, China conducted other tests. On December 28, 1966, China held a nuclear test that had some thermonuclear material. Finally on June 17, 1967, China announced: "The success of the hydrogen bomb test represents another leap in China's nuclear program." In the United States, neoconservative Republicans cited China and North Korea as rogue states requiring an antimissile defense system. Nevertheless, China faced many problems in obtaining ICBMs able to hit the continental United States. As of 1999, China had only outmoded liquid fuel missiles deployed without fuel in their tanks and with warheads stored nearby waiting to be loaded. These missiles were China's DF-5 (CSS-4) with a range of 8000 miles. China's solid fuel DF-31 road mobile missile had a range of 5000 miles but a DF-41 with a 7500 mile range might be ready for use between 2002 and 2005. For details see Gordan H. Chang, *Friends and Enemies: The United States, China and the Soviet Union* (1990); Richard Dean Burns, and Lester H. Brune, *The Quest for Missile Defenses, 1944–2003* (2003); and McGeorge Bundy, *Danger and Survival* (1988).

June 25, 1967

President Johnson and Premier Kosygin conclude meetings at Glassboro, New Jersey, addressing two primary issues: Middle East and strategic nuclear weapons.

The hastily arranged, Soviet-American summit at Glassboro took place because Kosygin was at the United Nations to support the Arab cause following the Six-Day War of June 5–11, 1967. Desiring to arrange talks on nuclear arms limitations, Johnson asked Kosygin to visit the White House. Kosygin did not wish to go to Washington because the Arabs might misconstrue such a meeting. Therefore, Johnson arranged to use the home of the president of Glassboro State College in New Jersey.

The American delegates arrived at the meeting with President Johnson ready to ask Kosygin to set a date for formal talks on the limitation of nuclear arsenals. It became evident Kosygin and other Soviet leaders had not decided on a negotiating position. Kosygin told Johnson he opposed linking offensive and defensive strategic arms, claiming that defensive missiles "don't kill people. They protect them." Secretary of Defense McNamara replied that a Soviet deployment of an antiballistic missile (ABM) system would "lead to the escalation of an arms race. That's not good for either one of us." At this point Kosygin pounded the table and shouted "Defense is moral; offense is immoral." Johnson and McNamara were dismayed, concluding Kosygin either failed to realize how an effective antiballistic missile system provided a first strike capability or they thought he could fool them by claiming ABMs had no strategic value. The Glassboro summit failed to achieve Johnson's hope to immediately begin negotiations. In Moscow, Soviet leaders initially resisted limits on missile defenses and members of Russia's scientific community were convinced "an effective ABM system was technically infeasible given the existing technologies." These specialists in weapons research realized that America's development of long-range missiles capable of carrying multiple independently targeted reentry vehicles (MIRVs) would soon enter the U.S. inventory and would saturate any antiballistic missile system. Thus the Soviets changed their mind within a year of the Glassboro meeting. For the ABM issue, see R.D. Burns and L. Brune, *The Quest for Missile Defenses* (2003).

While Johnson focused on Vietnam and arms control, Kosygin wanted to discuss the Middle East crisis. He said "the direction that U.S. policy was taking was not clear to him. . . ." Referring to Johnson's change on June 6 regarding an immediate Israeli withdrawal, Kosygin commented "the positions of the two countries calling for a cease-fire and a return to the original armistice lines had been as one. But then, four hours later, as the military situation had changed, the President had also changed his view." Johnson disputed Kosygin's charge, claiming Washington supported "preserving the territorial integrity of all countries."

"It was clear," Kosygin maintained, "that Israel would have to withdraw its forces back to the original armistice line. If this were not done, hostilities were certain to break out again; the Arabs were an explosive people and no other solution to this problem was possible." Johnson used "questions of security" to justify links between Israel's right to exist and its withdrawal: "the Israelis felt that they had been asked to do this very same thing in the past without gaining any security. Therefore, along with the troop withdrawal someone had to provide that security for them."

Johnson said he favored arms limitations in the region stating that "if we refrain from furnishing arms to Middle Eastern countries, at most they could fight with their hands, which certainly would not be as bad as an armed conflict." Kosygin was not impressed with Johnson's reasoning, insisting "Middle Eastern countries would find someone to sell them weapons no matter what the great powers do." The

Glassboro session ended with no specific agreements. For U.S.-Soviet positions, see Candace Karp, *Missed Opportunities* (2004).

August 25, 1967

The Senate Armed Forces Committee supports the JCS, strongly opposes McNamara's ideas, and blames Johnson for not using the "unanimous weight of professional military judgment."

Following a June 1, 1967 rebuttal of Secretary McNamara's May 19 report, the Joint Chiefs, led by Chief of Staff General Earle G. Wheeler and U.S. Commander, Pacific Vice Admiral U.S.C. Sharp Jr., contacted their friend Senator John Stennis, who chaired the Senate Armed Services Committee. Between August 9 and August 25, Stennis arranged secret committee hearings to review the military aspects of the Vietnam War. Wheeler and Sharp presented the JCS views on the war. They admitted the air war was not effective but blamed this on Johnson's bombing restrictions. They wanted the air targets enlarged and wanted permission to make the U.S. air presence felt over Hanoi and Haiphong.

They gave the subcommittee a list of 57 targets that should be bombed in North Vietnam. Although McNamara testified on behalf of his proposals, the Stennis report was a foregone conclusion. The senators could not comprehend Enthoven's computer analysis or differentiate between attrition and counterinsurgency strategy. As usual, the Armed Services Committee gave the military what they wanted. The Stennis Report, which came after the hearings ended on August 25, reflected that attitude. It urged Johnson to end his restriction on troops and bombing targets. Most surprising, it attacked the president, their fellow Democrat, for not following the opinions and recommendations of military experts. Because Johnson cherished the support of the generals and the Senate, the president and Secretary McNamara had reached the parting of the ways.

September 3, 1967

The South Vietnamese presidential election is won by the Thieu-Ky slate, although the election was "managed."

Unlike the 1966 election for the constituent assembly, the election for control of the government was managed by Ky and Thieu to keep the "delicate balance" that the military junta had established during the summer of 1965. The constituent assembly had designated 12 candidates for the presidency, one for each political faction in the assembly. Only Ky and Thieu seemed capable of winning, but a problem developed because both wished to be president. South Vietnam's military commanders met to resolve the conflict, persuading Ky to be a vice presidential candidate, while Thieu became their presidential nominee.

The campaign and election were considered by most observers in South Vietnam to be a farce. Two of the 12 assembly nominees could not run: one, because he advocated a neutrality agreement with North Vietnam; the other, Big Minh, was in exile. An effort to get the eight civilian candidates to unite against Ky and Thieu did not succeed. Thus, Thieu's victory on September 3 was no surprise. The surprise was his campaign manager's ineptness in stuffing the ballot boxes. In Saigon, where U.S. observers congregated, Ky and Thieu ran poorly. As a result, their advocates stuffed thousands of ballots into the boxes after the polls closed. Following the election, the eight losing candidates accused Thieu of fraud and tried to invalidate the vote. Before 1967 ended, however, Thieu retaliated by imprisoning 20 of his leading political, religious, and labor opponents. Despite the questionable election, Thieu provided a semblance of political order in South Vietnam. Political calm and a lack of *coups d'état* in Saigon had become equated with a politically sound government. Thieu's system did not, however, encourage the South Vietnamese to vigorously support anti-Communism as a way of life. Rather, it spawned apathy, immorality, and corruption in South Vietnam.

September 29, 1967

President Johnson says the United States will stop bombing North Vietnam when the Communists accept "productive discussions" for peace: the San Antonio formula.

During the summer of 1967, demonstrations to stop the U.S. bombing intensified in the United States and Europe, eventually culminating in the protest of 500,000 in Washington, D.C., on October 21. In a speech to the National Legislative Conference on September 29, Johnson publicly announced a proposal that he had privately agreed to with French intermediaries during August 1967. In July, two Frenchmen,

Herbert Marcovich, a scientist, and Raymond Aubrac, who knew Ho Chi Minh, returned from Hanoi with news that Hanoi would negotiate as soon as the U.S. bombing ended. The Frenchmen contacted Henry Kissinger, then a Harvard professor and adviser to the governor of New York, Nelson Rockefeller, asking him to find out if Washington would accept Hanoi's offer. Johnson agreed that the United States would halt the bombing if "productive discussions" followed and if North Vietnam agreed not to build up its forces and supplies during the truce. To persuade Hanoi that the French delegates were authentic representatives, Johnson informed Kissinger that the two men could inform Hanoi that the United States was reducing its bombing in the Hanoi area as a signal of Washington's intent. The effort of the two Frenchmen failed.

On August 24, Johnson learned that Hanoi would not renew visas for Marcovich and Aubrac. Later, Hanoi's delegation at Paris informed the two Frenchmen that there could be no negotiations until the United States stopped bombing and removed its forces from Vietnam. Subsequently, Johnson decided to announce publicly the formula that he had previously given to the two Frenchmen, although he did not mention the French effort during the San Antonio speech. While observers in September thought Johnson had made a new proposal, it was one that Hanoi had already rejected.

October 9, 1967

Reports from Bolivia are that Che Guevara has been killed by Bolivian troops.

Che, who symbolized the radical, Castro-type of Communist reform for Latin America, had been leading guerrillas in Bolivia against the government when he was reported to have been killed. While the initial stories of Che's death appeared dubious, they were later confirmed.

October 12, 1967

Rusk says America's vital interest in Vietnam is due to the danger from Chinese Communist aggressive policies.

Rusk had previously told the journalists that the United States was in Vietnam to "defend our vital national interests." Because the Johnson administration often used this term but never defined it, Jon Finney of the *New York Times* asked Rusk what the United States had at stake in Vietnam. Rusk referred to the future threat of China, saying Beijing had nominated itself as an enemy by proclaiming a "militant doctrine of the world revolution." Beijing had inspired the Vietnamese to engage in the war against the South. Rusk's words surprised many U.S. commentators because it ignored the long history of Vietnamese-Chinese conflicts.

Most leading Far Eastern scholars in academies and in the Far East Section of the State Department did not see China as a menace. Beijing's leaders always passionately denounced the Western powers, but Mao Tse-tung usually acted with caution. Rusk appeared to be intentionally raising the specter of the Chinese threat. However, if China were truly the enemy, then wasting U.S. resources in Vietnam would appear to be nonsense. The United States should have been planning responses to the Chinese threat, not Hanoi. Rusk seemed therefore simply to be repeating the anti-Chinese rhetoric that had been popular among the political right in the United States since 1949.

November 2, 1967

Johnson confers with the "wise men" regarding McNamara and the Vietnam War strategy.

President Johnson assembled this group of advisers for a White House meeting because he faced McNamara's opposition to his plan to escalate the war. Following the Stennis Report of August 25, 1967, Johnson decided in October to increase U.S. forces by 45,000, compared with McNamara's recommendation for 30,000 and the JCS's desire for 100,000. More important, Johnson rejected the secretary of defense's proposal to place a ceiling on future force increases. He also ordered Rolling Thunder to target 52 of the 57 targets listed by the JCS for the Stennis Committee. On October 31, McNamara discussed his opposition to the JCS with Johnson and prepared a memo that essentially summarized the arguments and proposals made on May 19, 1967. McNamara recommended a troop ceiling and suggested a cut in bombing raids coupled with a truce appeal to Hanoi. Finally, he asked for a study of military operations to reduce U.S. casualties and to persuade South Vietnam's army to assume more responsibility for self-defense.

The "wise men" met with Johnson to discuss McNamara's recommendations and future policy in

Vietnam. The group included Dean Acheson, George Ball, Maxwell Taylor, and McGeorge Bundy. These advisers believed the war was going well and thought the gradual escalation should continue. They could not accept McNamara's proposal to cut Rolling Thunder because they believed North Vietnam should be ready to surrender soon. In addition to the wise men, Johnson asked his future secretary of defense, Clark Clifford, and the Associate Justice of the Supreme Court, Abe Fortas, to comment on the secretary's proposal. They both agreed with Johnson. Significantly, however, none of these men had been informed of McNamara's views, of Enthoven's systems analysis studies, or of any explanation of the difference between the attrition strategy and counterinsurgency efforts that McNamara made. On the basis of these talks with other advisers, Johnson agreed to have McNamara resign.

November 22, 1967

U.N. Security Council Resolution 242 states terms for a long-term solution to the Six-Day War of June 5, 1967.

From June 11 to November, a variety of proposals to settle the Middle East crisis had been debated in the United Nations. Because the cease-fire agreement did not establish boundaries, the Soviet Union and the Arab nations demanded that Israel withdraw to its borders of June 4, 1967, evacuating the strategic military areas Israeli forces won during the fighting. Backed by the United States, Israel refused to withdraw without long-term security guarantees. U.N. Resolution 242 was based on suggestions by President Johnson and offered a peace favorable to all parties. It provided for free navigation of international waterways, justice for refugees (i.e., Palestinians), recognition of the sovereignty of all states with secure borders, and withdrawal of Israel from all occupied territories. The Arab world was critical of the Americans for backing Israel against them in the Middle East and looked to the Soviet Union for political and military assistance.

November 26, 1967

The People's Republic of South Yemen is proclaimed.

On November 5, President Sallal of Yemen was deposed and a three-man presidential committee formed. The radical left group had gained power and adopted a Communist style of government, aided by the Soviet Union.

November 28, 1967

McNamara resigns but agrees to stay until Clark Clifford can replace him on March 1, 1968.

Between May 19, when the secretary outlined his detailed recommendations for action in Vietnam, and October 31, when he stated his opposition to the Joint Chiefs, relations between the president and the secretary had grown increasingly tense. After meeting with the "wise men" and others in November, Johnson decided to replace the secretary. As Johnson later confessed to his biographer, Doris Kearns, he once thought McNamara had become a loyal friend. In November, however, the president realized the secretary was too much of a Kennedy man who imbibed Robert Kennedy's dissenting ideas. On November 28, McNamara tendered his resignation to Johnson, who arranged for him to become the head of the World Bank. In his memoirs, Johnson says he decided on December 18, 1967, to write himself a special memorandum giving his personal views on McNamara's October 31 proposals. The memo is reproduced in the appendix to Johnson's *The Vantage Point* (1971). While it responds to the secretary's proposals, the memo is notable as evidence that Johnson lacked the ability to visualize the strategic implications of McNamara's counterinsurgency ideas compared with the military's strategy of attrition.

November 30, 1967

Senator Eugene McCarthy announces he will be a "peace candidate," seeking the Democratic presidential nomination in 1968.

Although Senator McCarthy of Minnesota agreed with Senator Fulbright's opposition to Johnson's policy in Vietnam, he had been reluctant to campaign against the president. In November, however, Allard Lowenstein, who headed a group of student dissenters, persuaded McCarthy to run because he could expect 7 million college students to assist in the campaign. Although McCarthy's "children's crusade" enlisted many young people, the senator's amateur politicians were not well organized. McCarthy played

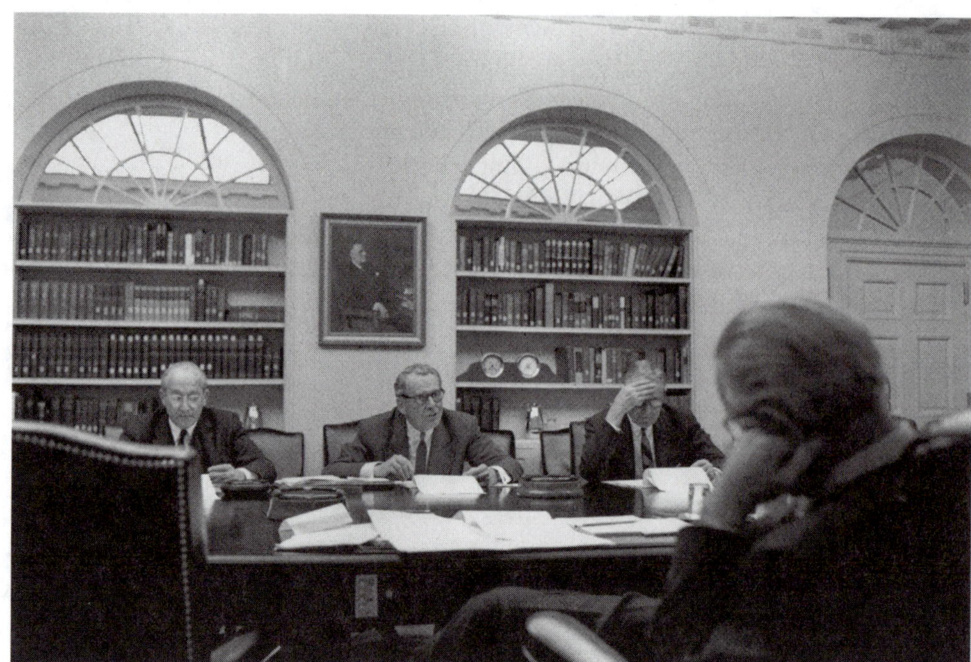

L-R: Walt Rostow, National Security Council, new Secretary of Defense Clark Clifford, Secretary of Navy Paul Nitze, President Johnson. Lyndon B. Johnson Library

one significant role in U.S. politics, however, in the New Hampshire primary.

December 1, 1967

France vetoes the admission of Great Britain into the European Economic Community (Common Market).

Prior to the British application for Common Market membership on May 11, the question of joining was a controversial political issue in England. France objected to the membership because it wanted Great Britain to end its British Commonwealth trade agreements before being admitted. For the second time, France opposed British membership in Europe's common market.

See January 29, 1963.

1968

January 16, 1968

The United Kingdom withdraws its forces from the Persian Gulf and the Far East.

The British government retreated further from its previous imperial commitments east of Suez, a not unusual decision inasmuch as its east coast African colonies had gained their independence between 1958 and 1967. Eventually, the United States would assume obligations in these regions.

January 23, 1968

North Korea seizes the USS *Pueblo*, a navy electronic spy ship, in international waters.

During the night of January 22–23, a North Korean submarine chaser and three patrol boats challenged the *Pueblo* and boarded the U.S. ship with an armed party. North Korea claimed the *Pueblo* was seven miles offshore. According to the Pueblo's commander, the ship was 15 nautical miles from shore, outside North Korea's 12-mile limit. During the foray, one American was killed and four injured. As a surveillance ship, the *Pueblo* was virtually unarmed and unprotected. North Korea also took 82 Americans captive. To obtain their release, President Johnson used diplomatic channels. Other more drastic methods were considered by the National Security Council but appeared too risky to the lives of the captives. Although Johnson sent 350 airplanes to bases in South Korea to deter further aggression, he worked through the United Nations, the Kremlin, and other nations to finally obtain the captives' release. It took

11 months to gain the freedom of the *Pueblo's* officers and crew.

January 26, 1968

General Westmoreland's year-end report for 1967 emphasizes the desperation of the Communist enemy in Vietnam.

Accurately or not, the U.S. commander in Vietnam and the U.S. ambassador to Saigon, Ellsworth Bunker, had been issuing favorable reports. In November 1967, the two leading U.S. figures in South Vietnam had visited Washington to spread the good word about U.S. successes. Before congressional committees and such luncheon groups as the National Press Club, they characterized the Vietnam struggle as nearing a victory. According to Westmoreland, the United States would soon "weaken the enemy and strengthen our friends until we have become superfluous." On invitations to the 1967 New Year's Eve party at the embassy in Saigon, the party message read, "Come and see the light at the end of the tunnel," the code words for winning the war.

Just before Westmoreland composed his annual report, the North Vietnamese attacked exactly where the U.S. military preferred, at Khe Sanh on the strategic border between Laos, South Vietnam, and the 17th parallel. Attacking on January 21, the North Vietnamese fought the type of battle favorable to U.S. firepower. In the north, away from urban areas, American forces could exploit their arsenals without concern for endangering the South Vietnamese population. Thus, Westmoreland's January 26 report reflected an added touch of optimism. He wrote that the enemy was "resorting to desperation tactics" to attain a "military/psychological victory" and had failed in these attempts since October 1967. From November to January 26, this optimistic news enabled President Johnson to look forward eagerly to the 1968 presidential campaign.

However, the euphoria reaped contrary results. Four days after Westmoreland reported, the Communists launched the Tet offensive.

January 30–31, 1968

The Tet Offensive begins in South Vietnam.

In retrospect, the North Vietnamese attack on Khe Sanh on January 20 had been only diversionary. While U.S. forces rushed north to engage the enemy at Khe Sanh, the Communists initiated their Tet offensive farther south. Its initial assaults appeared successful and, thereby, damaged Johnson's credibility for having publicized the recent optimistic reports of U.S. successes. During the first days of Tet in its attacks on Saigon, the Vietcong hit the U.S. embassy, the Presidential Palace, the South Vietnamese military headquarters, and Saigon's air bases. Although they were supposed to have been subdued, the Vietcong soon appeared to be everywhere. Communist troops overran Vietnam's former capital city and religious centers in Hue and raided 39 provincial capitals and 76 other cities and towns.

Unfortunately for North Vietnam's General Giap, the South Vietnamese did not rise up to join the Communists, as he had believed they would. The southern populace was apathetic to both Communist and American appeals. During Tet, this helped the United States because without their anticipated local support, the Communists had to withdraw or be driven from the cities after February 13. Giap had miscalculated. Using Mao's doctrine of protracted

Smoke covers areas of Saigon during attacks by the Vietcong. National Archives

war, Giap believed the time had come to employ his rural armies to gain control of the urban areas, but Tet 1968 was not the time.

As a result, the Tet offensive eventually cost the Communists heavily. It made new enemies for Communists in the South, and it caused the loss of 45,000 Communist soldiers and much equipment. Khe Sanh and Hue held out for several weeks until mid-March, but documents captured from Giap's forces showed that Tet failed to meet Giap's basic objectives. Nevertheless, if Tet proved to be a blow to the Communists, it was also a disaster for the American perspectives on the war. Although the full implications of Tet 1968 may always be controversial, Tet probably paved the way for both North Vietnam and President Johnson to initiate negotiations.

March 12, 1968

Senator McCarthy nearly defeats President Johnson in the New Hampshire primary.

Senator McCarthy's near victory surprised Johnson and most observers because the "children's crusade" of antiwar volunteers had not been well organized after November 30, 1967. Moreover, Johnson's campaign experts had predicted an easy victory with landslide figures of 70 to 80 percent. Johnson obtained only 49.5 percent of the vote to McCarthy's 42.2 percent. Political pundits interpreted McCarthy's near victory as a blow to the president's Vietnam policy.

March 16, 1968

Senator Robert Kennedy of New York announces he will campaign for the presidential nomination.

In November 1967, some Democratic liberals had urged Kennedy to campaign against Johnson, but he refused. Traditionally, party loyalty ruled that insiders should not challenge an incumbent president, and Kennedy's advisers preferred to wait until 1972. McCarthy's near victory in New Hampshire on March 12 and the disaster that appeared to befall the United States in the Tet offensive of January-February convinced Kennedy that he should challenge the president. Kennedy's candidacy surprised and dismayed Johnson and probably was one factor that influenced the president's decision to withdraw as a nominee on March 31.

March 25–26, 1968

Johnson meets with the "wise men" to decide future Vietnam policy after the Tet debacle.

North Vietnam's Tet offensive, Eugene McCarthy's near victory in New Hampshire, and Robert Kennedy's announced candidacy left President Johnson in a quandary. The JCS wanted more troops and more extensive bombing in Vietnam, while a report by the new secretary of defense, Clark Clifford, sought a compromise. Finally, economic problems over taxes and an unfavorable trade balance added to Johnson's problems. To help him decide on a course of action, Clifford persuaded the president to convene the "wise men," his trusted advisers from outside the bureaucracy. The Tet offensive had been quelled by mid-March, but its psychological effects on the American public had been disastrous. The optimistic reports of Westmoreland and Bunker at the end of 1967 had led Americans to believe that the Communists were nearly wiped out, but Tet demonstrated that the Communists' fighting capabilities remained substantial. Johnson compounded this problem because two days after the Tet offensive began, he asserted that the U.S. military had prior knowledge of the attacks and would immediately counterattack. His analysis was wrong. For the next 10 days, Communist advances continued and Hue was captured. Johnson lost the backing of American moderates during the Tet offensive. In the newspapers, cartoonists poked fun at the president, depicting him weeping crocodile tears because of destruction in Vietnam. Humorist Art Buchwald wrote a parody of Johnson as General George Custer just before the Little Big Horn massacre. Custer (Johnson) asserted: "We have the Sioux on the run," because the battle "had just turned the corner" and he could see "the light at the end of the tunnel." Of course, the massacre of Custer's men followed.

There were other causes of U.S. disillusionment in Vietnam. A U.S. army major at Ben Tri remarked: "It became necessary to destroy the town to save it." *Life* magazine published the gruesome picture of Saigon's police chief shooting a Vietcong prisoner in cold blood on the street. The president's press secretary claimed that Walter Cronkite, America's most prominent television news anchorman, had turned against Johnson when he stated "we weren't winning the war," despite Johnson's statements to the contrary.

Reportedly Johnson remarked, "Well, if I've lost Cronkite, I've lost Middle America."

Unlike Cronkite, the military officers' reaction to Tet was to seek fewer restraints on their battle tactics. As early as February 3, the JCS asked Johnson to give air force commanders complete authority to select targets. Generals Wheeler and Westmoreland wanted 206,000 additional troops as well as the mobilization of all military reserves. Wheeler's mobilization request alarmed Johnson. The president knew the difference between a limited military action and an all-out World War II–type war. He was never prepared to support the latter in South Vietnam because that nation was not that vital to the United States. Thus, as previously, Johnson rejected proposals to call up the National Guard and reserve units. Wheeler's request so disturbed Johnson that he asked secretary of defense designate, Clifford, to organize a committee to study the problem "from A to Z."

The Clifford Committee's report of March 4 further startled the president. Unlike McNamara, who the president believed had been tainted with Kennedy's influence, Clark Clifford was a longtime Washington friend of Johnson. In November, Clifford had counseled Johnson to follow his own policy, not McNamara's. Yet between November and March, Clifford changed his perspective on Vietnam. Looking back later, Clifford remembered that his first doubts about U.S. policy in Vietnam had been planted during the summer of 1967. During a trip to Asian nations, Clifford discovered that none of America's allies shared Washington's great fear of Communism in Vietnam. His requests for more troops to conduct the war in Vietnam had largely been shunned by the leaders of Australia, New Zealand, Thailand, the Philippines, and South Korea. Each of them sent token forces to South Vietnam only to placate the United States, not because they feared Hanoi's victory. By March 1968, Clifford altered his Vietnam analysis completely, largely because of the Tet offensive, General Wheeler's request for greater military control, and the findings of the policy review board he headed from February 26 to March 4. During the review, Clifford became familiar with the civilian-military division inside the Pentagon. He talked with and studied the computer data used by McNamara's advisers—Paul Nitze, Paul C. Warnke, and Alain Enthoven. He began to grasp the political dimensions of South Vietnam's problem, realizing that U.S. military strength could not solve the country's internal problems. At the same time, he heard total war opinions of Generals Wheeler and Taylor, and National Security Adviser Walter Rostow, as they sought full mobilization of U.S. forces.

The Clifford Committee's report of March 4 represented a compromise, not the new attitudes of its chairman. Because it was a composite of the civilian and military proposals, the March 4 report simply made Johnson less certain of how to proceed. While Johnson pondered the report and observed the final defeat of the North Vietnam's Tet offensive, he experienced a new crisis during mid-March—an economic one. Johnson's attempted guns-and-butter economy began to come unhinged by early 1968. In 1967, the president sought an income tax surcharge to finance his programs, but the Democratic leaders in Congress rejected the tax. In January 1968, Johnson again asked Congress for a 10 percent tax surcharge. This time Southern Democrats, led by Wilbur Mills of the House Committee on Ways and Means, preferred to spend more on the war but less on Johnson's social programs as the best method to cut the budget deficits. In March, the tax conflict became complicated by the rapid decline in the value of the dollar on the gold market. The U.S. international trade balance had been experiencing trouble since the 1960s. The Kennedy Round of trade and tariff reforms tried to band-aid the problem, but by 1967 the imbalance became more acute. During the last quarter of 1967, U.S. trade imbalances were $7 billion and this trend continued into 1968.

The Tet offensive caused a flurry of international speculation, and during the first 10 weeks of 1968, the dollar's value declined on the gold market by $327 million. To stem the gold dollar decline in March, the United States and its European allies arranged temporary relief by buying dollars to raise their value artificially. Because other "free world" currencies were pegged to the dollar, U.S. economic shortfalls affected the currency and budget of many countries. The instability of the dollar was temporarily rectified in March, but the international financial community informed the United States that it must correct its budget and tax problem. Both the "Great Escalation" and the Great Society were jeopardized by financial problems in 1968.

Johnson's call upon the wise men to meet on March 25 came at a difficult time militarily, diplomatically, economically, and with regard to domestic dissent. Clifford had urged Johnson to consider a bombing halt and negotiations; the wise men, he said, could focus on this issue as the central problem requiring an answer. Clifford handled the wise men's March meeting discreetly. For their first meeting on March 25, Clifford gave Johnson's advisers a briefing at the State Department. During this session, Clifford familiarized them with detailed computer data prepared by Nitze, Enthoven, and Warnke, as well as with the military proposals of Wheeler and Westmoreland. Their data were updated to reflect the Tet offensive information. As a result of the March 25 briefing, Johnson's White House meeting with the advisers took a divergent turn on March 26. During a breakfast session, the advisers heard an up-to-date report on Tet by General Wheeler, who had just flown in from Saigon at 6:00 A.M. Wheeler was optimistic. Tet had damaged the Communist forces. The South Vietnamese army had fought "commendably." Although Wheeler avoided mentioning his request for full mobilization, which he knew Johnson disliked, he asked for only 13,000 troops to aid the pacification effort. Johnson had already agreed to send an additional 30,000 combat troops. Following Wheeler's report, General Taylor spoke strongly in favor of escalation of the bombing targets and of providing more combat troops for Vietnam. But Taylor stood almost alone.

Most of the wise men told Johnson that a new counterinsurgency strategy was necessary. The military, they believed, had prevented the fall of South Vietnam. Now the United States should stabilize its combat role by emphasizing internal reform in that country. In addition, they said, the political divisions and dissent at home were serious disturbances of national harmony. Although each adviser emphasized different concepts, the same men who backed the military attrition strategy in November now supported the Pentagon civilians who stressed counterinsurgency. Johnson was distraught. Someone, he said, "had poisoned the well." The men whose opinions Johnson most respected had changed their views, but Johnson could not believe that Tet alone had done this. Clifford later remarked: "The meeting with the Wise Men served the purpose that I hoped it would. It really shook the president." At first, Johnson was angry. He asked to hear the briefing that the wise men received at the State Department on March 25. He learned they had been fully informed of both the civilian and the military perspectives in the Pentagon. He also learned that his good friend Clark Clifford agreed not with Wheeler but with McNamara. Johnson was resilient, however. His long political experience permitted him to change his policy.

March 31, 1968

Johnson announces dramatic changes: a bombing halt, a request for North Vietnam to negotiate, and his withdrawal as a 1968 presidential candidate.

Sometime after the wise men's meeting of March 25–26, the president decided to salvage what fame he might as a statesman. Although he never admitted any past errors nor directly proposed the counterinsurgency strategy desired by McNamara and Clifford, he changed the terms of U.S. involvement in Vietnam between March 31, 1968 and January 1969. The change began with a television address on March 31. The most dramatic part of Johnson's address came last, his decision not to run for reelection. Exactly when Johnson decided not to be a nominee is not certain. In his memoirs, the president said he had decided early after 1964 but waited for the right moment to announce it. Various sources indicate he mentioned retirement between 1965 and 1968.

On March 31, Johnson believed his decision to retire would be a special signal of his sincerity in seeking negotiations with Hanoi. The proposal to talk would not be seen as a political tactic. The other two announcements on March 31 were vital to developments in Vietnam, demonstrating that Johnson had not wavered since 1965 in his determination to fight a limited war there. First, he announced that U.S. aircraft and naval ships would no longer attack North Vietnam except in the "area of the demilitarized zone," that is, between the 17th and 20th parallels. He called on Ho Chi Minh to "respond positively and favorably" by agreeing to negotiate. Second, the president announced the moderate increase of U.S. troop strength in South Vietnam. This moderate increase (30,000) would protect South Vietnam. Our first priority, Johnson said, would be to improve South Vietnam's ability to defend itself militarily and politically. Although he did not specify this, his statement reflected the counterinsurgency policy that the civilians in the Defense Department had been advocating. Without saying so, Johnson ended the policy of escalation that governed the years 1965–1968. He privately rejected the JCS's full mobilization plan and retained presidential control of the war to attain political objectives. His subsequent activity in striving to open negotiations with Hanoi indicated both his presidential control and his desire to make certain that North Vietnam did not perceive his March 31 speech as a sign of weakness.

May 13, 1968

U.S. and North Vietnamese delegates open discussions in Paris to talk about negotiations.

Although on April 4 North Vietnamese officials denounced Johnson's speech of March 31 as an imperialist plot, they secretly contacted the United States to indicate their willingness to talk. They wanted the United States to stop all bombing and other acts of war, but Johnson refused. Finally, the two sides agreed to talk about conditions for beginning talks. They held their first session at Paris on May 13. W. Averell Harriman represented the United States at Paris; Xuan Thuy represented North Vietnam. Neither the Vietcong nor the Saigon regime had direct representation.

June 5, 1968

Robert F. Kennedy is assassinated on the day of his presidential primary victory in California.

Kennedy was shot by the Palestinian extremist Sirhan B. Sirhan, who opposed Kennedy's pro-Israel views. His death left Vice President Hubert Humphrey as the likely nominee.

July 1, 1968

Nuclear Non-Proliferation Treaty signed and, with other components, forms the basis of nuclear non-proliferation.

In 1965 the U.N. General Assembly urged the Eighteen-Nation Disarmament Committee (ENDC) to devise a treaty structured to end the proliferation of nuclear weapons. According to the General Assembly an agreement should rest on "an acceptable balance of mutual responsibilities and obligations of the nuclear and non-nuclear powers," including the continued progress on nuclear disarmament. In 1965, both the Americans and Soviets submitted draft proposals that were reconciled by 1967. The nonaligned and non-nuclear members of the ENDC wanted equal responsibilities of all nuclear parties and to stop increasing their quantity and quality of nuclear weapons if non-nuclear nations suspended their efforts to obtain nuclear weapons. The non-nuclear nations urged nuclear power to take steps in the following order: (1) a comprehensive nuclear test ban; (2) a halt to the production of fissionable material for weapons use; (3) a halt to the building of, and progressive reduction of, nuclear weapons and delivery systems; (4) outlawing the use of nuclear weapons; and (5) superpower assurances for the security of non-nuclear states. Although the nuclear powers only pledged "good faith" in seeking nuclear disarmament "at an early date," the non-nuclear powers accepted the superpower pledges.

On July 1, 1968, the Nuclear Non-Proliferation Treaty (NPT) was signed in the White House by the United States, the USSR, Britain and 50 other countries. Later, France and China also signed the treaty. Eventually, 150 nations signed the NPT. By the 1990s, only Israel, India, and Pakistan had joined the nuclear club; North Korea and Iran became possible members. The U.S. Senate ratified the treaty on March 13, 1969.

The NPT was the centerpiece of Cold War nonproliferation efforts that includes: (1) the International Atomic Energy Agency (1957) to monitor peaceful uses of atomic energy; (2) the Partial Nuclear Test Ban Treaty (1963); (3) various Nuclear Weapons-Free Zones; and (4) the Nuclear Suppliers Group (1974). Together these comprise an arms control regime at least equal to the superpower's strategic arms limitation treaties.

July 1, 1968

U.S.-Soviets will discuss nuclear arms limitations, but the meeting falls victim to the Czech crisis.

President Johnson sought U.S.-Soviet talks about nuclear arms limitations since he met with Alexsei Kosygin at Glassboro, New Jersey, from June 22 to 25, 1961. Kosygin was initially unprepared to encourage possible negotiations since the matter was still being discussed in Moscow. On June 30, 1968, Kosygin informed Johnson that a Soviet broadcast on July 1 would announce that U.S.-Soviet negotiations on arms limitations would be held in the near future. Thus, the same day Johnson signed the NPT, he announced future negotiations to consider both ABM and ICBM limitations. On August 19, the Soviet Ambassador to the United States Anatoly Dobrynin informed Secretary of State Dean Rusk that arms limitation talks could begin on October 15, 1968, and President Johnson could announce his trip to Moscow to inaugurate the arms talks.

Unfortunately, Johnson never made the trip. On August 20 at 8:00 A.M., Dobrynin informed Johnson that Warsaw Pact nations, including the USSR, had accepted a Czechoslovak "invitation" to end a "conspiracy" against the Czech "social order." Although Dobrynin's message concluded that the Czech events should not prevent Johnson's October visit nor damage U.S.-Soviet relations, Johnson disagreed. Secretary Rusk informed Dobrynin that the president could not visit Moscow because of Warsaw Pact members' intervention in Czechoslovakia. The ABM and ICBM limitation negotiations were delayed until Richard Nixon became president.

See November 17, 1969.

July 1, 1968

President Thieu accepts responsibility for the conduct of the American CIA's Operation Phoenix to eliminate the Vietcong's leadership infrastructure (VCI).

This project had been designed by the CIA as a means of reducing the Vietcong's operational ability in an area after the United States had withdrawn its troops. Thieu's officials would arrest and punish captured Vietcong who directed the insurgency efforts in South Vietnam. About 50 U.S. civilian CIA advisers and 600 U.S. military men assisted Thieu's government. The clandestine Phoenix operations used strong-arm methods to eliminate the Vietcong. Paid informants were recruited, normal search and arrest procedures were avoided, and torture was used to interrogate suspects. There was a large number of killings in the process.

Other Vietcong suspects were imprisoned or "rallied" to support the Saigon government. In 1970 information on Phoenix was leaked to American journalists, and the morality of its methods became controversial. Although the White House–CIA view was that the Vietcong were terrorists who deserved their fate, the critics charged that Phoenix methods were not only wrong but also punished or "neutralized" many innocent people. Reporters uncovered a number of gruesome stories of assassination and misinformation that caused persons to be killed because of a grudge or of homes broken into at night. Robert Komer's 1971 study of Operation Phoenix, *The Lessons of Vietnam*, concluded that although 20,000 Vietcong leaders were allegedly killed or otherwise neutralized, the project was a "largely ineffective effort."

August 20, 1968

Warsaw Pact forces invade Czechoslovakia: The Brezhnev Doctrine.

Although Moscow accepted Alexander Dubcek as Czechoslovakia's leader early in 1968, the Soviet Presidium became alarmed by Dubcek's reforms during what became known as the "Prague Spring." These reforms included the ending of Communist censorship, the abolishing of the secret police, and the relieving of restrictions on non-Communist political parties. According to Stephen F. Cohen's *Rethinking the Soviet Experience* (1985), Dubcek's "socialism with a human face" resembled Khrushchev's reform program after 1956. In 1964, Leonid Brezhnev and Aleksey Kosygin ousted Khrushchev, abandoned his reforms, and adopted conservative practices including "the preeminent symbol of the past, Stalin himself."

Between 1992 and 1998, the *Cold War History Project's Bulletins* published documents declassified from Communist archives in the Soviet Union, East Germany, Poland, and Ukraine. These documents indicated that Communist leaders in those countries feared Dubcek's reforms would spill over into their nations. In addition, reports from hard line Communists in Czechoslovakia alerted Soviet leadership regarding Dubcek's "dangerous" reforms. Because the Soviets had few military bases in Czechoslovakia, Brezhnev wanted to place more troops and Soviet controlled nuclear weapons on Czech territory. Previously, Dubcek had refused a "temporary deployment" of Soviet forces as part of the Warsaw Pact strategy. After Dubcek rejected several of Brezhnev's offers to compromise, the Soviet leaders decided to invade with 300,000 Soviet and Warsaw Pact troops, excepting Romania. When they invaded on August 20, Warsaw Pact forces easily overcame the Czech defenders. According to the declassified documents, the invading Communist forces killed 100 armed Czechoslovakian citizens and seriously wounded 335. In addition, 433 unarmed Czechoslovak civilians were killed, although they had opposed the invaders. Warsaw Pact forces experienced only one death from combat, while another 19 were killed in traffic accidents or by "friendly fire."

In addition to delaying the arms limitation talks with the United States, the Soviet invasion heralded the Brezhnev Doctrine, under which the Soviet Union arrogated to itself the right to intervene militarily against any Warsaw Pact socialist state. Between 1968 and 1991, 75,000 to 80,000 Soviet troops remained on Czech soil. In early 1969, Dubcek resigned as Chairman of the Czechoslovakian Communist Party and was replaced by Gustav Husak.

August 28, 1968

The Democratic Party convention nominates Hubert Humphrey for president while police fight demonstrators in downtown Chicago.

While the Democratic Party divided seriously on foreign policy during the convention, 11,900 Chicago police, 7,500 members of the Illinois National Guard, and about 1,000 FBI and Secret Service agents tried to protect the delegates and the city from radical groups. Right-wing Democrats did run another candidate in the Dixiecrat style of 1948. Governor George Wallace of Alabama formed the American Independent Party.

October 31, 1968

The United States and North Vietnam agree to conduct formal negotiations for peace; President Johnson halts all bombing in North Vietnam; Hanoi agrees to stop rocket attacks and raids on cities in South Vietnam.

From May 13 to October 30, Johnson's personal representative Averell Harriman and North Vietnamese diplomat Xuan Thuy pursued a joint process of formal and secret talks to try to arrange a cease-fire and the beginning of formal truce agreements. Unofficially, these talks were opposed by the JCS in Washington and Thieu's government in Saigon, both of whom thought that peace discussions and bombing restrictions benefited Hanoi. President Johnson tended to support the JCS view that Thieu had to be satisfied and grow stronger. Harriman and the Democratic presidential nominee, Hubert Humphrey, wanted a more complete turnaround in U.S. policy, hoping for a return to the divided Vietnam of 1954. They believed the first steps in this process were to stop the bombing, start negotiations, and move to a complete cease-fire in Vietnam. Until October 15 Johnson would not accept any concession in addition to those he had made on March 31. The talks had become stymied by October, indicating that Johnson would not end his administration on a positive note unless he agreed to halt the bombing. To accomplish this, Harriman got Hanoi to agree that Thieu's government could have a direct role in the peace negotiations while the National Liberation Front (NLF?) represented the Vietcong. Having arranged this compromise, Johnson reported on October 31 that all bombing would cease in North Vietnam; that is, the bombing from the 17th to the 20th parallel, which had continued after March 31. The president announced that peace talks would begin, involving four parties but with two sides in negotiations: the United States/South Vietnam as one side; the NLF/Hanoi as the second. On the negative side, there was no cease-fire or truce. Negotiations would proceed while fighting continued, except for the restrictions against Rolling Thunder's bombing of the North and Hanoi's attacks on South Vietnam's cities. In line with these agreements, Johnson ordered the bombing halt that North Vietnam required before the peace talks would begin. South Vietnam's President Thieu had privately agreed to participate in the talks after Hanoi promised to respect the demilitarized zone (DMZ) and not attack South Vietnamese cities. Yet the peace talks never took place.

Two days after the bombing halt began on October 31, Thieu announced the South Vietnamese would not take part in the talks because they could not sit down with the Vietcong. Thieu's reasons for refusing to participate quickly became controversial. Nixon claimed the bombing halt was negotiated for political reasons to help Humphrey's candidacy. In fact, Nixon had his campaign manager contact Anna Chan Chennault, the Chinese widow of the wartime hero General Claire Chennault, to tell President Thieu that Nixon would "see that Vietnam gets better treatment from me than under the Democrats." Democratic candidate Humphrey had told Thieu that prolonged U.S. aid was "not in the cards." Although historians such as Stephen Ambrose's *Nixon: The Triumph of a Politician* (1989) offered much evidence of Nixon's deceptive practice in persuading Thieu to reject peace talks, Anthony Summers's *The Arrogance of Power: The Secret World of Richard Nixon* (2000) provides evidence that Nixon secretly sabotaged the peace talks then kept the fighting going for five more years, with more than 20,000 Americans and about 1 million Vietnamese being killed during that period. In 1969, Nixon renewed negotiations with the North Vietnamese.

November 5, 1968

Richard Nixon is elected president.

Nixon had won an easy Republican nomination for president, winning many primaries by cultivating a new image of maturity after his political loss to Kennedy in 1960 and the California governorship in 1962. The split in the Democratic Party over Vietnam policy caused many liberal Democrats to boycott the election. In addition, George Wallace's party cost Humphrey votes in the South. Although Humphrey broke with Johnson on Vietnam in October, his late surge in public opinion polls came too late for a victory. In the November 5 ballot, Nixon's popular vote was 31,785,148; Humphrey's was 31,274,503; Wallace received 9,901,151. The electoral college vote was Nixon, 301; Humphrey, 191; Wallace, 46. The Democratic Party retained control of Congress.

1969

January 20, 1969

Nixon's inaugural address indicates his desire to change U.S. policy to more "realistic" diplomacy.

Although Nixon had explained some of his foreign policy views in an October 1967 article for the quarterly *Foreign Affairs*, his inaugural address and his selection of Henry Kissinger as National Security Adviser led a wider group of persons with international interests to realize that a major new approach to U.S. foreign relations was to be attempted. Nixon's inaugural speech outlined some of the attitudes of the power politics that the Nixon Doctrine later asserted more definitely. Thus, the president stated:

> After a period of confrontation, we are entering an era of negotiation.... We seek an open world—open to ideas, open to the exchange of goods and people—a world in which no people, great or small, will live in angry isolation.... We cannot expect to make everyone our friend, but we can try to make no one our enemy.... [But] let us leave no doubt that we will be as strong as we need to be for as long as we need to be.

Kissinger agreed with Nixon's basic policy views on balance-of-power diplomacy, being a scholar of the two leading nineteenth-century power balance diplomats, Prince Metternich of Austria and Otto von Bismarck of Germany. Kissinger and Nixon

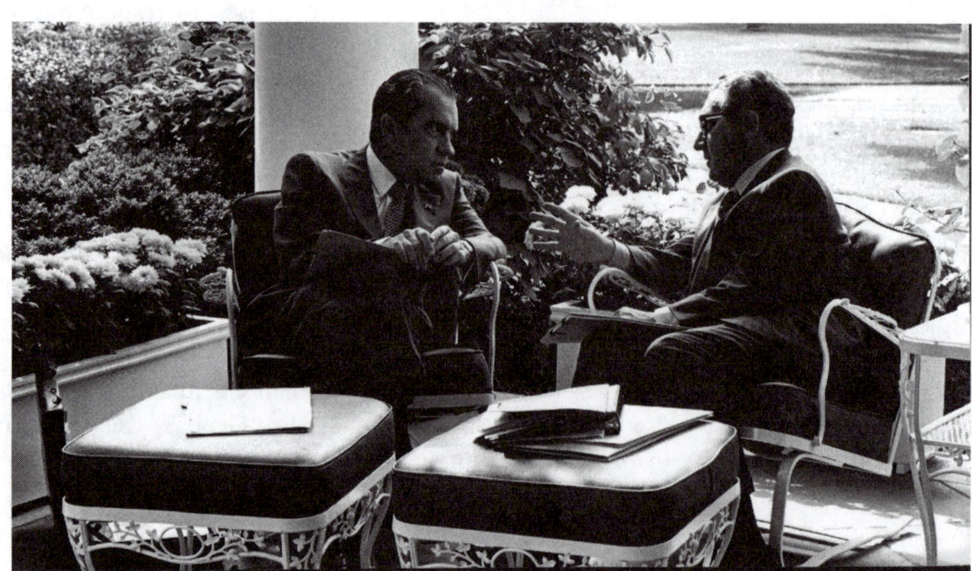

President Richard Nixon and his National Security Advisor Henry Kissinger discuss policy issues. National Archives

moved immediately on January 20 to give the White House direct access to American ambassadors abroad. He and Nixon drafted messages to the ambassadors and personal letters to 15 leaders of foreign governments, including the Soviet Union's Leonid Brezhnev. Kissinger obtained Rogers's consent to directly address the various ambassadors, often informally as a "back channel" method of operation. For the usages of the "back channel" with Nixon and other presidents, see Anatoly Dobrynin, *In Confidence: Moscow's Ambassador to America's Six Cold War Presidents* (1995).

January 21, 1969

William Pierce Rogers is commissioned as Secretary of State in President Nixon's cabinet.

Nixon selected Rogers not for his foreign policy expertise but for his talents at handling Congress and the press. President Nixon made it clear he was going to direct foreign policy, and chose Henry Kissinger as his National Security Adviser to centralize international policy-making in the White House. Consequently, in decision-making, the State Department was generally bypassed and Nixon and Kissinger consulted Rogers only when he could be useful.

February 23, 1969

Nixon emphasizes his desire to consult more with America's European allies as he leaves on a one-week visit to European nations.

When the president embarked on his European trip on February 23, he told dignitaries at Andrews Air Force Base that he believed progress in settling world affairs made it "necessary to consult with our friends." The grave problems he wished to discuss with other leaders included Vietnam, the Middle East, monetary affairs, and others. Nixon's itinerary included Brussels, where he visited King Baudouin and the NATO Council; London, to renew assurance of the Anglo-American "special relation'; Bonn and West Berlin; four days with de Gaulle in Paris; and Rome and Vatican City to meet Italian leaders and Pope Paul VI. Nixon returned to the United States on March 2, having launched his term of office with a gesture he hoped would gain better U.S. relations with its European allies.

March 2, 1969

Soviet and Chinese troops clash on the border at the Ussuri River.

This was one of several border skirmishes in 1969–1970 that indicated the nadir of the Sino-Soviet relations. The Sino-Soviet split had began in 1960 (see December 5, 1960) and escalated when their negotiations on border issues were terminated by the Chinese in 1964. From 1964 to February 1969, there were several minor border clashes before the attacks escalated between March 2 and the end of August 1969. On March 2, Chinese forces carried out plans to ambush Soviet troops and killed 31 Russians. The Soviets retaliated on March 15 in a battle that engaged large numbers of troops with both sides losing many soldiers. Between April and August, there were frequent attacks along the border, the most serious attacks being on the Xinjiang-Kazakhstan border.

As early as March 21, Soviet Prime Minister Kosygin tried to reopen border negotiations but Mao refused to resume talks that had been broken off in 1964. Eventually on September 3, Kosygin and Chinese Foreign Minister Chou En-lai attended the Vietnamese leader Ho Chi Minh's funeral, but rather than discussing the border issues at that time, Kosygin agreed to visit Beijing on September 11. Subsequently on October 7, Mao announced the two sides would resume the 1964 talks of border issues.

March 14, 1969

Nixon requests the approval of Congress for the Safeguard ABM system.

Early in March, Kissinger's NSC staff completed NSSM-3, a study of the U.S. military posture regarding the strategic arms limitation talks (SALT), which President Johnson had wanted to begin with the Soviet Union prior to the invasion of Czechoslovakia. Relying on NSSM-3, Nixon decided to seek ABM funding to buy time prior to the SALT negotiations and to gain a bargaining chip against the USSR's ABM defenses under construction around Moscow. As a result, on March 14 Nixon announced he would ask Congress for a Safeguard ABM system to replace President Johnson's plans for a "thin line" ABM Sentinel system allegedly for defense from a Chinese nuclear attack. Because Secretary of State Rusk and President Johnson had attempted to solicit better relations with Moscow in 1967–1968, they had announced that the Chinese "menace" required the Sentinel ABM defense.

Nixon's Safeguard ABMs would begin their deployment around two Minuteman ICBM sites in North Dakota, increasing further deployments as warranted by Soviet responses. By defending America's second-strike capability at the Minuteman bases, Nixon said the United States demonstrated it did not have a first-strike nuclear strategy. The second-strike strategy required that U.S. ICBMs be able to survive a Soviet first strike to retaliate in kind. Thus, Nixon argued, the Soviet ABM defense of Moscow was creating a first-strike capacity because the Soviet defenses of their cities protected them from the U.S. second strike aimed at the centers of Soviet population. Here, as was frequently the case, the United States grossly overestimated the effectiveness of Soviet ABM systems.

In reality, the rhetoric of first- and second-strike tactics partly obscured the fact that, as Secretary of Defense McNamara had indicated in 1967, MAD had given each side sufficient weaponry and warheads to destroy much of the world should a nuclear war begin. Nevertheless, in the nuclear limitation game that the United States and the USSR played from 1969 to 1979, ABM and other tactical claims and preparations became part of the complex methodology by which the United States and the Soviet Union sought to stabilize their nuclear arms competition.

March 18, 1969

President Nixon orders the first secret bombing attacks on Cambodia.

President Nixon's secret orders to extend the Vietnam War into neutral Cambodia led to the first in a series of bombings between March 18, 1968, and April 1970. The secrecy of the operations was maintained until 1973, when congressional investigations followed a report on the operation by Major Hal Knight, a radar officer near Saigon, who objected because he thought the falsification of records violated Article 107 of the Military Code of Justice. Nixon, Kissinger, and other high U.S. officials had conspired to keep information on this extension of the war from Congress and the public. Prince Sihanouk of Cambodia and Soviet, North Vietnamese, and Chinese officials and most Western European leaders knew about it, but not the American public. Nixon did not want to risk the criticism of dissenters at home. Or, as some analysts claim, the secrecy was to demonstrate to Moscow President Nixon's willingness to use American power and to do so secretly to accomplish his goals.

The Cambodian bombings had been recommended for some time by U.S. military officers who contended that Communist "sanctuaries" in eastern Cambodia were the principal base of supplies for North Vietnamese and Vietcong forces in the southern delta area. President Johnson had tried to obtain Prince Sihanouk's permission to eliminate the sanctuaries, but he would not permit the Pentagon to attack without Cambodian approval. In January 1969, Nixon asked the Joint Chiefs for recommendations on Cambodia, indicating his willingness to violate Cambodian neutrality if necessary. On February 9, General Abrams, the U.S. Commander in Vietnam, recommended "a short-duration, concentrated B-52 attack of up to 60 sorties" to destroy the central headquarters of the Communists (COSVN) in eastern Cambodia. Pentagon intelligence located the headquarters at Base Area 353 in the "fishhook" area of Cambodia, which geographically jutted into South Vietnam northwest of Saigon. Abrams believed that the B-52 attacks would minimize the violation of Cambodian territory to one minute per sortie and that few Cambodian civilians would be killed. The destruction of COSVN, Abrams said, would "have a very significant effect on enemy operations throughout South Vietnam."

President Nixon approved Abrams's proposal but insisted on strict secrecy, objecting to Secretary of Defense Laird's desire to inform congressional leaders. To maintain secrecy, a "dual reporting" system was devised by the Pentagon. The B-52s would leave Guam for Vietnamese targets. Once over South Vietnam, ground radar controllers would redirect the planes to Cambodia without the pilot or navigator realizing the location of the new target. The radar controllers knew, however, and would send two reports to General Abrams, one for the original targets and one for the revised target. Officially, the bombs fell on Vietnam. Major Knight was a radar controller who had first appealed to his superiors to amend the false documents. When they refused to follow

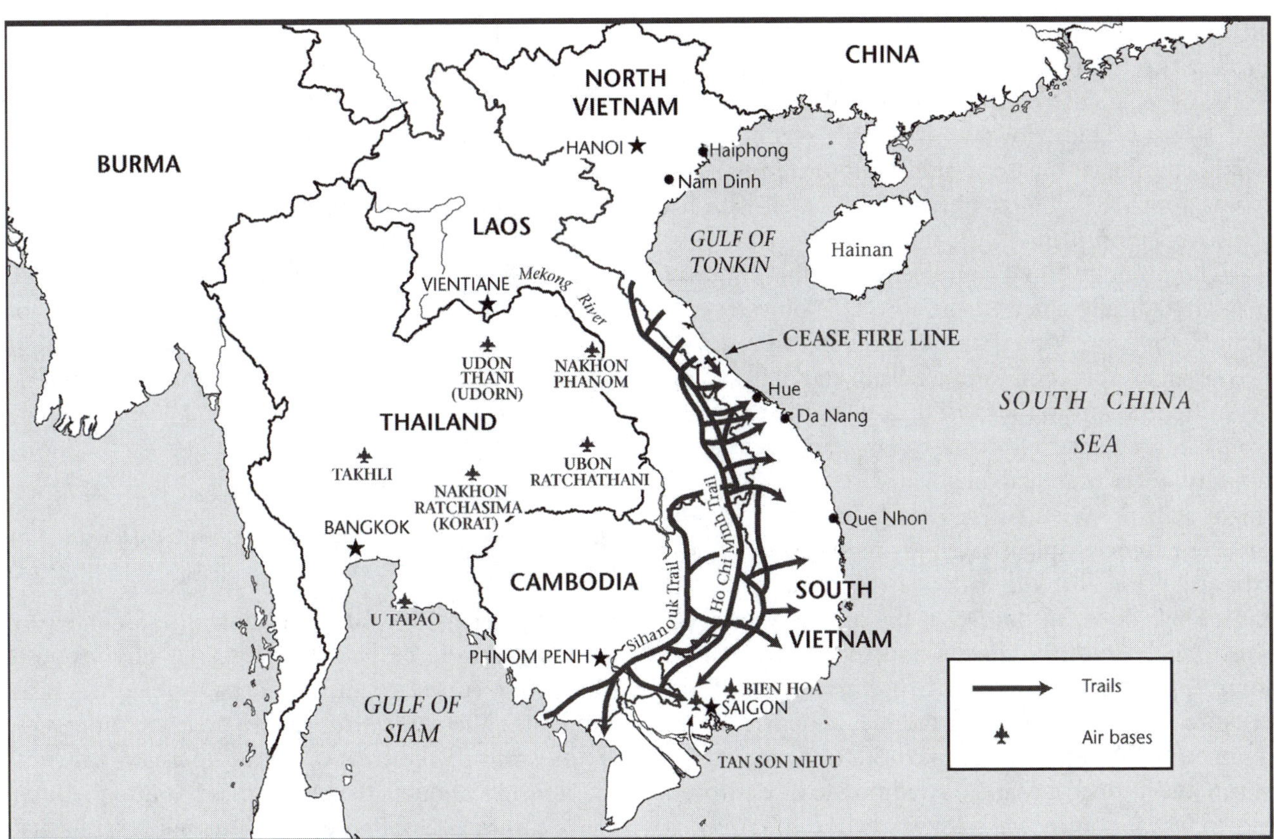

Cambodia, Laos, and Vietnam

through, Knight later appealed to Congress. General Abrams's February 9 recommendation for a few low-level attacks never accomplished its objective, assuming his assumptions about the sanctuaries were correct.

Following the March 18 bombing of Base 353, a U.S. Special Forces team code-named Daniel Boone entered the area to survey the damage. The team of 12 men commanded by Captain Bill Orthman flew helicopters to the area, but after they landed and moved toward the jungle, the enemy attacked. Nine men were killed; three Vietnamese and Orthman were wounded but got back to the helicopter and survived. Overlooking Abrams's miscalculation, Nixon ordered additional bombings, but the objectives of these attacks were never fulfilled. During the next year there were 3,875 sorties in which the B-52s dropped 108,823 tons of bombs. The Communist bases survived, being relocated farther inland. Only Cambodian civilians suffered from the bombings. The U.S. incursion into Cambodia in April 1970 led to the end of Cambodian neutrality.

May 10, 1969

In Vietnam, Operation Apache Snow indicates the U.S. army has not adjusted to the use of General Abrams's "area security" strategy.

Although General Abrams, who succeeded Westmoreland as U.S. commander in Vietnam on April 10, 1968, had introduced new strategic methods for the war, Abrams's "area security" plan broke so severely with the U.S. army's traditional attrition warfare that U.S. officers either could not or would not forsake the attrition strategy. As designed by Abrams and approved by President Nixon early in 1969, the United States and the Army of the Republic of Vietnam (ARVN) would cooperate with the local South Vietnamese People's Self-Defense Forces (PSDF) to clear and secure an area of Vietcong (VC) influence. Because the PSDF had knowledge of local conditions, the United States and ARVN would work closely with them. These would be small-unit actions that would emphasize every effort to avoid devastating the local area and thus the PSDF could avoid the dislocation and killing of the local people such as occurred from attrition firepower. Together ARVN and PSDF would protect the future security of a region step by step. Thus, Abrams's methods deemphasized "body count" and stressed "local loyalty." The area security plan would counteract the Communist-protracted warfare. It was approved by Nixon because it fit well with his Vietnamization plans.

There was one major problem with the Abrams's plan. It radically changed the way U.S. officers were trained to fight. West Point taught big-unit action, firepower, and attrition through death and destruction. From the Indian frontier to Korea these methods had won. Thus, U.S. army doctrine eschewed political goals: military goals were ends in themselves. Area security might win the Vietnamese "hearts and minds," but as Major General Julian Ewell wrote in 1969, "I guess I basically feel that the 'hearts and minds' approach can be overdone. In the Delta, the only way to overcome VC [Vietcong] control and terror is by brute force applied against the VC." Another senior officer criticized Abrams's methods more succinctly: "I'll be damned if I'll permit the United States Army, its institutions, its doctrine, and its tradition to be destroyed just to win this lousy war." As Guenter Lewy's *America in Vietnam* (1978) concludes: "Abrams' campaign plan, for the most part, remained a paper exercise."

About one year after Abrams took command, Operation Apache Snow, including the famous battle of Hamburger Hill, represented U.S. "old-style" heroism and the inability of the United States or its trained ARVN units to accept Abrams's plan. Apache Snow was a big-unit action by the U.S. 101st Airborne Division and the First ARVN Division in the 30-mile-long A Shau valley near the borders of South Vietnam, Laos, and the 17th parallel. The first day, B-52s, artillery, and naval guns bombarded the valley. The second day, U.S. airborne troops and ARVN helicopters entered the valley and eventually reached Hill 937, where a strong enemy force held out. Lodged on a rugged, densely forested, heavily fortified hill, the Vietcong held out for 10 days. The U.S. Field Commander, Major General Melvin Zais, threw more and more men into battle, where they were "chewed up like meat" on "Hamburger Hill." The U.S. air force flew 272 sorties and dropped 1 million pounds of bombs including napalm. The artillery fired 21,732 rounds at the hill. Finally, fighting bunker to bunker, the U.S. soldiers secured Hill 937. U.S. losses were 56 killed, 420 wounded; the enemy lost 505 troops.

Once Hill 937 was secured, however, it was abandoned. The search-and-destroy operation had killed the enemy. Hill 937 had no political or military value such as Abrams had prescribed. In fact, the U.S. pacification agency reported that Vietcong terrorism increased in formerly "pacified" areas while the battle of Hamburger Hill raged. Abrams's area security plans collapsed before the search-and-destroy attrition methods. Old army methods still needed to be attuned to new world conditions. American soldiers fought heroically, but their gallant efforts provided no lasting results.

May 14, 1969

Nixon offers peace terms unacceptable to North Vietnam.

Speaking on nationwide television, President Nixon announced a peace plan for Vietnam. His proposal called for a cease-fire, the withdrawal of all American and North Vietnamese troops, an exchange of prisoners of war, and the creation of an international commission to conduct free elections in South Vietnam. News commentators noted that this proposal had no chance to be accepted by North Vietnam. Its terms would have accomplished what the United States had not achieved during the last five years: the withdrawal of Vietcong forces and an election to divide Vietnam, with Thieu in charge in the South. At best, Nixon's so-called eight-point plan expressed the extreme bargaining position for U.S. truce negotiations at the Paris peace talks.

June 8, 1969

President Nixon and President Thieu announce the initial withdrawal of U.S. forces from South Vietnam: the Vietnamization process begins.

Nixon had approved the initial "Vietnamization" plans on May 14 but waited to announce the decision until after a meeting at Midway Island during which Thieu had little choice but to accept the plan. Significantly, the initial study—NSSM-1—drafted by Kissinger's national security team in January 1969 recommended plans for the gradual U.S. withdrawal from Vietnam. These plans were reviewed and redesigned slightly in NSSM-36 and -37 during April before Nixon accepted them. Thus, following talks with Thieu and General Creighton Abrams, Nixon announced the Vietnamization program on June 8.

On Thieu's recommendation, Nixon told reporters that 25,000 U.S. combat troops would be withdrawn as the first step in allowing South Vietnamese forces to take over their nation's self-defense.

Thieu and Abrams agreed that with proper training by U.S. officers and with U.S. equipment, the ARVN could protect their country from Communism. Training of the Vietnamese had begun under Abrams's orders in 1968, and it showed signs of success. Nixon did not give a precise timetable for withdrawal of U.S. troops. He said the situation in Vietnam would be reviewed regularly and future withdrawals would be in accord with ARVN's capacity to take charge. The initial secret plans of the NSC indicated that the summer of 1972 would be the earliest date when South Vietnam might be able to defend itself. As Nixon explained to reporters at Guam on July 25, Vietnamization fitted the Nixon policy by which local defense forces would be aided, trained, and equipped to defend themselves.

Not stated, but a part of the Nixon-Kissinger strategy, Vietnam was no longer considered a vital interest of the United States in global relations.

June 15, 1969

Georges Pompidou is elected president of France following de Gaulle's resignation.

French economic problems increased in 1968, prompting student riots in Paris and the Paris suburb of Nanterre. To strengthen presidential power, President de Gaulle suggested reforms of the French Senate, but in a referendum the majority rejected this by 52.87 percent on April 28, 1969. De Gaulle resigned and Pompidou was elected president on June 15. The new prime minister was Jacques Chaban-Delmas. On August 10, Pompidou devalued the franc to solve some of the country's economic difficulties.

July 15, 1969

Nixon sends a secret letter to Ho Chi Minh.

Although U.S. negotiations with North Vietnam had been conducted in Paris since January 25, these were public meetings with both South Vietnamese and NLF delegates present, as agreed to in October 1968. Nixon had designated the former Senator from Massachusetts Henry Cabot Lodge to head the U.S. delegation, replacing Averell Harriman and the team Johnson had appointed in May 1968. Kissinger suggested to Nixon in February that the open Paris sessions could never reach an agreement. But he believed that high-level secret discussions in Paris with a North Vietnamese delegate could achieve success. To do this without Ambassador Lodge's knowledge, Kissinger arranged for Jean Sainteny, a retired French diplomat and friend of Kissinger, to deliver to Xuan Thuy, Hanoi's delegate in Paris, an oral message urging secret talks as well as a letter from Nixon to Ho Chi Minh.

President Nixon and French President Georges Pompidou. National Archives

Following Nixon's world tour and the beginning of Vietnamization in July, the president accepted Kissinger's proposal of using Sainteny to act as the go-between. Although Ho did not respond to Nixon's letter for more than four weeks, he responded immediately to the suggestion for secret talks. The first session began in Paris on August 4, 1969.

July 20, 1969

U.S. astronauts make the first moon landing.

Neil A. Armstrong and Edwin E. Aldrin Jr. landed the lunar module *Eagle* on the moon. Armstrong became the first man to walk on the moon's surface. After 21 hours on the moon, the *Eagle* rejoined Apollo 11, which had been orbiting the moon after ejecting *Eagle* for the landing. Astronaut Michael Collins commanded Apollo 11. Live television broadcasts sent pictures of the landing back to the earth for viewers around the world to watch. A second U.S. moon landing was made on November 19–20, 1969. Four more moon visits were made by Americans between 1970 and 1972. Only one moon mission experienced difficulty: Apollo 13. This mission was aborted but the three astronauts landed safely in the Pacific Ocean on April 17, 1970.

The moon landing program was the consequence of John F. Kennedy's call for a U.S. program to land the first man on the moon to surpass Soviet space achievements.

July 25, 1969

At Guam, Nixon informally tells reporters the policies that will become basic to the Nixon Doctrine regarding Asia and, by implication, other regions of the world.

Unlike the Truman Doctrine, which derived essentially from a presidential speech on March 12, 1947, the Nixon Doctrine was first casually disclosed by the president in July and November 1969, before it was formally defined in a report to Congress during January 1970. Nixon arrived in Guam as part of a world tour during which he greeted the U.S. astronauts on their return from the first moon flight.

During the evening of July 25, he met with news reporters for an off-the-record conversation that the White House later made public. In somewhat rambling fashion, Nixon told the reporters that nationalism had changed the world, especially Asia. The United States needed to recognize this fact and, while keeping commitments, let other countries develop in their own fashion. The United States had to avoid policies that made others "so dependent on us that we are dragged into conflicts such as the one that we have in Vietnam." During later questioning by reporters, Nixon summarized his ideas more precisely.

He said the United States in its Asian relations must be quite emphatic on two points:

> One, that we will keep our treaty commitments-for example, with Thailand under SEATO; but, two, that as far as the problems of internal security are concerned, as far as the problems of military defense, except for the threat of a major power involving nuclear weapons, that the United States is going to encourage and has a right to expect that this problem will be increasingly handled by, and the responsibility for it taken by, the Asian nations themselves.

The president also said that the policy of letting x Asians protect themselves would be effective only after the Vietnam War ended. Until then, the United States had of necessity to remain in command.

During his subsequent visits to Manila, Djakarta, Bangkok, and Saigon, Nixon made much the same point regarding Asians eventually assuming control of their own internal and defense needs. On July 31, Nixon flew to India, where relations with the United States were not satisfactory, and continued on to Pakistan and Romania before flying back to Washington.

August 3, 1969

Nixon returns from a world tour that ended with a visit to Romania.

Following a trip to greet the moon astronauts in the Pacific and visit Guam and four capitals of Southeast Asia, Nixon made final stops in India, Pakistan, and Romania. Relations in neutralist India were tense because of that country's close ties with Moscow and its desire for the United States to leave Vietnam. Pro-American Pakistan was more congenial, giving Nixon the nation's highest medal, the Nishan-e-Pakistan.

The visit to Bucharest, Romania, impressed Nixon the most. On August 2, thousands of citizens in this Communist state greeted the president. The Romanian enthusiasm was subtly more anti-Soviet than pro-American because the government of Nicolae Ceauşescu wanted to show the nation's limited independence of the Soviet Union. Both Nixon and Ceauşescu expressed the desire for open contacts with all nations. Having traveled around the world, Nixon arrived back at Andrews Air Force Base near Washington on the evening of August 3.

August 4, 1969

Kissinger and Xuan Thuy conduct their first secret negotiations in Paris.

On July 26, Ho Chi Minh sent word to President Nixon that North Vietnam would empower Xuan Thuy to hold high-level secret talks in Paris. Nixon selected Kissinger to represent him, and bypassing Lodge and the State Department, Nixon entrusted the secret arrangements to his old friend Lieutenant General Vernon A. Walters, the U.S. defense attaché at the Paris embassy. On August 3, Nixon's plane *en route* from Romania had stopped briefly in London for a presidential visit with Prime Minister Wilson. Kissinger and two of his aides, Anthony Lake and Helmut Sonnenfeldt, left the presidential plane Air Force One and boarded a U.S. military aircraft for Paris. The Americans spent the night at General Walters's Neuilly apartment and Kissinger met publicly with President de Gaulle to brief him on Nixon's recent trips. De Gaulle also agreed to help Kissinger preserve the secrecy of his future talks with Xuan Thuy in Paris.

On the afternoon of August 4, Kissinger and his assistants visited Jean Sainteny's apartment, where they were introduced to Xuan Thuy and his aide. The first talks led to an agreement to hold future secret talks, although no date was set for the next meeting.

August 13, 1969

Fighting breaks out on the Sino-Soviet border.

This border clash was the last in a series of Chinese-Soviet border incidents during 1969, highlighting the year as a low point in relations between Moscow and Beijing. Following a clash on March 2 along the Ussuri River border, the two governments exchanged heated accusations intermixed with border engagements. The most serious fighting took place on March 15, June 11, and August 13. Soviet Premier Kosygin stopped in Beijing on September 11 following the funeral of Ho Chi Minh in Hanoi. (See September 3, 1969.) Talks to resolve the border problems began on October 19 but were not resolved during the next month.

September 3, 1969

Ho Chi Minh dies, soon after answering Nixon's personal letter on August 25.

Although Nixon and Kissinger believed Ho's death was good news for the United States because it would leave Hanoi leaderless, they had, as was often true of other Americans, underestimated the North Vietnamese political structure. The North Vietnamese leaders were united in their devotion to expelling the Americans and reuniting Vietnam. On August 25, Ho had sent his reply to Nixon's letter of July 15, 1969.

Ho's response showed the gulf between the perceptions of the two leaders regarding Vietnam. Whereas Nixon believed the United States was rightfully fighting in Vietnam to defend its Saigon ally, Ho saw the U.S. role as that of direct aggression to preserve imperialism and in violation of the "fundamental rights" of the Vietnamese people. He told Nixon that only if the United States left Vietnam could Vietnamese rights and peace be secured. The letters exchanged between Nixon and Ho were released by the State Department for publication on November 4, 1969.

October 21, 1969

In West Germany, Willy Brandt becomes chancellor, leading the Social Democratic Party.

Brandt was an exponent of building better relations with Eastern European countries and the Soviet Union.

October 21, 1969

The Shah of Iran visits with President Nixon. The president tells the Shah that Iran should become the dominant power in the Persian Gulf.

Although the visit to Washington of Reza Shah Pahlavi was largely ceremonial, Nixon stressed to the shah Iran's important role in the Middle East. National Security Council Study NSSM-66 indicated that as Great Britain abdicated more and more power east of

Suez, the United States needed allies such as Iran to control the Straits of Hormuz in the Persian Gulf oil region.

November 17, 1969

The United States and the Soviet Union begin SALT I negotiations in Helsinki.

On January 20, the day Nixon was inaugurated, Moscow announced it was ready to begin discussing limits of offensive and defensive nuclear weapons. Seven days later, Nixon told reporters he was ready to begin talks on these topics as soon as he and Henry Kissinger had reviewed American military strength and a new ABM proposal. On August 6, the U.S. Senate authorized ABM construction and Nixon was ready to start talks.

Finally on October 25, 1969, the two governments jointly announced discussions covering offensive and defensive weapons would begin at Helsinki on November 17. From the U.S. viewpoint, the principal issues for Strategic Arms Limitations Talks I (SALT-I) were ABM, MIRV warheads, and verification methods. Nixon and Kissinger had agreed the United States wanted to eliminate ABM systems if possible, having sought ABM funds as a bargaining chip to be given away during the talks. The Pentagon's greatest concern was to retain leadership in MIRV technology. MIRVs could be deployed on the Minuteman and U.S. submarine launchers. Considered by technicians to be the biggest breakthrough since the hydrogen bomb, MIRV would give the United States at least a temporary advantage over the Soviet Union and stimulate a new stage in the nuclear arms race.

Nixon believed the USSR delayed SALT discussions to perfect its own MIRV system. In fact, there was a dispute within the Nixon administration between Secretary of Defense Melvin Laird and Richard Helms of the CIA. Laird insisted that the Soviets already had minimum MIRVs available with three separate warheads. Helms's intelligence data indicated it would be 1972 before the Soviets had this capability. Although the Soviets did not gain MIRV technology until 1973, Kissinger assumed Laird was correct and obtained limits on Soviet offensive missiles. The verification issue was always one of the most problematic for U.S. negotiators. Here again, Laird and Kissinger differed with Helms. The CIA believed that electronic surveillance and telemetry permitted the United States to keep aware of Soviet weapons including such capabilities as MIRV. Kissinger, who apparently disliked Helms personally, argued that Helms and the CIA had a "vested interest" in verification and could not therefore be relied on to judge the requirements of it.

Thus when the SALT talks convened, the principal U.S. concerns were to stop ABM systems, to protect U.S. advantages in MIRV, and to seek the most satisfactory verification methods possible. To conduct the U.S. discussions, Nixon named as special ambassador, Gerard C. Smith, director of the U.S. Arms Control and Disarmament Agency. The first round of talks lasted until December 22, 1969.

November 21, 1969

The United States agrees to return Okinawa to Japan as a result of discussions in Washington between President Nixon and Japan's Prime Minister Eisaku Sato.

During 1969, two issues disturbed relations between Japan and America: Japan's desire to regain Okinawa and the importation of Japanese textiles. As a lawyer for U.S.-owned corporations during the 1960s, Nixon had often visited Tokyo and liked the conservative political-business circles of that country. He was eager therefore to satisfy Japan's major request in 1969—the return of Okinawa. Nixon had convinced the Joint Chiefs of Staff that U.S. planes and nuclear weapons requirements would not be damaged if they later had to be removed from Okinawa. Consultation with Tokyo on these affairs was necessary. Thus, when Sato reached Washington on November 19, Nixon was prepared to agree on details of the U.S. withdrawal from Okinawa. Sato stated that the U.S. Treaty of Mutual Cooperation would be extended to Okinawa.

Thus, U.S.-Japanese consultations on air bases in Okinawa would have the same terms as those in the Japanese home islands. In addition, the prime minister approved the continued use of B-52 bases on Okinawa for action in Indochina, where the United States fought for "self-determination for the people of South Vietnam." The treaty on Okinawa was finalized in April 1970. The textile issue was not easily resolved;

in November 1969, Sato told Nixon he would place self-limits by Japanese on their textiles. Sato's promise was vague, however, and this trade issue was not resolved for two more years.

November 25, 1969

Nixon proclaims U.S. ratification of the Nuclear Non-proliferation Treaty and announces that the United States will renounce chemical-biological weapons by having the U.S. Senate ratify the Geneva protocol of 1925.

The Non-Proliferation Treaty had been signed by the United States on July 1, 1968, but was not ratified by the U.S. Senate until March 1969. In the interim, 108 nations (but not China or France) signed the treaty that Nixon accepted for the United States. On the same day, Nixon committed the United States not to make first use of chemical, incapacitating, or biological weapons. He would submit the 1925 protocol to the Senate because the United States had not previously accepted this pact. Henceforth, said Nixon, America would confine its chemical-biological research to "immunization and safety methods." In 1975, U.S. Senate investigators found that the CIA had ignored Nixon's 1969 suggestion to destroy its stocks of toxins used in biological warfare. It had retained stocks of cobra venom and Saxitonit, a toxin causing instant death. The 1925 protocol was not ratified until 1975.

December 8, 1969

In a press conference, President Nixon refers to the My Lai "massacre" as an isolated incident not representing U.S. policy.

The My Lai massacre had taken place on March 16, 1969, but had not been reported by U.S. newspapers until November 16. During this action, U.S. troops led by Lieutenant William L. Calley shot 450 unarmed South Vietnam villagers. Although there were other reports of individual atrocities in North Vietnam, My Lai and the Phoenix operations of 1968–1972 became the most notorious illustrations of the type of horrific incidents frequently associated with guerrilla warfare. During his press conference, Nixon was asked to react to the My Lai report. He said, "We cannot ever condone or use atrocities against civilians" to bring security to Vietnam. He hoped this event would not "smear the decent men that have gone to Vietnam" on a vital mission.

December 19, 1969

Secretary of State Rogers explains his October plan for the Middle East has been rejected by the USSR and Egypt.

Nixon and Kissinger had decided in March 1969 to have Secretary Rogers conduct discussions with the Soviet Union regarding a solution to the Arab-Israeli quarrels that continued following the Six-Day War of 1967 and U.N. Resolution 242's interpretation. Nixon believed the two superpowers should determine a plan for their client states—Israel and Egypt—that would have to be accepted by them. With Joseph Sisco of the State Department's Near Eastern Division conducting most of the day-to-day negotiations with Soviet Ambassador Dobrynin during the spring and summer of 1969, the so-called Rogers Plan emerged by September and was "signed off on" (approved) by the National Security Council on October 19.

Although the White House never fully supported the Rogers Plan, its principal features were that (1) the Sinai would be demilitarized with Israel's security guaranteed in the Strait of Tiran; (2) after Israel withdrew from the occupied territory, the Arabs and Israelis would negotiate details of peace "in some manner"; and (3) special discussions would settle the issue of the Gaza Strip. The precise definition of where Israel would withdraw was not provided. When Israel's Prime Minister Golda Meir visited Washington on September 25–26, Nixon did not confide in her about the Rogers Plan or U.S.-Soviet discussions. He told her the White House fully supported Israel but that he had trouble dealing with others in the State Department and the NSC.

After the NSC approved the Rogers Plan on October 19, the secretary held extensive talks with Soviet Foreign Minister Andrei Gromyko in New York. The two worked out an agreement for the approval of Egypt and Israel. By their terms, the territories that Israel would withdraw from were those taken from Egypt in 1967 except for "insubstantial alterations," which was one of Rogers's phrases. In return, Egypt would assure the security of Israeli borders. The Rogers Plan, as he explained in December, did not survive long. Late in October, after the United States had orally explained the plan to Israel, Tel Aviv announced that the Soviet-American plan called for "direct negotiations" between Israel and Egypt. Egypt's foreign minister, Mahmoud Riad, objected to this phrasing. At best, he told Moscow, he would participate only in "indirect talks," which itself was a concession because of strong Arab opposition to talks that would appear to recognize Israel's right to exist as a state. Although the Rogers plan might have survived if Nixon had fully supported it, he did not. By December, Dobrynin informed Rogers and Sisco that the Soviet Union no longer backed the plan because of Egyptian opposition. Before the speech of December 19, in which Rogers explained the failure of his proposal, Rogers had neglected to inform Israel of the Soviet notification. Abba Eban, Israel's foreign minister, objected strongly to any effort of outside parties to impose a peace on Israel. As a result, U.S.-Israeli relations were strained by the end of 1969.

1970

January 8, 1970

President Thieu of South Vietnam informs reporters that it would be "impossible and impractical" to withdraw all U.S. troops from Vietnam in 1970.

Since the announced Vietnamization program of June 8, 1969, there had been extensive speculation in South Vietnam and the United States regarding the time of America's complete withdrawal. A vital part of Vietnamization was the question of South Vietnam's preparations to take charge of local defense. During the summer of 1968, President Thieu had called a general mobilization in South Vietnam. All army reserves were called up and a draft began of men 18 and 19 years old. In addition, men aged 16–17 and over 38 years could be drafted into Socialized People's Self-Defense Forces (PSDF). By 1972, the ARVN and other regular South Vietnamese forces totaled 516,000, fewer than the American total of 542,000 at its peak in January 1969. U.S. military advisers expected that a trained and equipped PSDF of nearly 500,000 would add to Saigon's total defense establishment. The critical problem was for the Saigon government to obtain the respect and loyalty of local leaders of the PSDF. Enlarging the PSDF was simple; achieving their allegiance and motivation was a different matter.

January 20, 1970

U.S. Ambassador to Poland Walter Stoessel Jr. and China's *Chargé d'Affaires* Lei Yang conduct talks in Warsaw.

The U.S. and Chinese representatives had held 133 sessions in Warsaw since 1955, but since 1965 these had dwindled to only one or two a year, with only one in 1968 (January 8). On November 26, 1968, the Chinese *chargé* had sent Stoessel a note suggesting a formal meeting with a U.S. representative on February 20, 1969. Later, Chinese diplomats said they had read president-elect Nixon's article in the October 1967 issue of *Foreign Affairs* and were impressed by his advocacy of normalizing U.S. relations with China. Although Nixon, through Secretary of State Rusk, agreed to a meeting with the Chinese in Warsaw in February, the session was canceled because a Chinese diplomat in the Netherlands defected to the West and Beijing blamed the United States.

Both Nixon and Kissinger were willing to hold talks with the Chinese and sought in various ways to encourage this during 1969. On May 24, Secretary of State Rogers visited Pakistan and, along with other matters, told Yahya Khan, who had good relations with China, that the United States desired to make diplomatic contact with Beijing. On July 21, the State Department announced that certain professional persons could obtain valid passports for China and that U.S. residents abroad or tourists could buy a limited amount of Communist Chinese goods to bring back with them to America. Finally, on December 12, Ambassador Stoessel, acting on instructions from Nixon, informally contacted Lei Yang at a Yugoslav reception, telling Lei's interpreter that the United States would like to arrange a meeting. Two days later, Lei sent Stoessel an invitation to visit him at the Chinese embassy on January 20, 1970. At the January meeting and again at a meeting in the U.S. embassy on February 20, Stoessel and Lei exchanged formal and polite views. Stoessel also suggested that perhaps a "high-level emissary" from America could visit Beijing. No firm agreement resulted from this overture, but Stoessel and Lei decided to hold monthly sessions thereafter.

February 18, 1970

The Nixon Doctrine is described in a report to Congress titled "Foreign Policy for the 1970s."

Although Nixon had informally commented on the principles of his policy during a news conference at Guam on July 25 and in a national television speech on November 3, 1969, the Nixon Doctrine was not precisely spelled out until his report to Congress of February 18, 1970. This report identified three basic points of the Nixon Doctrine: (1) The United States would keep all of its commitments to its allies; (2) The allies should provide their own troops for self-defense against Communism; and (3) The United States would provide a nuclear shield and economic aid for its allies.

Despite the Nixon Doctrine's resemblance to Eisenhower's "new look," Nixon did not offer to decrease U.S. defense expenditures or rely principally on U.S.'s nuclear capabilities. In fact, Nixon was negotiating with the Soviets on ICBM and ABM limitations. Nixon principally wanted the United States to "participate" but no longer undertake all of the defense efforts for its allies. To provide U.S. aid, funds for the Military Assistance Programs increased in 1971 by $2 billion over Johnson's last budget. The United States also increased its sale of arms to its allies. For example, from 1953 to 1973, the United States sold Iran $205 billion worth of weapons, a sale helping to offset the balance of payments due to the increase in oil prices during the 1970s. Nevertheless, American allies would, said Nixon, "define the nature of their own security and determine the path of their own progress."

March 18, 1970

Prince Sihanouk of Cambodia is overthrown by his prime minister, Lon Nol.

Since becoming leader in Cambodia on June 5, 1960, Sihanouk often irritated U.S. officials because of his desire to remain neutral in both the Cold War and the Vietnam conflict. U.S. claims of Communist sanctuaries in eastern Cambodia were shrugged off by the prince as "illegal" or "under control." Essentially, Prince Sihanouk believed his people would fare best if he kept his nation as aloof as possible from direct involvement in the north-south conflict in Vietnam. As William Shawcross's *Sideshow* (1979) explains, Sihanouk's policies toward North Vietnam's sanctuaries in Cambodia were unacceptable to Premier Lon Nol and Deputy Premier Sirik Matek. In particular, Matek, a cousin of the king, opposed Sihanouk because in 1941 the French crowned Sihanouk as King of Cambodia, passing over Matek's family. Thus, while Sihanouk vacationed in France during March 1970, Matek persuaded Lon Nol to seek American support to replace Sihanouk as king. Hoping to obtain U.S. backing, Matek and Lon Nol promoted anti-Vietnamese demonstrations along the border with Vietnam and in front of Phnom Penh's embassy of the Provisional Government of South Vietnam (Vietcong). They not only canceled the trade agreement with North Vietnam, closing the port of Sihanoukville for Hanoi to buy Cambodian products, but also ordered Hanoi to withdraw all its troops from Cambodia in 72 hours. On March 17–18, they completed their coup by arresting Sihanouk's supporters in and near Phnom Penh. Although President Richard Nixon's decision to begin bombing Cambodia on March 18 undoubtedly influenced Sihanouk's ouster, Shawcross found no evidence that America's CIA was directly involved in the Cambodian events staged by Matek and Lon Nol. Indeed, if Sihanouk had immediately come home from France on March 18, Shawcross believes his supporters would have rallied to his side because the new government was on shaky ground in opposing North Vietnam as well as Sihanouk. Rather than risk going to Phnom Penh, Sihanouk flew to Beijing and organized resistance against Matek and Lon Nol. While President Nixon recognized Lon Nol's regime, Sihanouk allied with Communists in Cambodia's Khmer Rouge and North Vietnam.

March 19, 1970

Government heads of East and West Germany meet at Erfurt.

After becoming chancellor of West Germany in October 1969, Willy Brandt announced the policy of *Ostpolitik* aimed at promoting détente with states of Eastern Europe. His initial step was to meet in Erfurt with East Germany's Prime Minister Willi Stoph. Following the March 19 session, delegates from the two German states began negotiations resulting in the signing of a treaty on December 22, 1972. This treaty entailed reciprocal recognition between East and West Germany. Brandt also sought a treaty with Poland.

April 6, 1970

Moscow views 1970 as a year of wait and see.

Gromyko sent a secret paper to the Politburo on April 6 to assess Soviet-American relations and suggest Moscow wait until the Nixon administration decided what direction it wished to take. After a year's experience with Nixon, the Kremlin should let Washington realize "the hopelessness of a policy of confrontation" with the Soviet Union and "understanding our country's readiness to promote Soviet-American relations on a mutually acceptable basis." As a result, the Kremlin adopted a wait and see policy.

In his memoirs, *In Confidence* (1995) Dobrynin refuted Kissinger's memoirs claiming that in exchange for a 1970 summit Moscow demanded an informal alliance with Washington against China, a strategic arms control agreement on Soviet terms, and a European security conference.

April 30, 1970

President Nixon tells the U.S. public that American and South Vietnamese forces have made an "incursion" against Communist sanctuaries in Cambodia.

The U.S.-ARVN attack on Cambodia began on April 29. To his television audience on April 30, Nixon explained that Cambodia had been neutral since 1954, and U.S. policy "had been to scrupulously respect the neutrality of the Cambodian people." Nixon asserted that only North Vietnam "has not respected that neutrality." The Communists, Nixon stated, had large bases in Cambodia for training, weapons, ammunition, air strips, prisoner-of-war compounds, and planning headquarters. Previously the United States had not moved against these bases, Nixon claimed, "because we did not wish to violate the territory of a neutral nation"—but he failed to acknowledge the U.S. bombings that began in Cambodia on March 18, 1969. Nixon noted that the Communists had recently stepped up their attacks on Cambodia and were encircling the capital city of Phnom Penh. Therefore, the U.S. and South Vietnamese forces had to clean out the Communist bases to secure the freedom of South Vietnam and permit the process of Vietnamization to be successful.

Nixon asked the American people to understand and support his decision. "Free institutions," he said, "are under attack from without and within." America cannot be a "pitiful, helpless giant" in a totalitarian world. "I would rather be a one-term president and do what I believe is right than to be a two-term president at the cost of seeing America become a second-rate power and to see this nation accept its first defeat in its proud 190 year history." America, he concluded, was being tested. If we fail, "all other nations will be on notice that despite its overwhelming power the United States, when a real crisis comes, will be found wanting."

The idea to send 74,000 troops into Cambodia originated in October 1969, when the U.S. Commanding General in Vietnam, General Abrams, and the Joint Chiefs of Staff recommended that ground forces invade both Cambodia and Laos to destroy the Communist bases. By October, Abrams realized that his February 9 bombing proposal had been incorrect. The military-bureaucratic game, however, does not admit mistakes. Nixon delayed action on the October request until April 1970. By then, many things had changed. The bombing had clearly failed, Sihanouk had been ousted, and in the secret Paris peace negotiations during early 1970, the North Vietnamese had not offered any significant compromises.

Nixon could not ally with Lon Nol because the Cambodian leader was as much anti-Vietnamese as he was anti-Communist. In April, Lon Nol had appealed to the United Nations to help Cambodia get rid of both the Communists and the South Vietnamese who operated on the western borders of his state. Kissinger claims in his memoirs that he obtained approval for the Cambodian "incursion" from Senator John Stennis, chairman of the Senate Armed Forces Committee. He wrote that Stennis, like other Southern senators "sometimes lagged behind the moral currents of their time, but on national security and foreign policy they were towers of strength." No other congressmen were told in advance about the April 29–30 decision. Both Secretary of State Rogers and Secretary of Defense Laird cautioned Nixon about the constitutional question involved in ordering a ground attack on neutral Cambodia, but the president ignored their advice.

The Cambodian incursion became a 90-day raid with, at best, limited success. As another "search and destroy" mission, there were some benefits. U.S. forces encountered little resistance in their 21-mile invasion. The tanks, planes, and armored vehicles destroyed small towns such as Snuol and Mimot. At Snuol, the 11th Armored Cavalry Regiment's tanks shelled the village for 24 hours. On occupying the village they found seven dead bodies, one a small Cambodian girl. Elsewhere, U.S. forces captured large caches of rice, arms, and ammunition. In addition, George Herring's *America's Longest War* (1996 edition) indicates that some 2,000 enemy troops were killed, 16,000 acres of jungle were cleared, and 8,000 enemy bunkers were destroyed. Generally, however, the U.S. objective of destroying significant sanctuaries failed. An August 1970 Defense Department study stated that Communist attacks had been disrupted "to some extent." The incursion had not "substantially reduced NVA capabilities in Cambodia." The Communists lost perhaps 25 percent of their supplies, but these would be replenished within 75 days or less. Neither Kissinger nor Nixon agreed with the Pentagon's August report. Kissinger claimed the attacks bought two years' time to carry out Vietnamization. The Communists did not launch another offensive action in Vietnam until 1972. Of course, the Communists may have simply been awaiting a better time to make their next major attack.

As in the case of the secret bombing, Cambodians suffered the most. The Khmer Rouge stepped up its attacks on Lon Nol's forces. Although the Nixon administration gave Phnom Penh $273 million of economic aid and military equipment for an army of 220,000, the new government was unable to sustain itself. During the next decade Cambodia experienced destruction, starvation, and genocide. First the Khmer Rouge under Pol Pot, and later the Vietnamese conquered the ancient kingdom.

May 4, 1970

At Kent State University, four students are killed by Ohio National Guardsmen. Ten days later, police at Jackson State College kill two antiwar demonstrators.

A major consequence of Nixon's "incursion" into Cambodia was the greatest outburst of antiwar dissent since the president took office. Demonstrations at colleges and universities began on May 1. In both Ohio and Mississippi, inspired perhaps by Nixon's claim that dissenters were disloyal, national guardsmen and police responded by shooting, and killed six dissenters. At Kent, Ohio, Governor John Rhodes denounced the demonstrators as "worse than brown shirts and the Communist element," ordering 750 guardsmen to the campus after someone set fire to an Army ROTC building. On May 4, Kent State students staged a peaceful assembly to protest the war. For still unclear reasons, a group of guardsmen moved to disperse the crowd, advancing in full battle gear and carrying loaded M-1 rifles. The guardsmen fired at the unarmed students, later asserting there was sniper fire, an unsubstantiated charge. Two young women and two young men died; nine students lay wounded, one permanently paralyzed. An investigation disclosed that the students had no weapons other than a few rocks.

On May 14, a protest at Jackson State College had similar results. Drawn to the campus by reports of rock and bottle throwing, city and state police found a large crowd protesting the Cambodian invasion. For reasons that a later investigation called "completely unwarranted and unjustified," the police fired 150 rounds of ammunition into the assembly and a nearby women's dormitory. Two students were killed, 12 wounded. The President's Commission on Campus Unrest found that a combination of racial animosity and pro-war feelings probably caused the police to open fire. During the spring of 1970, over 448 colleges experienced some form of protest. At the end of May, 100,000 dissidents marched in Washington. Police used tear gas and made mass arrests to stop the protestors.

June 9, 1970

A crisis erupts in Jordan when the Palestinian Liberation Front rebels and holds a group of Americans hostage at Amman's Intercontinental Hotel.

The crisis in Jordan began as a conflict between the Popular Front for the Liberation of Palestine (PFLP) and King Hussein of Jordan. Hussein was a moderate and usually pro-Western Arab ruler. Because Jordan had become a major haven for Palestinian refugees after the Arab-Israeli war of 1948–1949, Hussein had increasing difficulty preventing the Palestinians in Jordan from conducting raids into Israel. This resulted in Israeli retaliatory attacks on Jordan and disrupted Jordanian society.

In 1970, Hussein used the army to prohibit future Palestinian raids. This caused anger among the PFLP as well as the more moderate Palestine Liberation Organization (PLO) headed by Yasser Arafat. When the Palestinian uprising began on June 9, members of the PFLP took some Americans hostage in the Intercontinental Hotel to express their opposition to U.S. support for Israel. Moreover, some American homes in Jordan were looted and Major Robert P. Perry, an embassy military attaché, was killed by shots fired into his house. The U.S. ambassador to Amman, Harry L. Odell, reported that it was too dangerous to evacuate U.S. personnel from the airport because of heavy fighting in the city. As a result, the White House undertook contingency discussions to prepare either a paratroop drop at Amman or to ferry Americans by helicopter to aircraft carriers in the Mediterranean Sea. Fortunately neither action was necessary because on June 12, King Hussein responded with force and the guerrillas accepted a truce. The hostages were released and the fighting ended. The uprising indicated a factor in Middle Eastern affairs not previously given much attention: the status of Palestinian refugees who had become organized and were ready to demand the right to a homeland in territory controlled by Israel.

June 18, 1970

Edward Heath becomes prime minister of Britain after a Conservative electoral victory.

June 22, 1970

The U.S. Senate terminates the Tonkin Gulf Resolution of 1964. This is one of several congressional attempts to challenge continued U.S. involvement in Southeast Asia.

Although the Senate repealed the Tonkin Gulf Resolution overwhelmingly, most congressional measures to restrict Nixon's activity were limited or unsuccessful. Included among these actions were the following: (1) May—Senate approved section of Cooper-Church amendment to prohibit funds for Cambodia after July 1, 1970, unless authorized by Congress. President Nixon had promised to have all troops out of Cambodia by July 1. (2) June 10—Senate rejected a proposal authorizing the president to send troops back into Cambodia if necessary to protect Americans in Vietnam. (3) June 23—Senate rejected the "end-the-war" McGovern-Hatfield amendment to ban all funds expended in Vietnam after December 31, 1970, unless Congress declared war. (4) June 29—Senate rejected a proposal to allow Nixon to aid "other nations such as Thailand" in helping Cambodia. (5) June 30—Senate approved Cooper-Church amendment to ban all funds for training Cambodians. This bill was rejected by the House of Representatives on July 7. Although none of these measures specifically tied the president's hands, they all represented a considerable dissatisfaction in Congress regarding Nixon's policy in Vietnam and Cambodia.

August 7, 1970

The United States arranges a cease-fire in the Middle East: Rogers Plan II.

Throughout the first seven months of 1970, border conflicts between Israel and three of its neighbors—Syria, Jordan, and Egypt—had steadily escalated to the status of an undeclared war. In addition, the Soviet Union extended its influence in the region by increasing its arms and missiles in Egypt as well as using Soviet "experts" to fly missions protecting Egypt. The United States wanted some means to lessen Soviet influence or, as Kissinger told reporters in a "backgrounder" in early July, to expel the Soviets. (A "backgrounder" was a remark that could not be publicly attributed to Kissinger but that, by mid-July 1970, most diplomats knew meant "Kissinger.")

Beginning as border skirmishes in 1969, the conflicts in the Middle East multiplied. On the Golan Heights border of Syria and Israel there often were heavy tank and artillery duels in addition to border raids. Along the Jordanian border, Palestinian raids became frequent until the Hussein-Palestinian dispute of June 9–12 finally reduced the PFLP-PLO raids. The Egypt-Israeli border became the most serious area, however, for a war of attrition had begun. After the breakdown of the 1969 Rogers Plan, the Soviets rapidly increased their delivery of modern weapons to Egypt. Advanced jet fighter bomber MIG-23s and SAMs (surface-to-air missiles) gave Egypt a new integrated air-defense system. Soviet personnel also manned the SAM-3 batteries, while Soviet pilots flew jets defending against Israeli planes. At the same time, Israel urged the United States to send Phantom and Skyhawk jets to bolster their defenses. Nixon and Kissinger restricted these deliveries, however, to persuade Moscow to limit arms to the area as a means of moving toward permanent peace arrangements.

Egypt and the Soviet Union had become closer allies after the Israelis launched "deep penetration" air raids against Egypt beginning in January 1970. By February, the Israeli air force controlled Egyptian skies from Alexandria to Aswân, even attacking Cairo-West air base. Reportedly, the Israelis shot down five MIGs flown by Soviets and killed a Soviet general during one air raid. The Soviets response between February and July was to rapidly deploy more planes and SAM bases in Egypt. Eventually Israeli raids became so risky that during April and May, they curtailed penetration attacks, limiting their air attacks to the Suez area. The situation became so tense that Israel considered large-scale invasion plans to destroy SAM bases along the Suez Canal before they were completed by Egypt and the Soviet Union.

Following the end of the Jordanian crisis on June 12, Nixon, Kissinger, and Rogers agreed to launch a new peace initiative in the Middle East. On June 25, after prior consultations without agreement by the various parties involved, Rogers announced his cease-fire plan. His hope was to obtain an Egyptian-Jordanian-Israeli cease-fire while the U.N. mediator, Gunnar Jarring, undertook negotiations to implement U.N. Resolution 242 or some other acceptable proposal. Syria was left out of the Rogers proposal because Damascus never accepted in principle the U.N. Resolution 242 of 1967. The same day he offered his proposal, Rogers announced that the United States would withhold plane shipments to Israel. Privately, Rogers explained to Israeli Ambassador Yitzhak Rabin that if the cease-fire did not work within a short time, U.S. aircraft deliveries would resume.

To pressure Moscow and Cairo to accept the cease-fire, Kissinger and Nixon made tough statements about expelling the Soviets or giving Israel huge new arms supplies. At the same time, Rogers, who was not fully aware of Kissinger's tactics, had qualified these tough statements by, for example, distinguishing between "expelling" the Soviets and "lessening" their influence. The Soviet Union demonstrated its own "toughness." While considering Rogers Plan II and encouraging Cairo and Amman to accept the plan, Kosygin delayed any commitment while rushing additional SAM-3s to be deployed along the Egyptian side of the Suez Canal. Moscow planned to protect its client by providing a more secure air defense if a cease-fire broke down.

By late July, Egypt and Jordan had accepted Rogers's June 25 plan in principle. Israel had to comply before the details could be worked out for a cease-fire arrangement. Before the August 7 cease-fire went into effect, the United States obtained a secret agreement that none of the parties would increase their arms or defense units during the cease-fire. Israel also wanted assurances that the Soviet Union would respect the agreements. Rogers talked with Soviet Ambassador Dobrynin, receiving a commitment from him, but not an absolute one, to respect the cease-fire as well as the arms "standstill" agreements. Finally, on August 7 the cease-fire went into effect. The situation remained precarious, however, and hardly had the arrangements begun before violations of the agreement took place.

September 6, 1970

The second Jordanian crisis of 1970: the PFLP hijacks three commercial airliners, holding 475 hostages near Amman.

Although the cease-fire of August 7, 1970, did not settle the difficulties in the Middle East, the Palestinian radicals wanted to prevent any settlement by disturbing the equilibrium of the region. To demonstrate their ability to disrupt the world community, the PFLP organized four skyjackings of airliners on September 6–7, 1970. Three of these succeeded, and the planes and passengers on Trans-World Airways, Swiss Air, and British Overseas Airways were commandeered and flown to an abandoned British airfield 35 miles from Amman, which the PFLP called Revolution Field. The fourth skyjack attempt, on an El Al (Israeli) plane, failed. In Jordan, the PFLP demanded the release of all Palestinian and pro-Palestinian prisoners jailed in Israel, West Germany, Switzerland, and Britain. While the Swiss complied, the United States joined Britain and Israel in rejecting the demands but offering to negotiate. They asked the International Red Cross to contact the PFLP for possible discussions.

Nixon agreed to preparations to intervene in Jordan if necessary. On September 9, he announced that the United States was delivering 18 Phantom jets to Israel. He also sent six C-130 U.S. air force transports to a Turkish base at Incirlik, 350 miles from Amman, where they would be ready to bring out the PFLP hostages. The U.S. Sixth Fleet was ordered to the Israeli-Lebanese coast and 25 U.S. air force Phantom jets were sent to Incirlik. At Revolution Field near Amman, the Red Cross negotiators achieved a compromise with the PFLP by September 12. Although the Palestinians blew up the three airliners, they took the hostages to a camp near the village of Zerqua preparatory to working out a deal with the Red Cross. Israel agreed to release 450 Arab prisoners it had taken since September 6 and the British agreed to release Khaled. In exchange, the PFLP released all but 55 Jewish passengers. The Jewish passengers were held until September 29, when the PFLP secured the actual release of the 450 Israeli-held Palestinians.

September 15, 1970

King Hussein of Jordan attacks the Palestinian refugee camps to abolish the PFLP and PLO power in Jordan.

While the last non-Jewish hostages of the PFLP were being released from the camp at Zerqua, King Hussein decided the moment was opportune to eliminate the Palestinian "state-within-a-state" that the PFLP and PLO had created in their refugee camps in Jordan. The Royal Army and tank corps moved to take over the camps, forcing the Palestinians to relocate or go into exile in Syria or Iraq. Hussein's action was a civil war with international repercussions. Both Syrian and Iraqi forces with Moscow's quiet support moved to their borders in a threatening menace to aid the Palestinians. The Israeli government of Golda Meir preferred a viable Jordanian government under the Hasemite King Hussein and considered the possibility of backing him against the Palestinians and other Arabs. In this context, the United States had to decide on a satisfactory response.

September 22, 1970

At the peak of the crisis over King Hussein's fight with the Palestinians, Nixon agrees to protect Israel if it will assist Jordan. Within 48 hours, the tensions abate.

Because the Soviet Union's client states of Syria and Iraq backed the Palestinian organizations in Jordan as a way to keep the refugees out of their own lands, King Hussein's campaign to eliminate the fedayeen caused widespread international concerns. President Nixon was ready to back Hussein as far as necessary but hoped he would not have to commit American troops to intervene. Initially, on September 16 and 17, the president publicly warned Moscow that the United States and Israel might intervene if Syria and Iraq attacked Jordan. He talked with Israeli Prime Minister Golda Meir, who was on a scheduled visit to the United States, telling her that the United States favored Hussein but that Israel should use restraint as

Kissinger, Nixon, and Israel Prime Minister Golda Meir during Washington visit in 1974. National Archives

long as possible. He also contacted the Soviet *chargé* in Washington (Ambassador Dobrynin was on leave) and asked the Soviets to restrain its two Arab associates. Although the Soviets said they would restrain Syria, they did not or could not. On September 19, 300 Syrian tanks attacked Jordan, bringing a severe world crisis. If Hussein fell, Israel and perhaps the United States would have to move to help Jordan. Hussein survived, however. On September 20, Hussein asked for Israeli air support to make an all-out offensive against Syria and the Palestinians.

The Israelis were reluctant to comply without U.S. guarantees of protection on their southern (Egyptian) border. Nixon and his staff reviewed their options. On September 19, the president had alerted American troops in the United States and Europe, while ordering emergency preparations by airborne battalions at Fort Bragg, and in West Germany. Now at Meir's request the president agreed on September 22 to protect Israel from the Soviet Union and Egypt if she helped Hussein maintain his authority in Jordan. Nixon's commitment brought the United States and the USSR to the brink of war.

Fortunately, the crisis stopped. All Hussein needed was enough encouragement to commit his tanks and air force to an all-out war on Syria and the Palestinians. The promises of Israel and America supplied this, and by September 23, Hussein's army turned the Syrians back. Perhaps Moscow, too, had pressured Damascus to stop the attacks. Consequently, tensions relaxed temporarily in Jordan. Hussein had established his position against the Palestinians. Soon after, however, the PFLP, PLO, and other Palestinian groups moved to reestablish a position of strength in Lebanon.

September 25, 1970

An alleged Cuban crisis arises about the possible construction of a Soviet nuclear submarine base at Cienfuegos, Cuba.

While there is some evidence that the Soviets had begun some new type of activity at Cienfuegos during the summer of 1970, exactly what was done is not clear. During July, Admiral E.P. Holmes of the Atlantic Fleet told a congressional committee that the Soviets might build a submarine base in Cuba. According to Kissinger, U-2 flights on September 10 showed construction activity that he interpreted to be a nuclear submarine base. He indicated this in a press background briefing on September 16. The article appeared in the *New York Times* on September 25, causing other congressmen to accuse Moscow of deception. Subsequently, Kissinger claimed a diplomatic triumph for putting pressure on the Soviets to stop their construction. After the *Times* story appeared, Ambassador Dobrynin denied it. Kissinger later claimed he confronted the ambassador with photo evidence and Dobrynin turned "ashen," asking to consult Moscow. On October 5, Dobrynin—followed on October 13 by the TASS news agency in Moscow—denied that the Soviet Union was building a submarine base in Cuba. The "crisis" disappeared as fast as Kissinger had introduced it during his September 16 briefing. In 1989, Raymond Garthoff's *Reflections on the Cuban Missile Crisis* (1989 edition) indicates the crisis ended because President Nixon pledged that the United States would not invade Cuba.

September 28, 1970

President Nasser of Egypt dies of a heart attack, Sadat takes over.

On September 29, Vice President Anwar Sadat was sworn in as acting president. On October 15, Sadat was elected president.

October 6, 1970

President Nixon announces a new peace initiative to North Vietnam that contributes nothing new. It is seen as a political ploy to help Republican congressmen in the November elections.

Nixon's much publicized "new initiative" called for a cease-fire-in-place in all Indochina, the convocation of an Indochina Peace Conference, and the "immediate and unconditional release of all prisoners of war held by both sides." Hanoi saw no advantages to these proposals and, on October 9, dismissed them as "a maneuver to deceive world opinion." Nixon used the plan as evidence of his desire for peace, asking voters to provide Republican congressmen to support him in his effort.

October 17, 1970

Great Britain makes a major oil find in the North Sea.

October 24, 1970

CIA efforts fail to influence the defeat of Salvador Allende as president of Chile.

As disclosed by the Senate Select Committee on Intelligence Activities in 1975, the CIA had been attempting to prevent the rise to power of left-wing liberal groups in Chile since at least the days of President Kennedy. Alarmed by the rise of Castro in Cuba, Kennedy apparently ordered the CIA in 1962 to use $180,000 to help the conservative Christian Democratic candidate Eduardo Frei Montalvo defeat the Socialist Salvador Allende Gossens. Frei won in 1964 and, perhaps boastfully, a CIA report said that U.S. funds of $3 million made the difference in the election. Additional funds were continually used in Chile to aid pro-American candidates, but by 1970 Allende's chances of victory appeared to increase. Both the U.S. business community and Ambassador Edward Korry, who backed U.S. business interests, feared that if elected, Allende would nationalize copper mines and other U.S. investments.

Thus, in March 1970, the Forty Committee of the NSC, which regulated covert intelligence operations, agreed to spend $135,000 to subsidize "spoiling" operations critical of Allende. In June, an additional $300,000 was authorized by the Forty Committee because Korry flooded the State Department with alarming messages that Allende's victory would be worse than Castro's. In addition to CIA funds, International Telephone and Telegraph and other U.S. business firms spent monies to assist the National Party candidate, Jorge Allessandri. On September 4, 1970, no candidate won a majority in the Chilean elections. Allende received 36.3 percent; Allesandri, 35.3 percent; and a third, left-wing candidate, Radomiro Tomic, received 28.4 percent. If one put Tomic's left-of-center vote with Allende's, the rightist candidate, Allesandri, clearly seemed likely to lose.

In accord with the Chilean constitution, the absence of a majority victory sent the names of the two leading candidates to the Congress to select the president. The ballot would be between Allende and Allesandri. Although a CIA report in September 1970 found that the United States had "no vital interests within Chile" and the world balance would "not be significantly altered by an Allende regime," it asserted that Allende's victory would be a "psychological setback to the U.S. as well as a definite advance for the Marxist idea." In reality, Allende was not pro-Soviet or a Communist, although many conservative U.S. cold warriors such as Ambassador Korry believed anyone left of center was a Bolshevik working for Moscow. Allende was an advocate of Marxian ideals. In Chile, he was the candidate of Unidad Popular, a coalition of several leftist parties advocating economic nationalism for Chile and broad social reforms.

Like many Mexican nationalists between 1911 and 1941, Allende antagonized U.S. business by espousing a program to use Chilean resources to benefit the Chilean people. This constantly translated into a candidate's being an advocate of Soviet Bolshevism when viewed through the prism of U.S. investors. Therefore on September 8 and 14, the Forty Committee authorized the CIA and Ambassador Korry to use $350,000 of covert funds to bribe moderate Christian Democratic congressmen who had backed Tomic. Their votes for Allesandri in the congressional balloting for president on October 24 would defeat Allende. On September 15, however, Nixon and Kissinger went one step further, ordering Richard Helms of the CIA to support military factions in Chile who opposed Allende. The CIA had considered backing a military leader in Chile since 1969. The political interference programs of the NSC were called "Track I" and the military coup plans, "Track II."

By September 15, Helms had evidently convinced Nixon and Kissinger that an Allende victory was akin to a Communist victory. Because Kissinger was notably lacking in knowledge of Latin America, he could easily be persuaded. Kissinger demonstrated his attitude during a news briefing on September 16. He told reporters that if Chile fell, then Argentina, Peru, and Bolivia would follow. What would happen to the "Organization of American States...is extremely problematical." These "domino" theories abounded in the United States after 1947. Nixon's September 15 approval of Track II aid to the Chilean military involved the CIA in a scenario that assured Allende's election. Although the exact connection of the CIA to the plot to kidnap General Rene Schneider is not known, this plan went awry. The Chilean military wanted Schneider out of the way because he was a strong constitutionalist. It was planned that his abduction would be blamed on the left, giving the right an excuse to seize power. Unfortunately, Schneider was killed during the kidnap attempt and the right wing was implicated, not the left. After anti-army protests arose, the Chilean generals showed their loyalty by joining to support the constitutional decision of Congress on October 24. Allende was elected president. The plans of the CIA and the NSC were not laid aside, however.

November 10, 1970

General de Gaulle dies in France.

To many of the French de Gaulle had been the symbol of France's pre-1940s glory as a great empire and civilization. He had created the stable Fifth French Republic and was its first president after 1957.

November 21–22, 1970

A group of American volunteers stages an unsuccessful attack on a POW camp in North Vietnam.

This raid against a POW camp at Sontay, 23 miles west of Hanoi, was made by volunteer troops from the U.S. army's Special Forces and the air force's Special Operations Force. Reportedly, 70 to 100 Americans were prisoners at Sontay, but when the U.S. helicopters landed, they found the place deserted. The POWs had been moved. Following a brief firefight with North Vietnamese in the area, the U.S. troops boarded their helicopters to return south. The raid was not reported in the United States until November 24. The POW issue became one of the principal concerns of many Americans as Nixon's Vietnamization program proceeded. The Communists knew this and used the POW exchange as a trump card in all negotiations.

November 21–22, 1970

U.S. fighter-bombers from Thailand stage heavy air attacks all over North Vietnam.

Secretary Rogers told Congress that these raids were retaliatory because the North Vietnamese and Vietcong had shelled Saigon and Hue in violation of the October 31, 1968, agreement. Some observers believed these attacks were designed to warn Hanoi because it had recently infiltrated about 200,000 troops into South Vietnam. Others related them to the U.S. attack on the Sontay POW camp on the night of November 21–22.

December 7, 1970

Poland and West Germany sign a treaty that recognizes the Oder-Neisse River line as the German-Polish border.

This treaty was signed by Polish Premier Józef Cyrankiewicz and West German Chancellor Willy Brandt. The border had been established as part of the Yalta compromise in 1944–1945 to award Poland with former German territory in the west as compensation for the extension of the Soviet Union's border into former eastern Polish land. Final ratification of this treaty was delayed because it was coupled with the Quadripartite Agreement on Berlin by the West German government.

December 14, 1970

Riots occur in Gdansk, Poland, as workers protest the government's economic policy.

Polish workers' complaints against Communist rule had steadily increased in 1970, leading to a large-scale uprising of shipyard workers in Gdansk. In response to these difficulties, the government promised to rectify some of the complaints. On December 24, the Polish Communist Party followed Soviet advice by naming Edward Gierek to replace Wladyslaw Gomulka as first secretary of the Communist Party.

December 16, 1970

A rebellion begins in Eritrea.

About 10,000 insurgents threatened to overthrow the government of this East African state. The conflict drew the attention of the West and the USSR and soon made the so-called Horn of Africa on Africa's northeast coast a new area of global strategic concern.

December 28, 1970

The United States persuades Israel to resume talks with U.N. mediator Gunnar Jarring.

The Middle East peace talks that resulted from the cease-fire of August 7, 1970, provided for mediation by the United Nations. Israel broke off these discussions on August 27 because it claimed Egypt had violated the cease-fire by basing more Soviet SAM-3s along the Suez Canal. CIA photos verified the Israeli charge and in September and October, the United States passed new legislation to send new weapons to Israel such as the Shrike missile, which could neutralize the SAM-3. Following the Jordanian events of September and October 1970, U.S. allies urged Washington to try again to keep peace by mediation in the Middle East. Finally, on December 28, under pressure from Washington, the Israeli government agreed to formal discussions with Jarring. The U.N. mediator hoped to shuttle between Israeli and Egyptian delegations to seek a method to solve the Sinai dispute.

1971

January 15, 1971

Egypt's Aswân High Dam is dedicated.

The construction of the Aswân Dam was a cooperative project between Egypt and the Soviet Union following the Suez Crisis of 1956. The dam began operations on July 21, 1970, when its final generators were turned on. On January 15, President Sadat of Egypt and the USSR's President Nikolay Podgorny led dedication ceremonies for the project. Soon thereafter, Moscow and Cairo signed a 15-year friendship pact.

February 8, 1971

South Vietnam's invasion of Laos to wipe out Communist sanctuaries and the Ho Chi Minh Trail becomes a disaster.

Code-named Lam Son 619 (Total Victory), the ARVN operation, aided by U.S. air strikes and helicopters, attacked the Laotian border in a planned five-to-eight-week invasion. During the first two weeks of battle, the ARVN succeeded. General Abrams reported the ARVN "are fighting...in a superior way." Nixon bragged to reporters about the qualities of South Vietnam's new army. Late in February, however, ARVN ran into trouble, first with the Laotian terrain, next with North Vietnamese forces. With tanks aligned in mass formation, the North Vietnamese forced Saigon's forces into a retreat that soon turned into a rout. ARVN suffered heavy casualties and lost large quantities of U.S. equipment in the retreat. This Laotian fiasco not only hurt Nixon's pride but also demoralized the ARVN troops.

February 11, 1971

Eighty nations sign the Seabed Arms Control Treaty that prohibits nuclear weapons or weapons of mass destruction on the ocean floor.

In 1967, Arvid Pardo, the Italian delegate to the U.N.'s First Committee, urged an arms control agreement prohibiting nuclear weapons on the seabed. Following the Soviet Union's introduction of a draft iniative in March 1969, the proposal underwent six periods of negotiations in the Eighteen Nation Disarmament Committee until it obtained treaty form in 1970. Under the treaty, signatory nations agreed not to place or implant "on or under the seabed beyond a 12-mile" zone off their coast "any nuclear weapons or other types of weapons of mass destruction as well as structures, launching installations, or any other facilities specifically designed for storing, testing, or using such weapons." The United States, the Soviet Union, and Great Britain were the most important nations among 80 nations signing the Treaty. France and China refused to sign it.

February 14, 1971

Western oil companies and six Persian Gulf oil nations agree to raise prices: the Tehran Agreement.

According to Tad Szulc's *The Illusion of Peace* (1978), President Nixon let U.S. oil companies work out deals with Libya and other Middle Eastern States, not being concerned until the Tehran Agreement's oil prices affected Americans in May 1971. By the Tehran Agreement, the Western oil companies accepted an immediate posted oil price increase from $1.80 to $2.15 per barrel for 1971 and an annual 2.5 percent increase between June 1, 1971, and January 1, 1975. The companies also accepted a 55 percent income tax. The Western oil companies said the pact increased the stability of the oil supply. They simply added the extra oil costs to their customers' bills in Western Europe and the United States. As inflationary prices resulted in the Western nations after 1971, the Arab nations and Iran required the oil companies to amend their agreements.

March 16, 1971

Secretary Rogers proposes a Mideast peace plan because U.N. discussions have broken down. Israel rejects it and another deadlock results.

Secretary of State Rogers offered a plan on March 16: if Israel withdrew to the pre-June 1967 borders, Egypt would guarantee peace in the Sinai and an international force, including U.S. troops, would monitor the region. Egypt rejected this plan. By March 1971, Prime Minister Golda Meir said Israel "cannot trust Rogers' offer, even if it is proposed in good faith." As a result, another deadlock occurred in the Middle East. Meir was especially upset that the United States was again restricting arms sales to Israel while the Soviet Union bolstered its military aid to Egypt.

April 6, 1971

Ping-Pong Diplomacy: while in Japan, Chinese ping-pong team members invite the U.S. team to China as soon as the Nagoya tournament ends.

Although the United States and China had been quietly and frequently sounding each other out to renew normal diplomatic relations, Beijing followed an unusual method to indicate its willingness to negotiate with Washington. Prior talks had begun in Warsaw (January 20, 1970) and through contacts by way of Lahore, Pakistan, and Romania. On March 15, 1971, the State Department again signaled Beijing because it completely lifted the travel ban by Americans to China that had been partly raised on July 21, 1970.

The April 6 invitation came from the Chinese ping-pong team, which had participated in an international tournament in Nagoya, Japan. On the last day, Chinese team members invited the Americans to come and play against them in China. Graham B. Steenhoven, president of the U.S. Table Tennis Association, contacted the American ambassador in Tokyo. By telegram, the State Department responded positively. The American group arrived in Beijing on April 10. It included nine team members, four officials, two wives, and three American journalists. Although the Chinese easily won at ping-pong, the U.S. team had an unusual reception at the Great Hall of the People.

Premier Chou En-lai told them: "You have opened a new page in the relations of the Chinese and American people. I am confident that this beginning again of our friendship will certainly meet with majority support of our two peoples." The U.S. team invited China's ping-pong team to visit the United States, and Chou accepted.

April 14, 1971

President Nixon picks up China's "ping-pong" overture and announces plans to end restrictions on travel and to "create broader opportunities for contacts between the Chinese and American peoples."

Nixon had eagerly awaited Chou En-lai's indication that better relations were needed. After learning of Chou's favorable speech to the U.S. table tennis team on April 14, he indicated that the NSC recommended, and he approved, the following actions that did not require legislation or negotiation: (1) to expedite visas for visitors from the People's Republic of China to America; (2) to relax U.S. currency controls on China; (3) to end U.S. restrictions on oil sales to Chinese-owned or chartered ships or aircraft; (4) to allow U.S. vessels to carry Chinese cargo again; (5) to create a list of nonstrategic materials that could soon be exported to China.

April 16, 1971

President Nixon explains two vital parts of his Vietnam strategy: (1) to use air power and small U.S. ground forces until peace is made; (2) to have all U.S. POWs released as a condition of withdrawing all U.S. forces.

On April 16, the president specified this particular part of his plan for Vietnam. Earlier, on April 7, Nixon announced on national television that 100,000 U.S. forces would be brought home between May 1 and December 1. This would leave about 175,000 men in Vietnam in 1975 with only 60,000 to 75,000 in combat units. Thus, Nixon explained to the American Society of Newspaper Editors on April 16 that he hoped after the peace treaty was made to bring all U.S. troops home so that the South's government could defend itself. Again, as he had more and more in 1970, Nixon stressed the POW issue as one the United States would insist on before it withdrew completely. In his speech of April 16, he made the POW release a *sine qua non* of final U.S. withdrawal.

May 3, 1971

A massive anti-Vietnam war demonstration in Washington, D.C., leads to the arrest of nearly 12,000 people.

May 27, 1971

Cairo and Moscow announce an Egyptian-Soviet treaty of friendship and cooperation.

Article 8 of this treaty pledged the Soviet Union to help Egypt in the military field. Since September 1970, Egypt had received 100 MIG-21 fighters and 16 MIG-8 troop-carrying helicopters.

June 13, 1971

The *New York Times* begins publishing texts of secret Vietnam documents: *The Pentagon Papers.*

Aides of Secretary of Defense McNamara had compiled the documents known as the *Pentagon Papers* in 1967–1968 as a systematic study of how the United States became involved in Vietnam between 1945 and 1968. In addition to an analytical text, it included copies of secret documents available in Pentagon files that included any circulated from the White House and State Department. Daniel Ellsberg, a former member of Kissinger's NSC staff who went to work in 1969 at the RAND Corporation, leaked these documents to the *Times.* In addition to the *Times* edition, which was a selected version of the papers, the Pentagon Papers were later published in a five-volume Senator Michael Gravel edition (1971) and a 12-volume Government Printing Office edition, United States-Vietnam Relations (1971).

July 9, 1971

NSC Chairman Kissinger secretly interrupts an around-the-world trip to fly to Beijing from Rawalpindi, Pakistan. In China, Kissinger consults with Foreign Minister Chou En-lai.

Arrangements for Kissinger's secret trip to Beijing originated late in April 1971. Chou's invitation—by way of Pakistan—for a high-level delegate to visit the Chinese capital had been made and accepted. A specific date for the visit was set in mid-June, and on July 1, Kissinger left on a world tour that took him to Pakistan by July 8. After visiting Saigon, Bangkok, and New Delhi, Kissinger arrived at Rawalpindi, where Pakistan's Foreign Minister Khan Sultan took great pains to assure the secrecy of Kissinger's departure to and return from China. On the evening of July 8, Kissinger canceled a dinner because of illness, slipping from his room to an automobile that took him back to the airport. The next morning a Secret Service agent disguised as the NSC chairman set out to recover from his illness by resting at Nathia Gali.

Kissinger visits with Chou En-lai to plan Nixon's visit to China. National Archives

Meanwhile, Kissinger flew by Pakistani Airlines to Beijing, where he met on July 9–10 with Chou En-lai. These sessions went splendidly as the personalities of the two officials were compatible. Their discussions included the following points:

1. The United States would recognize that Taiwan was part of China; the issue would be settled by the Chinese themselves. Kissinger accepted this because on April 26, a special U.S. presidential commission recommended that the United States approve the seating of the People's

Republic in the United Nations, but without expelling Nationalist China. This commission included fairly conservative Republicans such as Henry Cabot Lodge and Senators Robert A. Taft Jr. and Bourke B. Hickenlooper.

2. Chou indicated that he expected the United States would some day sever relations with the Nationalist government, but he set no date or precondition on this.
3. Kissinger said Nixon could not break with Chiang Kai-shek immediately but hoped for good relations with Beijing anyway.
4. The People's Republic would be accepted in the United Nations, but the precise status of Nationalist China was left unsettled.
5. Kissinger said the United States believed, as Nixon had stated in a speech on July 6, 1971, that mainland China was one of the five great power centers of the world.
6. Chou invited President Nixon to visit China in 1972; Kissinger accepted.
7. Future contact would be through the U.S. and Chinese embassies in Paris.

July 15, 1971

President Nixon announces on television that he will visit the People's Republic of China before May 1972.

Kissinger returned to Washington from his Beijing visit on July 13. Following extensive discussions, the president decided to announce the visit on July 15, as Chou and Kissinger had agreed. Nixon relaxed most of the day, then flew to California to make the broadcast from San Clemente. This sequence of events is important because until he reached Los Angeles about 5:30 P.M. California time, he did not notify Secretary of State Rogers so that U.S. allies could be contacted in advance. When Rogers phoned the State Department, its Asian specialist, Marshall Green, was concerned that Japan must know in advance. He telegraphed Ambassador Armin Meyer in Tokyo but the message arrived too late. Nixon was on television and the Armed Forces radio station while Meyer was having his hair cut. Rogers did call the ambassadors of Japan, Nationalist China, and the USSR in advance. Nationalist Chinese Ambassador James C.H. Shen was shocked, calling Nixon's move a "shabby deal."

Although American allies generally concurred with Nixon, they all felt dismayed by not being consulted, especially the Japanese. Nixon and Kissinger's style, however, was often to work outside the normal diplomatic apparatus and protocol channels of the State Department. Moreover, Nixon surprised many Americans when he announced his proposed visit—he had changed a U.S. policy that dated back to October 1949. He told his audience that the United States sought "friendly relations with all nations." The visit would reduce tensions with China and promote peace "not just for our generation but for future generations on this earth we share together."

August 9, 1971

India and the Soviet Union sign a 10-year treaty of friendship and cooperation.

For some time, Moscow hoped to use India as a balance to China's growing power and independence. With Beijing and Washington supporting Pakistan and with trouble brewing in Pakistan's eastern provinces, India turned to Moscow to restrain both China and the United States. Similar to the Soviets' May 27 treaty with Egypt, this pact provided for Soviet military aid to India. Although both nations claimed the pact was to maintain peace in South Asia, the United States and Pakistan believed it was aimed at Pakistan where a threat of war loomed. The Cold War now influenced affairs in South Asia.

August 12, 1971

The Soviet Union and West Germany sign a treaty making the European frontiers established in 1945 "inviolable" as part of Brandt's *Ostpolitik*.

While Nixon and Kissinger gradually promoted links to develop a Soviet-American détente, the Western European nations sought to improve relations with the Soviets. The European motivation sought to reduce tensions that might lead to hostilities in Central Europe and to begin exchanges of commerce, ideas, and travelers. West German Chancellor Willy Brandt's *Ostpolitik* led the way in improving relations with the Eastern bloc by establishing diplomatic relations with Romania in 1967 and Yugoslavia in 1968. To normalize relations with Poland in 1970, West Germany accepted the Oder-Neisse border between Poland and Germany. In 1971, Brandt normalized relations with Moscow aimed at promoting détente. By 1974, West Germany also exchanged diplomats with Czechoslovakia, Bulgaria, and Hungary.

Nixon and Kissinger were not pleased with Brandt's activities. Kissinger believed America's allies should follow Washington's lead in seeking détente. The administration planned to link foreign policy strands so that Soviet concessions would relate not only to European questions such as the status of Berlin and conventional arms reductions but also issues of strategic arms control and Vietnam.

August 15, 1971

President Nixon announces a "new economic policy" that includes a 10 percent import tax surcharge, but it has international consequences.

The U.S. foreign trade imbalance had been growing since March 1968, and European nations wanted the United States to devalue the dollar in terms of gold to a more realistic ratio. Gold had held at $35 per ounce since 1933. By 1971, the speculative gold exchange no longer valued dollars sufficiently, causing the currency and trade of all nations based on the dollar to suffer. Following a lengthy meeting of the NSC, the Treasury Department, and others, Nixon decided to take three important actions on August 15: (1) A wage-price freeze was set up for the United States. (2) The convertibility of the dollar to gold was temporarily suspended. (3) There would be a 10 percent import surcharge.

Nixon claimed the surcharge would stabilize the dollar better than devaluation. He announced it would be temporary but did not specify for how long. The trade surcharge shocked America's allies, who had not been consulted before the announcement by Nixon. In reality, these policies were temporary expedients that delayed a crisis in which the United States would be unable to exchange gold for dollars on the international market. Later in 1971, delegates at an international conference discussed arrangements to handle the world's monetary affairs.

September 3, 1971

The Quadripartite Agreement on Berlin solves some of the past tensions in that divided city.

Ambassadorial-level talks regarding Berlin began among the four powers during February 1970. The talks dragged on until May 14, 1971, when Soviet First Secretary Brezhnev agreed to discuss possible mutual reductions of Warsaw Pact and NATO forces if the West would discuss the confirmation of the postwar European borders. Following detailed discussions between June and August, the four-power pact was signed in Berlin on September 3. The agreement's main clauses were as follows: (1) Traffic to and from West Berlin would be unimpeded. (2) West Berliners could visit East Berlin and East Germany for up to 30 days per year. (3) East Berliners could enter the West, but their departures were to be controlled by East Germany. (4) The three Western powers agreed that Berlin's western sectors were not a "constituent" part of West Germany and would not be governed by it. (5) Four-power rule was retained in Berlin.

The Berlin accords were ratified by East Berlin and West Germany on December 17, by West Berlin and East Germany on December 20. The Berlin Wall remained as a symbol of East Germany's need to keep its people locked in. The force reduction talks did not begin as scheduled in October 1971 because the Soviets would not receive the NATO delegation in Moscow. The final protocols on the Quadripartite Agreement of 1971 were not ratified until 1972.

September 5, 1971

A *New York Times* report mistakenly indicates that the Soviet Union has developed an intercontinental supersonic bomber, the Backfire.

The Backfire would have been the world's first supersonic bomber. The White House learned of its successful testing in March 1971, but there was disagreement and misinformation regarding capabilities of the bomber and its role in subsequent strategic arms negotiations.

The *New York Times* mistakenly reported that the Soviet Union's Backfire was an intercontinental supersonic bomber. This information was based on a CIA study that had drawings of the plane, although the Pentagon refused to discuss "sensitive" intelligence about the Backfire whose Soviet designation was the Tu-22M bomber. Coming at a time when Nixon's administration was negotiating ABM and SALT treaties with Moscow, the report was probably leaked by critics opposing such negotiations. During the SALT I negotiations, the United States insisted that the Backfire might refuel in flight and thus become an intercontinental bomber.

After Henry Kissinger became President Ford's secretary of state in 1974, Kissinger agreed with the Soviets that the Backfire's range was just over 2000 miles, a little over one-third the U.S. B-52's intercontinental range. Thus at best it was a medium range bomber and the Soviets agreed not to use refueling tactics. Details on the Backfire are in the memoirs of *Henry Kissinger: Years of Renewal* (1999) and in Pavel Podvig, *Russian Strategic Nuclear Forces* (2001).

September 30, 1971

The United States and the USSR sign two agreements to try to avoid an accidental nuclear war.

These two agreements state that (1) the nation under nuclear attack would try to ascertain if it were an accidental launch or not. This pact tried to strengthen fail-safe procedures, although no specific actions in case of an attack could be precisely predetermined; (2) the Washington-Moscow hot line was connected to space satellite communications to make it faster and less vulnerable to disruption in case of an accidental launch.

See June 22, 1973; September 15, 1987, and September 23, 1989.

October 3, 1971

President Thieu wins reelection in South Vietnam with 82 percent of the vote.

Although Thieu staged the election to please his U.S. advisers, the campaign threatened for a while to become a real contest, with former South Vietnamese politicians Marshal Ky or General Big Minh. In particular, Big Minh ran as an advocate of neutrality and negotiations with Hanoi, a program that found favor with the North Vietnamese. On August 5, the Supreme Court of the Republic of Vietnam ruled that as a former vice president, Ky could not run for election. Big Minh first tried to get the United States to guarantee a fair election. The Americans claimed to be "neutral" in the election and, therefore, unable to interfere. On August 20, Minh withdrew from the race, charging that the election process was corrupt.

By 1971, most observers of Thieu's government either criticized or excused his political methods. Critics said his government had less support than that of Diem in 1963; at least Diem had the Catholic backing that Thieu had lost by 1971. After 1968, Thieu talked about political, economic, and military reform but never took any significant action in these areas.

October 12, 1971

Washington and Moscow announce that Nixon will visit the Soviet Union in May 1972.

While reporters believed the signing of SALT I was near, the president cautioned that the pact might not be achieved by that time. In other respects, the announcement of Nixon's visit was no surprise. Since his July 15 decision to visit China, most observers believed the visit to the USSR would come sooner or later.

October 25, 1971

The People's Republic of China is admitted to and the nationalist government of Taiwan expelled from the United Nations.

Although the U.S. State Department would have liked to have both Chinese governments in the United Nations, Chou En-lai told Kissinger in July that the Beijing regime could not be represented unless Taiwan left the United Nations. Beginning on August 2, however, Secretary Rogers stated that the United States would support the seating of the mainland regime but oppose Taiwan's expulsion. The United States submitted such a resolution to the U.N. General Assembly on August 20 and solicited votes to support Taiwan. Until September 16, the United States left undisclosed its view of the Chinese seat as one of the Big Five permanent members of the Security Council if Taiwan remained. Then Nixon announced that the United States would vote for Beijing's position on the council because it reflected "realities."

After that statement, the United States lost all but a small hard core of followers on the U.N. vote. The U.N. action on October 25 was essentially a foregone conclusion. In the General Assembly, the U.S. vote to keep the Nationalists as members lost by 59 to 54. Ninety minutes later, an Albanian resolution to admit the People's Republic and expel Nationalist China carried by a vote of 76 to 35. The United States voted for this resolution. Taiwan's delegation, led by Liu Chieh, quietly gathered its papers and left the hall. The Beijing delegation arrived in New York on November 12.

October 26, 1971

Henry Kissinger leaves China with news that Nixon's 1972 visit is arranged.

Kissinger made his second visit to Chou En-lai on October 20, realizing that the details of the president's visit could be finalized following the U.N. vote on October 24 or 25. Thus, on the day after the U.N. vote that expelled the Taiwanese government, Beijing was assured that the United States had complied with its July request. Officially, the White House announced on November 29 that Nixon's visit to China would begin on February 21, 1972.

December 3, 1971

War begins between India and Pakistan.

There had been a buildup of tension between these two antagonists since 1970 following the outbreak of a rebellion in Bengal, East Pakistan. Because of Pakistani persecution, 5 million refugees fled from Bengal to India, where Prime Minister Indira Gandhi championed their cause. The rebels had proclaimed the independent republic of Bangladesh on March 26, 1971, causing the Pakistanis to take further measures to suppress the rebellion. On December 3, Indian troops invaded Bengal and with help from the rebels trapped 90,000 Pakistani troops. In West Pakistan, Indian armies took over some land in the disputed areas of Kashmir.

The Cold War caused strange partners in the South Asia conflict. Both the United States and China had pacts with Pakistan, and now an "understanding" with each other; while the Soviet Union had treaty arrangements with India. Fortunately, it was a short war.

See December 17, 1971.

December 17, 1971

The Group of Ten agrees on new international monetary arrangements by which the U.S. dollar is devalued and exchange rates "float."

Because America's major economic partners could no longer accept the 10 percent surcharge and continued declining value of the dollar—which Nixon permitted in his August 15 "new economic policy"—the United States as one of the leading financial nations had to work out a new exchange program with the European Community, Canada, and Japan. Secretary of Labor George Shultz argued for floating currency rates. Nixon and Kissinger accepted the floating currency concept and dollar devaluation during the Azores sessions, an idea with which Pompidou agreed.

This basic pact was announced as the Azores Pact on December 14 and ratified by the other European nations, Canada, and Japan on December 17. The agreement permitted all national currencies to float on the exchange market within "broader permissible margins" around a devalued dollar. The United States ended the 10 percent import surcharge and the nonconvertibility of the dollar decreed on August 15.

December 17, 1971

Pakistan and India agree to a cease-fire, partly owing to U.S. action to prevent a wider war.

After war broke out on December 3, President Nixon sought a truce through the United Nations and took action that "tilted" toward Pakistan to limit the war. The U.N. Security Council resolutions did not gain a truce because the Soviet Union vetoed three attempts to pass them. Although publicly claiming U.S. neutrality on December 6, Nixon acted in a fashion that prevented a disastrous defeat for Pakistan. He persuaded Jordan and Iran to send obsolete F-5, F-86, and F-104 jets to Pakistan. Meanwhile, China began massing troops on its frontiers with Sikkim and Bhutan—two Indian protectorates. Nixon also ordered a naval task force led by an aircraft carrier to move from the Pacific to the Bay of Bengal. This act indicated to India and its Soviet ally that the United States might aid Pakistan if necessary. Whether Nixon would have employed military force is unclear. U.S. public opinion favored the Bengalis as victims of Pakistani persecution. Thus, presidential action would have been difficult to justify.

The Soviets responded to the Sino-American actions by shifting their naval forces into the Indian Ocean and suggesting to the Chinese that the Soviets were prepared to use nuclear weapons. Despite the threat to China, Moscow played a cautious game because the Soviets were more concerned with improving their relations with Washington. A few days later, the Soviets informed Washington that the Indians would end military operations in East Bengal and the United States did not need to send troops to Pakistan. The Soviets' U.S. Ambassador Dobrynin notes the absurd nature of the affair: "after taking Pakistan's side as a payoff for helping open up China, Nixon and Kissinger had to rely on Moscow's word that India would not attack West Pakistan." Subsequently, India agreed to a cease-fire in East Bengal on December 14 and in Pakistan on December 17. The major result of the war was to make Bangladesh an independent nation.

1972

January 22, 1972

The United Kingdom is accepted as a member of the European Economic Community Common Market.

Because French President de Gaulle had vetoed the British membership application on December 18, 1967, Prime Minister Heath held discussions with President Pompidou of France on May 21 to agree on terms of Britain's admission. As a result the EEC voted in favor of English membership on June 23, 1971. On October 28, the British Parliament approved the terms of membership, and on January 22, 1972, the EEC formally voted to admit the British. On the same day, Ireland and Denmark also were accepted as members of the Common Market. The membership of these three nations became effective on January 1, 1973.

January 25, 1972

To a national television audience, Nixon outlines a plan to end the Vietnam War and discloses Kissinger's secret talks in Paris.

President Nixon told the public he was presenting a plan for peace to North Vietnam that should "end the war now" because it was "both generous and far-reaching." In reality, the proposal Nixon described was a slightly revised version of an offer made to Le Duc Tho in Paris on October 11, 1971. The proposal included withdrawal of all U.S. forces within six months of an agreement, new elections in South Vietnam after Thieu's prior resignation, an independent body to conduct elections in which the Communists could run candidates, and a U.S. aid program to help rebuild Vietnam. To impress his fellow Americans with his willingness to "try to break the deadlock in the negotiations," Nixon informed the public about Kissinger's secret talks in Paris since August 4, 1969. The national security adviser had met 12 times with Le Duc Tho, Xuan Thuy, or both.

Nixon reported that until recently, the secret talks had appeared to progress, but the Communists late in 1971 again became reluctant to compromise on any point. Nixon's speech indicated that, contrary to public impressions, he had been making extra efforts to seek peace. North Vietnam appeared for the first time to have been the party blocking a successful truce arrangement.

January 30, 1972

Pakistan withdraws from the British Commonwealth after Great Britain recognizes the independence of Bangladesh.

Although the truce with India of December 1971 virtually assured the independence of Bangladesh, Pakistan refused to recognize the loss of its eastern territory. As a result, London's recognition of the government of Prime Minister Sheikh Mujibur Rahman was opposed by Pakistan. On April 18, 1972, Bangladesh became a member of the British Commonwealth.

February 17, 1972

President Nixon leaves for China, making his entire journey a television spectacular.

Nixon used the China tour to promote his 1972 presidential campaign. After stopping in Hawaii and Guam, Air Force One reached Peking at 11:40 A.M. on February 21. Nixon and Kissinger went immediately to visit with Chairman Mao Tse-tung. Subsequently, live television reports carried into American homes his visits to the Great Hall of the People, the Great Wall, Hangchow, and Shanghai. On the final day in Shanghai, Nixon and Chou En-lai issued what became known as the Shanghai Communiqué, which described the working relations between Washington and Beijing.

The important parts of this message were as follows:

1. On Vietnam, the United States declared that after a truce the U.S. forces would withdraw and permit the peoples of Indochina

President Nixon visits with Chairman Mao Tse-tung. National Archives

The Nixons at the Great Wall. National Archives

to "determine their destiny without outside intervention." America, the message incorrectly stated, had always sought "a negotiated solution" to the Vietnam War.

2. The United States said it would retain strong ties with South Korea and Japan.
3. In South Asia, Nixon promised U.S. support for the rights of peoples in India, Pakistan, and

elsewhere to "shape their own future in peace, free of military threats, and without having the areas become the subject of great power rivalry."

4. Chou declared China wanted all nations to be treated as free and equal; "it opposes hegemony and power politics of any kind."
5. China supported the "peoples of Vietnam, Laos and Cambodia in their efforts" but said nothing about the U.S. presence in the area.
6. China opposed any Japanese "revival and outward expansion" of "militarism," favoring a "peaceful and neutral Japan."
7. China said it backed Pakistan in its "struggle to preserve...its independence and sovereignty." This referred indirectly to China's alliance against India.
8. The United States and China agreed to conduct relations on the "principles of respect for the sovereignty and integrity of all states, non-interference in the internal affairs of other states, equality and mutual benefits, and peaceful coexistence."
9. Regarding Taiwan, China stated that it could have no full diplomatic relations with the United States as long as Washington recognized the Taiwan regime. Without a definite date, Nixon promised the gradual U.S. withdrawal of its forces from Taiwan, agreeing that there is but one China and Taiwan is part of it.
10. China and the United States promised to broaden "people to people" exchanges, bilateral trade, and exchanges in science, technology, sports, and journalism. The two nations would remain in direct contact and establish "liaison missions" in lieu of normal diplomatic representation.

February 25, 1972

Secret bombings of North Vietnam are disclosed in a letter to Senator Hughes of the Senate Armed Services committee.

Similar to the secret Cambodian bombings of 1969–1970, the aggressive U.S. air force attacks on North Vietnam between November 1971 and March 1972 by General John D. Lavelle's Seventh Air Force were made public after February 25. Air Force Sergeant Lonni Douglas Franks told Senator Harold E. Hughes of these actions and requested a public investigation. Subsequent hearings of the Senate committee between June and September 1972 indicated that the Nixon administration had condoned, if not approved, these violations of the 1968 agreement with Hanoi. To justify the attacks, air force personnel filed reports that reconnaissance planes had been attacked and the fighter escorts had retaliated. A second set of reports for General Lavelle would list only the planes and the targets struck by the B-52s. The targets were not the surface-to-air missile (SAM) bases but truck parks, petroleum depots, troop concentrations, and other suitable targets. General Lavelle claimed he designed the attacks and the report system to impede the pre-invasion buildup of Communist forces. He said "higher authorities" encouraged him to use "protective air strikes" to attack other targets. He considered his method similar to the navy's practice of sending an aircraft as bait over North Vietnam's coast and retaliating after the North's fire had been provoked.

General John D. Ryan told the committee that the Defense Department had issued "liberal interpretations" of Communist targets during 1971 and that by January 1972, the revised regulations justified the targets Lavelle had hit. Thus, the committee tried to locate exactly by whom the changes in guidelines had been ordered. They could not obtain the secret documents either to corroborate or to refute that a "higher authority" was responsible. General Lavelle was relieved of command, reduced in rank, and retired from the service. According to the Senate committee report, he had ordered 28 unauthorized missions with 147 sorties by B-52s in a three-month period of 1971–1972.

March 13, 1972

The United Kingdom grants full diplomatic recognition to the People's Republic of China.

In their agreement with China, the British raised their recognition to the ambassadorial level for the first time since 1950. They also withdrew their consulate from Taiwan. The British were one of many nations granting the mainland government formal recognition during 1972.

March 30, 1972

North Vietnam begins offensive action in South Vietnam that lasts until early June.

When the Communists began their 'Easter offensive' on March 30, only 6,000 U.S. combat troops remained in South Vietnam. As a result, ARVN bore the brunt of the March–June offensive. Giap's forces attacked on three fronts: across the demilitarized zone and the Laotian border into the northern and central highlands, then, later, after ARVN forces moved north from Saigon, into the southern delta region near Saigon. By April, An Loc and Kontum were besieged and the Communists had nearly cut the country into two parts. After Thieu sent ARVN troops north, other Communists attacked the delta regions.

Lacking ground forces, General Abrams ordered B-52s from Guam to hit the delta. Previously, the United States had avoided B-52 raids in the populous delta. Now these planes struck in this area, destroying many peasant villages and homes as much as they hurt the Communists. The B-52 attacks and the Vietcong attacks severely damaged America's pacification program in the South. In June, ARVN counterattacks began to succeed. Some ARVN forces did commendably well; others did not hold up, however. The People's Self-Defense Force functioned well in the north but seemed to be demoralized in the delta region. The military consensus was that U.S. air support was the decisive factor in the successful defenses. How the ARVN would do without U.S. air cover remained unclear.

April 4, 1972

Nixon renews B-52 raids on North Vietnam; he believes large Communist Easter offensive justifies his action.

Since President Johnson halted Rolling Thunder on October 31, 1968, the only authorized U.S. air attacks on North Vietnam had been low-level retaliatory fighter-bomber attacks. After General Giap's March 30 offensive, Nixon reaffirmed U.S. resolve by responding with a strong attack against the enemy. The initial B-52 bombing raids were limited to the area from the 17th to the 20th parallel. Nixon decided also to test Moscow's link to Hanoi by additional bombings plus the mining of Haiphong Harbor. To enact this maneuver, Nixon sent Henry Kissinger on a special mission to Moscow before the new escalation began.

April 20, 1972

Kissinger begins secret meetings with Brezhnev; the focus is escalation of U.S. activity against North Vietnam and new conditions for the peace negotiations in Paris.

Kissinger's secret mission to Moscow from April 20 to 24 was summit politics in its most dramatic fashion. Nixon and Kissinger achieved two objectives during these secret talks. First, they learned that détente with the United States took precedence for Moscow over the events in Vietnam. This became evident when Kissinger told Brezhnev that Nixon believed he had to do two things to punish North Vietnam for the Easter offensive: (1) begin a general bombing of North Vietnam, and (2) mine Haiphong Harbor as the strongest U.S. action yet taken against Hanoi. Brezhnev accepted this necessity, although Moscow had protested the B-52 attacks of April 4 as a formality. In addition, Brezhnev would not interfere with the U.S. escalation in the north but would continue to supply Hanoi. Brezhnev agreed to receive Nixon on his long-planned visit to Moscow on May 22, 1972.

The second objective was to gain Brezhnev's backing for a U.S. proposal to break the deadlock in Kissinger's secret peace talks with Le Duc Tho. Because Brezhnev had yielded regarding the bombing escalation as a sign of Soviet interest in détente, Kissinger showed the U.S. desire for big-power détente by yielding on a significant point in the truce talks with Hanoi: the United States would agree to a cease-fire-in-place on the basis of North Vietnam's troops in the South before the March 30 Easter offensive. This meant that Hanoi could keep 100,000 North Vietnamese in the South after the truce and until a final settlement between North and South Vietnam. Kissinger asked only that Hanoi permit Thieu to remain in power in Saigon from the time of the cease-fire until the final settlement. Brezhnev realized that Kissinger made a major concession to allow Hanoi's troops to remain in the South. The Thieu matter appeared inconsequential to the Kremlin leaders. Therefore, Brezhnev accepted Kissinger's offer. He immediately dispatched Konstantin Katushev, the Politburo member in charge of allied relations, to Hanoi to deliver Kissinger's new proposal and to arrange a renewal of the secret Paris talks between Kissinger and Le Duc Tho. Kissinger was elated. On April 24, before leaving Moscow, he called Ambassador Beam and told him that not even the State Department must know about the secret visit. Beam would be Kissinger's contact point with Brezhnev in working out arrangements for the new truce talks via Katushev.

May 8, 1972

President Nixon orders the mining of Haiphong Harbor and renews large-scale B-52 attacks on North Vietnam as Linebacker I.

Whereas the April 4 B-52 attacks were limited to the 20th parallel, Linebacker I duplicated many of Rolling Thunder's North Vietnamese targets. Only the 30-mile limit of China's border was restricted. New targets included the Paul Doumer bridge in Hanoi, bridge and rail lines leading to China, fuel dumps, power plants, pipelines to China, and all missile or antiaircraft sites. The B-52s now had television and laser-guided bombs for more accuracy and fewer plane losses. Linebacker I continued until October 23, 1972. The order to mine Haiphong Harbor was the most critical escalation ordered by Nixon. The Joint Chiefs had urged the mining of Hanoi's port since 1965, but heretofore the risk of possible war with China or the Soviet Union seemed too great in case one of those nations' ships were hit.

Nixon's détente policy negated the previous risks. His February 1972 visit to China and Kissinger's secret talks in Moscow of April 20–24 guaranteed that those two major powers would not interfere but would accept the closing of the harbor. Not knowing of the secret arrangements made by Nixon with Brezhnev, dissenters warned nuclear war was being risked with the Soviet Union. Not until Nixon arrived in Moscow to begin talks on May 22 did dissenters concede President Nixon had gained Soviet approval for the mining.

Soon after May 8, the mining of the sea areas around North Vietnam began. U.S. planes laid the mines in the water, setting them to explode at various depths. The aircraft placed over 8,000 mines in the coastal port areas and 3,000 in the inland waterways. Prior to the aerial mining, foreign ships had been given three days' notice to leave the area. The warning was effective. All ships, including Communist-bloc vessels, left the region without serious incident. Only General Giap and Hanoi's Communists were surprised that neither Beijing nor Moscow did more than issue mild protests to Washington. While U.S. planes completed the mining process late in May, Brezhnev and Nixon wined and dined in Moscow and China's diplomats arranged new trade deals with the United States. Hanoi's Communist Party newspaper, *Nhan Dan*, bitterly complained that Brezhnev's reception of Nixon was like "throwing a life preserver to a drowning pirate." Nevertheless, the Joint Chiefs' expectation that mining the harbor would seriously hurt Hanoi was another miscalculation.

Much of North Vietnam's foreign trade simply went overland. Highways from China to Hanoi became clogged with trucks carrying supplies. New oil pipelines kept fuel plentiful, and a French news correspondent in Hanoi found no evidence of a critical lack of supplies during the summer of 1972. As some observers had previously told the JCS, 90 percent of North Vietnam's supplies always came overland, making the mining the waterways unimportant. For hawks in America, however, mining the North Vietnamese port areas had come to symbolize the hard line against the Communists.

May 25, 1972

U.S.-USSR sign agreement to prevent incidents at sea.

During the 1960s and early 1970s, American and Soviet warships and aircraft engaged in harassing each other at sea. Despite international "rules of the road" to avoid sea collisions, the activities included using aircraft to buzz the other's vessels, ship guns aimed at other ships, nudging or "shouldering" the opponent's ships, or a game of "chicken" where two rival ships threatened to ram each other before moving away at the last moment. There always was a possibility of an undesired or inadvertent incident involving the loss of life and vessels, or of creating serious political/military clashes that eventually drew high level attention.

While naval professionalism prevented a serious mishap, the United States wanted to establish a bilateral accord to reduce such incidents as early as 1967. The Soviets had ignored the idea but in 1970 offered to open discussions. Delegations from both countries began negotiations in October 1971, led by Undersecretary of the Navy John W. Warner and first deputy commander of the Soviet Navy Admiral Vladimir A. Kasatonov. Although the Soviets wanted to restrict the distance between opposing ships, the Americans did not want arbitrary limits on surveillance activities such as locating and following submarines. Thus the two sides agreed negotiations would deal with surface ships and aircraft but ignore submarine operations.

The discussions were completed during May 3–17 and the agreement signed by the heads of the delegations on May 25. The treaty followed the "rules of the road" in providing wide berths during maneuvers, especially aircraft landings and takeoffs. It also prohibited other acts such as simulated attacks, shining searchlights on bridges, and buzzing by aircraft. Communications were improved between opposing ship and channels established for regular consultation or prior notification of activities at sea. The immediate impact reduced incidents from over 100 a year prior to May 1972 to 40 in 1973. (See July 15, 1986.) For details see David F. Winkler, *Cold War at Sea* (2000).

President Nixon and Soviet Premier Brezhnev. National Archives

May 26, 1972

Nixon and Brezhnev sign the ABM Treaty and SALT I agreement in Moscow.

President Nixon was the first U.S. president to visit Moscow (May 22–30), although Nixon had visited as vice president. (See July 24, 1959.) The 1972 visit was part of Nixon's triangular policy to play off the USSR against the Chinese. His visit with President Brezhnev would also allow Nixon to claim credit for the arms control agreement. To complete that agreement, Nixon made concessions to Brezhnev that baffled American nuclear arms control experts who were critical of Nixon's ignorance about essential details of ABM missiles and strategic armaments. Detailed information on the Moscow meeting and agreements is provided in Raymond Garthoff's *Détente and Confrontation* (1985).

To summarize the sessions, Nixon and Brezhnev signed two arms control agreements and several agreements for cultural exchanges. First, the two arms control pacts were an Anti-Ballistic Missile Treaty (ABM) and a Strategic Arms Limitation Agreement (SALT I). Both agreements had been prepared during secret talks that began in 1969. (See November 17, 1969.) The discussions were completed between March and May 1972 by chief U.S. negotiator Gerard Smith and the Soviets' Vladimir Semenov. Smith was assisted by National Security Adviser Henry Kissinger's visit with Brezhnev in April. (See April 20, 1972.) The ABM Treaty limited each side to two ABM sites, separated by no fewer than 1300 kilometers so that they would not overlap. Later, Nixon and Brezhnev reduced ABM sites from two to one. (See July 3, 1974.) The limited ABM sites were essential to the SALT I agreement that was based on the concept of mutual assured destruction (MAD). Under MAD, if one side launched a nuclear attack, the other side would retain sufficient nuclear weapons to destroy the aggressor in a second strike; thus, both sides would suffer vast nuclear devastation.

Agreement on the ABM Treaty enabled Nixon and Brezhnev to sign the Interim Agreement on Certain Measures with Respect to Strategic Offensive Arms. The term interim indicated both sides proposed to continue negotiations for a SALT II treaty while each side restricted its existing launching sites for intercontinental missiles (ICBMs). The SALT I clauses may be summarized as follows: (1) a freeze banned the start of any new ICBM launching sites after July 1, 1972. (2) Existing launching sites could not be moved or replaced by new ones. (3) Small ICBM launchers could not be converted to large ICBM sites. (4) ICBM silos under construction could be completed. (5) Except as otherwise limited, modernization and replacement of strategic missiles and launchers were permitted. As Garthoff explains, SALT I failed to define small or light and large or heavy ICBM missiles and to limit increases in the size of silos being modernized. U.S. negotiator Smith wanted to resolve these issues but Nixon did not wish to delay news about the signing of an arms control agreement, an event to enhance his campaign for a second term as president. In the long term, the most critical factor ignored by SALT I was consideration of the development of multiple independent targetable reentry vehicles (MIRVs). MIRV technology permitted each launcher to carry as many as 10 nuclear warheads aimed at 10 different targets. The US had already tested and deployed some MIRV launchers, but Soviet MIRVs were from three to five years behind the American program. Although the Senate ratified the ABM Treaty and Congress approved funds for implementing it under Public Law 92-448, which Nixon signed on November 15, 1972, many Republican politicians later criticized SALT, the ABM Treaty, and Nixon's détente policy. In particular, the Committee on the Present Danger was formed in 1976 to oppose the agreements and détente. In addition to arms control, Nixon and Brezhnev signed a "Basic Principles of Relations" for both nations to live in peace and security. Other agreements were to improve trade and cultural relations and cooperation in science and technology, including a joint Apollo-Soyuz orbital space mission.

May 29, 1972

Brezhnev and Nixon sign "The Basic Principles of Relations between the Soviet Union and the United States of America."

This agreement was initiated by the Kremlin and while virtually ignored in America, was considered by Soviet officials as "an important political declaration." As Ambassador Dobrynin's memoirs note, it was "the foundations of the new political process of détente in our relations." Soviet leaders believed the document was of special importance because it jointly told the world the basic "principles of international conduct we had long been striving to have recognized." The Principles of Relations recognized the Soviet doctrine of peaceful coexistence and acknowledged the "principle of equality as a basis for the security of both countries."

Kissinger was the only American involved in drafting the Principles but paid little attention to the document even though it meant a great deal to Soviet officials and the Soviet public. The Russians saw it as validating peaceful coexistence and creating a friendly atmosphere rather than confrontation between the two countries. The Principles never had the effect its sponsors hoped for because neither side defined its scope and boundaries. To the Soviets it meant the superpowers would cooperate in resolving basic issues despite "minor" differences in the Third World.

In contrast, Americans interpreted détente as cooperation or "hands off" in the Third World. Subsequently, they linked disputes in Africa, the Middle East, and Central America with bilateral negotiations on issues like controlling strategic arms. The failure to develop détente's boundary and gain public acceptance doomed it in America's domestic political arena.

June 3, 1972

The Quadripartite Agreement on Berlin is fully ratified.

The final exchange of the agreement's ratification was signed on September 3, 1971, but awaited the ratification of West Germany's 1970–1971 treaties with the Soviet Union and Poland. The 1970–1971 treaties were delayed by West Germany's Bundestag because opponents of the treaties wanted to be certain that Germany retained its right to self-determination, to membership in the European Common Market, and to future reunification with East Germany. After those doubts were satisfied, the Bundestag ratified the two treaties on May 19. The Soviet Union and Poland ratified the treaties by May 31, 1972. This action cleared the way to exchange ratification on the Berlin pact on June 3. A new relationship was formalized between the two Germanys and Poland.

June 17, 1972

The Watergate break-in at the Democratic National Headquarters is linked to the Committee to Re-elect the President (CREEP).

Watergate is an apartment-hotel complex in Washington, D.C. Initially a relatively small incident, Nixon's denials of involvement prevented it from affecting his 1972 campaign. However, further investigation resulted in disclosures that led to his resignation as president in August 1974.

July 18, 1972

Egypt's President Sadat expels 20,000 Soviet "advisers."

Ostensibly, Sadat was upset with Moscow because First Secretary Brezhnev refused to supply him with modern military technology to prepare for war with Israel. The only Soviets Sadat permitted to remain were 200 advisers on SAM missile sites.

July 19, 1972

Henry Kissinger and Le Duc Tho renew truce negotiations in Paris that finally lead to a settlement.

The renewed discussions in Paris came 10 months after Kissinger and Le Duc Tho reached an impasse during a session on September 13, 1971. Kissinger's April 20–24, 1972 talks with Brezhnev opened the door for both to renew negotiations and to find a settlement in the formal and secret discussions that had been held intermittently in Paris since May 1968. The formal talks in Paris had become a sideshow because of the many secret and separate discussions that Kissinger held with either Le Duc Tho or Xuan Thuy.

The talks were important as a symbol of the four parties negotiating and as the group that would finalize any treaty resulting from the secret talks. The U.S. head of the formal delegation in July 1972 was William Porter. The first head of the delegation, Henry Cabot Lodge, resigned on November 20, 1969. From July 1, 1970 to July 1971, Ambassador to London David Bruce led the U.S. delegation. Finally, Porter took over for Bruce in July 1971. Kissinger's secret talks had resulted in 12 meetings between August 1969 and September 13, 1971, when the talks became deadlocked. His first discussions with Le Duc Tho were in February 1970. The lengthiest series of secret discussions occurred between May 31 and September 13, 1971. On at least six different trips to Paris in 1971, Kissinger and Le Duc Tho exchanged various proposals, but all talks broke down by September 13. Although Kissinger made another proposal on October 11, 1971, the North Vietnamese refused to meet again until more substantive changes were made by the United States.

The principal deadlock in 1971 resulted from U.S. insistence on two points: (1) mutual withdrawal of all "foreign" troops from South Vietnam, because to Kissinger "foreign" included North Vietnamese; and (2) leaving President Thieu in charge in South Vietnam to negotiate a final settlement with the Communists. The second proposal had particularly concerned Hanoi during 1971 because Hanoi did not want the United States to allow Thieu to be reelected again as president of South Vietnam during the October 11 elections. By July 1972, both Kissinger and North Vietnam had become aware of the need for each side to compromise. Kissinger had outlined a new U.S. position on the cease-fire-in-place when he talked with Brezhnev on April 20, 1972. During a press conference in Paris on May 12, Le Duc Tho indicated his willingness to make a major concession: to permit Saigon to be represented on a three-party "government of broad national concord reflecting the real political situation in South Vietnam." Tho's only qualification was that Thieu could not be chosen by the South Vietnamese as a representative.

Before July, a variety of developments enabled the new discussions to begin. The Communists' spring offensive, Nixon's retaliatory B-52 strikes, and the successful defense of their territory by the ARVN with U.S. air support were factors causing the North Vietnamese to become more conciliatory when the July 19 meetings began. The most vital reality to North Vietnam, however, was that both Beijing and Moscow urged Hanoi to negotiate a U.S. withdrawal from Vietnam. Hanoi had hoped China and the USSR would reject Nixon's détente overtures unless the United States stopped all military action in Vietnam. By canceling the Moscow summit and halting Chinese-U.S. trade discussions, Hanoi's Communist allies could have pressured Nixon to withdraw more rapidly from Vietnam. This policy had been rejected by the Soviet Union and China, each of which had its reasons for encouraging détente with America. North Vietnam, therefore, had both military and diplomatic reasons for moving toward a truce. Until U.S. air support was taken away from Saigon, the Communists could not win in Vietnam. Without Soviet or Chinese diplomatic backing, a coalition government in the South would have to precede a definite Communist victory.

For Nixon and Kissinger, the desire to pull out of Vietnam was part of their realistic global strategy and part of the president's 1972 campaign strategy at home. Détente and satisfactory relations with Moscow and Peking required that the United States relinquish its exaggerated concern for the minor issue of Vietnam in its big power relations, that is, to release the U.S. foothold in Southeast Asia that the Chinese disliked. Vietnam, not Taiwan, was the primary obstacle to Nixon and Kissinger's rapprochement with Beijing. At home, the increased dissent against the prolonged war in Vietnam that Nixon had promised to end during the 1968 campaign and the belief that George McGovern was a serious contender for a presidential victory required Nixon to demonstrate that the Vietnamization process was nearly fulfilled. As Nixon's exaggerated concern in planning the Watergate burglary of June 17 demonstrates, the president wanted to avoid all possible risks of defeat in 1972. On July 19, therefore, Le Duc Tho and Kissinger began what became their final round of discussions for truce arrangements.

October 26, 1972

Kissinger announces that "peace is at hand" in Vietnam. The only remaining issues are the American requirement for the precise language needed for an "honorable withdrawal" and to protect President Thieu's government.

In light of the draft treaty that Kissinger negotiated with Le Duc Tho between July 19 and October 26, Kissinger's remarks to the press conference misled reporters. The real issue delaying the peace process was Nixon's need to convince Thieu to accept the proposals drawn up by Kissinger in Paris. Although Kissinger tried on August 15 and from October 16 to 22 to gain Thieu's approval, the National Security Adviser did not persuade Thieu to concede. Kissinger had tried to persuade Nixon not to give Thieu veto power over the treaty, but Nixon refused. For political reasons, the president could not risk loud protests from Saigon because the "peace with honor" concept required Thieu's acceptance of any truce.

Nevertheless, the basic framework of the January 1973 truce terms had been worked out by October 16. Briefly summarized, the agreements and the controversial points accepted by Le Duc Tho and Kissinger between July 19 and October 16 were as follows:

1. Cease-fire-in-place. The important terms influencing this agreement were that all U.S. troops would withdraw within 60 days of the cease-fire, and all U.S. prisoners of war would be released within 60 days of the cease-fire. Although the agreement did not so specify, omission of withdrawal terms for the North Vietnamese meant that those forces would remain in place in South Vietnam.
2. "Two-party" National Council of Reconciliation and Concord to implement truce terms and reunify Vietnam. The original Kissinger plan for a Tripartite Commission to be formed by Thieu's regime, the Provisional Revolutionary Government (formerly the National Liberation Front), and South Vietnamese neutralists was rejected by Thieu. To attempt to satisfy Thieu, Kissinger on October 11 changed the name to "National Council" and referred only to the "two parties" in South Vietnam. Between October 11 and 26, however, Thieu also rejected this proposal. Thieu wanted to be the only government recognized in the South, a position that would have prevented any truce accord. On October 26, therefore, Thieu had not accepted this idea.
3. United States to stop bombing first. The October 16 agreement called for the United States to stop bombing by October 23 so that the treaty could be signed on October 30–31. Linebacker I bombings ceased on October 23, but the treaty was not signed because of Thieu's objections.
4. Replacement of war matériel. When the first treaty draft was accepted on October 11, there was no agreement on this. Kissinger wanted loose terminology that would permit the United States to keep Thieu well supplied after

the cease-fire; Tho wanted a narrow definition to prevent replacements as much as possible. The North Vietnamese accepted Kissinger's terms on replacement on October 22, 1972. Because Thieu refused to sign the treaty on October 23 as provided for in the Kissinger-Tho plan of October 11, Hanoi broadcast a report that announced the terms it had agreed to and condemned Washington and Saigon for breaking their promise to sign and disturbing world peace. Beijing and Moscow joined Hanoi's opposition to U.S. actions. The Communist protests unintentionally helped to smooth over the Nixon-Kissinger problems with Thieu. Thus, at the press conference on October 26, Kissinger could appear to make the Nixon administration the champion of peace but also the champion of the Thieu government's rights. Kissinger's "peace is at hand" statement indicated that only technical details needed to be resolved. One more round of talks with Le Duc Tho should resolve the matter, Kissinger said. At the same time, by requiring Thieu's agreement before signing, Nixon and Kissinger appeared to be defenders of "peace with honor," making certain that the technicalities of the truce would preserve the independence of South Vietnam. In this manner, Nixon's reelection campaign was not damaged but assisted on the eve of U.S. balloting.

November 7, 1972

President Nixon is reelected by a large margin.

Following his nomination on July 13 by the Democratic National Convention, George McGovern waged an ineffectual campaign that emphasized the immediate end to the Vietnam War and a guaranteed income for the poor. The Republicans nominated Richard Nixon and Spiro T. Agnew on August 23, with a platform supporting Nixon's foreign policy, advocating welfare reform, and opposing the busing of school children to achieve racial integration. The war issue became insignificant after Henry Kissinger's "peace is at hand" statement of October 26. Nixon won 520 electoral votes to 17 for McGovern, who carried only Massachusetts and Washington, D.C.

November 9, 1972

The United States, France, Great Britain, and the Soviet Union agree that both the East German and the West German governments may join the United Nations.

As a follow-up to the Berlin agreement ratified on June 3, 1972, delegates of the four powers met in Berlin to decide on a method for accepting both governments as U.N. members. This was part of an overall arrangement by which the East and West Germans cooperated to improve their relations as part of détente in central Europe. As early as March 19, 1970, Chancellor Willy Brandt of the Bonn government had visited Erfurt to conduct talks with Prime Minister Willie Stoph of East Germany.

December 16, 1972

Kissinger claims the Paris peace talks are at an impasse because of Hanoi's intransigence. The United States may need to renew air attacks.

Between Kissinger's October 26 "peace is at hand" statement and his December 16 press conference, close observers realized that the differences between the negotiators in Paris were greater than "technical details." After the peace talks were renewed in Paris on November 20, Saigon's demands for 69 changes in the draft treaty and Kissinger's initial attempt to support Saigon nearly brought the negotiations to an end. Nixon's attempts to placate Thieu to get his agreement had been unsuccessful during November. Nixon demonstrated U.S. support by speeding a rapid increase of military supplies to South Vietnam through Projects Enhance and Enhance Plus, which began on October 14. But the rapid delivery of 70 tanks and 600 helicopters and fighter planes by early December did not persuade Thieu to yield. Nixon also sent a personal letter to Thieu on November 14 telling him the United States would take "swift and severe retaliatory action" against the Communists if they violated the truce terms. Moreover, he warned Thieu that his best security would be the sympathy of American and world opinion, a benefit that Thieu sacrificed by being an obstacle to the peace process. The South Vietnamese leader held firm; the destiny of all the people of South Vietnam was his to protect, Thieu claimed.

Because Saigon's demands precluded a truce solution, Kissinger asked Le Duc Tho to renew secret and separate discussions on December 4. Kissinger was willing to return to the October draft treaty but he demanded a timetable by which the treaty would be signed on December 22, 1972. Kissinger wanted several changes in the October treaty to placate Thieu, but Le Duc Tho charged that the new concepts were complicated and could not be answered in the 48-hour limit that Kissinger desired. Kissinger became frustrated. First Thieu, now Le Duc Tho, was being difficult. By December 11, the Kissinger-Tho talks had reached an impasse. The national security adviser returned to Washington on December 13. Kissinger and Nixon agreed that they must vigorously bomb North Vietnam as Kissinger frequently had threatened during the November 1972 negotiations to make their points. Hanoi was sent a 72-hour ultimatum. It must agree to the issues pending during the December 4–11, 1972 peace talks or it would be bombed again. At his December 16 press conference Kissinger never mentioned the ultimatum to Hanoi or the problem of Saigon's 69 demands. He emphasized that North Vietnam was responsible for the negotiating problems. Le Duc Tho, he stated, had raised "one frivolous issue after another." Because Hanoi rejected these peace terms, the security adviser feared that the United States might have to renew its bombing raids on the North. On December 18 these attacks began on a larger scale than ever before.

December 18, 1972

The United States begins bombing raids on North Vietnam: the "Christmas Bombing" by Linebacker II.

Nixon and Kissinger decided to undertake the "Christmas" bombing raids with no outside advice. Although Secretary of Defense Laird wrote the president opposing a military response to the Paris deadlock, neither he nor Secretary of State Rogers was brought into the discussion by Nixon and Kissinger. In addition, since the Cambodian incursion of April 1970, Kissinger had lost most of the highly competent NSC staff he recruited in 1969. Those who had resigned included Morton Halperin, Roger Morris, Anthony Lake, and William Watts. When, as expected, Hanoi rejected Nixon's 72-hour ultimatum, Nixon ordered the Linebacker II attacks to begin on December 18. For these attacks, Nixon released the air force from almost all previous restrictions. The purpose of the bombing was allegedly to cripple daily life in Hanoi and Haiphong, the two major cities of North Vietnam. Between December 18 and 29, except for Christmas Day, incessant air raids were launched from Guam by 200 B-52s aided by F-4s and F-111s from Thailand and South Vietnam. Using carpet-bombing tactics, every three-plane B-52 mission attacked a target area one and one-half mile long and one-half mile wide. The planes dropped 15,000 tons of bombs on their section of target, and little but rubble remained except for a few houses with roofs or windows remaining. For example, on the night of December 27–28, whether by design or accident, the Khan Thieu residential district of Hanoi was hit. Fortunately, most of the 28,198 people had evacuated that area. After the raid only a few houses still had roofs or windows.

The bombing attacks of December 18–29 were controversial. Critics such as Telford Taylor argue that they hit civilian areas and were largely indiscriminate "terror" attacks. Military authorities emphasized that they targeted only military areas, but that "spillage" caused residences and hospitals to be hit off-target. In addition, Guenter Lewy's analysis shows that the 11-day attack was not as severe as the attacks on Dresden and Tokyo during World War II. In North Vietnam, reported deaths from the raids were 2200 to 5000 compared to the 35,000 or more who died at Dresden and the some 87,000 killed in Tokyo raids. Undoubtedly, the bombings were denounced in America because the public had been told "peace is at hand" and "only technical details" had to be worked out. The U.S. Vietnamization process seemed to be nearly completed and U.S. military advisers in Saigon were optimistic about the capabilities of the troops they had been training since 1968.

Given these expectations, the Christmas bombings appeared to be purposeless and vengeful attempts to coerce Hanoi to accept some technicalities in Paris. The results of the bombings are also controversial. Nixon and Kissinger claim the bombings brought the North Vietnamese delegates back to agree at the bargaining table. Their critics argue that public opposition to the bombing caused Nixon to agree to negotiate again. Somewhat paradoxically, Lewy claims the bombings were not terroristic but did force Le Duc Tho to return to Paris. Bombing critics such as Gareth Porter and Alan Goodman say the bombings were terroristic but were not the reason that negotiations began again. Whatever the reason, on December 30, President Nixon announced that the bombings above the 20th parallel had stopped and negotiations would begin again in Paris in January.

Later, the White House said it acted in response to Hanoi's pleas to stop bombing; the North Vietnamese said they had never broken off the talks, and Kissinger returned to Paris because of world opinion and the "fact" that 34 B-52s had been lost. The U.S. Air Force acknowledged 15 losses. Perhaps the greatest effect of the December Linebacker II raids was that Nixon and Thieu lost the sympathy of a majority of U.S. congressmen. A poll of senators on December 20 indicated they opposed the bombing 45 to 19 and favored legislation to end the war 45 to 25. When Congress returned to the Capitol in January, most members were ready to cut off funds for the war, a measure they had previously rejected. World opinion blamed both Thieu and Nixon for the "terror" attacks. None of the NATO nations approved, and Pope Paul VI deplored the "resumption of harsh and massive war action" in Vietnam. Thieu's regime could no longer be seen by most as an unwilling victim or an embattled republic; this new attitude lasted until the fall of Saigon in April 1975. As a commentator remarked, Kissinger violated one of the principal rules of Bismarck's nineteenth century realistic politics: never punish a weaker enemy when his surrender is near.

1973

January 27, 1973

In Paris, four delegations in the Vietnam negotiations sign truce agreements.

The Paris talks between Kissinger and Le Duc Tho resumed on January 8, 1973. President Nixon wanted a truce before his second inauguration but did not quite achieve that goal. Although the Paris delegates did not initial the draft treaty until January 23, Nixon had ordered an end to all war action by the United States on January 15 because Kissinger informed him the treaty was practically agreed to. The cease-fire in Vietnam officially began at 24:00 Greenwich Mean Time on January 27, 1973. Actually, two separate treaties were signed in Paris because Thieu's delegation refused to sign a document that specifically mentioned the Provisional Revolutionary Government (PRG). One treaty was signed by two parties, the Democratic Republic of (North) Vietnam (DRV) and the United States. This treaty had the concurrent agreement of the other two parties. The second treaty was a four-party treaty signed by the DRV, the United States, the PRG, and the Republic of South Vietnam. During the last week of negotiations, Kissinger had yielded most disputed points to North Vietnam although, of course, he never admitted this.

The two scholars of the truce process, Allan Goldman and Gareth Porter, agree that the January truce differed in no substantial ways from the October draft. Despite Thieu's objections, the most critical clauses of the October draft were intact:

1. North Vietnamese troops would remain in place in South Vietnam, but the United States was to withdraw in 60 days.
2. Both sides were to exchange prisoners of war in 60 days, but Saigon's political "detainees" would be handled after the truce.
3. Military equipment could be replaced on a one-to-one basis.
4. An International Control Commission of 1,160 persons would implement the truce terms.
5. The National Council on Reconciliation and Concord would carry out elections and negotiate to reunite Vietnam. In the two-party treaty, both the Provisional Government and Thieu's Republic of Vietnam were included. In the four-party treaty the Council consisted of the "two parties in South Vietnam."
6. Contrary to Thieu's wishes, the 17th parallel was not a boundary between states but remained, as in the 1954 Geneva Treaty, a "provisional and not a political or territorial boundary" until Vietnam was united as one nation. Nixon had forced Thieu to agree to the treaty.

The same day the December bombing began (December 18), Nixon sent Alexander Haig, a member of the National Security Staff, to Saigon to inform Thieu that he must accept the settlement agreed to by Nixon or each party would go his "separate way." Haig had been instructed not to negotiate. Thieu had to decide whether "to continue our alliance" or whether Nixon should "seek a settlement with the enemy which serves United States interests alone." On January 5, Nixon again put pressure on Thieu. Nixon wrote him that his "best guarantee" for survival was unity with Washington. This, he said, "would be gravely jeopardized if you persist in your present course." Nixon also promised to make certain that the North Vietnamese would not violate the truce terms. This and other personal promises by Nixon held little substance in future years as his actions in the Watergate cover-up would lead to his resignation as president in August 1974.

February 9, 1973

The United States resumes bombing of Cambodia, claiming Communists have not respected a cease-fire agreement.

Between February and August 1973, Nixon and his opponents in Congress argued continually regarding the renewed bombing of Cambodia after the Vietnamese truce went into effect on January 27. The administration contended that North Vietnamese troops and the Khmer Rouge continued fighting in Cambodia and that Lon Nol, the prime minister of Cambodia, requested U.S. aid. Congressional critics such as Senator Stuart Symington pointed out that in every military appropriations bill since October 1970, a proviso forbade the bombing of Cambodia except to protect Americans in Vietnam. Therefore, the continued bombing after the 1973 Vietnam truce was illegal. Henry Kissinger endeavored during the final Paris peace talks of 1972–1973 to arrange cease-fires in Laos and Cambodia as well as Vietnam. Le Duc Tho assured him this could be done in Laos because Hanoi had control over the Laotian Communists.

The same, Le Duc Tho said, could not be done for Cambodia because the Khmer Rouge was too independent. In fact, the traditional enmity between the Khmer and Vietnamese ethnic groups caused the Cambodians to distrust all Vietnamese—who reciprocated these feelings. Kissinger, however, was ill informed about Cambodia and apparently did not understand or believe Le Duc Tho's assertion. On January 23, 1973, during the final discussions in Paris, Kissinger read a unilateral statement saying that Lon Nol would suspend offensive attacks and the United States would stop bombing Cambodia. If the Khmer Rouge and North Vietnamese reciprocated, there would be a *de facto* cease-fire. If not, the U.S. Air Force would resume bombing until there was a cease-fire. Kissinger did not advocate or engage in any talks between the Khmer Rouge and Lon Nol. For Kissinger and other U.S. officials, Cambodia was a "sideshow" to sustaining South Vietnam. Although he urged Lon Nol and the Communists to negotiate, Kissinger never actively fostered this process. Lon Nol would have profited from a cease-fire because the Khmer Rouge were on the verge of victory. Le Duc Tho and Hanoi encouraged the Khmer to stop fighting. The Khmer leaders and, in Beijing exile, Prince Sihanouk believed Hanoi simply wanted to damage the cause of Cambodia so that the Vietnamese could conquer that country at a later date. Therefore, the Khmer ignored Hanoi's requests.

By February 9, the *de facto* cease-fire had not materialized. Thus, Nixon and Kissinger agreed to renew the bombing of Cambodia. This action would not only support Lon Nol but demonstrate to Hanoi that Nixon was determined to require North Vietnam to fulfill the 1973 truce. Indirectly, therefore, the White House viewed the Cambodian bombing as continuing evidence of its backing of Thieu. Nixon did not, however, ask Congress to repeal its prior legislation against the Cambodian bombing as Symington suggested he should do. The renewed bombing of Cambodia after February 9 was not a token bombing to indicate dissatisfaction to Hanoi but a large-scale, massive series of bombing attacks by B-52s from Guam and fighter bombers from Thailand. During the 12 months of 1972, B-52s dropped 37,000 tons of bombs on Cambodia. In March 1973, they dropped 24,000; in April 35,000, and in May 36,000 tons. The fighter-bombers had dropped 16,513 tons in 1972. In April 1973, these aircraft dropped 15,000 tons; the figure rose to 19,000 tons in July. The U.S. bombings of Cambodia in 1973 prevented the fall of Lon Nol's government, but, as in the case of Thieu in Vietnam, U.S. military action weakened rather than strengthened Lon Nol's support among the people. Internally, the Khmer Rouge successes between 1971 and 1973 caused the government of Lon Nol and Prince Sirik Matak to use repressive methods. Consequently, those Cambodians who opposed the Khmer Rouge sought the return of Sihanouk. This tactic never succeeded because Sihanouk increasingly preferred an alliance with the Khmer Rouge against Lon Nol as the best way to regain control of Cambodia. In July 1973, when Kissinger offered to talk with Sihanouk, it was too late. The exiled prince could not risk association with the United States.

February 15, 1973

Cuba and the United States sign an antihijacking agreement.

The number of incidents in which U.S. aircraft were hijacked and forced to fly to Havana caused difficulty for both nations. By this agreement, each country would try or extradite hijackers who forced aircraft to land in either the United States or Cuba.

March 19, 1973

Talks between the Republic of Vietnam (RVN) and the Provisional Revolutionary Government of Vietnam (PRG) begin at St. Cloud, France.

The first conference agenda item concerned setting a date for elections to the National Council on Reconciliation and Concord (NCRC). Disagreement occurred immediately. The RVN wanted North Vietnamese troops to withdraw from the South before the election; the PRG wanted all fighting, including frequent skirmishes along the cease-fire line, to stop before elections. The NCRC was never elected. Formal but infrequent meetings continued at St. Cloud until January 25, 1974, when the delegates adjourned because their meetings were superfluous.

March 21, 1973

The United States vetoes U.N. Security Council resolution favoring the restoration of Panamanian sovereignty in the canal zone.

In order to change the issue of the Panama Canal from a bilateral question with the United States to an international issue, Panama's head of state, General Omar Torrijos, invited the U.N. Security Council to conduct a meeting in Panama between March 15 and March 21. As a result, the council, with strong backing from all Latin American and other developing nations, offered a resolution stating that the United States should restore Panamanian national sovereignty over its entire territory. In the vote, 13 council members approved, Great Britain abstained, and the United States vetoed the resolution.

March 29, 1973

The last U.S. soldier leaves Vietnam. All American prisoners of war are returned but the fate of many missing in action is not known.

By March 29, about 1,000 POWs had returned to the United States, as had the last of the 6,000 combat troops who remained at the end of 1972. More than 2.5 million Americans served in Vietnam between 1961 and 1973. During the conflict, over 50,000 Americans were killed, and 300,000 wounded, and MIAs numbered 2,300. When the last U.S. soldier left on March 29, the war effectively ended for the United States.

U.S. POWs/MIAs in Four Wars

POWs	Total	WWI	WWII	Korean	Vietnam
Captured/ Interned	142,227	4,120	130,201	7,140	766
Died as POW	17,034	147	14,072	2,701	114
Returned to U.S. Control	125,171	3,973	116,169	4,418	651
Missing in Action	92,693	3,350	78,773	8,177	2,338

June 16, 1973

Soviet leader Brezhnev arrives in the United States for summit meeting with President Nixon.

The main achievement of this visit was a pact to prevent nuclear war; Leonid Brezhnev and Nixon signed a treaty titled "Prevention of Nuclear War" on June 22. The Treaty would reduce an outbreak of nuclear war anywhere in the world. The two nations would not threaten or use forces against another party and would conduct "urgent conversations" between themselves or with a third power if needed to avert nuclear war. Nixon and Brezhnev also signed agreements on agricultural cooperation, oceanographic research, and cultural exchanges.

See September 30, 1971; September 15, 1987, and September 23, 1989.

June 30, 1973

The U.S. Selective Service Act expires.

On President Nixon's recommendation, Congress did not renew the law providing for drafting of men into the armed forces. For the first time in 25 years, the armed forces became entirely voluntary.

July 1, 1973

Congressional legislation prohibits the use of funds to bomb Cambodia or to engage in further military action in Indochina without prior approval of Congress after August 15, 1973.

The arguments between Nixon and his critics about the renewed bombing of Cambodia on February 9, 1973, added to the president's difficulties with the hearings of Senator Sam Ervin's Watergate committee during the spring of 1973. The first indication that Congress no longer accepted Nixon's explanation of the Cambodian bombings came on May 10, when the U.S. House of Representatives voted 219-188 in the Supplemental Appropriations Bill to stop funds for bombing Cambodia. This bill also passed the Senate, but Nixon vetoed it on June 26. The House did not have sufficient votes to override the veto.

Because Nixon needed the Supplemental Appropriations Bill, he agreed to compromise, accepting a statement on the Cambodian bombing that permitted it to continue until August 15 so that truce arrangements could be worked out. Although some congressmen objected to the compromise, the majority accepted it as a "realistic" solution. The bill was approved on June 30; Nixon signed it on July 1. Later, both Nixon and Kissinger claimed the peace talks on Cambodia in 1973 failed because Congress had abrogated the bombing powers of the president on June 30. Kissinger said that "delicate negotiations" for a truce were underway, but he never revealed any details of these transactions. In his book *Sideshow,* which was based on extensive research in documents secured under the Freedom of Information Act as well as interviews with various participants, William Shawcross could find no evidence of such talks. Nevertheless, the U.S. bombing of Cambodia stopped on August 15. At a farewell press conference in Phnom Penh on September 4, U.S. Ambassador Emory C. Swank said the war in Cambodia after 1970 was Indochina's most "useless war."

July 12, 1973

Hearings on Nixon's secret bombing of Cambodia begin after the Senate Armed Services Committee learns that they occurred.

Major Hal Knight, a radar operator who had handled the "dual bombing" reports on the Cambodian bombings, wrote Senator William Proxmire of Wisconsin in October 1972, about the secret bombing tactics and believed that the American people should know about this. Knight protested the false record system to his commanding officer. His objections first brought him low efficiency ratings and finally the news that he would be discharged. Thus, he asked Senator Proxmire to investigate the bombings. Proxmire gave Knight's letter to Senator Harold Hughes, on the Senate Armed Forces Committee, and between March 28 and July 1973, Hughes secured versions of the 1969–1970 bombing reports that were the sanitized official reports to which Knight had objected. On July 12, Hughes searched further into the matter. During committee hearings at which General George Brown testified on his appointment to become air force chief of staff, Hughes asked Brown if the United States had conducted air strikes in Cambodia before May 1970. Requesting that the committee go into secret session, Brown told them that B-52s had bombed Cambodia in 1969–1970. Brown knew that because he had been in Saigon as General Abrams's deputy for air operations from August 1968 to August 1970.

Following the hearings on July 12, Brown returned to the Pentagon, reflected on his secret testimony, and decided to send the committee an explanation of the Cambodian raids. The "dual reports," he said, were not technically falsified reports because "they were not intended to deceive those with a security need to know." This admission was hardly sufficient. During July and August, the Senate Armed Services Committee hearings disclosed Nixon's secret orders as well as information on the bombings between March 1969 and April 1970.

August 19, 1973

Greece proclaims a republican government.

Since the rebellion against King Constantine on April 21, 1967, the provisional leaders had elected a constituent assembly that ended the monarchy and approved a republican form of government. George Papadopoulos was elected president of Greece.

September 11, 1973

A military coup in Chile overthrows President Allende, who dies. Later, a U.S. Senate investigating committee indicates that Nixon and Kissinger had used CIA operations to destabilize Chile's economy and assist anti-Allende groups.

The military coup against Allende was Chile's first overthrow of a democratic government since 1932, a record unparalleled in recent Latin American history. U.S. authorities had feared that Allende's electoral victory in 1970 was a victory for Communist-inspired takeovers in Latin America. As a result, the CIA used funds to buy anti-Allende votes and to aid opposition candidates. The Nixon administration also suspended negotiations with Chile to roll over its external debt. The United States wanted the debt to include funds covering Chile's expropriation of U.S. property in copper mines and the ITT Company. By mid-1973, the Chilean economy was in disarray. In June, miners, teachers, physicians, and students went on strike. On June 21, Allende supporters and opponents fought a bloody pitched battle in Santiago. Prior to the September 11 coup, Allende had averted several rebellions by diverse military factions. In August, shopkeepers, taxi drivers, truck owners, and professional groups staged strikes. Allende had lost the support of the middle classes and his overthrow appeared to be imminent.

After General Carlos Gonzáles resigned as defense and army chief on August 23, Allende chose General Augusto Pinochet Ugarte to replace him. Although Pinochet said he was loyal to Allende, his loyalty soon proved shallow. The occasion for the military coup was Allende's announcement of his intention to seek a national referendum creating a unicameral congress to replace the two-house legislature. Pinochet now turned against Allende, taking charge of an organization that aimed to overthrow the president. On September 11, army forces took over Moneda Palace. Whether Allende was killed or committed suicide is uncertain; his widow claimed the military murdered him. Following the coup, the CIA (according to the Senate Select Committee on Intelligence Activities) spent $34,000 to finance a public relations campaign that would give Pinochet a "positive" image and gain support for the new regime. This was difficult because during the next months Pinochet executed many opposition leaders and enforced repressive measures against all dissenters.

September 21, 1973

The Senate confirms Henry A. Kissinger as Secretary of State.

On September 3, Secretary Rogers resigned to return to his law practice. The appointment of Kissinger was no surprise because as assistant to the president for national security affairs, Kissinger worked closely with Nixon to control U.S. foreign policy. Secretary Rogers had carried out assignments in special areas such as the Middle East, but generally Kissinger's NSC staff took over most of the significant diplomatic activity usually carried out by the State Department. Kissinger's appointment as secretary returned the policy development apparatus to the State Department. Nevertheless, the power he had wielded as head of the NSC allowed later appointees to this post to challenge the role of the Secretary of State.

October 6, 1973

An Arab-Israeli conflict breaks out: the Yom Kippur War.

Throughout September there were intelligence reports of war preparations in Egypt, Jordan, and Syria. According to Ambassador Dobrynin's memoir Moscow warned Washington "several times of the rising danger of an Arab-Israeli military conflict" but Secretary of State Kissinger misread the signals. At 9:00 P.M. on October 5, Ray Cline of the State Department's Bureau of Intelligence and Research concluded war would break out soon but Kissinger relied on former NSC staffers, who discounted Cline's report. Later, Kissinger's memoirs claimed the Soviet warnings were rejected "as psychological warfare because we did not see any rational military option that would worsen the Soviet and Arab positions." As a result, Kissinger did not accept the imminence of war until receiving a telegram from Ambassador to Israel Kenneth Keating on October 6 that reported Prime Minister Golda Meir expected a Syrian-Egyptian attack that day.

The timing of Kissinger's information was vital because at the last moment he realized the Soviet Union was not following the administration's détente prescription to influence the Arab states to avoid war. The Soviets viewed the situation differently and were dismayed that Brezhnev's June discussions with Nixon at San Clemente stressed the mounting danger of an Arab-Israeli war but did not prompt joint action. Soviet officials fequently urged the administration to join them in seeking peaceful solutions to festering Middle Eastern issues, but were ignored in Washington where putting pressure on Israel to make concessions risked adverse public reactions, particularly from America's pro-Israeli community.

Kissinger had contacted Prime Minister Meir to agree not to make a preemptive strike although Israel's previous strategy was to strike first. Now, Meir altered Israeli tactics and only took defensive action in the Sinai and the Golan Heights when the Egyptian-Syrian attacks began. At 8:00 A.M. on October 6, Egyptian forces crossed the Suez Canal into the Sinai while Syrians attacked the Golan Heights. King Hussein of Jordan accepted the role of simply mobilizing his army on the Israeli border to provide a threat that required Israel to maintain some defensive units along the Jordan River. Although Kissinger believed the Israeli army and air force would quickly turn back the Arabs, this did not happen during the first week of the war. Using Soviet-supplied surface-to-air missiles, tanks, and MIG jet fighters, the Egyptian forces broke through the Bar-Lev defense lines in the Sinai and made significant advances between October 6 and 15. In addition, the Soviet Union airlifted huge quantities of arms to Damascus and Cairo. Israel urged Washington to reciprocate by rushing Phantom jets and other military equipment to Tel Aviv, but Nixon and Kissinger were slow to respond.

October 10, 1973

Spiro Agnew resigns; Gerald Ford confirmed as Vice President.

Long the rhetorical champion of law, order, and "good faith," Agnew had been implicated in bribery and accused of income tax evasion. Nixon nominated Gerald Ford for vice president and Congress confirmed him. Constitutional provisions for this unusual process had been provided by the 25th Amendment (ratified in 1967) to the Constitution. Ford was sworn in as vice president on December 6.

October 13, 1973

Nixon authorizes a full-scale airlift of equipment to Israel following a week of delay.

During the first week of the Arab-Israeli war, the United States failed to provide Tel Aviv with military supplies equaling those Moscow sent to Syria and Egypt. Exactly why there was a delay is controversial. President Nixon was deeply involved in a crisis over the Watergate tapes and Vice President Agnew's resignation. Therefore, most observers believe Secretary of State Kissinger played the leading role—with Nixon's backing—in the U.S. decisions. Kissinger, however, blamed Secretary of Defense James Schlesinger and his deputy, William Clements, for the delay in aiding Israel. More probable, however, is the view that Kissinger hoped to make sure Israel realized its dependence on the United States so that it would follow the secretary's plans to obtain a broad settlement between Arabs and Jews in the Middle East.

In addition, Kissinger had mistakenly counted on Brezhnev's desire to maintain the détente relationship to restrain the Soviet Union's Arab allies. Moscow had sent large quantities of military supplies to Egypt and Syria during the two weeks before October 6 to maintain its relations with the Arab world. Between October 6 and 13, Kissinger chose to seek a cease-fire resolution in the United Nations and to avoid sending Israel the equipment it desired. When talking with Israel's ambassador to the United States, Simcha Dinitz, Kissinger implied that he was willing to send aid to Israel but that the Defense Department's bureaucracy hampered prompt action. On one occasion, Kissinger asked Dinitz if Israel would pick up U.S. equipment in El Al aircraft whose tail emblem of the Star of David would be painted over. On another occasion, he told Dinitz he was seeking charter planes to fly equipment to the Portuguese Azores, from where Israel could transport the equipment to Tel Aviv. Apparently, Kissinger's "games" were designed to make him appear the champion of Israel even though his objective was to demonstrate that he controlled Israel's fate.

Not until October 13 did Kissinger and Nixon agree to use U.S. military aircraft to rush supplies to Israel. During the first week of the war, Israeli forces had not been able to turn back the Egyptians, and the Soviet Union was rushing around-the-clock airlifts of equipment to Cairo and Damascus. In addition, proposals for a cease-fire had been rejected by Egyptian

President Sadat. Finally, Ambassador Dinitz had threatened to go public regarding Washington's delay by appealing to friendly senators and the American Jewish community. Once the White House approved aid to Israel, the State Department quickly received Portugal's permission to refuel U.S. military planes in the Azores, and the Pentagon worked 24 hours a day to send Phantom jets, tanks, 155 mm shells, and other equipment.

Moreover, as soon as Israel knew the United States would replenish its military equipment, its army proceeded with plans for a bold attack across the Suez. This attack began on October 16 and quickly turned the war to Israel's favor.

October 16, 1973

The Arab states begin an oil embargo the same day Israel launches an offensive across the Suez Canal.

Although the United States was not informed of the Arab oil embargo until October 17, U.S. oil companies began receiving telegrams on October 16 informing them that oil shipments to the United States, Western Europe, and Japan would soon cease. The Arab states had warned Secretary Kissinger that, if necessary, they were prepared to use oil as a weapon on behalf of Syria and Egypt. After the U.S. airlift of supplies began for Israel, the Arab leaders began to apply the embargo. On October 17, the Arabs announced a 10 percent cut in oil production. On October 18, Abu Dhabi instituted its oil embargo. Libya did likewise on October 19. On October 20 and 21, Saudi Arabia, Kuwait, and Algeria inaugurated oil embargoes.

As plans for the Arab oil embargo proceeded, Israel launched an offensive into Egypt on the night of October 15–16. Using rafts to cross the Suez Canal, Israeli commandos reached Egyptian territory in force on the morning of the October 16 and began their attack on Egypt. Led by General Ariel Sharon, the Israelis advanced rapidly. After 72 hours they were within 50 miles of Cairo. At the same time, Israel began a counteroffensive against Syria, soon reaching within artillery range of Damascus. The tide of battle had turned. By October 18, Syria, Egypt, and the Soviet Union desired a cease-fire as quickly as possible.

October 25, 1973

A cease-fire is finally achieved in the Arab-Israeli War: Nixon puts the U.S. military on alert.

Within 48 hours after General Sharon's forces attacked Egypt on October 16, President Sadat and the Soviet Union's leaders realized that an early cease-fire was needed. On October 18, Ambassador Dobrynin gave Kissinger a copy of a Soviet proposal for a cease-fire and total withdrawal of Israel from all occupied Arab lands, including the Old City of Jerusalem. This proposal was quickly rejected by the secretary of state. Kissinger agreed to fly to Moscow, however, where he could work in consultation with Brezhnev in solving the Middle East crisis. Arriving in Moscow on October 20, the day that Nixon fired Archibald Cox as the Watergate special prosecutor, Kissinger worked out a cease-fire proposal with Brezhnev that the United Nations passed on October 22 (Resolution 338).

The cease-fire was soon violated because Egypt's Third Army Corps tried to break free of the Israeli army's encirclement. The Egyptian action and the arrival of more Soviet equipment in Cairo permitted Israel to tighten its grip on the Egyptians, preparatory to a possible complete decimation of Egypt's forces. Thus, another crisis occurred between October 22 and 25. A second cease-fire was approved on October 23, but it also failed on October 23. Blaming Israel for the violations, Brezhnev sent a personal message to Nixon that Ambassador Dobrynin read to Kissinger at 10:00 P.M. on October 24. The message seemed ominous. After urging that a joint Soviet-American force go to Egypt to restore peace, Brezhnev concluded: "I will say it straight, that if you find it impossible to act together with us in this matter, we should be faced with the necessity urgently to consider the question of taking appropriate steps unilaterally. Israel cannot be allowed to get away with the violations."

About this time, U.S. intelligence reported that seven Soviet airborne divisions had been alerted in the USSR and Hungary and that additional Soviet ships had entered the Mediterranean Sea, where the Soviets currently had 85 ships. Although the accuracy of these reports was uncertain, Kissinger and Nixon assumed the worst, i.e., that the Soviet Union was ready for unilateral action in the Middle East. Considering there was a "high probability" of Soviet action, Nixon took military and diplomatic action between 11:30 P.M. and 1:30 A.M. on October 24–25. He ordered a global alert of most U.S. forces.

There are five degrees of U.S. alerts ranging from Defense Condition (Def Con) 5, the lowest form, to Def Con 1, which means war. At 1:30 A.M. Def Con 3 went into effect for all U.S. Army, Air Force, and naval stations, while Def Con 2 applied to the U.S. Mediterranean fleet. At the same time, Nixon dispatched an answer to Brezhnev. He said Israel had not "brazenly" violated the cease-fire, asserting there was no need for a U.S.-Soviet force in the region. The United States could not permit unilateral Soviet action. "Instead," he said, "non-veto and non-nuclear powers should comprise the peace force sent to the Middle East by the United Nations."

One flap of the Kissinger process on October 24–25 was his failure to consult with any NATO allies until the U.S. alert was underway. The British ambassador was piqued and reportedly told the secretary: "Why tell us, Henry? Tell your friends—the Russians." Other NATO allies were equally distressed, particularly because Nixon and Kissinger had frequently treated them in such cavalier fashion. If there was a genuine Soviet threat as on October 25 as Kissinger later argued, the NATO allies might have to bear the brunt of Soviet action. Indeed, many observers thought Nixon conjured the Soviet threat and the alert to divert attention from Watergate and to show his decisiveness in dealing with Moscow. In such a context, there was no "probable" threat and no need for an alert. Nixon's letter to Brezhnev would have sufficed.

Later, Ambassador Dobrynin wrote that the Politburo had no intention of unilaterally intervening in the war because to do so "would have been reckless both politically and militarily." Moscow had insufficient forces for such an undertaking. Even if they had intervened "it would have transformed the Arab-Israeli War into a direct clash between the Soviet Union and the United States. Nobody in Moscow wanted that." Some historians label this episode as being as deadly as the Cuban missile crisis; however, there was little possibility of a military clash between the two superpowers. The crisis did not disrupt American-Soviet relations or impair détente.

Whatever the circumstances resulting from the cease-fire, it was achieved on October 25. U.N. Security Council Resolution 340 was passed 14-0 and accepted by the belligerents. The resolution provided for a cease-fire, a small-powers U.N. force to patrol the problem areas, and an international conference to finalize an armistice. The cease-fire became effective on October 26. The U.S. Defense Department ended its alert as quickly as it had called it. Whether or not the alert was connected to Watergate, on October 26 Nixon implied in a news conference that it should be. In his usual rambling style, the president claimed the Soviets miscalculated because of Watergate. Nevertheless, he said, the Soviet leaders knew how Nixon had acted in Cambodia and in the mining of Haiphong Harbor in 1972. Thus, he argued on October 25, Brezhnev knew he had to yield when Nixon ordered the alert on October 24.

November 7, 1973

Nixon informs the nation that it must change its consumption of oil and gas to achieve oil independence by 1980.

The Arab oil embargo, which began on October 16, had reduced the U.S. oil supply by 13 percent, which would reach 17 percent during the winter of 1973–1974, Nixon told the nation in a television address. Americans, he said, must conserve oil by reducing airplane flights, reducing home heating to 65 degree or 68 degree and reducing automobile speed (50 to 55 miles an hour maximum). On November 8, Nixon asked Congress for legislation to provide $10 billion for Project Independence, so that the United States could become self-sufficient in oil and therefore better able to conduct its foreign policy. In addition to oil shortages, the Arab oil embargo led to large increases in oil prices. Iran did not join the embargo, but the shah more than doubled the price of Iranian oil. Other OPEC countries such as Venezuela and Nigeria followed the shah's lead. These increases continued after the oil embargo ended in 1974, placing a new burden on America's already unfavorable balance of trade.

November 7, 1973

Both houses of Congress override Nixon's veto of the War Powers Act.

For some time, opponents of the U.S. war in Vietnam had sought legislation to limit presidential authority to involve the United States in war without the approval of Congress or a declaration of war. President Truman, they said, set the precedent in acting against

North Korea in June 1950; but the Vietnam conflict clearly indicated what they deemed to be the excessive power of the executive to act without the concurrence of the legislative branch. The bill approved on November 7 began its legislative enactment on July 18, when the House passed the bill. This act required the president to report to Congress within 48 hours after he committed U.S. troops to hostilities anywhere in the world. The president would have 60 days to gain congressional approval for the commitment. If he did not do so, the hostile action by the United States would have to stop. Congress retained power to act on its own to support ordering the commitment before 60 days passed.

Because the Senate version of this bill differed in details, it did not get through a conference committee to be approved until October 12. On October 24, President Nixon vetoed the bill. His veto did not hold, however. On November 7, the House overrode the veto by a vote of 284-135 (barely two-thirds); the Senate overrode the veto by 75-18.

November 25, 1973

In a bloodless coup, Greek President George Papadopoulos is overthrown.

A military government was set up under General Phaidon Gizikis. On August 19, 1973, Greece had become a republic under President Papadopoulos.

November 30, 1973

Defense Secretary Schlesinger announces the Pentagon will seek new weapons programs to preserve the "essential equivalency" of U.S. nuclear systems relative to the Soviets.

The Middle East crisis and a perceived Soviet violation of its détente pledges during the fall of 1973 prompted the Department of Defense to believe that the second round of the Strategic Arms Limitation Talks (SALT II) would not succeed. Therefore, as reinsurance, the United States had to equal or exceed the Soviet missile systems. From this perspective, Schlesinger announced that the Pentagon desired the following: 1. a larger ICBM weapon because Soviet ICBM weapons now had MIRV capabilities; 2. a mobile land-based missile system; 3. MIRV missiles for all existing U.S. missiles; 4. an accelerated production of ballistic missile submarines.

By the term "essential equivalency," Schlesinger indicated he wanted U.S. weapons to be equal or superior to the USSR's in every nuclear category—land-based, manned bombers, and submarines. Opponents of this new concept, including the NSC staff, calculated nuclear parity in terms of the overall equivalency of missiles possessed by the Soviet Union and the United States. Schlesinger's concept became popular with U.S. politicians who opposed détente and talked of Soviet superiority in land-based ICBMs—the one category of ballistic missiles that the Soviets possessed in greater numbers than the United States. For this group, the mobile land-based MX missile system became the essential weapon for U.S. defenses between 1974 and the early 1980s.

December 13, 1973

The Vienna (MBFR) Conference to reduce conventional forces in Central Europe adjourns with no progress.

The Vienna Conference of 19 nations opened on October 30. Its object was to achieve a mutual balanced-force reduction (MBFR) of conventional forces between NATO and Warsaw Pact nations. After a month and a half of sessions, no agreements could be reached. On December 17, an article in the Soviet Communist Party newspaper *Pravda* claimed that the Vienna conferees had developed more distrust because the NATO representatives proposed an alteration in existing force levels that would benefit the Western European nations.

December 20, 1973

Secretary Kissinger's last meeting with North Vietnam's Le Duc Tho.

This session, which proved to be Kissinger's final meeting with Le Duc Tho, achieved no results. Kissinger urged that Vietnam pull its forces out of Cambodia but Tho refused. Following the session, the State Department sent a circular letter to all U.S. diplomatic posts summarizing North Vietnam's frequent violations of the January 1973 truce. The message concluded: "while we cannot predict their decision, the Communists clearly have a viable option to launch another major offensive [in Vietnam]."

December 21, 1973

The conference on the Middle East convenes in Geneva. For the first time Arab and Israeli officials exchange views in the same room.

Following the October 25 cease-fire agreement, Secretary Kissinger became the key figure in bringing together representatives of Israel, Egypt, and Jordan. On November 7, Kissinger met Egypt's President Sadat in Cairo. The meetings led to full-scale U.S.-Egyptian diplomatic relations as well as Sadat's agreement that Egypt would negotiate with Israel. Kissinger also visited Damascus, where he persuaded Syria's President Hafiz al-Assad to offer a list of Israeli prisoners held by Syria. This gesture enabled Israel to justify the Geneva talks even though Syria refused to attend the December 21 sessions. The formal Geneva sessions lasted only two days. With Kissinger and Soviet Foreign Minister Gromyko as observers, Egypt and Israel agreed that their military officers would meet on December 26 to settle the military problem along the Egyptian-Israeli borders of the Suez Canal. This was the beginning of a series of talks that returned those borders to their place as of October 5, 1973.

December 23, 1973

The Shah of Iran announces increased oil prices.

Rumors had begun circulating in October 1973 that Iran and other nations that had not joined the Arab oil boycott after October 16, 1973, would increase their crude oil prices. On December 23, the Iranian government announced that its oil prices would increase from $5.10 to $11.65 per barrel. Other non-Arab members of OPEC (Nigeria and Venezuela) also adopted the $11.65 price. Thus, U.S. oil shortages since November were now matched by the doubling of the price of available oil. The Shah had initially increased Iran's oil prices on October 16 when the Arab boycott began.

1974

January 10, 1974

Secretary of Defense James Schlesinger suggests the doctrine of limited nuclear warfare.

Suspicious of détente and a Kissinger critic, Schlesinger urged Nixon to approve a new doctrine to

President Nixon meets with the Shah of Iran. National Archives

retarget U.S. strategic nuclear weapons from Soviet urban areas to its military forces and ICBM sites. While trumpeted as sparing civilian population centers, Soviet military leaders saw the strategy as aimed at destroying their ballistic missile sites that would eliminate the essential deterrence system of a second or retaliatory nuclear strike as was currently offered by Mutual Assured Destruction (MAD).

Schlesinger denied the plan would create a first-strike advantage but Ambassador Dobrynin's memoir indicates "that was exactly how it was received in the Kremlin, to say nothing of the way it contradicted the recently concluded agreement on the prevention of nuclear war." Since the announcement came as SALT II talks were scheduled to begin and Nixon was preparing for the Moscow summit, the Kremlin viewed it as a Pentagon effort to retard strategic arms limitations and downgrade efforts to improve Soviet-American relations.

January 18, 1974

Israeli and Egyptian Chiefs of Staff disengage their armies in the Sinai. Following five days of shuttle diplomacy, Secretary Kissinger obtains an agreement between Egypt and Israel.

After the Geneva Conference of December 21–22, Israeli and Egyptian officials began discussions on December 26. When in early January the peace process became stymied, Secretary Kissinger undertook a series of trips between Jerusalem and Aswân, where Sadat spent the winter months, to achieve a peace formula. The final agreement grew out of a proposal by Israeli Defense Minister Moshe Dayan. It was based on the following five zones in the Suez area: 1. an Egyptian zone 10 miles east of Suez in the Sinai with limited forces to patrol the area (about 7,000 men); 2. a U.N. buffer zone patrolled by a small-power U.N. force; 3. an Israeli zone in the Sinai; 4. two zones on each side of the Sinai in which no SAM missiles would be allowed for either Egypt or Israel; and 5. the west bank of the canal, from which Israel would withdraw all forces. In secret agreements, Kissinger gave Israel a memorandum saying that Egypt would clear the Suez Canal, rebuild cities, and resume peacetime activities along the canal. The United States also agreed to "make every effort to be fully responsive on a continuing and long-term basis to Israel's military equipment requirements." Sadat also agreed that Israel's nonmilitary barges could use the Suez Canal. Finally, both nations permitted the United States to conduct aerial surveillance over the disengaged area. On January 18, Israeli and Egyptian troops began withdrawal according to the zonal plan.

February 7, 1974

Secretary Kissinger visits Panama, where he signs a statement of principles for negotiations on the canal issue.

Following the U.S. veto of the U.N. Security Council resolution on Panama on March 21, 1973, Secretary Kissinger decided to provide for a more conciliatory U.S. policy in Latin America. Consequently, in September 1973, he appointed Ambassador-at-Large Ellsworth Bunker to renew discussions on the canal with Panama. Bunker's discussions with Juan Antonio Tack, Panama's minister of foreign affairs, resulted in a Statement of Principles signed by Tack and Kissinger on February 7, 1974.

These principles are summarized below:

1. A new treaty will replace the 1903 treaty.
2. The United States will abandon the 1903 concept of "perpetuity" so that a fixed termination date can be negotiated. This was the most critical U.S. concession.
3. The treaty will provide for terminating U.S. jurisdiction in the future.
4. The new treaty shall return all canal territory to Panama but will provide for American transit and defense of the canal.
5. Panama shall have an equal share of the canal's benefits.
6. The new treaty will permit Panama to join in the canal's administration.
7. Panama and the United States will jointly protect and defend the canal.
8. The United States and Panama will agree on joint studies to enlarge the canal's capacity for new, larger ships.

Detailed negotiations to prepare the process for implementing these eight points would be continued between U.S. and Panamanian officials until a treaty was attained.

February 11, 1974

A Washington conference to unify the Western powers on an oil consumer action program is unsuccessful.

On January 9, President Nixon invited the foreign ministers of Canada, West Germany, France, Italy, Japan, the Netherlands, Norway, and Great Britain to meet on February 11. The meeting's purpose was to unite the industrialized nations on a policy regarding oil supplies and prices. The nine nations could not agree, however, and disputes among them caused some bitterness, especially between the United States and European nations such as France, which preferred to arrange an independent deal with the Arab nations.

February 13, 1974

The Soviet Union deports and revokes the citizenship of Aleksandr Solzhenitsyn, a Nobel prize-winning author and dissident.

Solzhenitsyn was sent to West Germany. Later he moved to the United States, where he continued to strongly criticize the Soviet government.

February 27, 1974

An army coup in Ethiopia forces the government to resign.

Led by radical Marxists, the new leaders of Ethiopia gained complete control of the country on June 29, deposing Emperor Haile Selassie on September 12, 1974. The Soviet Union and Cuba soon become embroiled with the United States regarding control of the Horn of Africa.

February 28, 1974

The United States and Egypt resume full diplomatic relations.

Diplomatic relations between the two nations had ended during the Six-Day War in June 1967. On November 7, 1973, Secretary Kissinger and Egypt's President Sadat agreed to reopen their respective embassies and consular offices. This process officially began on February 28, 1974.

February 28, 1974

Britain's general elections give no party a majority. On March 4, Labour Party leader Harold Wilson forms a minority government.

Neither the Conservative nor Labour Parties gained 51 percent of the seats in Parliament. Harold Wilson created a minority Labour government with the assistance of Liberals that gained sufficient votes to be installed on March 4.

March 17, 1974

The Arab oil producers lift their oil embargo.

The Arab oil embargo had been set up in October 1973 as a form of political pressure against the Western powers that tended to support Israel in wars against Arab nations, in this instance the current war between Israel, Egypt, and Syria. At a meeting at Tripoli, Libya, on March 5, the Saudi Arabian delegation proposed lifting the ban since the Israeli-Egyptian settlement indicated the crisis had ended. Libya and Syria wanted to retain the embargo but were outvoted. Officially, the end of the embargo was announced on March 17.

April 25, 1974

A Portuguese revolution overthrows dictatorial regime of Premier Marcello Caetano.

Caetano and his predecessor, dictator Antonio de Oliveira Salazar, had fought for 14 years to keep control of Portugal's colonies of Angola, Mozambique, and Guinea-Bissau. The costly wars exhausted Portugal's economy. In addition, its young army officers had begun to sympathize with the leftist ideas of the colonial nationalists. One of the revolution's first acts was to suspend the colonial wars and to grant independence to Portugal's imperial possessions, to be effective at the end of 1975. Black rulers, most of them claiming to be Marxists, would gain control of Portugal's three African states. The Cold War was poised to open a new theater in Africa.

May 18, 1974

India explodes a nuclear device.

Using waste from the nuclear power plant's fuel supplied by Canada, India developed the capabilities for producing nuclear weapons. India had been one of several nations that had refused to sign the Nuclear Non-Proliferation Treaty. While India's primary objective was to match China and reestablish some military balance, unfortunately, this action also prompted Pakistan to launch a nuclear weapons program.

May 31, 1974

Israel and Syria agree to disengage their armies in the Golan Heights following 32 days of talks with Secretary of State Kissinger, who shuttles between Damascus and Jerusalem.

Although the Egyptians made peace with Israel on January 18, President Assad of Syria was adamant

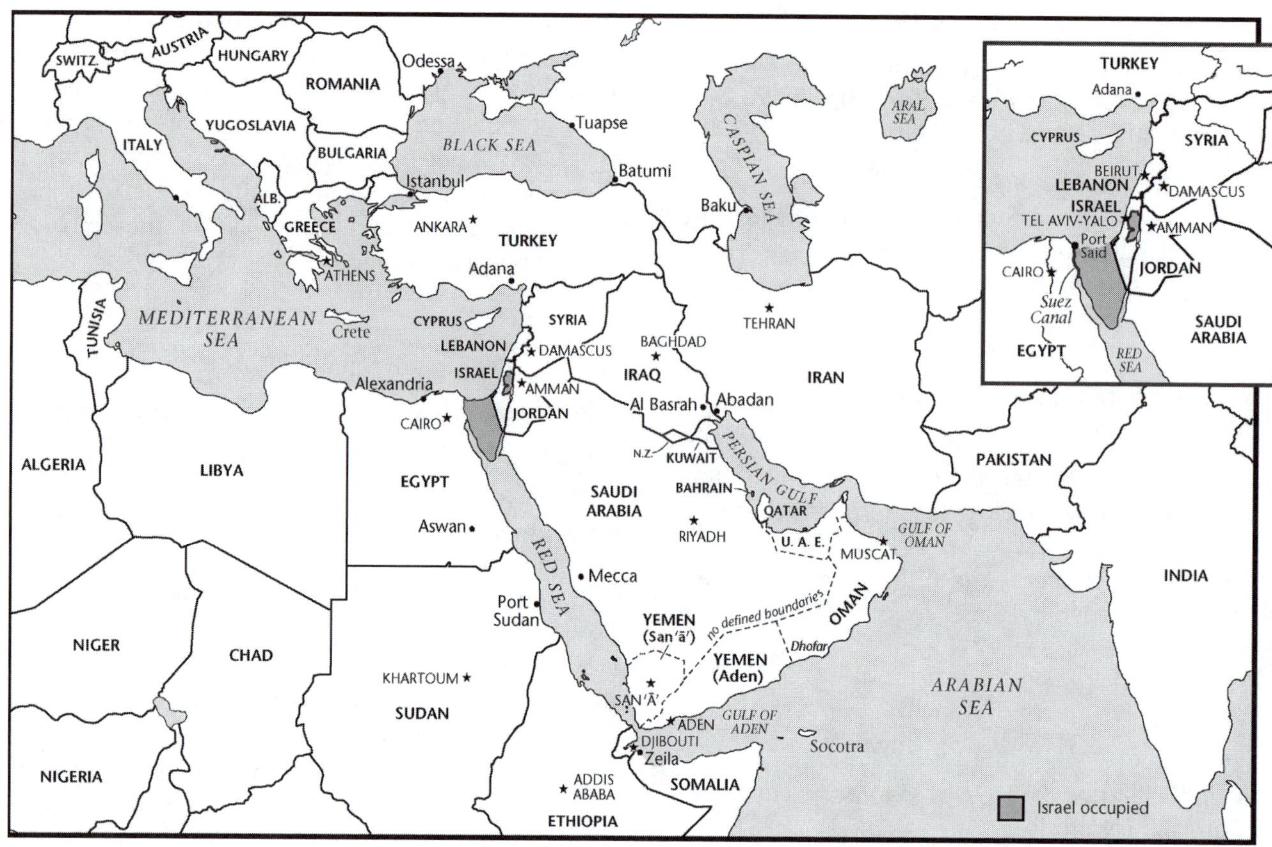

The Middle East, 1974

about his desire to obtain some territory, such as the town of Quneitra from Israel. The Israeli government was not willing to give up any hard-won territory. As a result, these two nations continued a war of attrition both on the ground and in the air in the region surrounding the Golan Heights until May 29. The agreement provided for a U.N.-protected buffer zone between the two states and for limited-forces zones along the immediate boundary of each nation. The Israeli army pulled out of Syrian territory occupied during the war of 1973.

June 14, 1974

The United States and Egypt sign a statement of principles of cooperation that contains a clause providing nuclear fuel to Egypt. Several days later, a similar promise is made to Israel.

On a visit to the Middle East, President Nixon stopped in Egypt to meet with President Sadat. Before Nixon left Cairo on June 14, the two leaders issued a statement on the Principles of Relations and Cooperation between Egypt and the United States. The controversial clause in this agreement provided U.S. aid in helping Egypt to develop nuclear power reactors and supplying fuel for this capacity. There were protests against this in both Israel and the United States. As Tad Szulc's *The Illusion of Peace* (1978) explains, Israel was concerned that Egypt might use the waste from the power plant to make a nuclear weapon just as India had in May 1974. Nixon and Kissinger claimed that Egypt would have obtained this technology from the Soviets unless the United States offered it under strict regulations to prevent the Egyptians from using nuclear waste to develop weapons. Nevertheless, as Szulc indicates, the reaction against Nixon's plan became so intense that the United States never fulfilled this agreement with Egypt.

In addition to the statement of principles, later reports alleged that Nixon told Sadat that it was the desire of the United States that Israel return to its pre-1967 boundaries. Reportedly, Nixon and Kissinger made similar statements to President Assad of Syria in a meeting in Damascus on June 15. Whether or not such verbal or written commitments on the Israeli borders were made has not been verified. If so, they were not considered binding on later U.S. presidents but were part of the Nixon-Kissinger plan to appear to operate evenhandedly with both Israel and the Arabs. Meeting on June 17 with Israeli Prime Minister Yitzak Rabin as part of his tour, Nixon agreed that Israel would have access to the same nuclear power fuel and technology as Egypt. In addition, Nixon urged Israel to negotiate with Jordan regarding the West Bank territory of the Jordan River. This was an emotional issue in Israel, however, because many Israelis believed the West Bank should, like Jerusalem, remain under their nation's control. Prime Minister Meir said she could not negotiate this issue with King Hussein without a specific mandate from her people. On June 17–18, Nixon met with King Hussein and explained the U.S. desire for Jordanian negotiations with Israel. Hussein was willing to conduct such talks but Israel was not. Nixon agreed to continue U.S. military and economic aid to Jordan.

July 3, 1974

President Nixon leaves Moscow, having signed the Threshold Test Ban Treaty.

Nixon's visits to Brussels for NATO talks and to Moscow from June 27 to July 3, 1974, had been designed largely to boost the president's political status. In talks with Brezhnev on SALT II agreements nothing could be accomplished since neither leader had cleared proposals in advance with his military leaders. However, the ABM agreement of 1972 was amended to permit only one rather than two ABM sites. A Threshold Test Ban Treaty (effective March 31, 1976) was signed prohibiting nuclear weapons tests having a yield exceeding 150 kilotons, thereby extending the 1963 Test Ban prohibitions. Agreements were signed to cooperate in energy, housing, and artificial heart research. But these pacts did not require a summit meeting. The concept of détente and goodwill was refurbished during the visit, but Nixon's future at home did not benefit, given the Watergate problem.

One incident during Nixon's visit caused him to be criticized on his return home. U.S. television networks covering the visit had prepared reports on Soviet dissidents to transmit to the United States. Just as a report began on Andrey D. Sakharov, the noted physicist and dissenter, the television screens went black. Soviet technicians had shut off the reports. However, Nixon did not comment on this or urge Brezhnev to do something about Soviet repression of human rights. As George Will, a U.S. columnist, said, perhaps Brezhnev knew Nixon's opinion of the press was not favorable.

August 8, 1974

President Nixon announces his resignation, effective at noon on August 9, 1974.

Following extensive investigations of the Watergate cover-up and other reports of the president's activity since 1969, the House Judiciary Committee found Nixon guilty of three impeachable offenses: obstruction of justice, violation of his oath of office, and defiance of the impeachment process. Subsequently, Nixon resigned on August 9.

The Soviet leaders were perplexed by how public opinion and intricate constitutional processes could force a strong president to resign over a trivial incident. Brezhnev wrote privately to Nixon: "On behalf

[Letter to Nixon after his resignation, August 10,1974]

On behalf of myself and my colleagues I should like to express kind feelings with regard to the fruitful cooperation and the spirit of mutual understanding that marked our joint efforts aimed at improving Soviet-American relations and normalizing the international situation. All that has been done over the last year in relations between the Soviet Union and the United States is highly appreciated in our country, in the USA, and the whole world. These truly great achievements cannot be regarded otherwise by all those who really care for peace and the future of mankind. I would also like you to know that we have received with satisfaction President Ford's statement of his intention to continue the course in our relations aimed at their further broadening and deepening.

As to the Soviet union, we are determined to further the cause of developing the relations of peace and cooperation between the Soviet Union and the United States, the cause we have started together with you. We have also communicated that to President Ford.

Our best wishes to you, your wife and the whole family.

Sincerely,
L. Brezhnev

Anatoly Dobryin, *In Confidence.* (Seattle: University of Washington Press, 1995, p. 317)

of myself and my colleagues I should like to express kind feelings with regard to the fruitful cooperation and the spirit of mutual understanding that marked our joint efforts aimed at improving Soviet-American relations and normalizing the international situation."

After Vice President Gerald R. Ford became president, he pardoned Nixon unconditionally on September 8. Using the 25th Amendment, Ford nominated Nelson A. Rockefeller for vice president. On December 19, Congress approved and Rockefeller was sworn in as vice president.

October 18, 1974

President Ford signs legislation threatening to cut off U.S. aid to Turkey. U.S. bases in Turkey close.

Although the Ford administration opposed the congressional threat to stop military and economic aid to Turkey, the movement to do so had begun in August 1974, following the second Turkish attack against Greek control of Cyprus. The first Turkish troops landed on Cyprus on July 20 following the Greek military overthrow of Cypriot President Makarios. Soon after a cease-fire in Cyprus on July 21, liberal opponents of the Greek military junta in Athens overturned the rule of General Ionnides, bringing back a civilian Greek regime under Konstantinos Karamanlis. Because the liberals continued Greek efforts to dominate the Cypriot government, hoping to make it part of Greece, Turkey broke the cease-fire on August 14, landed reinforcements, and sought to conquer additional territory on Cyprus.

Greeks in Athens and Greek-Americans strongly protested the Turkish invasion and blamed Secretary Kissinger for not restraining Turkey. Pro-Greek lobbyists in Washington persuaded the House of Representatives to pass an amendment to a funding bill for federal departments, cutting off aid to Turkey. President Ford vetoed the House amendment on October 14 and because the House could not override the veto, a compromise was reached. Accordingly, U.S. aid to Turkey would continue until December 10, 1974, provided Turkey did not send additional military equipment to Cyprus. This October 18 law did not end the crisis in U.S.-Turkish relations.

The Cyprus crisis continued, and on February 5, 1975, U.S. aid to Turkey halted. Turkey retaliated by closing down all NATO and U.S. bases on its territory. The U.S. bases had the vital function of monitoring weapons and missile activity in the Soviet Union.

November 24, 1974

President Ford and Soviet leader Brezhnev place a ceiling on offensive nuclear weapons in a meeting at Vladivostok; Brezhnev has a seizure at the meeting.

Since 1972, U.S. and Soviet negotiators had sought some formula to limit strategic nuclear weapons. As late as July 3, when President Nixon left Moscow, the United States wanted to limit the number of Soviet MIRV warheads. Between July and October, negotiators sought to attain some limit on offensive weapons because both nations already held overkill proportions of such weapons, but for reasons of prestige neither wanted to have a total lower than that of the other. In October, Kissinger visited Moscow to propose a formula granting each side parity in overall offensive warheads.

During their sessions the secretary of state and Brezhnev reached an agreement that became the basis of the Vladivostok formula. The Soviets agreed not to count the 500 U.S. bombers based in Europe as part of the U.S. strategic arsenal. This was a significant Soviet concession because U.S. aircraft in Europe could reach Soviet territory and, heretofore, Brezhnev had insisted that they be counted in the total of U.S. warhead launchers. On the part of the United States, Kissinger conceded that the USSR could continue to fit its missiles with MIRVs. The United States had been ahead in MIRV weapons, and as part of the overall parity, the Soviets could now build as many MIRV weapons as the United States held. The Vladivostok formula as signed by Ford and Brezhnev was based on overall nuclear parity for the United States and the USSR.

Specifically, the agreement was an *aide–mémoire* designed to be the basic framework for a SALT II agreement. The agreement included the following: (1) Each nation would have a 2,400 aggregate limit on nuclear delivery vehicles (ICBMs, SLBMs, and heavy bombers). (2) Each nation would have a 1,320 aggregate limit on MIRV systems. (3) No new land-based ICBM launchers would be built. (4) There would be limits on new types of strategic offensive weapons. (5) The new agreement would extend through 1985.

Following the summit, President Ford expected that SALT II might be finalized in 1975. As negotiators began drafting a treaty to suit the Vladivostok formula, however, difficulties arose. The two critical

President Ford and Soviet Premier Brezhnev. National Archives

concerns that prevented the conclusion of SALT II in 1975 were (1) how U.S. cruise missiles would be counted, and (2) whether the new Soviet Backfire bomber should be counted as a heavy bomber under SALT II. These questions were not addressed again until 1977, after President Carter had succeeded Ford.

Apparently unknown in the West, Brezhnev suffered a seizure soon after his initial meeting with Ford. This was the first sign of Brezhnev's atherosclerosis of the brain. In recounting the event, Ambassador Dobrynin believes this was a "definable turning point" in history because détente reached its zenith. Following his seizure, Brezhnev showed less interest in foreign policy and did not exert influence in Moscow to sustain détente.

December 20, 1974

Congress refuses to grant the Soviet Union the most-favored-nation trade status, placing restrictions on U.S. trade with the Soviets pending liberalization of their Jewish emigration policy.

Opponents of détente with the Soviet Union complained that U.S. trade helped Moscow but brought no reciprocal advantages to the United States. They contended that the 1972 grain treaty resulted only in higher costs for U.S. consumers, although U.S. farmers also profited from higher grain prices. Senator Henry Jackson, an outspoken opponent of détente, proposed that U.S. trade policies be linked with Soviet emigration policy, in particular its limitations on exit visas for Jews desiring to leave the Soviet Union. Thus on December 20, 1974, Congress approved the Trade Reform Bill with amendments that permitted lower tariffs for the Soviet Union only after Moscow eased its emigration restrictions. Both Jackson and Secretary Kissinger thought the Soviets were in sufficient need of U.S. trade to be convinced to increase the number of Jewish emigration visas. Thus, the USSR was not given most-favored-nation status, an international trade principle that would have given the Soviets the trade benefits awarded to other nations friendly to the United States. In addition, the bill limited Soviet credits through the Export-Import Bank to $300 million, a sum that Secretary Kissinger denounced as "peanuts." Senator Jackson and Kissinger miscalculated the Soviets' reaction to the U.S. trade amendments.

On January 14, 1975, the Soviets rejected the trade agreement because its emigration policy was an internal issue. Soviet Ambassador Dobrynin faults "misguided" Kremlin "hawks" for viewing Jewish emigration "as a reproof to our socialist paradise. That anyone should have the temerity to want to leave it was taken as a rank insult!" Even worse, Dobrynin's memoirs state the Kremlin failed to distinguish between Soviet Jews who wanted to go to Israel and dissident Jews such as Andrey Sakharov and Aleksandr Solzhenitsyn who "all were lumped together as enemies of the Soviet state, a heavy heritage of Stalin." The Kremlin hawks saw any suggestion to ease restrictions on Jewish emigration as "a concession to the anti-Soviet Zionists."

Consequently, rather than ease Jewish emigration restrictions, the Soviets tightened them, cutting such visas to 13,200 for 1975, down from 35,000 Jewish visas in 1973. Additionally, the Soviets halted payments on the old, World War II lend-lease debts—an agreement that had been reached three years earlier. The Jackson amendments were a grave blow to the détente policy of Nixon and Kissinger.

1975

January 8, 1975

Twenty nations agree in Washington to recycle petrodollars to avoid a global recession.

Unlike the Washington Conference of February 11, 1974, which failed to deal with the oil problem, the 1975 session was attended by representatives of the developing nations and oil-producing nations as well as the industrial powers. The 20 nations agreed to add a $6 billion oil facility to the International Monetary Fund (IMF) to help consuming nations pay their oil bills and to give interest rate subsidies to 30 poor nations. The $6 billion would be borrowed from oil producers to recycle the assets those nations held as a consequence of the greatly increased oil prices since October 1973. During a separate session, 10 industrial nations agreed to set up a $25 billion "safety net" fund for emergency use by the "poor" nations. In future meetings, the quota payments for each industrial country would be established. The United States would contribute the greatest single amount, about $7 billion.

January 8, 1975

North Vietnam's General Van Tien Dung learns of unexpected successes by his forces in South Vietnam and decides to step up his attacks.

During 1974, the truce of 1973 had completely broken down in South Vietnam. The disputes at St. Cloud between the conflicting parties ended on January 25, 1974, and the International Control Commission could not persuade either the North Vietnamese or President Thieu to cooperate in settling the disputes and the constant skirmishes along the cease-fire line. Initially, from February 1973 to February 1974, Thieu seized additional territory and extended his control over the South. U.S. analysts estimated in February 1974, that the RVN had seized 15 percent of the land controlled by the PRG in January 1973, including 779 hamlets and 1 million people. Thieu also tightened his controls in the South, which did not endear him to the people.

During 1974, however, the Communist leaders moved from a passive to an aggressive effort to counteract Thieu's actions. Once American forces had withdrawn and U.S. bombing stopped in Cambodia, Hanoi secured a major advantage because U.S. air support had been Thieu's biggest asset. Although in 1974 Nixon asked Congress to give more money to Saigon, he could offer little evidence to support his views because all reports from Vietnam indicated that both sides violated the truce and that until the fall of 1974, Saigon was the major violator. Before the fall of 1974, Hanoi had built a long-term logistical system for its efforts against Saigon. Where the Ho Chi Minh trail had existed, it built a road eight meters wide through the Truong Mountains. It laid a pipeline into the central highlands of South Vietnam and recruited North Vietnamese to help "unify" the nation.

Subsequently, while Americans experienced the unusual historic events of Nixon's resignation and Ford's ascension to power, the North Vietnamese undertook small-scale probing actions in the South during the fall of 1974 that disclosed weak support for Thieu among the local populace and the People's Defense Forces in South Vietnam. On January 8, General Dung learned that all of Phuoc Long Province had fallen under Communist control. Surprised but pleased, Dung accelerated his plans for a 1975 offensive. He hoped to make sufficient inroads into the South in 1975 to win a victory in 1976. These plans, which Dung published in a 1976 account of the war, miscalculated the weakness of the Army of the Republic of Vietnam. After Dung began his large-scale offensive on March 1, 1975, ARVN's defense efforts crumbled quickly.

January 22, 1975

President Ford approves the Geneva protocol of 1925 and the 1972 Biological Convention, with U.S. affirmations on the scope of chemical or biological uses under the protocol.

Unlike the United States, most nations had ratified the 1925 agreement on chemical and biological war weapons much earlier. In 1969, President Nixon decided to resubmit the treaty to the Senate; however, until 1974, the protocol was not ratified by the Senate because of interpretations about its application to nonlethal chemical herbicides and tear gas. To resolve these questions, President Ford affirmed in 1974 that under the protocol America would renounce first use of herbicides in war excepting use "applicable to their domestic use" or their riot-control use in "defensive military modes to save lives." Under these guidelines, the Senate ratified the Geneva Protocol on December 16, 1974. President Ford signed the ratification on January 22, 1975.

At the same time that the Senate ratified the Geneva Protocol, it also approved the Convention on the Prohibition of the Development, Production, and Stockpiling of Bacteriological (Biological) and Toxin Weapons and on Their Destruction. This treaty had been signed by the USSR, Great Britain, and the United States on April 10, 1972, but its ratification had been delayed by the Senate until the U.S. position on chemical weapons was clarified. Following the guidelines adopted by the Ford administration for the Geneva pact, the Senate ratified the 1972 convention on December 16, 1974; Ford signed it on January 22, 1975.

March 14, 1975

President Thieu of South Vietnam decides to withdraw his forces from the highland areas and concentrate them along the coast leading to Saigon. This becomes a critical decision because ARVN commanders have no precise plans for the retreat that became a rout.

President Thieu's decision reflected the quick success of the Communist offensive that began on March 1, 1975. After cutting Highways 19 and 21 between the coast and the central highlands, North Vietnamese forces captured Ban Me Thuot and threatened Pleiku and Kontum. Pleiku, the former center of a large U.S. support base, had prospered during the war. The local populace was not secure, however, because General Nguyen Van Toan, whom Thieu appointed in 1972, controlled the heroin trade and ARVN troops had been corrupted by this illegal traffic, as well as by the addiction of a third of the soldiers. On March 14, after conferring with other ARVN officers, Thieu decided to retreat from Pleiku and Kontum and concentrate the ARVN defenses along the coastal areas. The retreat from the two cities was a disaster. The upper-ranked officers left quickly; the lower-ranked officers had no plans for retreat. Command of the troops disintegrated. Soldiers mutinied, looted, raped, and left Pleiku burning as the Communists arrived. Many ARVN troops had their families with them, and they fled in trucks or wagons, or by backpacking down Highway 19 toward the coast. About 250,000 people fled the highlands. General Dung followed his advantage as quickly as logistical control allowed. In the north on March 18, Communists captured Quang Tri and moved south.

Between March 24 and 28, the Pleiku chaos was repeated at Hue and Danang. At Danang's docks, refugees and troops vied for the last boats to Saigon, while Communist forces shelled the beaches. Between March 1 and March 28, Thieu's forces lost two-thirds of their territory, half of their 1.1 million man army and local defense forces, and most of the air force. Former U.S. military equipment at Pleiku and Danang fell into Communist hands because the retreating ARVN troops did not take time to destroy it.

March 29, 1975

Soviet Ambassador Dobrynin asks Kissinger if the United States was raising a Soviet submarine.

According to Soviet Ambassador Dobrynin, he received an anonymous tip that "certain authorities of the United States are taking measures to raise the Soviet submarine sunk in the Pacific Ocean." Soviet navy officials did not believe a salvage operation at that depth was possible. Yet Dobrynin asked Kissinger about press reports that Americans tried to raise a Soviet submarine that had sunk off Hawaiian shores in 1968 and that some of the crew's bodies were dumped into the sea. Dobrynin demanded an explanation, insisting all salvage work be halted as a violation of maritime law for a warship to be raised without the consent of its government.

Kissinger replied, "This whole problem has already caused extensive debate inside the government," but said nothing else. In his memoir, *A Time to Heal* (1979), President Ford indicates that on his second day as president, the State Department and CIA asked permission to proceed with salvage operations. He gave permission but the submarine broke in half when it was raised and only one portion was retrieved. Later, NSC Advisor Brent Scowcroft told Dobrynin six bodies had been found, of which three were identified and buried with full military honors. The Soviet pressed for more information and several years later it became known that the CIA built a special vessel, the *Glomar Challenger*, that cost over $300 million, to raise the submarine from 16,000 feet below the surface with its nuclear-tipped missiles to obtain technical information. When the Cold War ended in 1991, the U.S. gave Russia a full report including a film that showed bodies of Russian seamen buried at sea with military honors. See Anatoly Dobrynin, *In Confidence* (1995).

April 5, 1975

Chiang Kai-Shek dies in Taiwan.

On April 6, Yen Chin-kar became the president of the Republic of China. Following Chiang's death, his son Chiang Ching-kuo gained primary power in Nationalist China.

April 17, 1975

Cambodia falls to the forces of the Khmer Rouge as Phnom Penh surrenders after a long siege.

Former President Lon Nol had left Cambodia for exile on April 1, turning the government over to General Saukham Khoy.

April 25, 1975

Portugal conducts its first free election in 50 years.

After the election, the Ruling High Council became a mixture of non-Communist military officers and Communists. This allowed the non-Communist Council members to press for less radical economic measures.

April 29, 1975

The last American "chopper" evacuates the U.S. embassy in Saigon.

The collapse of the South Vietnamese forces and government of President Thieu came faster than anyone, even the Communists, anticipated. Thieu's apparently trained and well-equipped armies of 1973 crumbled, owing in large measure to the corruption, decay, and self-centeredness of the high-level officer corps that Generals Ky and Thieu created in 1967. While a few ARVN soldiers showed skill and bravery during the final weeks, they could not make up for the general decay of South Vietnam's military and political structure, which the United States had been unable to influence between 1954 and 1973. Throughout most of March 1975, President Ford and Secretary of State Kissinger worried more about Cambodia than about Saigon. Phnom Penh had been surrounded for some time and the Khmer Rouge tightened its grip on the city early in 1975. Eventually, Phnom Penh fell on April 17 after the United States evacuated the embassy on April 12.

Regarding Vietnam, Washington officials were beguiled by an alleged successful Vietnamization program from 1968 to 1973. Even after Pleiku fell, the Pentagon expected "well-trained" ARVN to counterattack as they had during the 1972 Easter offensive. On March 24, *Time* magazine quoted U.S. military officials as predicting that Saigon would soon establish "battle-field equilibrium." On March 31, *Time* praised Thieu for his "gritty gamble to evacuate the highlands" and save the "body of South Vietnam." U.S. experts gave Thieu "high marks for his strategy of retreat." In retrospect, Saigon would have fallen earlier except for the gallant defense of ARVN units at Xuan Loc on Highway 4 near Saigon. On April 28, the RVN National Assembly announced that General Duong Van Minh had replaced President Thieu. Because the North Vietnamese had previously offered to negotiate with a neutralist advocate such as Minh, the assembly hoped Saigon would be spared.

But it was too late for negotiations. The Communists refused to negotiate with Minh but accepted his surrender on April 30. The U.S. embassy and its "friends" completed their evacuation late in the evening of April 29. U.S. Ambassador Graham Martin delayed the evacuation to provide exit for pro-American Vietnamese. On April 20, President Ford ordered the immediate departure of U.S. personnel, and until

April 29, helicopters relaying refugees to U.S. ships tried to carry all the people they could. American television cameras relayed the chaotic evacuation scenes back to U.S. firesides. Less influential Vietnamese "friends" climbed the embassy walls and sought to reach a departing helicopter. Finally, the last U.S. helicopter left. Saigon had fallen to the Communists, following a "decent interval" of 27 months since the truce of January 1973.

May 15, 1975

The *Mayaguez* incident ends after U.S. Marines rescue the ship's crew from Cambodia.

This incident began on May 12 when President Ford learned that a private U.S. cargo ship, the *Mayaguez*, had been fired on, boarded, and captured by Cambodian patrol boats 55 miles off their coastline in the Gulf of Thailand. Because the United States had no diplomatic relations with the Pol Pot regime in Phnom Penh, Washington found it difficult to learn exactly what Cambodia intended. Cambodian patrol boats had harassed two other foreign boats recently, but there had been no warnings sent to keep ships out of the region. On Tuesday, May 13, the president ordered 1,000 marines to fly from Okinawa to Utapao air base in Thailand, although the Thai government, which had not been consulted, protested this action. In addition, the aircraft carrier *Coral Sea* and two destroyers were sent to the Gulf of Thailand. On Wednesday, Ford appealed to U.N. Secretary-General Kurt Waldheim for assistance.

At the same time, however, the president and the NSC decided to take military action as soon as possible. Thus, without waiting for the United Nations to act, the United States began an assault against Cambodia on the evening of May 14 (morning of May 15 in Cambodia). While U.S. helicopters carried Marines to Koh Tang, the island where the *Mayaguez* had been taken, the destroyer USS *Holt* approached the cargo ship and marines boarded the vessel. They found it was empty. At 11:13 A.M. Cambodian time, a Thai fishing boat approached the destroyer. The fishing boat flew a white flag and carried the 39 *Mayaguez* crew members.

Ralph Wetterhahn's 2001 book *The Mayaguez Incident and the End of the Vietnam War* offers new evidence about the events of May 12 to May 15, 1975. The book shows that the *Mayaguez*'s 40-member crew was never held on Koh Tang island, invaded by the U.S. Marines, but on Rong Sam Len island. In addition, Wetterhahn found that more U.S. servicemen were killed during the operation than the Ford administration admitted, including 23 men killed when a helicopter crashed in Thailand and three Marines who were inadvertently left behind on Koh Tang island, where they were captured and murdered by the Khmer Rouge. The assault may not have been necessary, however, because from 7:07 to 7:26 A.M. (Cambodian time) a Phnom Penh radio message received in Bangkok indicated Cambodia would surrender the *Mayaguez*. The Marine assault had begun at 6:20 A.M.

June 5, 1975

President Sadat reopens the Suez Canal to international shipping.

The canal had been closed since the 1967 Six-Day War with Israel. During his discussion with Secretary Kissinger in November 1973, Sadat had agreed to return the Suez operations to normal and to permit nonmilitary Israeli ships to use the canal.

June 10, 1975

The Rockefeller commission's report on the CIA finds its overall record good but notes some areas of illegal action that must be remedied.

Because there were extensive claims of illegal CIA activities, President Ford appointed Vice President Nelson Rockefeller on January 5 to head an investigative commission to review the organization's activity. Following five months of study, the commission report, entitled "CIA Activities Within the United States," found that the agency overstepped the bounds of legality in some areas. The violations involved errors of judgment, not crimes, in seeking to protect the national security. The areas where the CIA overstepped its bounds included (1) opening the mail of private citizens since 1959; (2) preparing computer files on the names and actions of over 300,000 citizens; (3) experimenting with mind-expanding drugs on unknowing subjects; (4) giving President Nixon secret data on the Kennedys that was used for political purposes; and (5) keeping a Soviet defector in solitary confinement for three years while checking on his credibility.

The commission also uncovered material regarding CIA plots of attempted or actual assassinations of foreign leaders during the Eisenhower and Kennedy administrations. President Ford directed that these data not be made public, but they were turned over to a congressional committee on the intelligence services. The Rockefeller Commission recommended that a joint congressional committee have oversight of intelligence agencies. The Rockefeller Commission recommended an administrative reorganization of the CIA to prevent a recurrence of what had occurred. It did not propose a fundamental alteration of the CIA's authority as the predominant U.S. agency for intelligence gathering. But critics of the CIA claimed that the Rockefeller Commission did not go far enough and that more serious actions and attitudes of the CIA needed to be corrected.

July 1, 1975

Vietnam is united as one nation.

Following the fall of Saigon on April 29 and the unconditional surrender of the Republic of Vietnam, the effort to unite an independent Vietnam that began in September 1945 became an accomplished fact 30 years later.

July 11, 1975

Black nationalists groups in Angola begin to fight for dominance as Portugal proceeds with plans to grant independence.

In January 1975, Portugal's plans to grant Angola independence by November 11 seemed to be going smoothly because the three nationalist factions said they would cooperate in forming an interim government. During the next four months fighting broke out, becoming more serious by July 11. In Luanda, the capital, the Marxist Popular Front for the Liberation of Angola had gained control. It expelled the Conservative National Front of the Liberation of Angola (FNLA) from the capital. The third group, the National Union for the Total Independence of Angola (UNITA) was much smaller and had not yet been involved in the fighting. Portugal tried to mediate the dispute but had failed. There was a minority of 400,000 white settlers in Angola, but many of these had fled into exile to avoid involvement in the fighting.

July 15–17, 1975

Apollo 18–Soyuz 19 represent a joint U.S.-Soviet space venture.

As one of President Nixon-First Secretary Brezhnev's détente achievements, a joint space program was agreed upon. This was completed in July 1975. The U.S. and Soviet spacecraft rendezvoused and docked while orbiting the earth, linking the two ships. Their crews exchanged visits and shared meals in space. Prior to the launching of the mission, the astronauts visited the space facilities of each other's nation. The American astronauts were Vance D. Brand, Thomas P. Stafford, and Donald K. Slayton. The Soviet astronauts were Aleksey A. Leonov and Valeriy N. Kubasov.

July 24, 1975

The House of Representatives rejects President Ford's request to lift arms embargo on Turkey.

Ford requested $185 million in military aid for Turkey to make up for the Turkish aid program that Congress cut off on October 18, 1974, after Turkey used U.S. weapons to invade Cyprus. Ford wanted the aid restored so that the activity of U.S. military installations in Turkey could return to normal. These bases monitored Soviet missile and troop movements. Arguing that Turkey violated the Foreign Military Assistance Act in using the weapons in Cyprus, House members refused to renew aid to Turkey. In Washington, a large Greek lobby opposed aid to Turkey; the Turks had no similar Turkish-American interest group. Immediately after the House rejected the aid bill, Turkey halted all activity at 20 U.S. military bases within its borders. At President Ford's urging, the House reconsidered the July 24 vote and on October 2 voted to ease the Turkish embargo. The Senate rejected the change, however. Congress continued the embargo until 1978.

August 1, 1975

Representatives of 35 nations sign the Helsinki agreements that legitimize the Soviet Union's territorial gains in Europe since 1940 and guarantee human rights and the free flow of ideas in both Eastern and Western Europe.

After several months of negotiation at Vienna in 1974–1975, the Helsinki document was finalized in a three-day conference on European security. It was called officially the "Final Act of the Conference on

Security and Cooperation in Europe." A principal part of the agreement confirmed the Eastern European boundaries established by the Red Army in 1945, a reality that President Franklin D. Roosevelt had conceded during World War II. These borders included the Soviets' absorption of the three Baltic states (Estonia, Latvia, and Lithuania); the Soviet takeover of Ruthenia (formerly part of Czechoslovakia) and Bessarabia (formerly Romanian territory); the westward shift of Poland's border, whereby Poland lost territory in the east to the Soviet Union but gained German territory in the west; Romania's acquisition of Transylvania (formerly Hungarian); and the partition of Germany. This "ersatz peace treaty" declared that the new frontiers were "inviolable." It also stated that borders might be changed by peaceful agreement, a clause West Germany desired in the hope that the two Germanys might one day reunite.

The second part of the Helsinki document was designed to guarantee certain human rights in Europe. All nations subscribed to the concept that they would permit more human freedom and free contacts between their peoples and those of other nations. To evaluate better the "human rights" accords, the security conference agreed to reconvene in June 1977 to assess the situation. The U.S. State Department emphasized the advantages of having the Soviets agree to improve these rights; the Soviets emphasized the Helsinki agreement that recognized the political boundaries existing since 1945.

The document's third portion dealt with confidence-building measures beginning with an agreement requiring signatories to give prior notification of military maneuvers involving more than 25,000 troops. The notification must include data regarding the type of activities and the voluntary invitation of foreign observers to a maneuver. The provision's basic purpose was to reduce fears that unannounced maneuvers might be a prelude to a surprise attack.

During the three-day meeting, the Helsinki Accord divided into what delegates called Baskets I, II, and III. The speeches by Soviet First Secretary Brezhnev and U.S. President Ford showed a divergence of interests of the two superpowers in signing the Helsinki Accords. Brezhnev's address emphasized that under the accord, states could no longer interfere in the internal affairs of another nation. Although some observers thought the Soviet Union might no longer interfere in the affairs of its Warsaw Pact allies, Brezhnev really meant that the United States should not complain about human rights in, or the emigration policies of, the Soviet Union. President Ford's message to the Helsinki delegates emphasized the accords as a method to improve the daily life of people living in both Eastern and Western Europe. Ford said, however, that the new agreement would be judged "not by promises made but by promises kept."

September 1, 1975

Egypt and Israel sign an additional agreement on buffer zones in the Sinai, setting up an early-warning system entrusted to the United States.

The agreement of September 1 was based on the January 18, 1974, Israeli-Egyptian pact. It provided a more sophisticated means of avoiding aggression by Egypt or Israel through the Giddi or Mitla Passes in the Sinai desert. At those locations the two nations would establish surveillance stations. The United States would erect three watch stations to be operated by 200 U.S. civilian personnel. Electronic sensor fields would be set up at each end of the pass. Any movement of armed forces other than the U.N. Emergency Forces would be reported by the American surveillance teams.

November 10, 1975

A U.N. General Assembly resolution condemns Zionism as a form of racism.

This U.N. action was a strong rebuff to both Israel and the United States, which had fought to prevent its passage. It indicated that the political makeup of the General Assembly had changed considerably since 1945. The United Nations had tripled its membership in 30 years, most of the new nations coming from former imperial and colonial regions previously dominated by the United States and Western European countries.

November 10, 1975

Angola obtains independence from Portugal.

Lisbon granted Angola independence even though the three factions seeking power in Luanda would not give the nation a united government. Soon the United States would be supporting a rival to the Soviet and Cuban-backed governments in Angola.

See December 9, 1975.

November 20, 1975

General Franco, Spain's Fascist leader, dies.

November 21, 1975

The Church committee of the U.S. Senate reports previous CIA involvement in plots to assassinate foreign leaders.

Between 1970 and 1974, there were many accusations that the Federal Bureau of Investigation and the CIA had engaged in illegal covert activity. Because CIA action directly affected U.S. foreign relations, the investigation of its activities particularly affected U.S. diplomacy. Two committees investigated the CIA during 1975. One, a "blue-ribbon" panel chaired by Vice President Rockefeller, began its investigation on January 5. On June 10, its report indicated that the CIA had exceeded its charter by conducting domestic surveillance of U.S. citizens.

The second, the Senate Investigative Committee, headed by Frank Church, delved into CIA activity abroad. The most sensational findings of the committee were the CIA's involvement in assassination plots. Among nations where the CIA's involvement was identified were Cuba, Zaïre, the Dominican Republic, South Vietnam, and Chile; the methods varied, usually encouraging or paying parties already willing to carry out an assassination. Later in December, the Church Committee cleared the CIA of direct responsibility for the overthrow and murder of Chile's Salvador Allende. But the CIA and the Nixon administration had assisted anti-Allende groups in Chile.

December 5, 1975

President Ford concludes a five-day visit to China.

There was no significant agenda for Ford to pursue in his talks with Chinese officials. The tour was largely designed to project a favorable public relations image for the president and to confirm prior U.S.-Chinese friendship. During this visit, Ford and China's leader, Deng Xiaoping, renewed the commitment of their two nations to the Shanghai communiqué of February 1972. Ford also restated orally the U.S. commitment to remain a major power in the Pacific.

December 9, 1975

Soviet Ambassador Dobrynin discusses serious Angola issue with President Ford.

After gaining independence from Portugal, Angola became a Cold War focal point in Africa. Several factions began fighting to gain independence with a similarity in names of the groups: the Movement for the Liberation of Angola (MPLA), the Front for the National Liberation of Angola (FNLA), and the National Union for the Total Liberation of Angola (UNITA). These factions began fighting a civil war to control the government with funds from oil reserves developed by U.S.-based oil companies. After some factions drew support from Cuba and the Soviet Union, other factions had help from the United States, South Africa, and China. This led Angola to become the center of an international contest beyond its importance to any foreign contributor. Most significantly, the situation caused problems for U.S.-Soviet relations and again was a challenge to détente.

President Ford told Ambassador Dobrynin that the United States had no strategic interests in Angola, but the American public saw it as a test of détente. Ford was concerned about being seen as yielding to the Soviets, who supported the MPLA faction to help Angolans gain independence. Ford indicated that U.S. intelligence agencies reported large shipments of Soviet arms and Soviet planes airlifting Cuban troops to assist the MPLA efforts to gain control of Angola's government. Ford admitted that the United States sent supplies to Angola and helped recruit foreign mercenaries to aid the FNLA faction.

Finally, Ford wondered if it was necessary for the Americans and Soviets to be involved in Angola where neither had vital interests at stake. Ford asked if the two superpowers might ask for a peaceful settlement among Angola's factions and call on all nations involved to stop sending arms to the combatants. Kissinger echoed Ford's query at a NATO foreign ministers' meeting in Brussels but used a harsh tone that implied that Soviet actions in Angola endangered détente.

On December 18, Brezhnev responded that Angola's fighting was not a civil war but a struggle caused by foreign intervention, especially by South Africa. He said the way to peace was to halt foreign intervention and agreed with Ford that the events should not be "a test of détente policy." Unfortunately, both Washington and Moscow denounced each other and Angola's affair worsened relations by challenging détente.

Ambassador Dobrynin's memoir, *In Confidence* (1995), describes Moscow's decision-making process for various issues. The Soviets' International Department of the Central Committee of the Communist Party, not the Soviet foreign ministry, was responsible for policies such as the case of Angola, where there were long established contacts with Portugal's Communist Party. The department head, Boris Ponomarev, argued that the United States was involved in many civil wars such as overthrowing Chile's socialist government. Thus, how could Washington view Moscow's support for a government in Angola as interfering with détente? Soviet leaders saw America's position as creating a double standard. Also, the Soviets' Politburo believed they must support Angola's MPLA to offset the Chinese who attempted to usurp Moscow's position in the region.

The Kremlin viewed Angola as an ideological conflict; Soviet leaders underestimated Cuba's role on American public opinion and the Ford administration. Since the 1962 missile crisis, Americans assumed Moscow directed Havana's policies and did not know about Dobrynin's claim that Fidel Castro initiated the dispatch of Cuban troops to back the MPLA. Because Castro dreamed about being a world figure, Dobrynin noted that Castro "liked to make things difficult for the Americans."

See January 26, 1976.

IV. CONFRONTATION AND CONCILIATION, 1976–1991

The détente policy was short-lived because Soviet and American policymakers could not reconcile their different definitions of détente. Soviet Ambassador Dobrynin believed détente was "to a certain extent buried in the fields of Soviet-American rivalry in the Third World." He lamented that Soviet "foreign policy was unreasonably dominated by ideology" and was therefore unable to assist effectively "the transition toward socialism in the Third World." Dobrynin believed Soviet policies in Cuba and Africa undermined "the foundations of détente even as we tried to build them" because they did not account for Washington's reactions. "In all fairness, Dobrynin concluded "the same criticism could be leveled at Washington" because the diplomacy of the administrations of Nixon, Ford, and Carter in places such as the Middle East ignored the Soviet Union except in times of crisis.

American leaders who followed public opinion about the Soviets were driven by their anti-Communist ideology and thought the socialist ideas of many Third World governments were part of the Soviet Union's plan to dominate the world, leading Presidents Carter, Reagan, and George H.W. Bush to engage in Afghanistan, Angola, El Salvador, Nicaragua, and Somalia. The U.S. Congress also annoyed Moscow by tying trade relations to an exit quota for Jewish emigration rather than granting the Soviets most-favored-nation status. The American leaders often used economic "sanctions" against the Soviet Union. For instance, President Reagan asked NATO members and Japan to level economic sanctions on Moscow in response to the Soviets' so-called repressive measures in Poland. Reagan also embargoed the export of high-technology products for a pipeline designed to bring oil and gas from the Soviet Union to Western Europe.

During these years, President Nixon's ABM and SALT I treaties, which limited both sides' armaments, were slowed down by Carter and Reagan. After the Kremlin proposed additional reductions of strategic weapons that would maintain parity, President Carter sought drastic cuts from Brezhnev without considering the compromises agreed to by President Gerald Ford in the Vladivostok agreement. In June 1979, Carter and General Secretary Leonid Brezhnev agreed to the SALT II pact, but after the Soviet intervention in Afghanistan, Carter asked the Senate to delay ratification of SALT II. Throughout the 1970s, many prominent Cold War hawks came together as the Committee for the Present Danger to claim that Presidents Ford and Carter allowed the Soviets to build a superior strategic nuclear force with ICBMs, thus endangering America. After 1981, President Reagan embraced the notion of Soviet military superiority and would not accept negotiations to further limit arms but launched a massive American military buildup. After General Secretary of the USSR Mikhail Gorbachev took power, Reagan agreed to a Strategic Arms Reduction Treaty (START) program for both sides to reduce their strategic armaments. Gorbachev agreed to participate in talks, where he made concessions beginning with a treaty to eliminate all intermediate range missiles, resulting in the INF Treaty of 1987.

Gorbachev's policies of *glasnost* and *perestroika* to reform the Soviet Union developed a momentum of their own and led to the breakup of the Soviet Union and its Eastern European satellites. After the Berlin Wall fell in November 1989, the Soviet satellites also asserted their independence. By December 1991, many republics in the Soviet Union also declared their independence. For the United States, President George H.W. Bush watched while the Soviets' unforeseen collapse took place in December 1991. Before Bush left office on January 20, 1993, he realized that the end of the Soviet Union in December 1991 did not end American foreign policy concerns in the former Soviet satellites and in other nations such as Iraq and Somalia. One of Gorbachev's final acts was to join the U.N. coalition that forced Iraq out of Kuwait.

1976

January 11, 1976

The Organization of African Unity (OAU) deadlocks on the issue of Angola's government.

The OAU called an emergency meeting to resolve the Angolan issue but adjourned with no results on January 11. Twenty-two African states favored recognition of the Soviet-backed government of the Popular Movement for the Liberation of Angola; 22 other African states opposed this government. The 50-50 split prevented the OAU from acting.

January 27, 1976

Congress rejects President Ford's request for aid to Angola. The House of Representatives concurs with prior Senate action in refusing to provide $28 million for Angola's anti-Communist factions.

Between May and December 1976, reports surfaced of the Ford administration's covert aid of $32 million to support Angolan rebels opposing the Luanda government, which held the dominant position in that African state. According to State Department officials, the Soviets had provided $200 million and 11,000 Cuban troops to support the Popular Movement in Angola. In December 1976, U.S. news reports indicated that the United States had given covert military aid to two Angolan groups opposing the Luanda government: the Bakongo tribal group, which led the National Liberation Front of Angola (NFLA); and the Ovimbudu tribal group, which formed the Union for the Total Independence of Angola (UNITA). The White House denied that Americans were recruited to fight in Angola but would not comment on reports that Cuban refugees were hired to fight on behalf of the U.S.-backed factions in that country. South Africa also supported the same factions in Angola, but the apartheid policies of the Johannesburg government only served to detract from the arguments that favored the U.S.-backed factions in Angola.

In December, President Ford asked Congress for additional military aid to Angola even though he and Secretary of State Kissinger refused to apply direct pressure on Moscow to stop assisting the Luanda government. The president rejected a proposal to restrict grain shipments to the Soviets, and Secretary of State Kissinger objected to suggestions that SALT II be halted unless Moscow cooperated in Angola. Thus, in presenting the case for Angola to Congress, Ford used only rhetoric to imply that the domino theory might lead to the spread of further Communist victories in Africa. Congress rejected these arguments, especially because the United States appeared to be backing the weaker side in Angola. The Bakongo and Ovimbudu tribal groups were not effective and refused to cooperate with each other against the Luanda government. The breadth of congressional opposition to Ford's request is seen in the House vote of 323 to 99. Votes to end aid to Angola were cast by 251 Democrats and 72 Republicans.

See December 9, 1975 and December 1, 1976.

March 1, 1976

President Ford tells newsmen he wants to drop the word détente from his political vocabulary.

Criticism from the right wing of the Republican Party, headed by Ronald Reagan, caused Ford to move away from détente because it was a concept that many Americans seemed unable to comprehend. President Nixon and his adviser, Henry Kissinger, had never been careful to school the U.S. public in the nuances of power politics and the advantages of reaching mutual agreements with the Soviet Union. Following Nixon's resignation in August 1974, Secretary of State Kissinger endeavored to deliver more speeches throughout the country to clarify his policies with the USSR.

From August 20, 1974, to early 1976, Kissinger made 16 such speeches. He also sent four of his principal advisers around the nation to conduct town-meeting sessions on foreign policy. Generally, however, these meetings convinced Kissinger and his aides that there was widespread disagreement with the administration's policies. Although experts on international affairs continued to laud détente and the emphasis on political realities espoused by Kissinger, the U.S. public did not. Nixon's radical change from the moralistic, anti-Communist rhetoric that began under President Truman was renewed by Ronald Reagan and Senator Henry Jackson who continued to rouse the anti-Communist pulse of conservative Americans. By January 1976, many European observers stated that Kissinger's rhetoric became more flamboyant as he spoke of "domino" Communist victories in Africa. One British editor stated that Kissinger's private comments were "reminiscent of John Foster Dulles" as he talked of dominoes in Europe if the Italian Communists should be elected, leading to Communist governments in Paris, Madrid, and Lisbon as well. These were signs that Kissinger and Ford wanted to end détente with the Soviets.

March 14, 1976

Egypt ends its 1971 treaty of friendship with the Soviet Union.

Prime Minister Sadat distrusted the Soviet advisers in Egypt. Soon after signing the treaty, Sadat undertook talks for a treaty with mainland China.

March 18, 1976

The United States stops aid to India.

The halting of U.S. aid to India resulted because negotiations about economic assistance broke down in February 1976. Washington was upset because Prime Minister Indira Gandhi accused the CIA of trying to undermine her government. The amount of aid involved totaled about $65 million for 1976.

March 28, 1976

Southeast Asian nations form a treaty of friendship and cooperation.

To replace the SEATO (Southeast Asia Treaty Organization), a new organization was formed of regional non-Communist nations: the Association of Southeast Asian Nations (ASEAN). The nations signing this agreement were the Philippines, Singapore, Malaysia, Thailand, and Indonesia. The U.S. gave its support to ASEAN.

April 5, 1976

James Callaghan replaces Harold Wilson as prime minister of the United Kingdom.

Wilson announced his retirement on March 16, 1976. On the third ballot at a Labour Party Convention, Callaghan received 176 votes to 137 for Michael Foot.

April 5, 1976

Cambodia's Prince Norodom Sihanouk resigns as head of state in favor of Khieu Samphan.

May 28, 1976

The United States and USSR sign a treaty on nonmilitary nuclear explosions.

The treaty limited any single underground nuclear test to the equivalent of 150,000 tons of TNT. If any explosion exceeded this limit, the other side had the right to an on-site inspection. In practice, no inspections were anticipated because neither nation planned larger explosion tests.

June 30, 1976

Europe's Communist Parties, after a two-day meeting, declare that each national party is independent and equal to other parties.

This conference should have ended the myth of a Communist monolith controlled by Moscow. Although the Soviet Union continued to exercise control wherever it had military forces in place, Communist parties outside the Soviet orbit followed, as they often had previously, their own national attitudes toward Communist methods and local policies. Nevertheless, the conference dramatized the new tactic of non-Soviet parties to emphasize separate programs for their respective nation's needs. This policy became known or condemned as "Euro-Communism."

July 20, 1976

The U.S. spacecraft Viking 2 lands on Mars and transmits photographs to Earth.

On September 3, Viking 2 landed on Mars.

August 18, 1976

At Panmunjom, Korea, North Korean forces attack and kill two U.S. army officers. The incident ends with a North Korean apology on August 21.

The North Koreans attacked a U.N. forces contingent in the Joint Security Area at Panmunjom. The U.N. group was trimming trees in the area to permit two U.N. command posts to see each other, when 30 North Korean soldiers appeared on the scene. They asked the U.N. officials to stop their work, and when they refused, the North Koreans attacked the U.N. forces personally, beating them with ax handles and clubs. The U.N. commanders suffered the worst beatings and died. They were Captain Arthur G. Bonifas and Lieutenant Mark I. Barrett. U.S. officials in Korea believed the incident was part of North Korea's attempt to publicize tensions between U.S. and Korean troops, hoping the United States would withdraw.

The American reaction was to move up U.S. F-4 and F-111 aircraft from Okinawa and Idaho. The Pentagon also sent the Midway naval task force into the area and raised the region's alert status to Def Con 3: war is likely but not imminent. In addition, on August 21, a U.N. work team under heavy guard went to the Security Defense Area at Panmunjom and cut down the tree that previously was only being trimmed. On August 21, North Korea's President Kim Il Sung sent an unprecedented message to the Korean U.N. headquarters. Kim expressed his regret at the incident and hoped such incidents could be prevented in the future. The U.N. command believed its response affirmed U.N. rights in the area and successfully calmed the incident.

September 9, 1976

Mao Tse-Tung dies; new Party Chairman Hua Guofeng arrests the "gang of four."

The Chinese Communist Party (CCP) chairman since 1927, Mao led the People's Republic of China since 1949. His death came soon after Chou En-lai died on January 8, 1976. Hua Guofeng replaced Chou as prime minister in January and became Deputy Chairman of the CCP on April 1, following a series of riots in Beijing. In November 1976, Hua launched attacks on the radical "gang of four" who had led the Cultural Revolution in the 1960s. The gang included Mao's widow, Chiang Ching, who was arrested by Hua along with three other radical CCP members. Joined by Li Hsien-nien as prime minister, Hua directed a modernization program for China in contrast to the "gang of four's" rural program.

November 2, 1976

James Earl Carter is elected President.

Running against Gerald Ford, whom the Republicans nominated on August 19, Carter advocated reforms in Washington to cut government costs and emphasized human rights in foreign affairs. Ford's platform upheld the Nixon-Kissinger policies except for deemphasizing détente with the Soviet Union. Ford's principal opponent before the August convention was Ronald Reagan, whose strong conservative group claimed that Nixon's détente policy had weakened the United States in relation to the Soviet Union. Carter avoided making public any definitive statements on détente, though informally he indicated a desire for cordial U.S.-Soviet relations. (See January 20, 1977.) On the November 2 ballot, Carter received 297 electoral votes to Ford's 241.

November 15, 1976

Vietnam is united but the United States vetoes its U.N. membership.

Following Communist elections in April 1976, Vietnam's two parts were united officially on June 24, 1976. Vietnam applied for membership in the United Nations, but on November 15, the United States vetoed the application. Washington claimed Hanoi was not cooperating in providing information about 395 Americans listed as missing in action (MIA) during

James (Jimmy) Carter. National Archives

the Vietnam War. Representatives of the two countries continued talks in Paris about the MIAs, but the United States was not satisfied about the data Hanoi provided.

December 1, 1976

With the United States abstaining, Angola becomes the 146th member of the United Nations.

Following the end of U.S. aid to the opponents of the government of President Agestinho Neto of Angola, the triumph of the Luanda regime became certain. By October 1, 1976, Portugal recognized Neto's government as the successor to the former Portuguese colony. On November 10, Neto and Soviet leader Leonid Brezhnev signed a 20-year friendship treaty in Moscow. Nevertheless, when Angola's membership in the United Nations was voted on, the United States decided to abstain rather than veto it because as early as February 21, 1976, the State Department had told Gulf Oil and Boeing Aircraft they could undertake business deals with Neto's government.

December 16, 1976

OPEC increases oil prices at a meeting in Qatar.

Although Saudi Arabia and the United Arab Emirates agreed only to a 5 percent increase, the other 11 OPEC members raised their oil prices by 10 percent. Saudi Arabia not only announced a smaller price increase but indicated it would increase oil production. Some observers believed that the Saudi oil minister, Sheik Ahmed Zaki Yamani, was indicating to President-elect Carter that he should pressure Israel to be more flexible in solving Middle East problems.

1977

January 18, 1977

Brezhnev tries to rejuvenate détente.

On December 1, 1976, former ambassador W. Averell Harriman passed a message from Carter to Brezhnev, via Ambassador Dobrynin, stating the new president would move promptly after his inauguration to conclude a SALT II treaty. Although Carter did not feel bound by Nixon or Ford's negotiations, he would consider accomplishments of past years and hoped a future summit would reach an agreement. Because Carter said he was not bound by previous negotiations, Harriman responded to Dobrynin by saying Carter wanted to offer new solutions to issues with the USSR, making Dobrynin apprehensive.

Subsequently, Brezhnev hoped to maintain détente through the SALT II process. During a speech at Tula, he said the Soviets did not seek military superiority but preferred a strategic capability sufficient to prevent any aggressor from attacking the USSR, Moscow's first statement acknowledging its military sufficiency was a goodwill signal to the Carter's administration. Brezhnev also offered a Soviet view of détente:

> Détente is above all an overcoming of the Cold War, a transition to normal, equal relations between states. Détente is a readiness to resolve differences and conflicts not by force, not by threats and saber-rattling, but by peaceful means, at the negotiating table. Détente is a certain trust and ability to take into account the legitimate interests of the other.

January 20, 1977

James Earl "Jimmy" Carter is inaugurated president and wants better relations with the Soviet Union although Moscow is uneasy.

As noted in the January 18, 1977 entry, W. Averell Harriman had an unofficial channel between Carter and Brezhnev following his September 1976 trip to Moscow. Brezhnev told Harriman that he would meet Carter at a future summit to discuss limits on strategic arms—SALT II. During a January 4 breakfast meeting, Kissinger arranged for Ambassador Dobrynin to talk with Cyrus Vance, Carter's new secretary of state, about what policies the Carter administration would promote. Kissinger also noted that Vance should use a private channel with the Soviet ambassador. Vance indicated Carter was eager for a summit meeting and SALT II was a high priority. Vance told Dobrynin that Carter had special concerns about human rights, a topic both sides knew would irritate Moscow. Vance said Carter had been concerned about human rights throughout the world for many years due to his religious convictions. Dobrynin replied that personal convictions were Carter's right but it was not appropriate to apply such convictions to foreign relations because this would interfere in a nation's domestic affairs.

National Security Adviser Zbigniew Brzezinski, President Carter, Secretary of State Cyrus Vance. Jimmy Carter Library

Vance's prior experience was as a New York lawyer who also held diplomatic posts in the Kennedy and Johnson administrations. Thus, he provided a link with the Eastern foreign policy establishment. For national security adviser, President Carter selected Zbigniew Brzezinski, a New York professor of international relations whose views often differed with Vance and Kissinger. Due to their contrasting foreign policy views, Vance and Brzezinski would compete regarding whose ideas would influence Carter's foreign policy.

January 26, 1977

Two young Americans are indicted for selling the Soviet Union data on U.S. space satellite systems used to gather intelligence about Soviet weapons.

Christopher Boyce and Andrew Daulton Lee of Palos Verdes, California, were indicted by a federal grand jury in Los Angeles on 12 counts of espionage. Lee had been arrested near the Soviet embassy in Mexico City on January 6, 1977. A heroin addict and fugitive from justice in California, Lee had relayed data obtained by Boyce to Soviet agents in Mexico between 1975 and January 1977. Boyce was a $140-a-week clerk at the TRW Defense and Space Systems Group in Redondo Beach, California. TRW was the Thompson-Ramo-Woolridge Corporation, which since 1959 had worked on U.S. intercontinental missile systems such as Atlas, Titan, Thor, and Minuteman. Since 1960, TRW had experimented with and operated for the Defense Department more than a dozen earth satellite projects in order to collect data about Soviet weapons. It also processed and analyzed the data for the Pentagon.

Within five months after going to work for TRW in 1974, Boyce had a security clearance for the highest TRW special project at the Redondo Beach plant: Project Rhyolite. This was a covert electronic surveillance system that monitored activity in the USSR and China. Boyce worked as a clerk in the code room, which linked ground stations placed secretly in Australia with the CIA in Washington. During the next two years, Boyce also had contact with Project Argus, an advanced Rhyolite system. He also handled plans for Project 20,030-Pyramid, a futuristic scheme for TRW space satellite systems. Following his arrest, Boyce cooperated with U.S. intelligence authorities in attempting to recall all the data he had photographed and given to the Soviets through Lee, but he had not kept a systematic account of the data he copied. At the least, the Soviets gained data to decode the telemetry reports used by the United States. They also changed all their codes for future messages sent from their satellites. On September 12, 1977, having been found guilty on eight counts of espionage and conspiracy to commit espionage, Boyce was sentenced to 40 years in prison. In a separate trial, Lee was also found guilty of espionage and sentenced to life imprisonment. Boyce's lesser sentence was due to his cooperation. On January 21, 1980, Boyce escaped from Lompoc Prison, California. He was recaptured on August 22, 1981.

The data Boyce and Lee gave to the Soviets seriously handicapped U.S. intelligence-gathering systems for the next several years. After SALT II was signed in 1979, the treaty's critics believed the American system to verify Soviet compliance with SALT I or later SALT II was violated by the USSR. Even though Project 20,030-Pyramid was canceled by TRW, knowledge of future U.S. expectations would assist Soviet intelligence operations in countering the U.S. satellite spy system. Prior to the Lee-Boyce case, U.S. satellite spy operations were secret until President Carter admitted their existence in October 1978.

See February 28, 1978.

February 17, 1977

President Carter's personal letter to Soviet dissident Andrey Sakharov supports Sakharov's dissenting beliefs.

In accordance with his 1976 campaign position on U.S. concerns for human rights, President Carter issued statements in February 1977 that criticized human rights restrictions in the Soviet bloc. Carter told Sakharov he would ask the U.N. Human Rights Commission to investigate the arrest of dissidents in the Soviet Union. The Soviet government denounced Carter for interfering in their internal affairs, declaring that the United States should first improve human rights in some of the dictatorships it supported in Latin America and Africa. Apparently, Carter believed he could separate comments on Soviet human rights abuses from fundamental American-Soviet issues but Carter's moralizing complicated American relations with the Kremlin to the same degree Ronald Reagan's "evil empire" speech had negative influences on Soviet policies.

March 9, 1977

President Carter announces the United States will withdraw about 30,000 troops from South Korea during the next three or four years.

Carter stated that during the past 25 years, South Korea's ability to defend itself had reached the point where the reduction in U.S. forces was feasible. The decision, he said, did not affect the continuing obligation of the United States to defend South Korea if necessary. He soon would be compelled by Congress to reconsider this move.

March 24, 1977

The United States and Cuba inaugurate official talks regarding fishing zones and normalizing relations.

During the next two months these talks made some progress in instituting new diplomatic ties. In early June, the two nations announced that Cuba would establish an "interest section" in Washington; the United States would do likewise in Havana. Nevertheless, the negotiations were tense, and each side seemed reluctant to go too far in the direction of friendship.

March 30, 1977

Secretary of State Vance informs reporters that the Soviets have rejected an arms limitation proposal the Carter administration prepared.

According to Vance, who met with reporters in Moscow after sessions with Soviet leader Brezhnev and Foreign Minister Gromyko, the Soviets simply rejected Carter's proposals as inequitable. Hoping to go beyond the Vladivostok formula of November 1974 to achieve a reduction of nuclear armaments, Vance and Carter made two proposals to Brezhnev: (1) to sign a SALT II treaty based on the Vladivostok formula but to defer for the future the controversy over cruise missiles and the Backfire bomber; (2) to proceed with SALT III discussions to obtain a comprehensive proposal for progress in arms control by reducing nuclear weapons. This second proposal would (a) substantially reduce the aggregate number of strategic delivery vehicles; (b) reduce the number of modern large ballistic missile launchers; (c) reduce the MIRV (multiple independently targeted reentry vehicles) missile launchers; and (d) limit the number of ICBM launchers.

According to Vance, the Soviets would not accept these proposals because they believed the deal would not be to their advantage. Vance stated the Soviet decision on arms was not connected to Carter's complaints about Moscow's violations of human rights.

Brezhnev opposed Carter's approach on two grounds: (1) it reopened issues previously resolved, and (2) it demanded too large a reduction in Soviet ICBMs. "If Carter wants to discuss new issues,"

Brezhnev said, "then the Soviet Union will again raise such problems as the American Forward-Based Systems in Europe and the transfer of American strategic weapons to its allies." Moreover, Moscow was not going to eliminate one-half of its heavy land-based ICBMs to satisfy the Pentagon and Congress. Soviet leaders were dismayed because they had hoped to carry on the gains made during the Nixon and Ford administrations.

May 17, 1977

In a significant political change, Israel's Labour Party loses an election after 29 years in office. The new prime minister is Menachem Begin of the Likud Party.

May 18, 1977

The United States, the USSR, and 32 other nations sign a U.N. agreement banning environmental warfare.

This pact prohibited experiments with or the use of military methods that would alter weather patterns or other environmental phenomena. From 1972 to 1974, the United States conducted a study of "environmental war" based partly on techniques employed during the Vietnam War that led to a Senate resolution urging the president to negotiate a treaty prohibiting such action. At a Moscow summit on July 3, 1974, President Nixon and Soviet leader Brezhnev approved a draft treaty that each nation submitted to the U.N. Conference of the Committee on Disarmament (CCD) in Geneva on August 21, 1975. This U.S.-Soviet draft became the basis for the treaty signed on May 18, 1977.

June 3, 1977

A series of conferences between rich and poor nations (North-South) ends with no significant results.

For over 18 months, dialogue had been conducted in Paris between eight industrialized nations including the United States and 19 developing nations. The rich nations wanted to pressure OPEC to cut its oil prices; the poor nations wanted drastic reforms of the world's trade structure to redistribute the world's wealth. The developing nations also requested a moratorium on the $200 billion of debts they had accumulated; the rich nations offered only $1 billion of funding. More North-South talks were scheduled for November 1977 in Geneva.

June 15, 1977

Spain conducts its first election in 40 years. Adolfo Suarez's Democratic Center Union receives a majority of seats in Parliament.

June 21, 1977

At a Communist conference in Warsaw, Soviet delegates condemn Euro-Communism as ideological heresy.

The Kremlin denounced Euro-Communism, a term that included the willingness of Western Communist parties to renounce revolution and pursue parliamentary methods to gain power. In addition, Euro-Communists such as Santiago Carillo of Spain and Enrico Berlinguer of Italy rejected Moscow's claim to dominate other Communist parties because the USSR was the world's first socialist country.

July 1, 1977

President Carter cancels production of controversial B-1 bomber program.

The president astounded newsmen at a press conference on July 1 by opening the session with the statement that the expensive B-1 program would be ended except for minimal testing developments in the unlikely event "that the cruise missile system had trouble." Carter told the press: "I think that *in toto* the B-1, a very expensive weapons system conceived in the absence of the cruise missile factor, is not necessary." Carter's decision was logical, not political, and aroused resentment from members of Congress who hoped the B-1 would provide economic benefits in their districts or who believed the United States had to be superior to the USSR in all categories of weapons. The B-1s would cost more than $100 million each. However, they would create 69,000 jobs directly and 122,700 jobs by ripple effect. In contrast to the B-1, the cruise missile was, according to its advocates, cheap, accurate, and powerful, and able to avoid Soviet detection systems after being launched from existing B-52 planes outside the Soviet defense perimeter. As a result, the cruise missiles could penetrate into the Soviet Union more effectively than manned bombers.

July 20, 1977

Vietnam is recommended for U.N. membership by the Security Council.

Vietnam's membership became certain because the United States announced in May that it would not use its Security Council veto again to prevent Hanoi from joining the United Nations. In May, Hanoi's delegates told U.S. diplomats in Paris they would intensify their search for 795 Americans missing in Vietnam. This number increased to 2,338 after all Pentagon records were released by 1990. By September 30, Hanoi delivered the remains of 22 U.S. servicemen to American representatives. About the same time, the U.N. General Assembly finalized Vietnam's admission to its organization.

August 8, 1977

Ethiopia and Somalia engage in full-scale war on the horn of Africa.

Each side claimed the other began this conflict, but Somalia appeared to be the aggressor. It captured most of the southern third of Ethiopia, which it claimed to be Somalia's territory. The Soviet Union had the most to lose in this conflict because Moscow supported Ethiopia's government and had naval facilities at the port of Berbera in Somalia.

September 7, 1977

The United States and Panama sign treaties on future operation and defense of the Panama Canal.

President Carter and the head of the Panamanian government, General Omar Torrijos, signed the treaties in the presence of representatives of 25 other American republics and Canada. The treaties resulted from negotiations begun in 1964 and conducted at various times under Presidents Johnson, Nixon, Ford, and Carter. The key decision permitting successful negotiations had been a statement of eight principles signed by Torrijos and Secretary of State Kissinger on February 7, 1974. The first treaty dealt with the transition of canal ownership over a period of 20 years, to end on December 31, 1999. The second treaty provided for U.S.-Panamanian relations after the Panamanians assumed full jurisdiction over the canal in the year 2000. The first treaty provided for a Joint Commission of five Americans and four Panamanians gradually to phase out U.S. control of the canal and prepare the way for Panama's operation of it. Until 1999, a Joint U.S.-Panama Defense Commission would regulate the defense of the canal. The second treaty provided for the neutrality of the canal, future canal toll charges, and the joint U.S.-Panamanian defense of the canal.

November 5, 1977

The United States withdraws from the International Labor Organization (ILO).

This U.N. agency had become politicized by Arab and Communist delegations. In 1974, the ILO voted a resolution to condemn Israel for "racism" in administering Arab territory under its control, and Secretary Kissinger warned the ILO that the United States would withdraw unless the group concerned itself only with labor conditions. President Carter decided to withdraw U.S. membership until the ILO changed its rules and policies.

November 13, 1977

Somalia expels 6,000 Soviet advisers and breaks diplomatic relations with Cuba.

Somalia had been a Soviet ally for eight years but was angered by Soviet aid to Ethiopia in the conflict that broke out on August 8, 1977, between the two African neighbors. Somalia obtained aid against Ethiopia from France and the conservative Arab states. Soon after, Washington changed support from Ethiopia to Somalia and began a Cold War contest on the Horn of Africa.

November 15, 1977

Prime Minister Begin invites Egypt's President Sadat to visit Israel. Sadat accepts, heralding a new relationship between Egypt and Israel.

Early in November, Sadat had suggested he would be willing to visit Israel. Nevertheless, Begin's invitation surprised most observers. After 29 years of enmity Egypt and Israel finally began a search for peaceful relations. On November 19, Sadat flew to Israel, where he talked with Begin. He addressed Israel's

Knesset (parliament) on November 20. When Sadat returned to Cairo on November 21, cheering crowds indicated many Egyptians lauded these new peace overtures.

December 2, 1977

Radical Arab leaders meet in Tripoli to unite against Egypt's moves toward peace with Israel.

Leaders of Libya, Algeria, Iraq, South Yemen, Syria, and the PLO opposed President Sadat's new policy of negotiating with Israel. On December 5, Egypt expelled the ambassadors of each of the radical Arab states except the one from Iraq.

December 14, 1977

A Cairo summit meeting of representatives of the United States, Egypt, and Israel convenes to discuss peace proposals.

Following his visit to Israel, President Sadat of Egypt offered to negotiate directly with Israel, and Prime Minister Begin agreed (November 27). As a result, sessions began in Cairo on December 14 and included U.S. representatives. Initially, Sadat had hoped to persuade the Soviet Union and the other Arab states to join the talks, but Syria led the Arab radicals in rejecting the Egyptian proposal. Moscow also refused to join a multinational meeting on the Middle East. Therefore, Sadat called for direct Israeli-Egyptian talks with only U.S. representatives involved in the discussions.

Although American diplomats preferred a multinational agreement on Middle Eastern problems, President Carter decided to encourage the new initiatives of Begin and Sadat. Nevertheless, both Sadat and Carter continued to seek support for the Cairo talks from moderate Arab leaders in Jordan, Saudi Arabia, and the Persian Gulf states.

December 29, 1977

President Carter arrives in Warsaw, his first stop on a tour to Poland, Iran, India, Saudi Arabia, France, and Belgium.

Carter made this trip for several reasons:

1. A desire for East-West accords with such Communist nations as Poland, Hungary, and Romania;
2. A desire to improve the image of the Shah of Iran in America. The United States depended on the shah as a major ally in the Middle East, although the shah had been severely criticized in the U.S. news media because of his repressive measures against dissenters;
3. A desire to improve relations with India, whose president, Morarji R. Desai, had indicated his desire to end the tensions created with America by Indira Gandhi's policies;
4. A desire to show Saudi Arabia that the United States welcomed its friendship as well as its "friendly" oil policies;
5. A desire to bolster continued good U.S. relations with French President Valéry Giscard d'Estaing;
6. A desire to visit NATO headquarters in Brussels and symbolically reaffirm the American commitment to NATO as the keystone of U.S. alliances.

1978

February 28, 1978

The State Department issues a Senate Foreign Relations Committee report that finds the Soviet Union has generally complied with the 1972 SALT I agreements.

The report on SALT I compliance had been prepared to counteract critics' arguments that Moscow had not fulfilled its agreements with President Nixon.

March 3, 1978

The United States and Hungary sign a trade agreement granting each other most-favored-nation status.

Paving the way for this trade arrangement with Communist Hungary, the United States had returned the Crown of St. Stephen to Hungary. On January 6, Secretary Vance in elaborate ceremonies delivered the crown to Budapest. The crown was Hungary's symbol of nationhood, having been given to King Stephen I by Pope Sylvester II in the year 1000. At the end of World War II, American troops were given the crown by a Hungarian colonel. It had been stored at Fort Knox, Kentucky, since that time. President Carter stated that he returned the crown to Hungary because it belonged to no regime but to the people of Hungary.

April 7, 1978

President Carter announces he has deferred production of the neutron bomb.

During the summer of 1977, the neutron bomb had become public knowledge when a budget item of the Energy Research and Development Administration included an outlay for an "Enhanced Radiation Warhead." This was the neutron bomb, an antipersonnel device that would damage humans more than buildings. It was an intense radioactive bomb that would be deployed in Europe for use against the tanks of the Warsaw Pact armies. In 1977, the neutron bomb became controversial. After Congress approved funds for its development, Carter had to decide whether to continue to prepare the weapon for deployment.

The bomb's critics claimed that using the bomb would begin an escalation of other nuclear weapons if war should begin. During a NATO meeting in March 1978, the European powers were divided on use of the neutron bomb. The NATO Council finally voted that the United States should produce the weapon. Its deployment in Europe, however, would be delayed to determine if the Soviet Union would restrain its development of SS-20 missiles aimed against Western Europe. Evidently, President Carter decided not to produce the bomb unless some European nations first agreed to deploy it. On March 20, he sent Deputy Secretary of State Warren Christopher to sound out England and West Germany. Neither nation would agree to deploy the bomb at that time. Therefore, Carter decided to delay its production. On April 19, 1978, the NATO Nuclear Planning Group decided to keep the neutron bomb option open for possible future use. Subsequently, after further discussions with the NATO governments, President Carter decided on October 18 that components of the neutron bomb would be produced by the United States.

April 20, 1978

Soviet jet fighter planes force a Korean Boeing 707 jetliner to land near Murmansk: Two passengers are killed.

A commercial Korean airliner *en route* from Seoul to Paris flew 1,000 miles off course, crossing into Soviet airspace. Fired on by Soviet planes, the airliner made an emergency landing on a frozen lake south of Murmansk, 390 miles northeast of Leningrad (present-day St. Petersburg). Soviet authorities claimed they forced the Korean plane to land but did not admit shooting at it, as the Korean pilot and his passengers averred. The passengers on the plane were immediately released by the Soviets, but the pilot and navigator were held for questioning until April 29, 1978.

April 27, 1978

Afghan military coup overthrows the Daoud regime: The "April Revolution."

Although Afghan Communists established the People's Democratic Party of Afghanistan (PDPA) in 1965, King Muhammad Zahir Shah experienced few problems while receiving aid from both the United States and the Soviet Union (see April 15, 1946). The nation's political problems began in 1973 when Muhammad Daoud Khan overthrew the king. Trying to unify competing Afghan political parties, Daoud appointed some PDPA members as government and military officials, especially favoring those from the Parcham faction of the PDPA rather than the Khalq members. In 1975, Daoud formed his own political party after a constituent assembly wrote a constitution to create a one-party state that excluded all parties including the PDPA. According to Henry S. Bradsher's *Afghan Communism and Soviet Intervention* (1999 ed.), Daoud's centralization of power in Kabul caused opposition groups to form, especially in rural areas where fundamentalist Muslims preferred King Zahir's royal government because it gave local power to villages and cities as well as Islamic mullahs. By 1978, opposition groups grew in strength with the PDPA's Parcham and Khalq factions uniting to get rid of Daoud. On April 23, Afghan police arrested seven Parcham and Khalq political leaders while Daoud declared that an "anti-Islamic" plot had been uncovered.

Alarmed by these arrests, Afghan Army Major Muhammad Aslan Watanjar persuaded the air force chief of staff to join in an attack on the palace during a meeting when Daoud was deciding on the fate of the seven PDPA leaders. Watanjar led a force of 60 tanks and 600 men in an attack on Daoud's residence while the air force strafed and fired rockets to disperse 1,800 presidential guardsmen. Because Daoud's loyal generals failed to rally loyal troops, the palace guard surrendered. Watanjar's men entered the palace, where they slaughtered Daoud, his family, and most of his ministers. Later, they also killed members of Daoud's Mohammadzai clan.

Following Daoud's death, PDPA leaders Nur Muhammad Taraki and Hafizullah Amin of the Khalq faction, and Babrak Karmal of the Parcham faction headed the government. The PDPA unity ended within three months with Amin as prime minister and Taraki as president and PDPA secretary-general forcing Karmal and other Parcham out of their political and military positions. The April revolution failed to satisfy the rural opposition, which increased after Amin instituted Communist methods of land, education, and social reforms to create a secular state. Although Afghanistan and the Soviet Union signed a Friendship Treaty on December 5, 1978, political disorders continued in Afghanistan.

May 16, 1978

War breaks out again in the Horn of Africa when Ethiopia invades Eritrea.

Following Somalia's withdrawal from fighting in Ethiopia on March 8, the Ethiopians were aided by the Soviet Union in preparing to regain territory Ethiopia claimed in Eritrea. By November 29, Ethiopia said it had crushed the Eritreans; however, rebels in Eritrea launched guerrilla warfare against Ethiopia. During 1978, the Horn of Africa brought a paradoxical realignment of superpower positions. Somalia took advantage of chaos in Ethiopia after the overthrow of the U.S.-supported Haile Selassie and the emergence of Mengistu Haile Mariam as a leader who professed ideas of Marxist-Leninism. Somalia took advantage of Ethiopia's problems by seizing Ogaden province and refusing to return it. Now the Soviets supplied Mengitsu with arms and airlifted about 2,000 Cuban troops to aid Ethiopia. In this role reversal, the United States backed Somalia and the USSR aided Ethiopia.

May 18, 1978

The United States, France, and Belgium rush aid to Zaire when a rebellion recurs in Shaba province.

President Mobutu of Zaire claimed that Cuba and the Soviet Union aided the Shaba rebels. President Carter quickly sent $17 million of nonlethal military aid to Zaire. He also ordered U.S. transport planes to shuttle French and Belgian forces to Kolwezi to rescue 3,000 stranded Europeans and Americans. The president disclosed the U.S. action on May 19. The conflict in Zaire ended quickly. The Belgian and French forces left the area by May 25. The United States charged that Cuba knew about the invasion, permitting the guerrillas to stage their operations in Angola before launching their attack on Zaire. On June 5, the United States airlifted another 1,500 Moroccan troops to Zaire. By July 29, the last Western forces evacuated Zaire after Zaire and Angola agreed to prevent future guerrilla outbreaks along their borders.

May 21–23, 1978

National security adviser Brzezinski visits China to expand the breach between Beijing and Moscow; Brezhnev is displeased.

Brzezinski's trip focused on the U.S.-Taiwan relations with China but also exploited the "China card" regarding U.S.-Soviet relations. Brzezinski rebuked China about its claim America was "soft" toward the Soviets. He also said China was wrong in insisting SALT talks would strengthen the USSR and criticized Soviet border disputes with China. See Zbigniew Brzezinski, *Power and Principle* (1983).

Moscow was not pleased with Brzezinski's criticism of Soviet policy toward China. In turn, Brezhnev criticized the Carter administration's use of the "China card" in an attempt to gain concessions from Moscow.

May 24, 1978

The Soviet Union successfully tests a hunter-killer satellite.

This test followed the USSR's agreement with Secretary of State Vance on April 10 to begin negotiations to suspend the testing of hunter-killer satellites. These earth satellites were capable of finding and blowing up enemy satellites in space. U.S.-Soviet negotiations for a ban on these space weapons began on June 8 at Helsinki with Paul Warnke heading the U.S. delegation.

June 7, 1977

Carter attempts to clarify U.S. policy on the Soviet Union: he fails.

Soviet leaders were confused by American press reports regarding foreign policy disagreements between Secretary of State Vance, who favored détente, and

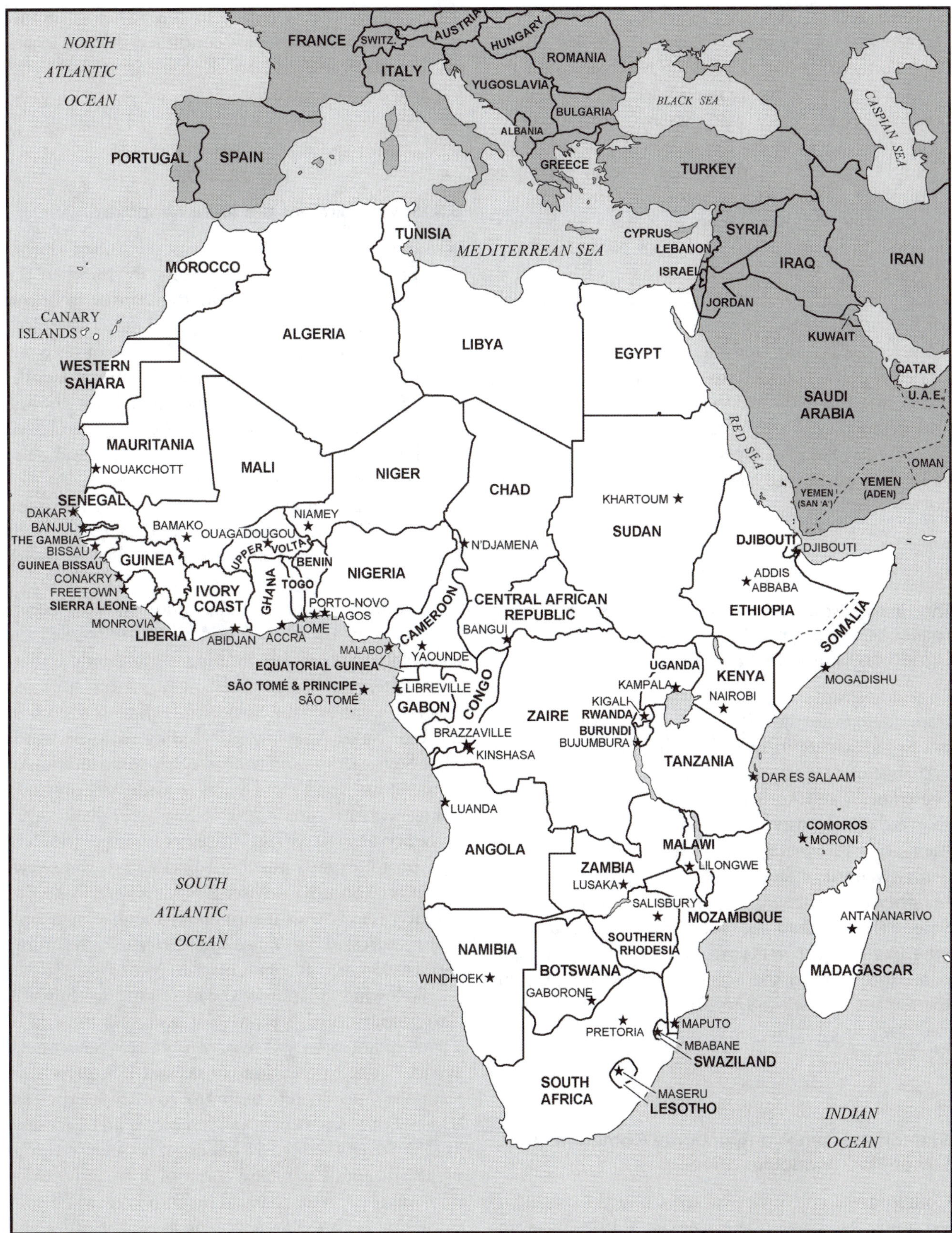
NORTH
ATLANTIC
OCEAN
FRANCE
SWITZ.
AUSTRIA
HUNGARY
ROMANIA
ITALY
YUGOSLAVIA
BULGARIA
BLACK SEA
CASPIAN SEA
ALBANIA
PORTUGAL
SPAIN
GREECE
TURKEY
TUNISIA
MEDITERREAN SEA
CYPRUS
LEBANON
SYRIA
ISRAEL
IRAQ
IRAN
JORDAN
MOROCCO
CANARY
ISLANDS
ALGERIA
LIBYA
EGYPT
KUWAIT
WESTERN
SAHARA
QATAR
SAUDI
ARABIA
U.A.E.
RED SEA
MAURITANIA
MALI
NIGER
OMAN
NOUAKCHOTT
CHAD
YEMEN
(ADEN)
YEMEN
(SAN 'A')
SENEGAL
KHARTOUM
DAKAR
NIAMEY
BANJUL
BAMAKO
OUAGADOUGOU
SUDAN
THE GAMBIA
UPPER VOLTA
DJIBOUTI
DJIBOUTI
BISSAU
N'DJAMENA
GUINEA BISSAU
GUINEA
BENIN
NIGERIA
ADDIS
ABBABA
CONAKRY
TOGO
FREETOWN
IVORY
COAST
GHANA
CENTRAL AFRICAN
REPUBLIC
SIERRA LEONE
PORTO-NOVO
ETHIOPIA
LAGOS
MONROVIA
LOME
CAMEROON
BANGUI
SOMALIA
LIBERIA
ABIDJAN
ACCRA
MALABO
YAOUNDE
EQUATORIAL GUINEA
UGANDA
KENYA
MOGADISHU
KAMPALA
SÃO TOMÉ & PRINCIPE
SÃO TOMÉ
LIBREVILLE
CONGO
NAIROBI
KIGALI
GABON
ZAIRE
RWANDA
BURUNDI
BRAZZAVILLE
BUJUMBURA
KINSHASA
TANZANIA
DAR ES SALAAM
LUANDA
COMOROS
MORONI
ANGOLA
MALAWI
ZAMBIA
LILONGWE
SOUTH
ATLANTIC
OCEAN
LUSAKA
SALISBURY
MOZAMBIQUE
ANTANANARIVO
SOUTHERN
RHODESIA
NAMIBIA
BOTSWANA
MADAGASCAR
WINDHOEK
GABORONE
MAPUTO
PRETORIA
MBABANE
SWAZILAND
SOUTH
AFRICA
MASERU
LESOTHO
INDIAN
OCEAN

Africa, 1978

National Security Adviser Zbigniew Brzezinski, who claimed the Soviets were engaged in a global offensive. Carter contributed to the Soviet confusion by mixing human rights in the Soviet Union's Cuban involvement in Africa with strategic arms negotiations. One solution to this problem became clear when 14 members of the House Foreign Relations Committee asked Carter to end the confusion.

On June 7, Carter tried to clarify his foreign policies during an address at the U.S. Naval Academy at Annapolis, Maryland. Before the speech, Carter asked Vance and Brzezinski to prepare separate drafts for his speech. Thus, the version of the speech Carter delivered was an odd mixture of viewpoints. Carter expressed a desire to cooperate with Moscow but he also was dedicated to promoting human rights and democracy. Carter's contradictory approach to Moscow led Soviet leaders to believe Carter wanted to be firm but leaned toward confrontation with the Soviets.

June 16, 1978

The United States and Panama exchange ratification of the two Panama Canal treaties signed on September 7, 1977.

To demonstrate U.S. goodwill toward Panama and its leader, Omar Torrijos, President Carter visited Panama to participate in special ceremonies for the final exchange of ratification of the canal treaties. Between September 7 and April 1978, the Panama treaties had to overcome intensive opposition from U.S. congressmen prior to Senate ratification. Led by Baker and Senate Majority Leader Robert C. Byrd, a two-thirds majority of the senators approved the treaty by one vote (68) more than necessary. The second and more vital treaty, which replaced the 1903 treaty, did not come to a vote in the Senate until April 18. Again the Senate vote was 68 to 32, barely the two-thirds necessary to ratify it.

June 29, 1978

Vietnam becomes a member of Comecon, the Soviet-Bloc economic alliance.

Comecon was the Soviet-backed Council for Mutual Economic Assistance. On November 3, 1978, Vietnam and the USSR signed a Treaty of Friendship and Cooperation that further solidified their alliance. The admission of Vietnam to the Soviet economic sphere indicated Moscow's continued interest in hegemony in South and Southeast Asia, a policy the Chinese disliked intensely.

July 18, 1978

U.S.-Soviet relations are further impaired.

Tensions in U.S.-Soviet relations intensified during the spring of 1978, climaxing on July 18 when the Soviet Union sentenced Anatoly Sharansky to prison for 13 years. Throughout May and June, President Carter's policy seemed to change because of his complaints about Soviet human rights violations. Unofficial U.S. protests and boycotts began on May 19 when the U.S. Committee of Concerned Scientists protested Yuri Orlov's imprisonment for seven years and delegates of the National Academy of Science canceled their participation in a Moscow scientific symposium. Several U.S. protests also denounced the convictions and imprisonment of other Soviet scientists or Jewish activists.

The first official U.S. opposition to these events came on July 10, when President Carter warned the Soviets that Sharansky's imminent trial would undermine détente relations. Previously, Carter appeared ready to confront the Soviets in a June 7 speech at the U.S. Naval Academy, concluding with the words "The Soviet Union can choose either confrontation or cooperation. The United States is adequately prepared to meet either choice." Carter's June 7 speech dismayed Secretary of State Cyrus Vance because the president seemed to express the hard-line anti-Soviet views of National Security Adviser Zbigniew Brzezinski. Apparently Carter was unsure about the divergent opinions expressed by Vance and Brzezinski regarding cooperation or confrontation with Moscow.

Following Sharansky's conviction on July 18, Carter confronted Brezhnev by canceling the sale of a $6.8 million Sperry Univac computer to Soviet news agency TASS. In addition, all sales of U.S. petroleum technology now had to be approved on a case-by-case basis by the Department of Commerce and Brzezinski. The Soviets wanted $1 billion of petroleum equipment but could purchase some of it in Europe. By mid-August, Carter changed his mind regarding confrontation with the Soviets. The president was angry on April 10 when Secretary of Commerce Juanita Kreps unilaterally approved a Dresser Industries

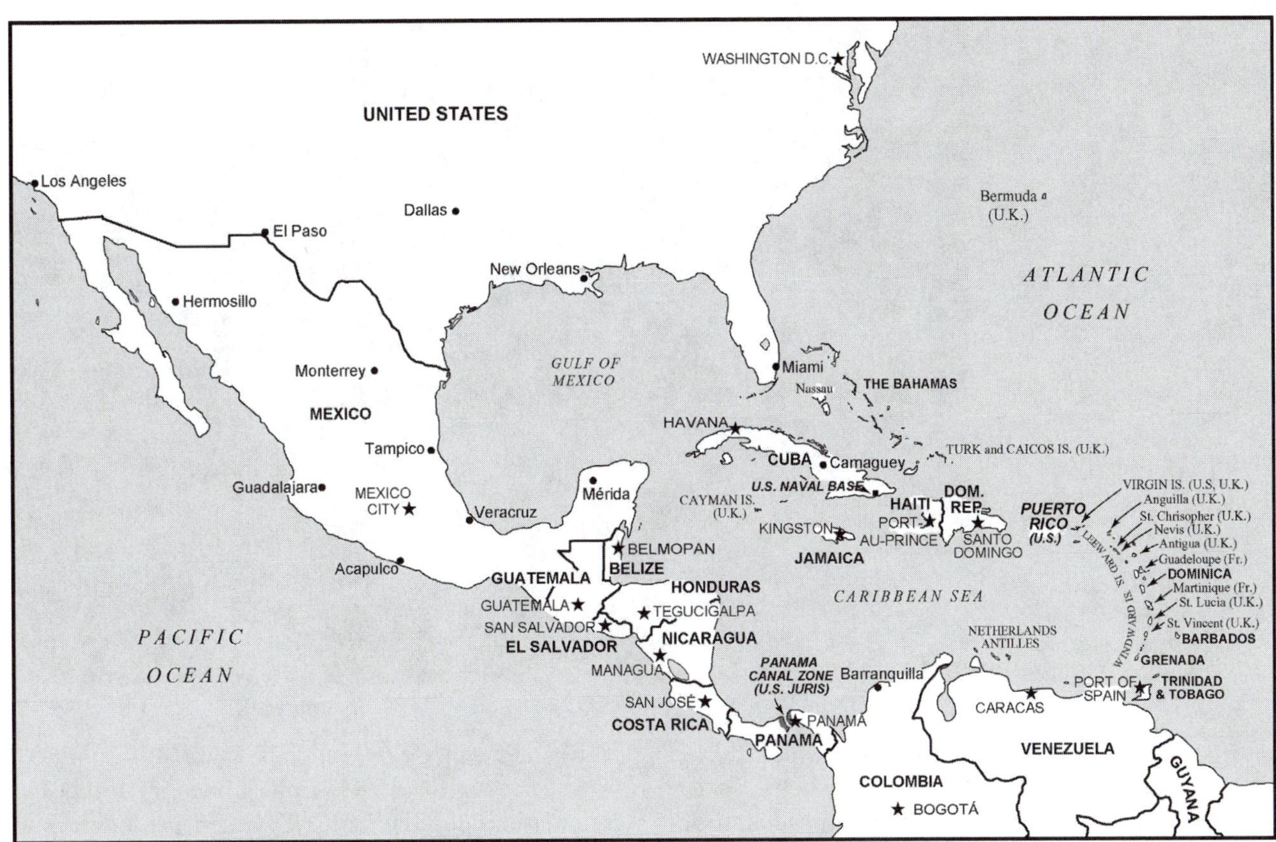

Central America and the Caribbean, 1978

application to sell a $145 million electron-beam welder and drill bits to the Soviets.

Soon after, he gradually shelved his human rights emphasis in favor of obtaining the SALT II agreement with President Brezhnev. In November, Carter reviewed the U.S. trade policy with Kreps and Vance, agreeing to normalize trade relations with Moscow. During the same period, Soviet authorities shifted their policies to permit dissidents to emigrate rather than be arrested and imprisoned. By the end of 1978, 30,000 Jews were allowed to emigrate, twice the average number for the four preceding years. These changes enabled Carter to justify his approval of oil drilling equipment he previously prohibited. On December 4, Secretary Kreps and Secretary of the Treasury David Blumenthal visited Moscow to announce that $65 million of oil equipment was approved for delivery to the Soviet Union. On April 5, 1979, the sale of the Sperry Univac computer was approved. For details about 1978 events see Raymond Garthoff's *Détente and Confrontation* (1985 and 1994).

July 18, 1978

The People's Republic of China closes its borders to ethnic Chinese fleeing from Vietnam.

Trouble began on the Chinese-Vietnamese border after the Socialist Republic of Vietnam expelled 70,000 ethnic Chinese citizens on May 24, 1978. In retaliation on June 9, China canceled 70 aid projects in Vietnam and recalled 1,000 Chinese technicians. Between August 8 and 27, 1978, Beijing and Hanoi attempted but failed to reach a settlement on the status of the ethnic Chinese in Vietnam, most of whom had lived in Indochina with their families for many generations.

September 17, 1978

Egypt and Israel sign two agreements designed to bring peace to the Middle East: The Camp David Accords.

President Sadat's visit to Jerusalem in November 1977 heralded improved prospects for peace in the Middle East. During the first half of 1978, however, these

Anwar Sadat and Menachem Begin with Carter at Camp David. Jimmy Carter Library

efforts became stalled as the two nations talked with U.S. and other leaders in an attempt to resolve *a priori* such questions as Israel's settlements in the land occupied on the West Bank and the Gaza Strip in 1967 and the status of the PLO. In addition, the March attack of terrorists against Tel Aviv and Israel's invasion of Lebanon caused further difficulties for the peace process. During the summer of 1978, several attempts to renew negotiations were unsuccessful or short-lived. On July 5, Egypt offered a six-point plan that Israel rejected. In July, Sadat held meetings in Austria with both Shimon Peres of Israel's Labour Party and Israeli Defense Minister Ezer Weizman. Finally, on July 18–19, the foreign ministers of Egypt, Israel, and the United States met at Leeds Castle in England.

Eventually, President Carter's August 8 invitation to Begin and Sadat to meet on September 5 at Camp David was accepted and proved to be fruitful. After 12 days of intense negotiations with Carter acting as mediator and prodder, Begin and Sadat agreed to sign two documents: "A Framework for Peace in the Middle East" and "A Framework for the Conclusion of a Peace Treaty Between Egypt and Israel." The first treaty sought a solution to the problems involving Israel, Jordan, and the Palestinians and proved to be the more difficult to carry out. The second called for an Israeli-Egyptian peace treaty to be concluded in three months and to provide for subsequent Israeli withdrawal from Egyptian territory in the Sinai. The treaties signed on September 17 in an atmosphere of hope and euphoria were only guidelines for peace. Negotiations for the Israeli-Egyptian peace treaty as well as agreements signed by Israel with other Arab states were required to carry out both treaties.

From Moscow, Brezhnev complained to Carter that the Soviets were excluded from Middle East negotiations. The Soviets believed Carter only called on them when there were serious problems in the region.

September 23, 1978

The radical Arab states reject the Camp David Accords and break diplomatic and economic relations with Egypt.

Meeting in Damascus, the Arab Front for Steadfastness and Confrontation strongly denounced Egyptian President Sadat's agreements with Israel. These Arab governments were Syria, Libya, South Yemen, Algeria, and the PLO, which claimed to be the provisional government for Palestinians.

September 26, 1978

The three-year-old Turkish arms embargo is lifted when President Carter signs the International Security Assistance Act of 1978.

Although President Ford had opposed the arms embargo in 1974 and 1975, Congress required it after

February 5, 1975, because of Turkey's intervention to help the Turkish minority on Cyprus against the Greeks. Subsequent attempts by Presidents Ford and Carter to end the embargo were resisted by Congress, owing largely to the influence of pro-Greek lobbyists in Washington. Although the Cypriot issue had not been resolved in 1978, the Carter administration persuaded Congress to end the embargo by citing evidence of U.S. military needs in Turkey as well as evidence that Greece prevented a Cypriot solution as much as Turkey did. Although the Senate vote in July 1978 required the certification that Turkey had contributed to settle the Cyprus issue, both Carter and the House voted to approve this limit so that the arms embargo could be ended for Turkey. Carter signed this legislation on September 26, 1978.

September 30, 1978

Following eight months of internal troubles in Nicaragua, President Anastasio Somoza accedes to U.S. demands that he accept the international mediation group to settle the disturbances.

Nicaragua's internal problems began on January 24, 1978, when business and labor groups joined the anti-Somoza Sandinista National Liberation Federation (FSLN) in protesting the assassination on January 10 of Nicaragua's leading newspaper *La Prensa's* anti-Somoza editor, Pedro Chamorro. For the first time since the beginning of the Sandinista's 45-year struggle against Somoza, a broad spectrum of middle-class bankers and business leaders acted against the Nicaraguan dictator. On August 28, a businessmen's strike took place, and fighting broke out between police and strikers. The conflict grew and, on September 13, Somoza declared martial law. To end the disturbances and investigate reports of Somoza's terrorist methods, Carter sent a special ambassador to Nicaragua, William Jorden. On September 25, Jorden informed Somoza that the United States would cut off its economic aid unless he accepted mediation by the United States, the Dominican Republic, and Guatemala. Somoza agreed to mediation on September 30, but during the next several months he sought to delay any reforms. On December 27, the Organization of American States (OAS) planned a plebiscite that opposition groups accepted but Somoza rejected on January 18, 1979. Somoza's intransigence eventually led to his exile in 1979.

October 1, 1978

President Carter concedes the United States has used spy satellites.

Public knowledge that the United States might have been using satellites in space to gather intelligence first surfaced widely during 1977, when two young Americans were accused of selling spy satellite data to the Soviets. In a speech on October 1, Carter indicated that the United States had covertly used spy satellites for more than a decade. This intelligence gathering, he said, was essential to national security.

October 23, 1978

The USSR tests a cruise-like missile.

The cruise missile had been rapidly developed by the United States as a possible substitute for a manned bomber. Until the announcement of this test, the United States had been the only power with cruise technology. The October 23 test indicated that the Soviets had developed such technology and might soon have these weapons in its arsenal.

December 3, 1978

Vietnam launches an invasion of Cambodia.

There had been reports of fighting between Cambodia and Vietnam since December 1977. On December 3, 1978, Hanoi radio said the Kampuchean (Cambodian) United Front for National Salvation had been formed to overthrow the tyrant Prime Minister Pol Pot, who had gained control after the Khmer Rouge overthrew Lon Nol's government in April 1975. By December 30, Vietnamese forces had joined Cambodian guerrillas in capturing the Cambodian town of Kratie. Pol Pot earned the enmity of Hanoi because he refused to be subservient to the Vietnamese and had purged Cambodia of all opponents in bloody executions in 1975–1976. By December 1978, the "Communist" states of Vietnam and Cambodia were engaged in war, Vietnam being backed by the Soviet Union, China giving some aid to Cambodia.

December 14, 1978

Egypt and Israel are unable to meet their three-month deadline for a peace treaty despite American mediation attempts.

The September 17 accords provided only a basis for peace; further diplomatic negotiations began at Blair House in Washington on October 12 in an attempt to reach a final agreement. In addition, Secretary of State Vance made frequent visits to Israel and Egypt to seek agreement on sticky points. In Vance's last attempt at reconciliation from December 10 to 14, he worked out a peace formula with Sadat, but the Begin government continued to reject Egyptian demands for clarity on the timing for Palestinian self-rule in the West Bank and Gaza, and for recognition that Egypt had to consider its defense pacts with other Arab states. Israel rejected the Egyptian demands, saying it could review the Sinai issue and the "target" date, not "fixed" date, for Palestinian self-rule but not those parts regarding Egypt's relations with other Arab nations.

Generally the dispute focused on a major flaw in the Camp David accords: there was no definite statement on the linkage between the Egyptian peace treaty and Palestinian self-rule. Cairo claimed they were linked; Begin said not necessarily. President Carter tended to agree with Sadat, thus worsening relations between Israel and America. On November 5, Carter and Vance insisted that linkage of the two agreements was essential. The next day, Israel's cabinet rejected this concept. Thus on December 14 there was an impasse on this issue.

December 15, 1978

Washington and Beijing issue joint communiqués announcing the establishment of diplomatic relations and the termination in 12 months of the U.S. Defense Treaty with the Republic of China (Taiwan).

President Carter announced that the United States and the People's Republic of China would establish normal diplomatic relations beginning January 1, 1979. At the same time, in Beijing, China's Premier and Communist Party Chairman Hua Guofeng read a similar statement to news reporters. It was Hua's first press conference. Although the normalization of U.S.-Chinese relations had been expected since President Nixon visited China in February 1972, the process was slowed because of Watergate, Mao's death, the Vietnam War, and the overthrow of the "Gang of Four" (see September 9, 1976).

On May 20–22, National Security Adviser Brzezinski had visited Beijing where he proposed, with the agreement of Deputy Premier Deng Xiaoping, to negotiate the normalization. Subsequently, in secret sessions, the U.S. liaison officer in Beijing, Leonard Woodcock, and the Chinese began discussions. In addition, Brzezinski met in Washington with Chinese envoys Han Tsu and Chai Tse-min. Early in December the negotiations moved quickly to a conclusion. On December 12, Woodcock visited with Deng, who accepted an invitation to visit the United States in 1979. This signaled the Chinese willingness to normalize relations soon, and both sides worked on a communiqué to be issued on December 15.

Prior to his television address, Carter briefed U.S. congressional leaders and met with Soviet Ambassador Anatoly Dobrynin to inform him that the U.S.-Chinese decision would not influence U.S. relations with Moscow. In his message, Carter said normal relations would begin on January 1, with each nation opening an embassy in the other's capital city. Carter indicated that while the United States would give Taiwan the necessary 12 months' notice required to end the 1954 mutual defense treaty, the normalization would not "jeopardize the well-being of the people of Taiwan." The U.S.-Beijing communiqué stated that "there is but one China, and Taiwan is part of China," a belief that Taiwan's government shared. Carter said that while the United States would recognize Beijing as the "sole legal government of China," Beijing had given assurances it would not seek to reunite Taiwan by force. The United States, Carter said, "will maintain cultural, commercial and other unofficial relations with the people of Taiwan." America could also continue to sell Taiwan "selective defensive weaponry" such as interceptor aircraft, antitank weapons, and artillery.

Following his speech, Carter told a press conference: "The interests of Taiwan have been adequately protected." Despite Carter's assurances on Taiwan, there remained a number of strong pro-Taiwan groups in the United States that protested strongly against Carter's move. Arizona Republican Senator Barry Goldwater called the president's action "cowardly." On December 22, Goldwater and 14 other legislators filed suit in U.S. District Court to prevent the termination of the 1954 treaty with Taiwan. Goldwater argued that the Senate had ratified the

1954 treaty; therefore, the president needed Senate approval to end it. Although a district court ruled on October 17, 1979, that the president could not abrogate the 1954 treaty, a Federal Appeals Court reversed the decision on November 30, 1979, upholding the president's action. On December 13, the U.S. Supreme Court upheld the appeals court ruling.

December 5, 1978

Afghan-Soviet treaty signed.

The Afghan-Soviet Treaty resulted from Afghanistan's request for the Soviets to provide economic and technical assistance. (See January 7, 1979.) The treaty gave Moscow a legal basis for Soviet intervention whenever requested by the Afghan government.

See January 7, 1979.

December 31, 1978

The United States and the Philippines sign a five-year agreement for continued U.S. use of Filipino military bases.

The agreement provided $500 million of U.S. economic and military aid for the Philippines.

1979

January 1, 1979

The United States and the People's Republic of China resume diplomatic recognition with ceremonies in Beijing and Washington.

On February 26, the U.S. Senate confirmed Carter's appointment of Leonard Woodcock as ambassador to China. Woodcock had been serving as the U.S. liaison officer in Beijing.

January 7, 1979

Vietnam and the Kampuchean National United Front conquer Cambodia as Phnom Penh falls.

The next day, Heng Samrin was named head of the Kampuchean People's Revolutionary Council. On January 15, the appeal of Prince Sihanouk of Cambodia to the U.N. Security Council resulted in a resolution asking Vietnam to withdraw from Cambodia (Kampuchea). The resolution was vetoed by the Soviet Union.

January 7, 1979

Soviet Politburo decides to assist Afghanistan's military.

As Chairman of the Council of Ministers, Kosygin confirmed a Politburo decision to send Soviet military specialists to assist the Democratic Republic of Afghanistan's armed forces. The only cost to the Afghans was to provide interpreters and living quarters for the Soviet specialists as well as transportation for official purposes and medical service. For the Soviets, the costs in Soviet rubles from accounts in the USSR's state budget that permitted free assistance to foreign governments from accounts that were appropriated in terms of Afghan currency. The Soviet ambassador to Kabul told the Afghans that shipments of civilian equipment, including auto-transports, civilian airplanes, and helicopters was a matter for the Ministry of Foreign Trade that governed commercial trade whether this equipment was used in the armed forces or other departments.

January 16, 1979

The Shah of Iran leaves for Aswân, ending his power in Iran.

Between 1953 and 1973, the United States had come to rely on Reza Shah Pahlavi of Iran as a strong anti-Communist, pro-Western power in the Persian Gulf region. Following the overthrow of the Mossadegh government in 1953, the shah enhanced his power by undertaking to increase Iran's share of its oil revenues. Following the first oil boycott of the West, the shah moved to acquire leadership in the Middle East's oil politics. The shah avoided the radical confrontation style of Libya's Gadhafi. Nevertheless, the February 4, 1971, Tehran Agreement, which the shah and other Persian Gulf countries made with the oil companies, established the dominant position for OPEC in future oil decisions. On March 20, 1973, the shah obtained the St. Moritz agreement from Iran's oil companies. This pact brought all Iranian oil production under National Iranian Oil Company (NIOC).

Neither President Nixon, Secretary Kissinger, nor subsequent U.S. presidents seriously criticized the shah for undermining the economic prosperity of the Western world. By 1973, the shah's anti-Communism required U.S. support at almost any cost. The U.S. backing for the shah continued even though his economic modernization program in Iran did not envisage political and social reforms. Claiming all opponents were "Communists," the shah organized the Savak (secret police), which used torture, imprisonment, exile, and other methods to suppress all his opponents. By 1977, Iran was experiencing high inflation and economic and social inequities.

In 1977, the shah appointed a new prime minister, Jamshid Amuzegar, who was expected to liberalize the government, end corruption, and establish the human rights desired by President Carter. These measures came too late, opening the way for underground opposition groups to rally public support against the shah. The Ayatollah Khomeini, the Shiite Muslim leader whom the shah exiled to France in 1978, returned to Iran. Khomeini was determined to overthrow the shah because he believed that Savak was responsible for the death of his son. The shah's decision to exile Khomeini on October 4, 1978, inflamed the masses even more, and his attempts to find ways to appease the opposition did not succeed.

Throughout 1978, President Carter supported the shah while urging him to establish a civilian government or become a constitutional monarch. The shah agreed to give most of his power to the National Front, appointing Shahpur Bakhtiar as head of a new government. In addition, the shah agreed to leave the country temporarily and not return as an absolute monarch. This arrangement was completed on January 16, and the shah left for a "holiday" abroad. The plan did not succeed. For the outcome.

See February 1, 1979.

January 30, 1979

China's Deputy Premier Deng Xiaoping begins a visit to Washington.

While visiting the United States, Deng signed scientific and cultural accords. He also made strong remarks against the Soviet Union, from which President Carter had to disassociate the United States.

February 1, 1979

Khomeini arrives in Iran from exile and forms his own provisional government.

Khomeini rejected the government that the shah had formed in Tehran before his departure on January 16. The United States hoped to maintain normal relations with Iran's new government. Discussions began for American businessmen to operate in Iran and for the United States to provide spare parts for the military equipment it had supplied to the shah. Because of the increased anti-Americanism in Iran, the establishment of normal relations became a slow process, because the new government distrusted the United States. This distrust built into active dislike when America permitted the shah to come to New York in October.

February 4, 1979

Chinese translations into pinyin adopted by Library of Congress and the *New York Times*.

In 1958, pinyin was devised by linguists in the People's Republic of China to simplify the translation of Chinese characters to roman letters. The People's Republic of China adopted the system for official translations in 1978. On January 28, when China's leader, Deng Xiaoping began a 10-day visit to the United States, Deng's presence made Americans aware of their lack of Chinese translators, partly owing to the failure to adopt pinyin. As a result, the Library of Congress decided in January 1979 to adopt pinyin to catalogue Chinese publications. On February 4, the *New York Times* announced it would begin using pinyin on March 5, 1979.

February 14, 1979

The U.S. Ambassador to Afghanistan, Adolph Dubs, is abducted and killed by right-wing Muslim terrorists.

Although the United States believed the Soviet Union was responsible for Dubs's assassination, later information showed that the events of February 14 were more complicated than at first believed. Dubs was abducted by four members of a dissident Tajik faction that wanted to exchange him for three imprisoned Tajik. U.S. diplomats in Kabul sought to meet the abductors' request but Prime Minister Amin refused to negotiate. As a result, Afghan police supported by Soviet advisers rushed the kidnappers' hideaway, an act that resulted in the deaths of the four abductors as well as Dubs. The United States did not appoint a new ambassador. For details of the event see Henry Bradsher's *Afghan Communism and Soviet Intervention* (1999 ed.).

February 17, 1979

Chinese forces invade Vietnam along a 480-mile border.

Although Beijing stated the Chinese incursion was limited and intended to punish Vietnam for its exile of ethnic Chinese and invasion of Cambodia, the Soviet Union threatened China, stating that it would support its Vietnamese ally. The hot line to Washington lit up with Brezhnev denouncing the Chinese aggressors and Carter claiming China reacted to Vietnam's invasion of Cambodia. Carter asked Soviet Ambassador Dobrynin to assure Brezhnev that the Chinese did not inform him of their intentions. The Soviets said they were suspicious because China's Deng Xaioping visited Washington less than a month before the assault. In response, Carter said he had warned Chinese leaders against military actions against Vietnam and agreed with Brezhnev that Chinese forces must withdraw from Vietnam.

On March 5, Chinese Premier Hua Guofeng announced Chinese troops would withdraw because their "punishment" of Vietnam had been completed. The Chinese reported on May 2 to have lost 20,000 soldiers; Vietnam claimed to have lost 50,000. The Chinese may have miscalculated the effectiveness of their forces against battle-hardened Vietnamese troops.

March 6, 1979

President Carter orders a U.S. naval task force to the Arabian Sea after fighting begins between the Yemen Arab Republic (YAR) and the Soviet-supported People's Democratic Republic of Yemen (PDRY).

The northern YAR had frequently exchanged harsh words with the southern PDRY. In 1979, however, intense fighting began along their border and the YAR asked the Arab League for help. While the league sought to arrange a cease-fire, President Carter sent a naval task force as a show of support. On March 9, the United States delivered $390 million of arms to the YAR. Carter acted to protect security in the region where Soviet support for the PDRY tried to expand, not only into north Yemen but into Ethiopia and Somalia. Under Arab League auspices, North and South Yemen agreed to a cease-fire on March 30. The two states also agreed to strive for cooperative relations.

March 10, 1979

Afghan military units mutiny in Herat, killing Soviet advisers and civilians; Soviet leaders face difficult decisions.

In mid-March, Afghan troops in the 17th infantry division of Herat mutinied to support Shi'ite Muslims. About 100 Soviet advisers and their families in Herat were killed by bombing that caused massive destruction and more deaths before Herat was recaptured by the Afghan army.

On March 17, Gromyko told the Politburo that "Bands of saboteurs and terrorists, having infiltrated from the territory of Pakistan, trained and armed not only with the participation of Pakistani forces but also of China, the United States of America, and Iran, are committing atrocities in Herat." An artillery regiment and one infantry regiment of that 17th division sided with the insurgents. According to reports, Gromyko said: "The insurgents infiltrating into the territory of Herat Province from Pakistan and Iran have joined forces with a domestic counter-revolution. The latter is especially comprised by religious fanatics. The leaders of the reactionary masses are also linked in large part with the religious figures."

Gromyko also stated that Afghanistan's foreign minister and premier Taraki's deputy, Amin, did not show any alarm when they spoke. Amin said "the situation was not all that complicated," that "the army was in control of everything," and so forth. In a word, he expressed the opinion that "their position was under control." When asked what assistance he might need, Amin made no requests and declared "that the help you have given will stand us in good stead, and that all of the provinces are safely under the control of lawful forces." Amin said there were no outside threats to his regime.

Not long after speaking with Amin, Gromyko learned Taraki had asked chief Soviet military advisor Gorelov and *Charge d'Affaires* Alekseev for military equipment, ammunition, and rations. Taraki also said, "perhaps ground and air support would be required." Gorelov and Alekseev reported that this meant a deployment of Soviet land and air forces was needed. When Gromyko addressed the Politburo, he said, "In my opinion, we must proceed from a fundamental proposition in considering the question of aid to Afghanistan, namely: under no circumstances may we lose Afghanistan. . . ." He concluded by saying "if the army is against the government and, as a result, against our forces, then the matter will be complicated indeed."

In response to Gromyko's analysis, Kosygin said Soviet arms and other supplies scheduled for shipment in April should be sent in March and the Politburo must provide "moral support to the leadership of Afghanistan." The issue was "really very serious," he said, it was vital they consider "the consequences that will flow" from Soviet assistance.

The KGB's Yuri Andropov agreed: "we must consider very, very seriously, the question of whose cause we will be supporting if we deploy forces into Afghanistan.... The economy is backward, the Islamic religion predominates, and nearly all of the rural population is illiterate." Andropov thought Lenin's teaching was for a revolutionary situation but Afghanistan was not that type of situation. He continued by saying: "In such a situation, tanks and armored cars can't save anything. I think that we should say to Taraki bluntly that we support all their actions and will render the kind of support that we agreed upon yesterday and today, but that in no case will we go forward with a deployment of troops into Afghanistan."

The next day Brezhnev concurred with Andropov saying: "In my view the Politburo has correctly determined that the time is not right for us to become entangled in that war.... We must explain to Comrade Taraki and our other Afghan comrades, that we can help them with everything that is necessary for the conduct of all activities in the country. But the involvement of our forces in Afghanistan would harm not only us, but first of all them." By March 20, the mutiny was quelled and Taraki visited Moscow.

See March 20, 1979.

March 12, 1979

The Central Treaty Organization breaks up when Pakistan withdraws on March 12, Turkey on March 15.

The United States had experienced increasingly poor relations with both Pakistan and Turkey. The latter disliked U.S. policy in the Cypriot crisis during which Congress cut off aid to Turkey. President Carter had criticized Pakistan for its arrest and later execution of former Prime Minister Zultikar Ali Bhutto on April 4. On April 6, the United States cut off all economic and military aid to Pakistan because of reports that the government was acquiring nuclear weapons capability.

March 20, 1979

Afghan leader, Mohammed Taraki, visits Moscow but is denied Soviet military forces.

When Taraki visited Moscow he asked the Soviet leaders to send ground troops to Afghanistan. Alexei Kosygin responded: "We believe it would be a fatal mistake to commit ground troops...if our troops went in, the situation in your country...would get worse." Despite the rebuff, Taraki did obtain support from Moscow in terms of armed helicopter gun-ships with Soviet pilots and maintenance crews, 500 military advisors, 700 paratroopers disguised as technicians to defend Kabul airport, and substantial food including 300,000 tons of wheat. Brezhnev warned Taraki that a full-scale Soviet intervention "would only play into the hands of our enemies—both yours and ours."

During 1979, many Afghans fled to Pakistan and Iran to begin organizing resistance groups. After the Soviet invasion in December 1979, the groups in Pakistan were be described by the Reagan administration as "freedom fighters" suggesting their objective was to establish democracy in Afghanistan. However, the groups were divided by ethnic, tribal, and religious beliefs and their agendas were far from democratic.

March 26, 1979

Egypt and Israel sign a peace treaty in Washington.

President Carter's persistent pressure on Egyptian President Sadat and Israeli Prime Minister Begin to conclude a peace treaty finally reached fruition on March 13. Following the president's consultations in Cairo and Jerusalem, the Egyptian and Israeli leaders reached agreement on the issues of the West Bank and Gaza Strip. These questions had caused negotiations to break down on December 14, 1978. Israel made the issue more difficult by announcing its approval of new Jewish settlements on the West Bank on January 15, 1979. Carter's successful diplomatic effort began on March 1–5 when, after meetings in Washington, Prime Minister Begin agreed to a set of U.S. compromises.

On March 8, the president flew to Cairo, where President Sadat accepted part of the agreement but desired several changes. On March 10, Carter flew to Jerusalem, where after three days of discussion he convinced Begin to compromise with Sadat. That same day, March 13, Carter stopped for two hours in Cairo and gained Sadat's approval before returning to Washington. Before boarding his plane in Cairo, the president indicated to newsmen that if the Israeli cabinet approved, the treaty agreement could be concluded. Formal drafts of the treaty were prepared and ready for Sadat and Begin to sign on March 26 after Israel's cabinet had approved Begin's recommendations.

The important points of the Israeli-Egyptian peace treaty were as follows:

1. Israel would submit to Egypt a detailed timetable to withdraw from the Sinai peninsula. The first stage would be in nine months, and over a three-year period Israel would withdraw all its troops and settlers from the Sinai. The area would generally be demilitarized, permitting Egypt to have only one division of troops there. Egypt could use the two existing airports only for civilian purposes. U.N. troops would remain along the Gulf of Aqaba and the eastern border of the Sinai.
2. One month after Israel made the first withdrawal behind the El Arish-Ras Muhammad line, the two nations would exchange ambassadors and establish normal diplomatic relations.
3. Egypt would end its economic boycott of Israel and grant Israel the right of passage through the Suez Canal. Israel could buy oil from the Sinai fields at nondiscriminatory prices. The United States would guarantee Israel a satisfactory oil supply for 15 years.
4. The two nations would conclude trade and cultural exchange arrangements and open their borders to each other's citizens.
5. Negotiations on Palestinian self-rule on the West Bank and Gaza Strip would be targeted for completion in 12 months. There would then be a five-year transition period to decide the final status of the West Bank and Gaza. These clauses did not set any deadline for settlement and later proved to be unworkable. The status of East Jerusalem was not mentioned in the peace treaty.

To help Egypt and Israel conclude their pact, President Carter promised that, with the consent of Congress, the United States would provide about $4.8 billion of aid to the two nations over three years. Egypt and Israel would each get about $2 billion of military aid plus $500 million for economic support. Some observers expected these costs to be higher in the future. Israel's cabinet formally ratified the treaty on April 1, Egypt on April 10. The two nations exchanged ratifications on April 25. The U.S. Senate approved the military-economic aid package on May 14; the House did so on May 30.

March 30, 1979

A western bank consortium announces loans of $300 million to Hungary and $550 million to Poland.

One consequence of détente was the increased number of loans from Western European and American bankers to Warsaw Pact countries, enabling Eastern European purchases in the West.

March 31, 1979

Meeting in Baghdad, the Arab League and PLO approve a complete break in economic and diplomatic relations with Egypt. They move the League's headquarters from Cairo to Tunis.

On March 27, anticipating the league's decision, Egypt announced it would freeze its relations with Arab League members. On April 8, the PLO Council announced it would intensify its violent attacks on Israel, Egypt, and the United States. On April 23, Saudi Arabia broke diplomatic but not economic ties with Egypt.

April 10, 1979

President Carter signs legislation establishing special U.S. ties with Taiwan: the Taiwan Relations Act.

This legislation established U.S. relations with Taiwan to replace Washington's previous recognition of the Taiwanese government as the Republic of China. Under the 1979 agreement, the embassies and consulates of the two countries were replaced by the Taiwan Coordinating Council for North American Affairs in Washington and the American Institute in Taiwan. The agreement permitted the United States to sell defensive arms to Taiwan and continued prior legal and economic relations between the United States and Taiwan.

May 3, 1979

In British general elections, Margaret Thatcher, the Conservative Party leader, becomes Britain's first woman prime minister.

May 14, 1979

The United States and China sign a trade treaty granting China most-favored-nation status.

This treaty was drawn up and signed in Beijing by Commerce Secretary Juanita Kreps and China's Trade Minister Li Qing. President Carter sent the Chinese Trade Treaty to Congress for approval on October 23, saying he hoped Congress would also grant the Soviet Union the same status. Congress approved the Chinese Trade Treaty on January 24, 1980; it became effective on February 1, 1980. The Soviet Union was not granted most-favored-nation status, however.

May 25, 1979

Israel returns El Arish to Egypt, the first step in its withdrawal from the Sinai peninsula.

On May 26, Secretary of State Vance, Israeli Prime Minister Begin, and Egyptian President Sadat met in Beersheba, Israel, to begin talks on an autonomy plan for the Palestinians.

June 8, 1979

President Carter approves full-scale development of the MX missile.

Carter reported on the status of the MX before leaving for the Vienna summit to sign SALT II. The MX was designed to modernize the U.S. ICBM system that in terms of land-based missiles, lagged behind the new Soviet land-based SS-18s and SS-19s. To make the MX less vulnerable to the Soviet first strike, U.S. plans were to make the MX a mobile force, moving it around on tracks in underground tunnels to varied launch sites in the southwestern United States. The MX was permitted under SALT II. On September 7, 1979, Carter announced that the United States would spend $33 billion to deploy 200 MX missiles that would be fully operational in 1989. The mobile MX missiles were never deployed. The Reagan administration continued the MX program but had to change to stationary MX missiles based in hardened silos because no realistic mobile basing system could be devised.

June 10, 1979

Elections for the first European Parliament are completed.

In direct elections where citizens of the European Union cast 110 million votes, 410 members were elected to form a European Parliament. On July 17, at the first session of the group in Strasbourg, Simone Weil, a French delegate, was elected president. Although the European Parliament had little political power, it was an additional, symbolic step in the direction of a united Europe.

June 18, 1979

At a Vienna summit meeting, President Carter and President Brezhnev sign SALT II, a five-year treaty limiting numbers of ICBMs and long-range bombers.

SALT II was negotiated for nearly seven years, having been intended to further restrict strategic missiles that the United States and the USSR limited in 1972. The final agreement on SALT II had been announced by Secretary Vance on May 9, although at the Vienna meeting, Presidents Carter and Brezhnev exchanged letters in which the Soviets agreed not to produce and deploy more than 30 Soviet TU-26 (Backfire) bombers in any one year. Because of earlier domestic criticism about SALT II, President Carter addressed Congress two hours after he returned to Washington from the Vienna meetings. In his speech and in later administration testimony to Congress on SALT II, Carter, Vance, and members of the JCS advocated ratification of SALT by emphasizing the following points:

1. SALT II would help maintain a stable balance of missile forces between the United States and the Soviet Union. According to SALT II each side would have an aggregate of 2,250 missiles and heavy bombers, 1,320 cruise carriers and MIRVed missiles, and 1,200 MIRVed ICBMs. Because the Soviets were above these numbers, they would destroy or dismantle 250 of their systems. While many of those destroyed would be old, they still had the power of America's Minuteman II or Polaris missiles. Without SALT II, the Soviets could keep and add to these 250 missiles or bombers.
2. Verification would continue to be based on U.S. systems, but for the first time there was

agreement not to encrypt telemetric information if it impeded compliance with the treaty. In addition, regular data would be exchanged on strategic forces, rules for counting weapons were simplified, and the USSR would ban its SS-16 mobile missile, which was difficult to verify because it could constantly be moved around.

3. Agreement on SALT II would open the way to negotiating further limits under SALT III.
4. Ratification was important to U.S. allies and U.S. leadership. The NATO allies did not want Soviet superiority or the political tensions and pressure stemming from lack of agreement.

June 28, 1979

As refugee problems become enormous in Southeast Asia, President Carter doubles U.S. refugee quota to 14,000 per month for the next year.

Other nations were also enlisted to assist the war refugees fleeing from Cambodia and Vietnam. Thailand became the principal base of operations for refugee programs because people fled there from the neighboring states. By November 18, the Thais had a camp for 200,000 refugees, which proved insufficient. On August 3, a Red Cross committee visited Cambodia, reporting that over 2.25 million Cambodians faced starvation because of the policies of the Pol Pot regime and the Vietnamese invasion. Emergency food relief operations began on August 28.

July 3, 1979

President Carter approves aid to opponents of Afghanistan's Communist government.

While Carter insisted the Soviet intervention in Afghanistan constituted "the most serious threat to world peace since the Second World War," his administration chose to intervene in Afghan politics when the Soviets had secretly dispatched helicopter gunships pilots and other equipment to the Afghan government. (See March 20, 1979) Zbigniew Brzezinski said the United States began supporting Afghan mujahideen six months before the Soviet intervention, because on July 3 Carter signed a directive approving non-lethal medical and propaganda aid for Afghans. (See January 10, 1980) At the same time, Brzezinski advised Carter that such aid might result in Soviet military intervention. (See Brzezinski, "les Révélations d'un Ancien Conseller de Carter: 'Oui, la CIA est entrée en Afghanistan avant les Russes. . .'," *Le Novel Observateur* [14 January 1998].) Allowing for Brzezinski's later exaggeration, William Maley later wrote: "the likely effects on ordinary Afghans of turning their country into Moscow's Vietnam seems to have weighed all too lightly on policy circles in Washington." See William Maley, *The Afghanistan Wars*, 2002.

See September 14, 1979.

July 14, 1979

Ethiopian forces launch an offensive against Eritrean rebels as war again breaks out on the Horn of Africa.

On August 3, U.S. officials estimated there were 11,000 to 14,000 Cuban troops and 1,000 to 1,200 Soviet military advisers and troops in Ethiopia.

July 17, 1979

Following U.S.-sponsored proposals, the Nicaraguan Congress accepts President Somoza's resignation. Congress names President Francisco Urcuyo Malaños to succeed Somoza.

Between October 1978 and January 1979, attempts by the Organization of American States (OAS) to mediate Nicaragua's internal problems failed. Consequently, Somoza became increasingly isolated from supporters at home and abroad because businessmen, the middle class, church leaders, and union members joined with the Sandanistas' FSLN group against the president. On June 4, a nationwide strike began and the rebels named a five-man junta to rule, headed by Sergio Ramírez Mercado. Between June 21 and 23, the foreign ministers of the OAS met in Washington, adopting a six-point plan proposed by U.S. Secretary of State Vance. The plan set up a peace force and asked for the "immediate replacement" of Somoza's government.

On June 27, U.S. Ambassador William G. Bowdlermet in Panama with FSLN leaders and demanded that two more moderates be added to the junta. With Bowdler satisfied that the junta represented many groups, the unified junta named an

18-man cabinet on July 14, asking Nicaragua's Congress to recognize this cabinet and to replace Somoza. On July 17, Nicaragua's Congress accepted the peace plan. It accepted Somoza's resignation and exile to the Bahamas. On July 19 rebel forces occupied Managua. The next day the junta's cabinet was sworn into office. The Somoza regime had ended.

July 20, 1979

President Carter halts the pullout of U.S. troops from South Korea.

On February 17, 1979, delegates from North and South Korea began meetings to seek cooperation and a process to reunite their nation. After these talks failed, Carter and President Park of South Korea proposed on July 10 that North Korea join them in a three-way discussion on national unity. Premier Kim Il Sung of North Korea rejected this proposal. In addition, the U. N. command at the 38th parallel truce zone reported that North Korea had built new fortifications within 100 yards of the truce border. As a result of the failure of unity talks and evidence of North Korea's defense buildup, President Carter announced that the United States would delay the withdrawal of American forces from South Korea until at least 1981. Carter had announced withdrawal plans on March 9, 1977.

August 1, 1979

The U.S. Department of Agriculture ends a secret session with Soviet delegates in London by announcing that the United States will sell the USSR an additional 10 million tons of both wheat and corn in the next 14 months.

This agreement was followed on October 3 by an Agriculture Department announcement that over the next year the USSR would buy a record 25 million metric tons of corn and wheat from the United States. It was also disclosed that Secretary of Defense Harold Brown had banned the sale of advanced computer technology to the Soviets.

August 6, 1979

The United States announces it has offered to deploy from 200 to 600 medium-range Pershing II and cruise missiles in NATO countries.

NATO had been considering the possible deployment of medium-range missiles since January 19, 1979. These nuclear-warhead missiles were to counteract the Soviets deployment of SS-20 missiles aimed at Western Europe. Medium-range weapons were not part of the SALT I or SALT II pacts. On October 4, the NATO High-Level Group approved deployment of these weapons, and between December 11 and 14, both the NATO defense ministers and the NATO Ministerial Council approved deployment of the missiles. There were some limitations on these NATO decisions. On December 6, the Dutch parliament rejected the stationing of Pershing II missiles on Dutch territory. West Germany accepted deployment of the Pershing II and cruise missiles on the basis that SALT II would be ratified and there would be new talks with the USSR on reducing nuclear forces in Europe.

On October 6, Soviet President Brezhnev offered to reduce the number of intermediate-range missile deployed in the western part of the Soviet Union and withdraw 20,000 troops and 1,000 tanks from East Germany if NATO would not deploy Pershing II missiles in Germany. Although West German Chancellor Helmut Schmidt urged NATO to accept Brezhnev's offer, on October 9 President Carter rejected Brezhnev's proposal because he considered it too vague on vital details.

September 4, 1979

The United States and the Democratic Republic of (East) Germany conclude a consular agreement after two years of negotiations.

September 7, 1979

President Carter asks the Soviet Union to respect America's concern about a Soviet military brigade stationed in Cuba. The president tells a national television audience the brigade is no threat to the United States.

Beginning on February 10, there were reports of increased Soviet military activity in Cuba. First the Defense Department confirmed that Cuba had received Soviet submarines and two torpedo boats. On March 28, there were reports that the USSR was building submarine bases in Cuba, and on August 31, the president stated that 2,000 to 3,000 Soviet combat troops had arrived in Cuba. On October 1, Carter announced the establishment of a new U.S.-Caribbean task force to offset Cuban-Soviet activity in that region. The president hoped this show of U.S. strength, plus President Brezhnev's statement that the Soviet forces were not in Cuba for combat purposes, would mollify senators who based their opposition to SALT II on this Soviet action. Carter's October 1 action did not gain any new converts for SALT II, however.

September 14, 1979

Soviets fail to replace Communist Afghan leadership; Amin is too radical.

Following the March uprising in Herat (see March 10, 1979), the Soviet Union tried to restore order in Afghanistan by ending disputes between Amin and President Taraki. Although the two Afghans claimed to be nonaligned in international affairs, Soviet military and political advisers had steadily increased due to rural and religious groups opposing the Kabul government. After the Herat uprising, Soviet advisers tried to persuade Amin to end reform programs or be replaced by someone willing to calm the rural opposition. On September 14, Moscow encouraged Taraki loyalists to assassinate Amin but they failed and on September 16, Amin had Taraki arrested and executed along with four of his loyalists.

Amin emerged from the affair with a small divided Afghan Communist party with political power only in Kabul. But Amin could not stop the escalation of guerrilla warfare outside the capital. In Kabul, Amin tried to moderate what other Afghans viewed as an anti-Islam regime. He promised more religious freedom, repaired mosques, presented copies of the Koran to religious groups, invoked the name of Allah in speeches, and declared that the Saur Revolution was "totally based on the principles of Islam." Yet many Afghans held Amin responsible for the regime's harshest measures.

Brezhnev and the Politburo became concerned about affairs in Afghanistan. They established a special commission on Afghanistan that in October reported Amin had purged his opponents, including Soviet sympathizers. Now, Brezhnev and the KGB were also concerned about a U.S. intervention in Iran following the Shah's overthrow. (See February 1, 1979) Andropov's KGB experts claimed Afghan's Amin was an American agent who would sell out in order for the United States to gain a foothold in Afghanistan. The American *Chargé d'Affairs* in Kabul, J. Bruce Amstutz, denied the KGB charge but neither Andropov nor Brezhnev believed Amstutz. However, reports from the Soviet Foreign Ministry's diplomatic corps in Kabul saw no probability of American intervention in Afghanistan.

September 19, 1979

The United States undertakes a larger role in the Sinai because the United Nations ended its emergency force in July 1979 and Israel rejected the U.N. Truce Supervisory Organization (UNTSO).

On July 24, the U.N. Security Council did not renew the emergency force and voted to install the UNTSO to oversee the Sinai situation. The United States and the Soviets had drawn up the UNTSO proposal on July 19 but could not obtain the approval of Israel. Prime Minister Begin objected to the UNTSO because he said unarmed observers could not perform the duties required of a U.N. neutral group. Moreover, the Israelis feared a possible repetition of an early U.N. withdrawal as had happened in June 1967, just before the Arab-Israeli war broke out. By September 1979, the U.N. forces were nearly withdrawn, necessitating a new plan to oversee the three stages of Israel's withdrawal and the Egyptian occupation of the Sinai.

In the trilateral agreement of September 19, the United States agreed to enlarge the duties of its Sinai Security Mission (SSM), which had been set up early in 1976 to operate an early-warning system in the Giddi and Mitla Passes. As the U.N. emergency force began its withdrawal, the SSM assumed more duties, although they were not to begin officially until February 1, 1980. Diplomatic arrangements were not completed until April 14, 1980, however, because the 1979 Trilateral Pact was not approved by the Israeli government until March 25 and by the Egyptians until April 2, 1980. Fortunately, no crisis occurred in the Sinai during the interim period from July 24, 1979 to April 1980.

September 27, 1979

Carter signs legislation to implement the Panama Canal treaties.

To operate through U.S.-Panamanian Committees under the two canal treaties that would become effective on October 1, 1979, the president asked Congress in January 1979 to pass the following legislation: 1. create a Panama Canal Commission; 2. form new bases for setting canal tolls; 3. arrange joint U.S.-Panamanian committees to carry out the treaties until 1999; 4. make special provisions for U.S. employees in the Canal Zone or for their emigration to the United States; 5. provide necessary funds to carry out the above provisions.

October 15, 1979

El Salvador's President Carlos Huberto Romero is overthrown in a bloodless military coup led by Colonels Adolfo Majano and Jaime Gutiérrez.

There had been fighting between leftist rebels of the Popular Revolutionary Bloc (PRB) and government forces since May 4, when the PRB occupied the French and Costa Rican embassies as well as the San Salvador Cathedral, holding 11 hostages. Following the coup of October 15, a ruling junta was set up in El Salvador on October 23, promising to solve the political and economic problems of the state. Nevertheless, guerrilla warfare continued in El Salvador. On October 30, a rebel attempt to capture the U.S. embassy in San Salvador was repulsed; the State Department blamed Cuba for backing the rebel attack.

October 24, 1979

In El Salvador, leftists occupy two ministries and take 130 hostages in protest against the new junta.

The Salvadoran leftists disliked the junta led by Majano and Gutiérrez that had gained power on October 15. Dramatizing their refusal to accept the regime, they occupied two ministries in San Salvador, asking for higher wages and an investigation of Salvador's treatment of political prisoners. On October 30, the leftists also raided the U.S. embassy but could not secure it or gain hostages. Subsequently, on November 6, they ended their occupation of the ministry quarters and released their hostages. The junta promised to increase wages.

October 26, 1979

The South Korean intelligence service (KCIA) chief assassinates President Park, his bodyguard, and four other Korean officials.

This incident resulted in a year of demonstrations, protests, and internal fighting in Seoul. Not until September 1, 1980, did President Chun Doo Hwan provide some degree of order in South Korean politics.

November 4, 1979

The U.S. embassy in Tehran is stormed by Iranian students who seize 60 hostages and demand the shah's return before they will be released.

In early October the State Department accepted pleas from Henry Kissinger and David Rockefeller to admit the former shah of Iran to the United States so that he could undergo treatment for cancer in New York. Iran's government had warned that such a decision would turn the Iranian people against America. Normally, a host country protects foreign diplomats, but the Iranian government would not take action to free the hostages. Rather, Khomeini and his followers supported the demand for the shah's return, using the crisis to rally the nation to oppose the United States and to back Khomeini and the fundamentalist Islamic republic that had been established in a national referendum on April 1, 1979.

Subsequently, between November 4 and the end of 1979, various unsuccessful attempts were made to end the U.S. embassy crisis or to negotiate with Iran. The crisis continued throughout 1980.

November 21, 1979

In Pakistan, the U.S. embassy is partly burned and a U.S. Marine guard is killed.

U.S. relations with Pakistan had deteriorated rapidly during 1978 and 1979. In addition, Muslim extremists in Pakistan had been inspired by the example of Khomeini in Iran to attack Western institutions, which allegedly corrupted the traditions of Islam. In this atmosphere, the U.S. embassy in Islamabad was attacked by a mob and partly burned. Marine Chief Warrant Officer Bryan Elis and two Pakistani employees were killed in the attack. But Pakistani troops fought the Muslim demonstrators and rescued 100 Americans from the embassy grounds, ending the mob activity.

November 28, 1979

Lt. General Viktor Paputin, the Soviet Union's deputy minister of interior, arrives in Kabul for a meeting concerning "mutual cooperation and other issues of interest."

Later many people speculated Paputin was the KGB official responsible for coordinating the Soviet invasion. The day after Paputin's arrival, the Soviet 105th Airborne Division led the intervention by deploying an advance group at Bagram Airbase, north of Kabul.

On November 29, Marshal Sergei L. Sokolov arrived in headquarters in Termez, Uzbeckistan, to direct the transfer of a sizable mechanized unit reinforced two weeks later. On December 24, 1979, the bulk of the 105th Airborne began arriving at Khwaja Rawash airport in Kabul.

See December 12, 1979.

November 29, 1979

The United States cuts Chile's military and economic aid because the government refuses to extradite three men accused of involvement in the assassination of Orlando Letelier in Washington.

Letelier had been Chile's foreign minister under Allende and was a critic of President Pinochet's military government before being assassinated in 1976. On October 1, the Chilean Supreme Court upheld Pinochet's refusal to extradite the Chileans as requested by the United States. President Carter's November 29 action halted a $6.6 million package of military spare parts for Chile. Loans to Chile were also canceled by the Export-Import Bank. President Carter's decision was based on human rights considerations, although he probably did not know about the continued CIA activity in Chile, even after the 1975 Senate investigation concluded the CIA assisted groups opposed to Allende.

As disclosed in a declassified report to Congress on September 18, 2000, the CIA not only helped Augusto Pinochet's dictatorial regime during the 1970s but also used U.S. funds to assist General Manuel Conteras, the head of Chile's infamous secret police (DINA). Conteras had ordered the 1976 car bombing in Washington, D.C., that killed former Chilean foreign minister Orlando Letelier and his American associate Ronnie Karpen Moffit. In the 2000 report on "CIA Activities in Chile," Congress learned the CIA not only knew about the killing of Letelier but also about DINA's killing of political opponents in other countries, known as Operation Condor. In 2000, Conteras was in a Chilean prison.

December 12, 1979

Soviet Politburo ratifies proposal to intervene in Afghanistan.

Using documents of the Soviet government declassified in 1995, Odd Arne Wested's essay in the *Cold War International History Project's Bulletin* (Winter 1996/1997) describes steps taken by Moscow's leaders in deciding to intervene on December 12. Despite opposition from Prime Minister Aleksei Kosygin and other Politburo members, Yuri Andropov of the KGB's secret police and Defense Minister Dmitri Ustinov convinced an ailing President Brezhnev of the need to intervene. To persuade Brezhnev, Andropov cited the danger of events in Iran (see November 4, 1979) and a possible U.S. deployment of short-range missiles in Afghanistan similar to those deployed in West Germany on December 6 (see August 6, 1979).

Theories about the Soviet intervention decision do not always agree. Probably, as Brezhnev stated the decision was "no simple decision." Two strategic factors that may have figured in Soviet estimates were the Allied interventions in Russia from 1919 to 1920 and the Kremlin's wish to establish a "cordon" of friendly or neutral states on all its borders including the southern border.. Perhaps equally important was the Brezhnev doctrine used against Czechoslovakia in 1968 that said the Soviets had a "right" to assist an endangered socialist country, and Afghanistan was a friendly regime that might not survive without Soviet assistance. Unfortunately, both Brezhnev and Kosygin were too sick to play meaningful roles in the decision making.

December 24, 1979

The Soviet Union intervenes in Afghanistan.

Substantial numbers of Soviet forces did not reach Afghanistan before December 24, 1979. Soviet troops began to arrive on October 7, when intervention seemed possible. (See November 29, 1979) At midnight on December 24, the Soviets began a massive military airlift involving an estimated 280 transport aircraft and three divisions of about 8,500 men each. In two days, they secured Kabul while motorized rifle units crossed the western border. By December 27, Soviet paratroops and two KGB units attacked Amin's residence where they overcame palace guards before Soviet troops executed Amin and several of his closest aides.

With Amin's death, Babrak Karmal—the exiled Parcham faction leader of Afghan's Communist party—was installed as the new leader. Karmal's regime faced many disabilities such as the question of legitimacy since a foreign power had installed it.

Moreover, Moscow miscalculated what Karmal required to crush the antigovernment mujahideen resistance. The Soviets expected the Afghan army to suppress the dissidents and to be quickly done with Soviet support. As the pacification war dragged on for years, Karmal's government was weakened by the army's poor performance that required the Soviets to send more armed troops.

December 28, 1979

President Carter calls Premier Brezhnev to warn of "serious consequences if the Soviets do not withdraw" from Afghanistan.

In the United States, after confirming the arrival of the Soviet forces, President Carter contacted Brezhnev on December 28 via the hot line to warn him of the "serious consequences" if the Soviet troops were not withdrawn. Carter also sent Deputy Secretary of State Warren Christopher to Europe for discussions with NATO allies.

Christopher learned that most European officials thought Carter had overreacted because the Soviet takeover did not threaten Europe's vital interests. Carter and National Security Adviser Zbigniew Brzezinski disagreed with the Europeans believing that Soviet control of Afghanistan confirmed the Soviet desire to expand into a strategic location, a view anticipating the Carter Doctrine. (See January 23, 1980) Details about the KGB and other Soviet decisions on this subject are in Henry Bradsher's *Afghan Communism and Soviet Intervention* (1999 ed.).

December 31, 1979

Kremlin insists the Afghan government requested Soviet forces.

On December 31, following Brezhnev's statement that the Afghan government asked Soviet troops to enter their country, Carter told reporters, Brezhnev's explanation was "obviously false." Throughout the 1980s, Soviet leaders continually maintained that Afghanistan asked Moscow to intervene. For example, the Soviet leader Mikhail Gorbachev's *Perestroika* (1987) indicates that Kabul asked 11 times "before we assented." Undoubtedly Kabul leaders asked several times for some Soviet units, but they never asked for the massive invasion in 1979. In October 1979, a KGB report warned Soviet leader Brezhnev that to send "Soviet troops to Afghanistan means war, and there is no way to win it without exterminating the entire nation."

1980

January 2, 1980

President Carter asks the Senate to delay its ratification of SALT II because of the Soviet invasion of Afghanistan.

Although the Senate Foreign Relations Committee voted 9-6 on November 9 to send the SALT II treaty to the full Senate with a recommendation favoring ratification, much opposition to the treaty had developed, especially among Republican members. On December 16, a group of 16 senators sent the president a letter requesting him to delay the Senate vote on SALT II until after the presidential elections. Carter did not comply with this request, but following the Soviet action in Kabul on December 27, he asked the Senate to delay voting on SALT II. On June 6, 1980, the State Department announced that SALT II and Afghanistan were "inseparable." Thus, the Senate never voted on the ratification of SALT II. Upon announcing the decision on SALT II on January 2, the White House indicated that the United States would continue to abide by the SALT I treaty, which had been extended in 1977 after its original expiration date. On May 9, President Carter told the Philadelphia World Affairs Council that he hoped eventually to have SALT II ratified, saying the United States would observe SALT II treaty terms as long as the Soviets did.

January 3, 1980

The United States agrees to sell the Republic of China (Taiwan) $280 million of defensive arms.

This deal did not include the advanced fighter jet planes requested by Taiwan.

January 4, 1980

President Carter announces measures against the Soviet Union because of its "invasion" of Afghanistan.

The détente relationship between the United States and the Soviet Union had grown shaky throughout 1979. Some observers attributed this to the fact that

Moscow feared Carter's decision to normalize relations with China in December 1978; others viewed it as due to U.S. concerns that the Soviets had violated the détente relationship in Angola, Ethiopia, and, finally, on December 27–28, in Afghanistan. Whatever the reason, Carter's announcement of retaliatory measures against the Soviet Union for invading Afghanistan indicated that a renewed Cold War relationship had developed between Washington and Moscow, a relationship disturbing to many European statesmen who cherished the results of détente between 1969 and 1979.

Asked on New Year's Eve 1979 whether the Afghanistan affair had changed his perceptions of the Soviets, President Carter candidly asserted: "This action of the Soviets has made a more dramatic change in my own opinion of what the Soviets' ultimate goals are than anything they've done in the previous time I've been in office." On January 4, the president announced that the United States was placing an embargo on sales to the Soviets of advanced technology, grain, and other strategic items. He also said he would seek a Western boycott of the Summer Olympic Games scheduled to be held in Moscow in 1980 if Soviet aggression continued. On January 2, the president wrote a letter to Senate Majority Leader Robert Byrd, asking the Senate to delay its vote on ratification of SALT II until "Congress and I can assess Soviet actions."

On January 8, Carter took additional measures to implement his hard line toward Moscow. He ordered the withdrawal of the American advanced consular group preparing to establish an office in Kiev and expelled 17 Soviet diplomats planning to open a consulate in New York. He also suspended current high technology licenses and shipments of such equipment to the Soviet Union. Carter's continuing reprisals in future weeks include the following actions:

1. On January 18, he ordered curbs on Soviet phosphate ammonia exports. Although on February 3 the White House said there might be future phosphate export licenses, Carter made this embargo indefinite on February 25.
2. On January 21, Carter sent personal messages to 100 foreign government leaders asking them to boycott the Olympics if the Soviets did not leave Afghanistan by February 20.
3. Carter banned the export of all computer spare parts for the Kama River truck plant on January 21. Carter's embargo actions were strongly criticized by some American politicians. As Senator Edward Kennedy said, "it's going to hurt the American farmer and taxpayer more than the Soviet aggressor." With regard to the embargo's effect on grain prices, the Carter administration pledged to buy up 14.5 million tons of corn, wheat, and soybeans (at a cost of $2.6 billion). On January 7–8, grain trading was suspended for two days to allow prices to stabilize, but then, on January 9, prices dropped as far as regulations permitted. The administration did nothing to assist manufacturers of machinery and technology or their employees.

Carter endeavored to persuade U.S. allies around the world to impose a similar embargo but failed to convince most of them. This enabled the Soviet Union to shop among other nations for replacements and needed commodities, especially corn and wheat. It also caused tension with Japan and the U.S.'s European allies who disagreed with the embargo.

January 6, 1980

Indira Gandhi's Congress Party returns to power in India by winning 350 of 542 seats in Parliament.

January 10, 1980

The United States provides secret military aid to Afghan rebels.

Because Carter provided nonlethal aid to the Afghan mujahideen prior to the Soviet intervention (see July 3, 1979), it was not surprising the United States soon developed a robust program of military aid to the rebels. After learning of the Soviet intervention, Carter issued a directive authorizing the shipment of lethal weapons to the mujahideen. A supply of old .303 Enfield rifles arrived on January 10 and throughout the 1980s the CIA supplied the mujahideen with weapons. The CIA tried to match types of weapons already used by the resistance in order to deny involvement with the rebels. This led to the U.S. purchase of Soviet weapons such as the AK-47 rifles, the RPG-7 anti-tank grenade launcher, DShK 12.7 mm heavy machine guns, and various mortars from various suppliers, especially Egypt and China. (For U.S. made Stinger missiles, see September 26, 1986.)

An estimate of U.S. aid during the war has been placed at $2 billion. The activities of the CIA and Congressman Charlie Wilson played an extraordinary role in obtaining money and weapons for the mujahideen. For details see George Crile, *Charlie Wilson's War: The Extraordinary Story of the Largest Covert Operation in History* (2003).

One downside of CIA operations was the decision insisted on by Pakistan President General Zia ul-Haq and his staff that all weapons and supplies would be distributed to the mujahideen by the Pakistani Army's Inter-Services Intelligence (ISI) agency. Many senior ISI members, unfortunately for U.S. interests, favored the young radical Gulbuddin Hekmatyar who would later lead Taliban forces in Afghanistan after 1991.

January 11, 1980

Soviet-backed Afghan regime creates secret police unit.

One key institution involved in the Soviet-Afghan War was the State Information Service (KhAD), established on January 11, 1980, and headed by Dr. Mohammad Najibullah until November 21, 1985. The unit's name was changed on January 11, 1986, to the Ministry of State Security and was lead by Ghuylam Faruq Yaqubi, who took over in November 1985 and remained director until the Communists collapsed in 1992. The KhAD had branch offices in cities of any size and was patterned after Soviet Union's KGB. The KhAD was responsible for counterintelligence, counterinsurgency operations in Pakistan and the surveillance of foreigners as well as party and government members and Afghan intellectuals.

The KhAD used ruthless enforcement tactics, especially in outlying offices that were considered more effective branches of the regime. Its efficiency was attributed to Najibullah who moved from police chief to Party Secretary to head of the government before he was murdered by the Taliban in 1996.

January 14, 1980

The U.N. General Assembly adopts resolution ES-612, demanding the immediate and total withdrawal of all foreign forces (Soviet) from Afghanistan.

The vote of the General Assembly was 104 to 18, with 18 abstaining and 12 absent. Although assembly votes are nonbinding, this vote was the first in which many "nonaligned" nations voted against the Soviet Union, which embarrassed Moscow, although Moscow's 18 allies voted against the resolution. Libya and Romania were absent when the vote was cast. This resolution became a model for measures adopted at General Assembly sessions until the Geneva Accords on Afghanistan were signed in 1988.

See August 14, 1988.

January 23, 1980

President Carter claims the Persian Gulf area is a "vital American interest": The Carter Doctrine.

In his state of the union message to Congress, the president extended U.S. global defense protection to the Arab oil states and the region along the Soviet Union's southern border. Specifically, Carter asserted that "any attempt by any outside force to gain control of the Persian Gulf region will be regarded as an assault on the vital interests of the United States.... Such an assault will be repelled by use of any means necessary, including military force." To implement the new U.S. defense perimeter, Carter asked Congress for a 5 percent increase in the defense budget for 1981, a sum he had resisted as "too much" during 1979. He also indicated that he would ask Congress for authority to register young Americans for selective service, although he added, "I hope that it will not become necessary to impose the draft." President Carter's message was warmly received by Americans, who had become incensed at the Iranian crisis and appalled at the Soviet intervention in Afghanistan. Thus, during the next several months, Carter continued to display his hard-line anti-Communist stance.

On February 11, the United States strengthened its presence in the Persian Gulf and the Indian Ocean by announcing agreements to obtain military facilities in Oman, Kenya, and Somalia. On April 8, Saudi Arabia refused to accept requests for U.S. military facilities but agreed (March 18) to provide financial aid for North Yemen to replace aid formerly received from Moscow. The United States also agreed to provide 60 F-15 fighter planes for the Saudi Arabian defense forces. Perhaps the most significant U.S. agreement in the Middle East was military cooperation with Egypt. On January 8, Cairo indicated that the United States had tested its Airborne Warning and Control (AWAC) planes by using Egyptian bases as a stopover for flights to Iran. On July 10, the United States and Egypt began a 90-day joint training exercise using American F-4E jet planes, paratroopers, and other forces of the two nations.

On November 12, 1980, the United States sent advanced units of its Rapid Deployment Force (RDF) to Egypt for 12 days of joint exercises. The RDF was designed by the U.S. armed forces as a unit that could be quickly sent to any crisis area to counteract enemy (Communist) activity. Thus, the RDF could carry out the Carter Doctrine with conventional forces in the Persian Gulf. The one aspect of the Carter Doctrine that was questioned the most by some U.S. politicians was the status of U.S.-Pakistani relations. One unidentified senator was quoted as saying: "If Russian troops chase Afghan rebels into Pakistan, do we want American boys up in the Khyber Pass trying to stop them?" U.S. defenses under such contingencies would operate at an extreme logistic disadvantage compared with Soviet home bases. In addition, Pakistan's stability and reliability were questioned. On January 13, Pakistan rejected a U.S. offer of $400 million in economic-military aid as "peanuts." Nevertheless, the United States continued to woo Pakistan, pledging on October 30 to assist that country in case of Soviet attack.

January 24, 1980

Congress approves the U.S.-Chinese Trade Act, giving China most-favored-nation status.

Although the Carter administration had previously requested most-favored-nation status for the USSR as well as China, this request no longer applied after the Soviet invasion of Afghanistan in 1979. Therefore, Congress granted Beijing a trade concession that the United States denied to Moscow.

January 29, 1980

The day after closing its embassy in Tehran, Canada discloses that it helped six U.S. Embassy employees escape.

After hiding the six Americans in its embassy for three months, Canada supplied them with forged Canadian diplomatic passports and smuggled them out on commercial air flights on January 26 and 27. Iran denounced the Canadian act and its foreign minister, Sadegh Ghotbzadeh, declared, "sooner or later, somewhere in the world, Canada will pay."

February 13, 1980

Carter announces the end of the 27-month U.S. boycott of the International Labor Organization. The United States rejoins the group on February 18, 1980.

The State Department stated that the ILO had ceased its previous practice of making statements on political and other nonlabor issues, a practice the United States had objected to in 1977.

February 19, 1980

The European Economic Community's Foreign Ministers reject President Carter's request to boycott the 1980 Moscow Olympics. Carter announces the U.S. boycott the next day.

Although the EEC members issued a resolution calling on the Soviet Union to pull its troops out of Afghanistan, the European ministers did not believe the Olympics should be mixed up with political questions. Without EEC support, President Carter announced on February 20 that the United States would boycott the Olympics in 1980. The EEC ministers also refused to support the U.S. embargo of high-technology equipment to the Soviet Union. They believed Carter overreacted to Moscow's actions on December 27, and did not consider the Afghan buffer state as "vital to European interests" compared with better relations with the Soviets.

February 22, 1980

Antigovernment uprising in Kabul challenges Soviet plans.

A significant antigovernment popular uprising that was stimulated by the circulation of so-called "night letters" took place on February 22 in Kabul. Troops fired on protesters using live ammunition and helicopter gunships launched rockets at them. It has been estimated that perhaps as many as 800 Afghan deaths resulted from the government forces' violent response. The opposition's spirit was not broken, however, because in April 1980 students at Kabul University marched in protest. Again the regime's forces fired on the protesters; however, the death of one of the victims—a girl named Nihad—became a symbol of anti-Communist defiance. The student revolt was eventually crushed and most of the student leaders were seized.

In January 1980 there also had been notable displays of opposition in Kandahar and Herat. Together these examples of determined resistance forced the regime to call upon the Soviets for assistance and revealed to the public just how dependent the government was on the USSR to sustain itself.

See April 7, 1980.

February 23, 1980

A U.N. commission of inquiry arrives in Tehran in hopes the hostage crisis may be settled.

The U.N. commission was established by the Security Council on January 11, at Iran's request, for an inquiry into Iran's demands for the return of the shah and his wealth to Iran. U.N. Secretary-General Kurt Waldheim, believed the U.N. group could settle the hostage crisis by discussions with Khomeini and Iran's foreign minister, Abolhassan Bani-Sadr. Following two weeks of interviews in Iran, the U.N. panel left on March 11; Secretary Waldheim admitted that its work had failed and that the commission was "suspended."

February 27, 1980

Leftist guerrillas occupy the Dominican Republic's embassy in Bogotá, Colombia, taking 80 hostages including U.S. Ambassador Diego Asencio.

Two dozen Colombians entered the Dominican embassy during a reception, occupied the building, and held the hostages. The rebels demanded $50 million, publication of a manifesto of their protests, and release of 311 "political" prisoners in Colombia. The hostages were held in Bogotá until the negotiation of their release on April 27. The Colombian government released nine rebel prisoners and agreed to have observers from the Human Rights Commission of the Organization of American States at the trials of the other prisoners. In addition, the guerrillas at the Dominican embassy were paid $2.5 million and allowed to take a plane to safety in Cuba.

March 4, 1980

Robert Mugabe's party wins the majority of seats in Zimbabwe's election. He becomes premier on March 11.

After Bishop Abel T. Muzorewa became President of Zimbabwe (formerly Rhodesia) on April 24, 1979 (see July 30, 1979), the United States and the Organization of African Unity insisted that the black Patriotic Front, headed by Robert Mugabe and Joshua Nkomo, be represented in the new government. To accommodate the United States and OAU, the British offered the "Lancaster House" proposals that Ian Smith's white government and the Patriotic Front accepted on November 15, 1979. The Soviet Union had assisted the Patriotic Front, and Soviet leader Brezhnev cooperated with the British and Americans in the transition to an independent Zimbabwe. Thus, on March 4, 1980, the British conducted elections for Zimbabwe's Parliament, in which 80 of the 100 seats were allotted to blacks. Of these 80, Mugabe's African National Front won 57 seats and Nkomo's African National Political Union won 20 seats; the other 3 seats went to smaller parties. Mugabe became Prime Minister of Zimbabwe and assured Rhodesian whites "there is a place for everybody in this country," naming Ian Smith to a cabinet position. On April 14, President Carter named Robert V. Keeley as ambassador to Zimbabwe and pledged $20 million in economic aid for both 1980 and 1981. On September 25, Zimbabwe joined the United Nations. Mugabe's conciliatory policies during the next year demonstrated that U.S. predictions of a Communist radicalization of Zimbabwe were incorrect. Over the years, however, Mugabe's behavior would become more dictatorial and less sensitive to his nation's needs.

March 6, 1980

El Salvador's junta, acting on U.S. advice, decrees land reforms, nationalizes the banks, and declares a 30-day state of siege.

The Salvador junta led by Colonels Adolfo Arnoldo, Majano Ramos, and Jaime Abdul Gutiérrez had gained power on October 15 with a promise to reform a nation in which previous military leaders had run the state to benefit the wealthy minority. As a U.S. official said, El Salvador was a "classic setting for social and political unrest" because 2 percent of the population owned 60 percent of the nation's arable land. The United States sought to head off further unrest in El Salvador by blocking a right-wing coup on February 23. In February 1980, Washington granted El Salvador $100 million in economic and military aid, asking the junta to make social reforms. Thus, on March 6, the government confiscated 376 estates covering 700,000 acres of land, promising to redistribute it to peasants. The government offered to pay the former landholders in government bonds.

The decree on the siege, which banned demonstrations to maintain order while the reforms were carried out, engendered much opposition from both left-wing and right-wing groups in Salvador, the left-wing because the payments for land were not in cash, the right-wing because they wanted to keep large estates.

March 24, 1980

El Salvador's liberal archbishop Oscar Romero is assassinated by right-wing terrorists.

Rather than ending violence by the left- and right-wing extremists in El Salvador, the junta's March 6 announcement of economic reforms caused greater disturbances. The right wing opposed the land reform as too radical; the Marxists denounced the reforms as too little, while also protesting the 30-day siege. The slaying of Archbishop Romero led to more violence. During the funeral on March 30, gunfire broke out near the cathedral, causing the 30,000 mourners to panic. More than 30 people were killed. Who began the gunfire was uncertain. Some people blamed Salvadoran armed forces occupying the National Palace near the cathedral; others blamed the leftists, who, the U.S. State Department claimed, had received aid from Cuba.

March 29, 1980

Agreement reached on U.S. bases in Turkey as well as on economic and military cooperation.

Following the Cypriot crisis, U.S.-Turkish relations seriously deteriorated. Throughout 1979, however, there was steady improvement owing partly to U.S. concern for the Middle East following the fall of the shah of Iran. Although Turkey rejected a U.S. request on May 15 to permit U-2 flights from Turkish bases as a means for verifying Soviet compliance with the SALT treaties, the renewal of talks between Greek and Turkish Cypriot leaders on May 18 enabled the United States to undertake negotiations to renew U.S. aid to Turkey. Talks began on August 13 that eventually resulted in the five-year agreement signed on March 29, 1980. In that agreement, the United States did not gain Turkish agreement to provide bases for U-2 flights over the USSR. It received one air base, four intelligence-gathering bases, and seven communications centers.

April 4–5, 1980

Over 10,000 Cubans jam Peru's embassy in Havana after Castro announces that all Cubans who enter the embassy peacefully are free to leave Cuba if they obtain foreign entry visas.

The Peruvian embassy had been harboring 25 Cubans who had crashed a bus through the embassy gates to get past a Cuban guard. Apparently to retaliate against Peru, Castro issued his offer, which permitted any Cubans who wished to emigrate to do so. On April 5, more than 10,000 citizens indicated they wanted to leave Cuba by arriving at the embassy. Castro's action caused difficulty for the Peruvians because they did not want 10,000 Cuban emigrés. Lima called on its Andean Pact neighbors to help. Peru also said most of the Cubans wanted to go to the United States. The initial U.S. reaction was that the Latin American countries should take the lead in opening their doors to the refugees.

April 7, 1980

President Carter breaks diplomatic relations with Iran and bans U.S. exports to that country.

From January to April 7, the United States conducted quiet diplomacy with Iran's President Bani-Sadr, hoping to reach a compromise on the hostage question. Following the failure of U.N. Secretary-General Kurt Waldheim's inquiry group on March 11, Bani-Sadr asked the United States for time until the Iranian Revolutionary Council met so that the government could persuade the militants to turn over the hostages. In this context, Carter believed a tough U.S. stance would hinder Bani-Sadr's efforts. On April 6, when the Revolutionary Council met, it placed the fate of the hostages in the hands of Khomeini, not the government of Bani-Sadr. Khomeini stated that the militants would continue to hold the hostages until the Majlis (parliament) met later in the summer. These circumstances caused Carter to break relations with Iran on April 7. He also imposed an economic boycott and asked the U.S. allies to join in these sanctions. He then proposed legislation to allow Americans who held debt claims against Iran to settle their bills by drawing on the $8 billion of Iran's frozen assets in the United States.

April 7, 1980

The role of Soviet forces in Afghanistan is redefined.

Soviet military leaders did not foresee how difficult the war against the insurgents would be. By the end of February, the rebellion against Afghan's government caused Moscow to issue orders to begin operations to destroy the armed opposition together with Kabul's armies. In early March, Soviet military units started operations in Kunar Province as part of an internecine Afghanistan war to suppress the rebels.

On April 7, Gromyko, Andropov, Ustinov, and Vadim Zagladin reported to the Politburo about new duties of the Soviet forces. These duties were not only "defending the revolutionary regime in the Democratic Republic of Afghanistan (DRA)" but also defending the Afghans from external threats by sealing off its borders to ensure safety for major cities and lines of communication. For details see William Maley, *The Afghanistan Wars* (2002).

While Afghans suffered many deaths, the CIA exploited a public relations situation that blackened the USSR. This was the first time the CIA used explicit, heart-wrenching accounts in foreign magazines, newspapers, and academic studies. The CIA's theme was that the rebels were "men of courage, armed only with their faith and love of freedom, being slaughtered by the full evil might of a Communist superpower." But Russian troops saw a different version of the Afghan war. Soviet troops were told anyone who surrendered or deserted to the enemy would be tortured and killed in a gruesome way. See George Crile, *Charlie Wilson's War: The Extraordinary Story of the Largest Covert Operation in History* (2003).

April 25, 1980

A U.S. rescue mission to liberate the American hostages in Iran aborts 250 miles from Tehran because of mechanical problems.

President Carter ordered the failed clandestine rescue mission, which resulted in the accidental deaths of eight U.S. servicemen. The U.S. operation had been planned since November as one means of rescue if negotiations failed. Volunteer antiterrorist specialists from U.S. army, navy, and Marine units had rehearsed their plan under the leadership of Colonel Charles Beckwith. President Carter did not give the operation a go-ahead until April 16. During the mission, six C-130 transport planes carrying a 90-man commando team left from an Egyptian base to Iran on Thursday evening, April 24.

The rescue operation never got beyond the initial salt desert rendezvous point. The landing team first had the unexpected interruption of capturing a busload of Iranians who came on the scene. Next, as the helicopters refueled, one developed a hydraulic problem. The mission plan called for a minimum of six helicopters. With only five remaining, Colonel Beckwith recommended aborting the mission; the president agreed. One consequence of the raid was that the Iranians scattered the U.S. hostages to various locations outside the U.S. embassy, making a second military rescue operation almost impossible. At home, the disaster caused further embarrassment for the president.

April 27, 1980

The Nicaraguan junta loses two moderate members who opposed the Sandinista policies.

Since the overthrow of Somoza on July 17, 1979, there had been frequent disagreements in the mixed moderate-radical junta the United States had sanctioned. The formation of a Sandinist Popular Army on July 28 and the political-economic accords signed with Moscow on March 20, 1980, were the two actions by the Sandinista members of the junta that were most criticized by Americans. The announcement by the National Council of State that the number of Sandinist members would increase from one-third to a majority resulted in the resignation of the two moderates, Violeta Barios de Chamorro (April 19) and Alfonso Callejas (April 22). De Chamorro resigned for "reasons of health." As the owner of *La Prensa*, the nation's leading independent newspaper, she had been troubled by a Sandinist-organized strike that shut down the paper. Callejas, a businessman, resigned to protest the April 21 decree giving the Sandinists a majority of council votes. On April 22, the council stated it would appoint other moderates to the junta. On May 19, two moderates, Rafael Rivas and Arturo Cruz, joined the National Council membership. Nevertheless, the new council moved rapidly to undertake radical measures for full Sandinist control of Nicaragua. Having gained a majority of council seats, the Sandinistas proceeded to obtain a firm hold on the nation.

April 29, 1980

Edmund Muskie is named secretary of state after Vance resigns in opposition to the aborted hostage rescue attempt.

Vance had submitted his resignation to President Carter on April 21, three days before the aborted raid against Iran, which the secretary had opposed. But he agreed not to announce his resignation until the raid ended. Some observers said Muskie was named secretary because, unlike Vance, he would not clash with the more aggressive proposals of National Security Adviser Brzezinski, to whom Carter had turned increasingly after the Afghanistan crisis. In his first significant speech as secretary, Muskie told the Foreign Policy Association on July 7 that the State Department would place less stress on human rights issues and provide essential economic, social, and military aid to non-Communist nations regardless of their civil rights record.

May 4, 1980

Marshal Tito of Yugoslavia dies.

Yugoslavia's 1974 constitution provided that upon Tito's death, the eight-member presidency would replace him. The constitution had created a nine-member presidency that, excepting Tito, had representatives from each of Yugoslavia's six republics and from the two autonomous regions of Vojvodina and Kosovo. The head of the presidency would rotate every May 15, a provision that weakened the federal government's power. This was not a problem as long as Tito was in control as chairman of Yugoslavia's Communist Party. After Tito's death, no leader came forward to assume his powerful role. The eight-member presidency caused the central government to slowly fragment before disintegrating after 1988.

May 5, 1980

President Carter announces the United States will welcome Cuban refugees "with an open heart and open arms."

On April 5, when Fidel Castro dropped all barriers to Cubans wishing to emigrate, the U.S. government had hesitated about the proper response. Washington agreed to take 3,500 of the 10,000 Cubans who went to Peru's embassy in Havana. Peru took 1,000; Venezuela and Spain, 500 each; Costa Rica and Canada, 300; and Ecuador, 200. On April 21, Castro suspended the airlift of refugees to Costa Rica and opened a ship-to-shore boat shuttle from Muriel, Cuba, to Key West. By May 5, about 30,000 Cubans had reached the United States, whose policy was to admit all Cubans who reached the mainland of the United States. Cuban-Americans attempted to free their relatives and bring them to the United States, but Castro decreed that of the passengers on each boat only one-third could be relatives; one-third would come from the group still at Peru's embassy; and one-third would be Castro's "trash'—political dissidents, criminals, and those the government wished to get rid of, including the mentally ill.

Carter's May 5 declaration meant that all Cuban American relatives might eventually come to Florida. Therefore, the president declared a state of emergency in Florida and set aside $10 million to feed and clothe the refugees. About this same time, refugees from Haiti began crowding onto boats to reach Florida and be accepted by the United States. Most Haitians, however, were declared economic, not political, refugees, even though it was as much Cuba's poor economy as Castro's dictatorship that caused most Cubans to flee. As a result, lawyers for the Haitians went to court, claiming that their clients had been discriminated against because they were black and had fled a dictatorship that was on good terms with the United States.

May 14, 1980

President Carter qualifies his "open arms" for refugees statement and orders limits on airlifts and sea-lifts to screen out undesirables.

From April 21 to mid-May, 60,000 refugees poured into Key West from Cuba. Many boat owners had overloaded their vessels to obtain more profits from charging each refugee for the transportation. In one instance, an overcrowded boat capsized, drowning 12 persons. Therefore, Carter proposed to Castro that he assist in making the refugee flow orderly and assist in first clearing people leaving Cuba for the United States. Castro chose to ignore Carter's suggestion and the exodus continued until September 26. Between April 21 and September 26, 125,262 refugees came to the United States from Cuba. Because Cuba did not screen its emigrants, the United States had to establish refugee centers to evaluate the status of each immigrant and assist each in locating work or other support after leaving the refugee center.

May 16, 1980

Secretary Muskie meets in Vienna with Soviet Foreign Minister Gromyko in the first high-level U.S.-Soviet meeting in eight months.

Secretary Muskie described the sessions as "introductory." During other meetings at Vienna that included British and French delegates, Muskie spoke bluntly in asserting that "an act of aggression [i.e., Afghanistan] anywhere threatens security everywhere."

May 18, 1980

In response to Carter's request for European action to oppose Iran's hostage policy, the European Economic Community places limited sanctions on Iran.

The economic sanctions voted by the EEC became effective on May 22 and applied to all contracts made with Iran since November 4, 1979. The British government accepted slightly different sanctions on Iran, limiting them to new contracts only, those made after May 22.

May 26, 1980

The target day for Egypt and Israel to complete West Bank autonomy talks ends with no results.

The 1979 Egyptian-Israeli peace treaty had scheduled autonomy talks to resolve the issue of Arab autonomy in lands occupied by Israel in 1967. Eight rounds of talks had been held, but like the ninth-round discussions from February 27 to March 4, 1980, they ended in disagreement. Efforts by President Carter to renew talks were rejected by Egyptian President Sadat on May 15, because Israel's Knesset (parliament) had approved a bill declaring that Jerusalem was the capital of Israel. On May 18, the Israeli cabinet also opposed another round of autonomy talks. Israel's relations with Egypt and the United States reached a low point during the spring of 1980. On May 8, the U.N. Security Council voted for the fourth time in three months to censure Israel.

May 27, 1980

The first Chinese head of state to visit Japan in 2,000 years, Hua Guofeng arrives in Tokyo.

Hua and Japanese Prime Minister Ohira met to discuss trade relations and joint cooperation against the USSR in East Asia.

May 30, 1980

West Germany and the Soviet Union sign a treaty on oil and gas exploration.

West German and other European statesmen wished to maintain the idea of détente in Europe and not get caught up in the rising U.S.-Soviet tensions that seemed to signal a renewing of the Cold War. Thus, the Germans signed the oil–natural gas proposals that were being negotiated with Moscow. Détente also continued to govern relations between East and West Germany. On April 30, the two German states signed a $282 million transportation agreement to permit road, railway, and water links between West Berlin and West Germany.

June 16, 1980

President Carter sends West German Chancellor Helmut Schmidt a letter warning him not to agree with Soviet President Brezhnev on freezing U.S. intermediate-range missile deployments in Europe.

Apparently the president felt European leaders were acting in concert with Moscow without consulting Washington. On May 19, French President Giscard d'Estaing met with Brezhnev in Warsaw without consulting the United States. Carter did not want Schmidt to do the same, even though the German leader had announced his meeting with Brezhnev as early as January 17, 1980. The publicity given to Carter's letter caused many Europeans to object to the president's interference, especially because Washington had frequently acted without first consulting its European allies. On June 21, Carter met with Schmidt prior to the Venice economic summit.

The United States was concerned its alliance with European nations was drifting apart. Reportedly, Carter and Schmidt did not get along personally and Carter's June 16 letter upset the German chancellor. Schmidt wanted NATO strengthened, but disagreed with U.S. proposals to stretch NATO forces into areas of the Persian Gulf. After their talks in Venice, the two leaders' disunity seemed to diminish. Carter said Schmidt supported NATO's 1979 decision to deploy intermediate-range missiles in Europe.

Nevertheless, Schmidt and Giscard d'Estaing of France expressed disappointment with U.S. policy. Between July 7 and 11, 1980, the two leaders met in Bonn and reaffirmed the German-French alliance.

Their communiqué on July 11 urged an independent European role in world affairs, a role that would not end the American alliance but would separate common European policies from Washington's authority to enact programs in the interests of Western European states.

June 17, 1980

Vietnamese forces attack across the Thai border, striking at refugee camps that hold Cambodians.

Following U.S. protests of these attacks, the Vietnamese withdrew from Thailand. The raids caused the death of 24 Thai and some 1,000 refugees. As these border incidents continued, the United States gave Thailand $32.5 million of military equipment on July 1. On October 22, the U.N. General Assembly passed a resolution calling for the Vietnamese to pull out of Cambodia. The United Nations still recognized Pol Pot's exiled government as Cambodia's legitimate rulers.

June 18, 1980

Following a visit to Washington, Jordan's King Hussein will join Mideast talks with Egypt and Israel if Israel agrees to return occupied territory.

Seeking to revive and extend the West Bank autonomy talks, President Carter hoped King Hussein would agree to participate, a maneuver that could end the Israeli-Egyptian deadlock. Hussein refused to join the discussions on autonomy without specific commitments from Israel. Nevertheless, the United States promised to sell Jordan 100 M-60 tanks with night-vision scopes and laser-range finders. Pro-Israeli groups in Congress opposed these sales, but the State Department said the arrangement was to prevent a Jordanian arms pact with the Soviet Union.

June 19, 1980

President Carter asks Congress to approve shipments of enriched uranium fuel to India; he hopes to wean India away from USSR.

On May 7, the president indicated that the United States had agreed to send India nuclear fuel for its Tarapur plant. Although the U.S. Nuclear Regulatory Commission (NRC) voted against the proposal on May 16, Carter overruled the NRC. The NRC objected because India refused to comply with international regulations on the use of nuclear power and on the development of nuclear weapons. The president favored the agreement to prevent closer ties between India and the Soviet Union. Congress held extensive debates before agreeing to allow the shipment of 38 tons of uranium fuel. The House had rejected the proposal on September 18, but the Senate removed the objection clauses, and a conference committee agreed to accept Carter's recommendation on September 24, 1980.

June 23, 1980

Soviet leaders blame the United States and China for trying to oust Afghan's Communist government and vow to stop it.

Brezhnev told the Soviet Plenum: "Not a day goes by when Washington has not tried to revive the spirit of the 'Cold War,' to heat up militarist passions." His recent example was Afghanistan where "the ruling circles of the USA, and of China as well, stop at nothing, including armed aggression, in trying to keep the Afghanis from building a new life in accord with the ideals of the revolution of liberation of April 1978." When the Soviets helped the Afghans "beat back the attacks of bandit formations which operate primarily from the territory of Pakistan, then Washington and Beijing raised an unprecedented racket." He concluded that "in the Soviet act of assistance to Afghanistan there is not a grain of avarice. We had no choice other than the sending of troops. And the events confirmed that it was the only correct choice."

Foreign Minister Gromyko agreed that in Soviet actions in Afghanistan "we fulfilled our obligation to international solidarity in relations to revolutionary Afghanistan, for the fact that the aggressor already has received a solid rebuff, the Soviet Union does not intend to make any excuses to anyone, and the inspirers of aggression against the Afghan state" should feel the same.

> Of course," Gromyko said, "it would be premature to believe that the complexity in relation to Afghanistan is already behind us. The external enemies of Afghanistan and the domestic reactionary forces will still make themselves known. But the matter is now on the correct path. Afghanistan will not return to the past.... Declaring our readiness to maintain normal relations with the USA, we proceed from the fact that hostility between the two powers is not only unwise, but also dangerous.

Thus, the Soviets have warned Americans the Soviet Union "will not permit anyone to trample on those interests." The Soviets tried to have peaceful co-existence with America, but "now the American administration has once again begun to veer wildly. The underlying cause of the current break in Soviet-American relations is Washington's attempt to do whatever it takes to achieve military superiority over us." See *Cold War International History Project's Bulletin* (Winter 1996/1997), "New Evidence on the Soviet Intervention in Afghanistan," or internet http://wwics.si.edu/).

June 25, 1980

Congress approves Carter's request for revival of the selective service system.

There had been discussions about reviving selective service and universal military training for several years because voluntary enlistments often fell short of armed forces requirements. Therefore, to indicate his continuing concern for the nation's defenses, President Carter asked Congress on February 8 to pass legislation for registering men and women under selective service for possible conscription "to resist further Soviet aggression." On February 26, the administration bill requested $45 million to make registration operative. The Senate approved this bill on the basis of $13.3 million on June 12; the House approved the bill on June 25.

June 26, 1980

France successfully tests a neutron bomb.

This French weapon was experimental. The French government said it would decide in two or three years about whether or not to produce such weapons in quantity and deploy them.

June 26, 1980

A U.N. Security Council resolution condemns South Africa's invasion of Angola, asking for its immediate withdrawal.

On June 13, South Africa said it had raided bases in Angola being used by Namibian rebels for raids into South-West Africa. On June 26, Angola claimed that 3,000 South African troops had occupied its southern towns and killed over 300 civilians. The Security Council backed Angola's demands for South Africa to withdraw. The vote was 12-0; the United States and two other members abstained.

July 1, 1980

West German Chancellor Schmidt and Soviet President Brezhnev meet in Moscow to discuss détente.

Following two days of talks with Soviet officials, the West German leader reported that the Soviets were prepared to negotiate with the United States on intermediate-range missiles to be stationed in Europe. He said he had asked the Soviet leader to pull Soviet troops out of Afghanistan but had received no commitment from Brezhnev. Finally, he said, the Germans and Soviets continued plans for the $13.3 billion natural gas pipeline to be constructed between Siberia and West Germany. Following the Moscow talks, Schmidt sent West Germany's foreign minister, Hans Dietrich Genscher, to Washington on July 2 to provide details of his conversations to President Carter.

July 4, 1980

The Organization of African Unity (OAU) demands that the United States remove its base on Diego Garcia and return the island to Mauritius.

The U.S. navy had occupied the Indian Ocean island of Diego Garcia during the early 1970s, gradually replacing the British fleet that previously used the island as a strategic naval base. The OAU protest was not acceptable to the United States because Washington believed the base was more vital than ever, owing to the Iranian and the 1979 Soviet intervention in Afghanistan and announcement of the Carter Doctrine.

July 19, 1980

As Olympics open in Moscow, 59 nations join the U.S. boycott of the games.

The Olympics were caught up in recent Cold War tensions. Carter persuaded nations such as West Germany, China, Japan, Canada, and Kenya to join Carter's boycott after the Soviets intervened in Afghanistan.

July 27, 1980

Mohammad Reza Pahlavi dies in Egypt.

The shah died from cancer and circulatory shock after 18 months of exile and a long illness.

August 5, 1980

White House administration aides disclose Carter approved Presidential Directive 59, providing a new American nuclear strategy that accepts the concept of a "winnable nuclear war."

After Nixon and Brezhnev signed SALT I and the 1972 ABM Treaty, Secretary of Defense James Schlesinger proposed that the United States adopt a nuclear utilization targeting system (NUTS) that would replace Mutual Assured Destruction (MAD). According to Schlesinger, the United States should plan to first target Soviet ICBMs, not the USSR's population centers. By first destroying the ICBM system, the Soviets would not be able to retaliate (see November 30, 1973). Schlesinger and other American hawks were part of the Committee on the Clear and Present Danger that claimed the Soviet Union adopted a similar strategy—a claim Soviet leaders denied.

While Directive 59 was not made public and Secretary of Defense Harold Brown said on August 10 it was not a "major break with past policies, but an evolutionary development," the implications of the directive were vitally significant to nuclear strategic, operational, and ultimately, political decisions. When Secretary of Defense James Schlesinger resigned in November 1975 after President Ford agreed with Secretary of State Kissinger on the defense budget for fiscal 1977, students of nuclear strategy knew their dispute was about the Pentagon's proposals to increase the American military establishment and to change from MAD to the NUTS strategy for a limited but winnable nuclear war.

In explaining Directive 59, Secretary Brown and President Carter insisted that the United States was not seeking a first-strike capacity. Brown said the U.S. strategy was to give the president options to use "countervailing" force, that is, the nuclear capacity to hit Soviet military targets or population centers and to do so at various levels of limited force that could be retaliatory but might be first strike. This selectivity of targets and force levels would permit U.S. and Soviet leaders to play a chess-like game during which each sought to calculate what level of nuclear attack would be sufficient to obtain the surrender of the enemy. Whether called "countervailing" or "counterforce," the strategy of Directive 59 sought to reverse the strategic concepts upon which nuclear parity, deterrence, and détente had rested.

Since being described as MAD by Secretary of Defense Robert Mc Namara in 1967, the U.S. nuclear strategy of mutual deterrence as well as the Nixon-Kissinger détente and SALT I and SALT II programs had been based on limiting strategic nuclear arms and U.S. parity with the Soviets. In this context, Directive 59 suggested that the Carter administration had accepted the concept contained in the Republican platform of Ronald Reagan adopted during the July 1980 national convention. This platform called for a "clear capability to destroy [Soviet] military targets." Both this statement and the terminology and rhetoric used by the Republican right wing and by Secretary of Defense Brown confused rather than clarified the strategic substance of the two nuclear strategies: MAD and counterforce. Pentagon officials erroneously claimed the Soviet military had also adopted NUTS that differed from the MAD doctrine where each side possessed sufficient nuclear weapons to sustain a first strike and retaliate against the other nation's population centers and would prevent either side from winning a nuclear war. The use of nuclear weapons during war was considered a lose-lose contest.

To military planners in the Kremlin and Pentagon, a counterforce NUTS strategy meant larger military budgets while MAD offered a stable nuclear budget. As a result, the Soviet and U.S. military searched for bigger and better weapons of greater accuracy and larger initial damage to be "certain" to destroy their opponent's "military targets"—weapons MAD strategy did not require. Even before approving Directive 59, Carter steadily moved in the direction of a new strategy by approving the MX-mobile missile system on September 7, 1979. The MX was one Pentagon answer to the Soviets' large SS-18 and SS-19 intercontinental missiles. The MX bases were to be mobile because the U.S. analysts expected that under the limited-war plan, the U.S. missiles would likely be used only on a second-strike basis. Mobility permitted the MX to evade destruction and required the Soviets to target more warheads to be certain to knock out all the MX weapons. In addition to the MX missiles, the Pentagon developed more powerful and more accurate submarine missiles for its Trident submarines, including advanced Ballistic Reentry Systems for accuracy. The U.S. air force developed the Precision Guided Reentry Vehicle to give the MX great accuracy. This accuracy would provide a greater capability of destroying the weapons of the opponent.

In strategic terms, opponents of SALT II used the counterforce strategy to justify their dubious claims that the Soviet Union developed new weapons and a strategy to "win" a nuclear war.

On August 5, Carter adopted NUTS as a strategy to reflect a hard-line anti-Communist attitude of the Committee on the Present Danger that the Soviets planned for NUTS in order to "win" a nuclear war. As a follow-up to PD-59, Secretary Brown told a Naval War College audience on August 20 that our ICBMs could be vulnerable to Soviet missiles. Brown ignored the large U.S. bomber forces and the navy submarine missiles that could launch missiles the Soviets could not knock out because they relied on land-based ICBMs and submarine missiles. Also on August 20, the Pentagon announced the development of "stealth aircraft," a bomber invisible to Soviet radar as a result of its aerodynamic and technical features for flying low and evading detection by the Soviet warning system. In "stealth" and cruise missile technology, the United States had an edge on the Soviets. For details see Raymond Garthoff, *Détente and Confrontation (1994)*; Henry Kissinger, *Years of Renewal (1999);* Gaddis Smith, *Morality, Reason and Power (1986);* and Zbigniew Brzezinski, *Power and Principle (1985).*

August 13, 1980

Polish strikes begin a crisis that lasts until December 1981.

In addition to earlier smaller strikes in Poland, the large-scale strike of 70,000 workers began on August 13 at the Gdansk shipyard on the Baltic Sea. The Gdansk workers demanded an independent union and the reinstatement of the leader Lech Walesa who had been dismissed during 1970 protest demonstrations. In 1970, after Polish leader Gomulka authorized Polish military units to fire on unarmed strikers, killing 45 of them, the Communist Party replaced Gomulka with Edward Gierek. In March 1980, a few dissidents protested working conditions, but serious turmoil began on July 18 after the government increased meat prices. On August 13, the Gdansk trade union began protests that drew more workers and protesters in other Polish cities during the next several months. At first, Moscow believed strikers were led by diverse but divided groups of workers. Soviet intelligence reported that Walesa's Solidarity trade union was the largest group but was more moderate than the radical Committee for Workers Defense (KOR). In light of these reports, Gierek decided to compromise with an Interfactory Strike Committee representing 21 factories, including the Gdansk shipyard. On August 17, Gierek agreed to increase workers' pay and later agreed that workers could form independent unions. Gierek's concessions alarmed Soviet leaders, who decided to replace him with Stanislaw Kania as the Polish Communist Party's first secretary. Kania accepted Gierek's compromises with the unions, enabling Walesa's union to form a charter and register officially in a Warsaw court as Solidarity. Walesa's charter was required to include a clause stating the Polish Communist Party had the "leading role" in union activities. Details on pos-Cold War declassified data about Poland's 1980–1981 crisis are in the *Cold War International History Project's Bulletins* (Winter 1995/1996, Winter 1998).

August 25, 1980

Ronald Reagan, the Republican party's presidential candidate, issues a "definitive" statement that he accepts the current unofficial relationship between the United States and Taiwan.

Candidate Reagan issued the statement following news reports that Chinese officials in Beijing, meeting with Republican vice presidential nominee George H.W. Bush, told Bush that Reagan's previous views on Taiwan endangered Chinese-American relations and world peace. Reagan had long been associated with right-wing Republican groups who supported Taiwan and opposed the recognition of mainland China. Until his statement of August 25, the presidential nominee's current views had not been clarified on the U.S. policy recognizing Beijing's status as China's government, and on the U.S. special legislation on Taiwan.

August 27, 1980

South Korean leader Chun Doo Hwan assumes the presidency.

Following student uprisings in Seoul, Kwangju, and other towns, Chun, who had been made head of the Korean Central Intelligence Agency on April 14, forcefully suppressed the riots, closed the universities, and extended martial law throughout South Korea. By August, Chun had solidified his power and conducted an election that guaranteed his selection as president on August 27. President Carter, who in his

Ronald Reagan. National Archives

early years in office championed human rights, told a *Boston Globe* reporter that Chun "favors complete democracy" but "the Koreans are not ready for that, according to their own judgment."

August 30, 1980

The Polish government grants workers the right to strike and form independent unions.

Attempting to meet some of the workers' demands and end extensive strikes, the Polish government yielded to two principal demands of the workers. These actions led Moscow to become more concerned about Poland's situation. On September 3, the Soviets loaned Poland $100 million in economic aid. They also decided that Edward Gierek should be dismissed as First Secretary of the Polish Communist Party. By September 22, the unions had prepared a labor charter and registered in a Warsaw court as a united organization known as Solidarity, with Lech Walesa as their leader. The Warsaw court legalized the union on October 24 with the provision that it recognized the Communist Party's "leading role" in Poland's unions. Yet workers were not satisfied. Strike activity was renewed in 200 plants in Czestochowa and other smaller cities on November 15. As a result, on November 19, under a threat of a national Solidarity strike, Poland's Supreme Court agreed to delete the lower court's wording on "the Communist Party's leading role," inserting the phrase in a separate protocol to the union charter. Solidarity's demands put more pressure on the Polish government from Moscow where Soviet leaders watched to make certain that the party's compromises with Polish workers did not weaken its leading role in Polish society.

September 4, 1980

Iraq and Iran go to war as the Iraqi Army seizes 90 square miles of territory north of the Shatt Al Arab waterway.

As the war began, there were immediate attempts by the PLO and the Arab League to mediate the boundary dispute, but to no avail. The United States, which later supported Iraq, and the Soviet Union both initially pledged neutrality in the conflict. The Iran-Iraq conflict became a lengthy war of attrition with neither side willing to compromise or able to launch a sustained major offensive to defeat the other.

September 19, 1980

Belgium government agrees to deploy 48 U.S. missiles if arms talks between the United States and the Soviets fail.

October 2, 1980

The British Labour Party backs unilateral disarmament to prevent nuclear war.

This was the first time in 20 years that the leftist faction gained sufficient votes in the Labour Party Convention to pass a resolution for unilateral disarmament. This vote was also a sign of the split developing between moderates and radicals in that party. On November 10, 1980, Michael Foot, a radical Labourite, was named as the British Labour Party Chief.

October 5, 1980

In West German elections, Helmut Schmidt's Democratic Coalition wins.

As a result, Schmidt was reelected as the West German chancellor on November 5, 1980.

October 17, 1980

The Soviet Union and the United States begin talks on limiting theater nuclear forces (TNF).

Although President Brezhnev told the State Department on January 3 that the TNF talks on long-range intermediate missiles in Europe could not be successful, discussions began on October 17, and the first round of discussions ended on November 17. The Soviets wanted the United States and NATO to renounce the December 1979 decision to deploy Pershing II and cruise missiles prior to negotiations. After the United States refused, the talks began but under difficulties that handicapped their success. Although no results were achieved by November 17, NATO's Nuclear Planning Group met on November 14 and approved the current U.S. nuclear strategy.

October 22, 1980

The United States signs a grain purchase agreement with China.

According to this grain accord, the Communist government of China would purchase up to nine million tons of grain annually over the next four years. The grain purchase pact helped Carter's presidential campaign because U.S. farmers had complained of price decreases resulting from the Soviet grain embargo imposed by the president in January 1980.

October 24, 1980

Greece rejoins NATO after its parliament approves a compromise agreement on Turkey.

The Cypriot crisis between Turkey and Greece had led Athens to withdraw its military cooperation with NATO to defend the Aegean Sea area in coordination with Turkey. Stressing the need to strengthen the Western alliance in light of the Iranian and Afghanistan conflicts, the U.S. and Turkish governments made concessions to Greece to obtain its reentry into NATO. Greece and Turkey still had to negotiate the details of their NATO cooperation in the Aegean.

November 4, 1980

Ronald W. Reagan is elected president, winning a clear-cut victory over Carter.

Former governor of California and spokesman for conservative groups in the Republican Party, Reagan won the nomination at the national convention in Detroit on July 17, while President Carter was renominated in New York on August 14. While Carter ran on his record, Reagan campaigned on a platform emphasizing the renewal of America's preeminent military position against the Soviets and the return to concepts of supply-side economics that would supposedly stimulate business investments, thereby revitalizing the economy. In the election, Reagan won 489 electoral votes to Carter's 49. The Republicans gained control of the Senate by a six-vote majority; the Democrats retained control of the House with a 57-vote majority.

November 11, 1980

Signs of a possible settlement with Iran appear as the United States begins talks in Algeria, which acts as an intermediary with Iran.

The initial indication that Iran might discuss a solution to the hostage crisis came on September 12, 1980, when the Ayatollah Khomeini announced four conditions for the release of the Americans. His terms were to return the shah's wealth, cancel U.S. claims against Iran, unfreeze Iranian assets, and promise future noninterference in Iran. On November 11, Deputy Secretary of State Warren Christopher went to Algiers for a 30-hour talk with Algerian representatives. Christopher explained the U.S. position; the Algerians agreed to convey the details of the U.S. response to Tehran. The process that finally gained the hostages' release had begun.

November 28, 1980

Senator Charles Percy meets with Leonid Brezhnev in Moscow, reporting the Soviets would like to start SALT III talks as soon as possible.

Percy, who became chairman of the Senate Foreign Relations Committee in January 1981, was the first high U.S. official to speak with Brezhnev since Carter signed SALT II in June 1979. During his week in Moscow, Percy talked for about 10 hours with Brezhnev and other officials. They discussed Poland, Afghanistan, and oil, as well as arms limitations. Percy also appeared on Soviet national television. Although the Illinois senator told the Soviets that SALT II was dead regarding Senate ratification, Brezhnev indicated he was ready to begin new talks on another strategic arms treaty.

December 3, 1980

President Carter is concerned about Poland because of rumors of Soviet intervention.

Although Poland's Supreme Court recognized Solidarity (see August 30, 1980), the Soviet Union closed Poland's borders with East Germany, and on December 1 the Polish Communist Party's Central Committee removed four members from the Politburo, ostensibly in response to orders from Moscow. In this tense atmosphere, U.S. support for Solidarity led President Carter to announce U.S. concern for the "unprecedented" build-up of 55,000 Soviet troops along Poland's borders. On December 12, NATO adopted a U.S. proposal to warn the Soviet Union that invading Poland would end the détente policies adopted in the 1970s, an ironic statement because neither Ford or Carter acted as if they believed détente was viable.

Meanwhile on December 5, Stanislaw Kania, the first secretary of Poland's Communist Party (Polish United Workers Party), met with Warsaw Pact members in Moscow. Although Poland's neighbors in the Warsaw Pact feared the spillover of Solidarity's independence, the allies agreed with Kania's proposal to resolve the crisis by making no more concessions to the "anti-socialist elements" in Polish society and using Polish security forces to "normalize" the situation. By December 12, Kania told union leaders to end the strikes and he would meet with union organizer Lech Walesa to discuss the union's future. In addition, Poland's Catholic Church asked dissidents to avoid provocative acts. Kania labeled the Western media reports of recent events a "hysterical campaign" with no factual basis, although Poland's crisis was ongoing. For declassified documents on Poland, see the *Cold War International History Project's Bulletin* (Winter 1998).

December 4, 1980

As right-wing violence increases in El Salvador, the bodies of four U.S. women missionaries are found near San Salvador.

The bodies found were those of three Roman Catholic nuns and one lay worker. Their van had been ambushed and the women killed. The Carter administration called for the suspension of $25 million in aid to El Salvador and asked for a thorough investigation because Salvadoran security forces were allegedly involved in the murder. Just six days before, rightist terrorists had attacked a meeting of the Democratic Revolutionary Front at a San Salvador high school. They dragged away 24 persons while 200 members of the National Guard and police stood by. The bodies of the six leftist leaders were dumped outside the city, including those of the front's president, Enrique Alvarez Córdova, and of the Popular Revolutionary Bloc's leader, Juan Chacon. Carter had been providing only nonlethal aid to El Salvador because of the government's human rights violations. There had been 8,000 political killings in El Salvador during 11 months of 1980.

In November, however, a group of right-wing Salvadorans had met with President-elect Reagan, reporting afterward that the new administration seemed more receptive to their military aid requests to combat left-wing guerrillas. On January 18, 1981, Carter authorized sending El Salvador $5 million of combat equipment. Reagan followed with another $25 million and 20 military advisers on March 2, 1981.

December 6, 1980

Reagan issues a statement backing the Camp David Accords as a basis for Middle East peace.

The U.S. Special Representative for the Middle East, Sol M. Lenowitz, indicated the president-elect assured him he backed the autonomy talks between Egypt and Israel, although they had not borne fruit in 1980.

December 16, 1980

Meeting in Bali, OPEC nations announce another increase of oil prices to a maximum of $41 per barrel.

This was the third significant oil price increase in 1980. On January 27, Saudi Arabia and other states had increased prices to $26; on May 14, the price went to $28; and on June 10, it rose to $30 per barrel.

1981

January 3, 1981

In El Salvador, right-wing assassins kill the head of the government's land reform program and two U.S. agricultural experts.

Those assassinated were José Rodolfo Vivera and two Americans, Michael P. Hammer and Mark David Pearlman. The three were killed while eating dinner in San Salvador's Sheraton Hotel. The killing of the land reform head in El Salvador raised questions about the success of the program during the nine months since it began. Thus far only 15 percent of the land was affected, leaving 85 percent of the coffee, 75 percent of the cotton, and 60 percent of sugarcane production in the hands of a few wealthy families. Most peasants were still landless, while others were members of cooperative groups formed to organize production on the former plantations. Apparently, some co-ops managed well, such as one at San Isidro. Others, such as one at El Penon, had to pay much of its profit in protection money to the local military commander and soldiers who "guarded" the ranch. Since March 1979, right-wing groups opposing land reform had killed 200 peasant cooperative leaders and five farm institute employees. With the slaying of Vivera, the rightists got rid of the principal architect of the land program.

January 20, 1981

The American hostages are freed and leave Tehran for Algeria just minutes after President Reagan is sworn in as president.

The use of Algerian officials as intermediaries between Tehran and Washington began on November 11, 1980, and proved successful on January 19, 1981. On December 30, the U.S. negotiator, Warren Christopher, met with the Algerians and worked out a plan to place $5 billion in an escrow account at the time the hostages were released. On January 3, the Algerians gave the U.S. proposal to Tehran. Khomeini accepted Algeria's offer to act as the guarantor of the hostage accord, and on January 14, Iran's Majlis (parliament) approved a bill authorizing the government to conduct binding negotiations with the United States. The accords were signed by Christopher on January 19. The next day, the 52 hostages flew from Iran to Algeria, ending 444 days of captivity. They were transferred to U.S. custody and flown to American military hospitals in Wiesbaden, Germany.

Carter and Walter Mondale meet returning hostages from Iran. Jimmy Carter Library

January 20, 1981

Ronald Wilson Reagan inaugurated president.

The inauguration of President Reagan occurred just minutes after Iran freed the U.S. hostages it had held since November 1979. In his inaugural address, Reagan pledged to renew U.S. military power and global prestige. His initial budget called for income tax reductions of 30 percent, cutting social programs, and rebuilding the nation's military power to assure superiority over the Soviet Union. In a speech at West Point on May 27, 1981, Reagan claimed the USSR was an "evil empire" that desired to destroy America.

January 21, 1981

Alexander Haig becomes secretary of state.

The U.S. Senate confirmed Alexander M. Haig Jr. as secretary of state. A West Point graduate, Haig served in Vietnam and at the National Security Council before becoming President Nixon's White House chief of staff in May 1973 and NATO commander in the fall of 1974. Haig shared President Reagan's belief that Soviet Communism was the source of all global problems.

January 24, 1981

South Korea ends martial law.

President Chun Doo Hwan announced the end of South Korea's martial law that he imposed on May 17, 1980, to end disorders following the assassination of President Tongsun Park. Chun's decision came just before he left Korea to visit the United States. At the White House on February 3, President Reagan praised the move toward democracy and promised to keep 39,000 U.S. troops in South Korea, an issue of concern to Seoul because President Carter had suggested withdrawing 30,000 of those troops. On February 25, 1981, President Chun was reelected to another seven-year term.

January 29, 1981

The United States is dissatisfied when Japan does not meet U.S. requests to increase its defense budget.

As the U.S. economy experienced hard times during the late 1970s and the 1980s, U.S. presidents looked for larger defense expenditures by its NATO allies and Japan to share the Cold War burdens. When the Japanese defense minister Joji Omura visited Washington at the end of January 1981, U.S. Secretary of Defense Caspar Weinberger informed him that the United States had expected Japan's current budget (approved in Tokyo on January 13) to increase by 11 percent. Yet it had been increased by only 7.6 percent, to $12 billion. Because Japan had spent so little on defense since 1945, U.S. defense managers believed immediate expenditures were essential.

American strategy envisioned a Japanese defense force able to defend a perimeter of 1,000 miles around the Japanese shores if the Soviet Union attacked. Both in Washington and upon his return home, Omura resisted demands for a more rapid defense buildup. Subsequently, Japan and the Reagan administration were often at odds over defense costs, especially after President Reagan greatly accelerated U.S. military expenditures from 1981 to 1984.

February 1, 1981

Ambassador to El Salvador Robert E. White is replaced because he publicly criticized El Salvador's government.

Ambassador White became increasingly dismayed with President José Napoleon Duarte's inept handling of land reform and his failure to keep the Salvadoran military from committing atrocities against peasants and the opposition. President Reagan then named a career officer, Frederic Chapin, to be ambassador. Similar to the Carter administration since 1979, Reagan's administration conceived of Duarte as a moderate non-Marxist. Duarte spoke like a reform moderate who realized that the rich fought to deny any benefits to the poor, and he advocated giving land to the peasants. But his efforts at land reform were limited. Even worse, rather than controlling the military, he collaborated with the generals who made him president in 1979. Other civilian reformers had resigned from the government to protest the continued personal power of the defense minister, Colonel José Guillermo García, who, in the view of many, used Duarte to hide military crimes and corruption.

Two rebel groups opposed the junta that gained power in 1979: the radical Farabundo Marti National Liberation Front (FMLN), made up of five guerrilla factions; and the Democratic Revolutionary Front (FDR), which coordinated efforts of forty groups ranging from priests and the professional middle class to Social Democrats and Christian Democrats, including some guerrilla forces. The FDR's first president was Enrique Alvarez Cordova, a wealthy landowner who resigned as minister of agriculture because the junta was dominated by the military. In November 1980, Alvarez and five other FDR leaders were assassinated by uniformed soldiers who attacked the Jesuit high school where the leaders met. The successor to Alvarez was Guillermo Manuel Ungo, a lawyer and professor at El Salvador's Catholic University. Because he had been threatened with assassination, Ungo traveled abroad to seek support for the FDR. Ungo claimed to favor socialist democracy but not Communism. In this context, Ambassador White became a critic of El Salvador's military order and of Duarte's inability to control them. Nevertheless, the Reagan administration believed Duarte was the most likely moderate candidate available for El Salvador.

February 9, 1981

Secretary of State Alexander Haig and Secretary of Defense Caspar Weinberger formulate a plan to cooperate in policy formulation.

In national security decisions, increased friction had arisen during the past 20 years between the roles of the Departments of State and Defense and the National Security Council. Hoping to avoid the disparities in policy planning that he experienced during his service in the Nixon administration, Haig obtained President Reagan's permission to clarify the role of the State Department in such undertakings.

Subsequently, on February 9, Haig and Weinberger agreed to give the State Department the leading role in most foreign policy matters, while the Defense Department retained some statutes by working through interagency committees operating out of the Pentagon. In addition, Haig and Weinberger agreed to schedule frequent meetings to discuss policies. In particular, this formulation delegated the National Security Council to the lesser role of coordinating preparations of the two departments. The new national security adviser, Richard Allen, accepted the lesser role, but the NSC staff disliked this subordination, and Allen's successor would seek to strengthen its position.

February 9, 1981

Polish Defense Minister Wojciech Jaruzelski becomes prime minister.

Since August 1980, the Solidarity trade union movement had staged strikes, and protests disrupted Poland, leading to the threat of Soviet military intervention. On January 5, Solidarity leader Lech Walesa met with government officials, but they failed to agree on worker's demands such as a five-day workweek. To end the disorder, Jaruzelski took the post of Prime Minister after firing Józef Pinkowski and asked the workers, students, and middle-class demonstrators to give him "ninety days of peace" to bring reforms. On February 18, some student groups gained the right to form a union, and some farmers reached accords with the government on farm prices.

February 18, 1981

President Reagan calls for tax cuts, lower welfare costs, and increased defense expenditures.

Pursuing his election campaign messages of an income tax cut, less welfare, and regaining military superiority over the Soviet Union, Reagan proposed to Congress in his state of the union message a 30 percent income tax cut over three years with rates on high incomes being trimmed the most to stimulate investment. He requested national defense outlays of $181.5 billion, increasing by $35 billion the amount President Carter had sought for fiscal year 1982. Between May 20 and August 13, Congress approved most of Reagan's request. Taxes were cut by 25 percent over three years, social programs cut by $36 billion, and military expenses increased by $25 billion to $188 billion for the year. The national debt reached a landmark during 1981. On September 29, Congress raised the debt ceiling to over $1 trillion—to $1,079,000,000,000. During the next four years this debt doubled to over $2 trillion.

February 23, 1981

The State Department reports the Soviet Union and Cuba give "massive" aid to rebels in El Salvador.

Release of the State Department report "Communist Interference in El Salvador" launched an extensive U.S. campaign to assist the government of El Salvador in defeating left-wing rebels. The report called the rebellion a "textbook case" of a major Soviet thrust in Central America. On February 22, the White House warned Cuba against sending arms to Salvadoran rebels, declaring a U.S. naval blockade would be used if necessary. Together, these actions implemented a decision Reagan reportedly had made in December to make El Salvador a testing ground for displaying U.S. willingness to counteract Communist aggression. Thus, El Salvador's rebellion became part of the larger East-West struggle. When the left-wing rebellion in El Salvador began during the 1970s, President Carter had assisted the government while urging it to enact economic, social, and political reforms. When a land-reform campaign began, however, right-wing groups in the army and government became active in limiting or stopping the reformers.

In 1980 and early 1981, advocates of reform including a Roman Catholic archbishop, four American missionary nurses, and two agricultural experts were assassinated. President Carter cut off U.S. aid after the murders, but on January 11, 1981, he resumed nonlethal aid after the rebels launched a new offensive against the government. On January 18, Carter released $5 million of military aid to help El Salvador fight the rebels. Against this background, Reagan decided to scrap Carter's emphasis on political and human rights reforms and to send more military aid to El Salvador. Thus, the State Department report justified Reagan's future aid program to El Salvador.

Although many investigative journalists, including one from the *Wall Street Journal*, argued that the report exaggerated Soviet involvement, the State Department defended its February 23 report in a subsequent report of June 18, 1981.

February 25, 1981

The United States vetoes a U.N. human rights report citing Chile and other U.S. allies for violations.

President Reagan appointed Jeane Kirkpatrick as America's U.N. delegate because Reagan accepted her belief that human rights shortcomings of right-wing "authoritarian" regimes were not as bad as those of a left-wing "totalitarian" government because the former permitted reform toward democracy. This position differed from that of the Carter administration that argued all violations were equally bad and advocated the adoption of reforms by U.S. friends as well as foes. The policy change began when Ambassador Kirkpatrick vetoed this U.N. report. Chile was one such authoritarian regime that Reagan preferred to assist rather than reform. On July 1, 1981, President Reagan used this rationale to provide development loans to Chile.

February 26, 1981

President Reagan affirms NATO's 1979 decision to modernize long-range theater nuclear forces parallel with arms control negotiations.

Based on the belief that recently deployed Soviet intermediate-range missiles gave the Communists strategic advantages in Europe, the North Atlantic Treaty Organization prepared to deploy Pershing II and cruise missiles while simultaneously conducting arms talks for reducing long-range theater nuclear forces (LRTNF) missiles. The Pershing II and the Soviets' SS-20s both had range estimates of about 5,000 kilometers, a distance so close to the 5,500 kilometers attributed to intercontinental ballistic missiles (ICBM) that the term LRTNF better described them. Missiles with ranges less than 5,000 kilometers were also called intermediate range missiles. The NATO "dual track" agreement had the support of Secretary of State Haig, who advocated close consultation with NATO allies, in contrast with Secretary of Defense Weinberger's desire to act unilaterally and ignore allied viewpoints, as well as to minimize arms control talks. In brief, Haig preferred the détente spirit of the 1970s; Weinberger wished to revive the Republican party's preference for unilateral action to achieve U.S. military primacy.

Reagan's statement to affirm the NATO dual track was made during a White House meeting with British Prime Minister Margaret Thatcher. According to the *Time* magazine reporter Strobe Talbott, the statement was inserted in the speech by one of Secretary Haig's friends on the National Security Council. Whatever the circumstances, Reagan's public statement clearly connected his administration with NATO's position that required the early continuance of arms talks with the Soviet Union. On May 20–22, during White House meetings with West German Chancellor Helmut Schmidt, Reagan repeated his support for the dual track. At Schmidt's urging, Reagan said the United States would begin arms talks before the year ended.

March 1, 1981

President Reagan considers sending U.S. armaments to help rebels in Afghanistan.

Although President Carter had previously sent $60 million of arms to the Afghan rebels opposing the Soviet intervention in their country, Reagan's first statement was to "consider sending" aid to the Afghan mujahideen rebels against Babrak Karmal's government, which had been installed by the Soviet army. Reagan's comment responded to Soviet leader Leonid Brezhnev's announcement on February 26 that Soviet troops would stay in Afghanistan until "outside aggression" ended. Brezhnev voiced Moscow's propaganda line that the United States used Afghan rebels to support Western imperialist expansion. In contrast to "consider sending," both Reagan and Carter sent CIA agents who infiltrated via Pakistan to assist the Afghan guerrillas. In addition to aiding the rebels, the Reagan administration charged that the Soviet Union used chemical weapons in Afghanistan.

March 2, 1981

The Reagan administration increases assistance for El Salvador's fight against left-wing rebels.

Acting according to prior assertions that Communists in Cuba and the Soviet Union were giving massive aid to El Salvador's rebels, the State Department stated that $25 million in military equipment and 20 additional military advisers would be sent to El Salvador. By March 22, there were 56 American advisers in that country. On March 4, after the Salvadoran right-wing leader Roberto d'Aubuisson boasted that the CIA aided him, Secretary of State Haig warned against a right-wing coup to overthrow President Duarte. On March 6, following public criticism that he was embroiling the nation in another foreign intervention, President Reagan defended his aid to El Salvador but said it would not be another Vietnam.

March 3, 1981

The State Department announces U.S. adherence to both strategic arms limitation treaties (SALT I and SALT II) provided the Soviet Union adheres.

The United States and the Soviet Union had ratified SALT I, but following the signing of SALT II in 1978, President Carter withdrew the treaty from Senate consideration after Soviet armies intervened in Afghanistan in 1979. Coming in the late stages of the Vietnam War, SALT I and the Anti-Ballistic Missile Treaty (ABM) of 1972 had not drawn much public attention. Based on the concept of MAD, in which no one could win a nuclear war, SALT I and the ABM treaty were intended as first steps to further missile limitation. By the time SALT II was signed by Carter and Brezhnev in 1979, many conservatives in the United States criticized the arms limits as benefiting the Communists, while some strategic theorists conjectured that in a carefully calculated nuclear exchange it was possible to "win" a nuclear war. This theory led its advocates to criticize SALT II as favoring the Soviets because, presumably, the Soviets had more advanced missiles with greater accuracy, which carried up to 10 separate nuclear warheads apiece. Consequently in 1979, Ronald Reagan and other conservatives had opposed SALT II, even before the Soviets intervened in Afghanistan. On March 3, however, the Reagan administration decided to abide by the SALT II agreements pending further strategic arms talks with Moscow, provided the USSR did the same.

March 3, 1981

President Reagan rejects the Law of the Sea Treaty negotiated by a U.N. commission during Carter's presidency.

At a conference in Geneva during which the U.N. Commission on Law of the Sea hoped to conclude a previously prepared treaty, President Reagan instructed the U.S. delegation to oppose the finalization of the work, saying the new president wished to review the document more thoroughly. George Taft, a State Department attorney who had worked on the treaty, told congressional committees that Reagan, in particular, wanted guarantees that U.S. companies would have access to seabed mining.

March 4, 1981

Mozambique expels three American diplomats it accuses of spying; the United States stops food assistance.

On January 30, 1981, South African armed forces had raided Maputo, the capital of Mozambique, where, they claimed, the African National Congress (ANC) had its headquarters. In Johannesburg, South African forces claimed they had killed many ANC "terrorists" and destroyed the headquarters of the group, which led the black South Africans' struggle for equality and the right of majority rule. Before cutting food assistance and revoking a $5 million credit line for Mozambique, the U.S. State Department offered an unusual explanation for the spying charge. On March 5, the United States said that Cuban agents had tried to force the three diplomats to obtain secret information, and when the ploy failed, Cuba pushed Mozambique into condemning the Americans, a scenario that Mozambique and Cuba denied. The three U.S. diplomats were Frederick Bryce Lundahl, Louis Leon Oliver, and Arthur F. Russel, whose wife, Patricia, was also expelled.

March 7, 1981

Chester A. Bitterman, a U.S. adviser in Colombia, is killed by the left-wing M-19 movement.

On January 19, Bitterman was abducted from an American language school, the Summer Language Institute, by five hooded gunmen. The M-19 group said Bitterman was a CIA spy who would be released if Colombia expelled the institute, for which Bitterman was an adviser. The leftists thought all U.S. missionaries should leave Colombia, and the institute was funded by the Southern Baptists Foreign Mission Board. The institute refused to close, and following several threats, the M-19 kidnappers executed Bitterman.

March 9, 1981

President Reagan rejects a Soviet request for a moratorium on deployment of medium-range missiles in Europe.

At a session of the 26th Communist Party Congress on February 26, Soviet leader Leonid Brezhnev proposed a ban on future missile deployment in Europe. Brezhnev then wrote letters to the United States and other NATO nations requesting a meeting to accept his missile freeze. President Reagan rejected such a meeting and Secretary of State Haig said a freeze would weaken the deterrent strength of Western Europe. On March 31, 1981, a NATO Special Consultative Group meeting in Brussels also opposed Brezhnev's request. The NATO communiqué said the USSR had already deployed 222 SS-20 missiles aimed at Western Europe. Therefore, a missile freeze would leave NATO without any means to deter the SS-20s.

March 19, 1981

President Reagan assures the People's Republic of China (PRC) that he will not jeopardize its ties with the United States.

Because President Reagan had been a staunch supporter of the Republic of China (ROC) on Taiwan prior to his 1980 election, the PRC viewed Reagan's policies with great suspicion. For example, when the Netherlands sold two submarines to the ROC on January 18, Beijing blamed the U.S. government. To stabilize or improve U.S. relations with the PRC, Secretary of State Haig urged the president to reassure the mainland Chinese. Thus, on March 19, Reagan met with PRC Ambassador Choi Zemin, to whom the president explained his desire for good relations with Beijing. As a follow-up to this session, former President Gerald Ford visited China on March 23, where he expressed the same desire for good relations to China's leader, Deng Xiaoping. Ford was reported to have recommended that the United States sell armaments to the PRC.

March 20, 1981

Initial meeting of the International Congress of Physicians for Prevention of Nuclear War takes place.

Because in both superpowers, the United States and the USSR, strategists sometimes talked about a winnable nuclear war, many groups in the early 1980s formulated plans to challenge the idea that any nation could win a nuclear war. Moreover, they hoped to convince their audiences that nuclear armaments were wasteful for all nations. One such group was made up of physicians headed by Harvard cardiologists Bernard Lown and James Muller, who prepared for this first conference to discuss methods for preventing war. Participants came from Japan, France, Britain, the United States, and the Soviet Union to discuss the medical effects of small atomic warheads dropped on the Japanese cities of Hiroshima and Nagasaki in 1945.

These specialists described the effects that thermonuclear war could have on human life and society. The U.S. experts pointed out that a 20-megaton nuclear warhead was 1,000 times as powerful as the bomb that flattened Hiroshima. If such a warhead were dropped on Boston, the blast would destroy everything in a four-mile radius and fire-storms would devastate everything within a 10-mile radius. Of Boston's 3 million metropolitan population, about 2.2 million would be killed, while the survivors would be maimed, burned, or in shock. Moreover, the survivors likely would develop new, virtually incurable ailments from radiation poisoning and contaminated food and water. Perhaps 900 out of 6,000 Boston physicians would survive, but their medical centers would not.

March 21, 1981

European antimissile demonstrations annoy the Reagan administration.

A pacifist and antinuclear movement had been growing in Western Europe ever since the NATO decision to follow the dual-track ruling of preparing to deploy Pershing and cruise missiles in Europe. In January and March, large demonstrations took place in many cities in Sweden, Norway, Denmark, Holland, and Belgium. In West Germany, plans were under way for an April 4 demonstration in Bonn, which attracted over 15,000 marchers. On March 21, National Security Adviser Richard V. Allen severely criticized the European protests.

March 24, 1981

Vice President George H.W. Bush is named to head a crisis-management team.

Although President Reagan told Secretary of State Haig that this announcement meant that Bush

Reagan foreign policy team, L-R: CIA Director Casey, Secretary of Defense Weinberger, Reagan, Vice President George Bush, Secretary of State Haig, National Security Adviser Allen, Presidential Adviser Meese. Ronald Reagan Library

would only chair the National Security Council in the president's absence, the arrangement was not satisfactory to Haig. The title "head of crisis-management team" appears to have been devised by President Reagan's White House "troika" of Edwin Meese III, Counselor to the President; James Baker III, Chief of Staff; and Michael Deaver, White House aide, to let Haig know he could not control the White House. In his memoirs, Secretary Haig claims that his agreement with Defense Secretary Weinberger was simply to clarify policies, plans, and lines of authority. Edwin Meese and many of Reagan's "California" friends disliked the Pennsylvanian Haig's attitudes and viewed his actions as his quest for increased power. Although Haig wrote a letter of resignation following the March 24 incident, Reagan reassured him that he should stay in office. Nevertheless, Haig did not fit in with Reagan's White House team and resigned in 1982.

March 30, 1981

Poland's Solidarity trade union cancels a strike because some of its demands are met.

Since Prime Minister Jaruzelski took office on February 9, 1981, there had been several wildcat strikes and confrontations between police and demonstrators, but Solidarity gave the prime minister time to meet its demands. Reforms came slowly, however, and the call for a national strike was designed to speed up a few changes, some of which were met; others were not.

April 1, 1981

The United States suspends $15 million of aid to Nicaragua.

In contrast to its support of El Salvador's government, the Reagan administration strongly opposed the rise to power of the Sandinista leaders in Nicaragua, claiming they were backed by Cuba and the Soviet Union and that they sent arms to El Salvador's rebels, the FMLN. Washington's claim about Soviet-Cuban aid seemed to be verified on April 24, when Nicaragua announced the receipt of 20,000 tons of grain from Moscow, a $100 million loan from Libya, and $64 million of technical aid from Cuba. The Reagan administration believed this was part of a Communist plot to dominate Central America.

April 2, 1981

The United States gives $70 million of surplus food to Poland.

The new ministry of Wojciech Jaruzelski inherited severe economic problems including insufficient food. On March 1, the government rationed sugar and, on April 1, meat. On April 14, butter and grain were rationed—the first food restrictions since 1945. U.S. food surpluses were sent as relief efforts to feed the Polish people. Other efforts to help Poland included 11 banks of Western Europe rescheduling $2.37 billion of long-term debt on June 25, and a

U.S. loan of $35 million on July 28 to purchase 350,000 tons of corn. Unfortunately, this assistance was not sufficient to solve the Polish problems.

April 6, 1981

The State Department proposes the "Zimbabwe formula" to obtain Namibia's (South-West Africa's) statehood, and removal of Cuban troops from Angola.

Assistant Secretary of State for African Affairs Chester A. Crocker and Secretary of State Alexander Haig announced new U.S. policies regarding Namibia's problems. Called the "Zimbabwe formula," it adopted the method that Zimbabwe used when, as Southern Rhodesia, it gained independence from Britain. Crocker wanted the competing parties in Namibia to agree on a state charter before holding elections. This proposal altered plans established by the Carter administration under which U.N. resolution 431 called for an immediate U.N.-supervised election to give Namibia independence, after which the political factions in that state could decide on a constitution.

It was revealed on May 31, 1981, that a Crocker memo of February 7, 1981, circulating in the State Department, indicated that America's Namibian strategy would be linked to the evacuation of Cuban troops from Angola and the requirement that Angola's government of Agastino Neto share power with the anti-Marxist Angolan rebel force headed by Jonas Savimbi, known as UNITA (National Union for Total Independence of Angola). Crocker's proposal was suspect to black Africans because the Reagan administration appeared to work with white-dominated South Africa.

Angola and Namibia, 1981

April 16, 1981

Six black African states condemn Reagan's policies for Africa.

Meeting in Luanda, Angola, representatives from Angola, Botswana, Mozambique, Tanzania, Zambia, and Zimbabwe condemned the Reagan administration's efforts to repeal the Clark Amendment and to forsake the U.N. policy for Namibian independence. Named for Senator Dick Clark, the Clark Amendment was approved by Congress in 1976 to prevent U.S. aid to any of the competing factions opposing Angola's government. The Reagan administration desired to repeal the amendment so it could renew aid to Jonas Savimbi's UNITA, which opposed the Angolan government. In addition, the African representatives wanted to use the U.N. formula for supervised elections in Namibia to force South Africa to grant independence. Their opposition to Chester Crocker's "Zimbabwe formula" came just before Crocker's April 23 visit to Angola.

April 23, 1981

The United States indicates Cuban troops must leave Angola before attempts can be made to secure Namibia's independence from South Africa.

From April 6 to 23, Assistant Secretary of State Chester Crocker toured Africa to seek support for his "Zimbabwe formula" on Namibia. His last stop was Luanda, Angola, where he told Angola's President Neto that Cuban troops must leave Angola before an effective Namibian solution could result. The Cubans had assisted Neto in gaining independence, but now, the United States claimed, they armed and trained

Namibian rebels known as SWAPO (South-West African People's Organization), who were led by Sam Nujoma. SWAPO's principal opposition in Namibia was the South African–supported all-white Democratic Turnhalle Alliance led by Dirk Mudge. Neither Angola nor other black African countries accepted Crocker's proposals, preferring U.N. resolution 431 for immediate elections and independence. On April 30, 1981, when the U.N. Security Council voted on resolutions to force South Africa to hold elections, the United States, France, and Britain vetoed the proposals.

April 24, 1981

President Reagan ends the U.S. grain embargo against the Soviet Union.

Following nearly a decade of profitable U.S. grain sales to the USSR, President Carter levied a grain embargo against the Soviet Union on January 4, 1980, to punish Moscow for intervening in Afghanistan. The Soviets, however, found other nations ready to sell grain to them, including some grain previously purchased from the United States. Consequently, the embargo hurt U.S. farm income most of all—a situation President Reagan now hoped to rectify. By ending the grain embargo, Reagan did not abolish all U.S. export restrictions on trade with the Soviet Union. There were still restrictions on fishing and high-technology products. In fact, Reagan tried to enforce restrictions on technology more vigorously than previous presidents. On August 5, U.S. and Soviet negotiators signed an agreement in Vienna that committed the Soviet Union to purchase from 6 million to 8 million tons of grain each year.

April 24, 1981

The Department of Defense announces creation of a Persian Gulf command with a unified rapid-deployment force.

This announcement by Secretary of Defense Caspar Weinberger established a military structure designed to carry out the "Carter Doctrine" of 1980, which pledged to protect the Persian Gulf as a "vital American interest." President Carter had sent Airborne Warning and Control System aircraft (AWACS) to Egypt, and on April 21, Reagan proposed to sell five AWACS to Saudi Arabia to help defend its oil fields. Neither Carter nor Reagan clarified how far the United States would go to protect land regions of the Persian Gulf, but both said it was America's responsibility to protect the area from Communism. Because Israel protested the sale of AWACS to Saudi Arabia, serious political problems faced the Reagan administration by September 1981.

April 27, 1981

Western bankers reschedule Poland's $2.4 billion debt.

To assist Poland in solving its economic problems without Soviet intervention, bankers from the United States and 14 other Western nations revised the terms of Poland's debt repayments—the first time this had been done for a Communist nation.

April 30, 1981

Retired Army General Edward L. Rowney is appointed as chief U.S. negotiator for the strategic arms talks with the Soviet Union.

Rowney had been a military representative on the delegation that negotiated SALT II with the Soviet Union. In 1979, after President Carter signed the agreement with Soviet President Leonid Brezhnev, Rowney resigned and lobbied in opposition to ratification of SALT II. This opposition endeared him to the Reagan administration, and after passing over Rowney for Eugene Rostow to head the Arms Control

President Reagan and General Edward L. Rowney. Ronald Reagan Library

and Disarmament Agency, Reagan appointed him to carry on arms discussions with the Soviet Union. The obvious intent of this maneuver was to retard movement toward any new controls on strategic nuclear armaments. The new secretary of state, George Shultz, would later replace Rowney with Paul Nitze in a move to gain control of the negotiations.

May 7, 1981

Mexico and Nicaragua sign a $200 million aid package.

In defiance of the Reagan administration's opposition to Nicaragua, Mexico agreed to help the Sandinista leader Daniel Ortega.

May 10, 1981

Socialist François Mitterrand is elected president of France.

In the second round of the French election designed to give one candidate a majority, Mitterrand won 51.76 percent of the vote; President Valéry Giscard d'Estang received 48.24 percent. In the first-round election on April 26, Communist Party leader Georges Marchais had 15.4 percent. For the first time since 1954, left and left-center parties ruled France. Mitterrand was inaugurated as president on May 22.

May 20, 1981

The United States votes against a World Health Organization (WHO) proposal to ban food companies from promoting infant formulas in preference to breast-feeding.

For several years, medical data collected by the WHO substantiated that the advertising of infant formulas in Third World countries and even in the United States caused thousands of infant deaths because parents misinterpreted the promotional messages. Consequently, babies did not get the nutrients they required—nutrients best acquired from breast-feeding. The two American doctors who worked on these studies at WHO, Stephen Joseph and Eugene N. Babb, favored the WHO proposal to prohibit misleading promotion of baby foods. The vote on the proposal at the WHO conference was 93 to 3 with 9 abstentions. The United States cast one of the three negative votes and was the only major nation to vote against the proposal. President Reagan's explanation was that regulations on such food companies would set a precedent and cause future WHO regulations to multiply. Joseph and Babb resigned as U.S. delegates in protest against Reagan's order to vote no. Ernst Lefever, Reagan's nominee for the assistant secretary for human rights, suffered from this decision and lost his nomination.

June 7, 1981

Israeli planes destroy a French-built nuclear reactor near Baghdad, Iraq.

The government of Israel said that F-15 and F-16 jets had flown from Israel to Iraq to destroy a plant capable of giving Iraq a nuclear bomb. Prime Minister Menachem Begin asserted that the attack was a "morally supreme act of national self-defense." While Israel was widely criticized for its action, Iraq announced its nuclear program would continue. Because it was building the reactor while fighting a war with Iran, the Iraqi government had assured Iran in October 1980 that the nuclear weapon was intended to attack Israel, not Iran. In other instances, Iraq said the research lab was only for training its scientists. The United States condemned Israel for its action but only mildly rebuked Begin's government. President Reagan held up the delivery of F-15 and F-16 planes to Israel until August 17, 1981. In the U.N. Security Council, U.S. Ambassador Jeane Kirkpatrick voted with the other 14 members to condemn Israel but only after obtaining a resolution that removed the economic sanctions that Iraq wanted against Israel.

June 15, 1981

Pakistan receives a $3 billion, five-year military and economic aid package from the United States; Pakistan insists it is not developing nuclear weapons.

Although some representatives believed Pakistan should receive no aid because, they alleged, it was building nuclear weapons, the Reagan administration favored the package to assist U.S. interests in the Persian Gulf and to help Afghan rebels who were fighting against Afghanistan's Communist-backed government. State Department spokesperson James L. Buckley told Congress that Pakistan had "absolutely assured" him that it was not developing nuclear weapons. Congress remained dubious, and on October 12, 1981, the Senate voted 57 to 46 to cut off aid to Pakistan or India if either tested a nuclear device.

June 15, 1981

Soviet-backed Afghan government seeks support from rebellious tribes.

President Karmal of Afghanistan sought to persuade various rural Afghan tribes by masking Communist atheism with an outward religious symbolism. To achieve this Karmal established an ill-fated "National Fatherland Front" on June 15. Led by Dr. Saleh Muhammad Zeray, they soon realized the Front was a cover for Afghan Communism.

June 16, 1981

Seeking better relations with Mainland China, the United States agrees to sell it arms.

Since March 19, 1981, the Reagan administration endeavored to cement relations with the PRC. The June 16 decision came after Secretary of State Haig told reporters that close U.S.-PRC ties were a "strategic imperative" because of a growing Soviet threat. The arms decision depended on future military-technological discussions to implement the agreement. The United States took two other actions in June 1981 that favored China. On June 2, the United States and the PRC agreed on the use of the Export-Import Bank to obtain Chinese credits. On June 4, Washington lifted trade curbs against China.

June 27, 1981

Organization of African Unity (OAU) condemns the United States for "collusion" with South Africa.

The OAU voted unanimously to protest America's Namibian policy because it favored South Africa.

June 29, 1981

The Central Committee of the Communist Party of the People's Republic of China concludes its sixth plenum session.

During the three-day meeting, the committee selected Hi Yaobang as party chairman with Zhao Ziyang as his deputy. China's real political leader was Deng Xiaoping, who headed the party's Military Commission.

June 29, 1981

Japan resists U.S. pressure to increase its national defense budget.

Generally, Japanese public opinion opposed spending more for defense purposes, even though Prime Minister Zenko Suzuki told President Reagan on May 8, 1981, that Japan would increase its defense budget (see also January 29, 1981). Two recent incidents stimulated Japan's opposition to a bigger defense establishment. On April 9, a Japanese freighter sank in the East China Sea after colliding with a U.S. nuclear submarine, killing two Japanese seamen. Second, on May 18, former U.S. Ambassador to Japan Edwin Reischauer disclosed that there was a secret U.S. accord with Japan in 1960 to allow the U.S. navy to carry nuclear arms in and out of Japan. These and other events caused two Japanese cabinet ministers to resign in May 1981 and strengthened Japan's will to resist U.S. proposals for large military budgets. On June 29, Japan's defense chief, Joji Omura, visited U.S. Secretary of Defense Caspar Weinberger in Washington to inform the United States that Tokyo would not increase national defense spending.

June 29, 1981

The United States agrees to help Egypt purchase two nuclear energy plants.

Egypt's 1979 peace agreement with Israel and the Persian Gulf–Iranian crisis since 1980 had brought the United States and Egypt to a close partnership. Because Egypt needed sources of energy in addition to the water-powered generators at the Aswân High Dam, Washington agreed to provide $2 billion to enable Egypt to obtain two large atomic reactors and fuel to generate electric power. Nuclear materials made available would serve only peaceful purposes, and the approval process of the International Atomic Energy Agency would follow.

July 12, 1981

An Israeli right-wing coalition government is formed by Menachem Begin following inconclusive elections.

July 12, 1981

El Salvador's bishop claims his nation's army has recently murdered 28 civilians, but President Reagan rejects the church's request for an investigation.

Bishop Arturo Rivera y Damos referred to the massacre of 28 peasants found in a crude grave on the banks of the Metayato River, 36 miles from San Salvador. He also blamed the army for the disappearance of 70 other civilians and for an attack on the church in Chalatenango. Riveray Damos had become acting archbishop following the assassination of Archbishop Oscar Amulfo Romero in 1980. The Reagan administration's staunch anti-Communist position toward the Salvadoran rebels caused it to ignore the Salvadoran Catholic Church leaders' claims against the government as well as their plans for negotiations between rebels and President Duarte. Washington approved Duarte's plans for elections in one or two years in which all who renounced violence could vote.

July 14–20, 1981

Polish Communist Party session reorganizes leadership and announces a wage freeze and a 110 percent price increase on most products.

The party reorganization strengthened the power of Prime Minister Wojciech Jaruzelski by ousting party leader Edward Gierek and six of his associates and by electing 200 Central Committee members by secret ballot.

July 20–21, 1981

Seventh annual economic summit reveals that the Reagan administration's policies diverge from those of Western Europe and Japan.

Meeting in Ottawa, Canada, the seven major industrial nations focused on high U.S. interest rates of up to 22 percent and President Reagan's desire to curb technological trade with the Soviet Union. Moreover, while the other six summit nations desired economic aid for Third World countries, Reagan believed Third World problems resulted because those nations needed to be hospitable to private capital investment. In addition to the United States, other nations attending the annual summit were Canada, France, West Germany, Great Britain, Italy, and Japan.

August 6, 1981

Neutron bomb production is resumed by President Reagan.

Reversing President Carter's decision to halt neutron bomb production, Reagan agreed with Secretary of Defense Caspar Weinberger's desire to prepare neutron bombs for European defense purposes. In his announcement, Reagan said the United States did not expect to deploy the bombs in Europe without consulting its European allies. Substantial European opposition to the neutron bomb arose early in 1981 after Weinberger stated on February 3 that he favored their deployment as the best means to counter Soviet tank superiority in Europe. In Holland, the two main political parties opposed deployment of the bomb, and the West German government wanted consultation on the issue with Washington.

August 13, 1981

The United States vetoes a loan of $20 million to Guyana.

Although the U.S. veto was hedged by economic technicalities, it was known that President Reagan wanted Guyana to accept a "free-market" economy before obtaining a loan from the Inter American Development Bank. In addition, Great Britain claimed that President Forbes Burnham of Guyana won his 1980 election in a corrupt manner. Since gaining power with U.S. help in 1968, Burnham had assumed near-dictatorial powers. But worse from the Reagan perspective, Burnham had nationalized 80 percent of the country's economy. Reagan wanted Guyana to use private loans and denationalize industry. Burnham claimed, in vain, that if he failed, his main opponent, a Marxist, Cheddi B. Jagan, could gain power.

August 18, 1981

Rejecting U.S. claims that it needed military aid, Costa Rica asks for economic assistance.

The U.S. ambassador to the United Nations, Jeanne Kirkpatrick, had remarked that Costa Rica needed arms to fight Communism, a statement Costa Rica's government denied. Often referred to as Central America's best democracy, Costa Rica opposed U.S. intervention in the affairs of Nicaragua and El Salvador and did not wish to be involved militarily.

August 19, 1981

U.S. navy planes shoot down two Libyan jets in the Gulf of Sidra.

Ever since the United States closed the Libyan mission in Washington on May 6, 1981, there was a continual flurry of charges and countercharges between President Reagan and Libya's Mu'ammar al-Gadhafi. Reagan claimed Libya supported terrorists. Gadhafi claimed that the entire Gulf of Sidra belonged to Libya, but the United States and other naval powers held that the northern section of the gulf lay within international waters. While flying in the disputed zone, two U.S. Navy F-14 jets were attacked by two Libyan SU-22s; the Americans shot down the Libyan planes with heat-seeking missiles.

August 27, 1981

Salvadoran authorities release the man accused of killing three agricultural advisers in January 1981.

Several weeks after the murder of two American and one Salvadoran agricultural experts, Ricardo Sol Meza, a wealthy landowner, was charged with the crime and put in prison. On August 22, he was released without bail because the judge ruled there was insufficient evidence against him. Originally, a waitress in the café where the men were killed had identified Meza as the gunman, but later she changed her testimony, denying she had seen Meza. One other man suspected of the murder, Hans Christ, was being held as a suspect by U.S. authorities in Miami, Florida. El Salvador had not asked for his extradition.

August 31, 1981

The United States vetoes a U.N. condemnation of South Africa's raid on Angola on July 12.

The South African forces had attacked a SWAPO base 90 miles inside Angola, where they left 114 persons dead. After Angola requested U.N. aid, South Africa argued it pursued SWAPO rebels who attacked South-West Africa. SWAPO was the South-West Africa People's Organization group advocating the independence of Namibia from South Africa. Following the U.S. veto of Security Council action, the U.N. General Assembly passed a resolution on September 14 that condemned South Africa and singled out the United States for blame in vetoing the Security Council action.

August 31, 1981

A bomb at Ramstein Air Force Base in West Germany destroys property and injures 20 people.

While the terrorist group Baader-Meinhof of the Red Army faction claimed credit for the bombing, the event symbolized the growing movement in West Germany and Europe that opposed U.S. missiles on their territory as well as dependence on the United States for their security. The Ramstein attack inaugurated a wave of terrorist incidents in West Germany where the Red Army faction had been quiescent for three years. On September 1, seven U.S. cars were set afire at Wiesbaden; on September 15, terrorists fired a grenade launcher but failed to injure the U.S. NATO commander in Heidelberg, General Frederick J. Kroesar; and on September 16, West German authorities defused two bombs at the U.S. base in Frankfurt. West German officials blamed a minority of 12 to 15 hard-core Red Army radicals and had 30 suspects on their wanted list. They said another 150 associates cooperated with the radicals by giving them supplies and safe houses.

September 5, 1981

The United States and the People's Republic of China sign a cultural exchange pact in Beijing.

This agreement permitted the exchange of students, teachers, and scholars of the arts and sciences, as well as art exhibits and visits by music groups.

September 13, 1981

Secretary of State Haig accuses Communist nations of using chemical weapons in Southeast Asia and Afghanistan.

During a visit to West Berlin, Haig made charges that began a lengthy controversy over so-called yellow rain that the Soviet Union allegedly used during conflicts in Asia. A variety of scientific studies of yellow rain resulted, with most scientists finding insufficient evidence to justify the Reagan administration's claims.

September 15, 1981

Egypt expels the Soviet ambassador, six aides, and 1,000 Soviets accused of subverting the government.

The Soviet ambassador, Vladimir P. Polyakov, his aides, and the Soviet technicians were ordered to leave Egypt. In retaliation, on September 17, Moscow expelled Egyptian officials.

September 15, 1981

U.S. aid package for Pakistan of $3.2 billion includes F-16 aircraft.

Washington had negotiated with Pakistan for nearly two years in reaching this agreement. Realizing the United States wanted his help in supplying aid to Afghanistan and providing security for the Persian Gulf, Pakistan's President Mohammad Zia ul-Haq sought the most favorable terms possible. He had rejected offers from President Carter and agreed to the $3 billion deal only if President Reagan wrote that this did not imply a security alliance with Pakistan. Among congressional leaders, a major issue was the possibility of Pakistan's development of nuclear weapons. The September 15 agreement ignored this issue, but Undersecretary of State James Buckley told the House Foreign Affairs Committee that Pakistan knew a nuclear detonation would end all U.S. aid. In approving the aid package on October 12, the U.S. Senate voted to cut off aid if a nuclear device were tested.

September 17, 1981

Funds for the United Nations Educational, Scientific, and Cultural Organization (UNESCO) are cut by the U.S. House of Representatives.

The solid House vote indicated most Americans' concern that nations of the Third World dominated committees of the United Nations. This opinion spread after May 17, 1981, when a UNESCO commission on mass communication voted for an International Information Order that permitted Third World countries to censor foreign information about themselves. These countries argued that the news media were a tool of industrial power that discriminated against them by publishing adverse data. Because censorship clashed with American concepts of a free press, UNESCO appeared to violate basic human rights.

September 23, 1981

Two American military advisers are wounded by gunshots in Honduras.

The U.S. advisers were training Honduran military to defend themselves. The Honduran radicals who wounded the Americans stated on September 24 that the shooting and the subsequent bombing of Honduras's parliament building began a drive to rid Honduras of "Yankee imperialists." It was later disclosed that the CIA used Honduran bases for training Contra units to attack Nicaragua.

See December 16, 1981.

September 24, 1981

The Western nations contact group prepares a revised plan for granting Namibia independence.

This group of representatives from the United States and four Western European countries offered a proposal for territory in South-West Africa under South African control to become the independent state of Namibia. The plan adopted resembled a three-year-old U.N. plan for a timetable to phase out South African control, conduct elections, and establish a Namibian government. The new government would be based on ideas of one person, one vote, the end of all racial discrimination, and a bill of rights. Both South Africa and Angola expressed reservations about the plan.

September 26, 1981

The Pentagon issues a booklet titled "Soviet Military Power" intended to promote greatly increased U.S. defense expenditures.

Since taking office in January 1981, Secretary of Defense Caspar Weinberger had argued that the United

States had fallen behind the Soviet Union in defense effectiveness and that the United States needed a five-year program to regain the military superiority held during the period from 1945 to 1965. Weinberger wanted $1.7 billion more than President Jimmy Carter proposed for fiscal 1982 and $158 billion more than Carter proposed for the next five years, figures that were understated compared to the cost of the new weapons systems the Pentagon desired in 1981.

To create an alarming vision of Soviet power, the widely criticized Pentagon booklet claimed the Soviets had leadership in army, navy, air force, and missile defenses, omitting data that, critics said, contradicted their exaggerated threat. For example, the text said the Soviets operated 377 submarines, including 180 nuclear-powered subs, compared with 115 U.S. navy submarines, but it only hinted at the U.S. navy's superior technology by saying that the Soviets were "reducing the U.S. lead in virtually every important basic technology." Generally, the booklet indicated that Soviet ground forces had increased since 1969 by 30 divisions to total 180 divisions and that they fielded 50,000 tanks, 20,000 artillery pieces, 5,200 helicopters, over 3,500 tactical bombers and fighter planes, and 7,000 nuclear warheads. It asserted that the Soviets spent 12 percent to 14 percent of their gross national product on defense, compared with America's 7 percent, but it did not mention that the U.S. GNP was at least twice that of the Soviets. It also left American allied forces out of the picture, ignoring the fact that together the United States, NATO members, Japan, and China spend more on defense than the Soviet Union, the Warsaw Pact countries, Cuba, and Vietnam. Nor did it relate China's threat on the Soviet border to any comparable threat on U.S. borders.

One of President Reagan's largest defense budget items was an attempt to "regain" U.S. naval superiority. In May 1981, U.S. Navy Secretary John F. Lehman Jr. indicated that an offensive-minded "maritime strategy" was the best deterrent to Soviet power. He convinced Reagan to increase the navy from 450 to 600 ships during the 1980s. Apparently, the Pentagon booklet originated from a briefing that Weinberger gave to NATO defense experts in April 1981. They urged such a document as a means to help them obtain greater defense funding from their national legislatures.

October 2, 1981

President Reagan's defense program is announced; it includes both stationary MX missiles in hardened silos and B-1 bombers.

Reagan's announcement caused much debate among defense experts in the U.S. Senate because of past expectations for the MX (Reagan called it the "Peacemaker") and the B-1. President Carter had proposed deployment of the MX in large underground tunnels designed to hide the MX in order to survive a first-strike and provide the ability to retaliate. In contrast, Reagan's proposal to put the MX in missile silos seemed to be predicated on a first-strike, or launch-on-warning, plan because now the MX would be more vulnerable to a Soviet first strike than under the Carter plan. And vulnerable missiles could not be second-strike weapons.

As for the B-1 bomber, both its use and its capability had been contested prior to its cancellation by President Carter, who favored the less expensive, more accurate cruise missile, whose flight pattern would be difficult for the Soviets to detect. In brief, Reagan's program favored the aggressive, offensive nuclear strategy that many of his supporters on the Committee for the Clear and Present Danger sponsored during the 1970s in claiming that a nuclear war could be fought and won with the proper weapons and a good civilian defense. As reported in interviews with Reagan and other members of his administration by Robert Scheer of the *Los Angeles Times*, the new president entered office advocating a nuclear program that was opposed to the on-going U.S. policy of deterrence to avert a nuclear war.

October 7, 1981

The President of the Republic of China (ROC) on Taiwan refuses to negotiate unity with Mainland China.

During 1981, Beijing made several overtures to conduct talks on unity with the ROC, but ROC president Chiang Ching-kuo claimed to be the leader of the real Chinese government. This government had fled to Taiwan in 1949 after the Communists defeated the Nationalist forces of Chiang Kai-shek.

October 19, 1981

Morocco's fight with Polisario rebels heats up in October.

Moroccan jet fighters chased rebels into neighboring Mauritania following an unsuccessful rebel attack. Six days earlier, the Polisario used Soviet-made surface-to-air missiles to shoot down two Moroccan planes. With aid from several Middle Eastern states, the Polisario tried to gain independence for the Western Sahara region.

October 22–23, 1981

North-South conference of rich and poor nations achieves nothing of substance.

Initiated in 1980 by an international development commission headed by West Germany's former Chancellor Willy Brandt, the idea of a dialogue between northern hemispheric industrial nations and southern hemispheric developing nations was intended to provide economic assistance to the poor southern nations. As a preliminary to the October session, the foreign ministers of 14 developing and eight industrial nations met in August 1981 to form an agenda for its leaders to follow. The agenda identified five basic areas for discussion in October: economic cooperation, trade, food reserves, alternative energy sources, and fiscal-monetary questions. During the October 22–23 meeting at the Mexican resort of Cancún, the three dominant figures were President Reagan, Prime Minister Margaret Thatcher of Great Britain, and Chancellor Helmut Schmidt of West Germany.

While the developing nations wanted all international economic issues to be decided by the United Nations, where each nation has one vote regardless of size or wealth, Reagan, Thatcher, and Schmidt rejected this concept. They insisted that key global economic decisions must continue to be made in the three organizations in which developing nations had no voice or vote—the World Bank, the International Monetary Fund, and the General Agreement on Tariffs and Trade organization. Moreover, the Cancún discussions revealed that the 14 developing nations had different economic interests to protect, making particular agreements hard to reach. At its final session, the 22 delegates agreed that North-South talks should continue, but they could not agree on a future date or agenda for a meeting.

October 24, 1981

Large-scale antinuclear rallies take place in Europe.

European groups opposing the U.S. deployment of nuclear weapons in Europe agreed on October 24 as a day to stage demonstrations. In London, 150,000 rallied; in Rome, 100,000 protested; in Paris and Brussels, thousands demonstrated against nuclear weapons. In Bonn, over 250,000 protested the presence of U.S. missiles in Germany. Peace marches occurred even in Eastern European countries during the fall of 1981. On October 20, protesters in Bulgaria called for a Balkan nuclear-free zone, and on November 12, over 100,000 marchers in Bucharest, Romania, staged an antinuclear protest.

October 28, 1981

The U.S. Senate finalizes the approval of the sale of American airborne warning and control system planes (AWACS) to Saudi Arabia.

Since April 21, when President Reagan proposed the sale of five AWACS aircraft to Saudi Arabia, political tension heated up not only between Israel and the Arab states but also between Congress and the White House. Pro-Jewish lobbyists opposed the sale because they feared the Arabs would use the planes against Israel. The Reagan administration argued that the AWACS early-warning planes were to assist reconnaissance in the Persian Gulf region and that Saudi Arabia would share its information with the United States. U.S. law stated that the president's approval of the sale of the radar planes could be stopped if both houses of Congress opposed it. On August 25, Reagan presented the formal request to sell $8.5 billion of planes and equipment to the Saudis, and public debate began. On October 14, the House of Representatives voted 301 to 111 to reject the sale, but Reagan hoped the Republican-controlled Senate would approve it.

In the Senate, the two issues were whether the United States would retain some control over the information gathered by the AWACS and whether the Saudis would prohibit their use against Israel. Saudi Arabian officials rejected the concept of joint control, but before the Senate vote, Reagan sent the Senate a letter certifying that the Saudis agreed not to use the planes against Israel. This sufficed to win the votes of some undecided senators and the vote favored the sale by 52 to 48. Since only one house of Congress was required to approve the sale, the House rejection was overruled by this Senate vote. During the Iran-Contra hearing in 1986–1987, a secret protocol of the U.S. sale to Saudi Arabia was revealed. As part of the deal, the Saudi government promised to give money to anti-Communist resistance groups when requested by Washington. Later, as part of the Project Democracy covert program, Saudi Arabia gave at least $30 million to help the Nicaraguan rebels.

November 10, 1981

Arab delegations meet in Saudi Arabia as the Gulf Cooperation Council seeks common policy regarding Israel.

Five nations plus Saudi Arabia, the host country, made up this council: Bahrain, Kuwait, Qatar, Oman, and the United Arab Emirates. This group had just been organized in 1980, and these oil-rich nations (with an estimated one-third of all world oil reserves) wanted to play some role in international decisions regarding the Middle East. In addition, they approved a Middle East peace plan proposed by Crown Prince Fahd of Saudi Arabia. It demanded a Palestinian state but provided for Israeli security under the Arabs' acceptance of Israel's right to exist. This was one of the first Arab plans for a peace settlement that recognized Israel as a state.

November 14, 1981

U.S.-Egyptian forces conduct Operation Bright Star military exercises, the biggest U.S. war game in the Middle East since 1945.

Preparing for a contingency of desert war, over 850 U.S. paratroopers bailed out over Egypt's desert area. Then 4,000 other U.S. military personnel arrived at Cairo West Air Base, transported by C-5A, C-141, and C-130 planes that carried trucks, personnel carriers, and 150 mm field guns, some of which also arrived on navy ships. On November 24, six B-52 bombers flew from North Dakota bases, refueled three times in midair, and skimmed across the desert to drop bombs. Principally, these war game results showed the continued inadequacy of America's rapid-deployment forces. Even with advanced planning, many problems arose during the 10-day event.

November 16, 1981

Visiting Washington, Venezuelan President Luis Herrera Campins opposes U.S. military intervention in Nicaragua.

Herrera's warning resulted from reports about possible U.S. military action against Nicaragua or Cuba, because those countries had aided Salvadoran rebels. Venezuela, Mexico, and other members of the Organization of American States generally opposed U.S. intervention in Nicaragua. On November 23, Mexico's foreign minister also warned U.S. Secretary of State Haig not to act against Nicaragua.

November 18, 1981

President Ronald Reagan calls for the "zero-option" on long-range theater nuclear forces (LRTNF) of the NATO and Warsaw Pact powers.

Reagan's televised address set the American agenda for the U.S.-Soviet arms control talks set to begin in Geneva on November 30, 1981. The "zero-option" meant that NATO would cancel its planned deployment of Pershing II and cruise missiles if the Soviet Union scrapped all its installed SS-20, SS-4, and SS-5 theater nuclear missiles. The zero-option evolved from the German term *null-losen* when the issue of basing intermediate-range missiles appeared between 1975 and 1980. Initially, as the Soviet Union deployed SS-20 missiles targeted at Western Europe, Chancellor Helmut Schmidt of West Germany proposed the introduction of U.S. Pershing II missiles as a countermeasure.

Subsequently, however, Schmidt and other Western European leaders feared that the deployment of SS-20s in the East and Pershing IIs in the West would make Europe a nuclear battleground between the two superpowers. As a result, Schmidt changed his mind, introducing the phrase null-losen to signify eliminating both the SS-20s and the Pershing IIs. Within the Reagan administration, zero-option had two diverging interpretations. Defense Secretary Caspar Weinberger and others who opposed the arms control agenda believed zero-option was a nonnegotiable U.S. requirement that the Soviets would never accept. Secretary of State Alexander Haig saw the zero-option covering all nuclear weapons with European targets and also as the maximum U.S. demand which, as in normal diplomacy, was flexible and open to negotiations to obtain mutual agreement with Moscow at some lower level. Tending to support Weinberger, President Reagan accepted the concept that the Soviets had to eliminate all their theater nuclear weapons, not just the SS-20s as Schmidt had proposed. In the context of a nonnegotiable demand, the arms control talks in Geneva were destined for stalemate.

November 19, 1981

West Germany and the Soviet Union reach accord on construction of a pipeline from Siberia to central Germany.

Designed to help Germany and other Western European countries secure natural gas as an alternative to Middle East oil, this project solidified on July 24, 1981, when West German banks agreed to a $10 billion loan to the Soviets to finance the pipeline's construction. The political accord finalized the project.

November 22, 1981

Andrey Sakharov and wife begin a hunger strike in Moscow, protesting that their stepson cannot join his fiancée in the United States.

This act by Sakharov, a physicist who was a Nobel Peace laureate, received international attention. It ended on December 8 when Soviet authorities permitted the stepson to leave.

November 22, 1981

Greek government announces a schedule to remove U.S. bases.

Elected to office following successes in the October 18, 1981, Greek vote, Prime Minister Andreas Papandreou of the Panhellenic Socialist Movement challenged the Western European alliances made by his predecessors. Thus, Papandreou set a timetable to remove U.S. naval bases in Piraeus, the port of Athens, and on Crete; to ban U.S. nuclear weapons from Greek soil; and to renegotiate Greece's role in NATO and the European Economic Community (EEC). The prime minister contended that NATO gave "unrestrained military aid to Greece's enemy, Turkey," and did not protect the nation's eastern border. He was ready to bargain for concessions from the United States but set the timetable to avoid delay. He also called for a Greek referendum concerning withdrawal from the EEC.

November 23, 1981

President Reagan issues National Security Decision Directive (NSDD) 17, which gives the CIA authority to fund a group rebelling against the government of Nicaragua: origin of the "Contra" movement.

NSDD 17 was a classified document whose contents were leaked to the *Washington Post* and *New York Times* in February and March 1982. The directive ordered the CIA to "work with foreign governments" to undermine the Sandinista government of Nicaragua. Reportedly, the CIA had already been working with Argentine military officers who trained Nicaraguan exiles and mercenaries in northern Nicaragua and Honduras. The CIA was given $19 million to assemble and arm 500 contras in addition to 1,000 exiles trained by Argentina.

November 24, 1981

West German Chancellor Schmidt tells Soviet President Brezhnev he doubts President Reagan's objectives in seeking the "zero-option."

Although initial American public reaction to Reagan's November 18 speech was favorable, Schmidt and other European political leaders reacted cautiously because of Reagan's previous harsh rhetoric against the Soviet Union. In addition, Schmidt was disturbed by Reagan's October 16, 1981, statement that a tactical nuclear exchange in Europe would not mean an all-out U.S.-USSR nuclear war. Although Reagan, on October 21, clarified his belief that any threat to Europe was a threat to the United States, Schmidt distrusted the president. Thus, during a four-day meeting in Bonn with Soviet leader Leonid Brezhnev, Schmidt sympathized with the Soviet desire for arms control, giving qualified support to the zero-option. Like U.S. Secretary of State Alexander Haig, Schmidt saw the zero-option as a starting point of talks because it should not be a final U.S. option for arms control.

November 29, 1981

In the first Honduran elections since 1971, Roberto Suazo Cordova is chosen president.

The United States had pressured the Honduran government of General Policarpo Paz García to end his corrupt nine-year reign and permit a free election.

November 30, 1981

Geneva missile talks begin between Paul H. Nitze of the United States and Yuli A. Kvitsinsky of the USSR.

Although President Reagan announced his zero-option on November 18, U.S. delegates had no specific treaty proposal to offer on November 30. The Soviet delegate offered a four-point program for a nuclear-free Europe that Soviet President Brezhnev shared with West German Chancellor Helmut Schmidt on November 24, 1981. The Soviets proposed (1) a moratorium on all 1,000 to 5,500 km–range missiles in Europe; (2) negotiations for reduction of these weapons; (3) reducing to zero all medium-range systems that threatened Europe, meaning British and French as well as U.S. and Soviet missiles; and (4) elimination of all tactical nuclear weapons in Europe with a range of fewer than 1,000 kilometers. In sum, the four points would have eliminated missiles but left Europe subject to the Soviets' superior position in conventional weapons. Both Reagan's (November 18) and Brezhnev's proposals appeared as political ploys, not genuine attempts at gaining arms control. The first round of talks achieved nothing and adjourned on December 17, 1981.

December 9, 1981

At a U.N. Law of the Sea Conference, the U.S. delegation again prevents completion of a treaty.

To the frustration of delegations from other nations, this third conference still failed to reach an agreement, which many member nations thought had been finished before Ronald Reagan became president. Striving to satisfy five U.S. business consortia wanting to profit from seabed mining, the Reagan administration wanted an international agreement limited to helping the consortia stabilize costs while avoiding conflicting claims to seabed rights.

Article 82 stated that the ocean's mineral wealth was a common heritage of humankind and therefore would give royalty payments to Third World countries for minerals mined in ocean areas more than 200 miles from their coastlines. For U.S. businessmen, Article 82 was, wrote William Safire in the *New York Times*, "a great rip off" to benefit the Third World.

The Reagan team also did not want an international cartel to mine such seabed minerals as copper, nickel, cobalt, and manganese, because they considered these minerals to be of strategic value; therefore, their extraction was essential to some sort of U.S. control.

December 11, 1981

Javier Pérez de Cuellar of Peru is chosen secretary-general of the U.N. Security Council.

The selection of Pérez de Cuellar ended a deadlock that began on October 27, 1981. In the dispute, one group favored the reelection of Kurt Waldheim of Austria and a second group, including the People's Republic of China and many Third World nations, preferred the Tanzanian foreign minister, Salim A. Salim. After Waldheim withdrew his candidacy, the two factions compromised by selecting Pérez de Cuellar. The U.N. General Assembly approved the selection on December 15, 1981.

December 11, 1981

Organization of Petroleum Exporting Countries (OPEC) ends a bad year by cutting oil prices.

After oil prices reached $41 per barrel in December 1980, some member countries began to renege on OPEC instructions by selling at lower prices, increasing production, or seeking higher prices on their own. The steady decline in world oil demand after 1979 also affected the national income of oil-exporting countries. On October 29 at Geneva, OPEC approved a price of $34 through 1982, but this did not hold. By December 11, OPEC unity was in disarray, but members again agreed to cut prices between $0.20 and $1.00 per barrel. These price cuts were good news to OPEC's customers and to President Reagan's economic program.

December 11, 1981

West and East German presidents meet for the first time since 1970.

Chancellor Helmut Schmidt's efforts to better West German relations with Eastern Europe seemed to pay off when President Erich Honecker welcomed Schmidt to East Germany to discuss trade relations.

December 13, 1981

Poland's Prime Minister Jaruzelski declares martial law.

Demonstrations, protests, and strikes continued in Poland after Jaruzelski's 90-day "period of peace" ended in May 1981, with no significant economic improvement. On October 13, three Polish cities had wildcat strikes, and 12,000 textile workers walked off the job. On October 20, steelworkers at Katowice occupied the steel mill, where they found a radio station to assist them. The Soviet Union had called for a crackdown against protesters on September 17, but strikes continued in October and November, with 190,000 students striking on November 12.

On December 12, the Solidarity trade union issued a new set of demands for the Polish government to fulfill. The next day Jaruzelski decreed martial law throughout Poland. The decree suspended all civil rights and labor union activity while Polish police arrested many union leaders and brought Solidarity leader Lech Walesa to Warsaw where he could be controlled. On December 30, Jaruzelski sought to demonstrate an interest in improving Poland's economic condition by appointing three groups to plan political, social, and economic reforms. (See December 23, 1981) Jaruzelski's reasons for calling martial law became controversial. On December 24, the prime minister said he chose martial law as the lesser of two evils, the alternative being a Soviet invasion. Later, Jaruzelski's statement was challenged by members of Solidarity as well as by the Soviet Union. The controversy continued in the post–Cold War era although Jaruzelski's reputation improved after 1981 when he showed concern for the Polish people's preferences. (See July 24, 1986)

After 1989, opened archives of Poland, the Soviet Union, and other Warsaw Pact members disclosed that Jaruzelski chose martial law even though the Soviet Union refused to intervene despite the prime minister's plea for military assistance. Details about declassified documents and other sources regarding Poland's 1980–1981 developments are in the *Cold War International History Project's Bulletin* (Winter 1998), especially Mark Kramer's article and Jaruzelski's response.

December 14, 1981

President Reagan reacts to Poland's martial law by suspending all aid to Warsaw and warning of "grave" consequences if repression continues.

Other Western countries also reacted strongly to the Polish repression. On December 16, foreign bankers refused further loans to Poland and insisted on payments and interest of prior loans. While the Soviet Union denied involvement in Poland, Western nations blamed Moscow as much as Jaruzelski for the Polish action.

December 14, 1981

Congress retains the Clark Amendment but authorizes $11.4 billion of foreign aid.

The Reagan administration had persistently asked for the repeal of the Clark Amendment, which restricted economic aid to rebels in Angola. The House of Representatives refused to repeal this amendment while the Senate approved. The report of a congressional conference committee accepted the House version of the bill, which retained the Clark Amendment. This amendment prevented the White House from assisting any faction in Angola. Reagan wanted to help the leader of UNITA, Jonas Savimbi.

December 14, 1981

Israel annexes the Golan Heights, which it took from Syria in 1967.

Since the Six-Day War of 1967, Israel had claimed that the Golan Heights was occupied territory. On December 14, the Knesset (parliament) voted to annex the area to Israel. The annexation increased problems between Israel and the United States. When President Reagan announced suspension of an agreement on strategic cooperation signed on November 30, 1981, Prime Minister Begin responded harshly, saying "no power on Earth" would make Israel repeal the annexation and that U.S. conduct in Vietnam gave Washington no moral ability to oppose Israel's bombing of Beirut or a PLO camp. The annexation was probably done to preempt U.S. demands that Israel withdraw from all territories it occupied in 1967.

December 15, 1981

Congress approves the largest peacetime military expenditure in the nation's history: $199.7 billion plus construction authorization of $7.1 billion for fiscal 1982.

Although Congress and the president had argued since July 1981 about budget allocations, the most crucial issue was not congressional support for a military buildup but about how deeply the federal government would cut social spending. President Reagan urged drastic cuts in social programs, while Democrats and many moderate Republicans in Congress resisted large cuts in nonmilitary programs. The dispute prevented passage of spending authorizations by the normal October 1 deadline for the 1982 fiscal year, and Congress and the president had agreed on stopgap spending provisions on October 2 and November 19. The budget dispute continued into December, and about the time another stopgap bill expired on December 15, Congress and the White House agreed on an omnibus appropriations bill. The military budget included large expenditures in new programs that would require continued large-scale funding in future years. Reagan accepted more social program funding than he desired and blamed Congress for upsetting his plans to balance the budget by 1984.

December 16, 1981

U.N. General Assembly resolution calls on El Salvador to negotiate peace with its rebels.

The United States opposed this resolution but it passed: 68 for, 22 against, and 53 abstaining. The United States argued that Cuba and Nicaragua supplied arms to the rebels, who would stop fighting if these shipments stopped.

December 17, 1981

Terrorists abduct the U.S. Commander of NATO forces for southern Europe.

Brigadier General James L. Dozier was kidnapped from his Verona, Italy, apartment by an Italian terrorist group, the Red Brigade. After 42 days in captivity, Dozier was rescued by Italian national police. The police had rounded up scores of suspects in December, one of whom gave information leading to the Red Brigade hideout in Padua. Dozier was not hurt and no shots were fired during the police raid.

December 23, 1981

President Reagan's economic sanctions punish the Soviet Union for Poland's martial law.

On December 23, after Poland's Prime Minister Jaruzelski decreed martial law, President Reagan announced restrictions on aviation and fishing imports and curbed loans to Poland. Previously on December 13, Reagan said he wrote to Soviet President Brezhnev, warning him the United States would take action if martial law continued. On December 29, Reagan added more sanctions by stopping future sales of electronic and computer equipment as well as oil and gas machinery including a $90 million sale of pipe-laying tractors essential to the building of a natural gas pipeline from Siberia to central Europe. However, Reagan neither ended U.S. grain purchases nor suspended arms talks scheduled for January 12, 1982. Although European leaders believed U.S. sanctions would not help Poland, the European Economic Community agreed not to undercut the sanctions.

Documents declassified after 1989 indicate that the CIA had contacts with four Polish officials who gave the Americans secret information about Polish events in 1980–1981. In particular, the CIA had reports from Colonel Ryszard Kuklinski, a high-ranking Polish army officer, that the Soviets told Jaruzelski the Red Army would not intervene even though there were many Soviet troops along the Polish border. Thus, the Soviet Union was not primarily to blame for Jaruzelski's invocation of martial law. Details about Kuklinski are in the *Cold War International History Project's Bulletin* (Winter 1998) in the article "Jaruzelski, the Soviet Union and the Imposition of Martial Law in Poland: New Light on the Mystery of December 1981," by Mark Kramer.

1982

January 4, 1982

William P. Clark replaces Richard V. Allen as national security adviser: the NSC role is enlarged.

With Haig as secretary of state and Weinberger heading the Pentagon, the NSC was seldom used during 1981. Allen had reported to Edwin Meese, the president's counselor, rather than directly to the president as previous national security advisers had. When

Allen came under public criticism for allegedly receiving cash and gifts from Japanese businessmen seeking access to the White House, he became a liability to Reagan.

In addition, President Reagan's close advisers believed that as national security adviser Clark would assume greater authority over foreign policy decisions, a role sought by Secretary of State Haig. However, Clark had little experience in foreign affairs, having been a judge for California's supreme court before Reagan was president. But as a long-time friend of the president, Clark did report directly to Reagan.

January 8, 1982

The United States refuses to grant an export license to General Electric Company to sell natural gas pipeline equipment to the Soviet Union.

Although President Reagan claimed that the restrictions on technology sales to the Soviets was punishment for Moscow's involvement in Poland, the Reagan administration actually hoped to weaken the Soviet economy by preventing the construction and sale of natural gas to Western Europe. In addition, many of Reagan's advisers did not like European leaders' attempts to pursue interests apart from the United States and thus opposed the natural gas project, which West Germany, France, and others had worked out with Moscow. To further assert the embargo in 1982, Reagan extended the ban to products that relied on the technology developed by General Electric and other U.S. companies. To do so, he tried to prohibit European technical products from being sold to the Soviets if the European industries had used a license from the Americans to employ U.S. technology. The Europeans, of course, objected to this policy. To placate Washington, the European Economic Community (EEC) voted on March 11 to reduce their 1982 imports from the USSR by $140 million, having first rejected a proposal to reduce imports by $350 million.

January 11, 1982

President Reagan's attempt to please two Chinas satisfies neither.

While the Reagan administration said it recognized China's only government as being the People's Republic (PRC), the president continued to assist the Republic of China on Taiwan (ROC) in order to mollify his right-wing supporters who insisted that the ROC was the legitimate Chinese government. On January 11, when Reagan approved the sale of F-5E jet planes to the ROC but refused to approve Taiwan's request for more advanced planes, the president pleased neither side. Senator Jesse Helms (R-N.C.) said the president had assured him that Taiwan would get more sophisticated planes. At the same time, the PRC objected to the sale of any U.S. planes to the ROC and asserted that Sino-American relations faced a severe test over this question.

January 14, 1982

President Reagan proposes a budget item to produce new binary nerve gas weapons, ending the nation's 13-year moratorium on making lethal nerve gas weapons.

Citing his administration's claim that the Soviet Union was using chemical weapons in Southeast Asia and Afghanistan, the president told Congress that developing binary chemical weapons was essential to deter Soviet use of such weapons. Defense Secretary Caspar Weinberger later explained that binary nerve gas would be used in Bigeye aerial bombs and in 155 mm artillery shells. Binary gases consist of two chemicals that alone are not lethal but, when mixed together as a bomb descends or as a shell is fired, become lethal on exploding. In February 1982, Reagan announced U.S. plans to end its 13-year moratorium on chemical weapons by producing binary weapons. Nevertheless, Reagan's proposal ran into serious debate in Congress.

January 19, 1982

Japan and Western European nations refuse U.S. request for economic sanctions against Poland and the Soviet Union.

To punish Poland and the USSR for the repressive measures taken by the Polish government on December 13, 1981, President Reagan asked a meeting of delegates from NATO nations and Japan to adopt similar economic sanctions, especially by embargoing the export of high-technology products to the Soviet Union. Meeting in Brussels, the United States and its major allies readily agreed that Poland's government should be condemned for decreeing martial law. However, the allies rejected the U.S. request for sanctions. Although only 4 percent of Western Europe's trade was with Eastern Europe, most of those products were high-technology equipment that required a stable source of customers because of their costly production. European banks also had made many loans to Eastern European countries, which repaid them through trading activity. Consequently, industrialists and bankers in France, West Germany, Italy, and Great Britain opposed U.S. sanctions as worthless in influencing the Soviets. European leaders pointed out that President Reagan did not stop U.S. grain shipments to the Soviet Union because he did not want to harm U.S. agriculture.

Subsequently, Western European governments continued their economic relations with the Communist countries. On January 13, the West German government told West German businessmen that it would not restrict natural gas pipeline materials to the USSR. On January 23, France signed a 25-year agreement to purchase 2,980 billion cubic feet of Siberian natural gas each year. On February 10, French banks agreed to loan the USSR $140 million to purchase French equipment for the pipeline.

January 25, 1982

Polish Prime Minister Wojciech Jaruzelski denounces U.S. economic sanctions and defends martial law.

Jaruzelski said that civil war would have erupted in Poland if he had not used martial law to quell the disturbances. Following his speech, the Polish government took three actions to demonstrate the prime minister's resolve: parliament approved the December 1981 martial law decrees; on January 28, Polish police released a film to "prove" allegations that nine Americans engaged in espionage in Poland; and on February 8, Jaruzelski's cabinet proposed plans to free Poland from economic dependence on the West. On April 6, Western banks indicated that Poland had paid interest due on its 1981 debt and rescheduled $2.4 billion of 1981 principal that Poland could not pay, a plan that was revised on November 3, 1982, to defer repayment of the $2.4 billion for eight years. More significantly, on January 31, 1982, to avert troubles for Western bankers, President Reagan declared that Poland was not in default on its debts. The United States decided to pay $71 million in interest that Poland owed on loans for American agricultural products.

January 26, 1982

Secretary of State Alexander Haig links the renewal of strategic arms talks to the settlement of Poland's crisis.

Although Soviet Foreign Minister Andrei Gromyko told Haig that Polish problems were internal affairs of a third country and inappropriate for U.S.-USSR discussions, his negative response did not delay strategic arms talks. During the interim, Secretary of Defense Weinberger and Assistant Secretary for International Security Policy Richard Perle proposed the United States and the Soviet Union should eliminate all intermediate range missiles known as the "zero-option." Haig opposed the zero-option but President Reagan accepted Weinberger's proposal. On November 18, Reagan told a national television audience: "The United States is prepared to cancel its deployment of Pershing II and ground-launched cruise missiles if the Soviets will dismantle their SS-20, SS-4, and SS-5 missiles." Of course, Weinberger and Perle were confident Moscow would reject this proposal and they did when talks resumed in Geneva in January 1982. Moreover, Reagan's reaction to the Poland's martial law was economic sanctions, a situation that disturbed U.S.-NATO relations but did not harm Moscow. For more information on sanctions see January 19, 1982; on Poland see February 6, 1989. For details see Strobe Talbott, *Deadly Gambits* (1984), Frances Fitzgerald, *Way Out Their in the Blue* (2000), Lou Cannon, *Ronald Reagan: The Role of a Lifetime* (2000).

January 28, 1982

To obtain more economic aid for El Salvador, President Reagan certifies that El Salvador has improved its human rights record during the past year.

Despite the alleged massacre of civilians by the Salvadoran military and reports of serious human rights abuses, Reagan reported human rights progress in that country, as required by Congress before economic aid could be sent. On January 27, a guerrilla attack on the country's largest air base destroyed four

U.S.-supplied helicopters and six other aircraft. This attack indicated to El Salvador's government the need for U.S. aid. On February 1, 1982, the Defense Department sent $55 million of emergency supplies to El Salvador, and Reagan asked Congress to approve an additional $100 million for 1982. Some data that contradicted Reagan's certificate of progress in El Salvador included a Roman Catholic Legal Aid Office report that 13,353 noncombatants were killed in 1981 and a Human Rights Commission report that 16,276 died in 1981. Both groups claimed that El Salvador's military groups were responsible for most of the murders. The U.S. State Department called these death reports insurgent propaganda. Evidence of El Salvador's progress, the department stated, was the arrest in January 1982 of six suspects for the murder of four American missionaries in December 1980. Previously, El Salvador had freed six suspects in this murder case.

January 29, 1982

France sells Nicaragua arms despite U.S. opposition.

Criticizing countries (i.e., the United States) that seek to impose their will on other nations, French Foreign Minister Claude Cheyson said France would not cancel its $15.8 million arms sale to Nicaragua. President Reagan wanted Europeans to embargo arms to Nicaragua and to aid the Contra rebels. France declared its sale made Managua less dependent on the Soviet Union.

February 2, 1982

A draft proposal of President Reagan's "zero-option" arms treaty is presented to Soviet delegates at Geneva.

The second round of intermediate-range arms talks in Geneva found the United States and the USSR offering different proposals, neither of which was acceptable to the other side. Reagan's zero-option proposal had not been ready to present during the November 1981 talks but was now formally offered. The Soviets said it was not acceptable because it did not include the elimination of French and British missiles and therefore would give NATO an advantage over the Soviets. On February 3, the Soviets proposed that each side cut two-thirds of its medium-range missiles. The United States rejected this idea, arguing that it would leave the Soviets superior in conventional and nuclear weapons in Europe.

February 11, 1982

MX missile-basing debate heats up after Defense Department says it will deploy the first 40 MX in vacated, nonhardened Minuteman silos.

Ever since the Reagan administration abandoned President Jimmy Carter's underground basing plan, the Department of Defense seemed uncertain what basing scheme to adopt, a critical matter because it involved the broader strategy of whether the MX would be a second-strike retaliatory weapon or a U.S. first-strike weapon because it could not survive a Soviet attack. In October 1981, Defense Secretary Caspar Weinberger talked about basing up to 36 MX in obsolete Titan missile silos in Arkansas, Kansas, and Missouri. In January 1982, however, Reagan officials indicated that existing Minuteman silos would be used, a decision announced on February 11. This choice would save $3 billion on rebuilding silos and would avoid the necessity of obtaining the Soviet Union's permission to harden the silos, a condition required by SALT II that, though unratified, both nations treated as being operative.

Critics of the old silo-basing mode immediately challenged the decision. Tom Wicker of the *New York Times* wrote that the use of existing silos would make the MX vulnerable and would be correctly perceived by Moscow as a new U.S. first-strike weapon. By March 19, the Senate Armed Services Committee voted to have Congress block the February 11 plan and deny any MX production funds unless permanent, hardened silos were used. Following this advice, the Senate committee deleted $2.1 billion from the defense budget for fiscal 1983. The debate on this question had only begun.

February 24, 1982

The Caribbean Basin Initiative (CBI) is announced by President Reagan.

This proposal was designed to provide nations of the Caribbean Sea and Central America with freer access to the U.S. market, giving them trade concessions not extended to other nations.

February 26, 1982

The United States relaxes its export restrictions on South Africa.

As part of its effort at "positive disengagement" to gain South African concessions in problem regions such as Namibia, President Reagan ended many restrictions that previous U.S. administrations had placed on South African trade. On March 11, 1982, Reagan also eased restrictions on South African military officials visiting the United States in search of arms; on November 11, Washington supported an International Monetary Fund loan of $1.1 billion to South Africa. Many spokespersons in the United States opposed Reagan's actions because they believed such benefits enabled South Africa to continue its apartheid policies at home and its military interference in Namibia (South-West Africa) and Angola.

March 4, 1982

The Reagan administration has difficulty finding evidence that Cuba and Nicaragua are helping rebels in El Salvador.

With White House mail running 10 to 1 against the president's policies in El Salvador and with over 100 congressmen urging Reagan to seek negotiations. Secretary of State Alexander Haig experienced difficulty in providing the "overwhelming and irrefutable" evidence that he told a congressional committee was available to prove that Salvadoran rebels were aided by Cuba and Nicaragua. In early March, two administration attempts to offer proof backfired. First, on March 4, after Haig told congressmen that the United States had captured a Nicaraguan officer sent to aid El Salvador's rebels, the captive escaped and obtained safe-conduct from the Mexican embassy. Mexican officials said the man was a 19-year-old university student who was "captured" on his way home to Nicaragua. On March 7, the State Department suffered more embarrassment when it called a press conference to present a Nicaraguan who would verify the U.S. claims of foreign intervention in El Salvador. Orlando José Tardencillas Espinosa was presented to the reporters, but he refuted the claims that he was supposed to verify. As a guerrilla captured in El Salvador, Espinosa said he was taken to the U.S. embassy and instructed to give evidence that Cubans were aiding the rebels. "They gave me an option," he said; "I could come here or face certain death. All my previous statements about training in Ethiopia and Cuba were false."

The State Department's only remaining option was to say it could not give all evidence because CIA sources would be damaged. Subsequently, William Casey, director of the CIA, gave a classified briefing to 26 "leakproof" former officials who reported his evidence was "very persuasive." CIA photos showed military bases similar to Cuba's, Soviet-type armored tanks, and four airfield runways being lengthened for jet planes. The Nicaraguan government said these were defense preparations resulting from the threat of a U.S. invasion, denying that it aided El Salvador's rebels.

March 7, 1982

In Guatemala, General Angel Anibal Guevara is elected president but is replaced within a month by General Efrain Ríos Montt.

Some observers believed that the guerrilla conflict was more widespread in Guatemala than in El Salvador. Preceding the election, competing guerrilla groups intensified their attacks while the army used a scorched earth program to eradicate guerrilla hideouts. Within 12 months, Amnesty International reported that at least 13,500 people had been killed in Guatemala. Even among Guatemalan politicians, there was intense preelection conflict. All four candidates for president were conservatives because the two liberal candidates had been assassinated. There were also charges of fraud in the election won by General Guevara. Finally, on March 23, a three-man army junta took over the government, ousting Guevara. General Ríos Montt headed the junta. On June 9, 1982, Montt deposed his two partners, suspended the constitution, named himself president, and declared a state of siege.

March 8, 1982

The Reagan administration claims Soviet forces have killed at least 3,000 people in Afghanistan with chemical weapons.

To substantiate this and previous claims that the Soviets used chemical weapons, Deputy Secretary of State Walter J. Stoessel offered evidence of 47 incidents with 3,042 deaths between 1978 and 1981. The data were based on accounts of Afghan defectors, including some who said they had been trained in chemical warfare by Soviet advisers. Stoessel admitted he had no samples of the chemicals or the weapons; nor did he have pictures showing toxic weapon use. He asserted, however, that the victims' physical symptoms and the dates of the alleged attacks supported his claims. Both on March 22 and on December 5, 1982, the State Department issued reports containing circumstantial evidence that Soviet, Laotian, and Vietnamese forces used chemical weapons causing over 10,000 deaths since 1975. These accounts of "yellow rain" chemicals were questioned by many scientists who argued that the incidents and symptoms could have resulted from the same type of herbicides the United States used in Vietnam. They argued that the State Department gave no hard, direct evidence of chemical attacks. In the 1987 article "Sverdlovsk and Yellow Rain: Two Classes of Soviet Non-compliance," published in volume 11 (Spring 1987) of *International Security*, Professor Elisa D. Harris reviewed all the Reagan administration claims since September 13, 1981, concluding that they were filled with errors and inconsistencies. She believed verification problems caused the difficulties but that those who favored the renewed U.S. production of chemical weapons used the false data to bolster their cause and to undermine the arms control process.

March 10, 1982

The U.N. Human Rights Commission votes to urge Poland to restore fundamental freedoms.

The United States voted with the 19-vote majority; 13 nations opposed the resolution, and 10 abstained. On March 2, 1982, Polish Prime Minister Wojciech Jaruzelski met with Soviet President Leonid Brezhnev, informing him that future challenges to Communism would be "cut short." Since December 1981, Poland's martial law kept a tight reign on domestic order, with demonstrators being arrested and strikes being prevented or broken.

March 14, 1982

During a major Contra attack in Nicaragua, the U.S.-backed rebels seriously damage bridges on the Negro and Coco Rivers by detonating explosives.

The Contras had been organizing throughout 1981 with the aid of the CIA and Argentina. This attack was made by the Nicaraguan Democratic Front (FDN), which consisted of many former military members of the dictatorial Somoza government that was overthrown in 1979. The leader of the FDN was Enrique Bermudez Varela, who had been a colonel in Somoza's National Guard and had served as Somoza's defense attaché in Washington in 1977. The FDN made continuous raids into Nicaragua following this first significant action. Most of the raids were on industrial, transportation, and agricultural targets to weaken the economy. Bermudez hoped to seize the whole eastern Costa de Mosquitos province, a goal he never achieved.

March 18, 1982

In Pusan, South Korea, unknown arsonists burn the American cultural center as anti-Americanism grows.

Although the extent of anti-Americanism in South Korea was unclear, this attack indicated some extensive opposition. Students at Seoul's National University circulated leaflets calling for the withdrawal of the 40,000 U.S. troops stationed in South Korea. But many Koreans feared such action would cause a war between the two Koreas. The two students arrested for the fire in Pusan said they opposed U.S. backing of the repressive regime of President Chun Doo Hwan.

March 26–31, 1982

Visiting Japan and Korea, Defense Secretary Caspar Weinberger asks Tokyo to increase its defense budget and Seoul to protect civil rights.

As Japan's astonishing economic growth made it the most prosperous nation in the world, Americans increasingly felt Tokyo should undertake a greater share of its defense burden, which the United States had funded since the end of World War II. The Japanese were reluctant to do so, but on August 1, 1982, Prime Minister Zeiko Suzaki announced there would be a $64 billion increase in the military budget over the next five years, a 60 percent increase. In South Korea, Weinberger expressed U.S. dissatisfaction with President Chun Doo Hwan's political repression. Early in March 1982, Chun granted amnesty to 2,863 prisoners, including 287 political prisoners, but he kept all opposition party leaders in jail. Chun's major achievement during his first year in office was securing the Olympic Games for Seoul in 1988.

March 28, 1982

El Salvador's election does not give the moderate Christian Democratic (CD) Party the majority preferred by the United States.

Although President José Napoleon Duarte's CD Party received a plurality of 35.4 percent, the right-wing National Republican Alliance of Roberto d'Aubuisson and other smaller right-wing groups gained 52.4 percent of the vote, as well as 36 of the 60 seats in the Constituent Assembly, which was elected to write a new constitution. The CDs had only 24 assembly seats. Because left-wing guerrillas boycotted the election, the 1.5 million votes were considered a large turnout, over which more than 500 foreign observers watched. Within a month of the election the American-backed CDs lost their leadership posts to d'Aubuisson, an alleged leader of the right-wing death squads, who became president of the Constituent Assembly and named a political nonentity, Alvara Alfredo Magaña, as president of El Salvador. Former U.S. Ambassador to El Salvador Robert E. White called d'Aubuisson a "pathological killer," but the Reagan administration now looked for virtues in d'Aubuisson, who received U.S. economic aid.

March 31, 1982

Deputy Undersecretary of Defense T.K. Jones finally testifies to Congress regarding his extremist survivalist claims during a nuclear war.

Since January 1982, the Senate Subcommittee on Arms Control of the Foreign Relations Committee had tried to get Jones to appear and describe the extremist claims he made publicly regarding a civil defense scheme to enable most of the population to survive a nuclear war. Jones failed to appear at a scheduled hearing, possibly because his extremist ideas embarrassed the Reagan defense department. In speeches to right-wing groups and in a January 16 interview with Robert Scheer of the *Los Angeles Times*, Jones claimed that if every American had a shovel to dig a hole and then cover himself with three feet of dirt, 98 percent of the population could survive a nuclear war.

Finally appearing before the committee, Jones claimed the United States should do this or something similar, because the Soviet Union's shovel program would permit the Soviets to initiate a nuclear war as they would be protected. Jones said Scheer misinterpreted his position, although the reporter's book *With Enough Shovels* includes the verbatim interview as tape-recorded by Scheer. Advocates of a protracted nuclear war who wanted the United States to survive rather than fear a nuclear conflict was part of the Committee on the Clear and Present Danger program that supported Reagan's 1980 election and Reagan's view that the Soviet threat had grown because the USSR violated arms control treaties. While Reagan sought votes from these groups and appointed Jones to office on behalf of those interest groups, Jones did not represent the general thought of the Defense Department. At the March 31 hearings, Richard N. Perle, the assistant defense secretary for international security, accompanied Jones and told the subcommittee that Jones did not speak for the Defense Department on civil defense methods. Perle said civil defense plans were designed to mitigate the consequences of a limited nuclear strike by one week's warning before an attack.

Reagan meeting with El Salvador's President Jose Napoleon Duarte. Ronald Reagan Library

March 31, 1982

Vietnam drops General Giap of Vietnam War fame from membership in the Communist Party Politburo.

General Vo Nguyen Giap had been the Communists' chief military planner for the war in Indochina from 1945 to 1975. He was one of six party leaders removed from a leadership role as younger party members gained authority.

April 18, 1982

Ground Zero Week is launched by antinuclear war advocates in the United States.

To publicize their campaign against the Cold War mentality of the Reagan administration and promote a freeze on all nuclear weapons as a first step toward complete nuclear disarmament, the National Nuclear Freeze Committee designated the week of April 18–25 as a nationwide campaign of seminars, lectures, teach-ins, and protest marches to point up the horrors of nuclear war. Several events related to nuclear war or disarmament preceded and inspired Ground Zero Week. Two of the important events were a Senate resolution for an immediate nuclear freeze, sponsored by Senators Edward Kennedy (D-Mass.) and Mark Hatfield (R-Oreg.) plus the efforts of former presidential advisers Mc George Bundy, George F. Kennan, Gerard Smith, and Robert S. Mc Namara to persuade the United States and its NATO allies to declare a "no first use" of nuclear weapons in the event of a European war. The Kennedy-Hatfield resolution called on the United States to seek agreement with the Soviets on a verifiable means to stop the production and deployment of nuclear weapons. It argued the Reagan administration's policy of seeking U.S. nuclear superiority to force the Soviets to accept arms reduction was "voodoo arms control, which says you must have more in order to have less." Opponents of the nuclear freeze, such as Republican leader Robert Michel of Illinois, argued that defending freedom, not the possession of nuclear arms, was the main U.S. issue. Freedom, he said, could be defended "only by the deterrent power of U.S. nuclear arms."

The "no first use" declaration sought by Bundy, Kennan, Smith, and McNamara was explained in the spring 1982 issue of *Foreign Affairs* magazine and during a Washington press conference on April 8, 1982. Although NATO retained the "first use" option for nuclear weapons since its founding in 1949, the four former presidential advisers argued that nuclear fighting would never be limited to Europe once it started, and Europeans doubted Washington would risk the nuclear destruction of the United States if Soviet tanks attacked West Germany. The strain between the United States and its European allies also fueled European antiwar protests, which preferred some alternative to a nuclear holocaust. Bundy and McNamara had been close advisers to Presidents Kennedy and Johnson; Smith had been President Nixon's chief negotiator for SALT I (1972); Kennan was the State Department official who conceived the containment policy in 1948. These former officials advocated a buildup of NATO's conventional forces as the best means of reducing the risk of Soviet aggression and avoiding the chance of nuclear war. "No first use" signified that NATO would retaliate with nuclear weapons if the Soviets used them, but NATO forces would not initiate the first nuclear strike.

Many advocates of the U.S. freeze movement had less explicit reasons for their support, but all agreed that President Reagan's antagonistic rhetoric toward the Soviet Union and his desire to regain U.S. military superiority increased the danger of nuclear war. The U.S. antinuclear sentiment probably had its greatest practical impact in Congress, where efforts were successful in limiting the large defense expenditures President Reagan advocated. Thus the Senate Armed Services Committee voted in April 1981 to cut $2.1 billion from funds to deploy 40 MX intercontinental ballistic missiles. The committee wanted to know how the president intended to deploy the missiles because he had abandoned President Carter's plans for a mobile underground base designed as a "second-strike" retaliatory basing mode. In contrast to the concerns of Congress, Secretary of State Alexander Haig stated on April 6 that the United States would not renounce the "first use" doctrine or agree to a nuclear freeze at present levels of weapons.

April 25, 1982

Israel withdraws from the Sinai Peninsula, returning the territory to Egypt; the United States assumes responsibility for early warning system.

By completing its withdrawal from the Sinai, Israel fulfilled the terms of the Egyptian-Israeli Treaty of 1979, leaving land it had occupied during the Six-Day War (1967). After Israel annexed the Golan Heights on December 14, 1981, U.S. diplomats feared Israel would also remain in the Sinai, where some Jewish settlers had to be forcibly evicted. Israel's Prime Minister Menachem Begin contended, however, that the Golan's annexation permitted Israel to forego security interests in the Sinai. In accordance with prior agreement, a U.S. Sinai Security Mission had been enlarged to operate an early-warning system in the Giddi and Mitlai passes into the Sinai. This system was coordinated with the U.N.'s multinational peacekeeping force in the Sinai. Although Israel's withdrawal fulfilled one part of the 1979 Camp David accords, Prime Minister Begin's policy of increasing Jewish settlements in the West Bank territory made fulfillment of the second part of the accords more difficult. The second part said Israel would grant "autonomy" to Palestinians living in the Israeli-occupied West Bank and Gaza Strip regions. To complicate the issue further, Begin had moved Israel's capital city to Jerusalem in violation of previous U.N. agreements. From January 12 to 28, Secretary of State Haig visited Cairo and Jerusalem several times but could not gain an agreement on the West Bank–Gaza "autonomy" issue for Palestinians.

April 30, 1982

The United States votes against the Law of the Sea Treaty after it rejects compromises suggested by other nations at the U.N. conference.

After changing the Law of the Sea Treaty to guarantee seabed mining rights for private enterprise and to prevent a global cartel from favoring Third World rights to future profits, U.N. conference delegates, who had been meeting since March 8, claimed they had "exhausted all possibilities of agreement" and decided to vote. Favoring the treaty were 130 nations, including Japan and France. The treaty was scheduled to be signed during a U.N. meeting at Kingston, Jamaica.

May 3, 1982

Jordanian volunteers go to help Iraq fight Iran.

Arab support for Iran and Iraq was divided; Jordan and most Arab states backed Iraq either covertly or overtly, while Syria and Libya helped Iran. Jordan's decision to permit volunteers to fight for Iraq was announced the day after U.N. mediator Olaf Palme reported that attempts to end the Iran-Iraq war had failed.

May 5, 1982

Hungary becomes the first Warsaw Pact nation to join the International Monetary Fund (IMF).

Hungarian agriculture and trade had increased remarkably under the liberalized economic program of its Communist leaders. During 1982, Budapest's Central European International Bank established good relations with six Western European banks and took steps to switch to free-market trade and investment activities. Hungary had applied for membership in the IMF on November 5, 1981, and by May 5, 1982, its application was approved.

May 9, 1982

President Reagan proposes strategic arms reduction talks (START) with the Soviet Union, which would not limit but would cut back on nuclear weapons.

Addressing graduates at Eureka College, Illinois, the president's alma mater, Reagan emphasized that in strategic arms talks the United States wanted nuclear weapons reductions, not limitations as in the 1970s SALT negotiations. He proposed a ceiling of 850 intercontinental launchers and 5,000 warheads with a sub-limit of 2,500 warheads on land-based missiles. Both sides would destroy some existing weapons—the Soviets eliminating more launchers and the United States, more warheads. From a U.S. perspective, Reagan's START prescription favored the views of the State Department and Secretary Alexander Haig, in opposition to proposals of the Defense Department and Secretary Caspar Weinberger. Using suggestions from Richard Perle, an undersecretary of defense, Weinberger wanted to reduce missile throw weights, which would have required deeper Soviet reductions. The State Department argued that this would be impossible for the Soviets to accept and would cause America's NATO allies to question the sincerity of the proposal. In part, Reagan's decision was a political response to the growing nuclear freeze movements in the United States and Europe. Several nuclear freeze resolutions were before Congress, and others would be on state ballots during the November 1982 elections. Although on May 18 Soviet Chairman Leonid Brezhnev criticized Reagan's proposal as a "one-sided" idea that would give the United States nuclear superiority, on May 30 the two powers agreed to begin strategic arms discussions on June 29 at Geneva.

May 9, 1982

After a visit to the People's Republic of China (PRC), Vice President George H.W. Bush failed to end Beijing's opposition to U.S. arms sales to the Republic of China on Taiwan (ROC).

Bush, who had been the U.S. ambassador to the PRC under President Nixon, believed he could explain to the Chinese the sale of U.S. F5-E fighter planes to the ROC in January 1982. He did not succeed because

Beijing considered Taiwan a province of China, not a separate nation. On June 2, Senator Howard Baker Jr. (R-Tenn.) visited China and found the Chinese angry about the U.S. arms sales to Taiwan. The situation became more difficult when President Reagan, on July 16, announced that Taiwan and the United States would cooperate in the production of the F5-E planes. Reagan wanted the political support of right-wing Republicans who favored Taiwan.

May 10, 1982

Hopes for U.S. Nicaraguan peace negotiations fade when Nicaragua signs a five-year, $166.8 million aid agreement with the Soviet Union.

Talks to improve Washington's relations with Managua seemed possible on April 14, 1982, after Nicaragua accepted U.S. proposals for negotiations. On April 18, Nicaragua requested immediate discussions, but the United States replied it was not yet prepared. Subsequently, the Soviet-Nicaraguan five-year pact confirmed the administration's opinions about the Communist threat in Central America, and hopes for talks disappeared.

May 16, 1982

Salvador Jorge Blanco is elected president of the Dominican Republic.

During the 1965 U.S. intervention, Jorge Blanco helped draft the agreement for U.S. Marines to leave the island. For the next 12 years, however, right-wing leader Joaquín Balaguer ruled before losing an election in 1978 to Antonio Guzmán Fernández, who was a member of Jorge Blanco's Dominican Revolutionary Party. In July 1982, the U.S. Senate voted to withhold $100 million in land reform funds because an audit disclosed that over $6 million of previous funds had been siphoned off to private farmers and military commanders.

May 20, 1982

El Salvador suspends its land reform program, alarming the U.S. Senate.

After Roberto d'Aubuisson became president of El Salvador's Constituent Assembly on April 22, he moved to eliminate or change the land reforms of former President Duarte. The May 20 action suspended the U.S. designed "land-to-the-tiller" program, which would have allowed 85 percent of sharecropping peasant families to purchase up to 17 acres of the land they worked. Earlier, the assembly had canceled Duarte's program for converting medium-sized farms into cooperatives. Because d'Aubuisson had done exactly what U.S. congressional leaders feared, the Republican-controlled Senate Foreign Relations Committee voted to cancel $100 million of the $166 million President Reagan had requested for military aid to El Salvador unless land reform was undertaken. D'Aubuisson said a new program would be enacted, and Senator Christopher Dodd (D-Conn.) called suitable land reform the "linchpin" in defeating guerrillas in El Salvador.

May 24, 1982

Expiration of the U.S.-Soviet space cooperation agreement of 1972.

The Reagan administration decided not to renew this agreement because relations with the Soviets had cooled during the Carter administration and had not improved since Reagan became president. The 1972 agreement's most dramatic result had been the 1975 Apollo 18–Soyuz 19 flight. Discussion of other joint space flights had ended in the fall of 1977 because the United States believed the scientific and technological return was minimal. More modest levels of cooperation had continued in biology and planetary science, which sent test animals into space as late as 1979. Under a separate agreement another biosatellite mission was set for 1983. On December 29, 1981, President Reagan had decided not to renew Soviet agreements on space, energy research, and space science and technology as part of the sanctions applied against the Soviet Union when Poland imposed martial law. The energy agreement expired on June 28, 1982; the agreement on science and technology expired on July 8, 1982.

May 27, 1982

The United States and Morocco agree the U.S. air force may use Moroccan air bases during emergencies in Africa and the Middle East.

An agreement for the possible use of Moroccan bases was concluded after King Hassan II of Morocco visited Washington, D.C. The Moroccan base agreement included radar facilities that were an important part of the rapid-deployment force that the Pentagon was preparing for Middle East contingencies.

May 29, 1982

The Department of Defense issues a defense guidance (plan) that explicitly prepares for "protracted nuclear conflict."

During early 1982, President Reagan asked the Joint Chiefs of Staff to revise the Single Integrated Operational Plan (SIOP) for fighting the next war so that the United States would prevail in a nuclear war as per the NUTS doctrine. While this task was not unusual, the chiefs were uneasy about the enthusiasm that Richard Perle and others in the administration showed for the enhancement of the nuclear war–fighting capacity that assumed a limited nuclear war could be fought and won. The chairman of the Joint Chiefs of Staff, General David Jones, said in June 1982 that he did not see "much of a chance" for any nuclear war to be limited. For a protracted nuclear war, the Reagan administration wanted the expensive infrastructure essential to nuclear war fighting, that is, not just superior weapons but also superior C3I—superior command, control, communications, and intelligence facilities—to survive all nuclear attacks.

In addition to a nuclear capacity "beyond deterrence," the 1982 defense guidance called for using economic warfare against the USSR, boosting China's military potential to threaten the Soviets, and developing capacities for guerrilla warfare against Eastern European and other Communist targets. As information about this plan leaked to the press and the public, Americans and Europeans became alarmed. When American leaders talked about fighting and winning a nuclear war, the potential destruction encouraged the promotion of a nuclear freeze as a step to nuclear disarmament.

June 1, 1982

The United States declares its willingness to help mainland China develop its nuclear power industry.

For China's modernization program, nuclear power plants would be an essential source of energy. This announcement sanctioned the desire of U.S. companies to build nuclear power plants in China. Deputy Secretary of State Walter J. Stoessel Jr. also began talks with Chinese representatives about nuclear cooperation. Not coincidental, perhaps, was the fact that on May 29 and 30, 1982, the *New York Times* reported recent plans of the Department of Defense proposed "measured military assistance" to China to keep as many Soviet forces tied down on the Soviet-Chinese border. China's development of nuclear power had a direct impact on these plans.

June 1, 1982

As a prelude to President Reagan's upcoming visit to West Germany, terrorists bomb four U.S. military bases in the Federal Republic of Germany.

The bombing attacks were conducted by a small organization, the Revolutionary Cells Terrorist Group. In contrast, large pro-American rallies were held in Munich and Bonn, where West Germans demonstrated their appreciation of the U.S. alliance with their country since 1948.

June 4–6, 1982

The annual summit of the seven major industrial nations is held at Versailles, France.

The summit discussions were conducted carefully because the European members did not want to embarrass President Reagan, whose large budget deficits were detrimental to the other G-7 nations' economies. Europeans blamed the high interest rates and budget deficit of the United States for their economic recessions. Although little agreement was reached, the seven leaders agreed to consult closely on their national economic policies.

June 6, 1982

Israeli forces invade Lebanon seeking to defeat Palestinian armies; U.S. and USSR asked to stop invasion.

Assisted by Christian armies led by Saad Haddad, a Lebanese army officer, the Israelis conducted eight days of intensive fighting against the forces of Palestinian refugees, Lebanese Muslim forces, and the Syrian army. By June 13, Israeli units reached the outskirts of Beirut, where they linked up with Christian Phalangist armies and captured the Beirut-to-Damascus highway; thereby, the Israelis sealed off men and supplies coming to Beirut from Syria. Hints of an impending Israeli invasion abounded since December 1981 because Israeli and Palestinian forces raided and counterraided along the south border of Lebanon following Israel's annexation of the Golan

Heights. On April 9 the United States expressed concern about Israel's military buildup along the Lebanese border.

On April 16 Lebanon's President Elias Sarkis asked the United States and the USSR to prevent an invasion. The incident that persuaded Israel's cabinet to launch an invasion was the attempted assassination of Ambassador Shlomo Argov by a Palestinian terrorist in London. Argov survived, although paralyzed, and British police captured the assassin, Hassan Said, and two other Palestinians from the Iraqi-backed Abu Nidal group. Although Israeli intelligence believed that Iraq wanted to provoke Israel to defeat the Syrians (an enemy of Iraq), Prime Minister Begin did not tell Israeli cabinet members about this possibility because Begin and his defense minister wanted to invade Lebanon. Thus, with cabinet approval, Defense Minister Ariel Sharon launched the attack on Lebanon in Operation Peace for Galilee, a bid to end the threat of the Palestine Liberation Organization (PLO) in Lebanon and to end PLO influence in the West Bank and Gaza, so that compliant Palestinian inhabitants would accede to Israel's annexation of those territories. To achieve this Sharon also planned Operation Big Pines to crush the PLO infrastructure in Beirut and drive them out of Lebanon. Initially, Sharon's plans went well. The U.N. interim forces, which since 1978 had failed to keep the border peace, did not resist the Israeli attack. By June 8, Israeli armies were beyond the 25-mile security zone of southern Lebanon that Sharon told the Israeli cabinet he wanted to control. Israel's army and air force did not stop, however. On June 9 and 10, Israeli planes wiped out 17 of the 19 surface-to-air missile sites that the Soviet Union had given the Syrians and shattered the Syrian air force by shooting down at least 72 Soviet-built MiG-25 fighter planes.

June 8, 1982

President Reagan announces Project Democracy in a speech to the British Parliament. The project evolves into two segments—one covert, the other overt.

Although receiving little attention immediately after President Reagan delivered his speech to members of the British Parliament, Project Democracy became a two-track program designed to fulfill the Reagan administration's attempt to promote democracy in countries where authoritarian regimes existed. Project Democracy became a reality after Congress funded a governmental agency called the National Endowment for Democracy on November 22, 1983. The Endowment's overt projects provided funds to support democratic elections outside the United States. For covert programs, the Reagan administration used Endowment for Democracy funds to oppose Soviet activity in nations such as Nicaragua during the 1980s. (See January 14, 1983.)

As part of his May–June trip to Europe, Reagan was invited by British leaders to speak at the Houses of Parliament, following his attendance at the G-7 sessions in Versailles, France. During the G-7 sessions, Reagan had tried to persuade other G-7 representatives to stop their trade credits and commercial activities with Warsaw Pact nations, especially the Soviet Union, but had failed to convince the Europeans to change their commercial activities because they favored increased trade with the Soviet Empire. In London, President Reagan's speech to Parliament focused primarily on his long-standing opposition to Marxism-Leninism as practiced in the Soviet Union. Reagan's speech expressed his firm belief that the forces of freedom would inevitably triumph over Communism, an ideology that would soon be thrown on "the ash-heaps of history." In conclusion, Reagan said "Let us now begin a major effort to secure the best—a crusade for freedom that would engage the faith and fortitude of the next generation."

Following Reagan's June 8 speech, some commentators called it a valuable statement about democracy's challenge to Communist rule; other pundits feared the Reagan administration was ready to take enormous risks designed to "roll back" the Soviet Empire. Yet Reagan's deeds did not fit his words. Reagan had lifted the embargo on grain sales to the Soviet Union imposed by President Carter in 1980 after the Soviet forces invaded Afghanistan. Also, he did little when General Jaruzelski declared martial law in Poland in December 1981.

See December 13, 1981.

June 12, 1982

Largest disarmament rally in American history assembles in New York in favor of a nuclear freeze.

Around the world, people conducted antinuclear weapons demonstrations during the spring and summer of 1982. In New York on June 12, crowds estimated at up to 750,000 rallied to promote disarmament. This event preceded the convening of a special United Nations Disarmament Conference, where Soviet proposals gained favor while President Reagan's responses brought condemnation from peace advocates in the United States and abroad. During the opening session the Soviet delegates pledged not to be the first to use nuclear weapons—a pledge that U.S. officials consistently rejected. In addition to opposing the Soviet pledge as "unverifiable and unenforceable," President Reagan, addressing the conference, denounced the Soviet Union for creating tyranny around the world.

June 16, 1982

The United States supports a Cambodian government-in-exile formed by three competing Cambodian groups.

Officially renamed Kampuchea in 1975, Cambodia had experienced many deaths under the Communist leader Pol Pot's government before Vietnamese armies defeated his regime, the Khmer Rouge, in 1978–1979. To unify groups fighting to force Vietnam's withdrawal, these rebel groups had joined under Prince Norodom Sihanouk and two of his rivals, former Prime Minister Son Sann and the Khmer Rouge spokesman Khieu Samphan. In 1978, the United States encouraged the unity of these groups against Vietnam. On October 29, 1982, a resolution of the U.N. General Assembly called on Vietnam to remove its 180,000 troops from Cambodia, but Hanoi ignored the request.

June 21, 1982

The U.S. air force forms a Space Command to expand U.S. military operations in space.

The decision to form a special division for space activity gave the air force an impetus to plan and operate military space missions of its own, as well as in cooperation with the National Aeronautics and Space Administration (NASA). As NASA's shuttle flights developed during the 1980s, there was an increased use of the shuttle for military missions of the Space Command.

June 24, 1982

A French astronaut joins the Soviet cosmonauts aboard the Soviet T-G spacecraft.

French Air Force Colonel Jean-Loup Chrétien became the first astronaut who was neither Soviet nor American. He joined the Soviets in a nine-day space flight.

June 25, 1982

George P. Shultz is nominated for Secretary of State to replace Alexander Haig, who resigned effective July 5.

Although Haig gave no public reasons for resigning, his differences in outlook with the rest of the Reagan administration—especially to adapt clear, consistent policy lines between the State and Defense Departments and the National Security Agency—probably determined his action. Haig often disagreed with Secretary of Defense Caspar Weinberger, who used confrontational tactics against U.S. allies. Shultz presented a guarded, taciturn personality and was not predisposed to freelance policy on his own. He was a conservative but not burdened with excessive the anti-Soviet characteristics of other members of the Reagan administration.

June 29, 1982

Strategic arms reduction talks (START) begin in Geneva between U.S. and Soviet delegates.

Since President Reagan's speech of May 9, 1982, the U.S. media had dubbed the U.S.-USSR negotiations on intercontinental nuclear weapons as START. These talks paralleled other U.S.-USSR negotiations on intermediate theater nuclear weapons that had begun on November 30, 1981. The U.S. delegation to START was headed by retired General Edward Rowney, who had represented the Joint Chiefs of Staff at the SALT II talks until he resigned in 1979 because of objections to the Carter administration's "weak" position on the talks. Rowney agreed with President Reagan that the United States had to regain its lost strategic nuclear superiority and generally disliked the arms control approach. The Soviet delegation was led by Viktor A. Karpov, who had worked on SALT II as the principal deputy to chief negotiator Vladimir Semyonov until the final stages of the talks. Although Karpov had been sent home for a while to treat his alcoholism, he returned in 1982 to demonstrate the Soviet view that START was a descendent of SALT I and SALT II. Just as Soviet President Brezhnev's May 18 response to Reagan's START proposal suggested a hard Soviet line to counter the U.S. hard line, the talks opened on June 29 with both sides more focused on propaganda rather than serious negotiations. In response to Reagan's START proposals, the USSR offered reductions in its long-range missile and bomber forces if the United States would end its plans to deploy medium-range missiles in Europe and restrict developments of its cruise missiles. This proposal linked the strategic missile talks with the intermediate-range talks, a proposition the United States did not reject but tried to avoid in 1982 and 1983. On July 20, the Reagan administration refused to renew talks with the USSR and Great Britain on a comprehensive nuclear test ban. The talks became stalemates in 1980 after the Soviet intervention in Afghanistan.

July 8, 1982

The Mutual and Balanced Force Reduction (MBFR) talks continue in disagreement in Vienna.

Delegates of the North Atlantic Treaty Organization (NATO) and of the Warsaw Pact countries had been sporadically negotiating reductions in their conventional European forces since 1973. Typical of their discussions was the NATO proposal of July 8 to put a ceiling of 900,000 men on each side, a suggestion that the Warsaw Pact delegates questioned but responded to with no enthusiasm. Many in the Reagan administration wanted to stall these talks until the U.S. military achieved superiority. This approach added to the distrust of both sides regarding each other's official data on existing forces and possible verification methods. Following the 1982 discussion in Vienna, Richard Starr, the chief U.S. negotiator, resigned and was told by Richard Perle, an assistant secretary of defense: "Congratulations! You have obviously done a good job, because nothing happened." Perle was one of the administration's major opponents of arms control efforts.

July 12, 1982

Somalia requests and receives U.S. aid against an alleged Ethiopian invasion.

Border tensions existed between Ethiopia and Somalia since 1977, when Somalia tried to assert its right to the Ogaden desert region in Ethiopia. Ethiopia was aided by the Soviet Union and Cuban soldiers, while the United States began aiding Somalia in March 1978. In 1982, Somalia said Ethiopia began an invasion on July 1 and 11 days later asked for help to halt Ethiopia's successful assault. Ethiopia argued that it only aided rebels of the Western Somalia Liberation Front, who desired to overthrow the Somali government. The rebels, backed by Ethiopia, also had military equipment from the Soviet Union, South Yemen, East Germany, and Cuba. The United States airlifted $5.5 million of military aid to Somalia on July 24, although by that time Somalia claimed it had driven the Ethiopians back across the border.

July 22, 1982

France defies President Reagan's embargo on Soviet gas pipeline equipment.

Although French President François Mitterrand supported the deployment of U.S. missiles in Europe, he agreed with other Western European leaders that the Soviet natural gas pipeline was needed and would not enhance the strategic position of the USSR. President Ronald Reagan, who on January 8, 1982, prohibited General Electric from selling pipeline technology to the Soviets, had on June 18 formally extended trade sanctions to include foreign subsidiaries or foreign companies licensed to use U.S. technology for their equipment. Not only had France defied Reagan's unilateral action but West Germany, Italy, and Great Britain rejected the president's attempt to control their export products.

August 16, 1982

A Senate-House conference committee opposes funding for nerve gas weapons.

Following President Reagan's decision to renew the U.S. production of nerve gas weapons, many in Congress opposed this step. While the Republican-controlled Senate voted 49 to 45 on May 14 to approve $54 million for chemical weapons, the House voted on July 22 against such weapon production by 251 to 159. On August 13, the Senate-House conference committee seeking to rectify budget differences voted to accept such funding, but on August 16 the joint committee removed the funds for nerve gas weapons. The issue of chemical weapons production was pursued again by the Reagan administration and finally passed.

August 16, 1982

The United States and the People's Republic of China (PRC) sign an agreement on their relations with the Republic of China (ROC) on Taiwan.

To stabilize relations between Beijing and Washington, the Chinese government agreed to use only peaceful means to regain Taiwan; the United States agreed to reduce the present level of its arms aid to the ROC, a decision Taiwan protested. Friction had arisen early in 1982 after the United States sold aircraft and arms to the ROC because neither Vice President Bush, who visited Beijing from May 5 to May 9, nor Senator Howard Baker (R-Tenn.), who visited from May 30 to June 2, could persuade China of the U.S. position toward Taiwan. Therefore, the two sides decided to make a formal agreement to follow.

August 17, 1982

The People's Republic of China rejects Vietnam's request for a cease-fire in their border war.

The failure of this cease-fire effort resulted in new PRC-Vietnam border skirmishes on September 13, 15, and 18. Border attacks between these two countries had been staged several times since the first in 1979.

August 26, 1982

The United States levies penalties against French companies that export gas pipeline equipment to the Soviet Union.

In accordance with its July 22, 1982 announcement that it would honor technology contracts with Moscow, a French freighter carried three compressors bound for the Soviet Union. In retaliation, the U.S. Commerce Department directed penalties against two French companies that furnished this equipment—the French Dresser subsidiary in Dallas, Texas, and the French-owned Creusot-Loire Company. Other European nations supported the French against the United States. West Germany urged its companies to continue their Soviet sales, and Britain's John Brown Engineering Company shipped three turbines to the Soviets on August 31, 1982. On October 5, President Reagan banned exports of U.S. materials to four U.S. subsidiaries in West Germany. Usually a supporter of Reagan, British Prime Minister Margaret Thatcher telephoned the president to say that 10,000 British jobs were involved in the $182 million Soviet deal for 21 turbines. This factor led Reagan to modify his stand. On September 1, Treasury Secretary Donald Regan said the United States would reduce British sanctions, and President Reagan later announced that the United States would simply prevent violators of the sanctions from buying U.S. oil and gas equipment but not other U.S. products. The United States continued to experience problems on this issue with its NATO allies.

September 8, 1982

A Helsinki Watch group in the Soviet Union disbands because of arrests and deportations.

This group of Soviet dissidents had formed to report on the Soviet Union's fulfillment of the Helsinki Accords. Because Moscow had sent 16 Helsinki Watch members to labor camps or internal exile, only three members remained by 1982.

September 17, 1982

In West Germany, Helmut Schmidt's government collapses when the Free Democrats withdraw support; Helmut Kohl becomes chancellor on October 7.

Schmidt's Social Democrat–Free Democrat coalition had been in office since 1969. His hold on the Free Democrats, a "classical liberal" group, steadily dwindled after 1980 when his health weakened and West Germany's relations with Eastern European countries became difficult because of the issues surrounding the deployment of U.S. Pershing II missiles in West Germany. In addition, the rise of the Green-Alternative List Party created a group that attracted votes from Schmidt's Social Democratic Party (SPD) by emphasizing a mix of pacifist and ecological issues. On October 7, Helmut Kohl of the Christian Democratic Party became chancellor, having obtained the support of the Free Democratic leader, Hans-Dietrich Genscher, who retained the position of foreign minister under Kohl.

September 24, 1982

The United States and other NATO nations withdraw from the International Atomic Energy Conference after Israel is denied a seat.

Secretary of State George Shultz stated that the United States would leave any U.N. agency that voted to exclude Israel from its deliberations; the United States said it would also withhold payment of $8.5 million assessed for the 1982 operations of the Atomic Energy Agency. Not until May 6, 1983, did the United States rejoin this U.N. group.

September 26, 1982

The Atlantic Richfield Oil Company (ARCO) wins a contract to drill for oil off the China coast.

On February 16, 1982, the People's Republic of China announced that bids would be open for oil exploration and production rights in its offshore waters. ARCO, a U.S. company, obtained the right to explore 3,500 square miles of the South China Sea, where experts predicted at least 30 billion barrels of oil could be located. China needed new energy sources to pursue its economic modernization program.

September 27, 1982

U.S. forces land at Beirut.

In line with Reagan's September 21 agreement to send U.S. Marines to join French and Italian forces in a peace-keeping operation, the U.S. Marines arrived to participate in Beirut but their presence had to be gradually enlarged in Lebanon.

See November 1, 1982.

October 8, 1982

Poland bans all trade unions, including Solidarity.

Since August 31, 1982, when demonstrators began celebrating the second anniversary of the founding of the Solidarity trade union, there had been numerous clashes between police and antigovernment groups. Banning the unions, Prime Minister Jaruzelski claimed, was the only way to solve the nation's problems. Solidarity strikes continued, however, and on October 11, the government arrested 148 people. In retaliation for the ban on Solidarity, President Reagan, on October 9, suspended Poland's most-favored-nation trade status, thereby restricting Polish exports to the United States.

October 22, 1982

The National Council of Catholic Bishops proposes a pastoral letter that opposes U.S. nuclear policy.

Titled "The Challenge of Peace" the Catholic bishops issued a statement that had been in preparation since July 1981, and was revised from an initial draft of June 1982. The October 22 draft stated that "stringent limits must be set on the government's use of nuclear weapons." It opposed the first use of nuclear weapons or any use against civilian targets and any concept that proposed to fight a "protracted nuclear war." Deterrence, the bishops said, is justified only if it is a step on the way to progressive nuclear disarmament. They called for a bilateral verifiable freeze on nuclear weapons and a comprehensive test ban treaty. Generally, the bishops' action reflected the widespread concern with President Reagan's harsh anti-Communist policies and his efforts to establish U.S. nuclear superiority. The nuclear freeze movement, which grew in Europe and the United States, led the bishops to issue a statement of the church's moral concern for actions the government took on behalf of its people.

October 22, 1982

The United States and the Marshall Islands conclude an agreement on future relations.

Located in the South Pacific, the Marshall Islands was one of a group of Pacific islands over which the United States held trusteeship after World War II. The Marshalls and the Micronesia Islands gained semi-independent status in 1980, but disputes continued over U.S. nuclear tests that were conducted at the Kwajalein atoll. Islanders demonstrated against missile and antimissile tests conducted in June 1982, and over the visits of U.S. navy ships that carried nuclear weapons. The October 22 agreement included clauses for U.S. payment to the Marshalls of at least $1.5 billion during the next 30 years when tests could be permitted.

October 23, 1982

The Reagan administration voices concern about right-wing activity in El Salvador.

The particular event that stirred President Reagan to criticize El Salvador was the abduction of five key political opponents of Roberto d'Aubuisson, who, since becoming president of El Salvador's Constituent Assembly in April 1982, had ended land reform and was alleged to support paramilitary groups in killing many opponents. Previously, U.S. Ambassador Deane R. Hinton had avoided criticism of the right wing. The abduction of the five non-Communist politicians occurred just after a Salvadoran court freed the army officials accused of killing two American land reform experts on January 3, 1981, saying there was "insufficient evidence" to hold them. On November 17, 1982, Washington saw signs of a slight change in El Salvador when a judge ordered the trial of five national guardsmen accused of killing four American missionaries on December 4, 1980.

October 28, 1982

Spain's Socialist Worker's Party wins control of parliament in a landslide election.

The Socialist victory made Felipe Gonzáles Marques prime minister. On December 16, Gonzáles informed U.S. Secretary of State Shultz that Spain would remain a loyal U.S. ally but that it was halting the integration of its forces into the NATO.

November 1, 1982

President Reagan expands U.S. peacekeeping duties in Lebanon.

Because negotiations for the withdrawal of Israeli and Syrian forces from Lebanon became stymied, Lebanon's President Amin Gemayel requested further assistance from Washington. On November 1, Reagan agreed to undertake army patrol duties in East Beirut. During the remainder of 1982, Reagan added other duties to the U.S. mission in Lebanon: on November 29, Reagan doubled the size of U.S. forces; on December 2, he agreed to rebuild the Lebanese army at a cost of $85 million; and on December 5, he extended the U.S. mission into 1983. Observers saw that U.S. forces were no longer a neutral peacekeeper but a force favoring Gemayel's government, a development opposed by the Muslims.

See November 26, 1982.

November 1, 1982

The Reagan administration states it is supporting covert operations against the Nicaraguan government from Honduran bases.

Following a *Newsweek* magazine report that the U.S. ambassador to Honduras, John D. Negroponte, was in charge of arming and training Nicaraguan exiles to fight the Sandinista regime, the Reagan administration admitted that the CIA assisted these exiles in Honduras. Argentina had helped the Nicaraguan exiles in 1981, but the Falkland Islands War halted aid from Buenos Aires. According to the White House, U.S. aid was not to overthrow the Nicaraguan government but to "keep it off balance" and halt the flow of military aid through Nicaragua to El Salvador's rebels. Thus, under U.S. auspices, Nicaraguan exiles began border skirmishes and hit-and-run raids from Honduras into Nicaragua.

November 2, 1982

In off-year U.S. elections, Democrats gain 26 seats in the House of Representatives; Republicans retain their eight-seat Senate majority; nuclear freeze movement wins.

In addition to the congressional elections, voters showed concern with the Reagan administration's hawkish nuclear policies and failure to promote arms control by approving referenda for a U.S.-Soviet nuclear weapons freeze in eight states, 30 cities, and the District of Columbia.

November 7, 1982

Turkish voters approve a new constitution and elect General Kenan Evren president.

Turkey's republican government ended temporarily in September 1980, when a military junta overthrew it. Although some European countries suspended economic aid to Turkey after the 1980 coup, the United States did not. In January 1982, U.S. Defense Secretary Caspar Weinberger visited Ankara to promise continued U.S. support for Turkey.

November 10, 1982

Soviet President Leonid Brezhnev dies and is replaced by Yuri A. Andropov on November 12.

During his early years in power, 1970–1974, Brezhnev readily dealt with international affairs and negotiations. During these years, Ambassador Dobrynin saw him as a man "eager for peace and accords" but he became a different person during the last years when his health declined and required him to withdraw from the direct shaping of Soviet foreign policy. Vice President George Bush represented the United States at Brezhnev's funeral on November 15.

Andropov was the former KGB head who was critical of Reagan's public attacks on the Soviet Union and thought Reagan would not ready to improve relations with the Soviets. In his memoir Dobrynin recalls that Andropov was "unlucky to get this American president to deal with." Yet Dobyrnin thought Andropov might improve Soviet-American relations because "his intellectual abilities were certainly a cut above those of Brezhnev and Chernenko." Unfortunately, Andropov, like Brezhnev, was in poor health and died on February 9, 1984.

November 11, 1982

Prime Minister Thatcher reveals that a British intelligence officer gave NATO secrets to the Soviet Union.

Margaret Thatcher indicated that Geoffrey Arthur Prime had pleaded guilty to passing secret data to the Soviets from his post at the Government Communications Headquarters. British officials admitted that the information Prime passed on was of "incalculable harm" to U.S. and NATO security interests. Prime was sent to prison for 35 years.

November 13, 1982

President Reagan lifts U.S. sanctions against foreign countries selling pipeline equipment to the USSR.

In applying sanctions against France and Great Britain on August 26 and September 9, Reagan created widespread protest and now had to save face. Britain's Prime Minister Thatcher deserted Reagan and warned that he damaged transatlantic relations in trying to forbid Europeans from shipping pipeline components to the Soviets. In October, Secretary of State George Shultz could not reach a compromise with the Europeans, while at home the Republican minority leader in the House of Representatives, Robert Michel, tried to overturn Reagan's policy because it damaged sales by Caterpillar Tractor Company, which was located in Michel's district.

In withdrawing U.S. sanctions against the European companies, Reagan stated that the allies had reached "substantial agreement" on economic strategy toward Moscow. Nevertheless, France, West Germany, and Great Britain all denied any deal with Washington. To further "save face" for Reagan, on December 13 the U.S. Defense Department warned Austria to stop transferring sensitive technology to the Soviets. On December 14, the United States and France agreed to study economic measures against the Warsaw Pact countries. These talks did not limit either side, but they were conciliatory. While Secretary of State Shultz read a six-point proposal on "realistic" ways to deal with Moscow, French Foreign Minister Claude Cheysson nodded but later said France did not limit its freedom of action on any points.

November 13, 1982

The Vietnam War Memorial is dedicated in Washington.

This monument to 57,939 U.S. soldiers killed or missing in the Vietnam War was intended to help Vietnam veterans receive the respect that they felt had not been previously shown to them.

November 17, 1982

West Germany says it has captured its foremost terrorist suspect, Christian Klar of the Red Army Faction.

The Red Army was the principal terrorist group that had bombed and harassed U.S. military installations and personnel in Europe for over 10 years. Klar's arrest followed the capture of two of his associates in Frankfurt who possessed coded plans of the terrorists. Klar was picked up in woods near Hamburg, where he was digging up an arms cache. Although the Red Army was hurt by the leader's capture, its terrorist activity continued for a while.

November 20, 1982

Leaders of Poland's Solidarity trade union cancel a December protest after Prime Minister Jaruzelski offers conciliatory terms.

Although Poland's martial law continued, Jaruzelski decided early in November to work with Solidarity's leaders by releasing Lech Walesa from internment on November 14. On November 29, he freed another 327 interned protestors. There was a step back toward repression when the Polish government prevented Walesa from delivering a speech in Gdansk, but conciliation continued after the Polish Council of State decreed that martial law would end on December 31, 1982. On December 23, the government released all but seven Solidarity leaders arrested for violating martial law.

November 26, 1982

Palestinian groups backed by Syria announce their opposition to President Reagan's September peace plan.

Pro-Syrian Palestinian leaders who opposed Yasser Arafat's leadership met in Damascus and condemned Reagan's September 1, 1982 plan because it did not recognize the Palestine Liberation Organization as the "sole and legitimate representative of the Palestinian people."

December 3, 1982

The UNESCO Commission on Mass Communications temporarily satisfies the United States and other Western nations regarding Third World censorship, but the dispute renews.

Since 1981, there had been a dispute about news reporting in the United Nations Educational, Scientific, and Cultural Organization (UNESCO). Developing Third World nations wanted to permit their governments to control information given by their media to Western newsmen, claiming that Western reporters held prejudices against their cultures. American delegates to the Communications Commission led other industrialized nations in arguing that government censorship limited free speech. The Reagan administration refused to finance UNESCO media projects but had offered economic aid to help Third World nations develop their own communications networks if they accepted standards of free speech and free press. To satisfy U.S. desires, the Communications Commission, on December 3, offered changes in prior proposals that allowed censorship.

Unfortunately, the changes discussed on December 3 did not prevail very long. On December 10, the U.N. General Assembly adopted a resolution that permitted governments to censor or ban television satellite broadcasts coming from abroad. The U.S. and Western European delegates opposed this decision, but as in the case of UNESCO, Third World delegates had more votes in the assembly. This was one of several disputes that led the United States to withdraw from UNESCO.

December 6–8, 1982

Pakistan's President Zia visits Washington to resolve issues on military aid and nuclear power.

Although the Reagan administration was eager to assist Pakistan as a conduit for aid to the Afghan rebels, the military aid had been in dispute for a year because of allegations that Pakistan was developing a nuclear bomb. At the request of Congress, the CIA made a report in January 1982 that predicted Pakistan would have nuclear weapons by 1985. On January 26, Pakistan's President Muhammad Zia ul-Haq had denied Pakistan was developing nuclear

Reagan meets with Pakistan's President Muhammad Zia ul-Hag. Ronald Reagan Library

weapons, but since the International Atomic Energy Agency had accused him as well of similar intentions, Zia visited Washington from December 6 to 8 to speak with Reagan, members of Congress, and Washington newsmen. Zia said Pakistan wanted nuclear energy only for peaceful purposes. Zia also had to settle misunderstandings about economic and military aid from the United States. The latter agreed that the F-16 planes Pakistan purchased would eventually have the advanced technology on which Zia insisted, and President Reagan confirmed the U.S. commitment to give Pakistan $3.2 billion over five years. Pakistan received its first six F-16 planes on January 15, 1983.

December 9, 1982

Nicaragua blames U.S. aid to the Contra rebels for the deaths of 75 children killed when Contras shoot down a helicopter evacuating Nicaraguans from Honduran border villages.

The helicopter that crashed in northern Nicaragua had been transporting people living in the area where Contras from U.S.-supplied Honduran bases had invaded to burn crops and destroy villages. Nicaragua's pleas for aid against the U.S. threat were partly answered on December 13 when a group of foreign bankers provided Nicaragua with $30 million to help meet payments on its $40 million foreign debt.

December 10, 1982

The United States refuses to sign the Law of the Sea Treaty.

Since taking office in 1981, President Reagan and his administration had opposed the seabed mining provisions of the Law of the Sea Treaty. Subsequent efforts failed to achieve a compromise on the treaty terms when it was voted on in April 1982. President Reagan said he firmly objected to the treaty because, in the terms of conservative *New York Times* columnist William Safire, it violated principles of free enterprise. One hundred seventeen nations signed the treaty. Representatives of Third World nations and U.N. Secretary-General Javier Pérez de Cuellar hailed the treaty as promising great benefits. In addition to regulations on seabed mining, the treaty had provisions on territorial waters, free passage, exclusive economic zones, and the use of straits and the continental shelf.

December 21, 1982

President Reagan signs legislation that prohibits using funds to "overthrow" the Nicaraguan government—the first version of the Boland Amendment.

Even though most members of Congress wanted to stop Nicaraguan aid to the rebels in El Salvador, they also opposed the use of American funds to help the Contra rebels in Nicaragua overthrow their government. Led by Edward P. Boland (D-Mass.) the House of Representatives Select Committee on Intelligence approved legislation in July 1982 that prohibited the CIA or the Department of Defense (DOD) from providing military equipment and training to groups whose purpose was "overthrowing the government of Nicaragua."

The Senate Select Committee on Intelligence also approved this restriction in August 1982. The select committee's prohibition remained secret until December 1982 to protect CIA operations, but after Boland read a November 1, 1982, *Newsweek* article about the CIA's expanding the war against Nicaragua, he confronted CIA director William Casey, who admitted that the Contras had grown from 500 to 4,000 men. Deciding to publicize the committee's amendment, Boland read it to the House on December 8, 1982. It was then incorporated into the 1983 Intelligence Authorization Act and approved by the House in a 411-to-0 vote. After Casey told the Senate committee there was no problem with the amendment, the Senate passed the bill, and President Reagan signed it on December 21, 1982. This amendment became part of the $230 billion military appropriation bill, the largest peacetime military legislation ever approved by Congress.

Casey was playing word games with Congress. Although one member of the Senate Select Committee, Daniel Patrick Moynihan (D-N.Y.), told Casey he expected the CIA to conform to the letter and spirit of the law, Casey used the ambiguity of the statement "to overthrow the government" to continue secret aid to the Contras, contending that the Contras' purpose was to harass the government, not overthrow it.

After consulting CIA lawyers, Casey instructed CIA agents to warn Contra leaders against the term "overthrow the government" and to denounce any Contra leader who publicly used those words. According to Casey, the Contra purpose should be called harassment, destabilization, interdicting arms to El Salvador, or "causing problems" for the Sandinista government.

December 21, 1982

President Reagan agrees to compromise on the MX missile.

Since Reagan announced on October 2, 1981, that the MX would be deployed in silos, not in a more protected underground track system, the president and congressional leaders argued over the program for the new U.S. intercontinental ballistic missile system. At the request of Congress, the U.S. air force on November 4, 1982, had presented plans for a "dense pack" deployment of the MX in Wyoming. The 100 MXs initially would be spaced 1,800 feet apart in Minuteman missile silos hardened to withstand a pressure of 10,000 pounds per square mile. Located within an area 1.5 meters wide and 14 miles long, the air force calculated that the first Soviet missile to explode would result in "fratricide," causing later Soviet missiles to destroy themselves before hitting other MX silos. They estimated that 50 U.S. missiles would survive and be fired as a retaliatory strike on the Soviet Union. Many experts disputed the air force scenario, arguing that the dense pack sacrificed survivability and claiming such deployment made the MX a first-strike weapon, not a retaliatory deterrent. As the dispute over MX deployment continued, President Reagan made a television speech on November 22 to defend the dense pack deployment as a survivable defensive weapon, which he had renamed "Peacemaker." The new MX name never caught on, however; Congress remained convinced that its first-strike potential raised the risk of nuclear war. Between December 17 and 20, Congress and the White House compromised on MX funding. Congress authorized $2.5 billion for research and development of the missile but eliminated production funds until it could approve a satisfactory basing plan. Reagan also appointed a special committee to study the MX basing problem before funds for production would be provided in 1984.

1983

January 8, 1983

The Contadora process begins as foreign ministers of four Latin American nations meet on Panama's Contadora Island to seek a peaceful end to conflicts in El Salvador and Nicaragua.

The nations sponsoring this peace process were Mexico, Venezuela, Colombia, and Panama. The Contadora Initiative gained great respect during the next several years, as diplomats from the four nations negotiated treaties within Central America to try to demilitarize the region and reconcile warring factions. It rejected President Reagan's view of its troubles as being fomented by the Soviet Union.

January 12, 1983

President Reagan's dismissal of Eugene Rostow as arms control director indicates influence of opponents in the White House.

Rostow was selected as director of the Arms Control and Disarmament Agency in 1981 because he was perceived as an opponent of all arms control agreements and would prevent Secretary of State Alexander Haig from compromising with Moscow. By the end of 1982, however, Rostow had incurred the dislike of Reagan and National Security Adviser William Clark because he was not a member of the president's California team and treated them like "not-very-bright" law students. In addition, Rostow now favored Paul Nitze's, Reagan's ambassador for long-range theater nuclear force negotiations, desire for firm but flexible arms control agreements with the Soviets—a position that other hawkish advisers of Reagan opposed. Consequently, when Rostow did not resign after the White House withdrew its support for Senate confirmation of Robert T. Grey as Rostow's deputy, Clark and Reagan decided to fire Rostow and nominate Kenneth Adelman, a known opponent of arms control. After the Senate Foreign Relations Committee rejected Adelman's nomination, Reagan lobbied hard to gain the Senate's approval for Adelman on April 14, 1983.

January 14, 1983

President Reagan secretly approves covert action by the National Security Council to promote Project Democracy.

Project Democracy had been announced by Reagan in a June 8, 1982, speech to the British Parliament. While the project's public side was funded by Congress on November 22, 1983, as the National Endowment for Democracy, its unannounced covert side was placed under the NSC by a document that Congress declassified as part of the Iran-Contra scandal in 1987. National Security Decision Directive 77 of January 14, 1983, was titled "Management of Public Diplomacy Relative to National Security." It set up several planning groups for "public diplomacy" that would support the growth of democratic institutions by foreign governments and private groups. While some NSC teams planned propaganda to promote anti-Communist groups such as the Nicaraguan rebels by planting stories in the press, other groups planned secret action to counter activity by the Soviet Union or its surrogates. Finally, one NSC team sought funds from private individuals or foreign governments to finance U.S. covert activity.

In October 1983, NSC Adviser Robert C. Mc Farlane appointed Lt. Col. Oliver L. North to head Project Democracy's covert arm. During the 1987 Iran-Contra hearings, Congress learned that taxpayer financing for Project Democracy was partly used by North for aid to the Nicaraguan Contras from 1984 to 1986.

January 15, 1983

The *New York Times* publishes the story of "walk in the woods" missile agreement between Paul Nitze and the Soviet negotiator, Yuli Kvitsinsky.

According to a news report leaked by Arms Control Director Eugene Rostow to Strobe Talbott for a *New York Time* magazine, Nitze and Kvitsinsky had concluded an informal "understanding" to limit medium-range missiles during a July 1982 private walk in the woods away from other delegates and "bugging" devices in Geneva. The two diplomats proposed a package deal by which the Soviets would reduce their SS-20s by two-thirds, giving them 75 SS-20s with 225 warheads; the United States would deploy no Pershing IIs but could deploy 75 Tomahawk cruise missiles with 300 warheads. When the two negotiators returned to their homes, however, neither the Reagan administration nor the Soviet leadership accepted the proposal. If accepted, the medium-range missile problem would have been resolved, and the deployment of U.S. missiles in Europe would cease. When negotiations began again in Geneva on January 27, 1983, the United States returned to its earlier "zero-option" and the USSR to its earlier plans for a nuclear-free central Europe.

January 17, 1983

Radical PLO factions reject President Reagan's September 1982 Middle East peace plan, but they disagree on other matters.

Following PLO leader Yasser Arafat's eviction from Lebanon in August 1982, anti-Arafat PLO groups secured help from Syria and Libya. Eventually, these groups became divided, but at Tripoli, Libya, they agreed in January 1983 to oppose Reagan's plan for the PLO and the "Jordanian solution" to the West Bank conflict.

January 19, 1983

Japanese Prime Minister Yasuhiro Nakasone visits the United States to discuss Japanese trade barriers and possible Japanese rearmament.

Since occupying the White House, the Reagan administration had made only slight headway in prodding Japan to loosen its trade restrictions and to spend more on defense. Before leaving Tokyo, Nakasone announced on January 13 that he would liberalize import restrictions on automobiles, pharmaceuticals, and other products. In practice, however, most American businesspeople had found that such orders did not effectively permit foreign competition in Japan.

In defense matters, Nakasone promised the president he would increase Japan's military budget and begin to share responsibility with the United States for the surveillance of Soviet planes and ships in the vicinity of the Japanese islands. As part of this promise, on February 8 Nakasone risked public displeasure in Japan by allowing nuclear-powered U.S. aircraft carriers to dock in Japanese harbors.

January 20, 1983

French President François Mitterrand and West German Chancellor Helmut Kohl reaffirm support for the Atlantic Alliance.

Mitterrand and Kohl met in Bonn to celebrate the twentieth anniversary of the French-German Friendship Treaty. During their meeting, they pledged to continue support of the Atlantic Alliance and warned others (i.e., the Soviet Union) not to try to split the friendship between the United States and Western Europe. Their statement solidified support for NATO's dual-track policy of preparing to deploy Pershing II missiles by the end of 1983 if U.S.-Soviet intermediate-range arms control talks did not succeed. On March 23, 1983, NATO's defense ministers also confirmed the dual-track policy.

January 21, 1983

President Reagan certifies El Salvador's progress in protecting human rights to make that nation eligible for U.S. economic aid.

For many observers, meeting the congressional requirement that nations receiving U.S. aid be certified by the president as protecting human rights was difficult to judge. An American medical team had recently visited El Salvador and found numerous human rights violations. Other groups concurred that there were violations. Nevertheless, by certifying that the Salvadorans had made progress, Reagan could ignore contrary findings and send the $60 million in aid that Congress appropriated in 1982. The president made a similar certification on July 20, 1983, to obtain more funding for El Salvador.

February 1, 1983

U.S. forces stage "war games" with Honduran forces in Central America—Operation Big Pine; Nicaragua protests.

U.S. military advisers had begun using Honduras as a supply and training base for the army of El Salvador and for Nicaraguan exiles who raided across the border against Nicaragua's Sandinista government. The 1983 war games involved over 6,000 troops, the largest such exercise ever held in Central America. Claiming that the exiles entered their country and killed 192 people during January, Nicaragua protested the war games and on March 23, 1983, complained to the United Nations, where it accused Washington of plotting to overthrow the Sandinista government. The Reagan administration ignored Nicaragua's protests and on July 20, 1983, announced new military exercises with Honduras.

These 1983 exercises were a culmination of U.S. aid provided to the Nicaraguan rebels through Honduras since 1981. In return for U.S. economic aid of $30 million in 1982, Honduras allowed the United States to train and supply the Nicaraguan rebels. The United States also "loaned" Honduras a fleet of 23 helicopters and other aircraft.

February 4, 1983

U.S. delegates at the U.N. Committee on Disarmament propose a ban on chemical weapons.

At the Geneva meeting of the U.N. Disarmament Committee, Vice President George H.W. Bush announced what the U.S. State Department called a "new initiative in the field" by describing the details for an effective weapons ban. The principal parts of the proposal were the following:

1. Systematic on-site inspection of chemical weapons stocks, production facilities, and plans to destroy stocks.
2. Inspection of the destruction of stock and production facilities.
3. Inspection of facilities for legal chemical production that could be diverted to weapons production.
4. A multilateral complaint mechanism for compliance issues.

The U.S. specifically objected to Soviet "self-inspection" proposals or to suggestions that satellite photography could do the job, because clandestine production could occur without being detected. As was frequently the case, the inspection issue sidetracked progress for four years. By the spring of 1987, the Soviets came to accept the idea of "quick challenge" inspections, while Americans modified their demand for "anywhere, anytime" inspections.

February 6, 1983

Secretary of State George Shultz concludes a four-day visit to China.

During its first two years, the Reagan administration experienced difficulties with the People's Republic of

China (PRC) because the president had been a staunch opponent of "Red" China throughout his political career. While the most serious issues between the two countries related to U.S. aid to Taiwan (Republic of China [ROC]) and mainland China's textile exports, other issues developed over minor affairs such as the "refugee status" of tennis star Hu Na and the attempts of nine American soldiers to obtain $41.3 million through U.S. courts to repay them for defaulting 1911 Imperial Chinese Railroad bonds. On February 10, 1983, a U.S. district court ordered The People's Republic of China to pay these bondholders.

Shultz's visit did not resolve any problems but clarified U.S. policy by indicating the Reagan administration would not stop its economic and military aid to Taiwan but might gradually reduce Taiwan's military aid if the PRC maintained friendly relations with America. In response to Shultz's question about China's relations with the Soviet Union, Chinese Communist Party Chairman Deng Xiaoping agreed to cooperate with the United States against Soviet aggression in Cambodia and Afghanistan.

February 8, 1983

Opening session of the Second Conference on Security and Cooperation in Europe begins in Madrid, Spain.

The most significant outcome of this meeting was an agreement between delegates of the NATO and Warsaw Pact nations to go beyond the 1975 Helsinki Final Act. The Final Act emphasized secure national borders and human rights as confidence-building measures (CBMs). Additional measures to reduce tension required binding, verifiable constraints on military movements, or a nonaggression treaty such as the Warsaw Pact nations proposed on January 5, 1983. At Madrid, 35 European nations plus Canada and the United States agreed to negotiate military CBMs and to meet in Stockholm in 1984 to conclude such measures.

February 8, 1983

The Israeli commission that investigated the September 1982 massacres at Sabra and Shatila reports that Defense Minister Sharon and three officers were guilty of not fulfilling their duties.

Chaired by Israel's Supreme Court President Yitzchak Kahan, the commission reported that the Christian Phalangist forces were directly responsible for the slaughters at the PLO refugee camps. However, high-ranking Israeli officials had general control over the region and their "indirect responsibility cannot be disregarded" since they were responsible for safety and public order. Sharon's responsibilities were greater and his "blunders constitute the nonfulfillment of duties." Sharon was not contrite. He denounced the Kahan report and claimed to be a martyr of insidious American plots to implement the Reagan plan for removing Israel from the West Bank and Gaza.

February 10, 1983

The Soviet Union withdraws from the World Psychiatric Association.

The Soviet delegates expected to be expelled as the result of an investigation by the association into allegations that Soviet psychiatrists used their professional position for political purposes. Although the issue was not voted upon and many members preferred to maintain contacts with their Soviet counterparts, the Soviet members decided to avoid further criticism. The Cuban and Bulgarian psychiatrists also withdrew. To critics of Soviet psychiatry, an incident in the spring of 1983 verified their claims of the political use of psychiatry. On May 28, Vladimir Danchev, a Moscow radio announcer, was fired because he criticized Soviet action in Afghanistan. On June 22, 1983, Danchev was committed to a psychiatric hospital for treatment. The Soviet Union remained out of the World Psychiatric Association until September 1989, when the Soviet group was given probationary membership.

February 18, 1983

Petroleum price war is stimulated when the British National Oil Corporation cuts prices by $3.00 per barrel to $30.50.

Throughout 1982, the Organization of Petroleum Exporting Countries (OPEC) had difficulty in maintaining prices at $34.00 per barrel. On March 14, OPEC negotiators agreed to cut prices to $29 per barrel and to limit their 1983 production to 17.5 million barrels per day, an action OPEC members endorsed on June 18.

February 25, 1983

An El Salvador peace commission is formed to urge all social and political sectors to participate in the democratic process to solve their nation's problems.

President Alvara Magana appointed this peace commission to prepare amnesty laws that might persuade left-wing guerrilla forces to end their opposition to the government. Members of the commission were the bishop of Santiago de Mariá, Rene Revelo; former foreign minister of El Salvador, José Trabanino; and a Populist Party leader, Francisco Quinonez. The peace commission's creation had been stalled by right-wing members of Roberto d'Aubuisson's National Republican Alliance (ARENA), which formed a coalition in March 1982 to control the Constituent Assembly. President Magana had joined with assembly moderates in January to cut back ARENA's power and demonstrate to the United States that the right-wing's notorious death squads might be controlled. On January 27, eight conservatives had defected from d'Aubuisson's coalition to vote with the Christian Democratic minority to limit ARENA's power. The moderates passed laws preventing ARENA from vetoing assembly decisions of which d'Aubuisson disapproved and abolishing d'Aubuisson's right to set the assembly's agenda. Magana's appointment of the peace commission intended to prepare methods for ending the civil war with the guerrillas.

March 5, 1983

The Australian Labor Party gains a parliamentary majority in elections; its leader, Robert Hawke, replaces the Liberal Party's Malcolm Fraser.

During the election, one of Hawke's principal platforms was to reevaluate the ANZUS Treaty regarding Australia's right to prohibit U.S. navy ships carrying nuclear weapons from visiting Australian ports under the ANZUS treaty.

March 6, 1983

Helmut Kohl's victory in West German elections solidifies his position as chancellor.

Kohl had succeeded Social Democrat Helmut Schmidt as chancellor in October 1982, and formed a Bundestag (lower house) coalition with the Free Democrats. In the March 6 elections, Kohl's Christian Democrats (CD) won 244 seats in the 498-member Bundestag; the Social Democrats won only 193 seats; the Free Democrats and minor parties, 34 seats; and the new left-wing Green-Alternative List, 27 seats. Kohl's CDs and the Free Democrats had sufficient votes to control proceedings in the Bundestag.

March 8, 1983

President Reagan tells a convention of Evangelical Christians that the Soviet Union is an "Evil Empire," the "focus of evil in the modern world."

Among various Christian organizations in the United States, the Evangelicals were recognized as the most conservative, right-wing group whose theology required that born-again Christians hate Communism as the Antichrist of the twentieth century. These groups promoted President Reagan's revival of Cold War antagonisms and desired to make the United States militarily superior to the USSR. Reagan's March 8 speech became known for its most virulent attack on the Soviet Union. It came just after a State Department report of February 14, 1983, contended that there were 4 million forced laborers in the Soviet Union, at least 10,000 of whom were religious or political prisoners. It came the day before the U.S. Defense Department released a booklet, "Soviet Military Power," that, claiming Soviet power was superior, said the United States had "begun to catch up" but was five years away from equality with the USSR. The Defense Department's report was criticized by many informed observers for using questionable data.

March 10, 1983

The United States redefines the International Law of the Sea Treaty.

After the Reagan administration rejected the 1982 Law of the Sea Treaty, the president unilaterally defined the rights of U.S. nationals for exploration of the seabed. The administration proclaimed the country had an exclusive zone to use all seabed resources up to 200 miles from U.S. coastlines.

March 10, 1983

Andropov reiterates support for the Soviet intervention in Afghanistan.

When Yuri Andropov assumed power in November 1982, President Reagan and other Western leaders hoped the Soviets would soften their stance on Afghanistan and negotiate the Red Army's withdrawal from that country. These hopes were negated on March 10 when Andropov denounced other nations for interfering with Moscow's attempt to stabilize Afghan's government. Andropov told the Politburo that "We are fighting against American imperialism which well understands that in this part of international politics it has lost its position. That is why we cannot back off." Obviously, the Soviets preferred to continue their intervention.

March 12, 1983

The convention of 101 nonaligned Third World nations issues a report that criticizes U.S. policy in Central America and urges economic assistance to Third World nations.

Meeting in New Delhi, India, the final declarations from this summit moved away from the pro-Soviet statements made during the 1979 sessions in Havana, Cuba. Chaired by Indian Prime Minister Indira Gandhi, the 1983 meeting emphasized the Third World's need for economic aid, urging both Moscow and Washington to stop the nuclear arms race. The group did, however, criticize U.S. policy in Central America and its support of South Africa in delaying independence for Namibia.

March 23, 1983

After President Reagan criticizes the Soviet militarization of Grenada, Grenada's prime minister charges the United States plans to overthrow his government.

President Reagan's speech to the National Association of Manufacturers emphasized the U.S. need to counter the Soviet threat in the Caribbean and Central America. He asserted that the Cuban-Soviet alliance was acting aggressively in the Caribbean, and he charged that the two Communist nations had financed the building of a 10,000-foot runway on the island of Grenada. Because Grenada had no air force, the president argued, the large airport was evidence of a Communist power projection "unrelated to any conceivable threat" to Grenada. Following the address, several American commentators noted that the airport was part of Grenada's plans to attract tourists, a recommendation of the European Economic Community in 1982 when it granted Grenada $16 million to boost its economy. The airfield compared to runways on Caribbean islands such as Aruba. Alarmed at the possibility of a U.S. attack, Prime Minister Maurice Bishop called the small Grenada army to full alert. Bishop's New Jewel Movement had gained control of Grenada's government in 1979 by overthrowing the military dictatorship of Eric Gairy, who fled to the United States, from whence he sought support for a return to power. The March 23 incident was hardly noticed in the United States, until President Reagan ordered an invasion of Grenada.

March 23, 1983

President Reagan calls for a strategic defense initiative (SDI) to permit the United States to defend itself from all Soviet intercontinental ballistic missiles: "star wars."

Coming about three weeks before a presidential commission on the MX missile reported that the "window of vulnerability" of U.S. defenses had never existed, President Reagan's speech transformed the 1982 disputes over the MX deployment to disputes over the viability of an SDI that might create what Reagan called a "dome-like protective umbrella to ward off Soviet nuclear warheads." Reagan's dramatic speech added the SDI to subsequent arms negotiations during his presidency. Originally known as an antiballistic missile defense (ABM), or a ballistic missile defense (BMD) system, the concept of missile protection had been considered since the 1950s. After the 1972 ABM treaty between the United States and the USSR restricted missile defense because it destabilized the practice of mutual assured destruction (MAD), slight public attention was given to the issue of missile defenses. Both sides conducted research and development of BMD as permitted by the 1972 treaty. In addition, while the 1972 agreement permitted each side to build one ABM site, the United States did not build its site.

Initial reports about Reagan's SDI decision focused on the role of Edward Teller, a Hungarian born physicist who had worked on nuclear weapons

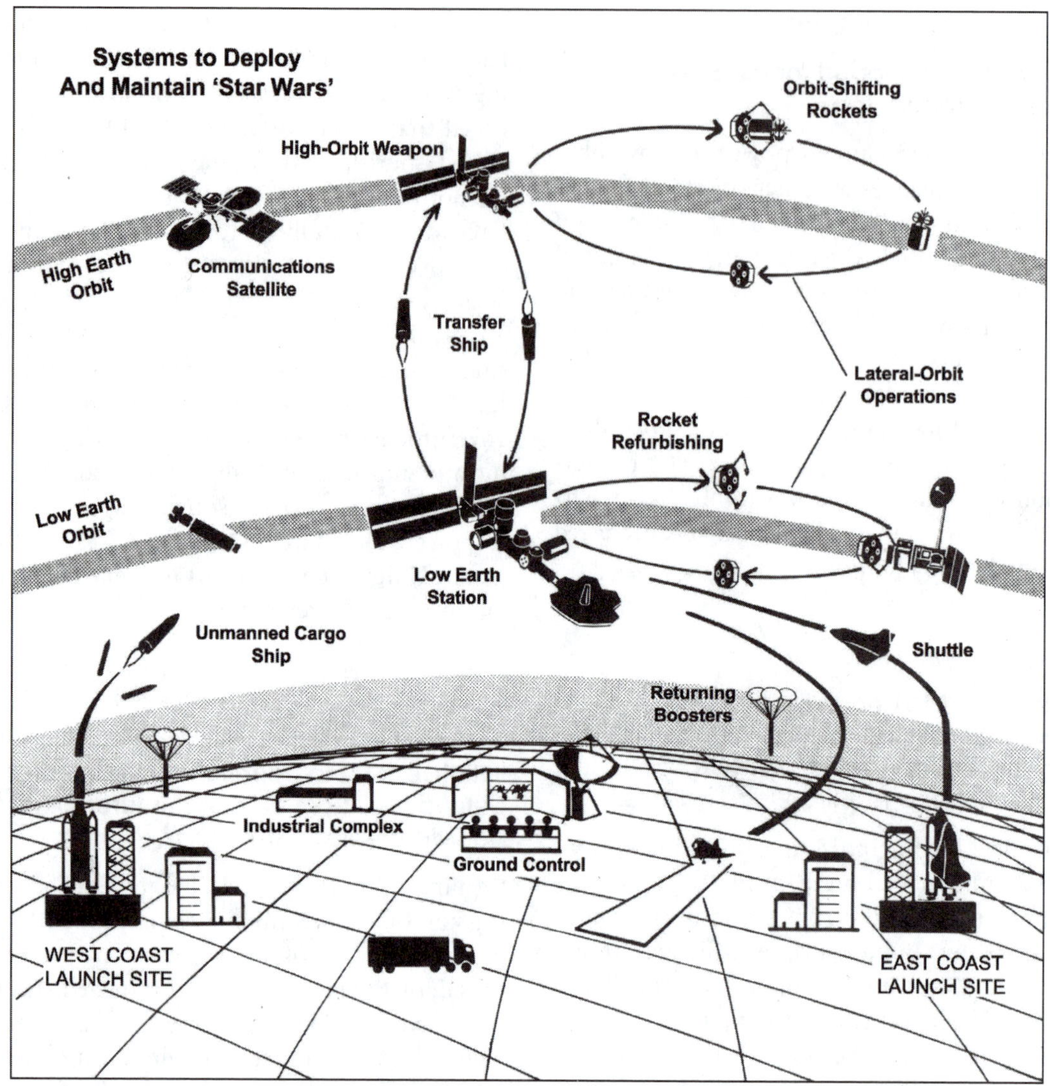

after World War II and who was a prominent scientist at California's Lawrence Livermore Laboratory. In contrast, Frances Fitzgerald's *Way Out There in the Blue* (2000) examined many early reports before concluding that neither the Livermore Laboratory, the State Department, Defense Department, nor the Joint Chiefs of Staff knew that President Reagan had tailored his March 23 speech to elicit a favorable response from his television audience. During the day before his 8:00 P.M. speech, Reagan made extensive changes in the draft written by his science adviser, George Keyworth. After deleting several phrases such as "no near-term panaceas," Reagan emphasized why the U.S. arms buildup was necessary. His speech ended with "I call upon the scientific community in this country, who gave us nuclear weapons, to turn their great talents to the cause of mankind and world peace, to give us the means of rendering these weapons impotent and obsolete."

Making nuclear weapons obsolete was precisely what most Americans wanted, especially those who found it difficult to interpret the complexities of nuclear arms control, which included esoteric terms such as SALT I, Anti-Ballistic Missile Treaty, and "nuclear war-fighting." On March 26, Michael Deaver, the White House deputy chief of staff, told Soviet Ambassador Anatoly Dobrynin that the SDI speech was simply a campaign effort to neutralize the nuclear threat by blunting Democrats who "attacked Reagan as a warmonger." In contrast, Secretary of

State George Shultz, Defense Secretary Caspar Weinberger, and Edward Teller disliked Reagan's edited speech but did not express their dissatisfaction to the president. Nevertheless, Reagan's March 23 speech captured wide public attention, resulting in ongoing scientific disputes about SDI's viability. While SDI might have some future potential to defend U.S. missiles from a first strike, this moderate concept became blurred by the Reagan administration's bloated claims that it had found a perfect way to defend the country from nuclear attack.

Thus, Reagan's SDI proposal preempted the problem of the United States making the MX a retaliatory second-strike weapon as proposed by a commission appointed by President Reagan in December 1982 and chaired by Brent Scowcroft to study the MX basing problem. In addition, it gave Reagan another card in the arms control game with the Soviet Union. The Soviets believed SDI was part of Reagan's effort to gain U.S. nuclear superiority for a first nuclear strike.

March 30, 1983

New U.S. proposals to limit intermediate-range missiles are offered in Geneva; the Soviets reject them.

To show America's NATO allies U.S. flexibility in seeking an agreement with the USSR, President Reagan had U.S. delegates propose an interim solution at Geneva on March 29, which he announced publicly on March 30, 1983. The White House also exchanged letters with West German Chancellor Helmut Kohl, British Prime Minister Margaret Thatcher, and other NATO leaders before making the proposal. The essence of the interim proposal was to begin cutting intermediate-range missiles by reducing Soviet SS-20s to a level of equality with the number of Pershing or cruise missiles NATO would deploy. Next, the Soviets would cut their worldwide deployment of intermediate-range missiles, which numbered 572, and the United States would match that number. Most crucial was that the new U.S. position involved global intermediate-range limits of U.S. and Soviet missiles, not just European-based missiles. On April 2, Soviet Foreign Minister Andrei Gromyko rejected the U.S. proposal because it did not allay Soviet concerns regarding French and British missiles capable of hitting Soviet territory and treated Asian missiles as part of European arms control without involving Chinese missiles. In the Soviet view, any missile capable of reaching the Soviet homeland would have destructive results, whatever its point of origin. The United States had no comparable non-Soviet intermediate-range threat to its home territory. Deployment of the Pershing IIs in Europe was, therefore, what the Soviets desired to prevent.

March 31, 1983

Vietnamese forces attack a Kampuchean refugee camp in Thailand, killing 200 civilians and five Thai soldiers.

In the Vietnamese-Cambodian War, Hanoi's forces had driven the Khmer Rouge armies to the border, where an estimated 45,000 Cambodian refugees had crossed into Thailand. Claiming that many of the Khmer Rouge army personnel were among the refugees, the Vietnamese staged this attack into Thailand. Thailand retaliated by bombarding Vietnamese positions in Cambodia, but more Vietnamese raids were expected. As an ally of Thailand, the United States sent additional military aid to that country on April 4, but there were no further large-scale Vietnamese attacks during 1983.

April 7, 1983

After the United States grants asylum to Chinese tennis star Hu Na, the People's Republic of China (PRC) cancels its sports and cultural exchanges with the United States for 1983.

During a 1982 Chinese tennis tour in California, Hu Na left her hotel and hid in a friend's house from Chinese authorities. The Chinese protested against her request for political asylum, and for eight months the Reagan administration delayed a decision. Although various U.S. groups supported Hu Na's request, the State Department did not want to damage relations with China, which were already tense over U.S. arms sales to Taiwan. Beijing would grant her immigration status but refused to concede that Hu Na had fled because of political persecution. Nevertheless, Washington decided to give Hu Na asylum. China retaliated by canceling 19 sports and cultural agreements planned with Americans for 1983. Despite the disagreements, President Reagan accepted the diplomatic credentials of China's new ambassador, Zhang Wenjin, on April 8, 1982.

April 9, 1983

The U.S. space shuttle Challenger has its first successful space flight.

The flight included time for the crew to have a four-hour space walk. One problem was encountered when a giant communications satellite that the shuttle deployed went out of control and had to be stabilized from the ground. The second Challenger flight took place on June 18, carrying the nation's first female astronaut, Sally K. Ride.

April 11, 1983

A presidential commission on the MX missile offers recommendations.

The Scowcroft Commission, named after its chairman General (retired) Brent Scowcroft, was appointed by President Reagan in accordance with an agreement with Congress on December 17, 1982. The Commission members were former Secretaries of State Henry Kissinger and Alexander Haig; six former Defense Department secretaries or undersecretaries, including James Schlesinger, Harold Brown, Melvin Laird, Donald Rumsfeld, William Perry, and William Clements; former CIA directors Richard Helms and John McCone; White House insider Thomas Reed; Massachusetts Institute of Technology scientist John Deutch; retired Vice Admiral Levering Smith; and the vice president of the American Federation of Labor, John Lyons.

The commission report denied that the 1970s arms control treaties would create a "window of vulnerability" during the mid-1980s, a claim made by President Reagan during the 1980 presidential election. Nevertheless, because the MX was nearly ready to be deployed, its use should be as a temporary weapon to prevent a Soviet attack. After deploying the first 100 MX missiles in silos, however, the commission wanted to deploy small Midgetman missiles carrying one warhead each, because they would be mobile and, therefore, better able to survive a first strike and act as a second-strike retaliatory force. The commission indicated that the Midgetman development and deployment would require at least 10 years and would cost about $40 billion to $50 billion. The Scowcroft report convinced Congress to release $625 million for the MX on May 25, 1983. On June 17, the MX had its first successful test launch.

April 15, 1983

A Sandinista war hero, Eden Pastora Gómez, announces plans to overthrow the Sandinista junta of Daniel Ortega.

Pastora was the legendary Commander Zero, who in August 1978, led the rebel unit that captured the National Palace in Managua, an event leading to the overthrow of the Somoza regime and the Sandinista victory. Pastora served as vice minister of defense in the Sandinista government until April 15, 1982, when he resigned in opposition to Ortega's Communist policies. He and Alfonso Robelo Callejas cofounded the Democratic Revolutionary Alliance (ARDE), which opposed Ortega. Organizing his rebel force, the Sandino Revolutionary Front (FRS) in southern Nicaragua, Pastora announced the start of a war of liberation. The "Contra group" of rebels, which had gained most of Washington's support, was based in northern Nicaragua and Honduras. Called the Nicaraguan Democratic Front, it was headed by Enrique Bermudez. Pastora disapproved of this rebel group because it had too many army officers from the Somoza regime.

April 18, 1983

Terrorists bomb the U.S. embassy in Beirut; 63 persons are killed, including 17 Americans.

A pro-Iranian Muslim faction claimed responsibility for this attack, which was well planned and targeted to alarm not only Americans but also those in Beirut who believed the United States guaranteed their security. About one-half of the Americans killed were CIA agents, including Robert C. Ames, the agency's principal Middle East analyst.

April 20, 1983

Brazilian authorities impound arms headed for Nicaragua aboard a Libyan cargo aircraft.

Planes flying from Libya landed to refuel in Brazil, where customs officials discovered arms that were not on the cargo list. Brazil unloaded the armaments, released the crew, and, on June 8, agreed to return the aircraft to Libya. The United States claimed that the military items came originally from the Soviet Union and, therefore, substantiated U.S. contentions that the Sandinistas were assisted by the Soviets.

May 3, 1983

Congress challenges President Reagan's Central American policy.

Disagreeing with the president's emphasis on a military solution to problems in Nicaragua and El Salvador, the House Permanent Select Committee on Intelligence on May 3 approved legislation to ban covert aid to the Nicaraguan rebels. Because the Senate Intelligence Committee wanted to aid the Contras, the two committees compromised by giving $19 million of the $36 million requested. The joint congressional committee also approved $80 million of covert aid to any friendly Central American country willing to help the United States stop Cuban arms shipments to Nicaragua or El Salvador. To secure the congressional compromise, President Reagan appointed Richard Stone, a former Democratic Senator from Florida, as a special envoy to visit Central America to seek peace negotiations and endorsed the Contadora Group's efforts to obtain peace. Reagan also agreed to appoint a special commission headed by Henry Kissinger to study U.S. policy in Latin America, especially focusing on Central America. Secretary of State George Shultz hoped the Kissinger Commission would provide Congress with a positive statement about Reagan's policy in Central America before Congress adjourned in 1983, but the Commission's work was not completed until January 1984.

May 6, 1983

U.S. representative returns to International Atomic Energy Agency (IAEA) meeting after Israel's membership is certified.

On September 24, 1982, U.S. delegate Richard T. Kennedy and several Western European delegates walked out of the IAEA meeting in Vienna after delegates voted 41–39 to expel Israel from the IAEA. African and Arab delegates to the IAEA had joined ranks in voting against Israel, claiming Israel violated IAEA guidelines by refusing to let IAEA inspectors examine all of its nuclear energy facilities, a claim Israel denied. On October 16, Secretary of State George Shultz commended Kennedy's decision to leave the IAEA meeting, adding the United States was withholding $8.5 million scheduled to be paid to the IAEA during 1982. Shultz also asked Kennedy to form a committee to thoroughly review U.S. membership in the IAEA. After the reassessment was completed in January 1983, Kennedy reported to Shultz that the IAEA played a key role in international relations by regulating nuclear energy facilities and preventing the proliferation of nuclear weapons in other countries.

The report concluded that some IAEA delegates damaged the IAEA's reputation by politicizing meetings such as that held in September 1982. The United States should not tolerate those who sought to play politics during IAEA meetings. After this report was made public, Kennedy met with IAEA Director General Hans Blix on February 22, 1983, and Blix agreed to certify Israel's membership at the next IAEA meeting. On May 6, 1983, Blix's promise was confirmed at the IAEA's general meeting. Following this action, Israeli, American, and all Western European delegates once again attended the IAEA sessions. Infact, Israel had developed nuclear weapons at secret locations not on the IAEA's list of nuclear sites.

See October 5, 1986.

May 10, 1983

President Reagan cuts Nicaragua's sugar quotas by 90 percent.

To punish the Sandinistas for what Reagan called "subversion and violence," the United States reduced its sugar imports from Nicaragua to 6,000 short tons from its current annual quota of 56,800 tons. Reagan indicated that this would reduce the Sandinistas' ability to support subversion in El Salvador. Managua's government said the reduction cost it $54 million and appealed to the Council of the General Agreement on Tariffs and Trade (GATT), claiming that the United States violated its treaty.

May 15, 1983

Japan seeks trade relations with both Koreas, welcoming a North Korean delegation to Tokyo.

As a first step toward better Japanese relations with Communist North Korea, North Korean judges visited Tokyo for an international judicial meeting. Japan made it a ceremonial occasion to impress the North Koreans with their goodwill. On January 11, 1983, Japan's interest in South Korea was demonstrated when Prime Minister Yasuhiro Nakasone visited Seoul, becoming the first Japanese leader to visit Korea since 1945.

May 27, 1983

The U.S. State Department removes two moderate diplomats from important positions in Central American affairs.

Thomas Enders, the Assistant Secretary of State for Inter-American Affairs, and Deane Hinton, the U.S. Ambassador to El Salvador, were replaced respectively on May 27 and June 2, 1983. Secretary of State George Shultz approved their dismissal in an attempt to prevent National Security Adviser William Clark from gaining control over policy making for Central America. In accordance with State Department policy in 1981, Enders and Hinton pursued a dual-track policy of persuading Central America to accept peaceful solutions to their problems. Using the dual-track, Enders proposed negotiations to solve disputes but employed the threat of possible U.S. military action as an incentive to enable diplomacy to resolve problems in El Salvador, Nicaragua, Honduras, and Guatemala.

On October 2, 1982, Enders organized a forum of Central American leaders in San Jose, Costa Rica, to discuss peaceful ways to resolve their mutual problems. Forum members prepared the San Jose Declaration, which called for each Central American country to create and maintain democratic governments based on the people's will as expressed in free and regular elections. The declaration also said each country should prevent the use of its territory to support, supply or train "terrorist or subversive elements" aimed at the overthrow of another government. According to Secretary Shultz's memoir, the San Jose principals were controversial among the Sandinistas and their supporters but were also opposed by CIA Director William Casey and "hard-liners on the NSC staff," including William Clark. Subsequently, Clark told President Reagan that Enders must be removed from his State Department position. Clark's opinion gained support from U.S. Ambassador to the United Nations Jeanne Kirkpatrick and from Casey, both of whom claimed Enders was "soft on communism."

Clark and Kirkpatrick advocated military and CIA action to aid the right-wing government of El Salvador and to send military and financial aid to Nicaragua's Contra rebels, who fought against the left-wing Sandinista government of Nicaragua that gained control in 1979 elections. (See July 17, 1979) Hoping to regain control of policy in Central America, Shultz tried to satisfy Clark by replacing Enders with Langhorne Anthony Motley, who was Ambassador to Brazil, and by designating Enders ambassador to Spain. As for Hinton, Clark and Casey claimed that his reports about the murders committed by men affiliated with El Salvador's government demonstrated Hinton's inability to support U.S. policy of assisting the government's campaign to defeat left-wing rebels supported by Cuban and Soviet Communists. (See October 23, 1982 and November 12, 1983) To satisfy Clark, Shultz replaced Hinton with Thomas Pickering, who was ambassador to Nigeria; Hinton became ambassador to Panama.

May 28, 1983

Leaders of seven major industrial nations hold annual summit at Williamsburg, Virginia.

This summit meeting of the leaders of the United States, Great Britain, Canada, France, West Germany, Italy, and Japan ended with no concrete results. Under pressure from the other six leaders, President Reagan agreed to some flexibility in arms control discussions with the USSR, and in return, the European leaders would deploy U.S. Pershing II and cruise missiles if no agreement were reached. On the economic front, the group's final communiqué glossed over the fact that the six U.S. allies blamed high U.S. interest rates and the growing American national debt for their economic problems. The official release simply noted the need to rectify the problem of high interest rates.

May 30, 1983

The Philippines and the United States sign an agreement on U.S. military bases in the islands.

To continue using Subic Bay Naval Base and Clark Air Force Base for another five years, the United States would pay the Philippines $900 million—$400 million more than the 1979 agreement required. Because some Philippine groups objected to using the bases for nuclear weapons, the agreement provided for joint consultation regarding base operations, including the stationing of intercontinental missiles. U.S. ambassador to the Philippines, Michael H. Armacost said the pact put U.S.-Philippine relations back on an "even keel." On June 25, Secretary of State George Shultz visited Manila, where he praised President

Ferdinand Marcos for his excellent leadership and reaffirmed U.S. support despite recent demonstrations against the Marcos government.

June 6, 1983

Tension increases between Nicaragua and the United States when Managua expels three U.S. diplomats it accuses of plotting to kill Sandinista officials.

The United States denied Nicaragua's June 6 allegation and retaliated by expelling 21 Nicaraguan consular officials and closing six Nicaraguan consulates in the United States. Nevertheless, ambassadorial relations remained intact with both sides finding advantages to retaining official contact.

June 17, 1983

First successful test launch of the MX missile.

Although Congress and President Reagan still argued over the production and deployment of the MX, it approached its final developmental stage with a 4,700-mile flight across the Pacific to drop six simulated warheads near Kwajalein Island in the Marshalls.

June 23, 1983

Libyan-supported rebels invade northern Chad, seeking to overthrow the government of President Hissen Habré.

Chad's troubles began on June 7, 1982, after Habré ousted President Goukouni Oueddei, who fled and gained support from Libya. On June 23, 3,500 rebel forces crossed from Libya to march against Chad's government. France and the United States backed the Habré government, and by August the rebel threat had dissipated.

June 24, 1983

The U.N.-sponsored Afghan peace talks achieve no results.

The June 24 meeting in Geneva concluded a second round of negotiations between parties involved in the Afghanistan war. The first round, on June 16, 1982, consisted of "proximity" talks conducted by U.N. mediator Diégo Cordovez, an Ecuadoran lawyer. In these "proximity" meetings, Cordovez shuttled between Afghan and Soviet diplomats in one room and Pakistani and U.S. diplomats in another room. This shuttle diplomacy reached no conclusions but determined that the chief problem was finding a method to withdraw foreign troops either before or after a cease-fire and peace agreement. The Soviet Union had urged the United Nations to supervise these negotiations.

After Soviet President Leonid Brezhnev died on November 10, 1982, the new Soviet leader, Yuri Andropov, wanted to end the Afghan conflict while the Soviets still held a strong position in Afghanistan. The Soviets' main problem was finding an Afghan leader willing to accept peace terms through compromise arrangements with Pakistan, the principal supporter of the Afghan rebels. The June 1983 sessions achieved no solutions to the Afghan conflict, which remained unsolved until 1988. Meanwhile, the United States continued to accuse the Soviet Union of using chemical weapons in Afghanistan.

June 27, 1983

After Italian elections, Socialist Bettino Craxi forms a five-party coalition government.

Although Craxi's Socialist Party won only about 10 percent of the vote, it was the largest of four minority parties and came to power because of irreconcilable differences between Italy's two largest parties—the Christian Democrats and the Communists—which each won about 30 percent of the vote. During 1982, the Socialists had forced three cabinet changes by leaving the Christian Democrats coalition. Now, Craxi formed his own coalition of Communists, Socialists, and members of other parties.

June 27, 1983

The Soviet Soyuz T-9 spacecraft is launched and successfully docks the next day with the orbiting Salyut 7 space station.

Despite this Soviet success, a Soviet spacecraft exploded during its launch on September 27, 1983. The Soviet cosmonauts were saved because their escape rocket fired safely.

July 8, 1983

A Caribbean Community (CARICOM) conference in Trinidad criticizes the United States for delays in granting economic aid promised in Reagan's Caribbean basin initiative; Congress approves part of Reagan's Caribbean request on July 20.

CARICOM—English-speaking nations in the Caribbean Community—met to discuss ways of ending their economic recession by accelerating their economic integration. They expected to be assisted by Reagan's proposed economic program. Despite the CARICOM leaders' desire for significant U.S. aid, the House of Representatives voted on July 14 to cut back the funds President Reagan had requested for the Caribbean area. Later on July 19, a Senate-House conference committee approved legislation to give the Caribbean nations duty-free access for certain products sold to the United States.

July 21, 1983

Poland's government ends martial law but expands Prime Minister Wojciech Jaruzelski's power to arrest and detain dissenters.

The number of demonstrations in Poland had grown after 2,000 protesters marched in Gdansk on March 13 and 14, 1983. The visit of Pope John Paul II from June 16 to 23 temporarily quieted the country because the pope met with Solidarity leader Lech Walesa, as well as with Jaruzelski. Walesa received the Nobel Peace Prize on October 5, 1983, because he used nonviolent methods in confronting the government. Ending martial law on July 21 did not satisfy most members of Solidarity because the Sejm (parliament) also enlarged the police power of the government. On November 22, the Sejm further enhanced Jaruzelski's power and named him chairman of a new National Defense Committee.

July 22, 1983

China denounces American plans to sell more weapons to Taiwan, claiming a violation of an agreement of August 1982.

After July 15, when the United States announced the sale to Taiwan of $530 million of military equipment, Beijing protested to U.S. Ambassador Arthur Hummel, Jr. These new sales would total $800 million of U.S. armaments to Taiwan in 1983. Since this exceeded the $600 million of sales in 1982, China asserted it was not the decrease in arms sales to Taiwan that the Reagan administration had agreed to in 1982. The U.S. State Department argued that high inflation rates made the 1983 figure an actual decrease in real value. The dispute further cooled China's relations with the United States during Reagan's first administration.

July 25, 1983

News is leaked in Washington that large-scale U.S. military exercises off the Atlantic and Pacific coasts of Nicaragua are under way to intimidate the Sandinistas.

On the eve of a congressional vote on aid to the Nicaraguan rebels, news reports said the U.S. navy aircraft carrier *Ranger* had arrived off the Atlantic coast of Nicaragua. This was part of "Big Pine 2," a six-month series of army and navy exercises along both coasts of Central America. Nineteen naval ships and about 4,000 U.S. Marine and army forces were deployed. Although President Reagan played down the news by saying it was simply one of many such exercises, one unidentified Pentagon official stated, "We want to persuade the bad guys in Nicaragua and Cuba that we are positioned to blockade, invade or interdict if they cross a particular threshold." An immediate response to the news was a House of Representatives vote to cut off aid to the U.S.-backed rebels fighting in Nicaragua.

July 28, 1983

The House of Representatives cuts off U.S. covert aid to the Nicaraguan rebels.

For some time, members of Congress and the American public had the impression that President Reagan was risking war in Central America by pushing military means to overthrow Nicaragua's Sandinista regime. Although the president called a televised news conference on July 26 to dispel such notions about his policy, he did not succeed. To exemplify the range of public concerns, Republicans Olympia Snowe of Maine and Lynn Martin of Illinois voted with the Democratic majority to prohibit aid to the Contras. Snowe said she was confused about the U.S. role in Nicaragua; Martin feared that Reagan wanted to overthrow the Sandinista government. Despite the House vote in favor of Massachusetts Democratic Senator Edward Boland's amendment to stop aid to the Contras, the Senate did not concur and some aid went to the Contras.

August 2, 1983

Lebanese factions fight civil war, with the heaviest fighting near Beirut; U.S. forces find new role.

Although it had made an agreement with Israeli troops to leave Lebanon, President Amin Gemayel's government experienced greater problems in restoring the political compromises that had maintained peace in Lebanon before 1975. The six factions fighting in early August included three Christian Phalangist groups, at least two PLO Muslim groups, and the National Front. By mid-September, U.S. forces in Lebanon undertook the new role of assisting Gemayel's Lebanese army.

August 20, 1983

President Reagan ends all controls concerning sales of U.S. gas pipeline equipment to the USSR.

This action ended a two-year argument between the United States and its Western European allies over supplying the Soviet Union with modern technology to construct a gas pipeline from Siberia to central Europe.

August 23, 1983

The United States withdraws AWAC planes aiding Chad's government after French forces arrive to help fight rebels supported by Libya.

After rebels based in Libya attacked northern Chad on June 23, 1983, France warned Libya it would send troops if Chad's President Hissen Habré was endangered. The United States gave Chad a $15 million increase in military aid and, on August 3, sent AWAC reconnaissance planes to Sudanese bases to monitor the Libyan-backed rebel movements. Because Libya bombed Chad's government forces, both the United States and France sent antiaircraft weapons to assist Habré's forces. As soon as 3,000 French troops arrived in August to assist Habré, the rebel advances stopped, and a stalemate developed between the government and the rebels. Thus, the United States decided to withdraw its AWACs from the Sudan.

August 24, 1983

Iran pays $419.5 million of U.S. claims to relieve its debts.

To meet its U.S. obligations, Iran transferred funds to the U.S. Export-Import Bank from the $1.42 billion escrow account set up when U.S. hostages were released in January 1981. So far, Iran had settled accounts with 20 U.S. banks and repaid nearly all of the $10 billion debt inherited from the shah's government in 1979. U.S. foreign sales to Iran continued, especially such items as Boeing transport jets and electronic and power plant equipment. During the first six months of 1983, U.S. exporters sold $97 million of goods to Tehran. Iran was expected to earn $20 billion in oil exports during 1983.

August 26, 1983

Soviet President Yuri Andropov offers to "liquidate" the SS-20s withdrawn from Europe as part of an arms agreement.

Because the United States and its allies feared that Soviet SS-20s could be moved to Asian targets if they were removed from Europe, the United States had talked about making a global agreement on intermediate-range nuclear forces (INF). Desiring to limit present INF discussions to Europe, Andropov stated that the Soviets would destroy any SS-20s that were restricted by arms reductions. This Soviet proposal looked like a breakthrough but was limited because Moscow insisted on counting French and British missiles in any agreement signed with the United States. By counting French and British missiles, Andropov said that the Soviets could retain 162 missiles while destroying 81 missiles if the United States did not deploy Pershing IIs to Europe. Then, a Soviet and NATO balance would be attained, he declared. Because Washington could not control the use of British and French missiles not under NATO authority, the U.S. negotiators argued that other nations' weapons could not be counted. Hence, the stalemate in the U.S.-Soviet INF talks continued.

August 28, 1983

Israeli Prime Minister Menachem Begin announces his resignation.

The transition to a new cabinet was completed on September 12, when the six parties in the Likud coalition named Yitzhak Shamir as prime minister.

September 1, 1983

The Soviets shoot down a South Korean passenger plane that strays into Soviet airspace.

The Soviet Union stated that an unidentified plane had intruded over Soviet territory on an espionage mission. The Korean Air Lines Boeing 747 aircraft was *en route* from the United States to Seoul, Korea, with 269 passengers, including 61 Americans, when it was shot down. The United States denied the allegation that KAL flight 007 was collecting data about Soviet air defenses but admitted the plane had strayed off course. President Reagan's reaction was milder than many observers expected. He expressed outrage at the killing of innocent victims and suspended all Soviet commercial aircraft flights to U.S. airports. His words were not matched by other punitive measures such as stopping arms control talks in Geneva or halting U.S. grain sales.

While there was increased tension, President Reagan contended that the United States should continue its dialogue with Moscow in a "quest for peace." This incident resulted partly from the recent Soviet buildup of army, navy, and air force units in eastern Asia. This activity countered Soviet fears of a Chinese attack as well as the recent U.S. plan to obtain naval supremacy. In 1981, President Reagan's secretary of the navy, John Lehman, announced a "maritime strategy" to develop a 600-ship U.S. fleet against the Soviet Union. Lehman's maritime strategy called for an offensive "force projection" against Soviet fleet and coastal targets.

This meant preparing several U.S. aircraft carriers and other forces to move into narrow waterways (choke points) surrounding the Soviet Union. One strategic choke point was the Sea of Japan, where five narrow straits leading into the open Pacific Ocean could be easily mined, blockaded, or bombed. This would bottle up the Soviet's Pacific-based fleet at Vladivostok. Combined with the air forces of the United States, South Korea, and Japan, the maritime strategy could give the United States distinct military advantages in the northwestern Pacific. It also contributed to Soviet suspicions about the off-course flight of KAL-007 as a spy mission. Thus, when KAL-007 skirted sensitive Soviet military installations between Japan and the Soviet Union, both U.S. and Japanese intelligence monitored the flight. These tapes indicated that the plane strayed hundreds of miles off course for unexplained reasons. Eight Soviet planes tracked the Boeing aircraft for over two hours before ground commanders ordered its fighter planes to fire the air-to-air missile that downed the plane. The Soviets said the KAL pilot did not respond to Soviet warnings or their efforts to make contact. Evidence regarding KAL's penetration of Soviet airspace is inconclusive despite many studies about the event.

September 8, 1983

Secretary of State Shultz has a stormy session with Soviet Foreign Minister Andrei Gromyko.

While denouncing the shooting down of KAL flight 007 by Soviet pilots, President Reagan minimized conflict with Moscow and kept the arms control talks active until the U.S. Pershing IIs were deployed in Europe. Consequently, Secretary Shultz kept an appointment with Gromyko in Madrid to discuss a Reagan-Andropov summit meeting in 1984. The deaths of the 269 passengers had infuriated Shultz, however, and his anger showed up in his meeting with Gromyko. The Madrid meeting was one of the most volatile between high-level U.S.-Soviet delegates in some time, making Secretary Shultz more combative and less willing to offer concessions on arms control with the Soviets. On September 26, however, President Reagan offered the Soviets a new intermediate-range nuclear forces (INF) missile proposal during a speech at the United Nations.

September 8, 1983

Greece permits four U.S. bases to remain on Greek soil for five years.

Since taking office on October 18, 1981, Greek Prime Minister Andreas Papandreou had threatened to abolish the U.S. bases because he desired an independent Greek foreign policy. Even while Greece negotiated with Washington on February 24, 1983, Papandreou met with Soviet Prime Minister Nikolay A. Tikhonov and joined the Soviets in calling for a nuclear-free zone and limited armed forces in the Balkans. Undoubtedly, Papandreou hoped to nudge the United States toward better terms for Greece, because on September 8, he signed an agreement concluded by negotiators on July 15, 1983. The pact retained four major U.S. bases in Greece in return for

$500 million per year, up from previous funding of $280 million annually. The United States also promised to maintain a balance of military power between Greece and Turkey, the historic rival of Greece even though both countries were NATO members.

September 9, 1983

Four Central American states approve the Contadora objectives for peace.

The Contadora process begun by four Latin American countries—Mexico, Colombia, Venezuela, and Panama on January 8, 1983, pursued a variety of proposals to end the Central American wars involving Nicaragua, El Salvador, and U.S.-based rebels in Honduras. At Cancún, Mexico, on July 17, they urged the Central American states, Cuba, and the United States to renew peace efforts. The Contadora diplomats now decided to spell out possible methods for peacemaking in the September 9 "Document of Objectives." This document favored regional negotiations, democratic pluralism, national compromises to reconcile rebel groups with national governments, a halt to support of paramilitary forces, agreement for arms limitations, withdrawal of all foreign advisers, and methods to verify the agreements concluded. Although none of the nations involved in Central America's conflicts formally rejected the September 9 proposals, the United States, Nicaragua, and El Salvador failed to take them seriously. Nevertheless, the Contadora nations continued their attempts to bring about peace.

September 13, 1983

U.S. forces in Lebanon are authorized to use naval gunfire and air strikes to defend themselves; the U.S. role escalates.

The U.S. role in Lebanon escalated because the multilateral peacekeeping force that returned to Lebanon after the massacres at Sabra and Shatila on September 16–18, 1982, had gradually tied itself to the defense of Amir Gemayel's Lebanese government after the civil war began during July and August 1983. On September 1, President Reagan ordered 2,000 Marine reinforcements to the eastern Mediterranean, and U.S. naval guns first fired at Druze positions east of Beirut on September 8. Thus, the September 13 order backed earlier naval action and approved future firing. The U.S. navy became more involved on September 17 and 18 when naval guns bombarded Syrian-controlled regions of Lebanon. French peacekeeping forces entered the fray on September 22, when French combat planes struck rebel camps outside Beirut after rebels shelled French positions in Beirut. During the fighting in Beirut between Christian and Muslim armies, two U.S. Marines and four French soldiers were killed between August 29 and 31, 1983.

September 26, 1983

President Reagan offers an INF missile proposal that the Soviets reject as deception.

As the November date drew near for deploying U.S. Pershing II missiles in Europe, the president presented a new plan to the Soviet Union. The U.S. proposal, which U.S. negotiator Paul Nitze offered to the Soviets at Geneva, stated that for any global limitation the Soviets established on intermediate-range missiles, the United States would deploy its intermediate-range nuclear forces (INF) in similar proportions, including those deployed in NATO countries. Thus, while some U.S. missiles would be stationed in Europe, they would decrease in proportion to the Soviets' willingness to decrease their SS-20s in Europe. The Soviets found nothing substantially new in the U.S. proposal. President Andropov said that Washington talked of flexibility but did not address the real issue of the number of French, British, and U.S. missiles able to strike Soviet territory. The breakdown of the INF talks seemed apparent and in November became a reality.

September 29, 1983

Congress permits U.S. Marines to remain in Lebanon for another 18 months.

Prior to August 1983, President Reagan avoided invoking the War Powers Act by telling Congress the U.S. forces did not face imminent hostilities. The renewal of large-scale civil war in Lebanon, the killing of two Marines on August 29, and Reagan's dispatch of another 2,000 Marines on September 1 caused congressional leaders to insist that the president invoke the War Powers Act to obtain congressional consent to keep forces in the eastern Mediterranean. It was clear to most members of Congress that the original U.S. peacekeeping role had changed, a belief reinforced by the September 13 U.S. decision to permit naval bombardment of rebel positions. Reagan's disdain for the limits that the War Powers Act placed on the executive was countered by his supporters who thought a congressional role avoided the analogy of Lebanon as another Vietnam conflict taking place without legislative approval. Republican congressmen such as Henry Hyde and Robert H. Michel (both R-Ill.) wanted to rid the nation of the self-doubt inherited from the Vietnam experience, while conservative Democratic Senator John Stennis of Mississippi said the American people were concerned about where their "boys" would fight and die. A New York Times/CBS poll indicated that two out of three Americans thought Lebanon resembled Vietnam and that Americans disapproved of Reagan's foreign policies by 47 percent to 38 percent, with 15 percent abstaining. Actually, most Congress members wanted to keep the Marines in Lebanon but insisted that Reagan use the War Powers Act. Reagan finally relented, and with little debate the congressional resolution to keep U.S. forces in the eastern Mediterranean passed on September 29.

September 30, 1983

World financial crisis leaves the World Bank and the International Monetary Fund (IMF) in need of $6 billion; President Reagan offers $3 billion.

A joint meeting of World Bank and IMF members in Washington, D.C., disclosed that their commitments to assist countries with debt problems would exceed their resources by $6 billion before the end of the year. Throughout the year many Third World countries could not meet their debt payments. As a result of the expected shortfall in financial resources, President Reagan asked Congress for an increase of $8.4 billion, including $3 billion in emergency funds, to help the IMF meet its commitments. Congress approved the appropriation on November 18, 1983.

October 9, 1983

In Rangoon, Burma, a North Korean bomb plot fails to kill South Korean President Chun Doo Hwan, but 20 persons die.

On October 10, Burma arrested two North Koreans for the bombing that killed four South Korean cabinet members and 16 other people. The bomb did not hit its intended target, President Chun Doo Hwan. On November 4, Burma broke diplomatic relations with North Korea, claiming it had proof that the North Korean government was involved in the bombing. On returning to Seoul after the bombing, Chun said "I cannot control the raging anger and bitter grief of this tragedy." This feeling was shared by U.S. Secretary of State George Shultz, who had developed close relations with South Korea's Foreign Minister Lee Bum Suh, one of the four cabinet ministers killed in Rangoon.

October 10, 1983

Nicaraguan rebels destroy oil and gasoline tanks in Corinto, forcing the evacuation of the city.

The Contra attack on Corinto, which was designed to damage the nation's economy, had been planned by the U.S. Central Intelligence Agency, a fact President Reagan later admitted. It occurred just one week after an American pilot, whom the Nicaraguans captured after shooting down his plane, described the CIA's involvement in Contra operations. Although President Reagan claimed the Contra attacks were designed to weaken and harass the Sandinista government, Nicaragua's leader, Daniel Ortega, called on "friendly governments" to help him defend Nicaragua against an impending U.S. invasion.

October 17, 1983

Robert C. McFarlane replaces William Clark as national security adviser.

McFarlane became Reagan's special envoy to the Middle East on July 22, 1983, and he was now elevated to head the National Security Council. Clark became secretary of the interior on October 13, 1983.

October 22, 1983

Rumors indicated that President Reagan has secret plans to organize a Jordanian strike force for the Middle East.

In early October, rumors from Israel indicated that the United States was organizing Jordanian commando teams. While details were not publicized, the Pentagon had been training 8,000 Jordanians during the past 30 months. Their mission would be to move to any Persian Gulf trouble spot to prevent rebellions. Allegedly, the Pentagon provided $220 million, three C-130 transport planes, and sophisticated weapons for the Jordanians. The Israeli government opposed such plans, and the disclosure ended the idea. Nevertheless, the ploy cast light both on Reagan's desire to involve Jordan deeply in his Middle East peace plans and on the shallow thinking of Reagan's advisers, who thought other Arab states would rely on Jordanians for help. Jordan denied that the plan existed.

October 23, 1983

A suicide truck-bomb destroys a U.S. Marine barracks in Beirut, Lebanon, killing 241 marines and naval personnel; a similar attack on a French compound kills 58 French paratroopers.

The U.S. Marine barracks was blown up by the driver of a truck who, at daybreak, smashed his vehicle past two Marine sentry posts, through an iron gate, over an 18-inch sewer pipe, through a row of sandbags, and past a second sentry before hitting the building housing the Marines. The truck contained 12,000 pounds of explosives. This tragedy caused a Pentagon investigation led by retired Admiral Robert Long. In its report issued on December 28, 1983, the Long Commission asked two basic questions: why was the barracks not suitably protected after the bombing of the U.S. embassy on April 18, 1983? And why was a terrorist attack not anticipated? The central answer was the failure of the Reagan administration to make a clear, definite change in military orders to the Marines and the U.S. public as Reagan shifted policy in Lebanon from a "passive" peacekeeping role to the aggressive policy of bombarding Muslim and Syrian positions in defense of President Amin Gemayel's government.

The Long Commission said the peacekeeping team could not by itself shore up the Gemayel government and urged President Reagan to reexamine alternative methods of achieving American objectives, including "a more vigorous and demanding approach in pursuing diplomatic alternatives." Two days before the report, Reagan attempted to minimize its potential negative impact by telling a press conference that the armed forces were not to blame but that the president's office was. The Marines' deaths shocked the public and Congress, leading the Reagan administration to withdraw the U.S. military from Lebanon as soon as politically feasible.

October 24, 1983

President Reagan says Americans should engage in subversive warfare if it serves the national interest.

During a news conference in which he admitted that the CIA helped Nicaraguan rebels who subverted the Sandinista government, the president asserted: "I do believe in the right of a country, when it believes that its interests are best served, to practice covert activity" that will bring change in a foreign country. Although Reagan did not clarify his precise goals in helping Nicaraguan rebels, the State Department said U.S. policy wanted the Sandinistas to stop their repression. Most commentators and members of Congress believed Reagan wanted to overthrow the Sandinistas, employing a policy resembling Soviet subversive tactics. This opinion about Reagan's policy spurred congressional leaders to challenge sending U.S. funds to the Contras.

October 25, 1983

Grenada is invaded by U.S. forces with allies from other Caribbean states.

About 6,000 American Army Rangers and Marines joined 400 troops from Jamaica, Barbados, and four members of the Organization of Eastern Caribbean States (OECS) to invade Grenada by air, land, and sea. American paratroopers landed on an airfield being built by Cuban workers, while the navy landed Marines and allied soldiers on the beaches of Grenada. Facing only 750 Cuban and Grenadian soldiers on an island with a population of about 110,000, the Americans and their allies had little trouble meeting their military objectives by October 28. The invaders evacuated 599 U.S. citizens who wanted to leave, mostly students at St. George's Medical School. American casualties totaled 18 killed and 116 wounded; the Cubans lost 24, and 59 were wounded; and 45 Grenadians were killed and 337 wounded, including 21 killed when a mental hospital was accidentally bombed.

By November 23, Communist representatives on the island were sent home, including all Cubans except one diplomat, 17 Libyans, 15 North Koreans, 49 Soviets, 10 East Germans, and three Bulgarians. By December 15, all U.S. combat forces had evacuated the island; a few troops remained to train a Grenadian militia and police and to provide medical and logistic

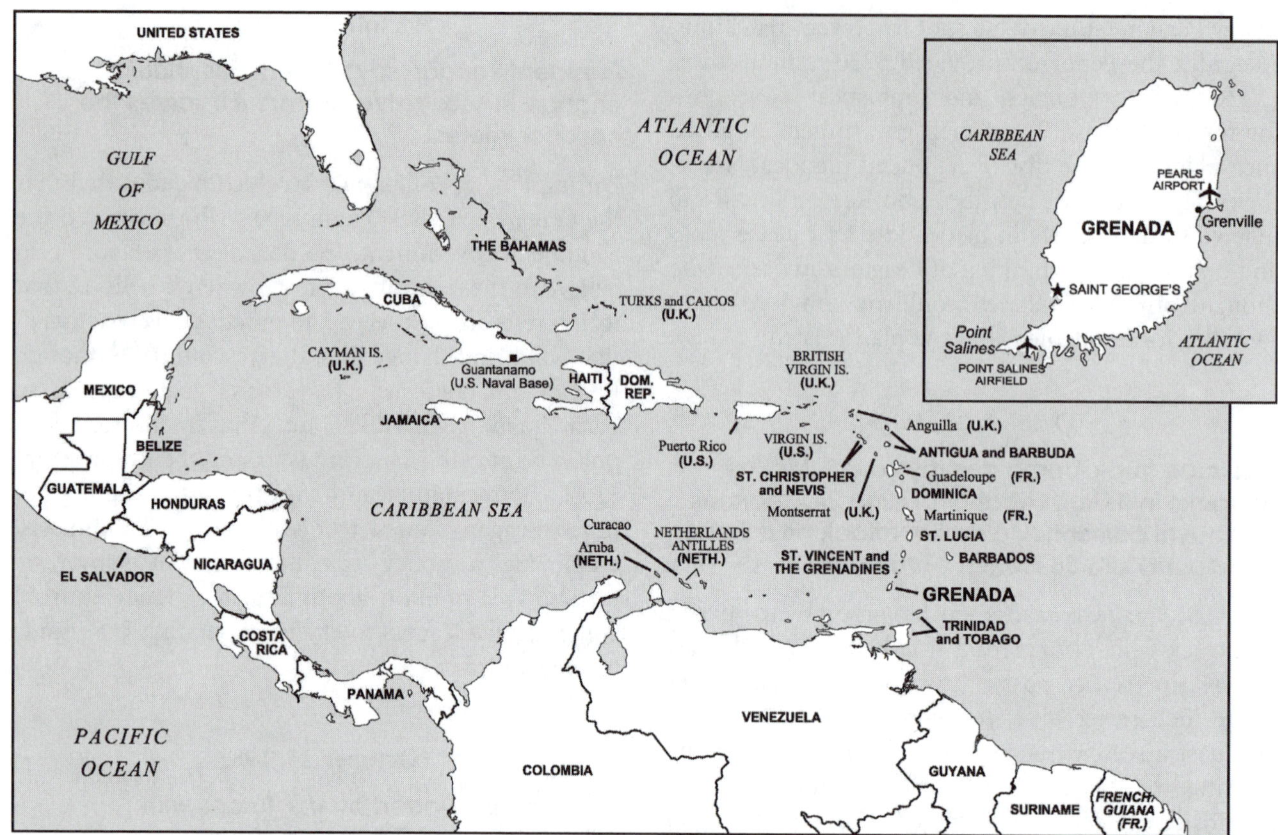

Grenada and the Caribbean, 1983

support for a new Grenadian government. The new regime was an Advisory Council appointed by Governor General Paul Scoon, who represented Great Britain's Queen Elizabeth as the official head of state of Grenada. Two major issues arose regarding the U.S. invasion: Why did Washington attack this tiny island? Were the U.S. military authorities justified in restricting newsmen seeking to report the war? The U.S. decision to invade went back to March when Grenada's Prime Minister Maurice Bishop said he feared a U.S. attack, a baseless but prophetic claim. Because the United States disliked the construction of a 10,000-foot runway on Grenada by Cubans, Prime Minister Bishop visited Washington in June 1983, where he was viewed as a moderate socialist. On his return to Grenada, however, Bishop became involved in disputes with radicals of the New Jewel Movement (NJM) at the NJM Central Committee meetings on July 13–19 and August 26.

Bishop was challenged by a pro-Cuban faction led by Bernard Coard, who, on September 14–16, gained control of the Politburo, which made party policy. Following a visit to Moscow and Havana, Bishop tried to regain control of the NJM, but he lost and was placed under house arrest by the Central Committee. Coard was named prime minister, while real power devolved on General Hudson Austin. On October 19, a crowd of 1,000 Bishop supporters freed him from house arrest and marched to Fort Rupert, where Bishop took over the central office. Within a few hours, however, Austin's People's Revolutionary Army (PRA) converged on the fort, fired into the crowd, and arrested Bishop and three of his former cabinet members. Austin's men executed these four and two union leaders who were in the fort's courtyard. Austin's Military Council gained control and announced an around-the-clock curfew with orders to the army to shoot violators on sight. Austin also closed the airport for several days. The diplomatic situation leading to President Reagan's invasion order evolved between October 13 and 20, 1983. As explained by the State Department, an interagency group reviewed the unrest in Grenada and on October 14 asked the Joint Chiefs of Staff to examine its contingency evacuation plans. Following the murder of Bishop on October 19, the interagency group considered using military force, and the next day, several U.S. ships heading for Lebanon were diverted to Grenada. Information about this diversion caused the governments of Cuba and Grenada to inform Washington that Americans would be protected on Grenada and to urge that negotiations precede any attack. The White House ignored these requests. Also on October 20, the day U.S. ships were diverted, the prime minister of Barbados, J.M.G. Adams, asked Washington to do something about the violence in Grenada. He found a receptive audience, and although Adams could not induce representatives of the larger Caribbean Community to join in any action, he persuaded representatives of the smaller OECS to meet in Barbados on October 21. The OECS asked the United States to help end the violence on Grenada. At the October 21 meeting, Grenada was not represented or heard from, but the six other OECS nations—Antigua and Barbuda, St. Lucia, St. Vincent and the Grenadines, Monserrat, Dominica, and St. Christopher and Nevis—favored U.S. action. Between October 21 and 24, Prime Minister Adams also obtained support from Jamaica and contacted Grenada's governor general, Sir Paul Scoon, who agreed to ask for U.S. assistance in restoring order. Adams informed the U.S. State Department of Scoon's agreement on October 24, even though Scoon's official appeal did not reach Washington until October 27. Scoon's appeal was a vital part of the U.S. justification for acting under a regional defense agreement.

In fact, President Reagan ordered the Pentagon to invade on October 22. State Department officials said the president's order was the reason that Cuban and Grenadian attempts to prevent the attack were ignored. In addition, the White House ignored Austin's opening of Grenada's airport on October 24. Austin had closed the airport from October 19 to 24, a decision cited as evidence that American students on Grenada could not get out. After evidence of the airport's opening on October 24 became known, Reagan stopped talking about the students' being captive in Grenada. Immediately following the attack, the Reagan administration offered two basic reasons for invading. Initially, the safety of the medical students and other Americans was emphasized. By October 29, this rationale was dropped and Reagan argued that the U.S. takeover prevented a Communist coup with Soviet and Cuban support. U.S. officials found thousands of documents on Grenada that allegedly proved that Cubans and Soviets directed the New Jewel Movement. Included in the documents deposited in the National Archives were proposals to raise the 600-man Grenadian army to 10,000, secret military agreements and arms purchase plans with East Germany and Czechoslovakia, and a variety of suggestions for making Grenada a Cuban-Soviet satellite. As long as these plans were not compared with the Pentagon contingency plans, the evidence seemed startling.

The Reagan administration believed the worst about all Communists in 1983, and treated the captured documents as if their plotting would come to pass if the United States had not invaded. If Reagan's advisers thought the worst of the plans in the documents, they also believed the worst of the American media. The Pentagon's success in restricting journalists from reporting the events in Grenada raised serious questions about a free press in a free society. During the first five days of the Grenadian "war," American military officials prevented full news coverage. For two days, no newspeople could go to Grenada, causing Haynes Johnson, a news columnist, to say it was the first war "produced, filmed and reported by the Pentagon." News releases and tapes for television were prepared and given to reporters by American military officers. Thus, information about how real the Communist threat was on October 25, how U.S. forces behaved, and what resulted, were presented only by Pentagon dispatches. When ABC-TV personnel hired fishing boats to reach Grenada, U.S. naval ships scared them off by dropping buoys in their path or unfurling the big guns of their ships. Vice Admiral Joseph Metcalf II, who had charge of the censorship, threatened reporters: "We'll stop you. We've got the means to do that." After 48 hours of the war, as fighting nearly ended, Admiral Metcalf allowed journalists to form a 15-reporter pool to visit the island and share the information with journalists not in the pool. Then, for two days, groups of 27 to 47 journalists were taken for two-hour guided tours of Grenada. Finally, on October 30, President Reagan told the Pentagon to ease up on reporters, and the next day journalists received free access to the island. When more than 200 journalists arrived on October 31, the Cuban fighters were gone, and only cheerful Grenadians welcomed them. Reporters had difficulties getting stories out because the island's radio transmission center had been bombed, and the U.S. military had severed all cable and telephone facilities. Prominent newsmen and many members of Congress criticized the news restrictions. The American Society of Newspaper Editors wired a protest to Defense Secretary Caspar Weinberger, and a Senate resolution calling for an end to news restrictions passed by a vote of 53 to 18.

Ironically, U.S. delegates to UNESCO opposed press restrictions that Third World governments and the Soviet Union favored. When debate on this issue took place at a UNESCO meeting in Paris during the week of November 7, 1983, the United States threatened to cut UNESCO funds if it imposed press limitations.

October 28, 1983

Britain's Prime Minister Thatcher strongly opposes President Reagan's action; the United States vetoes a U.N. Security Council resolution condemning the Grenada invasion.

Many European allies of the United States were dismayed by Reagan's use of force rather than diplomacy against this small island. Chief among Reagan's critics was Britain's Prime Minister Margaret Thatcher, usually one of his strongest supporters. In an interview on January 21, 1984, Thatcher repeated her strong disagreement with the U.S. invasion of Grenada refuting every justification used by the president. She said British citizens on Grenada felt no danger and did not believe Americans were in danger, that the airstrip being built was just like those on at least three other tourist islands, and that the United States could tolerate a Communist government on the tiny island, assuming it was Communist. Above all, she believed there must be an overwhelming case to justify using force. All other political channels should precede the use of the military. "In the free world," she said, "we do not pursue our objectives by force, whereas we have always said that the difference was that the Soviets did." Unlike some American "conservatives," the prime minister added, the British conservative tradition recognized the dangers of permitting right-wing extremists to extol military power.

While the United States vetoed a U.N. Security Council resolution denouncing the Grenada invasion, the U.N. General Assembly condemned the United States by a vote of 108 to 9, with 27 abstentions.

October 30, 1983

Military rule ends in Argentina when the Civic Union candidate is elected president.

The election of Raul Alfonsin ended the dominance of Argentina's Peronist Party as well as its military rulers. The new civilian leaders organized a military commission that recommended trials for military officers who led the 1982 Falkland Islands War and a special investigating commission to learn about the disappearance of 6,000 persons during the eight years of military rule.

November 1, 1983

An international scientific conference receives a study that claims a limited nuclear war could cause a "nuclear winter" and the end of human life.

During a two-day meeting in Washington, D.C., 50 scientists discussed the findings from teams of U.S. and Soviet scientists who reported on studies of "The World after Nuclear War." Both teams concluded that nuclear war would alter the climate of the Northern Hemisphere, causing months of darkness and freezing weather known as "nuclear winter." The U.S. group headed by Richard P. Turco, an atmospheric chemist, included Owen B. Toon, Thomas J. Ackerman, James B. Pollack, and Carl Sagan; the group used the acronym TTAPS from their last names. Based on a detailed computer study, the TTAPS report hypothesized a nuclear war involving 10,400 explosions for a total of 5,000 megatons—less than half of the existing nuclear arsenal, which was 12,000 megatons.

The TTAPS results included 1.1 billion people dead; 1.1 billion seriously wounded but having no medical service; and 100,000 tons (90,700 metric tons) of soot and dust blown into the upper atmosphere for each megaton exploded. Because of the soot and dust, the Northern Hemisphere's normal heat and light would be blocked, allowing only 5 percent normal sunlight even in mid-July. Noncoastal temperatures would fall to 13 degrees Fahrenheit (minus 25 Celsius) for months. The impact of the climate change would last for several years and carry some soot and dust to the Southern Hemisphere. Surviving plants would be unable to photosynthesize food from light, so the natural food chain would be destroyed. When the darkness ended, the earth would receive high levels of ultraviolet radiation because of the depleted ozone layer around the globe.

Conducting their experiments at the Moscow Academy of Science, the Soviet team offered a more grim report than TTAPS. Using the same 5,000-megaton model as TTAPS, the Soviets found that in 40 days temperatures at Murmansk would drop 100 degrees Fahrenheit (56 degrees Celsius); those in the United States would fall 60 degrees Fahrenheit (34 degrees Celsius). During discussions, none of the scientists found significant points for disagreement. The American ecologist Paul Erlich said that a full-scale nuclear war would leave the Northern Hemisphere uninhabitable, and if it spread south, "we could not preclude the extinction of homo sapiens." The U.S. report was published in brief in *Science* 222 (December 23, 1983, pp. 1283–92). For a list of articles and studies on nuclear winter, see Carl Sagan's letter to the editors *of Foreign Affairs* 65 (Fall 1986: 163–68).

November 6, 1983

Turgut Ozal's Independent Motherland Party wins 212 seats in Turkey's 400-member parliament.

This election ended the rule of the military junta that had taken power during a 1980 coup. Ozal became prime minister of a civilian cabinet on December 13, 1983.

November 8, 1983

Vice President George H.W. Bush's vote enables the Senate to approve funds for binary nerve gas weapons; funds are cut 10 days later.

Although on September 15 Congress authorized funds to produce and stockpile nerve gas, the MX missile, and the B-1 bomber, debate on the need for nerve gas continued. On October 31, the Senate Appropriations Committee eliminated the nerve gas funds. However, Vice President Bush's tie-breaking vote restored these funds on November 8. A joint congressional committee on November 18 eliminated the chemical weapons funds once again because the House delegates also opposed nerve gas. As a result, the appropriated funds for the $249.8 billion defense bill for 1984 did not include nerve gas.

November 8–9, 1983

The Soviet's KGB command center fears possible Western attack during U.S.-NATO exercise.

At the height of the U.S. and NATO's wide-ranging and high-level strategic exercise in early November 1983, KGB headquarters ordered its officers to report all information that might indicate American preparations for a nuclear attack on the Soviet Union. NATO's week-long exercise called Able Archer 83 was designed to test "command and communications procedures for the release and use of nuclear weapons." Although such activities were not uncommon, the autumn of 1983 was a time of heightened tensions between Washington and Moscow because senior intelligence officers on both sides were watching the other side's activities for any potential threat. Although many KGB officers disagreed with headquarters that a U.S. first-strike was imminent, Able Archer 83 caused concern in Moscow. According to Raymond Garthoff, "Soviet military doctrine had long held that a possible design for launching an attack would be the conversion of an exercise simulating attack into a real attack." Subsequently, Soviet fighter planes were place on alert in East Germany after Soviet intelligence erroneously reported certain NATO troops were being moved.

After British intelligence reported Moscow's alert to Washington, American intelligence agencies reviewed the episode in early 1984 and concluded the KGB probably had adequate reasons for being alarmed. When he was informed, President Reagan found it hard to believe the Soviets could imagine he would order a first strike. Subsequently, the superpowers established the Nuclear Risk Reduction Centers (see September 15, 1987) and a pact calling for reciprocal notification of strategic exercises (see September 23, 1989), that would reduce situations that could escalate to nuclear confrontation. See Raymond L. Garthoff, *The Great Transition* (1994).

November 12, 1983

Congress votes to limit aid to El Salvador unless the murderers of four American missionaries are convicted.

The four American nuns had been killed in December 1980. Upon taking office in 1981, the Reagan administration acted with indifference toward the murders even though these deaths aroused great concern among the U.S. public. The U.S. ambassador to El Salvador, Dean Hinton, charged El Salvador's government with a cover-up to protect its military leaders. In April 1981, six former national guardsmen had been arrested as suspects, but they were released on January 10, 1983, due to insufficient evidence. Similarly, on April 29, 1982, El Salvador released three men who had been indicted for killing land reform agents on January 3, 1981. The "nuns' case" became stalemated until 1983, when Senator Arlen Specter (R-Pa.) visited El Salvador, where local Catholic priests and others persuaded him that the government was protecting high-level military men who ordered the killing. Specter decided not to try to end all U.S. aid to El Salvador but proposed to limit aid until El Salvador convicted the killers. He added an amendment to PL-98-151, an act to continue existing foreign aid bills for 1984, which stated that 30 percent of the $64.8 million for El Salvador would be withheld until the murderers were convicted. Specter's amendment had more influence on El Salvador than congressional amendments, which required the president to certify El Salvador's progress in human rights.

November 17, 1983

Retaliating for the October 23 bombing of its Beirut barracks, France aircraft attack pro-Iranian rebels in eastern Lebanon.

The French jets struck a pro-Iranian Shiite militia base near Baalbek, causing heavy casualties. The French said the retaliatory raid was to discourage fresh terrorist attacks even as unidentified terrorists fired grenades at French positions in Beirut—retaliation for retaliation.

November 23, 1983

The Soviet Union walks out of INF negotiations to protest U.S. deployment of Pershing IIs and cruise missiles.

Although negotiations to limit intermediate-range missiles continued on a regular basis during 1983, the Geneva sessions uncovered no grounds for agreement. Although suggestions to renew the "walk-in-the-woods" proposal or interim reductions were sought, none came close to agreement. The United States proposed some global limit on intermediate range nuclear forces (INF), but the Soviets were concerned about counting French and British missiles capable of hitting the USSR. The two sides could not resolve these basic matters. Despite widespread public protests in Europe against the deployment of Pershing IIs and cruise missiles, the United States began installing cruise missiles in England on November 14 and Pershing IIs in West Germany on November 23. On November 16, the Italian Chamber of Deputies endorsed the NATO deployment of nuclear missiles, and on November 22, the West German Bundestag did the same by a vote of 286 to 226, with one abstention.

As the U.S. deployment of Pershing II and Tomahawk cruise missiles began, the current status of intermediate-range missiles was as follows:

1. Soviet missiles: While its antiquated SS-4 and SS-5 missiles were active, the Soviets had deployed 360 modern solid-fueled SS-20s in the past six years, scattered over 38 sites. Of these, about two-thirds were west of the Ural Mountains, aimed at European targets with a range of 3,100 miles. Each was "MIRVed" with three 150-kiloton warheads and had reloadable launchers. They could hit West Germany after a 20-minute flight.
2. U.S.-NATO missiles: The United States had 108 Pershing Is in Europe with a range of 500 miles. These would be replaced by the 1,000-mile-range Pershing IIs, which were solid-fueled and carried one 250-kiloton warhead with a terminal guidance system that provided great accuracy. It could not hit Moscow from West Germany but could hit many other parts of the western Soviet Union. Tomahawk cruise missiles would replace manned bombers. These mobile launchers fired four cruise missiles, each having one 200-kiloton warhead. The Tomahawk flew at a slow speed of 500 miles per hour but could fly below radar at 50 to 200 feet above ground on a zigzag course and strike within 10 to 20 yards of its target. NATO planned to deploy 464 Tomahawks in Britain, West Germany, Belgium, Italy, and the Netherlands.

November 28, 1983

Launching of U.S. space shuttle Columbia includes a European on the six-man crew.

The Columbia launched a European-built space laboratory that performed scientific experiments before returning to Earth on December 8. The Spacelab's prime contractor, from West Germany, put up half of the $1 billion cost.

November 29, 1983

President Reagan and Israeli Prime Minister Yitzhak Shamir establish a joint committee to coordinate military plans.

Reagan and Shamir signed this agreement when the Israeli prime minister visited Washington seeking ways to cooperate in supporting the Lebanese government, which was engaged in conflict with Syria as well as with various Muslim and Druze groups. Many moderate Arab nations protested the formation of this joint committee with good reason. U.S. news sources disclosed that Reagan had signed the highly classified paper "Middle East National Security Decision Directive 111" on October 29, 1983. While details of the November 29 agreement were not revealed, the proposed cooperative efforts included joint military exercises, stockpiling U.S. military equipment in Israel for use in the Middle East, sharing intelligence data, planning jointly for military contingencies, and the use of Israeli ports by naval ships of the U.S. Sixth Fleet in the Mediterranean.

November 30, 1983

President Reagan vetoes legislation requiring that U.S. aid to El Salvador depends on the president's certifying that El Salvador improved human rights.

Disdainful of the need to certify human rights progress, the president wished to end this annoyance. He did so one day after the State Department denied a U.S. visa to Roberto D'Aubuisson, president of El Salvador's Constituent Assembly and the notorious head of the right-wing ARENA party associated with death-squad killings of guerrillas as well as moderate political and religious leaders. Moreover, on November 25, 1983, the U.S. ambassador to El Salvador, Thomas R. Pickering, condemned the right-wing groups whose actions, he said, threatened to bring a cut off of future U.S. economic and military aid. Reagan's veto appeared to signal that right-wing violations of human rights did not matter. Senator Claiborne Pell (D-R.I.) denounced Reagan's veto, saying that Congress would not allow U.S. aid to be "poured into a nation that has not demonstrated a will to undertake basic reforms." El Salvador's Human Rights Commission had estimated that 40,000 people had been killed by death squads in the last four years. These reports led Deputy Secretary of State Kenneth W. Damto tell a group of Latin American leaders at a Miami, Florida, conference that "the death squads are enemies of democracy every bit as much as the guerrillas." Congress continued to challenge Reagan's disdain for certifying human rights progress.

December 4, 1983

A day of serious combat ensues between U.S. and Syrian forces in Lebanon.

After Syrian planes attacked U.S. reconnaissance aircraft on December 3, carrier-based U.S. aircraft raided Syrian positions. Two of 28 American planes were lost with one pilot killed and one captured; Syria said two persons died in the U.S. attack. About the same time, eight U.S. Marines were killed by artillery fired from Druze militiamen east of Beirut. Although the U.S. air raid caused consternation among some parliamentarians in Great Britain and Italy, whose peacekeeping forces in Lebanon seemed to be endangered, the British, Italian, and French foreign officers agreed at a NATO session in Brussels to keep their forces in Lebanon. On December 20, 1983, however, Italy announced plans to reduce its forces, and on January 2, 1984, France indicated it planned to withdraw 482 of its 1,700-man contingent. The United States announced withdrawal plans on February 15, 1984.

December 6, 1983

West Germany and the United States agree to replace Nike Hercules antiaircraft missiles with Patriot missiles.

At a NATO meeting, U.S. Defense Secretary Caspar Weinberger and West German Defense Minister Manfred Worner signed an agreement to spend $3 billion for U.S. Patriot missiles and West German Roland missiles to improve Western European defenses against Soviet intermediate-range missiles. Weinberger's spokesperson said the Patriot and

Roland missiles used conventional warheads and would replace the U.S. Nike Hercules missiles in Germany that used nuclear warheads. The Patriot-Roland antimissile system would complement U.S. Pershing II offensive missiles, which began to be deployed in Britain and West Germany in November 1983.

December 8, 1983

Soviet delegates end the START negotiations and refuse to schedule a date to resume talks.

As a follow-up to its abandoning the INF negotiations on November 23, Moscow told the American delegates at the Strategic Arms Reduction Talks (START) in Geneva that the recent deployment of U.S. missiles in Western Europe required extensive reconsideration of its START positions. The Soviet delegate refused to set future meeting dates for strategic arms talks.

December 9, 1983

President Reagan signs a bill to aid Nicaraguan rebels, which eliminates the Boland Amendment but restricts Contra aid to $24 million for 1984.

The Boland Amendment, which Congress approved in 1982, seemed obsolete by December 1983 because several incidents indicated that the Nicaraguan rebels could not overthrow the Sandinista government. President Reagan said the Contras' purpose was to stop Sandinista aid to Salvadoran rebels and to persuade the Sandinistas to amnesty the Contras so they could participate in the political processes and not have to resort to violence. Finally, in November 1983, a national intelligence estimate given both to the House's Select Committee on Intelligence and the Senate's Intelligence Committee stated that the Contras could never overthrow the Sandinista government. Subsequently, Boland (D-Mass.) lost support for the renewal of his amendment but persuaded the House and Senate select committees to agree that $24 million appropriated for Contra aid would be the absolute ceiling spent in 1984 fiscal year. President Reagan signed this legislation as part of the 1984 military authorization bill. While Boland's prohibition was temporarily ended, the Reagan administration disliked the ceiling placed on aid and looked for other methods to help the Contra rebels.

December 19, 1983

Japanese Prime Minister Nakasone forms a coalition cabinet to remain in office because his Liberal Democratic Party lost its parliamentary majority.

December 24, 1983

South African forces invade Angola to wipe out Namibian guerrilla bases; U.S. concurs.

Although on June 23 the Reagan administration reaffirmed its commitment to a pro–South African policy of "constructive engagement," it continued to speak out against the South African apartheid that oppressed the non-white population and to seek independence for South-West Africa. The "constructive engagement" policy made little headway because it also demanded the withdrawal of Cuban troops from Angola prior to negotiations on Namibia. The year ended with another South African incursion into Angola, even though on December 15, South Africa said it would withdraw its troops from Angola beginning on January 31, 1984. Johannesburg's pledges were offset by its constant military action in Angola and its takeover of the South-West African government on January 18, 1983.

December 28, 1983

The United States announces it will withdraw from UNESCO in 1985, protesting the group's politicization.

Officially, the United States gave one year's notice of intention to withdraw. In a letter to UNESCO Director General M'Bow, Secretary of State Shultz said the United States was concerned about the "trends in the management, policy and budget of UNESCO," which made the group ineffective. Among many reasons for the U.S. action was dissatisfaction with UNESCO's commission on mass communication, which advocated restrictions on press access to events in Third World nations. Assistant Secretary of State for International Organization Affairs Gregory Newell broadened the U.S. complaint, stating "UNESCO has extraneously politicized virtually every subject it deals with. It has exhibited hostility toward a free society, especially a free market and a free press, and it has demonstrated unrestrained budgeting expansion."

The United States claimed that UNESCO's high ideals had been forgotten since Third World nations gained a controlling influence over the organization. In 1974, the U.S. Congress suspended UNESCO aid after the U.N. agency excluded Israel from a regional group. Aid was resumed in 1977 after UNESCO readmitted Israel. In 1980, UNESCO made it difficult for American journalists by permitting Third World governments to censor their reports, while refusing to help educate Third World refugees. Finally, Washington disliked the rapid increase of the UNESCO budget from $165.1 million to $374.4 million in the past 10 years. The United States paid 25 percent of this budget but had no effective control over its expenditures. The U.S. withdrawal became effective after December 31, 1984.

December 28, 1983

U.S. Defense Department commission blames military commanders for serious errors in Beirut bombing of the Marine barracks.

Both the House Armed Services Committee and a five-member Defense Department commission investigated the Beirut bombing that killed 241 Americans on October 23, 1983. On December 19, the House panel charged Marine commanders with "serious errors" that permitted the terrorists to get past U.S. security posts. The December 28 Defense Department report agreed that the military commanders made serious security and intelligence mistakes. It also suggested that the Reagan administration reconsider the military mission's role in Lebanon and its political options in the Middle East.

1984

January 1, 1984

Natural gas from the Soviets' trans-Siberian pipeline is delivered to France for the first time.

Because President Reagan opposed the sale of Western technology to the Soviets, the construction and completion of this link between Soviet Central Asia and Western Europe became a symbol of French and German willingness to override Reagan's anti-Communist fervor to benefit their countries' economies. Natural gas from the USSR made Western Europeans less dependent on oil from the Middle East.

January 4, 1984

Thirty-three Democrats in the House of Representatives challenge President Reagan's pocket veto of the law requiring reports on El Salvador's progress in human rights.

On November 30, 1983, the president delayed signing legislation on aid to El Salvador in order to eliminate the requirement of reporting to Congress on human rights. El Salvador's right-wing death squads frequently killed political opponents despite U.S. protests. After the 33 representatives went to court, the U.S. Senate voted on January 26 to join the suit, arguing that the president had acted unconstitutionally. While these representatives went to court, other House members introduced a bill to require the president to certify human rights progress in El Salvador.

January 10, 1984

A bipartisan commission on Central America recommends military aid to El Salvador and denounces Cuba and the Soviet Union for aiding rebels.

Former Secretary of State Henry Kissinger headed this commission whose report provided data that both proponents and opponents of President Reagan's Central American policy used in debate. The report recommended increased military aid to the Salvadoran government, whose war with left-wing rebels was stalemated. But despite Reagan's wishes, the commission wanted this aid tied to the president's certification of human rights progress in El Salvador. While devoting less attention to Nicaragua, the report stated that the consolidation of a Marxist-Leninist regime there would pose a constant security threat to Central America. In particular, Nicaragua was a threat because it received arms and military advisers from the Soviet Union, Cuba, and other Communist countries, while supplying weapons to left-wing rebels in El Salvador. Although the commission reached no consensus on Reagan's support for the Nicaraguan rebels, it endorsed the Contadora peace efforts for Central America.

On February 3, President Reagan used the commission findings to ask Congress for a five-year $8 billion aid package for Central America. The commission believed the region's unrest was due to poverty, injustice, and closed political systems. It advocated reforms that were prevented by the intrusion of outside powers such as Cuba and the Soviet Union, who, it claimed, exploited the people for strategic political advantages. Central Americans themselves should solve their problems. Generally, the report was not acceptable to many Washington politicians and did not establish the bipartisan support President Reagan desired. Democrats and many Republicans in Congress opposed Reagan's emphasis on military solutions to problems in El Salvador and Nicaragua. Moreover, the American public did not believe, as the commission did, that there was danger of a Soviet takeover in Central America. Commission members were former Republican Senator Nicholas F. Brady, San Antonio mayor Henry G. Cisneros, former Texas governor William Clements, Yale economics professor Carlos F. Dias Alejandro, National Federation of Independent Business President William S. Johnson, A.F.L.-C.I.O. President Lane Kirkland, political scientist Richard M. Scammon, Boston University President John Silber, former Democratic Party Chairman Robert S. Strauss, the medical care Project Hope President William B. Walsh, and Henry Kissinger as chairman.

January 12, 1984

During a visit to the United States, Chinese Prime Minister Zhao Ziyang accepts cooperation in trade and scientific exchanges.

American-Chinese relations had chilled considerably since 1980 because of trade problems and especially because the Reagan administration sent military aid to the Chinese regime on Taiwan. Nevertheless, as part of their triangular relations with the Soviet Union, both China and the United States had common interests in maintaining friendship. China needed U.S. technology and capital investments for its modernization program.

January 16, 1984

President Reagan sets a new tone in U.S.-Soviet relations, offering compromise and flexibility in future arms talks.

The collapse of all U.S.-Soviet nuclear arms control talks on November 23, 1983, alarmed many of America's European allies and many members of the U.S. Congress. Other commentators saw the advice of the President's wife, Nancy Reagan, at work when her husband began to talk more like a peacemaker than a warmonger on January 16. Whatever the reasons for his shift, the president's address became the first of several messages that stopped calling the Soviet Union an evil empire and used terms such as "mutual compromise" or making 1984 a "year of opportunity for peace." The president and his advisers argued that the nation's three years of defense expenditures now gave the United States a greater deterrent power so that Moscow would be willing to accept arms control. Nevertheless, the January 16 speech was made in an atmosphere of tension, not agreement.

On January 11, NATO officials accused the Soviets of deploying more SS-20 missiles in Europe, and on January 23, the Reagan administration issued a report alleging that Moscow had violated at least seven arms control agreements. Perhaps Reagan viewed an election year as a time to balance appeals to peace with warnings about the dangers of Communism to satisfy both moderate Americans and hawks.

January 17, 1984

Conference on Confidence and Security-Building Measures (CBM) opens in Stockholm, Sweden, including delegates from NATO and Warsaw Pact countries.

Meeting as agreed at the Madrid Conference on Security and Cooperation in September 1983, the sessions began with U.S. Secretary of State George Shultz offering a six-point proposal of NATO member nations regarding the exchange of military data and activities that could reduce East-West tensions. On January 18, Soviet Foreign Minister Andrei Gromyko attacked the Reagan administration for its obsession with military power but listed six alternative proposals on confidence-building measures emphasizing a nuclear-free zone in Central Europe. NATO's proposals included exchanging military data annually, notifying about future military exercises and military movements, permitting observation of military activity, providing for inspection of suspected activity, and developing better ways to communicate.

January 23, 1984

U.S. Congress is told that the Soviet Union has violated arms control treaties. Sixdays later, the USSR protests against U.S. violations.

In its 50-page report, the Reagan administration described an "expanding pattern of Soviet violations or possible violations" of arms agreements. The two major U.S. charges were the testing of the PL-5 (or SSX-5) missile, which violated SALT II if it had the 10 warheads suspected by U.S. intelligence, and a giant radar station under construction at Abalakova, in the Krasnoyarsk region of central Siberia. This latter discovery was considered more serious because the radar base's inland location violated parts of the 1972 Anti-Ballistic Missile (ABM) Treaty. Other U.S. allegations regarded the Soviet use of chemical weapons and the encoding of missile test signals so that the United States could not verify them. The administration issued a similar report on October 10, 1984. On January 29, the Soviet Union protested U.S. violations, such as conducting nuclear tests above the threshold limit and upgrading radar stations on the Atlantic and Pacific coastlines in violation of the 1972 ABM Treaty. See Richard Dean Burns and Lester H. Brune, *The Quest for Missile Defenses, 1944–2003* (2004).

It is also of interest to note that the Reagan administration's reports of alleged Soviet violations were challenged by arms control experts. These specialists reported that most U.S. charges appeared to be contrived or exaggerated to align with Reagan's anti–arms control views. Both supporters and critics were unaware of the CIA's secret experiments and the Soviets biological weapons program, both of which were revealed after the end of the Cold War. See Gloria Duffy, *Compliance and the Future of Arms Control* (1988) and Judith Miller, Stephen Engelberg, and William Broad, *Germs: Biological Weapons and America's Secret War* (2001).

January 25, 1984

Japan increases its military budget by 6.55 percent, taking another step in defense burden sharing at U.S. request.

The 1984 budget of Prime Minister Nakasone sought a compromise on defense expenditures that would be large enough to placate Washington but small enough to avoid upsetting those Japanese, who thought that the military already received too much funding. U.S. Secretary of Defense Caspar Weinberger was only partially placated. He welcomed the increase but wanted Tokyo to increase military costs at an "even greater pace in future years." On December 28, 1984, Nakasone again increased Japan's defense expenditures by another 6.9 percent.

January 25, 1984

Defense Secretary Weinberger informs Congress that the "Midgetman" ICBM could be ready for deployment in 1992.

As a follow-up to the 1983 Scowcroft Report, the Defense Department developed the smaller, single-warhead missile as a successor to the 10-warhead MX missile. Weinberger said the Midgetman system would have 1,000 missiles with each weighing 30,000 pounds and carrying 1,000-pound nuclear warheads up to a range of 6,000 miles. The manned truck to transport the missiles would be reinforced to withstand winds of 600 to 900 miles per hour arising from nearby enemy explosions. A major problem was to obtain a lightweight guidance system accurate enough to hit a Soviet ICBM silo. The Pentagon estimated that the 1,000 Midgetmen would cost from $65 billion to $75 billion. It requested $715 million in the 1985 budget to develop the missile, a 50 percent increase over its 1984 allocation.

See May 1, 1988.

January 29, 1984

The Reagan administration completes grants of economic aid to three "authoritarian" governments of Latin America.

In contrast to President Carter's refusal to aid dictators of the right or the left who violated human rights, the Reagan administration differentiated between "authoritarian" right-wing dictators and totalitarian left-wing rulers because the former were capable of reform, while the latter ruled without hope of possible reform. Reagan had adopted the distinction between left and right rulers from U.S. Ambassador to the United Nations Jeanne Kirkpatrick's "Dictatorships and Double Standards," *Commentary* (November 1979). Between January 25 and 29, the United States provided aid to the three "authoritarian" powers in Latin America. On January 25, Chile's military regime restructured its $1.6 billion debt to make repayment easier. On January 27, Brazil obtained foreign loans of $6.5 billion, and the administration lifted U.S. export controls on technology to benefit Brazil's arms industry. Finally, on January 28, the United States sold $2 million worth of helicopter parts to Guatemala after its dictator, General Oscar Mejia Victores, announced that elections could be held on July 1, 1985.

President Reagan honors Ambassador Jeanne Kirkpatrick for service at the United Nations. Ronald Reagan Library

February 1, 1984

Norway expels five Soviet diplomats accused of espionage after it arrests a Norwegian civil servant.

Norway based its espionage claims on data obtained from Arne Treholt, who spied for the Soviet Union and Iraq. Treholt had access to sensitive data as the chief of information of the Foreign Ministry and a Norwegian delegate to the United Nations. The U.S. Federal Bureau of Investigation assisted the Norwegians on the case for over three years before Treholt was arrested at Oslo's airport on January 21, 1984, on the way to give more information to the Soviet secret police. Allegedly, he also sold classified documents to Iraq for $50,000.

February 5, 1984

U.S-backed Lebanon government collapses because of Muslim groups fighting Lebanon's army.

After Israeli troops withdrew from Lebanon, Lebanon's President Amin Gemayel was unable to restore Lebanese Christian relations with many Muslim factions, which were being helped militarily by Syria and Iran. As fighting grew between competing Lebanese groups in early 1984, the United States suffered more casualties and U.S. congressional members became concerned. On January 8, two Marines were wounded and one was killed; on January 30 another Marine was killed and several were wounded. Subsequently, on February 1 and 2, the Democratic caucus in the House and Senate approved resolutions asking President Reagan to withdraw the U.S. Marines from Lebanon. Although the United States tried to assist President Gemayel, his government collapsed on February 5 when moderate Muslim cabinet members resigned. This took place just as American, French, British, and Italian troops prepared to withdraw from Lebanon. On February 6, dissident Muslim forces took control of West Beirut while 1,400 U.S. Marines left Beirut's airport to embark on American naval ships along the Lebanese coast from which U.S. naval aircraft and guns could bombard Muslim and Syrian military positions. Throughout February, Israeli aircraft joined U.S. naval planes and guns to assist Gemayel's Christian armies.

Meanwhile on February 15, 1984, the White House announced plans to withdraw U.S. forces from Lebanon by March 18, 1984. British and Italian forces left the area on February 7. On February 22, Reagan told reporters the Marines would not just "bug out and go home" but might return if it served the cause of peace in Lebanon. Peace, however, was a long distance away in Lebanon. At the end of the month, Gemayel contacted Syria's President Hafez Assad to negotiate better relations with the Muslims.

See March 5, 1984.

February 9, 1984

Soviet President Yuri Andropov dies; he is replaced by Konstantin U. Chernenko.

Illness caused Andropov's death at age 69. His February 14 funeral was attended by most high-ranking world leaders. Vice President George H.W. Bush represented the United States. On February 13, the Communist Party's Central Committee elected the 72-year-old Chernenko as general secretary. A protégé of Leonid Brezhnev, Chernenko appeared to be a compromise candidate between Politburo members favoring military build-ups and those wanting economic reform. In Ambassador Anatoly Dobrynin's assessment, Chernenko "was the most feeble and unimaginative Soviet leader of the last two decades." Soviet foreign affairs decisions were guided by Foreign Minister Gromyko.

February 15, 1984

Terrorists in Rome assassinate U.S. General Leamon R. Hunt.

General Leamon R. Hunt, director general of the 10-nation Sinai peacekeeping force, was shot by a group identifying itself as the Fighting Communist Party, a faction linked to the Red Brigade in Italy. The caller said they wanted all "imperialist forces to leave Lebanon."

February 18, 1984

China and the Soviet Union sign a $1.2 billion trade agreement, increasing their 1984 trade by 50 percent.

This trade deal had been completed in January, but the announcement was delayed owing to Soviet President Yuri Andropov's death. He had sought better relations with the Chinese. China's Deputy Prime Minister Min Wan-li attended Andropov's funeral, after which the deal was jointly announced.

February 21, 1984

The United States tells a Geneva arms control meeting the Soviets had used chemical weapons in Laos, Cambodia, and Afghanistan.

Although the United States contended that the Soviets had used chemical weapons in Southeast Asia and Afghanistan, many scientific investigators argued that there were other, perhaps better, explanations for the toxic materials causing illness in refugees who fled from the conflicts in those two areas. During the 1984 Geneva Conference on Disarmament, both the United States and the USSR offered proposals to control chemical weapons. On January 10, Moscow proposed that both Warsaw Pact and NATO members ban chemical weapons. On February 21, the Soviets also offered to permit inspection rights to verify a chemical weapons arms control system. The U.S. proposal was made in April.

March 5, 1984

Lebanon abrogates its 1983 withdrawal agreement with Israel and seeks compromise with Syria.

The 1983 Lebanese-Israeli agreement achieved few results because Israel's evacuation of Lebanon depended on a Syrian troop withdrawal (see May 17, 1983). Although Syria's President Hafiz al-Assad denied that he had forced Gemayel to abrogate the Israeli agreement, the president of Lebanon did so on March 5.

March 13, 1984

The GATT council upholds Nicaragua's contention that the United States violated GATT rules by cutting Nicaragua's sugar quotas.

The Reagan administration had ordered the cut in Nicaraguan sugar imports to the United States in 1983. This action reduced the quota from 56,800 tons in 1982 to 6,000 tons in 1983. Nicaragu acomplained to the General Agreement on Tariffs and Trade (GATT) Council in Geneva that it lost $54 million because of Reagan's action. Drawing on the report of its study panel, the 90-member GATT Council ruled that the United States violated trade rules and should either renew Nicaragua's sugar quota or restrict all foreign sugar suppliers on the same basis. The Reagan administration rejected the GATT ruling, refusing to rescind its action against Nicaragua. Although the United States had been a principal advocate of GATT since its inception, President Reagan's unilateral action overrode the council's effectiveness in pushing for "free trade" principles.

March 14, 1984

Jordan's King Hussein rejects American proposals for talks with Israel, saying Washington is pro-Israel; asks USSR for aid.

President Reagan wanted King Hussein to represent Palestinian interests and establish a Jordanian protectorship over the West Bank Arab sectors. The U.S. proposal was made in 1982 but Hussein delayed a decision. Apparently, his meeting with Yasser Arafat, chairman of the Palestine Liberation Organization (PLO), from February 26 to March 1 persuaded Hussein to join other Arab states in opposing the U.S. plan. Hussein told a *New York Times* reporter that during election years, U.S. politicians had no principles but succumbed to the "dictates of Israel." He disliked America's refusal to condemn Jewish settlements on the West Bank, believing Israel would never end its West Bank occupation unless the United States cut off its economic assistance, something the United States would not do. Hussein claimed the United States praised Afghan rebels as freedom fighters but called Palestinian rebels terrorists.

The King's remarks anticipated President Reagan's decision on March 21 to cancel the sale of Stinger antiaircraft missiles to help Jordan defend itself from Iran and Syria. King Hussein claimed that the Jewish

King Hussein and Queen Noor are entertained at the White House by President and Mrs. Reagon. Ronald Reagon Library

lobby in the United States told members of Congress that Jordan would use these weapons against Israel. Under similar circumstances, after the United States refused to sell AWACS to Saudi Arabia, the Saudis purchased a $4 billion air defense system from France on January 16, 1982. King Hussein asked the Soviet Union for help and received it.

March 18, 1984

U.S. surveillance planes in Egypt monitor trouble between Libya and the Sudan.

There had been tension between Libya and the Sudan for some time because Sudanese President Gaafar al-Nimeiry accused Libya's Mu'ammar al-Gadhafi of assisting Sudanese rebels fighting against Nimeiry's regime. This tension verged on war after an unidentified plane flew over the Sudanese city of Omdurman and dropped five bombs, killing five people and wounding two others. Libya denied sending the aircraft and claimed that the United States had fabricated the incident to justify sending aid to Egypt and the Sudan in opposing Libya. Egypt had been helping the Sudan to construct a defense network, and the American AWACS supplemented those facilities. The crisis subsided, however, and by April 19, the AWACS could be withdrawn.

March 23, 1984

Japanese Prime Minister Nakasone visits China and offers the Chinese a $2.1 billion industrial development loan.

Although Chinese-Japanese relations grew friendly after Japan renewed diplomatic relations with Beijing in 1972, Prime Minister Yasuhiro Nakasone promoted economic ties with China and South Korea. He also hoped these two nations would improve their relationship with each other. In addition to arranging the $2.1 billion low-interest loan for China, Nakasone discussed with his Chinese hosts the future of East Asian relations with the United States and the Soviet Union. China's leader, Deng Xiaoping, indicated that China hoped for better ties with Washington but Deng could not predict improved ties with Moscow.

March 31, 1984

In Honduras, the pro-American General Gustavo Alvarez Martínez is exiled to Costa Rica; he is replaced by Air Force General Walter López Reyes.

Under General Alvarez Martínez, the United States had built Honduran airstrips and military bases to train and supply anti-Sandinista rebels to fight in

Nicaragua. The United States increased its military aid to Honduras from $9.1 million in 1981 to $41 million in 1984, and its economic aid from $47 million to $108.5 million. After the United States announced on February 9 that its forces in Honduras would double in order to carry out new military exercises, these plans caused complaints among the Honduran army and air force. While not anti-American, the new commander of the Honduran armed forces, General López Reyes, said he would adjust the nation's economy by spending less on defense and more to stimulate export. He also promised full support for the Contadora process to bring peace to Central America.

April 3, 1984

Secretary of State George Shultz approves preemptive action against terrorists—the "Shultz Doctrine."

Believing that terrorist acts in Lebanon had upset U.S. policy and cost American lives, Shultz was eager to have the U.S. government use antiterrorist tactics. In a public address, he stated that the best way to combat terrorism was to retaliate against terrorists or to strike preemptively against groups planning terrorist raids. In a national security directive of 1982, President Reagan gave the State Department jurisdiction over terrorist activity. Subsequently, in March 1984, Shultz tried to involve the Pentagon and the Central Intelligence Agency in attacking the terrorists. Lt. Colonel Oliver North of the National Security Council staff drafted a plan to kill potential or verified terrorists. Although previous executive orders prohibited U.S. involvement in foreign assassinations, *Washington Post* reporter Bob Woodward indicated that Colonel North thought it was "time to kill the . . . terrorists by using CIA trained teams of foreign nationals to neutralize them."

Although Shultz probably did not agree with North's extreme remedy, the colonel expressed the attitude of many Americans. Shultz probably intended that the CIA should obtain intelligence to prevent a terrorist attack. In some cases this happened, but tracking every terrorist cell was impossible. Because the Beirut bombings of the U.S. embassy and U.S. Marine barracks in 1983 had heightened public awareness of the terrorist threat, the "Shultz Doctrine" of preemptive or retaliatory strikes gained much attention in 1984. Following President Reagan's reelection in November 1984, invoking the Shultz Doctrine seemed more likely, leading Defense Secretary Caspar Weinberger to prepare criteria for deploying the U.S. armed forces by limiting circumstances for the State Department to call for military action. American military officers believed the use of clandestine force incited terrorists to retaliate in greater force.

In contrast to the Pentagon's caution, the CIA under William Casey seemed willing to use any methods to achieve its end. Moreover, the National Security Council gained wide authority from President Reagan. Thus, NSC staff members such as Colonel North were anxious to engage in clandestine attacks on those who opposed U.S. policy as well as terrorists. George Ball became a severe critic of the Shultz Doctrine. A former adviser to President Lyndon Johnson and one of the few in the Johnson White House to oppose the 1965 Vietnam escalation, Ball argued in the *New York Times* on December 16, 1984, that Shultz forgot the basic concepts that American leadership traditionally reflected. Rather than reduce the United States to the lowest level of terrorist behavior, Ball wanted other nations to follow a U.S. leader who sought collective international action against all forms of group or state sponsored terrorism.

April 4, 1984

U.S. complicity in mining Nicaraguan seaports is revealed.

After the Nicaraguan Contra rebels announced on January 8, 1984, that they had mined their nation's seaports, minor news stories appeared of ships being damaged by the mines. On February 25, three Nicaraguan fishing trawlers were hit near the El Bluff port on the Atlantic coast. Next, a Dutch cargo ship and freighters from Panama, Japan, and Liberia were damaged off the Pacific coastal waters near Puerto Corinto and Puerto Sandino. Finally on March 20, a Soviet tanker was struck. On March 30, Nicaragua appealed to the United Nations, claiming that the United States had been involved in the mining operation. Within the week news leaked that the CIA had helped plan and carry out the mining. When the U.N. Security Council voted to condemn the mining on April 4, the United States vetoed the resolution. The next day, French Foreign Minister Claude Cheysson offered to cooperate with other European countries in sweeping the mines from Nicaraguan ports. France had voted for the Security Council resolution, and although the British delegate abstained in the vote, British Prime Minister Margaret Thatcher strongly protested the mining as a dangerous precedent against trade on the high seas.

On April 7, information leaked by the Reagan administration confirmed the CIA role in mining Nicaragua's harbors. President Reagan approved the operation in December 1983, and the CIA supervised Contra forces, who laid mines along both seacoasts of Nicaragua and in Lake Nicaragua. Since the CIA wanted only to frighten foreign ships entering Nicaraguan ports, its operatives located a Martin Marietta plant that made "firecracker" mines that created mostly noise and splash and would damage but not sink a ship. This detail had been kept secret because the purpose was to cut off trade to Nicaragua or to increase insurance rates for ships using Nicaraguan ports. News of direct U.S. involvement in the mining operation shocked many members of Congress, America's NATO allies, and other international observers. Although Deputy Secretary of State Kenneth W. Dam called the mining "collective self-defense" to stop Nicaragua's supply of weapons to El Salvador, both the House of Representatives and the Senate passed resolutions on April 10 and 11, respectively, that condemned the Reagan administration's action. In the Senate, 41 Republicans joined the Democrats in approving the resolution. Senator Barry M. Goldwater (R-Ariz.) wrote a critical letter to CIA Director William Casey saying that such action was an "act of war," and was deplorable.

April 7, 1984

Vietnam reports that it repelled a Chinese invasion of 2,000 troops.

Since the Vietnamese conquest of Cambodia (Kampuchea) in 1979, warfare had sometimes erupted on the Chinese-Vietnamese border. On April 2, 1984, China shelled Vietnamese border forces in retaliation for a Vietnamese attack and later reported killing or wounding 35 Vietnamese alleged to have planted land mines on Chinese soil. Vietnam accused China of attacking on April 6, but stated that China had failed. These incidents may have been a Chinese attempt to bolster the Khmer Rouge forces of Pol Pot in Cambodia. The Khmer armies rallied against Vietnam by gaining supplies from Thailand, where many Cambodians fled as refugees.

The United States was indirectly involved in these Southeast Asian conflicts. The United States sent aid to the Cambodian refugees, and the Reagan administration increased military assistance to Thailand, which included 40 M-8 tanks and some advanced F-16A fighter aircraft. This equipment was supposedly to help Bangkok defend its border areas.

April 11, 1984

Mikhail Gorbachev may be Chernenko's successor.

The April 11 Politburo meeting was auspicious because Gorbachev, the Politburo's youngest member and one who favored reform, nominated Chernenko as the Supreme Soviet President. This was a performance to signify he would be Chernenko's heir apparent.

See March 10, 1985.

April 13, 1984

With Congress in recess, President Reagan uses emergency powers to send $32 million of military aid to El Salvador.

After Congress left for its Easter recess, the president sent helicopters, ammunition, medical equipment, and spare parts to El Salvador. Congress had refused to fund military aid until the Salvadoran election was finalized in May. Reagan took the $32 million from funds appropriated for other countries. The president said he waited until the recess to avoid a confrontation with Congress, telling his weekly radio audience that he could not turn his back "on this crisis at our doorsteps." He wanted Congress to approve another $62 million for El Salvador when it returned from recess, a request made more difficult because of Reagan's emergency action that, legally, Congress did not have to approve. Despite Reagan's desire to aid El Salvador and Nicaragua's Contra rebels, many members of Congress and the public disagreed. A Louis Harris poll found on May 17, 1984, that 74 percent of Americans opposed U.S. aid to El Salvador.

April 15, 1984

Senator Daniel Patrick Moynihan symbolically resigns in protest from the Senate Select Committee on Intelligence because the CIA mined Nicaraguan waters, but rejoins after CIA director William Casey apologizes.

Moynihan (D-N.Y.) and Senator Barry Goldwater (R-Ariz.) accused the CIA of not informing them of the covert mining of Nicaragua's harbors. Initially, Casey argued that he had told congressional intelligence committees about the mining. Meeting with the Committee on Intelligence, Casey read briefings of March 8 and 13 that mentioned the mining, and Senator Malcolm Wallop (R-Wyo.) contended that these comments made clear the CIA's intentions. Moynihandis agreed. He said that on March 8 the only reference was the word "mine" in a 27-word sentence. On March 13, the word "mines" appeared once in a 26-word sentence. Casey mentioned this in the midst of other Contra actions and never said the CIA was involved or that Reagan had authorized the mining. On April 26, Casey admitted to the committee that he had not kept the group adequately informed in the timely manner required by legislation.

April 17, 1984

Nicaragua takes complaints against the United States for aiding Contra rebels to the International Court of Justice, whose restraining order the United States ignores.

Nicaragua pursued action against American assistance to the rebels not only in the United Nations but also at the International Court of Justice at The Hague, a body whose opinions the United States had heretofore respected. Nevertheless, on April 8, the Reagan administration stated that it did not recognize the court's jurisdiction over the Nicaraguan issue, calling it a "domestic" issue and a propaganda ploy of the Sandinista regime. The court disagreed with the U.S. view and, after hearing Nicaragua's case, issued a restraining order on May 10. It declared that the United States should halt its mine blockade of Nicaraguan harbors while the court investigated other allegations of the case. Although the Reagan administration said it had stopped mining operations before May 10, it rejected the court's jurisdiction and said it would do so for the next two years.

The U.S. decision led foreign leaders to question the International Court's values relative to other nations. In 1946, when the U.S. Congress recognized the International Court's authority, it reserved the right to reject the court's involvement in "domestic issues," a term that, as in the Nicaraguan case, could be interpreted broadly. Over two-thirds of the 158 nations that recognized the court refused to grant it full authority over internal issues. For example, in 1970, Canada refused to accept the court's jurisdiction over a U.S. complaint on marine pollution caused by Canadians. Nevertheless, the American Society of International Lawyers, during a convention in Washington, D.C., adopted a resolution opposing the Reagan administration's position on the Nicaraguan issue. In international law, the blockade of a nation's coast is an act of war, and mining a nation's harbors is a principal means of an effective blockade. During the 1962 Cuban missile crisis, President John F. Kennedy's administration not only did not mine Cuba's harbors, but the U.S. navy patrolled the sea at some distance from Cuba's coast, where it carefully selected ships to inspect for nuclear missile material. Whether Kennedy's tactics were considered by Reagan is not known. Senator Malcolm Wallop (R-Wyo.), who usually backed Reagan's policies, suggested that a better course of action would have been to countersue Nicaragua for supporting El Salvador's rebels.

April 18, 1984

Vice President Bush proposes a ban on chemical weapons that seems designed to precipitate Soviet objections.

During March 1984, President Reagan accepted a draft treaty that would prohibit the use of chemical weapons as proposed by Secretary of State George Shultz. On March 30, President Reagan told a press conference that Vice President George H.W. Bush would offer this draft treaty during the United Nations Disarmament Conference to begin on April 18 in Geneva. Reagan said the draft would be a "bold" initiative for a comprehensive ban on chemical weapons. In its April 16 edition, *Time* magazine reported the U.S. proposal was "framed in terms guaranteed to invite Soviet objections" because the treaty required strict verification of each nation's chemical facilities. Produced by a compromise between the U.S. State and Defense Departments, the plan called for $1.126

billion to finance a chemical weapons buildup, while Bush traveled to Geneva to ask the U.N. Conference on Disarmament to adopt a procedure permitting inspection of all government-owned or -controlled facilities on 24 hours' notice. This terminology exempted privately owned plants from inspection, the very kind the United States used for its production. Because Soviet "government-owned" industry produced all defense material, the U.S. proposal would open Soviet industry to inspection. As expected, the Soviet delegates objected. President Reagan's attempt to begin production of nerve gas weapons was temporarily blocked by the House of Representatives, which deleted funds for the project on June 1, 1984.

April 19, 1984

Egypt and the Soviet Union renew diplomatic relations.

Diplomatic relations were severed in 1981 by Egyptian President Anwar al-Sadat, who accused the Soviet delegation of subverting his government. Believing relations should be restored, Egyptian President Hosni Mubarak contacted Moscow, and on April 19 both governments announced their agreement. The process was finalized on July 6, when the Soviet Ambassador Aleksandr V. Belonogov reached Cairo, and Egypt's Ambassador Salah Bassiouni went to Moscow.

April 22, 1984

Jonas Savimbi takes responsibility for bombing Cuban barracks in Huambo, Angola.

Savimbi, the head of the National Union for Total Independence of Angola (UNITA), which had been fighting against the government, claimed that over 200 people were killed when a jeep loaded with dynamite was driven into a Cuban military barracks and exploded. Among the dead, he said, were 37 Cuban officers and two Soviet army officers. Angola reported that 14 Cubans and 10 Angolans died while 70 people were injured. Although the U.S. Central Intelligence Agency rejected Cuban complaints that the United States had assisted the terrorists, the Reagan administration not only assisted Savimbi but also praised him for using the same tactics that the White House had denounced when the U.S. Marine barracks in Lebanon were bombed on October 25, 1983. On March 19, Cuba had offered to withdraw its 25,000 troops from Angola, but the United States and South Africa objected because Cuba wanted the United States and South Africa to stop aiding UNITA.

May 1, 1984

President Reagan concludes a five-day visit to China, where he signs accords on nuclear cooperation and cultural relations.

The Reagan administration wanted to improve relations with China, which had deteriorated badly

China's leader, Zhao Ziyang, entertains the Reagans. Ronald Reagan Library

because the president had dispatched arms to Taiwan and tried to restrict Chinese textile imports. In addition to approving agreements on nuclear cooperation and cultural and scientific exchanges during his visit from April 26 to May 1, Reagan applauded China's desire to reunite peacefully with Taiwan and agreed to send advanced U.S. computer technology to China. China's leader, Zhao Ziyang, urged Reagan to stop deploying missiles in Western Europe and to negotiate arms control agreements with the USSR. Although Reagan addressed the Chinese people on television, his speech was taped, and when the tape was broadcast, the Chinese had deleted Reagan's anti-Soviet rhetoric and references to the Soviets' shooting down a Korean Air Lines plane in September 1983.

May 5, 1984

José Napoleon Duarte wins the runoff election in El Salvador.

This was a runoff election because no candidate won a majority on March 25. U.S. officials approved of Duarte's victory because the Christian Democratic Party leader was considered the "democratic-moderate," while Roberto d'Aubuisson, the National Republican Party candidate, was known as the power behind the right-wing death squads that terrorized the populace. Although Duarte won 52 percent of the vote, d'Aubuisson's showing revealed the strength of landowners, the military, and their allies. On February 2, former U.S. Ambassador to El Salvador Robert White told a congressional committee that d'Aubuisson oversaw the assassination of Archbishop Oscar Romero, which was confirmed on March 21 by former Salvadoran intelligence officer Roberto Santivanez. Because the Christian Democrats lacked a majority in the National Assembly, they formed a coalition cabinet that weakened Duarte's position. During his campaign, Duarte promised what the U.S. Congress wanted to hear—to stop the death squads, to pursue land reform, and to negotiate peace with the rebels. Reports were that the CIA spent $2.1 million to help Duarte's campaign. Duartee spoused the same goals as when he was El Salvador's president from December 1980 to April 1982; he did little then to reform the military or support land reform. Nevertheless, Duarte's election enabled President Reagan to persuade Congress to continue to provide military aid to El Salvador.

May 6, 1984

Panamanian election is won by Nicolas Ardito Barletta in a close race against Arnulfo Arias Madrid; wins approval of White House.

The close race caused disputes about the vote count and delayed Barletta's taking office officially until October 11, 1984. Arias Madrid had been elected president three previous times but was overthrown each time by the military because he tried to reorganize the corrupt National Defense Forces, controlled by General Manuel Noriega. Barletta was Noriega's "front man" but won the election by only 1,713 votes out of 600,000 accepted ballots. During the counting, over 200,000 ballots had been challenged. After the Electoral Commission named Barletta the winner, he visited Washington, D.C., on July 27, where he received praise from the Reagan administration that it later regretted extending. For details, see R.M. Kocter and Guillermo Sanchez, *In the Time of the Tyrants: Panama*, 1968–1990 (1990).

May 7, 1984

The Soviet Union refuses to participate in the summer Olympic Games, held at Los Angeles.

Although claiming there was inadequate security for its athletes, Moscow was disturbed because President Carter withdrew Americans from the 1980 Olympics in Moscow and because on March 1, 1984, the United States denied a visa to Oleg Yermishkin, a Soviet Olympic official who, Washington said, was in the Soviet secret police (KGB). The Soviets had denounced this U.S. action but did not announce their withdrawal from the 1984 summer games until they persuaded other Communist nations to join the boycott. Soon after, Bulgaria, East Germany, Czechoslovakia, Vietnam, Laos, and Mongolia refused to participate in the games. The absence of these countries enabled the United States to dominate the 1984 Olympics.

May 9, 1984

Libyan leader Mu'ammar Al-Gadhafi accuses the United States and Britain of attempting to assassinate him.

Gadhafi complained that a May 8 attack was planned in Washington and London. Twenty gunmen attacked the barracks where Gadhafi usually resided, but they failed to kill the leader because loyal Libyan troops killed 15 of the gunmen.

May 9, 1984

On a visit to Japan Vice President George H.W. Bush urges the Japanese to lower their import restrictions and liberalize their financial markets.

Bush's visit with Prime Minister Nakasone and other Japanese officials dramatized the ongoing U.S. effort to blame Japan for the unfavorable U.S. trade balance and to seek changes in Japanese commercial policy. On January 30, 1984, Japan signed an agreement to let U.S. telecommunications firms compete with Japanese firms on an equal basis in its domestic market. On April 21, Tokyo deregulated some of its financial markets so that foreign bankers and investment firms could operate in Japan. Later, on May 29, the two nations agreed to strengthen the yen and create an international euro-yen market for European currency. Japan steadily invested more in U.S. corporations. On April 24, 1984, Nippon Kokan bought a 50 percent share in U.S. Intergroup Steel, a subsidiary of National Steel.

May 10, 1984

The Danish parliament refuses to deploy U.S. missiles that NATO had assigned; the Dutch delay deployment.

In Denmark, the antinuclear missile movement was successful in electing its candidates to parliament. Denmark became the first NATO country to reject plans to deploy U.S. intermediate-range missiles as a countermeasure to the Soviet Union's SS-20 missiles. More serious to NATO plans, the Dutch decided on June 13 to delay their scheduled deployment of 48 cruise missiles. The Dutch parliament voted 79 to 71 to delay deployment for two years, pending a possible arms control agreement between the Soviet Union and the United States.

May 14, 1984

President Reagan certifies that Haiti has improved its human rights record and can receive U.S. economic aid.

Although the Haitian dictator Jean-Claude Duvalier promised to guarantee a free press and respect human rights, as soon as an opposition newspaper criticized the government, Duvalier banned all opposition activity on May 10. Opposition to Duvalier continued, and on May 30, 1984, the U.S. Federal Bureau of Investigation arrested 13 people in Sidell, Louisiana, for plotting to overthrow Haiti's government. Nevertheless, the Reagan administration certified that Haiti had improved its performance in protecting human rights and thus was eligible to obtain U.S. aid. American corporations had considerable investments in light industry in Haiti and supported Duvalier because he kept Haitian labor costs low.

May 15, 1984

The Senate rejects President Reagan's appointment of Leslie Lenkowsky as deputy director of the U.S. Information Agency (USIA).

Lenkowsky's confirmation failed because he had blacklisted prominent Americans from speaking in the USIA's overseas program. News of the blacklist became public on February 9, 1984, after Lenkowsky admitted to a congressional committee that the Reagan administration had a list of 81 liberals and anti-Reaganites who should not be accepted for the agency speakers program. The *New York Times* published 84 names on March 15, including those of Ralph Nader, David Brinkley, Walter Cronkite, and Coretta Scott King. Although Lenkowsky denied preparing the list, he was refuted by two USIA officials, W. Scott Thomson and John Moshen. Members of Congress objected to the blacklists as restricting free speech and making the USIA program contradictory to American ideals of free expression of opinion.

May 16, 1984

Mexico's president warns against using force in Central America and urges support of the Contadora group.

While visiting Washington, President Miguel de la Madrid Hurtado addressed a joint session of Congress to explain that the Communist threat was not serious in Central America. Because Mexico led the Contadora effort of Latin American nations seeking a negotiated peace in that region, de la Madrid wanted U.S. policy to give primary attention to that effort, something the Reagan administration had not done. In addition to asking Congress to support Contadora, de la Madrid said that U.S. budget deficits caused higher interest rates, which lowered standards of living in Mexico and other debtor nations. Every 1 percent increase in U.S. interest rates, he stated, added $3.5 billion a year to the interest that developing nations paid on their debts. Because of de la Madrid's criticism, President Reagan gave him a cold reception at the White House. The only agreement they reached was Mexico's promise to end direct export subsidies if the United States showed proof of injury before Mexico levied tariffs to protect key trade items.

May 20, 1984

The Arab League condemns Iran for attacking Saudi Arabian and Kuwaiti oil tankers in the Persian Gulf but rejects a U.S. offer of naval protection.

Since early 1984, Iraq had attacked Iranian ships at the Kharq Island Oil Terminal, while Iran retaliated against pro-Iraqi ships in the Persian Gulf. The United States offered to protect the oil lanes and the Strait of Hormuz if the Arab League provided naval bases in the Gulf. An American battle group headed by the aircraft carrier *Kitty Hawk* was in the Arabian Sea and ready to operate. At this time, however, the Arab League preferred to keep U.S. ships at a distance.

May 20, 1984

The Soviet Union announces recent missile deployment in retaliation for U.S. military buildups in Western Europe.

Over a period of six days, Moscow took steps to counter U.S. military activities. First, on May 14, the Soviets deployed more intermediate-range nuclear missiles in East Germany in response to the U.S. deployment of Pershing IIs in West Germany beginning in November 1983. Second, on May 20, Soviet officials increased the number of nuclear missile submarines patrolling off the coast of the United States.

May 24, 1984

Two days after acquitting an army officer of killing three agricultural advisers, a Salvadoran court convicts five national guardsmen for killing four American Catholic nuns.

These two events in May highlighted the limits on U.S. policy in getting El Salvador to prosecute death squads in its army who committed terrorist acts. On May 22, Salvadoran courts freed the army officer accused of slaying two Americans and one Salvadoran land reform official in January 1981. On May 24, however, the court sentenced killers of the Catholic nuns to 30 years in prison. The conviction was based on evidence pieced together for the prosecutor by the U.S. Federal Bureau of Investigation. This case was not closed, however, because Salvadoran President José Napoleon Duarte had not followed up on allegations that Defense Minister Carlos Eugenio Vides had "quite possibly" covered up for the leaders who ordered the four women shot.

May 27, 1984

Egyptian President Hosni Mubarak's party wins 391 of 448 parliamentary seats.

While President Mubarak's National Democratic Party remained dominant in Egyptian politics, the election indicated the revival of the liberal New Wafd Party, which gained 57 seats in parliament.

May 30, 1984

Eden Pastora Gómez, a Nicaraguan rebel leader, is wounded by a bomb that kills three journalists including one American. Later investigations implicate the CIA in the assassination plot.

Pastora had led rebels in the 1979 overthrow of Nicaragua's Somoza regime. After breaking with the Sandinistas in 1982, he formed a rebel group in southern Nicaragua but refused to work with the U.S.- backed northern rebels, the FDN Contras, because their leaders had been national guard officers under the Somoza regime. Initially the United States provided funds for Pastora's ARDE group, but by 1984, the CIA wanted Pastora to unite with the Contras to end congressional complaints that they were a right-wing military organization, compared with Pastora's more "democratic" group. Because Pastora refused to join the Contras or be subservient to the CIA, the agency gave him a deadline of May 30, 1984, to change his mind or be cut off from future U.S. funds. According to investigative journalist Leslie Cockburn, the CIA not only enticed another ARDE commander, Alfonso Robelo, to break with Pastora but also plotted to kill Pastora if he refused to join the Contras. On the day that the CIA deadline ran out, a professional killer from Libya, Amal Galil, disguised as a photojournalist, tried to kill Pastora during his press conference in La Penca, a town on the Costa Rican border. After the La Penca bombing, the ABC News stringer Tony Avirgan and the *New York Times* stringer Martha Honey investigated the bombing. Avirgan described his presence at the bombing: "I was just sitting on a box, actually not very far from where the bomb was planted, drinking a cup of coffee. And I mean it's not even nice to think about, but one of the reasons I wasn't killed was because there was another journalist, a good friend [Linda Frazier], who was standing right in front of me and took the major impact of the blast and she was killed."

Avirgan's experience led him to join with Honey to investigate the bombing. Although the U.S. State Department attributed the bombing to a Spanish Basque terror group and claimed that Frazier had planted the bomb, the Avirgan-Honey investigation proved that the State Department had misled reporters in Washington. Their investigation showed that Galil traveled to Costa Rica on the stolen Danish passport of Per Anker Hansen, a freelance photographer. Galil (Hansen) carried a metal photographer's box when the group of journalist went to La Penca on May 30 and placed it near Pastora just before the blast. The next day Galil disappeared from Costa Rica, having been aided by John Hull, an American rancher whose farm was a staging ground for the delivery of CIA weapons to the Contras. Hansen's escape was also planned by Costa Rica's Directorate of Intelligence and Security (DIS). Pastora himself blamed Lt. Colonel Oliver North of the National Security Council staff, who frequently criticized Pastora as a drug dealer and praised the FDN rebel leaders despite their Somoza connections. In July 1984, after recovering from his wounds, Pastora visited Washington but was told by the U.S. State Department that his rebel group would receive no more economic or military aid from the United States.

June 5, 1984

Saudi planes shoot down an Iranian plane over the Persian Gulf.

Defending its interests against Iranian attacks on oil tankers in the gulf, Saudi F-15 fighter planes directed by American AWACS reconnaissance planes attacked an Iranian plane preparing to hit a Kuwaiti tanker near Al Arabiyah in the Persian Gulf. On June 10, both Iran and Iraq told U.N. Secretary-General Javier Pérez de Cuellar that they would stop attacks on civilian targets. They did not end attacks on shipping, however, because both countries sought to use these attacks to win the war they had waged since 1980.

June 6, 1984

The fortieth anniversary of World War II, D-day, is celebrated by President Reagan and Western leaders.

Veterans of the D-Day 1944 landing joined President Reagan, Great Britain's Queen Elizabeth, and France's President François Mitterrand to celebrate the event beginning the liberation of Western Europe from the Germans. Mitterrand stated that Nazis are foes of all people but that the German people have been reconciled with their present-day allies. President Reagan paid tribute to the at least 20 million Soviet citizens who died in the war but criticized the Soviet Union for dominating its Eastern European neighbors.

June 9, 1984

Leaders of the seven largest industrial democracies end their annual summit in London.

This annual summit, in which President Reagan and other leaders discussed economic affairs, achieved no significant results. The final communiqué focused on the Third World debt problem and the need to liberalize trade regulations. The European leaders urged President Reagan to cut the U.S. budget deficit and lower interest rates. The president replied that he disliked high interest rates but resisted efforts to raise U.S. taxes to cut the deficit and high interest costs.

June 10, 1984

The SDI program claims a significant advance when a homing device intercepts and destroys a mock ballistic missile warhead in midcourse flight.

Following President Reagan's call to develop the Strategic Defense Initiative (SDI), the Defense Department established an SDI Organization in January 1984 to determine the feasibility of such a program. Following three tests, which failed for "mechanical reasons," the SDI team launched a rocket from Meck Island in the Kwajalein Archipelago, a part of the Marshall Islands, that struck a Minuteman I intercontinental missile launched 30 minutes before from Vanderbilt Air Force Base, California, that was flying 100 miles above the earth. The Defense Department said this exercise involving Homing Overlay Experiment (HOE) showed that the homing guidance system and kinetic energy weapons could destroy enemy missiles by colliding with them at great speed.

SDI's rockets were designed to intercept Soviet missiles or warheads at one of three phases of flight—in the boost phase, where missiles were most vulnerable after being fired; in the midcourse phase, where MIRV warheads separated but were harder to detect; and in the reentry phase, as the warheads returned to the earth's atmosphere heading for their targets. The June 10 test demonstrated how a missile in the midcourse or reentry phase might be hit. Critics of SDI contended that the June 10 test greatly oversimplified the problems involved in tracking, finding, and striking 10 warheads per launcher speeding through space and reentering to hit U.S. targets.

Nearly a decade later, on August 18, 1993, the *New York Times* reported that four former members of the Reagan administration acknowledged the 1984 SDI's HOE test had been rigged to make the test appear that a "bullet hit a bullet in space." The *Times* article led the Pentagon and the General Accounting Office (GAO) to examine these charges. A year later, on July 23, 1994, the *New York Times* reported the investigation showed Pentagon officials installed a small bomb to explode in the dummy warhead when the HOE interceptor flew past. The Pentagon claimed the idea was to deceive the Soviet Union about SDI's capabilities but, of course, it also fooled American news reporters, Congress, and the public.

June 20, 1984

The Nunn Amendment to reduce U.S. troops in Western Europe is defeated.

A member of the Senate Armed Services Committee, Senator Sam Nunn (D-Ga.) wanted Western Europeans to pay a larger share of their defense costs. The NATO nations, he argued, had agreed in 1978 to increase these expenditures by 3 percent a year, but most did not do so. Except for the United States, only Canada increased its defense budget (by 5 percent), and Great Britain increased its budget by 3 percent in 1983. In contrast, West Germany's increase was 1.9 percent, Italy's 1.1 percent, and France's 0.9 percent. The Nunn Amendment required the withdrawal of 30,000 American soldiers from Europe each year that the NATO members failed to fulfill the 3 percent increase. The United States had assigned 326,414 troops to NATO. Although Nunn wanted to encourage larger NATO defense expenditures, the NATO leaders were dismayed with the amendment because they had already taken great political risks by deploying American missiles on their territory.

Moreover, the Europeans contended that since 1970 their increase had been 44 percent (averaging over 3 percent a year), while Washington's increase was only 27 percent in 14 years. Their economies, they argued, suffered because of high U.S. interest rates. West German leaders added that their compulsory military service created an essential strategic reserve, while the United States had canceled its draft in 1973. The Reagan administration lobbied to defeat Nunn's amendment, and Senator William Cohen (R-Me.) proposed a substitute amendment urging the NATO allies to increase their defense contributions but omitting clauses about troop withdrawals. On June 20, the U.S. Senate voted 55 to 41 to defeat the Nunn Amendment but approved Cohen's amendment of the U.S. concern about the burden of sharing NATO defense costs.

June 22, 1984

A plot by El Salvador's right-wing ARENA Party to kill U.S. Ambassador Thomas R. Pickering is thwarted.

Reagan administration officials revealed that members of Roberto d'Aubuisson's ARENA Party had planned to kill Ambassador Pickering in May 1984. The d'Aubuisson group disliked the CIA's role in helping El Salvador's President José Napoleon Duarte win the election of May 5, 1984. Although d'Aubuisson denied any involvement in the plot, President Reagan sent his roving ambassador General Vernon Walters to El Salvador to warn right-wing ARENA leaders of serious consequences if their "death squads" tried to kill Pickering. The plan was aborted (see June 25, 1984). President Duarte never fulfilled his preelection promise to investigate the military-connected death squads but did appoint Colonel Rinaldo Golcher to clean up the Treasury Police. Golcher found that intelligence division S-2 of the Treasury Police was linked to a 2,000-man force that had carried out executions and other abuses. One result of Golcher's investigation was the removal of Colonel Nicolas Carranza as head of the Treasury Police. Carranza, who was in the pay of the CIA, was connected to the death squads and implicated d'Aubuisson in the murder of El Salvador's Archbishop Romero in 1980. He was sent to West Germany as a military attaché on May 24, 1984.

June 25, 1984

The United States and Nicaragua conduct peace talks at Manzanillo, Mexico, the first of a series of nine rounds of talks.

The Manzanillo talks resulted from Secretary of State George Shultz's surprise visit with Nicaragua's President Daniel Ortega in Managua on June 1, 1984. Shultz stopped there after attending the inauguration of El Salvador's President Duarte. During the discussions on June 25, the United States said it hoped the bilateral talks could coordinate with the Contadora process in obtaining a broad regional agreement. Nicaragua was most interested in preventing U.S. or Contra rebel attacks.

June 25, 1984

El Salvador's Roberto d'Aubuisson visits several U.S. senators who prefer his methods to those of El Salvador's president.

Although d'Aubuisson was a leader of right-wing death squads and had been implicated in attempts to assassinate Thomas Pickering, the U.S. ambassador to El Salvador, the Reagan administration granted him a visa. A conservative group, the Young Americans for Freedom, sponsored d'Aubuisson's visit, and Senator Jesse Helms (R-N.C.) hosted receptions with about a dozen members of Congress. Helms stated that he admired d'Aubuisson's use of terror to wipe out the rebels in El Salvador, tactics that had caused killings on both sides for the past five years despite extensive U.S. aid. Because the Reagan administration had denied visas to liberal and left-wing foreigners desiring to visit the United States, many critics believed d'Aubuisson should also have been prevented from entering the country. Although U.S. State Department officials admitted that d'Aubuisson probably knew in advance of the plot against Ambassador Pickering, they claimed he was not directly involved.

June 29, 1984

The Soviet Union seeks negotiations to ban weapons in space but rejects counterproposals by the United States.

In a formal diplomatic note, the Soviet Union offered to conduct talks on banning space weapons. The Reagan administration stated that space weapons should be part of broader arms control talks. On July 21, the USSR made a second offer, while the United States made two counteroffers on July 24 and July 28. Moscow rejected the suggestions for broader talks and negotiations did not begin. On July 17, Moscow and Washington did agree to modernize the hot line communications system between the White House and the Kremlin.

June 29, 1984

The Reverend Jesse Jackson, a Democratic presidential candidate, returns from Cuba, bringing 22 Americans and 26 Cuban political prisoners freed by Cuban leader Fidel Castro.

This lead to Cuban-American talks. Soon after Jackson returned, U.S. and Cuban representatives began talks on July 12 in New York City about returning to Cuba the Cuban criminals and mental patients who arrived in the United States during the 1980 boatlift.

July 17, 1984

Vietnam returns the remains of eight American servicemen killed during the war.

Although on July 11 Secretary of State George Shultz announced that negotiations with Vietnam had been stalemated because Hanoi was not willing to provide data on all the 2,489 American personnel listed as missing in action (MIA), Hanoi returned some of the bones it believed to be Americans' remains. Because of the POW/MIA attention given to the Vietnam War, on July 2, the U.S. State Department said a total of 2,489 men were unaccounted for in Vietnam, while 8,177 were unaccounted for from the Korean

War (1951–1953). Richard Nixon precipitated the Vietnam POW issue on April 16, 1971, when he made the return of all American POWs a condition for North Vietnam to fulfill before American troops would leave Vietnam. Nixon's conditions did not mention American troops listed as MIA. His omission became clear in March 1973, when the POWs returned home.

July 18, 1984

The U.S. Drug Enforcement Agency (DEA) claims Nicaraguan leaders engage in drug smuggling; the Sandinistas deny charges.

The DEA filed affidavits in Miami's district court that Nicaragua was directly involved in the cocaine traffic from South America. They arrested six suspects in Miami and charged them with handling cocaine that allegedly came from Colombia through Nicaragua. On July 28, a federal grand jury indicted one Nicaraguan, Frederico Vaughan, and 10 others, including three top-level Colombian cocaine traffickers. One Colombian official, Pablo Escobar, was in a photograph released on August 8 that allegedly showed him loading cocaine onto a plane in Nicaragua. Although DEA evidence implicated Vaughan, an aide to Nicaragua's interior minister, the agency had no firm evidence for its accusations against Interior Minister Tomás Borge or the Defense Minister Humberto Ortega. On August 2, a defector, Antonio Farach, told a Senate committee that Humberto was involved in drugs but could provide no indictable evidence.

July 21, 1984

A congressional report says U.S. military forces are not combat ready, a claim the Defense Department denies.

The Democratic-controlled House Appropriations Committee issued a report that claimed the U.S. armed forces were less combat ready than they had been before the Reagan administration's large defense buildup. Because most defense spending of the Reagan administration was on elaborate new weapons systems and naval construction, the preparedness of the armed forces for conventional war had been neglected. Several field commanders, the report said, complained of being shortchanged on such essentials as spare parts and communications equipment. This report caused much controversy, and in August the Pentagon denied the report's findings, declaring that there were sufficient supplies for 30 days of conventional combat. Moreover, it stated that this capacity would double if Congress did not cut future defense funding.

July 21, 1984

The United States praises Poland for granting amnesty but declines to lift U.S. economic sanctions.

The Reagan administration continued the sanctions placed on Poland when the government declared martial law on December 13, 1981. Although Poland had recently freed 652 political prisoners and 35,000 common criminals, the president wanted evidence that the Polish Communists improved their human rights practices before ending the sanctions. Nevertheless, on August 3, 1984, Reagan lifted the ban on cultural and scientific exchanges with Poland and restored the rights of Poland's airline (LOT) to land in the United States. Agricultural and trade sanctions remained in place.

July 28, 1984

As the Olympic Games begin in Los Angeles, the Soviet Union and 11 of its "friends" do not participate.

Without the participation of the Soviet Union and East Germany, two major Olympic "powers," the United States had little competition in winning 83 gold medals. The games became a celebration of U.S. nationalism. On August 18, 1984, the 11 nations that joined the Soviet Olympic boycott were invited to Moscow for the Friendship Games.

August 2, 1984

A U.S. mine-sweeping team arrives in the Red Sea to clear mines that had damaged 15 ships since July 9, 1984; the Pentagon's response time is slow.

When Suez Canal traffic slowed because of the mines, the mystery was who laid them. Although an extremist religious group, Islamic Jihad, claimed it had done so, Iran, which sponsored Jihad, said it was not responsible. Iran's opponent, Iraq, also denied any involvement. Britain and France sent mine-sweeping ships to the Red Sea, and President Reagan acted at the request of Egyptian President Hosni Mubarak by dispatching 200 sailors and four Sea Stallion helicopters to the area. Because the helicopters required 10 days to reach the Red Sea, the Pentagon's rapid-deployment capability was questioned. The Defense Department explained that it decided not to use an Egyptian land base and, therefore, the helicopters needed a ship for operations. This required sending 200 sailors to Rota, Spain, to board a refitted marine assault ship, the Shreveport, for transportation to the Red Sea. Nevertheless, the response time raised questions about the effectiveness of Reagan's enormous defense buildup since 1981.

August 5–6, 1984

At the U.N. Conference on Population, the United States opposes funding of abortions.

This U.N. conference met in Mexico City, in a country where, despite a family planning program, the population had doubled in 10 years. In his opening address, Rafael M. Salas, the Filipino who chaired the meeting, predicted an overcrowded world of 10.5 billion people in which scarce resources would drastically lower the quality of life: 42 percent of children under five would be malnourished; 25 percent of families would be inadequately housed; and 600 million people would live in poverty. Although leaders of developing nations realized the need for family planning, the Reagan administration not only maintained a U.S. prohibition on aid for abortion but also refused to permit private agencies to receive assistance if they performed or promoted abortions. The chief U.S. delegate, James L. Buckley, said the free-market economy should follow the "natural mechanism for slowing population growth." This late-nineteenth-century Social Darwinistic formula meant, in practice, that poor children would be born to starve and suffer through a short life. Although Buckley did not say so, the "natural mechanism" assumed that the unfit would die. The final conference report recommended international efforts to improve the status of women, end forced marriages, and delay childbearing in cultures where giving birth at an early age was common.

August 10, 1984

A House-Senate committee approves $70 million in military aid to El Salvador.

Following elections on March 25 in El Salvador, Congress rejected President Reagan's request for aid because a runoff vote was held in May, and El Salvador's policies were uncertain. In May the moderate Christian Democrat won, and during July, President José Napoleon Duarte visited Washington to gain support from the two leading House Democrats—Majority Leader James Wright of Texas and House Appropriations Committee Chairman Clarence D. Long of Louisiana. On August 8, President Reagan at a press conference, showed infrared film and other intelligence data to "prove" that Nicaragua had sent arms to rebels in El Salvador. Duarte wanted funds either to fight the rebels or to persuade them to negotiate peace. Although on January 16, 1984, President Reagan reported that death squad killings in El Salvador increased significantly in 1983, on July 13, 1984, the State Department said there were "only" 93 killings per month in 1984. Some members of Congress feared that Duarte could not control the right wing and gain peace. Consequently, the House-Senate committee allocated only $70 million, not the $117 million of El Salvador military aid that Reagan had requested. The committee also provided $112 million of economic aid.

August 11, 1984

Believing the microphone he used is being tested, President Reagan broadcasts a joke about bombing Moscow.

Preceding his Saturday radio show, President Reagan thought only a voice check was under way and quipped, "My fellow Americans, I am pleased to tell you I just signed legislation which abolished Russia forever. The bombing begins in five minutes." Because the radio lines were open, many listeners heard the president's words. America's European allies were embarrassed by the president's black humor; the Soviet media interpreted the comment as typical of Reagan's hostility. But Republican supporters on Reagan's presidential campaign trail applauded lustily whenever Reagan repeated his jest.

August 13, 1984

Morocco and Libya sign a treaty that disturbs the United States.

Although King Hassan II of Morocco and Libyan leader Mu'ammar al-Gadhafi had common interests in allying against Algeria, Tunisia, and Mauritania, this treaty surprised the United States. The State Department viewed King Hassan as a special friend and Gadhafi as a dedicated enemy. The agreement was a nonaggression pact between Libya and Morocco, setting up regular meetings on defense preparations. Therefore, Secretary Shultz warned Morocco not to permit U.S. arms to reach Libya.

August 20, 1984

Greece withdraws from military exercises with United States.

Greek Prime Minister Andreas Papandreou announced that Greek forces would not carry out military exercises with NATO forces set for September 1984 because of Turkish threats to Greek security. The long tradition of Greco-Turkish antagonism caused problems between these two NATO members. There had been tension between Washington and Athens since July 8, 1984, when the United States blocked the sale of Norwegian planes to Greece. After Papandreou threatened to shut down the Voice of America station in Greece, the United States approved the sale. The exercise cancellation was one of several anti-American incidents reflecting the Greek public's belief that the United States favored Turkey and dominated Greek policy.

Papandreou had denounced U.S. imperialism and defended the Soviet Union as a faithful opponent of capitalism. He claimed in 1983 that the Korean Air Lines flight KAL-007, which the Soviets shot down, was on a CIA spy mission. He angered Washington by freeing a suspected Arab terrorist. Later, in October 1984, he denounced Poland's Solidarity trade union and praised Polish leader Wojciech Jaruzelski for trying to crush them with martial law. Of course, Solidarity was not crushed. Anti-Americanism won Papandreou votes. Papandreou did, however, renew the treaty permitting U.S. bases to remain in Greece (see September 8, 1983). His close associates said he was not anti-American but that he only boosted both Greek independence from Washington and Greek national self-esteem.

August 23–24, 1984

Colombia's government and two rebel groups agree to fight drug lords; but NLA rejects plan.

To wage war on Colombia's drug lords, two rebel groups agreed to a cease-fire on March 28, 1984. Only one smaller Cuban-backed Communist group, the National Liberation Army (NLA), rejected the cease-fire and truce. Colombian President Belisario Betancur now was ready to fight the cocaine dealers in Colombia. He inaugurated this drug war on May 1, 1984, but it was to be a long, difficult effort for Colombia and the United States.

August 25, 1984

The Soviet Union successfully tests a new long-range ground-launched cruise missile.

This test report caused Soviet and U.S. spokesmen to ask who had the cruise missile first. TASS, the Soviet news agency, said the cruise missile was a response to Washington's deployment of cruise missiles in Western Europe since November 1983. The U.S. State Department said Moscow had developed cruise missile technology long before the United States deployed its missiles. On August 28, the Congressional Office of Technological Assessment reported that if cruise missiles could evade radar and other defenses as U.S. experts argued, then their use could make all ICBM land-based missiles vulnerable and obsolete.

August 29, 1984

A U.S. court of appeals rules against President Reagan's pocket veto of a bill requiring a report on El Salvador's human rights progress.

In November 1983, President Reagan had not signed, and therefore vetoed, congressional legislation that prohibited economic aid to El Salvador unless the president reported that human rights had been improved during the past year. On January 4, 1984, 33 members of Congress, led by Congressman Michael D. Barnes (D-Md.) filed suit to challenge the constitutionality of Reagan's pocket veto. The appeals court upheld the congressional view, ruling that the president's action was not valid. Subsequently on September 14, Secretary of State George Shultz followed legislative requests by certifying that El Salvador had made progress in curbing human rights violations.

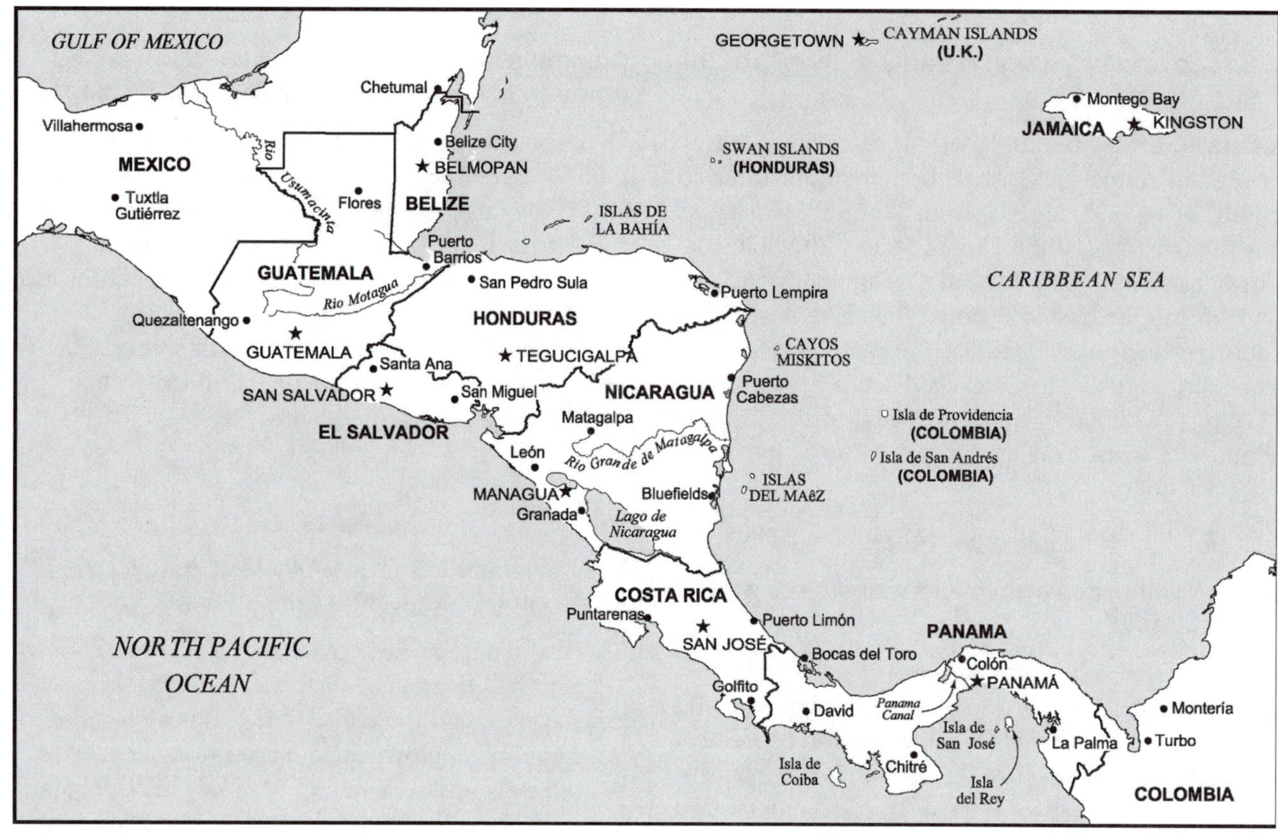

Central America, 1984

That same day, Reagan sent new jet aircraft and helicopters to El Salvador.

September 1, 1984

Nicaraguan soldiers shoot down a rebel helicopter, killing two Americans.

Proving that American citizens were in combat in Nicaragua, this incident took place when three American Cessna planes and one Hughes 500 MD helicopter flew from a CIA-controlled base in Honduras, crossed into Nicaragua, and fired 24 rockets at a military school in the small town of Santa Clara. Nicaraguan anti aircraft guns shot down the helicopter, killing two Americans and one Nicaraguan rebel. The two Cessna planes returned safely to Honduras. The two Americans were Dana Parker and James P. Powell. Parker was an undercover detective for the Police Department in Huntsville, Alabama, and a member of the Twentieth Special Forces Group of the Alabama National Guard. A Huntsville official told the CBS News reporter Leslie Cockburn that Parker was a "paid assassin, who had killed three Cuban government officials." Powell was a pilot from Memphis, Tennessee, who never told his family or friends of his connections. Later, Tom Posey, an Alabama grocer and head of the Civilian Military Assistance group, claimed that the two Americans worked for him.

Evidence from the Iran-Contra hearings of 1986–1987 indicated that Lieutenant Colonel Oliver North was in Honduras on August 31 and wanted to postpone the raid because the helicopter was the only one the Contras had. North called the Americans "nonofficial assistants," but the CIA said they were private mercenaries with no official ties. In reality, they were part of the so-called private group organized by North, an aide to the National Security Council. The origin of the two Cessna planes also became a political issue. On September 14, Senator Jim Sassor (D-Tenn.) told reporters that the planes belonged to the New York National Guard but were declared "excess" in December 1983 and flown to the Air Force Logistics Command at Andrews Air Force Base in Washington, D.C. In February 1984, the U.S. Air Force gave them to "Project Elephant Herd," which in turn gave them to

Summit Aviation, a Delaware company that converted them for military use. Summit Aviation had a reputation for aiding CIA operations. Elephant Herd was an interagency task force of the U.S. military—in this case, the Defense Department and the CIA. The political question raised by the transfer of the Cessnas was the violation of the December 1983 legislation that restricted funding to the Contras to $24 million.

September 4, 1984

Hope for better relations between East and West Germany fades after East German leader Erich Honecker postpones visit to West Germany.

Honecker was scheduled to visit Bonn on September 23, but pressure from Moscow apparently caused him to cancel the meeting. Previous events in 1984 had improved relations between the two German states. On January 22, East Germany permitted six citizens who sought asylum in the U.S. embassy in Berlin to go to West Germany. During Soviet President Yuri Andropov's funeral on February 13, West German Chancellor Helmut Kohl met Honecker for the first time. On July 27, however, Moscow showed dissatisfaction with the German developments. After East and West German negotiators agreed to ease restrictions on their trade and travel, the Soviet Union protested that Bonn was trying to weaken socialism in East Germany. Thus, Honecker's cancellation indicated that the Soviet Union had put a brake on changes in East Germany's relations with West Germany.

September 4, 1984

Canada's Progressive Conservative Party ousts the Liberal Party.

Because of the Liberals' defeat, Brian Mulroney replaced John N. Turner as Canada's prime minister. Turner had replaced Pierre Trudeau as the Liberal leader on June 18, 1984.

September 5, 1984

Prime Minister P.W. Botha is elected as the first executive president under South Africa's new constitution.

Under the constitution approved on November 3, 1983, the mixed-race "coloreds" elected representatives to a third chamber of parliament, principally made up of South Africans of Indian origin. The new constitution increased the power of President Botha, who now had authority to veto legislation and to summon or dismiss parliament.

September 6, 1984

The United States vetoes a U.N. resolution that demands Israel's withdrawal from Lebanon.

The Security Council resolution asked Israel to evacuate its armed forces from Lebanon and to lift all restrictions on Lebanese civilians in southern Lebanon. As on prior occasions, the United States appeared as Israel's only friend on the council. Lebanon and Israel negotiated a troop withdrawal on October 31, 1984.

September 11, 1984

President Reagan says the Soviet Union can purchase 10 million metric tons of U.S. grain.

Because of an abnormally hot, dry season, the Soviet Union had its worst harvest since 1975. Although Reagan increased the amount of grain the Soviets received, U.S. farmers requested such purchases to relieve their surplus. Between June 29 and October 18, the USSR purchased about 15.2 million metric tons of U.S. corn and wheat. This was the president's second effort in 1984 to help the Soviets as well as American economic interests. On July 25, he ended the ban on Soviet fishing in U.S. waters imposed by President Jimmy Carter in 1980.

September 19, 1984

A General Accounting Office (GAO) investigator tells Congress about defects in the navy's air-to-air missiles.

Testifying before the House Subcommittee on National Security of the Government Operations Committee, GAO investigator Frank C. Conahan indicated that thousands of the navy's air-to-air missiles were useless because of defects. Upto 33 percent of the Sparrow and 25 percent of the Sidewinder missiles were listed in recent navy records as "unserviceable." In earlier testimony, on September 12 Assistant Defense Secretary Lawrence J. Korb admitted that many air combat missiles could not be used but estimated the number to be about 21 percent. Korb blamed

Congress because it insisted on competitive bidding in defense contracts. As one reporter observed, this was odd because Korb represented an administration that extolled competitive free enterprise. Other defense experts blamed the problem on the military's insistence on technologically complex weapons that were prone to serious maintenance problems.

September 21, 1984

The Coordinadora group refuses to participate in Nicaragua's November elections.

On March 16, 1984, Nicaragua announced an election for November and revised the law to encourage opposition parties to participate. On July 25, 1984, Arturo Cruz and other Sandinista opponents formed the Coordinadora group and sought negotiations to clarify the election terms for eligibility of participants. The European-based Socialist International mediated these efforts. On August 22, the attempt to hold an election nearly failed when the Sandinistas said three opposition groups could not participate because they had not registered their candidates. On September 21, Sandinista leader Daniel Ortega gave the opposition until September 30 to meet candidate requirements. When the Coordinadora rejected this proposal, further talks occurred with the Socialist International but did not succeed. As a result, Cruz and his followers boycotted the November 4 elections. While prodemocracy groups in Nicaragua and the United States wanted Cruz to run, hard-liners among the Contra rebels and the Reagan administration preferred to discredit the elections. These hard-liners won by claiming that since Ortega refused the terms laid out by Cruz, the elections could not be democratic and free.

September 23, 1984

The United States closes School of the Americas to comply with the 1978 Panama treaty.

For 38 years, the School of the Americas trained Latin American military officers. Although it was intended to teach these officers respect for democracy as well as military instruction, the school provided better training in killing and clandestine warfare than in inculcating respect for the principle of civilian control of the military as an essential of a democratic society.

September 24, 1984

In U.N. speeches, President Reagan urges renewed arms control talks, but Soviet Foreign Minister Gromyko criticizes U.S. policies.

Even compared with his January address, Reagan's U.N. speech had a distinct tone of moderation toward the Soviet Union. He appealed to Moscow to establish "a better working relationship" to "shorten the distance" from the United States on arms control. The president concluded, "We recognize that there is no sane alternative to negotiation on arms control and other issues between our two nations which have the capacity to destroy civilization as we know it." Although Gromyko avoided Soviet demands for the withdrawal of U.S. missiles from Europe, he stated that "concrete deeds and not verbal assurances are necessary to the normalization of relations with America."

Gromyko thought Reagan's moderation was part of a presidential campaign to calm the fears generated by Reagan's earlier tough stances. Referring to Reagan's previous speeches, Gromyko told the U.N. General Assembly: "all we hear is that strength, strength, and above all strength is the guarantee of international peace. In other words, weapons, weapons, and still more weapons." Thus, Gromyko did not believe that Reagan sincerely sought better relations. Following the U.N. session, Gromyko met with Secretary of State George Shultz and visited Washington, D.C. President Reagan had never before met with a high-ranking Soviet official. Gromyko also took the unprecedented step of meeting with Walter Mondale, the Democratic candidate in the November 1984 presidential election.

The World Bank approves $2 billion for sub-Saharan African nations but has funding problems.

Agreed to by delegates from both developing and developed countries at the World Bank meeting, the $2 billion for emergency aid was to relieve the desperate economic conditions of sub-Saharan African nations. During the meeting, the United States opposed a West German plan to give investment funds for African economic reforms. Under President Reagan's guidelines, the U.S. delegates wanted Africans to seek private-sector investment initiatives rather than state-controlled programs. On September 24, the

World Bank delegates approved the West German plan but were unable to find governments willing to pledge the $2 billion. The United States refused to contribute, and Treasury Secretary Donald T. Regan said the Africans should obtain funds from the International Development Association. The World Bank, whose official name was the International Bank for Reconstruction and Development, needed not only the $2 billion of emergency aid but also $9 billion for the regular programs approved on May 24, 1984. At the end of 1984, the World Bank was still searching for $1 billion to fully fund emergency aid to Africa.

September 25, 1984

Nicaragua and the United States disagree on the Contadora peace proposals at the sixth round of talks in Manzanillo, Mexico.

Although Nicaragua initially rejected Contadora proposals made on September 7, 1984, the Sandinista delegates offered them as the basis for the sixth round of U.S.-Nicaraguan talks at Manzanillo on September 25. The Contadora proposition was to eliminate all foreign military schools, bases, and advisers as well as military-based political parties in Central America. The Reagan administration refused to accept the Contadora proposals, stating that the Sandinistas deceived the public by their alleged acceptance. The U.S. State Department wanted the proposals to provide adequate verification methods and to avoid an immediate cut off of all U.S. aid to the Contras and Honduras. At Manzanillo, the U.S. delegation offered to limit U.S. military exercises in Central America and to agree to a step-by-step phasing out of military forces in the region. However, the Nicaraguan delegates maintained their support for the September 7 Contadora proposals. Thus, the sixth meeting at Manzanillo since June 25, reached no solutions.

September 25, 1984

Hong Kong's future status is agreed on by China and the United Kingdom.

In 1997, Great Britain's 99-year lease on Hong Kong would end, and the territory would revert to the People's Republic of China. For two years, London and Beijing had negotiated the transfer of authority before reaching a settlement. On September 18, the British and Chinese embassies announced a draft agreement that the British cabinet approved on September 21, and British and Chinese representatives signed on September 25. Finally, the British Parliament approved it on December 19, 1984. The pact allowed the people of Hong Kong to retain "all the rights and freedoms they now have until 2047." It preserved Hong Kong's own convertible currency and its property, trading, and travel rights. The present school system would continue, as would freedom of the press and religion. In 2000, China would become responsible for defending the territory of Hong Kong.

September 28–29, 1984

Foreign ministers of 12 European and nine Latin American states support the Contadora effort in Central America.

Western European and Central American leaders met in San José, Costa Rica, to bypass U.S. efforts to isolate Nicaragua from European trade and commerce. U.S. NATO allies opposed President Reagan's enmity toward Nicaragua's government and believed that Central America needed economic aid to improve living standards and solve the region's problems. Reagan had isolated the United States from world opinion when he mined Nicaraguan waters.

October 3, 1984

Over the course of two days, two Americans, including an FBI agent, are arrested for selling secrets.

On October 1, a naval intelligence analyst, Samuel L. Morison, was arrested for selling secret photos of a Soviet aircraft carrier to the British journal *Jane's Defense Weekly*. Two days later, an FBI agent, Richard W. Miller, was charged with selling secret documents to the Soviet Union, which gave a detailed picture of U.S. intelligence activity. Miller was to receive $65,000 in gold and cash from two Soviet émigré—Nicolay and Svetlana Ogorodnikov—whom the FBI also arrested. Svetlana Ogorodnikov claimed to be a KGB major in Soviet intelligence, but U.S. authorities claimed she was an amateur spy.

On October 17, 1985, a federal grand jury found Morison guilty of selling secrets, he received only a two-year prison sentence because his lawyers portrayed him as a patriotic American seeking more funds for the U.S. navy by disclosing secret data about Soviet naval power. Miller was convicted on June 19, 1986, and sentenced to life in prison. The Ogorodnikovs pleaded guilty on June 26, 1985; he received an eight-year prison sentence and she, an 18-year sentence.

October 9, 1984

Israeli Prime Minister Shimon Peres accepts President Reagan's offer of U.S. economic aid.

After becoming prime minister on September 13, Peres visited Washington from October 7 to 10 seeking assistance for a five-year plan to restructure Israel's debt. Israel currently suffered from 800 percent inflation and was having difficulty in paying foreign debts. Reagan released immediately all of the $1.2 billion Congress had appropriated and agreed to give $2.6 billion in nonrepayable grants for 1985. Israel began austerity measures that included freezing wages and prices and halting the importation of 50 luxury items.

October 10, 1984

The Defense Department rules for a journalists' pool to cover U.S. combat operations; journalists gain some changes.

The Defense Department wanted a pool of reporters to accompany troops during the first stages of combat and share data with the media. There would be no provisions for individual journalists to collect independent information. After protests from daily newspapers that had no representation in the pool, the Defense Department increased the pool from six to 12 persons— one each from television network, CBS, NBC, ABC, and CNN; two television crewmen; one photographer; one from a radio network; one each from AP and UPI; one for weekly news magazines; and one for daily newspapers. The secretary of defense made final allocations of reporters to the pool.

October 12, 1984

A second Boland Amendment prohibits U.S. government agencies from aiding Nicaragua's Contra rebels.

For the fiscal year 1985 beginning October 1, the Reagan administration not only failed to obtain the $28 million it sought for the rebels but also was prohibited from sending any type of aid to the Contras. An earlier Boland Amendment (1982) that banned aid to "overthrow" the Nicaraguan government was easily ignored by the CIA. In December 1983 all that Congressman Edward Boland (D-Mass.) could do was limit U.S. aid to $24 million for 1984. By September 1984, evidence of the CIA's double-dealing with Congress and stories of the Contras' terrorist methods persuaded many Republican members of Congress to join Democrats in opposing President Reagan's policy. Most damaging to the president was the CIA's mining of Nicaraguan waters and evidence that the overthrow of the Sandinistas was the real purpose of the Contras despite Reagan's statements to the contrary. Initially, the House and Senate deadlocked on ending all Contra aid. On June 25, however, the Senate voted 88 to 1 to separate the Contra aid issue from the 1985 supplemental appropriations bill, and Reagan's request for $20 million for the Contras seemed doomed.

In July and August, however, Reagan released intelligence data designed to revive Contra aid. On July 18, a State Department report described Nicaragua's military buildup and support for subversive activity in Central America. On August 2, an alleged Nicaraguan defector told the Senate Subcommittee on Drug Abuse that Nicaraguan officials, including the president's brother, Humberto Ortega, were smuggling drugs. On August 8, Reagan showed a press conference infrared film and other CIA data that allegedly proved that Nicaragua had transferred military equipment to rebels in El Salvador. On June 18, the U.S. Drug Enforcement Agency (DEA) had firm evidence against only one aide to the Nicaraguan interior minister. During the Iran-Contra hearings of 1986–1987, evidence indicated that the Contras and CIA agents condoned drug sales to finance the rebels. According to the Georgetown University professors Robert Parry and Peter Kornbluh in the 1988 issue of *Foreign Policy*, this aspect of the Iran-Contra investigation was not pursued. Although the Iran-Contra disclosures were secret in 1984, there was enough evidence to raise doubts about the Contras among members of Congress. Moreover, most congressional members and the American public seemed immune to Reagan's exaggerated support for the Contra "freedom fighters." Consequently, after the October 1 deadline for the Continuing Appropriations Resolution passed, Senate members of the joint House-Senate conference committee yielded to Boland's persistent request to cut off Contra funds. Those in Congress who supported Reagan felt the president had not kept them informed of events while his appointees deceived them about the Contra situation, which the recent downing of the Contra helicopter demonstrated.

On October 10, the Senate accepted Boland's amendment, and on October 12, Congress approved the bill. The senators' only concession to the president was that the White House could again request Contra funds after February 28, 1985. In contrast to the 1982 Boland Amendment, the 1984 version applied to any accounting procedure of any government agency, even restricting the "transfer of equipment acquired at no cost." Rather than simply prohibit aid intended to "overthrow the government," as in December 1982, the 1984 Boland Amendment stated:

> No funds available to the Central Intelligence Agency, the Department of Defense, or any other agency or entity of the United States involved in intelligence activities may be obligated or expended for the purpose of which would have the effect of supporting, directly or indirectly, military or paramilitary operations in Nicaragua by any nation, group, organization, movement, or individual.

During floor debate, Boland said the provision meant that "if you are engaged in support of the Contras, you are involved in intelligence activities. So you are covered [by the ban]." President Reagan signed the law on October 12, 1984, but his legal counselors later argued that the National Security Council (NSC) was not covered by the prohibition. Opponents of this interpretation cited Reagan's Executive Order 12333 of December 4, 1981, which defined the NSC as providing guidance for "all national foreign intelligence, counterintelligence, and special activities."

October 15, 1984

A CIA manual instructs Nicaraguan rebels on assassinating and blackmailing leaders.

The Associated Press revealed the existence of the CIA manual. Titled "Operaciones sicologicas en guerra de guerrillas" ("Psychological Operations in Guerrilla Warfare"), this 89-page pamphlet advocated tactics such as the public execution of government officials, arranging the deaths of Sandinista politicians, killing rebel leaders to make them martyrs, blackmailing citizens to work for the rebels, and other forms of terror and sabotage against the Nicaraguan government. Some beneficial methods were also cited, such as helping to harvest crops, teaching peasants to read, and improving village hygiene. Nevertheless, as one reporter said, it read like a manual for the Vietcong in Vietnam or Communist rebels in El Salvador. Because it was prepared by a U.S. agency, it undercut President Reagan's moralistic statements against state-sponsored terrorism as in Libya, Syria, and Iran. For the United States, the difference was that the press and Congress could challenge the chief executive to stop such activity.

The disclosure resulted in four government investigations of the manual and CIA tactics in Central America. In addition to Senate and House investigations, the General Accounting Office investigated the manual, and on October 18, President Reagan ordered an investigation. The president, however, did not heed House Speaker Thomas (Tip) O'Neill's demand to fire CIA director William Casey. The CIA claimed that the manual helped rebels avoid combat and use persuasion, a claim readers of the manual could not find. It had been prepared by a low-level contract employee of the CIA. The 2,000 copies were published and distributed by a Contra leader, Edgar Chamorro. On November 10, a CIA investigation said publication of the manual violated no law but recommended penalties to punish six mid-level CIA agents. CIA director Casey said he never reviewed or approved the manual.

October 15, 1984

Salvadoran President Duarte meets with rebel leaders, agreeing to form a joint peace commission; there are few results.

Fulfilling a campaign promise and encouraged by the United States, President José Napoleon Duarte met with rebel leaders Guillermo Ungo, Rubén Zamora, Ternan Cienfuegos, and Nidia Díaz at a Roman Catholic church in La Palma, El Salvador. Talks achieved only a 13-day cease-fire for the Christmas holidays. On October 16, Roberto d'Aubuisson, El Salvador's right-wing leader, opposed the talks.

October 19, 1984

An unarmed American plane crashes in El Salvador, killing four CIA agents.

The agents were on a surveillance mission that had been cleared by the CIA director, William S. Casey, who had previously informed the Senate Select Committee on Intelligence about the flight. Although the rebels claimed to have shot down the plane, the exact reasons for the crash were unknown—apparently a mechanical failure caused the accident. The CIA's informing the senators spared the Reagan administration some embarrassment.

October 29, 1984

Food relief for widespread Ethiopian famine faces political problems.

Politics impeded efficient distribution of international food deliveries for Ethiopia while a million people faced starvation. By mid-November, the slow arrival of food became a political controversy. Ethiopia blamed anti-Communists in Britain and the United States for delaying the shipments to make Ethiopia's Communist regime collapse. The United States blamed Addis Ababa's rulers, citing the government's expenditure of $100 million to celebrate the regime's tenth anniversary and its use of famine to fight rebels in the three provinces where food was most needed—Tigre, Eritrea, and Wollo. Other observers noted that Ethiopia's lack of trucks and adequate roads slowed the shipment of food to the hinterlands.

October 29, 1984

Japanese Prime Minister Yasuhiro Nakasone is elected to a second term as head of the Liberal Democratic Party.

Although party leaders traditionally retired after one two-year term, the top leaders reelected Nakasone.

October 30, 1984

A Polish priest who favored the Solidarity trade union is murdered by state security forces.

The body of the Reverend Jerzy Popieluszko, who had been abducted on October 19, was found on October 30. The priest became a martyr to the cause of Solidarity. Eventually, the priest's death came to be blamed not on Polish leader Wojciech Jaruzelski but on hard-liners in the state security network who opposed compromise with Solidarity leaders. Since July, Jaruzelski's policy of amnesty and cooperation with Solidarity had disturbed Polish Stalinists. After the priest's body was found, Jaruzelski ordered an investigation and suspended a general and two colonels of the Interior Ministry, which controlled the state security office. On February 7, 1985, after a trial, Colonel Adam Pietruszka and Captain Grzegarz Piotrowski received 25-year prison terms. Two police lieutenants, Leszek Pekala and Waldemar Chmielewski, received sentences of 15 years and 14 years, respectively. Piotrowski said his orders came from a very high level. The two policemen said they never intended to kill Popieluszko but only tried to persuade him to stop working for Solidarity.

October 31, 1984

Indian Prime Minister Indira Gandhi is assassinated by two Sikh bodyguards; her son Rajiv Gandhi replaces her.

November 4, 1984

Nicaraguan elections give the Sandinista National Liberation Front 63 percent of the vote—61 of 90 National Assembly seats.

Although the Coordinadora opposition groups boycotted and tried to discredit the election, many foreign observers praised the election and the "national dialogue" that the government conducted with Coordinadora groups ranging from the Marxist-Leninist Party led by an idealistic Communist, Domingo Sánchez Salgado, to the Roman Catholic hierarchy. Both the newspaper *La Prensa* and Catholic bishops were allowed to publish reports that criticized Sandinista policies. While Sandinista Vice President Sergie Ramírez Mercado wanted the elections to reflect a popular consensus, hard-line Sandinistas used threats of a U.S. invasion to propose strong attacks on enemies of the government. Arturo Cruz and other pro-U.S. candidates who boycotted the elections denounced the restrictions that prevented a fair election. Yet, for general world opinion the 1984 Nicaraguan elections legitimatized the rule of Daniel Ortega's Sandinista party.

November 6, 1984

Ronald Reagan is reelected president by a landslide over Walter Mondale.

Although President Reagan's electoral count of 525 votes was the largest total in history, his 60 percent of the popular vote was less than the 61.1 percent that Lyndon Johnson won in 1964.

November 6, 1984

The U.S. State Department claims Soviet MiG-21 fighter planes are going to Nicaragua.

The "crisis" began on November 6, when the State Department warned Moscow not to permit fighter planes to reach Nicaragua. Although Nicaragua denied the report, President Reagan sent 25 warships to the area of Puerto Corinto and SR-71 spy planes on reconnaissance flights with unmuffled sonic booms that could be heard throughout Nicaragua's countryside. Normally, the SR-71 flights were secret and muffled, but Reagan wished to make a show of U.S. power for the Sandinistas. The noise also seemed to confirm Ortega's claim that the United States planned to invade Nicaragua. Ortega called up 50,000 Nicaraguan reservists. In addition to the reservists, thousands of Nicaraguan students rallied to defend their nation. The tension continued for three days until the Soviet freighter, which was allegedly carrying the MiG-21s, arrived at Corinto. The Sandinista government escorted carloads of reporters from Managua to Corinto, where boxes of unassembled helicopter parts—not MiGs—were loaded into military trucks.

In Washington, the State Department tried to explain that an unidentified official had leaked false information, which Secretary of State George Shultz called a "criminal act." Yet the State Department never found and punished anyone. Secretary of Defense Caspar Weinberger said the flow of helicopters and surface-to-air missiles had increased because Nicaragua planned to invade a neighbor. Ortega said the weapons were defensive because Nicaragua would fight hard if the United States attacked.

November 12, 1984

Secretary of State George P. Shultz says the United States deplores Chile's declaration of a state of siege.

For the second time in 1984, Chile's President Augusto Pinochet took emergency measures to silence public protests. On March 23, he closed the universities and imposed press censorship because of opposition demonstrations. Pinochet's November 6 measures were more drastic. He imposed a curfew, assumed new arrest and censorship powers, sent the army to raid slum areas, and rounded up the entire male population to screen for suspected terrorists. In Santiago, over 2,000 suspects were singled out as troublemakers or Marxist subversives and sent to exile in villages. Despite these actions, Chile received a $448 million loan from the International Development Bank on December 12, 1984.

November 20, 1984

Salvadoran courts halt proceedings against an army officer accused of murdering three land reform experts.

El Salvador's supreme court upheld a May 22, 1984, appeals court ruling that acquitted an army officer in the 1981 murder of two American and one Salvadoran land reform experts. Although two men convicted of the murder testified that Lieutenant Isidro López Sibrian ordered the killings and supplied weapons for the job, they could not identify Sibrian in a police lineup. Other witnesses disclosed that the police let Sibrian dye his red hair black and shave off his mustache before the lineup. Both the appeals court and the supreme court ruled against the prosecutor's charge that Sibrian should not have been allowed to change his appearance before the police lineup. On November 29 President Duarte announced that Sibrian had been discharged from the army with no pension.

November 22, 1984

Washington and Moscow announce that new arms talk will begin on January 7, 1985.

The first signs that arms talks, which ended in 1983, when the Soviet delegates walked out, would begin again came on November 7, when President Reagan told a postelection press conference that he wanted progress on an arms control treaty. On November 14, the Soviet Union expressed interest in a broadened series of talks. The official announcement on November 22 said U.S. Secretary of State Shultz and Soviet Foreign Minister Gromyko would discuss "the entire complex of questions concerning nuclear and space weapons" and set objectives for future talks. The Soviets argued that the discussions were not a return to the status quo of 1983 but totally new talks encompassing all types of nuclear weapons.

November 22–29, 1984

PLO National Council backs Yasser Arafat; King Hussein of Jordan calls for Palestinian self-determination in Israeli-occupied territory.

Meeting in Amman, Jordan, 261 delegates of the Palestine Liberation Council voted for Arafat and called for an "escalation of the military struggle against Israel." During the conference, Jordan's King Hussein asked the PLO to negotiate with Israel on the basis of U.N. Security Council Resolution 242, which stipulated that Israel should withdraw from territories it had occupied. The PLO rejected resolution 242 because it failed to mention a separate Palestinian state.

November 24, 1984

Edgar Chamorro is dismissed as a Contra leader because he criticized U.S. policy.

The Miami, Florida-based Nicaraguan Democratic Force, which was the exiles' largest anti-Sandinista group, expelled Chamorro because the CIA disliked his public criticism of their covert operations in Nicaragua. On October 19, Chamorro publicly disputed the White House explanation of the CIA's guerrilla manual as being designed to lessen the guerrillas' harsh attacks on the Nicaraguan population. On October 31, Chamorro elaborated on his CIA connections and CIA director William Casey had ordered the Contras to disavow any member who publicly stated that the Contras purpose was to overthrow the government of Nicaragua because such statements antagonized the U.S. Congress. Chamorro was a moderate among Contra leaders because many were former officials of the pre-1979 Somoza government.

November 26, 1984

The International Court of Justice rules it has jurisdiction over Nicaragua's suit against the United States.

While the World Court ruled 15 to 1 to consider Nicaragua's complaint that U.S. support for the Contra rebels violated international law, the Reagan administration believed a great power could not allow the court to limit its military options, a view contrary to America's traditional championing of the rule of law to settle disputes. In 1980, for example, the United States condemned Iran for ignoring a World Court decision to release U.S. hostages in Tehran. The Reagan administration acted unilaterally not only at the World Court but also with its vetoes in the U.N. Security Council and at meetings of UNESCO and the Organization of American States.

Columbia University law professor Richard N. Gardner said the president isolated the United States from the world forums and its traditional allies regarding the value of international law. To justify the Reagan administration stances, U.S. Ambassador to the United Nations Jeanne J. Kirkpatrick argued that World Court justices from Communist or Third World countries were not neutral toward the United States.

November 26, 1984

The United States (and Soviet Union) reestablish diplomatic relations with Iraq.

During the Iraq-Iran war, which began in September 1980, the United States gradually sympathized with Iraq. During a Washington visit by Iraqi Foreign Minister Tariq Aziz, these developments led to restoration of relations between Baghdad and Washington by the exchange of ambassadors. Since October 1984, Iraqi President Saddam Hussein performed the difficult task of improving relations with both the United States and the Soviet Union. Moscow also renewed formal diplomatic relations with Baghdad during 1984.

The United States renewed relations with Iraq despite clear evidence that Iraq had used chemical weapons against Iran. A team of U.N. experts reported on March 26, 1984, that there was evidence that Iraq used chemical weapons against Iran. On March 5, the U.S. State Department asserted even more firmly that Iraq had used chemical weapons. At Washington's request, the West German government took steps to stop its chemical industries from exporting chemicals to Iraq. Nevertheless, Reagan ignored such evidence of Iraq's illegal acts when he decided to recognize that country. Reagan also encouraged European and U.S. business interests and arms dealers to assist Iraq. As a result, Saddam Hussein's armed forces obtained new weapons from many parts of the world, becoming militarily stronger than

Iran or any Arab power. In 1987, when an Iraqi missile damaged a U.S. naval ship in the Persian Gulf, Reagan blamed Iran.

November 28, 1984

Defense Secretary Caspar W. Weinberger cites six criteria for using U.S. military force.

In a speech delivered with President Reagan's approval and the endorsement of the National Security Council, Weinberger enunciated six criteria to be met before the nation would resort to military force, as follows:

1. Do not commit forces unless it is in our vital interest or that of our allies.
2. Forces should be committed only with the "clear intention of winning."
3. There should be clear objectives with forces used to fulfill those objectives.
4. The relationship between forces and objectives must be "continually reassessed and adjusted if necessary."
5. There must be assured support of the "American people and their elected representatives in Congress."
6. "The commitment of U.S. forces to combat should be a last resort."

Weinberger said these criteria evolved from past doubts and debates and should guide the nation's leaders in meeting future national security threats.

December 3, 1984

The Union Carbide pesticide plant in Bhopal, India, leaks poisonous gas.

The accidental leak of carbon monoxide at Bhopal raised general questions about global environmental standards because nations such as India had inadequate codes and understaffed agencies to protect its citizens. President Jimmy Carter had issued an executive order for American companies to meet strict requirements in exporting dangerous substances, but President Reagan canceled the order in 1981. The Bhopal accident killed over 2,000 people and injured some 50,000 more. It was considered as severe as the Chernobyl accident.

See April 26, 1986.

December 4, 1984

In Grenadian elections, the New National Party wins 14 of 15 seats in parliament; U.S.-backed Herbert A. Blaize becomes prime minister.

Blaize was Washington's choice from the outset of the election campaign. American diplomats hinted that the United States would have to reconsider its $50 million aid package if the leftist New Jewel party of Sir Eric Gairy won the election. The new Blaize government needed economic assistance and foreign investment to lower Grenada's 40 percent unemployment rate.

December 5, 1984

Paul H. Nitze is named special arms control adviser to Secretary of State Shultz.

Larry Speakes, President Reagan's White House spokesman, announced Nitze's appointment, a significant gesture because it indicated the president backed George Shultz's somewhat more flexible attitude toward arms control talks scheduled to begin with the Soviet Union on January 7, 1985. Nitze was recognized as more willing to compromise with the Soviet Union than were former Defense Department arms control spokesmen such as Richard Perle. Previously, Nitze's so-called walk-in-the-woods proposals of 1982 had been rejected. Having Nitze as an adviser was unusual, but it gave Shultz a means to bypass the Arms Control and Disarmament Agency, the National Security Council, as well as Perle. Insiders saw this appointment as a victory by Shultz over Defense Secretary Caspar Weinberger, who opposed arms control.

December 8, 1984

The Reagan administration approves a visa for El Salvador's right-wing leader Roberto d'Aubuisson, having refused visas earlier for four Salvadoran human rights leaders.

Because the Reagan administration had made an issue of denying U.S. visas to "undesirable" political persons, critics protested when d'Aubuisson, an alleged leader of El Salvador's death squads, received a visa in June 1984 and again in December. This latter visa was particularly criticized because on November 12 the Reagan administration denied visas to four

Salvadorans who had been invited to Boston to receive the Robert F. Kennedy Human Rights Award for their work among El Salvador's poor and underprivileged who had suffered at the hands of the "death squads."

It was to D'Aubuisson's advantage that he was the guest of Senator Jesse Helms (R-N.C). Helms was a leading figure among the right-wing fundamentalists who supported Reagan's presidential campaigns. A view opposed to that of Helms had been expressed on February 2, 1984, by former U.S. Ambassador to El Salvador Robert E. White, who told a congressional committee that d'Aubuisson was involved in the 1980 murder of Archbishop Oscar Arnulfo.

December 10, 1984

Nicaragua and the United States conclude a round of talks at Manzanillo, Mexico.

Since failing to agree on peace procedures during a series of talks after June 25, 1984, Nicaraguan and U.S. delegates continued to disagree at talks on November 19 and on December 10. After returning to Washington, the American delegates recommended a halt to further talks, and on January 18, 1985, the Reagan administration suspended discussions at Manzanillo. Generally, Nicaragua wanted to limit agreements to disarmament, and the United States wanted Nicaragua to accept obligations to democratize the government and be reconciled with its rebel groups. Nicaragua claimed those issues were internal matters not subject to international negotiation.

December 14, 1984

Successful northern Afghan guerrilla commander killed.

A former school teacher, Abdul Qader who went by the name Zabiullah, had been successful in waging an active guerrilla campaign against government and Soviet forces in northern Afghanistan. Reportedly, he commanded a force of about 20,000 combatants around the northern city of Mazar-e Sharif and regions southeast of Baghlan, east of Kunduz, and west of Balkh. His forces staged spectacular operations such as destroying the control tower of Mazar's civilian airport in May 1983. The 30-year-old Zabiullah was killed on December 14 after his vehicle hit a mine but it was not clear whether his death accidental or an assassination. He would be hard to replace.

December 14, 1984

The United States and Cuba agree to exchange persons involved in the 1980 boatlift.

According to the agreement, Cuba would repatriate 2,746 Cuban criminals and mental patients sent to the United States in 1980; the United States would admit more political refugees and political prisoners, with preference being given to relatives of U.S. citizens or of Cubans with permanent resident status in the United States. The agreement did not indicate whether Cuba would prosecute those returned under the agreement. This became an issue in the federal court of Atlanta, Georgia, where the return of excludable immigrants had stopped because of fear that they would be punished by Castro's government.

December 18, 1984

A California aerospace worker is arrested for offering Stealth bomber technology to the Soviet Union.

Thomas Patrick Cavanaugh, a 40-year-old Northrop Corporation engineer, tried to sell the Stealth secrets to pay the heavy debts he owed. Cavanaugh was sentenced to life in prison on May 23, 1985.

December 18, 1984

U.S. Defense Department officials report that two U.S. reconnaissance planes provoked a major Soviet response.

The U.S. reconnaissance planes were from two American aircraft carriers participating in the fleet's naval maneuvers in the Sea of Japan near the main Soviet Far Eastern base at Vladivostok. They provoked a Soviet response of more than 100 aircraft and warships to defend their far eastern bases. During November 1984, Soviet military maneuvers had disturbed Japanese authorities. After seven Soviet bombers flew into international airspace near South Korea and Japan, Japan's Defense Agency scrambled 32 jet planes to warn the Soviets, and Tokyo protested to the Soviet Union for violating Japan's airspace.

December 18, 1984

Soviet leader Mikhail Gorbachev visits Great Britain, gaining plaudits for advocating arms reductions.

The 53-year-old Soviet leader, who was considered to be second in command in the Kremlin, won praise from the British public. Even Prime Minister Margaret Thatcher declared, "I like Mr. Gorbachev. We can do business together." American diplomats were concerned about Britain's favorable reception of Gorbachev's talk about limiting the Strategic Defense Initiative (SDI) program promoted by President Reagan. French President François Mitterrand vigorously opposed Reagan's Strategic Defense Initiative (SDI), referring to it as unnecessary "over-arming" and stimulating the militarization of space. President Reagan frequently stated the "Star Wars" program was not a negotiating topic with the Soviet Union. On December 29, White House officials said the United States would not limit SDI research but might restrain it if future negotiation limited both offensive and defensive weapons.

December 19, 1984

The United States reaffirms its decision to withdraw from UNESCO on December 31, 1984.

As was the case one year earlier when the Reagan administration announced the U.S. withdrawal, the White House said UNESCO's politicization continued because its leadership showed an "endemic hostility" toward a free society, especially to "those that protect a free press, free markets, and above all, individual human rights." Only if UNESCO returned to its original principles would the United States renew its membership. Although Great Britain joined the United States by leaving UNESCO in 1985, UNESCO's secretary-general, Amadou-Mahtar M'Bow of Senegal, said the loss of U.S. revenue would have no adverse effect on the agency. Before December ended, West Germany and Singapore also left UNESCO.

December 25, 1984

Vietnam invades four Khmer Rouge rebel camps near the Thai border.

During 1984, frequent skirmishes took place between Vietnamese and Khmer Rouge rebel forces along the Thai borderlands. On January 27 and 28, the Khmer captured Siern Reap before withdrawing to Thailand. On April 14, a Vietnamese offensive chased 100,000 Kampuchean (Cambodian) refugees fleeing over the border to Thailand. On December 25 and 26, the Vietnamese raided other Khmer camps, hoping to destroy them before the spring monsoons prevented the use of tanks and trucks to move Vietnam's army. The largest camp attacked was at Rithisen, from which 60,000 civilians fled to Thailand.

1985

January 2, 1985

President Reagan and Japanese Prime Minister Nakasone discuss opening Japan's markets to more U.S. goods.

As the U.S. trade imbalance reached more than $150 billion per year and the U.S. national debt soared from $1 trillion in 1981 to nearly $2 trillion during 1985, the United States needed to export more manufactured goods.

January 5, 1985

Jordan buys Soviet antiaircraft weapons and denounces the United States for refusing to sell to it.

Jordanian army Chief of Staff General Sharif Zaid bin Shaki said this purchase was made because the United States refused to sell weapons to Jordan for its mobile defense force. Jordan obtained Soviet shoulder-fired antiaircraft weapons resembling the Stingers whose sale President Reagan had canceled owing to opposition from Congress and the Israeli lobby.

January 8, 1985

The United States and the Soviet Union agree to resume arms control negotiations.

Secretary of State George P. Shultz and Soviet Foreign Minister Andrei A. Gromyko concluded two days of talks in Geneva by announcing that their nations would renew negotiations on nuclear weapons, which had broken off in 1983. The new talks would combine discussions on intermediate-range (INF) and intercontinental (ICBM) nuclear weapons, as

Secretary of State George Shultz, Reagan, and Secretary of Defense Caspar Weinberger. Ronald Reagan Library

the United States preferred. As a U.S. concession, the talks would include the arms race in space, an issue prompted by President Reagan's Strategic Defense Initiative (SDI). In September 1984, Reagan indicated that the United States could accept restrictions on antisatellite tests (ASAT) if the talks included both offensive and defensive weapons. During December 1984, news leaks from Reagan administration officials reported a controversy over the future SDI program. Several officials told reporters that the advanced SDI program might be abandoned if the Soviets made concessions on offensive missiles. On December 22, Reagan's science advisers reported that SDI had been scaled back to the more modest goal of protecting U.S. ICBM missiles.

The next day, however, Secretary of Defense Caspar Weinberger denied this report, reaffirming that SDI's objective was to defend the entire nation from enemy nuclear missiles, and it was not a bargaining chip in arms talks. At present, SDI's only function was to defend the ICBMs by destroying Soviet missiles entering the earth's atmosphere over North America. This made it an antiballistic missile (ABM), which was restricted by the 1972 ABM treaty. Weinberger did not want the ABM question raised with the Soviets, even though major scientific and technological breakthroughs were necessary before SDI could destroy enemy missiles immediately after launching or while in their midcourse trajectory in space. Gromyko seemed ready to discuss other missiles without agreement on SDI even though, on January 13, he told a television interviewer that an arms agreement depended on U.S. limitations on SDI. Neither Shultz nor Gromyko made statements about ASAT tests.

January 10, 1985

The United States and the European Economic Community set new quotas on European steel tubes and pipes exported to America.

U.S. Special Trade Representative William Brock negotiated this agreement with representatives of the 10-member European Economic Community (EEC). It ended an embargo that President Reagan had placed on the importation of European steel pipes and tubing.

January 11, 1985

Canada denies reports U.S. nuclear weapons would deploy in Canada during a war.

Following a report from U.S. experts that nuclear weapons would be based in Canada if war broke out involving the United States, opposition to the plan spread throughout Canada. The Canadian government stated that it had not known about these plans, but opposition parties remained skeptical. At this time, U.S. and Canadian military leaders conducted talks about modernizing the Arctic Circle network of North American radar stations. On January 24, 1985, they agreed to spend $1.2 billion on improving the radar network to detect low-flying aircraft. Some Canadians opposed this action, largely because they feared that the U.S. Strategic Defense Initiative had destabilized relations with the Soviet Union and endangered Canadian security.

January 14, 1985

Rights of political asylum challenged when federal prosecutors arrest 16 persons assisting Central American refugees.

The Reagan administration welcomed refugees fleeing from the Sandinistas in Nicaragua and Fidel Castro's Cuba, but when underground groups in the United States helped refugees fleeing persecution from the governments of Guatemala and El Salvador that were aided by Washington, the Department of Justice harassed and finally arrested those who provided sanctuary to the refugees. On January 14, federal officials arrested three nuns, two priests, a Protestant minister, and 10 volunteers accused of helping "illegal immigrants" in regions from Arizona to New York. They also arrested 60 aliens as unindicted co-conspirators for violating the law.The Reagan administration claimed refugees from Guatemala and El Salvador came to the United States for economic reasons, not from fear of persecution. On May 1, 1986, the defendants were convicted of smuggling illegal immigrants. The Reverend John Fife, the Presbyterian minister who founded the Sanctuary Movement, received five years in prison; eight others got lesser sentences; all said they would continue their Christian mission.

January 15, 1985

Brazil chooses its first civilian president in 21 years.

Leader of the opposition Democratic Alliance Party, Tancredo de Almeida Neves defeated the Social Democratic candidate, Paulo Salim Maluf. Neves's term of office was cut short, however, by his death on April 21. Vice President Jose Sarney replaced him.

January 20, 1985

Ronald Reagan is sworn in to begin second term as president.

President Reagan's second inaugural address focused on his popularity in winning a second term and having overseen two years of economic growth. He proposed to continue America's military buildup against "totalitarian darkness," while at the same time hoping to see all nuclear weapons eliminated from the earth—seemingly incompatible goals.

January 23, 1985

The 24-hour delay of the *Discovery* space shuttle mission dramatizes its shift to military missions.

Discovery's military mission had been discussed since December 19, 1984, when a *Washington Post* article used "leaked" information describing the electronic intelligence signals that would come from a satellite carried into space. After Secretary of Defense Caspar Weinberger accused the *Post* of "irresponsible journalism," its editors replied that all published data came from sources outside the Pentagon and the *Post* had, in fact, withheld data it found sensitive to the national security. On January 22 and 23, U.S. army generals in Florida were dismayed when the military mission was delayed by cold weather because military missions should be operable whenever required. More crucial, observers noted Reagan's "Star Wars" program caused overall expenditures for space programs to be military missions. Prior to 1982, the National Aeronautics and Space Administration's (NASA) budget aimed primarily at civilian and scientific projects. After that time, the Defense Department spent $12.9 billion on space shuttle projects. NASA had $6.8 billion for projects, of which one-fourth supported Pentagon needs.

January 24, 1985

President Reagan denounces Iran's foreign minister for aiding Nicaragua's military buildup.

When Reagan denounced Iran about Nicaragua, the news media paid little attention because it was connected to the "Reagan Doctrine" that the president announced regarding subversive warfare to overthrow totalitarian Communist regimes in Nicaragua and other Third World countries (see October 24, 1983). What Reagan did not disclose in October 1983 were his secret plans to use a few National Security Council (NSC) members to bypass the State Department and the Central Intelligence Agency. In 1982, this inner circle NSC staff undertook secret parts of Reagan's "Project Democracy" to take private initiatives that would not be reported to Congress as part of the CIA's annual report on its activities.

Secretary of State George Shultz first heard of these secret projects during the spring of 1985, three months after Reagan denounced Iran's aid to Nicaragua. In mid-April 1985, Shultz learned Israel told the White House Iran wanted American-made TOW antitank missiles to use in its war against Iraq (see September 4, 1980). Shultz also learned the White House NSC staff had already sent 100 TOW missiles to Iran in exchange for the release of American hostages (see January 8, 1985). In memoirs published in 1993, Shultz indicates he opposed the White House policy regarding the exchange of arms to Iran for the release of hostages. "In four major battles between mid-1985 and Fall 1986," Shultz writes, "I had fought to stop such a deal and each time I felt—or had been assured that—my view had prevailed. But this snake never died, no matter how many times I hacked at it." The final story of Reagan's "Project Democracy" for Iran and Nicaragua was not revealed until 1986.

See November 3, 1986 and successive entries.

January 26, 1985

Pope John Paul II visits Latin America, and denounces "liberation theology" that many Roman Catholic priests advocate.

The pontiff visited Venezuela, Ecuador, Peru, and Trinidad between January 26 and February 5, 1985. During the visits it became clear that John Paul emphasized hierarchical organization by which the Roman Catholic Church decided what teachings were to be communicated to the faithful. This view had prevailed for centuries until the Second Vatican Council of the 1960s, which viewed the church as "the people of God," with a theology that developed from problems people experienced. The latter view was accepted by Catholic "liberation theologians" such as Friar Leonardo Boff of Brazil and priests and layworkers working to improve the economic security of lower class people.

February 4, 1985

New Zealand bans U.S. Navy destroyer USS *Buchanan* from its ports unless it carries no nuclear weapons. Australia also opposes U.S. nuclear policy.

Under the ANZUS Treaty of Mutual Security (Australia–New Zealand–U.S. alliance), U.S. naval ships frequently visited New Zealand's ports during naval exercises in the South Pacific. Recently, however, intense opposition developed in New Zealand and Australia to the potential danger of nuclear weapons. Thus, Washington realized that those nations might close their ports to ships using nuclear weapons, but it had refused to indicate which of its vessels carried those weapons. On July 14, 1984, New Zealand's Labor Party, headed by Prime Minister David Lange, was elected on a platform that opposed nuclear weapons on New Zealand territory. Consequently, after Lange blocked the U.S. destroyer, the value of the ANZUS alliance became doubtful. On February 26, 1985, the United States canceled naval exercises scheduled with New Zealand and reduced its military and intelligence cooperation with that country. The United States subsequently suspended diplomatic relations with New Zealand, not to renew them until August 2001.

Australia also opposed U.S. nuclear policy. On February 5, it abrogated a pledge to assist tests of U.S. MX missiles; on March 4, it canceled a meeting of the ANZUS Security Council scheduled for July.

February 7, 1985

Because of Chile's human rights violations, the United States abstains from approving a loan to Chile.

Although the Reagan administration tried quiet diplomacy to persuade Chile's President Augusto Pinochet to make his regime more democratic, the efforts had failed thus far. Washington disapproved of a proposed bank loan because of Chile's human rights violations.

February 8, 1985

President Reagan names General Vernon Walters as U.S. ambassador to the United Nations.

The former ambassador, Jeanne J. Kirkpatrick, resigned on January 30, 1985. The U.S. Senate confirmed Walters on May 16, 1985. Walters shared Kirkpatrick's hard-line views against the Soviet Union but was less independent-minded than his predecessor in expressing extreme prejudices against those with whom he disagreed.

February 11, 1985

President Reagan declares the SDI program will continue even if an offensive arms control agreement is reached with the Soviet Union.

Although the January 8 communiqué of Secretary of State George Shultz and Soviet Foreign Minister Andrei Gromyko indicated an arms race in space should be avoided, President Reagan defended the need to pursue the SDI to provide a defense against enemy missiles aimed at the United States. Reagan contended that space defense should not be confused with nuclear arms control, even though many strategic analysts said that SDI would offset Soviet offensive ICBMs. In a dubious analogy, Reagan said that SDI resembled gas masks in the 1930s because after the 1925 ban on chemical weapons, nations still prepared for poisonous gas attacks if war were to begin. He did not continue the analogy by saying the masks were superfluous despite all the destruction of World War II.

February 12, 1985

In South Korean elections, the New Korea Democratic Party wins 67 seats.

The elections not only affirmed the leadership of President Chun Doo Hwan but also signaled the rise of Kim Dae Jung's newly formed New Korea Democratic Party.

February 21, 1985

The USSR permits the International Atomic Energy Agency (IAEA) to make on-site inspection of its nuclear plants.

For the first time, the Soviet Union allowed the IAEA to inspect civilian power plants that were using nuclear reactors. Although some critics indicated the agreement permitted inspection only of older plants and not the most advanced Soviet models, the United States praised the new policy as a step toward opening Soviet society.

February 25, 1985

President Reagan calls Nicaraguan rebels "the moral equal of the Founding Fathers."

In early 1985, Reagan undertook a major public relations campaign to obtain congressional backing for the Contra rebels fighting Nicaragua's Sandinista government. His most exaggerated effort came on February 25, when he told a group of conservative supporters that the Contras were the equivalent of America's Founding Fathers. Such language left members of Congress skeptical of Reagan's motives and his deficient knowledge of American history in comparing George Washington to the Contra leader, who was a former officer of Nicaragua's dictator Anastasio Somoza's National Guard and who used the guerrilla manual compiled by the CIA. In other speeches during February, Reagan called the Contras "our brothers" and "freedom fighters" like Simón Bolívar. In contrast to his support for the Contras, on February 28 Reagan criticized Nicaragua for sending 100 Cuban advisers home as an attempt to influence the U.S. Congress, not as a step for peace.

March 1, 1985

Defense Department report says a nuclear war could cause climatic disaster, but this does not affect defense policies.

A 17-page study titled "The Potential Effect of Nuclear War on Climate" was issued by the Pentagon in response to claims about "nuclear winter" raised by the astronomer Carl Sagan and other environmentalists. Although admitting climatic disaster was possible, the booklet said the Soviet Union used the concept of "nuclear winter" as propaganda, a veiled implication that some American scientists were "tools" of Moscow. Moreover, the Pentagon claimed its current nuclear deterrent policy, including the development of a spaced-based defense, was the best means to prevent a nuclear war.

March 3, 1985

The Pentagon abandons plans for civil defense evacuation of U.S. cities.

Although some Reagan administration advisers in 1981 desired to match the Soviet Union's alleged plans to evacuate cities to survive a "protracted nuclear war," previous funds spent on this were wasted when the Pentagon dropped the Crisis Relocation Plan. Defense Department officials said that congressional budget cuts prevented further expenditures. The "Crisis Relocation Plan" was designed to accelerate the evacuation of America's largest cities prior to a nuclear attack. This was part of a larger Pentagon plan to build blast shelters and concrete underground structures to withstand the impact of a nuclear bomb. Originally, the Pentagon estimated the cost of real estate and bomb shelters at $10 billion, a large portion of the Department of Defense budget.

March 5, 1985

In Cambodia (Kampuchea), Vietnam wins a third major victory on Thailand's border.

Supporting its appointed Cambodian government, Vietnam continued fighting against guerrilla forces of the Khmer Rouge in the jungles along the Thai border. On January 8, the Vietnamese captured the main headquarters of the Khmer People's National Liberation Front, forcing them to retreat into Thai refugee camps. On February 15, the Vietnamese took over the Khmer Rouge headquarters camp near Thailand. Finally, on March 5, the Vietnamese overran the headquarters of Cambodian guerrillas who supported the exiled Prince Norodom Sihanouk, causing Thailand to denounce Vietnam for crossing its border, a charge Hanoi denied. These Vietnamese victories led to U.S. aid to "noncommunist" rebels in Cambodia. President Reagan requested assistance from Congress on April 9, 1985. Subsequently, the foreign aid bill signed on August 8 allocated funds to Cambodian guerrillas.

March 10, 1985

Soviet leader Konstantin Chernenko dies of heart failure and is replaced by Mikhail S. Gorbachev the next day.

President Chernenko had been ill throughout his 13 months as Soviet leader. His state funeral was perfunctory. Only hours after his death Soviet Foreign Minister Andrei A. Gromyko, one of the few surviving Stalinists, nominated Gorbachev as Communist Party General Secretary. To Vice President George H.W. Bush, who represented the United States at Chernenko's funeral, and to other foreign dignitaries, Gorbachev indicated that his first priority would be to improve the Soviet economy. He wanted to return to the détente spirit of the early 1970s by having better relations with the United States and Western Europe. Gorbachev also sought to restructure the Soviet economy (perestroika) and to promote more openness (glasnost) in Soviet society.

March 24, 1985

A Soviet sentry kills an American officer on surveillance in East Germany.

Major Arthur D. Nicholson Jr. was shot by a Soviet sentry near a small town outside Berlin. Nicholson and a companion, Sergeant Jesse G. Schatz, were on a routine reconnaissance mission permitted by the Big Four power accords with Germany at the end of World War II. The shooting was debated for several months afterward because U.S. and Soviet versions of the event differed. The Soviets said Nicholson was spying in an off-limits zone. When warned by the Soviet guard, Nicholson was said to have fled and was shot. Sergeant Schatz was in a nearby car. To the contrary, the Americans claimed the two Americans were in a car 300 to 500 yards outside a zone whose off-limits status had ended on February 20, 1985. It was not known why the Soviet guard fired three shots at the American car, killing Nicholson. For over one hour, the Soviets did not allow the U.S. major to receive first aid. Although President Reagan expressed outrage at the shooting, he told reporters that plans for a summit with Soviet leader Mikhail Gorbachev would continue. He declared that such incidents made meetings with Gorbachev even more essential.

March 29, 1985

Spain and Portugal admitted to the European Economic Community (EEC).

Discussions about the admission of these two countries to the EEC had been under way for six years before agreement was reached on March 29. A treaty formalizing this act was signed on June 12, and their admission became effective on January 1, 1986. With the addition of Spain and Portugal, the EEC had 12 member nations.

March 31, 1985

In El Salvador, President Duarte's Christian Democratic Party defeats right-wing parties, gaining 33 of 60 National Assembly seats.

Although there were charges of corruption in this election, the Salvadoran army backed Duarte's claim that the errors were of little significance. The right-wing party of Roberto d'Aubuisson was the loser, although it retained influence among the military. The United States had promoted Duarte's reelection as a sign that El Salvador was more democratic. Duarte said he would try to negotiate peace with his opponents.

April 2, 1985

The Defense Department's fourth edition of *Soviet Military Power* accuses the USSR of a large-scale military buildup.

As in three previous reports during the Reagan administration, the Pentagon warned of the Kremlin's aggressive military expansion. Defense Secretary

Caspar Weinberger presented portions of the 143-page report on a satellite television hookup with Western Europe and Japan. Important parts of the report said that the Soviets were ready to deploy SS-24s launched from railroad cars, each carrying 10 nuclear warheads; had launched two new Delta-IV class submarines with 16 SS-NA-23 missiles each; had added five divisions to their ground forces; and supplied Nicaragua with 17,000 metric tons of military supplies. On February 1, 1985, and again on December 23, the Reagan administration issued reports on Soviet violations of arms control agreements. Most knowledgeable observers recognized the reports as having inflated the so-called disparity between the two superpowers and as being Defense Department propaganda aimed at influencing the American people and Congress to support Reagan's military buildup and avoid arms control agreements.

April 7, 1985

Soviet leader Mikhail Gorbachev declares a moratorium on deployment of Soviet intermediate-range missiles; the United States objects.

In an interview with the Communist Party paper *Pravda*, Gorbachev said he wanted to speed up Geneva arms talks by ending the deployment of Soviet SS-20s targeted for Europe. Gorbachev's interview was part of a peace offensive that made him popular in Western Europe. On May 27, he followed the interview by blaming the Reagan administration's Strategic Defense Initiative for making arms control impossible. Gorbachev also expressed a desire to meet with President Reagan in the near future. Though the Reagan administration opposed joining the moratorium because it would leave Moscow with an eight-to-one advantage over the United States in intermediate-range missiles, meeting Gorbachev was acceptable to the president because he had written Gorbachev a letter in March 1985 to suggest such talks.

April 11, 1985

Albanian leader Enver Hoxha dies and is replaced by Ramiz Alia.

Under Hoxha, Albania became isolated from the rest of the world for over 40 years. An orthodox Communist, Hoxha broke with the Soviet Union in 1961 and supported mainland China. The new ruler, Ramiz Alia, continued the policy of isolation; no foreigners were invited to Hoxha's funeral.

April 11, 1985

The United States cancels a naval visit to China, denying it promised to send no ships that carried nuclear weapons.

On January 11, 1985, in response to an invitation from the People's Republic of China, Washington scheduled a naval visit for May 13, 1985. The United States canceled the visit on April 11, the day after Beijing reported a U.S. pledge to send no ships with nuclear weapons. The U.S. navy was sensitive about identifying which warships carried nuclear weapons. Identification became an issue because U.S. allies such as Japan, New Zealand, and Australia allowed non-nuclear ships to visit their ports but wanted to block those carrying nuclear weapons.

April 24, 1985

The House of Representatives rejects President Reagan's request for Contra aid.

Despite Reagan's public promotion of the Contra rebels as freedom fighters, Congress rejected these efforts. Reagan's claim to support Pope John Paul II and Latin American leaders in seeking peace in Nicaragua was denied by the Vatican and the Latin Americans, a ploy that further polarized Reagan's opposition. Finally, Congress received a secret report implying U.S. forces might be used if "other policy alternatives failed" had the negative effect of justifying the worst fears of Congress that a new "Vietnam" was being readied. For these reasons, the House voted against President Reagan's request for $14 million of aid to the Contras. As it turned out, Nicaraguan President Daniel Ortega's decision to visit Moscow on April 28 enabled Reagan to get the aid.

See May 1, 1985.

April 26, 1985

Warsaw Pact members agree to 20-year extension of their alliance.

Soviet leader Mikhail Gorbachev presided over the meeting of the Communist-bloc powers. During the session, Gorbachev called on Western European nations to restrain their deployment of missiles and to help eliminate the danger of "nuclear extinction" if war should occur.

May 1, 1985

President Reagan places a trade embargo on Nicaragua.

Alleging that Nicaraguan policies were an "extraordinary threat" to the nation, Reagan stopped all trade to that country effective May 7, 1985. He also prohibited Nicaraguan aircraft or ships from entering the United States. While this action hurt the Nicaraguan economy, it also helped the Sandinista government obtain economic aid not only from the Soviet Union but also from U.S. allies who disagreed with Reagan's policies.

May 2, 1985

Annual economic summit of seven industrial nations convenes in Bonn to discuss trade agreements.

As in recent annual summits, this meeting of seven heads of state symbolized their cooperative economic efforts even though they disagreed on policy details. President Reagan wanted a commitment to schedule a new round of GATT trade liberalization talks, but the French objected and refused to accept a specific date to begin negotiations. The French wanted to clarify a specific agenda to precede formal trade talks. Reagan also failed to get allied support for his Strategic Defense Initiative program. Although West Germany and Italy were interested in the proposal, neither the French nor British would make a commitment as "subcontractors." Reagan had offered to distribute some research projects to U.S. allies to gain their backing.

May 5, 1985

President Reagan visits military cemetery at Bitburg, Germany, arousing a storm of controversy.

Widespread controversy began on April 11, 1985, when Reagan's White House spokesman announced Reagan would visit a German cemetery in Bitburg during his European trip in May. In reaction to this announcement, Nathan Perlmutter, the National Director of the Anti-Defamation League of B'nai B'rith told a *Washington Post* reporter "I think this visit to a cemetery of German soldiers is an act of grace because it is good to express friendship to a former enemy. But the asymmetry of doing this while choosing not to visit the graves of that enemy's victims is insensitive, and is not a healing act."

Secretary of State George Shultz's 1993 memoir has details about the controversy surrounding the Bitburg visit. He explains how Reagan decided to visit the graves of Holocaust victims at Bergen-Belsen as well as Bitburg cemetery. Reagan also visited the U.S. Air Force Base at Bitburg where he told crowds "Some old wounds have been reopened, and that I regret very much because this should be a time of healing." To Holocaust survivors, Reagan said, "Your terrible suffering has made you ever vigilant against evil. I promise we will never forget."

May 20, 1985

The U.S. Information Agency begins broadcasting on Radio Marti, sending news programs to Cuban audiences.

At President Reagan's requested in 1983, Congress approved broadcasting of Voice of America programs to Cuba. The radio's opening was delayed due to problems of getting a director and qualified staff. On May 20, Radio Marti began Cuban broadcasts for 14 hours per day. Cuba's government objected to the invasion of its air and communications space and retaliated in two ways. First, by jamming broadcasts and second by suspending a 1984 agreement allowing up to 20,000 Cuban immigrants per year to enter the United States while accepting the return of 2,746 Cuban criminals and mental patients sent to the United States in the 1980 boatlift.

See December 10, 1984.

May 20, 1985

The spy ring of retired naval officer John A. Walker Jr. is broken up after 15 years of selling material to the Soviets.

The Walker spy ring was uncovered by the Federal Bureau of Investigation (FBI) after Walker's wife provided the essential information. Initially, while serving as a navy chief warrant officer aboard a submarine; later, after retiring, Walker led a group of two relatives and a friend who sold Soviet agents classified data on U.S. communications and keycode methods. On May 20, the FBI arrested Walker for selling classified documents. Two days later, they arrested his son, Seaman Michael Walker, who was aboard the USS *Nimitz.* Subsequently, they arrested a third relative, Navy Lieutenant Commander Arthur

J. Walker, and a family friend, retired Chief Petty Officer Jerry A. Whitworth. In court, John A. Walker pleaded guilty and was sentenced to life in prison. He plea bargained to get his son a 25-year prison term in exchange for giving a complete accounting of the material sold to the Soviets. Arthur Walker was fined $250,000 and sentenced to life in prison for espionage and conspiracy.

June 1, 1985

Alan García Pérez is declared president of Peru after chief opponent withdraws from a runoff election.

June 2, 1985

Greek Prime Minister Papandreou retains control of Parliament.

The victory of Andreas Papandreou and the Pan Hellenic Socialist Movement was greater than expected. The Socialists won 45.8 percent of the vote and 161 seats in the 300-member parliament; the conservative New Democracy won 125 seats; the Communist Party, 13 seats. In 1981, Papandreou stated he would close all U.S. naval bases in Greece but eventually negotiated a new treaty with Washington. The U.S. State Department was upset because Papandreou's anti-American rhetoric led Greek terrorists to bomb a military base near Athens on February 2, 1985, injuring 57 Americans. Privately, Greek officials said Papandreou sought independence from Washington.

June 6, 1985

Israeli troops complete evacuation of Lebanon, leaving advisers to aid Lebanese.

Israel and Lebanon had agreed to a troop withdrawal on October 31, 1984, which Israel's cabinet approved on January 14, 1985. The first stage of withdrawal began on February 16; the last took place on June 6.

June 10, 1985

President Reagan says United States will abide by SALT II by dismantling a Poseidon submarine.

Arms control experts thought Reagan would exceed the SALT II limit when the U.S. navy launched a new Trident submarine armed with 24 missiles but the president had ordered the navy to dismantle one Poseidon with 16 nuclear missiles to keep the United States under the limit of 1,200 multiple warheads agreed to in 1979. Reagan told reporters this action would encourage restraint in the deployment of nuclear weapons and success for the Geneva arms talks. He called on the Soviet Union to show restraint and end its violation of previous arms treaties.

June 11, 1985

Indian Prime Minister Rajiv Gandhi begins a visit to the United States.

Although Washington expected India to continue its neutral stance between the Soviet Union and the United States, Gandhi pleased many American politicians during a speech to Congress in which he urged the creation of an independent, nonaligned Afghanistan. India, he said, backed U.N. and U.S. efforts to get Soviet troops out of Afghanistan.

June 11, 1985

Criticizing poor Soviet economic performance, Mikhail Gorbachev proposes Soviet economic reform.

In a major address, Gorbachev followed up previous statements that urged better economic performance (April 8) and actions to combat alcoholism (May 16) and claimed broad changes were needed in the Soviet economy. Revealing to Communist Party officials that the Politburo had rejected his draft of a five-year plan for 1986–1990, Gorbachev said the Soviet Union must renovate its existing industry and obtain better consumer products to sell at home and abroad. He berated economic managers, singling out Soviet steel makers for manufacturing poor products and squandering their use of metals. On October 15, Gorbachev announced a five-year plan that the Communist Party Congress reviewed in February 1986.

See February 25, 1986.

June 12, 1985

Mujahideen in Herat region clash with government and Soviet forces.

Sunni guerrilla fighters in western Afghanistan were a vast distance from supply lines coming from Pakistan but were able to challenge opposing forces. Shindand air base south of Herat and the city of Herat were tempting targets. Herat's violent outbreak first began in March 1979, followed by rebel challenges in October 1981, December 1981, and January 1982.

In 1984, Soviets troops changed tactics by using planes and helicopters to bomb the area to scatter or kill people who supported the guerrillas. The bombing caused substantial casualties but failed to prevent the June 12, 1985, rebel attack on Shindand airfield that destroyed about 20 Soviet aircraft. During July, another Herat uprising forced the regime's governor to flee the city.

June 19, 1985

Salvadoran terrorists kill 13 people including six Americans at sidewalk cafés.

The attack was aimed at four off-duty U.S. Marine guards who were among the victims. A leftist rebel group attacked three outdoor cafés, firing machine guns at patrons. One of the 10 terrorists was killed immediately. On August 27, El Salvador announced that three suspects in the killings had been arrested. They were members of the Central American Revolutionary Worker's Group, one of five Salvadoran guerrilla organizations.

June 23, 1985

Sikh terrorists stage two aircraft bombings, one over the Atlantic, another at Tokyo airport; other terrorists are also busy.

There seemed little doubt that Sikh terrorists from India had planted the bomb that exploded on an Air India plane crossing the Atlantic Ocean to London, killing 329 persons on board. The second bomb exploded in the baggage area of Tokyo International Airport, having been in a suitcase on board a Canadian Pacific Airlines plane that arrived ahead of schedule.

July 2, 1985

Eduard A. Shevardnadze becomes Soviet foreign minister, replacing Andrei Gromyko, who becomes the Soviet president.

At a meeting of the Supreme Soviet, Communist Party First Secretary Mikhail Gorbachev announced that Gromyko would become the president of the Soviet Union, a largely honorific title. By selecting Shevardnadze, who had no experience in foreign affairs but was a long-time friend, the new Soviet leader could formulate his own international policy knowing the new foreign minister would carry it out. Gromyko had been a leading Soviet figure throughout 40 years of the Cold War.

July 4, 1985

In Zimbabwe's first election, the Zimbabwe African National Union (ZANU) wins 63 of 80 black parliamentary seats.

Robert Mugabe, head of the ZANU, became prime minister. He wanted to scrap the 1980 constitution, which guaranteed the nation's white minority a role in the government, and create a one-party socialist state under ZANU, but he did not receive 70 percent of the the parliamentary votes necessary to amend the constitution.

July 7, 1985

Vietnam returns remains of 26 Americans.

At the invitation of Hanoi, a U.S. research group made a three-day mission to Vietnam to discuss evidence of American POWs and MIAs from the Vietnam War. In June, another American team visited Laos to excavate the wreckage of an AC 130 gunship shot down in 1973. The State Department hoped that talks with Hanoi might reveal the whereabouts of the remaining 2,464 Americans unaccounted for since 1975. The Pentagon pointed out, however, that 8,100 Americans were unaccounted for from the Korean War and 78,000 from World War II, even though the United States had access to World War II battlefields and crash sites. Neither of these conflicts had stirred the American public about POW-MIAs as did the Vietnam conflict.

July 8, 1985

President Reagan says Iran, Libya, North Korea, Cuba, and Nicaragua sponsor world terrorism.

Addressing the American Bar Association, Reagan denounced these five nations as outlaw states who undertook a "new international version of Murder, Inc." by sponsoring terror groups that they trained, financed, and directed, especially against the United States. Notably, Syria was no longer on Reagan's list, probably because its president had helped to free TWA hostages.

July 8, 1985

Canada imposes economic sanctions on South Africa, protesting apartheid.

Because many Canadians opposed South Africa's racial policies, Canada's minister of external affairs, Joe Clark, took action to limit trade with South Africa. The government prohibited Canadian firms from processing uranium and asked all companies doing business with South Africa to employ nondiscriminatory personnel policies. On September 13, Clark announced sanctions that embargoed air traffic to South Africa and called for a voluntary ban on new bank loans and crude oil trade.

July 10, 1985

Congress repeals the Clark Amendment, ending restrictions on U.S. aid to Angolan rebels.

When approved by Congress in 1976, the Clark Amendment opposed the Central Intelligence Agency's secret aid to anti-Communist rebels in Angola. On June 11, the Senate repealed the Clark Amendment followed by the House on July 10, 1985. Since becoming president, Ronald Reagan sought to repeal aid to Jonas Savimbi, who headed the National Union of Total Independence for Angola (UNITA) guerrillas seeking to overthrow the government that received aid from Cuba. Congress approved $30 million for UNITA on August 8, but Reagan withheld half of it while trying to persuade Angola to send Cuban troops home. After November talks with Angola failed, Reagan released all UNITA funds on December 10, 1985.

July 10, 1985

China and the Soviet Union double their trade to $14 billion over four years.

In addition to establishing bartering agreements worth an estimated $14 billion, the Chinese and Soviets also made an economic and technical cooperation agreement by which the USSR would construct seven new factories in China.

July 12, 1985

President Reagan reinstates regulations on export of military technology.

The president signed the 1985 Export Administrative Extension Act to carry on a 1979 act that expired in 1983. In 1983–1984, Reagan used the International Emergency Economic Powers Act to control exports of U.S. technology. The law relaxed restrictions on high-technology exports to Japan and America's NATO allies. The Commerce Department and U.S. Customs Agency would draw up guidelines for export controls that the Defense and Justice Departments would review.

July 16, 1985

Senator Jesse Helms protests Secretary of State Shultz's anticonservative policies.

During 1985, the right-wing Heritage Foundation and its champion, Senator Jesse Helms (R-N.C.), claimed President Reagan's administration had stopped its hard-line anti-Communist policies because of Secretary of State George Shultz. To publicize this view, Helms vowed to block 29 pending State Department appointees unless six conservatives were assured of jobs. Shultz was also castigated on July 2 at a Heritage Foundation forum where three former Reagan-appointed ambassadors claimed Shultz was "undermining" Reagan's foreign policy. David Funderbunk, former ambassador to Romania, Charles Lichenstein, former U.N. delegate, and Curtin Winsor Jr., former ambassador to Costa Rica, each said Shultz had purged conservative appointees in favor of career Foreign Service personnel. After delaying a Senate vote on the 29 appointees from June 20 to July 16, Helms talked with Reagan and Shultz and agreed to permit Senate votes that approved all 29. Helms said his wishes were met but the incident pointed to the defection of right-wing ideologues during Reagan's second term.

July 23, 1985

Chinese President Li Xiannian signs nuclear power agreement but criticizes charges against China's population policy.

During his July 23 visit with President Reagan at the White House, Li was most agreeable, and the two leaders announced a pact for nuclear power cooperation, which could involve the sale of U.S. nonmilitary nuclear reactors to China. Earlier, on July 11, Li spoke harshly against a House of Representatives vote that cut $56 million from a U.N. fund helping nations to control their rapid population growth. Li said U.S. reports of China's forced abortions and sterilization of women were "based on fabrications and distortions of Chinese policy." U.S. opposition, he argued, interfered in China's internal affairs. The House of Representatives denied the funds on July 10.

July 23, 1985

South and North Korean officials meet for the first time in 40 years to discuss unification.

This meeting at Panmunjom on the 38th parallel met with little success in fostering unity but provided for the reunion of some Korean families who had not met for 40 years. After planning by the Korean Red Cross on September 20, 1985, 151 North Koreans and 157 South Koreans from various families visited Seoul or Pyongyang for reunions with family members.

July 26, 1985

The United States abstains on U.N. resolution to suspend new investments in South Africa.

France sponsored this resolution in the U.N. Security Council as a reaction to South Africa's imposition of emergency controls on its citizens on July 20, 1985. Its emergency decrees gave police and the army powers to quell the opposition to the regime, including searches at will and detaining people without charge or legal aid. Although the United States and Great Britain abstained, the resolution passed. On August 1, 10 European Economic Community nations, including Spain and Portugal recalled their ambassadors from South Africa to protest the state of emergency. In Washington, President Reagan preferred "quiet diplomacy" toward South Africa rather than sanctions. Nevertheless, the House of Representatives voted 380 to 48 for a "mild" package of economic sanctions.

July 29, 1985

The Soviet Union places moratorium on nuclear tests until January 1986, to be extended if United States agrees.

During 1985, Soviet leader Mikhail Gorbachev made various proposals to commit the Reagan administration to arms control so the Soviets could divert more funds to economic development. Reagan called these Soviet proposals "propaganda" and refused to follow suit, saying the nuclear tests were not verifiable. Gorbachev said ending of nuclear tests would be a "major contribution to consolidating strategic stability and peace on earth." Gorbachev's messages made him popular among many Europeans who lived under the threat of nuclear war between the two superpowers. On September 10, Gorbachev suggested a chemical-weapons-free zone in Central Europe. Again, the White House said this would have to be verifiable.

August 6, 1985

West German incidents disclose presence of East German spies in Bonn.

On August 6, the disappearance of the secretary of the West German economics minister, Sonja Lueneburg, began a month in which other Bonn officials disappeared or defected to East Germany. Margaret Hoecke, a secretary in West German President Richard von Weizsacker's office, confessed to being a spy. Soon after, two political lobbyists defected to East Germany. On August 14, Bonn's third-ranking intelligence officer, Hans Joachim Tiedge, vanished and turned up in East Germany. Finally, on September 16, a secretary in Chancellor Helmut Kohl's office, Herta Astrid, and her husband defected to the East. Of these, Tiedge's spying was the most serious because he knew West German agents in East Germany and had access to NATO operational data.

August 8, 1985

President Reagan signs foreign aid bill that includes many congressional restrictions on the executive, although the Clark Amendment is abolished.

This was the first time since 1981 that the foreign aid bill was not simply a continuing resolution of Congress, although those resolutions often contained amendments to restrict U.S. funding for military or nonmilitary purposes. The 1985 bill authorized $6.26 billion in military aid for 1986 and 1987, the total of $12.77 billion being a 5 percent increase over 1985; Reagan had requested a 13 percent increase. The bill limited the president's authority to waive restrictions on arms sales to $750 million per year, with no more than $50 million to one country being waived. Thus, a maximum of 15 countries could receive $50 million per year. Other highlights of the bill were the following:

1. The United States could not negotiate with the Palestine Liberation Organization.
2. The President need not certify El Salvador's human rights progress.
3. Guatemala received no military aid until it elected a civilian government and ended human rights abuses.
4. Nicaraguan rebels received $27 million in non-military aid, but the CIA could not administer it.
5. The Philippines received $70 million in "non-lethal" equipment but was warned to begin human rights reforms.
6. Increased aid was granted to anti-Communist rebels in Afghanistan and Cambodia.
7. The Clark Amendment, which banned aid to Angolan rebels, was repealed.
8. Aid to Libya and any other nation linked to terrorism was prohibited.
9. Aid to Pakistan was barred unless the president certified that it had no nuclear weapons.

August 8, 1985

Two Americans are killed by a terrorist bomb at a West German air base; more terrorist activity.

The worst bomb explosion at a West German base since 1981 (see August 3, 1981 and June 1, 1982) occurred at the U.S. military installation—Rhein-Main Air Base. In addition to killing Americans, 20 other persons were injured. The terrorist groups claiming responsibility for the attack were the West German Red Army Faction and the French Direct Action Group. On August 13, German police disclosed that the terrorists had also killed an off-duty American soldier to steal his papers and gain admission to the base. Other terrorist attacks occurred in West Germany in July and August. On July 10, six British soldiers were injured in a bomb explosion near a British base. On August 15, a terrorist bomb damaged a radio tower at the U.S. Armed Forces radio base.

August 26, 1985

President Reagan says South Africa has a "reformist government," provoking complaints against his "racist" views.

The president made comments in a radio interview that were favorable toward South Africa. Although President P.W. Botha imposed a state of emergency in South Africa on July 20, Reagan said Botha had a "reformist administration." President Reagan later issued a statement saying that he "carelessly gave the impression he believed racial segregation was eliminated." South Africa's Archbishop Desmond Tutu later told reporters that the president "is a racist, pure and simple."

August 30, 1985

Poland's Solidarity leader, Lech Walesa, calls for new talks with the government to benefit the nation.

Although Solidarity demonstrations protested Prime Minister Wojciech Jaruzelski's austerity measures on February 13 and May 1, no results were achieved. Initiating a new approach on the fifth anniversary of Solidarity's founding, Walesa issued a 500-page report containing a plan for ending Poland's social and economic difficulties. He urged the government to consult with Solidarity to achieve such a program.

September 9, 1985

President Reagan imposes limited trade sanctions on South Africa, prompting the Senate to postpone consideration of a sanctions bill.

Although President Reagan previously opposed sanctions, he said some action might pressure South Africa to end apartheid. The president's sanctions included restrictions on exports of nuclear technology, a ban on the sale of computers for security agencies, and prohibitions on most U.S. bank loans. These mild measures achieved a compromise with congressional advocates of stronger sanctions.

September 10, 1985

The daughter of El Salvador's president is kidnapped.

The oldest daughter of President José Napoleon Duarte, Inés Duarte Duran, and a friend were abducted by gunmen who killed one bodyguard and wounded another during the fracas. The rebels freed Duran and her friend unharmed on October 24, as well as 23 mayors and other government officials in exchange for the release of 22 political prisoners and safe conduct out of the country for 101 guerrillas disabled in the fighting. The guerrillas changed to new tactics because the American-supplied Salvadoran army was too strong to defeat in a conventional war. A longer, more disruptive war seemed to be under way in El Salvador.

September 12, 1985

The United Kingdom exposes a major Soviet intelligence network, expelling 25 Soviet agents.

Great Britain discovered this spy network following the defection of a British-based Soviet agent, Oleg Gordievsky, a veteran of 23 years with the KGB, the Soviet secret police. Following the British expulsion of the Soviets, Moscow expelled 25 British diplomats on September 14. This led to another round of retaliatory expulsions—the British sent six Soviet diplomats home on September 16, and Moscow returned six British on September 18. Britain revealed that Gordievsky had been a "double agent" with British intelligence for over 20 years. He defected because his activity was discovered by the KGB.

September 12, 1985

The World Court begins hearings on Nicaragua's complaint of U.S. military operations against it. The United States alters its tradition favoring international law.

Although on January 18 the United States rejected the World Court's invitation to defend itself against Nicaragua's accusations, the court held hearings from September 12 to 20. While the World Court heard evidence such as the March 5 American Human Rights Watch report accusing Contra rebels of atrocities, the most critical testimony against the United States was the report of former Contra leader Edgar Chamorro, who stated the CIA encouraged rebels to use a terrorist campaign against civilians to turn them against .the Sandinista government. On October 7, the State Department asserted that the United States would not comply with World Court decisions, because the court served "political ends" hostile to the United States. This contention altered traditional U.S. policy to support the rule of law in international affairs. Senator Mark Hatfield (R-Ore.) criticized the Reagan administration's position, noting that "Khomeini, Qaddafi and all other world-class thugs who thrive on the rule of the jungle will no doubt welcome this decision."

September 12, 1985

The Contadora nations propose "final" peace plan for Central America.

The four major Contadora states of Mexico, Venezuela, Colombia, and Panama had tried since 1983 to obtain peace in Nicaragua, El Salvador, and Guatemala (see January 8, 1983). The present Contadora peace concept proposed removing all foreign military advisers from all states in the region and prohibiting foreign nations from supporting any group trying to overthrow a Central American government. The Contadora members asked each Central American government to respond to their plan by November 21, but Nicaragua rejected the plan on November 11 because it required neither the withdrawal of U.S. military advisers nor end the enlargement of guerrilla forces in the region. Nicaragua's rejection of the plan required Contadora representatives to meet again on November 19.

See December 18, 1986.

September 13, 1985

The U.S. air force successfully tests an antisatellite missile.

Despite Soviet objections that this test violated nuclear arms treaties, the air force proceeded with it because the White House stated on April 7, 1985, that the antiballistic test did not violate the 1972 ABM treaty. During the test, a missile from an F-15 fighter plane hit and destroyed an orbiting derelict satellite flying 290 miles above the Pacific Ocean. The missile's ability to hit a space satellite was an essential step to pursue Reagan's Strategic Defense Initiative.

September 16, 1985

The Chinese Communist Party (CCP) appoints younger members to replace older Politburo and Central Committee members.

At its annual session in Beijing, the CCP made the most extensive leadership changes since 1949. Ten retiring Politburo members and 64 of 340 Central Committee members were replaced. Earlier, on June 18, Chinese leaders had replaced nine senior ministers with younger men. During its September 16–22 meeting, the party also approved a four-year economic plan that continued the market-oriented program begun by Chinese leader Deng Xiaoping.

September 22, 1985

The "Plaza Accord" among five industrial nations lowers dollar's value.

The Group of Five industrial powers met at the Plaza Hotel in New York to conclude three months of negotiations on trade and currency. The agreement said the five nations would intervene in the currency market to devalue the dollar, whose value had risen because of high U.S. interest rates financing the national debt, which reached $2 trillion by the end of 1985. Secretary of the Treasury James Baker and Federal Reserve Board Chairman Paul Volker represented the United States at the Plaza meeting, having persuaded President Reagan to reverse policies that let the dollar float freely on the currency markets. Baker believed a lower dollar value would lower U.S. export prices and encourage foreign sales of U.S. goods. Representatives of Great Britain, France, West Germany, Japan, and the United States agreed to sell dollars when necessary to drive down the dollar value. The other leaders urged Baker to reduce U.S. budget deficits and interest rates to stabilize currency values. The day after the accord was announced, the value of the dollar dropped by 5.2 percent, a record one-day decline. During the next four years, the U.S. trade balance improved but not enough to correct the trade imbalance with Japan. It became cheaper for Japan to invest in U.S. business enterprises and to build Japanese assembly plants in the United States while importing Japanese auto parts for its U.S. plants. Before the Plaza Accord, the Japanese yen was 263 per dollar and by 1989 it was 132 yen per dollar. Similar results enhanced the ability of the Germans and the British to invest in America. The alternative would have been to balance the U.S. budget by raising taxes and lowering interest paid on the national debt. American politicians, especially Republicans, had avoided this "sacrifice" and campaigned instead on a policy of no new taxes.

September 26, 1985

A top KGB agent defects to the United States—the curious case of Vitaly Yurchenko.

Assumed to be the fifth-highest officer of the Soviet secret police (KGB), Yurchenko disappeared from his Rome post in early September and was reported to have defected to the United States, where the CIA secretly debriefed him. On November 4, 1985, Yurchenko unexpectedly appeared for a news conference at the Soviet embassy in Washington. He told reporters the CIA had drugged and abducted him from Italy, bringing him to the United States, where he was held and questioned. He escaped and came to the embassy to return home. The U.S. State Department claimed Yurchenko had willingly defected and given the CIA valuable information. After the Soviets permitted a State Department official to interview Yurchenko privately, the officer said Yurchenko wanted to return home, and he did so on November 6. CIA spokesmen said Yurchenko divulged the names of several Americans who spied for the Soviet Union, and these persons were under investigation. On November 25, 1985, Ronald Pelton, a National Security Agency official, was arrested on the basis of Yurchenko's revelations. On June 5, 1986, Pelton was convicted and sentenced to life in prison.

September 28, 1985

The State Department announces a program for U.S. embassies.

This $5.5 billion five-year program was planned to make American ambassadorial residencies around the world secure from terrorism and to counteract Soviet espionage efforts. On August 21, the State Department reported that its Moscow Embassy staff had discovered that the Soviet Union used a compound called "spy dust" picked up by the shoes or hands of U.S embassy personnel and visitors. The Soviets could then follow the individuals by using ultraviolet light to make their tracks visible.

September 29, 1985

Roberto D'Aubuisson resigns as head of El Salvador's right-wing National Republican Alliance.

Although this announcement ostensibly removed the notorious d'Aubuisson from El Salvador's rightist party, most U.S. observers doubted the resignation ended his control over military groups (death squads) that carried out attacks on left-wing radicals in El Salvador.

September 30, 1985

Four Soviet diplomats are kidnapped in West Beirut.

The first Soviet citizens to be abducted in Lebanon, the Islamic Liberation Organization said, would be executed unless Syrian-backed militia stopped attacks on Tripoli. Although one Soviet captive was found dead in West Beirut on October 2, the other captives were released unharmed. On October 30, 1985, some commentators claimed that strong Soviet threats gained their release. Two more probable factors were that the kidnappers were moderate Sunni (not Shiite) Muslims, and Syria produced the hostages because it depended on Soviet arms.

October 1, 1985

Israeli planes bomb PLO headquarters in Tunis, killing over 70 people.

Although President Reagan initially called the Israeli raid "a legitimate response" in retaliation for three Israelis killed in Cyprus, he modified the statement on October 2 by saying it "cannot be condoned" because many innocent people died in the Tunis air raid. Although the U.N. Security Council voted to condemn Israel's attack with the United States abstaining, such resolutions did not influence Israel.

October 10, 1985

U.S. navy planes intercept an Egyptian airplane carrying the *Achille Lauro* hijackers, forcing it to land in Sicily, where Italian police arrest the terrorists.

On October 7, Egyptian authorities obtained the release of the 400 passengers on the cruise ship *Achille Lauro* by promising safe-conduct to the four hijackers. The hijackers hoped to fly to Tunisia, where the Palestine Liberation Organization was headquartered. Although Tunisia refused to admit them, they boarded an Egyptian commercial aircraft for Tunis. Soon after the plane left Egyptian territory, President Reagan ordered U.S. fighter planes from the carrier *Saratoga* to intercept the airliner, forcing its pilot to land the Boeing 737 in Sicily. American and Italian troops from a Sicilian base took over the plane and Italian authorities arrested the four Arabs for murder and kidnapping. Seventeen American *Achille Lauro* passengers were flown from Port Said, Egypt, to Sicily where they identified the hijackers.

Italy's Prime Minister Bettino Craxi complained about the high-handed U.S. tactics. In addition, he contended U.S. fighter planes had violated Italian airspace by following the Egyptian airliner bringing the arrested hijackers from Sicily to Rome. On July 19, 1986, 11 of the 15 men charged in the hijacking were sentenced to life in prison by a court in Genoa, Italy. The judge also imposed life sentences in absentia on Muhammad Abbas and two others for planing the hijacking.

See October 17, 1985.

October 11, 1985

At the IMF-World Bank conference in South Korea, Secretary of the Treasury James Baker proposes aid to debtor nations.

The conference of 149 member countries of the International Monetary Fund (IMF) and the World Bank advanced the question of how industrial nations could help Third World countries obtain private investments while developing market-oriented economies. The Baker Plan proposed establishing a $30 billion fund, in addition to the $50 billion already allocated, over three years to allow debtor countries to develop market policies that would boost domestic savings, investments, and growth.

October 15, 1985

Nicaraguan President Daniel Ortega declares national emergency, blaming the "brutal aggression by North America and its internal allies."

Ortega suspended, for one year, free expression, public assembly, privacy of mail and home, and the right to strike, claiming that some religious institutions and media outlets were allies of Washington. He was also troubled by workers demonstrating in Managua to obtain their unpaid year-end bonuses. Ortega had substantial reasons for thinking that Washington continued to help the Contras, even though Congress had restricted military aid to them in 1984 and 1985. On August 8, 1985, President Reagan admitted that a

New York Times article was correct in stating that National Security Council officials advised the rebels. Neither Reagan nor the *Times* disclosed the full extent of this clandestine aid until the Iran-Contra scandal surfaced in 1986.

October 17, 1985

Italian Prime Minister Bettino Craxi resigns after a dispute growing from the *Achille Lauro* incident.

Following the arrest of the hijackers of the Italian cruise ship *Achille Lauro*, Craxi's government allowed Islamic Jihad terrorist Abu Abbas to go free because he was not directly involved in the hijacking of the vessel. On October 30, Craxi formed a five-party coalition that urged the Palestine Liberation Organization to pursue peaceful negotiations.

October 24, 1985

President Reagan meets with leaders of allied nations to discuss Geneva summit preparations.

Reagan met with the leaders of the United Kingdom, Canada, Italy, West Germany, and Japan. French President François Mitterrand declined an invitation, while leaders of Belgium and the Netherlands were upset not to have been invited. Generally, the Europeans expected little from the first Reagan-Gorbachev meeting but hoped the U.S. president would not cause the summit to fail by pushing his Strategic Defence Initiative (SDI). Recently, National Security Adviser Robert C. McFarlane startled both Bonn and London by remarking that the 1972 Anti-Ballistic Missile Treaty might be abandoned so that the SDI system could be tested and deployed. Europeans saw the SDI as destabilizing the deterrent nuclear policies already in place. Because Reagan and his advisers were seldom sensitive to the advice of European leaders, most observers doubted that their views were influential. Reagan gave his U.N. speech the same day, and both West German and British officials privately expressed dismay that the president talked tough against the Soviet Union but offered no arms control proposals to seize the peace initiative from Soviet leader Mikhail Gorbachev. On November 1, 1985, Reagan tried to mollify his European critics by proposing to cut nuclear warheads by 50 percent, with a ceiling of 4,500. But this plan contained nothing new from prior proposals.

October 24, 1985

President Reagan calls for a "fresh start" in U.S.-Soviet relations while blaming Moscow for conflicts.

Speaking before the U.N. General Assembly, Reagan stated a desire to lead peace efforts and end difficulties with the Soviet Union. Nevertheless, Reagan's "fresh start" consisted mostly of old criticisms of Soviet involvement in conflicts in Angola, Afghanistan, and elsewhere, his implication being the Soviets were untrustworthy.

October 24, 1985

A Soviet seaman jumps ship and causes friction in U.S.-Soviet relations before he is returned to the USSR.

A 22-year-old sailor, Miroslav Medved, precipitated a dispute with the Soviets by jumping into the Mississippi River near New Orleans to escape Soviet control, but then changed his mind about defecting. Initially, on White House orders, American officials and doctors examined Medved, keeping him in a naval facility overnight to make sure he was not ill or drugged. Then the defector signed a statement that he wanted to return to his ship. A U.S. air force psychiatrist who interviewed Medved believed the Soviet ship's captain had indicated to Medved that his parents might be harmed if their son did not return. Although a U.S. Senate resolution opposed the forced return of political asylum seekers, President Reagan decided that all evidence showed Medved wanted to go home. Reagan told Republican leaders that he resented the suggestion of Senator Jesse Helms (R-N.C.) that he "threw this guy to the wolves because we're getting ready for Geneva," where Reagan was to meet with Soviet leader Mikhail Gorbachev.

October 27, 1985

A press report indicates the Soviet Union would stop work on its illegal Krasnoyarsk radar base if the United States stopped modernizing radar stations in England and Greenland.

The *London Times* reported on October 27 that at the Geneva arms talks, the chief Soviet delegate, Yuli Kvitsinsky, offered to stop building the Krasnoyarsk

Radar Station, which, the United States claimed, violated the 1972 Anti-Ballistic Missile Treaty because it was an early-warning defense system. Heretofore, the Soviets had denied these charges. The Soviets wanted the United States to stop modernizing its 20-year-old radar bases at Thule, Greenland, and Fylingdales Moor, England. They said such changes violated the 1972 treaty, a claim that some British politicians accepted. On October 29, the U.S. State Department expressed doubt that Moscow would forsake its Central Asian facility and announced that the United States would modernize its bases. It claimed the U.S. bases did not violate the 1972 agreement. The Soviet offer was Gorbachev's attempt to gain favorable public opinion before his November summit meeting with President Reagan.

November 1, 1985

The Netherlands says it will deploy U.S. medium-range missiles in 1988.

Rejecting Soviet leader Mikhail Gorbachev's request to delay the vote on U.S. missile deployment, the Dutch parliament approved deployment but delayed it until 1988 to determine whether a U.S.-Soviet treaty might restrict these missiles. In contrast to the Netherlands' policy, the Belgian parliament on March 20, 1985, had approved deployment of 48 U.S. cruise missiles, and 16 were deployed during March 1985. Italy, Great Britain, and West Germany also deployed cruise or Pershing II missiles after November 1983.

November 12, 1985

The European Economic Community signs an economic cooperation pact with six Central American states including Nicaragua.

Meeting in Luxembourg, EEC members increased their assistance to Costa Rica, El Salvador, Honduras, Panama, Guatemala, and Nicaragua. A West German proposal to link any nation's part of the $33 million to its observance of human rights was voted down. The Europeans urged all foreign nations to withdraw their troops from Central America and adopt the Contadora peace plan. Just the previous day, Nicaragua had rejected the most recent Contadora plan.

November 14, 1985

The U.S. national debt reaches $2 trillion as President Reagan signs a stopgap finance bill.

Soon after becoming president in 1981, Ronald Reagan promised to balance the budget by 1984, a promise that his 1981 tax cut and a huge military buildup had doomed to failure. The national debt reached $1 trillion in 1981. Reagan's distinction was to double the debt in four years, leading Republican conservatives to propose a constitutional amendment to require a balanced budget. Instead, Reagan signed the Gramm-Rudman Bill designed to balance the budget by 1991. Meanwhile, the national debt moved toward $3 trillion while annual interest rates on the debt grew larger. Japan was the leading nation in purchasing U.S. Treasury bills to finance the deficit.

November 15, 1985

Peace efforts by Israeli Prime Minister Shimon Peres and Jordanian King Hussein are stymied by Israel's right wing.

Since February 24, 1985, Middle East peace plans seemed possible after Egyptian President Hosni Mubarak suggested a summit meeting among the United States, Egypt, Israel, and Jordanian-Palestinian representatives. After Israel indicated its willingness, quiet discussions took place, highlighted by Mubarak's visit to the United States from March 9 to 13 and King Hussein's visit with President Reagan on May 29. On October 28, Israel's Knesset (parliament) approved Peres's peace proposal by a vote of 68 to 10. In early November, however, hopes faded when members of the Israeli right wing became upset over the *New York Times* report that Peres had agreed to an international conference on the Middle East to which King Hussein would bring Palestinians acceptable to Israel. The report incensed Israeli Minister of Trade Ariel Sharon, and the Labor-Likud coalition that governed Israel nearly collapsed on November 15, 1985.

November 20, 1985

Poland's creditors agree to reschedule debt payments due in 1985.

Known as the Club of Paris, 17 Western nations that had loaned $12 billion to Poland between 1982 and 1984 agreed to reschedule $1.3 billion over a 10-year period with a five-year grace period to assist the Polish economy. After Prime Minister Wojciech Jaruzelski resigned on November 6, 1985, Polish leaders talked about changing its controlled economy to a market economy. Prime Minister Zbigniew Messner told parliament he wanted to link wages to productivity, stimulate individual initiative, and increase investment. Previously, conservative forces in the Communist Party had prevented changes, but Messner and Jaruzelski, who was also Communist Party First Secretary, promised to overcome this problem.

November 20, 1985

Yelena Bonner, wife of Andrey Sakharov, receives permission to visit the United States; 10 others get exit visas.

Sakharov, a dissident Soviet physicist, and his wife had been sent to internal exile in Gorky in 1980. On several occasions, they had requested visas to visit relatives in the United States or to receive medical treatment for Bonner's glaucoma and heart disease. A report that Bonner had received permission to leave was announced by U.S. Secretary of State George Shultz on October 31, and on November 20, Bonner reported that she could visit the United States in December but not talk with reporters. She reached the United States on December 6, 1985. Following Bonner's return to the Soviet Union in 1986, her children told reporters that photographs brought to the United States by Bonner showing Sakharov in good health had been faked by the Soviet photographer to hide the fact that Sakharov's health had deteriorated due to his hunger strikes protesting Soviet policies.

November 21, 1985

Reagan-Gorbachev summit ends with six minor agreements and good rapport between the two leaders.

At the first U.S.-USSR summit since 1979, President Reagan and Communist Party First Secretary Gorbachev signed six bilateral agreements. The agreements covered cultural and scientific exchanges; the opening of consulates in Kiev and New York; air safety in the North Pacific to prevent incidents such as the Korean Air Line destruction in 1983 (see September 1, 1983); and resuming civil aviation ties; magnetic fusion research; and environmental protection. Although there were no breakthroughs on arms control or human rights issues, the summit promised future good relations because the two leaders got along well. Reagan and Gorbachev spent five hours in private talks—more than scheduled. These talks were described as frank, cordial, and businesslike, but both leaders later expressed optimism about ensuring peaceful relations—Gorbachev remarking that "the world has become a more secure place" and Reagan informing Congress that the two leaders understood each other better and "that's a key to peace."

Following the sessions on November 21, Reagan flew to Brussels, Belgium, to brief America's NATO allies on the meetings; Gorbachev went to Prague, Czechoslovakia, for meetings with the USSR's Warsaw Pact members. On November 16, the *New York Times* disclosed one glitch in the summit came when Defense Secretary Caspar Weinberger urged the president to take a tough line on arms control, to make no concessions on the Strategic Defense Initiative, and not to extend SALT II. Reagan learned about the letter while en route to Geneva and told reporters he would have preferred to read it in his office not in the *New York Times.*

November 21, 1985

A U.S. navy analyst and his wife are charged with spying for Israel.

Jonathan Jay Pollard, a civilian who worked as a counterintelligence specialist in the U.S. navy, was arrested in Washington near the Israeli embassy, where he and his wife were attempting to seek political asylum. Pollard sold intelligence data to Israel; his wife, Anne L. Henderson-Pollard, was charged with possessing "unauthorized" documents. According to the *New York Times*, the Israeli government, on December 21, fired Rafael Eita, the Israeli intelligence official involved in the Pollard case, but later promoted him to a high army post. On March 4, 1987, Pollard was sentenced to life in prison and his wife to five years.

November 23, 1985

A former CIA agent, Larry Wu-tai Chin, is arrested on charges of spying for China.

According to charges against China filed by FBI investigators, Chin gave the Chinese highly classified data during the 30-year period that he worked for the Central Intelligence Agency. Chin was convicted on February 15, 1986, but committed suicide on February 21.

November 28, 1985

GATT members agree on multilateral trade liberalization talks in 1986.

The principal feature of the eighth round of talks since 1947 would be discussions on trade rules to cover services such as insurance, banking, and communications, an agenda desired by the United States. There were 90 member nations, and Mexico applied for membership on November 24, 1985.

December 2, 1985

European Economic Community member states revise the 1957 Treaty of Rome and agree to remove their final trade barriers by 1992.

Meeting in Luxembourg from December 2–4, 1985, the 12 EEC nations (including 1986 members-to-be, Spain and Portugal) revised the 1957 treaty to eliminate their remaining trade barriers in 1992.

December 4, 1985

John M. Poindexter replaces Robert C. McFarlane as national security adviser.

According to White House observers, McFarlane resigned because he found it difficult to "fight over turf" with President Reagan's chief of staff, Donald T. Regan. Poindexter, a navy admiral, was McFarlane's deputy, but his policy views were not known outside official circles.

December 5, 1985

Great Britain announces its withdrawal from UNESCO at the end of 1985.

The British government of Prime Minister Margaret Thatcher followed the lead of the United States, which had abandoned UNESCO in 1984. Although in October 1985, UNESCO officials had reformed some of the methods the Reagan administration deemed "hostile" to a free society, neither Great Britain nor the United States thought the changes sufficed.

December 5, 1985

Mikhail Gorbachev offers on-site inspections at nuclear test sites; President Reagan rejects offer.

President Reagan disclosed the Soviet leader had offered an inspection system for test sites in a letter he received. Reagan rejected the proposal on December 19, 1985, although U.S. policy had sought on-site inspection for many years. Reagan's only positive comment was to suggest bilateral talks for halting nuclear tests. Since 1981, the Reagan administration had opposed test restrictions because the United States was developing advanced nuclear weapons technology.

December 5, 1985

The Organization of American States (OAS) gives its secretary-general greater power; U.S. prevents readmission of Cuba.

Meeting in Cartagena, Colombia, from December 2 to 5, 1985, the 31 delegates of the OAS revised its original charter to grant more authority to the secretary-general. In particular, the secretary could convene members whenever matters affecting the hemisphere's peace and security needed action. On other agenda items, the U.S. delegate, Secretary of State George Shultz, prevented the readmission of Cuba and rejected proposals of other OAS members for further peace talks between Shultz and representatives of Nicaragua.

December 8, 1985

At the Geneva talks, the U.S. delegate is mistaken about United States support to Afghan rebels.

From 1982 through 1984 there had been extended international discussions to end the fighting in Afghanistan. Washington suspected the Soviets deliberately prolonged negotiations in an effort to buy time while suppressing the Afghan resistance. Infact, there were several issues that were difficult to reconcile, one being when and how to stop external assistance to the warring parties.

In a December 8 letter to Diego Cordovez, U.N. Under-Secretary General for Special Political Affairs, U.S. Deputy Secretary of State John Whitehead wrote the administration would halt aid to Afghan rebels at the *beginning* of a Soviet military withdrawal from Afghanistan. Perhaps White was mistaken, because in December 1987, President Reagan rejected the idea of ending shipments before the Soviets withdrew. On March 4, 1988, Reagan's view was presented to the State Department.

See April 14, 1988.

December 10, 1985

The Nobel Peace Prize is awarded to the International Physicians for the Prevention of Nuclear War.

Founded in December 1980 by Soviet and American medical doctors concerned about public ignorance of the effects of nuclear war, the physicians' group seldom gained much media coverage. It was notable, however, as a joint venture of medical experts from the Soviet Union and the United States. Its cofounders were Dr. Bernard Lown, a cardiologist at Harvard School of Public Health, and Dr. Yevgeny Chazov, director of the Soviet Union's Cardiological Institute and a member of the Central Committee of the Communist Party. Just after Lown and Chazov arrived in Norway to receive the award, a newsman disclosed that Chazov had signed a 1973 letter denouncing Soviet physicist Andrey D. Sakharov, who won the Nobel Peace Prize in 1975 for advocating human rights in the USSR. Chazov refused to discuss the 1973 letter, but Lown defended him as an "honest guy" and said the crucial issue was the right of survival against a possible nuclear war. Unfortunately, this incident marred the ceremony, designed to publicize the cooperative efforts of U.S. and Soviet medical doctors trying to prevent the nuclear conflict. The group said it had 135,000 physician members who represented 47 different nations.

December 16, 1985

Belgian police arrest four terrorists for bombing NATO installations and U.S. bank.

The Belgian police arrested three men and one woman who belonged to the Communist Combatant Cells, accusing them of committing 27 bombing incidents during the past 14 months. These bombings included the December 4, 1985, attack on a Bank of America branch in Antwerp and the December 6 bombings of NATO installations west of Brussels and at Versailles, France.

December 18, 1985

Secretary of State George Shultz visits Eastern Europe.

Shultz visited Eastern European leaders to encourage better relations with the United States. With President Reagan's approval, Shultz visited leaders of Romania, Hungary, Bulgaria, and Yugoslavia even though hard-line anti-Communists in the White House, such as Patrick Buchanan, urged Reagan to avoid all contacts with Eastern European Communists. Shultz began his visit by flying to Romania to visit Nicolae Ceauşescu. He asked Ceauşescu to stop Romania's discriminatory policies against Jews and German Christians living in Romania and to allow any of these minorities to emigrate if they desired. Ceauşescu made no promises to Shultz on these affairs but agreed to accept Shultz's offer to obtain the most-favored-nation trade status for Romania (see June 2, 1987). Next, Shultz visited Budapest where he talked with Hungary's Communist leader Janos Kadar. Shultz had kind words for Hungary's successful economic reforms but Kadar asked Shultz not to talk in public about how Hungary's policies differed from the Soviet Union's economic policy. Kadar also accepted Shultz's offer to obtain a most-favored-nation trade status for Hungary.

During his visit with Yugoslav Foreign Minister Raf Dizdarevic, Shultz strongly condemned Yugoslavia for releasing Muhammad Abbas Zaida (Abu Abbas), whom U.S. authorities blamed for masterminding the attack on the *Achille Lauro* cruise ship (see October 10, 1985, and October 17, 1985). Dizdarevic told reporters Yugoslavia condemned terrorism but said we "must also view the causes that lead to it," because terrorism can only be eliminated if the causes are ended. Enraged by Dizdarevic's remarks, Shultz asserted: "Hijacking the Italian ship, murdering an American, torturing and holding" other Americans is not justified by any cause. In his memoir, Shultz says he was more angry with Iraq for allowing Abu Abbas to live in Baghdad after he left Yugoslavia. The United States had been supporting Iraq in its war against Iran during the 1980s.

See September 4, 1980.

December 20, 1985

The White House announces lie detector tests will be used on government officials suspected of espionage.

For some time, the Reagan administration had sought methods to end leaks of information that it considered sensitive to national security. On November 1, a presidential order stated that government officials with access to classified data might be required to take a polygraph test. Many persons disliked the general nature of this order, and on December 19, Secretary of State George Shultz opposed it, saying he would resign if he had to be tested. The December 20 announcement toned down the original directive by limiting tests to people who were suspected of leaking classified data.

1986

January 11, 1986

Afghan regime's "secret police" is reorganized along the lines of the KBG.

The Afghan regime's "State Information Service" or KhAD (see January 11, 1980) that served as a secret police force is reconstituted as the Ministry of State Security.

February 2, 1986

El Salvador convicts two national guardsmen who murdered land reform agents; higher officials are not arrested.

The killing of three agricultural workers in 1981 had been investigated reluctantly by El Salvadoran police because high-level politicians associated with the ARENA Party led by Roberto d'Aubuisson were involved in the murders (see January 3, 1981). On February 2, 1986, the two National Guardsmen who confessed to the murders were convicted and sentenced to 30 years in prison. Nevertheless, the Salvadoran government had not prosecuted two army officers associated with the ARENA Party and wealthy landowner Ricardo Sol Meza, who were said to have ordered the three assassinations.

February 11, 1986

A prominent Soviet dissident Anatoly B. Shcharansky is freed in an exchange of nine prisoners in Berlin.

An East-West prisoner exchange at the Berlin Wall included Shcharansky, whom the Soviets had convicted of spying for the West in 1978. Shcharansky was an outspoken critic of the Soviet Union's anti-Jewish policies. After his release, he went to Israel, where his wife, Avital, lived. He visited the United States in May 1986, to describe his ideas of and his treatment by the Soviet Union.

February 15, 1986

Nine members of Congress visit Vietnam; they return with the remains of possible MIAs.

A congressional delegation headed by Gerald Solomon (R-N.Y.) arrived in Hanoi (January 6–7) one month after Assistant Secretary of Defense Richard L. Armitage had met with Vietnamese officials in Hanoi to discuss the MIAs. On April 10, the remains of 21 soldiers were turned over to U.S. officials, but Foreign Minister Hoang Bich Son denied that any MIAs were still alive in Vietnam. These talks ended when Hanoi suspended them following the U.S. air attack on Libya on April 15, 1986.

February 18, 1986

The Senate Foreign Relations Committee is told that President Reagan wants $15 million for Angolan rebels.

The Angolan government had combatted rebels since the early 1970s after it obtained independence from Portugal. In August 1985, Congress had, at President Reagan's urging, repealed the Clark Amendment, which since 1976 had made secret aid to the rebels illegal (see July 10, 1985). Congress also allocated $30 million for aid to the National Union for the Total Independence of Angola (UNITA). From January 28 to February 8, Jonas Savimbi, the leader of UNITA visited Washington. Savimbi hired a lobbying agent for $600,000 to gain favor with the U.S. public, and Reagan gave him a red carpet reception. Reagan did not promise him aid, deciding not to ask

Congress for funds until later. Savimbi had many critics. All black African nations supported the existing Angolan government. South Africa was his one ally, supplying UNITA with weapons and often staging raids against Angola's army. Cuban volunteers served in Angola and their presence was a major reason the Reagan administration disliked Angola's government. Under the "Reagan Doctrine," Savimbi was hailed as a freedom fighter despite his ill repute in Africa.

February 19, 1986

After delaying for 37 years, the U.S. Senate approves the U.N. Convention on the Prevention and Punishment of the Crime of Genocide.

Proposed by the United Nations National Assembly in 1948 in the wake of the Nazi genocide against the Jews and other peoples, this treaty was signed by the United States but the Senate had not approved it. Ninety nations including the Soviet Union had approved it, but certain senators prevented approval because it supposedly compromised U.S. sovereignty. In 1986, a bipartisan group led by Senators Robert Dole, William Proxmire, and Rudy Boschwitz offered the treaty for Senate approval and President Reagan's ratification. It passed by a vote of 83 to 11. To prevent a filibuster, the Senate added an amendment that the treaty could not interfere with the U.S. Constitution, and that the International World Court at the Hague had no automatic jurisdiction over the United States.

February 20, 1986

President Reagan admits to representatives of various Caribbean nations that two years of the Caribbean Basin Initiative (CBI) achieved little.

At a conference of Caribbean nations in Grenada, President Reagan stated that his CBI had not worked well. The program to encourage a free-market economy with U.S. investments had actually damaged their economies. The U.S. Commerce Department reported that the CBI exports to the United States declined 23 percent in two years, while U.S. imports from the rest of the world increased 36 percent. Moreover, there had been no progress in gaining U.S. investments, raising unemployment to 25 percent. Finally, the U.S. farm bill for 1985 reduced sugar imports from the islands, damaging Caribbean sugar producers. The president told the conference that the United States would try to improve the CBI by offering more favorable quotas for Caribbean sugar and other products.

February 25, 1986

"People power" claims victory in the Philippines; President Marcos is exiled, and Corazon Aquino becomes president.

February 25, 1986

The 27th Congress of the Communist Party of the Soviet Union opens. Soviet leader Gorbachev seeks economic reforms.

The congress met from February 25 to March 6. Its principal agenda was the approval of a five-year economic plan that First Secretary Mikhail Gorbachev had unveiled in October 1985. In addition, major changes in the party's Central Committee membership were announced.

After Gorbachev blamed economic stagnation on the 18-year rule of Leonid Brezhnev and offered his policy of economic reforms, called "*Perestroika*" the Congress passed a resolution calling for "truly revolutionary changes." One major change began on November 19, 1986, when the Supreme Soviet approved the use of private enterprise to manufacture some consumer goods and to provide services such as women's hairdressing.

February 25, 1986

Iran launches attacks on northern Iraq, extending the front lines of the conflict.

These Iranian attacks on the Kurdistan region of Iraq were part of a series of offensive movements in the five-year-old war. On February 11, Iran captured the Iraqi port of Fao. In May, Iraq took offensive measures, bombing a Tehran oil refinery on May 7 and overrunning the town of Mehran on May 17 before Iran counterattacked to retake its territory.

February 28, 1986

Swedish Prime Minister Olof Palme is assassinated in Stockholm.

Palme was killed while he and his wife were walking home from a movie theater at 11:30 P.M. He was replaced as prime minister by Ingvar Carlsson. Christer Pettersson, a local alcoholic, was tried and convicted of murder on July 27, 1989, but a Swedish appeals court voided the conviction.

March 14, 1986

A U.N. report says Iraq used chemical weapons against Iran.

This report by U.N. Secretary-General Javier Pérez de Cuellar was based on the findings of international experts who visited Iran but were refused permission to visit Iraq. This was the first report to specifically blame Iraq for using such weapons, especially mustard gas and nerve gas. The report said more extensive use of chemical weapons had been made by Iraq since 1984. Secretary-General Pérez de Cuellar condemned Iraq for violating the 1925 Geneva Protocol ban on chemical weapons.

March 14, 1986

President Reagan offers a major policy change: he will oppose dictatorships on the right as well as on the left.

In a foreign policy message to a joint session of Congress, Reagan urged democratic reforms of right-wing as well as left-wing governments. This decision moved him away from the so-called Kirkpatrick doctrine. Reagan's former U.N. representative, Jeanne Kirkpatrick, stressed that right-wing "authoritarian" regimes differed significantly from left-wing "totalitarian" regimes. Reagan now discarded this distinction, indicating that Haiti, the Philippines, and South Africa were examples of governments where democracy could replace right-wing rule. Nevertheless, Reagan emphasized the need to combat Communist governments and rebels, especially in Central America. He ended the speech to Congress by asking Congress to provide $100 million for the Contra rebels fighting Nicaragua's Sandinista government.

March 18, 1986

The Soviet Union protests the incursion of two U.S. navy ships into its territorial waters near the Crimea.

The U.S. vessels were the *Yorktown*, a guided-missile cruiser, and the *Caron*, a destroyer, which entered the Black Sea on March 10, traveling within six nautical miles of the Soviet coastline near the Crimean peninsula. The Soviet Union claimed territorial rights of 12 nautical miles. The White House said the U.S. ships simply tested the right of innocent passage. A Pentagon spokesman said the ships gathered intelligence data as Soviet ships did off the U.S. coastline.

March 27, 1986

West Germany agrees to participate in SDI research; Britain, Italy, Israel, and Japan also join SDI research.

At first, West Germany's Bundestag (Parliament) opposed any government role in America's SDI program because Chancellor Helmut Kohl's coalition partner, the Free Democrat Party, would not consent to have the German government fund missile defense research. To obtain a majority of Bundestag votes favoring a German role in SDI, Kohl and U.S. Defense Secretary Caspar Weinberger reached a compromise satisfactory to the Free Democrat Party. The agreement permitted West Germany's private companies and private research institutes to obtain U.S. contracts for SDI research, but no federal government funds could be used for such research. When the full text of the U.S.-German agreement became public on April 8, 1986, members of Germany's Social Democratic Party and Green Party (environmental) criticized the agreement because West German companies having SDI contracts would be restricted on the sale of technological products to Eastern European countries. West Germany was the second U.S. ally to join SDI research. On December 8, 1985, the United Kingdom's Defense Minister Michael Heseltine signed an agreement with Weinberger whereby British companies and research institutes could obtain contracts for SDI research, although the British Labour Party, a minority in Parliament, opposed the agreement.

On May 6, 1986, Israel and the United States signed an agreement for Israeli companies to participate in SDI research. On September 9, Japan and the United States signed an agreement for Japanese institutes and companies to perform SDI research, and on September 19, Italy signed an agreement by which Italy became the fifth U.S. ally to participate in SDI research. France was the principal European nation rejecting an American offer to cooperate in SDI research. France established an antimissile defense program called EUREKA, hoping members of the Western European Union (WEU) would help fund EUREKA. France was not successful in its quest for WEU funds because West Germany, Italy, and the United Kingdom rejected the French plans.

April 2, 1986

President Reagan reorganizes the U.S. military.

The president's changes were based on the February 28, 1986, report of the Blue Ribbon Commission on Defense Management chaired by former Deputy Secretary of Defense David Packard. The president enacted some reforms by executive order, such as overhauling the military procurement process, which took too long and cost too much. In other cases, Congress enacted legislative measures, such as making the chairman of the Joint Chiefs of Staff an independent adviser of the president, speaking for all the armed services.

April 8, 1986

Soviet Ambassador Anatoly F. Dobrynin meets for the last time with President Reagan.

Dobrynin, who was Soviet ambassador to the United States for 24 years, left on March 6 and had his last official visits with the president and Secretary of State George Shultz. On May 20, Yuri V. Dubinin was appointed as the new ambassador. Although a former Soviet ambassador to the United Nations, Dubinin was neither trained in U.S.-Soviet relations nor fluent in English as was Dobrynin.

April 14, 1986

U.S. aircraft bomb five Libyan targets in retaliation for Libyan leader Mu'ammar al-Gadhafi's support for terrorists.

Early in the morning of April 15 (April 14 at 7:00 P.M. Eastern Standard Time), American planes from aircraft carriers and bases in Great Britain attacked five targets in Libya: a military base and installation,

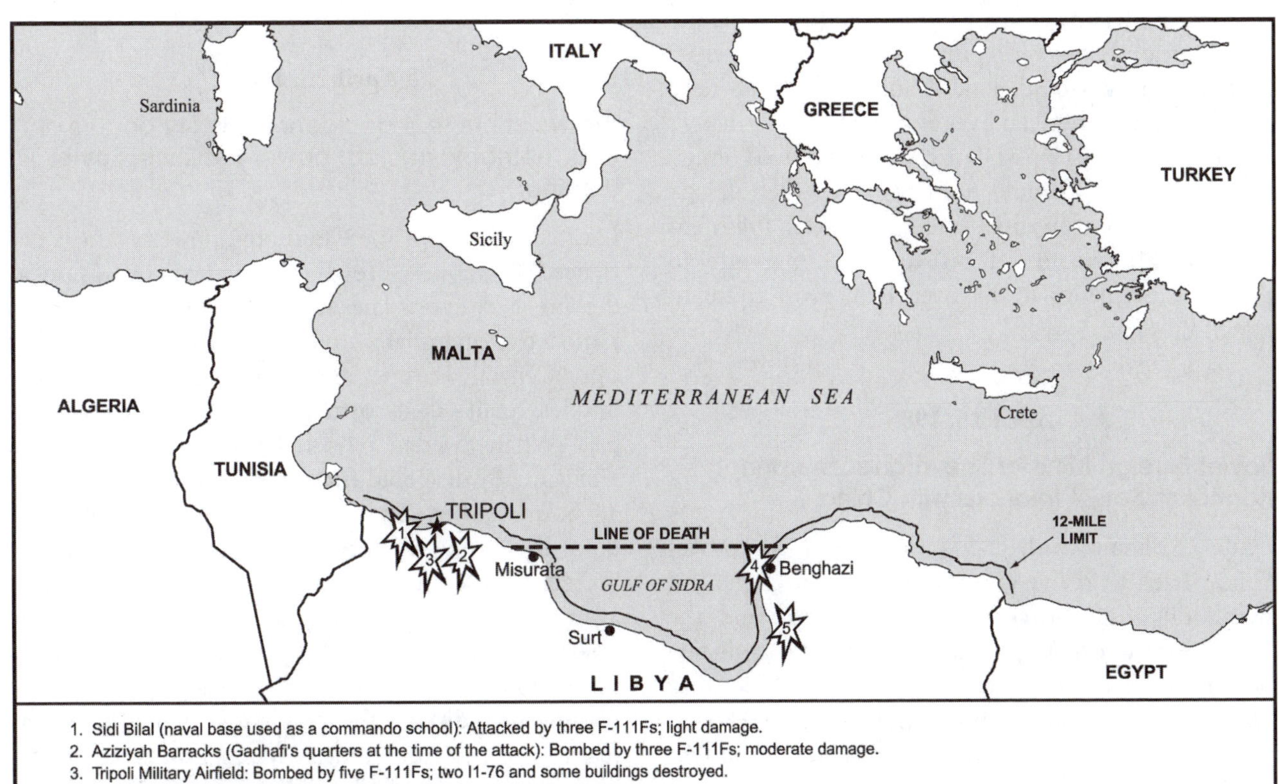
ITALY
Sardinia
GREECE
TURKEY
Sicily
MALTA
ALGERIA
MEDITERRANEAN SEA
Crete
TUNISIA
TRIPOLI
LINE OF DEATH
12-MILE LIMIT
Misurata
Benghazi
GULF OF SIDRA
Surt
LIBYA
EGYPT
1. Sidi Bilal (naval base used as a commando school): Attacked by three F-111Fs; light damage.
2. Aziziyah Barracks (Gadhafi's quarters at the time of the attack): Bombed by three F-111Fs; moderate damage.
3. Tripoli Military Airfield: Bombed by five F-111Fs; two I1-76 and some buildings destroyed.
4. Benghazi: Attacked by six A-6E bombers from the America; moderate damage.
5. Benina Airfield: Attacked by six A-6Es from the Coral Sea; four MiG-23 Floggers, two Mi-8 Hip helicopters, and two prop planes destroyed; moderate damage.

U.S. air raid on Libya, 1986

the port at Sidi Bilat in Tripoli, and a military barracks and an air base near Benghazi. Bombs also struck the French embassy and buildings in the Bin Ashur district of Tripoli. Bombs hit near a residence of Gadhafi, killing his infant adopted daughter and seriously injuring two of his sons. Gadhafi was absent at the time of the bombing. President Reagan had launched a campaign of vilification against Gadhafi, whom Reagan blamed for these and other terrorist raids.

On April 9, Reagan called Gadhafi a "mad dog," saying the United States is "certainly going to take action in the face of specific terrorist threats." After consulting with leaders of the U.S. Congress, Britain, France, West Germany, Spain, and Italy, President Reagan decided to attack Libya on the night of April 14–15.

After the U.S. attack, a New York Times/CBS poll found that 77 percent of those polled backed the president, but European opinion was mixed regarding the bombing and its results. While British Prime Minister Margaret Thatcher approved the attacks and granted permission for the U.S. use of air bases in England to make the attack, a British opinion poll showed two-thirds opposed the raid. The London *Observer's* pundit Patrick Scale wrote that the attack would make Gadhafi an "Arab hero and put more American lives at risk." West Germany's Foreign Minister Hans-Dietrich Genscher told Shultz the United States should not have taken such drastic action and Europeans lauded French President François Mitterrand for resisting U.S. pressure to permit U.S. planes to fly over France on route to attack Libya.

April 16, 1986

Soviet Foreign Minister Shevardnadze cannot normalize Soviet relations with China.

Under Mikhail Gorbachev's leadership, the Soviet Union tried to revive good relations with China but with only slight success. Although China and the USSR agreed on March 21 to exchange engineers and technicians, on January 15 China rejected a Soviet proposal for a nonaggression pact. Soviet Foreign Minister Eduard Shevardnadze proposed on April 16 that China and the Soviets have a summit conference to normalize relations. In response, China's Vice Foreign Minister Qian Qichen, who was visiting Moscow, replied that a summit was unrealistic until Soviet policy removed the "three obstacles"—lessening tension on the Chinese border by reducing the number of Soviet troops, withdrawing Soviet troops from Afghanistan, and ending support for Vietnam's occupation of Cambodia. In a speech on July 28, Gorbachev took steps to eliminate these three obstacles.

April 18, 1986

A Titan 34-D rocket carrying a secret military payload explodes after liftoff in California.

This accident was a setback to the military launching of such payloads (the Titan 34-D was believed to be carrying a reconnaissance satellite), adding to the problems of the U.S. space program since the *Challenger* exploded on January 28, 1986. Less than a month later, on May 3, 1986, a third space mission failed when a U.S. Delta rocket exploded after liftoff. The Delta carried a weather satellite, and after the rocket's power failed, ground control destroyed it.

April 26, 1986

The worst nuclear accident in history occurs at the Chernobyl nuclear power facility in Soviet Ukraine.

Located near Kiev, the Chernobyl power plant experienced a graphite fire that caused an explosion at the no. 4 reactor. The accident sent high levels of radioactive material into the atmosphere, reaching into Central Europe and Scandinavia, where the Swedes reported abnormal levels of radioactive debris. When Sweden reported this on April 28, the USSR finally disclosed that the accident had occurred 48 hours earlier. The Soviets rejected foreign assistance in fighting the reactor fires, but on May 4, First Secretary Mikhail Gorbachev proposed a four-point agenda to cooperate with the International Atomic Energy Agency. On August 25 and 26, Soviet scientists and engineers met with 500 delegates from 50 countries to discuss the accident, which the Soviets blamed on an unauthorized test that was further exacerbated by the faulty design of the reactor plant. On June 15, *Pravda*, the Communist Party newspaper, reported that several high officials had been dismissed, including the head of the Soviet nuclear power industry and the head of the State Committee for Atomic Safety.

May 4, 1986

Najibullah replaces Karmal as general secretary of the People's Democratic Party of Afghanistan.

Babrak Karmal resigned as party head because of his health. Najibullah had been head of the secret police in Afghanistan.

May 6, 1986

West German and Italian police implicate Syria, not Libya, in the Rome-Vienna airport attacks of December 1985.

Evidence collected in Germany and Italy indicated that President Reagan and other U.S. leaders had been too hasty in implicating Libya in the December airport bombings. Italian police told the Central Intelligence Agency in December 1985 that the surviving Rome terrorist, Muhammad Sarhan, had been trained in Syria and brought by Syrians through Eastern Europe to Rome before the incident. British authorities also believed that Syria, not Libya, was the central base of terrorist operations. They could not, however, persuade U.S. officials to act on this premise.

May 16, 1986

As the Contra rebels move to unify their opposition to Nicaragua's government, Eden Pastora Gómez retires from the struggle.

Early in 1986 as the Reagan administration struggled to improve the public image of the Contra leaders and to bring unity to the movement, the United Nicaraguan Opposition (UNO) was formed under Alfonso Robelo Callejas, Arturo José Cruz, and Adolfo Calero Portocarrero. They received President Reagan's blessing at a March 3 meeting in Washington but needed the support of the southern group of anti-Sandinistas, which had been set up by Pastora Gómez. Pastora refused to work with the former Somoza National Guard's military leaders who dominated the northern Contra group. Pastora gradually lost influence after the United States cut his economic aid in 1984, but in 1986, the southerners were enticed by Washington's promise to renew aid if they joined the UNO. Pastora refused, but on May 9 his top officers accepted U.S. aid. As a result, on May 16, Pastora gave up the struggle and sought exile in Costa Rica, where he formed a political party. Costa Rica granted him asylum on June 3.

May 22, 1986

NATO defense ministers approve the U.S. production of chemical weapons, but congressional opponents say the full NATO council must do so.

The Reagan administration had pushed for the renewed production of chemical weapons but found Congress reluctant to fund the project. In the defense bill approved on December 19, 1985, Congress inserted a clause requiring the approval of NATO before binary nerve gas weapons were produced. Subsequently, the Defense Department found it difficult to get NATO approval, but they finally convinced NATO defense ministers to do so despite the reluctance of NATO political leaders. No NATO nation permitted U.S. chemical weapons to be stored or used from its territory with the exception of West Germany, which allowed the United States to store some of its 30,000 tons of chemical weapons on its soil. West Germany also supported the U.S. binary nerve gas production provided that the United States would withdraw its existing stock from West German soil when the new weapons production began. On May 22, NATO defense ministers approved U.S. production of chemical weapons provided they were not deployed in Europe. In Washington, members of Congress who opposed chemical weapons argued that the full NATO Council, not the defense ministers, must approve. The U.S. State Department disagreed, contending that the intent of the congressional legislation had been fulfilled. Congressional opponents still sought to delay production of the nerve gas. Although Congress approved $35 million for the nerve gas bombs and artillery shells, the omnibus spending bill that passed on October 3, 1986, stated that chemical weapon production could not begin before October 1, 1987.

June 25, 1986

Congress approves aid to the Contra rebels after previously refusing aid in 1986.

Although the Iran-Contra hearings of 1987 indicated that the National Security Council had agreed on May 16, 1986, to solicit Contra funds from other friendly countries, President Reagan simultaneously urged Congress to approve $100 million of assistance. On March 20, the House of Representatives rejected Reagan's $100 million request by a vote of 222 to 210. By June, however, six swing Democrats in the House, who wanted some type of Contra aid, proposed $300 million in aid to other Central American countries, thereby delaying the delivery of weapons until September 1 and requiring reports on Contra reform and peace talks. With these additions, the House gave $100 million for the Contras on June 25, the first time the House approved both military and economic aid. The vote was 221 to 209. The $300 million for the other Central American countries was never released by President Reagan.

June 27, 1986

The International Court of Justice rules that the United States violated international law and Nicaragua's sovereignty; the United States rejects the ruling.

Although the United States had previously rejected the World Court's jurisdiction over the Nicaraguan complaint, the court conducted 26 months of hearings before ruling against the United States. By a vote of 12 to 3, the jurists said the United States should pay reparations to Nicaragua and cease all violations of international law in coercing Nicaragua. On October 8, 1986, the United States vetoed a U.N. Security Council resolution urging it to comply with the World Court ruling.

July 9, 1986

The U.S. ambassador to Chile attends the funeral of a U.S. citizen killed by Chile's police force and indicates dissatisfaction with the government's human rights record.

Following President Reagan's decision to oppose both right-wing and left-wing dictators, U.S. policy toward Chile became a symbol of the new policy. The first evidence of Reagan's change came on March 12, when the U.S. ambassador to the United Nations offered a resolution criticizing President Pinochet's violations of human rights.

On July 13, Senator Jesse Helms (R-N.C.) criticized Ambassador Barnes for attending the funeral. While visiting Chile, Helms praised his friend, General Pinochet, as a strong defender of freedom over Communism. The State Department issued a statement on July 14 that supported Barnes's attendance as a humanitarian gesture.

July 15, 1986

Britain and the Soviet Union seek to prevent potentially dangerous naval incidents.

The British and Soviets signed a Prevention of Incidents at Sea Treaty. It was modeled after a similar agreement between the United States and the Soviets (see May 25, 1972) that sought to prevent untoward incidents between warships and naval aircraft of the two nations.

July 15, 1986

Great Britain and the Soviet Union settle a 69-year dispute over the debt of Czar Nicolas II.

This agreement was completed between Soviet Foreign Minister Eduard A. Shevardnadze and British Foreign Secretary Sir Geoffrey Howe. Essentially, each side dropped its claims against the other. With interest accumulated since 1917, the British claims totaled £82 billion; the Soviets' claim for British damage inflicted during its civil war was over £2 billion.

July 24, 1986

Jerry Whitworth of the Walker spy ring is convicted of espionage.

Whitworth was the former U.S. navy radioman who worked for spymaster John Walker from 1975 to 1985. Affidavits released by the court indicated that the KGB (Soviet secret police) thought the Walker-Whitworth operation was the most important in KGB history. The director of U.S. Naval Intelligence, Rear Admiral William Studeman, said the secrets had "potential. . .war-winning implications for the Soviet side," because they dealt with navy codes and communications. Whitworth had collected the most crucial secrets sold to the Soviets. Whitworth was sentenced to 365 years in jail and fined $410,000. John Walker and his son received a better deal by plea bargaining: on November 6, John was sentenced to life in prison (parole possible in about 10 years); his son Michael received a 25-year sentence (parole possible in about eight years). John Walker's brother, Arthur, had previously been sentenced to three life terms (parole possible in 10 years).

July 24, 1986

Poland begins an amnesty program to release political dissidents.

During the Congress of the United Workers (Communist) Party on July 24, First Secretary Wojciech Jaruzelski approved an amnesty to solve Poland's political and economic problems. He released 369 criminal and political prisoners on July 24 and another 225 on September 13. The group included Solidarity leaders such as Bogdan Lis, Adam Michnik, and Zbigneiw Bujak. Nevertheless, when Bujak formed a seven-member Provisional Council of Solidarity on September 30, the government declared it illegal, a sign that Polish political activity continued to be forbidden.

July 28, 1986

At Vladivostok, Soviet First Secretary Gorbachev promises Soviet troop withdrawals from Mongolia and Afghanistan.

Visiting eastern Asia, Gorbachev sought better relations between the Soviet Union and the People's Republic of China. China often cited the need to remove Soviet troops on the northern Chinese border, in Afghanistan, and in Cambodia. To eliminate these obstacles, Gorbachev agreed to withdraw about 60,000 of the 450,000 Soviet troops on China's border; to take six regiments from Afghanistan (i.e., about 6,000 of 120,000 troops); and to obtain peace in Cambodia where the Soviet ally, Vietnam, controlled the anti-Pol Pot regime. Neither China nor the United States believed these steps were significant. The Chinese reacted coolly, saying the acts were insufficient. The Reagan administration said Gorbachev should give a timetable for total withdrawal, especially from Afghanistan. By December 1986, the Soviets had withdrawn the six regiments.

Gorbachev threw his support to a policy of "national reconciliation" and endorsed the Communist Afghanistan government efforts in that direction. In doing so, he was acknowledging that years of military action had failed to solve the regime's political problems.

August 1, 1986

Prodded by Congress, President Reagan subsidizes wheat sales to the Soviet Union.

Reagan's subsidy covered up to $4.4 million of wheat (about 3.85 million metric tons). He increased the farm subsidy from $12 to $15 per metric ton to boost Soviet purchases of U.S. grain at a lower price. The U.S. Senate passed an Export Enhancement Program on July 22 to subsidize grain sales to the USSR and China, but Reagan opposed this action as contrary to free trade. Although the senators accepted the August 1 compromise, the desired result was not achieved. Even with the subsidy of $15 per ton, U.S. wheat prices remained above world market prices.

August 26, 1986

Mujahideen guerrillas carry the war to Kabul.

Some of the more spectacular guerrilla activities took place in and around Kabul. On August 26, for example, 107-mm and 122-mm rockets launched by the mujahideen caused large explosions that greatly damaged an ammunition depot at Kargha. While the Communist regime said the blasts were caused by technical problems, Soviet television attributed responsibility for the destruction to the guerrillas. Several months later, such rocket attacks became routine. Car bombings inside Kabul also became an increasing problem for the government.

August 22, 1986

Although Cuba began releasing political prisoners in June, President Reagan tightens trade restrictions on Cuba.

There had been increasing evidence that Cuba circumvented the 26-year-old U.S. embargo by obtaining U.S. goods through Panama. One report said over 118 U.S. companies and individuals transshipped goods to Cuba through Panama. The Reagan administration wanted to stop this trade. Despite this trade problem, Reagan overruled a State Department decision on June 8, 1986, to prevent Cuba from releasing 67 political prisoners to the United States. Most of these had been officials in the government of Fulgencio Batista, whom Castro overthrew in 1959. During 1986, the Castro regime also released the last two Cubans who fought under U.S. support at the Bay of Pigs in 1961. On June 8, Richard Montero Duque was released, and on October 18, Ramón Conte Hernández was freed. Both were aided in their release by Senator Edward Kennedy (D-Mass.).

August 25, 1986

The Reagan administration begins a disinformation campaign against Libyan leader Gadhafi.

Based on a White House leak, the *Wall Street Journal* reported that U.S. intelligence believed Mu'ammar al-Gadhafi was "off his rocker" and had sponsored additional international terrorist attacks since April 15, a policy placing Libya and the United States on another collision course. On October 3, White House spokesman Larry Speakes said the administration did not lie but only "shaped the content" of stories about Libya. President Reagan later admitted approving a plan "to make Gadhafi go to bed every night wondering what we might do." On October 8, Bernard Kalb, the assistant secretary of state for public affairs, resigned because he refused to support American disinformation policy. According to Kalb, this practice damaged American credibility in world opinion more than it damaged Gadhafi.

August 30, 1986

Nicholas S. Daniloff is arrested in Moscow.

Daniloff, the Moscow correspondent for *U.S. News and World Report*, was arrested after giving a Soviet acquaintance a package containing two maps marked "top secret." The Reagan administration claimed Daniloff had been framed in retaliation for the August 23 arrest in New York City of Soviet U.N. staffer, Gennadi F. Zakharov, who the Federal Bureau of Investigation charged with purchasing classified documents. Because an exchange of letters between President Reagan and Soviet leader Gorbachev did not resolve the situation, the United States expelled 25 members of the USSR mission to the United Nations. A deal was now worked out. On September 29, the Soviet Union dropped its charges against Daniloff and released him. On September 31, Zakharov was permitted to leave for home. Following the Icelandic summit on October 19, the Soviets expelled five U.S. diplomats; Washington expelled 55 Soviets.

September 5, 1986

A Pan Am airplane is hijacked in Pakistan; 21 die after a 16-hour ordeal.

The Pan Am 747 jumbo jet had arrived at Karachi from Bombay, India, and was to fly via Frankfurt, Germany, to New York, when four Pakistani dissidents dressed as airport security guards stormed aboard the plane and demanded to be taken to Cyprus. Twenty-one were killed, including two Americans, and over 100 were wounded. Miraculously, nearly 300 had escaped. In retrospect, two factors seemed clear: first, the Pakistani authorities bungled the affair; second, the U.S. Delta Force, a quick strike commando force that flew from Fort Bragg, North Carolina, arrived too late. Some U.S. leaders wanted to scatter Delta Force bases around the world.

September 6, 1986

Arab terrorists attack a synagogue in Istanbul, killing 21.

The two armed gunmen entered the synagogue during worship services disguised as photographers. They blocked the door with an iron bar then opened fire on the congregation, killing 21 and wounding four others critically, then poured gasoline on several bodies and set them ablaze. As the terrorists left, Turkish police arrived, chasing the two men back inside. The gunmen committed suicide by detonating a grenade with a short fuse. This was the first attack on Jews in Turkey that anyone could remember.

September 9, 1986

After a trip to Angola, Senator Orrin Hatch praises rebel leader Jonas Savimbi.

During Savimbi's January 28, 1986, visit to the United States, Senator Hatch (R-Utah) was one of Savimbi's principal supporters. Thus, it was no surprise that Hatch reported favorably on visits to rebel camps in

Angola. The surprise was his video tapes of Savimbi's troops using Stinger missiles to shoot down Soviet planes used by Angola's army. There had been controversy over giving Stinger missiles to Afghan rebels while refusing them to Saudi Arabia. Now, Stingers had been given to the National Union for Total Independence of Angola (UNITA), although the chances of their being captured by Cuban forces helping Angola's government were great. This gave Stinger technology to other nations. The United States later discovered Stingers in Iran.

September 9, 1986

The United States again charges that the Soviets promote chemical warfare; but U.S. evidence is unconvincing.

Since 1981, when Secretary of State Alexander Haig charged the Soviets with using chemical weapons in Southeast Asia and Afghanistan, the United States had repeated these charges even though the available scientific data disproved them. In a 1987 article for *International Security,* Elisa D. Harris reviewed the charges, evidence, and studies made about "yellow rain." She concluded: "the errors and inconsistencies in the Reagan administration's case for Soviet-sponsored toxin warfare are beginning to be recognized by more than just its critics." Some U.S. Defense Department studies concluded that the charges were unfounded. Most scientists believed that yellow-colored bee feces found in Southeast Asian jungles caused illness that Haig and others called the "yellow rain" of chemicals. Harris indicated that these charges were designed by the Reagan administration to justify the renewed production of chemical weapons by the United States. She urged an international agreement on verification methods for the future.

September 13, 1986

Brazilian President Sarney visits Washington in an effort to ease tensions with the United States.

Between September 9 and 13, President Jose Sarney addressed a joint session of Congress and met with President Reagan. A variety of disputes hampered U.S.-Brazilian relations including Brazil's diplomatic recognition of Cuba, Brazil's opposition to U.S. support of the Nicaraguan Contras, and the concern for Brazil's limits on U.S. imports.

September 14, 1986

Peace talks between rebels and Salvadoran President Duarte are canceled for security reasons.

From April 26 to August 23, contacts among leaders of El Salvador's left wing rebels, the Farabund Marti National Liberation Front (FMLN), and President José Napoleon Duarte resulted in a scheduled meeting for September 19 in the town of Sesori. On September 14, however, the FMLN indicated that the talks could not be held unless the government removed an army battalion that had recently moved to Sesori. Duarte refused, condemning the guerrillas for avoiding a chance for peace. The rebels distrusted the Salvadoran army and believed the troop presence in Sesori endangered the safe-conduct they had been promised.

September 26, 1986

Afghan rebels destroy two soviet helicopters using American made Stinger missile.

The story of the Stingers use in Afghanistan began in March 1985, when President Reagan approved National Security Decision Directive 166 (NSDD) while National Security Advisor Robert McFarlane signed the 16-page Top Secret Annex. The Annex to NSDD 166 allowed the CIA to escalate its role in Afghanistan by employing advanced military technology, intensified training of Islamic guerrillas in the use of explosives, and sabotage techniques to target Soviet military officers. Following the signing, the interagency intelligence group proposed using the Stinger missile to shoot down the Soviet's Spetsnaz's helicopters, weapons that would fly low to shoot and kill many Afghan mujahideen rebels. The helicopter attacks were so effective that rebel activity had begun to decline significantly by 1985, and the Stinger missiles might be effective against the aircraft weapons. The U.S. designed and produced Stinger weighed about 4.5 pounds and was a shoulder fired missile with a battery-powered, heat-seeking guidance system that could hit a target, especially slow flying aircraft such as helicopters and transport planes, with great accuracy.

After NSDD-166 and its Annex were signed, some CIA officials were reluctant to send the Stingers to Afghanistan because they might fall into the hands of the Soviets and other rogue states. In contrast, the State Department's intelligence chief Morton Abramowitz and other interagency members wanted to send the Stinger as soon as possible. Finally, after secret negotiations with China and Pakistan, the CIA relented and began sending some agents to train mujahideen in the use Stingers, especially along Afghan's eastern border with Pakistan. On September 26, 1986, Afghan's guerrilla commander Engineer Ghaffar and two of his colleagues fired three Stingers at Soviet helicopters operating out of Afghanistan's Jalhabad Airport. Although the first shot misfired and only hit some rocks, the second and third Stinger missiles destroyed two Soviet helicopters, killing their pilots and crew members. Ghaffar's team was supplied with Sony video-cameras to record the Stingers. Because CIA Director William Casey knew President Reagan preferred watching a movie to reading a report, the CIA showed Reagan the movie version of the Stingers success. The CIA also showed the movie version to a few leaders of Congress.

The three Stingers used by Ghaffar's team were the first of about 2,300 Stingers used by Afghan rebels to destroy Soviet helicopters and large transport aircraft. To avoid the Stingers range of 12,500 feet, Soviet aircraft flew so high that they no longer lingered over targets so they could be accurate in their expected missions in Afghanistan. By 1988, the Stinger's success made a valuable marketing product to be sold to Iranians and others who could afford to pay premium prices up to $15,000 per Stinger. After the Soviet Union's troops left Afghanistan, the Taliban had at least 53 Stingers that, in 1996, they refused to sell to the United States. Details about Stinger are in Steve Coll, *Ghost Wars*, published by Penguin Press (2004) and Henry Bradsher, *Afghan Communism and Soviet Intervention* published by Oxford University Press, 1999. (Also see January 10, 1980 and May 27, 1988)

September 29, 1986

The Senate refuses $200 million in aid to the Philippines but later approves it.

Although Congress had provided an additional $150 million for the Philippines in the supplemental appropriations Bill of July 2, 1986, senators proved stubborn about adding $200 million to legislation for fiscal 1987. Their concerns were about whether President Corazon Aquino could handle the Communist threat and her willingness to renew the U.S. leases at Clark Air Force Base and Subic Bay. In the vote on the 1987 omnibus spending bill on October 3, the Senate Republicans rallied their votes, approving $200 million for the Philippines.

October 1, 1986

President Reagan signs the defense reorganization bill.

This law resulted from congressional studies in 1985 and from the studies of the Commission on Defense Management chaired by Deputy Secretary of Defense David Packard, which reported on February 28, 1986. The changes would centralize the president's military advice by designating the chairman of the Joint Chiefs of Staff as his adviser and by consolidating the staffs of the three service secretaries (army, navy, air force). The purpose was to cut down interservice rivalries and improve the Defense Department established in 1947, but its success seemed doubtful because Secretary of Defense Caspar Weinberger and the Joint Chiefs opposed the reform.

October 2, 1986

Congress overrides President Reagan's veto of sanctions against South Africa.

During 1986, conflict escalated between South Africa's white government and black Africans opposing the apartheid program. On July 22, Reagan had argued that economic sanctions would not work, even though he used them against Nicaragua and Libya. However, on September 29 and October 2, each house of Congress overrode the president's veto. The congressional act banned new U.S. investment in South Africa, prohibited the importation of certain products including coal and steel, and canceled landing rights of South Africa's airline.

October 4, 1986

Nicaragua shoots down a U.S. plane over Nicaraguan airspace near Costa Rica, capturing the American survivor, Eugene Hausenfus.

The downed plane had a crew of four men and military supplies for the Contra rebels. Although U.S. officials denied that the Central Intelligence Agency (CIA) had organized air shipments, Hausenfus told a press conference on October 9 that the flights and other rebel supplies were supervised by the CIA operating from El Salvador. In particular, he named Félix Rodríguez, alias Max Gómez, and Ramón Medina as CIA agents. Hausenfus was tried in Managua by Nicaragua's Popular Anti-Somocista Tribunal and found guilty of terrorism and other crimes. He was sentenced to 30 years in prison but was pardoned by Nicaragua and set free on December 17, 1986.

October 5, 1986

A *London Times* report that Israel possesses a nuclear weapons arsenal results in the affair of Mordechai Vanunu.

An Israeli nuclear arms technician, Vanunu, was brought from Australia to London to be debriefed by a British physicist, who confirmed the *Times* photos and details of Israel's underground nuclear weapons plant. Vanunu said the secret plant in Israel's Negev desert had been started by French nuclear experts between 1957 and 1964, a fact confirmed by the "father" of the French atomic capability, Francis Perrin, who built the Dimona Nuclear Research facility in Israel. Vanunu revealed that Israel was the sixth nation with nuclear weapons capacity, although the Israeli government denied it. The Vanunu mystery developed after Vanunu disappeared from London on September 30. On November 9, Israel revealed that Vanunu had been charged with espionage for "pretending" to disclose state secrets. Vanunu had been kidnapped by Mossad, the Israeli intelligence agency, in Rome on September 30, having been lured there by a female Mossad agent. After a secret trial in Israel, which ended on March 24, 1988, Vanunu was found guilty of treason and espionage. Being remorseful and cooperative, he received a lenient sentence of 18 years in prison. Israel's handling of Vanunu gave every indication that it indeed had a nuclear arsenal.

October 10, 1986

Britain's Conservative Party resolves to maintain the nation's nuclear deterrent; the Liberal and Labour Parties offer qualified support for the deterrent.

During the early 1980s, antinuclear advocates in Britain created a large following, causing political parties to divide on proposals for national security measures. The ruling Conservative Party under Prime Minister Margaret Thatcher favored Britain's independent nuclear force and cooperation with U.S. nuclear forces based in the British Isles to deter the Soviets. On September 23, the Liberal Party Conference overrode its leadership in the Liberal-Social Democratic Alliance by opposing a British nuclear force, including all U.S. forces. The Labour Party conference on October 2 took a middle position. It called for ending nuclear forces in Britain but maintaining nonnuclear U.S. forces and intelligence assistance for Great Britain. Soon after the Labour Party conference, however, its leaders realized that its policy needed to change before the next general election, or Labour could not win.

October 11, 1986

Vice President Bush and his adviser deny connections with the downing of a U.S. plane in Nicaragua.

On October 10, the *San Francisco Examiner* published a story on Eugene Hausenfus, claiming that George Bush and his aide, Donald Gregg, were associated with Félix Rodríguez as the CIA agent who directed operations from El Salvador. Because on October 1, Congress had extended the previous ban on a CIA secret fund for the Contra rebels, CIA assistance to Hausenfus would be illegal. An ex-Marine from Wisconsin, Hausenfus said he flew at least 10 flights in the C-123K cargo plane out of Ilopang Air Force Base in El Salvador. The two crew members who died in the crash had worked for the CIA, as Hausenfus confirmed. Rodríguez was the CIA field agent who directed the activity. Bush claimed he had met Rodríguez, but they talked generally about El Salvador, not about private arms for the Contra rebels. There was extensive private U.S. assistance to the Contras as well as aid from Lt. Colonel Oliver North, a fact disclosed during the Iran-Contra hearings after November 1986. While Bush's role seemed marginal at best, following a briefing by CIA director William Casey in October 1986, Senator David Durenburg (R-Minn.) said he believed Ronald Reagan "sponsored all of this private action in aiding the Contras."

October 11–12, 1986

The Reagan-Gorbachev Iceland summit achieves no agreement, but changes U.S.-USSR perspective toward arms control.

The summit meeting at Reykjavík, Iceland, was preceded by a variety of U.S. disagreements between the

President Reagan holds serious discussion with Soviet leader Mikhail Gorbachev. Ronald Reagan Library

State Department and the National Security Council regarding arms control since the Geneva meetings (see November 21, 1985). On January 11, 1986, the Soviets extended the moratorium on nuclear tests, urging Reagan to stop U.S. testing. Despite appeals from international leaders and 60 members of Congress, Reagan approved a series of underground tests on March 22 that totaled 13 by the end of 1986. The president argued that underground tests could not be verified. Hoping to prove Reagan wrong, the New York National Defense Council agreed with the Moscow Academy of Science to jointly monitor Soviet tests and on July 13 arrived in the Soviet Union to prepare to monitor future tests. Yet when the October 11 Iceland meetings began, the monitor testing had not begun, and the testing issue was not yet resolved.

Regarding intermediate and intercontinental missile reductions, talks were under way after January 16 but each side differed on how to achieve reductions. The Soviets proposed to ban all nuclear weapons by 2000 in three stages. The U.S. delegates offered a modified version of Reagan's zero option, first to reduce medium-range missiles over a three-year period. These sessions adjourned without compromises on March 3. After renewing the Geneva talks on May 8, the second round also failed to reach agreement, adjourning on June 26. The Geneva talks failed principally because U.S. delegates feared Gorbachev would link the nuclear reduction talks to limits on the Strategic Defense Initiative program.

Eventually, the linking of nuclear reduction to SDI became a key issue at the Iceland talks. Although the Soviets saw the SDI as a first-strike strategy, Reagan insisted it was only a defensive program, even though the logical conclusion would make the SDI illegal under the 1972 ABM treaty. Although the U.S. Congress began limiting the funds for SDI, Reagan wanted to spend as much as possible even though after four years SDI laboratories had achieved no significant technological breakthroughs. As a result, neither the United States nor the Soviet Union was prepared to finalize any of these prior issues during the Iceland meetings.

Without a prepared agenda, largely due to Washington's internal bickering, Gorbachev offered a package of concessions at the first Iceland session on October 11. These included concessions on underground testing, long- and medium-range missiles, the 1979 SALT II, and the relationship of SDI to the 1972 ABM treaty. To counter Gorbachev's concessions and prevent Reagan from having to say no, the president's hard-line staff, which opposed any arms control, devised more "sweeping proposals" that "they thought" Gorbachev would have to reject. These provided for a 50 percent reduction of strategic nuclear arsenals by 1991 during which period ABM research and development was permitted. In addition, during the years from 1991 to 1996, the remaining 50 percent of nuclear missiles would be eliminated, after which either side would be free to deploy defensive missiles. Thus, at the final Iceland session, Reagan put forward these sweeping proposals, but when Gorbachev accepted them, Reagan had to reject his own proposals and walk out of the last session, returning immediately to Washington.

Apparently, Reagan did not want to wait until 1996 to deploy the SDI. Because reporters in Iceland believed Reagan's "sweeping proposals" were genuine and not merely deceptive, America's NATO allies became concerned about losing a deterrent to the Soviet's superiority in conventional weapons. After the Iceland meetings, the Reagan administration began a blitz campaign to emphasize that the administration stood firm on SDI, while Gorbachev argued that Reagan had backed down on his "sweeping proposals to abolish all nuclear weapons by 1996." Although the SDI, test ban, and missile issues perplexed both sides, an INF missile treaty emerged the next year.

October 18, 1986

President Reagan signs the 1987 omnibus spending bill including $291.8 billion for the military and $100 million for the Nicaraguan Contra rebels.

The congressional compromises on the defense budget were linked to the Gramm-Rudman deficit limitations; those on Contra aid, to the reluctance of the House of Representatives to vote for assistance to the rebels. The fiscal 1987 defense authorization was 11 percent below 1986 and $28.5 billion less than President Reagan requested in February. The $100 million for the Contras was divided into $27 million for nonlethal aid and $3 million for human rights enforcement officers to monitor the behavior of the rebels. Reagan certified that the Contras would try to end human rights abuses and agreed to the enforcement oversight. The Gramm-Rudman limits were reached by accounting procedures. For example, the defense budget was reduced more than 11 percent because $3.8 million was taken out by assuming a lower inflation cost for 1987 than Reagan's original budget request assumed in February 1986.

October 24, 1986

Great Britain breaks diplomatic relations with Syria for aiding terrorists.

Britain condemned Syria for assisting in a terror bombing against the Israeli El Al Airlines at London's Heathrow Airport on April 17, 1986. Britain said the evidence implicated Syria in the bomb attempt and broke diplomatic relations. The United States and Canada did not sever relations but withdrew their ambassadors.

November 2, 1986

A U.S. hostage David P. Jacobsen, is released just before President Reagan's secret deal with Iran is revealed.

Jacobsen was the third hostage held by the pro-Iranian Islamic Jihad in Lebanon. Benjamin Weir was released in 1985, and Lawrence Jenco was freed on July 26, 1986. When Jenco was released, his captors called it a "good will gesture"; when Jacobsen was released, his captors attributed it to "certain approaches that could lead, if continued, to a solution of the hostage crisis." Evidently, the "certain approaches" referred to Reagan's arms for hostages deal with Iran. As Lou Cannon's 2000 edition of *President Reagan: the Role of a Lifetime* explains, Reagan's diary entry for January 17, 1986 was "I agreed to sell TOWs to Iran." This entry refers to a secret finding Reagan signed that day permitting members of the National Security Council staff to use covert operations that continued until mid-November 1986. These covert ventures sent 2,004 TOW antitank missiles and 220 spare parts for ground-launched HAWK antiaircraft missiles to Iran in exchange for Iran's releasing American hostages held in Lebanon by pro-Iranian terrorist groups. Reagan's decision to send weapons to Iran violated Reagan's proclaimed policy of withholding weapons from nations sponsoring terrorist groups and a specific U.S. arms embargo on Iran.

November 3, 1986

The Iran-Contra scandal begins with reports that the United States exchanged arms for hostages.

An article published on November 3, 1986, in the Lebanese magazine *Al-Shiraa* provided information about the Reagan administration's arms-for-hostages deal with Iran. The magazine's editor received word from Iran's Ayatollah Hussein Ali Montezari, a political opponent of Iran's speaker of the Majlis (parliament) Hojatolislam Hashemi Rafsanjani. On November 4, Rafsanjani told Iran's parliament that Reagan's National Security Adviser Robert McFarlane and four other Americans visited Tehran in October 1985, although both Rafsanjani and Al Shiraa later corrected the date of McFarlane's visit to May 1985. *Al-Shiraa*'s report indicated the five Americans arrived in Tehran carrying Irish passports and were detained for five days, during which they offered to send Iran the TOW missiles requested by Rafsanjani if Iran released American hostages in Lebanon. On November 6, McFarlane called the magazine's report "fanciful," and on the same day Reagan denied there was a deal with Iran. Reagan told reporters the story from the Middle East "has no foundation" and such reports made it more "difficult for us in our efforts to get other hostages free."

November 4, 1986

The Northern Mariana Islands becomes a U.S. commonwealth state; other U.S. trusteeship islands gain independent status in 1986–1987.

After World War II, the United States assumed control of Micronesia as a trusteeship under the United Nations. By 1986, these islands evolved into four groups: the Marshall Islands and the Federated States of Micronesia, which became independent but "freely associated" with the United States on October 29, 1986; Palau, whose independent status as an "associated" state was delayed until August 4, 1987; and the northern Marianas, whose voters chose to become a U.S. commonwealth—the same as Puerto Rico in the Caribbean.

All these islands depended on economic aid from Washington and accepted a U.S. military presence; in the case of the Marshalls, Kwajalein Island was a missile testing range for U.S. weapons. The delay in the status of Palau resulted because its constitution forbade nuclear weapons unless 75 percent of the voters chose otherwise. Because this conflicted with the U.S. policy of not identifying which U.S. naval vessels carried nuclear warheads, the voters had to change their constitution to permit nuclear weapons. Voters approved by 71 percent in a referendum on August 4, 1987.

November 13, 1986

Soviet Politburo recognized that their policy in Afghanistan has failed.

If there was a decisive moment in the Kremlin's questioning of its policy in Afghanistan, it came during the November 13 Politburo meeting. During the frank discussions at this meeting, the participants examined political calculations and strategies. Gorbachev declared: "In Afghanistan we have already been fighting for six years. If the approach is not changed, the fighting will go on for another 20–30 years." It was his proposal, drawing on discussions of the October 17, 1985 Politburo meeting, that Moscow should withdraw its forces from Afghanistan over a two-year period, with 50 percent being withdrawn during 1987 and the remaining forces the next year. The other members of the Politburo agreed.

The Soviets were not prepared to withdraw their support for the Communist Afghan regime of Dr. Najibullah. Gorbachev once again reiterated his support for broadening the social and political base of the Kabul regime, while Foreign Minister Shevardnadze acknowledged that Najibullah's government would require some "practical" assistance. The Soviets were also searching for a coalition government, but it would be in vain.

November 14, 1986

Great Peace March ends as 1,000 walk from Los Angeles to Washington, D.C.

The peace advocates began the walk on March 1, 1985, with 1,400 participants. Lacking enough funds, the trek ended near Barstow, California. After being reorganized, however, the walk continued to November 14.

November 22, 1986

India seeks $3 billion in damages from Union Carbide for the 1984 Bhopal accident.

Although the Union Carbide Company offered families of the Bhopal victims $350 million on March 24, 1986, India rejected the offer, and lawyers for the victims sought relief by suit in U.S. courts. A settlement was reached on December 22, 1988, when India accepted $470 million for the Bhopal victims, who numbered 3,289, according to Indian authorities.

November 25, 1986

President Reagan discloses pertinent aspects of the Iran-Contra affair during a televised press conference.

After denying the existence of an arms-for-hostage deal on November 4, American newspapers headlined the story of a deal based on Rafsanjani's admitting to Iran's parliament that the Americans visited Tehran (see November 3, 1986). Although on November 6, Reagan refused to comment on these news reports, congressional leaders became concerned that Reagan had rewarded Iranian terrorists. On November 25, when Reagan met with reporters for a televised briefing, Reagan announced that National Security Adviser John Poindexter and Oliver North, a Marine working for the National Security Council, would no longer work for the Reagan administration and that he would appoint a presidential panel to investigate the National Security Council's role in assuming duties usually associated with the CIA, the State Department, or the Defense Department.

Apparently between $10 million and $30 million had been paid for arms sent to Iran, and there was a special account at Credit Suisse Bank used by North to assist Nicaragua's Contra rebels during a period when the Boland Amendment limited or stopped aid to the Contras. McFarland, Poindexter, and North had transshipped arms to Iran through Israel by using former Marine General Richard Secord's Enterprise Corporation. Secord worked with North to send arms to Iran, whose payments for the TOW missiles and other armaments were used to purchase arms that were sent by air transport to the Contras. Despite these and other disclosures about the arms-for-hostages deal, President Reagan continued to argue that the arms deal with Iran had nothing to do with the release of hostages. Reagan told *Time* magazine columnist Hugh Sidney in an article published by *Time* on December 8, 1986, that North was a "national hero" and that this "whole thing boils down to a great responsibility on the part of the press" in preventing the release of more hostages. On December 9, North and Poindexter invoked the Fifth Amendment during a hearing of the Senate Intelligence Committee, claiming their testimony might incriminate themselves.

In contrast, McFarland told the Senate Committee that in August 1985, President Reagan had approved the transfer of Israel's TOW missiles to Iran and the replenishing of Israel's TOWs with U.S. stocks, testimony Reagan confirmed before the presidential commission (the Tower Commission, named for its chairman former Senator John G. Tower) on January 26, 1987. In addition to the Tower Commission, both the Senate and the House appointed separate Special Select Committees that conducted joint hearings in investigating the Iran-Contra affair. Also, on December 19, three judges of the Washington, D.C. Federal District Court appointed Lawrence E. Walsh as an independent counsel to investigate this affair.

November 27, 1986

Communist rebels in the Philippine Islands accept a cease-fire.

This cease-fire ended a third attempt to unseat President Corazon Aquino since she gained office in February 1986. On November 23, Aquino asked her cabinet to resign. She replaced Enrile with Deputy Defense Minister Rafael Ileto. She feared Enrile might try another *coup d'état.* Ileto and Aquino took special pains to get a cease-fire with the rebels, achieving this on November 27. Peace talks with the rebels began on December 23.

December 7, 1986

U.S. helicopters ferry Honduran troops to defend against Nicaragua.

U.S. helicopters answered a request from Honduran President José Azcona Hoyo, who said that since December 4, Nicaraguan troops had overrun a border post at Las Mietes and penetrated three miles into Honduras, near the area where 20,000 Contra rebels and their families lived. President Reagan ordered nine U.S. helicopters to carry 1,000 Honduran soldiers to the border, but it had become quiet by December 8. Nicaragua claimed it held war games in December but since this involved 6,500 troops, Azcona said they were "provocative." In response, on December 29, 1986, the United States started Big Pine '87 in Honduras, a four-month U.S.-Honduran military exercise.

December 12, 1986

U.S. nuclear reactor in Richland, Washington, is closed for safety.

This reactor at the Hanford Nuclear Reservation had been ordered shut down by the Department of Energy on October 8, 1986. Opened in 1963 and producing most U.S. weapons-grade plutonium, it resembled the reactor that failed at Chernobyl in the Soviet Union. Although cited for 54 violations in two years, the plant did not close immediately because politicians feared the effect on Richland's economy and the future of nuclear reactors. Critics wished to close all plants designed like Chernobyl's.

December 18, 1986

The Soviet Union proposes a nuclear test moratorium.

The Soviet Union's General Secretary Mikhail Gorbachev initially proposed a moratorium on nuclear testing in July 1985 (see July 29, 1985), but President

Reagan refused to accept the moratorium because he claimed such tests could not be verified. The United States continued nuclear tests and conducted another nuclear test on December 13, 1986, just two months after Reagan's summit meeting with Gorbachev in Iceland (see October 11, 1986). On December 18, 1986, Gorbachev again urged Reagan to accept a nuclear test ban agreement. If not, the Soviet Union would renew its nuclear testing after the first 1987 nuclear test by Americans. On December 19, Soviet Ambassador to the United States Yuri V. Dubinin indicated that if both countries renewed nuclear testing, U.S. scientists from the Natural Resources Defense Council, an independent environmental group, could use the Soviet monitoring station in the Soviet Republic of Kazakhstan to monitor Soviet tests.

Disregarding Moscow's warning, the Reagan administration staged another nuclear test on February 3, 1987. Two days after the U.S. test, Soviet Deputy Foreign Minister Vladimir Petrovsky called the U.S. test "provocative," indicating the Soviet Union would renew its nuclear testing. On February 26, 1987, the Soviets conducted their first nuclear test since Gorbachev announced a unilateral moratorium on nuclear tests in July 1985.

December 18, 1986

The Contadora group criticizes the United States for preventing peace in Central America.

Throughout 1986, the four Latin American nations of the Contadora group—Mexico, Venezuela, Colombia, and Panama—and five support members—Costa Rica, Nicaragua, El Salvador, Honduras, and Guatemala—were frustrated in peace attempts for Central America. As early as January 12, the nine nations urged Nicaragua and the United States to accept peace negotiations. After proclaiming a "last version" peace draft on June 7, the group obtained what seemed to be Nicaragua's approval, but because acceptance depended on the withdrawal of U.S aid to the Contras, no results followed. The U.S. State Department rejected Contadora plans unless Nicaragua agreed to negotiate with the Contras, who gained more aid from the U.S. Congress in 1986. Thus, meeting at Rio de Janeiro, Brazil, on December 18, the nine nations particularly criticized the United States for sustaining a war. They called on the United States and Nicaragua to negotiate for peace.

1987

January 8, 1987

Secretary of State George Shultz begins an eight-day tour of six African nations.

This journey covered six pro-Western black African countries—Senegal, Kenya, Nigeria, Ivory Coast, Cameroon, and Liberia. Generally, Shultz praised Africa's trend away from socialism but offered no new U.S. aid programs.

January 10, 1987

A U.S. investigation discloses Soviet electronic devices are in the new U.S. embassy in Moscow; the United States bugs Soviet embassy in Washington, D.C.

The investigation of the U.S. embassy situation was precipitated on January 10, 1987, by the arrest of U.S. Marine Corps Sergeant Clayton Lonetree, a member of the Marines who guarded the embassy. Lonetree was charged with giving secret information to a female agent of the KGB (the Soviet Union's secret police) with whom he had sexual relations. Lonetree was court-martialed, found guilty of espionage, and sentenced to 30 years in prison on August 24, 1987. After Lonetree cooperated by giving detailed information about his recruitment as a spy and disclosing Soviet secrets he knew about, a Marine Corps appeals court granted clemency to Lonetree and reduced his sentence by five years. The information Lonetree gave to U.S. authorities provided essential data enabling U.S. investigators to find the electronic bugs placed inside the new U.S. embassy building being built in Moscow.

When the Soviet embassay was completed in 1979, Soviet ambassador Dobrynin reported in his memoirs that they found "more than two hundred listening devices secreted inside." He informed Secretary of State Vance but received no response. Because the American embassy in Moscow was used to intercept official Soviet telephone and radio conversations, the KGB used electromagnetic devices to jam the intercept system. In December 1991, according to, Dobrynin, the KGB had informed the U.S. ambassador of "the design and location of the Soviet bugging equipment" in America's new embassy building in Moscow. Dobrynin's comment was "Well, what about returning the favor?" to which the American ambassador laughed and said Washington officials were not ready for such openness.

January 15, 1987

The United States lifts controls on exports of oil-drilling equipment to the Soviet Union.

The Commerce Department ended the limitation that President Jimmy Carter began in July 1978 to punish the Soviets for the trial and imprisonment of two human rights dissenters—Aleksandr Ginzberg and Anatoly Shcharansky. U.S. business firms were hurt more than the Soviets, who found other suppliers for the oil-drilling equipment. In 1978, Carter's action cost U.S. manufacturers $2 billion in contracts. Some U.S. oil-drilling equipment was advanced in 1978, but by the mid-1980s such equipment was widely available from other countries.

January 25, 1987

West German Chancellor Kohl is reelected.

While Helmut Kohl's Christian Democratic Union and the Free Democrats maintained their coalition, both Kohl's party and the Social Democratic Party lost seats in the Bundestag (lower house of parliament) while the Free Democrats and the Green Party increased their votes. Voter concern about the basing of nuclear-tipped missiles played a large role in the results.

January 27, 1987

The Soviet Union's Communist Party Central Committee meeting approves General Secretary Mikhail Gorbachev's proposed reforms.

As described in his 1995 *Memoirs*, General Secretary Gorbachev began in December 1986 to change the Soviet Union's direction toward democratizing both the Communist Party of the Soviet Union (CPSU) and the structure of the Soviet government in order to implement his perestroika (reforms) and revitalize the country. Prior to the January 27 meeting of the Central Committee, Gorbachev's ideas about democratizing the country were discussed with CPSU Politburo members. Somewhat to Gorbachev's surprise, all the Politburo members, including Andrei Gromyko and Boris Yeltsin, supported his proposals. The Politburo was the policy making body of both the CPSU and the Soviet government. Its proposals could be questioned or revised by the Party's Central Committee, although this seldom occurred regarding major political and economic affairs.

When the Central Committee members met on January 27, 1987, the Central Committee approved Gorbachev's reform program with little debate. The reforms allowed more than one candidate to be on the ballot in secret elections for Party representatives and officials. Other significant reforms permitted Communist Party members to file grievances against Party officials and granted greater regional control in Party affairs. Having gained approval from the CPSU Central Committee, Gorbachev was able to begin carrying out political reforms on June 21, 1987, when representatives of the Party's Council of Representative Delegations were elected in secret ballots. The June elections permitted multiple candidates on the ballots, but only 76 of the 3,912 Council seats were contested with two or more candidates. Nevertheless, Gorbachev believed the precedent was set for multiple candidates to be on future ballots. When the Supreme Soviet of the USSR (a parliament) met to approve the legislation recommended by the Central Committee, the Supreme Soviet enacted the necessary legislation in two working days: June 29 and 30, 1987.

January 28, 1987

Secretary of State Shultz meets with Oliver Tambo of the African National Congress (ANC).

Tambo represented the leading black South African group fighting the apartheid policies of South Africa. On January 8, 1987, the State Department had issued a report claiming the ANC was "deeply beholden" to the South African Communist Party, a charge Shultz asked Tambo to refute. The ANC, like other black African rebel groups, found Moscow ready to help when Western powers refused to do so. Because of Tambo's Communist connections, the State Department emphasized that his meeting with Shultz was only symbolic of the ANC role in any South African settlement. Shultz urged Tambo to cut Soviet ties and avoid the use of violence. Nevertheless, conservatives in the United States opposed the meeting.

January 29, 1987

A Senate Intelligence Committee report contradicts President Reagan's claim that sending arms to Iran sought better relations.

During December 1986, the Senate Intelligence Committee had briefings with Central Intelligence Agency Director William Casey and others to learn details of the Iran-Contra affair. The major issue was Reagan's purpose in selling arms to Iran, using the money to support the Contras, and negotiating the hostages' release. Anticipating the Senate report, on January 9 the White House had released an intelligence finding of January 17, 1986, signed by Reagan and stating that the arms sale had the strategic goal of a more moderate Iranian government. At the bottom of the document National Security Adviser John Poindexter noted that Reagan signed but did not read it. During his January 27 State of the Union speech, Reagan argued that the Iranian effort was worthy, and his major regret was that it did not improve Iranian relations and get the release of all the hostages. On January 29, the Senate Intelligence report was released. One of its principal findings was that the main purpose of the affair had not been to improve Iranian relations or to aid moderate Iranians.

The Senate found no evidence that Reagan knew about Oliver North's diversion of funds to the Contras. Other new Senate information on the affair was that the Reagan administration had solicited aid for the Contras from at least six countries. One was the sultan of Brunei, who put $10 million in secret Swiss accounts for North to use in Central America. The Senate Intelligence Committee was the only investigative group obtaining testimony from Casey. They heard Casey on December 10, five days before he was hospitalized for a cerebral seizure. After surgery to remove a malignant brain tumor on December 18, Casey died on May 5, 1987. Regarding news about soliciting aid for the Contras from other sources, the White House issued a statement on May 14, 1987, declaring that while Congress could limit the federal monies, nothing limited the "constitutional and historic power of the president" to decide foreign policy and raise private money for the Contras. On May 15, Reagan told journalists it was his idea to obtain private aid for the Contras because Congress had restricted it.

President Reagan meets with CIA Director William Casey. Ronald Reagan Library

February 9, 1987

The United States is alarmed by the Soviets naval buildup at a Vietnamese base; Australian authorities disagree.

During the Reagan era, the U.S. navy moved toward a "maritime strategy" to control narrow "choke points" of the world's sea lanes to gain naval superiority. Inline with this, the United States argued that the USSR sought to dominate the Pacific Ocean through its Vietnamese base at Cam Ranh Bay. The Reagan administration indicated that the Soviets had quadrupled their base size in a major effort to dominate the region. This U.S. assessment was questioned by Australian Defense Minister Kim Beazly, as reported in the *Far East Economic Review* for June 18, 1987. Using American photographs as proof, Beazly argued that the Soviets had none of their "first line craft" at Cam Ranh Bay. Moreover, he claimed, the U.S. navy's recent expenditures had checkmated all Soviet efforts in the Pacific.

February 18, 1987

Returning from Iraq, Representative Robert G. Torricelli (D-N.J.) says Iran benefited greatly from the U.S. sale of arms.

The Iran-Contra impact on the Iran-Iraq war was overlooked by many U.S. commentators. Reports, however, suggested that there were benefits to Iran and costs to Iraq resulting from these sales. After a five-day visit to Baghdad, Torricelli learned from Iraqi Foreign Minister Tariq Aziz that because of the sale of U.S. Hawkanti aircraft missiles, Iraq lost 45 to 50 warplanes—10 percent of its air force. In addition, during a recent Iranian offensive, Iraq blamed its extremely high tank losses on the U.S. sale of TOW antitank missiles to Iran. According to Reagan administration officials, two types of weapons were sent to Iran: parts for the Hawk antiaircraft missiles sold to the shah before 1979, and 2,008 TOW tube-launched, optically tracked, wireguided antitank missiles. Although President Reagan said he had authorized only "small amounts of defensive weapons" that did not affect the Iran-Iraq military balance, military experts said these two weapons caused considerable damage to Iraq and could determine the war's course.

February 19, 1987

President Reagan lifts economic sanctions from Poland.

In 1984, Reagan had removed some of the sanctions levied in December 1981 because the Polish government instituted martial law to break the Solidarity trade union led by Lech Walesa. He now removed the last sanction by ending a ban on U.S. trade credits and granting Poland most-favored-nation status, which lowered U.S. tariffs on Polish exports. The United States took two other steps in 1987 to encourage Poland to grant greater political and economic reform. On September 22, diplomatic relations were restored when Ambassador John Davis went to Warsaw. Second, from September 26 to 28, Vice President George Bush visited Poland and indicated that Washington would help Poland reschedule its foreign debt to help rebuild its economy.

February 26, 1987

The Tower Commission claims that President Reagan's management style caused the Iran-Contra debacle.

Appointed by Reagan on November 26, this commission consisted of former Senator John G. Tower (R-Tx.) as chairman, former Secretary of State Edmund S. Muskie, and former National Security Adviser Brent Scowcroft. After reviewing the secret events of the Iran-Contra affair and the National Security Council's procedures, the report concluded that the president had not insisted on accountability for NSC activity. It believed no criminal activity was involved but recommended reviewing NSC procedures so that "loose cannons" such as Lt. Colonel Oliver North could not act independently, as he had done during these operations. On March 4, President Reagan told a television audience that he accepted full responsibility for the affair, conceding that his honorable intentions deteriorated into an arms-for-hostages deal. This was the closest Reagan came to admitting a mistake or apologizing for action contrary to his public posturing about no deals with terrorists. The Tower Commission report included a chronology of major events of the scandal, which historians may compare to publicized events at particular moments. As a note of historical interest, the president's wife, Nancy, had since December 1986 marshaled forces to blame the White House chief of staff, Donald T. Regan, for the affair and to seek his resignation. An expert in domestic matters, Regan seems to have had little direct role in the Iran-Contra deal, but he did not monitor NSC staff members Poindexter and North. On February 27, Regan resigned and was replaced by former Senator Howard Baker (R-Tenn.). On July 30, 1986, Regan told the House-Senate committee on the Iran-Contra affair that Mrs. Reagan thought he "let Ronnie down."

February 28, 1987

Soviet First Secretary Mikhail Gorbachev offers a plan to eliminate Intermediate-Range Nuclear Forces (INF) in Europe: President Reagan reacts favorably.

Mikhail Gorbachev's February 28 proposal to eliminate Intermediate-Range Nuclear Forces (INF) was based on his decision to separate negotiations on INF from such arms control issues as President Reagan's Strategic Defense Initiative (SDI). Following Gorbachev's offer, subsequent negotiations resulted in the December 1987 INF Treaty (see December 8, 1987). Before announcing his proposal, Gorbachev began a "peace offensive" to convince Americans and Europeans he wanted to end the Cold War. On February 4, he convened a meeting in Moscow that was co-sponsored by the Council on Foreign Relations, a private group located in New York City. The American delegation included former U.S. Cabinet officials Harold Brown, Henry Kissinger, Peter

Peterson, and Cyrus Vance. From February 14 to 16, Gorbachev hosted an international meeting on peace and disarmament attended by 700 artists, scientists, business leaders, and politicians.

The most important result of this international meeting was a speech by physicist Andrey Sakharov to a meeting of scientists. Sakharov called on Gorbachev to stop linking negotiations on INF and arms reduction treaties to Reagan's SDI program. Sakharov said no SDI system would be effective against a massive attack by Soviet intercontinental ballistic missiles (ICBMs). SDI, he argued, was only a "Maginot line in space," a reference to France's ineffective 1940 Maginot line defenses. By February 28, Gorbachev had concluded Sakharov and other Soviet scientists who made similar comments about SDI were correct. Thus, the December INF Treaty could be finalized as the first of other strategic arms reduction treaties (START) made between the Soviet Union or Russia with the United States during the 1990s.

March 3, 1987

Secretary of State Shultz visits China and learns about the Chinese interest in Western-style free markets.

When Shultz arrived in China on May 1, he met with the leader of the Chinese Communist Party Deng Xiaoping, who told Shultz that China's political difficulties had slowed down its economic modernization program. The party, Deng said, wanted Western help in economic affairs but not in China's political and cultural matters. The political problems Deng referred to included the forced resignation of the Communist Party's General Secretary Hu Yaobang, who, in the Chinese tradition following the overthrow of the "gang of four" and the 1960s cultural revolution (see August 18, 1966 and December 15, 1978), had confessed to his mistakes in being too pro-Western and his failure to prevent the extensive student demonstrations from January 1 to 5, 1987. Hu's mistakes also led the Chinese Communist Party to expel Wang Ruowang, a university Marxian theorist, and Liu Binyan, a journalist for China's *People's Daily*. Hu was replaced by Premier Zhao Ziyang while the Communist Party's Politburo came under the influence of Deputy Premier Li Peng, who opposed political reforms in China.

April 1, 1987

British Prime Minister Thatcher visits Moscow; British-Soviet relations are improved.

Prime Minister Margaret Thatcher spent five days in the USSR and had a lengthy visit with Soviet leader Mikhail Gorbachev. As when Gorbachev visited London in 1984, Thatcher and he got along splendidly. Minor agreements were made to upgrade the telephone hot line between London and Moscow and to exchange scientific and cultural personnel.

April 13, 1987

Secretary of State George Shultz and Soviet Foreign Minister Eduard Shevardnadze discuss INF weapons and space probes.

Meeting in Moscow for three days, the two diplomatic delegations discussed the Soviet proposal of February 28, 1988, to eliminate intermediate-range nuclear forces (INF). They also signed an accord to share data obtained from unmanned planetary space flights. On April 27, the Soviet Union formally presented a draft treaty to eliminate INF in Europe.

April 20, 1987

PLO meeting in Algiers unifies hard-line approach to Israel; Syria seeks aid from Moscow.

Meeting in Algiers from April 20 to 26, the PLO's leader, Yasser Arafat, wanted dissident factions to unite against Israel. To obtain support, Arafat adopted a tougher approach toward Israel, which damaged his relations with Egypt and Jordan.

While Arafat sought to rebuild the PLO's strength, Syrian President Hafiz al-Assad visited Moscow on April 23 and 24 to request advanced armaments and to reschedule Syria's debt to the Soviet Union. Soviet leader Mikhail Gorbachev told Assad he would aid Syria if it ended its antagonism toward Arafat and helped pro-Syrian Palestinians reunite with the PLO. Gorbachev favored an Arab-Israeli peace conference to settle Middle Eastern problems.

April 23, 1987

East German leader Erich Honecker rejects the Soviet Union's economic and political reforms.

East German Communist Party leader, Honecker, was one of the few Eastern European leaders who refused to adopt the reform practices of the Soviet Union under Mikhail Gorbachev. Honecker told a trade union congress that the East German economy worked well and needed no change. His desire to maintain the status quo was demonstrated on June 6–8, when East German security forces broke up a large group of young people at the Berlin Wall trying to listen to a rock concert on the West Berlin side. While East German police used weapons to restrain the students and arrested 30, many of the youths chanted, "Gorby, Gorby, we want freedom."

May 5, 1987

Joint hearings begin for the House-Senate investigation of the Iran-Contra affair.

These hearings lasted until August 4, 1987. The following are highlights of the testimony other than those recorded in the Tower Commission report:

May 11, 1987: Robert McFarlane testified that he frequently briefed President Reagan on Contra aid.

May 19, 1987: Adolfo Calero, the principal Contra leader, gave North $90,000 in blank traveler's checks in 1985 to finance Drug Enforcement Agency attempts to contact hostages. He did not say where he obtained the $90,000.

May 28, 1987: Lewis Tambs, former U.S. ambassador to Costa Rica, was asked by North in 1985 to develop a southern Contra front.

June 25, 1987: Assistant Attorney General Charles Cooper explained at a meeting on November 20, 1986, that CIA Director Casey, Lt. Colonel North, and National Security Adviser Admiral John Poindexter planned false testimony to conceal sending Hawk missiles to Iran.

July 7–10, 1987 Lt. Colonel Oliver North shredded documents before President Reagan's television address about the Iran-Contra affair on November 22–23, 1986; he recommended the diversion of Iranian funds to the Contras, leaving a small space on the bottom of the page for the president to initial but giving the memos to Poindexter; he stated that Iranian arms merchant Adnan M. Ghorbanifar proposed diverting funds to the Contras while Poindexter approved it and CIA Director Casey was "very enthusiastic."

July 15, 1987: John Poindexter, national security adviser until November 25, 1986, testified that Reagan authorized the Iran arms sale but that it was Poindexter's decision to divert funds to the Contras. On other matters, Poindexter had many memory lapses.

July 23, 1987 Secretary of State, George Shultz, described a "battle royal" with Casey, McFarlane, and Poindexter, who lied to him and withheld data from President Reagan. Shultz said he opposed the deal with Iran and disliked National Security Council (NSC) officers directing State Department officials to report to them, as were John H. Kelly, U.S. ambassador in Beirut, and Lewis Tambs in Costa Rica.

May 13, 1987

The United States stages combined air-sea exercises near Nicaragua's border.

U.S. support for the Contra rebels fighting against the Nicaraguan government included extensive displays of U.S. forces in the Contra sanctuary territory located in Honduras. The Big Pine '87 U.S. military exercise begun in Honduras on December 29, 1986, lasted beyond the original plan of four months and became part of the larger military exercise called Operation Solid Shield. Deploying 40,000 troops in a landing assault at Trujillo, Honduras, near the Nicaraguan border gave U.S. troops practice while at the same time threatening Nicaragua. One U.S. official said Operation Solid Shield would "wave a big stick at Nicaragua" while defending Honduras and the Contra bases.

May 15, 1987

Japanese government bans Toshiba Machine Company from selling to the Soviet Union because it sold the Soviets sensitive technology.

Toshiba sold the Soviets a computer program for milling submarine propeller blades in June 1984, and tools for manufacturing these blades in December 1982. U.S. Secretary of Defense Caspar Weinberger stated that the security of both Japan and the United States was damaged because these sales permitted the Soviets to acquire quieter submarines, making their detection more difficult. On July 1, the chairman and president of Toshiba resigned because of the government ban.

May 17, 1987

Iraqi missiles hit a U.S. navy ship, killing 37 Americans; President Reagan accepts Iraq's apology.

While patrolling in the Persian Gulf, the U.S. navy guided missile frigate USS *Stark* was hit by two missiles launched from an Iraqi plane. One missile exploded, and the unexploded missile was defused by the *Stark*'s crew. Thirty-seven of the *Stark*'s 220-man crew died in the explosion. Ironically, although Iraq was responsible for over two-thirds of the attacks on 300 ships in the Persian Gulf during the Iran-Iraq war and the *Stark* attack killed 37 Americans, President Reagan blamed Iran for the incident. Iraqi President Saddam Hussein accepted the blame for the incident and informed Washington that Iraq would pay compensation for the American lives and damage to the ship.

May 19, 1987

President Reagan agrees to fly U.S. flags on Kuwaiti oil tankers in the Persian Gulf escorted by the U.S. navy.

After discussions with Kuwait that began in early 1987, on March 23, the United States offered Kuwait naval protection, and on April 4, the U.S. Navy added a naval battle group to the existing U.S. aircraft carrier *Kitty Hawk* in the Persian Gulf. The Gulf problem arose after Iraq started attacking commercial ships headed for Iranian ports while Iran retaliated against both Iraqi and Kuwaiti ships because Iran claimed that Kuwait had assisted Baghdad. On April 6, Kuwait proposed that its oil tankers be registered under the U.S. or the Soviet flag for protection. The Soviet Union agreed on April 14 to lease three of its tankers to Kuwait while Soviet naval ships escorted those tankers. This led the Reagan administration to reconsider the situation, but until the USS *Stark* was hit on May 17, the president had not decided to accept Kuwait's offer. Congress now became involved. On May 21, the Senate voted 91 to 5 to request a detailed report on the reflagging plans, causing Reagan to delay the process.

May 29, 1987

Soviet air defenses fail when a West German lands a small plane in Red Square.

Mathias Rust, a young West German who said he was on a "peace mission," flew a Cessna 172 plane 500 miles from Finland into Moscow, where, after buzzing Red Square, he landed near the Kremlin Wall. He got out and talked with people in the square before being arrested. Coincidentally, he did this on the day the Soviets celebrated Border Guards Day. During his journey, only one Soviet plane passed Rust's plane but did not interfere with him. The main consequence of this exploit was that Soviet leader Mikhail Gorbachev dismissed the defense minister and air defense commander. Gorbachev then appointed a personal political ally, Dimitry Yazov, as the new Soviet defense minister. Rust was tried by a Soviet court and sentenced to four years in a Soviet labor camp. His plane was returned to the Hamburg, West Germany, flying club that owned it. On August 3, 1988, at the order of the Presidium of the Supreme Soviet (parliament), Rust was freed and returned to West Germany.

June 2, 1987

President Reagan renews most-favored-nation status for Romania, Hungary, and China.

Despite constant reports of human rights violations in Romania and student dissent in China, Reagan granted these countries the trade status they desired to compete favorably in exporting products to the United States. Notably excluded from Reagan's list was the Soviet Union, whose leader, Mikhail Gorbachev, had urged the United States to grant it status equal to that of other "friendly" U.S. trading partners. The United States used this as a bargaining chip to seek other Soviet concessions such as changing Soviet emigration policy.

June 8, 1987

A special State Department panel recommends eliminating the three top floors of the U.S. embassy in Moscow.

Since the arrest of a U.S. embassy guard in Moscow (see January 10, 1987), not only were Marine guard practices examined, but an investigation of embassy security disclosed that the U.S. embassy building under construction was implanted with electronic listening devices by the Soviets. After two members of Congress visited the embassy unannounced in April, they reported that the Soviet electronic devices "fully compromised" the integrity of the embassy building. Headed by former Secretary of Defense James Schlesinger, a special panel of experts visited Moscow and reported its findings on June 8, with the final report released June 26. The panel recommended razing the top three floors, although congressional visitors to Moscow wanted the entire building torn down and rebuilt. On October 26, 1988, President Reagan ordered the entire building razed.

June 11, 1987

Economic summit of seven major industrialized nations meets in Venice.

The meeting in Venice was attended by the leaders of the industrial nations of the United States, Great Britain, France, West Germany, Japan, Italy, and Canada. They praised Soviet First Secretary Mikhail Gorbachev for his economic reforms. Regarding the Venice Summit, the *Washington Post* reported on June 11, 1987, that President Reagan's stature had diminished among the other six leaders, owing to the Iran-Contra affair and the fact that the United States had become the world's largest debtor nation by 1986. Most of the American debts were held by the other six nations at the summit.

June 11, 1987

British Prime Minister Thatcher wins a third term.

Margaret Thatcher was the first British prime minister to win a third term in 160 years.

June 25, 1987

At a Communist Party Central Committee plenum, party First Secretary Gorbachev calls for ending central economic controls and subsidized prices.

At the plenum, Mikhail Gorbachev proposed detailed guidelines for restructuring the Soviet economy, the policy of *perestroika.* These included decentralizing the economy to allow more local responsibility and making state-owned enterprises self-sustaining and competitive. Previously, on May 1, 1987, Soviet laws were changed to allow citizens to be licensed to sell their skills privately in 40 business categories.

June 25, 1987

Hungary announces two leaders will retire.

Both President Pál Losonczi and Prime Minister György Lazar retired from their posts. The Communist Party announced they would be replaced by Karoly Nemeth as president and Karoly Grosz as prime minister. These changes occurred because Hungary began economic austerity programs to rectify its hard currency trade deficit with Western European nations. On July 20, 1987, the government raised prices of consumer goods, reduced subsidies to certain businesses, and levied a value-added tax.

July 21, 1987

Israel tests a new intermediate-range missile.

Known as Jericho II, it replaced Jericho I, which Israel had developed in the 1960s with French help. The new missile range was between 500 and 900 miles, capable of hitting most Middle Eastern targets and the Soviet Union. After the report was published, the Soviets warned Israeli leaders against deploying such weapons. Moscow radio said the Soviets might give Syria SS-23 surface-to-surface missiles if Israel threatened its neighbors.

July 22, 1987

Two reflagged Kuwaiti oil tankers are escorted into the Persian Gulf—one hits a mine.

Although Congress held up the U.S. flagging of Kuwaiti ships, which President Reagan had proposed on May 19, Reagan rejected further delays and ordered the navy to reflag and escort Kuwaiti ships. On July 22, three U.S. ships began escorting two reflagged Kuwaiti ships through the Strait of Hormuz into the Persian Gulf, while U.S. navy planes patrolled the skies. On July 24, just before reaching Kuwait's port, the tanker *Bridgeton* hit a sea mine, but the 400,000-ton ship was not damaged enough to stop, and it soon reached port. The U.S. navy was embarrassed because on July 19 it had swept the area for mines and said it was clear.

On July 29, Defense Secretary Caspar Weinberger ordered eight minesweepers to the gulf and asked West Germany, Britain (who had the best mine sweepers), and other European nations to send minesweeping equipment. Obtaining U.S. minesweepers was not simple because it was a weapons system the U.S. navy had allowed to deteriorate. The best sweepers available were eight RH-53D Sea Stallion helicopter minesweepers, which were dispatched on July 29.

July 28, 1987

Bulgaria's Todor Zhivkov joins the reform program advocated by Soviet First Secretary Mikhail Gorbachev.

First Secretary of Bulgaria's Communist Party Todor Zhivkov adopted Gorbachev's perestroika reform program. During a July 28 speech to Bulgaria's Communist Party's Central Committee, Zhivkov called for the Central Committee to restructure Bulgaria's State Assembly and the Communist Party's policy making Politburo. Zhivkov said Bulgaria should adopt a free market economy that would give Bulgaria's currency—the lev—a value equal to the Soviet Union's ruble, and approve free-trade relations for the nation's enterprises. Zhivkov's speech brought few immediate changes in Bulgaria but in 1988, the Central Committee allowed more than one candidate to run for each local office and on July 20, 1988, Zhivkov told a Communist Party Plenum to initiate specific economic reforms to implement those called for in 1987.

August 4, 1987

The Reagan administration offers a peace plan for Nicaragua.

Anticipating the meeting of Central American presidents on August 7 to sign the Arias Peace Plan, President Reagan and U.S. Speaker of the House James Wright (D-Tex.) announced a proposal for peace in Nicaragua. The proposal called for an immediate cease-fire, the end of all foreign military support to either side, the restoration of Nicaraguan civil rights and open elections, talks between the Central American leaders and the United States, and amnesty for the Contra rebels. The proposal threatened the resumption of U.S. military aid to the Contras if no progress was made by September 30, 1988. Reagan's plan provoked criticism both in the United States and abroad. Conservatives such as Senator Jesse Helms (R-N.C.) said the plan was a dream especially since the Contras were starting to win the war; liberals such as Senator Edward Kennedy (D-Mass.) said it was a show to justify renewal of U.S. military aid to the Contras on October 1, 1988, if the Sandinistas rejected the plan. The president wanted $150 million in aid for the Contras for the next 18 months. Reagan's plan never got off the ground because, as Cynthia Arnson's *Crossroads* explains, the Arias Peace Plan of 1986 gained support from Central America's Contadora, as well as peace groups in Latin America and Europe.

August 7, 1987

The Arias Peace plan is signed by five Central American governments.

President Oscar Arias Sánchez of Costa Rica drafted a peace plan for Central America early in 1987, and lobbied extensively to achieve agreement on August 7. Beginning on January 7, Costa Rica's Foreign Minister Rodrigo Madrigal Nieto met in Miami with Assistant Secretary of State Elliott Abrams and Special Presidential Envoy Philip Habib to describe the peace initiative for ending civil wars in Nicaragua, El Salvador, and Guatemala. The Arias plan assumed greater significance after a January 19–20 meeting of the Contadora group failed to make progress on peace. President Arias and his colleagues quietly met with many groups throughout Latin America and Europe to promote the proposal and prepare for the August meeting in Guatemala City. Although the United States acted indifferently toward the plan, President Reagan's August 4 proposal for peace in Nicaragua did not conflict seriously with Arias's concepts except for the deadline of September 30 for Nicaragua to act. Assigned on August 7, the Arias Peace Plan included timetables for cease-fires in the three civil wars to be verified by an international commission, negotiations with unarmed guerrilla groups, freedom of the press and free elections, and ending the various states of emergency. On August 13, El Salvador offered to meet with leftist rebels if they renounced violence; and on August 21, the Contras accepted the plan, provided the Nicaraguan government began direct negotiations with them.

Guatemalan rebels of the National Resistance Union met with government delegates in Madrid, Spain, in October.

August 11, 1987

The United States and the Soviet Union accept "challenge inspections" of each other's chemical weapons facilities.

This agreement permitted chemical weapons experts to visit each nation's chemical production facilities on 48 hours' notice to determine what weapons if any were being made. The first Soviet delegation visited the U.S. chemical storage facilities at Tooele, Utah, on November 19, 1987. In addition to this bilateral agreement, the Soviet Union permitted a U.N. delegation to visit its chemical weapons complex at Shikhany on October 3, 1987. The U.N. delegates watched the Soviets destroy a 550-pound chemical bomb containing nerve gas. Final agreements on chemical weapons were still pending, however. On October 5, the Soviet U.N. delegate denounced the United States for undertaking new chemical weapons production. The U.S. delegate responded that the United States began new production only because the Soviet arsenal of chemical weapons was so much larger than the American. He claimed that in addition to Shikhany, the Soviets had 14 to 20 secret chemical production facilities.

August 23, 1987

The three Soviet Baltic republics stage protest marches for independence.

Nationalist protest demonstrators in Estonia, Latvia, and Lithuania claimed that the Nazi-Soviet Pact of August 23, 1939, gave the Soviet Union illegal control over their territory. Subsequently, in reaction to Soviet leader Mikhail Gorbachev's policies of glasnost and perestroika, the native inhabitants of these three Soviet republics demanded their independence from Soviet control. The August 1987 demonstrations were put down by local police but the national opposition did not disappear. In 1989, the Baltic states' nationalists adopted nonviolent methods and political measures to fulfill their desire for independence (see July 1, 1989); Gorbachev faced similar nationalist stirrings among its Warsaw Pact allies of Eastern Europe (see January 15, 1989).

August 28, 1987

A right-wing attempt to overthrow Philippine President Aquino fails; claims Aquino not forceful enough with left-wing rebel groups.

In this second right-wing attempt to oust Aquino in 1987, Colonel Gregorio Honasan led 1,350 rebel soldiers in attacks on Manila and Cebu City. The right-wing groups believed Aquino had not dealt forcefully enough with left-wing rebel groups. She had held peace talks with rebel leaders for nearly a year. The talks were suspended on January 22, 1987, and on March 22, Aquino called for the military to combat both Communist and right-wing rebels. To further counter left-wing groups, she announced plans for a land reform program on July 21, 1987.

September 4, 1987

U.N. Security Council resolution 598 fails to end the Iran-Iraq war; the United States finds evidence of Iranian sea mines on September 21.

Although the Security Council resolution for a cease-fire was approved, it had only a slight immediate effect. On September 8, Iraq struck at two oil tankers near the Iranian island of Kharq and bombed 13 Iranian cities. Libya offered, on September 10, to send Iran more sea mines. On September 21, the United States obtained the first definite evidence that Iranian ships were laying sea mines, a charge Tehran had denied. After U.S. ships saw an Iranian vessel mining the sea near Bahrain, a U.S. helicopter fired on the ship, but it again began planting its mines. Although a U.S. navy video-camera filmed the ship as it was dropping mines, the film came out blank, and reporters could be shown only some captured mines.

Nevertheless, on September 22, Iranian President Sayyed Ali Khamenei addressed the U.N. General Assembly, claiming Iraq had refused to accept Iran's peace terms.

September 7, 1987

Pakistan and Afghanistan meet with a U.N. mediator to try and end the Afghanistan war.

Generally, the rebel forces in Afghanistan were stalemated in their civil war against the government, which was backed by Soviet troops and equipment.

The rebel forces benefited from Pakistani and U.S. aid. Particularly after the Reagan administration sent the rebels shoulder-fired Stinger antiaircraft missiles, the rebels operated effectively against Soviet helicopters and Afghan troop transports. On February 9, a Stinger downed a transport plane, killing 37 troops, and on June 11, another downed a troop plane, killing 53 of the 55 aboard. The Soviet Union wanted to withdraw its troops, but agreements among the rebels, Pakistan, and the United States would be necessary to protect the Kabul government.

At the September 7 meeting with U.N. mediator Diégo Cordovez, the principal issue concerned coordinating outside assistance to the rivals in Afghanistan with the pullout of Soviet troops. While the Afghan government wanted to stretch the Soviet withdrawal over a 16-month period, Pakistan wanted only eight months. The two sides ended their meeting on this difference.

September 7, 1987

East German leader Erich Honecker visits West Germany for the first time.

The general secretary of East Germany, Erich Honecker, made a four-day visit to West Germany to meet with Chancellor Helmut Kohl on September 7–8. Although a few agreements on trade, nuclear safety, and the environment were made, the visit was a first step toward more cooperation. Honecker had planned a visit in 1984, but incidents in East-West relations caused him to cancel it.

September 11, 1987

The Organization of African Unity (OAU) mediates a cease-fire between Chad and Libya.

Kenneth Kaunda, president of Zambia and chairman of the OAU, used his office to obtain a cease-fire in a conflict waged since 1983 between Chad and Libya, with Libyan-backed rebels.

September 15, 1987

U.S.-USSR agree to establish Nuclear Risk Reduction Centers.

Senators Sam Nunn and John Warner, in a bipartisan move, sponsored a resolution calling for the creation of Nuclear Risk Reduction Centers in Washington, D.C., and Moscow in 1984; the Senate endorsed it, but initially the administration was cool to the idea. After several months of study, the administration accepted the concept but the Defense Department rejected the joint American-Soviet operation of the centers that the initial proposal sought. Also dropped was the idea that the centers prepare contingency plans for the possible use of nuclear weapons by terrorist groups.

When Secretary of State Shultz and Foreign Minister Shevardnadze signed the treaty it was the first arms control agreement entered into by the Reagan administration. The Nuclear Risk Centers in Washington, D.C., and Moscow would exchange pertinent information and notifications demanded by various arms control agreements. The basic purpose of this activity was to reduce the possibility of a miscalculation or misunderstanding by either superpower. The centers were not, however, intended to supplant the "Hot Line" links that provided direct communications between the heads of state, nor were the centers to become involved in crisis management.

The centers in Moscow, located in the General Staff headquarters, and Washington, D.C., located in the State Department, became operational on April 1, 1988.

September 18, 1987

The FBI brings a hijacker to the United States for trial.

Using a Middle Eastern CIA agent to lure Fawas Younis, a Syrian terrorist, onto a yacht sailing in international waters, Federal Bureau of Investigation agents captured Younis and brought him to the United States. In 1986, Congress had passed legislation giving the United States jurisdiction over terrorists who endangered U.S. nationals. The FBI claimed Younis was involved in the 1985 hijacking of a Jordanian airliner on which four Americans were aboard. On February 23, 1988, a U.S. federal court judge dropped several charges against Younis, after ruling that the FBI had obtained his confession illegally. Younis had not been advised of his constitutional rights and had been detained too long before arraignment. Younis's wrists were broken and FBI agents had refused to treat him; Younis said that FBI agents broke his wrists in gaining his confession. Eventually, Younis was tried by a federal court and convicted on March 14, 1989. He was sentenced to 30 years in jail. According to *Newsweek*, a Pentagon source said that millions of dollars were spent to prosecute Younis, and a major CIA source in the Middle East was revealed so President Reagan and the Justice Department, according to the Pentagon, could "look good at the height of Iran-Contra disclosures."

September 21–24, 1987

French and West German forces hold joint military exercises in West Germany.

Known as Bold Sparrow, these exercises involved 20,000 French and 55,000 West German troops in war games to counteract an attack by Warsaw Pact nations. According to reports from France and West Germany, these countries planned to form a Joint Defense Council by 1989 to supplement their defenses because since 1966 France had refused to coordinate its military with NATO.

September 30, 1987

Treasury Secretary Baker tries to revive interest in the Baker Plan of 1985.

On September 29, Secretary of the Treasury James Baker met with board members of the World Bank and International Monetary Fund (IMF). Baker sought to revive interest in the Baker Plan's approach to relieving the enormous debts of Third World nations. Since March 27, 1985, the Baker Plan created a pool of $3.1 billion plus another $9 billion added to loans for an African fund. These funds had not only relieved the debts of Argentina, Mexico, and several African nations, but also enabled these countries to achieve averaged annual growth rates of 3.7 percent for the last two years, their best growth rates in six years. Despite the Baker Plan's success in several Third World countries, the IMF/World Bank board members decided the Baker Plan would be used only as one option in the IMF/World Bank's case-by-case decisions about a particular nation's needs. Secretary Baker disapproved of the IMF/World Bank members' decision to continue working on a case-by-case system because it slowed down the transition of each Third World nation's movement from a regulated state-controlled economy to a free market economy. On August 5, 1988, Baker resigned as Secretary of the Treasury and his successor Nicholas Brady continued to support the Baker Plan. After George H.W. Bush became president in 1989, Brady introduced the Brady Plan that attempted to help developing nation's reduce their debts.

See March 10, 1989.

October 2, 1987

Japan ends plans to build a new fighter plane and agrees to buy the U.S. F-16 fighter modified as an "FSX."

Japan's Defense Minister Yuko Kurehare announced this decision after meeting in Washington with U.S. Defense Secretary Caspar Weinberger. Although Japan considered purchasing the McDonnell-Douglas F-15 on November 29, 1988, it announced that the General Dynamics F-16 would be used as the basis for the advanced fighter FSX, with Japan's Mitsubishi Corporation as the main contractor in a joint U.S.-Japanese project. In part, the FSX would improve submarine detection, which had been impaired by the Toshiba scandal. But a separate antisubmarine project was also to be set up at the U.S. naval base in Yokosuka, Japan. The formal accord on the joint U.S.-Japanese production of a new jet fighter was signed on November 29, 1988.

October 4, 1987

Salvadoran rebels begin peace talks with government representatives.

Following many preliminary proposals to act in accordance with the Arias Peace Plan, Salvadoran President José Napoleon Duarte and rebel delegates met from October 4 to 6 but disagreed regarding the withdrawal of foreign military advisers and left-wing participation in the government. They formed two commissions to negotiate peace but accomplished little in 1987, largely because of right-wing opposition. For example, Defense Minister, Hector Alejandro Gramajo rejected all talks with the rebels until they laid down their arms.

October 7, 1987

Guatemalan rebels and the government hold unsuccessful peace talks.

Acting in accord with the Arias Peace Plan (see August 7, 1987), Guatemalan President Marco Cerezo Arevalo met in Madrid, Spain, with members of the left-wing National Resistance Union. The Guatemalan conflict received less attention in the United States than Nicaragua's warfare because Guatemala's President Arevalo's armed forces avoided atrocities in their combat with left-wing rebels.

October 8, 1987

President Reagan obtains congressional agreement on arms sales to Saudi Arabia by withdrawing Maverick antitank missiles.

On May 29, President Reagan notified Congress of his intention to sell 1,600 Maverick missiles to the Saudis, but on June 11, he withdrew the offer because of congressional opposition. Events in the Persian Gulf and the Iranian violence at Mecca on July 31 made the U.S. Defense Department believe more than before that Saudi Arabia needed defensive weapons. Subsequently, the Reagan administration renewed overtures to Congress regarding the supply of advanced weapons to the Saudis. The compromise, which Reagan and Congress reached on October 8, permitted the administration to sell 12 F-15 fighter planes to the Saudis plus $1 billion worth of other arms. However, Reagan withdrew the Maverick missile offer because Israeli lobbyists did not want antitank missiles to reach Arab armies. War in the Middle East usually involved tank battles.

October 19, 1987

U.S. stock market crash occurs: the Dow Jones Industrial Average falls 508.32 points.

The market dropped 22.6 percent in one day, the largest single decline since 1914.

October 19, 1987

Secretary of State Shultz visits the Middle East without results for peace process.

U.S. policy sought an international conference on the Middle East that might move Israel and the Palestine Liberation Organization toward peace. Shultz had no success largely because Israeli Prime Minister Yitzhak Shamir opposed talks with the Palestinians.

October 19, 1987

U.S. destroyers bombard an Iranian oil rig after an Iranian missile strikes a U.S.-flagged tanker near Kuwait; President Reagan bans Iranian imports.

The Kuwaiti tanker flying the U.S. flag as the *Sea Isle City* was hit by an Iranian Silkworm missile on October 16. Eighteen U.S. crewmen were injured and the ship's captain, John Hunt, was blinded by glass fragments. President Reagan ordered a "measured response." On October 19, U.S. ships bombarded an offshore Iranian oil rig for 85 minutes. In retaliation, Iran fired a Silkworm missile at an offshore Kuwaiti oil terminal on October 22, seriously damaging the structure.

On October 8, U.S. helicopter gunships attacked four Iranian patrol boats that had allegedly fired on another U.S. helicopter. After capturing the gunboats, they found U.S. Stinger missiles in Iranian possession. The Stingers, which the United States supplied to rebels in Afghanistan and Angola, had reached the Iranians. On October 26, President Reagan used an executive order to ban all Iranian imports.

October 22, 1987

Following lengthy debate, the U.S. Senate asks President Reagan to report on Persian Gulf policy in 30 days.

Ever since President Reagan proposed reflagging Kuwaiti ships with U.S. flags on May 19, Congress had debated what action it should take to limit the president. At best, perhaps, Senate debate made the president cautious because he had begun reflagging on July 22, and neither house of Congress found a suitable way to restrict him. Democratic members of Congress preferred to invoke the War Powers Act, debating with Republicans and each other about its applicability to escort vessels. In the Senate, all efforts to vote on results dealing with the War Powers Act of 1973 were filibustered by the Republicans; after the United States attacked an Iranian oil rig on October 19, 1987, the filibuster stopped. A Senate compromise resolution regarding Reagan's unilateral decisions asked the administration to clarify its intentions in the gulf region in 30 days.

October 22, 1987

The Reagan administration acts against China for selling Iran missiles but defends the presence of Chinese forces in Tibet.

Because the Reagan administration alleged that China sold Silkworm missiles to Iran for use in the Persian Gulf, the United States prohibited the sale of high-technology products to China. Early in October, however, President Reagan had defended China for using force to suppress demonstrations in Tibet by Buddhist monks against the Chinese government. The U.S. Senate differed with Reagan, voting 98 to 0 on October 10 to condemn China for its conduct in Tibet.

November 5, 1987

Defense Secretary Caspar Weinberger resigns and is replaced by Frank Carlucci; Colin Powell becomes national security adviser.

Weinberger resigned because his wife had cancer. He pointed out that he did not object to the arms control treaty being finalized by the United States and the USSR. To replace Carlucci, who had been Reagan's national security adviser, President Reagan selected a Jamaican-born, naturalized citizen, Lt. General Colin L. Powell. Carlucci assumed office after Senate approval on November 20, 1986. Although Weinberger was often involved in conflicts with Congress, Carlucci, a pragmatic career official, knew how and when to compromise.

November 7, 1987

The prime minister of Tunisia removes President Habib Bourguiba from office.

Because Bourguiba was mentally incompetent, Prime Minister Ben Ali removed Bourguiba to avoid a civil war.

November 8, 1987

An Arab League meeting makes a major realignment of Arab states in the Middle East.

The session of 16 Arab heads of state and five other Arab state delegates condemned Iran for refusing to negotiate peace and backed Iraq in the gulf war. The moderate leaders wanted an international conference on the Middle East as a means to bring Israel and the Palestine Liberation Organization to negotiate peace.

November 16, 1987

Japanese Prime Minister Nakasone is replaced by Noboru Takeshita.

Yasuhiro Nakasone proposed a new sales tax, which the Japanese Diet defeated on May 12, 1987. Subsequently, on October 20, Nakasone selected Takeshita, a former finance minister, to become his successor. The Diet confirmed this action on November 16.

November 17, 1987

President Reagan and congressional leaders compromise on interpretations of the 1972 ABM treaty in relation to the SDI.

As experimental work proceeded on the Strategic Defense Initiative (SDI), the Reagan administration's proposal for a broad interpretation of the 1972 Anti-Ballistic Missile (ABM) treaty in order to test and partially deploy an SDI system was contested by congressional leaders as well as students of the 1972 treaty. Beginning with a letter to President Reagan on February 7, 1986, Senator Sam Nunn (D-Ga.), the chairman of the Senate Armed Services Committee, warned the president against a unilateral broadening of the 1972 ABM treaty. House speaker James Wright (D-Tex.) and other House leaders sent a similar letter, which emphasized that a broad interpretation would erode House support for SDI funds.

On May 13, President Reagan sent Congress two new studies by Abraham Sofaer, legal counsel of the Department of Defense, of the 1972 treaty. Sofaer had analyzed declassified records of the 1972 negotiations and of the U.S. Senate ratification hearings on the treaty. He concluded that the Soviets told negotiators that unknown devices on future technology should not be limited and that no Senate action or statement prevented the United States from testing future technology. This interpretation was immediately challenged by several arms control and international law specialists, including those in the Nixon administration who had negotiated the ban. John Rinelander, who had served as the

President meets with Secretary of Defense Frank Carlucci and National Security Adviser Lt. General Colin L. Powell. Ronald Reagan Library

legal adviser to the ABM treaty negotiations, complained that the reading of the treaty by the Regan administration was "absurd as a matter of policy, intent, and interpretation."

Neither Senator Nunn nor other congressional Democrats were convinced of the Sofaer interpretation. Nunn offered an amendment to the defense appropriations bill for 1988, which required the president to obtain congressional permission before conducting any SDI tests that might violate the strict interpretation of the 1972 treaty, a tactic that caused Senate Republican leaders to begin a four-month filibuster to prevent a vote on the Nunn Amendment. Because the 1988 fiscal year budget could not operate after October 1 without funding, Republican Senate minority leader Robert Dole (R-Kans.) stopped the filibuster, and on September 27, the Nunn Amendment passed by a 58-to-38 vote. President Reagan argued that such congressional action hampered negotiations with the Soviet Union and vowed to veto the final 1988 spending bill if the Nunn Amendment was retained. This led to a November 7 meeting between the president and congressional leaders during which a compromise was approved. In the final appropriations bill, the 1972 treaty was not mentioned. The bill prohibited the administration from purchasing any equipment for testing SDI that required a broad interpretation of existing arms control measures. Thus, Congress obtained some control over future SDI tests.

On December 13, Secretary of State Shultz told reporters that the Reagan administration would no longer push for a broad interpretation of the ABM treaty. It would instead seek specific funds from Congress whenever individual tests were proposed.

November 18, 1987

House and Senate committees on the Iran-Contra scandal release their final report.

Drawing on evidence and public hearings, the committees said they could not determine President Reagan's precise role in the decisions, partly because of the documents shredded by Lt. Colonel Oliver North. They concluded, however, "if the President did not know what his National Security Advisers were doing, he should have." The report criticized North, John Poindexter, and Robert McFarlane for subverting the nation's democratic process. The report said profits from the Iran sale were $16 million, but only about $3.8 million reached the Contras. The private funding network established to help the

Contras raised $10 million, but only $4.5 million was spent on the Contras.

November 20, 1987

President Reagan and congressional leaders agree on budget reduction tactics to cut the annual deficit.

Under the compromise achieved, a reduction of $30 billion would be made in 1988 and $46 billion in 1989. For 1988, military expenditures were cut $5 billion, and domestic spending, $6.6 billion. There would be a tax increase of about $9 billion by charging user fees for federal facilities, increasing corporate and individual taxes on the wealthy, and charging for Medicare insurance.

November 20, 1987

The United States and the Soviet Union agree to hold joint nuclear underground tests in 1988 to study test verification procedures.

This agreement resulted from talks between the two nations that began in Geneva on November 9. If verification methods for such tests could be agreed upon, it was expected that a comprehensive test ban treaty could be negotiated.

November 23, 1987

The United States pays $90 million to help resolve the U.N. budget crisis.

The U.N.'s inability to meet its staff payroll in December 1987 had been reported to President Reagan in a private letter from the secretary-general on October 26. The United States had paid only $10 million of its 1987 assessment, and, after having agreed to pay $90 million, it still owed $112 million. The United States also owed $147 million from 1986 and $61 million for U.N. peacekeeping forces in the Middle East. The United States and other nations had urged the United Nations to cut back its staff and other "exorbitant" expenditures but to no avail. Nations having small assessments benefited by voting to increase the budget. On December 21, 1987, the U.N. General Assembly approved a budget of $1.77 billion for 1988–1989. The United States, Japan, and Australia abstained from the vote to protest the high expenditures voted with insufficient revenues.

November 23, 1987

Two Salvadoran rebel leaders test peace possibilities.

Under previous plans, El Salvador's rebel leaders had hoped the Arias Peace Plan would work despite the opposition of right-wing groups. Following the October 4 negotiations, the rebels canceled scheduled talks because right-wing death squads assassinated human rights activist Herbert Anya Sanabria on October 26. On October 27, the Salvadoran National Assembly granted amnesty not only to leftist guerrillas but also to soldiers accused of murder, except those who killed Archbishop Oscar Romero in 1980. As to the archbishop's death, President Duarte on November 22, 1987, accused his right-wing political rival, Roberto d'Aubuisson, of ordering Captain Alvaro Rafael Saravia to kill Romero. Police arrested Saravia on November 24, 1988, but most observers believed d'Aubuisson would never be successfully prosecuted. Because of the amnesty, two leaders of the rebel Democratic Revolutionary Front returned to El Salvador. On November 21, the group's vice president, Rubén Zamora, returned. Two days later, its president, Guillermo Ungo, returned. They stayed only until December 2 because Duarte refused to negotiate with them.

November 25, 1987

The U.N. Security Council condemns South Africa for intervening in Angola to aid rebel forces.

South Africa sent armed forces into Angola on November 2 to help Jonas Savimbi's UNITA rebels. Savimbi launched an offensive against Angolan government forces on October 22 using U.S.-supplied TOW antitank missiles and Stinger antiaircraft missiles to win a large battle early in November. South Africa aided UNITA by diverting Cuban and Soviet forces that assisted Angola. The U.N. resolution condemning South Africa was significant because the United States did not veto the resolution. Nevertheless, South Africa ignored the resolution and refused to withdraw its troops from Angola on December 20, 1987.

November 28, 1987

Soviet-Afghan forces launch the largest military operation of the war.

While Soviet-Afghan military activities in 1983 had been designed to drive the people off the land, later this strategy changed to ensuring Kabul's control of the towns. There were several military campaigns designed to accomplish this objective. In August 1986, for example, combined Soviet and Afghan forces made a number of major incursions into Logar and, on May 20, 1987, they drove off guerrillas who had surrounded the garrison in Jaji in Paktia. They continued to meet with such heavy resistence in the area that less a month later they withdrew.

Starting on November 28, some 10,000 Soviet and 8,000 government forces undertook what has been called the largest operation of the war in Operation Magistral that was designed to lift the siege of Khost. On December 29, 1987, the combined assault finally opened the road to Khost from Gardez for supply convoys; however, at the end of January 1988, the Soviet forces protecting the road were withdrawn.

This campaigning in eastern and southern Afghanistan highlighted the inability of the Soviet-Afghan forces to hold the territory they won.

November 29, 1987

A national referendum in Poland on economic reforms disapproves the proposals.

In addition to releasing almost all political prisoners in 1986–1987, Poland's leader, Wojchiec Jaruzelski, wanted popular backing to enact stringent economic measures to improve the nation's economic performance. He failed, however, to get the backing of the Solidarity trade union, which asked its members to boycott the referendum. Poland needed the union's backing to enact economic reforms.

December 1, 1987

U.S. and British officials criticize France for making a deal with Iran to free French hostages.

Circumstantial evidence since November 27 seemed to indicate that France had made a deal with Iran. On November 27, two French hostages were freed by the pro-Iranian Revolutionary Justice Organization. On November 29, an Iranian terrorist, Wahid Gordji, was allowed to leave his haven at Iran's Paris embassy and fly to Tehran, where a French consul, Paul Torri, was released by Iran. Of course, after President Reagan's Iran-Contra disclosures, U.S. criticism was difficult to justify.

December 2, 1987

Nicaraguan Contras begin peace talks with the Sandinistas without success.

Following the signing of the Arias Peace Plan, Nicaragua took steps toward making peace with the Contra rebels, whom the United States backed. On October 1, the opposition newspaper *La Prensa* resumed publication, and the next day the Roman Catholic Church's radio station resumed broadcasting. (Both had been shut down in 1980.) On October 7, an amnesty for the Contras began, with Sandinista troops leaving 1,500 square miles of territory to Contra control. The Contra response, however, was to attack five towns on October 15. The December 2 talks in Santo Domingo, Dominican Republic, began only after the Sandinistas freed 985 political prisoners and 200 former members of former President Somoza's National Guard on November 22. Mediated by Nicaragua's Cardinal Miguel Obando y Bravo, the discussions lasted less than two days because the Sandinistas demanded that U.S. aid to the Contras stop before a cease-fire began.

Following reports that the Soviet Union agreed to supply Nicaragua with more armaments on December 13–14 and a brief Sandinista offensive and Contra counterattack on December 20–21, a two-day Christmas truce was accepted on December 22. Only gradually did the rebels and the government move toward a settlement.

December 8, 1987

President Reagan and Soviet leader Mikhail Gorbachev sign a treaty eliminating their nations' intermediate-range missiles: the 1987 INF treaty.

During a three-day Washington, D.C., summit meeting, Reagan and Gorbachev met in the East Room of the White House to sign the INF treaty, which resulted from six years of bilateral negotiations, finalized on November 24, when Secretary of State

George Shultz met with Soviet Foreign Minister Eduard Shevardnadze in Geneva. By the terms of the treaty, the two superpowers would destroy 2,611 intermediate-range missiles with flight ranges from 300 to 3,400 miles (500 to 5,000 kilometers). Principally, these would include U.S. Pershing II and ground-launched cruise missiles and Soviet SS-4s, SS-12s, SS-20s, and SS-23s. It excluded 72 West German–based short-range Pershing IA missiles.

A significant part of the treaty provided for detailed verification procedures by which each power could inspect the other's facilities. Over the next 13 years, both resident and short-notice on-site inspections would be conducted at 140 INF-related facilities in the two countries. On December 8, it was reported that Soviet inspectors would be located outside a Hercules Aerospace plant in Magna, Utah, where Pershing II and the MX strategic missile were assembled. This was one of nine sites in the United States and 12 sites in five NATO countries that the Soviets could inspect. U.S. inspection teams could visit 70 sites in the Soviet Union and seven sites in East Germany and Czechoslovakia.

On December 9, American reporters disclosed that a secret appendix to the treaty revised the previously publicized numbers of INF weapons that each side possessed. The United States had 429 Pershing IIs and ground-launched cruise missiles in Western Europe, not the previously cited 364. The Soviets had 470 deployed SS-4 and SS-20 missiles and 105 SS-4 and SS-20s that were not deployed, plus 387 deployed SS-12s and SS-23s, with another 506 undeployed missiles of these categories. President Reagan launched a campaign in favor of the INF treaty during a television speech on December 3. Referring to it as a historic treaty, he claimed that those who opposed it were either ignorant of advanced verification techniques or believed that a nuclear war was inevitable. Throughout his meetings with Gorbachev, Reagan would repeat the phrase "the wisdom in an old Russian proverb… *doveryai no proveryai.* Trust but verify."

Gorbachev also promoted the treaty. In a November 30 television interview, he called the INF treaty a step to more vital strategic long-range missile reduction treaties. He also admitted that the Soviet Union engaged in secret space-based missile defense research to counteract the U.S. Strategic Defense Initiative program (the "Star Wars" program). In order to meet with members of the U.S. Congress, Gorbachev entertained them at the Soviet embassy in Washington, D.C., on December 9 because right-wing Republicans had persuaded President Reagan not to schedule Gorbachev for an address to Congress, which would normally be the proper protocol. Democratic leaders wanted Gorbachev to speak in a joint session, but on November 19, 75 members, mostly Republicans, opposed this idea. Therefore, senators and representatives were invited to the Soviet embassy to talk with the Soviet leader about the INF and other matters. On December 11, 1987, NATO foreign ministers met in Brussels to support the INF treaty and urged the U.S. Senate to ratify it. (For treaty ratification, see May 26, 1988, and June 1, 1988.) Although Reagan and Gorbachev avoided comments about Soviet opposition to the SDI program, two post-summit announcements revealed the continued disagreement. On December 13, Secretary of State Shultz said the administration would not seek congressional approval for the "broad" interpretation of the 1972 ABM treaty but would seek funds for SDI tests on a case-by-case basis. On December 29, National Security Adviser Colin Powell said the Soviets had reserved the option of revoking strategic arms reduction proposals if the United States violated the 1972 ABM treaty by testing SDI in space.

December 9, 1987

The beginning of Palestinian protests known as the intifada begins in the West Bank and Gaza Strip, occupied by Israeli forces since 1967.

Tensions had steadily built up in the occupied territories not only because Israeli authorities mistreated Arab Palestinians but also because Israel supported and financed the growth of Jewish settlements in the occupied territory. Some Israelis advocated displacing all the Palestinians so that the Jewish state could possess its historic biblical lands of Judah and Samaria. The first protest by young Palestinians, who had spent their entire lives under the occupation authorities, soon grew and gained widespread sympathy as Israeli forces tried to subdue them. As rioting spread into Jerusalem on December 21, Palestinians living in Israel staged a one-day sympathy strike in favor of the Palestinian cause. On December 22, the U.N. Security Council passed a resolution deploring the handling of the protests by Israeli troops and police. The council vote was 14 to 0; the United States abstained rather than cast its usual veto on Israel's behalf. The State Department said the United States deplored the "excessive use of live ammunition" against innocent people who had no guns. The intifada demonstrations had just begun, however.

December 14, 1987

The United States accepts Israel as a major "non-NATO" ally.

U.S. Defense Secretary Frank Carlucci and Israeli Defense Minister Yitzhak Rabin signed a 10-year agreement giving Israel this special position—an agreement held previously only by Australia and Sweden. Under this arrangement, Israel could purchase certain U.S. advanced weapons systems and compete with American firms for U.S. defense contracts. President Reagan suggested this idea on February 18, 1987, when Israeli Prime Minister Yitzhak Shamir visited him at the White House.

December 14, 1987

Summit meeting of the Association of Southeast Asian Nations declares its region a nuclear-free zone and seeks peace in Cambodia.

This was only the third meeting of the leaders of ASEAN nations since 1967. The two main concerns on which the leaders agreed was to make Southeast Asia a nuclear-free zone of peace and neutrality and, second, to urge a settlement of the Cambodian conflict by having Vietnam withdraw its forces in favor of a negotiated peace. Because there were three competing groups in Cambodia, peace was difficult to obtain. On December 2, 1987, Prince Sihanouk, the former ruler and leader of one faction, met with Hun Sen, whom the Vietnamese had made prime minister of Cambodia. This meeting achieved no results because Sihanouk wanted Hun Sen to allow the third political group to be represented in negotiations. Hun Sen refused to talk with delegates from Pol Pot's Khmer Rouge because they had killed millions of Cambodians before Vietnam attacked in 1978.

December 16, 1987

Roh Tae Woo wins election as president of South Korea.

December 17, 1987

The U.S. Defense Department announces it has begun production of chemical weapons.

President Reagan decided that the United States should renew its chemical weapons production despite much opposition at home and abroad. The House of Representatives had delayed action on production of such weapons until October 1, 1987, when the president could renew production if he declared it to be in the interest of national security. On October 16, Reagan certified the need for the United States to begin producing binary gas weapons because no chemical weapons had been produced since 1969, and the Soviets held large quantities of lethal gas weapons. Inline with this, the Defense Department prepared to spend the $35 million authorized by Congress in producing binary artillery shells at a plant in Pine Bluff, Arkansas. The shells would hold only alcohol while in storage but could be used in battle after adding the organic chemical known as DF. When combined, these substances gave off lethal nerve gas. The Defense Department said it would begin production of Bigeye bombs and rockets early in 1990 as two other binary weapons.

December 18, 1987

President Reagan and Congress compromise on aid to the Nicaraguan Contra rebels.

The perennial issue of U.S. aid for the Contras arose again in 1987, lasting until a compromise was reached after Reagan threatened to veto the omnibus spending legislation if no Contra assistance was included. The Reagan administration wanted at least $9 million of military and nonlethal aid, while Speaker of the House James Wright (D-Tex.) argued that a cease-fire was near under the plan of Costa Rica's President Arias. On October 13, Arias won the Nobel Peace Prize for his efforts to settle the dispute, leading Wright to assert that a vote for aid would damage the process. On September 30, 1987, Reagan signed a stop-gap appropriation of $3.5 million in nonlethal aid to the Contras that maintained U.S. aid until a final bill for fiscal 1988 was approved. Subsequently, on December 18, Congress compromised with Reagan's demands, providing $8.1 million of nonlethal aid to operate until February 29, 1988, when the peace agreement was expected to be completed.

December 22, 1987

Congress passes the 1988 spending bill.

The deficit-reduction bill had been worked out during a November 20 conference between President Reagan and congressional leaders. This bill and the spending bill were both approved by Congress on December 22 and later signed by the president. The 1988 spending authorization was for $603.9 billion and included $270.5 billion for the military, $12.2 billion for foreign aid, and $7.7 billion for military construction.

December 26, 1987

Arab leaders in the gulf region meet to discuss the Iran-Iraq war and attacks on ships in the Persian Gulf.

The six-member nations of the Gulf Cooperative Council met in Riyadh, Saudi Arabia, whose King Fahd wanted to take strong action against Iran. However, because the United Arab Emirates and Oman feared antagonizing Iran, the only result was a weak statement by the council that urged the U.N. Security Council to levy sanctions against Iran for refusing to accept a cease-fire in the Iran-Iraq war.

1988

January 12, 1988

A Honduran official who had testified about compliance with the Arias Peace Plan is murdered.

Miguel Pavon of the Honduran Human Rights Commission had testified, just before his murder, to the International Verification Commission about the Honduran military's abuse of human rights. Pavon was the second witness to be killed. On January 5, Sergeant José Isaias Vilario was killed by four gunmen before he could testify to the commission. On November 1, the *Washington Post* reported that a Honduran army defector, Sergeant Fausto Reyes Caballero, disclosed that the Honduran military had murdered Pavon. The International Commission had been part of the Arias Peace Plan agreed to by Central American nations on August 7, 1987. When it met with a Central American summit on January 16, its report harshly criticized U.S.-backed regimes in Honduras and El Salvador, as well as the Nicaraguan rebels. Because the Reagan administration decided the commission was pro-Sandinista, it was dismissed in Washington and its report ignored.

January 15, 1988

Complying with a congressional restriction on aid to Pakistan, President Reagan exempts Pakistan from the Nuclear Non-Proliferation Treaty.

President Reagan issued this exemption because he said that ending aid to Pakistan would jeopardize U.S. national security.

February 11, 1988

Armenians in the Soviet Republic of Azerbaijan demonstrate to join the Armenian Republic.

Various nationalities in the Soviet Union began to demand autonomy after Soviet leader Mikhail Gorbachev broadened political participation. Armenians in the autonomous region of Nagorno- Karabakh in Soviet Azerbaijan became one of the first groups to seek changes, by demonstrating to become part of the Soviet Armenian Republic. Subsequently, both the Armenian and the Azerbaijani Republics agitated for greater autonomy. On February 27, Gorbachev persuaded the Armenians to suspend their demonstrations, but on February 28, members of the two ethnic groups rioted in the Caspian Sea town of Sumgait in Azerbaijan, leaving 32 Armenians dead. On March 26, Gorbachev sent troops to Armenia's capital, Yerevan, to prevent mass demonstrations of support for Armenians living in Nagorno-Karabakh.

February 17, 1988

An American army officer serving the United Nations in Lebanon is kidnapped by a pro-Iranian Shiite group.

Lt. Colonel William Richard Higgins was kidnapped in southern Lebanon, and two days later the

Organization of the Oppressed on Earth, a group linked to the pro-Iranian Hezbollah (Party of God), claimed responsibility. Higgins was a commander of a U.N. peacekeeping group; on July 31, 1989, the pro-Iranian Hezbollah released a video-tape showing they had hanged Higgins.

February 22, 1988

France and West Germany establish joint councils on defense and economics.

A step in Franco-German cooperation resulted from this agreement signed by French President François Mitterrand and West Germany Chancellor Helmut Kohl. Their agreement included a 2,000-man joint brigade to be stationed in Boblingen, West Germany. This was important to European defenses because France had terminated integration of its forces with NATO during the 1960s.

See February 6, 1966.

February 23, 1988

Balkan nations agree to foster better relations, but Turkey opposes making the region a nuclear-free zone.

An unusual meeting took place when the foreign ministers of Albania, Bulgaria, Greece, Romania, Turkey, and Yugoslavia met in Belgrade, Yugoslavia, to discuss ways to establish better relations. Bulgaria, in particular, promised to end mistreatment of its ethnic Turkish minority. Greece proposed an agreement to declare the Balkans a nuclear-free zone. Although Greece, like Turkey, was a member of NATO, Turkey's leaders opposed it because NATO and the United States objected to creating such zones without superpower agreements making them effective through nuclear arms control.

February 26, 1988

Romania relinquishes its most-favored-nation trade status with the United States because the United States criticizes its human rights record.

Romania announced it did not need U.S. special trade rights after Deputy Secretary of State John Whitehead visited Bucharest to explain to Romanian leader Nicolae Ceausescu why Romania should improve treatment of its ethnic Germans and Jews who wanted to emigrate. Ceausescu, Whitehead said, told him not to meddle in Romania's internal affairs. If Romania had not ended its special trade status, the United States might have taken such action because many members of the U.S. Congress opposed President Reagan's granting Romania special trade status.

March 2, 1988

A congressional attempt to close PLO offices in New York is opposed by U.N. groups.

On March 2, the U.S. Justice Department announced that the PLO had to leave its offices in New York by March 21, 1988, because of a congressional amendment to the 1988 budget bill passed on December 22, 1987. American Jewish groups had pressured legislators to close PLO offices in Washington and New York, and the congressional amendment required the U.S. Justice Department to do so despite State Department opposition.

The U.N. General Assembly voted its opposition on March 2 by a vote of 143 to 1; and the International Court of Justice gave an advisory opinion against the U.S. action on April 26, 1988. The issue reached a federal district court in New York City. On June 29, the court ruled that the Justice Department had no legal authority to close the PLO mission because the 1987 amendment violated the 1947 Headquarters Agreement ratified by the United States when U.N. headquarters were established in New York.

March 9, 1988

The United States lifts sanctions on high-technology goods to China.

On the final day of talks among China's Foreign Minister Wu Xuequian, President Reagan, and Secretary of State Shultz, the United States announced the lifting of sanctions on high-tech goods to China, which were imposed in October 1987, because the Chinese had sold Silkworm antiship missiles to Iran. The sanctions were lifted because China agreed to support a U.N. arms embargo against Iran if the U.N. Security Council approved it. The Chinese still sent some arms to Iran but claimed these fulfilled old contracts. China did not keep its agreement. On April 22, it vetoed a U.N. arms embargo resolution, claiming to do so because of U.S. clashes with Iran after a U.S. frigate was sunk.

March 16, 1988

After visiting Soviet Defense Minister Dmitry Yazov, U.S. Defense Secretary Frank Carlucci claims the Soviets have not changed defense force structures.

An important issue for U.S. national security policies relative to Soviet leader Mikhail Gorbachev's policy of *perestroika* (restructuring) was whether the Soviet armed forces had significantly shifted from offensive to defensive strategies in case of future war. Some U.S. military analysts had described the shift in Soviet policy between 1977 and 1986. Led by writings of Soviet Marshall Ogarkov, whose works Gorbachev preferred to the ideas of other Soviet military officials, the Soviet armed forces doctrine had concluded that a nuclear war could not be won and that high-technology conventional weapons were so destructive that the best doctrine would be defending the homeland rather than pursuing an offensive action if war began. Not unexpectedly, the U.S. Defense Department wanted definite proof of the Soviet changes before decreasing the U.S. defense budget. Thus, following talks with Yazov in Bern, Switzerland, Carlucci concluded that there was no evident change in Soviet policy.

Yazov and Carlucci met again from August 1 to 4, 1988, when Carlucci visited the USSR to inspect the Soviet's Blackjack bomber and other aircraft at the Kubinka Air Base near Moscow. This August meeting was preceded on July 6 to 11 by the visit to the United States of the Soviet Union's chief of staff, Sergey Akhromeyev. He met with President Reagan and also inspected the B-1 bomber and a U.S. aircraft carrier. These exchanges of high-level U.S. and USSR defense officials set a new precedent, allowing each side to inspect the other's advanced weapons.

March 23, 1988

Nicaragua and the Contra rebels sign the Sapoa truce.

Meeting at Sapoa, Nicaragua, representatives of the Sandinista government and the Contra rebel leader Adolfo Calero Portocarreo signed a cease-fire and provisions for a return to normal civilian life. Under a 60-day truce, Contra forces would move to special zones, and the Sandinistas would grant amnesty to former army officers of the former dictator Anastasio Somoza Debayle. A national dialogue on reconciliation would begin with "unrestricted freedom of expression," humanitarian aid to the Contras, and the release of political prisoners.

Although Congress had been divided on providing aid to the Contras requested by Reagan, the House and Senate changed their view after Contra leader Calero reached a cease-fire agreement with the Sandanista rebels. The House and Senate approved aid for the Contras on March 30 and Reagan signed the bill on April 1, 1988.

See July 11, 1988.

March 23, 1988

On the SDI's fifth birthday, ground is broken for its National Test Facility (NTF).

The NTF would be the coordinating point for regional facilities doing research on the Strategic Defense Initiative (SDI). On March 14, President Reagan told a conference on SDI that the United States was moving toward its goal to make SDI a "truly comprehensive defense." He said, "as it becomes ready, we will deploy it." To achieve this technology required a major breakthrough to make space defense viable. During their 1987 meeting, President Reagan and Soviet leader Mikhail Gorbachev agreed to observe the 1972 ABM treaty while continuing research on antiballistic missile defenses. Despite Reagan's vision of a comprehensive defense, most advocates of SDI believed it would be primarily a defense for U.S. ICBM missiles, not the entire nation.

April 13, 1988

China's National People's Congress concludes a three-week session during which more economic reforms are passed.

Although the sessions were notable for reelecting Deng Xiaoping to his office of chairman of the Central Military Commission and confirming Li Peng as premier, the Communist Party's call for continued economic reforms was the highlight of the congress. During the remainder of 1988, the government undertook several significant reforms. On May 15, it moved toward a market economy by ending price controls on eggs, pork, vegetables, and sugar in Beijing and Shanghai. Price controls were removed from cigarettes and alcohol on July 25. On August 17, the Communist Party's Politburo approved a five-year plan to liberalize price controls on many other products. Because of the inflation resulting from the end of price controls, the government retreated a bit on September 26. Party General Secretary Zhao Ziyang gave orders to freeze prices on some consumer goods and to reduce investments in fixed assets. He said these steps were essential because inflation was running as high as 50 percent. One other notable economic change in China took place on March 22, 1988, when the government began receiving foreign bids for long-term land-use leases in Shanghai, the first time the Communist Chinese had permitted foreigners to lease Chinese land.

April 14, 1988

Geneva accords are signed for Soviet troop withdrawal from Afghanistan.

On April 7, 1988, Soviet General Secretary Gorbachev met with the Afghan Communist Party's General Secretary Najibullah (Najib) in Tashkent. According to Soviet documents in the April 2004 *Cold War International History Project's Bulletin*, Gorbachev told Najib he could expect Soviet aid in reconstructing Afghanistan's economy if Najib carried out a policy for national reconciliation for all Afghan factions including Pakistani exiles. Najib noted several Afghan Politburo members were unwilling to join a reconciliation project, but he hoped they would change their minds when they learned the Geneva Accords required Soviets troops to begin withdrawing from Afghanistan.

Following lengthy Geneva negotiations, the United States, the Soviet Union, Pakistan, and Afghanistan signed agreements providing for Soviet forces to leave Afghanistan between May 15, 1988, and February 15, 1989. Two other separate agreements were signed. First, Pakistan and Afghanistan agreed not to interfere in each other's affairs and to repatriate Afghan refugees from the conflict. Second, the United States and the USSR agreed not to interfere in the signatories' internal affairs and to act as guarantors of the agreements. The crucial decision making the Geneva accords possible was announced on February 8, 1988, when Soviet leader Mikhail Gorbachev said that Soviet troops would follow the withdrawal of the May 15-February 15 timetable if the Geneva settlement were reached. Gorbachev also accepted terms on which the United States had insisted—a major pullout should be at the beginning and that the withdrawal should not depend on keeping a pro-Soviet regime in power in Kabul.

May 8, 1988

French president François Mitterrand wins reelection.

Gaining 54 percent of the national votes, the Socialist Party's Mitterrand defeated Jacques Chirac, who had been French Premier after his center-right coalition parties gained control of parliament in 1986.

May 11, 1988

After a failed Midgetman test, funding for it ends in January 1992.

After the failure of Midgetman's first test on May 11, the Reagan administration asked Congress to stop funding the missile because the Department of Defense wanted those funds for the SDI and MX ICBM programs. Despite Reagan's request, the Democratic majority in Congress restored $250 million for additional research and development of the Midgetman—an amount that was never spent. After Reagan signed the 1987 Intermediate Range Missile (INF) Treaty (see December 8, 1987) and George H.W. Bush signed START I Treaty with the Soviet Union (see July 31, 1991) all the Midgetman funds were eliminated from the Department of Defense budget for fiscal year 1993 with the approval of Congress.

May 11, 1988

Polish parliament grants government emergency powers to resolve strikes.

About two months after Poland's government undertook austerity measures to raise prices and devalue the currency to promote a Western-style market economy, demonstrations and strikes disrupted many Polish cities. When transportation workers in Bydgoszcz struck on April 25, the government quickly raised their salaries by 63 percent. But when steelworkers at Nowa Huta began a strike for better pay on April 26 and shipyard workers at Gdansk went on strike, the government could not fulfill their demands. By May 13, police and demonstrators had fought in 15 cities. Riot police ended the strikes by May 11, and the next day parliament gave Communist Party First Secretary Wojciech Jaruzelski more authority to try to solve the economic problems.

May 12, 1988

Vietnam appeals for aid because of a food shortage leaving 3 million near starvation.

Vietnam's appeal for help was correlated with its efforts to improve international relations by beginning to withdraw its armed forces from Cambodia and releasing data on more Americans missing in action during the Vietnam War. Nevertheless, Vietnam had acute food shortages since 1987 because drought, typhoons, and insect infestations had reduced the rice crop by over 1 million tons. On June 25, the United Nations announced it would send Vietnam $9.1 million of food to offset its shortages.

May 25, 1988

Libyan leader Mu'ammar al-Gadhafi recognizes Chad's government; peace results.

Having agreed to a cease-fire between Chad's rebels and Chad's government, Gadhafi avoided further conflict in Chad by dropping his support of the rebels and recognizing the government of Habré, which French forces and the United States had supported. On October 3, 1988, the two nations reestablished formal diplomatic relations.

May 26, 1988

The Senate places a binding condition on approving the 1987 INF treaty.

During Senate hearings on the Intermediate Nuclear Forces Treaty (see December 8, 1987), several Democratic senators raised questions about future treaty interpretations because the Reagan administration had altered interpretations of the 1972 ABM treaty to justify experiments with the SDI program (see November 17, 1987). Initially in February 1988, Senators Sam Nunn (D-Ga.) and Robert C. Byrd (D-W. Va.) asked Secretary of State Shultz to make all administration testimony to the Senate on the treaty legally binding for future interpretations. On February 9, Shultz gave the Senate qualified support for their concerns about testimony. Some senators were satisfied but Senator Joseph Biden (D-Del.) proposed a "binding condition" should be passed to assert the Senate's constitutional power of treaty interpretations. Although Biden became ill in April and was absent from Senate discussions, Senator Robert C. Byrd proposed a modified form of Biden's amendment that the Senate passed on May 26. Byrd's amendment stated the "binding condition" only referred to the 1987 INF treaty. If questions arose about which the Senate and the president could not reach agreement, the president could make that interpretation. On May 29, the Byrd amendment was included when the Senate approved the treaty by a vote of 93 to 5.

May 27, 1988

Stinger antiaircraft missiles that President Reagan gave Afghan's rebels reach many countries.

While various sources reported Stingers had been sold by U.S.-supplied rebels, a *London Times* article provided details of Afghan guerrillas (mujahideen) selling them at $300,000 each. These shoulder-fired antiaircraft weapons provided by the United States to rebels in Angola and Afghanistan were much desired. Their sale to U.S. enemies was first confirmed when the U.S. navy discovered some on Iranian gunboats on October 19, 1987. Subsequently, on December 3, 1987, the U.S. Senate sought to ban Stinger sales to Persian Gulf nations but President Reagan insisted on selling 70 to Bahrain to defend against Iranian aircraft. On March 31, 1988, the *Los Angeles Times* reported Qatar purchased Stingers from Iran and Afghan rebels sold 33 to Iran plus 10 more to drug smugglers in Central America. Stingers in the hands of drug lords meant Reagan's clandestine aid had come full circle to damage his "war on drugs" program at home.

June 1, 1988

President Reagan and Soviet leader Mikhail Gorbachev sign documents of ratification for 1987 Intermediate Range Nuclear Forces Treaty.

Gorbachev showed eagerness to fulfill terms of the INF treaty of 1987 on February 27, 1988, when the Soviets began dismantling 30 SS-12 medium-range

Reagan and Gorbachev sign the INF treaty eliminating intermediate range missiles. Ronald Reagan Library

missile bases in Waren and Bischofswerda, East Germany. On March 2 and 3, NATO leaders met in Brussels to approve the INF treaty and discuss upgrading the American-made Lance tactical missiles in West Germany. There was no agreement on the Lance because some NATO members believed they were obsolete. The U.S. Senate approved the treaty on May 29, acting two days before President Reagan met with Gorbachev. Reagan visited Moscow from May 29 to June 2 and signed INF documents of ratification on June 1. Although Reagan spoke out against Soviet human rights violations, most of his visit was pleasant. He strolled with Gorbachev in Red Square, addressed students at Moscow University, and signed nine other agreements on arms control, student exchanges, nuclear power research, maritime rescues, fisheries, transportation, and radio navigation.

June 7, 1988

Secretary of State George Shultz makes no progress on Middle East peace plan despite four months of effort.

Beginning on February 25, 1988, Shultz proposed to hold elections to give autonomy to Palestinians in the occupied territories. This would be followed by peace talks between Israel and its Arab neighbors to decide territorial matters. On June 7, after his last stop in Cairo to see Egyptian President Hosni Mubarak, Shultz gave up. He said that everyone liked what he was trying to do but that no one would clearly back his plan or any other.

June 14, 1988

Canada expels eight Soviet diplomats for spying to obtain advanced technology.

Canada claimed the Soviets tried to steal secrets from a Montreal defense contractor, Paramax Electronics, a subsidiary of the U.S. UNISYS corporation. The USSR denied the charges and retaliated by expelling two Canadian diplomats and denying reentry to three others.

June 21, 1988

Annual "Group of Seven" economic summit ends in Toronto after reaffirming existing policies.

These annual meetings enabled the leaders of the United States, Britain, France, West Germany, Japan, Canada, and Italy to demonstrate their cooperation even though few policy changes resulted. At the end of this summit, the leaders reaffirmed the need for a stable U.S. dollar, for expanded East-West trade, and for continued reductions in the nuclear arsenals of the two superpowers.

July 3, 1988

U.S. navy ship in Persian Gulf shoots down Iranian passenger liner, killing 209 persons.

Iran Airlines Flight 655 had just left the coastal city of Bandar Abbas to fly across the Strait of Hormuz to Dubai in the United Arab Emirates, when the cruiser USS *Vincennes* destroyed it with a heat-seeking surface-to-air missile. There were no survivors; the victims included 66 children, 16 crew members, and citizens of several different nations. On December 2, 1988, the International Civil Aviation Organization's team of experts blamed the U.S. navy for poor planning. Not only was the crew unprepared for battle, but the navy's ships, unlike the ships of other nations, did not bother to monitor civil aviation flights. Moreover, Flight 655 was in the center of the known commercial airway and was ascending. (When a Pan Am airliner exploded later on December 21, 1988, pro-Iranian terrorists said it was revenge for Flight 655.) After Iran sought compensation in a suit filed against the United States at the World Court on May 17, 1989, the U.S. State Department offered to pay families of the victims. Five nations of the victims accepted, but Iran did not drop its suit.

July 4, 1988

A general strike in Soviet Armenia requires Soviet troops to intervene.

Since February, Armenians in the Armenian Soviet republic and in the Nagorno-Karabakh region of the neighboring Soviet republic of Azerbaijan had developed more antagonism toward the Azerbaijanis and the Soviet government (see February 11, 1988). On June 15, the Supreme Soviet of the Armenian Republic passed a resolution urging the reunification of Nagorno-Karabakh with Armenia. After the strike began on July 4, some 400 protesters clashed with Soviet troops at the Yerevan airport, and the legislature of Nagorno-Karabakh voted to secede from Azerbaijan. Sporadic violence continued while Soviet soldiers attempted to keep order. On December 7, 1988, an earthquake diverted attention in Armenia to other difficulties because it leveled two Armenian towns and killed an estimated 25,000 people.

July 8, 1988

Great Britain sells Saudi Arabia $12 million to $30 billion of modern armaments.

In 1987 and again in April 1988, the U.S. Congress opposed President Reagan's request to sell arms to Saudi Arabia because of pressure from pro-Israeli lobbyists. Thus in 1988, the Saudis purchased missiles from China and France, but the largest Middle East arms purchase to date was the British sale announced by the Saudis on July 8. One Saudi official said his country preferred U.S. armaments but was "not going to pay billions of dollars to be insulted." President Reagan called the deal a blow to U.S. political and economic interests. The Saudis had decided to make Great Britain their main arms supplier for the next decade. The sale included 50 Tornado jet fighters, 50 Hawk jet trainers, over 80 helicopters, six mine-hunting ships, and the construction of two new air bases. This deal saved thousands of British jobs. The purchase from China was for intermediate-range (1,000 to 2,000 miles) missiles using conventional warheads; the French sold the Saudis helicopters armed with Exocet missiles as well as fast patrol boats. After the Chinese sale, Israel threatened a preemptive strike against the Saudis, however, both the United States and Egypt warned Israel against such a move. On July 7, the U.S. Senate blocked Reagan's request to sell Kuwait $1.9 billion of arms because it included Maverick air-to-ground missiles. Kuwait purchased $300 million of armored carriers from the Soviet Union on July 9 and said it would ask Britain for other weapons it wished to purchase.

July 11, 1988

Nicaragua expels U.S. ambassador, claiming he incited rebellion.

The Sandinistas' decision to expel U.S. Ambassador Richard Melton and seven other U.S. diplomats came after a protest march of 3,000 people in Nicaragua became violent. The government asserted that Ambassador Melton and his colleagues incited the violence, hoping it would renew the Contra rebellion against President Ortega. On July 13, Melton, a senior administration official who had become ambassador in May 1988, wanted opposition groups to gain greater freedom under terms of the cease-fire and the Arias Peace Plan of 1987.

See July 19, 1988.

July 13, 1988

For the third time, Vietnam returns remains of Americans missing in action (MIA) from Vietnam War.

The Vietnamese returned to U.S. officials the remains of 25 MIA service personnel. This followed the return of 17 remains on March 2 and 27 more on April 6. The remains of 23 MIA were returned on November 3 and those of 38 MIA on December 15. As usual, American officials came to Noi Boi airport in Hanoi to receive these remains.

July 19, 1988

As Nicaraguan Contras come under right-wing control, seven commanders resign and others form new organizations.

While Nicaragua's Sandinista government moved toward political changes to extend the cease-fire and resolve conflict with Contra rebels, Contra leaders directing rebel operations from Miami, Florida, had internal disputes. The CIA backed Valerie Enrique Bermudez, whose hard-line attitude caused tension and prevented a peaceful settlement. Subsequently,

Bermudes promoted his candidacy for the directorate, and on July 18 a meeting of the Contras' National Resistance Assembly elected Bermudes after voting Pedro Chamorro out of office.

A wider split now developed in the Contra organization. On July 19, seven Contra field commanders on the "southern front" near Costa Rica resigned from the National Resistance because of Bermudes's election. Later, on October 14, Alfredo César, another opponent of Bermudes, formed the Democratic Center Coalition. Made up of three Nicaraguan political factions, César's group advocated political, not military, confrontation with the Sandinistas. César said the right-wing tactics of the National Resistance failed to bring peace, and on November 8 he sought new peace talks with the Sandinistas.

See October 14, 1988.

July 25, 1988

Cambodian opposition groups meet in Indonesia after Vietnam begins troop withdrawals from Cambodia.

Because Vietnam began withdrawing troops from his country early in 1988, Cambodian Premier Hun Sen agreed to meet with leaders of three rebel groups to decide on a future government. Although the four factions agreed to a four-party "national reconciliation council" to arrange free elections, the three rebel groups disagreed with Hun's demand that his regime be allowed to rule until elections.

The second problem involved a timetable for all Vietnamese troops to leave. This was assigned between Soviet and Chinese representatives from August 28 to September 2 but they could not agree. Despite disagreement on Cambodia's final form of government, Vietnam began withdrawing its forces as early as February 1988. On February 23, a Japanese news agency reported that Vietnam pledged to withdraw all of its 125,000 troops from Cambodia by 1990. Other sources said Vietnam had withdrawn another 40,000 of its troops from Laos by early 1988.

July 31, 1988

Jordan relinquishes claims to the West Bank in favor of the Palestine Liberation Organization.

Before Israeli troops occupied the West Bank of the Jordan River and Jerusalem in 1967, Jordan made claims to that area. King Hussein now surrendered all Jordanian claims, announcing that he would end Jordan's legal and administrative ties to the Israeli-occupied lands. On August 4, the PLO said it would maintain its responsibility as sole legitimate representatives of the Palestinians.

August 8, 1988

While Secretary of State Shultz visits Bolivia, a bomb explodes near his car.

While on a tour of several South American nations, Shultz was traveling in a car from the La Paz airport to town when a bomb, set off by remote control, exploded alongside his limousine. His special security car suffered no real damage and no one was hurt. Although Bolivia had difficulty shutting down coca farms, the United States helped fund its effort to combat the cocaine industry.

August 14, 1988

Soviet troop withdrawals from Afghanistan meet interim goals.

As required by the Geneva accords, the Soviet Union withdrew 100,000 of its troops by August. The U.N. Good Offices Mission monitoring the withdrawal reported that one-half of the Soviets' "limited contingent" was withdrawn on schedule. Despite the Soviet withdrawal, leaders of Afghanistan's mujahideen rebels said they would continue fighting because they were not represented at Geneva and the Kabul government of the Communist-backed President Mohammad Najibullah remained in control. Almost immediately, the rebels captured two provincial capitals, Qalat and Mohammad Agha. The rebels' early success did not last because disputes ensued between rival guerrilla factions. In addition, the Soviet Union attempted to make the rebels accept peace terms. (See December 3, 1988) In Kabul, President Najibullah tried to broaden his power base by naming Muhammad Hapsan Sharq as prime minister. He also convened the first Afghan parliament since 1973, but no rebel leaders attended. Najibullah's difficulties with the mujahideen rebels multiplied.

See December 3, 1988.

August 17, 1988

Pakistani President Zia ul-Haq and the U.S. ambassador to Pakistan are killed when their plane crashes.

Exploding just minutes after leaving Bahawalpur airport for Rawalpindi, the transport plane carrying President Zia ul-Haq, U.S. Ambassador Arnold Raphel, and 28 other U.S. and Pakistani officials crashed, killing everyone aboard. The chairman of the Pakistani Senate, Ghulam Ishaq Khan, became acting president and promised to carry out the mandate of the November elections. On October 16, a Pakistani military board reported that the crash was a "criminal act of sabotage" but did not accuse anyone or explain how it happened.

August 19, 1988

North and South Korean delegates begin unification talks.

These talks between the two Koreas were inspired by student demonstrations in both regions. The demonstrations in the south had been especially large since May 15, when a South Korean student jumped to his death from a Seoul building to dramatize his desire for unification while blaming the United States for blocking that goal. Subsequently, persistent student protest marches, ranging in size from 25,000 to 100,000 demonstrators, on 78 university campuses in South Korea caused thousands of injuries and arrests, which the government wanted to avoid because of the forthcoming Olympic Games in September. As late as August 14, students had to be prevented from marching north to the 38th parallel to meet North Korean students who advocated unity. In this atmosphere, the unity talks took place from August 19 to August 26 at Panmunjom, a village on the border between North and South. Although North Korea's delegates withdrew their demand that U.S. forces leave South Korea before meaningful talks could begin, the two sides soon became stalemated regarding the process and goal of unification talks, and their sessions ended on August 26. On December 28, prime ministers of the two Koreas agreed on talks, but they were canceled on March 2, 1989. South Korea conducted the 24th Summer Olympic Games in Seoul from September 17 to October 2 without serious incident.

August 20, 1988

Iran and Iraq officially begin a cease-fire, but peace talks face problems.

A cease-fire ending the eight-year Iran-Iraq war was negotiated by U.N. Secretary-General Pérez de Cuellar. Even though fighting had been intensive since February 1988, Pérez de Cuellar persuaded Iran's Ayatollah Khomeini to reverse earlier demands that Iraqi President Saddam Hussein resign. On July 19, Khomeini said the decision to stop fighting was "more deadly than taking poison," but he accepted U.N. resolution 598. Iraq now grew reluctant, saying that it wanted peace talks as well as a cease-fire. This was agreed upon, and on August 8, Pérez de Cuellar announced the August 20 cease-fire agreement, with peace talks to start on August 25. The peace talks became stymied over the future possession of the river Shatt al Arab, which Iraq wanted to control when it first invaded Iran in 1980. The cease-fire returned the Shatt al Arab to its status under the 1975 Algiers convention, which divided the waterway between the two nations. Iran and France had restored diplomatic relations on June 16, 1988. Britain resumed diplomatic relations on September 30.

August 24, 1988

Turkey admits Kurdish refugees who allege Iraq used chemical weapons.

As the Iran-Iraq war moved to a cease-fire on August 20, Iraq attacked Kurdish tribes on its northern border because Iran had incited them to rebel during the war. Iraqi President Saddam Hussein wanted to punish the Kurds, and as early as March 15, Kurds claimed that up to 4,000 people had died from poison gas when Iraq's army destroyed the village of Halabja. Iran flew 30 Kurd victims to several hospitals in Europe and a New York hospital for treatment as evidence of Iraq's use of chemical weapons. On August 23, the U.N. team reported that Iraq had used mustard gas principally, but also cyanide and Tabun nerve gas. The next day, Turkey said 100,000 Kurdish refugees had flocked across its border, but later reports said only one-half that number had fled. On March 29, 1989, the *New York Times* reported that while several hundred returned, and some went to Iran, 36,000 Kurds remained in Turkey, living in tents.

Since 1983, the Reagan administration had played down Iraq's use of chemical weapons. Congress, however, proposed sanctions against Iraq. On September 9, 1988, the Senate voted unanimously to levy economic penalties on Iraq, and on September 27, the House of Representatives passed a similar but weaker resolution. President Reagan approved these measures and strong White House lobbying prevented final passage before Congress adjourned on October 22. Reagan continued to believe Saddam Hussein could be a moderating influence whom the United States could manipulate. Reagan's successor, George H.W. Bush, followed a similar policy until Iraq invaded Kuwait on August 1, 1990.

August 31, 1988

ABM review talks end in disagreement.

The success of future arms control agreements between the Soviet Union and the United States seemed to depend on the settlement of disputes about the U.S. Strategic Defense Initiative (SDI) program and its connection with the 1972 ABM treaty. The Soviet Union wanted to limit the SDI and objected to the Reagan administration's broad interpretation of the 1972 treaty. On August 8, 1988, President Reagan agreed to abide by the narrow interpretation of the treaty while new reviews of the agreement took place. From August 24 to August 31, 1988, negotiations between United States and Soviet delegates failed to produce agreement on the proper interpretation of the 1972 ABM Treaty.

Following President Ronald Reagan's announcement of SDI in 1983 (see March 23, 1983), the Reagan administration reviewed the status of the ABM Treaty and decided a broad interpretation of the treaty would permit the development and deployment of an "exotic" space-based missile defense system. Reagan's broad interpretation contrasted significantly with previous interpretations by the administrations of Presidents Richard Nixon, Gerald Ford, and Jimmy Carter. Congressional leaders such as Senator Sam Nunn questioned the validity of Reagan's broad interpretation of the ABM Treaty, as did General Secretary of the Soviet Union Mikhail Gorbachev (see November 17, 1987). In 1987, Gorbachev agreed to separate the issue of the ABM Treaty's interpretation from negotiations on the Intermediate Nuclear Forces (INF) Treaty that was signed in 1987 (see December 8, 1987) and the strategic arms reduction talks (START). Nevertheless, during the August 31 ABM review conference, U.S. delegates continued to insist that the broad interpretation of the ABM treaty was valid and that the SDI program could develop and deploy an effective antimissile system that could be used to destroy Soviet ICBMs in space.

Yet, five years after Reagan's 1983 speech, the SDI program had not developed an effective missile defense system. In addition to reaffirming their differences on the 1972 ABM treaty's interpretation, the 1988 conference delegates discussed the Reagan administration's claim that the Soviet Union's Krasnoyarsk radar station violated the 1972 ABM Treaty. The Soviet delegates denied the radar station violated the treaty but offered to dismantle the radar station if the United States accepted the narrow interpretation of the 1972 ABM Treaty. The American delegates not only refused this offer because it might prevent tests and deployment of any SDI system under development, but also stated that neither the START negotiations nor other arms control agreements would be signed until the Soviets dismantled the Krasnoyarsk radar station. Subsequently, the ABM interpretation issue stalled START negotiations until September 1989, when the Soviets agreed to dismantle their radar station.

August 31, 1988

Polish Solidarity leader Lech Walesa ends strikes, bringing changes in the government.

In April, May, and August, Poland suffered waves of demonstrations and strikes by coal miners, dock workers, and Gdansk shipyard workers seeking better wages and the legalization of Solidarity as the workers' union. Finally, on August 31, after Walesa met with Interior Minister Czeslaw Kiszizak, they agreed to negotiate. Solidarity called an end to strikes, and by September 19, a parliamentary investigation criticized the government's economic policy. A new premier, Mieczyslaw Rakowski, was appointed on September 27, but he proved to be disappointing. Rakowski shut down the Gdansk shipyard because it lost $3.5 million in 1987. Another nationwide strike was averted only when new talks began between the government and Solidarity delegates on November 17, 1988.

September 13, 1988

A major policy change for the Reagan administration: U.S. dues to the United Nations to be fully paid.

Reagan began displaying an appreciation of the U.N.'s role that conservatives generally disdained. Thus, when the White House announced that it would make full payments on upcoming U.N. budgets as well as make up the $467 million the United States already owed, it was a significant policy change. The United Nations had made an effort to decrease its often extravagant budget.

Also, Secretary of State Shultz persuaded Reagan that the United Nations played a vital role in U.S. global diplomacy. In particular, U.N. officials cooperated with Washington in solving problems in the cease-fire between Iran and Iraq, the Afghanistan cease-fire, and the Namibia-Angola problems. There were still U.S. areas of disagreement with UNESCO and other agencies, but generally the Reagan advisers saw its salutary role as worthy of support and agreed to help it finance operations.

September 14, 1988

American and Soviet scientists monitor underground nuclear tests in Kazakhstan.

In accordance with a November 20, 1987, agreement, U.S. and Soviet experts monitored two underground nuclear explosions, one on August 17 in Nevada, the other on September 14 in Kazakhstan. Intended to permit the calibration of instruments for verification purposes, both the Soviet seismic method and the American Corrtex measuring system were used. In both 1988 experiments, the seismic system proved superior.

The U.S. experts were especially embarrassed after their Corrtex system measured 163 kilotons at the Nevada tests, making the test exceed the 150-kiloton limit, which was the agreed upon testing limit. The Soviets' seismic system measured it more accurately at 140 kilotons. According to Western analysts, the less effective Corrtex system was one reason that the United States previously complained about Soviet violations, which Moscow denied.

September 23, 1988

Secretary of State Shultz and Soviet Foreign Minister Shevardnadze fail to break strategic arms talks deadlock but express concerns on chemical weapons.

In December 1987, when the intermediate-range missiles reduction treaty (INF) was signed, Moscow and Washington had hoped to conclude a strategic arms reduction treaty (START). By September, however, talks became stymied over divergent proposals by each side. Although Shultz and Shevardnadze did not resolve the issues, they said they had made some progress. Later, Shultz told reporters that START was unlikely to be completed before the November 1988 elections. Shultz and Shevardnadze did take another step toward abolishing chemical weapons. The United States had previously listed the sites where it produced chemical weapons, and the Soviets said they would prepare a list of their own sites. Shultz also agreed to disclose the current size of the U.S. chemical arsenal.

September 28, 1988

Spain and the United States sign an eight-year agreement for military bases after the United States moves 72 aircraft to Italy.

During more than two years of negotiations for U.S. military basing rights in Spain to replace an agreement due to expire May 14, 1988, the two key issues were Spain's desire to close the base at Torrejon, near Madrid, and whether U.S. naval ships should be allowed to visit Spanish ports if they carried nuclear missiles. The first question was resolved on January 15, when the United States agreed to remove 72 F-16 fighter-bombers from Torrejon. Italy agreed to base the planes in its southern city of Crotone to protect NATO's southern flank. The Italian parliament approved this move on June 30, 1988. Regarding the visits of U.S. ships, Spain agreed not to inspect them when they made calls at their ports, even though antinuclear advocates in Spain wished to prevent visits by nuclear missile-carrying ships. One additional change in the new agreement required no U.S. economic or military aid to be paid to Spain. The usual practice had been to require compensation, but as a member of NATO, Spain waived such payments.

September 29, 1988

President Reagan signs a $299.5 billion defense authorization bill that Defense Secretary Carlucci planned with Congress.

Although on August 3, the president vetoed a defense bill authorizing $299.5 billion, Defense Secretary Frank Carlucci and Congress adjusted the funding to increase allowances for the MX missile and the

Strategic Defense Initiative as desired by Reagan. The MX received $600 million and the "Star Wars" program $4.1 billion. The Reagan administration's defense expenses escalated between 1981 and 1988 while outlays for other international programs decreased.

October 5, 1988

Chileans oust President Pinochet.

Augusto Pinochet had ruled Chile since the overthrow of President Allende Gossens in 1973. An October 5 plebiscite went against Pinochet by a vote of 54.7 percent to 43 percent.

October 14, 1988

President Reagan ends an attempt to get $16.3 million of military funds for the Nicaraguan Contras.

The Contras had received no military aid from the United States since 1985, and most observers, including pro-Contra Assistant Secretary of State Elliott Abrams, believed the Contra military effort had ended. On November 8, Abrams said a "post-Contra era" had begun. In December, President-elect George H.W. Bush indicated that he would emphasize diplomatic methods to end the Nicaraguan civil war.

October 17, 1988

The Philippines extend rights to U.S. military bases through 1991.

Since the overthrow of President Ferdinand Marcos on February 25, 1986, the outcome of the issues regarding U.S. bases had been uncertain because some Philippine nationalists wanted the Americans to leave. On October 17, an interim agreement to extend U.S. use of the base at Subic Bay and Clark Air Base for three years was signed in Washington by Secretary of State George Shultz and Philippine Foreign Minister Raul Manglapus. In this agreement, the United States gave the Philippines $500 million in export credits through 1991, as well as $481 million in military and economic aid in 1990 and 1991. Philippine President Corazon Aquino needed U.S. support because her government faced threats from the left and the right.

November 8, 1988

George H.W. Bush is elected president, defeating Massachusetts Governor Michael Dukakis.

Bush and his running mate, Senator Dan Quayle (R-Ind.), defeated Dukakis and Senator Lloyd Bentsen (D-Tex.).

November 8, 1988

Kosovo Protests oppose policies of Serb Republic's President Slobodan Milosevic.

The United States had given financial aid to Yugoslavia after General Secretary of the Yugoslav Communist Party Marshall Tito (Josip Broz) broke with General Secretary of the Soviet Union Joseph V. Stalin (see November 14, 1951). In 1982, the Reagan administration sopught to cut off all financial aid to Yugoslavia after Yugoslav leaders declared martial law in the Serb Republic's autonomous province of Kosovo following violent and bloody student. Yet, as Susan Woodward's *Balkan Tragedy* claims, the International Monetary Fund, an organization using some U.S. money, gave

George H.W. Bush. National Archives

financial aid to Yugoslavia until 1987. Most historians attribute Yugoslavia's demise to Serbian President Slobodan Milosevic, who gained control of the Republic of Serbia in 1987 by raising the banner of Serbian nationalism. By the end of 1987, he had gained control of Serbia's Communist Party and the government of the Serb Republic. The Kosovo protests eventually led to U.S. and NATO attacks on the Serb Republic in 1999.

November 22, 1988

Australia and the United States agree on maintaining U.S. intelligence bases in Australia for the next 10 years.

This pact renewed existing agreements but gave Australian personnel a greater role in base operations and full knowledge of the facilities related to the nation's interests and sovereignty. One base, at Pine Gap in the north, helped monitor arms control agreements; the other, at Nurrungar in the south, was a ground station for U.S. satellites in the defense support program.

November 25, 1988

America's Watch gives Guatemala and El Salvador low marks for violation of human rights.

The activities of El Salvador's right-wing death squads received more publicity in the United States than did the more subtle tactics used by Guatemala's President Marco Cerezo and his military leaders in punishing political dissenters.

December 1, 1988

Benazir Bhutto becomes Pakistan's first woman prime minister.

General elections had been held on November 16, but the assembly did not meet and elect Bhutto until December 1.

December 2, 1988

President Reagan reports to Congress that Moscow complies with the 1987 INF treaty, except for a few technicalities.

In his annual report to Congress on Soviet compliance with arms control treaties, Reagan cited five minor violations of the intermediate-range nuclear missile treaty of 1987. Overall, the Soviets complied, having destroyed 80 of their 654 SS-20s and removed all their shorter-range missiles and launchers to sites for their destruction.

December 3, 1988

Soviet delegates meet with Afghan rebels in Saudi Arabia to seek peace in Afghanistan.

To secure a more broadly based Afghan government following Soviet troop withdrawals, Soviet Deputy Foreign Minister Yuli Vorontsov headed a delegation to Taif, Saudi Arabia, to meet with Afghan rebels. The Soviets urged the rebels to participate in a new Afghan government but also wanted to guarantee safe passage for the withdrawing Soviet forces. The rebels promised not to attack major cities until the Soviets had departed.

December 6, 1988

During a U.N. address Mikhail Gorbachev indicates he will reduce Soviet forces by 500,000 men.

Soviet leader Gorbachev said Soviet forces in the USSR and Eastern Europe would be cut by 10,000 tanks, 8,500 artillery pieces, and 800 combat planes by 1991. He claimed that the USSR's military doctrine followed a strictly defensive stance. Gorbachev's U.N. address was the first by a Soviet leader since Premier Nikita Khrushchev spoke in 1960. He stated: "Today, we face a different world" from that in 1917 (the era of the Russian Revolution) and there must be a "consensus as we move forward into a new world order." Western analysts estimated that the troop cutback for Eastern Europe represented about 500,000 troops. Gorbachev also said he would withdraw four of the 57 divisions on the Sino-Soviet border and pledged a broadening of human rights in the Soviet Union. Gorbachev visited New York City from December 6 to 8, meeting with President Ronald Reagan and President-elect George Bush. The State Department said this was not a summit but a symbolic "passing of the torch" from Reagan to Bush. Gorbachev planned to visit Cuba and Great Britain on his way home, but a massive earthquake in Soviet Armenia on December 8 caused him to fly directly back to Moscow.

December 13, 1988

Angola, Cuba, and South Africa agree on Namibian independence and Cuba's withdrawal from Angola.

At a meeting in Brazzaville, Congo, the three previous competitors signed the prologue to a protocol that allowed for Namibia's transition to independence from South Africa and for Cuba to withdraw its 50,000 troops gradually from Angola. Half of the 50,000 would leave by November 1, 1989; another 25,000 would move north from Namibia's border. The final 25,000 would leave by July 1991, although Angola had to resolve its civil strife with Jonas Savimbi's rebel group, UNITA. South Africa agreed to reduce its forces in Namibia from 60,000 to 1,500 by July 1989. The United Nations would supervise elections in Namibia on November 1, 1989, after which all South African forces would leave.

The one problem in Namibia was to persuade the rebel group, the South-West African People's Organization (SWAPO), to accept these terms. Namibia's plans succeeded in 1989, while Angola had to contend with the rebel forces of UNITA, led by Jonas Savimbi, to whom the United States continued to give military aid. Namibia held elections from November 7 to 11, 1989, and SWAPO, led by Sam Nujoma, won 41 of 72 seats for the constituent assembly. Savimbi agreed to a truce with Angolan President Jose Eduardo dos Santos, effective June 23, 1989. However, fighting broke out again on August 23, and dos Santos blamed the United States for urging Savimbi to fight. The Bush administration had decided to continue arming Savimbi until peace was finalized. After meeting with President Bush on October 5, 1989, Savimbi agreed to another cease-fire.

December 14, 1988

PLO leader Arafat recognizes Israel's right to exist, and the United States begins discussions with PLO.

The Reagan administration's decision to begin a dialogue with the PLO followed an intricate series of maneuvers leading Arafat to accept U.N. resolutions 242 and 338, which recognized Israel's right to exist as a state. In addition, he denounced terrorism and accepted U.N. resolutions 242 and 338. Within hours, the State Department agreed to "diplomatic dialogue" with the PLO and on December 16 designated U.S. Ambassador to Tunisia Roberto Pelletreau as its liaison. Talks began but reached no quick resolution of the problem because Israel refused to talk with the PLO.

December 21, 1988

A terrorist bomb explodes on Pan American Boeing 747 flying over Scotland, killing 259 people on board and 11 people on the ground.

Following this explosion, a pro-Iranian terrorist group called news media and disclosed that it had planted the bomb to avenge the Iranian passenger plane shot down by a U.S. warship on July 3. An extensive investigation of the crash began with preliminary evidence showing that the bomb may have been placed aboard the plane at its originating point in Frankfurt, West Germany. A sophisticated bombing device, probably made by a terrorist in Syria and smuggled to West Germany, triggered the explosion by a timing device that relied on barometric pressure to set it off as the plane rose to a higher altitude following its stop in London. The plane was *en route* across the Atlantic to New York.

December 21, 1988

The U.N. General Assembly streamlines 1988 and 1989 budgets after the United States takes steps to pay back dues.

During the General Assembly sessions that began on September 20, the organization drew up a budget that cut excess staff and reduced expenses. Previous budgets for 1988 and 1989 were revised to meet the U.N. goal of cutting waste in the budget. In conjunction with this U.N. action, President Reagan ordered the release of the U.S. dues of $44 million owed to the United Nations. They had been held in escrow. He also ordered the State Department to draw up a schedule to pay the organization $520 million of past dues owed by the United States.

December 21, 1988

President Reagan reveals the United States is investigating a possible chemical arms plant in Libya.

As early as September 14, 1988, the U.S. Department of State found evidence that Libya was on the verge of producing chemical weapons at a chemical plant being constructed near Rabat, Libya, by West Germany's Imhausen-Chemil's chemical firm. When West German Chancellor Helmut Kohl visited Washington on November 15, 1988, Secretary of State George Shultz and National Security Adviser General Colin Powell briefed Kohl on the evidence involving Imhausen-Chemil. Early in 1989, West Germany's Imhausen-Chemical firm stopped its construction of Libya's chemical plant and withdrew its personnel from Libya.

December 22, 1988

Soviets consider closing naval operations at Cam Ranh Bay.

Following a meeting in Manila with Soviet Foreign Minister Eduard Shevardnadze, Foreign Minister Manglapus told reporters that the Soviet Union was considering closing its naval base at Cam Ranh Bay in Vietnam. U.S. authorities cited the Soviet base as proof the Soviets increased its Pacific Ocean naval power, an act to justify U.S. Philippine bases.

See October 17, 1988.

1989

January 4, 1989

U.S. fighter planes shoot down two Libyan aircraft.

On January 4, two U.S. F-14 combat aircraft were patrolling the northern part of the Gulf of Sidra, which the United States considered part of the Mediterranean Sea, when two Libyan fighter MiG-23s appeared, "armed and hostile," and were shot down by the American pilots. Although Libya claimed its aircraft were unarmed, the U.S. Defense Department released some film on January 5 that showed that the Libyan Mi Gs had, in fact, been armed.

January 6, 1989

Cambodia's president indicates Vietnamese forces will leave by September if a peace agreement is reached.

Vietnam had begun its troop withdrawal in 1988, but Hanoi awaited plans for a new Cambodian government to end the civil war. Cambodian President Heng Samrin wanted to encourage truce discussions by making his January 6 announcement. On July 6, 1989, an important step was made when U.S. Secretary of State James Baker supported talks between Heng's government and Prince Norodom Sihanouk, who represented the opposition. Previously, Washington refused to recognize the Cambodian regime backed by Vietnam.

January 7, 1989

Delegates from 149 nations reaffirm Geneva protocol against chemical weapons.

French President François Mitterrand called this meeting to revive a 10-year U.N. effort to gain agreement on curbing or abolishing all chemical weapons. The Geneva Protocol of 1925 was an agreement not to use these weapons, but it did not ban their production or stockpiling. At this Paris meeting all nations present agreed not to use chemical weapons, but some raised qualifications. U.S. Secretary of State George Shultz failed in his attempts to stop the export of chemical weapons technology, such as that which Libya had recently obtained from West Germany. In addition, an attempt by Arab delegates to ban nuclear as well as chemical weapons was not accepted. Many Third World nations argued that poison gas was the "poor man's atomic bomb," but the superpowers rejected this comparison.

During the meeting, Soviet Foreign Minister Eduard Shevardnadze announced the USSR would unilaterally destroy its chemical stockpile of 50,000 tons and urged others to do so. Although the United States claimed the Soviets had 200,000 tons, a revised 1990 CIA study suggested the Soviet total was indeed 50,000. Under President George H.W. Bush, the United States produced binary nerve gas weapons until June 1, 1990, when Bush and Soviet leader Gorbachev agreed to stop production of chemical weapons, and awaited its ratification. Thus, the January 1989 Paris meeting did not yet end chemical weapon production.

January 15, 1989

The Soviet Union reports its last troops have left Afghanistan.

While the United States gave military assistance to the Afghan rebels, the Soviets continued to aid the Afghan government. When President George H.W. Bush took office in 1989, he insisted that Afghanistan President Najibullah and his aides go into exile before supervised elections chose a new government. The Soviet Union rejected this position and fighting in Afghanistan continued between rebels and government forces.

Since agreeing to withdraw its forces, the Soviet Union kept its fixed timetable. Kabul government attempts to negotiate with the rebels had not been successful and the United States continued supplying rebels even though they failed to unite. During a January 10 meeting in Islamabad, Pakistan, negotiations were suspended due to disputes between Pakistan-based and Iran-based rebels.

After their troops withdrew, Moscow placed Soviet military casualties during the intervention at 13,833 killed (62 percent under 20 years of age), 49,985 wounded, and 404,414 cases of sickness. Afghan combat and noncombat losses were at best estimates: 876,825 killed and 1,500,000 wounded. About six million Afghan refugees fled to Pakistan and Iran. See William Maley, *The Afghanistan Wars* (2002).

January 15, 1989

Police use water cannons to disperse protest demonstrations in Czechoslovakia led by Václav Hável.

Havel was the leader of Charter 77 that formed in 1977 following the signing by Czechoslovakia and 34 other nations (including the United States) of the Helsinki Accords (see August 1, 1975). Charter 77 members accused the government of discrimination in education, employment, and violation of human rights cited in the Helsinki Accords. Throughout the 1980s, the Stalinist old guard Communists led by Gustav Husak harassed or arrested many Charter 77 members. When Gorbachev instituted reform (*perestroika*) polices in the Soviet Union, Charter 77 rallied other Czechs to demonstrate against Milos Jakes who had replaced Husack in 1987. Following a series of small protests in December 1988, Charter 77 called for massive demonstrations in January 1989 in Prague to celebrate the 20th anniversary of a student's suicide in protest against the August 1968 Soviet-led Warsaw Pact invasion of Czechoslovakia (see August 20, 1968). The January protests continued for six days with Havel and about 400 protesters being arrested by the police. Havel was sentenced to eight months in prison but other demonstrations persuaded the government to release him in May 1989.

During the January protests, the Soviet's General Secretary Gorbachev was attending meetings in Moscow, including a January 20 session with Moscow's City Party Committee. Apparently, Gorbachev was misinformed about the events in Prague. On January 20, *Pravda*, the Communist's official newspaper simply reported data from Czechoslovakia's press agency CTK whose report claimed the demonstrations were undermining "the incipient process of democratization." Of course, Jakes Stalinist hard-liners were the ones who undermined Czech democracy, and the Czech protests heralded 1989 as the year during which the Czechs and other Warsaw Pact nations moved to end their Communist regimes and promote democratic reforms. Gorbachev began the process of making these nations independent by gradually withdrawing Soviet troops from Czechoslovakia and other Eastern European nations.

See April 25, 1989.

January 15, 1989

Thirty-five nations approve comprehensive agreement on human rights in Europe and North America.

The third follow-up meeting to the Helsinki Accords of 1975 began on November 4, 1986, in Vienna and concluded on January 15. The first sessions in Helsinki and the second sessions in Madrid prepared the way for specific agreements on all forms of human rights and government performance to respect them. In the 79-page agreement, provisions were made to continue meetings on confidence and security-building measures among all European states and negotiations to reduce conventional armed forces between the NATO and Warsaw Pact alliances.

January 19, 1989

President Reagan permits U.S. oil companies to resume business in Libya but still blames Libya for supporting terrorism.

Reagan permitted five U.S. oil companies to resume business to prevent Libya from nationalizing them and to stop Libyan leader Mu'ammar al-Gadhafi from receiving the oil profits. Reagan's orders permitted the U.S. managers to operate, sell, or transfer ownership of the companies.

On January 18, the State Department reported that Libya continued to assist terrorists. According to the report, since the U.S. air raid of April 15, 1986, Libya had supported an average of one terrorist attack each month and was linked to attacks on U.S. information libraries in Colombia, Peru, and Costa Rica, using Panama as a base.

January 20, 1989

George H.W. Bush is inaugurated as the 41st president of the United States.

Unlike President Reagan, whose first inaugural of 1981 shared headlines with Iran's release of American hostages, Bush faced domestic economic problems, the waning of the Cold War, and decisions about Soviet leader Mikhail Gorbachev's policies of *glasnost* and *perestroika*, that sought, among other things, cooperation between East and West.

January 27–29, 1989

Delegates at a Moscow conference reveal that U.S. President Kennedy made concessions to the Soviets during the Cuban missile crisis of 1962.

The Moscow conference was one in a series of meetings featuring the 1962 crisis participants and scholars to record and analyze their statements at the time. American officials participating in the crisis initially met at Hawk's Cay, Florida, in January 1987. They also joined three Soviet participants at a Cambridge, Massachusetts, session in October 1987. Because the Cold War was winding down, the January 1989 conference in Moscow included Americans, Russians, and a Cuban delegation.

The meeting was especially revealing by disclosing that President John F. Kennedy took a more flexible position with Soviet Premier Nikita Khrushchev than traditional accounts had claimed. On October 27, 1962, Kennedy offered concessions to Krushchev with a definite pledge to withdraw U.S. nuclear missiles from Turkey in exchange for the withdrawal of Soviet missiles from Cuba. Although scholars previously hinted at Kennedy's willingness to compromise, The odore Sorensen told the Moscow delegates that he deleted Kennedy's promise to remove the Turkish missiles when editing Robert Kennedy's memoir of *October's Thirteen Days*, published in 1969. Robert had promised the president would withdraw the Turkish missiles during an October 27 meeting with Soviet Ambassador Anatoly Dobrynin. The Soviet ambassador agreed the promise would be kept secret for fear of the reaction of the NATO allies of the United States and to avoid exposing President Kennedy to domestic political criticism in a congressional election year.

In addition to meetings at Hawk's Cay, Cambridge, and Moscow, Havana, Cuba, sponsored a conference in January 1992. At Havana, the Soviets revealed that contrary to CIA estimates in October 1962, they had 35 nuclear warheads in Cuba between October 16 and 28, 1962, which could be used if the United States tried to invade Cuba. These sessions were supplemented with declassified documents by the United States, the Soviets, and Cuba that provided other details about the 1962 Cuban missile crisis. These conferences stimulated a renewed interest in the missile crisis. See Lester H. Brune, *The Cuba-Caribbean Missile Crisis of October 1962* (1996).

February 6, 1989

The Polish government agrees to hold talks with opposition leaders.

The Polish government inaugurated talks with opposition groups to negotiate political and economic reforms. An agreement was reached during a January 27 meeting among government representatives, leaders of the Roman Catholic Church, and Solidarity trade union leader Lech Walesa.

February 23, 1989

The United States approves formation of rebel government in Afghanistan.

The Afghan exile government in Pakistan consisted of seven rebel leaders who elected moderate Sibghatullah Mojaddidi president and radical Muslim Abdul Rasul Sayaf premier. In February, President Bush rejected Soviet leader Mikhail Gorbachev's offer to embargo arms shipments to Afghanistan because he claimed the Soviets left stockpiles of arms for Afghanistan's pro-Soviet government when they withdrew on January 15, 1989.

February 25, 1989

Soviet troops disperse demonstrators in the Soviet Republic of Georgia.

In Tbilisi, Georgia, 15,000 people led by the National Democratic Party staged protests against the Soviet

Union on the anniversary of Georgia's annexation by the Soviets in 1921. To quell protests, Soviet police arrested over 500 dissidents. Between April 9 and April 14, 1989, Soviet soldiers killed 20 demonstrators and arrested many more before forcing Georgia's Communist Party leader to resign. He was replaced on April 14 with Georgia's KGB chief, Givi Gumbaridzhe.

February 27, 1989

President Bush attends burial services for Japanese Emperor Hirohito and visits China and Korea.

Bush began a week's visit to East Asia by joining 700 foreign dignitaries for burial ceremonies for Emperor Hirohito, who died on January 7. Hirohito's position was filled by Crown Prince Akihito. Following the ceremonies, Bush visited China and South Korea.

In China, Bush received assurances that Soviet leader Mikhail Gorbachev's forthcoming visit to Beijing would not result in a new Sino-Soviet alliance. Bush's visit was marred by China's refusal to allow the dissident Fang Lizhi to attend a banquet hosted by Bush. In Seoul, Bush urged South Korea's National Assembly to promote a free-market economy by ending its protectionist trade policies.

March 10, 1989

The United States seeks to reduce debts of developing countries and nations adopting free-market reforms.

U.S. Treasury Secretary Nicholas F. Brady suggested a plan under which international financiers would reduce debts of developing countries and the IMF/World Bank would aid debt reductions in countries adopting free-market reforms and austerity policies comparable to the Reagan program introduced in the 1980s.

March 11, 1989

The United States and Israel announce a peace plan to moderate intifada uprising.

Hoping to bring peace to its occupied territories on the West Bank and in Gaza, Israel agreed to stop detaining and deporting Palestinians in the territories and to reduce its troops in Palestinian areas. At the same time, the United States urged Yasser Arafat's PLO to moderate the intifada uprising and stop PLO raids from south Lebanon into Israel. On March 15, Israel also encouraged peace by returning Taba beach to Egypt, a part of the Sinai retained by Israel under the 1979 agreement.

March 17, 1989

The Senate approves Bush's foreign policy team.

President Bush's national security team was completed when the Senate approved Richard Cheney as secretary of defense. The Senate had previously approved James A. Baker and Brent Scrowcroft as secretary of state and national security adviser, respectively.

March 20, 1989

The State Department says U.S. relations with El Salvador require its new government to respect human rights and democracy.

Because El Salvador's March 19 elections had problems with dissidents protesting El Salvador's human rights violations, the United States said future diplomatic relations depended on the newly elected President Alfredo Cristiani's policy on human rights. On February 3, 1989, U.S. Vice President J. Danforth (Dan) Quayle visited Salvador to emphasize U.S. concerns for human rights and to urge the FMLN and other parties to participate in the elections. After the FMLN refused, the civil war continued between the rebels and the government despite additional cease-fire negotiations in Mexico City on September 7 and in Costa Rica beginning on October 16.

President Bush with his major foreign policy adviser, Brent Scowcroft, and R. John Sununu. George Bush Presidential Library

March 23, 1989

Serbia employs illegal terms to claim Kosovo's assembly approved amendments to Serbia's constitution. This marks the beginning of the breakup of the Communist state.

Kosovo and Vojvodina were two autonomous provinces within the Serb Republic as established by the Federated Republic of Yugoslavia's 1974 constitution. Under this constitution, six of the eight seats on the Yugoslav Presidency were occupied by one delegate from each of the six Yugoslav Republics: Serbia, Slovenia, Croatia, Bosnia-Herzegovina, Montenegro, and Macedonia plus two seats of one representative from Kosovo Province and one from Vojvodina Province. In October 1988, Milosoevic had no problem in getting Montenegro and Vojvodina to accept his nominees for the presidency but he had problems in Kosovo. First he had the Serb Republic's assembly approve constitutional amendments giving the Serbs control of Kosovo's courts and police but he still had to get Kosovo's assembly to accept the Serb's constitutional amendments. On March 23, Kosovo's Assembly met in a building surrounded by Serbian troops while other Serb official mingled with the delegates to discover how they voted. When the vote of the amendments was completed, a majority but not the required two-thirds of assembly members approved the amendments. Despite lacking the required of two-thirds vote, Milosevic said a majority was sufficient, an illegal step that the Yugoslav troops prevented Kosovars from protesting further. Thus by the end of March 1989, Milosevic had gained control of four seats on Yugoslavia's eight-member presidency. By April 1989, Milosevic was on the way to completing his dream of a Greater Serbia, but leaders of Croatia, Slovenia, and Bosnia-Herzegovina waged a war against Serbia to prevent him from obtaining a Greater Serbia. For details see Lester H. Brune, *Kosovo Intervention and United States Policy* (2000).

March 26, 1989

Multicandidate elections in Soviet Union result in mixed results for Communist Party candidates.

First Secretary of the Communist Party Mikhail Gorbachev decided to call for multiparty election in March 1989, as another step toward his program to democratize the Soviet Union's shift to a civil society. As defined by the Communist Party's Central Committee, the March elections would choose members for a new Soviet Congress of People's Deputies as a parliament to meet twice a year. Of the 2,250 members being elected for the Congress of People's Deputies, 1,500 would represent people from all of the Soviet republics. The Communist Party's Central Committee selected the other 750 members during its January 10, 1989 meeting in Moscow.

In the March 26 elections, Communist Party members won 1,200 of the 1,500 at large seats in the Congress of People's Deputies. Of the remaining seats in Congress, 300 represented various parties scattered throughout the Soviet Union and, of course, the Central Committee's candidates made up the remaining 750 members, giving a total of 2,250 delegates to the Congress of People's Deputies. Notably, Leningrad's Communist Party chief, Yury F. Solovyev, lost in the election because 130,000 voters used their right to cross out Solovyev's name on the ballot while only 110,000 people voted for Solovyev. Boris Yeltsin chose to run for one of Moscow's seats, correctly believing he could win because of his popularity among Muscovities.

April 25, 1989

The Soviet Union's troops begin pulling out of Eastern Europe.

On April 25, the Kremlin announced 1,000 battle tanks had been withdrawn from Hungary as part of the Soviet program to withdraw 10,000 tanks and 56,000 personnel carriers from Eastern Europe. By May 5, it also withdrew 1,000 tanks from East Germany. During 1990 and 1992, the Soviets gradually withdrew remaining troops and military equipment from Eastern Europe. The withdrawal was completed in January 1992, after Gorbachev resigned as the Soviet's General Secretary on December 25, 1991.

See July 7, 1989.

April 30, 1989

President Bush thanks Iran for releasing U.S. hostages held in Lebanon.

President Bush thanked Iran for assisting the release of Frank Reed, who had been held hostage in Lebanon by the Iran-backed Hezbollah since 1986. The first information that Iran would assist in the hostage release came on February 22, when a Tehran *Times* editorial urged Lebanese Muslim groups to release its hostages. Subsequently, on April 22, both Reed and Robert Pohill were released by Islamic Jihad. Pohill was an American University of Beirut professor captured in January 1987. Bush indicated there was no deal with Iran for the hostage release.

May 4, 1989

Hungary dismantles fence on border with Austria.

Since October 18, 1988, when Hungary adopted a constitution guaranteeing human rights, its government moved toward democracy. Now, a significant change of policy for Eastern Europe came when Hungary's government ordered troops to dismantle barbed wire fencing that separated the country from Austria. This opened the "iron curtain" that had been dividing Europe since the late 1940s.

May 4, 1989

Oliver North is found guilty of obstructing Congress in the Iran-Contra affair.

A U.S. federal court found Oliver North guilty of obstructing the congressional investigation of the Iran-Contra affair, which arose under President Reagan. In January 1989, Special Prosecutor Lawrence Walsh dropped the more serious charge of U.S. Marine Colonel Oliver North's illegally diverting $14 million to Nicaragua's Contra rebels because the Reagan administration refused to declassify materials Walsh requested that might prove North guilty.

Despite the scandal involving the Nicaraguan Contras during the 1980s, President Bush sought and received $49.9 million in "non-lethal" aid for the Contras, who were trying to overthrow the socialist regime of Daniel Ortega, even though Nicaragua was working with the United Nations to plan for democratic elections in 1990.

May 11, 1989

The United States sends more troops to Panama following a fraudulent election.

President Bush sent an additional 2,000 U.S. troops to Panama to bolster the 12,000 U.S. army personnel already there after a fraudulent election renewed the power of Panama's military leader, General Manuel Antonio Noriega. International observers overseeing the May 7 elections claimed that the Democratic Alliance's candidate, Guillermo Endara, won by a margin of 3-to-1 before government troops raided the vote-counting centers and Noriega's candidate, Carlos Duque, claimed victory. Because violence erupted after popular demonstrations Bush denounced the elections and sent more U.S. forces to Panama.

May 13, 1989

The United States and Iran settle small claims from the 1979 Iranian Revolution.

The United States and Iran signed an agreement to settle 2,000 small claims that resulted from the 1979 Iranian Revolution. The U.S. claims went to the Claims Tribunal of the International Court of Justice in The Hague. Iran agreed to pay the United States $105 million as a settlement.

May 25, 1989

The Soviet Congress of People's Deputies elects a new Supreme Soviet with Mikhail Gorbachev as president.

The 2,250 members of the Congress of People's Deputies elected in March convened its first session in Moscow on May 25 (see March 26, 1989). During the two-week session of the People's Deputies, some delegates made unprecedented public criticism of Soviet Chairman Mikhail Gorbachev, the Soviet Communist Party, and the KGB's secret service operations. Before adjourning on June 9, the People's Deputies elected a new Supreme Soviet with 542 members as a standing legislature and elected Gorbachev as the Supreme Soviet's President. In the People's Deputies election, Gorbachev gained 95 percent of the votes with some hard-line Communists casting blank ballots because they opposed Gorbachev's reform program. The blank ballots made the deputies' votes more democratic than the automatic 100 percent votes of the old Supreme Soviet but, as Garthoff indicates in *The Great Transition*, a "long step" away from a popular democratic vote for the presidency. The People's Deputies also elected Nikolai I. Ryzhkovas prime minister of the new Supreme Soviet.

May 29–30, 1989

NATO accepts U.S. proposals to reduce Europe's short-range missiles and U.S.-USSR conventional forces.

After Secretary of State James Baker visited European allies and Moscow, he realized the issue of conventional forces in Europe (CFE) was closely linked to short-range nuclear missile forces (SNF) that were not part of the 1987 intermediate-range nuclear forces (INF) treaty. On March 5, Baker was in Vienna when the negotiations on CFE began. The CFE talks involved members of NATO and the Warsaw Pact seeking to determine how many combat aircraft, tanks, armored personnel carriers, and artillery each side should retain for "purely defensive purposes." After the first round of CFE talks failed to reach an agreement, Baker returned to Washington where he persuaded President Bush to link CFE with SNF during NATO's May 29–30 sessions.

To prepare for future CFE negotiations, President Bush and other NATO leaders held a summit to develop a strategy for future talks with the Warsaw Pact. An immediate NATO concern was NATO plans to deploy America's newest Lance missiles in Germany. Although Chancellor Helmut Kohl had opposed deploying the new missiles in West Germany, he finally accepted a U.S. proposal for "partial reductions" in NATO's SNF as well as a 20 percent reduction of U.S. and Soviet troops in Europe. The 20 percent would be an initial CFE reduction for CFE negotiators' consideration. Any remaining U.S. Lance missiles in West Germany would be pulled out after the CFE agreement was finalized.

June 3–4, 1989

Chinese troops kill hundreds of protesters in Tiananmen Square; U.S.-Chinese relations strained.

U.S. relations with China were severely tested after hundreds of Chinese demonstrators were killed in the "Tiananmen massacres." Protests against Chinese police who killed four bicyclists brought thousands of Chinese to Beijing's Tiananmen Square on June 3, where army troops and tanks assaulted the protesters, killing hundreds and wounding many more.

Student demonstrations had begun on April 15 following the death of Communist Party leader Hu Yaobang, who was considered a party reformer. Protests grew during the days leading to Hu's burial on April 22, and students presented their grievances to Premier Li Peng that included demands for more democratic politics and punishment of corrupt Communist Party officials. The students accepted the party's authority because Premier Li promised to continue Hu's reforms. Zhao Ziyang, who replaced Hu as party leader, was sympathetic to the students' reform proposals but other party leaders, including Deng Xiaoping—China's actual ruler—opposed political changes.

On May 15, Soviet Communist Party First Secretary Mikhail Gorbachev visited Beijing, and with television cameras and other world media reporting the visit, Chinese students publicized their cause by staging a hunger strike at Tiananmen Square. After Gorbachev departed, Deng dealt harshly with the students, declaring martial law and bringing in local army troops. The troops fraternized with demonstrators and many army officers signed a student letter against using violence to disperse demonstrators.

By June 3, these local troops had not cleared the square of protesters and Premier Li brought army units from outside Beijing to replace them. The new units led an assault to disperse the protesters, which took place after midnight on June 3 when foreign television cameras and reporters quickly transmitted the bloody events by satellite around the world, sending pictures of soldiers bayoneting civilians. During the next month, Deng continued persecuting dissidents and purged the party of all prodemocracy members, including party General Secretary Zhao Ziyang. The government executed seven dissidents in Beijing, 17 in Janin, and three in Shanghai.

June 5, 1989

President Bush responds to Tiananmen massacres with stringent measures.

In response to the Tiananmen massacres, President Bush took punitive actions, short of severing relations, to demonstrate U.S. disapproval of China's tactics. On June 5, he announced sanctions against China suspending all military sales and high-level contacts and asking the IMF and World Bank to postpone Chinese loan applications. He also declared that the U.S. embassy in Beijing was correct in giving refuge to Chinese dissident Fang Lizhi and his wife.

At the same time, Bush arranged secret meetings of U.S. officials with the Chinese to prevent the complete breakdown of diplomatic and trade relations.

June 5, 1989

President Bush and Pakistani Prime Minister Bhutto discuss Afghanistan.

President Bush met with Prime Minister Benazir Bhutto to discuss methods of achieving peace in Afghanistan as rebel factions continued a civil war there. In Washington, Bhutto also spoke before a joint session of Congress to assure its members that Pakistan's nuclear program was intended only for peaceful purposes.

June 12, 1989

The United States and the USSR sign Prevention of Dangerous Military Activities Agreement.

This treaty committed each country to prevent four types of dangerous military activities during peacetime when their armed forces might be operating in each other's proximity. First, the two sides were to avoid unintentional or emergency entry into national territory of the other side. Second, each side was to be careful in using lasers and notifying the other party in advance if they believed the use might be hazardous. Third, either party may ask to create a "Special Caution Area" but both sides must avoid disruption of military operations in the area. Fourth, both sides must prevent interference with command and control networks of the other side.

June 27, 1989

European Community members agree to join the European Monetary Union.

Meeting in Madrid, European Community (EC) ministers agreed their countries would join the European Monetary System in July 1990. Although British Prime Minister Margaret Thatcher was expected to oppose a movement toward EC unity, she helped formulate a compromise to broaden the European Monetary System during the next year in establishing a central bank and common currency.

July 1, 1989

U.S. officials make secret trip to Beijing to sustain contacts with Chinese leaders.

Despite China's massacre of protesters in Tiananmen Square on June 4, President Bush sent secret emissaries to Beijing for a day of clandestine talks. Believing contacts with Beijing were essential to retain some semblance of favorable trade and diplomatic relations despite widespread congressional opposition, Bush decided secret contacts were worth the risk and sent National Security Adviser Brent Scowcroft and Deputy Secretary of State Larry Eagleburger to Beijing. Previously, Bush wrote to Chinese leader Deng Xiaoping asking the Chinese to accept the secret dispatch of two U.S. envoys.

As Bush and Scowcroft explain in their book *A World Transformed* (1998), the Americans flew to Beijing to avoid a complete rupture in U.S. relations with China. Scowcroft carried a message to Deng Xiaoping that President Bush had to protest the massacres by imposing sanctions because American public opinion expected it; but he did not want to destroy the good relations with China that existed previously. U.S. relations with China could revive if Deng stopped the arbitrary executions of dissidents and ended martial law. The secret visit was not disclosed to the U.S. public until December.

July 1, 1989

Soviet leader Mikhail Gorbachev sees ethnic nationalism as a danger to the Soviet empire.

Gorbachev saw evidence of nationalism's danger in demonstrations held in the Soviet Republic of Georgia in February and April, in Georgia's autonomous province of Abkhazia during March, and in Soviet Uzbekistan in June. Gorbachev's television address failed to halt the rise of nationalism as it grew stronger in 1989.

Although Gorbachev complained again about "separatist" nationalism in a speech on September 19, words proved incapable of stopping the division among the Soviet republics. The local governments of Lithuania and Estonia passed laws to introduce free-market policies and on July 30, 1989, the Russian Republic under Boris Yeltsin formed the 300 members of its Congress of People's Deputies into an Inter-Regional Group of Deputies.

July 6, 1989

The United States accepts Communist leader Hun Sen as part of the Cambodian government.

Before the summer of 1989, the United States refused to recognize Cambodia's government of President Heng Samrin and Foreign Minister Hun Sen because Vietnam backed that regime. On June 6, Secretary of State James Baker said he was willing to recognize the legitimacy of Heng Samrin's government as a "fact of life" especially because Vietnam was withdrawing its troops from Cambodia. Nevertheless, Baker said the United States would not allow any Cambodian government to have any Khmer Rouge leaders who were part of the Pol Pot regime that killed millions of Cambodians during the 1970s (see December 14, 1987).

Thus, Baker revised U.S. policy and supported negotiations between Hun and opposition leader Prince Norodom Sihanouk that began on May 2, 1989. By July, Sihanouk and Hun formed an alliance and international discussions regarding Cambodia moved to Paris on July 23. The Paris talks had delegates from 19 nations including the United States and the Soviet Union, but they could not resolve the disputes among Cambodia's main factions, largely because China insisted on giving the Khmer Rouge a role in a new government. The peace talks collapsed on August 28 while heavy fighting continued between the Khmer Rouge and Hun Sen's army.

July 7, 1989

Soviet leader Mikhail Gorbachev recognizes that Communist nations have varied ways to solve their economic problems.

As Soviet leader in 1985, Gorbachev found ways to begin reforming the Soviet economy. On July 7, he suggested these reform ideas to the USSR's Warsaw Pact allies at their annual meeting in Bucharest, Romania. Gorbachev called for tolerance among Communist leaders who had "independent solutions of national problems." The summit's final press release said there were "no universal models of socialism." Some Warsaw Pact nations had already begun instituting reforms. On June 24, 1989, Hungary reformed the Communist Party's Central Committee by establishing a four-member presidium headed by reform advocate Rezso Nyers, who became party chairman. Other Presidium members were Party General Secretary Karóny Grósz, Premier Miklós Németh, and Minister of State Imre Poszgay.

In Poland, the reformist Solidarity Union was making rapid headway by moving to invigorate Poland's private sector of the economy.

July 13–19, 1989

President Bush offers economic aid to Poland and Hungary and attends the G-7 summit.

During an extensive European tour, President Bush's trip was highlighted by visits to Poland and Hungary. Because both nations had undertaken market-oriented economic reforms to improve trade relations with the Western powers, Bush promised the two nations financial aid from the United States and the World Bank.

On July 14, Bush attended the annual G-7 meeting in Paris, where there were celebrations for the 200th anniversary of the French Revolution. The G-7 members agreed to provide financial aid to Hungary and Poland but condemned China's military action against its prodemocracy demonstrators on June 3–4. They also called for restrictions on ozone-depleting chemicals and for international efforts to control drug traffic.

July 18, 1989

Poland's legislature elects Wojciech Jaruzelski president of a democratic government.

Since 1988, when Solidarity leader Lech Walesa ended strikes against the government, Poland had moved toward democracy. Beginning in January 1989, First Secretary of the Polish United Workers Party General Jaruzelski met with Walesa's Solidarity movement/union and on April 5 agreed to abandon the existing unicameral legislature. The new parliament consisted of a Senate with 100 seats and a lower house (Sejm) with 460 seats. The United Workers (Communist) Party and its allies would have 65 percent of the Sejm seats with the remainder as well as all Senate seats filled by free elections. Elections were held on June 4 with runoffs conducted on June 18.

Solidarity won 99 of the 100 Senate seats as well as all 161 opposition seats in the Sejm. The Communist Party had 294 Sejm seats reserved for them. On July 18, a joint session of parliament elected Communist Party First Secretary Jaruzelski as president. Former Interior Minister Czeslaw Kiszczak was to be premier but could not form a coalition to govern.

July 28, 1989

Israel captures Hezbollah's spiritual leader in Lebanon.

Israeli commandos captured Sheik Abdul Karim Obeid, the spiritual head of the Hezbollah Muslim militia. Israeli officials offered to release Obeid and 100 other Lebanese detainees in exchange for all Israeli and Western hostages held in Lebanon. Rejecting the offer, Hezbollah kidnapped and hanged U.S. Marine Colonel William R. Higginson July 30 and threatened to, but did not kill, American hostage Joseph James Cicippio.

August 17, 1989

President of the Supreme Soviet Mikhail Gorbachev plans economic autonomy for all Soviet republics.

According to his *Memoirs*, Gorbachev wanted to resolve Soviet problems in 1989 by democratic discussions and tolerance, but at the same time to warn the Soviet people about extremists who sought to destroy the Soviet Union's unity. After consulting with the Central Committee of the Communist Party of the Soviet Union (CPSU), Gorbachev issued a publication titled, "The nationalities policy of the Party under modern conditions" on August 17, 1989. The publication emphasized the need for a "radical renewal of nationality policy" that would make "meaningful political and economic" changes, expand the opportunities of all forms of national autonomy, and guarantee equal rights for all people without infringing on the "rights of citizens because of nationality."

At the same time, Gorbachev warned that extremists might try to tear apart the Soviet Union as a "living organism." The Soviet Communist Federation must not allow extremists to "begin destroying what we have created." In brief, Gorbachev and the Communist Central Committee offered some degree of autonomy for each of the 15 Soviet republics, while keeping the Central Committee's control over foreign affairs, defense, and internal security. Gorbachev believed the August 17 document was "outstanding" in trying to resolve the nationality problem, but leaders of the Baltic Republics and other Soviet republics saw the Central Committee offer of some autonomy as a half-way measure that came too late to satisfy their local nationalism.

Previously, on November 16, 1988, Estonia's Supreme Soviet had amended the Republic of Estonia's constitution by adding a Declaration of Sovereignty. On November 18, 1989, the Supreme Soviet of the Soviet Union declared Estonia's action was unconstitutional, but Estonia's nationalists ignored that decree. By August 1989, Latvia and Lithuania had joined Estonia in issuing Declarations of Sovereignty that led toward independence. Leaders in the three Baltic republics also held a memorial remembrance of the 50th anniversary of the 1939 Nazi-Soviet pact that annexed the three Baltic states to the Soviet Union's sphere of influence (see August 23, 1939). The celebration was designed to promote the independence movement in the three Baltic Republics.

August 24, 1989

Polish Communists join with Soldarity members to form a coalition ministry.

Between June 18 and August 23, 1989, Communist party leader Czeslaw Kiszczak was unable to form a cabinet with enough votes in Poland's parliament (Sejm). To resolve this political situation, Soviet leader Gorbachev telephoned the Chairman of the Communists Polish United Worker's Party (PUWP), Mieczyslau Rakowski. During the call, Gorbachev advised Rakowski that because national reconciliation was the best way to proceed in Poland, Rakowski should have Kiszczak join a coalition government led by Tadeusz Mazowiecki, a Solidarity member proposed by Solidarity leader Lech Walesa. As Raymond Garthoff's *The Great Transition* explains, Solidarity originated as a trade union movement in Gdansk but in 1989 campaigned as a political party to encourage all Polish workers and peasants to join Solidarity and campaign for local candidates for parliament. These efforts enabled Solidarity to win 99 of the 100 seats in Poland's senate and all 161 opposition seats permitted in the Sejm, the lower house of parliament (see July 18, 1989).

After Rakowski received approval to follow Gorbachev's advice from the PUWP's Politburo, Solidarity's Mazowiecki formed a cabinet that was confirmed by Poland's Senate and Sejm on September 12. The 23-member cabinet had 11 Solidarity members, 11 members from the Communist Party and its allies, and one independent member.

September 9, 1989

Boris Yeltsin, a Soviet politician, begins a U.S. visit.

Yeltsin, a former Communist Party official who was elected mayor of Moscow on March 26, disagreed with many of Soviet leader Gorbachev's policies. He visited the United States to explain his beliefs that Gorbachev's political and economic reforms were not moving ahead as fast as they should be. Hemet with President Bush at the White House and visited New York, Baltimore, Chicago, and other cities.

September 10, 1989

Hungary acts to open its borders to Western Europe.

On May 4, when Hungary began dismantling its fences along the border with Austria, Hungary told East Germany's leaders to work out a solution to the emigration problem because East Germans often vacationed in Hungary. During the next three months, the East German government did nothing to resolve the emigration problem. Subsequently, on September 10, Hungary's Foreign Minister Gyula Horn announced East Germans could leave Hungary in any way they wished. Subsequently, during the next 36 hours an estimated 10,500 East Germans crossed Hungary's border with Austria before moving on to West Germany.

Although East Germany protested, the Soviet Union did not. By October 1, about 30,000 East Germans took the Hungarian route to the West.

September 21, 1989

In a speech at the United Nations, President Bush emphasizes the need to regulate chemical weapons.

President Bush's speech to the U.N. General Assembly emphasized the need for the world organization to help prevent the spread of chemical weapons, a project designed to complement a January 7, 1989 meeting in Paris at which 149 nations, including the USSR, reaffirmed their adherence to the 1925 Geneva Protocol opposing chemical weapons.

September 21, 1989

The United States and the USSR agree that with six months' notice either side could end the ABM treaty.

Soviet Foreign Minister Shevardnadze visited Washington to deliver a letter from Soviet leader Gorbachev, asking if Bush would agree that either country could stop observing the Anti-Ballistic Missile (ABM) treaty of 1972 by giving six months' notice. In addition, Gorbachev said the Soviets would destroy their Krasnoyarsk radar station, which the Reagan administration said violated the treaty.

In part, Gorbachev offered these terms after learning from Soviet dissident physicist Andrei Sakharov that the Soviets were wasting money on their missile defense research (SDI) that, Sakharov said, resembled the French Maginot Line in the 1930s. Sakharov had first stated these opinions at a secret meeting of U.S. and Soviet scientists in Moscow in 1987. Most U.S. scientists, whom the Reagan administration ignored, concurred with Sakharov's opinions.

September 23, 1989

The United States and the USSR agree to notify each other prior to any strategic exercises.

This pact endorsed the idea "that a nuclear war cannot be won and must never be fought;" consequently, it sought "to reduce and ultimately eliminate" the possibility that an outbreak of hostilities might occur "as a result of misinterpretation, miscalculation, or accident." The treaty, therefore, required the two superpowers to provide reciprocal advance notification of major strategic exercises and was intended to expand the responsibilities undertaken by their agreement in 1987 to establish Nuclear Risk Reductions Centers (see September 15, 1987).

The possibility of one side misreading the intent of strategic exercises during a time when tensions are high was not all that far-fetched. In early November 1983, the U.S. and NATO forces counducted an exceptionally wide-ranging and high-level strategic exercise, called Able Archer 83, which tested "the command and communications procedures for the release and use of nuclear weapons." Although such activities were not uncommon, this was a time of particularly heightened tensions between Washington and Moscow.

September 30, 1989

East Germans seek to leave for West Germany via Prague.

After Hungary opened its Austrian border for East Germans to cross, Czechoslovakia experienced problems because over 5,500 East Germans had taken refuge in West Germany's Prague embassy and asked to go to the West. East German authorities agreed that the East Germans at their Prague embassy could go by train to the West, a decision precipitating the flight of East Germans who boarded trains in Dresden coming from Prague *en route* to the West. In Dresden, East German police clashed with an estimated 10,000 Germans who tried to board the trains. The Berlin Wall was now bypassed and a crisis arose in East Germany.

See November 9, 1989.

October 6, 1989

Soviet leader Gorbachev tells East Germans to reform their government.

As some of its citizens were fleeing to West Germany, East Germany celebrated the 40th anniversary of its founding with Soviet leader Mikhail Gorbachev as the celebration's key speaker. Although the East German Communist Party's Politburo hoped for Soviet backing in suppressing protesters, Gorbachev told them to solve their problems by adopting Soviet-style reforms. His advice precipitated larger demonstrations in East Germany's main cities, with the police resorting to violence to beat and arrest protesters. Owing to protests, East German leader Eric Honecker decided to "retire" from the Socialist Unity (Communist) Party (SED) on October 18. State Security Chief Egon Krenz was appointed SED chairman but protests continued in Berlin, Leipzig, Dresden, and elsewhere.

October 9, 1989

The Soviet Union fails to end protests by recognizing workers' right to strike.

Hoping to end Siberian miners' strikes, the Supreme Soviet (parliament) passed legislation recognizing the worker's right to strike but restricted circumstances for a strike and prohibited strikes in transportation, communication, defense, and power-supply sectors. The concessions failed to end Siberian unrest. Instead, workers staged protests, trying to implement the few concessions offered by Gorbachev, as chairman of the Supreme Soviet in July 1989.

October 18, 1989

South Korea asks United States not to reduce troop strength in Korea's peninsula.

During a six-day U.S. visit, South Korea's President Roh Tae Woo asked a joint session of Congress not to cut back American troop strength in South Korea. Despite his efforts to build better relations with North Korea, Roh also approved U.S. plans for South Korea's purchase of 120 advanced fighter jets. On December 20, Seoul announced Mc Donnell Douglas would be South Korea's partner in constructing these planes.

October 18, 1989

Hungarian National Assembly ends Communist Party's powers and inaugurates the Republic of Hungary.

Hungary's governmentsal changes began in early October at a special Hungarian Socialist Workers (Communist) Party Congress, when delegates voted 1,005 to 159 to change their name to the Hungarian Socialist Party with a new party platform. The congress adjourned on October 9 after abolishing the party's four-member presidium and its Central Committee. It formed a 24-member presidium and elected reformer Reszo Nyers as president. The congress also divested the party of most of its property holdings and abandoned all Workers' Militia and party factory cells.

When the National Assembly met on October 18, it voted to delete the Hungarian constitution's references to the Communist Party's leading role. The assembly also approved laws to allow political parties, codify civil and human rights, and form separate executive, legislative, and judicial units. On October 23 at a rally celebrating the 33rd anniversary of the 1956 uprising against Soviet forces, Hungarian President Mátyás Szuros fulfilled the National Assembly's desire by declaring the "free Republic of Hungary" to replace the "People's Republic of Hungary." On November 16, a national referendum decided Hungary's president should be elected by parliament, not by popular vote. Hungary's first free elections for parliament were on March 28, 1990.

October 21, 1989

President Bush disrupts Nicaraguan plans for democratic elections.

By approving legislation granting $9 million aid to Nicaragua's Contra rebels, President Bush disrupted Nicaragua's plans for elections scheduled for February 1990. In cooperation with the United Nations, presidents of five Central American countries (Guatemala, Honduras, El Salvador, Costa Rica, and Nicaragua) had agreed to close Contra bases in Honduras and relocate rebels so Nicaragua could hold democratic elections.

On April 18, 1989, Nicaragua's socialist government of President Daniel Ortega approved laws for "free and fair" elections, and on September 2, the moderate Coalition National Opposition Union (UNO) named Violeta Barrios de Chamorro, owner of the opposition's *La Prensa* newspaper, as its presidential candidate. These U.N. plans were ruptured after Bush approved aid to Contras who ambushed and killed 19 Nicaraguan soldiers. Because the Contras violated the U.N.-brokered cease-fire, Ortega said new military operations would continue against the Contras until the United States stopped financing them. On November 9, Ortega spoke with Contra representatives at a U.N. meeting but they could not agree on details about the demobilization and withdrawal of Contra rebels from Honduras before elections were held.

On December 12, the presidents of Guatemala, El Salvador, Honduras, and Nicaragua met in Costa Rica. They agreed to link the status of Nicaraguan Contra rebels with El Salvador's left-wing rebels and asked the United States to stop aiding the Contras. The linkage failed because an airplane carrying arms for Salvadoran rebels was shot down in eastern El Salvador. Apparently, the plane shot down was coming from Nicaragua.

November 7, 1989

U.N. observer group is formed for Central America.

The U.N. Security Council unanimously approved the creation of a U.N. observer force in Central America to monitor cease-fire accords in Nicaragua and elsewhere, demobilize rebel armies in the region, and work with the U.N. International Commission of Support and Verification.

November 9, 1989

The Berlin Wall falls.

Since being constructed in 1961, the Berlin Wall symbolized totalitarianism and the "iron curtain" that separated democratic Western Europe from Communist regimes of the East. The Wall began to be torn down after East Germany's government announced exit visas would be granted to all citizens wishing to leave the country at any border. This decision followed the resignation of East German Premier Willi Stoph and his entire cabinet on November 7, which led to changes when the Communist Party's Politburo evicted 11 hard-liners and added four dissenters.

After several nights of Berlin celebrations between East and West Germans, Hans Modrow, Dresden's reform leader, was confirmed as premier by the Volkskammer (parliament) on November 13. Modrow called for elections in December and abolished the Ministry for State Security (Stasi), reforming it as the Office of National Security.

November 20, 1989

The U.S. budget provides foreign aid for new democracies and old military rulers.

President Bush signed legislation for foreign aid that gave economic assistance not only to new democracies in Europe but to authoritarian regimes in the Americas. This bill provided funds to Hungary and Poland, nations in transition from socialist to market economies. At the same time the bill assisted El Salvador's military regime in fighting left-wing guerrillas.

November 28, 1989

Prague demonstrations lead to power-sharing talks between Communists and the Civic Forum.

In Czechoslovakia, antigovernment demonstrations led to negotiations between the Communist regime and Václav Hável's Civic Forum. Since January 15, when demonstrators were arrested or dispersed

West side of the Berlin Wall, looking toward East Berlin. Brune photo

by police, more citizens both inside and outside Prague had staged protests. In May, Hável was released from prison, where he served a nine-month sentence for disturbing the peace. During the summer, protests grew larger on a regular basis. On October 28, 100,000 protesters filled Prague's streets with riot police beating demonstrators and arresting 355 people.

On November 17, another round of antigovernment demonstrations preceded a meeting of opposition leaders, including Hável. The opposition decided to unite with the Civic Forum on November 19. Four days later, Alexander Dubcek, the Czech leader during the 1968 Prague Spring, joined protests and told a Bratislava rally to back prodemocracy opposition. Millions of workers throughout the nation supported democracy by staging a two-hour work stoppage on November 27.

Meanwhile, the Communist Party Central Committee instituted political changes enabling moderates to remove hard-liners from the Politburo. The new Communist leader, Premier Ladislav Adamec, opened power-sharing discussions with Civic Forum leaders on November 28. The next day, the Czech parliament changed the constitution by removing clauses regarding the Communist Party's "leading role" in government.

See December 18, 1989.

December 1–3, 1989

At Malta, President Bush and First Secretary Gorbachev discuss arms limitations.

Meeting near the island of Malta aboard the Soviet cruise ship Maxim Gorky, President Bush and Soviet leader Gorbachev discussed Europe's conventional forces as well as strategic arms reductions and tactical nuclear missiles. Bush told Gorbachev he would change U.S. policy that had denied the Soviets most-favored-nation trade status since 1974 (see December 20, 1974) and would have a Soviet delegate observe GATT meetings. Above all, the Malta talks demonstrated the Bush administration supported Gorbachev's *perestroika* and democratic values he promoted in Eastern Europe. After the Malta talks ended, Bush visited Brussels to brief NATO leaders on his discussions with Gorbachev and they considered methods to reunite Germany.

December 6, 1989

Secretary of State Baker proposes plan for Israeli-Palestinian talks.

After a year in which the United States tried to renew the peace process between Israelis and Palestinians, Secretary Baker prepared a five-point plan called the Baker Plan. He proposed that foreign ministers from the United States, Israel, and Egypt meet to set guidelines for negotiations in Cairo between Israelis and Palestinian, delegates regarding elections in the occupied territories. Egypt and Israel accepted the plan but Israel insisted that the Palestinian delegation could not include members of the Palestine Liberation Organization (PLO).

December 8, 1989

East German socialists are divided on issue of a united Germany.

The East German government planned reforms but the Socialist Unity (Communist) Party (SED) was ambivalent about uniting Germany. After the East German parliament repealed the SED's "leading role" in government on December 1, the SED's Central Committee expelled 12 members accused of bribery and corruption, including former President Eric Honecker and Premier Willi Stoph. On December 9, the SED congress elected Gregor Gysi as chairman but voted to reject West German offers of reunification. Many members of the SED and Dresden's New Forum preferred to be separate from West Germany to devise their own path to socialism. The socialist plans were never fulfilled because demonstrations in Dresden and other cities demanded German unity as proposed by West German Chancellor Helmut Kohl.

December 9, 1989

High-level U.S. officials visit China and Japan.

To brief leaders of China and Japan on his Malta talks with Soviet leader Mikhail Gorbachev, President Bush sent National Security Adviser Brent Scowcroft and Deputy Secretary of State Lawrence Eagleburger to Tokyo and Beijing. In Beijing, they discussed the best means to improve U.S.-Chinese relations but achieved no immediate results. The Chinese claimed that their treatment of prodemocracy demonstrators in Tiananmen Square on June 4 was an internal matter. On October 31, when former President Richard Nixon had visited China, Chinese leader Deng Xiaoping blamed the United States for encouraging the dissidents who caused the Tiananmen massacres. Nevertheless on December 19, Bush appeased China by waiving the June 1989 ban imposed on Export-Import Bank loans to firms doing business with China. In Tokyo, Scowcroft and Eagleberger simply told Japan's foreign minister details about Bush's arms control discussions with Gorbachev.

December 14, 1989

Pinochet's candidate loses Chilean presidential election to Patricio Aylwin.

Aylwin won Chile's first multiparty presidential election since 1970 (see September 11, 1973). As the candidate of a 17-party Coalition for Democracy, Aylwin defeated Augusto Pinochet's former finance minister, Hernán Buchi. The multiparty elections were required by Chile's constitutional changes that Pinochet and the leaders of the Coalition for Democracy accepted in May 1989. Under the agreement, Pinochet would be army commander in chief for four years but would relinquish the presidency to Aylwin in March 1990.

December 19, 1989

With U.S. backing, West German Chancellor Kohl and East German Prime Minister Modrow agree on process for German reunification.

As early as October 8, Secretary of State Baker told reporters U.S. policy always supported Germany's peaceful reunification and the fall of the Berlin Wall required specific ideas about achieving unity. On November 28, Kohl outlined a 10-point plan for German unity, but Britain and France were skeptical about uniting the country.

To clarify U.S. positions on German unity, Bush and Secretary Baker adopted four points for unification: pursuing self-determination without preconceived ideas; unification in the context of Germany's commitment to NATO and the European Community; peaceful step-by-step procedures; and respecting borders as outlined in the Helsinki human rights agreements. West German leaders appreciated the U.S. position explained by Baker in a Berlin speech on December 12 and during a meeting with Modrow.

Then Baker told President Bush that Modrow wanted early reunification because East Germany needed West German economic assistance.

On December 19, Kohl and Modrow discussed future ties between East and West Germany. The first items they accepted were to open Berlin's Brandenberg Gate before Christmas 1989, and to establish cultural and economic ties in the next several months.

December 20, 1989

A U.S. invasion overthrows Panamanian President Noriega.

Following the fraudulent May 7 election, Panama experienced continuous difficulties after General Manuel Noriega annulled the presidential victory of Guillermo Endara. On October 3, Major Moisés Giroldi Vega led a coup that failed to overthrow Noriega. President Bush admitted that the United States knew about coup plans but denied that the United States had aided dissidents who protested against Noriega's fraudulent election of May 7, 1989. The coup involved about 300 Panamanian soldiers, 10 of whom, including Giroldi, were killed or executed. Following the coup, U.S. Senator Jesse Helms (R-N.C.) proposed a resolution authorizing U.S. forces to overthrow Noriega, but the Senate defeated it by a vote of 74 to 25.

On December 15, the Panamanian National Assembly named General Noriega "maximum leader" and declared that a state of war existed with the United States. After a U.S. soldier was killed in Panama City on December 16, President Bush mobilized American troops in Panama. Soon after midnight on December 20, a Panamanian judge administered to Endara the oath of presidential office before U.S. forces attacked. American troops seized Panama's airfields, power stations, and the headquarters of the Panamanian Defense Force, but Bush had to send 2,000 additional troops to Panama before order was restored on December 23. In a televised speech to Americans on December 20, Bush said he intervened to protect American citizens and uphold U.S. rights under the Panama Canal Treaty.

While Panama officially disbanded its army in favor of a public security force, Washington announced 23 American troops and three civilians were killed and another 323 wounded. Panamanian losses were 314 soldiers killed and 124 wounded as well as an estimated 500 to 1,000 civilian who were or killed. Later estimates placed the civilian losses at nearly 2,500; together with millions of dollars of property damage. Meanwhile, General Noriega eluded capture and took refuge in the residence of the Vatican nuncio, who would not turn him over until Noriega agreed.

See January 1, 1990.

December 20, 1989

Soviet leader Mikhail Gorbachev opposes Lithuanian independence.

Lithuania's Communist Party Congress withdrew from the Central Committee of the Communist Party of the USSR because Lithuania's government wanted to declare an independent Lithuania. Gorbachev replied that he opposed secession because it would bring "discord, bloodshed and death." Gorbachev agreed to visit Lithuania to talk with its party leaders.

See April 24, 1990.

December 22, 1989

Romania's army joins protesters to overthrow President Ceausescu.

In Bucharest, key Romanian army leaders joined crowds to attack the Communist Party's Central Committee building. During the attack, President Nicolae Ceausescu and his wife tried to flee by helicopter but were captured. After a counterattack by army units loyal to Ceausescu failed, dissident leader Ion Iliescu announced plans for a non-Communist government. A military field court martial ordered Ceausescu to be executed on December 25 for crimes of genocide and sending $1 billion abroad for his personal use. Iliescu became interim president with elections slated for 1990.

December 27, 1989

Bulgaria abolishes Communist Party's leading role in the life of the nation.

Following a protest movement by an environmentalist Eco-Glasnost group beginning on November 3, Communist Party General Secretary Todor Zhivkov resigned and Bulgaria's government began negotiations with the opposition Union of Democratic Forces. On December 27, the government and nine opposition groups agreed to abolish the Communist Party's leading role in society, to hold free elections, to expel President Zhivkov from the Communist Party, and to appoint Petar Mladenov as party leader.

December 28, 1989

Czechoslovakian Elections end the Communist government.

Following the November 28 meeting between Czechoslovakia's Communist Party Premier Ladislav Adamec and members of the Civic Forum led by Václav Hável, Adamec resigned his position (see November 28, 1989). On December 10, Marian Calfa became Czechoslovakia's premier and formed a cabinet of 10 Communists and 11 non-Communists. The final step ending the Communist Party's rule came on December 28, when the Czechoslovakian Federal Assembly elected Václav Hável president of Czechoslovakia and Alexander Dubcek chairman of the Assembly. In 1968, Dubcek had been replaced by the armed forces of the Soviet Union and Warsaw Pact because his government initiated reforms opposed by the Soviet's General Secretary Leonid Brezhnev (see August 20, 1969). Hável was a writer and poet who often had been jailed by Czechoslovakia's Communist regime because of his dissidence (see January 15, 1989).

After Dubcek and Hável were elected to their new positions, they instituted reforms to confirm the end of the Communist Party's leading role in government. Among the first reforms, Czechoslovakia's Federal Assembly dropped the Marxist-Leninist curriculum from schools and approved elections for a new Federal Assembly to be held in 1990.

1990

January 1, 1990

Afghan refugee population is 6.2 million.

The political-military upheavals in Afghanistan were demonstrated by the enormous growth of refugees fleeing to surrounding territories. The Office of the United Nations High Commissioner for Refugees (UNHCR) estimated that by December 1979, about 600,000 refugees were outside of Afghanistan, with two-thirds in Pakistan and the remainder in Iran. By January 1, 1990, the refugee number reached 6.2 million with about 3.3 million in camps on Pakistan's border.

January 1, 1990

Panama gains new administrator for the canal; Panama's General Noriega is flown to Florida.

Acting in accord with the 1977 U.S.-Panama Canal Treaty, Fernando Manfredo Bernal became acting administrator of the canal. On January 3, by prior agreement Noriega left the papal mission and the United States flew him to Florida, where on May 4 he was arraigned on drug charges in a Miami district court. President Bush sought funds to aid Panama's recovery and Congress approved $420 million for Panama on May 24 as part of a foreign aid package that gave $355 million to Latin American nations plus a $400 million loan guarantee to Israel.

January 23, 1990

The Yugoslav League of Communists is dissolved.

Disputes among the Yugoslav republics of Slovenia, Croatia, and Serbia increased in 1989 after Serbian President Slobodan Milosevic enlarged Serb control over the "autonomous" provinces of Kosovo and Vojvodina. On September 17, 1989, Slovenia's assembly adopted legislation that gave it the right to secede from Yugoslavia if Serbia tried to gain control over Yugoslavia's six republics. In Croatia, Franjo Tudjman formed an anti-Serb party of Croatian nationalists (HDZ) to counter Milosevic's propaganda appeals to the Serb minority in Croatia.

More frictions among these three republics arose during a convention of the Yugoslav League of Communists (YLC) because delegates from Slovenia and Croatia challenged Milosevic's attempt to enact constitutional "reforms" to enhance the power of Yugoslavia's central government. Following disputes with Serbia's delegation about constitutional changes, Slovenia's delegates seceded from the YLC and walked out of the convention. Although Milosevic called on the convention to continue by forming a "new quorum," the Croatian delegation joined Slovenia in leaving the meetings. Unable to proceed, Convention Chairman Momir Bulatovic called for a 15-minute break he later said "lasted throughout history." Yugoslavia's disintegration had begun, although it was not completed until June 1991.

February 2, 1990

South Africa legalizes African National Congress and other parties.

South African President F.W. de Klerk launched changes in South Africa by legalizing the African National Congress (ANC), the South African Communist Party, and the Pan-African Congress. De Klerk also promised to free ANC leader Nelson Mandela, who had been in jail for 27 years. Mandela was freed on February 11. In May, the ANC and De Klerk's government began talks about releasing political prisoners and granting immunity to returned exiles. On August 6, the ANC called a cease-fire in its armed struggle with South Africa's government.

February 12, 1990

The reunification of Germany will be decided by two plus four (2+4) negotiations.

Since November 28, 1989, when West German Chancellor Helmut Kohl suggested ways to reunite Germany, U.S. Secretary of State Baker sought to foster Germany's reunification while reassuring the British, French, and Soviets that Germany would maintain its cooperation with other European nations. In January, Baker and other State Department personnel devised a plan to conduct talks between East and West Germany regarding Germany's internal political and economic relations. At the same time, the four powers (United States, France, Great Britain, USSR) occupying Germany after World War II would negotiate with East and West Germany regarding external relations with Germany's allies and neighbors. The four powers plan became known as the 2+4 plan.

Anticipating that the six nations could approve the 2+4 plan at a February conference in Ottawa, Canada, Baker contacted British, French, Soviet, East and West German and other European leaders to explain his proposal. In addition, West German Chancellor Helmut Kohl met with Soviet leader Mikhail Gorbachev in Moscow to assure the Soviets that Germany would remain part of the European Community and negotiate future borders with Poland. Subsequently, the 2+4 plan was finalized at an Ottawa Conference, where 23 members of NATO and the Warsaw Pact discussed Germany's future and control of Europe's conventional weapons. Baker announced the plan by saying negotiations would begin after East German elections on March 18.

February 25, 1990

The U.S. favorite wins Nicaraguan elections.

In Nicaraguan elections, the U.S.-favored candidate, Violeta Barrios de Chamorro, defeated the incumbent, President Daniel Ortega. Because the United States opposed Ortega's Sandinista National Liberation Front (FSLN), Washington was delighted that Chamorro was elected and that her National Opposition Union (UNO) gained control of 52 of the 90 seats in the National Assembly. The FSLN received only 38 seats. On March 13, President Bush assisted Chamorro by lifting U.S. economic sanctions and requesting $300 million emergency aid that Congress approved on May 24. The remaining issue was the demobilization of the U.S.-sponsored Contra rebels who continued to fight Nicaragua's government. In November 2004 elections, the Sandinistas returned to power via the ballot box by taking over control of the larger cities.

February 25–27, 1990

U.S. Deputy Secretary of State Lawrence Eagleburger urges the European Community to solve Yugoslavia's problems.

After President Bush took office in 1989, his administration decided Yugoslavia was no longer vital to U.S. interest as it had been during the Cold War. Reaching Belgrade in 1989, U.S. Ambassador Warren Zimmermann learned about Yugoslavia's recent political and economic problems and persuaded Deputy Secretary of State Lawrence Eagleburger to visit Belgrade. From February 25 to 27, Eagleburger met Yugoslav Prime Minister Ante Marcovic, representatives of Yugoslavia's six republics, and opposition group leaders. After Marcovic was elected prime minister in March 1989, he tried to establish free-market reforms to obtain IMF loans.

Under IMF guidelines, the long-term benefits of reforms required short-term cuts in social welfare programs and workers' wages while state-owned industries were privatized. Slovenia, Serbia, and Croatia opposed the IMF reforms because they caused unemployment, less income for retired people and wage-workers, and the loss of jobs in state-owned businesses. In addition, Serbia's President Slobodan Milosevic wanted constitutional changes to centralize the federal government's power, but leaders of Slovenia and Croatia wanted each republic to control its own economy. After leaving Belgrade, Eagleburger instructed U.S. ambassadors in Europe to call their host countries' attention to the danger of Yugoslavia's disintegration.

President Bush focused his attention on German unity and watched Mikhail Gorbachev's reforms in the Soviet Union while the State Department hoped the European Community could deal with Yugoslavia's problems.

See April 8, 1990.

March 7, 1990

President Bush denies the United States set fire to a Libyan factory producing mustard gas.

After an ABC news broadcast reported that Libya was producing mustard gas in a factory near Tripoli, the White House confirmed the accuracy of the report. A week later, the Libyan factory producing the gas was reported to have been burned down and Libya blamed CIA agents. Bush denied any U.S. role in setting the fire.

March 13–15, 1990

The Soviet Union's People's Congress repeals Communist Party's power monopoly.

The first step toward ending the Communist Party's monopoly of power was taken by the Plenum of the Central Committee of the Communist Party on February 7, when the members approved party First Secretary Gorbachev's proposal to end the party's monopoly of political power. The Plenum's decision was recommended to the Third Soviet Congress of People's Deputies at its March meeting. On March 14, the deputies voted 1,817 to 133 to repeal the constitutional guarantees of the Communist Party's monopoly. The Congress also created the office of executive president, electing Mikhail Gorbachev president. Popular elections would choose future presidents. On March 24, Gorbachev appointed a 16-member Presidential Council to assist him.

March 15, 1990

The Baker Plan disrupts Israel's coalition cabinet.

Although in December Israel agreed to proceed with the Baker Plan, events in early 1990 made it difficult to continue. On January 14, Prime Minister Yitzhak Shamir said Israel needed the occupied territories to house Soviet Jewish immigrants. On February 4, the terrorist Islamic Jihad for the Liberation of Palestine ambushed a bus in Egypt, killing 16 Israeli tourists.

On February 12, Ariel Sharon of the Likud Party resigned from the cabinet and 10 days later, the Labor Party threatened to leave the coalition unless Shamir accepted their interpretation of the Baker Plan requiring some type of Palestinian representation. These actions split Israel's cabinet over the differences about the U.S.'s peace plan between the Likud Party's Prime Minister Shamir and Labor's Finance Minister Shimon Peres. After Shamir removed Peres from office, all other Labor Party ministers resigned. Shamir had to form another coalition ministry.

March 18, 1990

East German elections confirm desire to reunite with West Germany.

In East German elections, the Alliance for Germany, which favored speedy reunification with West Germany, won 48.1 percent of the vote. Its rival, the Social Democrats, received only 21.8 percent and the former Communist Party, the Party of Democratic Socialism (SED), gained 16.3 percent of the votes. Following the election, the Alliance for Germany and the Social Democrats formed a "grand alliance" coalition government.

On April 28, a European Community meeting approved a united Germany as a member, setting the stage for German reunification.

March 21, 1990

Secretary of State James Baker represents the United States at Namibia's presidential inauguration.

Baker represented the United States at the inauguration of Sam Nujoma as Namibia's first president. Namibia had received independence from South Africa in 1988 after several years of struggle.

March 23, 1990

Nicaragua and Contras agree to a cease-fire, overseen by observers.

Sponsored by the United States and the United Nations, Nicaragua's Contra leaders met with Nicaraguan president-elect Chamorro. The Contras agreed to dismantle rebel camps in Honduras and accepted a cease-fire monitored by a multinational U.N. Observer Group. In turn, former President Daniel Ortega's Sandinista Party recognized Chamorro's right to control Nicaragua's army and security forces. Chamorro was sworn in as president on April 25. The Contras soon raised other questions about Chamorro's policies, and the rebels' disarmament was not ended until June 29, 1990.

March 27, 1990

U.S. television MARTI begins broadcasting into Cuba.

An American-financed station, TV MARTI, began trial broadcasts into Cuba, which decided not to jam the station's broadcasts. On August 26, President Bush said the television station was successful in bringing music and news to Cubans and its operation would continue.

March 28, 1990

British and U.S. customs agents prevent nuclear detonators from reaching Iraq.

U.S. customs officers were on this case after Iraq ordered specially designed nuclear detonator-capacitors from CSI Technologies of San Marcos, California. When the detonators arrived at London's Heathrow airport on March 28, British police arrested the Iraqi Airway's manager and four other Iraqis who worked for the Iraqi Ministry of the Interior's explosives research division. The five Iraqis were arrested for smuggling atomic weapons parts into Iraq. President Saddam Hussein denied the detonators were for nuclear weapons, claiming they were for laser research.

The London incident was one of three in March 1990, that led Saddam Hussein to assert that the United States and Israel conspired against Iraq. The first was a report of the growing number of Jews emigrating from the USSR to Israel. The second was the assassination of a Canadian ballistics expert, Gerald Bull, in Brussels. Bull had developed a long-range artillery weapon for Iraq and was developing a new super gun for Iraq at the time of his murder.

April 1, 1990

Iraqi President Saddam Hussein threatens to destroy half of the Israeli population with binary nerve gas.

Denouncing the United States and Britain, Hussein threatened to use binary nerve gas weapons to destroy half of Israel if it made a preemptive attack on Iraq as it did in 1981. Following the end of the Iraq-Iran war in 1988, Hussein tried to become the Arabs' primary leader against Israel and the Western powers who, he said, assisted the "Zionists." Although neither the Reagan nor the Bush administration immediately recognized Hussein's anti-Americanism, the U.S. Congress opposed a $350 million Export-Import Bank credit to Iraq that President Bush bypassed with an executive order in January 1990.

In February 1990, President Hussein told a meeting of Arab leaders to put Arab unity ahead of petrodollars and to force the United States to remove its ships from the Persian Gulf. In March, Hussein was further incensed by three events involving Israel and the West. Together, these developments led to Hussein's April 1 tirade against Israel as part of a policy to be the great leader of all Arabs opposing Israel's military power.

April 7, 1990

A federal court convicts John Poindexter for obstructing justice in the Iran-Contra affair; Oliver North's conviction is suspended.

The federal court convicted President Reagan's former national security adviser, John M. Poindexter of obstructing justice and lying to Congress about the Iran-Contra affair. On June 11, he was sentenced to six months in prison. In contrast, on July 20, a federal appeals court suspended Oliver L. North's three felony convictions in the Iran-Contra affair because he had been given immunity by Congress.

April 8, 1990

Yugoslav unity threatened when Slovenian and Croatian nationalists win elections.

The first blow to the Yugoslav Federation of Socialist Republics came in January 1990, when the Slovenian and Croatian delegates walked out of the annual meeting of the Yugoslav League of Communists due to disputes with Serbian delegates regarding the future power of Yugoslavia's federal government (see January 23, 1990). Slovenian Communists led by Milan Kuchan, and Croatian Communists led by Franjo Tudjman wanted the Yugoslav Federation to allocate more authority in economic affairs to each of the Yugoslav Republics, while Serbian President Slobodan Milosevic planned to enhance the central role of the Yugoslav presidency. These differences between Yugoslavia's largest and most prosperous republics precipitated the break-up of the Yugoslav League of Communists in January and led to the victories of Slovenian and Croatian nationalists who opposed Milosevic's nationalistic program for a Greater Serbia.

In early April, before the Slovenian and Croatian election date, the pro-Serb Yugoslavian Defense Minister, Veljko Kadijevic, visited Slovenia and Croatia, where he openly threatened to retaliate against any group that questioned the territorial integrity of Yugoslavia. As Laura Silber and Allan Little's *Yugoslavia: Death of a Nation* (1997) concludes: General Kadijevic's threat backfired because Slovenian and, especially, Croatian voters resented the general's threat. One Croat Communist Party leader told Kadijeic the Slovenians and Croatians were not breaking Yugoslav apart but "It is Milosevic and your refusal to resist him." In April 8 elections for the Republic of Slovenia's Assembly and president, Slovenia's Communist Party leader Michael Kuchan won 60 percent of the votes, defeating Joze Pucnik, the nominee of the DEMOS coalition of seven parties that included the Christian Democrats and Greens (environmental) Party. Before the election Kuchan's followers changed the party name from Communist to the Party of Democratic Reform, while hard-line Communists were on the ballot under the name of the Communist Party. In Slovenia's Assembly election, reformers in the DEMOS and the Party of Democratic Reform won 55 percent of the votes, the Communist Party 17 percent. Smaller parties won the remaining 28 percent.

On April 22, the Republic of Croatia's elections were won by members of the Croatian Democratic party (HDZ), a party established in February 1989, under the leadership of former General of the Yugoslav National Army Franjo Tudjman. HDZ's political campaign was based on Croatian nationalism and a pledge to make Croatia independent. In Croatia's elections, Tudjman was elected president with 66 percent of the votes, and after runoff elections on May 6 and 7, 1990, HDZ members won 205 of the 356 seats in Croatia's parliament (Sabor), the Communist Party won 73 seats, and eight smaller parties won the remaining 78 seats. Primarily, the HDZ victory was due to the Communist Party's support for Serbian nationalists who favored the Serb Republic's Slobodan Milosevic. Both Tudjman and Kuchan opposed Milosevic's plans for a Greater Serbia.

See October 1, 1990.

April 24, 1990

President Bush faces crisis regarding Lithuania and the Soviet Union.

Because Bush favored self-determination for the Soviet republic of Lithuania, he faced a crisis after Lithuania tried to secede from the Soviet Union. In March 1990, when Lithuania's Supreme Soviet declared independence, Soviet President Gorbachev rejected its decision and, on April 19, placed an economic embargo against Lithuania that shut off its oil and natural gas from the USSR. President Bush favored Lithuanian self-determination but realized Gorbachev would not allow any Soviet republic to secede because other republics would follow.

In an agreement with British Prime Minister Margaret Thatcher, French President François Mitterrand, and German Chancellor Helmut Kohl, Bush proposed negotiations between Gorbachev and Lithuania's President Vytautas Landsbergis as the best way to accommodate both sides. The situation also benefited when on April 26 Mitterrand and Kohl sent Landsbergis a letter urging Lithuania to suspend its declaration of independence and negotiate with the Soviets.

Amid this crisis and against Bush's wishes, the U.S. Senate led by Senator Jesse Helms (R-N.C.) passed legislation on May 1 to withhold trade benefits from Moscow. Although the Senate action upset the Soviets, the Franco-German appeal to Lithuania got Landsbergis's attention. During a summit meeting in June, Bush persuaded Gorbachev to negotiate with Lithuania as the best way to end the crisis. After discussions in Moscow between Gorbachev and Landsbergis, Lithuania suspended its independence declaration on June 29 and the Soviets reopened the oil and gas pipelines to Lithuania.

April 24, 1990

China and Soviet Union sign a 10-year economic cooperation agreement.

During Premier Li Peng's visit to Moscow, China and the Soviet Union signed a 10-year agreement to cooperate in economic and scientific affairs. Li was the first Chinese leader to visit the USSR since 1964. Li Peng and General Secretary Mikhail Gorbachev also agreed to decrease the size of military forces along their mutual borders.

April 24, 1990

Chilean courts order investigation of Letelier's assassination in Washington, D.C.

Acting at the request of Patricio Aylwin, who became president on March 11, Chile's Supreme Court ordered the military to review its investigation of the 1975 assassination of Orlando Letelier, Chile's former ambassador to the United States who was assassinated in Washington by a car bomb (see November 29, 1979). On May 12, Chile formed a commission to investigate human rights violations by the military government of General Augusto Pinochet Ugarte and to determine what compensation Chile should pay the United States for the bombing that killed an American citizen Ronnie K. Moffett who rode in the car with Letelier.

May 2, 1990

The 2+4 talks result in Germany's having a single currency.

During an initial series of talks between East and West Germans, the delegates finalized terms for ending the circulation of the East German currency and replacing it with the German mark, to become effective on July 1, 1990. Talks on German political unity were also under way in "2+4" negotiations between German states plus four allies from World War II.

See September 12, 1990.

May 14, 1990

Philippine Islands face problems in closing U.S. bases and defeating rebel groups.

Throughout 1990, Philippine President Corozon Aquino dealt with two demanding issues. First, to meet popular demands, she asked the United States to remove its navy and air force bases from the islands. Second, she ordered the Philippine army to defeat the rebel groups seeking to overthrow the government.

On April 10, President Bush appointed Assistant Secretary of Defense Richard L. Armitage to negotiate the future of U.S. bases in the Philippines. When Armitage arrived in May, he faced serious threats from protesters against American personnel. On May 1, the Communist New People's Army staged protests during which they killed a U.S. Marine sergeant at Subic Bay naval base and two U.S. airmen at Clark Air Force Base. Following preliminary talks in May Armitage returned from September 19 to 22, but talks failed over disagreements about phasing out U.S. bases.

The Philippine army and police had to deal with militant soldiers and also the New People's Army. The most serious soldiers' rebellion began on October 4, when 200 rebels captured a Mindanao outpost to set up an independent state. After the Philippine air force bombed the rebel stronghold on October 10, most of the militant soldiers surrendered, including their leader, Colonel Alexander Noble. The guerrillas proved more dangerous to Aquino. Although on August 29 she offered to negotiate a cease-fire, the rebels refused. The Philippine army faced the difficult task of trying to defeat the guerrilla New People's Army, whose members hid in mountains and jungles scattered throughout the islands.

May 20, 1990

Romanian acting president is elected in a landslide victory.

In Romanian multiparty elections, acting president Ion Iliescu was victorious when his National Salvation Front (Communists) received 85 percent of the vote and 67 percent of the seats in each house of Romania's bicameral parliament. Despite his election, many students opposed Iliescu, staging massive protests in Bucharest. To end the demonstrations on June 14, Iliescu brought in 10,000 coal miners from northern Romania who successfully beat the students into submission. Although the United States expressed disapproval of Iliescu's method and the European Community suspended economic relations with Romania, Iliescu was sworn in as president on June

20, promising a commitment to free markets, pluralism, and "traditional democracy."

May 29, 1990

Boris Yeltsin is elected president of the Russian Federation.

Campaigning on a platform of political and economic sovereignty for the Russian Federation, the largest of the republics in the USSR, Yeltsin defeated Alexsander V. Vlasov, who was the Soviet Communist Party's candidate. Yeltsin's victory was followed by moves to gain the federation's independence. On June 19, a conference of the Russian Federation's Communist Party established an organization separate from the Soviet Communist Party and elected Ivan K. Polozkovto head the Federation's party. On August 10, the Russian Federation's parliamentary Presidium declared the federation's sovereignty over its natural resources.

Alarmed by these developments, Soviet President Mikhail Gorbachev sought a compromise on the rights of the central Soviet government's compared to the Russian Federation. Between August and December 1990, Gorbachev and Yeltsin discussed various plans to restructure political and economic power of each entity. But they were unable to agree on a solution to keep all Soviet republics in the Union.

See December 17, 1990.

May 30, 1990

The United States vetoes U.N. resolution calling for U.N. observers to be stationed on the Israeli-occupied West Bank.

The U.N. Security Council resolution was designed to send U.N. observers to Palestinian land occupied by Israel in the Six-Day War (1967). Riots by the PLO intifada in the West Bank and Gaza erupted in bloody confrontations from May 20 to 22 after a discharged Israeli soldier killed seven Palestinian laborers near Tel Aviv. On May 25, PLO leader Yasser Arafat asked the U.N. Security Council to send U.N. observers to the West Bank and Gaza and to protect Palestinians from the Israel Defense Forces (IDF). The United States vetoed the resolution, claiming the U.N. observers would violate Israel's internal sovereignty.

June 3, 1990

Presidents Bush and Gorbachev provide a basis for arms reduction treaties.

President Bush and Soviet President Gorbachev concluded a Washington, D.C., summit that began on May 30. During the sessions, they discussed a variety of issues before signing bilateral accords providing a basis for further negotiations to reduce strategic nuclear weapons, end the production of chemical weapons, and give the Soviets most-favored-nation trade status.

At a meeting in Irkutsk, Siberia, on August 2, Soviet Foreign Minister Eduard Shevardnadze and U.S. Secretary of State James Baker took another step to avoid nuclear war. Shevardnadze told Baker the Soviets would stop producing SS-24 rail-mobile ICBMs, the Soviet Union's SS-24 counterpart of America's MX ICBM missile that carryied multiple warheads (MIRVs).

If President Ronald Reagan's Strategic Defense Initiative (SDI) were combined with an MX system, the United States would have a superior nuclear war-fighting capability to force any opponent to surrender. In 1980, President Carter enunciated a nuclear war-fighting strategy in Presidential Directive 59 (see August 5, 1980), a strategy that caused tensions between the Soviets and the United States. By 1987 Soviet General Secretary Mikhail Gorbachev ended Soviet concerns regarding SDI or other U.S. missile defenses (see February 28, 1987). Rather than rely on a missile defense for the Soviet Union, Moscow developed the Topol-M ICBM's with the ability to penetrate and destroy any nation's missile defenses.

Presidents Bush and Gorbachev discuss arms limitations. George Bush Presidential Library

Despite Soviet views of America's antimissile defense, the Bush administration continued to spend $3 billion to $4 billion per year on variations of Reagan's original SDI. In 1989, the Pentagon claimed the technology of Brilliant Pebbles was a viable missile defense system to deploy within three years. Brilliant Pebbles consisted of several thousand small interceptors in space orbits above the earth. Each Pebble would carry computerized data that would locate an ICBM target on its mid-course trajectory from the Soviet Union and send a kill vehicle to ram and destroy the ICBM. By 1991, Brilliant Pebbles had failed several tests and the Pentagon had replaced Brilliant Pebbles with a plan called Global Protection Against Limited Strikes (GPALS).

See September 17–23, 1991.

June 8, 1990

Israeli Prime Minister Shamir announces new Israeli cabinet dominated by Likud Party members; U.S. Secretary of State Baker's peace plan is now hopeless.

Following the March 15 crisis ending the Likud-Labor coalition government, Prime Minister Shamir formed a Likud-dominated cabinet that excluded Labor Party members Shimon Peres and Yitzhak Rabin, on whom Secretary of State Baker depended to persuade Shamir to adopt his December 1989 peace plan. The formation of Shamir's new cabinet, added to recent conflicts between Palestinians and Israelis, made it clear that Baker's proposals could not be revived. Although President Bush and Secretary Baker believed Shamir was responsible for the failure of the peace talks, Bush suspended the U.S. dialogue with the PLO after its leader, Yasser Arafat, refused to condemn an attempted Palestinian raid on Israel on May 30, 1990.

The United States had encouraged a dialogue between the Palestinians and Israel since 1988. As James A. Baker III's *Politics of Diplomacy* (1995) indicates, Shamir was as unreliable as Arafat in seeking peace. Despite U.S. opposition to Jewish settlements in occupied territory, Shamir continued building new settlements that precipitated conflicts with the PLO before and after the Iraqi invasion of Kuwait on August 2, 1990.

See October 19, 1990.

June 9, 1990

Elections for Czechoslovakia's parliament are won by reformers.

In free elections, the alliance of President Václav Hável's Civic Forum and its Slovak Republic counterpart, Public Against Violence, won 170 of the 300 seats in the bicameral Federal Assembly. The other assembly seats were divided among the Communists (47 seats), the Christian Democratic Union (40 seats), and the separatist Slovak National Party (10 seats).

June 17, 1990

Bulgaria's former Communists win elections but protests continue.

In December 1989, protest demonstrations led to the overthrow of Bulgaria's Communist Party General Secretary Todor Zikov and the establishment of a coalition government to end the Communists' leading role in Bulgaria. The coalition government also called for free multiparty elections in 1990 and the Communist Party changed its name to the Socialist Party (see December 27, 1989). When the Bulgarian elections for parliament were held on June 17, 1990, the newly named Socialist Party of former Communists gained a majority 211 of the 400 seats in parliament.

The Union of Democratic Forces won 144 seats and smaller parties had the remaining 45 seats in parliament. On August 7, 1990, Bulgaria's parliament elected Socialist Party leader Andrei Lukanov as President and Socialist Zhelya Zhelan as Premier.

The June 17 elections did not end opposition protestors who complained Bulgaria's old secret police controlled internal affairs and gave opposition groups no access to the state controlled media outlets of radio, television, and newspapers. Protests continued for the next four months before President Lukanov agreed to resign.

See December 7, 1990.

June 27, 1990

The United States lifts retaliatory tariffs on Brazilian products; President Bush proposes a hemispheric free-trade zone.

During the 1980s, the Reagan administration had a variety of disputes with Brazil about Brazil's restrictions on American imports before the United States levied tariffs on many Brazilian products. After President Bush took office, a series of talks with Brazil enabled U.S. Special Trade Representative Carla A. Hill to report that the United States would lift retaliatory tariffs on Brazil's products. Her announcement reflected Brazil's willingness to reduce tariffs on all foreign imports and to protect foreign intellectual property rights.

Also on June 27, President Bush proposed a U.S. initiative to create a Western Hemispheric free-trade zone. Bush's Enterprise for the Americas Initiative (EAI) would encourage Latin American economic growth by forgiving up to 50 percent of the Latin American debts owed the United States and creating a hemispheric free-trade zone. The EAI complemented Bush's movement toward a North American free trade agreement with Mexico and Canada.

June 29, 1990

The United States joins 92 other nations for Aid to Third World countries in reducing the amount of their ozone-depleting gases.

During a U.N. meeting in London, the United States joined with representatives of 92 other countries to find methods to end the production of chlorofluorocarbons (CFCs) by the century's end and to help developing nations reduce their use of CFCs. At a May 9 U.N. conference, the United States opposed direct aid to Third World nations but reversed this policy on June 15, when it agreed to spend $256 million to fund the project over three years.

July 5, 1990

By dissolving Kosovo's parliament, Serbia assumes direct control over the province.

In 1989, the Serb Republic took over Kosovo's seat on the Federation of Yugoslavia's eight-member presidency (see March 23, 1989). One year later, on March 24, 1990, the Serbian Ministry of Internal Affairs took control of Kosovo's police force, expelling all Kosovo policemen who were ethnic Albanians. Finally, on July 5, 1990, the Serb Republic's National Assembly officially dissolved Kosovo's provincial parliament and assumed direct control of the province.

This action was another step in Serb President Slobodan Milosevic's call for a Greater Serbia. Despite these Serbian actions to suppress Kosovo's Albanian (Kosovars) who were 90 percent of the province of Kosovo's population, the Kosovars in the provincial parliament continued to oppose Serbian authority.

Three days before the Serb National Assembly voted to abolish Kosovo's parliament, Kosovo's provincial parliament voted on July 2 to declare Kosovo's independence of the Serb Republic. Throughout the period from July 1990 to 1998, Kosovars adopted nonviolent methods to deal with Serbia's harassment. In 1990, the President of Kosovo's Association of Writers, Ibrahim Rugova, founded the Democratic League of Kosovo (DLK). With Rugova's leadership, Kosovars organized secret meetings of an Albanian Assembly to draw up a constitution for the Republic of Kosovo. Meeting secretly in private homes or deserted buildings, the Kosovars held a referendum to approve a constitution, elect a parliament, and choose Rugova as President of the Republic of Kosovo. In addition to the DLK, other Kosovar parties included the Christian Democrats, the Social Democrats, and the Liberal Party.

Because Serb President Milosevic became involved in warfare with Croatia and Bosnia from 1990 to 1996, the unofficial Kosovo Republic was able to conduct day-to-day affairs in the lives of Kosovars, including functions such as keeping hospitals and schools open for Kosovars. In addition, most Kosovars adopted Rugova's nonviolent methods as the best means for Rugova to seek international backing from Western Europeans and the United States in opposing Serbia's illegal take over of Kosovo province.

In 1990, the plight of Kosovars gained attention from the U.S. Ambassador to Yugoslavia Warren Zimmermann, and U.S. congressional leaders who sympathized with the Kosovars. United States Representative Joseph Dioguardi, a Democrat from New York and an Albanian- American, became concerned about Kosovo in 1988, and after losing his campaign for re-election in 1988, became a lobbyist in Washington who called attention to Serb violations of Albanian human rights. In particular, Dioguardi gained attention from Senators Robert Dole (R-Kans.), Alfonse D'Amato (R-N.Y.), and Don Nickles (R-Okla.). In August 1990, these three senators visited Belgrade to talk with leaders from each of Yugoslavia's republics before visiting Kosovo to meet Rugova and other Kosovar leaders.

According to Ambassador Zimmermann's memoir *Origins of a Catastrophe* (1996), Dole, D'Amato, and Nickles believed Kosovo should be independent from the Serbs, who used abusive methods against the Kosovars. On returning to Washington, Senator Nickles added an amendment to foreign aid legislation for fiscal year 1991. Supported by Dole and D'Amato, the Nickles Amendment would cut U.S. economic assistance to Yugoslavia down to $5 million in May 1991, if Yugoslavia did not stop suppressing the Kosovars. The legislation passed Congress, but Bush and Ambassador Zimmermann opposed the Nickles Amendment because it did not affect Milosevic's Serb Republic, the real culprit. By May 1991, the Nickles Amendment was no longer relevant because the Yugoslav Federation collapsed in June 1991.

See October 1, 1990.

July 5, 1990

Poland's austerity program disrupts its government.

On January 1, 1990, Poland adopted the advice of U.S. economists to implement austerity methods that included price increases, wage freezes, and currency deregulation. Because inflation increased while wages fell, the reforms caused widespread discontent. In May, members of Lech Walesa's Solidarity union won local elections in which the Communists received only 2 percent of the votes, a sign of popular dismay with the economic reforms. To relieve the discontent, on July 5 Premier Mazowiecki removed three former Communists from his cabinet: the defense, interior, and transportation ministers. He also held meetings with Walesa to "preserve social peace" prior to the national elections scheduled for November.

July 8, 1990

The United States agrees to close military bases in Greece.

On July 8, the United States and Greece signed an agreement to close two U.S. army bases near Athens, although the United States could maintain an air and naval base on the Greek island of Crete. The United States also reaffirmed its military aid to Greece and Turkey that favored Greece by a seven-to-ten ratio.

July 11, 1990

Meeting in Houston, Texas, G-7 nations agree on three important issues.

President Bush hosted the four-day session of the seven leading industrial nations. The G-7 leaders agreed to study possible economic aid to the USSR to encourage a Soviet free-market economy; to end Soviet agricultural subsides; and to accept President Bush's suggestion to delay decisions about limiting the reduction of "greenhouse gases" until 1992.

July 18, 1990

The United States ends recognition of Cambodia's rebel coalition.

During the year after U.S. Secretary of State James Baker changed policy to promote peace in Cambodia, Baker reversed his peace effort by withdrawing U.S. diplomatic recognition of Cambodia's rebel coalition and its right to U.N. membership. Baker announced this new effort because the Khmer Rouge boycotted the U.N.-sponsored talks in Tokyo and another round of intense fighting began.

Baker also offered to negotiate with Vietnam, and on September 29, Baker and Vietnamese Foreign Minister Nguyen Co Thach discussed Cambodia but found no solutions for the problems. Although China was disappointed with Baker's decision to involve Vietnam in Cambodia, the U.N. Security Council agreed to provide an interim Cambodian government if the four Cambodian factions accepted a peace plan. The U.N. plan could not be implemented and Cambodia's fighting intensified near the end of 1990.

July 29, 1990

Mongolia's reform Communist Party retains control of parliament.

In Mongolia's first multiparty election, the Communist Party was victorious, keeping 75 percent of seats in the Great Hural (upper house) and 60 percent of the seats in the Small Hural (lower house). On March 14, the reformist chairman of the party's Politburo, Gombojavyn Ochirbat, promised to develop democracy and protect human rights. Parliament also amended Mongolia's constitution to end the Communists' power monopoly and allow direct elections.

August 2, 1990

Iraq invades Kuwait, easily conquering the small Arab state.

When news of Iraq's invasion of Kuwait reached Washington late in the evening of August 1, 1990, Iraqi forces had already conquered Kuwait City, three and one-half hours after crossing the border. The White House immediately issued a statement condemning Iraq's attack and President Bush ordered the U.S. Treasury Department to freeze all the financial assets of Iraq and Kuwait held in the United States.

The Bush administration also adopted the suggestion Soviet Foreign Minister Eduard Shevardnadze made to Secretary of State Baker in Siberia to have the United Nations issue a condemnation of Iraq's aggression and order Iraq to end its occupation of Kuwait. United Nations support not only would avoid a Soviet veto of any unwarranted U.N. Security Council resolutions against Iraq but also justify international economic sanctions against Iraq until Baghdad withdrew its forces from Kuwait.

Persian Gulf

Between August 2 and November 29, 1990, the United Nations Security Council approved 10 resolutions as part of a U.S.-led international coalition to evict Iraq from Kuwait. The first two of the 10 resolutions were U.N. Security Council Resolution 660, which condemned Iraq's conquest of Kuwait, and resolution 661, which levied economic sanctions on Iraq see August 25, 1990.

In addition to seeking U.N. backing, the Bush administration consulted with NATO members and officials of Saudi Arabia, Jordan, Egypt, and other Middle East countries near Iraq to obtain their support in evicting Iraq from Kuwait. Most important of all these contacts was sending a team of U.S. military advisers to consult with Saudi Arabia's King Fahd and Saudi Lieutenant General Prince Khalid Bin Sultan al-Saud, who worked with U.S. General Norman H. Schwarzkopf until the Iraqi conflict ended in March 1991. Headed by Defense Secretary Richard Cheney and Commander of U.S. Central Command for the Middle East General Schwarzkopf, these U.S. advisers gave King Fahd specific intelligence data regarding Iraq's threat to countries such as Saudi Arabia, Qatar, and Jordan.

Despite Saddam Hussein's denunciation of U.S. policies between January and August 1990, Bush had failed to perceive the Iraqi leader's rising anger during the week before the invasion. On July 25, U.S. Ambassador to Iraq, April Glaspie met with Hussein, who claimed Kuwait was a lackey of Washington and waged economic warfare on Iraq.

Glaspie tried to placate Hussein by saying she had insufficient time to prepare a response but the United States wanted Iraq's friendship. Glaspie told him problems could be handled by diplomacy although the United States had no security commitments with Kuwait. Glaspie's attitude was clarified in her recommendation to the State Department to relax its public criticism of Iraq. In response, Bush composed a letter for Glaspie to convey to Hussein that "in a spirit of friendship and candor," the United States would help find a peaceful solution to Iraq's problems with Kuwait. Some historians think Glaspie and Bush gave Hussein the impression that the United States would not oppose an Iraqi invasion of Kuwait.

August 2, 1990

Secretary of State Baker and Soviet Foreign Minister Shevardnadze condemn Iraq's invasion of Kuwait.

In a fortuitous circumstance, U.S. Secretary of State Baker was meeting with Soviet Foreign Minister Eduard Shevardnadze in Irkutsk, Siberia, where they learned about the invasion of Kuwait. The two ministers condemned Iraq's invasion in a mutual understanding that became the basis for U.S.-USSR cooperation in meeting Saddam Hussein's challenge and avoiding a Soviet veto in the U.N. Security Council. Shevardnadze's decision worried the Kremlin because some Soviet officials sympathetic to Iraq argued that the USSR had helped Iraq in the past. The Soviet Union had over 7,000 advisers in Baghdad.

See August 25, 1990.

August 6, 1990

Using U.N. Security Council resolutions against Iraq, President Bush orders U.S. forces to protect Saudi Arabia as a Desert Shield operation.

Adopting Soviet Foreign Minister Shevardnadze's suggestion to use the U.N. Security Council to force Iraq to leave Kuwait, President Bush consulted with European and Arab leaders. He also sent U.S. military advisers to determine whether Saudi King Fahd should request U.S. assistance. With King Fahd's approval, on August 6 Bush ordered U.S. forces to begin an operation known as Desert Shield. The United States immediately dispatched 2,300 paratroopers in addition to AWAC, B-52, and F-111 aircraft to provide an early defense for the Saudis prior to the arrival of an aircraft carrier task force and army ground forces. On August 8, Great Britain, Egypt, and other nations joined the multinational force to deter further Iraqi aggression and enforce U.N. economic sanctions against Iraq.

On August 8, Bush's televised broadcast informed Americans he accepted King Fahd's request for protection from Iraq's expansionism as a "wholly defensive operation." On August 10, Bush notified Congress about troops sent to defend Saudi Arabia without invoking the 1973 War Powers Act because "war is not imminent." Later, on October 1–2, the House and Senate voted to support the president's defensive actions toward Iraqi aggression.

August 22, 1990

West and East Germany renounce use of nuclear, chemical and biological weapons; a united Germany continues this commitment.

At the Fourth Non-Proliferation Treaty Review Conference, the two German governments affirmed their contractual commitments not "to manufacture, possess or control nuclear, biological and chemical weapons." They also declared the united Germany would abide by this obligation.

See September 12, 1990.

August 25, 1990

The U.N. Security Council authorizes naval and air blockades of Iraq.

To enforce the economic sanction levied against Iraq on August 2, the Security Council approved resolution 665 by a vote of 13–0 (Cuba and Yemen abstaining). Resolution 665 authorized U.S. and allied ships blockading Iraq to use force if necessary to carry out the sanctions. The vote was delayed until August 25 because the Soviet Union thought Saddam Hussein would negotiate a settlement and leave Kuwait. On September 25, resolution 670 extended the Iraqi embargo by ending air flights to and from Iraq.

On September 9, after Moscow realized Saddam Hussein intended to stay in Kuwait, Soviet President Mikhail Gorbachev met with Bush in Helsinki to declare U.S.-USSR solidarity in condemning Iraq's invasion and calling for Iraq's unconditional withdrawal from Kuwait. On October 15, Gorbachev received the Nobel Prize for his reforms leading to the end of the Cold War.

September 12, 1990

The 2+4 talks result in a final treaty for German reunification.

In Moscow, a final treaty resulted from six months of 2+4 talks before being signed by representatives of the United States, the Soviet Union, Great Britain, France, West Germany, and East Germany, plus a representative from Poland. In addition to providing for the political reunification of Germany, the agreements included these key clauses:

1. Germany guaranteed the Oder and Neisse Rivers as its eastern border with Poland;

2. Soviet troops would leave East Germany by 1994, with the West German government paying the cost of the Soviet withdrawal;
3. Germany would be a member of NATO but with limits on the size of the German army (370,000), with no nuclear weapons in eastern German territory, and with Germany as a signatory of the Nuclear Non-Proliferation Treaty.

During the six months of talks on Germany's future, NATO adopted policies to show that the Warsaw Pact and NATO nations were not adversaries. The two blocs would reduce their front-line defenses and make the use of nuclear weapons "a last resort," a phrase modifying the "first-use" strategy of previous years. Finally, NATO invited Warsaw Pact leaders to establish a diplomatic liaison at NATO's Brussels headquarters.

See September 20, 1990.

September 18, 1990

The Salvadoran government and rebels fail to get a cease-fire; President Bush sends El Salvador more aid.

Having negotiated in Costa Rica since July 26, representatives of El Salvador and the *Farabundo Marti para la Liberacion Nacional* (FMLN) rebels failed to agree on a cease-fire by September 18. Rebel leaders announced a new "political offensive" to change the government, and fighting increased during the next two months. On December 7, Bush announced the United States would rush $8 million to assist the Salvadoran government.

September 20, 1990

East and West Germany reunite in accordance with the 2+4 talks.

German reunification was completed when the East and West German parliaments ratified the treaty. The ratified agreement was the Settlement with Respect to Germany signed in Moscow on September 12, 1990. The unity was solidified on October 14 when elections were held in five new states formed from former East Germany. In elections for the united German Bundestag (lower house of parliament), Chancellor Helmut Kohl's Christian Democratic Union Party won either a majority or plurality of votes in all states except Brandenburg, where Social Democrats won a plurality.

In line with 2+4 talks, East Germany withdrew from the Warsaw Pact on September 24. On November 9, Germany and the Soviet Union signed a nonaggression pact and friendship treaty. On November 14 Germany and Poland signed a treaty making their current boundaries permanent along the Oder and Neisse River.

October 1, 1990

Slovenia and Croatia take steps against Serb dominance of Yugoslavia.

On September 28, Slovenia, one of six Yugoslav republics, amended its constitution to make the republic's laws superior to Yugoslav laws. Slovenia also assumed control of its territorial defense forces. In contrast to Slovenia, where few Serbs lived, Croatia's attempt to end Serb dominance was complicated by the large number of Serbs living in the northeast border region of Croatia known as the Krajina. On July 25, 1990, Milan Bobic, a Serb dentist who lived in Knin, the Krajina's largest city, began organizing Serb protests to gain autonomy from Croatia and, perhaps, become part of the Serb Republic. Bobic and many other Croatian Serbs were inspired by Slobodan Milosevic's propaganda calling for a Greater Serbia. To verify that the people of Krajina desired autonomy, Bobic called for a referendum to be held in the Krajina on August 18, 1990.

Two days before the referendum, Croatia's President Franjo Tudjman declared the Krajina referendum unconstitutional and ordered Croatian police to march on Knin and enforce Croatia's constitution by preventing the referendum from taking place. Croatia's Minister of the Interior also ordered three helicopters loaded with Croatian police reservists to back up the police objectives. As Laura Silber and Allen Little's *Yugoslavia: Death of a Nation* (1995) explains, Tujdman's attempt to stop the referendum was a fiasco. After learning the police were on the way to Knin, Bobic telephoned Belgrade and asked Serb President Milosevic for help against Croatia's police. Milosevic immediately dispatched the Yugoslav National Army's (YNA) aircraft to fly across the Croatian border, frighten the Croatian police, and attack the helicopters if necessary.

After the YNA's MiG fighter planes buzzed the helicopters to scare them away from Knin, the MiG pilot radioed the helicopters, telling the helicopter pilots to return directly to their bases or be shot down. The helicopter's turned homeward while the Croatian police stopped their march toward Knin and retreated to their home bases. After the confrontation ended and despite President Tudjman's complaints against Milosevic, the Krajina referendum was held with 99 percent of the Croatian Serbs voting in favor of autonomy for Krajina. Tudjman failed to suppress Serb nationalism but took action to revitalize Croatia's Territorial Defense Force (TDF) and to purge Serbian officers of the YNA stationed in Croatia. Compared to Croatians, the disproportionate number of Serbs in the TDF and the YNA were expelled from the services and Croatians were recruited to replace the reserves. Tudjman built a national Croatian army to prepare for Croatia's secession from the Yugoslav Federation and gain independence.

October 19, 1990

President Bush rejects a proposal to compromise with Iraq.

To placate hard-liners in the Soviet Foreign Ministry who criticized Foreign Minister Shevardnadze's cooperation with U.S. Secretary of State Baker on the Kuwait conflict, President Gorbachev sent former *Pravda* correspondent Yevgeny Primakov to Baghdad, Washington, and London in search of a diplomatic solution. In Baghdad, Primakov discussed Saddam Hussein's August 12 proposal to combine a conference on Kuwait with a conference to settle all Arab-Israeli disputes. Primakov next came to Washington to tell Bush that Hussein was "flexible" in working out details of the Kuwait and Arab-Israeli meetings. But Bush refused to link the Kuwait issue with the Arab-Israeli conflict, telling Primakov to make sure Hussein understood Iraq must unconditionally leave Kuwait.

Finally, Primakov visited London to talk with Prime Minister Margaret Thatcher but learned Thatcher would not compromise. Thatcher lectured Primakov on Hussein's treachery, saying there was no option but war, not only to free Kuwait but also to destroy Iraq's military power. Primakov's failure did not end criticism of Shevardnadze in the Kremlin.

November 8, 1990

President Bush moves to take the offensive against Iraq.

Two days after congressional elections, President Bush announced U.S. forces in the Middle East would be doubled to obtain "an adequate offensive military option." Bush's plan to increase troops began in October when the White House adopted rhetoric to condemn Saddam Hussein as a new "Hitler" who placed foreign hostages as human shields near military bases, terrorized the Kuwaiti population, looted Kuwaiti banks, and prepared to use chemical and nuclear weapons. Bush and Secretary of State James Baker also contacted friendly nations to ask for their support in future action against Iraq. Bush's increase of U.S. forces in the Persian Gulf led many members of Congress to be skeptical of his rhetoric against Hussein, and Senate hearings examined his decision.

See November 27, 1990.

November 17, 1990

The Treaty on Conventional Forces in Europe (CFE) is signed.

In Paris, leaders of NATO and Warsaw Pact nations signed the CFE Treaty. Resulting from meetings of the Commission of Security and Cooperation in Europe (CSCE), the pact limited each alliance to 20,000 battle tanks and artillery pieces, 30,000 armored combat vehicles, 6,800 combat aircraft, and 2,000 attack helicopters.

Two days later, the CSCE members signed the Charter of Paris for a New Europe, declaring an end to Europe's military and economic divisions and affirming democratic freedoms and human rights.

November 18, 1990

Saddam Hussein offers to release all foreign hostages in Iraq and Kuwait.

Hoping to divide the alliance opposing Iraq, Saddam Hussein offered to release foreign hostages in Iraq and Kuwait over a three-month period if no war began. Although President Bush rejected this ploy, Hussein released German hostages because, he said, Chancellor Helmut Kohl had made helpful remarks about peace. On December 4 without receiving U.S. or U.N. concessions, Hussein released the remaining Soviet hostages and approximately 3,000 Western hostages, including 163 Americans, the U.S. ambassador to Kuwait, and his four staff members. On December 11, the State Department said about 500 Americans chose to remain in Iraq or Kuwait.

November 27, 1990

The Senate Armed Forces Committee examines Iraqi economic sanctions.

Because of congressional opposition to President Bush's November 8 decision to increase troops in the Persian Gulf, the Senate Armed Services Committee under Chairman Sam Nunn (D-Ga.) conducted hearings on military action as compared to continuing economic sanctions. Appearing before the committee, Bush administration officials such as Defense Secretary Richard Cheney and Secretary of State James Baker argued that military action might be the only way to get Iraqi forces out of Kuwait.

Opponents of Bush's policy, such as former Chairman of the Joint Chiefs of Staff Admiral William Crowe, did not deny the need to get Iraq out of Kuwait but contended that economic sanctions would achieve this goal if sufficient time were given for them to work. Nevertheless, Bush feared the coalition of Western and Arab countries might fall apart if sanctions took too long to compel Saddam Hussein to leave Kuwait. The debate on war or sanctions continued until the eve of war.

November 28, 1990

Britain's Conservative Party selects John Major as Prime Minister.

The Conservative Party was divided on the issue of Margaret Thatcher's policy toward economic unity with the European Community. Although a plurality of Conservative Party members favored Thatcher, she resigned on November 24, with Major replacing her.

November 29, 1990

The U.N. Security Council authorizes "all means necessary" to get Iraq out of Kuwait.

After President Bush ordered 20,000 additional U.S. troops to the Persian Gulf on November 8, his rhetoric emphasized Iraq's atrocities in Kuwait and Iraq's preparations for nuclear war. Visiting U.S. troops in Saudi Arabia on Thanksgiving Day, Bush said experts thought it would be years before Iraq had nuclear weapons but they "may be seriously underestimating the situation." Each day, Bush said, brought Iraq "one step closer" to having a nuclear arsenal to use.

As revealed in Khidhir Hamaz's *Saddam's Bombmaker* (2000), Iraq had tried since August 1990 to speed up the construction of a nuclear warhead small enough to mount on an Iraqi missile. But Iraqi scientists only completed a nuclear bomb too big to be carried by a missile, so Saddam Hussein ordered the nuclear experimental units hidden in case U.S.-led forces attacked. Iraq also planted thousands of chemical and biological weapons in southern Iraq near Basra, where bombs of an invader would release their contents in the air, a possible reason for the postwar Gulf War syndrome experienced by veterans of the 1991 war.

Without knowing Saddam's precise plans, Bush and Secretary of State Baker contacted over 20 heads of state and all U.N. Security Council members to seek approval for a deadline to attack Saddam Hussein.

Baker's crucial task was to obtain wording satisfactory to Soviet Foreign Minister Shevardnadze. Baker and Shevardnadze finally agreed the U.N. resolution should avoid the term "use of force," but after the resolution passed, Baker would call it an "authority to use force" as part of the U.N. record. Baker also accepted President Gorbachev's suggestion to call the interval before the January 15 deadline a "pause of goodwill" for diplomacy that might prevent war.

Having the diplomatic cards in place, the United States proposed U.N. resolution 678, which Security Council members approved by 12 to 2, with Cuba and Yemen opposing while China abstained. The resolution authorized states "cooperating with the government of Kuwait" to use "all means necessary" to obtain Iraq's withdrawal from Kuwait and gave Iraq until January 15 to comply.

November 30, 1990

President Bush invites the Iraqi foreign minister to negotiate in Washington.

Following passage of U.N. resolution 678 on November 29, President Bush invited Iraqi Foreign Minister Tariq Aziz to Washington for negotiations and offered to send Secretary of State Baker to Baghdad for discussions. Although the offer disturbed U.S. allies because Bush did not contact them in advance, Bush simply planned to avoid war by telling Iraqi officials that the January 15 deadline for their unconditional withdrawal from Kuwait must be met.

Subsequently, Washington and Baghdad made frequent attempts to schedule a time and place for meeting, with the United States insisting the date must be well before January 15. Baker finally met with Tariq Aziz.

November 30, 1990

President Bush again seeks to improve U.S.-Chinese relations.

President Bush met with Chinese Foreign Minister Qian Qichen at the White House in an effort to improve U.S. relations with China following the 1989 Tiananmen Square massacres. On June 25, the Chinese permitted dissident Fang Lizhi, who in 1989 had sought safety in the U.S. embassy in Beijing, to leave the country for London. At Secretary of State Baker's request, China abstained from the November 29 U.N. resolution 678 on Iraq.

December 2, 1990

Reunited Germany holds its first general elections; Chancellor Kohl's alliance wins.

Reunited Germany's first general election was a victory for Chancellor Helmut Kohl's governing Christian Socialist Union (CSU)/Christian Democratic Union (CDU) coalition and his allied Free Democrats. East Germany's former Communist party, renamed the Party of Democratic Socialism (PDS), won 17 of the 672 seats in the Bundestag (lower house) and East German Greens received eight seats. German's Social Democratic Party remained the main opposition party.

December 3, 1990

President Bush begins a six-day visit to five Latin American states.

On the first stop of a tour of South America, President Bush addressed Brazil's Congress to praise President Fernando Collor de Mello, who, since his inauguration on March 15, had attracted international financial officials by beginning an economic austerity program. Collor's program reduced government spending and inflation, froze wages and prices for 30 days, and changed the currency from the cruzado to a cruzeiro. He also halted Brazil's secret nuclear weapons program and on November 28 joined with Argentine's President Menem to renounce the use of nuclear weapons.

After a brief visit to Uruguay, Bush met in Argentina with President Carlos Saul Menem on December 4. This meeting took place just two days after army forces loyal to the president put down an uprising of dissident troops who had seized army headquarters to demand the appointment of Colonel Mohammed Ali Seineldin as chief of staff. The loyalists regained control of all sites seized by the rebels, although 21 persons were killed in the conflict. After showing U.S. backing for Menem's government, Bush made short visits to Chile and Venezuela before returning home.

December 6, 1990

U.S. aircraft assist France in evacuating its citizens from Chad.

Washington and Paris had hoped Libyan dissidents would help Chad's President Hissene Habré defeat a rebel army backed by Libyan leader Mu'ammar al-Gadhafi. Instead, rebels led by General Idriss Deby captured Chad's capital, N'Djamena on December 2 and Habré fled into exile. At French request, U.S. planes airlifted 700 Libyan dissidents from Chad to Nigeria. The French also evacuated over 1,000 of their nationals from Chad.

December 7, 1990

Bulgaria moves toward a more democratic government.

Although Bulgaria's Communist Party was renamed the Socialist party and won Bulgaria's June elections, protests against Socialist Premier Lukanov broke out and led to his resignation in November. The Bulgarian parliament approved Ditmar Popov, a politically independent judge, as Bulgaria's premier. Popov organized a multiparty cabinet that included many Socialist Party members.

December 9, 1990

Poland's Communists lose in national elections.

Although Communist Premier Mazowiecki tried to alleviate Poland's social discontent in July 1990, his austerity policies were unpopular. They led to the presidential victory of the Solidarity Party's Lech Walesa, who won 74 percent of the votes in a runoff election.

On December 12, outgoing president Jaruzelski apologized for the "pain and injustice" the people suffered under the Communists. Walesa was sworn in as president on December 22.

December 12, 1990

The Czechoslovak National Assembly specifies the powers of the country's two republics.

Because leaders of the Slovak Republic desired autonomy, President Václav Hável asked the National Assembly to define the federal powers related to the authority of Slovakia. The assembly passed legislation that retained federal power over defense, foreign affairs, economic policy, and the protection of national minorities. The Czech and Slovak Republics held the remaining powers.

December 14–15, 1990

The European Community (EC) provides aid to the Soviets and asks Iraq to withdraw from Kuwait.

During a regularly scheduled session, EC leaders agreed to provide the USSR with $2.4 billion of aid. They also called on Iraq to withdraw peacefully from Kuwait and proposed future talks to coordinate EC policies on foreign and security affairs.

December 17, 1990

The Soviet Congress of People's Deputies approves President Gorbachev's plan to revise the central authority; Eduard Shevardnadze resigns as foreign minister.

On December 17, President of the Supreme Soviet Mikhail Gorbachev sought to maintain Soviet unity by presenting a plan to the Congress of People's Deputies that consisted of 2,250 delegates from each Soviet republic who were elected in 1989 (see March 26, 1989 and May 25, 1989). Gorbachev was concerned about Soviet unity because throughout 1990, Soviet republics such as Lithuania (March 11), Estonia (March 11), Latvia (May 4), the Russian Federation (August 10), Armenia (August 5), and Ukraine (October 24) had proclaimed various degrees of independence from the Soviet Union.

On October 16, 1990, Gorbachev sought to meet the challenge of maintaining Soviet unity by offering his plan to the Supreme Soviet, the standing legislative body consisting of 542 delegates elected by the People's Deputies in May 1989. Gorbachev's plan would restructure the economy and preserve the central government's authority over foreign policy, banking, taxes, and currency, but would also give each republic autonomy in domestic affairs. The plan also called for a referendum to be held in each of the Soviet republics to obtain the people's approval for maintaining Soviet unity. In October, the Supreme Soviet approved Gorbachev's plan although some hard-line Communists such as the chief of the KGB's secret police Vladamir A. Kryuchkov opposed Gorbachev's plan as "Western economic involvement." After obtaining the Supreme Soviet's approval, Gorbachev sought approval of his unity plan by the Congress of People's Deputies. After the Deputies convened on December 17, Gorbachev presented the plan approved by the Supreme Soviet, asking the delegates to assist Moscow in conducting the referendums in each of the republics. Before adjourning on December 24, the People's Deputies approved Gorbachev's reform plan and agreed to conduct the referendum. Also during the week of the congress, Soviet Foreign Minister Shevardnadze resigned.

Although President Gorbachev said Shevardnadze simply needed a rest, President Bush and his advisers believed Shevardnadze was dismayed because hard-line Communists such as Yevgeny Primakov had gained ascendancy in Moscow after Gorbachev placated them. This belief became reality when Primakov undertook efforts to help Saddam Hussein gain concessions from the United States in February 1991.

December 31, 1990

Israeli bombers hit PLO bases in southern Lebanon.

Although Israel realized it should avoid trouble in the Middle East to maintain President Bush's coalition against Iraq, Prime Minister Yitzhak Shamir wanted to keep the PLO from strengthening its position in south Lebanon. Hezbollah guerrillas continued to attack Israeli forces despite the peace among Lebanese factions. To retain Israel's position in south Lebanon, Shamir ordered Israeli fighter-bombers to attack Palestinian bases near Sidon, killing 12 persons. For similar reasons on December 29, Israeli troops put down demonstrations in the Gaza Strip that killed four Palestinians and wounded 125.

1991

January 5, 1991

Somalia's civil war requires United States and Italy to rescue foreigners in Mogadishu.

American officials first became concerned about Somalia in 1978 (see May 16, 1978) because Soviet and Cuban forces assisted Ethiopia in defeating Somalia in a war caused by Somalia's claim to Ogadan province on the border with Ethiopia. Following the war, President Carter sent $7 million of food aid to Somalia. In 1982, President Reagan sent military aid to assist Somalia in another Ethiopian conflict, during which Cuban leader Fidel Castro sent 18,000 Cuban soldiers to help Ethiopia.

During the 1980s, the Soviets and Cubans also helped rebel groups in Somalia seeking to overthrow the government of General Muhammad Siad Barre, who had taken power in 1969. By 1988, Barre was fighting various rebel forces. Rebel sin northern Somalia such as the Somalia National Movement and the Somalia Democratic Salvation Front were well organized. In southern Somalia near Mogadishu, competing clans and subclans carried on their civil war, causing more trouble for Barre and surrounding the capital by January 1991.

The fighting near Mogadishu prompted the United States and Italy to combine their forces in air and sea operations to rescue American, Soviet, Italian, and other foreigners in Mogadishu. U.N. groups providing food relief to Somalia also evacuated Mogadishu. To permit the safe rescue of foreign personnel, Somalia's warring factions accepted a temporary cease-fire while the evacuation took place.

Following the rescue, civil war resumed, with the rebels overthrowing President Siad Barre on January 26. Intense fighting continued as two warlords, Mohammad Farah Aideed and Mohammad Ali Mahdi, competed for control of Somalia.

January 9, 1991

Secretary of State Baker fails to persuade Iraq to evacuate Kuwait.

Throughout December 1990, attempts at negotiations between the United States and Iraq fell through. Finally on January 9, Iraqi Foreign Minister Tariq Aziz agreed to meet in Geneva with Secretary of State James Baker. At the first of two meetings with Aziz on January 9, Baker gave Aziz a copy of a letter addressed from President George Bush to Iraq's President Saddam Hussein. Baker asked Aziz to read the letter and respond to its contents. In part, Bush wrote: "We stand today at the brink of war between Iraq and the world. This is a war which (sic) began with your invasion of Kuwait; this is a war that can only be ended by Iraq's full and unconditional compliance with U.N. Security Council Resolution 687." As described by Baker's memoir *The Politics of Diplomacy*, after reading the letter Aziz told Baker "it is full of expressions of threat" and "alien" to "communications between the heads of state." Aziz also threw the letter on a table, saying he would not deliver such a letter to President Hussein. During his conversations with Aziz that morning and again after lunch, Baker reiterated contents of Bush's letter, although using different words in trying to convince Aziz that Iraq must withdraw its forces from Kuwait.

"If you do not leave," Baker told Aziz, "then we'll find ourselves at war" and "you will surely lose" because Iraq will face "devastatingly superior fire power." Baker also warned Aziz that if Iraq should use chemical or biological weapons against our forces Americans will "demand vengeance." The United States, Baker said, has the means to eliminate the "current Iraqi regime." Brushing off Baker's statement, Aziz said Iraq is not afraid of a war with America, describing a U.S. invasion of Iraq as simply an "alliance among the United States, Israel and former rulers of Kuwait." If the United States attacked, Aziz said, "Iraq will be justified in attacking Israel, an event that would rally all Arabs to the side of Iraq."

Aziz not only refused to accept Bush's letter but refused to fear Baker's warnings about America's superior fire power. In a final attempt to avert war, U.N. Secretary General Javier Pérez de Cueller visited Saddam Hussein in Baghdad on January 12, where he too learned Hussein would not withdraw Iraqi forces from Kuwait.

January 12, 1991

Congress approves use of military force against Iraq, if necessary.

Following two days of debate on whether the United States should attack Iraq or allow more time for economic sanctions to compel Iraq to withdraw its forces from Kuwait, Congress authorized the use of military force against Iraq if necessary. The Senate approved the resolution by 52 to 47; the House, by 250 to 183.

The vote for war was the closest since Congress approved James Madison's call for war against the British in 1812, but, unlike the Federalists in 1812, who continued opposing Madison, the Democrats in 1991 rallied behind President Bush. As Senator Sam Nunn (D-Ga.) said: "We may disagree in this chamber but when the vote is over... we are going to stand united."

January 16, 1991

Directed by the United States, a multinational U.N. force launches a Gulf War.

Almost immediately after Iraq's deadline to leave Kuwait ended, the U.S.-led 28-nation multinational force attacked. On January 16 at 4:50 P.M. Eastern Standard Time (early morning of January 17 in Iraq), U.S. and allied aircraft began a 38-day blitz against Iraq. During this period, allied planes flew over 100,000 sorties while 284 U.S. navy Tomahawk missiles struck Iraq. The U.S. aircraft and Tomahawk missiles targeted Iraq's air defense system and communication centers, tried to find and destroy Iraq's nuclear and chemical-biological weapons, and sought out the launching pads for SCUD missiles. Air raids also struck targets near the Kuwaiti border, where Iraqi tanks and troops were preparing to engage the allied ground forces.

Allied planes dominated the air. Iraqi aircraft that initially sought combat were shot down, and Iraq's remaining combat planes sought sanctuary in Iran. On January 28, after some allied planes were lost, Iraq television broadcast videos of seven airmen captured by Iraq (one American) and said the pilots would be dispersed to potential allied targets where they would risk death if those targets were bombed.

Bush participates in a Joint Chiefs of Staff briefing, with Secretary of Defense Richard Cheney, and General Colin Powell at the Pentagon. George Bush Presidential Library

The air raids succeeded but were insufficient to end the war.

January 17, 1991

Iraq uses unorthodox tactics against U.N. forces.

Iraqi President Saddam Hussein responded to allied air attacks by a series of unorthodox retaliatory tactics. On January 17, Iraq's SCUD missiles attacked Israel. Hussein hoped the SCUD attack would force Israel to retaliate, destroying the U.S. alliance with the Arab states. Israel did not strike back and the United States sent a Patriot antimissile system to help defend Israel from SCUDs. On January 20, Iraq began launching SCUDs targeted on military locations in Saudi Arabia. On February 24 a SCUD hit the U.S. barracks in Dhahran, killing 28 U.S. soldiers.

In a second unorthodox move, Iraq set fire to Kuwaiti oil wells, which generated oil spills from Kuwaiti facilities into the Persian Gulf. Iraq's only ground attack during the period of allied air raids was a surprise raid against the Saudi town of Khafji on January 29. The attack failed, and within 36 hours, Saudi and Qatar armies assisted by U.S. Marines drove out the Iraqi forces.

February 22, 1991

President Bush rejects Iraq peace proposals sought by the Soviet Union.

After rejecting two peace proposals that Moscow brokered with Iraq, President Bush informed Iraqi President Saddam Hussein that Iraq had until noon on February 23 to begin withdrawing from Kuwait or allied ground forces would attack. The Soviet peace effort began on February 12 when Politburo member Yevgeny Primakov visited Hussein and returned with proposals that Bush and other allied leaders called a "hoax." Iraqi Foreign Minister Tariq Aziz then flew to Moscow to make a second peace offer that President Gorbachev sent to Bush. Gorbachev said Iraq offered to withdraw unconditionally from Kuwait, but details of Iraq's message indicated Hussein would be absolved from all responsibility for invading Kuwait.

On February 22, Bush rejected both offers and gave Hussein 24 hours to demonstrate a desire for peace by withdrawing his forces from Kuwait or a ground war would begin.

February 25, 1991

The Warsaw Pact disbands its military and economic institutions.

Meeting in Budapest with East Germany no longer a member, the six remaining Warsaw Pact members agreed to disband their military structure by March 31, 1991. The members signed agreements providing for Soviet troops to withdraw from Poland, Czechoslovakia, and Hungary by June 21, 1991. At a second Budapest meeting on June 18, 1991, the Warsaw Pact disbanded its economic organization, Comecon.

February 28, 1991

In a 100-hour ground war, Iraq's forces are evicted from Kuwait.

At 5:00 A.M. Kuwaititime, within 100 hours after U.S. and allied U.N. forces began an offensive, Iraq's armies were defeated. On February 28, President Bush announced a cease-fire and Iraq's Foreign Minister Aziz accepted prior U.N. resolutions regarding Iraq's withdrawal.

As Bush had warned, the U.S.-led ground assault began soon after the deadline of February 23. French, British, and U.S. forces struck along the Saudi-Iraqi border while Saudi, Egyptian, Syrian, and other Arab forces advanced into Kuwait with U.S. Marines paving the way through Iraqi obstacles on the road to Kuwait City. Because Iraq useded inexperienced soldiers in front-line trenches, many of these troops surrendered *en masse.* Elsewhere, some Iraqi elite Republican Guard units engaged allied forces on Iraqi territory while others withdrew to safe positions to avoid destruction and enhance President Hussein's efforts to remain in power.

In a post-conflict analysis, critics said President Bush stopped the war a few hours too soon because allied forces were prepared to encircle two Republican Guard divisions near Basra. Bush's cease-fire order prevented the defeat of those units and left Saddam Hussein in power.

March 3, 1991

Iraqi military leaders sign official U.N. cease-fire terms.

U.S. General Norman Schwarzkopf, Saudi Prince General Khalid bin Sultan, and other allied commanders met Iraqi generals at Iraq's Safwan Air Base to sign a cease-fire. Under the cease-fire terms of U.N. resolution 686 of March 2, Schwarzkopf did not negotiate with Iraqi generals, who simply accepted U.N. terms. The agreement dealt with POW exchanges, avoiding future military incidents, and Iraq's acceptance of final peace terms to be drawn up by the U.N. Security Council. In retrospect, Schwarzkopf said his major mistake was failing to stop Iraqi helicopter flights that Iraq used to savagely put down anti-Saddam Hussein uprisings after the war ended by southern Iraqi Shiites and northern based Kurds.

During the war, President Bush had urged Iraqis to overthrow Saddam Hussein. In response, Shiite and Kurdish dissidents staged uprising against Iraq's government after the cease-fire was declared. They expected Bush to order American troops in Saudi Arabia to help them but Bush ignored the uprisings although he hailed the start of a "new world order" on March 6, 1991.

March 4, 1991

Chile reports on Pinochet's human rights violations.

In April 1990, Chilean President Patricio Aylwin Azócar formed a commission to investigate the human rights abuses that took place during the 17-year regime of General Augusto Pinochet Ugarte. On March 4, President Aylwin released the commission report that provided details about the murder, torture, and disappearance of over 2,000 Chileans by the military junta and secret police. Pinochet rejected the report and Chile's military leaders backed him. The complicity of Chile's government in the murder of many citizens did not become public for 10 more years.

March 6, 1991

President Bush heralds the start of a "new world order."

In a "victory" speech to Congress after Iraq surrendered, Bush called for a "new world order" of justice and fair play to protect weak nations. Applied to the Middle East, Bush's program would stabilize the region by achieving peace between Arabs and Israel, sharing security measures, promoting economic development, and eliminating weapons of mass destruction. Despite Bush's optimism, his ideals were difficult to fulfill even in post-war Iraq when Saddam Hussein had sufficient troops and helicopters to defeat uprisings by Iraqi Shiites and Kurds.

March 17, 1991

Referendum shows most Soviet citizens prefer a united Soviet Union.

The results of a national referendum indicated 77 percent of the voters wanted to preserve Soviet unity. President Gorbachev conducted the referendum after several republics held demonstrations to demand independence. The ballot was flawed because the republics of Estonia, Latvia, Lithuania, Georgia, Armenia, and Moldavia boycotted the referendum. In the Ukraine and Russian Federation, miners were on strike to oppose Gorbachev's reforms because they disputed the central government's power. His problems with the miners continued.

See August 19, 1991.

March 27, 1991

The United States withdraws medium-range missiles from Europe.

Acting in accordance with the 1987 Intermediate Range Nuclear Missile Treaty (INF) with the Soviet Union, the United States announced that its last medium-range nuclear missiles had been removed from the European continent.

April 4, 1991

The Salvadoran government and rebel forces accept reforms to end the civil war.

Following March 10 elections in which the governing National Republican Alliance (ARENA) won only a plurality of National Assembly seats, delegates of the government and rebel *Farabundo Marti para la Liberacion Nacional* (FMLN) met in Mexico City to agree on reforms to end the civil war.

On April 29, the National Assembly approved reforms that cut back the power of the military, created a nonmilitary police force, strengthened the judiciary, and instituted electoral reforms. Although the Mexico City reforms did not include a cease-fire, the two sides took steps to establish one.

April 5, 1991

Iraq accepts stringent cease-fire terms set by U.N. Security Council Resolution 687.

From the cease-fire of March 3 to early April, Security Council members debated various terms for Iraq. On April 3, the Council set terms contained in resolution 687, and on April 5, Iraq's Revolutionary Command Council ratified the agreement. Because multinational forces remained in southern Iraq, President Hussein submitted, although he soon discovered ways to circumvent the cease-fire terms. Iraq not only accepted resolution 687 but also resolutions made before the January conflict.

The resolution's principal terms were as follows: (1) U.N. inspection teams would oversee the destruction of Iraq's nuclear, chemical, and biological weapons as well as its missiles and launchers having a range over 90 miles; (2) Iraq could not import offensive weapons and dual-use technologies; (3) economic sanctions remained on Iraq until all the terms of resolution 687 were fulfilled; (4) a U.N. committee would supervise Iraq's imports of food and medicine.

April 18, 1991

Saddam Hussein begins deceptive practices about Iraq's weapons of mass destruction.

After accepting terms of U.N. Security Council Resolution 687 (see April 5, 1991), Iraq complied by giving the U.N. Special Commission on Weapons (UNSCOM) a list of its nonconventional weapons After inspectors checked the list on April 29, the United States claimed Iraq failed to include all of its nuclear weapons. Iraq finally admitted to the International Atomic Energy Agency (IAEA) that it failed to account for all its weapons-grade nuclear materials. This was the first of Iraq's efforts to deceive UNSCOM and the U.N. Security Council.

See June 22, 1991.

April 25, 1991

President Gorbachev and leaders of nine Soviet republics agree to cooperate.

Hoping to retain unity among the Soviet Union's republics, Soviet President Mikhail Gorbachev met with leaders of nine Soviet republics including Russia's Boris Yeltsin. During the meeting, Gorbachev persuaded the nine leaders to cooperate in restructuring the Soviet Union's government. Under these agreements, the Soviet Union would revise its constitution to give each republic a greater role in Soviet political decisions. In return, leaders of the nine republics agreed to honor the central government's existing economic arrangement and enforce Soviet laws within their borders.

On June 17, negotiations between the Soviet central government and representatives of the nine republics finalized plans to revise the Soviet constitution in accordance with the April 25 agreements. Unfortunately for Gorbachev's plans, Soviet Communists opposing his plans tried to overthrow him.

See August 19, 1991.

May 13, 1991

President Bush proposes an international ban on chemical weapons.

To encourage other nations to prepare a treaty prohibiting the use of chemical weapons, President Bush pledged that the United States would not use chemical weapons and asked other leaders to join him in drafting a treaty to ban them. If a treaty were approved, the United States would destroy its chemical weapons stockpile.

To prevent the spread of chemical weapons, Bush proposed restrictions on exporting chemicals needed to make chemical weapons. On May 30, 19 industrial nations agreed to restrict the export of these chemicals.

May 29, 1991

President Bush proposes to ban all weapons of mass destruction in the Middle East.

In a speech at the U.S. Air Force Academy, President Bush proposed to ban weapons of mass destruction and create a system to control conventional weapons in the Middle East. His basic suggestions for the Middle East were create a nuclear-free zone, ban surface-to-surface missiles, prohibit chemical and biological weapons, set up methods to regulate materials for nonconventional weapons, and establish methods for arms exporters to notify other nations about arms exports.

Following his speech, Bush held meetings with the Big Five—the United States, France, Britain, China, and the Soviet Union—but they failed to agree on methods to freeze the transfer of conventional weapons in the Middle East. There were meetings of arms negotiators in Paris in July 1991, in London in October, and in Washington from February to May 1992. During the three meetings in 1991 and 1992, the delegates from the Big Five powers were unable to prevent future armament sales to Middle East nations.

Although the Big Five delegates said they opposed an arms buildup in the Middle East, not one of the five delegates was willing to risk the loss of profits their armament manufacturers made by selling weapons to their Middle East customers. The United States was the biggest arms supplier, selling $32.2 billion of armaments to Middle Eastern nations during the period from August 1990 to August 1992.

May 31, 1991

Angola gains a cease-fire based on proposals by U.S. Secretary of State Baker and Soviet Foreign Minister Shevardnadze.

Angola's cease-fire resulted from a U.S.-Soviet proposal of December 13, 1990, when Secretary of State Baker and Soviet Foreign Minister Shevardnadze presented the plan to representatives from Portugal, Angola's government, and UNITA (National Union for the Total Independence of Angola) rebels. The United States and USSR agreed to end all arms shipments to Angola and UNITA. In addition, the 50,000 Cuban troops that Moscow supported left Angola before May 25. As a result, Angola's government and the UNITA rebels led by Jonas Savimbi accepted a cease-fire to end their 16-year war and prepare democratic elections in 1992.

Despite Baker's role in Angola's peace effort, the U.S. House of Representatives voted on June 11 to continue covert aid to UNITA, although it reduced the aid from $60 million to $20 million. On July 15, the Angolan government approved an amnesty for persons jailed for crimes against the state, and on September 29, Savimbi returned to Luanda to run for president. As of 2000, these and other U.S. and U.N. attempts to end Angola's civil war were not accepted by the competing factions in the country.

June 14, 1991

After Secretary of State Baker and the Soviet Foreign Minister resolve problems, CSCE members agree on limiting conventional weapons.

On June 14, members of the Commission on Security and Cooperation in Europe (CSCE) approved amendments to the initial Conventional Forces in Europe (CFE) treaty. Because disputes arose about the size of Soviet armored personnel carriers and that some Soviet military units moved beyond the Ural Mountains outside the treaty's Atlantic to Ural definition, U.S. Secretary Baker met with Soviet Foreign Minister Aleksandr Bessmertnykh on June 1 to solve the problems. After the United States and the Soviet Union agreed on the interpretation of these issues, NATO and Warsaw Pact members met to sign the final CFE agreement.

June 22, 1991

Secretary of State Baker visits Albania, whose Communist regime is floundering.

Secretary of State Baker arrived in Tirana, Albania, where large crowds shouted "U.S.A.! U.S.A.!" Baker's car needed an hour to go four miles from the airport to downtown. He visited Albania to promote democracy in a country whose Stalinist regime had kept it isolated from the outside world since World War II.

Since February 6, 1991, Albanian students advocating reform had demonstrated against the Communist regime, but in an election on March 31, the Communist Party allegedly won 66 percent of the vote to keep control of the People's Assembly. Protesters led by Sali Berisha, a heart surgeon who became the leader of opposition to the Communist regime, claimed the elections were fraudulent, and their demonstrations escalated after Premier Fatos Nano appointed a cabinet excluding all opposition parties.

Because of the unrest, the government resigned on June 4, and Nano appointed a nonpartisan interim government that scheduled elections for 1992. That government ended 47 years of despotic Communist rule under Enver Hoxha and his successor, Ramiz Alia.

June 22, 1991

Iraqi soldiers disrupt U.N. inspectors trying to locate nuclear weapons.

Iraqi soldiers obstructed and fired warning shots at U.N. weapons inspectors who seized documents indicating Iraq's nuclear capacity was further along than previously believed. Iraqi forces also interfered with U.N. inspectors at a factory building for a week during which U.S. intelligence satellites detected trucks hauling materials away from the factory's rear door. The U.N. Security Council fixed a deadline for Iraq to comply with the inspectors' demands. On July 25, President Saddam Hussein allowed inspectors to "see and inspect whatever they will." Saddam Hussein's deception in the June incident was duplicated in September 1991, when a joint team of U.N. Special Commission (UNSCOM) and International Atomic Energy Agency (IAEA) inspectors moved into a high-rise building in downtown Baghdad to find files about Iraq's atomic bomb program. On leaving the building, the inspectors were stopped by Iraqi troops in the parking lot, beginning a three-day confrontation. The crisis ended with a compromise that Iraq could inventory the documents before they were taken away. But, as Khidhir Hamaz's *Saddam's Bombmaker* (2000) explains, Iraq found a way to fool the inspectors. While inventorying the documents, Iraqi officials slipped them to Iraqi scientists who removed some documents or erased critical data to mislead inspectors when they were handed back. Thus, the inspectors took away tainted documents, leading UNSCOM and Washington to believe Iraq's nuclear weapons program was less advanced than it actually was.

Despite Hussein's deceptions throughout the 1990s, UNSCOM and the IAEA were able to find and destroy almost all Iraq's WMDs. During that time, President William Clinton and the U.K.'s Prime Minister Tony Blair frequently used threats or bombing of military installations to gain Iraq's compliance. In December 1998 for example, Clinton and Blair used the bombing mission called Operation Desert Fox that destroyed many of Iraq's best military installations but resulted in Hussein's refusal to permit anymore UNSCOM and IAEA inspections.

The U.N. Security Council replaced UNSCOM with resolution 1284 on December 17, 1999, to establish the U.N. Monitoring, Verification and Inspection Commission (UNMOVIC). From 1999 to November 2002, UNMOVIC Director Hans Blix led a team that studied UNSCOM documents to prepare for future inspections. From November 27, 2002 until March 17, 2003, UNMOVIC and the IAEA conducted inspections but found none of the stockpiles of WMD that President George W. Bush and Secretary of State Colin Powell, the CIA and Iraqi exiles—such as Ahmad Chalabi—claimed were in Iraq. Blix found and destroyed a few illegal Sahmoud-2 ballistic missiles.

After invading and occupying Iraq in March 2003, the Bush administration had the CIA send thousands of inspectors to Iraq in search of WMDs. First, David Kay's team searched but found no WMDs by January 2004. Next Charles A. Duefer's team searched, but in October 2004 agreed with Kay that Iraq had no WMDs. President Bush's primary reason for attacking Iraq proved to be a costly mistake when Iraq insurgents began to kill many U.S. soldiers and any Iraqis collaborating with the Americans. For details see Hans Blix, *Disarming Iraq* (2004), Richard Butler, *The Greatest Threat* (2000), and Scott Ritter, *Endgame* (1999).

June 25, 1991

Despite Secretary of State Baker's objection, Slovenia and Croatia declare independence from Yugoslavia.

Four days after meeting with Secretary of State Baker in Belgrade, Slovene President Kuchan and Croatian President Tudjman declared the independence of their republics. Baker had urged them to maintain Yugoslav unity, but their efforts to obtain reforms failed and in 1990 the two republics voted for independence.

Following a meeting with European Union representatives on June 28, Slovenia and Croatia suspended their independence declarations, but after they were attacked by the Yugoslav National Army (YNA), dominated by Serbia, each republic declared independence on September 7. The next day the Republic of Macedonia declared its independence.

See September 25, 1991.

July 11, 1991

The United States lifts economic sanctions against South Africa.

Because President F.W. de Klerk's government had fulfilled five conditions set by Congress in its 1986 Anti-Apartheid Act, President Bush lifted U.S. economic sanctions against South Africa.

July 31, 1991

Presidents Bush and Gorbachev sign a strategic arms reduction treaty (START I).

At the first post–Cold War summit in Moscow, Presidents Bush and Gorbachev signed START I, a treaty to be in effect for 15 years and be renewable. It limited each nation to 10,000 nuclear warheads and 1,600 intercontinental ballistic missile delivery systems. START I was the first of President Bush's efforts to reduce the number of nuclear weapons.

See September 17–23, 1991 and December 18, 1991.

August 16, 1991

Saddam Hussein rejects a U.N. Security Council oil-for-food program.

Although President Bush wanted to link the U.N. oil-for-food program to Hussein's fulfillment of the April cease-fire accords, reports of Iraq's starving and sick women and children impelled Bush and the Security Council to reach a compromise embodied in resolution 706. The resolution permitted Iraq to sell oil to buy food and medicine and begin paying reparations to Kuwait. Although the $1.6 billion of oil fell short of the $2.6 billion recommended by the U.N. relief agency, Saddam Hussein rejected the offer.

Reports from Baghdad indicated Iraq's wealthy had revived their luxurious living but Hussein allowed less fortunate people to bear the burden of suffering by rejecting the oil-for-food program. Nevertheless, some critics blamed the United States for the suffering in Iraq because Washington insisted on economic sanctions until Hussein eliminated Iraqi weapons of mass destruction. Other observers blamed Hussein's refusal of oil-for-food programs and flaunting the U.N. weapons inspections required by the April 1991 agreement. His persistent refusal to accept oil-for-food programs continued until 1998.

August 19, 1991

A coup attempt fails to overthrow Soviet President Gorbachev.

During the year before the attempted coup against Soviet President Mikhail Gorbachev, the central authority of the Communist Party of the Soviet Union (CPSU) had lost much of its policy making power. In addition, Gorbachev's *glasnost* policy permitting freedom of speech led to criticism of the CPUS and of Gorbachev for weakening the Soviet military organization and accepting reductions in tactical and strategic missiles and in conventional forces stationed in Europe. Soviet Defense Minister Marshall Dimitry Yazov complained that Gorbachev did not recognize that the Western powers continued to regard the Soviet Union as the "enemy" while they encouraged Gorbachev to disarm the Soviet Union. Moreover, hard-line conservatives like Yazov believed Gorbachev permitted various Soviet Republics to gain influence that weakened Soviet relations with the Western world (see December 17, 1990). Finally, Yazov believed Gorbachev's acceptance of a second strategic arms reduction treaty with U.S. President George Bush in July 1991 was further evidence that Soviet power was withering away see July 31, 1991.

Following his July meeting with Bush, Gorbachev left Moscow to relax for two weeks at his dacha in the Crimea, expecting to return to Moscow on August 19. One day before his scheduled return, Gorbachev was visited by a delegation from Moscow. The delegates were Gorbachev's Deputy on the Council of Defense Oleg Baklanov, Communist Party Secretary Oleg Shenin, Deputy Minister of Defense Valentin Varennikov, and Gorbachev's former Chief of Staff Valery Boldin. The delegates told Gorbachev that Communist Party leaders wanted a state of emergency declared, and asked him to sign the directive on the emergency or resign and turn his authority over to Vice President Gennady Yanayev. After Gorbachev refused to sign the directive or resign, the Moscow delegation cut off his ability to communicate with the outside world, leaving Gorbachev and his family with only a radio and television set to learn what was happening in Moscow. The delegates placed Gorbachev under house arrest with a small number of his bodyguards to protect him.

That night, August 18–19, Gorbachev heard Radio Moscow announce that Gorbachev's illness required him to remain in the Crimea, a lie of course, and that

Gennady Yanayev had assumed Gorbachev's duties. Gennady's first act was to issue a Declaration of the State of Emergency in the Soviet Union and to transfer authority to a newly organized Council for the State of Emergency. The State Council members were Gennady, Prime Minister Valentine Pavlov, KGB Chairman Vladimir Krychkov, Minister of the Interior Boris Pugo, Defense Minister Marshall Dmitry Yazov, Deputy Chairman of the Defense Council Oleg Baklov, Representative of the Industrial Sector Aleksander Tizyakov, and Representative of the Agricultural Sector Vasily Starodubtsev.

In Moscow, Russian President Boris Yeltsin rallied the resistance to Gennady and the Council for the State of Emergency. After declaring the Council for the State of Emergency unconstitutional, Yeltsin built a stronghold in the Soviet parliament building. From this fortress, Yeltsin made a televised speech that denounced the traitors and urged Muscovites and other Russians to demonstrate against Gennady's Council. In Moscow, Yeltsin joined 50,000 Russians protesting against the coup; in Leningrad, thousands of Russians demonstrated against Gennady.

Later, Gorbachev learned the coup leaders had failed to get key military officials to join their plot. After Yeltsin's televised speech, Soviet Marshall of Aviation Yevgeny Shaposhnikov opposed the State Council and was joined in condemning the Council's action by Chief Soviet Naval Officer Admiral Vladimir Cherrnavin, Commander of the Strategic Missile Forces Yury Maksimov, and Commander of the Soviet Airborne Troops Lieutenant General Pavel Grachen.

By the third day of the coup (August 21), State Council members had weakened their resolve. After Marshall Yazov resigned from the State Council, he told Deputy Chairman of the Defense Council Oleg Baklov to withdraw all Soviet troops from Moscow or resign from the State Council. On August 21, Yeltsin's success in resisting the State Council became clear when the State Council commandeered Soviet armed vehicles that failed to disperse protesting crowds in front of the Soviet parliament. After three men were killed by army gunfire, Soviet soldiers refused to attack fellow citizens and some army troops joined the protesters. Yeltsin's victory over the State Council was assured on August 22, when the KGB's special forces, the elite division of the Minister of the Interior's troops, and the Soviet army guarding Moscow's airport refused to move into the city and attack the demonstrators.

On August 22, a delegation from the Russian Federation's Supreme Soviet led by Russia's Vice President Alexsander Rutskoi flew to the Crimea to escort Gorbachev back to Moscow. Marshal Yazov and KGB Chief Krychkov asked Gorbachev to pardon them but they were arrested and imprisoned. With Gorbachev's approval, Russian police arrested the other members of the State Council including Gennady on charges of high treason. On August 24, Gorbachev resigned as the General Secretary of the Communist Party and disbanded the Central Committee of the Communist Party of the Soviet Union.

August 20, 1991

Three Soviet Baltic republics declare independence.

During the three-day coup in Moscow, the Soviet republics of Estonia, Latvia, and Lithuania affirmed their national independence and expropriated Communist Party property. Russian Federation President Boris Yeltsin quickly recognized the three nation's independence. On September 2, the United States and the European Union also recognized the Baltic nations' independence. On September 6, the new Soviet State Council also approved the independence of the three Baltic states.

September 12–14, 1991

Secretary of State Baker visits Moscow and the newly independent Baltic states.

During a human rights conference in Moscow, Secretary of State Baker met with the new Soviet foreign minister, Boris Pankin, and military chief of staff General Vladimir Lobov. Among other matters, Baker and Pankin agreed to encourage peace in Afghanistan, announcing that the United States and the USSR would end military aid to both warring sides by the end of the year. Baker visited Estonia, Latvia, and Lithuania and promised them a total of $14 million of U.S. assistance.

September 17–23, 1991

The U.N. General Assembly admits new members and hears President Bush introduce an arms control initiative.

The U.N. General Assembly's 46th session admitted seven new members: South Korea, North Korea, the

Marshall Islands, Micronesia, Latvia, Lithuania, and Estonia.

On September 23, President Bush's address to the assembly was highlighted by an offer to unilaterally eliminate naval cruise missiles, tactical nuclear missiles, and 24,000 nuclear warheads including the multiple warheads carried by MX missiles for which the Pentagon never found suitable basing on railroad rails or hardened underground silos. Bush also invited Soviet President Gorbachev to join the United States in developing a new version of the SDI missile defense system, a plan known as Global Protection Against Limited Strikes (GPALS).

Since 1991, SDI research had changed from the complex Brilliant Pebbles missile defense system to GPALS, a system of only 1,000 Pebbles in space combined with 1,000 ground-based missiles at seven sites in the United States. GPALS would allegedly protect the United States and other nations from attacks by "rogue nations" such as Iraq and North Korea as well as an accidental ICBM launch from the Soviet Union or China. Bush asked Gorbachev to join in developing GPALS, a joint venture allowing the termination of the 1972 ABM treaty.

On September 27, Bush implemented his promise to take all American bombers off alert. Although on October 3, Gorbachev ignored Bush's GPALS proposal, his response exceeded Bush's initiative by announcing Soviet plans to unilaterally deactivate 503 intercontinental missiles and all short-range nuclear weapons from Soviet ships, submarines, and land-based naval aircraft. Gorbachev also ordered a ban on Soviet nuclear testing for one year. Bush's initiative exempted nuclear weapons on submarines but any deal with the Soviets became complicated when the Soviet Union was divided into separate republics in December 1991.

See December 18, 1991.

September 25, 1991

The U.N. Security Council embargoes arms to Yugoslavia.

The U.N. Security Council embargo on Yugoslav military weapons intended to end the war between Croatia and Serbia that began in July 1991, but it was based on an unrealistic notion that Yugoslavia still existed and became an obstacle to nations wanting to help Bosnia and Herzegovina by sending arms after Serb military forces attacked Bosnia in 1992. Unlike the Slovene, Croatian, and Serbian republics, Bosnia wanted Yugoslavia to reunite and was unprepared for war when Serbia's army attacked its capital, Sarajevo in 1992. This was the beginning of a violent military contest that involved the massacre of thousands of Bosnian Muslims at Srebrenica in 1993. The United States did not get involved until 1994. See Lester H. Brune, *The United States and Post-Cold War Interventions* (1998) and *Kosovo Intervention and United States Policy* (2000).

October 1, 1991

Bush extends aid to Soviet Union.

The president granted an additional $585 million of credits to the Soviet Union. Later, on December 20, he approved another $1.25 billion in grain credits and $1 million in humanitarian aid. Earlier the White House approved insurance guarantees to assist trade with the Soviets and to help diminish the reluctance of American lending institutions to supply funds to Moscow.

October 4, 1991

The 1959 Antarctica treaty is extended for 50 years.

Meeting in Madrid, 24 nations extended the 1959 Antarctica treaty by levying a 50-year moratorium on mining and military activity and setting guidelines for scientific research.

October 13, 1991

Bulgaria's democrats win elections against the Communist Party.

In national elections, Bulgaria's anti-Communist Union of Democratic Forces (UDF) won 111 seats in parliament and joined with the Movement for Rights and Freedom's 24 seats to provide a majority in the 240-seat parliament. Although Bulgaria's government unveiled a new constitution on July 14, many Bulgarians were dissatisfied. On November 8, parliament elected UDF leader Filip Dimitrov as premier.

October 23, 1991

Cambodia's four factions sign a peace agreement.

A U.N. proposal succeeded when Cambodia's government and three rebel factions signed a Paris peace treaty providing for the United Nations to share power with four factions during a transition to democracy. The treaty named Prince Sihanouk provisional leader while rebels disarmed, and the peace process moved toward democratic elections. Sihanouk returned after 13 years in exile to become president, but trouble began in Phnom Penh on November 28 when the Khmer Rouge's leader, Khieu Samphan, who was notorious for having killed many Cambodians, returned. He soon fled to Thailand after mobs nearly lynched him. On December 30, Cambodia's factions requested the immediate deployment of U.N. peacekeeping forces.

October 30, 1991

A Middle East peace conference convenes in Madrid.

Sponsored by the United States and the USSR, an ill-fated peace conference launched a process to end 40 years of conflict in the Middle East. Following the Gulf War, President Bush and Secretary of State Baker made concerted efforts to hold the meeting by convincing Syria, Lebanon, Jordan, the PLO, and Israel to attend. Israel agreed after Bush withheld a U.S. loan guarantee of $10 billion and Palestinians accepted Israel's condition that PLO delegates would initially be part of Jordan's delegation, without PLO leader Yasser Arafat attending.

When the Madrid meeting began, Baker had no fixed agenda, intending that face-to-face sessions would be a first step toward future bilateral talks. After the Madrid sessions adjourned, negotiations began in Washington in December 1991, but bogged down when the Israeli election campaign began in the spring of 1992. Although the Madrid meeting led to the Oslo Accords in 1993, the struggle for peace between Israel and the Palestinians continues in 2005.

November 5, 1991

China and Vietnam normalize diplomatic relations that were perfunctory since a 1979 border conflict.

In 1979, China and Vietnam severed their diplomatic relations after Chinese forces invaded Vietnam's northern border, alleging that Vietnam was being punished for sending Vietnamese armed forces to fight the Khmer Rouge guerrilla movement led by Pol Pot. China's government supported the Communist Khmer Rouge's attempt to gain control of Cambodia's government (see February 17, 1979).

Throughout the 1980s, the two Communist countries continued political disputes that often ended in border clashes. Vietnam's decision to remove its armed forces from Cambodia (see July 6, 1989) enabled Chinese and Vietnamese delegates to negotiate the basis for renewing their peaceful relations. These negotiations brought about the formal renewal of diplomatic relations on November 5, 1991.

November 8, 1991

NATO approves post-Cold War strategic concepts.

NATO leaders meeting in Brussels approved post-Cold War strategic concepts prepared by their defense ministers in May. The new concepts ended earlier doctrines of "forward defense" and "graduated response." They emphasized collective planning for operations, NATO's primacy in European security, and keeping nuclear forces to a minimum. NATO also reaffirmed the role of the United States and Canada in the alliance and called for diplomatic and security contacts with the Soviet Union. Military plans provided for 70,000 NATO troops including a British led rapid reaction force, six multinational defense forces, and one all-German force.

November 8, 1991

U.S. nuclear weapons are removed from South Korea; the two Koreas move toward reconciliation.

As part of his September 27 program to eliminate U.S. nuclear warheads, President Bush announced that the

United States would remove all nuclear weapons from South Korea by April 1992. Because the United States was concerned about North Korea's nuclear complex at Yongbyon, the removal of U.S. nuclear weapons was designed to thwart North Korea's claim to need nuclear weapons as protection from South Korea. On November 8, South Korean President Roh Tae Woo announced his government would not store or possess nuclear weapons, and he asked North Korea to eliminate its existing nuclear weapons and abandon its program to produce new ones. While visiting Seoul on November 21, U.S. Secretary of Defense Richard Cheney said the United States would delay pulling more U.S. army personnel out of South Korea until North Korea clarified its activity regarding nuclear weapons.

After the United States began withdrawing its nuclear weapons from South Korea on November 29, the two Korean states moved toward better relations.

On December 13, North and South Korea signed agreements regarding trade, reconciliation, nonaggression, and peaceful coexistence between the two nations. On December 26, North Korea said it would sign the International Atomic Energy Agency (IAEA) agreement and permit IAEA inspections of its research center at Yongbyon. On December 30, the two Koreas agreed to free their peninsula of nuclear weapons.

November 15–17, 1991

Secretary of State Baker visits China to discuss nuclear technology and human rights.

Secretary of State Baker visited Beijing to discuss nuclear weapons and China's human rights record.

During Baker's visit, Chinese officials agreed to support a nuclear-free Korean peninsula; to ask the Chinese People's Congress to ratify the Nuclear Non-Proliferation Treaty; to "intend" to stop exporting medium-range missile technology to Pakistan and other states; and to continue discussions with U.S. representatives about improving China's human rights record. According to Baker's *Politics of Diplomacy* (1995), he thought China's concessions would prevent the U.S. Congress from removing China's most-favored-nation status.

November 21, 1991

Congress approves the Nunn-Lugar program to help destroy Soviet nuclear weapons.

Senators Sam Nunn (D-Ga.) and Richard Lugar (R-Ind.) proposed bipartisan legislation by which Congress authorized $400 million to defray the costs of destroying the former Soviet Union's nuclear, chemical, and biological weapons as required under treaties with the United States. Funds were also allocated to the Department of Defense to transport, store, and safeguard these weapons prior to their destruction.

The legislation was intended to prevent these weapons falling into unfriendly hands. On June 17, 1992, the United States and Russia signed an agreement for Russia to accept the Nunn- Lugar assistance. Later, other former Soviet republics agreed to accept similar U.S. aid: Belarus on October 22, 1992; Ukraine on October 23, 1993; Kazakhstan on December 13, 1993.

In subsequent years, Congress expanded the 1991 legislation to include defense conversion, joint military contacts, housing for military personnel, and environmental restoration at former Soviet military sites.

November 22, 1991

The United States and Vietnam seek to normalize relations.

The process leading to American-Vietnamese talks began on April 9, 1991, when Washington outlined plans to end Vietnam's trade embargo and seek its cooperation in ending Cambodia's civil war. On April 25, the United States sent Vietnam $1 million of financial aid, and on October 23 Secretary of State Baker lifted some restrictions on trade with Vietnam and said American tourists could visit Vietnam. In turn, Vietnam allowed 60,000 Vietnamese refugees to return home from Hong Kong if Hong Kong officials would confirm that they were economic, not political, refugees.

December 4, 1991

The U.N. General Assembly elects Egyptian Boutros Boutros-Ghali as secretary-general to replace Javier Pérez de Cuellar.

December 8, 1991

Three former Soviet republics form the Commonwealth of Independent States (CIS).

Following the August 1991 attempt by hard-line Communist Party members to overthrow Soviet President Mikhail Gorbachev (see August 19, 1991), Gorbachev proposed that all republics in the Union of Soviet Socialist Republics should form a confederation.

The confederation of republics would allow each republic to elect local officials responsible for conducting day-to-day domestic affairs while an all-Soviet State Committee dealt with foreign affairs, security issues, banking regulations, and essential economic matters such as maintaining the value of the ruble. The proposed confederation had some merits, but leaders of the republics rejected Gorbachev's plan, probably, as Gorbachev admits in his memoir, because the confederation plan was proposed in 1991, not 1989, after many republics already chose independence from any centralized authority.

Rather than accept Gorbachev's confederacy, the republics of Russia, Belarus, and Ukraine declared independence from the Soviet Union. On October 22, the Ukraine parliament created an independent army, navy, and air force. On November 1, the Russian Federation's Congress of People's Deputies gave President Boris Yeltsin power to end price controls on Russian products and to cut funds the Russian Federation's budget previously provided for Soviet foreign aid and for 70 Soviet ministries that no longer were relevant to Russia's needs. Two weeks later, Yeltsin asked Russian officials to assume control of the Soviet Union's natural resources, such as coal and lumber, within the boundaries of the Russian Federation. Belarus and Ukraine followed Russia's lead regarding natural resources within their boundaries.

By November 25, 1991, all Soviet republics had rejected Gorbachev's plans for a confederation. On

Post-Cold War Era

December 8, 1991, Russian President Yeltsin, Ukraine President Leonid Kravchuk, and Belarus President Stanislav Shushkevich met to form the Commonwealth of Independent States (CIS) and to issue invitations to former Soviet republics to join the CIS. By December 12, the parliaments of Russia, Ukraine, and Belarus ratified the agreement to form the CIS. Between December 8 and December 14, CIS membership was accepted by the republics of Kazakhstan, Kirghizia, Tajikistan, Turkmenistan, Uzbekistan, Armenia, Moldavia, and Azerbaijan.

Only the Baltic republics of Estonia, Latvia, and Lithuania did not join the CIS.

December 17, 1991

The European Community (EC) votes to recognize the independence of Croatia and Slovenia.

Despite opposition from former U.S. Secretary of State Cyrus Vance and former General Secretary of NATO, Britain's Lord Carrington, EC members agreed to recognize the independence of Slovenia, Croatia, and other former Yugoslav republics that met "humanitarian standards." Although in September 1991 Vance and Carrington were appointed by the United Nations and the EC to negotiate with Croatia, Slovenia, and Serbia to resolve problems regarding the disintegration of Yugoslavia, Vance and Carrington ignored Yugoslav Premier Ante Markovic's attempts to preserve Yugoslav unity.

On November 23, Vance persuaded Serbia and Croatia to accept a cease-fire monitored by a U.N. Protective Force (UNPROFOR). At the same time, Carrington prematurely believed Yugoslavia's factions had agreed to accept Vance's cease-fire between Croatia and Serbia. Carrington was premature because Serbian President Milosevic refused to withdraw the Yugoslav National Army units from Croatia.

Both Carrington and Vance warned EC members not to recognize the independence of any former Yugoslav republic because it would damage the cease-fire and peace proposals. Nevertheless, an EU commission examined the situation and reported Yugoslav unity could not be restored and the EC should set standards to recognize former Yugoslav republics. The EC formally recognized the independence of Slovenia and Croatia on January 15. The EC also favored Macedonia's independence but delayed because Greece objected to the name "Macedonia," a Greek province associated with the ancient empire of Alexander the Great.

December 18, 1991

Eleven members of the CIS agree to respect the Soviet Union's international treaties, especially on arms control.

When Secretary of State Baker visited Moscow and several Central Asian cities between December 14 and 16, he wanted to ascertain that the new commonwealth republics would carry out the START I and CFE treaties made with the USSR. In Moscow, Russian President Boris Yeltsin assured Baker that Russia would control the use of nuclear weapons in consultation with other CIS an assurance finalized on December 18 when leaders of 11 former Soviet republics met at Alma Atta, the capital of Kazakhstan. The leaders of Russia, Kazakhstan, Belarus, and Ukraine—the states having nuclear weapons or ICBM missiles on their soil—promised to fulfill the cuts in nuclear weapons agreed to in START I by President Gorbachev and allow U.S. advisers to help dismantle their weapons. After Gobachev resigned as General Secretary on December 25, 1991, the START I Treaty was pending until Yelstin agreed to carry out its terms. After Yeltsin met with Secretary James Baker at Camp David in February 1992, he not only agreed to fulfill START I terms but also proposed a START II treaty that would reduce nuclear warheads from 10,000 to 2,500 warheads. Lateron May 23, 1992, Russia and the three other members of the new Commonwealth of Independent States (CIS)—Ukraine, Belarus and Kazakastan—agreed to comply with START I.

December 25, 1991

Mikhail Gorbachev resigns as president of the Soviet Union.

After Gorbachev's televised speech, the Communist red flag was lowered from the Kremlin and replaced by Russia's white, blue, and red flag. On December 30, Commonwealth of Independent States (CIS) leaders agreed to control jointly the nuclear weapons previously under the control of the Soviet Union, but still had to decide how to handle their economic and military affairs. They also agreed to let Russia have the USSR's permanent seat on the U.N. Security Council.

V. EPILOGUE

When Mikhail Gorbachev resigned on December 25, 1991, the Cold War ended with a whimper, not a big bang, leaving historians and policymakers to ponder who, how, why, and what was responsible for the more than 40 years of the Cold War. During the first decade of the twenty-first century, these questions—four, in particular—remain the subject of scholarly and partisan debate. First, what was the role of the 1975 Helsinki Accords? Second, why were Central and Eastern European Warsaw Pact members able to gain independence prior to Gorbachev's abdication in December 1991? Third, did President Ronald Reagan's policies have a primary role in ending the Cold War? Fourth, was a long-term American or Soviet factor, such as George Kennan's containment policy, at work in ending the Cold War?

First, the Helsinki Accords, the result of months of talks, were signed in 1975 by leaders from 35 nations including U.S. President Gerald Ford and the Soviet's General Secretary Leonid Brezhnev. As described in the entry for August 1, 1975, the accords stated that the existing European borders could be changed only by peaceful means and that human rights permitted people of all nations to speak freely, to travel abroad, and to enjoy the rights of civil liberties. These accords resulted in the growth of human rights groups; for example, Czechoslovakia's Václav Hável organized Charter 77 in 1977 to report on human rights in his country. A Human Rights Watch group was also formed in the Soviet Union, although its members were harassed or imprisoned by Soviet authorities until Gorbachev took over in 1985. Notably, after President Ford signed the Helsinki Accords, California's Governor Ronald Reagan, who sought the Republican presidential nomination in 1976, criticized Ford for signing the pact. Reagan said: "I think all Americans should be against it." Other conservative Americans argued that Ford's Secretary of State Henry Kissinger had made a deal that was "forced down the president's throat."

Second, after Gorbachev took office in 1985, he told Warsaw Pact members to improve their countries by reforming their economic plans and their military defense forces because he did not accept the Brezhnev Doctrine that authorized Soviet forces to intervene as they did in Czechoslovakia during 1968. During 1989, Gorbachev's policy was the major factor when popular demonstrations overthrew Communist regimes in Hungary, Poland, Czechoslovakia, East Germany, and Romania.

Third, despite Reagan's opposition to the Helsinki Accords, did he have a leading role in ending the Cold War? Both Peter Schweizer and Reagan's former expert on Soviet affairs Jack F. Matlock Jr., claim Reagan's military, economic, political, and psychological policies set the stage for the West's "victory" over the Soviet Union. Reagan right-wing supporters celebrated his speech at Berlin's Brandenberg Gate outside the Berlin Wall, which had been built by the East Germans in 1961. After asking Gorbachev to obtain prosperity by seeking peace, Reagan concluded by saying "Mr. Gorbachev, take down this wall." Of course, Reagan's words did not take down the wall. East German reform advocates tore the wall down on November 9, 1989, after Hungarians tore down the fences that blocked their path to Austria and the Western world.

Fourth, authors such as former CIA Director Robert Gates and Richard J. Barnet claim that George F. Keenan's 1946 proposal to contain the Soviets played a vital role. Kennan's containment policy prevented new Soviet conquests and weakened the Soviets' Communist influence, leading to its downfall in December 1991. These authors specifically point to the United States' mediation in Poland and other Eastern European countries as well as consistent efforts to allay the fears of Soviet leaders about the rapid pace of change in the region.

To summarize, historians and political scientists hold various views about the end of the Cold War. But they will not be able to obtain accurate information about "who, how, why and what ended the Cold War" until many documents are declassified not only in Russia but also from American archives including those of presidents Ford, Carter, Reagan, and George H.W. Bush.

After the end of the Cold War, the year 1992 saw resolutions of several issues carried over from the Cold War years. These included ending military assistance to Afghan factions that began when Carter and Brezhnev led their nations; the end of El Salvador's civil war that was prominent in the Reagan years; and gaining control over chemical, conventional, and strategic weaponry that were under negotiation for many years before 1991. During the decade after 1991, controversial issues escalated to plague the United States, Russia, China, and former Communist nations liberated from Soviet control. Throughout the 1990s, problems resulted from Yugoslavia's breakup; the Talibans emergence Afghanistan; the Cambodia dilemma; American trade problems with China; tensions in Korea where North Korean Communists continued the Cold War; and worldwide environmental dangers.

(For an introduction to these problems, see Volume Three of the *Chronological History of U.S. Foreign Relations* [Routledge, 2003]).

1992

January 1, 1992

The United States and the former Soviet Union end military aid to Afghanistan; Moscow plans a peace agreement for the Afghans.

As agreed in September, the United States and the former USSR stopped all their military aid to the Afghan government and the Afghan mujahideen rebels. To promote peace in Afghanistan, Soviet Foreign Minister Pankin met with Afghan rebel leader Burhanuddin Rabbani to finalize a peace agreement on November 15, 1991. The accords provided for a transitional working group to transfer political power from President Najibullah's Communist regime to a unified government. A U.N. mediator and the Islamic Conference Organization would oversee the peace process expected to begin by April 1992.

January 16, 1992

Peace treaty ends El Salvador's civil war.

Representatives of El Salvador's government and the rebel FMLN (Farabundo Marti National Liberation Front) signed a treaty to end the 12-year civil war. On January 24, El Salvador's legislature approved laws granting amnesty to the war's participants excepting those involved in the worst massacres.

The next day, Salvadoran courts sentenced two army officers to 30 years in prison for the 1989 murder of six Jesuit priests, their housekeeper, and her daughter. On December 8, 1992, El Salvador's army abolished the Atlacal Battalion, which human rights groups blamed for most of the massacres since 1981.

January 23, 1992

Fifty-four nations agree to send food and medicine to former Soviet republics.

In planning for the January 23 meeting, U.S. Secretary of State James Baker began by dramatizing the need for a humanitarian aid conference known as Operation Provide Hope by first having the U.S. air force airlift 38 million pounds of food and medicine to the former Soviet republics. Next, when the conference convened in Washington, D.C., President Bush announced the United States would provide $645 million of humanitarian aid to the newly independent states.

Representatives of 47 nations and 7 humanitarian organizations attended the conference, and each offered to send some form of humanitarian assistance to the former Soviet states. On January 30, British Prime Minister John Major gave Russia £280 million of export credits and investment insurance; on February 7, France donated $392 million to allow Russia to import French grain and technical assistance. Other nations and groups offered various types of aid to the former Soviet republics during the next three months.

January 26, 1992

President Bush's proposed budget for 1993 cuts defense spending over five years.

In presenting a 1993 budget to Congress, President Bush included a post-Cold War cut in defense appropriations of $50 billion over the next five years. The proposed budget total of $1.5 trillion would result in a 1993 deficit of $268.7 billion, an amount higher than the record deficit of 1992. The final congressional defense budget signed in October 1992 allocated $253.8 billion.

January 31, 1992

The U.N. Security Council plans a greater U.N. role in collective security.

During a summit to discuss post–Cold War policies, the U.N. Security Council members accepted a greater U.N. role in maintaining peace. The Security Council also recognized nonmilitary causes of international instability and asked Secretary-General Boutros-Ghali to make recommendations regarding preventive diplomacy, peacemaking, and peacekeeping.

February 1, 1992

The CIS agrees to withdraw former Soviet troops from the three Baltic states.

The Commonwealth of Independent States (CIS) agreed to withdraw 100,000 former Soviet troops from the three Baltic states of Estonia, Latvia, and Lithuania. The agreement was not fulfilled in 1992 because Estonia and Latvia adopted laws limiting the civil rights of ethnic Russians living in their territory. The Baltic leaders also questioned their need to pay Russia to help finance the troop withdrawal.

On October 29, Russia suspended its troop withdrawal.

February 11, 1992

Secretary of State Baker visits former Soviet republics to discuss their problems.

Following a February 1 meeting between President Bush and Russian President Yeltsin at Camp David, Secretary of State Baker agreed to visit Russia and other former Soviet republics to determine the situation regarding nuclear arms control and the need for food and medicine.

During the Camp David meetings, Yeltsin assured President Bush that Russia had full control of the former Soviet Union's nuclear weapons, including the nuclear weapons in Belarus, Ukraine, and Kazakhstan. Yeltsin also proposed a second arms reduction treaty (START II) with the United States to reduce nuclear warheads from the 10,000 warheads allowed under START I to about 2,500 warheads, especially by removing all multiple and independent retargetable vehicles (MIRVs) from all land based ICBMs and sea based SLBMs. Although he would negotiate reductions in ICBMs, President Bush told Yeltsin the United States would not accept reductions of SLBMs because they were part of the U.S. triad of bombers, ICBMs, and SLBMs with nuclear warheads designed to deter an enemy (see June 17, 1992).

On February 11, following the Camp David meeting, Secretary of State James Baker left Washington to visit seven former Soviet republics. From February 12 to 14, Baker made brief visits to talk with the leaders of Armenia, Azerbaijan, Turkmenistan, and Tajikistan before reaching Yekaterinberg, Kazakhstan, early on February 15.

Secretary Baker was concerned about the CIS's nuclear facilities and the future employment of hundreds of former Soviet nuclear scientists who had not been paid their salaries for the past two or three months. Baker's Kazakhstan host drove him from Yekaterinberg to the isolated and previously secret city of Chelyabinsk-70, where the Research Institute of Technical Physics was the center for developing and testing nuclear weapons. Known as the "Los Alamos" of Soviet nuclear technology, Chelyabinsk-70 was one of the four CIS's nuclear facilities, the others being Belarus, Ukraine, and Russia. Meeting with 25 of the Institute's senior nuclear scientists, Baker asked how the United States and other Western nations could provide job security for them. One scientist told Baker there were many difficulties for them that were "tied to economics." He informed Baker that the nuclear scientists had many ideas for future products, such as developments in fiber optics or improvements in nuclear magnetic resonance, that could be valuable for peaceful purposes.

Other scientists told Baker that Iranians and North Koreans had approached them about hiring them to help build nuclear weapons or long-range ballistic missiles. To alleviate their concerns, Baker told them about his plan to organize a joint scientific center that would match the nuclear scientists with individuals prepared to invest money in research projects that would challenge their scientific abilities.

March 3, 1992

The U.N. Human Rights Commission votes 23 to 8 to condemn Cuba for human rights violations.

The Human Rights Commission's vote to condemn Cuba's violations of human rights was a sign that former Communist nations in Eastern Europe were taking positions in the United Nations that differed from the Warsaw Pact's uniform acceptance of Moscow's positions before the Soviet Union collapsed in December 1991. The resolution to condemn Cuba for violating the human rights of its people was cosponsored by Poland and Czechoslovakia. Other Eastern European delegates on the Human Rights Commission who joined the U.S. and Western European delegates by voting to condemn Cuba were from Hungary and Bulgaria.

March 14, 1992

North and South Korea agree to inspect each other's nuclear sites.

North Korea agreed to the mutual inspection of each nation's nuclear arms sites by mid-June. On January 30, North Korea had signed the International Atomic Energy Agency (IAEA) inspection agreement, a condition the Bush administration linked to canceling the U.S.-South Korean military exercises. On May 7, the two countries agreed to unite Korean families who had been separated since 1953, and on July 28 they agreed in principle to establish land, sea, and air links and scientific cooperation.

March 17, 1992

The United Nations fails to stop war between Armenia and Azerbaijan.

As the Soviet Republic of Armenia and the Soviet Republic of Azerbaijan, the two countries had been fighting sporadically for more than four years. In 1988 Armenian Christians living in the Azerbaijan *oblast* (province) of Nagorno-Karabakh staged protests during which Azerbaijan police killed 32 Armenians in forcefully breaking up the demonstrations (see February 11, 1988). Following more large Armenian demonstrations in July 1988, the Soviet Union's General Secretary Mikhail Gorbachev sent Soviet army units to the *oblast* to maintain order, but they were unable to prevent fighting between the Armenian Christians and Azerbaijani Muslims (see July 4, 1988).

Early in 1992, the United Nations sent former U.S. Secretary of State Cyrus Vance to seek a cease-fire and peace settlement between Armenia and Azerbaijan. By March 17, Vance admitted that neither side was willing to compromise on the future status of Nagorno-Karabakh. Soon after Vance left, Armenian forces launched an attack on Azerbaijan. By August 9, Azerbaijan's armed forces chased most Armenian Christian forces out of Nagorno-Karabakh. The potential of a complete victory for Azerbaijan led Armenian officials to ask the Commonwealth of Independent States (CIS) to intervene.

March 22, 1992

Sali Berisha becomes president of Albania by defeating his Communist opponent with 62 percent of the vote.

After Albania's Communist Party leader Enver Hoxha died in 1985, Ramiz Alia replaced him as party leader and president of Albania. Alia continued to serve until March 23, 1992. When students staged prodemocratic demonstrations in Albania, Alia offered to hold multiparty elections. On March 22, Sali Berisha defeated Alia in the election for president.

March 25, 1992

Commission on Security and Cooperation nations sign an "open skies" treaty.

At a meeting of the Commission on Security and Cooperation in Europe (CSCE), 25 nations signed the "open skies" treaty, permitting reconnaissance flights over their territory. The treaty affected North America, Europe, and the former Soviet republics.

April 1, 1992

Under U.N. supervision, Cambodia forms a Supreme National Council.

After the civilian chief of a U.N. peacekeeping force arrived on March 15, a coalition of Cambodian parties formed a Supreme National Council. Its members signed two agreements with the U.N.'s peacekeepers. The first was the Universal Declaration of Human Rights (see December 9, 1948); the second was an agreement to repatriate Cambodian exiles in Thailand. Refugees began returning from Thailand on March 30, but the United Nations had problems because the exiled Khmer Rouge refused to occupy camps in Cambodia designated for them by U.N. peacekeepers.

April 26, 1992

Prior to Russia's joining the International Monetary Fund (IMF), the G-7 nations approve aid to Russia.

On January 2, Russian President Boris Yeltsin issued economic reforms to end state subsidies for most products and permit price increases. These free-market reforms were required to receive an IMF loan but brought complaints from many Communists, who proposed a vote of no confidence to remove Yeltsin as president. Yeltsin survived when the Russian Congress of People's Deputies rejected the no-confidence proposal by a vote of 447 to 412 with 70 abstentions.

Although Russia's Congress declared conditional support for Yeltsin's reforms, IMF officials approved Yeltsin's reforms.

On April 1, President Bush and German Chancellor Helmut Kohl proposed an aid package to stabilize the ruble, making it convertible to Western currencies, provide export credits, and give financial assistance to the Russians. These events permitted the finance ministers of the seven major industrial nations (G-7) to endorse an aid package of $24 billion to Russia under IMF auspices. On June 1, Russia formally joined the IMF.

April 28, 1992

The Afghan Communist regime ends but the peace process is disrupted.

In 1989, President Bush rejected Soviet leader Mikhail Gorbachev's offer for both nations to embargo arms to Afghanistan. Because conflict escalated in Afghanistan, Secretary of State Baker changed U.S. policy and obtained a Soviet agreement for the two countries to cut off all military aid to both warring sides in Afghanistan. Military aid was cut off and the possibility of a new Afghan regime arose in 1992 because of a Soviet agreement with Afghan rebels.

In early April, U.N. mediator Benon V. Sevin supervised the transfer of power from Communist leader Najibullah to a six-member commission led by Ahmed Shah Massoud. Several Islamic nations gave diplomatic recognition to the new regime. In Washington, the State Department welcomed the new government, urging it to resolve all conflicts with militant factions. Although many militant factions accepted peace on May 25, hard-line guerrilla leaders and mercenaries previously paid by Najibullah rejected the new regime and fighting continued.

May 18, 1992

An American oil company agrees to invest in Kazakhstan oil fields.

The Chevron Oil Corporation and the government of Kazakhstan signed an agreement for Chevron to develop the Tengiz oil fields with an investment of $20 billion over 40 years.

May 22, 1992

Three former Yugoslav republics are admitted to the United Nations.

On May 22, the U.N. General Assembly voted to admit Croatia, Slovenia, and Bosnia and Herzegovina as U.N. members but on May 30, the Security Council refused to accept Serbia and Montenegro as being Yugoslavia. The Council not only condemned Serbia for giving military aid to Bosnian Serbs who rebelled against the government, but also levied economic sanctions on Serbia and Montenegro, including a trade embargo and freeze on the former Yugoslavia's foreign assets.

On April 27, the Republics of Serbia and Montenegro proclaimed a new Federal Republic of Yugoslavia to replace the former Yugoslav federation. The Belgrade ceremony celebrating the "new Yugoslavia" was boycotted by diplomats of the European powers, Canada, and the United States, who refused to recognize the "Serb-Montenegrin Yugoslavia." On September 22, 1992, the United Nations expelled the rump Yugoslavia because of Serbia's role in the Bosnian war.

May 22, 1992

Russia and Poland sign a friendship treaty.

Russian President Boris Yeltsin and Polish President Lech Walesa signed a Polish-Russian treaty of friendship. In addition, Yeltsin indicated 40,000 Soviet troops would leave Poland by November 5, 1992.

May 23, 1992

The United States and four CIS republics agree to comply with the START I treaty of 1991.

The United States and the four Commonwealth of Independent State (CIS) countries with nuclear arms signed the Lisbon Protocol to comply with the 1991 START I treaty negotiated with the Soviet Union.

Since January, U.S. Secretary of State Baker had negotiated with leaders of the Ukraine, Kazakhstan, and Belarus, which joined Russia in agreeing to fulfill START I. In addition, all except Russia agreed to sign the Nuclear Non-Proliferation Treaty (NPT) as non-nuclear states. One problem developed because on November 18, 1993, Ukraine's parliament approved Start I but refused to sign the treaty.

May 24, 1992

The Pentagon issues a defense policy guidance program for the post-Cold War era.

Following a review of U.S. strategic defense policies, the Department of Defense issued a Defense Policy Guidance paper that emphasized the U.S. commitment to collective military action. Notably, the May 24 guidance paper deleted a March 8 draft including phrases urging the United States to remain the world's only superpower by preventing competitor nations from challenging U.S. primacy in Western Europe and East Asia. These phrases raised extensive criticism, leading the Pentagon to delete them from the final Defense Policy Guidance.

Defense Secretary Richard Cheney was also concerned about updating the Pentagon's Single Integrated Operations Policy (SIOP) for using nuclear weapons. The seldom publicized SIOP had not been altered since October 1981, following President Reagan's announcement of a "launch on warning" nuclear strategy. During the next decade, the SIOP added more and more targets in the Soviet Union for U.S. nuclear warheads before Cheney ordered a reduction in targets from 40,000 to 10,000.

Significantly absent from the Pentagon's guidance report was mention of the SDI program. In March 1992, the Government Accounting Office (GAO) reported that neither GPALS nor Brilliant Pebbles was a viable antimissile defense. Although a single GPALS ground-based system might comply with the 1972 ABM treaty, the Senate Armed Services Committee learned that two GPALS tests failed and in July 1992, the committee found GPALS could not be deployed by 1996, as scheduled.

June 2, 1992

President Bush extends China's most-favored-nation trade status.

Despite disputes with Congress over China's trade status, President Bush extended China's most-favored-nation status for another year. On February 21, Bush lifted sanctions blocking U.S. exports to China of high-tech material, but Congress passed legislation requiring China to stop sending nuclear arms to countries such as Iran and to improve its human rights record, a measure Bush vetoed on March 3. Subsequently, Congress took action against renewing China's most-favored-nation trade status.

June 8, 1992

The U.N. Security Council orders UNPROFOR to protect Sarajevo's airport.

UNPROFOR "peacekeepers" were sent to Croatia as part of former U.S. Secretary of State Cyrus Vance's cease-fire agreement between Croatia and Serbia. On June 8, UNPROFOR forces were sent to occupy and protect Sarajevo's airport, which the Yugoslav National Army (YNA) and Bosnian Serbs had surrounded to stop humanitarian aid from reaching the besieged city.

Since April 5, superior Serb forces assisted by the YNA committed "ethnic cleansing" against Bosnia's Muslims and Croats by killing, torturing, and imprisoning males and raping many women, atrocities that were reported by the BBC and U.S. reporter Roy Gutman.

June 14, 1992

An environmental conference agrees to reduce greenhouse gases.

At the Rio de Janeiro Conference on Environment and Development, delegates of 178 countries agreed to promote economic development that would protect the earth's nonrenewable resources and signed a treaty to reduce emissions of carbon dioxide and greenhouse gases. During the meeting, U.S. delegates were criticized for refusing to support a treaty protecting endangered plants and animal species.

June 17, 1992

Presidents Bush and Yeltsin agree on the basis for START II.

At a two-day Washington meeting, Presidents Bush and Yeltsin agreed to draft a second strategic arms reduction treaty leaving each side one-half the number of nuclear warheads proposed under START I. By 2003, the United States would have 3,500 warheads, Russia 3,000. Bush and Yeltsin also agreed to cooperate in space operations, sign a friendship treaty, provide a global protection system, and allow U.S. businesses to avoid double taxation if they operated in Russia. Bush told Yeltsin that Russia would receive most-favored-nation trade status and a $610 million aid package, agreements Congress approved on August 6. On September 14, Russia opened its biological research buildings to let U.S. and British inspectors verify its adherence to the 1972 germ warfare treaty.

July 2, 1992

NATO announces all U.S. tactical nuclear missiles have been withdrawn from Europe.

August 30, 1992

The United States will purchase enriched Russian uranium.

To prevent Russia's high-grade enriched uranium from falling into "unfriendly hands," President Bush agreed to purchase up to 500 metric tons of it to prevent Russia from selling it to other nations. The uranium could make 30,000 nuclear bombs. The U.S. Department of Energy would transform the high-grade uranium into a lower-grade for use in U.S. nuclear power plants.

September 3, 1992

Geneva conference delegates approve a chemical weapons convention.

On September 3, delegates to a Geneva disarmament conference agreed to a Chemical Weapons Convention (CWC) and forwarded it to the U.N. General Assembly. After the assembly approved the CWC, the United Nations held a meeting in Paris on January 13, 1993, where each nation's delegate could sign the CWC treaty. The agreement would become effective in 1995 in order to liquidate chemical weapons by 2005. The United States and Russia had the largest stockpiles of weapons such as mustard gas and nerve gases, but experts believed 23 other nations also possessed chemical weapons.

The United States signed the treaty, but Senate ratification was delayed for over four years.

September 15, 1992

Commercial trade problems continue between China and the United States.

Although President Bush extended China's most-favored-nation trade status on June 2, Congress passed legislation on September 15 that conditioned China's most-favored-nation status on improving human rights, lowering trade barriers, and curbing nuclear and missile exports. After bilateral trade talks broke down in August 1992, Bush threatened to place 100 percent tariffs on Chinese imports, but on October 10 China agreed to lower some import barriers. Sino-U.S. trade issues continued after Deng Xiaoping opposed political reforms at the Communist Party congress on October 21.

September 16, 1992

Russia will withdraw its troops from Cuba.

Russia said it would withdraw its 1,500 troops from Cuba by mid-1993. Two months later, on November

11, the two nations signed agreements on trade relations and retained Russia's electronic intelligence gathering facilities in Cuba.

October 2, 1992

The 1993 U.S. budget includes a ban on nuclear tests.

When President Bush signed budget authorizations for fiscal 1993, the $274 billion defense budget was $6.7 billion less than he requested. The budget legislation also included a measure banning U.S. nuclear tests. Because President Bush threatened to veto a bill prohibiting tests, Congress inserted a clause to ban tests in legislation authorizing funds for energy and water including $517 million for a super-colliding beam machine that Bush wanted to build in Texas.

The congressional bill banned nuclear tests for nine months, after which a restricted number of tests could test safety measures for existing nuclear weapons until 1996. After September 1996, tests were banned unless another country conducted them.

October 17, 1992

Angolan election returns are challenged by Jonas Savimbi.

In Angola's runoff elections for president, the Popular Movement's Jose Eduardo dos Santos defeated UNITA's Jonas Savimbi, who claimed election fraud. On November 26, fighting again broke out between the two groups, but on December 7, U.N. peace monitors persuaded Santos and Savimbi to form a coalition government.

October 23, 1992

Vietnam cooperates in a search for American MIAs.

Vietnam provided U.S. Department of Defense investigators with documents, photographs, and personal effects of U.S. personnel from the Vietnam War.

These data were to help the DOD determine what happened to 2,265 Americans listed as missing in action (MIA) from the Vietnam War. In response to Vietnam's cooperation, on December 14 the United States lifted its 17-year trade embargo on Vietnam, permitting American companies to do business with Vietnam.

November 9, 1992

Touring both West and East, Russian president Yeltsin signs friendship agreements.

Visiting London on November 9, Russian President Boris Yeltsin met with British Prime Minister John Major to sign a friendship treaty. Later, Yeltsin flew to South Korea, where on November 18, Russian and South Korean officials signed a treaty of friendship.

South Korea also resumed Russia's $3 billion in aid, suspended in December 1991, when the future of the Soviet Union was uncertain.

November 23, 1992

Russian President Yeltsin and his critics compromise on economic reforms.

After the demise of the USSR in December 1991 (see December 25, 1991), Russian President Boris Yeltsin inherited the Congress of People's Deputies, whose members were elected in 1989 (see May 25, 1989). Throughout the months from January to November 1992, hard-line Communists whom Yeltsin referred to as "Stalinists" criticized President Yeltsin for weakening Russia by agreeing to withdraw from the Baltic states (see February 1, 1992), accepting strategic arms treaties that would eliminate many of the former Soviet Union's ICBMs (see May 23 and June 17, 1992), and withdrawing troops from Cuba that the Soviet Union used as a military base in the Western Hemisphere (September 16, 1992). To reduce Yeltsin's power and increase the Congress of People's Deputies' power, the "Stalinists" wanted to amend the constitution that was last approved by the Soviet Union in 1977.

On November 23, 1993, Yeltsin received enough votes from critics in the Congress of People's Deputies to achieve a compromise on his proposed legislation to create a free market economy and stabilize the ruble. Before the Congress of People's Deputies adjourned on December 1, 1992, the members voted to reject amendments to the 1977 constitution proposed by Yeltsin's critics. In addition, Yeltsin offered to draft a constitution for the Russian Federation that would replace the 1977 Soviet Constitution and hold a referendum on the new constitution in 1993.

November 30, 1992

France and Germany say their military unit will not hinder NATO.

On May 22, 1992, France and Germany announced the formation of a 35,000-member military force.

Intending the joint force to be a pillar of Western European defense forces, the French and Germans reassured NATO that if European security were threatened, the joint force would be under NATO's operational command. German Chancellor Kohl proposed the joint force to calm French fears about the status of a united Germany.

The creation of a Franco-German army was the first instance since 1949 of two Western European nations planning to act outside the Atlantic alliance. The 1999 Kosovo conflict revived additional European efforts to create armed forces separate from U.S. control.

November 30, 1992

The United Nations fails to keep Cambodia's Khmer Rouge from disrupting the peace process.

Although in March 1992, U.N. peacekeepers seemed to make progress, on June 10 the Khmer Rouge refused to occupy camps under U.N. supervision. With the peace process stalled on November 30, the U.N. Security Council tried to punish the Khmer Rouge by prohibiting trade with rebel territory and excluding them from forthcoming elections. In response, on December 17 the Khmer seized 46 U.N. peacekeeping troops. Obviously, the U.N. was a peace-making group, not "peacekeepers."

Bibliography

Personalities

(Other biographies and memoirs are listed in separate divisions)

Abramson, Rudy. *Spanning the Century: The Life of W. Averell Harriman, 1891–1986.* New York: William Morrow, 1992.

Callahan, David. *Dangerous Capabilities: Paul Nitze and the Cold War.* New York: Harper and Row, 1990.

Carlton, David. *Churchill and the Soviet Union,* 1917–1955. New York: Manchester University Press, 2000.

Clifford, Clark, and Richard C. Holbrook. *Counsel to the President: A Memoir.* New York: Random House, 1991.

Dobrynin, Anatoly. *In Confidence: Moscow's Ambassador to America's Six Cold War Presidents.* New York: Times Books, 1995.

Fromkin, David. *In the Time of the Americans: FDR, Truman, Eisenhower, Marshall, MacArthur: The Generation That Changed America's Role in the World Since 1938.* 8th ed. New York: Penguin Books, 1997.

Garthoff, Raymond L. *A Journey Through the Cold War.* Washington, DC: Brookings, 2001.

Sakharov, Andrei D. *Moscow and Beyond.* New York: Knopf, 1991.

General Accounts of the Cold War Era

Bailey, Thomas A. *America Faces Russia: Russian-American Relations from Early Times to Our Day.* Ithaca, NY: Cornell University Press, 1950.

Baylis, John. *Anglo-American Defence Relations, 1939–1984: The Special Relationship.* 2nd ed. New York: St. Martin's Press, 1984.

Becker, Jasper. *The Chinese: An Insider's look at the Issues which Effect and Shape China Today.* New York: Oxford University Press, 2000.

Boyle, Peter G. *American-Soviet Relations: From the Russian Revolution to the Fall of Communism.* New York: Routledge, 1993.

Brands, H.W. *The Devil We Knew: Americans and the Cold War.* New York: Oxford University Press, 1993.

Bulletins of the International Cold War History Project from # 1, Spring 1991 to 2004 and beyond. Washington, DC: Woodrow Wilson Center and http://cwihp.si.edu had declassified documents from various former communist nations.

Cohen, Warren I. *America in the Age of Soviet Power, 1945–1991.* Vol. 4. *The Cambridge History of American Foreign Relations,* 4 vols. Warren Cohen, ed. New York: Cambridge University Press, 1993.

Costigliola, Frank C. *France and the United States: The Cold War Alliance since World War II.* New York: Twayne Publishers, 1992.

Fleming, Denna Frank. *The Cold War and Its Origins, 1917–1960.* 2 vols. Garden City, NY: Doubleday, 1961.

Gaddis, John Lewis. *The Long Peace: Inquiries into the History of the Cold War.* New York: Oxford University Press, 1987.

———. *Strategies of Containment: A Critical Appraisal of Postwar American National Security Policy.* New York: Oxford University Press, 1982.

———, Philip H. Gordon, Ernest R. May, and Jonathan Rosenberg, eds. *Cold War Statesmen Confront the Bomb: Nuclear Diplomacy Since 1946.* New York: Oxford University Press, 1999.

Gorodetsky, Gabriel, ed. *Soviet Foreign Policy, 1917–1991: A Retrospective.* Portland, OR: Frank Cass, 1994.

Hanrieder, Wolfram F. *Germany, America, Europe: Forty Years of German Foreign Policy.* New Haven, CT: Yale University Press, 1989.

Iriye, Akira, *The Cold War in Asia: A Historical Introduction.* Englewood Cliffs, NJ: Prentice Hall, 1974.

Kaufman, Victor S. *Confronting Communism: U.S. and British Policies toward China.* Columbia: University of Missouri Press, 2001.

Kovrig, Bennett. *Of Walls and Bridges: The United States and Eastern Europe.* New York: New York University Press, 1991.

LaFeber, Walter. *America, Russia, and the Cold War, 1945–1996.* 8th ed. New York: McGraw-Hill, 1997.

Larson, Deborah Welch. *Anatomy of Mistrust: U.S.-Soviet Relations during the Cold War.* Ithaca, NY: Cornell University Press, 1997.

Laski, Harold J. *American Democracy: a Commentary and an Interpretation.* New York: Viking Press, 1947.

Libbey, James K. *American-Russian Economic Relations, 1770s–1990s: A Survey of Issues and Literature.* Claremont, CA: Regina Books, 1989.

Lukcas, John. *A New History of the Cold War.* 3rd ed. Garden City, NY: Anchor Books, 1966.

Lundestad, Geir. *East, West, North, South: Major Developments in International Politics since 1945.* 4th ed. Trans. by Gail Adams Kvam. New York: Oxford University Press, 1999.

McCormick, Thomas J. *America's Half Century: United States Foreign Policy in the Cold War and After.* 2nd ed. Baltimore: Johns Hopkins University Press, 1995.

Painter, David S. *The Cold War: An International History.* New York: Routledge, 1999.

Patterson, Thomas G. *Meeting the Communist Threat: Truman to Reagan.* New York: Oxford University Press, 1988.

Powaski, Ronald E. *The Cold War: The United States and the Soviet Union, 1917–1991.* New York: Oxford University Press, 1998.

Prados, John. *Presidents' Secret Wars: CIA and Pentagon Covert Operations from World War II through the Persian Gulf.* Rev. ed. Chicago, IL: I.R. Dee, 1996.

Radosh, Ronald. *Prophets on the Right: Profiles of Conservative Critics of American Globalism.* New York: Simon & Schuster, 1975.

Ruddy, T. Michael, ed. *Charting an Independent Course: Finland's Place in the Cold War and in U.S. Foreign Policy.* Claremont, CA: Regina Books, 1998.

Sakwa, Richard. *The Rise and Fall of the Soviet Union, 1917–1991.* New York: Routledge Press, 1999.

Seppain, Hélène. *Contrasting US and German Attitudes to Soviet Trade, 1917–1991: Politics by Economic Means.* New York: St. Martin's Press, 1992.

Sherwin, Martin J. *A World Destroyed: The Atomic Bomb and the Grand Alliance.* New York: Vintage/Random House, 1977.

Smith, Tony. *America's Mission: The United States and the Worldwide Struggle for Democracy in the Twentieth Century.* Princeton, NJ: Princeton University Press, 1994.

Stevenson, Richard W. *The Rise and Fall of Détente: Relaxations of Tension in U.S.-Soviet Relations, 1954–1984.* Urbana: University of Illinois Press, 1985.

Stone, David. *Wars of the Cold War: Campaigns and Conflicts, 1945–1990.* London: Brassey's, 2004.

Ulam, Adam B. *The Rivals: America and Russia Since World War II.* New York: Viking, 1971.

Weihmiller, Gordon R. *U.S.-Soviet Summits: An Account of East-West Diplomacy at the Top, 1955–1985.* Lanham, MD: University Press of America, 1986.

Williams, William Appleman. *American-Russian Relations, 1781–1947.* New York: Holt, Rinehart & Winston, 1952.

Wittner, Lawrence S. *Cold War America: From Hiroshima to Watergate.* New York: Praeger, 1974.

Wohlforth, William Curtis. *The Elusive Balance: Power and Perceptions during the Cold War.* Ithaca, NY: Cornell University Press, 1993.

Zubok, Vladislav M. and Constantine Pleshakov. *Inside the Kremlin's Cold War: From Stalin to Khrushchev.* Cambridge, MA: Harvard University Press, 1996.

Communism & Anticommunism in America

Belknap, Michal R. *Cold War Political Justice: The Smith Act, the Communist Party, and American Civil Liberties.* Westport, CT: Greenwood Press, 1977.

Buckingham, Peter H. *America Sees Red: Anticommunism in America, 1870s to 1980s: A Review of Issues and References.* Claremont, CA: Regina Books, 1988.

Draper, Theodore. *American Communism and Soviet Russia: The Formative Period.* New York: Viking Press, 1960.

Heale, M.J. *McCarthy's Americans: Red Scare Politics in State and Nation, 1935–1965.* Athens: University of Georgia Press, 1998.

Isserman, Maurice. *Which Side Were You On?: The American Communist Party during the Second World War.* Middletown, CT: Wesleyan University Press, 1982.

Klehr, Harvey, John Earl Haynes and Fridrikh Igorevich Firsov. *The Secret World of American Communism.* Trans. by Timothy D. Sergay. New Haven, CT: Yale University Press, 1995.

Schrecker, Ellen W. *Many Are the Crimes: McCarthyism in America.* Boston: Little, Brown, 1998.

Sherry, Michael S. *In the Shadow of War: The United States since the 1930s.* New Haven, CT: Yale University Press, 1995. Militarism in America.

Special Aspects of the Cold War

Burrows, William E. *By Any Means Necessary: America's Secret Air War in the Cold War.* New York: Farrar, Straus and Giroux, 2001.

Pedlow, Gregory W. and Donald E. Welzenbach. *The CIA and the U-2 Program, 1954–1974.* Washington, DC: Central Intelligence Agency, 1998.

Sagan, Scott D. *The Limits of Safety: Organization, Accidents, and Nuclear Weapons.* Princeton, NJ: Princeton University Press, 1993.

Winkler, David F. *Cold War at Sea: High-Seas Confrontation between the United States and the Soviet Union.* Annapolis, MD: Naval Institute Press, 2000.

The Cold Peace, 1917–1940

Personalities

Ellis, L. Ethan. *Frank B. Kellogg and American Foreign Relations, 1925–1929.* New Brunswick, NJ: Rutgers University Press, 1961.

Mayers, David. *The Ambassadors and America's Soviet Policy.* New York: Oxford University Press, 1995.

Pratt, Julius W. *Cordell Hull, 1933–1944.* 2 vols. New York: Cooper Square, 1964.

General Accounts

Bennett, Edward M. *Recognition of Russia: An American Foreign Policy Dilemma.* Waltham, MA: Blaisdell Publishing, 1970.

Browder, R. P. *The Origins of Soviet-American Diplomacy.* Princeton, NJ: Princeton University Press, 1953.

Clubb, O. Edmund. *Communism in China, as Reported from Hankow in 1932.* New York: Columbia University Press, 1968.

Filene, Peter G. *Americans and the Soviet Experiment, 1917–1933.* Cambridge, MA: Harvard University Press, 1967.

Hoff, Joan. *Ideology and Economics: U.S. Relations with the Soviet Union, 1918–1933.* Lexington: University Press of Kentucky, 1977.

Kennan, George F. *Russia and the West under Lenin and Stalin.* Boston: Little, Brown, 1960.

Leffler, Melvyn P. *The Specter of Communism: The United States and the Origins of the Cold War, 1917–1953.* New York: Hill & Wang, 1994.

McFadden, David W. *Alternative Paths: Soviets and Americans, 1917–1920.* New York: Oxford University Press, 1992.

Mayer, Arno. *Politics and Diplomacy at Peacemaking: Containment and Counterrevolution at Versailles, 1918–1919.* New York: Knopf, 1967.

Murphy, Paul L. *World War I and the Origin of Civil Liberties in the United States.* New York: Norton, 1979.

Murray, Robert K. *Red Scare: A Study in National Hysteria, 1919–1920.* Minneapolis: University of Minnesota Press, 1955.

Saul, Norman E. *War and Revolution: The United States and Russia, 1914–1920.* Lawrence: University Press of Kansas, 2001.

Schild, George. *Between Ideology and Realpolik: Woodrow Wilson and the Russian Revolution, 1917–1921.* Westport, CT: Greenwood Press, 1995.

Siegel, Katherine A.S. *Loans and Legitimacy: The Evolution of Soviet-American Relations, 1919–1933.* Lexington: University Press of Kentucky, 1996.

Tarulis, Albert N. *American-Baltic Relations, 1918–1922: The Struggle over Recognition.* Washington, DC: Catholic University of America Press, 1965.

Thompson, John M. *Russia, Bolshevism, and the Versailles Peace.* Princeton, NJ: Princeton University Press, 1967.

Ullman, Richard H. *Anglo-Soviet Relations, 1917–1921.* 3 vols. Princeton, NJ: Princeton University Press, 1961–1972.

Weissman, Benjamin M. *Hebert Hoover and Famine Relief to Soviet Russia, 1921–1923.* Stanford, CA: Hoover Institution Press, 1974.

U.S. Intervention in Russia, 1917–1922

Bradley, John F. N. *Allied Intervention in Russia.* New York: Basic Book, 1968.

Foglesong, David S. *America's Secret War against Bolshevism: U.S. Intervention in the Russian Civil War, 1917–1920.* Chapel Hill: University of North Carolina, 1995.

Kennan, George F. *Soviet-American Relations, 1917–1920.* 2 vols. Princeton, NJ: Princeton University Press, 1956–1958.

Rhodes, Benjamin D. *The Anglo-American Winter War with Russia, 1918–1919: A Diplomatic and Military Tragicomedy.* Westport, CT: Greenwood Press, 1988.

Unterberger, Betty Miller. *America's Siberian Expedition, 1918–1920. A Study of National Policy.* Durham, NC: Duke University Press, 1956.

Spanish Civil War

Howson, Gerald. *Arms for Spain: The Untold Story of the Spanish Civil War.* New York: St. Martin's Press, 1999.

Little, Douglas. *Malevolent Neutrality: The United States, Great Britain and the Origins of the Spanish Civil War.* Ithaca, NY: Cornell University Press, 1985.

Thomas, Hugh. *The Spanish Civil War.* New York: Harper & Row, 1961.

Traina, Richard P. *American Diplomacy and the Spanish Civil War.* Bloomington: Indiana University Press, 1968.

Coming of World War II

Bennett, Edward M. *Franklin D. Roosevelt and the Search for Security: American-Soviet Relations, 1933–1939.* Wilmington, DE: SR Books, 1985.

Carley, Jabara. *1939: The Alliance That Never Was and the Coming of World War II.* Chicago: Ivan Dee, 1999. Deals with the British-French relationship with the USSR.

Dallek, Robert. *Franklin D. Roosevelt and American Foreign Policy, 1932–1945.* New York: Oxford University Press, 1979.

Jacobs, Travis Beal. *America and the Winter War, 1939–1940.* New York: Garland Publishing, 1981.

Maddux, Thomas R. *Years of Estrangement: America's Relations with the Soviet Union, 1933–1941.* Tallahassee: University Presses of Florida, 1980.

The Strange Alliance, 1941–1945

Personalities

Berezhkov, Valentin M. *At Stalin's Side: His Interpreter's Memoirs from the October Revolution to the Fall of the Dictator's Empire.* Translated by Sergei M. Mikheyev. Secaucus, NJ: Carol Publishing Group, 1994.

Birse, A.H. *Memoirs of an Interpreter.* New York: Coward-McCann, 1967. British translator at wartime conferences.

Blake, Robert, and William Rogers Louis, eds. *Churchill.* New York: W.W. Norton, 1993.

Blechman, Barry. *The Politics of National Security: Congress and U.S. Defense Policy.* New York: Oxford University Press, 1990.

Charmley, John. *Churchill, The End of Glory: A Political Biography.* New York: Harcourt Brace, 1993.

Deutscher, Isaac. *Stalin: A Political Biography.* 2nd ed. New York: Oxford University Press, 1966.

Dunn, Dennis J. *Caught Between Roosevelt & Stalin: America's Ambassadors to Moscow.* Lexington: University Press of Kentucky, 1998.

Gardner, Lloyd C. *Architects of Illusion: Men and Ideas in American Foreign Policy, 1941–1949.* Chicago, IL: Quadrangle Books, 1970. Chapters on Truman, Byrnes, Marshall, Will Clayton, Lucius Clay, Bernard Baruch, James V. Forrestal and George F. Kennan.

Maisky, Ivan M. *Memoirs of a Soviet Ambassador: The War, 1939–1943.* Trans. by Andrew Rothstein. New York: Scribner, 1968.

Resis, Albert, ed. *Molotov Remembers: Inside Kremlin Politics; Conversations with Felix Chuey.* Chicago: Ivan R. Dee, 1993.

Volkogonov, Dmitri A. *Stalin: Triumph and Tragedy.* Trans. by Harold Shukman. New York: Grove Weidenfeld, 1991.

General Accounts

Beitzell, Robert. *The Uneasy Alliance: America, Britain, and Russia, 1941–1943.* New York: Alfred A. Knopf, 1972.

Feis, Herbert. *Churchill, Roosevelt, Stalin: The War They Waged and the Peace They Sought.* Princeton, NJ: Princeton University Press, 1957.

Folly, Martin H. *Churchill, Whitehall and the Soviet Union, 1940–1945.* New York: St. Martin's Press, 2000.

Lane, Ann, and Howard Temperley, eds. *The Rise and Fall of the Grand Alliance, 1941–1945.* New York: St. Martin's Press, 1995.

Miner, Steven Merritt. *Between Churchill and Stalin: The Soviet Union, Great Britain and the Origins of the Grand Alliance.* Chapel Hill: University of North Carolina Press, 1988.

Nadeau, Remi. *Stalin, Churchill and Roosevelt Divide Europe.* New York: Praeger, 1980.

Neumann, William L. *After Victory: Churchill, Roosevelt, Stalin and the Making of the Peace.* New York: Harper and Row, 1967.

Reynolds, David, Warren F. Kimball and A.O. Chubarian, eds. *Allies at War: The Soviet, American and British Experience, 1939–1945.* New York: St. Martin's Press, 1994.

Smith, Denis. *Diplomacy of Fear: Canada and the Cold War, 1941–1948.* Toronto: University of Toronto Press, 1988.

United States

Alperovitz, Gar. *Atomic Diplomacy: Hiroshima and Potsdam. The Use of the Atomic Bomb and the American Confrontation.* New York: Vintage Books, 1967.

Bennett, Edward M. *Franklin D. Roosevelt and the Search for Victory: American-Soviet Relations, 1939–1945.* Wilmington, DE: SR Books, 1990.

Herring, George C., Jr. *Aid to Russia, 1941–1946: Strategy, Diplomacy, the Origins of the Cold War.* New York: Columbia University Press, 1973.

Gaddis, John Lewis. *The United States and the Origins of the Cold War, 1941–1947.* Rev. ed. New York: Columbia University Press, 2000.

Levering, Ralph B. *American Opinion and the Russian Alliance, 1939–1945.* Chapel Hill: University of North Carolina, 1976.

Martel, Leon. *Lend-Lease, Loans, and the Coming of the Cold War: A Study of the Implementation of Foreign Policy.* Boulder, CO: Westview Press, 1979.

Sirgiovanni, George. *An Undercurrent of Suspicion: Anti-Communism in America during World War II.* New Brunswick, NJ: Transaction Publishers, 1990.

Stoler, Mark A. *The Politics of the Second Front: American Military Planning and Diplomacy in Coalition Warfare, 1941–1943.* Westport, CT: Greenwood Press, 1977. Deals with Second Front issue.

Soviet Union

Conversino, Mark J. *Fighting with the Soviets: The Failure of Operation FRANTIC, 1944–1945.* Lawrence: University Press of Kansas, 1997. Americans use Soviet airbases.

Erickson, John. *Stalin's War with Germany.* 2 vols. London: Weidenfeld and Nicolson, 1973–1983.

Linz Susan J., ed. *The Impact of World War II on the Soviet Union.* Totowa, NJ: Rowman and Allanheld, 1985.

Mastny, Vojtech. *Russia's Road to the Cold War: Diplomacy, Warfare, and the Politics of Communism, 1941–1945.* New York: Columbia University Press, 1979.

Paul, Allen. *Katy'n: The Untold Story of Stalin's Polish Massacre.* New York: Charles Scribner's Sons, 1991.

Raack, R.C. *Stalin's Drive to the West, 1938–1945: The Origins of the Cold War.* Stanford, CA: Stanford University Press, 1995.

Taubman, William. *Stalin's American Policy: From Entente to Détente to Cold War.* New York: Norton, 1982.

Europe

Iatrides, John O. *Revolt in Athens: The Greek Communist "Second Round," 1944–1945.* Princeton, NJ: Princeton University Press, 1972.

Kitchen, Martin. *British Policy towards the Soviet Union during the Second World War.* New York: St. Martin's Press, 1986.

Rabel, Roberto G. *Between East and West: Trieste, the United States and the Cold War, 1941–1954.* Durham, NC: Duke University Press, 1988.

Rothwell, Victor. *Britain and the Cold War, 1941–1947.* London: Jonathan Cape, 1982.

Smith, Arthur L., Jr. *Churchill's German Army: Wartime Strategy and Cold War Politics, 1943–1947.* Beverly Hills, CA: Sage Publications, 1977.

Asia

Carter, Carolle J. *Mission to Yenan: American Liaison with the Chinese Communists, 1944–1947.* Lexington: University Press of Kentucky, 1997.

Denning, Margaret B. *The Sino-American Alliance in World War II: Cooperation and Dispute among Nationalists, Communists and Americans.* Bern, Switzerland: Peter Lang, 1986.

Hsiung, James C., and Steven I. Levine, eds. *China's Bitter Victory: The War with Japan, 1937–1945.* Armonk, NY: M.E. Sharpe, 1992.

Lensen, George Alexander. *The Strange Neutrality: Soviet-Japanese Relations during the Second World War, 1941–1945.* Tallahassee, FL: Diplomatic Press, 1972.

Reardon-Anderson, James. *Yenan and the Great Powers: The Origins of Chinese Communist Foreign Policy, 1944–1946.* New York: Columbia University Press, 1980.

U.S. Department of Defense. *The Entry of the Soviet Union into the War Against Japan: Military Plans, 1941–1945.* Washington, DC: GPO, 1955.

Varg, Paul A. *Closing of the Door: Sino-American Relations, 1936–1946.* East Lansing: Michigan State University Press, 1973.

Yu, Maochun. *OSS in China: Prelude to Cold War.* New Haven, CT: Yale University Press, 1996.

Espionage and Intelligence

Albright, Joseph, and Marcia Kunstel. *Bombshell: The Secret Story of America's Unknown Atomic Spy Conspiracy.* New York: Times Books, 1997.

Hartgrove, J. Dane, ed. *The OSS-NKVD Relationship, 1943–1945.* New York: Garland, 1989.

Smith, Bradley F. *Sharing Secrets with Stalin: How the Allies Traded Intelligence, 1941–1945.* Lawrence: University Press of Kansas, 1996.

Weinstein, Allen, and Alexander Vassiliev. *The Haunted Wood: Soviet Espionage in America; The Stalin Era.* New York: Random House, 1999.

Containment and Détente, 1946–1975

Personalities

Callahan, David. *Dangerous Capabilities: Paul Nitze and the Cold War.* New York: Harper Collins, 1990.

Chace, James. *Acheson: The Secretary of State Who Created the American World.* New York: Simon and Schuster, 1998.

Dallek, Robert. *Lone Star Rising: Lyndon Johnson and His Times, 1908–1960,* New York: Oxford University Press, 1991.

——— *Flawed Giant: Lyndon Johnson and His Times, 1961–1973.* New York: Oxford University Press, 1998.

De Santis, Hugh. *The Diplomacy of Silence: The American Foreign Service, the Soviet Union, and the Cold War, 1933–1947.* Chicago: University of Chicago Press, 1980.

Djilas, Milovan. *Conversations with Stalin.* Trans. by Michael B. Petrovich. New York: Harcourt, Brace and World, 1962.

Donovan, Robert J. *Conflict and Crisis: The Presidency of Harry S. Truman, 1945–1948.* New York: Norton, 1971.

——— *Tumultuous Years: The Presidency of Harry S. Truman 1949–1953.* New York: Norton, 1982.

Friedman, Leon and William F. Levantrosser, eds. *Cold War Patriot and Statesman: Richard M. Nixon.* Westport, CT: Greenwood Press, 1993.

Gorlizki, Yoram and Oleg Khlevniuk. *Cold Peace: Stalin and the Soviet Ruling Circle, 1945–1953.* New York: Oxford University Press, 2004.

Gromyko, Andrei. *Memories.* Trans. by Harold Shukman. New York; Doubleday, 1989.

Guhin, Michael. *John Foster Dulles.* New York: Columbia University Press, 1972.

Hammond, Thomas T., ed. *Witnesses to the Origins of the Cold War.* Seattle: University of Washington, 1982.

Hixson, Walter L. *George F. Kennan: Cold War Iconoclast.* New York: Columbia University Press, 1989.

Isaacson, Walter, and Evan Thomas. *The Wise Men: Six Friends and the World They Made.* New York: Simon & Schuster, 1986. (John McCloy, Charles Bohlen, Dean Acheson, Robert Lovett, Averell Harriman, George Kennan)

Kearns, Dorothy. *Lyndon Johnson and the American Dream.* New York: Harper and Row, 1976.

Keith, Ronald C. *The Diplomacy of Zhou Enlai.* New York: St. Martin's Press, 1989.

Kennan, George F. *Memoirs.* 2 vols. Boston: Little, Brown, 1967–1972.

Haldeman, H.R. *The Haldeman Diaries: Inside the Nixon White House.* New York: G.P. Putnam's Sons, 1994.

Immerman, Richard H., ed. *John Foster Dulles and the Diplomacy of the Cold War.* Princeton, NJ: Princeton University Press, 1990.

Kalb, Marvin, and Bernard Kalb. *Kissinger.* Boston: Little, Brown, 1974.

Khrushchev, Nikita. *Khrushchev Remembers: The Glasnost Tapes*, Boston: Little, Brown, 1990.

——— *Khrushchev Remembers: The Last Testament.* Boston: Little, Brown, 1974.

Khrushchev, Sergei. *Nikita Khrushchev and the Creation of a Superpower.* Trans. by Shirley Benson. University Park: Pennsylvania State University Press, 2000.

Kissinger, Henry. *White House Years.* Boston: Simon & Schuster, 1979.

——— *Years of Upheaval.* Boston: Simon & Schuster, 1982.

——— *Years of Renewal.* New York: Simon & Schuster, 1999.

Miscamble, Wilson D. *George F. Kennan and the Making of American Foreign Policy, 1947–1950.* Princeton, NJ: Princeton University Press, 1992.

Montefiore, Simon Sebag. *Stalin: The Court of the Red Tsar.* New York: Knopf, 2004.

Nitze, Paul H., Steven L. Rearden and Ann M. Smith. *From Hiroshima to Glasnost: At the Center of Decisions, A Memoir.* New York: Weidenfeld and Nicolson, 1898.

Nixon, Richard. *RN: The Memoirs of Richard Nixon.* New York: Grosset and Dunlap, 1978.

Ognibene, Peter J. *Scoop: The Life and Politics of Henry M. Jackson.* New York: Stein & Day, 1975.

Robertson, David. *Sly and Able: A Political Biography of James F. Byrnes.* New York: Norton, 1994.

Schoenbaum, Thomas J. *Waging Peace and War: Dean Rusk in the Truman, Kennedy and Johnson Years.* New York: Simon and Schuster, 1988.

Schulzinger, Robert D. *Henry Kissinger: Doctor of Diplomacy.* New York: Columbia University Press, 1989.

Short, Philip. *Mao: A Life.* New York: Henry Holt, 2000.

Stoler, Mark A. *George C. Marshall: Soldier-Statesman of the American Century.* Boston: Twayne Publishers, 1989.

Taubman, William. *Khrushchev: The Man and His Era.* New York: Norton, 2003.

Walker, J. Samuel. *Henry A. Wallace and American Foreign Policy.* Westport, CT: Greenwood Press, 1976.

Origins of Cold War

Aronsen, Lawrence, and Martin Kitchen. *The Origins of the Cold War in Comparative Perspective: American, British, and Canadian Relations with the Soviet Union, 1941–48.* New York: St. Martin's Press, 1988.

Etzold, Thomas H., and John L. Gaddis, *Containment: Documents on American Policy and Strategy, 1945–1950,* New York: Columbia University Press. 1978 has full texts of NSC-68 and other documents of that time.

Gormly, James L. *From Potsdam to the Cold War: Big Three Diplomacy, 1945–1947.* Wilmington, DE: SR Books, 1990.

Harbutt, Fraser J. *The Iron Curtain: Churchill, America, and the Origins of the Cold War.* New York: Oxford University Press, 1986.

Hinds, Lynn Boyd, and Theodore Otto Windt, Jr. *The Cold War as Rhetoric: The Beginnings, 1945–1950.* New York: Praeger, 1991.

Hogan, Michael J. *The Marshall Plan: America, Britain, and the Reconstruction of Western Europe, 1947–1952.* New York: Cambridge University Press, 1987.

Leffler, Melvyn P. *The Specter of Communism: The United States and the Origins of the Cold War, 1917–1953.* New York: Hill and Wang, 1994.

Messer, Robert L. *The End of an Alliance: James F. Byrnes, Roosevelt, Truman, and the Origins of the Cold War.* Chapel Hill: University of North Carolina Press, 1982.

Offner, Arnold A. *Another Such Victory: President Truman and the Cold War, 1945–1953.* Stanford, CA: Stanford University Press, 2002.

Reid, Escott. *Time of Fear and Hope: The Making of the North Atlantic Treaty, 1947–1949.* Toronto: McClelland Publishers, 1977.

Senarclens, Pierre de. *From Yalta to the Iron Curtain: The Great Powers and the Origins of the Cold War.* Trans. by Amanda Pingree. Washington, DC: Berg, 1995.

Simpson, Christopher. *Blowback: America's Recruitment of Nazis and Its Effects on the Cold War.* New York: Weidenfeld and Nicolson, 1988.

Siracusa, Joseph M. *Into the Dark House: American Diplomacy and the Ideological Origins of the Cold War.* Claremont, CA: Regina Books, 1998.

Ward, Patricia Dawson. *The Threat of Peace: James F. Byrnes and the Council of Foreign Ministers, 1945–1946.* Kent, OH: Kent State University Press, 1979.

Yergin, Daniel. *Shattered Peace: The Origins of the Cold War.* Rev. ed. New York: Penguin Books, 1990.

Soviet Union

Firth, Noel E. and James H. Noren, *Soviet Defense Spending: A History of CIA Estimates, 1950–1990.* College Station, TX: Texas A & M Press, 1998.

Kaplan, Karel. *The Short March: The Communist Takeover in Czechoslovakia, 1945–1948.* New York: St. Martin's Press, 1987.

Kennedy-Pipe, Caroline. *Stalin's Cold War: Soviet Strategies in Europe, 1943–1956.* New York: St. Martin's Press, 1995.

Mastny, Vojech. *The Cold War and Soviet Insecurity: The Stalin Years.* New York: Oxford University Press, 1996.

Podvig, Pavel, ed. *Russian Strategic Nuclear Forces.* Cambridge, MA: MIT Press, 2001.

Roman, Eric. *Hungary and the Victor Powers, 1945–1950.* New York: St. Martin's Press, 1996.

Sokov, Nikolai. *Russian Strategic Modernization: Past and Present.* Lanham, MD: Rowman and Littlefield, 2000.

Ulam, Adam B. *Expansion and Coexistence: Soviet Foreign Policy, 1917–1973.* 2nd ed. New York: Praeger, 1974.

United States

Alexander, Charles. *Holding the Line: The Eisenhower Era, 1952–1961.* Bloomington: Indiana University Press, 1975.

Ambrose, Stephen E. *Eisenhower: Soldier and President.* New York: Simon and Schuster, 1990.

Beschloss, Michael. *The Crisis Years: Kennedy and Khrushchev, 1960–1963.* New York: Edward Burlingame Books, 1991.

Bills, Scott L. *Empire and Cold War: The Roots of US-Third World Antagonism, 1945–1947.* New York: St. Martin's Press, 1990.

Bowie, Robert R. and Richard H. Immerman. *Waging Peace: How Eisenhower Shaped an Enduring Cold War Strategy.* New York: Oxford University Press, 1998.

Bundy, William. *A Tangled Web: The Making of Foreign Policy in the Nixon Presidency.* New York: Hill and Wang, 1998.

Cohen, Warren I. and Nancy Bernkopf Tucker, eds. *Lyndon Johnson Confronts the World: American Foreign Policy, 1963–1968.* New York: Cambridge University Press, 1994.

Doenecke, Justus D. *Not to the Swift: The Old Isolationists in the Cold War Era.* Lewisburg, PA: Bucknell University Press, 1979.

Freedman, Lawrence. *Kennedy's Wars: Berlin, Cuba, Laos and Vietnam.* New York: Oxford University Press, 2000.

Friedberg, Aaron L. *In the Shadow of the Garrison State: America's Anti-Statism and Its Cold War Grand Strategy.* Princeton, NY: Princeton University Press, 2000.

Garthoff, Raymond. *Détente and Confrontation: American Soviet Relations from Nixon to Reagan.* Rev. ed. Washington, DC: Brookings Institution, 1994.

George, Alexander L., ed. *Managing U.S.-Soviet Rivalry: Problems of Crisis Prevention.* Boulder, CO: Westview Press, 1983.

Hogan, Michael J. A *Cross of Iron: Harry S. Truman and the Origins of the National Security State,* 1945–1954. New York: Cambridge University Press, 1998.

Kaplan, Lawrence S. *NATO and the United States: The Enduring Alliance.* Rev. ed. New York: Twayne Publishers, 1994.

Kuntz, Dianne B., ed. *The Diplomacy of the Crucial Decade: American Foreign Relations during the 1960s.* New York: Columbia University Press, 1994.

Leffler, Melvyn P. *A Preponderance of Power: National Security, the Truman Administration, and the Cold War.* Stanford, CA: Stanford University Press, 1992.

Lucas, Scott. *Freedom's War: The American Crusade Against the Soviet Union.* New York: New York University Press, 1999.

Melanson, Richard A., and David Mayers, eds. *Reevaluating Eisenhower: American Foreign Policy in the 1950s.* Urbana: University of Illinois Press, 1987.

Nixon, Richard, "U.S. Foreign Policy for the 1970's: Building for Peace," *Department of State Bulletin,* March 22, 1971 for the Nixon Doctrine.

Paterson, Thomas G., ed. *Cold War Critics: Alternatives to American Foreign Policy in the Truman Years.* Chicago, IL: Quadrangle Books, 1971.

Rose, Lisle A. *The Cold War Comes to Main Street: America in 1950.* Lawrence: University Press of Kansas, 1999.

Schlesinger, Arthur M. *A Thousand Days: John F. Kennedy in the White House.* Boston: Houghton Mifflin, 1965.

Snead, David L. *The Gaither Committee, Eisenhower, and the Cold War.* Columbus: Ohio State University Press, 1999.

Solberg, Carl. *Riding High: America in the Cold War.* New York: Mason & Lipscomb, 1973.

Szulc, Tad. *The Illusion of Peace: Foreign Policy in the Nixon-Kissinger Years.* New York: Viking, 1978.

Walton, Richard J. *Cold War and Counter-Revolution: The Foreign Policy of John F. Kennedy.* New York: Viking, 1972.

Détente

Litwak, Robert S. *Détente and the Nixon Doctrine: American Foreign Policy and the Pursuit of Stability, 1969–1976.* New York: Cambridge University Press, 1984.

Nelson, Keith, *The Making of Détente: Soviet-American Relations in the Shadow of Vietnam.* Baltimore, MD: Johns Hopkins University Press, 1995.

Sobel, Lester A., ed. *Kissinger & Détente.* New York: Facts on File, 1975.

Stevenson, Richard W. *The Rise and Fall of Détente: Relaxations of Tension in U.S.-Soviet Relations, 1953–1984.* Urbana: University of Illinois Press, 1986.

Thornton, Richard C. *The Nixon-Kissinger Years: Reshaping America's Foreign Policy.* New York: Paragon House, 1989.

Espionage and Intelligence

Aldrich, Richard J., ed. *British Intelligence, Strategy and the Cold War, 1945–1951.* New York: Routledge, 1992.

Coldby, William E., and Peter Forbath. *Honorable Men: My Life in the CIA.* New York: Simon and Schuster, 1978.

Darling, Arthur B. *The Central Intelligence Agency: An Instrument of Government to 1950.* University Park: Pennsylvania State University Press, 1990.

Jeffreys-Jones, Rhodri. *The CIA and American Democracy.* 2nd ed. New Haven, CT: Yale University Press, 1998.

Mangold, Tom. *Cold Warrior: James Jesus Angleton; The CIA's Master Spy Hunter.* New York: Simon and Schuster, 1991.

Marchetti, Victor, and John D. Marks. *The CIA and the Cult of Intelligence.* New York: Alfred A. Knopf, 1974.

Randlagh, John. *The Agency: The Rise and Decline of the CIA.* Rev. ed. New York: Simon and Schuster, 1987.

Thomas, Evan. *The Very Best Men: Four Who Dared; The Early Years of the CIA.* New York: Simon and Schuster, 1995.

Atomic Weapons and Arms Control

Divine, Robert. *Blowing in the Wind: The Nuclear Test Ban Debate, 1954–1960.* New York: Oxford University Press, 1978.

Herken, Gregg. *The Winning Weapon: The Atomic Bomb in the Cold War, 1945–1950.* New York: Knopf, 1980.

Holloway, David. *Stalin and the Bomb: The Soviet Union and Atomic Energy, 1939–1956.* New Haven, CT: Yale University Press, 1996.

Lehman, John F., and Seymour Weiss. *Beyond the SALT II Failure.* New York: Praeger, 1981.

Miller, Richard L. *Under the Cloud: The Decades of Nuclear Testing.* New York: Free Press, 1986.

Moulton, Harland B. *From Superiority to Parity: The United States and the Strategic Arms Race, 1961–1971.* Westport, CT: Greenwood Press, 1973.

Payne, Samuel H. *The Soviet Union and SALT.* Cambridge, MA: The MIT Press, 1980.

Seaborg, Glenn T., and Benjamin S. Loeb. *Kennedy, Khrushchev and the Test Ban.* Berkeley: University of California Press, 1981.

Sims, Jennifer E. *Icarus Restrained: An Intellectual History of Nuclear Arms Control, 1945–1960.* Boulder, CO: Westview Press, 1990.

Smith, Gerald C. *Doubletalk: The Story of the First Strategic Arms Limitation Talks.* New York: Doubleday, 1980.

York, Herbert F. *The Race To Oblivion: A Participant's View of the Arm Race.* New York, 1970.

Arms and Strategies

Aliano, Richard. *American Defense Policy from Eisenhower to Kennedy: The Politics of Changing Military Requirements, 1957–1961.* Athens: Ohio University Press, 1975.

Ball, Desmond, and Jeffrey Richelson. *Strategic Nuclear Targeting.* Ithaca, NY: Cornell University Press, 1986.

Baratta, Joseph Preston. *International Peacekeeping: History and Strengthening.* Washington, DC: Center for UN Reform Education, 1989.

Barnhart, Michael, ed. *Congress and United States Foreign Policy: Controlling the Use of Force in the Nuclear Age.* Albany, NY: State University of New York Press, 1987.

Craig, C. *Destroying the Village: Eisenhower and Thermonuclear War.* New York: Columbia University Press, 1998.

Dyson, Freeman. *Weapons and Hope.* New York: Harper Colophon Books, 1984.

Feldbaum, Carl B., and Ronald J. Bee. *Looking the Tiger in the Eye: Confronting the Nuclear Threat.* New York: Harper & Row, 1988.

Fischer, David, and Paul Szasz, *Safeguarding the Atom: A Critical Appraisal.* Ed. Jozef Goldblat. London: Taylor & Francis, 1985.

Graebner, Norman A., ed. *The National Security: Its Theory and Practice, 1945–1960.* New York: Oxford University Press, 1986.

McNamara, Robert. *Blundering Into Disaster: Surviving the First Century of the Nuclear Age.* New York: Pantheon Books, 1986.

Roman, Peter J. *Eisenhower and the Missile Gap.* Ithaca, NY: Cornell University Press, 1995.

Stone, David. *Wars of the Cold War: Campaigns and Conflicts, 1945–1990.* London, UK: Brassey's, 2004.

Wenger, Andreas, *Living with Peril: Eisenhower, Kennedy and Nuclear Weapons.* Lanham, MD: Rowman and Littlefield Publishers, 1997.

Africa

Borstelmann, Thomas. *Apartheid's Reluctant Uncle: The United States and Southern Africa in the Early Cold War.* New York: Oxford University Press, 1993.

Brzezinski, Zbigniew, ed. *Africa and the Communist World.* Stanford, CA: Stanford University Press, 1963.

Emerson, Rupert. *Africa and United States Policy.* Englewood Cliffs, NJ: Prentice Hall, 1967.

Gleijeses, Piero. *Conflicting Missions: Havana, Washington and Africa, 1959–1976.* Chapel Hill: University of North Carolina Press, 2002.

Jackson, Henry F. *From the Congo to Soweto: U.S. Foreign Policy toward Africa since 1960.* New York: W. Morrow, 1982.

Larkin, Bruce D. *China and Africa, 1949–1970: The Foreign Policy of the People's Republic of China.* Berkeley: University of California Press, 1971.

Mahoney, Richard D. *JFK: Ordeal in Africa.* New York: Oxford University Press, 1983.

Nielsen, Waldemar A. *The Great Powers and Africa.* New York: Praeger Publishers, 1969.

Noer, Thomas J. *Cold War and Black Liberation: The United States and White Rule in Africa, 1948–1968.* Columbia: University of Missouri Press, 1985.

Asia and Pacific Rim

Borg, Dorothy, and Waldo H. Heinrichs, eds. *Uncertain Years: Chinese-American Relations, 1947–1950.* New York: Columbia University Press, 1980.

Buhite, Russell D. *Soviet-American Relations in Asia, 1945–1954.* Norman: University of Oklahoma Press, 1981.

Chang, Gordon H. *Friends and Enemies: The United States, China and the Soviet Union, 1948–1972.* Stanford, CA: Stanford University Press, 1990.

Foot, Rosemary. *The Practice of Power: US Relations with China since 1949.* New York: Oxford University Press, 1995.

Gallicchio, Marc S. *The Cold War Begins in Asia: American East Asian Policy and the Fall of the Japanese Empire.* New York: Columbia University Press, 1988.

Hunt, Michel H. *The Genesis of Chinese Communist Foreign Policy.* New York: Columbia University Press, 1996.

Knaus, Kenneth. *Orphans of the Cold War: America and the Tibetan Struggle for Survival, 1951–1974.* New York: Public Affairs, 1999.

Lee, Steven Hugh. *Outposts of Empire: Korea, Vietnam, and the Origins of the Cold War in Asia, 1949–1954.* Montreal: McGill-Queen's University Press, 1995.

Lerner, Mitchell B. *The Pueblo Incident: A Spy Ship and the Failure of American Foreign Policy.* Lawrence: University Press of Kansas, 2002.

Mayers, David. *Cracking the Monolith: U.S. Policy against the Sino-Soviet Alliance, 1949–1955.* Baton Rouge: Louisiana State University Press, 1986.

McIntyre, W. David. *Background to the Anzus Pact: Policy-making, Strategy and Diplomacy, 1945–1955.* New York: St. Martin's Press, 1995.

Korean War

Baum, Kim Chull, and James I. Matray, eds. *Korea and the Cold War: Division, Destruction and Disarmament.* Claremont, CA: Regina Books, 1993.

Brune, Lester H. ed. *The Korean War: Handbook of The Literature and Research.* Westport, CT: Greenwood Press, 1996.

Chen Jian. *China's Road to the Korean War: The Making of the Sino-American Confrontation.* New York: Columbia University Press, 1994.

Cumings, Bruce. *The Origins of the Korean War, 1947 to 1950.* 2 vols. Princeton, NJ: Princeton University Press, 1990.

Foot, Rosemary. *The Wrong War: American Policy and the Dimensions of the Korean Conflict, 1950–1953.* Ithaca, NY: Cornell University Press, 1985.

Goncharov, Sergei N., John W. Lewis and Xue Litai. *Uncertain Partners: Stalin, Mao and the Korean War.* Stanford, CA: Stanford University Press, 1993.

Halliday, Jon, and Bruce Cummings. *Korea: The Unknown War.* New York: Pantheon Books, 1989.

Simmons, Robert R. *The Strained Alliance: Peking, Pyongyang, Moscow and the Politics of the Korean Civil War.* New York: Free Press, 1975.

Stueck, Willam W., Jr. *The Korean War: An International History.* Princeton, NJ: Princeton University Press, 1995.

South and Southeast Asia

Levine, Alan J. *The United States and the Struggle for Southeast Asia, 1945–1975.* Westport, CT: Praeger, 1995.

McMahon, Robert J. *The Cold War on the Periphery: The United States, India and Pakistan.* New York: Columbia University Press, 1994.

O'Balance, Edgar. *Malaya: The Communist Insurgent War, 1948–1960.* Hamden, CT: Archon Books, 1966.

Vietnam Conflict

Anderson, David L. *Trapped by Success: The Eisenhower Administration and Vietnam, 1953–1961.* New York: Columbia University Press, 1991.

Berman, Larry. *No Peace, No Honor: Nixon, Kissinger, and Betrayal in Vietnam.* New York: Free Press, 2001.

Brune, Lester H., and Richard Dean Burns, *America and the Indochina Wars, 1945–1990: A Bibliographical Guide,* Claremont, CA: Regina Books, 1992.

Goodman, Allan. *The Lost Peace: America's Search for a Negotiated Settlement of the Vietnam War.* Stanford, CA: Hoover Institution, 1978.

Halberstam, David. *The Best and the Brightest.* New York: Random House, 1972.

Herring, George C. *America's Longest War: The United States and Vietnam, 1950–1975.* 4th ed. New York: John Wiley, 1979.

Kaplan, Lawrence S., Denise Artaud and Mark R. Rubin, eds. *Dien Bien Phu and the Crisis of Franco-American Relations, 1954–1955*. Wilmington, DE: SR Books, 1990.

Kiernan, Ben. *The Pol Pot Regime: Race, Power, and Genocide in Cambodia Under the Khmer Rouge, 1975–1979*. New Haven, CT: Yale University Press.

Lawson, Eugene K. *The Sino-Vietnamese Conflict*. New York: Praeger, 1984.

Lewy, Guenter. *America in Vietnam*. New York: Oxford University Press, 1978.

Logevall, Fredrik. *Choosing War: The Lost Chance for Peace and the Escalation of the War in Vietnam*. Berkeley: University of California Press, 1999.

McNamara, Robert S., and Brian Van DeMark. *In Retrospect: The Tragedy and Lessons of Vietnam*. New York: Times Books, 1995.

———., James G. Blight, and Robert K. Brigham. *Argument Without End: In Search of Answers to the Vietnam Tragedy*. New York: Public Affairs, 1999.

Moise, Edwin E. *Tonkin Gulf and the Escalation of the Vietnam War*. Chapel Hill: University of North Carolina Press, 1996.

Porter, Gareth. *A Peace Denied: The United States, Vietnam and the Paris Agreement*. Bloomington: Indiana University Press, 1975.

Schandler, Herbert. *The Unmaking of the President: Lyndon Johnson and Vietnam*. Princeton, NJ: Princeton University Press, 1977.

Schulzinger, Robert D. *A Time for War: The United States and Vietnam, 1941–1975*. New York: Oxford University Press, 1997.

Shawcross, William. *Sideshow: Kissinger, Nixon and the Destruction of Cambodia*. New York: Simon & Schuster, 1979.

Stevenson, William, and Monika Jensen-Stevenson. *Kiss the Boys Goodbye: How the United States Betrayed Its Own POW's in Vietnam*. New York: Plume, 1991.

U.S. Department of Defense. *The Pentagon Papers: The Defense Department History of United States Decision Making on Vietnam. The Senator Gravel Edition*. 5 vols. Boston: Beacon, 1971–1972.

Caribbean, South, and Central America

Avirgan, Tony, and Martha Honey. *La Penca: On Trial in Costa Rica, the CIA vs. the Press*. 2nd ed. San Pedro, Costa Rica: Editorial Porvenir, 1988.

Cullather, Nick. *Secret History: The CIA's Classified History of Its Operations in Guatemala, 1952–1954*. Stanford, CA: Stanford University Press, 2000.

Haines, Gerald K. *The Americanization of Brazil: A Study of U.S. Cold War Diplomacy in the Third World, 1945–1954*. Wilmington, DE: SR Books, 1989.

Immerman, Richard H. *The CIA in Guatemala: The Foreign Policy of Intervention*. Austin: University of Texas Press, 1982.

Rabe, Stephen G. *Eisenhower and Latin America: The Foreign Policy of Anti-communism*. Chapel Hill: University of North Carolina Press, 1988.

Scheman, L. Ronald, ed. *The Alliance for Progress: A Retrospective*. New York: Praeger, 1988.

Sigmund, Paul E. *The Overthrow of Allende and the Politics of Chile, 1964–1976*. Pittsburgh, PA: University of Pittsburgh Press, 1977.

Slater, Jerome. *Intervention and Negotiation: The United States and the Dominican Revolution.* New York: Harper and Row, 1970.

Castro and Cuba

Bonsal, Philip Wilson. *Cuba, Castro and the United States.* Pittsburgh: University of Pittsburgh Press, 1971.

Higgins, Trumbull. *The Perfect Failure: Kennedy, Eisenhower, and the CIA at the Bay of Pigs.* New York: Norton, 1987.

Kornbluh, Peter, ed. *Bay of Pigs Declassified: The Secret CIA Report on the Invasion of Cuba.* New York: New Press, 1998.

Paterson, Thomas G. *Contesting Castro: The United States and the Triumph of the Cuban Revolution.* New York: Oxford University Press, 1994.

Welch, Richard E., Jr. *Response to Revolution: The United States and the Cuban Revolution, 1959–1961.* Chapel Hill: University of North Carolina Press, 1985.

Wyden, Peter. *The Bay of Pigs: The Untold Story.* New York: Simon and Schuster, 1979.

Cuban Missile Crisis, 1962

Allison, Graham T., and Philip D. Zelikow. *Essence of Decision: Explaining the Cuban Missile Crisis.* 2nd ed. New York: Longman, 1999.

Blight, James G., and David A. Welch. *On the Brink: Americans and Soviets Reexamine the Cuban Missile Crisis.* New York: Hill and Wang, 1989.

Brune, Lester H. *The Cuba-Caribbean Missile Crisis of October 1962.* Claremont, CA: Regina, 1996.

Divine, Robert A., ed. *The Cuban Missile Crisis.* Chicago: Quadrangle, 1971.

Frankel, Max. *High Noon in the Cold War: Kennedy, Khrushchev, and the Cuban Missile Crisis*, New York: Ballantine Books, 2004.

Fursenko, Alexsandr and Timothy Naftali. *"One Hell of a Gamble": Khrushchev, Castro, and Kennedy, 1958–1964; The Secret History of the Cuban Missile Crisis.* New York: W.W. Norton and Company, 1997.

Kennedy, Robert. *Thirteen Days: A Memoir of the Cuban Missile Crisis.* New York: Norton, 1969.

Nathan, James A., ed. *The Cuban Missile Crisis Revisited.* New York: St. Martin's, 1992.

Europe

Andrianopoulos, Gerry Argyris. *Western Europe in Kissinger's Global Strategy.* New York: St. Martin's Press, 1988.

Berdal, Mats. *The United States, Norway and the Cold War, 1954–1960.* New York: St. Martin's Press, 1997.

Bischof, Günter. *Austria in the First Cold War, 1945–1955: The Leverage of the Weak.* New York: St. Martin's Press, 1999.

Boll, Michael M. *Cold War in the Balkans: American Foreign Policy and the Emergence of Communist Bulgaria, 1943–1947.* Lexington: University of Press of Kentucky, 1984.

Davis, Lynn Etheridge. *The Cold War Begins: Soviet-American Conflict over Eastern Europe.* Princeton, NJ: Princeton University Press, 1974.

Deighton, Anne, ed. *Britain and the First Cold War.* New York: St. Martin's Press, 1990.

Frazier, Robert. *Anglo-American Relations with Greece: The Coming of the Cold War, 1942–1947.* New York: St. Martin's Press, 1991.

Gori, Francesca, and Silvio Pons, eds. *The Soviet Union and Europe in the Cold War, 1943–1953.* New York: St. Martin's Press, 1996.

Heuser, Beatrice. *Western "Containment" Policies in the Cold War: The Yugoslavia Case, 1948–1953.* New York: Routledge, 1989.

Hitchcock, William I. *France Restored: Cold War Diplomacy and the Quest for Leadership in Europe, 1944–1954.* Chapel Hill: University of North Carolina Press, 1998.

Kovrig, Bennett. *The Myth of Liberation: East-Central Europe in U.S. Diplomacy and Politics since 1941.* Baltimore: John Hopkins University Press, 1973.

Krebs, Ronald P. *Dueling Visions: U.S. Strategy toward Eastern Europe under Eisenhower.* College Station: Texas A&M University Press, 2001.

Large, David Clay. *Germans to the Front: West German Rearmament in the Adenauer Era.* Chapel Hill: University of North Carolina Press, 1996.

Mawby, Spencer. *Containing Germany: Britain and the Arming of the Federal Republic.* New York: St. Martin's Press, 1999.

Morgan, Roger. *The United States and West Germany, 1945–1973: A Study in Alliance Politics.* London: Oxford University Press, 1974.

Naimark, Norman M. *The Russians in Germany: A History of the Soviet Zone of Occupation, 1945–1949.* Cambridge, MA: Belknap Press of Harvard University Press, 1995.

Reynolds, David, ed. *The Origins of the Cold War in Europe: International Perspectives.* New Haven, CT: Yale University Press, 1994.

Risse-Kappen, Thomas. *Cooperation Among Democracies: The European Influence on U.S. Foreign Policy.* Princeton, NJ: Princeton University Press, 1997.

Sodaro, Michael J. Moscow, *Germany and the West from Khrushchev to Gorbachev.* Ithaca, NY: Cornell University Press, 1990. Good insights on Soviet leadership.

Stavrakis, Peter J. *Moscow and Greek Communism, 1944–1949.* Ithaca, NY: Cornell University Press, 1989.

Berlin Crises

Morris, Eric. *Blockade: Berlin and the Cold War.* New York: Stein and Day, 1973.

Schick, Jack M. The Berlin Crisis, 1958–1962. Philadelphia: University of Pennsylvania Press, 1971.

Tusa, Ann, and John Tusa. T*he Berlin Airlift.* New York: Atheneum, 1988.

Middle East

Alteras, Isaac. *Eisenhower and Israel: U.S.-Israeli Relations, 1953–1960.* Gainesville: University Press of Florida, 1993.

Brands, H.W. *Into the Labyrinth: The United States and the Middle East, 1945–1993.* New York: McGraw-Hill, 1994.

Cohen, Michael J. *Palestine and the Great Powers, 1945–1948.* Princeton, NJ: Princeton University Press, 1982.

Gasiorowski, Mark J. *U.S. Foreign Policy and the Shah: Building a Client State in Iran.* Ithaca, NY: Cornell University Press, 1991.

Gerges, Fawaz A. *Superpowers and the Middle East: Regional and International Politics, 1955–1967.* Boulder, CO: Westview Press, 1994.

Glassman, John D. *Arms for the Arabs: The Soviet Union and War in the Middle East.* Baltimore: Johns Hopkins University Press, 1975.

Goode, James F. *The United States and Iran, 1946–1951: The Diplomacy of Neglect.* New York: St. Martin's Press, 1989.

Kass, Ilana. *Soviet Involvement in the Middle East: Policy Formulation, 1966–1973.* Boulder, CO: Westview Press, 1978.

Kuniholm, Bruce R. The *Origins of the Cold War in the Near East: Great Power Conflict and Diplomacy in Iran, Turkey and Greece.* Princeton, NJ: Princeton University Press, 1980.

Kyle, Keith. *Suez.* New York: St. Martin's Press, 1991.

Lesch, David W., ed. *The Middle East and the United States: A Historical and Political Reassessment.* 2nd ed. Boulder, CO: Westview Press, 1999.

Persson, Magnus. *Great Britain, the United States and the Security of the Middle East: The Formation of the Baghdad Pact.* Lund, Sweden: Lund University Press, 1998.

Confrontation & Conciliation, 1976–1991

Personalities

Baker, James A., III. *The Politics of Diplomacy.* New York: G.P. Putnam's Sons, 1995.

Brzezinski, Zbigniew. *Power and Principle: Memoirs of the National Security Adviser, 1977–1981.* New York: Farrer, Strauss & Giroux, 1985.

Bush, George, and Brent Scowcroft. *A World Transformed.* New York: Alfred A. Knopf, 1998.

Canon, Lou. *President Reagan: The Role of a Lifetime.* New York: Simon & Schuster, 1991.

Carter, Jimmy. *Keeping the Faith: Memoirs of a President.* New York: Bantam, 1982.

Chernyaev, Anatoly S. *My Six Years with Gorbachev.* University Park: The Pennsylvania State University Press, 2000.

Clifford, Clark, and Richard Holbrooke. *Counsel to the President.* New York: Random House, 1991.

Ford, Gerald R. *A Time to Heal: The Autobiography of Gerald R. Ford.* New York: Harper and Row, 1979.

Gates, Robert M. *From the Shadows: The Ultimate Insider's Story of Five Presidents and How They Won the Cold War.* New York: Simon & Schuster, 1996.

Haig, Alexander M., Jr. *Caveat: Realism, Reagan and Foreign Policy.* New York: Macmillan, 1984.

Hartmann, Robert T. *Palace Politics: An Inside Account of the Ford Years.* New York: McGraw-Hill, 1980.

Helms, Richard, and William Hood. *A Look Over My Shoulder: A Life in the CIA.* New York: Random House, 2003.

McFarlane, Robert C., and Zofia Smardz. *Special Trust.* New York: Cadell & Davies, 1994.

Reagan, Ronald. *An American Life.* New York: Simon & Schuster, 1990.

Rearden, Steven L. *The Evolution of American Strategic Doctrine: Paul H. Nitze and the Soviet Challenge.* Boulder, CO: Westview Press, 1984.

Shultz, George Pratt. *Turmoil and Triumph: My Years as Secretary of State.* New York: Scribners, 1993.

Talbott, Strobe. *Master of the Game: Paul Nitze and Nuclear Peace.* New York: Knopf, 1988.

Vance, Cyrus. *Hard Choices: Critical Years in America's Foreign Policy.* New York: Simon & Schuster, 1983.

Weinberger, Caspar. *Fighting for Peace: Seven Critical Years in the Pentagon.* New York: Warner Books, 1990.

General Accounts

Bialer, Seweryn. *The Soviet Paradox: External Expansion, Internal Decline.* New York: Knopf, 1986.

Blacker, Coit D. *Hostage to Revolution: Gorbachev and Soviet Security Policy, 1985–1991.* New York: Council on Foreign Relations Press, 1993.

Blinken, Anthony S. *Ally Versus Ally: America, Europe, and the Siberian Pipeline Crisis.* New York: Praeger, 1987.

Cahn, Anne Hessing. *Killing Détente: The Right Attacks the CIA.* University Park: Pennsylvania State University Press, 1998. On "Team B" critique of intelligence.

Dumbrell, John. *The Carter Presidency: A Re-evaluation.* 2nd ed. New York: St. Martin's Press, 1995.

Fink, Gary M. and Hugh David Graham, eds. *The Carter Presidency: Policy Choices in the Post-New Deal Era.* Lawrence: University Press of Kansas, 1998.

Fitzgerald, Frances, *Way Out There in the Blue: Reagan, Star Wars and the End of the Cold War,* New York: Simon and Schuster, 2000.

Garthoff, Raymond L. *The Great Transition: American-Soviet Relations and the End of the Cold War,* Washington, DC: Brookings Institution, 1994.

Greene, John Robert. *The Limits of Power: The Nixon and Ford Administrations.* Bloomington: Indiana University Press, 1993.

Hyland, William G. *Mortal Rivals: Superpower Relations from Nixon to Reagan.* New York: Random House, 1987.

Meneges, Constantine C. *Inside the National Security Council: The True Story of the Making and Unmaking of Reagan's Foreign Policy.* New York: Simon and Schuster, 1988.

Mower, A. Glenn, Jr. *Human Rights and American Foreign Policy: The Carter and Reagan Experiences.* New York: Greenwood Press, 1987.

Smith, Gaddis. *Morality, Reason and Power: American Diplomacy in the Carter Years.* New York: Hill & Wang, 1986.

Strong, Robert A. *Working the World: Jimmy Carter and the Making of American Foreign Policy.* Baton Rouge: Louisiana State University Press, 2000.

Tyroler, Charles II, ed. *Committee on the Present Danger: Alerting America; The Papers of the Committee on the Present Danger.* Washington, DC: Pergamon-Brassey's, 1984. Attacks Carter's arms control policies.

Arms Control

Adelman, Kenneth L. *The Great Universal Embrace: Arms Summitry; A Skeptic's Account.* New York: Simon and Schuster, 1989. Reagan's Director of the Arms Control & Disarmament Agency.

Carnesale, Albert, and Richard H. Haass, eds. *Superpower Arms Control: Setting the Record Straight.* Cambridge, MA: Ballinger, 1987.

Duffy, Gloria. *Compliance and the Future of Arms Control.* Cambridge, MA: Ballinger, 1988.

Freedman, Lawrence. *Arms Control: Management or Reform.* Chatham House Papers, No. 31. London: Routledge, 1986. Re: SALT, START, INF, MBFR & CSCE.

Foerster, Schuyler. "The Reagan Administration and Arms Control: Redefining the Agenda." In *Defense Policy in the Reagan Administration.* Ed. William P. Snyder and James Brown. Washington, DC: National Defense University Press, 1988, pp. 5–44.

Kartchner, Kerry M. *Negotiating START: Strategic Arms Reduction Talks and the Quest for Strategic Stability.* New Brunswick, NJ, 1992.

Mosher, David, and Michael O'Hanlon. *The START Treaty and Beyond.* Washington, DC: Congressional Budget Office, 1991.

Scheer, Robert. *With Enough Shovels: Reagan, Bush and Nuclear War.* New York, 1982. Insight into their attitudes toward arms control.

Shimko, Keith L. *Images and Arms Control: Perceptions of the Soviet Union in the Reagan Administration.* Ann Arbor: University of Michigan Press, 1991.

Talbott, Strobe. *Endgame: The Inside Story of SALT II.* New York: Harper & Row, 1979.

———. *Deadly Gambits: The Reagan Administration and the Stalemate in Nuclear Arms Control.* New York: Knopf, 1984.

Arms and Strategy

Carney, John T., and Benjamin F. Schemmer, *No Room for Error: The Covert Operations of Special Tactics Units From Iran to Afghanstan.* New York: Ballantine Books, 2003.

Gervasi, Tom. *The Myth of Soviet Military Supremacy.* New York: Harper & Row, 1986.

McGwire, Michael. *Military Objectives in Soviet Foreign Policy.* Washington, DC: Brookings, 1987.

Mendel, Richard A. *The Defense Game: An Insider Explores the Astonishing Realities of America's Defense Establishment.* New York: Harper & Row, 1986.

Nolan, Janne E. *Guardians of the Arsenal: The Politics of Nuclear Strategy.* New York: Basic Books, 1989.

Odom, William E. *The Collapse of the Soviet Military.* New Haven, CT: Yale University Press, 1998.

Pratt, Erik K. *Selling Strategic Defense: Interests, Ideologies, and the Arms Race.* Boulder, CO: Lynne Rienner, 1990.

Biological and Chemical

Alibek, Ken, and Stephen Handelman. *Biohazard: The Chilling True Story of the Largest Covert Biological Weapons Program in History: Told from the Inside by the Man Who Ran It.* New York: Random House, 1999. Soviet biological warfare program.

Miller, Judith, Stephen Engelberg, and William Broad. *Germs: Biological Weapons and America's Secret War.* New York: Simon & Schuster, 2001.

Schaefer, Henry W. *Nuclear Arms Control.* Washington, DC: National Defense University Press, 1986.

Seagrave, Sterling. *Yellow Rain.* New York, 1981.

Sims, Nicholas Roger Alan. *The Evolution of Biological Disarmament.* Oxford and New York: Oxford University Press, 2001.

Missile Defenses

Burns, Richard Dean and Lester M. Brune, *The Quest for Missile Defenses, 1944–2004.* Claremont, CA: Regina Books, 2004.

Lakoff, Sanford and Herbert F. York. *A Shield in Space? Technology, Politics, and the Strategic Defense Initiative.* Berkeley, CA: University of California Press, 1989.

Pressler, Senator Larry. *Star Wars: The Strategic Defense Initiative Debates in Congress.* New York: Praeger, 1986.

Waller, Douglas C., James T. Bruce, and Douglas M. Cook. *The Strategic Defense Initiative: Progress and Challenge; A Guide to Issues and Reference.* Claremont, CA: Regina Books, 1987.

Afghanistan

Bradsher, Henry S. *Afghanistan and the Soviet Union.* Durham, NC: Duke University Press, 1983.

Bradsher, Henry. *Afghan Communism and Soviet Intervention.* New York: Oxford University Press, 1999.

Coll, Steve. *Ghost Wars: The Secret History of the CIA, Afghanistan, and Bin Laden from the Soviet Invasion to September 10, 2001.* New York: Penguin Press, 2004.

Crile, George. *Charlie Wilson's War: The Extraordinary Story of the Largest Covert Operation in History.* New York: Atlantic Monthly Press, 2003.

Grau, Lester W. *The Bear Went Over the Mountain: Soviet Combat Tactics in Afghanistan.* London: Frank Cass, 1998.

Kakar, M. Hassan. *Afghanistan: The Soviet Invasion and the Afghan Response.* Berkeley: University of California Press, 1995.

Maley, William. *The Afghanistan Wars.* New York: Palgrave Macmillan, 2002.

Africa

Clough, Michael. *Free at Last? U.S. Policy toward Africa and the End of the Cold War.* New York: Council on Foreign Relations Press, 1992.

———., ed. *Reassessing the Soviet Challenge in Africa.* Berkeley: Institute of International Studies, University of California, 1986.

Dickson, David A. *United States Foreign Policy towards Sub-Saharan Africa.* Lanham, MD: University Press of America, 1985.

Klinghoffer, Arthur J. *The Angolan War: A Study in Soviet Policy in the Third World.* Boulder, CO: Westview Press, 1980.

Korn, David A. *Ethiopia, the United States and the Soviet Union.* Carbondale: Southern Illinois University Press, 1986.

Laïdi, Zadi. *The Superpowers and Africa: The Constraints of a Rivalry, 1960–1990.* Trans. by Patricia Baudoin. Chicago, IL: University of Chicago Press, 1990.

Lefebvre, Jeffrey A. *Arms for the Horn: U.S. Policy in Ethiopia and Somalia, 1953–1991.* Pittsburgh, PA: University of Pittsburgh Press, 1993.

Makinda, Samuel M. *Superpower Diplomacy in the Horn of Africa.* New York: St. Martin's Press, 1987.

Marte, Fred. *Political Cycles in International Relations: The Cold War and Africa, 1945–1990.* Amsterdam: VU University Press, 1994.

Smock, David R., ed. *Making War and Waging Peace: Foreign Intervention in Africa.* Washington, DC: United States Institute of Peace Press, 1993.

Windrich, Elaine. *The Cold War Guerrilla: Jonas Savimbi, the U.S. Media and the Angolan War.* New York: Greenwood Press, 1992.

Asia-Pacific Rim

Camilleri, Joseph A. *The Australia, New Zealand and US Alliance: Regional Security in the Nuclear Age.* Boulder, CO: Westview Press, 1987.

Kux, Dennis. *The United States and Pakistan, 1947–2000: Disenchanted Allies.* Baltimore: Johns Hopkins University Press, 2001.

Landais-Stamp, Paul, and Paul Rogers. *Rocking the Boat: New Zealand, the United States and the Nuclear-Free-Zone Controversy in the 1980s.* New York: Berg Publishers, 1989.

Nelson, Harvey W. *Power and Insecurity: Beijing, Moscow and Washington, 1949–1988.* Boulder, CO: Lynne Rienner Publishers, 1989.

Perkins, John H. *Geopolitics and the Green Revolution: Wheat, Genes and the Cold War.* New York: Oxford University Press, 1997.

Pugh, Michael. *The ANZUS Crisis, Nuclear Visiting and Deterrence.* New York: Cambridge University Press, 1989.

Ross, Robert S., ed. *China, the United States, and the Soviet Union: Tripolarity and Policy Making in the Cold War.* Armonk, NY: M.E. Sharpe, 1993.

———. *Negotiating Cooperation: The United States and China, 1969–1989.* Stanford, CA: Stanford University Press, 1995.

Tucker, Nancy Berkopf, ed. *China Confidential: American Diplomats and Sino-American Relations, 1943–1996.* New York: Columbia University Press, 2001.

South and Southeast Asia

Brady, Christopher. *United States Foreign Policy towards Cambodia, 1977–1992: A Question of Realities.* New York: St. Martin's Press, 1999.

Brown, Frederick Z. *Second Chance: The United States and Indochina in the 1990s.* New York: Council on Foreign Relations Press, 1989. Covers since 1972.

Chadda, Maya. *Paradox of Power: The United States in Southwest Asia, 1973–1984.* Santa Barbara, CA: ABC-CLIO, 1986.

Elliott, David W.P., ed. *The Third Indochina Conflict.* Boulder, CO: Westview Press, 1981.

Hurst, Steven. *The Carter Administration and Vietnam.* New York: St. Martin's Press, 1996.

Morley, James W., and Masashi Nishihara, eds. *Vietnam Joins the World.* Armonk, NY: M.E. Sharpe, 1997.

Caribbean, South and Central America

Adams, Jan S. *A Foreign Policy in Transition: Moscow's Retreat from Central America and the Caribbean, 1985–1992.* Durham, NC: Duke University Press, 1992.

Arnson, Cynthia J. *Crossroads: Congress, the President and Central America, 1976–1993.* 2nd ed. University Park: Pennsylvania State University, 1993.

Burrowes, Reynold A. *Revolution and Rescue in Grenada: An Account of the U.S.-Caribbean Invasion.* New York: Greenwood Press, 1988.

Coleman, Kenneth M., and George C. Herring, Jr., eds. *Understanding the Central American Crisis: Sources of Conflict, U.S. Policy and Options for Peace.* Wilmington, DE: SR Books, 1991.

Kagan, Robert. *A Twilight Struggle: American Power and Nicaragua, 1977–1990.* New York: Free Press, 1996.

Landau, Saul. *The Guerrilla Wars of Central America: Nicaragua, El Salvador and Guatemala.* New York: St. Martin's Press, 1993.

Miller, Nicola. *Soviet Relations with Latin America, 1959–1987.* New York: Cambridge University Press, 1989.

O'Shaughnessy, Hugh. *Grenada: An Eyewitness Account of the U.S. Invasion and the Caribbean History That Provoked It.* New York: Dodd, Mead, 1984.

Pavlov, Yuri I. *The Soviet-Cuban Alliance, 1959–1991.* New Brunswick, NJ: Transaction Publishers, 1994.

Central American Interventions

Adkin, Mark. *Urgent Fury: The Battle for Grenada.* Lexington, MA: D.C. Heath, 1989.

Armstrong, Robert, and Janet Shenk. *El Salvador: The Face of Revolution.* Boston: South End Press, 1983.

Arnson, Cynthia. *Crossroads: Congress, the Reagan Administration and Central America.* New York: Pantheon, 1989.

Beck, Robert J. *The Grenada Invasion.* Boulder, CO: Westview Press, 1993.

Burrowes, Reynold A. *Revolution and Rescue in Grenada.* Westport, CT: Greenwood, 1988.

Byrne, Hugh. *El Salvador's Civil War.* Boulder, CO: Lynne Rienner, 1996.

Cockbury, Leslie. *Out of Control: The Story of the Reagan Administration's Secret War in Nicaragua.* New York: Atlantic Monthly Press, 1987.

Cohen, William S., and George J. Mitchell. *Men of Zeal: A Candid Inside Story of the Iran Contra Hearings.* New York: Viking, 1988.

Donnelly, Thomas, Margaret Roth, and Caleb Barker. *Operation Just Cause: The Storming of Panama.* New York: Lexington Books, 1991.

Konbluh, Peter. *Nicaragua: The Price of Intervention.* Washington, DC: Institute for Policy Studies, 1987.

LeoGrande, William M. *Our Own Backyard: The United States and Central America, 1977–1992.* Chapel Hill: University of North Carolina Press, 1998.

Moreno, Dario. *U.S. Policy in Central America: The Endless Debate.* Miami: Florida International University Press, 1990.

Walker, Thomas W., ed. *Reagan versus the Sandinistas: The Undeclared War on Nicaragua.* Boulder, CO: Westview, 1987.

Europe

Allin, Dana H. *Cold War Illusions: America, Europe and Soviet Power, 1969–1989.* New York: St. Martin's Press, 1995.

Blinken, Antony J. *Ally versus Ally: America, Europe and the Siberian Pipeline Crisis.* New York: Praeger, 1987.

Costigliola, Frank C. *France and the United States: The Cold Alliance since World War II.* New York: Twayne Publishers, 1992.

Goldstein, Walter, ed. *Reagan's Leadership and the Atlantic Alliance: Views from Europe and America.* Washington, DC: Pergamon-Brassey, 1986.

Kirk, Roger, and Mircea Raceanu. *Romania versus the United States: Diplomacy of the Absurd, 1985–1989.* New York: St. Martin's Press, 1994.

Zelikow, Philip D., and Condoleezza Rice. *Germany Unified and Europe Transformed: A Study in Statecraft*. Cambridge, MA: Harvard University Press, 1995.

Middle East

Brune, Lester H. *America and the Iraqi Crisis, 1990–1992*. Claremont, CA: Regina Books, 1993.

Freedman, Lawrence, and Efraim Karsh. *The Gulf Conflict, 1990–1991: Diplomacy and War in the New World Order*. Princeton, NJ: Princeton University Press, 1993.

Freedman, Robert O. *Moscow and the Middle East: Soviet Policy since the Invasion of Afghanistan*. New York: Cambridge University Press, 1991.

Golan, Galia. *Soviet Policies in the Middle East: From World War Two to Gorbachev*. New York: Cambridge University Press, 1990.

Hiro, Dilip, *The Longest War: The Iran-Iraq Military Conflict*. New York: Routledge, 1991.

———, *Desert Shield and Desert Storm: The Second Gulf War*. New York: Routledge, 1992.

Jentleson, Bruce W. *With Friends Like These: Reagan, Bush and Saddam, 1982–1990*. New York: W.W. Norton, 1994.

Keddie, Nikki R., and Mark J. Gasiorowski, eds. *Neither East nor West: Iran, the Soviet Union and the United States*. New Haven, CT: Yale University Press, 1990.

Quandt, William B. *Peace Process: American Diplomacy and the Arab-Israeli Conflict since 1967*. Washington, DC: Brookings Institution Press, 2001.

Saikal, Amin. *The Rise and Fall of the Sha*h. Princeton, NJ: Princeton University Press, 1980.

Sick, Gary. *All Fall Down: America's Tragic Encounter with Iran*. New York: Random House, 1985.

Smolansky, Oles M., and Bettie M. Smolansky. *The USSR and Iraq: The Soviet Quest for Influence*. Durham, NC: Duke University Press, 1991.

Epilogue: End of the Cold War

Beschloss, Michael R., and Strobe Talbott. *At the Highest Level: The Inside Story of the End of the Cold War*. Boston: Little, Brown, 1993.

Carrere d'Encausse, Helene. *The End of the Soviet Empire: The Triumph of the Nations*. New York: Basic Books, 1993.

English, Robert D. *Russia and the Idea of the West: Gorbachev, Intellectuals and the End of the Cold War*. New York: Columbia University Press, 2000.

Hogan, Michael J., ed. *The End of the Cold War*. New York: Cambridge University Press, 1992, See especially Richard J. Barnet, "A Balance Sheet: Lippman, Kennan and the Cold War," and Denise Artaud, "The End of the Cold War: A Skeptical View."

Hough, Jerry F. *Russia and the West: Gorbachev and the Politics of Reform*. New York: Simon and Schuster, 1987.

Hutchings, Robert S. *American Diplomacy and the End of the Cold War, An Insider's Account of U.S. Policy in Europe, 1989–1992.* Baltimore, MD: Johns Hopkins University Press, 1997.

Kaiser, Robert G. *Why Gorbachev Happened: His Triumphs and His Failure.* New York: Simon and Schuster, 1991.

LeBow, Richard, and Janice Gross Stein. *We All Lost the Cold War.* Princeton, NJ: Princeton University Press.

Lundberg, Lirsten. *The CIA and the Fall of the Soviet Empire: The Politics of "Getting it Right."* Cambridge, MA: Kennedy School of Government, Harvard University, 1994.

Matlock, Jack F. *Autopsy of an Empire: The American Ambassador's Account of the Collapse of the Soviet Union.* New York: Random House, 1995.

Matlock, Jack F., Jr. *Reagan and Gorbachev.* New York: Random House, 2004.

Rowen, Henry S., and Charles Wolf, Jr. eds. *The Impoverished Superpower: Perestroika and the Soviet Military Burden.* San Francisco, CA: Institute for Contemporary Studies, 1990.

Schweizer, Peter. *Victory: the Reagan Administration's Secret Strategy that Hastened the Collapse of the Soviet Union.* New York: The Atlantic Monthly Press, 1994.

Shelton, Judy. *The Coming Soviet Crash: Gorbachev's Desperate Pursuit of Credit in Western Financial Markets.* New York: Free Press, 1988.

Summy, Ralph and Michael E. Salla, eds. *Why the Cold War Ended: A Range of Interpretations.* Westport, CT: Greenwood Press, 1995.

Zubok, Vladislav M. "New Evidence of the End of the Cold War." *The Cold War International History Bulletin,* Issue 12/13 (Fall/Winter 2001): pp. 5–23. (An excellent overall source on the Cold War's end.)

Prologue 1992

Brune, Lester H. *The United States and Post-Cold War Interventions: Bush and Clinton in Somalia, Haiti, and Bosnia.* Claremont, CA: Regina Books, 1998.

Dijlas, Aleksa. *The Contested Country: Yugoslav Unity and the Communist Revolution.* Cambridge, MA: Harvard University Press, 1996.

Goldgeier, James H. *Not Whether but When: The U.S. Decision to Enlarge NATO.* Washington, DC: Brookings Institution Press, 1999.

Halbestam, David. *War in a Time of Peace: Bush, Clinton and the Generals.* New York: Scribner, 2001.

Heymann, Philip B. *Terrorism and America: A Commonsense Strategy for a Democratic Society.* Cambridge, MA: M.I.T. Press, 1998.

Litwak, Robert S. *Rogue States and U.S. Foreign Policy: Containment after the Cold War.* Washington, DC: Woodrow Wilson Center Press, 2000.

Oakley, Robert B., and David Bentley. *Peace Operations: A Comparison of Somalia and Haiti.* Washington, DC: National Defense University Press, 1995.

Tow, William T. ed. *Building Sino-American Relations: An Analysis for the 1990s.* New York: Paragon House, 1991.

Woodward, Susan. *Balkan Tragedy: Chaos and Dissolution after the Cold War.* Washington, DC: Brookings, 1995.

Reference Works

Beisner, Robert L., ed. *American Foreign Relations since 1600: A Guide to Literature.* 2nd ed. 2 vols. Santa Barbara, CA: ABC-Clio, 2003.

Burns, Richard Dean, ed. *Encyclopedia of Arms Control and Disarmament.* 3 vols. New York: Scribners, 1993.

DeConde, Alexander, Richard Dean Burns, Fredrik Logevall, and Louise Ketz, eds. *Encyclopedia of American Foreign Policy.* 2nd ed. 3 vols. New York: Scribners, 2002.

Haines, Gerald K., and J. Samuel Walker, eds. *American Foreign Relations: A Historiographical Review.* Westport, CN: Greenwood Press, 1981.

Higham, Robin, and Donald J. Mrozek, eds. *A Guide to the Sources of United States Military History* and Supplements I to IV. Hamden, CT: Archon Books, 1975 to 1998.

Appendix

Soviet Premiers/General Secretaries

Source: Joseph L. Wieczynski, editor, *The Modern Encyclopedia of Russian and Soviet History, 1976–1987*, New York: Academic International Press, 1987, 45 volumes.

Lenin, Vladimir Ilyich Ulyabov Born on April 9, 1870, in the town of Simbirsk, later called Ulanovsk. Lenin's father was a schoolmaster, his mother the daughter of a doctor named Berg. A vital factor in Lenin's life was the execution of his eldest brother in 1891, following the brother's involvement in an unsuccessful revolutionary terrorist (Narodovoltze) plot to assassinate Czar Alexander III. After graduating from a Simbirsk school, Lenin studied law at Kazan University as well as the works of Karl Marx in a local Marxist circle. After passing his law examinations at St. Petersburg University, he became a lawyer for the defense for several trials in Samara but his main endeavors were to study how Marx's ideas could be practiced in Russia's political and economic affairs.

Lenin moved to St. Petersburg in 1894, where he engaged in printing polemic manuscripts against the city's popular political parties in pamphlets that where distributed from hand to hand. The next year, he formed an illegal group called the Union for the Liberation of the Working Class (ULWC) to carry out propaganda among workers. In December 1895, he and four other ULWC members were arrested and sent into exile for five years. While in exile, Lenin wrote an economic tract called *The Development of Capitalism in Russia.* He also married N. K. Krupskaya who was his devoted companion for the rest of his life. In 1900, Lenin went to Switzerland where he began publishing papers known as *Iskra* (The Spark). The Spark provided ways for Social Democrats to form a revolutionary party that would create the dictatorship of the proletariat for the working class.

In August 1903, Lenin, Trotsky, and other Russians attended a Congress of Social Democrats in London but the meeting ending in turmoil due to serious divisions between Bolsheviks and Mensheviks. Lenin's Bolsheviks wanted to align Russian peasants with the workers while Mensheviks thought workers should join with the bourgeoisie. After the 1905 workers and peasants uprising failed against Czar Nicholas II, Lenin used its consequences as a guide for his Bolshevik overthrow of Russia's Provisional Government in 1917. By 1924, Lenin's health was compromised by hard work that resulted in sclerosis of his cerebral arteries. He died on January 24, 1924.

Stalin, Joseph Vissarionovich Born in 1879 to a Georgian peasant shoemaker, Stalin was educated at a Russian Orthodox religious seminary but he was soon expelled for being "unreliable." In 1896, he joined a Social Democratic group for whom he organized a group called the Georgian Worker's Class (GWC). After leading the GWC in protest demonstrations against the government, Stalin was arrested and sentenced to three years of exile in eastern Siberia. He escaped from Siberia in January 1904, and renewed his revolutionary activities in Georgia before again being arrested and sent to exile in Volgoda province for three years. In 1912, he was an editor for the Bolsheviks' journal *Sviezda* (Star) and the *Pravda* newspaper before being arrested and sent to exile in northern Siberia's Turukhansk, where he remained until Russia's first revolution began in March 1917. After Lenin took charge in November 1917, Stalin was a member of the Communist Party's Central Committee as Commissar for Nationalities. From 1920 until Lenin's death in 1924, he was a member of the CP's Military Council. After using this position to expel Trotsky from the CP, Stalin became the powerful general secretary of the Central Committee of the Communist Party.

As general secretary, Stalin became widely known for his purges of CP members in the "Great Terror" of the 1930s. After World War II, he split with his former allies from the United States and Great Britain and even Tito in Yugoslavia as the Cold War began. He died on March 5, 1953.

Malenkov, Georgi Maximilianovich Born in Chakalov in the Ural Mountain area to middle-class parents on January 8, 1902, Malenkov joined the Red Army during the civil war in 1919 and served as the CP's political officer for the Red Army from 1920 to 1922. He attended Moscow's Higher Technical School from 1922 to 1925 before serving as Stalin's secretary from 1925 to 1930. Next, he led the province of Moscow's Communist Party Organization until 1934, where he played a considerable role in Stalin's purges from 1936 to 1938. He was elected an alternate Politburo member in 1940 and directed the Soviet's military production team during World War II. In 1949, Malenkov provided a scenario for the Soviet future by saying "Can there be any doubt that a Third World War will become the grave for world capitalism?" Following Stalin's death in 1953, Malenkov became premier of a five-member Presidium (former Politburo) that included Deputy Premier Larenti P. Beria (soon to be executed), Viacheslav Molotov as foreign minister, Nikolai Bulganin, and Lazar M. Kaganovich. Malenkov was premier until he was ousted by Khrushchev on February 8, 1955. He then became chairman of the Stavropol Economic Council until his death on February 1, 1988.

Bulganin, Marshal Nikolai Alexandrovich Born on June 11, 1895, to a middle-class family in Gorki, he joined the CP shortly before the November 7, 1917 revolution. After working as a secret policeman from 1918 to 1922, he shifted to economic work, finally becoming manager of the USSR's main electrical equipment plant from 1927 to 1931, when he was elected Mayor of Moscow. After serving as mayor for six years, he became a deputy premier and chairman of the USSR's State Bank until 1941. During World War II, he was the chief political officer in the Red Army before becoming a member of the Politburo in 1946. Bulganin was named a full Soviet marshal and vice premier in 1947. In that post, he directed the Defense Ministry until Stalin's death in 1953. After Stalin died, Bulganin became a member of the Presidium headed by Malenkov. When Malenkov was ousted in February 1955, Bulganin became Premier of the Presidium. On March 27, 1958, Khruschev overthrew Bulganin who later became Chairman of the USSR State Bank until his death on February 24, 1975.

Khrushchev, Nikita Sergeevich In 1894, Khrushchev was born the son of a coal miner in Kalinovka, Ukraine. After being an apprentice fitter at the Kharkov machine plant in Donbas from 1911–1917, he became chairman of several minor Soviet organizations between 1917 and 1919. During the civil war against the White Armies in the Ukraine, he was political commissar for the CP. From 1922 to 1925, he studied at the Donetsk Industrial Institute and at the Stalin Industrial Institute in Moscow from 1929–1931. After graduating, he served as the secretary of various CP groups such as the secretary of Moscow's Oblast from 1935 to 1938. During World War II, he returned to the Ukraine, where he was First Secretary of the Communist Party Central Committee from 1938 to 1947. He transferred to Moscow in 1948 to again be a member of Moscow's Oblast from 1949 until Stalin's death in 1953, after which he was Secretary General of the All-Union Communist Party Central Committee. He held this position until Leonid Brezhnev and cohorts removed him from his official positions on October 14, 1964. He lived under virtual house arrest outside Moscow where he began to make tape recordings of his memoirs, which were published and translated into English as *Khrushchev Remembers* in 1970. Although he died in September 1971, another volume titled *Khrushchev Remembers: His Last Testament* was published in 1974. Following a series of talks with Khrushchev's son Sergei, a third volume was published in 1990 as *Khrushchev Remembers: The Glasnost Tapes.*

Kosygin, Aleksei Nikolaevich Born on February 10, 1904, the son of a lathe worker in Leningrad (St. Petersburg at that time), Kosygin joined the Red Army during the civil war from 1919 to 1922. After the defeat of the White Armies, Kosygin studied at Leningrad's Cooperative Technicum from 1922 to 1926. After graduation, he became an instructor and board member of Irkutsk, Siberia's Oblast Consumers' Cooperative until 1930. During the 1930s, he returned to Leningrad where he became a shop supervisor at the Zhelyabov Plant and member of the Communist Party's Vybork Rayon Committee. Later, Kosygin chaired the Executive Committee of Leningrad's City Soviet. During World War II, he served as Deputy Chairman of the USSR's Council of People's Commissars and Chairman of the Russian Soviet Federated Council of Commissars. From 1946 until 1953, he was Deputy Chairman of the USSR Council of Ministers. Following Stalin's death, he held various positions including Deputy Chairman of the State Economic Commission and Chairman of Gosplan. When Khrushchev was exiled in 1964, he became Premier of the Council of Ministers, a position he held until he resigned due to illness on October 23, 1980. He died on December 18, 1980.

Brezhnev, Leonid Illich Born the son of a steelworker in Dneprodzerzhinsk, Ukraine on December 12, 1906, Brezhnev attended the Kursk Technical School from 1921 to 1927 while also working at the local steel mill. After graduating, he went to the city of Dzerzinsky in the Urals to head the Land Utilization Department until 1931, when he began four years of study at the Dneprodzerzhinsk Metallurgical Institute. After graduation, he became an engineer at the city's metallurgical plant and deputy chairman of the city's Soviet Worker's Deputies. In 1938, he returned to the Ukraine and became the deputy chairman of the Oblast Committee of Ukraine's CP, a position he held when Khrushchev was head of Ukraine's CP. During World War II, he was chief of the 18th Army's political department on the 4th Ukrainian front against the Germans, where he was made a major general in 1943. After the war, he was first secretary of Ukraine's CP until 1950, after which he served as first secretary of Moldavia's CP Central Committee until 1953. After Stalin's death, he became First Deputy of the USSR Defense Ministry until 1957 when he became a member of the CP Presidium of the Supreme Soviet that he chaired after 1960. In 1964, he led a group of Presidium members who exiled Khrushchev. Brezhnev became First Secretary of CP Central Committee, a position he held until his death in 1982.

Andropov, Yuri Vladimirovich Born on June 15, 1914, the son of a railway worker in the village of Nagutskaya in the Northern Caucasus, Andropov worked as a telegraph operator and film projectionist before going to study at Petrozavodsk University. Although never graduating from the university, he was sent to head the Young Communist League in the newly formed Karelo-Finnish Republic in 1940. During the German occupation of the area in World War II, Andropov organized guerrilla activity behind the German lines. After the war, he became the CP chief and Second Secretary of the Petrozavodsk Republic from 1946 to 1950. In 1951, he moved to Moscow to join the staff of the CP Central Committee before serving as ambassador to Hungary during the tragic days of the Hungarian uprising between 1954 and 1957. After returning to Moscow, he headed the Communist Secretariat's liaison with Communist parties in other countries and was a member of the CP Central Committee Secretariat from 1958 until 1966. In 1967, he began a 15-year tenure as the head of the KGB intelligence service and a full voting member of the CP Central Committee. He resigned from his KGB post in May 1982, before replacing Brezhnev as General Secretary of the CP Central Committee on November 12, 1982. Following many days in hospital, Andropov died of a heart attack on February 9, 1984.

Chernenko, Konstantine Ustinovich Born on September 24, 1911, the son of a peasant family in the Siberian village of Bolshaya Tyes, he first worked as a farm hand. During the 1930s, he became active in the Young Communist League, rising to become Party Secretary for the Krasnoyarsk region in 1941. After World War II, he moved to the newly formed Moldavian Republic to head the CP's propaganda department. Fortunately, Leonid Brezhnev was also in Moldavia and became Chernenko's good friend. When Brezhnev went to work in Moscow in 1956, Chernenko joined the propaganda section of the CP Central Committee in Moscow. In 1960, Brezhnev promoted Chernenko to be the office manager and chief of staff for the Presidium of the Supreme Soviet (parliament) and secretary of the CP Central Committee, positions he retained until Brezhnev died in 1982. As Secretary of the Central Committee, Chernenko nominated Andropov to replace Brezhnev and Central Committee members unanimously endorsed Andropov. Thus, when Andropov died from a heart arrack, Chernenko was selected to become General Secretary of the Communist Party Central Committee on February 13, 1984. His term of office only lasted 13 months. He died of heart failure on March 10, 1985, being replaced the next day by Mikhail Gorbachev.

Gorbachev, Mikhail Sergevich He was born in 1931 to a poor peasant family in the northern Caucasus town of Stavropol. After World War II, he joined the CP while a law student at Moscow State University. After graduating in 1955, he decided to change from the practice of law to emphasize agriculture and received a degree from the Stavropol Agricultural Institute in 1967. During the years from 1955 to 1967, he rose steadily in the ranks of the local CP, becoming first secretary of the Communist Youth League in 1956 and first secretary of the Stavropol region in 1970. With the backing of the Party's chief ideologist Mikhail Suslov, Gorbachev became a member of the Communist Party Central Committee in 1971. In 1978, he became the Central Committee's Secretariat as supervisor of the USSR's troubled agricultural section. In 1980, Gorbachev became a full member of the Politburo. After Andropov replaced Brezhnev as General Secretary of the Politburo in 1982, Gorbachev often chaired Politburo meetings due to Andropov's poor health. Because General Secretary Chernenko also suffered from poor health, Gorbachev had to carry out many of the Politburo's duties. In December 1984, the Western world got their first look at Gorbachev when his wife Raisa joined him on a visit to London. In addition to the British press being impressed by his sense of humor and relaxed manner, British Prime Minister Margaret Thatcher offered some memorable word about Gorbachev by saying: "He's a man you can do business with." After the death of Chernenko on March 10, 1985, the Politburo selected Gorbachev as General Secretary of the Communist Party's Central Committee. Gorbachev was the Soviet Union's last leader. In December 2001, he resigned from office. The USSR was replaced by a Commonwealth of Independent State (CIS). The Cold War had ended with Boris Yeltsin becoming president of Russia, the largest state in the CIS.

Foreign Commissars/Foreign Ministers

Trotsky, Lev Davidovich In 1879, he was born into a middle-class Jewish family named Bronstein in the village of Elizavtgrad. After being educated at Odessa's Peter and Paul School (Real Schule) and the city's university, he was arrested for radical activity in 1898, and exiled to eastern Siberia. Before escaping from Siberia in 1902, he changed his name from Bronstein to Trotsky on his passport and went by boat to Istanbul (Constantinople) before boarding a larger ship that took him to England. In London, he collaborated with Lenin in publishing the *Iskia* (Spark) newspaper. Three years later, Trotsky returned to Russia where he was elected to St. Petersburg's Soviet of Workers Deputies. For his activities in recruiting workers to the St. Petersburg Soviet, he was arrested and sent to exile in Siberia. He escaped again and traveled to Vienna to work as a correspondent for the *Arbeiter Zeitung* (Worker's Newspaper) and *Pravda*. In 1914, he went to Zurich where he wrote a book on the origins of World War I before going to Paris. Because he opposed the war in public writings, French police arrested and expelled him in 1916. He tried to enter Spain but was arrested by border guards after crossing the border. Spanish authorities allowed to him to board a boat leaving for America. In New York, he spent one year as editor of a Russian revolutionary tract called the *Novy Mir* (New World). When Russia's first revolution against Nicholas II broke out in March 1917, his New York friends collected money for his boat trip home but British authorities arrested him when he reached Halifax, Nova Scotia. He was interred in Halifax until Russia's Provisional Government asked for his release. Upon arriving in Petrograd (St. Petersburg), he joined Lenin in organizing the revolution that overthrew the Provisional Government in November 1917.

In early 1918, Trotsky served as the Bolshevik's foreign minister and negotiated the Treaty of Brest-Litovsk with Germany. During the civil war against the czar's White Army, Trotsky yielded the foreign minister's post to Chicherin and became Commissar for War. In this position, Trotsky organized the Red Army, whose forces were victorious over the White Army as well as the French, British, and American troops who intervened in Russia at various times between 1918 and 1920.

Following Lenin's death in January 1924, Trotsky was strongly criticized by Stalin and other long-time Bolsheviks; they forced Trotsky to forfeit his role as Commissar of War and accept a low level position as head of a committee on electric power in Russia. In November 1927, he was expelled from the CP for antiparty activities and exiled to Turkestan. After a brief period in Istanbul, Trotsky went to Mexico in 1937. On August 20, 1940, a "Stalinist agent" attacked Trotsky in his Mexican home and Trotsky died the next day.

Chicherin, Georgii Vasil'evich Born on November 12, 1872, at his wealthy parents' estate in Karaul, he was part of the Naryshkin clan whose nobility could be traced back five centuries. During his early years, his mother, a governess, and a tutor educated him at home. In 1885, the family moved to St. Petersburg where he attended gymnasium before enrolling at St. Petersburg University, where he studied history and foreign languages, including English. After graduation, he joined the archival section of the Ministry of Foreign Affairs where he helped prepare the Centennial history of the Foreign Ministry, published in 1902. After the 1905 general strike of Russian dissidents collapsed after Czar Nicholas II granted Russians some civil liberties, Chicherin joined the Mensheviks who elected him Secretary of the Foreign Bureau of the Russian Social Democratic Labor Party. As World War I approached, he became disillusioned with the Mensheviks and fled to England where he published a series of antiwar essays. In August 1917, British police arrested Chicherin, imprisoning him at Brixton jail. After Lenin took control in Russia in November 1917, Russia's Foreign Commissar embarrassed the British by appointing Chicherin as Ambassador to the Court of St. James, a ploy leading the British to release him from jail and deport him to Russia. As Trotsky's deputy, Chicherin began the process of training a new Soviet diplomatic corps during the civil war against the White Armies. During the 1920s, he gained international attention by representing the Soviets in negotiations at Geneva and Locarno and by making the Rapallo Treaty of friendship with Germany's Weimar Republic. After Lenin's death, Chicherin had to deal with Stalin and his Deputy Foreign Minster Maxim Litvinov, both of whom disagreed with his efforts at friendship with Germany and other European nations. From 1928 to 1930, Litvinov was in charge of the Foreign Office while Chicherin went to Germany for medical treatment regarding diabetes. He returned in 1930 to retire. He died on July 7, 1936.

Litvinov, Maxim Maksimovich Born on July 13, 1876, of Jewish parents (his original name was Meyer Wallach) in Bielostok, Russian Poland. Litvinov was educated at Realschule in Bielostok where he learned the Russian language (they spoke Yiddish at home). He joined the army when he was 17 years old and was assigned to Baku where he had clerical duties but also time to read the works of Karl Marx. In 1898, he was discharged from the army because he refused to fire on a demonstration of local workers who wanted better work conditions and wages. He was sent to work at a sugar factory in Kiev where he joined the Social Democrat Labor Party (SDLP). During an SDLP demonstration in 1901, he was arrested and sentenced to two years in prison. The next year he escaped from prison and traveled to London where he attended the SDLP conference that divided the party into Mensheviks and Bolsheviks. After the 1905 uprising failed to unseat Czar Nicholas II, he sought refuge in England as the Bolshevik Party's chief representative until 1918. After Lenin gained power, Litvinov was appointed as Russia's *charge d'affaires* in London on December 30, 1917. He returned to Russia in 1921 to serve as a deputy in Chicherin's Office of Foreign Affairs. As the deputy, his most important task was as Russia's delegate to the League of Nations Disarmament Conference in Geneva. At the conference, he proposed the total disarmament of all nations, including the abolition of defense budgets, all military service, and munitions factories. Of course his proposal failed because the other delegations thought the proposal was Communist propaganda. When Chicherin became ill in 1928, Litvinov became Minister of Foreign Affairs, a position he officially took over in 1930. As Minister of Foreign Affairs, Litvinov visited Washington to finalize talks whereby President Franklin D. Roosevelt ended American's boycott of Russia by formally recognizing the USSR in 1933. Litvinov persuaded Stalin to formally join the League of Nations in September 1934, and formed defensive alliances with France and Czechoslovakia against Germany. His policy of "collective security" with Western powers failed in 1938, when England and France signed the Munich pact with Germany. Subsequently, Litvinov was forced to resign as Minister of Foreign Affairs on May 3, 1939, and was replaced by Viacheslav Molotov. After Germany invaded the USSR in June 1941, Stalin called on Litvinov to revive good relations with the United States. He arrived in Washington a few hours before the December 7 Japanese attack Pearl Harbor and remained in the United States until May 1943 when Stalin called him home "for consultation" because Roosevelt and Churchill rejected Stalin's pleas to open a second front in Europe. He became a deputy to Molotov until the war ended in August 1946. He died of natural causes on December 31, 1951.

Molotov, Viacheslav Mikhailovich Born in Kazan, Russia, on March 9, 1890, he was the son of a store clerk whose family name was Scriabin, a name he changed to Molotov ("the Hammer") while imprisoned in Siberia in 1915. He joined the Bolshevik branch of Russia's Social Democratic Party in 1906. After studying at St. Petersburg's Vologda Technical Institute, he joined the local Bolshevik group. When he came to help Lenin direct the November revolution, he was arrested and imprisoned in Siberia until 1917. After advancing through several Communist Central Committee positions, he succeeded Litvinov as foreign minister in 1939, and held that position while also holding the post of vice premier to Stalin during World War II. After the war, he personified the Soviet's "just say no" policy toward U.N. proposals made by the U.S. and Western European powers. On March 4, 1949, he yielded the foreign minister's post to Andrei Vishinsky, who had been his deputy. After Stalin's death in 1953, he again became foreign minister, a post he retained until June 1, 1956, when he yielded that office to Dmitri Shepilov. Nikita Khrushchev expelled him from the Party's Central Committee in 1957, but in 1960, he became the Soviet representative to the International Atomic Energy Agency until 1964. He was not readmitted to the CP until 1984. He died on November 8, 1986.

Vishinsky, Andrei Yanuarievich Born on December 10, 1883, he was the son of a well-to-do notary in Odessa, Russia. Although he sided with the Menshevik's before 1917, he was accepted into the Bolshevik ranks of the CP in 1920 because of his legal talents. After working on lesser issues as a public prosecutor, he became prominent as Stalin's main prosecutor during the purge trials from 1936 to 1938. In 1940, he became Vice Commissar for Foreign Affairs. After World War II, Vishinsky was known as a "master of invective" in public diplomacy during U.N. General Assembly meetings in 1947 and 1948. For example, he denounced Americans as "warmongers" and alleged the United States had plans to drop atomic bombs on cities in the Soviet Union. Thus, Americans and other countries were surprised when Vishinsky replaced Molotov as the Soviet Foreign Minister on March 4, 1949, a position he held until Shepilov replaced him in 1956. He then became the Soviet's permanent Ambassador to the United Nations. He died in New York City in 1970.

Shepilov, Dmitri Trofimovich Born in Krasnodar province on November 5, 1905, Shepilov went to schools in his home province where he joined the local CP during the 1930s. After moving to Moscow, he directed the Communist Central Committee's Department of Agitation and Propaganda before becoming editor of *Pravda* (Truth) newspaper in 1952. After Stalin's death in March 1953, the CP's General Secretary Nikita Khrushchev had Shepilov join him and Soviet Premier Nikolai Bulganin on a trip to China and Yugoslavia. Because Marshall Tito of Yugoslavia believed Soviet Foreign Minister Molotov was a persistent opponent of Yugoslavia, Khrushchev appointed Shepilov to replace Molotov as foreign minister two days before Tito visited Moscow in June 1956.

As foreign minister, Shepilov played an important role during Tito's three-week visit to the USSR. He also helped Egypt's President Nasser celebrate Egypt's independence after Britain withdrew its troops from the Suez Canal. Soon after, Khrushchev claimed Shepilov was part of Bulganin's antiparty faction that tried to depose the General Secretary. On February 18, 1957, Khrushchev dismissed Shepilov and appointed Andrei Gromyko as foreign minister. In December 1958, Shepilov became Director of the Kirghiz Scientific Institute, a position he held until his death in 1970.

Gromyko, Andrei Andreyevich Born in 1910 to a poor peasant family near Minsk, White Russia, Gromyko was an outstanding student majoring in economics at the Soviet Institute of Economics, where he became an economics professor in 1937. In 1938, he joined the American division of the Foreign Ministry. In 1939, he joined the Soviet embassy staff in Washington before becoming Ambassador to the United States from 1943 to 1946. In 1946, he was deputy foreign minister and the Soviet's permanent delegate to the U.N. Security Council until returning to Moscow in July 1948. Following Stalin's death in 1953, Khrushchev selected him as foreign minister on February 15, 1957, a position he held until July 1985 when Eduard Shevardnadze replaced him. He died on July 2, 1989.

Shevardnadze, Eduard Amvrosiyevich After Gorbachev became general secretary of the USSR in March 1985, he considered how to change Soviet foreign policy from old guard Soviet leaders to those with a new perspective (glasnost) on dealing with the United States and other Western powers. Thus, in July 2, 1985,

Gorbachev shifted Foreign Minister Andrei Gromyko to the honorific position as President of USSR's Supreme Soviet (parliament) and chose Shevardnadze as Foreign Minister. Born in 1928, near the Northern Caucasus Republic of Georgia, Shevardnadze led the Young Communist League in Georgia where he became friends with Gorbachev who had the same office in Stavropol. After Gorbachev moved to Moscow, Shevardnadze was the CP's chief of police in Georgia, where he successful cracked down on corrupt officials. He also was first secretary of the CP in Georgia. Before becoming foreign minister, he became a full member of the Politburo on July 1, 1985. As foreign minister, Shevardnadze joined with Gorbachev in establishing better relations with President Reagan and Vice Preseident George H.W. Bush. Most notable was Shevardnadze's assistance to President Bush's administration after Iraqi forces invaded Kuwait in 1990. Following this assistance, Shevardnadze announced his resignation as foreign minister during the December 20, 1990 session of the Congress of People's Deputies. During the Congress meeting, he warned the members that conservatives in the party were trying to create a "dictatorship." Later, Shevardnadze was elected president of the Republic of Georgia.

Bessmertnykh, Aleksandr Born in 1934, Bessmertnykh became a career diplomat as a U.S. embassy counselor and specialist in U.S. relations under Ambassador to the United States Anatoly Dobrynin. After Dobrynin resigned as ambassador in 1990, Bessmertnykh became U.S. ambassador. After resigning as foreign minister in December 1990, Shevardnadze stayed on until the Supreme Soviet confirmed Bessmertnykh as foreign minister on January 15, 1991. He retained that post until Gorbachev resigned as President in December 1991.

Chinese Leaders (Nationalist/Communist)

Source: Jasper Becker, *The Chinese: An Insider's Look at the Issues which Affect and Shape China Today* (New York: Oxford University Press, 2000).

Sun Yat-sen (Sun Zhongshan) Born in Canton in 1866, Sun became a Western-style Doctor of Medicine after studying in Macao. In 1894 he founded the Revive China Society but went into exile abroad after the failure of the Society's 1895 uprising in Guangzhou province. In exile, he formed an anti-Manchu rebellion that overthrew the Qing (Manchu) Dynasty. On January 1, 1911, he returned to China where he was elected President of the Republic of China's Provisional Government until resigning the next year after an unsuccessful revolt against him by more conservative opponents such as Yuan Shika. He again went into exile, ending up in the Soviet Union whose Red Army helped him regain power in 1923. As President of the Chinese Republic, Sun formed the Nationalist Party known as the Kuomintang (KMT) to espouse the three principals of nationalism, democracy, and the people's livelihood. He died in 1925.

Chiang Kai-Shek (Jiang Jieshi) Becoming prominent as head of the Military Academy at Whampoa, Chiang was appointed commander of the KMT Army after Sun Yat-sen died in 1925. As KMT commander, Chiang led a successful campaign against China's northern warlords but divided the KMT by ordering the massacre of Shanghai's Communist wing in 1927. The next year, Chiang's forces put down a Communist uprising in Xi'an province. Yet, his luck ran out when a group of Communists kidnapped him in 1936, forcing his KMT to form a United Front with the Communists in fighting the Japanese invasion of China from 1937 until Japan surrendered in August 1945. During World War II, the United States sent the KMT a large supply of aircraft, arms, and ammunition but Chiang's corrupt KMT officials made poor use of the equipment when they waged a civil war against the Communists' People's Liberation Army after 1945. In 1949, Chiang's ragtag forces fled to Formosa (Taiwan) where Chiang became a military dictator until his death in 1975. His son, Chiang Ching-kuo, succeeded him as ruler of Formosa.

Mao Tse-tung (Mao Zedong) Born in 1892 as the son of a well-to-do peasant family in Hunan province, Mao was educated at Changsha before becoming librarian at the University of Peking (Beijing). After reading books by Karl Marx, he became a Marxist and one of the founders of the Chinese Communist Party (CCP) in 1921. Mao participated in a peasant uprising in 1928, but had to retreat to form a Soviet cell in Jianqxi province. After Chiang's KMT forces surrounded Jianqxi, Mao joined others in the Long March to Shanxi province, where he emerged as leader of the People's Liberation Army at Yun'an. In 1937, Mao allied with Chiang's KMT to fight the Japanese. During the anti-Japanese conflict, Mao's army received enough arms and ammunition from Moscow to build a strong Red Army in the post-1945 conflict with Chiang's KMT. By 1949, Mao's armies had defeated the KMT, causing Chiang and his forces to flee to the island of Formosa (Taiwan). During the 1950s, Mao succeeded in preventing Stalin from imposing his own Moscow-trained Chinese leadership while building up a Maoist cult in China, which became known as Mao Zedong Thought. After Mao's Great Leap Forward failed to improve China's agricultural production, he blamed other Chinese officials and launched the so-called Cultural Revolution to persecute those who had opposed his policies. In the years before his death, Mao became convinced that a massive military buildup was essential to prevent the Soviet Union from attacking China, a buildup that left China bankrupt at the time of his death in 1976.

Chou En-lai (Zhou Enlai) Chou was born in Jiansen province in 1898 and educated in Tianjin before going to study in Paris, France, where he joined the CCP. After return to China in 1928, Chou joined with Mao to establish a Soviet regime in Ruijin, Jiangxi province. In 1932, Chou established the first "Labor Persuasion" camp in Communist controlled areas of China. Such camps were designed to reform the thinking of socialist workers by having them perform "hard labor." From the 1930s until his death in 1976, Chou not only assisted Mao by serving as premier and foreign minister of China, but helped to negotiate a friendship treaty with the Soviet Union . He also supported Mao during the 1960s Great Leap Forward and the Cultural Revolution. Finally in the early 1970s, his work as foreign minister led the Chinese to negotiations with President Nixon, leading to friendship treaties with the United States during the administrations of Presidents Carter and Reagan.

Deng Xiaoping Born in 1904 to a wealthy peasant family in Guang'an province, Deng went to study in Paris in 1920, where he joined the CCP in 1925. After studying briefly at Sun Yat-sen University in Moscow, he returned to China in 1926. He served as political commissar at a military school and held the same position for Mao's Red Liberation Army during the anti-Japanese conflict from 1937 to 1945. When Mao resumed a civil war with the KMT, Deng was in charge of China's southwest frontier. After the Red Army chased Chiang Kai-shek's forces to Formosa (Taiwan), Deng moved to Beijing to become General Secretary of the CCP in 1956. During the 1960s Great Leap Forward, he advocated a free market economy, a claim that contradicted Mao's beliefs and made Deng Xiaoping a target for persecution during the so-called Cultural Revolution. After a period of exile, he was reinstated as vice premier in 1973. After Mao's death, Deng obtained help from two Red Army generals and staged a *coup d'etat* in 1976 by arresting the Gang of Four lead by Mao's widow, Jiang Quing. The coup enabled Deng to become the controlling force in the CCP. In 1979, Deng initiated China's program of the Five Modernizations of agriculture, industry, science, technology, and defense. He also introduced the open door policy for special economic zones. In contrast to the modernization, he opposed any political changes in China and was responsible for the Tiananmen Square massacre of hundreds of Chinese in June 1989. He fell into an irreversible coma in 1995 before his death in 1997.

Jiang Zemin Born in 1926 to a wealthy household in Jiangsu province, he was adopted by a Communist martyr, Jiang Shangsu. He studied electrical engineering at Shanghai's Jiatong University where he joined the CCP in 1946. In 1955, he went to Moscow to train Russians workers at the Stalin Automobile Works before returning to train Chinese at China's state-owned enterprises. After serving as Shanghai's mayor and Party secretary, Jiang was chosen by Deng to replace Zhao Ziyang as general secretary of the CCP in 1989. Jiang continued to hold a vital Chinese position as chairman of the Central Military Commission in charge of China's massive Liberation Army until he resigned on September 19, 2004. His successor, Hu Jintao, took over the Military Commission in addition to being China's president and first aecretary of the CCP.

Hu Yaobang He was born to a poor peasant family in Hunan province. Hu joined the Communist Youth League when was 14 years old. He was wounded in battle during Mao's Long March before becoming political commissar of the People's Liberation Army. He supported Mao during the Great Leap Forward but was persecuted during Mao's Cultural Revolution. Deng Xiaoping rehabilitated Hu in 1975, asking him to recreate the Chinese Academy of Social Sciences and later the Central Party School. In 1979, he became a member of the Politburo as the Party's general secretary. In that position he rehabilitated millions of Chinese persecuted by Mao. He was the CP general secretary from 1982 until 1987, when he was dismissed because he was accused of advocating "bourgeois liberalism" and supporting student protests in favor of more democracy in China. His sudden death from a heart attack in 1989 set off the Tiananmen Square demonstrations by pro-democracy students. Because Deng opposed any political changes, army units from outside Beijing massacred hundreds of Chinese during pro-democracy demonstrations.

Index

A

C

D

F

H

I

J

K

M

N

P

R

S

T

U

V

Y

Z